AMERICAN URBAN HISTORY

AMERICAN URBAN HISTORY

An Interpretive Reader with Commentaries

EDITED BY

ALEXANDER B. CALLOW, JR.
UNIVERSITY OF CALIFORNIA, SANTA BARBARA

NEW YORK
OXFORD UNIVERSITY PRESS
LONDON 1969 TORONTO

To my mother and father

Acknowledgments

I would like to thank the Oxford staff, especially Byron Hollinshead and Helen Richardson, for their encouragement, skill, and assistance. Thanks are also due my resourceful graduate research assistant, Robert M. Mullins.

Contents

Introduction

This is a book about what O. Henry called "a ragged purple dream, the wonderful, cruel, enchanting, bewildering, fatal, great city." It is an attempt to achieve a perspective on a phenomenon that in the past was a critical unifying force in our history and in the present has been described as our No. 1 problem—the American city.

American Urban History is neither a narrative textbook, a collection of primary documents, nor a combination of "conflicting" interpretations. It is an attempt to bring together, chronologically and topically, widely scattered interpretive essays that illuminate important themes and problems in American urban history and encourage an analytical approach to the study of the city. Some selections are broad in scope; others tackle specific topics; none are definitive, but most are provocative and well written. This is, then, largely a book of ideas, introducing what Daniel Boorstin calls "organizing ideas," concepts that fashion the bony, intellectual anatomy of American urban history and give shape to the countless "facts" about the American city.

Each of the nine chapters is preceded by a commentary that introduces the major ideas of the readings, correlates them with the central historical theme of the chapter, underscores notions of particular analytical interest, and raises further questions suggested (or ignored) by the selected essays, in the hope they will not only serve as guidelines but also that they and the selections will be the hors d'oeuvres to a larger feast if the student is excited to plunge deeper, through independent reading and research. Taken together, the commentaries and the selections themselves—especially the last essay in the book, the excellent survey of the literature of American urban history by Charles N. Glaab—will suggest ideas and sources for research papers, joint research projects, critical book reviews, and themes for class discussions.

This book is predicated upon the proposition that urban history should have an inter-disciplinary approach. Consequently, the selections include some of our best American urban historians as well as some of our ablest students of other phases of urban affairs, sociologists like Herbert Gans and Robert Merton, political scientists like Scott Greer, and city planners like Charles Abrams—men who have something to say, say it well, and, importantly, have an historical orientation.

This book is also based upon a few underlying principles that I feel should characterize the study of the American city. Broadly defined, there are two schools of thought concerning the best way to approach and to understand the history of the American city. One group sees the city as a reflection of national history—indeed, as one of the main currents in the mainstream of American history. Its members seek to reveal the impact of the city upon American history and the impact of history upon the city. The other group stresses the importance of the city as a singularly important phenomenon in itself. To this group the city has coherence, unity, muscles, and sinews of its own. They avoid stitching urban history into the conventional periodization of American history, such as the City and Jacksonian Democracy, the City and the Civil War, the City and the New Deal, insisting that such an approach is archaic and myopic for at least two reasons: the characteristics of urban developments do not always coincide with developments in national history, and such an approach obscures developments that we urgently need to know more about, namely, the various processes of urbanization. I occupy a middle position between these two approaches, not unmindful of both the smugness that moderation implies and the fact that one can get run over in the middle of the road. It seems to me that the two views are not necessarily contradictory and that a better perspective is achieved by trying to balance the two, and I have made my selections accordingly. In a day when we still do not have consensus on what the city is, as well as what we really mean by *urban,* the door should be open to all kinds of approaches. Our future depends upon it.

AMERICAN URBAN HISTORY

I THE CITY IN HISTORY

It has been said that the history of civilization "from Memphis, Egypt, to Memphis, Tennessee," is written in the rise and fall of cities. Perhaps, paradoxically, the city in history has been both inseparable from the course of human history yet a separate historical phenomenon of its own. It has mirrored some of the major tensions of the human condition—rich *vs.* poor, greed *vs.* compassion, change *vs.* tradition, the individual *vs.* the mass, ideology *vs.* ideology. It has reflected the best and worst in man—the hospital and the tenement, the clearinghouse of ideas, music, and the arts, and the refuge of filth, disease, and misery. Indeed, few of man's other creations have been so bewilderingly complex, so infinitely diverse, so compounded by extremes and contradictions.

There is no better example of this than the American city, until recently the scene of unprecedented rapid urbanization. In comparison with the European urban heritage, which stretches back roughly 5500 years, the American transformation from village to city was achieved in a dazzlingly short space of time. From the eighteenth century on, Americans experienced the painful yet rewarding metamorphosis of an agrarian nation becoming an urban-industrial giant that left few of her political, economic, and social institutions untouched, be they the farm, the factory, or the family. In 1790, for example, only a little over 4 per cent of the American population lived in cities; today 70 per cent of Americans live in urban areas. Richard Hofstadter summed it up well: "The United States was born in the country and has moved to the city."

All of this, of course, begs several questions. How do we account for the rise of the city? What historical forces, what processes of urbanization played determining roles? What was the impact of the rise of the city upon American society? It is the purpose of this chapter to grapple with these questions by showing that behind the maze of complexities, were patterns—political, economic, social, technological—in as well as outside the city, that shaped the rise of urban America and gave its history some coherence.

We begin with three essays, each broad in scope, each analytical and synthetical in nature, each bristling with organizing ideas that illuminate successively the rise of the city, major themes in American urban history, and the internal generating forces behind the city itself. We begin, then, with generalizations, hoping to sketch guidelines which from the very beginning may help one to steer a course through the sea of "facts" about American urban history.

Oscar Handlin sets the course by providing a historical background, without which the history of the American city is incomprehensible. For the American city was heir to a clutch of forces that generated one of the main turning points in world history: the conversion of the medieval pre-industrial city into the sprawling, creative, and disruptive modern city. His thesis is that this transformation constituted not a simple process of evolution, but a drastic break from the past. The continuity of history was ruptured by the emergence of something singularly new, the modern city. Handlin sees the catalysts of this remarkable phenomenon as the rise of the centralized nation-state, technological innovations, the novel developments in production and capital constituting the rise of modern industry, and the subsequent explosion in the urban population. If one major characteristic of the emerging modern city must be underscored, however, it is the change and disruption of the heart of the medieval pre-industrial social system—the traditional, corporate, communal organization of households, at once a social and economic institution.[1]

The American city, then, was born and grew into adolescence during the transitional stage between the pre-industrial and modern industrial city. In a pioneer essay Arthur Schlesinger, Sr., evaluates the evolution of over two hundred years of the American urban experience. This essay is to American urban history what Frederick Jackson Turner's essay was to American western history. It is a sweeping synthesis that provokes attention to a neglected field, and it is a reassessment of American history. It has the strengths and weaknesses of the Turner essay—imaginative insights and a tendency toward exaggeration, perhaps an occupational hazard for pioneer historians. It is, in fact, anti-Turnerian in character, an attempt to balance Turner's thesis that the national character and American institutions were created out of the successive frontiers of the westward movement. "The city," Schlesinger declares, "no less than the frontier, has been a major factor in American civilization. Without an appreciation of the role of both the story is only half told." Essentially,

---

1. For interesting, and conflicting, interpretations of the city in history, see Henri Pirenne, *Medieval Cities* (Princeton: Princeton University Press, 1925); Max Weber, *The City* (Glencoe, Ill.: The Free Press of Glencoe, 1958); Lewis Mumford, *The City in History* (New York: Harcourt, Brace and World, 1961); and especially, Gideon Sjoberg, *The Preindustrial City* (New York: The Free Press, 1960).

Schlesinger is saying that the city was a frontier as important and dynamic as that of the western wilderness.

The essay is particularly valuable as an introduction to some of the main organizing ideas of American urban history. With the finesse of the gifted generalizer, Schlesinger isolates some of the critical themes that accounted for the rise and particularly the impact of the city upon American history, such as urban rivalry, urban imperialism, a sense of collective responsibility, and the city's contributions to American cultural and economic life. Schlesinger may have underplayed the darker side of urban history, overstated the rift between farm and city, and elevated city dwellers at the expense of agrarians, but he has exposed some of the anatomy of the American city in history.[2]

Also taking as his departure point the celebrated Turner thesis, W. Stull Holt seconds Schlesinger's motion that the role of the city has been sorely underrated by American historians. While his presentation is not as panoramic as Schlesinger's, his imagination is provocative especially regarding his insistence that historians must pay more attention to the processes of urbanization. He argues that the "most pregnant result" of urbanization from the late 1800's to the late 1940's, was a declining birth rate and its ramifications, particularly as they affected women, the family, and an aging population. In evaluating this thesis, one should note that it is more relevant to the period before World War II, after which the birth rate increased and the average age of the population decreased. His most provocative idea, however, is that there is an intimate relationship between the city and its sense of collective responsibility and the growth of the welfare state. It is a stimulating theory, fraught with possibilities for a new view of American reform, but highly vulnerable to overstatement.

Less concerned with the historical "impact" approach, Leo F. Schnore examines the city as a phenomenon in itself by asking, what is a city? It is a confounding yet necessary question to any discussion of the city in history, and so far there has been no consensus on definition among students of urban affairs. Political scientists stress political and legal aspects; economists emphasize the economic factors; sociologists, depending upon their school, single out the physical, social, and psychological characteristics; and historians often dodge the question.[3] Since there are all kinds of cities in all kinds of places with all kinds of varying characteristics, perhaps we never will nor never can

2. For a more detailed criticism of the Schlesinger essay, see William Diamond, "On the Dangers of an Urban Interpretation of History," in Chapter 9 of this book.

3. For a series of valuable essays by a number of social scientists, discussing the methods and literature of their respective disciplines, see Philip M. Hauser and Leo F. Schnore (eds.), *The Study of Urbanization* (New York: John Wiley, 1965). Also profitable is Emrys Jones, *Towns and Cities* (London and New York: Oxford, 1966).

If there is one definition of the city, while not inclusive, that could be accepted, at least in part, by historians and social scientists, it could be that of Gideon Sjoberg. He defines the city as the residence of non-agrarian specialists.

agree upon a monolithic definition that satisfies everyone. But we still must ask the question in order to get a clearer conceptual pattern of the city and to measure with more precision such hazy concepts as "urban," "urbanized," and the "urbanization process."

Convinced that the heart of the question involves man himself, especially the extraordinary growth of the urban population,[4] Schnore sees the city as a social organism. He is fascinated by the internal structures of the city, the development of urban space, the web-like interdependence of the city's muscles, sinews, and nervous system. Indeed, he finds a close analogy between the internal structure and growth of the human body and the internal social development of the city. Some may argue that this is a strained oversimplified analogy, smacking of old-fashioned, nineteenth-century Social Darwinism painfully and unrealistically moulded to fit modern conditions. Others may say it leaves out too many other critical factors—political, economic, geographic, psychological, technological. But it is a view that many sociologists of the ecological tradition have, with variations, taken seriously. Schnore is not rigid about it; he presents it as a hypothesis, admitting that the city is open to a host of interpretations. In fact, the questions he raises regarding what we don't know but need to know about the city make up one of the most provocative sections of the essay.

Debatable (as any theory is), Schnore's essay is valuable to the historian for several reasons. It suggests a different way of thinking about the city, rather than being just a straight narrative, especially in terms of the internal growth of the city. Or to put it another way, if the saga of the agrarian frontier must be balanced by the saga of the urban frontier, the approach that measures the influence of the city upon American history must be balanced by an approach that seeks to understand the urbanization processes that make the city a phenomenon unto itself. Above all, it suggests that historians may profit by selectively using sociological techniques and insights in a historical context.

4. The impact of urban growth and its chilling implications, is further explored in Kingsley Davis's thoughtful essay, "The Urbanization of the Human Population," *Scientific American,* September 1965, pp. 40-53.

The Modern City as a Field of Historical Study

OSCAR HANDLIN

Seen from above, the modern city edges imperceptibly out of its setting. There are no clear boundaries. Just now the white trace of the superhighway passed through cultivated fields; now it is lost in an asphalt maze of streets and buildings. As one drives in from the airport or looks out from the train window, clumps of suburban housing, industrial complexes, and occasional green spaces flash by; it is hard to tell where city begins and country ends. Our difficulties with nomenclature reflect the indeterminacy of these limits; we reach for some vague concept of metropolis to describe the release of urban potential from its recognized ambit.

Contrast this visual image with that of the ancient or medieval city. It is still possible, coming up the Rhone, to see Sion in the Valais much as it looked four hundred years ago. From a long way off, one can make out its twin castles jutting into the sky. But the vineyards and orchards, the open fields and clumps of woodland, reach along the roadside to the edge of town. There, we cross a boundary to enter another universe, one which is whole and entire to itself. The record of sieges that lasted for months on end confirms the impression of self-containment. It is much so that Paris must once have been, and Athens.

The cities of the past were, of course, vulnerable to external assault and to disruptive changes that emanated from without. Wars, shifts in patterns of production and trade, and cultural innovations gathered force outside their walls and yet decisively altered their history. But even when they held agricultural lands and even when some residents tilled the soil, those earlier communities possessed an individual life of their own in a sense that their modern successors do not. The ancient world had been a world of cities, but each had been a world unto itself. The towns of the Middle Ages and the Renaissance, even those of the eighteenth century, were self-contained entities walled off from their surroundings, with which they had only precisely defined contacts. They provided a marketplace for the products of rural craftsmen and husbandmen; but the main lines of their trade ran to distant, often overseas, places. They were centers of administration. But the governmental and ecclesiastical functionaries existed apart in detachment. The distance between London and Westminster, between Paris and Versailles, even between Milan and the castle of the Sforzas, was more than symbolic; it measured the genuine isolation of the life of the bourgeois.[1]

On the map today London and Paris and Milan occupy the same sites as did the places which bore those names three

From Oscar Handlin and John Burchard (eds.), *The Historian and the City* (Cambridge: The M.I.T. Press, 1963), pp. 1-26. Copyright © 1963 by the Massachusetts Institute of Technology and the President and Fellows of Harvard College. Reprinted by permission of The M.I.T. Press, Cambridge, Massachusetts. Oscar Handlin is Winthrop Professor of History at Harvard University. John Burchard is Emeritus Dean of the School of Humanities and Social Sciences of the Massachusetts Institute of Technology.

hundred years ago; and subtle institutional and cultural ties run across the centuries. But it would be a mistake to regard the later communities as merely, or even primarily, the descendants of the earlier ones. The modern city is essentially different from its predecessors, and the core of the difference lies in the fact that its life is not that "of an organism, but of an organ." It has become "the heart, the brain, perhaps only the digestive stem, of that great leviathan, the modern state." Its history cannot be understood apart from that of the more comprehensive communities of which it is a part.[2]

The distinctive feature of the great modern city is its unique pattern of relations to the world within which it is situated. Large enough to have a character of its own, the modern city is yet inextricably linked to, dependent upon, the society outside it; and growth in size has increased rather than diminished the force of that dependence. Out of that relationship spring the central problems of urban history—those of the organization of space within the city, of the creation of order among its people, and of the adjustment to its new conditions by the human personality.

It is, of course, perfectly possible to approach the history of these communities in a purely descriptive fashion—to prepare useful accounts of municipalities, markets and cultural centers on an empirical basis. But such efforts will certainly be more rewarding if they are related to large questions of a common and comparative nature. These introductory remarks aim to define some of those questions.

The forces that made the modern city what it is took form outside its own limits. Hence the increases were always unexpected and unanticipated. In the sixteenth and seventeenth centuries London, the first truly modern city, was repeatedly forbidden to grow; men who knew it as it was could not conceive what it would become. For the same reason, projections of future trends—whether prophetic or scientific—almost without fail fell far short of actuality, even in the most optimistic cultures. It was rare indeed that the facilities of a community anticipated its later needs, as those of Los Angeles did. The direction and rate of expansion were not foreseen because the generative impulses were not contained within the older urban society of merchants, artisans, and functionaries. They sprang from three profound and interrelated changes in the society external to them —the development of the centralized national state, the transformation of the economy from a traditional, household, to a rational, capital-using basis, and the technological destruction of distance.[3]

The political changes were first to show themselves; here the medieval cities were at their weakest. Few of them had ever disposed of substantial military force. Venice and Ragusa were unusual in this respect, perhaps because of their relation to the sea. Most other towns, at best, found protection from a stadtholder, or at worst, remained the victims of *condottieri* or feuding barons. Often they welcomed the security of monarchical authority, but they had no illusions about the extent to which that would increase their own power. In the face of any assertion of royal or national will, they could only acquiesce.[4]

That dependent situation has persisted to this day. Despite their wealth and their critical economic position, the great cities do not control themselves;

indeed most of them remain underrepresented in their ability to influence state policy. Their subordination in the polity has decisively shaped many aspects of their development.

The economic metamorphosis from which the modern city emerged is conventionally referred to as industrialization—an inappropriate designation because factory production was only slowly, and late, incorporated into the urban economy and was, in any case, only one aspect of a more general development. The eye of the change occurred outside the city rather than within it. First in agriculture and then in industry, old household-oriented modes of production gave way to large-scale rationalized forms, ultimately mechanized, that immensely increased output. The need to distribute the products to territorially wide, rather than to local, markets directly implicated the city.

The influence of technological change upon communications needs little comment. The evidences are all about us; and the development that led from the early roads and canals to the railroad, the telephone, the wireless, and the airplane permitted the speedy concentration of goods, messages, and persons at the focal points of ever wider areas. The simultaneous acceleration in managerial skills that permitted the organized deployment of great numbers of men and materials was equally impressive. The pace of innovation was particularly rapid in the half century after 1875 when the character of the modern city was most precisely defined. Why there should have been so striking an outburst of creativity in those years is as elusive a question as why there should have been so striking a failure of creativity thereafter.

The centralized national state, the new productive system, and vastly improved communications created the modern city. Together they increased its population, they endowed it with novel economic functions, and they imposed upon its way of life a fresh conception of order.

The initial manifestation of the change was a rapid growth in urban population. The centralizing tendencies of the emerging states of the sixteenth and seventeenth centuries brought significant groups of newcomers to the capitals and to regional subcenters. Operations, formerly dispersed in particular units of administration, were now concentrated; and the steady growth of state power created many additional places. Numerous functionaries carried on the expanded volume of government business and brought with them their families and retainers. Moreover many noblemen found it necessary to live close to the focus of authority, either through choice to be near the source of favors as in Bourbon France, or through compulsion to be subject to control as in Tokugawa Japan. Ancillary educational and religious institutions gravitated in the same direction. All the people thus drawn to the city created a market for trade, crafts, and services which swelled the economy of their place of residence.[5]

These developments had subtle, long-term effects. Channels of communication with the rest of the country were established that deepened through use and that conditioned the routes of later railroad and telephone lines. In some places the extensive fiscal transactions of the central government laid a basis for subsequent banking developments. As important, the seat of power acquired a symbolic value that later acted as a magnet for other detached elements in the society; and national citizenship facilitated their free entry.

Urban population expanded preponderantly by immigration. Cataclysms of many types outside the city borders precipitously swelled the streams that flowed into it. A stroke of fortune such as the discovery of gold near San Francisco and Johannesburg, or population pressure in the hinterland, or a disaster such as the migrations into Bombay and Calcutta after partition quickly raised the number of residents. Colonial trade contributed to the same effect in London and Amsterdam. Most important of all, structural changes in agriculture and industry involved a total reorganization of the labor force and effectively displaced great numbers of human beings for whom the city was the only refuge.[6]

From these sources was derived the rapid increase in numbers characteristic of the metropolis. Through the nineteenth century the pace accelerated, with the very largest places growing more rapidly than the smaller ones. In 1800 the twenty-one European cities with a population of 100,000 or more held, in all, somewhat more than four and a half million souls, one thirty-fifth of the total. In 1900 there were 147 such places with a population of 40,-000,000 or one-tenth of the total; and thirteen and one-fourth million lived within the narrowly defined political limits of the six largest cities. Were there means of estimating the true size of the urban districts involved, the number would be larger still. The same cities in 1960 had a population of about 24,000,000—again a gross underestimation of their genuine numbers. Meanwhile places of comparable dimension had appeared in America and Asia. In 1961 well over 85,000,000 persons lived

in the world's twenty largest cities, each of which contained 2,500,000 or more residents. And the process was not yet over.[7]

Mere accretions of population, however, changed the fundamental character of the city but slightly. New people came in, but their presence in itself called for few radical accommodations on the part of the old residents who generally prospered from the increased demand for their services. The city spread through the addition of new areas to its living space. But the organization of life for some time remained much what it had been earlier. Growth to great size was a necessary precondition, but did not in itself bring the modern city into being. Edo (Tokyo) in 1868 is said to have had a population of about a million, London in 1660 held more than one-half million people; yet these places were but extended towns which functioned according to patterns set long before. Their nobility, mercantile pursuits, and artisans' handicrafts formed larger aggregates than before, but they were aggregates of units that were essentially unchanged. Characteristically, in such places the building trades occupied a large part of the total labor force, and they altered but little with the passage of time. Other pursuits remained much as they had been earlier. The number of smiths and tailors, or drapers and merchants grew; but the mere multiplication of stalls and shops did not change the character of the bazaar, of the lane or of the exchange.[8]

Nor did the new needs thrust upon the city by the transformation of agriculture and industry after the eighteenth century alone give it its modern identity. Viewed simply on the economic plane, there was nothing inherently novel in the relationship of the city to these changes. It had long been accustomed to receiving the placeless men who sought its shelter and it had always provided a market for the products of the countryside. What was new was the desire, and the ability, to impose a rational order upon the relations created by the new productive system. The evolution of that order not only brought the city into intimate dependence upon the surrounding society; it also entailed a thoroughgoing transformation in the urban way of life.

Earlier markets had been dominated by the characteristics of the fair; buyers and sellers had approached in the expectation that they might meet one another, but the actual encounters had been shot through with chance. Monopolies and other political controls, various systems of correspondence and intelligence, and numerous other devices had aimed to impart some regularity to these transactions, particularly in the exchange of the great staples—wine, wool, and later, spices, tea, tobacco, and sugar. But distance and the vagaries of household production had limited the utility of these efforts. In effect, the movement of goods came to a halt, started and stopped, within the city, and that discontinuity gave the entrepôt a considerable degree of autonomy.

That situation ceased to be tolerable after the eighteenth century. The new techniques resulted in a large and growing capacity for production far beyond local need; they involved heavy capital investments and considerable risk; and they entailed difficult administrative problems. The success of any enterprise hinged upon the ability to anticipate with some precision a favorable relationship between cost of production and selling price. It could only survive by planning, however primitive the means by later standards; and planning required dependability and predictability in access both to markets and to supplies.

The city supplied the essential mechanism: from it radiated the communications network—increasingly more extensive and more rapid—and within it were situated the facilities for transshipping, storing, and processing commodities on their way from producer to consumer. Here, too, was the apparatus of accounting and credit that made the movement of goods possible. The task of the city was that of speedy transmission. The more sensitive communications became, the more thoroughly the city was entangled in a mesh of relations that deprived it of autonomy and integrated it into a larger economic and social whole.[9]

The new role had profound consequences for the internal life of the city. Its effectiveness in the productive system of which it was a part depended upon its ability to create an appropriately functioning order within its own boundaries. The pressures toward doing so were critical in its development.

One can discover premature efforts to create such novel economic relationships in the role of Milan in Lombardy and in the experience of other Renaissance cities with their hinterlands. Such developments were abortive, not only because of their restricted territorial scope and because of technological limitations, but also because the corporate life inherited from the middle ages survived, indeed grew stronger; and that life significantly inhibited further changes. The seventeenth-century syndics who sat for Rembrandt's corporation portraits were custodians of communal organizations which resisted untoward changes. The destruction of their way of life was the necessary preliminary to the creation of a new urban order more in accord with the developing productive system.[10] Where that corporate life was weak or nonexistent to begin with, as in the United States, the process was all the faster.

Destruction of the older way of life was achieved through a convergence of political and economic forces. The national state eroded traditional elements of control and created new loci of power that dominated the city from outside it. The local aristocracy dwindled in importance; the old corporations were drained of influence; privileges were reshuffled; and new people rose to prominence. More generally, the national state undermined all traditional affiliations. It recognized only the indiscriminate relationship of citizenship. In its eyes there were only individuals, not members of clans, guilds, or even of households.

The changes in the productive system redistributed wealth to the advantage of men who could cast aside inherited modes of action to capitalize on fresh opportunities. The new economy encouraged the pursuit of individual profit rather than of status within a defined community; and the city housed a pack of people seeking after gain:

> Where every man is for himself
> And no man for all.[11]

The result was a new concept of orderly city life, one that no longer rested on a corporate organization of households, but instead depended upon a complex and impersonal arrangement of individuals. The process was already at work in the sixteenth century in England; it was immensely stimulated by the American and the French revolutions and was complete by the end of the nineteenth century.

We shall better be able to understand the character of the inner order of the modern city by regarding some of its specific manifestations.

An entirely new pattern for disposing of space appeared. The layout of the old city was altogether inappropriate. The population had already spread beyond the encircling walls and waters but it was inefficiently organized by a cumbersome and anachronistic plan. Churches, palaces, and other monumental structures occupied central places; squares and plazas pockmarked the limited area; and the streets ran but the short distances between nearby termini.

There was no reason why they should do more, for men had little need to travel since the household was both residence and place of work. Various districts were differentiated by occupational, class, or religious distinctions. But in each case, the basic unit was a self-contained familial entity that had a precisely defined place in the corporate life of the city. An increase in numbers was accommodated by multiplying the units, not by altering their character. In those unusual situations, as in the ghettoes, where space was constricted, the buildings rose upward and expansion was vertical. More frequently, where room was available, new clusters of settlement split off from the old and expansion was lateral. But until well into the nineteenth century growth in most places had simply multiplied the number of clusters; it had not altered their essential character.[12]

Reconstruction of the city plan depended upon the differentiation of living and working quarters. Such specialized use of space, reflecting the growing impersonality of business and its separation from the household, became prevalent everywhere except in professions like medicine, and in the service crafts where a personal relationship survived. Elsewhere, the dispersal of the population went hand in hand with the destruction of the household and was eased by the engulfment of suburb after suburb. The father and mother and children lived together but their life was detached from work. The categories of experience they shared in the home were unrelated to those of the job. Each individual left after breakfast to take up a separate task in the counting house or the shop or on the scaffold, to return in the evening to his residence some distance away, for each was an integer subject to a separate reckoning in the accounting of the productive system.[13]

The division of function was economical. Every productive or distributive operation became more efficient when it selected the individual employee according to his talents or cost apart from considerations of kin and clan, of family or ethnic grouping. Of course, no society fully realized the ideal of total fluidity that permitted its population to be sorted out in this manner; but the separation of work from residence encouraged an approach in that direction. The fact that single men and women always constituted a large proportion of the migrants into the city stimulated the trend as did related alterations in the behavior of settled families.

As a result space was released from all sorts of traditional expenses. The enterprise no longer had to bear the charge on land of high value, of wasteful drawing rooms and gardens. Precious urban acreage was withdrawn from farming. And the distribution of

population by income levels permitted a rational valuation of space in terms of an abstract, calculated, rent. Speculation was the incidental by-product, rather than the cause, of this development.[14]

Specialization required and facilitated the construction of an entirely new urban plant, a good part of which was built with the aid of a remarkable burst of innovation that began shortly after 1820 and which reached its peak between 1875 and 1925. Space was reallocated with an eye toward its most profitable use; and buildings directed toward a single function—trade, industry, or residence—went up with ruthless efficiency. The process of differentiation created demands for services which theretofore had been unneeded or had been supplied within the household, for fresh foods, milk, water, waste disposal, light, transportation, and recreation. In the frenzy of construction, the city was entirely recast and its ties to the past obliterated. Even topography ceased to be an obstacle; hills were razed, marshes and lakes filled in, and shore lines extended to make way for the limitless grid. Goethe could still make out medieval Frankfurt in place names, markets, buildings, fairs, and topography. By 1870, hardly more than a few of these monuments and ceremonies survived.[15]

Now begins the time of travel, at first on foot. Dickens' characters still walk across London, and at about the same time a resident of Tokyo thinks nothing of tramping five miles to and five miles from his destination every day. Even in twentieth century Rio or Tokyo an inefficient transport system compels workers to spend six hours a day between home and job.[16] But in cost-conscious societies speed is an important consideration; in its interest new streets are driven through the city, straight and wide to carry an ever heavier stream of vehicles—at first horse drawn, later, motor propelled. The wheels roll above and below as well as on the ground and inconvenient rivers are bridged over and tunneled under. The critical breakthrough comes with the appearance of the common carrier. At the beginning of the nineteenth century, every conveyance still bears the appearance of the personal or family carriage or litter —even the long distance stages that take fare-paying passengers. It is not at all clear, when the first railroads are built, that they will follow a different line of development. But the carriages are thrown open for all to enter; mass travel becomes possible; and the meanest laborer moves on wheels.

The pace and ingenuity of this work were impressive by any standard. That the subways of London, Paris, New York, and Boston were built faster than those of Moscow, Stockholm, or Rome fifty years later must mean something, although it would be hazardous to try to make the meaning precise. Any such comparison is to some degree arbitrary and perhaps far-fetched. Yet the standard of achievement certainly was not lower a half century ago than now, if we take into account the presumed improvement in technology since then. Travelers to New York today are aware that it will take seven years (1957- 1964) to reconstruct La Guardia Airport and that Idlewild has been more than a decade in the building. Their predecessors fifty years ago were likely to reach the city through one of the largest buildings ever theretofore constructed at one time, one covering eight acres of ground, with exterior walls of one half a mile. They could enter through two tunnels under the Hudson River and

four under the East River extending more than eighteen miles from Harrison, New Jersey, to Jamaica, Long Island. Work on this project began in June 1903; the Hudson tunnels were finished in three years, the East River tunnels in less than five and the Pennsylvania station in less than six. In September, 1910, the whole complex was in operation.[17]

The modern city demanded an immense number and variety of new buildings. Already in the eighteenth century architects like Claude-Nicholas Ledoux were compelled to devise new shapes for warehouses, for banks, for other commercial structures, and for dwellings appropriate to various classes of residents. Considerations of cost compelled them to adhere to the rule of geometry, and to stress functionalism and the rational organization of materials and space. In doing so they struggled against counterpressures toward tradition and individualism, against counterpulls toward exoticism and a romanticized view of nature. By the second half of the nineteenth century, they had begun to work out the styles that accommodated the life of the modern city.[18]

Certainly the New York tenement block of 1900 was an unlovely object. Having dispensed with the old central court, it could pile its residents up in suffocating density. The reformers of the period were altogether right to attack overcrowding there and elsewhere and to complain that the cities had not adequately met their housing needs. Only, one must remember that overcrowding and need are relative concepts; and few later efforts have been notably more successful.[19] Comparison with the experience of Moscow in the 1930's, to say nothing of Calcutta in the

1950's, puts the achievements of a half-century ago in better perspective.[20]

The altered situation of the city called also for a new conception of time. In the rural past, years, months, days, and hours had been less meaningful than seasons, than the related succession of religious occasions, than the rising and setting of the sun. Small communities had their own flexible conceptions of chronology. Such habits had extended to the city as well. Each household had a large margin within which to set its own pace, for the tempo of all activities was leisurely. An analysis of the course of an eighteenth-century merchant's day, for instance, revealed long disposable intervals so that even when he was busy, it was upon terms he could shape for himself.[21]

The complex interrelationships of life in the modern city, however, called for unprecedented precision. The arrival of all those integers who worked together, from whatever part of the city they inhabited, had to be coordinated to the moment. There was no natural span for such labor; arbitrary beginnings and ends had to be set, made uniform and adhered to. The dictatorship of the clock and the schedule became absolute.[22]

No earlier human experience had made such demands. The army camp, plantation labor, and the ship's crew which came closest to it were coherent, closed societies, the members of which lived close together and in isolation from outsiders; the tasks involved had a rhythm of their own that regulated their budgets of time. But the modern city could not function except under the rule of a precise and arbitrary chronological order which alone could coordinate the activities of thousands of individuals whose necessary encounters with one another were totally impersonal. By the same token, literacy or some alternative code of signals was essential to the coexistence of people who did not know one another.

The new uses of space and time were indicative of what order meant in the modern city. Its complex life demanded myriad daily contacts of such sensitivity that it could not depend, as earlier, upon well-established and static connections among the stable households and the fixed corporate groups in which its population had been distributed. Instead it required its residents to behave individually and impersonally in terms of their function, and it assured regularity of contacts by rigid allocations of space and time.

That order made it possible to bring manufacturing, like other large-scale activities, into the cities. The planners of the early great factories thought of the only models of disciplined activity familiar to them, the barrack and the army camp; their sites—visionary or actual—were therefore invariably in the countryside, where the tolling bell from the clock tower of the mill replaced that of the village church. The similarity in design of factories and prisons was by no means coincidental.[23]

The urban factory was conceivable only well in the nineteenth century when it was possible to imagine that a labor force would come to work regularly and dependably. The process of transition in actuality took a number of forms. Some factory centers, like Manchester, grew into cities. In other cases, as in Pittsburgh or Zurich, a commercial center expanded to engulf nearby industrial communities. Elsewhere industry was drawn in by the attractions of superior transportation facilities, or by the presence of an abundant labor supply, as in Berlin, or Chicago; or the shift was a product of conscious government decisions as in Moscow after 1928. But whatever the immediate impulse, the necessary condition was the order that permitted the factory to function.[24]

The way of life of the modern city created grave social and personal problems. Any increase of size had always complicated the police of the community. But so long as the family, the clan, or the guild remained accountable for the behavior of its members, so long as the normal ambit of activities was restricted to a familiar quarter, the primary danger of deviant behavior came from strangers. When the decay of the household weakened the sense of collective security, the initial response was to control or exclude outsiders, to arrive at some accommodation with violent elements, and to maintain the isolation of the district within which its residents felt safe. At the end of the eighteenth century, as large a place as London had not moved beyond this point.

But these expedients were not long useful. The modern city was no *colluvies gentium*—a fortuitous accumulation of unfused populaces—as were ancient Rome, or Alexandria. Extended travel and promiscuous contacts were essential to it; and the frequent mingling of men unknown to each other generated the need for holding each individual responsible for his behavior. The ultimate goal was some sort of total index that would precisely identify and infallibly locate each person so that he could be called to account for his obligations and punished for his delinquencies. The steady development of governmental power, the contrivance of numerous devices for registration, and the appearance of a professional corps of administrators were steps toward an approximation of that goal.

More was involved than the containment of criminality. The urban resident had positive as well as negative responsibilities. He had not merely to refrain from such actions as were injurious to others; he was expected, in ways that were difficult to define explicitly, also to contribute to the total well-being of the community by civic actions. The collective tasks of the old household and guild could not be left in abeyance. Someone had to provide care for dependent persons, education for children, facilities for worship, media for cultural and sociable expression, and commemorative monuments and objects of awe and beauty. The police of a city thus included a wide range of functions connected with its health and security. The state assumed some of these obligations, but the scope of its activity varied widely from country to country. Although we cannot yet explain convincingly the differences in the depth of its involvement, it is clear that it nowhere preempted the field entirely. Much remained to be done through other forms.[25]

It was not possible, although men often longed to do so, to revive the old corporate institutions or the solidary rural communities from which so many residents had migrated. The modern city contained too many disparate elements, too often thrown together, and in too fluid a pattern of relations to permit such regressions. Instead, where abstinence by the state left a vacuum, the characteristic device of a voluntary association, directed toward the specific function, met the need. The rapid proliferation of such organizations drew together memberships united by common interests, common antecedents, or common point of view. The wide expanse of the city and the continuing migration which peopled it, shaped such groupings. In some places the effective modes of organization fell within territorial, neighborhood lines; the *quartier*, ward, *ku*, or *favela* was the matrix within which associations formed. Elsewhere cultural or ethnic affiliations supplied the determining limits of cooperative action.[26]

For a long time, the cost of this adjustment was recurrent, overt conflict. Leadership was effective only within limited circles, and there were few means of resolving the frequent crises that led easily into outbreaks of violence. Bread riots in the West and rice riots in the East expressed the desperation of the uncared-for elements in the community; and racial or social antipathies, smoldering beneath the surface, erupted at the least disturbance.[27]

By the end of the nineteenth century, the instruments for controlling such dangerous disorders were at least available, if not always effectively used. The reconstruction of the great cities permitted a strategic disposition of power to contain the mob. The maintenance of an armed police force deterred overt lawbreakers. Moreover, by then a complex of philanthropic, religious, educational, and cultural institutions had begun to elicit the acquiescence of the urban masses through persuasion. Thereafter conflicts took more negotiable forms, in the bargaining of labor unions and employers, and in politics which was less a partisan contest for power than an instrument of group accommodation. Disputes were increasingly subject to conciliable resolution through the mediating efforts of recognized leaders. However, the issues which could be confronted on the municipal level were limited and concrete; and the deeper economic and emotional grievances of the population were likely to be displaced into other channels.[28]

The life of the modern city created subtle personal problems. Here were distilled many of the general effects of change in the past two centuries: the break with tradition and the dissolution of inherited beliefs, the impact of science and technology, and the transformation of the family and of the productive system. In the city, as elsewhere, such decisive innovations were a source of both release and tension in the human spirit. Only, concentrated as they were in their urban form, these new impulses were far more volatile than elsewhere. Furthermore, the man of the city passed through experiences unique to his setting. The number and variety and speed of his contacts, the products of an original conception of space and time, the separation from nature, the impersonality and individuality of work all were novel to the human situation.

Evidence of the negative consequences was painfully abundant. On the Bowery or in Brigittenau drifted the uprooted masses who had lost personality, identity, and norms and who now were trapped in every form of disorder. The deterioration of man to bum was all too familiar in every modern city. Even the less desperate were heedless of the restraints of church and family; in London, Berlin, and New York of the third quarter of the nineteenth century, a majority of marriages and burials were unsolemnized by the clergy. The most prosperous tore at each other in vicious competition except when they indulged in fierce and expensive debauchery. High rates of mortality, suicide, alcoholism, insanity, and other forms of delinquency showed that men reared in one environment could not simply shift to another without substantial damage to themselves.[29]

At the high point of change, in the half century after 1875, there were two distinct, although not contradictory, interpretations of the effects of the modern city upon the human personality. Those who focused their attention upon institutional developments, like Georg Simmel, Emile Durkheim, and, to some extent, Max Weber, took particular note of the decay of old forms which left the individual unsheltered, unprotected, and isolated, and therefore prone to deterioration. The later exaggerations of Spengler and Mumford distend these insights into a vision of imminent catastrophe.[30]

Exaggeration was easy because personal disorders were more visible in the city than in the country. But these observers were also limited by a fixed preference for what the city had been, a total systematic unit comprehending a defined order of institutions that no longer existed. It is significant that their views mirrored somber predictions, made long before. Rousseau and others had already warned of the inevitable results of urban detachment from nature before the process had even taken form. "Of all animals man is least capable of living in flocks. Penned up like sheep, men soon lose all. The breath of man is fatal to his fellows. . . . Cities are the burial pit of the human species."[31]

The personal hardships of adjustment to city life were genuine but they were distorted when examined in the perspective of the corporate, rural past. Other observers, whose gaze was fast-ened on the residents as human beings, made out a somewhat different pattern. "What can ever be more stately and admirable to me," asked Whitman, "than mast-hemm'd Manhattan?" Observing the curious procession of the ferry riders leaving work behind for their thousands of homes, he felt and expressed the wonder of their each being a person.[32] This was often the response of compassionate onlookers. At first regard, the city was totally inhuman; jungle, wilderness, hive, machine—these were the terms of the metaphors that sprang spontaneously to mind. But those sensitive enough to look more deeply found marvelous assertions of the human spirit even under these unpropitious circumstances. Here life was real and hard, and tested the human heart and mind so that emotions were deeper and reason more acute than elsewhere. Social scientists influenced by Darwinian conception of the survival of the fittest readily assumed that the city was the new environment within which a new, superior man would develop. And some who began half to understand the character of that life were tempted to idealize and romanticize even its least lovely aspects, the slums, the ruthless competition, and the grinding order.[33]

The two responses were not irreconcilable; indeed, in retrospect, they seem almost complementary, or perhaps, they were but different ways of describing the identical process. The decay of familiar institutions was another way of saying the release from traditional restraints; the unsheltered individual was also the liberated individual. The breakdown of the household and the attenuation of all the relationships formerly centered in it were the conditions of the liberation of modern man to all his painful tensions, all his creative opportunities. The hard stone of the city streets provided the stage for this drama; and it is the task of historical scholarship to explain its triumphs, its defeats, and its conflicts.

The modern city provided the scene for great outbursts of cultural creativity. Georgian London, Paris in the first decades of the Third Republic, Vienna toward the end of the reign of Franz Joseph, and Berlin of the 1920's were the settings of great achievements of the human spirit, in literature, in art, in music, and in science. Yet these were also, and at the same time, the scenes of bitter struggles for existence, of acute hardships suffered by hundreds of thousands of ill-prepared newcomers beaten down by insoluble problems. John Gay and William Hogarth, Anatole France and Honoré Daumier, Robert Musil and Berthold Brecht, and Charlie Chaplin and René Clair compiled a record of personal disasters, of moral disintegration, of human costs so high it could only be contemplated under the palliative gloss of humor. The laughter of their audiences did not conceal, it recognized the harsh truth. Yet the withering away of traditional guides to life, so debilitating in many ways, also set the individual free, left room for spontaneity and discovery, brought together selective new combinations of people, ideas, and forms, that permitted man to catch unsuspected glimpses of an unknown universe and an unfamiliar self.

Every aspect of the development of the modern city generated conflicts not resolvable within its own boundaries; that was a condition of its intimate relations with the society beyond its borders. The urban residents were divided among themselves, and they had to reckon with outsiders in their midst and beyond the walls, whose interests were intimately bound up with their own. Disputes of great importance were the result.

The city plan was therefore never simply the realization of an abstract design. Even in places created entirely afresh, as in Washington or St. Petersburg, it was the product of inescapable compromises. Within the city, the primary interest of the entrepreneurial groups and of the laboring population was to economize on the use of space. They wanted low rents, an efficient, functional allocation of the resources, and speedy interior transportation.

Such people met the determined, and sometimes effective, resistance of other elements, whose conceptions were still dominated by the static images of the rural landscape. The aristocracy—genuine and putative—wished to bring with them the commodious features of their landed estates. They expected the city to provide them with elegant squares to set off their homes, with picturesque monuments, and with parks and boulevards that would supply a back drop for the May Corso, for the Spring Parade, for the *ausflug* or Sunday excursion, for the gentleman on horseback and the lady in her carriage. Public transportation concerned them not at all.[34]

Immigrants who prospered to a lesser degree clung to the rural village as the model of home; they built wasteful villas in the sprawling suburbs and sought a restricted transport system that would take them conveniently to their desks and counters, yet prevent the city from engulfing them. Often their dogged struggles for autonomy hopelessly complicated any effort at urban reorganization, a problem as troublesome in Vienna, Leipzig, Manchester, and Liverpool in 1890 as in Boston and Nashville in 1960.[35]

The persistence of the rural model prevented these people from thinking of the city as a whole and as it was. From Robert Owen, Fourier, and the utopian socialists, to Ebenezer Howard, Frank Lloyd Wright, and Lewis Mumford, a good-hearted but illusory plea went forth for the rebuilding of urban life in garden cities or multiplied suburbs, where adults would not be tempted to squander their resources in the pub or music hall, nor children theirs in the sweetshop; and all would have access to the salubrious and moral air of the countryside.[36]

To such pressures were added those of agriculturists and industrialists in the hinterland concerned only with lowering the cost of transshipment, and of the state, increasingly preoccupied with security against insurrection or lesser threats to order. The great planners, like Baron Haussmann in Paris, found room for maneuver in the play of these forces against one another. But rarely did they find the city material they could mold into a unified and coherent whole.[37]

Urban elements were at a disadvantage in the determination of both municipal and national policies. The level of tariffs in the 1880's and 1890's, the routes of canals and railroads, and the character of the banking system vitally affected all cities. Yet their influence was perilously weak, underrepresented in the councils of state and divided, while the rural interests were monolithic and well entrenched. Paris, Rio, Rome did not govern themselves; and voices from the Platteland or Upstate were more likely to command than those from Johannesburg or New York. The political power of the country generally outweighed the economic power of the city.[38]

The clash of interests took its most subtle and most significant form in the contact of the diverse cultures that converged on the modern city. The folk traditions of the old bourgeois did not survive the disintegration of the corporate bodies in which it had been embedded; it was totally disrupted by the pressure from both above and below of alien elements.

The aristocracy surrendered its isolation and shifted some of its activities to the city. Still stabilized by its landed estates, it also drew support from new wealth and, in the nineteenth century, began the quest for a uniform, hierarchical culture at the peak of which it could stand. It wished more than indulgence in a lavish style of life; it wished also general acquiescence in its position. Indeed, to some extent it flouted the conventions of inferiors precisely in order to demonstrate its superiority. Legally recognized rank as in England and Prussia, the pretense of ancient lineage as in Austria and France, or arbitrary registers of inclusion as in the United States, asserted its claims to pre-eminence. In addition, it transformed the theater, the opera and the museum into institutions to display its dominance. The aristocracy turned music into classics, art into old masters, and literature into rare books, possessions symbolic of its status.[39]

The problems of other migrants into the city were of quite another order. The mass of displaced peasants were eager to transplant their inherited culture but the soil was inhospitable. Folk wisdom, inappropriate to the new conditions, took on the appearance of superstition; and folk art, detached from its communal setting, lost much of its authenticity. However these people fared, they were driven by anxiety—to retain the rewards of success, to avoid the penalties of failure. Some escaped through alcohol; others found moments of relief in the excitement of the yellow press, the music hall, and the popular theater.[40]

Above all, they needed to interpret their lives by seeing themselves as actors in a meaningful drama, and since it was inconceivable that they should be conquering heroes, they most readily visualized themselves as victims.

Of whom? Rarely of the aristocrat. Peasant and gentleman had a long history of accommodation; and their roles in city life engendered few direct conflicts. The lowly felt no compulsion to ape the high born, and gaped at the splendor of the carriages on the way to the opera without envy.

More often the villains were the capitalists, big business, whose wealth was abstract, was located in no communal context, and was attached to no responsibilities of position. Or sometimes, the enemy was the stranger—the Slav or the Jew or the Catholic or the Protestant Masons or the barbaric foreigner—who could be blamed for the ills of the city. Inhuman materialism, disregard of traditional faith, sensuality and obscenity were crimes against man; and for crimes, criminals were responsible; and they who came were guilty so that we who left home were but the innocent victims.[41]

The factory workers and craftsmen who held places in disciplined organizations found belief in socialism; the class struggle explained their present situation and offered them the hope of an acceptable future. But millions of place-less men could not so readily tear themselves away from the past. The shopkeepers and clerks, the casual laborers, the chaotic mass of men without function did not want the future; they wanted the security of the homes and families and blood communities they had never had or had lost in migration. That is, they wanted a miracle; and in their eagerness they became the gullible victims of nationalistic, racist, religious and quasi-religious fantasies of every sort. There is a particular interest, in Europe, in the ease with which these people allied themselves with some sectors of the aristocracy under the banner of a universal faith—Ultramontane Catholicism, pan-Germanism, pan-Slavism. Drumont and the royalist officer corps in France, Luëger and Prince Alois Liechtenstein in Austria, illustrated the attractiveness of tradition and authority for the demagogue and his mob. Perhaps analogous elements were involved in the revival of Shinto in Japan after 1868; they were certainly present in the history of fascism.[42]

The true miracle, however, was the emergence of a sense of civic consciousness connected with the old burgher traditions but responsive to the new character of the modern city. Its characteristics were tolerance to the point of latitudinarianism, rationalism, cosmopolitanism, pragmatism, and receptivity to change. It attracted the settled middle-class elements of the city, the leaders of organized labor and even demagogues suddenly charged with responsibility, as Luëger was in Vienna and La Guardia in New York; its essence was a creative reaction to the problems of the place; its achievement was the monumental building of the city to which I earlier referred.

Some decades ago—and I am deliberately vague about the date—a significant change appeared. The immediate local causes seemed to be the two wars, the depression, and new shifts in technology and population. However, these may be but manifestations of some larger turning in the history of the society of which the modern city is a part.

The differences between city and country have been attenuated almost to the vanishing point. The movement of people, goods, and messages has become so rapid and has extended over such a long period as to create a new situation. To put it bluntly, the urbanization of the whole society may be in process of destroying the distinctive role of the modern city. It is symptomatic of this change that, in western societies, most migrations now originate, as well as terminate, in the modern metropolis.

This change may be related to a general slackening of urban spirit. The worldwide movement to the suburbs is not in itself new; this was always one of the ways in which the city expanded. What is new is the effective motivation—the insistence upon constructing small, uniform, coherent communities, and the surrender of the adventure of life in the larger units with all the hazards and opportunities of unpredictable contacts. Increasingly the men who now people the metropolis long for the security of isolation from the life about them. They strive to locate their families in space, with a minimum of connections to the hazards of the external world.[43]

Finally, there has been a perceptible decline in urban creativity. The regression to private transportation is indicative of what has been happening in other spheres as well. Despite other advances in technology and despite refinements in methods, the last thirty or forty years have witnessed no innovations to match those of the thirty or forty years earlier. We have done little more than elaborate upon the inherited plant; nowhere has there been an adequate response to the challenge of new conditions.

We console ourselves with the calculation that if the modern city has ceased to grow, the metropolitan region continues to expand. What difference that will make remains to be seen. In any case, it seems likely that we stand at the beginnings of a transformation as consequential as that which, two hundred years ago, brought the modern city into being.

Therein lies the historian's opportunity to throw light on the problems of those involved with today's city, either as practitioners or as participants. His task is not to predict, but to order the past from which the present grows in a comprehensible manner. He can illuminate the growth of the modern city from the eighteenth to the twentieth centuries to make clear what was permanent and what transient, what essential and what incidental, in its development.

Such an account as this essay has presented has perforce touched upon a few themes abstracted from a large number of cases. Yet the historian must deal with particulars, not with generalities. Certainly the stress, laid here upon the connections between the modern city and the surrounding society points to the decisive role of political, cultural, and economic variants, widely different from place to place.

Comparisons crowd immediately to mind. Did the differences between

Washington and St. Petersburg in 1900, new capitals of expanding nations, emanate from the hundred-year disparity in their ages or from discernible differences between the United States and Russia? Did Shanghai and Singapore become what they did because they were perched on the edge of Oriental societies or because they were colonial enclaves? Did a tropical situation set the experiences of Rio and Havana apart from those of cities in the temperate zone; did their European population distinguish them from other tropical cities? Why did some cities fail to grow as others did, why were some more successful than others in resolving their problems?

No amount of theorizing about the nature of the city will answer questions such as these. We need fewer studies of the city in history than of the history of cities. However useful a general theory of the city may be, only the detailed tracing of an immense range of variables, in context, will illuminate the dynamics of the processes here outlined.[44] We can readily enough associate such gross phenomena as the growth of population and the rise of the centralized state, as technological change and the development of modern industry, as the disruption of the traditional household and the decline of corporate life. But how these developments unfolded, what was the causal nexus among them, we shall only learn when we make out the interplay among them by focusing upon a city specifically in all its uniqueness.

In the modern city, the contest between the human will and nature assumed a special form. Here man, crowded in upon himself and yet alone, discovered his potentialities for good and evil, for weakness and strength.

Compelled to act within a framework of impersonal institutions, he was forced to probe the meaning of his own personality.

In the balance for two centuries now has lain the issue of whether he will master, or be mastered by, the awesome instruments he has created. The record of that issue deserves the best energies of the historian.

NOTES

1. Max Weber, *The City* (Translated and edited by Don Martindale and Gertrud Neuwirth; Glencoe, [1958]), 70 ff.; Raffaele d'Ambrosio, *Alle Origini della città le prime esperienze urbane* (Napoli, 1956); A. Temple Patterson, *Radical Leicester* (Leicester, 1954), 3, 165.

2. George Unwin, *Studies in Economic History* (London, 1927), 49.

3. Norman G. Brett-James, *Growth of Stuart London* (London, [1935]), 67 ff., 105 ff., 296 ff.; Walter Besant, *London in the Time of the Tudors* (London, 1904), 83; Boyle Workman, *The City that Grew* (Caroline Walker, ed., Los Angeles, 1935), 266 ff.

4. William A. Robson, *Great Cities of the World: Their Government, Politics and Planning* (New York, [1955]), 78 ff.; Société Jean Bodin, *Recueils*, VI (1954), 265 ff., 367 ff., 434 ff., 541 ff., 612.

5. See, e.g., Franklin L. Ford, *Strasbourg in Transition 1648-1789* (Cambridge, 1958), 159 ff.; Lewis Mumford, *The City in History. Its Origins, Its Transformations, and Its Prospects* (New York, [1961]), 386 ff.; *Golden Ages of the Great Cities* (London, 1952), 192.

6. Adna F. Weber, *The Growth of Cities in the Nineteenth Century* (New York, 1899), 230 ff.; Besant, *London in the Time of the Tudors*, 226 ff.; Walter Besant, *London in the Eighteenth Century* (London, 1903), 213 ff.; Percy E. Schramm, ed., *Kaufleute zu Haus und über See Hamburgische Zeugnisse des 17., 18., und 19. Jahrhunderts* (Hamburg, 1949), pt. II; Emile Vandervelde, *L'Exode rural et le retour aux champs* (Paris, 1903), 39 ff.; Robson, *Great Cities*, 112 ff., 141, 683.

7. *Information Please Almanac, 1961*, 658; Edmund J. James, "The Growth of Great Cities," *Annals of the American Academy of Political and Social Science*, XIII (1899), 1 ff.; Weber, *Growth of Cities*, 20 ff., gives extensive nineteenth-century statistics. See also for more recent data, International Urban Research, *The World's Metropolitan Areas* (Berkeley, 1959); Kingsley Davis, "The Origin and Growth of Urbanization in the World," *American Journal of Sociology*, LX

(1955), 429 ff.; Norton S. Ginsburg, "The Great City in Southeast Asia," *ibid.*, LX, 455 ff.; Robert I. Crane, "Urbanism in India," *ibid.*, LX, 463 ff.; Donald J. Bogue, "Urbanism in the United States, 1950," *ibid.*, LX, 471 ff.; Irene B. Taeuber, *Population of Japan* (Princeton, 1958), 25 ff., 45 ff., 96 ff., 126 ff., 148 ff.; Kingsley Davis, *Population of India and Pakistan* (Princeton, 1951), 127 ff.; Vandervelde, *L'Exode rural,* 16 ff.; Edmond Nicolaï, *La Dépopulation des campagnes et l'accroissement de la population des villes* (Bruxelles, 1903); R. Price-Williams, "The Population of London, 1801-81," *Journal of the Statistical Society,* XLVIII (1885), 349 ff.

8. For the population of earlier European cities, see Roger Mols, *Introduction à la démographie historique des villes d'Europe* (Louvain, 1955), II, 502 ff. See also M. Dorothy George, *London Life in the XVIIIth Century* (London, 1925), 155 ff.

9. Robert M. Fisher, ed., *The Metropolis in Modern Life* (Garden City, 1955), 85 ff.; Weber, *Growth of Cities,* 170 ff. For earlier market relations see, "La Foire," Société Jean Bodin, *Receuils,* V (1953), *passim.*

10. See Douglas F. Dowd, "Economic Expansion of Lombardy," *Journal of Economic History,* XXI (1961), 143 ff.; *Storia di Milano* (Milan, 1957-1960), VIII, 337 ff., XIV, 835 ff.; Jakob Rosenberg, *Rembrandt* (Cambridge, 1948), I, 70 ff.; Weber, *The City,* 91 ff.; Mumford, *City in History,* 269 ff., 281 ff.; Société Jean Bodin, *Receuils,* VII (1955), 567 ff.; Schramm, *Kaufleute,* 185 ff.

11. Robert Crowley, quoted in Mumford, *City in History,* 343.

12. Gideon Sjoberg, *The Preindustrial City Past and Present* (Glencoe, [1960]), 100 ff.; Martin S. Briggs, "Town-Planning," Charles Singer, *et al.,* eds., *History of Technology* (New York, 1957), III, 269 ff.; *Golden Ages,* 31-34, 67, 230; Mumford, *City in History,* 299 ff.

13. See Otis D. and Beverly Duncan, "Residential Distribution and Occupational Stratification," *American Journal of Sociology,* LX (1955), 493 ff.; R. P. Dore, *City Life in Japan. A Study of a Tokyo Ward* (Berkeley, 1958), 91 ff.

14. Mumford, *City in History,* 421 ff.; Fisher, *Metropolis in Modern Life,* 125 ff.; Weber, *Growth of Cities,* 322 ff.

15. *The Auto-Biography of Goethe. Truth and Poetry: From My Own Life* (John Oxenford, transl., London, 1948), 3, 4, 7-10, 12 ff.

16. Fukuzawa Yukichi, *Autobiography* (transl. by Eiichi Kiyooka, Tokyo, [1948]); Robson, *Great Cities,* 510; Brett-James, *Stuart London,* 420 ff.

17. Pennsylvania Railroad Company, *The New York Improvement and Tunnel Extension of the Pennsylvania Railroad* (Philadelphia, 1910).

18. Emil Kaufmann, "Three Revolutionary Architects," *Transactions of the American Philosophical Society,* XLII (1952), 494 ff.; Helen Rosenau, *The Ideal City in Its Architectural Evolution* (London, [1959]), 79 ff.

19. Mumford, *City in History,* 465 ff.; Dore, *City Life in Japan,* 40 ff.; Reinhard E. Petermann,

Wien im Zeitalter Kaiser Franz Joseph I (Vienna, 1908), 128 ff.

20. Alec Nove, ed., *The Soviet Seven Year Plan* (London, [1960]), 75 ff.; Harry Schwartz, *Russia's Soviet Economy* (2 ed., New York, 1954), 453 ff.; Robson, *Great Cities,* 384 ff.

21. Arthur H. Cole, "The Tempo of Mercantile Life in Colonial America," *Business History Review,* XXXIII (1959), 277 ff.; *Golden Ages,* 44, 45.

22. On the problem of time, see Pitirim A. Sorokin and Robert K. Merton, "Social Time: A Methodological and Functional Analysis," *American Journal of Sociology,* XLII (1937), 615 ff.

23. Kaufmann, "Three Revolutionary Architects," 509 ff.; Rosenau, *Ideal City,* 121, 133.

24. See, e.g., Catherine E. Reiser, *Pittsburgh's Commercial Development 1800-1850* (Harrisburg, 1951), 28, 191 ff.

25. Louis Wirth, "Urbanism as a Way of Life," *American Journal of Sociology,* XLIV (1938), 20 ff.; Patterson, *Radical Leicester,* 222 ff.; Dore, *City Life in Japan,* 71 ff.

26. See, in general, Lloyd Rodwin, ed., *The Future Metropolis* (New York, 1961), 23 ff. For specific illustrations see Louis Chevalier, "La Formation de la population parisienne au XIXe Siècle," Institut National d'Etudes Démographiques, *Travaux et Documents,* X (1950); Alphonse Daudet, *Numa Roumestan—Moeurs parisiennes* (Paris, 1881), ch. iii; Dore, *City Life in Japan,* 255 f.; Alexander Campbell, *The Heart of Japan* (New York, 1961), 3 ff.; William A. Jenks, *Vienna and the Young Hitler* (New York, 1960), 4.

27. Société Jean Bodin, *Receuils,* VII (1955), 398 ff.; J. B. Sansom, *The Western World and Japan* (New York, 1958), 242; J. D. Chambers, *Nottinghamshire in the Eighteenth Century* (London, 1932), 40 ff.; Besant, *London in the Eighteenth Century,* 475 ff.; George Rudé, *The Crowd in the French Revolution* (Oxford, 1959), 232 ff.

28. Robson, *Great Cities,* 210 ff.

29. See Petermann, *Wien,* 331 ff.; Jenks, *Vienna and the Young Hitler,* 11; George, *London Life,* 21 ff.; Besant, *London in the Eighteenth Century,* 140 ff., 263 ff.; Fisher, *Metropolis in Modern Life,* 18 ff.

30. Georg Simmel, "Die Grosstädte und das Geistesleben," *Jahrbuch der Gehe-Stiftung zu Dresden,* IX (1903), 187 ff.; Kurt H. Wolff, ed., *Georg Simmel, 1858-1918,* (Columbus, Ohio, [1959]), 100 ff., 221 ff.; Emile Durkheim, *De la Division du travail social* (5 ed., Paris, 1926), *passim,* but especially the preface to the second edition; Oswald Spengler, *The Decline of the West* (New York, 1950), II, 92 ff.; Mumford, *City in History, passim.* See also Wirth, "Urbanism as a Way of Life," *loc. cit.,* 20 ff.

31. J[ean]. J[acques]. Rousseau, *Emile ou de l'éducation* (Paris, 1854), Book I, p. 36; Robert A. Kann, *A Study in Austrian Intellectual History* (New York, 1960), 63; see also the point of view

implicit in such novels as E. M. Forster, *Howard's End* (London, 1910).

32. Walt Whitman, *Complete Writings* (New York, 1902), I, 196.

33. See also Weber, *Growth of Cities*, 368 ff., 441 ff.

34. See Percy E. Schramm, *Hamburg, Deutschland und die Welt* (Hamburg, [1952]), 350 ff.; Mumford, *City in History*, 395 ff.

35. Robson, *Great Cities*, 30 ff., 60 ff., 75 ff.; Sam B. Warner, *Street Car Suburbs* (Cambridge, 1962); Weber, *Growth of Cities*, 469 ff.; H. J. Dyos, *Victorian Suburbs* (Leicester, 1961).

36. Rosenau, *Ideal City*, 130 ff.; Robert Owen, *Book of the New Moral World* (London, 1842), II, 16; Ralph Neville, *Garden Cities* (Manchester, 1904); G. Montague Harris, *The Garden City Movement* (London, 1906); Mumford, *City in History*, 514 ff.

37. David H. Pinkney, *Napoleon III and the Rebuilding of Paris* (Princeton, 1958), 25 ff.

38. Robson, *Great Cities*, 685; Schramm, *Hamburg*, 187 ff.

39. Oscar Handlin, *John Dewey's Challenge to Education* (New York, [1959]), 33 ff., George D. Painter, *Proust; the Early Years* (Boston, 1959), Robert Musil, *The Man Without Qualities* (London, 1953); Hans Rosenberg, *Bureaucracy, Aristocracy and Autocracy* (Cambridge, 1958), 182 ff.; Hannah Arendt, *The Origins of Totalitarianism* (New York, [1951]), 54 ff.; Norman Jacobs, ed., *Culture for the Millions?* (Princeton, 1961), 43 ff.; Kann, *Austrian Intellectual History*, 146 ff.

40. Jacobs, *Culture for Millions?* 64 ff.

41. Oscar Handlin, *Adventure in Freedom* (New York, 1954), 50 ff., 109 ff.

42. Dore, *City Life in Japan*, 291 ff.; Arendt, *Origins of Totalitarianism*, 301 ff.; Jenks, *Vienna and the Young Hitler*, 40 ff., 74 ff., 126 ff.

43. Mumford, *City in History*, 511 ff.; Louis Wirth, *Community Life and Social Policy* (Chicago, [1956]), 206 ff.

44. Weber, *The City*, 11 ff.; Wirth, "Urbanism," 8 ff.; Sjoberg, *Preindustrial City*, 4 ff., 321 ff.

The City in American Civilization

ARTHUR M. SCHLESINGER

"The true point of view in the history of this nation is not the Atlantic Coast," declared Frederick Jackson Turner in his famous essay of 1893, "it is the Great West." Professor Turner, writing in Wisconsin, had formed his ideas in an atmosphere of profound agrarian unrest, and the announcement of the Superintendent of the Census in 1890 that the frontier line could no longer be traced impelled him to the conclusion that "the first period of American history" had closed. His brilliant paper occasioned a fundamental reappraisal of the mainsprings of national development.

Today, however, it seems clear that in the zeal to correct older notions he overlooked another order of society which, rivaling the frontier even in the earliest days, eventually became the major force. The city marched westward with the outposts of settlement, always injecting exotic elements into pioneer existence, while in the older sections it steadily extended its dominion over politics, economics and all the other interests of life. The time came, in 1925, when Turner himself confessed the need of "an urban reinterpretation of our history." A true understanding of America's past demands this balanced

From Arthur M. Schlesinger, *Paths to the Present* (New York: Macmillan, 1949), pp. 210-33. Copyright 1949 by The Macmillan Company. Reprinted by permission of the publisher. The late Arthur M. Schlesinger was Francis Lee Higginson Professor of History at Harvard University.

view—an appreciation of the significance of both frontier and city. The broad outlines of the particular role of the city are here suggested.

I

The Atlantic shore constituted the original frontier. Though the great bulk of colonists took up farming, the immediate object of the first settlers was to found a village or town, partly for mutual protection and partly as a base for peopling the near-by country. Other advantages presently gave these places more lasting reasons for existence. There persons could enjoy friendly intercourse with their neighbors as in Europe and there, too, ply a variety of occupations. These communities, besides taking in farm produce for consumption and export, developed local manufactures, arts and crafts and carried on fisheries and an active overseas trade. Without the articles so provided—hardware, firearms, medicine, books and the like—the colonial standard of living would have greatly suffered.

In time the coastline became beaded with towns, many of them so well situated with respect to geographic and trading advantages as to grow into the great cities of today. The establishment of settlements like Albany, New York, and Lancaster, Pennsylvania, moreover, foreshadowed the rise of urban communities inland. If colonial towns seem small by modern standards, it is well to remember that this was also true of contemporary English provincial towns, for industrialization had not yet concentrated populations in the homeland. Philadelphia with thirty thousand people on the eve of Independence was one of the metropolises of the British Empire.

From the outset townsfolk were plagued with what would today be called urban problems. There were disadvantages as well as advantages in living closely together, and as these disadvantages became flagrant, the citizens were moved to action. Though they seldom assumed community responsibilities willingly, their record compares favorably with that of provincial cities in the mother country. To combat the increase of crime the public-spirited in some places maintained night watches out of their own purses, while in others the city fathers required persons to take turns guarding the streets by night on pain of fines. Sooner or later, however, the taxpayers accepted such policing as a normal municipal charge. The fire hazard early prodded the authorities to regulate the construction of chimneys, license chimney sweeps and oblige householders to keep water buckets; and when these measures fell short of the requirements in the eighteenth century, the people formed volunteer companies which, long after the colonial period, continued to be the chief agency of fire fighting. The removal of garbage generally devolved upon roving swine and goats, while drainage remained pretty much an unsolved problem, though occasional individuals laid private sewers. The pressure of urban needs also fertilized American inventiveness, producing Franklin's lightning rod and the fireplace stove.

Thanks to the special conditions of town life, the inhabitants developed a sense of collective responsibility in their daily concerns that increasingly distinguished them from the individualistic denizens of the farm and frontier. Other circumstances served to widen the distance. As cities grew in size and substance, they engaged in economic rivalry with one another which tended to ignore the interests of the intervening countryside. Boston, New England's metropolis, possessed special mercantile advantages which enabled her for nearly a century to maintain a position of primacy in British America, with New York, Philadelphia and lesser centers hardly more than commercial satellites. These other ports, however, contended as best they could for their share of ocean-borne traffic and briskly cultivated their local trading areas.

New Yorkers, for example, successfully fought the proposal of the East New Jersey authorities to erect a competing port at Perth Amboy, and for a time prevailed upon the provincial legislature to tax and otherwise hinder Boston's commerce with eastern Long Island. The fur trade with the Iroquois brought Manhattan and Albany businessmen immense profits, but watchful of every advantage, the New Yorkers contested with Philadelphia for the trade of the Susquehanna region. Farther to the south, Charleston and Virginia merchants staged a similar struggle for the deerskins of the back country, with the South Carolinians emerging victorious. An unpremeditated result of this fierce competition for pelts was a notable stimulus to westward exploration and settlement.

As the eighteenth century advanced, Boston's rivals came to stand securely on their own feet, aided by their rapidly developing hinterlands. New York now completed its sway over western Connecticut and eastern New Jersey, while Philadelphia merchants annexed western Jersey, Delaware and northern Maryland. So eager was the pursuit of business that the chambers of commerce of New York and Charleston, formed respectively in 1768 and 1774,

antedated all others in English-speaking lands. Meanwhile, in the tributary areas, these early indications of urban imperialism bred jealousies and resentments which were to reach critical intensity in later times. The metropolis of a given region became a symbol of deception and greed. "A Connecticut Farmer," venting his spleen against New York in the *New-London Gazette*, August 17, 1770, expressed the fervent hope that "the plumes of that domineering city may yet feather the nests of those whom they have long plucked."

Happily for America's future independence, Britain's new revenue policy after 1763 struck deeply at the roots of urban prosperity. The business classes rallied promptly to the defense of their interests and, heedless of the dangers of playing with fire, secured the backing of the artisan and mechanic groups. Throughout the decade of controversy the seaports set the pace of resistance, supplying most of the militant leaders, conducting turbulent demonstrations at every crisis, and mobilizing farmer support when possible. Even in rural commonwealths like Virginia and Maryland the most effective steps of opposition were taken when the colonists consulted together at the provincial capitals while attending legislative sessions. Boston's foremost position in the proceedings may well have arisen from the fact that, having recently fallen behind Philadelphia and New York in the commercial race, she was resolved at any cost to stay the throttling hand of Parliament. With the assembling of the First Continental Congress the direction of the movement shifted to Philadelphia, the principal city, presently to become first capital of the new Republic.

The colonial town, however, was more than an embodiment of political and economic energies or a means of gratifying the gregarious instinct. Cities, then as now, were places where one found a whole gamut of satisfactions. Ports of entry for European settlers and goods, they were also ports of entry for European thought and standards of taste. At the same time their monopoly of printing presses, newspapers, bookstores and circulating libraries exposed the residents to a constant barrage of mental stimuli. Hence the spirit of innovation expressed itself quite as much in intellectual as in commercial undertakings. It was townsfolk who led in founding schools and colleges. The protracted battle to establish inoculation as a preventive against smallpox was fought out in the cities. The first great victory for freedom of the press was won by a Philadelphia lawyer defending a New York editor. Besides, mere numbers of people made it possible for the professions to become more clearly differentiated, so that a merchant need no longer plead cases before the courts nor a clergyman practice medicine. Before the colonial period ended, bar associations and medical societies were flourishing in New York, Boston and elsewhere, and medical schools were drawing students to Philadelphia and New York.

The man whom a biographer has called the "first civilized American" was the scion of not one but many cities. Boston, Philadelphia, London and Paris, all contributed to Benjamin Franklin's intellectual growth and social understanding. Few elements of American culture but are indebted to his fostering care: printing, publishing, journalism, belles-lettres, education, the postal service, theoretical and applied science. All these achievements rested in final analysis on that interest, encouragement and financial support which a populous community alone could provide. How diligently Franklin utilized these advantages appears in his autobiography, which reveals, for instance, how he set about arousing his fellow Philadelphians to the need of such projects as a lending library, a hospital and the American Philosophical Society.

Yet Franklin with all his many-sidedness was less "civilized" than urban society as a whole: his ambit of interests did not embrace the theater, architecture or an active concern with art. In all these lines the pre-Revolutionary town, with the steady increase of wealth and leisure, showed a growing maturity. Cities, for example, vied with one another for the services of outstanding portraitists. Robert Feke, a Newport artist, painted also in Boston, New York and Philadelphia. John Singleton Copley of Boston found on a visit to New York "so many that are impatient to sit that I am never at a loss to fill up all my time." Like the Philadelphian Benjamin West, however, Copley eventually removed to London.

The city, both in its internal life and external relations, deeply affected colonial society politically, economically and culturally. Though in 1776 only about one in twenty-five Americans dwelt in places of eight thousand or more, the urban influence, thanks to its concentrated character, carried far greater weight than its fractional representation in the population indicated. Moreover, city residents evolved a pattern of life which not only diverged from, but increasingly challenged, that of countryside and frontier. These restless, aspiring urban communities foreshadowed the large role that cities would play in the years ahead.

II

That role townsfolk began to assume in the struggle for a strong central government following the Revolution. As a contemporary newspaper observed, "The citizens in the seaport towns . . . live compact; their interests are one; there is a constant connection and intercourse between them; they can, on any occasion, centre their votes where they please." Faced by interstate trade restrictions, stay laws and growing social turmoil, the urban business and cerditor classes feared for their future welfare and the sanctity of property rights. The framing and ratification of the Constitution represented in considerable degree their triumph over the debtor groups and small farmers of the interior. In the circumstances the first Congress under the new instrument was greeted with petitions from Philadelphia, New York, Boston and Baltimore for a tariff to protect American manufactures.

The underlying strife between city and country led also to the formation of the first national parties under the Constitution. Hamilton's famous financial plan, intended to benefit urban capitalists and thus indirectly the nation, formed the rallying point of the Federalists, while Jefferson, imbued with physiocratic notions, organized the Republican opposition. The Virginia planter, unlike the New York lawyer, dreaded the growth of a powerful moneyed class, and in the spread of cities he foresaw a repetition of the social miseries typical of the Old World. "For the general operation of manufacture," he declared, "let our work-shops remain in Europe." He could even regard calmly the destructive yellow-fever epidemics in Philadelphia and other ports in the 1790's, since the pestilence might teach people to avoid populous centers.

The contrasting social ideals and economic motives reflected in this early alignment of parties evoked differing views of constitutional interpretation and of particular measures. From that day to this the chief business of American politics has been to reconcile these interests in furtherance of the national welfare. True, the relative purity of the original groupings gradually became diluted. With the multiplication of urban voters through the years, Jefferson's political progeny, confident of the agricultural South, sought also to appeal to city wage earners. By the same token, the opposition party tended to be a coalition of city businessmen and Northern farmers. Hence each party came in time to constitute a battleground of contending urban and rural elements within its own ranks, a situation which continues to characterize American politics.

III

The westward surge of population beginning shortly after the Revolution has obscured the fact that the leading Atlantic cities, though hard hit by the war, soon resumed their growth, and that with the coming of the nineteenth century the rate of urban development in the nation at large far surpassed that of rural development. Between 1800 and 1860 the number of townsfolk increased twenty-four times while the rural population merely quadrupled. By 1810 one out of every twenty Americans lived in communities of eight thousand or more, by 1840 one out of every twelve, and by 1860 nearly one in every six.

Paradoxically enough, westward migration itself helped to bring this about, for the transappalachian region bred its own urban localities. Serving at first chiefly as distributing centers for commodities from the seaboard, these raw settlements quickly developed into marts where local manufacturer and farm dweller exchanged products. Pittsburgh early began to make glass, shoes, iron castings, nails and textiles, and already in 1814 the *Pittsburgh Gazette* was complaining of the sooty atmosphere. By that time Cincinnati, farther down the river, boasted of two woolen mills and a cotton factory, and its meatpacking business was winning it the sobriquet of Porkopolis. Emboldened by such achievements, apparently every cluster of log huts dreamed of equal or greater eminence. The Indiana pioneers, for example, hopefully named their forest hamlets Columbia City, Fountain City, Saline City, Oakland City and Union City or, setting their sights still higher, called them New Philadelphia, New Paris, Rome City and even New Pekin.

Meanwhile, in the East, scores of cities sprang into being, generally at the fall line of the rivers, where water power was available for manufacturing. As the budding industrialists looked about for new worlds to conquer, they, together with the Eastern merchants and bankers, perceived their El Dorado in the settling West. Soon New York, Philadelphia and Baltimore were racing for the trade of the transappalachian country. This clash of urban imperialisms appeared most strikingly perhaps in the rivalry for transportation routes to the interior. The Baltimoreans led off by building a turnpike to tap the eastern terminus of the Cumberland Road, which the federal government by 1818 had completed as far as Wheeling on the Ohio. In order to counter this move, Pennsylvania promoted Philadelphia's wagon trade with the West by subsidizing a chain of roads to Pittsburgh. New York City, utilizing her natural advantages, now secured state backing for an all-water artery through upstate New York from the Hudson to Lake Erie.

The instant success of the Erie Canal, opened in 1825, forced a change of strategy on Manhattan's competitors. Philadelphia with legislative help promptly instituted a part-water, part-land route through the mountains, while Baltimore pushed the project of a Chesapeake and Ohio canal. Other citizens in the Maryland metropolis, however, conceived a bolder plan. Just as the canal had bested the turnpike, why should not the newly invented railroad best the canal? The construction of the Baltimore and Ohio Railroad, begun in 1828, once more altered the major weapons in the contest. In the next quarter of a century Baltimore and Philadelphia completed their rail connections with the West, New York acquired two lines, and Boston, which had lagged behind during the turnpike and canal eras, recovered some of the lost ground with a railroad linking up with the eastern extremity of the Erie Canal.

Middle Western towns, following the Eastern example, meanwhile entered upon a somewhat similar struggle, each seeking to carve out its own economic dependencies and spheres of influence and to profit from the new ties with the seaboard. By 1840 a network of artificial waterways joined Cleveland and Toledo on Lake Erie with Portsmouth, Cincinnati and Evansville on the Ohio. As in the East, however, the arrival of the steam locomotive changed the situation. Now every up-and-coming municipality strove by hook or crook to become a railroad center, sometimes plunging heavily in debt for the purpose. And looking to the commercial possibilities of the remoter West, Chicago, St. Louis, Memphis and New Orleans concocted rival plans for a Pacific railroad—a maneuvering for position that had political repercussions in Congress and contributed to the passage of the Kansas-Nebraska Act in 1854, which it was thought would facilitate the building of a transcontinental line from St. Louis. This law, by authorizing slavery by "popular sovereignty" in a region hitherto closed to it, helped to set the stage for the Civil War.

The progress in transportation facilities, confined largely to the North, spurred urban development throughout that part of the country. The Erie Canal, reinforced by the rail arteries to the West and the magnificent harbor at the mouth of the Hudson, established conclusively New York's pre-eminence on the seaboard and in the nation. From only sixty thousand inhabitants in 1800 its population (not counting Brooklyn) climbed to eight hundred thousand by 1860, outdistancing Philadelphia and placing it next to London and Paris in size, while Philadelphia with more than half a million was in 1860 larger than Berlin. Brooklyn, Baltimore and Boston came next in size. Indicative of the westward movement of the urban frontier was the fact that at the latter date all the other places of over a hundred thousand—New Orleans, Cincinnati, St. Louis and Chicago—were in the heart of the country. Chicago, though the smallest of these cities in 1860, had already gathered the economic sinews which would make it New York's chief rival before the century closed. Anthony Trollope, observing the Midwest in 1861, remarked that except for a few

river and lake sites "settlers can hardly be said to have chosen their own localities. These have been chosen for them by the originators of the different lines of railway." Urban communities greatly augmented the demand for farm products, accelerated the invention of labor-saving implements like the steel plow and the reaper and thus furthered commercial agriculture, which in turn speeded city growth.

To master the new complexities of urban living demanded something more than the easygoing ways of colonial towns. Enlarged populations called for enlarged measures for the community safety and welfare, whether by government or otherwise. As might be expected, the bigger cities set the pace. After the lethal yellow-fever visitations of the 1790's frightened Philadelphia into installing a public water works, other places fell into line, so that more than a hundred systems came into existence before the Civil War. Unfortunately, ignorance of the yet to be discovered germ theory of disease fastened attention on clear water instead of pure water, thus leaving the public health still inadequately protected. To cope with the growing lawlessness the leading cities now supplemented night watches with day police. In 1822 Boston instituted gas lighting and in 1823 set the example of a municipally owned sewerage system. About the same time regular omnibus service was started on the streets of New York, to be followed in the next decade by horsecars running on tracks.

Fire fighting, however, continued generally in the hands of volunteer companies. Though Boston organized a paid municipal department in 1837 and Cincinnati and other Western towns greatly improved the apparatus by introducing steam fire engines in the 1850's, New York and Philadelphia, thanks to the political pull of volunteer brigades, resisted changes in equipment and waited respectively till 1865 and 1871 to municipalize their systems. The cities did nothing at all to combat the evil of slums, an unexpected development due to the great inrush of foreign immigrants into the Atlantic ports in the forties and fifties. Even more serious for the ordinary citizen was the growth of political machines, rooted in the tenement-house population, the fire companies and the criminal classes, and trafficking in franchises for the new public utilities. Appointments to government office for partisan services, first practiced in Eastern cities, preceded and led directly to the introduction of the spoils system into state and national politics.

The "diversities of extreme poverty and extreme wealth," which Edwin H. Chapin etched so sharply in *Humanity in the City* (1854), distressed the tenderhearted and gave rise to most of the reform crusades of the pre-Civil War generation. Compact living facilitated the banding together of such folk and also the collection of funds. Never before had America known so 'great an outpouring of effort to befriend the poor and the handicapped. Under urban stimulus arose the movement for free schools, for public libraries, for married women's property rights, for universal peace, for prison reform, for a better deal for the insane. The new conditions of city life begot a social conscience on the part of townsfolk which would be lasting of effect and which increasingly differentiated them from their brethren on the farm and frontier.

In these crowded centers, too, the labor movement took form, for the vaunted safety valve of the frontier failed to work for the mass of the wage earners. "The wilderness has receded," declared Orestes A. Brownson in 1840, "and already the new lands are beyond the reach of the mere laborer, and the employer has him at his mercy." Early in the preceding decade trade-unions began to appear, first along the seaboard, then at such inland points as Buffalo, Pittsburgh, Cincinnati and St. Louis; and for a short time a national federation flourished. But the long economic slump following the Panic of 1837 shattered most of the organizations and turned the thoughts of men like George Henry Evans, a New York labor editor, to plans for siphoning excess urban inhabitants into the federal domain by means of free farms. During the discussions over the homestead bill of 1852, even an Alabama member urged Congress "to help the cities to disgorge their cellars and their garrets of a starving, haggard, and useless population." But the House measure failed in the Senate, and until the Civil War further attempts went awry because of Southern fears that anti-slavery Northerners would fill up the Western territories. In any event the farm population would have been the chief beneficiaries, for it is unlikely that urban workingmen could have been enticed to exchange known ills for the hazards and uncertainties of pioneering.

Besides, along with the known ills went cultural opportunities and advantages absent from the countryside. The fast-growing cities afforded the largest public America had yet known for the appreciation and patronage of letters and the arts, and greatly increased the chances for the discovery and recruitment of talent in all fields. Townsfolk, moreover, were the first to feel the bracing impact of new currents of European thought. A varied and vital intellectual life resulted which directly or indirectly affected all members of the community, including the children, for whom municipal authorities now began to provide free high schools.

Newspapers and magazines proliferated. The first modern publishing houses sprang up. The theater became firmly established, native players like Charlotte Cushman and Edwin Booth winning additional laurels in England. Artists multiplied, being at last assured of adequate support at home, and the founding of the National Academy of Design in 1826 raised New York to the position of the country's chief art center. In literature also this richly creative period demonstrated urban superiority, with Boston, Cambridge and Concord largely responsible for the "flowering of New England," and New York and Philadelphia, even Cincinnati and St. Louis, making their own bids for fame. Only in architecture did the city botch the possibilities, for the mushroom growth of population forced new construction at a pace that ignored aesthetic considerations. The typical city, even in its wealthy residential sections, exhibited a fantastic patchwork of styles.

Whatever the attractions of town life, the elevenfold leap in urban population between 1820 and 1860 aroused increasing dismay and foreboding among rural folk who saw their own sons and daughters succumbing to the lure. "Adam and Eve were created and placed in a garden. Cities are the results of the fall," cried Joseph H. Ingraham, a popular religious novelist. Country preachers joined in denouncing these human agglomerations "cursed with immense accumulations of ignorance and error, vice and crime," while farm journals implored the young not to sacrifice their manly independence in order "to fetch and carry" and "cringe and flatter" for a miserable pittance. Political attitudes further mirrored the deepening distrust. Western opposition to the Second United States Bank sprang largely from alarm at the control of credit facilities by the "great cities of the Northeast, which," according to Missouri's Senator Thomas Hart Benton, "have been for forty years, and that by force of federal legislation, the lion's den of Southern and Western money— that den into which all the tracks point inward; from which the returning track of a solitary dollar has never yet been seen."

Since, however, the West was growing its own towns and cities, it was becoming steadily more like the Northeast, whereas the South, chained by Negro slavery to agriculture, contained few sizable cities and those mostly at its edges. The widening breach between North and South was in no small part due to these divergent tendencies. Every year sharpened the contrast between the urban spirit of progress animating the one section and the static, rural life of the other. Few important industries existed below the Mason and Dixon line. Though illiteracy prevailed among the mass of whites as well as blacks, little or nothing was done to further free schools, and the North's humanitarian crusades were derided as Yankee fanaticism. Moreover, the Southerners, lacking the nerve centers for creative cultural achievement, fell behind in arts, letters and science. "It would have been surprising had they not desired secession," remarked Anthony Trollope, in America shortly after Fort Sumter. "Secession of one kind, a very practical secession, had already been forced upon them by circumstances. They had become a separate people, dissevered from the North by habits, morals, institutions, pursuits and every conceivable difference in their modes of thought and action." Beyond the tie of language, he went on, "they had no bond but that of a meagre political union in their Congress at Washington."

In addition, their economic life lay under thrall to the Northern business community. "It is a hopeless task," affirmed the South Carolinian William Gregg, "to undertake to even approximate to the vast sums of wealth which have been transferred from the South to the North by allowing the Northern cities to import and export for us." For twenty years before the war, Southern commercial conventions sought ways and means to escape this bondage, but the hope of creating their own trading and financial centers was vain so long as lands and Negroes held a superior attraction for capital. It was no mere coincidence that Charleston, dropping rapidly behind the Northern ports, initiated every disunionist movement in the entire South from Jackson's time onward; and the *Charleston Mercury's* bitter comment in 1858 that "Norfolk, Charleston, Savannah, Mobile, are suburbs of New York" suggests that other places shared the bitterness.

Withdrawal from the Union coupled with free trade with England seemed the answer, since then, it was believed, "Charleston in the course of ten years will become a New York"; and other localities nursed similar hopes. Under the circumstances the leading towns and cities strongly supported the movement for separation. Even New Orleans, despite its large infusion of Northerners and foreign-born, chose twenty secessionists and only four unionists to the state convention summoned to take action. Not surprisingly, the Confederate authorities on assuming power invalidated the private indebtedness—estimated variously at forty to four hundred millions—owing to Northern merchants, bankers and manufacturers. But the North's industrial might and greater man power overwhelmed the South in war as well as in peace.

IV

In the generation following the Civil War the city took supreme command. Between 1860 and 1900 the urban population again quadrupled while the rural merely doubled. With one out of every six people inhabiting communities of eight thousand or over in the earlier year, the proportion rose to nearly one out of four in 1880 and to one out of three in 1900. Considerably more than half of the urban-moving throng gravitated to places of twenty-five thousand and upwards. Since every town dweller added to his effectiveness by association with his fellows, even these figures understate the city's new role in the nation. Nevertheless the sheer growth of particular localities is amazing. By 1890 New York (including Brooklyn) had about caught up with Paris, while Chicago and Philadelphia, with over a million each as compared with New York's two and a half million, then outranked all but five cities in Europe. In the Far West, Los Angeles jumped from fewer than 5000 in 1860 to more than 100,000 in 1900, and Denver from nothing at all to 134,000, while in the postwar South, Memphis with a bare 23,000 in the former year surpassed 100,000 in the latter. "The youngest of the nations," wrote Samuel L. Loomis in 1887, "has already more large cities than any except Great Britain and Germany." Thanks to the progress of settlement in the West and the burgeoning of industry in a South emancipated from slavery, the city had at last become a national instead of a sectional institution.

As urban centers grew in size and wealth, they cast an ever stronger spell over the American mind. Walt Whitman, returning to Greater New York in September, 1870, after a short absence, gloried in the "splendor, picturesqueness, and oceanic amplitude of these great cities." Conceding that Nature excelled in her mountains, forests and seas, he rated man's achievement equally great "in these ingenuities, streets, goods, houses, ships—these hurrying, feverish, electric crowds of men." (More tersely, Dr. Oliver Wendell Holmes, weary of hearing Cowper's line, "God made the country and man made the town," retorted, "God made the *cavern* and man made the *house!*") Little wonder that the young and the ambitious yielded to the temptation. "We cannot all live in cities, yet nearly all seem determined to do so," commented Horace Greeley, adding that with "millions of acres" awaiting cultivation "hundreds of thousands reject this and rush into the cities."

The exodus from the older countryside was especially striking. While the cities of Maine, Vermont, Massachusetts, Rhode Island, New York, Maryland and Illinois gained two and a half million people between 1880 and 1890, the rural districts of these states lost two hundred thousand. The drain of humanity from backwoods New England left mute witnesses in deserted hill villages and abandoned farms. In the nation as a whole, 10,063 townships out of 25,746 in thirty-nine states and territories shrank in population during the decade. Some of the rural decline was due to the shifting of agriculturists from older regions to the free unworked lands of the trans-Mississippi West, but the phenomenon was so widespread—and, indeed, as characteristic of Europe during these years as of America—as to evidence the more potent and pervasive influence of the city. True, the 1880's merely climaxed a historic trend. In the century from 1790 to 1890 the total population had grown 16-fold while the urban segment grew 139-fold. Hence the celebrated announcement of the Superintendent of the Census in 1890 that a frontier line no longer existed can hardly be said to have marked the close of "the first period of American history." Rather it was a tardy admission that the second period was already under way.

The lusty urban growth created problems which taxed human resourcefulness to the utmost. Though European precedent helped solve some of the difficulties, American ingenuity in most respects outdistanced that of Old World cities. The record is extraordinary. Hardly had New York in 1870 opened the first elevated railway than San Francisco contrived the cable car, and hardly had the cable car begun to spread over the country than Richmond demonstrated the superiority of the electric trolley system, and Boston at the end of the century added the subway. The need for better lighting prompted the invention of Brush's outdoor arc lamp and Edison's incandescent bulb for indoors, and in another application of electric power the telephone brought townsfolk into instant communication. By means of the apartment house and the department store cities simplified problems of housing and shopping, while by means of the steel-framed skyscraper they saved further ground space by building their business districts upward. Density of population also led to more effective protection of the public health by turning to account the principles of the germ theory of disease just being discovered abroad. Before the century's close nearly every municipality of ten thousand or over had one or more officials charged with the duty of charting and checking communicable maladies. The bigger cities had become healthier places to live than many rural sections.

These civic advances, however, came at a price already beginning to be evident before the Civil War. Americans had developed their political institutions under simple rural conditions; they had yet to learn how to govern cramped populations. Preyed upon by unscrupulous men eager to exploit the expanding public utilities, municipal politics became a byword for venality. As Francis Parkman wrote, "Where the carcass is, the vultures gather together." New York's notorious Tweed Ring denoted a sickness that racked Philadelphia, Chicago, St. Louis, Minneapolis and San Francisco as well. "With very few exceptions," declared Andrew D. White, "the city governments of the United States are the worst in Christendom—the most expensive, the most inefficient, and the most corrupt."

Though an irate citizenry succeeded now and then in "turning the rascals out," the boss and the machine soon recovered control. Nevertheless, the good-government campaigns ventilated the abuses of municipal misrule and aroused the humane to the worsening plight of the urban poor. Under reform prodding, the New York legislature from 1865 onward adopted a series of laws to combat the slum evil in America's metropolis, though with disappointing results. More fruitful were the steps taken by private groups in Manhattan and elsewhere to establish social settlements and playgrounds and to replace the indiscriminate almsgiving of earlier times with a more rational administration of charity. Religion, awakening to the social gospel, helped out with slum missions and institutional churches. In the city, too, trade-unions made a new start, organizing the swelling army of urban workers on a nation-wide basis, joining with the reformers in securing factory legislation and gradually winning concessions from the employing class. Occasional voices with a foreign accent advocated socialism or anarchism as the remedy for the city's gross disparities of wealth and want, while Edward Bellamy in *Looking Backward* offered a home-grown version of communism in his fanciful account of Boston as it would be in the year 2000.

The increasing tension of living was evidenced in a variety of ways. Masses of people reared in a rustic environment had suddenly to adapt themselves to the frantic urban pace. One outcome was a startling growth of neurasthenia, a word coined by Dr. George M. Beard of New York in his work *American Nervousness* (1881), which traced the malady to the hurry and scurry, the din of the streets, the frenzied struggle for existence, the mental excitements and endless distractions. From the ranks of the high-strung, Mary Baker Eddy gathered most of her converts to the new religion of Christian Science, and for much the same reason townsfolk now gave enthusiastic support to organized sports. Flabby muscles unfitted most persons for direct participation, but they compromised by paying professional contestants to take their exercise for them. If, as a magazine writer said, nervousness had become the "national disease of America," baseball, partly as an antidote, became America's national game.

The stress of existence seemed only to enhance creative powers, however. The cities, re-enacting their role of the "fireplaces of civilization"—Theodore Parker's phrase—provided compelling incentives to cultural achievement, multiplying colleges, public libraries and publishing houses and founding art museums, art schools and conservatories of music. A Henry James might still find Europe an intellectually more congenial milieu, but William Dean Howells, Mark Twain and Joel Chandler Harris discovered the needed stimulus at home; and the same held true of all or nearly all the leading painters, sculptors, architects, composers, playwrights and scholars. A statistical study showed that localities of eight thousand and more gave birth to almost twice as many men of note as their proportionate share, and that in fields like science, engineering, art and literature the ratio was far greater. But even such computations do less than justice to the city, for there, too, gifted newcomers from the countryside and foreign shores entered their Promised Land. Civic pride prompted the holding of two great expositions, one at Philadelphia in 1876 and the other at Chicago in 1893. That the second and grander took place in an inland metropolis revealed how decisively urbanization had altered the face of traditional America.

The new age of the city rested upon an application of business enterprise to the exploitation of natural resources such as mankind had never known. The city, as insatiable as an octopus, tended to draw all nutriment to itself. Railroads, industrial combinations, investment capital, legislative favors, comprised the means. There arose a complex of urban imperialisms, each striving for dominion, each battling with rivals and each perforce yielding tribute to the lord of them all. "Every produce market, every share market," observed James Bryce, "vibrates to the Produce Exchange and Stock Exchange of New York."

As the city forged ahead, imposing its fiat on less developed regions, the rift between country and town widened portentously. Historians speak of a new sectionalism aligning West and South against East in these years, but Charles B. Spahr in *The Distribution of Wealth in the United States* (1896) pointed out more acutely that the antagonism "only exists in so far as the East is the section of the cities, while the South and West are the sections containing the great body of the farmers." Everywhere rural life was in chains: "The people on the farms and in the villages in the East have shared no more in the advancing wealth of the past quarter of a century than the people on the farms and villages of the South and West." He estimated that city families possessed on the average almost three times as much as country families.

The passage of years heightened the husbandman's conviction of being a second-class citizen, of losing out in the technological and cultural progress that dowered townsfolk. He lacked the telephone, electric lights, central heating, plumbing, sewerage, street cars, recreational facilities. Herbert Quick in after years remembered the women as "pining for neighbors, for domestic help, for pretty clothes, for schools, music, art, and the many things tasted when the magazines came in." The drift of youth to the cities emphasized the shortcomings, embittering those who stayed behind, even though they loved the land and would not have left if they could. The farmer, moreover, accepted too readily the urban estimate of his calling. Once acclaimed by orators as the "embodiment of economic independence," now, remarked a magazine writer, he was the butt of humorists: "The 'sturdy yeoman' has become the 'hayseed.'"

This feeling of rural inferiority, this growing sense of frustration, underlay the political eruptions in the farming regions: the Granger movement in the 1870's, the Farmers' Alliances of the eighties and the Populist conflagration in the nineties. Each time specific economic grievances like steep freight rates, high interest charges and low crop prices stirred the smoldering embers into blaze. These were tangible hardships which the farmers demanded the government remove by such measures as railroad regulation and silver inflation. It fell to the greatest of the agrarian champions, addressing the Democratic national convention in 1896, to hurl the ultimate challenge at urban imperialism. "Burn down your cities and leave our farms, and your cities will spring up again as if by magic," cried William Jennings Bryan of Nebraska in a speech that won him the nomination, "but destroy our farms and the grass will grow in the streets of every city in the country." In the election that followed, the big cities of the East and Midwest, including New York which for the first time went Republican, responded by casting decisive majorities against the Democrats and free silver.

V

No one in 1900 could have foreseen the transformation which the twentieth century was to effect in both town and country. In the cities the reformers made steady progress in bridling the predatory forces which, in James Bryce's familiar phrase, had made municipal government "the one conspicuous failure of the United States." Early in the century a crusading type of mayor rode into power—men like "Golden Rule" Jones and Brand Whitlock in Toledo, Tom Johnson in Cleveland and Emil Seidel in Milwaukee—who aroused the citizens from their apathy and showed that elected officials could zealously promote the public good. Even more important was the introduction of the commission-manager plan of government, which by 1948 came to prevail in nearly eight hundred places. A radical departure from the clumsy older form, which imitated the checks and balances of state governments, the new system copied the streamlined structure of business corporations, with the commission corresponding to the board of directors and the city manager resembling the president or general manager named by the board to conduct detailed affairs. In nearly every case the reform quickly justified itself, though eternal vigilance by the voters continued to be the price of ensuring the best results.

Alongside these improvements occurred the first sustained attempts at city planning. Instead of letting urban communities evolve in hit-and-miss fashion, the endeavor now was to guide their growth in the interests of sightliness and the people's convenience, safety and health. By an extensive use of zoning ordinances, appropriate locations were mapped for business and factory districts, residential neighborhoods, recreational facilities; and the New York legislature's adoption of an effective tenement-house code in 1901 inspired other states and municipalities to a vigorous attack on the slum evil, though it was not till the 1930's that the federal authorities took a hand in the matter. Already by 1922 a hundred and eighty-five towns and cities had set up official bodies to chart over-all programs of development, and by 1940 the number had risen to well over a thousand. City planning, moreover, stimulated interest in county planning and state planning and helped create the atmosphere for the New Deal's ventures in regional and national planning.

These advances went hand in hand with a further piling up of townsfolk. By 1930 approximately half the nation dwelt in localities of eight thousand or more and nearly a third in centers of one hundred thousand or more. Urban dominance was further enhanced by the emergence of great metropolitan districts or regions. These "city states" had begun to form in the nineteenth century as swifter means of transportation and communication flung the inhabitants outward into the suburbs, but it was the coming of the automobile and motor truck and the extension of electricity and other conveniences into the surrounding territory that gave these supercommunities their unprecedented size and importance.

Each consisted of one or more core cities with satellite towns and dependent rural areas, the whole knit together by economic, social and cultural ties. The hundred and thirty-three metropolitan regions in 1930 grew to a hundred and forty by 1940, when they contained almost half the total population. New York's region overlapped four states, an irregular tract twice the area of Rhode Island with 272 incorporated communities and intervening farm lands. Chicago's embraced 115 incorporated places, and San Francisco's 38. Subdivided into independent municipalities, the people faced enormous difficulties in looking after such common governmental concerns as policing, sewage disposal, public health and schooling. Some students, despairing of any other solution, proposed separate statehood for the larger metropolitan regions. New and unanticipated strains have been placed on a federal system framed in the eighteenth century for a simple agrarian economy.

Of all the new trends in urban development, however, none had such profound effects as the altered relationship of country and city. Historians generally attribute the decline of the free-silver movement in the late nineties to the discovery of fresh sources of gold supply and an uptrend of crop prices, but probably the more fundamental cause was the amelioration of many of the social and psychological drawbacks of farm existence. The introduction of rural free delivery of mail after 1896, the extension of good roads due to the bicycle craze, the expanding network of interurban trolleys, the spread of party-line neighborhood telephones after the basic Bell patents expired in 1893, the increase of country schools—all these, coming shortly before 1900, helped dispel the aching isolation and loneliness, thereby making rustic life pleasanter.

Yet these mitigations seem trifling compared with the marvels which the twentieth century wrought. The automobile brought farm families within easy reach of each other and of the city; the motorbus facilitated the establishment of consolidated schools with vastly improved instruction and equipment; while the radio introduced new interests and pleasures into the homes themselves, shedding its benefits impartially on country and town. At the same time the mechanical energy used in agriculture grew eightfold between 1900 and 1935, thus lightening the husbandman's toil and adding to his opportunities for leisure. Moreover, the state and national governments increasingly employed their powers to improve the farmer's economic and social status. The Smith-Lever Act, passed by Congress in 1914, provided for agricultural-extension work in rural communities through county agents; the Federal Farm Loan Board, created in 1916, offered long-term loans at relatively low rates of interest; and the Smith-Hughes Act of 1917 appropriated public funds for teaching vocational agriculture and home economics in country high schools. Such enactments reached a climax in the 1930's when the New Deal embarked upon far-reaching programs of rural betterment like the Tennessee Valley and Columbia River developments, the Triple-A, government-aided electrification and measures to boost farm tenants up the ladder to ownership. Though inequalities remained, the tiller of the soil had come to share many of the comforts and refinements once belonging only to townsfolk. He had attained a position in American society of which his Populist forebears could hardly have dreamed.

Just as rural life became more urbanized, so urban life became more ruralized. Wooded parks, tree-shaded boulevards, beautified waterfronts, municipal golf courses, athletic fields and children's playgrounds multiplied, while an increasing army of white-collar workers and wage earners piled into motorcars and buses each night to go farther and farther into the suburbs. Within the metropolitan regions population actually grew faster in the rustic outskirts between 1930 and 1940 than in the central cities. Retail trade too felt the centrifugal tug, and even factories showed a tendency to move into outlying villages where taxes, rent and food cost less. The extension of giant power will doubtless speed the trend, affording more and more townsfolk a chance to live and work and bring up their children in country surroundings. The dread specter of atomic-bomb attacks may operate to the same end in the interests of national military security.

Thus the twentieth century has been spinning a web in which city and country, no longer separate entities, have been brought ever closer together. When the city encroaches sufficiently on the country and the country on the city, America may hope to arrive at a way of life which will blend the best features of both the traditional ways. The people will have within grasp the realization of Plato's vision of a society in which "youth shall dwell in a land of health amid fair sights and sounds and imbibe good from every quarter; and beauty, the emanation of noble works, will flow into the eye and ear like an invigorating breeze from a purer region and imperceptibly woo the soul from infancy into harmony and sympathy with the beauty of reason."

From humble beginnings in the early seventeenth century the city thus traced a varied course. In Europe the modern urban community emerged by gradual stages out of the simple town economy of the Middle Ages; by comparison, the American city leaped into being with breath-taking speed. At first servant to an agricultural order, then a jealous contestant, then an oppressor, it now gives evidence of becoming a comrade and co-operator in a new national syn-thesis. Its economic function has been hardly more important than its cultural mission or its transforming influence upon rural conceptions of democracy. The city, no less than the frontier, has been a major factor in American civilization. Without an appreciation of the role of both the story is only half told.

Some Consequences of the Urban Movement in American History

W. Stull Holt

About twenty-five years ago I had what I thought was an original idea. It was a new interpretation of American history which would bring understanding and give meaning to the meaningless. I remember distinctly that I had been contemplating the achievement of Frederick Jackson Turner and that I asked myself if another hypothesis could not be found to give significance to otherwise unrelated facts and to give reputation to its originator. Were there not other movements comparable to the westward movement? I do not know anything about the psychological explanations of creative thinking but with "a jar, a shock of the cerebral processes," or a flash of clarity, or what you will, I saw the answer to my inquiry.[1] There had been another movement, the urban movement. The more I thought of it the greater the significance it as-sumed.[2] If the westward march of the American people had been the key to American development, as Turner said, it was a key that worked only during the agricultural period of American history. For the more recent period the key was the cityward march of the American people. That and that more than anything else could explain the transition from the United States of Thomas Jefferson to the United States of Franklin Roosevelt.

Alas, my pride in having conceived this tremendously important, fertile, and valid generalization was soon to be rudely shocked. I reread Channing's fifth volume. There he has a chapter entitled "The Urban Migration" and it begins with these sentences, "The westward movement forms a distinct picture in our annals. No less distinct, but much less known, is the rise of manu-

From *Pacific Historical Review*, Vol. XXII (November 1953), pp. 337-51. Reprinted by permission of the publisher. W. Stull Holt is Professor of History at the University of Washington.

facturing and commercial cities and towns, principally in the Northeast, and the development therein of classes and of an industrial social system." That is all the generalization he gives, as the balance of the chapter is devoted to the details of city life in the period 1815 to 1846, but when I reread this passage I remembered the deep impression it had made on me the first time I had read it and I knew where my original idea had originated. More disturbing developments were to follow because it soon became apparent that other students were considering the influence of the urban movement on American history. Notable among them was Arthur M. Schlesinger of Harvard who in 1933 published *The Rise of the City* as Volume X of *A History of American Life*. In this he tried to use the urban movement to synthesize the events of American history from 1878 to 1898, when the United States "was trembling between two worlds, one rural and agricultural, the other urban and industrial."[3] His attempt was by no means completely successful but it was a remarkable pioneer effort and certainly showed he had the hypothesis in mind. A more direct expression of it appeared in an article by him in 1940 entitled "The City in American History" in which he formulated some generalizations but did not consider what I believe to be the most significant consequences of the urban movement.[4]

Of course, the fact that many Americans had been moving to the cities was a phenomenon which had long been observed by all sorts of people. Novelists were aware of it and popular writers turned from western cowboy fiction to stories of city adventure.[5] Those of us who are old enough to have read the numerous Horatio Alger books

—our equivalent of the more recent "comics" and especially of Orphan Annie—will remember how often the impossibly virtuous and priggish young men went to the wicked cities to prove that virtue is rewarded. Popular songs also recorded the urban movement. One such, entitled "In the Heart of the City That Has No Heart" announced that "She wanted to roam so she left the old home" and went "to the city of no pity."[6] Statisticians measured the growth of cities. Sociologists, more than any other group, studied the process and developed the subject of urban sociology with a large literature which historians have neglected to their cost. But few of these people, even of the sociologists, saw more than isolated facts and none used urbanization as the basis for a new synthesis. The work of the historians has so far only scratched the surface. Indeed most of their efforts have been histories of individual cities or of some small part of the urban movement. Thus Bessie Pierce's *A History of Chicago*, Bayrd Still's *Milwaukee*, or Constance McL. Green's *Holyoke, Massachusetts*, to name no others, are like the various histories of sections of the frontier such as Roosevelt's *Winning of the West* before Turner in his famous essay saw the forest as well as the trees.[7]

The failure of the historians to study the process of urbanization and its consequences is in truth curious. One would think that after several generations of writing and study of the westward movement someone would have looked for an eastward movement. Had that been done the problem of the growth of cities in the United States must have been confronted, since urbanization and the eastward movement have been intimately related.[8] That the cities have increased and since 1830 at a more rapid rate than the entire population is known and is readily established by the census reports which show that between 1790 and 1940 the total population increased 33 times while urban population increased 369 times.[9] The growth of the cities must have resulted from one, or several, of all of four processes: surplus of births over deaths, immigration from abroad, immigration from rural areas within the United States, and the expansion of city boundaries by the annexation of surrounding territory. It is impossible to determine the exact contributions of each of these to the remarkable growth that American cities have experienced. Yet it is reasonably certain that the migration from farm to city has furnished most of the large numbers involved. Fred A. Shannon has estimated that for the period between 1860 and 1900 for every urban dweller who moved to a farm there were 20 farmers who moved to a city. This conclusion leads him to suggest that Turner made a colossal mistake in describing the frontier as an avenue of escape for the oppressed city laborers and that the roles were reversed with the cities acting as a safety valve for the dissatisfied rural population.[10] The facts seem to support Professor Shannon's version of the safety valve theory.

One of the important questions, the answer to which would add significantly to our understanding, if we but knew it, concerns the quality of the migrants to the cities. Have they been the most energetic, ambitious, and intelligent or have the successful and intelligent remained in agriculture while the shiftless and stupid turned from failure on the farm to possible betterment in the city? Speculation is tempting and easy. While not enough to carry conviction, the little real evidence I have found is contained in a number of studies of small samples by sociologists. For example 2,544 high school students in rural Kansas who had been given intelligence tests in 1922-1923 were studied in 1935. It was found that those who had moved to cities were those who had been measured superior in the tests of thirteen years earlier and those who had gone to the largest cities had made the highest rating. Out-of-state migrants had been superior to those who remained in Kansas.[11] Comparable studies made in various sections of the country point to the same conclusion, namely, that the urban movement has taken away the abler rural inhabitants.

Whatever the facts on this point may be, and however much the entire and neglected history of the urban movement needs to be told, I wish to bring to your attention some of its significances, some of the ways in which the urban movement explains important facts not otherwise fully understood or reveals hitherto unsuspected relationships. The first and what I believe to be the most pregnant result of the urban movement has been its effect on the birth rate. This, in turn, by a chain reaction has radically altered life in America. The crude American birth rate, i.e., the number of live births per thousand of population (and this is the best figure we can have for most of the period of United States history) was in the fifties from 1790 to 1830, in the forties until 1860, had dropped to thirty by 1900, to twenty by 1930 and then fluctuated between 16.6 and 18.9 until World War II. The dramatic reversal of this steady decline which resulted from the war is apparently a temporary phenomenon and even at its peak in 1947 the birth rate only equalled that of 1915.

The amazing drop in the birth rate by which it was cut in half between 1860 and 1930 is a revolution of the first magnitude with consequences reaching every phase of American history. It is also a direct result of urbanization. Had Theodore Roosevelt said "urban suicide" instead of "race suicide" he would have been describing the process accurately. It is in the cities that the greatest decline in the birth rate has regularly occurred.[12] A most thorough and convincing study based on the census of 1920 shows that the birth rate for every group—native white, foreign-born white and Negro—was lower in the cities than in the rural areas and that the larger the city the lower the birth rate.[13] The same fact is revealed by other studies at different dates. The most accurate index to population change is what is known as the net reproduction rate which has been ascertainable in the United States only during the last generation or so when reliable birth and death records have been kept. The net reproduction rate gives the number of girl babies born to 100 mothers living through the ages 15 to 50 who will also live through the ages 15 to 50. Obviously a rate of 100 would mean a stationary population. The figure for 1940 for the entire United States was 96. This means that the American people were not reproducing themselves and that in spite of deceptive yearly increases the population was actually declining. The reason for this situation was the very low net reproduction rate of the urban portion of the population. It was only 74 compared to 114 for the rural non-farm rate and 144 for the rural farm rate.[14] In

1940, as in 1930, all the cities and in 1920 all cities above 25,000 were parasites. They could maintain their population, or grow in size, only because of the steady influx of people from the rural sections. Growth by the annexation of surrounding territory or by immigration since 1920 have been negligible factors.

The consequences of the drop in the birth rate resulting from urbanization are far-reaching and numerous. I propose to suggest only three of them to which historians have as yet given no attention.[15] The first is that the American population has grown older, or, more accurately, a steadily increasing percentage of the population is in the older age brackets.[16] America is no longer remarkable for the youthfulness of its leaders, as it was to European observers in the first part of the nineteenth century. The median age for members of the House of Representatives climbed from 41.81 in 1825 to 47.48 in 1875 and to 53.56 in 1925 and for Senators from 46.5 to 51.5 to 57.5 in the same years. Indeed, leaders of all types—judicial, diplomatic, military, naval, religious, and educational—are significantly older than their predecessors in the same positions.[17] If the widely held belief regarding age and conservatism is correct, both the American voters and their political leaders have been more and more inclined to conservative thinking and action. A parallel trend to older men in the leadership of the American economy may have meant that there has been less and less willingness to expand or experiment and more and more a desire to preserve the existing situation.

Conclusions on these points cannot be established by the historian's usual documentation so he generally ignores them completely. Yet surely the fact that in 1850 only 8.9 per cent of the total population were over 50 years of age and as late as 1880 only 11.8 per cent while in 1940 the figure was 20.4 per cent has implications which cannot be disregarded. Businessmen have not failed to note that the changing age composition of the population means a constantly expanding market for the goods and services older people desire. Politicians have been keenly aware of the situation. A good case could be made for the proposition that pensions for "senior citizens" have been a greater political issue during the past several decades than pensions for veterans in spite of the two world wars that produced so many veterans. The medical profession has shown its awareness of the aging population by developing a new field of specialization known as geriatrics. We who study and write history must take cognizance of this meaningful change even though we must go to unaccustomed sources for evidence.

Documentation is still more difficult in the second consequence of the reduced birth rate to which I wish to allude. This is the novel psychological experience of the Americans who grew to maturity in the period of the low birth rate. The difference between a childhood in a family where there are five or more other children and one in a family containing one or no brother or sister must be great. When the one- or two-child family became typical for so large a proportion of the population it would seem inevitable that changes in behavior and attitudes would be noticeable. Perhaps the fact that the new family pattern has produced more egocentric individuals helps to explain the high rates of divorce and of mental maladjustment which have been char-

acteristic of urbanized America. It is not possible to speak with assurance of any of the effects of the small family on the social history of the United States since, as far as I know, no psychologist, sociologist, or historian has isolated the facts and told the story.

The facts are more easily discerned in the only other result of the drop in the birth rate to which I will refer. This is the freedom that urbanization and its birth rate have brought to American women, a freedom which has nothing to do with legal status but which is nonetheless real. In the period before the urban movement transformed life in America, woman spent her middle years, or those between 20 and 45, either pregnant or taking care of young children. The women who have gone through those years in urban America have had a vastly different experience and have known a physical and temporal freedom previously inconceivable in any human society except for a very small minority. The numerous labor-saving devices contributed by the industrial revolution, itself both a cause and an effect of the urban movement in Western civilization, merely exaggerated the freedom conferred by the small families. It is perhaps correct to say that the urban American woman has "known" rather than "enjoyed" this freedom. As a group they were caught unprepared to devote the unaccustomed leisure to activities which would yield mental, physical, or spiritual satisfaction. They have been frustrated and bored to the point of having to kill time by shopping, going to the movies, playing bridge, or in the other ways which are readily observable, and which have sometimes been seriously treated by novelists and more frequently facetiously by male cartoonists. But the historians, even those who have written social history, have yet to deal with the new phenomenon of urbanized women, though it involves directly approximately half of the American people and indirectly all the others.

The older population, the psychological patterns accompanying small families, and the altered life of American women are only some of the results of the drop in the birth rate which in turn resulted from the urban movement. Lest it be thought that the urban movement leads only down the garden path to the strange and tangled fields of psychology and sociology, let us turn to the familiar and broad highway of political history. Here the historian feels securely at home. Yet even here much will be missed and much misunderstood if not interpreted in the light of the urban movement. The most obvious facts are well known. The political opposition between urban and rural sections and the decisive part played by urban voters during the past generation have been so notorious that every radio commentator and every textbook in political science refers to them as something that every sophisticated adult knows.[18] It was in the big cities that Franklin D. Roosevelt received his huge majorities. An analysis of Roosevelt's majority of 11,000,000 in 1936 shows that with the South omitted he received 67 per cent of the votes in all cities of over 25,000 population but only 56 per cent of the rest of the votes. Nine large cities with 15 per cent of the total population gave Roosevelt 28 per cent of his majority.[19] Since Roosevelt also carried most of the rural districts in 1936, the importance of the urban vote may have been obscured. It was to be made clearer in 1940 when Roosevelt received 60.3 per cent of the votes in all

the cities of over 400,000 population and when he carried every one of them except perhaps Cincinnati, where the vote was reported with that of the rest of Hamilton County as a Willkie majority of less than 7,000. In most of the large states it was clearly the city vote which gave Roosevelt the vote of the state. Thus his majority of 230,000 in New York State resulted from his majority of 730,000 in New York City. He carried Illinois by 94,000 because he carried Chicago by 295,000. In Missouri his majority of 90,000 was possible because St. Louis and Kansas City gave him majorities of 65,000 and 30,000. In Ohio his state majority was approximately equal to his majority in Cuyahoga County in which most of the voters live in the city of Cleveland. He received the vote of Wisconsin because his majority of 73,000 votes in Milwaukee overbalanced a Willkie majority of 52,000 in the rest of the state. He failed by a narrow margin to win the vote of Michigan although Detroit gave him a majority of 173,000.[20]

The repetition of this political phenomenon has made practically everyone aware of its existence, but historians have not yet begun to seek illumination and meaning in political events by looking for a possible urban-rural conflict. Was the Progressive party of 1912 primarily an urban affair as one scholar has intimated but as none has demonstrated?[21] Was the Bryan campaign of 1896 actually a movement of agrarian discontent as it is usually pictured? The one study of urban and rural voting in that election shows that in the states which McKinley won, Bryan had greater strength in the cities than in the rural areas, while in the states which Bryan carried his strength was rural.

This, at least, proves an urban-rural tension in all sections.[22]

How necessary it is to consider urban-rural differences in politics can be appreciated by an examination of the election of 1860. As is well known, an interpretation of the Civil War has been widely accepted, especially through the writings of Charles A. Beard, which states that the controversy over slavery was largely superficial and that in essence the war was a struggle between an agricultural society and a rising industrialized or capitalistic society. There is no doubt that as one result of the war the government was dominated and its policies were fixed by the industrial, commercial, and financial groups acting through the Republican party. There is also some evidence to support the thesis that the conflict between these rival interests located in separate geographical regions brought on the war. But when the election of 1860 is analyzed by urban and rural voting some facts emerge which seriously challenge if they do not destroy this thesis. With minor exceptions, the cities of the Northeast voted against Lincoln or, if they gave him a majority it was a smaller majority than the surrounding rural area. This was true of industrial cities like Lowell and Worcester, Massachusetts, as well as of Boston or New York where commercial interests may have prevailed over industry. The rising capitalistic and industrialized society was located in these northeastern cities. Clearly the people there did not recognize Lincoln and the Republican party as their champions. It was the rural northeast that gave Lincoln the votes of those states. Curiously a comparable situation existed in the South where the extremists had their greatest strength in the rural areas. Most of the

few cities there were in the South gave majorities to the moderates, Douglas or Bell, or if to Breckinridge it was a smaller majority than the surrounding rural area gave him.[23] Some explanation other than the conflicting economic interests of agriculture and industry is required.

Indeed none of the political history of the United States since the Civil War can be considered adequate if the possible implications of an urban-rural interpretation have not been explored. National politics in America is always significantly affected and is frequently determined by its constituent elements of state politics. And in state after state the vital fact has been the continuous conflict between urban and rural voters. For years all political activity in New York State has had meaning only when interpreted in terms of New York City versus up-state. In Illinois politics has been a reflection of the antagonism between Chicago and down-state. The same situation is duplicated widely. In state after state the split between urban and rural groups is the dominant theme and in many cases the words are the same. There is scarcely a state where the urban population has not just grounds for complaining of the rotten borough system that prevails. In Ohio the census of 1940 showed that there were 698,000 people in the 22nd congressional district, most of them in the city of Cleveland, and only 163,000 in the rural 5th district. There had been no revision of congressional districts in Ohio since 1913. Some citizens of Cook County, Illinois, tried in 1946 to secure corrective action by legal means. In a suit they complained that Cook County, which meant Chicago, with 52 per cent of the population of the state had only nine of the twenty-five seats in Congress. The Supreme Court rejected their plea by a vote of four to three.[24] In the minority opinion, Mr. Justice Black pointed out that the complaining citizens lived in congressional election districts with populations ranging from 612,000 to 914,000, while nineteen other districts had populations under 400,000 and seven of the latter had under 200,000. The districts had been established in 1901 on the basis of the census of 1900 and there had been no redistricting in the subsequent forty years in spite of shifts in population. The local political tensions symbolized in this fashion are sometimes as important in determining who is to be elected to the Senate or to Congress as are national party labels and are often the decisive factor in deciding nominations for office within the party.

Great as is the significance of urbanization for an understanding of political activity, it is of still greater significance in accounting for the revolution in American political thought. The urban movement, more than any other development, contains the explanation of the shift from Jeffersonian democracy to the Franklin D. Roosevelt conception of democracy. Probably I should not identify the contemporary concept of democracy with Franklin D. Roosevelt for what I refer to is the very broad political philosophy to which the other Roosevelt and both Tafts also subscribed. The American people, conservatives as well as liberals, once believed that that government is best which governs least. They now believe, in varying degrees perhaps but nonetheless believe, that government should not be limited to the bare police protection of life and property but should take positive action to promote the well-being of the people. No historian, or

other type of scholar, has yet given an adequate account of how this revolution in political thought has occurred. It resulted, I suggest, chiefly from the fact that the American people moved to cities, in that new environment sought solutions to pressing problems and then adjusted their theory to fit the facts.[25]

The earliest instances in the expansion of urban governmental activity were concerned with the protection of health and with the fundamental utilities. Water was supplied by private companies until complaints about service or the magnitude of the problem created sufficient pressure to compel the city to take over the task. This history repeated itself in practically every large city in the United States. The persons involved did not think in the language of political philosophy. Neither did authorities of Naugatuck, Connecticut, consider the question of socialized medicine when they provided for a daily health inspection of school children and appointed a public school nurse and a dental hygienist.[26] In rural America where the farmer milked his own cow the government felt no responsibility for the sanitary conditions of milking. In urban America the protection of milk from contamination became a necessity and an operation in which government exercised control over both farmer and city resident.

The same cycle of new urban problem, pressure, and expanded political authority took place again and again. In 1864 a wealthy New Yorker named Henry Bergh, who had been shocked at the sight of brutality to animals, organized a society for the prevention of cruelty to animals. He and the other members of the society did not rely on education or moral appeals but turned to government and persuaded the legislature of New York to pass a law. Then Mr. Bergh would halt overloaded street cars that some poor horse was trying to pull, would make passengers alight and even knock protesters into the gutter.[27] The movement spread to other cities where branches of the society were established and where in every case the solution of the problem was the extension of the government into a new area. In rural America each man could do with his animals what he would. When men and animals moved to the city the treatment of the animals became a problem for others and then for the government. The sphere of unrestricted freedom of individual action had been limited and the sphere of governmental activity expanded.

The solution of one problem would often be adapted to another. In 1874 a little girl was found in New York City beaten and starved by a foster mother. Since the law permitted no interference between parent and child short of mayhem or murder, she was brought as an animal to the Society for the Prevention of Cruelty to Animals. At once a society for the prevention of cruelty to children was organized and it successfully asked government to expand its activities so as to come between parent and child. In other cities similar demands led to similar action. Conceivably cruelty to children in rural areas might have produced the same results but in fact it did not.[28]

In rural America a man could spit on the ground wherever and whenever he wished. This rural habit became a public nuisance in the cities and again the scope of governmental authority was extended. The lady who led the successful agitation for an antispitting ordinance in Milwaukee urged every club woman to "carry a little silver bell to be rung at every offender, so that the man who dares to transgress will be greeted by a veritable chorus of bells at every expectoration."[29] But she and the others really depended on the power of government to correct this social and distinctively urban problem.

In rural America a man could always build any kind of a shelter or building he wished and could do with his property what he wanted, at least after Jeffersonian ideas of personal liberty supplanted the earliest mercantilist policies which tried to compel him to grow certain crops. But when more and more Americans lived in cities and when the results of unrestricted use of property became increasingly unsatisfactory a demand arose for social control. Zoning ordinances, building codes, tenement house laws, and all the other exercises of control over property by government to prevent slums or to solve urban problems represented departures from earlier standards or justifiable political action.

So it was with a host of problems which existed only when people lived in cities. None of the reformers who agitated for more government did so for principle's sake or under the influence of any political philosophy. Most of them would have denied emphatically that they wanted what we call a welfare state. All they saw was an existing evil or problem for which the obvious solution was the exercise of power by political society. Although it is not amenable to proof by documents or statistics, surely the belief is reasonable that a half century of such action must have been a major factor in the subsequent shift in theory to an open recognition of the fact of the welfare state.

These then are some of the significances of the urban movement in American history from 1850 to 1950. Yet valid and fruitful as the thesis may be, this generalization like Turner's about the frontier can easily be misused. This hypothesis rests on the assumption that city people are alike, or at least manifest some uniformities, and are different in some respects from people living in rural areas. There is evidence to support this assumption.[30] There are also weaknesses in it. A city contains not just one but many environments as well as many groupings of people and for many human actions more meaningful conclusions can be obtained by not treating city populations as a unit. For instance, in studying elections it is profitable to look for voting by economic classes or ethnic groups within a city.[31] There are also certain powerful forces which tend to obliterate urban-rural differences. Nationalism does so. Sectionalism too may dominate over the influences tending to differentiate a city population from its rural neighbors. One has only to compare the attitude of both urban and rural South on FEPC proposals with those of the North to appreciate that sectionalism is to be reckoned with. A further limitation is that there is no reason to expect the urban-rural differences or tensions to remain indefinitely. Indeed the automobile, good roads, the telephone, radio, national advertising, and an amazing concatenation of other developments have been steadily urbanizing the rural areas.

Nevertheless and in spite of all qualifications, it is true, I believe, that for an understanding of American life and American history from the Civil War to the present no more fruitful interpretation exists than the significance of the urban movement.

NOTES

1. Fulmer Mood uses these terms in describing Turner's achievement ("Turner's Formative Period," in The Early Writings of Frederick Jackson Turner [Madison, 1938], 5).

2. May I at once anticipate much criticism by saying I know that the urban movement has been closely associated with the industrial revolution, indeed, in some respects the two have been so closely integrated that it is impossible to attribute certain consequences to one or the other of these phenomena. The urban movement accompanied the industrial revolution in other countries than the United States and to be correctly understood should be studied in all its manifestations. It may also be used to cast new light on the history of other peoples. There were, of course, cities and urban populations and possibly urban consequences prior to the industrial revolution.

3. P. xiv. He was anticipating the sociologist who later wrote that "By placing the urbanization of the Western world in the center of our perspective, there is some promise that novel understandings will emerge," that the city is the center from which the influences of modern civilized life radiate to the ends of the earth, and that the problems of modern civilization are typiclly urban problems (Louis Wirth, "The Urban Society and Civilization," American Journal of Sociology, XLV, [1940], 743-755).

4. Mississippi Valley Historical Review, XXVII, (1940), 43-66.

5. George A. Dunlap, The City in the American Novel, 1789-1900 (Philadelphia, 1934); John Levi Cutler, Gilbert Patten and his Frank Merriwell Saga (Orono, Maine, 1934), 26.

6. For this one I am indebted to Dr. William A. Diamond. Anyone seeking the motives of the urban migrants could well ponder the words of "How Are You Gonna Keep 'Em Down on the Farm?"

7. The most recent and best summary of the work of the historians in this field is Blake McKelvey, "American Urban History Today," American Historical Review, LVII, (1952), 919-929.

8. The shift of population to the cities has also resulted from a northern and northeastern movement. In this the Negroes have had a prominent but not dominant part. From 1900 to 1920 Negro urban population of the country increased by more than a million and a half while Negro rural population increased by less than 72,000. Some of the Negroes went to Southern cities, but most went to the North (T. J. Woofter, "The Negro Migration to Cities," The Survey, LIX, [February 15, 1928], 647-649). There has also been a westward rural-urban movement, but since most of the cities in the United States, especially during the nineteenth and early twentieth centuries, have been in the East, the eastward movement has been the most important.

9. This, following the recent practice of the Bureau of the Census, counts places with 2,500 or more population as urban. Schlesinger points out that between 1790 and 1890 the total population had grown 16-fold and the urban population 139-fold ("The City in American History," p. 58). His calculations used a population of 8,000 as the test for a city, as was done in the census of 1790.

10. Fred A. Shannon, *The Farmer's Last Frontier* (New York, 1945), 55, 356-359. A more detailed analysis can be found in his article "A Post Mortem on the Labor-Safety-Valve Theory," *Agricultural History*, XIX (1945), 31-37. John M. Gillette and George R. Davis in a study of the period 1900-1910 estimate that immigration contributed more than rural migration ("Measure of Rural Migration and Other Factors of Urban Increase in the United States," *American Statistical Society Publications*, XIV, [1915], 642-653). A contrary estimate for the same period is given by Earle Clark ("Contributions to Urban Growth," *ibid.*, 654-671). A good account can be found in the Report of the Committee on Population Problems to the National Resources Board (*The Problems of a Changing Population*, [Washington, 1938], 83-118). It is not possible to trace the steps by which people migrated from rural to urban America. Did they first move to small towns and then to large cities, as was done in Sweden, or did they jump immediately from farm to metropolis? In the census of 1940 the American people were for the first time asked where they had previously lived, in this case in 1935, so that some picture of internal migration is possible for those years. (*Sixteenth Census of the United States: 1940. Population. Internal Migration 1935 to 1940* [Washington, 1943]). See also, Warren S. Thompson, *Migration Within Ohio, 1935-40* (Oxford, Ohio, 1951); Calvin F. Schmid and Manzer John Griswold, "Migration Within the State of Washington: 1935-40," *American Sociological Review*, XVII, (1952), 312-326. Dorothy Swaine Thomas, *Research Memorandum on Migration Differentials*, Social Science Research Council Bulletin 43 (1938), is an important study and contains an annotated bibliography of

many of the most important sociological studies of the subject. A curious thesis bearing on urban growth can be found in Mark Jefferson, "The Law of the Primate City," *Geographical Review*, XXIX, (1939), 226-232.

11. Noel P. Gist and Carroll D. Clark, "Intelligence as a Selective Factor in Rural-Urban Migrations," *American Journal of Sociology*, XLIV, (1938), 36-58; Thomas C. McCormick, "Urban Migration and Educational Selection—Arkansas Data," *ibid.*, XXXIX, (1933), 355-359; Wilson Gee and Dewees Runk, "Qualitative Selection in Cityward Migration," *ibid.*, XXXVII (1931), 254-265; Wilson Gee, "A Qualitative Study of Rural Development in a Single Township: 1900-1930," *ibid.*, XXXIX, (1933), 210-221; W. Parker Mauln, "Selective Migration from Small Towns," *American Sociological Review*, V (1940), 748-758. For a different conclusion see Carle C. Zimmerman, "The Migration to Towns and Cities," *American Journal of Sociology*, XXXIII, (1927), 105-109, and *ibid.*, 237-241. Here it is stated that the cities attract the extremes, unskilled labor and professional groups, while the farms attract or retain the mean strata of society. See also Pitram Sorokin and Carle C. Zimmerman, *Principles of Rural-Urban Sociology* (New York, 1929).

12. A. J. Jaffe, "Urbanization and Fertility," *American Journal of Sociology*, XLVIII, (1942), 48-60, asserts that the differential in fertility between urban and rural areas has existed not only in Europe but among the populations of Latin American countries, among at least some of the native Asiatic populations, among the Moslems in Palestine, in Europe during the entire nineteenth century, and in Sweden as early as 1760. Dennis W. Brogan has called my attention to the fact that this statement is not true for Ireland. There the extreme poverty on the small farms so often prevented a son from marrying until his father died that the birth rate in the rural areas was lower than that in the cities.

13. Warren S. Thompson, *Ratio of Children to Women, 1920*. Census Monograph XI (Washington, 1931). He gives the following figures on pp. 142 and 177:

Children under 5 per 1,000 Women Aged 20 to 44

	Urban				Rural
	Over 100,000	25,000 to 100,000	10,000 to 25,000	2,500 to 10,000	
Native white	341	390	434	477	721
Foreign-born white	679	766	861	873	998
Negro	257	294	338	370	743

14. Philip M. Hauser, "Population," *American Journal of Sociology*, XLVII (1942), 816-828.

15. There are, of course, others which might be mentioned. For instance, one has only to compare the houses built in the 1870's when six or more children were the normal expectation with the houses built recently to appreciate the effect

of the drop in the birth rate on American architecture.

16. I do not mean that the drop in the birth rate was the sole cause of this phenomenon. Obviously the reduction in the death rate was also a factor in producing it.

17. Harvey C. Lehman, "The Age of Eminent

Leaders: Then and Now," *American Journal of Sociology*, LII (1947), 342-356. He gives the median and mean ages of these and many other types of leaders at various periods throughout the nineteenth century.

18. One of the first textbooks to show an awareness of the significance of urban politics was Arthur N. Holcombe, *The Political Parties of To-day*, published in 1924. His later textbook, *The New Party Politics*, published in 1933, placed great stress on urban politics.

19. David Lawrence, *Who Were the Eleven Million* (New York, 1937).

20. Seattle *Post Intelligencer*, November 9, 1940. In his stimulating book on *The Future of American Politics* (New York, 1952) Samuel Lubell points out (pp. 31-34) that the big city pluralities won for the Democrats in 1940, 1944, and 1948 and that the Republican hold on the largest cities as a group was broken in 1928.

21. George E. Mowry, *Theodore Roosevelt and the Progressive Movement* (Madison, 1946), 280.

22. William Diamond, "Urban and Rural Voting in 1896," *American Historical Review*, XLVI, (1941), 281-305.

23. Ollinger Crenshaw, "Urban and Rural Voting in the Election of 1860," in Eric F. Goldman, ed., *Historiography and Urbanization* (Baltimore, 1941), 43-66.

24. Colegrove et al. v. Green et al., 328 U.S. 549. An appendix gives the congressional districts in each state with the largest and smallest populations for 1897, 1928, and 1946.

25. This does not mean that only an urbanized society will produce a government with a jurisdiction extending beyond the basic protection of life and property. Primitive societies have done so. Sumptuary laws have been known in rural societies. The mercantilist governments expanded the scope of their operations. Even in the period of Jefferson and Tom Paine there were individuals who accepted the current doctrine but urged departure from it by the government if they were to benefit. All that is meant here is that in the nineteenth and twentieth centuries, in America at least, the changes in practice and thought resulted from the fact that more and more Americans lived in cities.

26. Constance McL. Green, *History of Naugatuck, Connecticut* (New Haven, 1948), 157. The experience of Chicago with the problem of supplying water, which agrees in essential outline with that of every other city whose history I have read, is summarized in Bessie L. Pierce, *A History of Chicago* (New York, 1937-) II, 330-334. How urban experience changed conceptions on public education is well described in Charles Hirschfeld, *Baltimore, 1870-1900: Studies in Social History* (Baltimore, 1941), chapter III.

27. Allan Nevins, *The Emergence of Modern America, 1865-1878* (New York, 1927), 332-334.

28. *Ibid.*, 334-335.

29. Bayrd Still, *Milwaukee: The History of a City* (Madison, 1948), 386.

30. The differences between the urban and rural birth rates and the voting records of the two groups constitute the best evidence. A prominent sociologist testing this point selected at random eighteen social characteristics on which data were available. They included such items as ratio of young to middle-aged, percentage of adults married, sex ratio of the single, death rate, amount of rent, home ownership, automobile per capita, postal receipts, church membership, percentage of children in school. He found that in fourteen of the eighteen characteristics the cities of the North and South were more alike than the cities of either section were like the rural area of the same section (William F. Ogburn, *Social Characteristics of Cities* [Chicago, 1937], chapter VII). Too many of the social characteristics are almost inherent in the nature of cities to make this test conclusive, yet it deserves the consideration of the historian.

31. This point is developed in an exceedingly good essay by William Diamond, "On the Dangers of an Urban Interpretation of History," in Eric F. Goldman, ed., *Historiography and Urbanization* (Baltimore, 1941).

The City as a Social Organism

LEO F. SCHNORE

In his discussion of the emergence of the first urban areas, Lewis Mumford speaks of "little communal village cells, undifferentiated and uncomplicated, every part performing equally every function, turned into complex structures, organized on an axiate principle, with differentiated tissues and specialized organisms, and with one part, the central nervous system, thinking for and directing the whole."[1] This is the image of the city as a social organism.

What is the justification for such a view? We might begin with some specification of basic terms—"city," "social," and "organism." The term "city," of course, has many meanings, but the most common conception is legal or political; that is, the city is regarded as a kind of corporate entity possessing certain delegated powers. Thus, Eric E. Lampard quite properly observes that "city" is "a name given to certain urban communities in English-speaking countries by virtue of some legal or conventional distinction."[2] For our purposes, however, such a conception is unduly restrictive.

We are interested in cities around the world, not just in English-speaking countries; and we are interested in cities of many forms, from the earliest urban islands that rose above the seas of agricultural villages, through city-states, through preindustrial and post-industrial cities to the Megalopolis of today. Thus, I think it is well to keep a certain looseness in our conceptions of the city, for the city is many things— political, economic and social, historical and geographic, physical, and even psychological. For present purposes, however, we can think of "city" as referring to a particular type of community—the urban community—a large, densely settled community devoted to nonagricultural activities.

Next, we will have to consider what "social" might mean. How shall we understand this term? It happens that the literature in sociology exhibits a very interesting tension or ambivalence between two fundamentally different views. In the first view, "social" has reference to what we shall call consensus—an explicit or implicit understanding based on some kind of exchange of meaning within a shared frame of reference or universe of discourse. This view takes man's capacity for symbolic communication of ideas as central, focussing upon mental interpenetration, and a meeting of minds is seen as the critical feature of human conduct. Thus the city, along with such social forms as family and society, is regarded as one expression of a uniquely human capacity for meaningful communication.[3] This view is unquestionably valuable. It points to an aspect or facet of city life that is worthy of study in its own right. Yet, an exclusive emphasis upon consensus misses a more fundamental sense in which the

From *Urban Affairs Quarterly*, Vol. I, No. 3 (March 1966), pp. 58-69. Reprinted by permission of the publishers, Sage publications, Inc., Beverly Hills, California. Leo F. Schnore is Professor of Sociology at the University of Wisconsin.

term "social" has a great deal of meaning—a sense that permits us to speak of infrahuman social animals such as the so-called social insects. Such animals may be able to communicate rudimentary "ideas," but they are certainly limited by genetically determined characteristics to exchanges far less complex than those made by human beings.[4]

This second view of "social" stresses symbiosis or interdependence, whether or not it is mediated by the use of symbols. The relevance of such a view to any examination of the city becomes clear when one reminds himself that the city is simply not a self-sufficient or wholly independent entity. Rather, it is dependent—dependent on other areas such as rural areas for food and fiber and (through most of history) for men, or migrants to the cities. When we say that the city is dependent on other areas, whether we are thinking of rural areas or of other cities, we understand it to mean interdependent—especially in an economic sense. Cities offer things in return for still other things received by cities, whether these "things" are tangible goods or intangible services. The city is caught up in a kind of web of exchange relationships, supplying goods and services of a wide variety, including, most importantly, direction, control, integration, and coordination.[5]

All of these things are quite evident on the external side, for the interdependence of the city with other areas is obvious. The internal counterpart is somewhat less obvious. But, interdependence does exist within cities as well as between cities and other places, especially in the contemporary world. There is a territorial or geographic division of labor between the sub-areas making up the city. Most broadly, the division is between homes and work-

places, producing and consuming areas, between which there is a continuous flow of commodities, information, and people. It is exemplified by the stream of commuters between home and work. On a finer grain, there is also a division between areas devoted to different land uses—industrial, commercial, and recreational. From the standpoint of interdependence, then, the city is a "social" entity *par excellence*, for it displays both internal and external forms of symbiosis. Simultaneously, it reveals itself as an expression of symbolic communication between men.

It happens that these two faces of the city, the symbiotic and the consensual, were probably most clearly perceived in the 1920's by a sociologist at the University of Chicago, Robert E. Park. Park's thinking laid the groundwork for a singularly creative series of works by a group that came to be called the "Chicago School" of urban sociology. Park himself was a newspaperman before he was a sociologist, and he carried on a lifelong love affair with the city. In fact, he liked nothing better than to roam the alleys of Chicago and other cities, exploring backyards and observing cities from such vantage points as the lobbies of second-rate hotels. This was his style of work. And this is how he achieved his insight, for out of this habit of observation of city life and city ways, Park came to see that the city manifests a high degree of order and a remarkable level of organization *without* a perfect and somehow all-enveloping consensus. That is, the city was seen as an interdependent entity functioning quite effectively in the face of its inhabitants' indifference to an ignorance of the system as a whole. The residents of the city carried on their daily rounds and lived out their lives in their own small worlds, largely unaware of the larger unity of the city. At the same time, the city was exhibiting a life of its own.[6] This leads us quite naturally to the idea of the city as a so-called organism.

The notion of the community or the society as an "organism" is very old. The idea was especially prominent in the late nineteenth century, when biological reasoning, evolutionary and organismic, was in vogue. It probably reached its fullest and most detailed expression in the writings of Herbert Spencer, a British philosopher and sociologist. It has to be added that this mode of reasoning has since been virtually abandoned and, in the minds of many people, it has been thoroughly discredited. The historian Crane Brinton, for example, has asked, "Who now reads Spencer?" His question has been repeated by sociologists and others.[7] Without entering into a debate on the merits and demerits of analogous reasoning, without listing anew all of its uncritical uses, and without enumerating all the questionable purposes for which this particular analogy has been used, let us consider some of the ways in which the city may be considered *like*, though not identical to, an organism.

This approach is one way of bringing out the city's unit character, and a way of stressing the interdependence of its parts. In the words of Amos Hawley, a sociologist:

The community has often been likened to the human individual organism. So intimate and so necessary are the interrelations of its parts, it has been pointed out, that any influence felt at one point is almost immediately transmitted throughout. Further, not only is the community a more or less self-sufficient entity, having inherent in it the principle of its own life process; it has also a growth or natural history with

well-defined stages of youth, maturity, and senescence. It is therefore a whole which is something different from the sum of its parts, possessing powers and potentialities not present in any of its components. If not an organism, it is at least a super-organism.[8]

This quotation sketches the main themes of organismic thinking about the community, and despite the questionable remark about the self-sufficiency of communities, the passage is a valuable summary of the organismic view.

I would like to underscore two points about the city as an organism. First, the parts, the individual human beings making up the city, can be regarded as replaceable and interchangeable. They are very much like cells and, as in the organism, cells may come and go and the organism itself may survive. One might ask if this is radically different from the fact that the city may live on, while people come and go. Secondly, the city may grow and there are young, middle-aged, and old cities. Cities are founded, or born. There are periods of rapid growth, as in "boom towns." Cities live and die. There are "ghost towns," or dead cities.

If all this seems a bit fanciful, or as simply playing games with words, I would remind you that a reversal of the procedure is frequently used. In other words, a "social-system analogy" is often employed in order to say something about individual organisms. Communication systems, for example, are likened to the nervous system, with wires as ganglia, trunk lines as the spinal cord, etc. Similarly, transportation systems are likened to the circulatory system, with roads representing veins and arteries. The city is compared to the brain and the heart. Consider the following discussion of the "nervous system" of the higher organisms in a popular encyclopaedia:

In the "division of labor" characteristic of multicellular animals, a nervous system has developed as a group of tissues and structures that function to regulate the activities of the body. . . . The nervous system may be compared to an extensive communications system. It transmits messages (impulses) from sense organs (receivers) to a central switchboard (the brain). . . . From the brain or lower centers the impulses are transmitted to the proper regions or organs in such a way that an action appropriate to the stimulus is initiated.[9]

If one compares this passage with Mumford's idea quoted earlier, one sees that the analogy can be turned in either direction.

These considerations lead us to some observations concerning the internal aspects of the cities. Think first about some very simple demographic attributes, or population characteristics, such as the city's size and rate of growth. Without a detailed review of the evidence, one may assert that some of the most imaginative contemporary urban research in sociology, economics, and geography consists of spelling out the implications of variations in growth rates among cities or of identifying the concomitants of differences in size.[10]

Fast and slow growing cities are different structurally, whether regarded from economic, social, or political points of view. Large and small cities are also dissimilar, organizationally speaking. Size operates as a kind of limit upon complexity of organization. Large places are at least potentially more heterogeneous and more complex. Spencer himself observed that "it is a characteristic of social bodies, as of living bodies, that while they increase in size, they increase in structure. . . . The social aggregate, homogeneous when minute, habitually gains in heterogeneity along with each increment of growth; and to reach great size must acquire great complexity."[11] While his language is archaic, Spencer's thought is quite modern, at least in the sense that these problems are still being explored today. These words—complexity, heterogeneity, and homogeneity—are essentially structural or organizational terms.

What do we know about the structural characteristics of cities? We are coming to know a great deal about the internal social and economic organization of cities. In part, the ease of acquiring this knowledge stems from a convenient fact—that some structural features are very clearly represented in the spatial arrangement of parts, the way things are distributed in space. Space acts as a kind of mirror, reflecting structural patterns. Recall our earlier reference to the city as composed of homes and workplaces. There are areas devoted to residential uses and there are others given over to employment or productive uses. You can regard these as multicellular parts or "organs," bound together by flows of every description. In the organism, there are flows of nutrients, blood, and impulses of different kinds constantly being transmitted. In the community, there are flows of commodities, information, and individual persons.

We are also coming to know a great deal about why certain "organs" are located where they are in cities. For example, we are learning why "central offices" are truly central, why manufacturing plants of one type tend to be bound to the city core, while other types tend to move toward the periphery; why there should be selective decentralization of services; and why retailers of different goods take up different locations. We are also beginning to understand why certain units are segregated with others like themselves, as in manufacturing areas and financial districts, as well as why some highly dissimilar units are clustered together, functionally and spatially linked, as in the case of flower shops clustering around hospitals.

This kind of knowledge comes from observations that are very much like those of a laboratory technician examining tissue in a microscopic slide. This represents a static or cross-sectional view. We are also gaining new knowledge in longitudinal or historical terms. For example, we are learning how certain technological eras have left "scar tissue" in cities of a certain age, such as in pre-automobile cities. The street pattern and many of the other contemporary features of cities are residues of the past.[12] We are also beginning to find regularities in the changing shapes of cities.

We know least about a process that might be called "cellular turnover." That is, we don't know much about the appearance and disappearance of households and firms, the entry and exit of individual cells. We have imperfect knowledge, for example, of the absorption and assimilation of immigrants. We know very little about the general impact of the city on the individual. We also know very little about "social selection," the sifting and sorting that goes on, distributing people between occupations and industries, and distributing families through space.

We know a little about residential segregation according to socioeconomic status, and there is a great deal of interest in segregation according to race or color; but research hasn't been pursued to the point that we can speak of these things in any knowledgeable manner.[13] We can't say much about the social-psychological aspects of these problems. One might ask whether or not there is a distinctively urban personality. We have to say we don't know, though we do have a whole family of hypotheses that have been in the literature at least since the publication of a very influential essay by another Chicago sociologist, Louis Wirth, regarding "urbanism as a way of life."[14] In the conventional textbook treatment of this subject, in urban sociology and elsewhere, many of the ideas which Wirth expressed in tentative and hypothetical form have been taken as known facts. We know far less about "urbanism"—the individual in the city setting —than we do about "urbanization," or population concentration. We know a fair amount about the massing of people in cities from a demographic standpoint. We know quite a bit about urban structure, but we have very little in the way of a social psychology of urban life. I should also add that we know more about all of these things in the West than we do for cities in the rest of the world, and we know more about the present than we do about the past.[15]

Though it is being reduced, there is still a kind of cultural bias in our thinking about cities, and I regret to say that there is a kind of historical bias still present in the urban literature, despite the efforts of many historians and others interested in the past. I would submit that the present challenge is to learn more about cities or urban communities and to learn more about societies—both urban and urbanizing societies. We do know enough to appreciate the importance of context. We know of important differences in those societies in which city dwellers are in the majority, as opposed to those in which city dwellers form a small but growing minority.

This matter of context is important. Within cities there are important differences depending on the larger societal setting. For example, preindustrial cities are notably more "segmented," made up of highly similar parts which remain relatively independent of each other. Many cities of Asia and Africa consist of subcommunities which are physically separated from each other by walls and connected only by gates, but which are very much like each other in form and content, containing the same kinds of trade outlets and services.[16] This is in contrast to the closely linked, highly differentiated, yet interdependent form of city in the industrial West. In the United States it is useful to think of the urban community as composed of formerly quasi-independent cities, arranged like a sun and its planets, with a large metropolis surrounded by smaller urban subcenters. It is a community composed of legally distinct cities. In contrast, the segmented type is a city (a legal entity) composed of communities. These social segments or subunits are the true communities in many parts of Asia and Africa.

So much for the internal side. I have stressed the importance of context and I have emphasized the need for understanding cities that are found in different contexts. Externally, too, cities stand in different relations to the outside world. Many entrepôt cities in underdeveloped areas emerging from colonialism actually have closer ties to the cities in Europe and America than to their own hinterlands.[17] In contrast, our cities are intimately linked to rural areas, as well as to other cities, at home and abroad. In a society like our own, heavily urbanized and industrialized, it becomes hard to distinguish the urban from the rural. The diffusion of culture via the mass media has apparently led to a kind of homogeneity that is the counterpart of the heterogeneity we have been discussing.[18]

One cannot overstate the importance of context. To speak of context is only to remind ourselves that any understanding of the nature of an organism, even so complex an organism as the city, requires attention to its environment. We might ask ourselves this question: What is the most salient aspect of the city's environment? After looking at the historical and comparative evidence that is available, I have been persuaded that the critical feature is the growth of the human species itself. The West has already passed through its rapid growth stage. It is no coincidence to find that the period of most rapid city growth in England and Wales was between 1811 and 1851, when Britain was achieving an unprecedented mastery over a far-flung environment. In the United States, the period of most rapid city growth was between 1860 and 1890; in Germany it was between 1870 and 1910. What about the rest of the world? The most rapid growth in Egypt has been since 1920, in Mexico since 1921, and in India since 1941.[19] These periods correspond very interestingly to the periods of tremendous national population growth in these underdeveloped lands.

As a consequence, there are very striking differentials in city growth around the world today. The cities in the West are growing relatively slowly, while those in the developing areas, themselves more numerous than Western cities, are manifesting explosive growth. Calcutta is an interesting case, because its growth has meant that roughly 650,000 of its inhabitants are "street-sleepers," living on the sidewalks or in the railroad stations. Housing has not kept up with population growth. Calcutta is already the tenth largest city in the world, with a population of 4.5 million. But projections of its current rate of growth would yield a population of between 35 and 36 million people by the year· 2000. It happens that if one took such a population and gave it the density of New York City, he would have a city that would envelop an area larger than the entire state of Rhode Island. One may ask if this is really possible. Actually, it may well be impossible, but these figures are really designed to illustrate the magnitude of current growth, the enormous speed of increase in Calcutta and other cities in the underdeveloped areas of the world.

To take another case, there is reason to believe that twenty million people left rural areas to go to the cities of China between 1949 and 1956. This number happens to be nearly equal to the combined population of the Benelux countries, i.e., Belgium, Netherlands, and Luxembourg. Enormous numbers were thus involved in the rural-urban stream. In roughly the same period the cities of China were growing very rapidly.[20]

Such facts underscore the importance of both national growth and world population growth. Consider the difference between the births and deaths that are occurring, i.e., the "natural increase" of world population. At current rates, something like 6,000 persons are added each hour, or around 144,000 persons per day; this is a larger number than the population of Madison, Wisconsin.

The world is gaining 4,320,000 people per month, a number larger than the current population of the entire state of Wisconsin. The world is increasing by 52 million people per year; this is roughly the size of the United Kingdom —England, Wales, Scotland, and Northern Ireland.

The emerging picture is one of an ever-more-crowded world, and one finds many expressions of concern about the implications of this "population explosion." It is useful to think for a moment about whether this increasingly crowded world will mean increasingly crowded cities. The answer is clearly in the affirmative. The world is not only growing in terms of human numbers, but these numbers are being more compactly arranged. This holds true for urban communities and for the world as a whole. Cities are multiplying, they are growing larger in area and in population size, and they are containing progressively larger proportions of mankind in every major country throughout the world.

Very generally, with respect to the context of urbanization today, the critical fact is the sheer growth of both urban and nonurban communities. Population increases are being registered not only within cities, but within rural areas, with this latter increase indirectly providing the major source of city growth—rural-urban migration. To state the matter somewhat differently, the most impressive thing about contemporary urbanization is the fantastic proliferation and multiplication of human *and* social organisms.

You may not find the organismic analogy very helpful, but the principal facts that we have been considering remain the same. We should be aware of our growing world and of the fact that it is an increasingly urbanized world. If only to demonstrate that even now someone does read Herbert Spencer, I shall close by adopting as my own the words that he wrote in 1876 in defense of the organismic analogy. As he said, "I have used the analogies elaborated but as a scaffolding to help in building up a coherent body of sociological inductions. Let us take away the scaffolding; the inductions will stand by themselves."[21]

NOTES

1. Lewis Mumford, *The City in History* (New York: Harcourt, Brace & World, 1961), p. 34.
2. Eric E. Lampard, "The City," in *Encyclopaedia Britannica* (1967 edition), vol. 5, p. 809.
3. Anselm Strauss, *Images of the American City* (New York: The Free Press, 1961).
4. Martin Lindauer, *Communication Among Social Bees* (Cambridge: Harvard University Press, 1961).
5. See Raymond Vernon, *The Changing Economic Function of the Central City* (New York: Committee for Economic Development, 1959).
6. Robert E. Park, "The City: Suggestions for the Investigation of Human Behavior in the Urban Environment," *American Journal of Sociology*, 20 (March, 1916), pp. 577-612.
7. Crane Brinton, *English Political Thought in the Nineteenth Century* (London: Ernest Benn, 1949); quoted in Talcott Parsons, *The Structure of Social Action* (New York: The Free Press, 1949), p. 3.
8. Amos H. Hawley, *Human Ecology: A Theory of Community Structure* (New York: Ronald Press, 1950), p. 50.
9. Alden Raisbeck, "Nervous System," in *The American Peoples Encyclopedia* (Chicago: The Spencer Press, 1954), Volume 14, p. 466.
10. Otis Dudley Duncan and Albert J. Reiss, Jr.,

Social Characteristics of Urban and Rural Communities, 1950 (New York: John Wiley and Sons, 1956).
11. Herbert Spencer, *Principles of Sociology* (New York and London: D. Appleton and Co., 1920 edition), Volume I, Part II, pp. 449 and 471.
12. Edgar M. Hoover and Raymond Vernon, *The Anatomy of a Metropolis* (Cambridge: Harvard University Press, 1959).
13. Otis Dudley Duncan and Beverly Duncan, "Residential Distribution and Occupational Stratification," *American Journal of Sociology*, 60 (March, 1955), pp. 493-503; Leo F. Schnore, *The Urban Scene: Human Ecology and Demography* (New York: The Free Press, 1965), Part 4; Stanley Lieberson, *Ethnic Patterns in American Cities* (New York: The Free Press, 1963); Karl E. Taeuber and Alma F. Taeuber, *Negroes in Cities* (Chicago: Aldine, 1965).
14. Louis Wirth, "Urbanism as a Way of Life," *American Journal of Sociology*, 44 (July, 1938), pp. 1-26.
15. Eric E. Lampard and Leo F. Schnore, "Urbanization Problems: Some Historical and Comparative Considerations," in *Research Needs for Development Assistance Programs* (Washington, D.C.: The Brookings Institution, August, 1961); Philip M. Hauser and Leo F. Schnore (editors), *The Study of Urbanization* (New York: John Wiley, 1965).
16. Gideon Sjoberg, *The Preindustrial City: Past and Present* (New York: The Free Press, 1960).
17. Hauser and Schnore, *op. cit.*
18. Walter Firey, Charles P. Loomis, and J. Allan Beegle, "The Fusion of Urban and Rural," in Jean Labatut and Wheaton J. Lane (editors), *Highways in Our National Life* (Princeton: Princeton University Press, 1950), pp. 154-163.
19. Kingsley Davis, "The Origin and Growth of Urbanization in the World," *American Journal of Sociology*, 60 (March, 1955), pp. 429-437; Jack P. Gibbs and Leo F. Schnore, "Metropolitan Growth: An International Study," *American Journal of Sociology*, 66 (September, 1960), pp. 160-170.
20. "The World's Great Cities," *Population Bulletin*, 16 (September, 1960), pp. 109-131.
21. Spencer, *op. cit.*, pp. 592-593.

II THE CITY IN COLONIAL AMERICA

American urban history began with the small town—five villages hacked out of the wilderness. Each of these villages was geographically endowed to profit from seaborne commerce; each an "upstart" town with no past, an uncertain future, and a host of confounding and novel problems; each faced with survival from fire, disease, and war, and with the mightiest of problems when men gang together, living and acting together with tolerance and responsibility.

From their first rude beginnings in the 1600's to the American Revolution, five towns became five cities, five cities in the wilderness became five cities in revolt. The rise of New York, Boston, Newport, Philadelphia, and Charlestown underscored one major theme in the history of the American city: size is disproportionate to influence. In its first 150 years, this was a profoundly agrarian country with only a small portion of the population living in the five major cities, yet the influence, the power, the vitality of the cities transcended their size. By the end of the colonial period the cities imperially dominated their own immediate hinterland; each had grown economically mature as distributing, producing, marketing centers that helped pierce the backcountry with a transportation system that forged new towns and cities; each acted as a magnet luring the native farmer and the foreign immigrant alike by its opportunities and amenities. The cities had become the intellectual and cultural centers of a new nation, the frontiers of social change. Above all, they were symbols of one underlying cause of the American Revolution: the growth of an embryo nation into political, economic, and social maturity that demanded its own identity.

This is the thesis of Carl Bridenbaugh, whose books have thrust the city into the mainstream of American colonial history. In the first two selections in this chapter, Bridenbaugh analyzes the growing pains of the major cities-in-the-making as they struggled into puberty confronted with problems strikingly contemporary—housing, health, sanitation, crime, poverty—all demanding public municipal services that reflected a fundamental necessity for urban living: the will for collective responsibility. Indeed, Bridenbaugh sees this as the theme that singularly sets the city apart from other forms of human settlement, such as those experienced by the frontiersman and the farmer. It suggests that many historians who have assessed the national character have overemphasized the characteristics of agrarian self-reliance and individualism and must balance them with the drive for collective action so pronounced in the achievement and failure in the history of the city, from the colonial period to the present.

Bridenbaugh finds the early 1740's to be the watershed for the colonial cities. They had survived their first rugged hundred years, and from this time to the Revolution, largely through a burgeoning urban growth that fostered affluence and an urban imperialism that dominated both the seaboard and the rural hinterland, a distinct urban society emerged in America. Bridenbaugh stresses the integrated character of the urban network, noting that while each of the five major cities had its own particular flair, their similarities far outweighed their differences. This accounts, in part, for their role in the Revolution, a preparatory role whereby the city harnessed and unleashed the energies and ideas necessary for revolution. Bridenbaugh argues that the heart of this preparatory function consisted of one of the main contributions of the city in this period: the emergence of an urban society introduced the new nation to modern times. He equates modernity with the Enlightenment, and to him the city was "the triumph of the Enlightenment." The city was the natural environment for the Age of Reason, with its pragmatic temper, its passion for novelty and new ideas that shattered the piety, provincialism, and feudal institutions of the seventeenth century. One wonders whether Professor Bridenbaugh didn't overstate his point a bit, tossing seventeenth-century traditions into a historical rubbish heap when in fact the flow of continuity made many of them persist throughout the eighteenth century. Be that as it may, Bridenbaugh's interpretations must be reckoned with by anyone concerned with colonial history, as well as by those whose concern is urban history. They suggest a provocative but admittedly "ify" question. Could there indeed have been an American Revolution without the emergence and impact of the cities?

One thing is sure, there could not have been cities without the small town. Aside from some pious nostaglia about the small town, historians have been little concerned with this critical aspect of urban history. After all, cities of whatever size began as small towns. And it is an intriguing question why some grew into cities, some did not, and many withered away. Until recently, it has been the tendency of some historians and sociologists to make too sharp a distinction between rural and urban, and it has led to black-and-white oversimplifications. We have sometimes forgotten that the small town was an in-between station, a filtering maze between farm and city. The small town is also important in understanding American attitudes toward the city, for thousands of small towners moved to the city and took their attitudes with them. Thus the small town has influenced the so-called urban spirit, just as the city has to some extent urbanized the small town. And, finally, the small town is a superb comparative device to understand the city better.

Page Smith provides an analysis of what he calls the "covenanted community," the first and classic model of the small town in America, the New England town. Not merely a haphazard collection of individuals, it had a remarkable internal unity and an intensity of spirit that reflected the dedication of Puritan ideals and aspirations. Like the city, its influence far exceeded its modest size. And where urban historians point to the city in arguing that we must go beyond our preoccupation with the farmer and the frontiersman in seeking a more balanced understanding of American development, Smith goes one step further in dramatizing the role of the small town. His thesis is that the covenanted community was the genesis for a new kind of community settlement which produced and reproduced a host of communities in the American march to the Pacific. In a word, it was the "cutting edge" of the westward movement. He does not give us an altogether balanced picture of the impact of the small town, failing to treat the southern and western towns, with their Baptist and Methodist influences, which also played a significant role in small-town America.[1] Nonetheless, this is one of the best interpretations of the pervasive effect of the New England town.

No romantic chronicler of cozy, small-town America, Professor Smith is particularly effective in exploding the myth that the small town, at least the New England type, was a generator of individualism, liberal attitudes, and progressive change. The town was the bastion of rigid conservatism; the liberal pioneer was in the city.

1. For comparison, see Lewis Atherton, *Main Street on the Middle Border* (Bloomington: Indiana University Press, 1954), and Duane A. Smith, *Rocky Mountain Mining Camps* (Bloomington: Indiana University Press, 1967).

One Hundred Years of Urban Growth

CARL BRIDENBAUGH

The first hundred years of town history on the American continent witnessed the foundation and gradual development of a truly urban society. The story of American life is customarily regarded as a compound of sectional histories, and in the early colonial period two sections are commonly considered,—the tidewater and the frontier. Yet the tidewater was itself divided, and if we consider the sections as social and psychological rather than as purely geographical entities, it is possible to distinguish three of them,—the rural, agricultural society of the countryside; the restless, advancing society of the frontier; and the urban, commercial society of the larger seaports. Beginning as small specks in the wilderness, the five communities grew from tiny villages into towns, and finally attained the status of small cities. With other village communities of similar interests and outlook which multiplied and grew in the eighteenth century, they emerged as a social and economic "section" extending the length of the Atlantic seaboard, and exhibiting definite urban characteristics in striking contrast to rural farming districts and wilder regions of the frontier. Life in urban areas produced its own peculiar problems to be faced, and the urban viewpoint, based upon continuous close contacts with Europe, derived less from agriculture than from trade. Commercially minded town society looked to the East rather

than the West, and was destined from the first to serve as the connecting link between colonial America and its Old World parents.

The future of the colonial towns became immediately evident from the conditions surrounding their birth. Designed as trading communities, they were established on sites most favorable for the pursuit of commerce. They were the western outposts of European commercial expansion in the seventeenth century. City-dwellers from the Old World formed the larger proportion of early town populations, and from the start commercial relations with England or Holland were maintained. Most significantly, the founding process occurred at a time when western Europe, under Dutch and English leadership, was gradually outgrowing and casting off the limitations of medieval feudal economy. Colonial towns grew to maturity in the era of world expansion attending the emergence of modern capitalism, and being new communities, with few irrevocably established customs or traditions, they frequently adapted themselves to the economic drift with more ease and readiness than did the older cities of England. Moreover, the colonizing movement was itself an expression of early capitalistic activity. It called forth organized rather than individual efforts and resources, created new and wider markets for economic development, and opened up

From Carl Bridenbaugh, *Cities in the Wilderness* (New York: Knopf, 1938), pp. 467-81. Copyright 1938 and renewed 1966 by Carl Bridenbaugh. Reprinted by permission of Alfred A. Knopf, Inc. Carl Bridenbaugh is Professor of History at Brown University.

seemingly unlimited territories for imperialistic exploitation. It thus produced a marked effect upon Old World economy, accelerating the breakdown of local units of business, and facilitating the formation of larger and more complex organizations of commerce and finance.

The problems which confronted town-dwellers in America were not only those of urban communities, but of a pioneer society as well. Urban development depends largely upon community wealth, and upon the willingness of the group to devote portions of it to projects for civic betterment, or to consent to taxation for this purpose. To a considerable extent the nature of town governments and the extent of authority vested in them conditioned the expenditure of town wealth for community enterprises. Here the colonists were hampered by the traditional nature of the charters of medieval English municipal corporations, whose limitations ill accorded with circumstances in seventeenth and eighteenth century America, especially with the imperious demands for expansion and immediate activity in the New World. In New England towns a new political organization, the town meeting, developed, which exhibited considerable efficiency in the handling of urban problems. This institution was more immediately susceptible to social wants and requirements than were the aristocratic, self-perpetuating corporations founded in America after the example of English municipal governments. Its greater powers of local taxation, and the fact that it placed the spending of public moneys and the enactment of civic ordinances in the hands of those directly affected by these operations, made it a far more effective form of government for dealing with community problems. These problems were the greater, because in the first century of their history the five colonial seaports enjoyed a much more rapid physical growth than did the cities of contemporary Europe. The individual enterprise of American town-dwellers, and the commercial expansion and prosperity they achieved, aided in the solution of these problems of town living, but much of the efficiency and success which attended their efforts may be attributed to the emergence in the New World of a relatively high sense of civic responsibility in the early eighteenth century, at a time when public consciousness in Europe had receded to an extremely low ebb.

The towns were primarily commercial communities seeking treasure by foreign trade, and their economic vitality and commercial demands led to their early breaking the narrow bonds of medieval economic practice to forge ahead on uncharted but highly profitable commercial adventures. All five, during their first century, developed from simple manorial organizations, completely dependent upon European connections, into full-fledged commercial centers, only partially tied to England, and in many cases competing with British cities for a share of imperial traffic. Boston entered early into the West Indian provision trade, thereby setting an example for other American commercial communities. Soon Massachusetts mariners were seeking to monopolize the colonial carrying traffic in ships of their own building, and the profits of carrier and middleman became the basis of the Bay town's prosperity. Her priority in this field gave her an advantage which other seaports did not begin to overcome until the fourth decade of the eighteenth century. A further foundation for urban economic prosperity lay in the existence of an expanding frontier society with its great need for manufactured products. This made possible an earlier development of the towns as distributing centers for a wide hinterland than was the case with English cities like Bristol, Norwich and Exeter, and became in this first century as important a factor in the economic growth of New York, Philadelphia and Charles Town as in that of the New England metropolis. As a producer of staple goods for exchange in trade, Boston, with its limited back country was at a disadvantage. More fortunate were New York with its flour and furs, Philadelphia, with its great staples of wheat, meat and lumber, and Charles Town, which after 1710 found prosperity in the important South Carolina crops of rice and indigo. Eventually the communities enjoying this sound economic backing rose to threaten the supremacy of Boston in colonial trade, while Newport and Philadelphia cut heavily into the Bay town's West India commerce. In the eighteenth century also Newport attained importance in shipbuilding and the slave trade. By 1742 Boston merchants were facing a period of relative decline, while their competitors in other colonial towns found the volume and profits of their traffic steadily mounting.

Continual increase in the volume of colonial trade and enlargement of the territory served by the towns led to greater complexity in commercial relations. In the early years merchants performed all types of business, but toward 1700 their functions began to be more specialized. Retail merchandising having definitely emerged by 1700, the great merchant now dealt chiefly with larger operations of exporting, importing and wholesaling, leaving much of the small trade to the shopkeeper. Demands of trade had by 1710 necessitated the issuance of paper currency in most of the colonies, and the establishment of the colonial post office to serve intercolonial communication. Growing business further led to the creation of insurance offices and some extension of credit facilities. Profits from trade, originally completely absorbed in shipbuilding ventures and industries subsidiary to shipping, now began to create a surplus which sought investment in land, or, in some communities, in the development of certain forms of manufacturing.

Economic prosperity thus made possible the rise of colonial cities. It led to physical expansion of town boundaries, and facilitated dealing with urban problems by corporate effort. Wealth wrung from trade, more than any other single factor, determined the growth of a town society, in which urban amusements and a colonial culture might thrive. This is not, however, to force the history of urban America within the narrow bounds of an exclusively economic interpretation. Social and intellectual development are dependent upon and conditioned by economic progress, but they are not its necessary and inevitable result. They are altered, encouraged or stifled by the action and influence of material forces, but they are not necessarily caused or even initiated solely by economic factors.

When we consider American urban society, apart from its economic aspects, we find it characterized by certain problems affecting it as a unit, and with which as a unit it had to deal. Such problems in general, or collective attempts for their control and regulation, are either absent from or unimportant in rural or frontier societies, but in the case of our urban section they are present, in rudimentary form at least, from its inception. They persist and grow with the maturing of that section, and the means taken for dealing with them further differentiate the urban from other types of society.

Logically, the first of these problems to appear are the physical, and of these the most immediate was housing. As in rural regions this remained for the most part an individual problem, and there are only a few cases on record where even indirectly, by sale or subdivision of land or by encouragement of artisans, the community stepped in to relieve a housing shortage. On the other hand, the laying out and maintaining of a highway system constituted a problem, perhaps the first, which transcended private initiative. Not that the community at any time scorned the assistance of private enterprise; a favorite device, at Boston and elsewhere, throughout the colonial era, was by remission of taxes or grant of other privileges to encourage individuals to open up streets and undertake paving operations for public use at their own charge. But from the beginning public authorities indicated the location of roads, supervised the opening up of new ones, ordered their clearing or partial paving by abutters, and strove to prevent encroachments upon them. At Philadelphia and Charles Town, where some prior power had surveyed and planned the thoroughfares, the first task of local authorities was light; it was more arduous in other communities, where there was no preliminary plan, and where the design had constantly to be expanded and altered to keep pace with town growth. The problems accompanying the mere existence of a highway system,—paving, cleaning and upkeep,—called for full exercise of municipal authority. Sometimes the community exacted from each inhabitant a yearly amount of labor on the streets; in other cases it hired this labor and paid for it outright. In either case it had to levy special taxes, for materials or labor or both. To insure some cleanliness in the streets, it passed mandatory ordinances restricting the conduct of townsmen, impressed the services of carters, and employed public funds for the hire of scavengers. Further to protect the public ways, it restricted and regulated the traffic upon them, especially the weight of cart loads and the width of their wheels. Less necessary but desirable improvements in the highways, like the construction of drains, first came about through private demand and initiative, but as the civic power matured and public funds became available, these too became public functions and responsibilities. In either the municipal or the individual approach to highway problems the towns had good precedent in the Mother Country. In actual execution, especially with regard to refinements like paving and drainage, they seem in some cases to have gone beyond contemporary English cities. With a few exceptions, this generalization does not apply to the corporation governed towns, or to the unfortunately ungoverned metropolis of South Carolina.

Highways may be said to constitute the most rudimentary of public utilities, but there were others,—bridges, wharves, and engineering projects,—of which colonial townsfolk almost immediately felt the need. In the beginning, while municipal authority was politically and financially feeble, these were almost solely the product of private enterprise, but with the gradual tendency of town development they became increasingly matters of public concern. Following Old World precedent, bridges were conceived as parts of the highway system, and hence undoubtedly under public control, but they were usually constructed and operated by private persons or companies, under grant from local or provincial authorities. As the century progressed, in a few cases, notably at Philadelphia and Boston, town governments directly managed the operation and upkeep of bridges. Land reclamation projects, and harbor facilities like lighthouses, pursued a similar history. In the case of wharves, they were either a municipal or a private concern. Most towns maintained a minimum of public docking facilities, while more ambitious wharf projects, like the Long Wharves of Boston and Newport, were only within the capacity of private capital. At Philadelphia public docking facilities were so excellent as to discourage employment of private capital in their erection; at New York, so poor as to require it. Toward the end of the era, when the demands of trade began to make regular transportation between communities desirable, stage and freight routes, too, were operated by private capital, under license, usually from the provincial government.

Fire constitutes a threat especially dangerous to urban communities, and as buildings in colonial towns were from the beginning placed close together, its imminence was immediately felt. The combatting and prevention of fire called forth more than individual efforts from the start. Municipal ordinances required the keeping of fire fighting equipment by all townsmen, regulated their chimneys, forbade bonfires, fire-

works, and the housing of explosives in crowded areas. Public authorities had also to make direct outlays for fire fighting equipment of their own, and hire companies for its care and operation. In Boston, Philadelphia and Newport private societies for the protection of property during fires were organized to supplement public agencies. Similarly, water supply for fire uses was a matter of public concern and regulation. Boston, with its crowded streets and buildings of inflammable construction, and its willingness to spend public money and enegry for public welfare, was in general far in the forefront with regard to its fire defenses, but by the end of the first century all towns possessed fire engines of the latest European model, and fire fighting regulations equal or superior to those of the average English town.

A distinctive urban function grew in part out of the fire hazards of crowded sections,—the enactment of building regulations. Only public authority could specify the nature of legal building materials as did Boston after the fire of 1679 and the South Carolina Assembly after the Charles Town fire of 1740. Exercise of municipal powers was also necessary to prevent imperfect construction and dangerous neglect of town chimneys and hearths. In addition, conditions of urban congestion led to party-wall regulations like those of Boston and Philadelphia.

Another, more subtle class of problems, those which involved the personal relationships of inhabitants, affected town society from its inception. Intensified by the peculiar conditions of urban life, they required collective rather than individual efforts and powers for their control. Old World experience had taught town-dwellers the immediate need for means of preserving the public peace in settled communities, and the early appearance of constables in all towns supplied the traditional response to that need. For their security after nightfall the towns appointed bellmen or watchmen of varying degrees of efficiency. New York, after developing a highly effective nocturnal police in the seventeenth century, allowed this institution to languish from unwillingness to devote the necessary public funds thereto; other towns were slower in supplying the need, though somewhat more successful by the end of the first century. Efficiency of the watch was in direct ratio to the availability of public funds for its support,—impressment of a citizen's watch having revealed its inadequacy by the turn of the century,—and here the New England towns, with their powers of local taxation, were at a distinct advantage. There are numerous instances, during periods of unusual danger or disturbance like wars or epidemics, when the towns entirely failed in their efforts to preserve nocturnal peace, and their functions had to be taken over by the military arm of the provincial government.

Existence of crime and disorder early became a community concern in urban settlements. Here invitations to lawbreaking existed in the inequalities of wealth and opportunity, and materials for its perpetration in the diverse and unruly elements of town and seaport society. The concentration of people, many of them hardworked and underprivileged, also made for mob disorders, which increased in violence and frequency with the growth of the towns. Presence of sailors, blacks, foreigners, paupers, unpopular religious sects, interlopers in trade, profiteers, and rival

political factions, all provided increasing incentives for disorder and violence as the period progressed. Town society clearly soon passed beyond the stage where individual efforts or the force of public opinion could deal with this problem; rather it required the sanctions of the law. Provincial governments passed legislation, and municipal authorities enacted ordinances outlawing offenses against society. Riot acts were drawn up by colonial assemblies, and the local constabulary did its best to round up and confine the perpetrators of disorder and violence. In general, the towns could do little to remove the causes of criminality, and the solution of this peculiarly vexing problem of city life remained as remote in the seventeenth centuries as today.

For punishments, colonial authorities followed a number of Old World precedents, favoring especially the speediest and least expensive methods,—fines, floggings, public humiliation, restitution of stolen goods, and, occasionally, mutilation. In general, their criminal codes were less brutal than those of contemporary Europe. Efforts to make the whole community a partner in the work of law enforcement appeared in the division with informers of the proceeds from fines. Prisons were still generally places of detention for those awaiting trial, though imprisonment as punishment for crime seems to have become more widespread as the period advanced, and save in the case of debtors was probably somewhat more in use in the colonies than in the Old World. The frequency of jail breaks indicates the inefficiency of all colonial prisons, and their inadequacy suggests the absence of more vicious criminal types that troubled older societies. Yet colonial prisons were probably no more inadequate than those of contemporary England, and certainly far less squalid and brutal. Save in the case of Philadelphia in the eighteenth century, the rudimentary penology of the times made no distinction between various classes of offenders, and absence of prison facilities led to frequent misuse of alms and workhouses, wherein pauper and lawbreaker were housed together.

Offenses against the moral and ethical standards which society imposes appear more flagrant in the comparative populousness and congestion of urban environments, and early forced themselves upon the attention of colonial communities. In addition, the psychology of the times made many aspects of the regulation of conduct, manners and dress a legitimate province for the public authority. Early appearance of prostitution in the towns shocked authorities into decreeing harsh penalties for it and similar offenses. With its increasing prevalence in a society which included growingly diverse and uncontrollable elements, they seem everywhere to have become less concerned with the actual offense than with the fear lest the illegitimate offspring become charges to the community. Drunkenness was a prevailing vice, and in all towns the authorities and the better elements fought to eradicate it. Excellent tavern legislation in several of the towns reduced this offense to a minimum, but illegal sale of liquor, and misuse of the legitimate product, continued to baffle municipal authority throughout the period. Sabbath legislation in every town,—as strict in the Anglican South as in Puritan New England,—attempted to insure the sacred character of the Lord's Day. Gambling, card-playing, idleness, extravagance in dress and behavior, and evidence of frivolity came

under the ban of public regulation, either through colony or municipal authority, or as at Philadelphia through the dominant religious group. Especially at Boston and Philadelphia many seemingly innocent amusements suffered from the disapproval of a stern and narrow religion, which served as a powerful and useful supplement to the civic power.

The existence and effects of crime and immorality are intensified in urban communities; so, too, the problem of pauperism. Reports of travelers as to the absence of poverty from colonial towns can only be regarded as comparatively true, for in each town numbers of those unable to care for themselves soon constituted a problem of which the community had to take cognizance. The generally excellent methods with which the towns met this problem indicate a considerable sense of civic maturity and responsibility. New York and Charles Town favored the out-relief method through most of the period, but Boston and Philadelphia had by the end of the century well-regulated and practically self-supporting workhouses, and Newport maintained an adequate almshouse. Considerable direct relief had to be granted, especially at Boston, and in all towns save New York private or religious organizations supplemented the public work of poor relief. Methods to forestall the growth of poverty were devised, such as compulsory apprenticeship of poor children, exclusion of strangers without obvious means of livelihood, and, especially in the New England towns, restriction of immigration. In times of particular stress special devices had to be resorted to, as the distribution of corn or firewood, or a temporary embargo on export of necessary commodities. At Boston, where the problem of poverty became acute in the 1670's and was never thereafter absent, careful registration of all aliens and dependents prevailed, and a public granary was maintained.

The general health, which in rural regions may be privately cared for, early became in urban communities a matter for public concern, and municipal ordinances soon restricted the conduct of inhabitants in matters which might affect the general well-being. Location of wells and privies, and of slaughterhouses and tan pits which might become public nuisances, removal of dumps and disposal of refuse were all subjects of municipal regulation. Similarly, public authorities directed inhabitants in their behavior during epidemics, and enacted quarantine regulations in an attempt to prevent visitations of infectious disease. Toward the end of the century excellent isolation hospitals appeared in several of the towns, erected and operated by the municipality. Despite failure in this period of all attempts to regulate the practice of medicine by town or colony, the medical profession in the towns attained a relatively high development for the times.

In their approach to the physical and social problems of urban life the towns were imitators, not originators. The townsmen came to America with a fund of European experience from which they seldom deviated, and new methods as they employed them had usually first to cross the Atlantic. Poor relief and tavern legislation were directly imported from Great Britain, and the towns might conceivably have done better with their police problem had not Old World precedent served them so exclusively as a guide. Yet it may be said that in several cases there are distinct improvements in the thoroughness with which old methods were employed, and which may usually be traced to the individual civic pride of townsmen, reflected in their municipal governments. This is especially true of communities which enjoyed the town meeting form of government, where, as we have seen, the direct demands of townspeople could effect greater thoroughness and efficiency in dealing with town business, but even in the corporation governments of America there is less indifference to the public welfare than may be noted in contemporary England or Europe. Visitors were impressed with the excellence of poor relief at Boston and Philadelphia, and with Philadelphia's model prison. Fire defences in the towns were a combination of English and Dutch examples, and, especially at Boston, probably unsurpassed for their time. Solution of urban problems in colonial towns was continually hampered by lack of public funds or of necessary authority for obtaining them,—the sad decline of New York's excellent watch is an illustration, —but it was assisted, where public power failed, either politically or financially, by an encouraging growth of civic consciousness among private individuals and non-political organizations. Establishment of private agencies for charity, education, fire protection, improvement of morals, and the like, and the appearance of individual benefactors to the public welfare of the community, in an age not distinguished for civic virtue or interest, is a remarkable and significant accomplishment of town society in colonial America.

Having as they all did a common model and experience, colonial towns exhibit a remarkable similarity in the solution of their urban problems. There are many instances of the failure of a community to provide the usual and accepted necessary solution, but, with the possible exception of Philadelphia's eighteenth century prison, hardly a single example of the development by one town of a unique institution. By the time that local divergences from the original plan might have been expected to appear, communication had sufficiently improved to permit of one town's borrowing from the successful experience of another. The same holds true for privately initiated supplements of municipal endeavor. The Scot's Charitable Society and the Fire Society appear in Boston, copied from European models, and at a later date are further copied by other American towns. In the eighteenth century, because of its long experience in dealing with urban problems, the greater efficiency of its form of government, and its willingness to spend public money for the public good, Boston became the great example, with respect to municipal institutions, for other towns on the continent, but it enjoyed no monopoly of this function. New Yorkers had the fire defences of Philadelphia held up to them as a model, Bostonians were shamed by the excellence of Philadelphia's market, while Charlestonians tried to fashion their city government after the example of the corporation of New York. By the end of the period under review this inter-city exchange of experience had resulted in a striking similarity in municipal institutions, as well as a fairly uniform level of their development. Boston, for the reasons enumerated above, was probably still somewhat in advance in matters of social and material concern, though with its humanitarian agencies Philadelphia

was running a close second. Charles Town, within the limits of its governmental incapacity, dealt in fairly efficient fashion with its problems; at Newport, a lesser development of these problems had not yet necessitated any great display of urban consciousness. Even at New York, where political factionalism, a selfish corporation, and the difficulty of amalgamating two languages and nationalities prevented a consistent and devoted attempt to solve the problems of urban living, a comparison of its municipal life with that of older provincial cities of the British Empire would not have resulted in discredit to the former.

The accumulation of economic resources and their concentration in urban units, their direction in commercial ventures which attracted and supported large populations within these units, and the problems of providing for the physical and social well-being of those who thus became city-dwellers, all these aspects of urban development succeeded in bringing forth in America a distinctive society. In constitution, spiritual life, recreational activities, and intellectual pursuits it differed from types of society to be found in other sections of the continent. In respect neither to national origins nor to economic status of their inhabitants did the towns long remain homogeneous. Settled originally by people of the same nation, usually of the same locality, they soon came to include children of other European countries and of another race. Early in their history there could be found small groups of Scots in Boston, French Huguenots in Boston, New York and Charles Town, Welsh in Philadelphia, and a few Jews in every town. Many Germans settled in the 1680's in the environs of Philadelphia, and New York from the time of the first English occupation presented the problem of two peoples, each with their own language, schools and churches, living side by side under government by the numerically weaker group. This incipient cosmopolitanism flowered with the renewed immigration of the early eighteenth century, when all towns received numbers of Scotch-Irish, and the middle and southern cities, especially Philadelphia, large accessions of German exiles. For the most part these strangers were allowed to settle peaceably in colonial towns, whose economic expansion enabled them easily to absorb the newcomers, and though recent arrivals seldom attained social recognition or overcame the barrier of language where it existed, still there was little nativism and small emphasis on the superior advantages of Anglo-Saxon nativity. Such bountiful immigration did, however, lead to many restrictions, especially in the north, where the labor market was well supplied and the poor rates overburdened, to establishment of special churches and social organizations, and in Philadelphia, at least, to common use of the German language in business transactions. By far the greater problem was created by the presence of African Negroes in all towns. In Boston and Newport, where they were used mainly as house servants, and where many of them were free, the problem was negligible. They were subject to various discriminatory rules, such as those which required them to work out their obligations to the community in menial labor rather than by watch or militia duty. But at New York and Charles Town their greater numbers kept constantly present the fear of servile insurrection. At the former town they were the unfortunate objects of such waves of hysteria as the Negro Conspiracy of 1741, and at Charles Town, where they at times equalled the white population in numbers, a severe slave code kept them in subjection.

Social stratification further differentiated urban society from the easy democracy of the back country, where any man might own land and all must work with their hands. Distinctions between the well-to-do and the not-so-rich were perhaps relatively unimportant in the beginning, when society was still so fluid that luck or diligence might elevate a man above his fellows in a short time, but with the accumulation of wealth and economic power in the hands of a few, and the coming in of numbers of artisans, indentured servants and immigrant laborers, class lines tightened and society crystallized into easily recognizable categories of better, middling, and poorer sorts. In all towns native aristocracies were commercial in origin, even at Charles Town where they later sought land as a basis for social distinction. They consolidated their position by means of wealth from successful trading ventures, collecting thereby social prestige and political influence. They lived grandly, dressed gaily, kept horses and coaches, and employed the labor of the less fortunate. The commercial, political and social leadership of the towns was in their hands. Later, as urban life became more sophisticated, they contributed to the development of secular amusements and to the relaxation of earlier strict moral codes. They gained further brilliance by alliance with representatives of British officialdom in America. Below them the middle class, professional people, tradesmen and artisans, lived comfortably but more plainly, enjoying in prosperous times many of the good things of life, but in hard times feeling the pinch far more than did their wealthy neighbors. Steady laborers might know periods of prosperity, but many of them could be squeezed out by the vicissitudes of the economic cycle. They performed the menial labor of the towns, enlisted as common seamen, and constituted a group from which much urban poverty and disorder were recruited. Negro and Indian slaves, mere unprivileged pieces of property, rounded out the caste system as it developed itself in metropolitan America.

Save Newport, each of the towns had originally been dedicated to a dominant Protestant religious organization, but after a century of growth diversity, indifference and actual unbelief came to characterize the religious scene. The complexities of town society were in large measure responsible for this development, for different national or social groups soon evolved their favored sects and denominations. When the ministry could no longer speak with one voice to all elements of town populations, it lost much of its influence, both social and clerical, and the appearance of agnosticism and irreverence was rapid. In general, at the end of the first century, Anglicanism was in all towns the religion of officials and aristocrats; Quakerism and Congregationalism, which had once in their own localities enjoyed this favored position, had joined the ranks of middle class religions, which further included Baptists and Presbyterians; while for the common man a religious refuge was just appearing in the enthusiastic, emotional revivalism of Whitefield. Absence of devotion penetrated all classes; the poorer sort were largely indifferent to

the attractions of religion, freethinking characterized such middle class groups as Franklin's Junto, and aristocrats indulged a fashionable Deism. In contrast, a stern and uniform religious fundamentalism for a much longer time characterized the rural communities of the countryside.

Much of their power the quasi-established churches had attained in an age when religious concerns so dominated men's thoughts as to exclude many other aspects of life. But the commercial success of colonial towns altered this singleness of outlook by acquainting townsmen with the delights of secular grandeurs and providing money for their enjoyment. As the age advanced the church step by step gave way before the institution of more attractive secular recreations. Most successful of these, appearing very early and appealing to all classes, was the tavern. Instituted originally as a necessary convenience for strangers and travelers, it soon showed itself to be the resort of all classes of townsmen, the place where much of their social life was passed. In the eighteenth century coffee houses became as in England the rendezvous of business men and the scene of many commercial transactions. Taverns served not only as places of casual conviviality, but as headquarters for the multifarious clubs into which town social life gradually organized itself. They also offered opportunities for cards, billiards and games of chance, and housed the many traveling shows and exhibitions which the better transportation of the eighteenth century made possible.

Games, contests, tavern recreations, and public celebration of holidays constituted the entertainment of the common man, but for the aristocrats mounting wealth and sophistication were creating more elaborate forms of amusement. To the hearty private dinners and occasional excursions of early days succeeded great public banquets, dances and balls, musical entertainments, and finally, in two of the towns, dramatic presentations. Gradually the commercial aristocracy of the towns, combining with royal officials, evolved a society whose entertainments were artificial, costly, sophisticated and exclusive. But for aristocrat or common man, the vicarious amusements that money could buy, and their variety and attractiveness, differentiated town society from that of the countryside with its simpler, spontaneous pleasures, and tended to draw town-dwellers away from a strict and narrow conception of life as a duty and a task. Copied as they were from the recreations of English society, they also tended to make social life in the towns more like that of the metropolis.

A final characteristic of town society was that it offered to its members a wider intellectual opportunity and challenge than was possible to the man whose life was bounded by his fields or by the hard necessity of clearing away the forest. From earliest childhood opportunities for education, free or otherwise, were open to the town-dweller. Especially was this true of the poor, whose educational needs were largely cared for by religious societies, charity schools, or compulsory apprenticeship. This last system enabled youth of the poorer classes to equip themselves for a trade. In other strata of society young men might fit themselves for business at private vocational schools, for a place in society with private masters, or for higher education for a learned profession at public or private Latin schools or with a private tutor. Young women,

too, in the towns might purchase instruction in various fields of learning or merely in the polite arts of feminine society. Also, in the northern English towns, Boston, Newport and Philadelphia, there was from the start a tradition of scholarliness and of respect for intellectual achievement. It followed that a society so trained, constantly in contact by ship with Europe, was alive and ready to adopt the intellectual fashions of the age. Hence, in this first century of American life, most of the intellectual activity, in science, literature and the arts, and what intellectual progress there was, took place in the towns. Only there were there material and opportunity for such activity. And rather than regard the results of that progress with condescension, we should, with James Franklin's subscriber, wonder at the contrary. In comparison with the Augustan Age of eighteenth century London, intellectual and social life in the colonies may seem bare and sterile, but in comparison with the intellectual barrenness of provincial life in England itself, its cultivation and sophistication appear revealed. Urban culture in the eighteenth century was provincial culture at its best, nourished during this period of faltering imitation, which had to precede that of native accomplishment, by constant contact with the vital intellectual currents of England and Europe.

In these various ways the developments of a hundred years of life under relatively urban conditions created a society at once distinct from that of rural regions, whether tidewater or back country, and even further removed from that of the westward reaching frontier. The communal attitude toward the solution of the physical and social problems of diversified populations dwelling together in close propinquity, and the constantly widening outlook which material progress, commercial expansion, and contact with the larger world of affairs made possible, were its distinguishing characteristics. In general, this society was more cooperative and social, less individualistic in its outlook toward problems of daily life, far more susceptible to outside influences and examples, less aggressively independent than the society of frontier America. At the same time it was more polished, urbane, and sophisticated, more aware of fashion and change, more sure of itself and proud of its achievements, more able to meet representatives from the outside world as equals without bluster or apology than the rural society of the colonial back country. Because its outlook was eastward rather than westward, it was more nearly a European society in an American setting. It had appropriated various points on the American continent and transformed them as nearly as possible into likenesses of what it had known at home. It was itself less transformed in the process than might have been expected, because the contact with the homeland never ceased, but rather increased with the passage of years. Its importance to American life as a whole was therefore great. Here were centers of the transit of civilization from Old World to New,—five points at the least through which currents of world thought and endeavor might enter, to be like other commodities assimilated and redistributed throughout the countryside. It was well for the future of national America that its society should not remain completely rural and agricultural, isolated and self-sufficient, ignorant of outside developments and distrustful of new ideas from abroad, as it might well have done had there been no cities. Instead, the five towns provided the nucleus for a wider and more gracious living in the New World.

Cities in Revolt: Conclusion

CARL BRIDENBAUGH

Between the founding of New Amsterdam in 1625 and the year 1742, five towns were established in the English colonies and gradually grew into small cities, together constituting a genuine urban society. Within this period of little more than a hundred years, chronicled in *Cities in the Wilderness*, there emerged an *urban section* along the Atlantic seaboard which was sharply differentiated from the settled *rural areas* of the agricultural countryside or the newer, wilder, and sparsely populated districts of the *back country*.

From Carl Bridenbaugh, *Cities in Revolt* (New York: Knopf, 1955), pp. 418-25. Copyright © 1955 by Carl Bridenbaugh. Reprinted by permission of Alfred A. Knopf, Inc.

Throughout the remainder of the colonial period, by means of their particular form of urban imperialism, the cities, in effect, came to dominate the other two sections.

Constant communication, arising out of the needs of commerce, served to forge these communities into an integrated urban society—the only segment of colonial population so fused. In each of the cities certain common physical, economic, cultural, and social characteristics accentuated the homogeneity whereas the other two sections exhibited vivid differences, north and south, in crops, architecture, people, and customs. The achievement of the integration of urban elements was an essential prelude to independence. Otherwise the meeting of the First Continental Congress appears as a cataclysmic event not subject to historical explanation.

In this volume it is evident that two persistent themes run through the history of the colonial cities, 1743-76. The first is the astonishing expansion of all the activities of urban existence, for in spite of and because of war conditions for almost half the period, population mounted and the residents clamored for and secured municipal services, and outwardly the evolution of an urban society went on apace and undisturbed. Nevertheless the towns were in revolt, and this constitutes the second theme. On all sides the citizens were coming face to face with new situations and the new ideas of what we know as the Enlightenment. Gradually, almost imperceptibly, familiar ways of doing things, inherited beliefs, old loyalties gave way before novel methods, exciting or unsettling new ideas, and strange gods. In the brief passage of time between the return of the survivors from the British expedition to Carthagena

and the Declaration of Independence, the inhabitants discarded forever their seventeenth-century traditions and fatefully and irrevocably accepted the symbols and ways of modernity. In so doing, moreover, they transformed their communities from English colonial into American cities. These communities represented the fact, the constructive accomplishment of the age, not merely its dreams, its theories or its attacks on outworn institutions; in 1776 the achievements of the American cities stood as the great triumph of the Enlightenment just as their leading citizen, Benjamin Franklin, personified it.

The spectacular physical growth of the five cities naturally attracted the attention of foreign visitors first. Although every community expanded its area, compactness if not congestion typified them all, even Newport; and this living together in close proximity, in the environment, was the marrow of urban existence. Under the pressure of growing numbers, agencies for maintaining life and services devised in former years needed enlarging or revamping, and new municipal responsibilities were thrust upon civic authorities. Housing and its accompaniment, building regulations, and fire-fighting and water supply posed problems perennially. Rapid growth created pressing demands for new streets, drainage, paving, traffic laws, wharves, and ferries; and in the train of urban expansion came a critical increase of the poor, criminals, moral laxity, each intensified by wartime conditions, to impose a heavy expense and police burden on each city. Public health also became a matter of concern for city fathers.

Inasmuch as the cities had ample wealth to meet their civic requirements, the success attending efforts to solve the problems of urban living depended upon the willingness of local governments to levy taxes and of the inhabitants to pay for the solutions. The town meetings of the two New England cities ordinarily responded to reasonable demands with generous grants of funds; the elected Corporation of New York usually complied, but that of Philadelphia had to be supplemented by bodies with taxing authority; while at Charles Town an assembly of planters interested in other concerns too frequently turned a deaf ear to the citizens' petitions. As a group, the townsmen quickly became more aware of public issues and of ways and means than their rural brethren; they grew more alert and well informed about local political matters, an advantage they improved when the time came for them to play politics on a provincial or imperial scale.

These five seaports were above all else commercial centers. Overseas, coastal, or internal trade determined the economic well-being of the inhabitants. As colonials their merchants had to conduct trade according to the rules laid down in the Navigation Acts. For seventy years they succeeded in accommodating themselves to the British colonial policy, but when rigid observance of the Molasses Act of 1733 was ordered, which would mean ruin for many of them, these same individualistic merchants did not hesitate to resort to illicit trading and manufacturing in defiance of Parliamentary prohibitions. Furthermore, they prospered—more so in fact than the farms or plantations.

An inevitable conflict of interests was inherent in the subordinate status in which the mother country kept these city states—for their unprecedented growth had made them the equals, in

some cases the superiors, of all the cities of Britain save London. It is not here asserted that no resolution of these differences was possible; rather that the British government, failing to perceive the nature of the issues, never attempted to resolve them. Economically the cities and the colonies they served had so matured by 1760 that the attempts of British authorities to impose restrictions on them brought on a series of political explosions that impelled the citizenry to re-examine the entire connection.

One inherited concept to which the citizens offered little challenge before 1760 was a belief in a hierarchy of classes based on status. A mercantile aristocracy had rooted itself in the cities and, grown rich and powerful, presumed to control in its own interest public policy, organizations of many kinds, religious bodies, and social life as well as most of the external relations with the provinces and the British Isles. Through patronage it exercised a determining influence on education and the entire range of urban intellectual activities, and, on the whole, had evolved a very promising and fruitful culture. In the five cities one could glimpse these aristocracies in action, and one could also detect the rise of their Nemesis, the up-and-coming middle class.

The craftsmen and shopkeepers, men of middle rank, shared in the new prosperity, and as their class moved upward in numbers and strength, they came to sense their importance as a group and to entertain ambitions for political power commensurate with their economic status. They had no wish to overthrow the gentry, but rather they desired to move up into their ranks and share the power and prestige. Economic and political freedom concerned them much more than the social equality bred to the westward; the career open to talent was the goal, and the past history of the cities offered an abundance of success stories to sustain their hopes. The average person believed that he carried the civilian equivalent of a marshal's baton in his knapsack; he had no need of a Bonaparte to tell him so.

Citizens of the lower class—seamen, day laborers, Negroes—composed a much smaller fraction of city populations, save at Charles Town, than one might suppose. Lacking the franchise, they had little to say in municipal affairs, but one thing is certain, their white members were not a depressed group. Many of them rose to middle-class standing and not a few became property-owners. Along with the tradesmen and artisans they had hopes of improving their status and their fortunes.

City life wrought changes in attitudes and behavior that set the residents farther than ever apart from the inhabitants of the rural and back-country sections. Worldliness, which was insidiously making its way against traditional piety as townspeople increasingly cultivated all sorts of amusements and recreations, was far more the outgrowth of urban life than of the advance of science. The English, Scots, Scotch-Irish, and Germans more readily discarded extreme provincial or national traits and assumed a more tolerant attitude toward strangers once they came under the cosmopolitanism of the cities. Furthermore, with the exception of Newport, the seaports grew less English as their populations mounted.

Despite the distances that separated the two continents and the demands made on the new arrivals to establish

themselves, the commercial and cultural bonds joining European and American peoples were such that probably not until after our first war with Germany was the average citizen of the New World again so much aware of his membership in the Atlantic community. Thousands of immigrants arrived at most of the ports each year: Englishmen of all conditions, but notably skilled artisans and craftsmen eager to exchange the low wages and insecurity of London and Bristol for higher pay and surer employment at Philadelphia, New York, or Charles Town; Palatines lured by promotion literature; and Scotch-Irish bitter against the Britons and in desperate need of a new start. These newcomers contributed intelligence and skills as well as brawn to the building of the cities. Conversely, more colonials were making the long voyage back to Europe—home, as many said of England. Masters and their crews were, of course, familiar with the ports of the Old World, and merchants too. Now young men began to travel to complete their education in the universities of England, Scotland, and Europe or to make the grand tour before they settled down in counting-houses or the professions.

Ideas as well as persons and material goods took passage with every vessel and helped to batter down provincialism and force colonials to sharpen their wits. In the American cities, less bound by tradition and superstition than those of the Old World and bourgeois to the very core, the seminal ideas of the Age of Reason found a warm reception; no accumulated rubbish of the past had to be cleared out before the revolutionary and liberating forces of the Enlightenment could be released. Changing from old ways to new did not entail such a wrench in the New World, where the experimental temper of the people, continually facing new situations in a new environment, nourished a new philosophy. The Protestantism of the colonials, their very dissent from the established church, prepared the ground for these new concepts; the psychological change had been in progress for over thirty years before the shot heard round the world gave notice of the fact.

The people, living in congested cities and in constant contact with one another, could not fail to acquire a host of traits that collectively comprised the urban character—a character quite as American as that which Crèvecœur discovered in the inland farmers. The average townsman seemed, to travelers, to be more intelligent than his European opposite, or perhaps gave that impression because the life he led was more untrammeled. By their public acts the citizens showed themselves outstanding humanitarians, and in their good works offered models to Europeans. Individually most of them were ambitious and energetic, assertive and often grasping, generally thrifty, and independent. Doubtless many immigrants failed to adjust to the strange new world, and frustration and pessimism must have gripped many others; still, experience apparently confirmed the optimism and hope of most of the citizens. In short, the colonial urban temperament had in it a mixture of imported theory and native experience. Above all, in such figures as Benjamin Franklin, Ezra Stiles, Charles Willson Peale, James Parker, and Henry Laurens, the cities produced leaders, men who became not only great citizens but great Americans, because they grasped the essentials of their own existence and that of their

fellows and set their sights on fixed and attainable goals.

With very few exceptions, the culture of the late colonial period was of urban origin. In the cities alone could the necessary conditions for a vital intellectual life be found: wealth and leisure for patronage, talent for performance, and an audience to enjoy, applaud, and encourage further efforts. The commercial aristocrat far more than the gentleman planter met the requirements for the patron, and he displayed the willingness to gather in the trophies produced by local talent. Passive in his attitudes toward the arts, he never became a professional, or, at the most, indulged in the dilettantism of a Francis Hopkinson. Nowhere save in these cities did there exist a vigorous middle class from whose "ingenious craftsmen" the practitioners of the arts and sciences might be recruited—a Franklin, a Copley, a Timothy, or a Harrison. The city offered better education and opportunities for persons of like minds to convene, discuss, and practice their arts amid friendly surroundings. Harvard, King's, and the College of Philadelphia did much to foster interest in the sciences. Finally, the cosmopolitan urban center served as the seedbed for the ideas of the Enlightenment, and in the long run, the social change, call it revolution, first took hold in the cities and their environs and proved more far-reaching and permanent than that begun in France and spread over continental Europe.

For the times, the accomplishments of the colonial urban centers were noteworthy and were admired abroad as well as applauded at home. The press, a purely urban phenomenon, enjoyed greater freedom than that of any other country, including England, and, in its role of formulating and swaying public opinion, was the fundamental fact of American culture. Through its support and encouragement, a vigorous prose style evolved, which culminated in the magnificent controversial literature and impressive state papers of the Revolution—a political literature almost unsurpassed in history. At least seven painters from the four Northern towns won foreign recognition after having succeeded in their craft on this side of the water. In architecture Peter Harrison and Robert Smith earned intercolonial reputations, and the work of many gentlemen amateurs, like Robert Crommelin, revealed a well-developed taste in this art. No musician of permanent worth appeared in the colonial towns, but a wide interest and participation in singing and playing testified to a forming taste, and a few such as Gualdo and Billings portended later accomplishment. The most significant performances came in science with the first-rate achievement of Franklin in electricity, the minor though sound astronomical work of John Winthrop and David Rittenhouse, and the botanical contribution of John Bartram. With the formation of the American Philosophical Society, scientific investigation on this continent entered into that co-operative phase which has characterized all subsequent investigation. The record of intercolonial and international traffic in culture by these new communities is impressive.

The Enlightenment took different forms in different parts of the Western World according to the nature of the society or the needs of its people. That which was universal in it was a corpus of ideas; votaries borrowed such of them as suited their peculiar wants. One could hardly expect, therefore, that the Enlightenment would take the same form in the cities as it did in the British Isles or in France. It had to be an American variant. What happened was that with discriminating selectivity the citizens took the ideas of the Old World as refurbished by the philosophers of the Enlightenment and, working out their own responses to such forces of modernity as intimately affected their existence in their own communities, translated them into action. Here were five points at which ideas became facts and thereby created history. The novel element, "the American thing," was not the philosophy or the system but the synthesis. In their indefeasible loyalty to the Enlightenment, the townsmen in their civic as well as their cultural undertakings insisted upon performance rather than talk or thought (perhaps too much so); they determined to set ideas in motion. By 1776 they had proved beyond all cavil their collective greatness by their capacity to borrow, not merely to imitate but successfully to adapt, to transform, and ultimately to assimilate current and older European elements. In so doing the people of these cities ceased to be colonials; they became Americans.

In 1743 the average citizen, when he thought about it at all, loved his native community for its age, its local traditions and associations, and as the place he called home. Nationalism in the modern sense did not then exist, even in England or in France; local patriotism absorbed the loyalties of most people. A series of negative reactions to imperial policies, however, served to arouse colonial pride concurrently with resentment of the mother country: the fiasco of Carthagena and the heedless loss of nine out of ten colonials, the return of hard-won Louisburg to France in 1748, the brutal activities (no matter how legal) of the press gang, the ill-concealed contempt of the British military for "Americans," Parliamentary prohibition of vitally needed paper money, the course and aftermath of the wars in general, and the detestation of placemen. These and other irritants played a prominent part in the growing realization that, as Goethe would later say:

> *Amerika, du hast es besser*
> *Als unser Continent. . . .*

Prior to 1763 such sentiments as these seldom rose to the surface of colonial thinking but remained, for the most part, in "the deep well of unconscious cerebration."

All of these issues between the colonials and the mother country hinged on attitudes toward overseas authority and the actions of its local representatives. A minority of American conservatives consistently supported British officialdom; they were now branded Tories. The Whig, or liberal majority view, stressed provincial rights. Both sides sought to guide public opinion through the press, but gradually the latter, with the support of the printers, won out. The newspapers began to single out anything "American" for unrestrained praise, which stimulated the burgeoning pride of the citizens. In 1760 Benjamin Franklin, a loyal British subject, welcomed the accession of George III; only fifteen years later he spoke with contempt of "that noble China-vase, the British Empire"—so far had loyalties shifted under provocation and self-stimulus. The contest of the

sixties forced the citizens to a recognition of the differences between Englishmen and Americans, to list their own strengths and virtues, to discount or overlook their weaknesses and defects, and above all to feel their own maturity as a society. The colonial world was a new place, it *was* different. Most people had come to live in it by choice, and they were, as Crèvecœur said, a new breed.

Notwithstanding their status as colonials and therefore somewhat restricted by British policy, the citizens had lived in a free society, the freest then known anywhere. During the war years and after 1763, suspicions that hard-won liberties were to be abridged or lost aroused fear and resentment, and at the same time there welled up a strange, new, but exhilarating emotion —Americanism. A majority of citizens determined to preserve these freedoms at any cost; and as the issues clarified with each new crisis, they proceeded from protest to opposition, from opposition to revolt, and ultimately, in 1776, to independence. This shift of loyalties and birth of nationalism occurred before Lexington; it was upon a sure knowledge of this powerful sentiment that Thomas Paine could, in *Common Sense*, make the great emotional appeal for independence. Provincial attachments had long been and would again continue to be foremost in the thoughts of rural inhabitants, especially in Virginia, but decades before independence the cities became the birthplace of American nationality.[1] Thinking men like John Adams saw this clearly: "The Revolution was effected before the war commenced. The Revolution was in the minds and hearts of the people. . . . This radical change in the principles, sentiments, and affections of the people was the real American Revolution." The primary role of the cities in the attaining of American independence was preparatory. They provided five centers where the essential conjunction of people, leadership, and events could occur and give concrete expression to what Thomas Jefferson with his customary felicity called "the unquestionable republicanism of the American mind." Revolt would never have succeeded—nay, it would hardly have been attempted—had there not been this silent social and intellectual preparation which sustained the sense of American nationality so evident in the cities after 1764. These communities composed a dynamic society, one bursting with pent-up forces which have often been thought to be the result of the War for Independence, whose true role was not to generate but to release them. When the final break came, the city dwellers succeeded in carrying their fellows of the rural and frontier sections with them. From this point of view, the uprising against Great Britain is seen as the culmination of a deeper, more subtle change that encompassed the entire colonial urban experience as the cities, so completely in harmony with the ideas of the Enlightenment, silently and persistently revolted against the tyranny of the past and cast their lot with modern times.

NOTES

1. No disparagement of the great and vital contribution of the Virginia planters to the revolutionary movement is here implied. Even in the Old Dominion the village of Williamsburg assumed during "publick times" certain urban attributes and exerted an influence similar to that of the large cities, as I have pointed out in *Seat of Empire* (Williamsburg, 1950), pp. 29, 33.

The Expansion of New England

PAGE SMITH

"The Expansion of New England" was the title chosen by Lois Kimball Mathews for her turn-of-the-century study of the spread of New England settlement and institutions to the Mississippi. Miss Mathew's book, published in 1909, marks a kind of watershed in American historiography. Most of the prominent historians of nineteenth-century America were New Englanders, bred and trained in a tradition-bound society and dedicated to the proposition that Old England had given birth to the greater part of what was estimable in the world and that New England had brought it to fruition.

The phrase "Anglo-Saxon" was often on the tongues of these historians, and through their genial monopoly of American history they spread the impression

From Page Smith, *As a City Upon a Hill* (New York: Knopf, 1966), pp. 37–54. Copyright © 1966 by Page Smith. Reprinted by permission of Alfred A. Knopf, Inc. Page Smith is Provost of Cowell College, University of California, Santa Cruz.

across the country that the finest flowers of our society had been nurtured in New England soil. There was, moreover, a good deal of evidence to back them up, and if they were sometimes inclined to bear heavily on the evidence in order to prove, for instance, that the Puritans were the fathers of American democracy, they were nonetheless high-minded, scholarly, and industrious gentlemen who contributed greatly to, if they did not in fact make up, American historiography in their century.

In the last decades of the nineteenth century a number of young historians rose to challenge what might be called the Anglo-New England interpretation of our past. Frederick Jackson Turner was the most effective spokesman of the thesis that it was to uniquely American factors, rather than to our English heritage, that the United States owed its remarkable development. Turner's brilliant essay on the role of the frontier in American history had symbolic as well as scholarly significance. It was received, not as proven fact—it was, as it turned out, not provable—but as revelation. The response that it evoked in the historical profession showed how inadequate the Anglo-New England version of our past had become in a world awakened to new intellectual currents. The hinterland could not forever be brought to worship at a temple whose high priests were Yankee historians. The Turner thesis was, perhaps primarily, the Midwest's declaration of intellectual and moral independence from the East. But there was more to it than that. The social and political attitudes of the older generation of historians had been thoroughly conservative. Their emphasis was on the persistence of tradition and the continuity of institutions; by dwelling on the Old World

roots of American culture, they ensured New England's eminence as its preserver and transmitter.

It was hardly to be expected that these claims would go forever undisputed. If a Weaver, a Bryan, or a La Follette appeared to challenge the political hegemony of the Northeast, there must be a Turner to provide the historical rationale for the new claims. But if it was the West that saw in Turner the prophet of intellectual and cultural equality, the East was also ready to embrace him. He preached a national doctrine. The younger generation of historians had been deeply affected by those currents of reform that manifest themselves in Progressivism. Turner became the preceptor of a generation of historians many of whom came, like their master, from the Middle West and most of whom were passionate crusaders for a wider social democracy. Turner taught them to look skeptically on the old gods and to examine their credentials with a ruthless disregard of the accepted pieties. The study and writing of American history profited enormously thereby. But the new schools inevitably produced their own distortions.

Lois Kimball Mathews stood between the two traditions—that of George Bancroft on the one hand and that of Turner on the other. She gave her scholarly allegiance without question to the exciting new spokesman of the West, but she had strong emotional ties with the Anglo-New England school. As a result the subject on which she chose to write her doctoral dissertation —the expansion of New England—was perfectly suited to elaborate the new dogma while propitiating the old gods. Her book professed to show how important New England had been in the settlement of the West; but at the same time it acknowledged the Turner doctrine by stressing the degree to which the frontier modified the ideas and institutions of the pioneers, and it accepted as a basic tenet that, in every New England town, it was the "radical," "progressive," and "independent" spirits who migrated westward.

Although a product of the new scholarship, Miss Mathews could not free herself of all vestiges of the older tradition. Thus we find frequent references to the marvelous properties of "Anglo-Saxon blood," the same blood that Miss Mathews's predecessors had exalted as having unique propensities for freedom—in the classic phrase "liberty-loving Anglo-Saxon blood"—blood whose individual corpuscles were imbued with zeal for civil rights and popular government. For Miss Mathews, it was also blood containing a "wanderlust" that helped to explain the migratory impulses of those through whose veins it flowed. The mysterious properties of this blood, which it may be feared will continue to evade chemical analysis, was the favorite *deus ex machina* of the earlier New England historians. Whatever was otherwise elusive and inexplicable might at last be traced to this magic fluid.

In Miss Mathews we might therefore discern a historian of New England, ready to join the new champions of the frontier, but on terms which enabled her to preserve a good measure of glory for the auld sod. The story of the frontier, she wrote, in the best Turner tradition, was "a study of institutions transplanted and transformed, the old ones influencing the new ones, the new ones reacting upon the old, making the latter broader and more flexible." Cramped by the conservatism of the

New England towns "the more radical spirits began to chafe, and turn to newer sections where they might be unhampered by either tradition or habit." In this way "the spirit of radicalism so conspicuous among the pioneer's motives" had contributed "immeasurably" to the development of the country, since the frontier showed thereby a "tendency to radicalism in all matters."

"The conservative element," by Miss Mathews's reading, remained in the "settled portions of the country" making those sections increasingly stodgy with each passing decade. The forces that influenced the pioneer to start on his westward trek were his "radicalism," his "sometimes excessive individualism," "the desire for greater material prosperity" and, of course, his wandering Anglo-Saxon blood. The classic pioneer was "a New Englander grown more independent and probably more tolerant under his new environment."

The pioneers were in the terms of the new dogma individuals who longed "for the open, for the free life of an unorganized community." But the fact was that the frontier town settled by New Englanders, far from being "a community where people might do as they pleased," was if anything more highly organized, more rigid and repressive than its parent community, while the forces of change, sparked by an expanding ocean commerce with its attendant prosperity, appeared first, as Carl Bridenbaugh has shown, in the large seacoast towns and cities. If there were any Puritans who founded communities "where people might do as they pleased" they have escaped this historian's notice.

The propositions about the migrating New Englander that are stated so confidently, Miss Mathews does not attempt to prove. They were part of the new dispensation, taken by her and by many of her contemporaries as articles of faith. Yet Miss Mathews, aware that theory is not entirely consistent with fact, reveals her own uneasiness when she notes of the pioneers that "curiously enough . . . when the malcontents found themselves in the majority instead of the minority (as they had been before their removal), they frequently became as intolerant as their comrades had been."[1] The key word in this passage is "curiously." That settlers on the frontier should be as intolerant as their cousins back home (or more so) was only "curious" if the historian saw the pioneer as the forerunner of Progressivism. The idea that the frontier was populated by individuals imbued with the ideals of twentieth-century liberal reform could be dismissed as simply naïve if it had not been accepted by so many historians. The myth of the "liberal" pioneer has been almost as enduring as the older image of the noble Anglo-Saxon, which it replaced.

The story of New England's expansion is far more complex than Miss Mathews suggests. The development of the American frontier has of course been continuous. From the earliest years of colonial settlement the older seacoast towns bred new communities deeper in the wilderness. The spectacular settlement of the West that took place in the nineteenth century had been preceded, and was indeed accompanied by the settlement of northern New England, New York, and Pennsylvania as well as the southern frontier of Kentucky and Tennessee. No radical change occurred in the motives of settlement from the colonial period through the early decades of the nineteenth century. The Puritans who had

pushed out from the Massachusetts Bay area had had for the most part the same motives as their descendants who moved into Ohio, Illinois, and Michigan two hundred years later. One of the principal causes of such migration was religious controversy.

Robert East has pointed out that "a distinctive force in the expansion of the New England frontier in the seventeenth century *and later* [italics mine] . . . is a certain explosive character in Calvinistic Puritanism itself. The dynamic church principle inherent in the doctrine of every man his own priest was in constant disharmony with the severe external authority attempted in practice by the Puritan clergy and elders."

The result was the constant fragmenting of the parent communities, but the secessions were of a group, rather than an individual, type. True, the group generally formed about a person of unusual force of character, but it was as a group that the dissenters departed, not as separate individuals; and a new covenant was invariably the first order of business. Certainly some of "the rag-tag and bobtail element" fled from settled communities to the frontier, but as East states it, "the effective spearhead of expansion was generally in the religiously discontented."

With such a figure as Roger Williams in mind we are inclined to think of these dissenters as being somehow "liberal," but in reality they were often the most rigidly orthodox members of the community, individuals who were alarmed at the softening of Puritan dogmas and who withdrew to the wilderness to recover the purity of the ancient faith. It was often, at least in terms of theology, the liberal elements who achieved dominance in the older towns and cities, precipitating the exodus of the conservatives. In East's words, again, the farther west one traveled "the more 'orthodox' was the Puritanism at work; contrarily, the more liberal and enlightened (or corrupt and defiled, according to one's point of view) did Harvard and Boston appear. . . . The forward-looking, the liberal religious element of the eighteenth century was invariably found in the older settlements of the seaboard and the [Connecticut] valley."[2]

It was, after all, Cotton Mather, the high priest of Boston Puritanism, who favored private examination for church membership as opposed to the traditional examination by the congregation. It was in Boston, too, that the Half-Way Covenant got its strongest backing. The church at Branford, Connecticut, offended by the union of the colonies of New Haven and Connecticut and at the spread of the Half-Way Covenant, moved en masse to Newark, New Jersey; a similar dispute in Stratford led to the founding of Woodbury, Connecticut. Bennington, Vermont, was settled from Hardwick, Massachusetts, by Captain Samuel Robinson who took twenty-two people with him, all of them conservatives who wished to preserve the old faith.

The records of one New England town after another disclose bitter and often protracted disputes over theological doctrines and even over the personalities of particular ministers. Wethersfield, Connecticut, alone colonized a number of towns as the result of splittings off from the original church. It might be argued that quarreling was one of the principal causes of the expansion of New England. It was then, as it is today, difficult to repair the unity of the town once it was shat-tered; it was generally easier for the minority to withdraw, and it did so. The emigrants were, however, no more radical, tolerant, or independent than their less mobile neighbors.

In essence, the process was this: as the original community began to break down—sometimes because of theological wrangles, sometimes because of progressive economic and social differentiation, sometimes because of its own inner tensions—individuals within the community coalesced around aggressive leaders and then broke off to found their own communities, hoping thereby to recapture the classic unity of their common life.

An example of this is Worthington, Ohio, formed by settlers from Granby, Connecticut, who "drew up articles of association, among which was one limiting their number to forty, each of whom must be unanimously chosen by ballot, a single negative being sufficient to prevent an election." It would be difficult to discover in such action any yearning for independence or any desire to be free of the tyranny of the community.

Colonization by congregations and kinship groups, fiercely exclusive in many instances, refutes the argument that the pioneers were champions of "individualism." The settler who wished to go his own way, free from the scrutiny of his neighbors, stood a better chance in the older towns than in frontier communities, unless, of course, he was willing to live the precarious life of an isolated trapper and hunter. While it is true that the emigrants often left their home communities pronouncing an anathema on them as being sunk in vice, vain presumption, and worldliness, these strictures were not related to "radical" or liberal political theories, or indeed related, in most instances, to politics at all. They referred to the community's failure to live up to the covenant, and thus they have a better claim to the title of "conservative" than of "radical."

The New Englanders who colonized towns, far from being conscious or unconscious innovators, sought to reproduce the institutions and values of their home communities. They wished in Norwalk, Ohio, to create a refined and purified version of Norwalk, Connecticut. A historian, discussing the founding of Hudson, Ohio, by colonists from New Haven, has written that while the town "might, in many ways, be more primitive and ruder than New Haven, yet, in another way, it was the Connecticut original in purer form, undiluted and undistracted by modern worldliness and the change encroaching on the east."[3]

It must be said that many communities did not have their origins in religious dissent and contention. The need for new land was undoubtedly the most persistent motive for emigration, and the strength of the ties between new town and old is suggested by the frequency with which the frontier settlement took the name of its parent community. Richmond, New Hampshire, was named after Richmond, Rhode Island. Lebanon, Lyme, and Plainfield of the Granite State were all offspring of Connecticut towns with the same names, and the list could be extended by the hundreds and indeed thousands.[4]

The settlement of Maine and Vermont was not halted by the Revolution. In 1780 nine new towns were founded in Maine and twelve in Vermont. Almost all the early settlers of Andover, Maine, migrated from Andover, Massachusetts, in protest of the relaxed theology of the Massachusetts town. New Vineyard was peopled from Martha's Vineyard, and Exeter, Maine, was settled from Exeter, New Hampshire. Vermont's Braintree was the offshoot of Massachusetts' Braintree, and Pittsfield and Groton were named after towns in the Bay State.

It was not, however, to northern New England that emigrating Yankees went in largest numbers. New York, Pennsylvania, and Ohio claimed tens of thousands. A Congregational church organized in Poultney, Vermont, moved in a body to East Springfield, New York, and became like many others with similar origins a model New England community. Wherever the settlers went they carried their politics with them as well as their religion. Luzerne County, New York, was a stronghold of New England Federalism and so it continued for more than a generation.

Hudson, New York, was settled in 1783 by thirty Quaker fishermen and their families from Martha's Vineyard; and from Plymouth, Massachusetts, to Plymouth, Connecticut, to Plymouth, Ohio, we can trace families, civil institutions, and church dogmas in an unbroken line; from Greenwich, Connecticut, to Greenwich, Ohio, and from the New England Deerfield to its western counterparts.

Religious revivals and "awakenings," perhaps more than any other single factor, were responsible for the establishment of colonized towns. The Great Awakening of the 1730's and 1740's led directly to the founding of a number of "New Light" communities and a half dozen colleges. The awakening which swept through Connecticut at the end of the eighteenth century scattered Connecticut towns through New York, Vermont, and Ohio. Hudson, Ohio, was just such a community; it was started by David Hudson, a native of Goshen, Connecticut, who, according to his own testimony, had been a Godless man and then was caught up in a revival, underwent a profound spiritual crisis and, pledging himself to God's service, vowed to found a community in the wilderness which would live according to God's ordinances. In the words of Richard Wohl: "From the very first he determined that his resolve should not be dissipated under the stress of a frontier life with its attendant hardships. He need not have feared. The isolation, the hard work done in common, sustained the original homogeneity of the group and served, indeed, to provide it with added vitality." Having established his covenanted community in the forest, Hudson went on to help found Western Reserve College.[5]

The story was a typical one. The older towns were like ripe seed pods which when heated by one of the periodic revivals would burst open and scatter seedlings wherever the winds of migration were blowing at the moment.

After the earlier period of migration, the increase in missionary activity—especially by the Congregationalists and Presbyterians—led to the settling of many new communities and to the gathering together of individual farm families into congregations.

When a group from Granville, Massachusetts, decided to move to the Ohio country, a 24-member Congregational church drew up a covenant and a constitution and transplanted pastor, deacons, and church members to Granville, Ohio. The emigrants numbered 176 and their first act upon reaching the new settlement was to hold a service of worship in the forest. One of the little band later wrote of how they wept when they heard their voices echoing among the lonely and forbidding trees; "they wept when they remembered Zion."

Oberlin, in Lorain County, was another classic example of the transplanted New England community. The colonists were asked to subscribe to a covenant which pledged them to "a life of simplicity, to special devotion to church and school, and to earnest labor in the missionary cause."[6]

Illinois and Indiana's earliest settlers were Southerners, many of them from North Carolina, Kentucky, and Tennessee. The great influx of New Englanders into Indiana came in the 1830's and the decades that followed. In Elkhart County, 213 out of 255 settlers in the years between 1828 and 1840 came from New England. Grange, Noble, and La Porte counties were largely settled by families from Massachusetts, Connecticut, and Vermont. A Connecticut colony was established in 1834 at Rockwell, Illinois, and in 1836 three New England colonies were founded, one at Tremont in Tazewell County, one in Knox County, and one at Lyons near Varna. A company from Gilmanton, New Hampshire, settled Hanover in 1835 and settlers from Pittsfield, Massachusetts, established a purified version of their hometown in Pittsfield, Illinois.[7] Wethersfield was founded by a pastor and his congregation from Wethersfield, Connecticut, while a church colony from Benson, Vermont, moved as a group to Du Page County. From Rhode Island in 1836 came forty families, members of the Providence Farmers' and Mechanics' Emigrating Society, who had organized a church and school before their departure.

A colony from Northampton, Massachusetts, was adjacent to one from Norwich, Connecticut. The so-called Hampshire colony organized its own church and academy and planted a town in Bureau County. By 1840 Illinois could count at least twenty-two colonies in northern or central Illinois, all of which had their origin in New England or New York. There was, to be sure, a great number of people who came at random into the state and who either joined established towns or formed loosely knit rural communities. But the colonized towns played a role in the history of the state that was out of all proportion to their numbers. In a few years these centers came to dominate the social and political life of Illinois. As a former governor wrote, the Yankee was "the most liberal in contributing to whatever is for the public benefit. Is a schoolhouse, a bridge, or a church to be built, a road to be made, a school or minister to be maintained, or taxes to be paid for the honor or support of the government, the northern man is never found wanting."[8]

The Southerners on the other hand, while more picturesque, were notoriously indolent, a vice which led to many others. "On a bright day," a traveler wrote, "they mount their horses and throng the little towns in the vicinity of their homes, drinking and trading horses until late in the evening." Toward education the Southerner had a humorous hostility. "He 'reckons' they should know how to write their names, and 'allows it's a right smart thing to be able to read when you want to' . . . but he don't 'calculate' that books and the sciences will do as much good for a man in these matters as a handy use of the rifle. . . . As for teaching 'that's one thing he allows the Yankees are just fit for'; he does not hesitate to confess that they are a 'power smarter' at that than the western boys. But they can't

hold a rifle nor ride at wolf hunt with 'em; and he reckons, after all, these are the great tests of merit."[9]

Sixty New Englanders came to Romeo, Michigan, in 1827 and gave that town a thoroughly Yankee character. By 1850 almost half of Michigan's population had come from New England by way of New York, and as much as a third or a quarter came directly from New England.

The Union Colony got its start in Poultney and Bennington, Vermont, where the Reverend Sylvester Cochrane recruited ten families, adding three more from Benson and Bellevue, Michigan. Before the Vermonters left home they signed a covenant which began:

> *Whereas,* The enjoyment of the ordinances . . . of the Gospel is in a great measure unknown in . . . the western country, and
> *Whereas,* We believe that a pious and devoted emigration is . . . one of the most efficient means, in the hands of God, in removing the moral darkness which hangs over a great portion of the valley of the Mississippi; and
> *Whereas,* We believe that a removal to the West may be a means of promoting our temporal interest, and we trust [may] be made subservient to the advancement of Christ's kingdom;
> *We do therefore,* form ourselves into . . . a colony with the design of removing into some parts of the western country which shall hereafter be designated, and agree to bind ourselves to . . . the following rules. . . .

The rules covered codes of behavior and, since the town wished to preserve equality among its members, the rules for the distribution of land. No settler was to be allowed to take more than "one farm lot of 160 acres, and one village lot of 10 acres, within the limits of the settlement."

A final injunction to the colonists of Vermontville, as the community came to be called, carried overtones of John Winthrop's "Modell of Christian Charity." "As we must necessarily endure many of those trials and privations which are incident to a settlement in a new country," the statement read, "we agree we will do all in our power to befriend each other; we will esteem it not only a duty, but a privilege to sympathize with each other under all our trials, to do good and lend, hoping for nothing again, and to assist each other on all necessary occasions."[10]

While the tide of colonizing by the purer type of covenanted religious community declined as the nineteenth century wore on, there continued to be many such towns founded. And those such as the temperance and antislavery towns that were established on some substitute version of the covenant were generally deeply imbued with religious feeling.

After the passage of the Kansas-Nebraska Bill in March, 1854, New England emigrants poured into Kansas. New Haven sent a band of seventy settlers known as the Connecticut Colony, a group which included tradesmen, teachers of music, tutors in Yale College, politicians, farmers, and ministers. The community, the forerunner of a number of future colonies, settled on the Wabaunsee River, armed with twenty-five rifles and twenty-five Bibles, gifts from Henry Ward Beecher's Brooklyn congregation.

Amenia, North Dakota, was founded by pioneers from Sharon, Connecticut, who planted their church at once and prided themselves on never having "sought for Eastern sources a single dollar in its support." Down to the end of the century, the Yale Divinity School dispatched its famous "Bands" of young ministers to the Far West and North-west, and many New Englanders followed them to California, Oregon, and Washington. Moreover town building went on in the unclaimed regions of the older Midwestern states as well as on the frontier, and New England contributed generously to such communities.[11]

As for the Turner-Mathews thesis, while it is undoubtedly true that much individual migration was motivated by a desire to escape from the restraints of organized society, myth has vastly exaggerated their number and importance. Such emigrants were certainly not town builders, though they became in many instances the nucleus for towns. They were the cutting edge of the westward movement (Timothy Dwight called them "foresters"), whose function it was "to cut down trees, build log-houses, lay open forested grounds to cultivation, and prepare the way for those who come after them. These men," Dwight wrote, "cannot live in regular society. They are too idle; too talkative; too passionate; too prodigal; and too shiftless; to acquire either property or character. They are impatient of the restraints of law, religion, and morality; grumble about the taxes, by which Rulers, Ministers, and Schoolmasters are supported; and complain incessantly, as well as bitterly, of the extortions of mechanics, farmers, merchants, and physicians; to whom they are always indebted."[12]

This is, to be sure, a somewhat jaundiced view of the classic pioneer figure. Nevertheless we know from many other accounts that the description is not far wide of the mark. Such individuals were the restless, the discontent, the psychologically and economically marginal portions of older communities. Yet the myth has associated them with a dream of romantic freedom. We might well recall the words of D. H. Lawrence: "Men are free when they are in a living homeland, not when they are straying and breaking away. Men are free when they are obeying some deep, inward voice of religious belief. Obeying from within. Men are free when they belong to a living, organic, *believing* community, active in fulfilling some unfulfilled, perhaps unrealized purpose."[13]

The lonely, wide-ranging frontiersmen bulk large in historical fiction and in the popular mind, but they counted for little in comparison with the town builders of the covenant.

If New England placed the stamp of its own spirit on the Middle West, it did so by dispatching what were by any reasonable standards its most conservative sons and daughters to fill up the vast empty spaces. The colonized communities of Puritans who occupied the frontier states were composed neither of "radicals," nor "independents," nor "lovers of freedom" as an abstract principle. Far from being "tolerant," they were highly intolerant of cities, of the big business of the day, of alien races and faiths, of drinking, of Sabbath-breaking, and indeed of a host of things. Those who remained in the Eastern towns and cities learned to live with the Irish, the French-Canadians, the Poles, the Italians, "the offscourings of the earth," and often to make profits from them. They learned to tolerate what they could not well evade. But in the iron soul of the Puritan town builder there was little tolerance for those who stood outside of the covenant of grace. These builders were the true believers, nerved by their faith to subdue the heartland of a continent in the name of a Jehovah who, if he was terrible in his wrath, was also wonderfully forgiving.

The transplanting of Eastern "culture" froze rather than liberated it. The new town "clung to traditional institutional forms and social practices; and it hungered after intellectual and social contact and parity with the East. A large part of western opportunity was the opportunity to imitate an older society." Before the West could claim parity, it had to prove that it could successfully emulate its supercilious parent. The frontier towns were thus an enormously conservative force since they clung tenaciously to "forms" and "practices" that were a generation old by city standards.

"Much has been said, and foolishly said, of Western character," wrote the Reverend Rufus Babcock. "Most people in the West formed their characters before they emigrated thither; and they have been slightly or not at all modified by their change of residence."[14] The great majority of those who came to the frontier were conservative to begin with. Their situation on a frontier where they felt that the forms and order of civilized life were threatened made them far more resolute in resisting change than their urban cousins.

NOTES

1. Lois Kimball Mathews: *The Expansion of New England* (Boston: Houghton Mifflin Company; 1909), pp. 4, 5, 6, 73, 72.
2. Robert A. East: "Puritanism and New England Settlement," *New England Quarterly*, XVII (June, 1944), 255, 256-7, 263.
3. Richard Wohl: "Henry Day," in William Miller, ed.: *Men in Business* (Cambridge, Mass.: Harvard University Press; 1952), p. 164.
4. Mathews: *Expansion*, p. 114.
5. Wohl: "Henry Day," p. 162.
6. Henry Howe: *Historical Collections of Ohio* (Cincinnati: Derby, Bradley & Co.; 1848), pp. 296, 297; James H. Fairchild: *Oberlin, the Colony and the College, 1833-1883* (Oberlin, Ohio: E. J. Goodrich; 1883), pp. 9-16.
7. Theodore Calvin Pease: *The Frontier State, 1818-1848* (Springfield, Ill.: Illinois Centennial Commission; 1918), pp. 178-9.

8. Thomas Ford: *A History of Illinois* (New York: Iverson & Phinney; 1854), p. 281; Albert Shaw: *Local Government in Illinois* (Baltimore: Johns Hopkins University; 1838), p. 11; Charles A. Church: *History of Rockford, Illinois, and Winnebago County* (Rockford, Ill.: W. P. Lamb; 1900), pp. 160 ff.; William V. Pooley: "The Settlement of Illinois from 1830 to 1850," *Bulletin* of the University of Wisconsin, no. 220 (1908).

9. Clyde E. Buckingham: "Early Settlers of the Rock River Valley," *Journal of the Illinois State Historical Society*, XXXV (September, 1942), pp. 242, 241 quoting Eliza W. Farnham: *Life in Prairie Land* (New York: Harper & Brothers; 1846).

10. Edward W. Barber: "The Vermontville Colony: Its Genesis and History," *Michigan Pioneer and Historical Collections*, XXVIII (1900); J. Harold Stevens: "The Influence of New England in Michigan," *Michigan Historical Magazine*, XIX (autumn, 1935), pp. 321-53.

11. Lois Kimball Mathews Rosenberry: "Migrations from Connecticut after 1800," *Tercentenary Commission of the State of Connecticut*, LIV (New Haven: Yale University Press, 1936), pp. 18, 19, 20, 29.

12. Dwight: *Travels*, II, 459.

13. D. H. Lawrence: *Studies in Classic American Literature* (London: M. Secker; 1933), p. 12.

14. Earl Pomeroy: "Towards a Reorientation of Western History," *Mississippi Valley Historical Review*, XLI (March, 1955), pp. 597, 593.

III THE CITY IN THE ERA OF MANIFEST DESTINY

The nineteenth century was "the century of cities." From Australia to Europe, urbanization was an international phenomenon, but it was seldom surpassed in the speed and size of its growth than in the United States. The popular conception of urban expansion usually associates it with the rise of the industrial giants in the forty years after the Civil War. But the first sixty years of the century were as dynamic as (and in some ways more dramatic than) the post-Civil War period. Cornfields, trading stations, forts, lake and river ports, construction camps, and whistle stops, developed into towns, small and large, and sometimes sank into ghost towns. It was a period of unprecedented optimism and wild speculation, where the enthusiasm of "manifest destiny" to conquer a continent was also poured into town and city building.

Perhaps never in our history have so many Americans shown such unbridled faith and competitive rivalry about their cities: undoubtedly, Athens, Ohio, would outshine her ancient Greek namesake, Chicago would outgrow New York, St. Louis would dominate the American heartland—all would be bigger and better than their wicked and dirty European counterparts. Never in our history has the United States experienced such rapid urban growth as the four decades preceding the Civil War. From 1820 to 1860 the total population of the country increased by 226 per cent, while the urban population increased by almost 800 per cent. Whereas roughly 6 per cent of Americans lived in cities in 1800, not only were 20 per cent urban dwellers by 1860, but Philadelphia was bigger than Berlin, New York was the third largest city in the world, and Chicago was the most spectacular of them all. A scruffy little village of fifty people in 1830, Chicago survived a panic and depression and, with little more than mud and a prayer, seized upon canal and railroad building to explode by 1853 into a city of 60,000 people with 150 hotels. Old and new cities in the East and South continued to grow, with the South, significantly for the later Civil War period, lagging behind. But nowhere was there more hope, lusty vitality, and

95

bigger dreams in the seventy years after the formation of the new nation than in the urban expansion in the new West.

Whereas Page Smith described the small town as the cutting edge of the wilderness, Richard Wade, in the first selection—a major essay in the literature of American urban history[1]—describes the cities of the trans-Appalachian West from 1790 to 1830 as the "spearheads of the frontier." To the familiar array of such western characters as the hunter and farmer, Wade adds the urbanite, many of whom moved west to settle good towns rather than to cultivate good land. His thesis of the urban frontier is another important revision of the frontier thesis of Frederick Jackson Turner, for Wade shows that the city dweller often preceded the farmer in the westward plunge of the early nineteenth century. Cities like Cincinnati, Lexington, Louisville, St. Louis, and Pittsburgh were not only spearheads of settlement, but spearheads of political, economic, and cultural leaderships as well. Although they worked in mutual dependence with the farm, the cities were more aggressive, more dynamic, and more creative than the farm in giving a frontier wilderness diversity, direction, growth, opportunity, and, above all, maturity. Like Bridenbaugh, Wade sees the cities forging a distinct urban society sharply distinct from the countryside and the farm; like Schlesinger, he concludes that without the role of the cities the story of American development is only half told. Indeed, it is interesting to note the continuity of themes established by previous essays that Wade carries forward into the early nineteenth century.

Whereas Wade is concerned with the history of the interior river and valley cities up to 1830, Bayrd Still analyzes the emergence of Buffalo, Cleveland, Detroit, Chicago, and Milwaukee, the five major cities of the Great Lakes region in the middle years of the nineteenth century. Like Wade, he sees the urban frontier as a major event in facilitating the westward movement; like Bridenbaugh, he sees more similarities than differences among cities. In discussing such patterns of urbanization as urban politics, municipal and cultural services, urban competition, and the transition from commerce to manufacturing, he is fascinated by the striking similarities that bound the lake cities in a common mould. In tackling the reasons for similarity, he demonstrates a delicate handling of the thorny balance between change and continuity.

What Still has done in this important essay is to see the lake cities of the mid-nineteenth century in a transitionary, intermediary stage of urban development between the old and the new, although one might want more evidence that they reflect other cities of the same period.

First, there was similarity because the lake cities were facing the same demands and problems that confronted the older coastal cities of fifty or more years before. The response was continuity, an intense imitation of the older

1. His thesis is more fully developed in his book, *The Urban Frontier, 1790-1830* (Cambridge: Harvard University Press, 1957), indispensable for the study of American urban history.

and tested ideas and institutions of the eighteenth-century city, from its charter to its municipal services. Yet, at the same time, the lake cities infused the
newer influences of Jacksonian democracy, such as manhood suffrage, to
eliminate some older, eighteenth-century restrictions on political authority.
Second, the lake cities shared the problem of size, the confounding difficulty
of rapid urbanization. The response to size was a burst of civic responsibility
centered around voluntary associations. Still makes one of his most insightful
points by showing that the response was not, however, one of seizing upon a
new philosophy that recognized the novel and changing character of urban
settlement, a view which emerged in the late nineteenth and early twentieth
centuries. Rather, it was one that was heavily saturated with older village and
agrarian attitudes which emphasized private, individual responsibility and the
sanctity of private property. It was not what he calls the "municipal consciousness" of the twentieth century, but a "group consciousness . . . still
very largely articulated by and pivoted around the individual." The response
to older village and agrarian values suggests that the city did not necessarily
transform by some uncanny urban magic a former farmer or villager who
moved to the city into a complete urbanite. Newcomers could tenaciously
cling to their former attitudes and prejudices despite the novel demands of
urbanization.

Up to this point, the readings have covered large chunks of time and a multitude of urban themes. The last two essays in this chapter, however, were
selected to achieve more depth by pinpointing two critical forces shaping the
city, urban rivalry and the urban entrepreneur.

Rivalry is a dynamic theme in American urban history. Like gladiators,
cities and towns fought each other for their lives and for a stake in the American bonanza. For the winners, urban rivalry built cities, enriched regions,
generated—among other things—a vast transportation network, and contributed to the economic prosperity of the nation as a whole. For the losers, it
stunted cities and created bankruptcy, depression, and broken dreams. The
two classic cases of rivalry in the nineteenth century were the eastern rivalry
over access to western markets, won by New York with her Erie Canal,[2] and
the famous battle between Chicago, Milwaukee, and St. Louis for control of
the Mississippi Valley. But these were examples of what was going on elsewhere on perhaps a less heroic scale, but of no less significant importance, as
Harry N. Scheiber indicates in his essay on urban rivalry in the Old Northwest.

In a vivid account, Scheiber catches the fierce competition, wild hopes, bitter disenchantment, enormous growth, and unbelieveable waste, as the cities
and towns of the Old Northwest, by means fair and foul, invested their pride,

2. See Julius Rubin's perceptive, *Canal or Railroad? Imitation and Innovation in the Response to the Erie Canal in Philadelphia, Baltimore, and Boston* (Philadelphia: American
Philosophical Society, 1961).

fortune, and future in a furious scramble for dominance over canal and railroad routes. He traces the tactics, often ruthless, the jockeying for position,
often chaotic, the ambitions, sometimes narrowly selfish, the results, often unanticipated and self-defeating, but in the large, beneficial, in this frantic contest for security. Above all, he analyzes its significance by showing that both
the "transportation revolution" and its result, a burgeoning economic growth,
were not merely the outcome of state and national efforts, but that they were
also a local and regional phenomenon, urban and regional rivalry. The key
factors of private financing, public aid, political and business promotion, were
expressly aimed and directed at local needs and ambitions. In a real sense,
Scheiber goes beyond linking the city intimately to the canal and railroad age.
He demonstrates how local history, if not blighted by provincialism and sentimentality, can illuminate the larger issues of state and national history.

Cities did not grow as a result of urban rivalry alone, or transportation, or
a convenient location, or the impersonal forces of urbanization. They were
also the creatures of the men and women who lived in them—their hopes, their
energy, their community spirit, their initiative, their adaptability. A railroad
could make a city, a fire could break a city, but ultimately whether a city
prospered through good luck or survived bad luck depended upon the spirit
of its citizens. Daniel Boorstin catches the flamboyant spirit of the human
element in urban manifest destiny by examining the roles and impact of three
men, William B. Ogden of Chicago, Dr. Daniel Drake of Cincinnati, and
William Larimer of Denver, who were representative of countless others in
cities everywhere.

These men were a new breed of the promotor extraordinary—the entrepreneur as the city booster, the dreamer as the city builder. They were "upstart
businessmen" who helped build upstart cities. They pinned their hopes and
fortunes to cities without a past and with only a future. They constituted a
perfect marriage of city booster and self-booster, fusing private interests to
community interests. Their energies at first directed to promoting real estate
and railroads, spread to building practically every aspect of city life, from
municipal services, hospitals, colleges, parks, and, not the least, politics. They
in turn reflected an attitude of the general community, the booster spirit—an
ethos, a state of mind, often a mystique, the intensity of or lack of which
sealed the success or failure of many a city in America.

Urban Life in Western America, 1790-1830

RICHARD C. WADE

The towns were the spearheads of the American frontier. Planted as forts or trading posts far in advance of the line of settlement, they held the West for the approaching population. Indeed, in 1763, when the British drew the Proclamation Line across the Appalachians to stop the flow of migrants, a French merchant company prepared to survey the streets of St. Louis, a thousand miles through the wilderness. Whether as part of French and Spanish activity from New Orleans or part of Anglo-American operations from the Atlantic seaboard, the establishment of towns preceded the breaking of soil in the transmontane West.

In 1764, the year of the founding of St. Louis, settlers made the first plat of Pittsburgh. Twelve years later and four hundred miles down the Ohio, Louisville sprang up at the Falls, and the following decade witnessed the beginnings of Cincinnati and Lexington. Before the century closed, Detroit, Buffalo, and Cleveland were laid out on the Great Lakes. In fact, by 1800 the sites of every major metropolis in the old Northwest except Chicago, Milwaukee, and Indianapolis had been cleared and surveyed.

Furthermore, these urban outposts grew rapidly even in their infant decades. By 1815 Pittsburgh, already a thriving industrial center, had 8,000 inhabitants, giving it a slight margin over Lexington. Cincinnati estimated its population at 4,000 at the end of the war with Great Britain, while farther west Louisville and St. Louis neared half that figure.

The speed and extent of this expansion startled contemporaries. Joseph Charless, the editor of the *Missouri Gazette*, who had made a trip through the new country in 1795, remembered the banks of the Ohio as "a dreary wilderness, the haunt of ruthless savages," yet twenty years later he found them "sprinkled with towns" boasting "spinning and weaving establishments, steam mills, manufactures in various metals, leather, wool, cotton and flax," and "seminaries of learning conducted by excellent teachers."[1] The great transformation moved a Cincinnati bard to a somewhat heroic couplet:

> Here where so late the appalling sound
> Of savage yells, the woods resound
> Now smiling Ceres waves her sheaf
> And cities rise in bold relief.[2]

Not all the towns founded in the trans-Allegheny region in this period fared as well, however. Many never developed much beyond a survey and a newspaper advertisement. Others after promising beginnings, slackened and settled down to slow and unspectacular development. Still others flourished briefly then faded, leaving behind a grim story of deserted mills, broken buildings, and aging people—the West's first harvest of ghost towns. Most of

From *American Historical Review* (October 1958), pp. 14-30. Reprinted by permission of the publisher. Richard C. Wade is Professor of American History at the University of Chicago.

these were mere eddies in the westward flow of urbanism, but at flood tide it was often hard to distinguish the eddies from the main stream. Indeed, at one time Wheeling, Virginia, St. Genevieve, Missouri, New Albany, Indiana, and Zanesville, Ohio, were considered serious challengers to the supremacy of their now more famous neighbors.

Other places, such as Rising Sun, Town of America, or New Athens, were almost wholly speculative ventures. Eastern investors scanned maps looking for likely spots to establish a city, usually at the junction of two rivers, or sometimes at the center of fertile farm districts. They bought up land, laid it out in lots, gave the place a name, and waited for the development of the region to appreciate its value. Looking back over this period one editor called it a "city-making mania," when everyone went about "anticipating flourishing cities in vision, at the mouth of every creek and bayou."[3] This speculation, though extensive, was not always profitable. "Of the vast number of towns which have been founded," James Hall declared, "but a small minority have prospered, nor do we think that, as a general rule, the founders of these have been greatly enriched by their prosperity."[4]

Despite many failures, these abortive attempts to plant towns were significant, for they reveal much about the motives of the people who came West in the early period. Many settlers moved across the mountains in search of promising towns rather than good land, their inducements being urban opportunities rather than fertile soil. Daniel Drake, who was among the earliest urbanites of the frontier, later commented on this process:

It is worthy of remark, that those who made these beginnings of settlement, projected towns, which they anticipated would grow into cities. . . . And we may see in their origins, one of the elements of the prevalent tendency to rear up towns in advance of the country which has ever since characterized Ohio. The followers of the first pioneers, like themselves had a taste for commerce and the mechanic arts which cannot be gratified without the construction of cities.[5]

Proprietors competed for these urban migrants, most of whom came from "those portions of the Union which cherish and build up cities."[6] In fact, the preference of some settlers for towns was so great that in 1787 Lexington petitioned the Virginia legislature for incorporation to be "an inducement to well disposed persons, artizens [sic] and mechanics who from motives of convenience do prefer Town life."[7]

The West's young cities owed their initial success to commerce. All sprang from it, and their growth in the early years of the century stemmed from its expansion. Since the Ohio River was the chief artery of trade and travel, the towns along its banks prospered most. Pittsburgh, where the Allegheny meets the Monongahela, commanded the entire valley; Cincinnati served the rich farm lands of Kentucky and Ohio; Louisville fattened on the transshipment of goods around the Falls; and St. Louis, astride the Mississippi, was the focus of far-flung enterprises, some of which reached to the Pacific Ocean. Even Lexington, landlocked in a country of water highways, grew up as the central mart of Kentucky and Tennessee.

Though these cities were firmly established by the first decade of the century, the coming of the steamboat greatly enhanced their size and influence.[8] By quickening transportation and cutting distances, steam navigation telescoped fifty years' urban development into a single generation. The flow of commerce down river was now supplemented by a northward and eastward movement, giving cities added opportunities for expansion and growth. "The steam engine in five years has enabled us to anticipate a state of things," a Pittsburgher declared enthusiastically, "which in the ordinary course of events, it would have required a century to have produced. The art of printing scarcely surpassed it in beneficial consequences."[9] The "enchanter's wand" not only touched the established towns but created new ones as well. A French observer noted that "in the brief interval of fifteen years, many cities were formed . . . where before there were hardly the dwellings of a small town. . . . A simple mechanical device has made life both possible and comfortable in regions which heretofore have been a wilderness."[10]

As these commercial centers grew, some inhabitants turned to manufacturing. Indeed, this new interest spread so rapidly in Pittsburgh that in 1810 a resident likened the place to "a large workshop," and already travelers complained of the smoke and soot.[11] Between 1803 and 1815 the value of manufactured goods jumped from $350,000 to over $2,600,000, and the city's iron and glass products became known throughout the new country.[12] Watching this remarkable development, the editor of *Niles' Register* exclaimed: "Pittsburgh, sometimes emphatically called the 'Birmingham of America,' will probably become the *greatest manufacturing town in the world*"[13] Lexington also turned increasingly to industry, her ropewalks and textile mills supplying the whole West. Beginnings were more modest in other places, but every city had at least a few ambitious enterprises.

Some of this urban expansion rested on a speculative base, and the depression of 1819 brought a reckoning. Lexington, already suffering from its landlocked position, received fatal wounds, while Pittsburgh, the West's foremost city, was crippled for a decade. Elsewhere, however, the setback proved only momentary and the mid-twenties saw the old pace renewed. Population growth again provides a convenient index of development. Cincinnati quickly overtook its faltering rivals, the number of its residents leaping from 6,000 in 1815 to over 25,000 in 1830. By the latter date the census recorded Pittsburgh's recovery. Though the figure had dropped to 7,000 during the depression, it rose to 13,000 in 1830. Farther west Louisville and St. Louis enjoyed spectacular expansion, the former boasting over 10,000 inhabitants at the end of the period, while the Mississippi entrepôt passed the 6,000 mark. Lexington alone lagged, its population remaining stable for the next two decades.

Even these figures, however, do not convey the real growth. In most places municipal boundaries could no longer contain the new settlers, and many spilled over into the suburbs. For instance, Allegheny, Bayardstown, Birmingham, Lawrenceville, Hayti, and East Liberty added nearly 10,000 to Pittsburgh's population, bringing the total to 22,000.[14] The same was true of Cincinnati where 2,000 people lived in the Eastern and Northern Liberties.[15] In Louisville, Preston's and Campbell's "enlargements" and Shippingport and Portland swelled the city's total to 13,-

000.[16] Ultimately, the urban centers annexed these surrounding clusters, but in the meantime local authorities grappled with early manifestations of the suburban problem.

As the cities grew they staked out extensive commercial claims over the entire West.[17] Timothy Flint calculated that Cincinnati was the central market for over a million people, while a resident asserted that its trade was "co-extensive with steamboat navigation on the western waters."[18] Louisville's economic penetration was scarcely less impressive. As early as 1821, a local editor declared that "the people of the greater part of Indiana, all Kentucky, and portions of Tennessee, Alabama, Illinois, Missouri, now report to this place for dry goods, groceries, hardware and queensware."[19] St. Louis' empire touched Santa Fe on the south, Canada on the north, and the Pacific on the west. "It is doubtful if history affords the example of another city," wrote Hiram M. Chittenden, "which has been the exclusive mart for so vast an area as that which was tributary to St. Louis."[20]

In carving out these extensive dependencies, the young metropolises overwhelmed their smaller neighbors. The rise of St. Louis destroyed the ambitions of Edwardsville across the Mississippi, which once harbored modest hopes of importance. Pittsburgh's recovery in the late twenties condemned Wheeling and Steubenville to minor roles in the upper Ohio region. And Louisville's development swallowed two Kentucky neighbors while reducing Jeffersonville and New Albany on the Indiana side of the river to mere appendages.

Not satisfied with such considerable conquests, the cities reached out for more. Seeking wider opportunities, they built canals and turnpikes and, even before 1830, planned railroads to strengthen their position. Cincinnati, Pittsburgh, and St. Louis tried to tap the increasing trade on the Great Lakes by water links to the North. Pennsylvania's Iron City also hoped to become a major station on the National Road, and for a decade its Washington representatives lobbied to win that commercial bond with the East. Lexington, suffocating in its inland position, frantically strove for better connections with the Ohio River. A turnpike to Maysville was dashed by Jackson's veto, technical difficulties made a canal to the Kentucky River impractical, but some belated hope rose with the possibility of a railroad to Louisville or Cincinnati.

The intensive search for new advantages brought rivalry and conflict. Though the commerce of the whole West lay untouched before them, the cities quarreled over its division. Thus Louisville and Cincinnati fought over a canal around the Falls of the Ohio. The Kentucky town, feeling that its strength depended upon maintaining the break in transportation, obstructed every attempt to circumvent the rapids. Only when Ohio interests threatened to dig on the Indiana side did Louisville move ahead with its own project. Likewise, harsh words flew between Wheeling and Pittsburgh as they contended for the Ohio River terminus of the National Road. Smaller towns, too, joined the struggle. Cleveland and Sandusky, for instance, clashed over the location of the Ohio Canal, the stake being nothing less than control of the mounting trade between the Valley and the lakes. And their instinct to fight was sound, for the outcome shaped the future of both places.

Urban rivalries were often bitter, and

the contestants showed no quarter. In the late twenties when only the success of Transylvania University kept Lexington's economy from complete collapse, Louisville joined the attack which ultimately destroyed the school. In a similar vein Cincinnatians taunted their upriver competitor as it reeled under the impact of the depression of 1819. "Poor Pittsburgh," they exclaimed, "your day is over, the sceptre of influence and wealth is to travel to us; the Cumberland road has done the business."[21] But even the Queen City found her supremacy insecure. "I discovered two ruling passions in Cincinnati," a traveler remarked, "enmity against Pittsburgh, and jealousy of Louisville."[22] This drive for power and primacy, sustained especially by merchants and articulated by editors, was one of the most consistent and striking characteristics of the early history of Western cities.

As they pursued expansive policies, municipalities also ministered to their own growing pains. From the beginning, urban residents had to contend with the problems of living together, and one of their first acts was to petition the territory or state for governing authority to handle them. The legislatures, representing rural interests and generally suspicious of towns, responded with charters bestowing narrow grants of power which barely met current needs and failed to allow for expansion. As localities grew, however, they developed problems which could be met only with wider jurisdiction. Louisville's charter had to be amended twenty-two times before 1815 and Cincinnati's underwent five major changes between 1815 and 1827. Others, though altered less often, were adjusted and remade until finally scrapped for new ones. Reluctantly, and bit by bit, the states turned over to the cities the responsibility of managing their own affairs, though keeping them starved for revenue by strict tax and debt limitations.

Despite inadequate charters and modest incomes, urban governments played a decisive role in the growth of Western cities. Since these were commercial towns, local authorities paid special attention to mercantile requirements. They not only constructed market houses but also extended municipal regulation over a wide variety of trading activity. Ordinances protected the public against adulterated foods, false measurements, and rigged prices. Some municipalities went even farther and assumed responsibility for seeing that "justice is done between buyer and seller."[23] In search of this objective, officials fixed prices on some goods, excluded monopolies from the market, and tried to equalize opportunities for smaller purchasers. To facilitate access to the exchange center, they lavished time and money on the development of wharves and docks and the improvement of streets.

Municipalities also tackled a wide variety of other problems growing out of urban life. Fire protection, at first casually organized, was placed on a more formal basis. Volunteer companies still provided the manpower, but government participation increased markedly. Local councils legislated against many kinds of fire hazards, and public money furnished most of the equipment. Moreover, some places, haunted by the image of Detroit's disaster in 1805, forbade the construction of wooden buildings in the heart of the city, a measure which not only reduced fire risks but also changed the face of downtown areas. The development of adequate police was much slower. By

1830 only Lexington and Louisville had regular patrols, and these were established with the intent more of control of slaves than the general protection of life and property. In other towns law enforcement was lax by day and absent at night, though the introduction of gas lighting in Pittsburgh and Cincinnati in the late twenties made the after-dark hours there less dangerous than before.

Congested living created new health hazards and especially increased the likelihood of epidemics. Every place suffered, but none like Louisville, which earned a grim reputation as the "Graveyard of the West" because of the constant visitations of yellow fever and malaria.[24] Cities took preventive measures, such as draining stagnant ponds and clearing streets and lots, and also appointed boards of health to preside over the problem. Municipal water systems, introduced in Pittsburgh and Cincinnati before 1830, made life healthier and certainly more comfortable, while the discussion of installing underground sewers pointed to still more extensive reform in sanitation.

In meeting urban problems, Western officials drew heavily on Eastern experience. Lacking precedents of their own, and familiar with the techniques of older cities, they frankly patterned their practice on Eastern models. There was little innovation. When confronted by a new question, local authorities responded by adopting tested solutions. This emulation characterized nearly every aspect of development—from the width of streets to housing regulations. No major improvement was launched without a close study of established seaboard practices. St. Louis' council, for example, instructed its water committee to "procure from the cities of Philadelphia and New Orleans such information

as can be obtained on the subject of conveying water and the best manner of clearing it."[25] When Cincinnati discussed introducing underground sewers, an official group was designated to "ascertain from the city authorities of New York, Philadelphia, Baltimore and Boston, how far the sinking of common sewers is approved in those cities."[26] Pittsburgh undertook gas lighting only after exhaustive research and "very full enquiries at New York and Baltimore."[27]

Though the young towns drew upon the experience of all the major Atlantic cities, the special source of municipal wisdom was Philadelphia. Many Western urbanites had lived or visited there; it provided the new country with most of its professional and cultural leadership; it was the model metropolis. "She is the great seat of American affluence, of individual riches, and distinguished philanthropy," a Pittsburgh edtiorial declared in 1818. "From her . . . we have everything to look for."[28] Newspapers often referred to it as "our mother city."[29]

From street plans to cultural activity, from the shape of market houses to the habits of people, the Philadelphia influence prevailed. Robert Peterson and John Filson, who had a hand in the founding of Louisville, Lexington, and Cincinnati, borrowed the basic grid pattern of the original plats from the Pennsylvania metropolis.[30] Market location and design came from the same source, as did techniques for fire fighting and police protection. Western towns also leaned on Philadelphia's leadership in street lighting, waterworks, and wharving. Even the naming of suburbs—Pittsburgh's Kensington and Cincinnati's Liberties—came from the mother city. The result was a physical likeness which struck many travelers and which Philadelphians themselves recognized. Gideon Burton, for instance, remembered his first impression of Cincinnati in the 1820's: "How beautiful this city is," he remarked, "how much like Philadelphia."[31]

The Quaker City spirit, moreover, went beyond streets, buildings, and improvements, reaching into a wide range of human activity. Businessmen, yearly visitors in the East, brought marketing and promotion techniques from there;[32] young labor movements lifted their platforms from trade union programs in the mother city; employment agencies were conducted "principally on the Philadelphia plan."[33] The same metropolis trained most of the physicians of the West and a large share of the teachers and ministers. Caspar Wistar's famed Sunday evening gatherings of the intelligentsia provided the idea for Daniel Drake's select meetings of Cincinnati's social and cultural elite. Moreover, Philadelphia furnished the model of the perfect urbanite, for the highest praise that Western town dwellers could bestow upon a fellow citizen was to refer to him as their own "Benjamin Franklin."[34] In short, Philadelphia represented the highest stage of urban development, and progress was measured against this ideal.

Such borrowing was a conscious policy. In 1825 Mayor William Carr Lane of St. Louis, the most able urban statesman of the period, provided the justification. "Experience is the best guide . . . ," he told his councilmen. "The records of other towns are a source from which we may expect to derive useful hints. . . . It is therefore incumbent upon us to examine carefully what other communities similarly situated have done."[35] The process, however, was selective, not slavish. Investigation usually revealed a wide variety of possibilities, allowing Western cities to choose the most appropriate technique. Nevertheless, young towns preferred to meet their urban problems by adopting the established ways of the East. The challenge of the new country, far from producing a bold and fresh response, led to greater dependence on the older sections of the Union.

As transmontane cities developed they created societies whose ways and habits contrasted sharply with those of the countryside. Not only was their physical environment distinct, but their interests, activities, and pace of life also differed greatly. In 1811 a farmer near Lexington expressed the conflict as contemporaries saw it in a dialogue between "Rusticus" and "Urbanus." The latter referred to the "rude, gross appearance" of his neighbor, adding: "How strong you smell of your ploughed ground and corn fields. How dismal, how gloomy your green woods. What a miserable clash your whistling woodland birds are continually making." "Rusticus" replied with the rural image of the town dweller. "What a fine smooth complexion you have Urbanus: you look like a weed that has grown up in the shade. Can you walk your streets without inhaling the noxious fumes with which your town is pregnant? . . . Can you engage in calm contemplation, when hammers are ringing in every direction—when there is as great a *rattling* as in a storm when the hail descends on our house tops?"[36]

One of the most conspicuous differences was in social structure. The stratification of urban societies was in marked contrast with the boisterous equality of the countryside. Social lines developed very quickly in the city. Though not as tightly drawn as in the East, they represented the meaningful distinctions in Western communities. The groupings were basically economic, though professional people were set apart by their interest and training, and Negroes by their color. No rigid boundaries divided the classes, and movement between them was constant. Yet differences did exist; people felt them and contemporaries thought them significant. It is suggestive in this regard that the first great literary product of the West, *Modern Chivalry*, satirized the notion of equality, and the author, Hugh Henry Brackenridge, was one of Pittsburgh's leading citizens.

These divisions deepened in the postwar years. As the cities grew the sense of neighborliness and intimacy diminished, giving way to the impersonality characteristic of urban living. To oldtimers the changing social configuration bred a deep nostalgia and raised the image of happier, simpler days. "We cannot help looking back with sorrowful heart, in that time of unaffected content and gaiety," a Pennsylvanian lamented, "when the unambitious people . . . in the village of 'Fort Pitt' in the yet unchartered town of Pittsburgh, were ignorant and careless of all invidious distinctions, which distract and divide the inhabitants of overgrown cities. Then all was peaceful heartfelt felicity, undisturbed by the rankling thorns of envy; and equality . . . was a tie that united all ranks and conditions in our community."[37] Town life in the West had never been that idyllic, but the distortion of the vision was itself a measure of the rapid change. "We have our castes of society, graduated and divided with as much regard to rank and dignity as the most scrupulous Hindoos maintain in defense of their religious prejudices," the same source admitted

in 1826. Moreover, social distances were great. "Between the . . . classes . . there are lines of demarcation drawn wide, distinct and not to be violated with impunity."[38] Nor was this stratification surprising. Having come from places where differences mattered, early city dwellers tried to re-create them in a new setting. The urge for status was stronger than the appeal of equality and as the towns expanded cleavages deepened.

Urban ways were further distinguished from rural habits by the collective approach to many problems. City living created issues which could not always be solved by the highly individualistic methods of agrarian society. Local governments assumed an ever wider responsibility for the conduct of community affairs, and voluntary associations handled a large variety of other questions. Merchants formed chambers of commerce to facilitate cooperation on common problems; professional people organized societies to raise the standards of their colleagues and keep out the untrained. Working people, too, banded together in unions, seeking not only greater economic strength but also fraternity and self-improvement. Religious and philanthropic clubs managed most charity and relief work, while immigrants combined to help new arrivals. In addition, other associations grew up to promote literature and music, encourage debating, advocate social innovations, support public causes, and conduct the welter of amusements which larger cities required. Just as conditions in the countryside placed greatest emphasis on individual effort, so the urban situation made cooperative action seem more appropriate.

Rural and metropolitan West were also separated by distinctive social and cultural developments. The towns very quickly produced a surprisingly rich and diversified life, offering opportunities in many fields similar to those of Eastern cities but lacking on the farm or frontier.[39] They enjoyed a virtual monopoly of printing presses, newspapers, bookstores, and circulating libraries. Theaters sprang up to encourage local players and traveling troupes, while in larger places museums brought the curious and the scientific to the townfolks.[40] In addition, every week brought numerous lectures and debates on all kinds of topics, keeping urban residents abreast of the latest discoveries and developments in every field. By 1815 these amenities had already lost their novelty. Indeed, some thought the civilizing process was getting out of hand. "Twenty sermons a week—," a Cincinnatian wearily counted, "Sunday evening Discourses on Theology—Private assemblies—state Cotillon parties —Saturday Night Clubs, and chemical lectures— . . . like the fever and the ague, return every day with distressing regularity."[41]

Of course, the whole transmontane region matured culturally in this period, but the towns played a strategic role. "Cities have arisen in the very wilderness . . . ," a St. Louis editor noticed in 1821, "and form in their respective states the *foci* of art and science, of wealth and information."[42] A Cincinnatian made a similar observation. "This *city*, in its growth and cultural improvements has anticipated the western country in general."[43] The hinterland, already bound to urban communities by trade, readily admitted its dependence. The *Pittsburgh Gazette* merely stated the obvious when it remarked in 1819 that the surrounding region "looks up to Pittsburgh not only as a medium

through which to receive the comforts and luxuries of foreign commodities, but also a channel from which it can most naturally expect a supply of intellectual wealth."[44] Thus while the cities' merchants staked out markets in the countryside, their civic leaders spread a cultural influence into the same area.

This leadership extended into almost every field. For example, the educational opportunities of town children greatly exceeded those of their rural neighbors. Every municipality developed a complex of private tuition schools topped by an academy and, in every place except Louisville, a college. Moreover, the cities organized movement of public schooling. Ohio's experience is illustrative. The movement for state legislation started in Cincinnati, received its major impetus from the local press, and was carried in the Assembly through the efforts of representatives from Hamilton county. It is also significant that the first superintendent of common schools in Ohio was Samuel Lewis of Cincinnati. Nor was this urban leadership surprising. The cities, as the great population centers, felt the educational pressure first and most acutely. In addition, they alone had the wealth needed to launch ambitious projects for large numbers of children. Hence the towns were ready for comprehensive public programs long before the countryside.

The most striking illustration of the cultural supremacy of the cities, however, was Lexington's unique reign as the "Athens of the West."[45] The area's largest town until 1810, it was early celebrated for its polish and sophistication and was generally conceded to be the region's capital of arts and science. But the coming of the steamboat and the depression of 1819 combined to undermine its economic position. To offset this commercial and industrial decline, Lexington's civic leaders inaugurated a policy of vigorous cultural expansion.[46] They built schools, subsidized Transylvania University, and advertised the many opportunities for advancement in learning and letters in the metropolis. Throughout the twenties this campaign was a spectacular success. The town became the resort of the most talented men of the new country. Educators, scientists, painters, lawyers, architects, musicians, and their patrons all flocked there. Transylvania University attained national eminence, attracting most of its faculty from the East and drawing students from better than a dozen states. Like a renaissance city of old Italy, Lexington provided the creative atmosphere for a unique flowering that for a decade astonished travelers and stimulated the best minds of the West.

In its golden age the town boasted the most distinguished collection of intellectuals the new country had ever seen in a single city. The central figure in this awakening was Horace Holley, a Unitarian minister from Boston and the president of Transylvania. Though not an accomplished scholar himself, he recruited a remarkable faculty and raised the institution from a small denominational college to a university of the first rank. The medical department achieved a special distinction. Its dean was Charles Caldwell, one of Benjamin Rush's favorite pupils, who turned down important posts in New York, Philadelphia, and Baltimore to join the Kentucky experiment. Members of the staff included the botanist, Charles Wilkins Short, Daniel Drake, later the author of a pioneering study of diseases in the Mississippi Valley, and the surgeon,

Benjamin Winslow Dudley. Among them, too, was the furtive and erratic, yet highly talented, Turkish-born naturalist, Constantine Rafinesque, whose most fruitful years were spent in Lexington.[47]

The graduating class of the medical school in 1826 demonstrated the extent of the university's reputation and influence. With sixty-seven degrees granted in that year, twenty-eight of the recipients came from Kentucky, ten from Tennessee, five each from Virginia, South Carolina, and Alabama, three from Ohio, two each from Mississippi, Illinois, and Louisiana, and one each from North Carolina and Georgia. During the twenties the college trained many of the West's most distinguished people. In politics alone it turned out at least seventeen congressmen, three governors, six United States senators, and the president of the Confederacy. In the same decade the school produced scores of lawyers, clergymen, and physicians, who did much to raise professional standards in the new country. Few universities have left such a clear mark on a generation; in its heyday Transylvania fully deserved its title of the "Harvard of the West."[48]

The college was the center of this wilderness renaissance, but around it moved other figures—artists, architects, musicians, and poets—who gave added luster to the movement. In Matthew Jouett the city had the West's most famous painter. A student of Gilbert Stuart and a portraitist of considerable gifts, he made his studio the exciting headquarters for a group of promising young artists. Gideon Shryock provided Lexington with an architect equal to its enlightenment. After studying with William Strickland in Philadelphia, he brought the Greek revival across the mountains. His work, especially the state capitol at Frankfort and Morrison College at Transylvania, brought him immediate fame and has led a modern critic to assert that he "was almost a decade ahead of his time even when judged by sophisticated eastern standards."[49] Music shared the upsurge, and in 1817 townsfolk heard Anthony Phillip Hennrich conduct the first performance of a Beethoven symphony in the United States.

The glitter of this city drew young people from all over the transmontane region, including many from the countryside. In doing so, it provoked a familiar lament from the rural areas whose children succumbed to the bewitchment of Lexington. "We want our sons to be practical men," wrote a Kentucky farmer, "whose minds will not be filled with those light notions of refinement and taste, which will induce them to believe that they are of a different order of beings, or that will elevate them above their equals."[50] Later, agrarian representatives in the legislature joined the attack on Transylvania by voting to cut off state financial assistance.

No less striking than cultural cleavages were the differences in rural and urban religious development. Progress in the cities was steadier and more substantial—though less spectacular—than in the back country. Traveling ministers might refer to Pittsburgh as "a young hell, a second Sodom,"[51] and Francis Asbury might complain in 1803 that he felt "the power of Satan in those little, wicked western trading towns,"[52] but both churches and membership multiplied rapidly in urban centers. Furthermore, the growth owed nothing to the sporadic revivals which burned across the countryside at the beginning of the

century. These movements were essentially rural, having their roots in the isolation of agricultural living and the spiritual starvation of people unattended by regular services. The city situation, with its constant contacts and settled church organizations, involved neither of these elements. Instead, religious societies proliferated, sects took on such additional functions as charity and missionary work, and congregations sent money back East to aid their seminaries. Far from being sinks of corruption, Western cities quickly became religious centers, supplying Bibles to the frontier, assisting foreign missions, and, in the twenties, building theological schools to provide priests and ministers for the whole region.

Political life also reflected the growing rural-urban division. Though the rhetoric of the period often obscured them, differences existed from the very beginning. Suspicion of the towns led states to avoid economic and cultural centers when locating their capitals. Nearly all these cities sought the prize, but none was successful. The *Missouri Gazette* candidly stated the issue in 1820. "It has been said that St. Louis is obnoxious to our Legislature—that its growth and influence . . . are looked on with a jealous eye, and its pretensions . . . ought to be discouraged."[53] The same clash had earlier occurred in Kentucky, where state leaders virtually invented Frankfort to keep the capital away from Louisville or Lexington.

As the region developed, however, the conflict became increasingly apparent, though it was still expressed cautiously. "We must be permitted to say," an editor asserted in 1829, "that in Cincinnati we have separate interests" from the countryside.[54] Likewise, a Pittsburgher prefaced a strong attack on the neighboring areas by declaring that "we think it wrong to stir up a jealousy between city and county."[55] Nevertheless, the split represented one of the fundamental facts of Western politics.

Of course, farm dwellers easily outnumbered urbanites, but the latter wielded disproportionate power. The case of Jefferson and Oldham counties in Kentucky was illustrative. In the mid-twenties the combined vote reached 3,-200, Louisville residents casting roughly a quarter of them. Yet the state senator and both representatives came from the city. In 1829 when a third assemblyman was added, the rural interests pleaded with Louisville leaders to name someone from the surrounding area. "It may seem strange," wrote an observer, "that it would be necessary thus to ask for the liberality of 800 voters in favor of 2,400. . . . Nevertheless, the concentrated energies of 800 do entirely outweigh the scattered influence of the 2,400—that all past experience teaches."[56] The situation was the same elsewhere. At one time all of Missouri's representatives in Washington—two senators and one congressman—as well as its governor came from St. Louis.

The cities' political influence rested on their ability to produce leadership. As the economic and intellectual centers of transmontane life they attracted the talented and ambitious in all fields. Politics was no exception. Nearly all the great spokesmen of the West had important urban connections and their activity often reflected the demands of their town constituents. Henry Clay was one of Lexington's most prominent lawyers when he went to the United States Senate in 1806. Thomas Hart Benton held local offices in St. Louis before moving on to the national scene,

and William Henry Harrison, though he lived in nearby North Bend, had deep roots in Cincinnati affairs through most of his long public life. Moreover, all were alive to the interests of their city. Benton's successful attack on government factories in the Indian territory culminated a long and intense campaign by St. Louis merchants to break federal trade control on the Missouri. Clay's enthusiasm for an ample tariff on hemp derived at least as much from the pressure of Lexington's manufactures as from that of the growers of the Blue Grass. And Harrison, as state senator, led the campaign for public schools in Ohio largely at the behest of his Cincinnati supporters. These were not isolated cases; an examination of the careers of these men demonstrates the importance of their urban connections.

By 1830, then, the West had produced two types of society—one rural and one urban. Each developed its own institutions, habits, and living patterns. The countryside claimed much the larger population and often gave to transmontane affairs an agrarian flavor. But broadcloth was catching up with buckskin. The census of 1830 revealed the disproportionate rate of city growth. While the state of Ohio had four times as many inhabitants as it counted in 1810, Cincinnati's increase was twelve-fold. The story was the same elsewhere. Louisville's figure showed a growth of 650 per cent compared with Kentucky's 50 per cent, and Pittsburgh tripled in size while Pennsylvania did not quite double its population. By 1830 the rise of these cities had driven a broad wedge of urbanism into Western life.

Though town and country developed along different paths, clashes were still infrequent. The West was large enough to contain both movements comfortably.

Indeed, each supported the other. The rural regions supplied the cities with raw materials for their mills and packinghouses and offered an expanding market to their shops and factories. In turn, urban centers served the surrounding areas by providing both the necessities and comforts of life as well as new opportunity for ambitious farm youths. Yet the cities represented the more aggressive and dynamic force. By spreading their economic power over the entire section, by bringing the fruits of civilization across the mountains, and by insinuating their ways into the countryside, they speeded up the transformation of the West from a gloomy wilderness to a richly diversified region. Any historical view which omits this aspect of Western life tells but part of the story.

NOTES

1. *Missouri Gazette* (St. Louis), July 13, 1816.
2. *Liberty Hall* (Cincinnati), June 11, 1815.
3. *Missouri Republican* (St. Louis), Aug. 29, 1825.
4. Hall, *The West: Its Commerce and Navigation* (Cincinnati, 1848), p. 227.
5. Drake, "Dr. Drake's Memoir of the Miami County, 1779-1794," Beverley Bond, Jr., ed., Historical and Philosophical Society of Ohio, *Quarterly Publications*, XVIII (1923), 58.
6. *Ibid.*
7. James R. Robertson, ed., *Petitions of the Early Inhabitants of Kentucky to the General Assembly of Virginia, 1769-1792* (Louisville, Ky., 1914), p. 106.
8. Louis C. Hunter, *Steamboats on the Western Rivers, An Economic and Technological History* (Cambridge, Mass., 1949), pp. 27-32.
9. Morgan Neville, "The Last of the Boatman," *The Western Souvenir for 1829* (Cincinnati, Ohio, n.d.), p. 108.
10. [Jean Baptiste] Marestier, *Mémoire sur les Bateaux à vapeur des États-Unis d' Amérique* (Paris, 1824), pp. 9-10.
11. Zadock Cramer, *Pittsburgh Almanack for the Year of Our Lord 1810* (Pittsburgh, Pa., 1810), p. 52.
12. Pittsburgh's industrial foundations are discussed in Catherine Elizabeth Reiser, *Pittsburgh's Commercial Development, 1800-1850* (Harrisburg, Pa., 1951), pp. 12-21.

13. *Niles' Register*, May 28, 1814.
14. *Pittsburgh Gazette*, Nov. 16, 1830.
15. *Cincinnati Advertiser*, Aug. 18, 1830.
16. United States *Census*, 1830, pp. 114-15.
17. For an appreciation of the economic importance of the cities in the growth of the West, see Frederick Jackson Turner, *Rise of the New West, 1819-1829* in *The American Nation: A History*, A. B. Hart, ed., XIV (New York, 1906), 96-98.
18. Flint, "Thoughts Respecting the Establishment of a Porcelain Manufactory at Cincinnati," *Western Monthly Review*, III (1830), 512; Benjamin Drake and Edward W. Mansfield, *Cincinnati in 1826* (Cincinnati, Ohio, 1827), p. 71.
19. *Louisville Public Advertiser*, Oct. 17, 1829.
20. Chittenden, *The American Fur Trade of the Far West* (2 vols. New York, 1902), I, 99.
21. *Pittsburgh Gazette*, Dec. 18, 1818.
22. *Pittsburgh Gazette*, Feb. 5, 1819.
23. *Pittsburgh Gazette*, Mar. 9, 1810.
24. Benjamin Casseday, *The History of Louisville from Its Earliest Settlement till the Year 1852* (Louisville, Ky., 1852), p. 49.
25. St. Louis City Council, Minutes, Court House, St. Louis, June 12, 1829.
26. Cincinnati City Council, Minutes, City Hall, Cincinnati, Oct. 6, 1827.
27. Pittsburgh City Council, City Council Papers, City Hall, Pittsburgh, May 10, 1827. The extent of Western urban indebtedness to the East is perhaps best illustrated in the establishment of the high school in Louisville. The building was "mainly after the plan of the High School of New York, united with the Public School Rooms of Philadelphia." Most of the teachers came from the East, while the curriculum and even reading assignments derived from "the High School of New York and some of the Boston establishments." *An Account of the Louisville City School, Together With the Ordinances of the City Council, and the Regulations of the Board of Trustees for the Government of the Institution* (Louisville, Ky., 1830), pp. 5 ff.
28. *Pittsburgh Gazette*, Oct. 27, 1818.
29. For example, see *Pittsburgh Gazette*, June 23, 1818.
30. For example, see Rufus King, *Ohio First Fruits of the Ordinance of 1787* (Boston, 1888), p. 209.
31. Burton, *Reminiscences of Gideon Burton* (Cincinnati, Ohio, 1895). The strategic location of Western cities in the life of the new country reminded some visitors of the regional supremacy of Philadelphia. Lewis Condict, for example, referred to Lexington as "the Philadelphia of Kentucky." "Journal of a Trip to Kentucky in 1795," *Proceedings of the New Jersey Historical Society*, n.s., IV (1919), 120.
32. *Cincinnati Enquirer*, Apr. 22, 1923.
33. *Pittsburgh Mercury*, Aug. 7, 1827.
34. The phrase was constantly used in characterizing John Bradford of Lexington and Daniel Drake of Cincinnati, but it was applied to others as well.
35. St. Louis City Council, Minutes, Court House, St. Louis, Apr. 25, 1825.
36. *Kentucky Reporter* (Lexington), July 2, 1811.

37. Samuel Jones, *Pittsburgh in 1826* (Pittsburgh, Pa., 1826), p. 43.

38. *Ibid.*

39. For a day-to-day account of the cultural offerings of a Western city between 1820 and 1830 see the highly informative but unpublished diary of William Stanley Merrill in the library of the Historical and Philosophical Society of Ohio (Cincinnati).

40. The development of the theater in Western cities is outlined in Ralph Leslie Rush, *The Literature of the Middle Western Frontier* (New York, 1925), I, 352-400. For a detailed study of a single town see William G. B. Carson, *The Theatre on the Frontier, The Early Years of the St. Louis Stage* (Chicago, 1932), pp. 1-134.

41. *Liberty Hall* (Cincinnati), Dec. 9, 1816.

42. *Missouri Gazette* (St. Louis), Dec. 20, 1820.

43. *Liberty Hall* (Cincinnati), June 29, 1819.

44. *Pittsburgh Gazette,* Apr. 30, 1819.

45. For Lexington's growth and brief supremacy see Bernard Mayo, "Lexington, Frontier Metropolis," in *Historiography and Urbanization,* Eric F. Goldman, ed. (Baltimore, Md., 1941), pp. 21-42.

46. See, for example, *Kentucky Reporter,* Oct. 4, 1820.

47. Transylvania's "golden age" is treated in de-

tail in Walter William Jennings, *Transylvania, Pioneer University of the West* (New York, 1955), pp. 99-124, and Niels Henry Sonne, *Liberal Kentucky, 1780-1828* (New York, 1939), pp. 160-242.

48. The reputation of Lexington in Cincinnati is charmingly portrayed in the letters of young Ohioans attending Transylvania University to their friends back home. See especially the William Lytle Collection in the library of the Historical and Philosophical Society of Ohio (Cincinnati).

49. Talbot Hamlin, *Greek Revival Architecture in America: Being an Account of Important Trends in American Architecture and American Life prior to the War between the States* (New York, 1944), p. 244.

50. *Kentucky Reporter* (Lexington), Feb. 16, 1824.

51. *Pittsburgh Gazette,* Sept. 23, 1803.

52. Francis Asbury, *Journal of Rev. Francis Asbury, Bishop of Methodist Episcopal Church* (n.p., 1821), III, 127.

53. *Missouri Gazette* (St. Louis), Dec. 6, 1820.

54. *Cincinnati Advertiser,* Sept. 16, 1829.

55. *Pittsburgh Statesman,* Aug. 26, 1823.

56. *Louisville Public Advertiser,* July 28, 1824.

Patterns of Mid-Nineteenth Century Urbanization in the Middle West

BAYRD STILL

Until recently a persistent preoccupation with the agrarian aspects of the westward march of American settlement has to some extent obscured the fact that the prospect of future towns and cities as well as the promise of broad and fertile acres lured settlers to the "sunset regions." On many a frontier the town builder was as conspicuous as the farmer pioneer; the western city, through the efforts of its founders to extend its economic hinterland, actually facilitated the agrarian development of the West; and the opportunities attending city growth as well as those afforded by cheap farm lands contributed to the dynamic sense of economic abundance felt by Americans of the mid-nineteenth century. As early as 1845 one middle western editor identified this urban growth with the rapid development of the West when he wrote:

From *Mississippi Valley Historical Review* (September 1941), pp. 187-206. Reprinted by permission of the publisher. Bayrd Still is Head of the Department of History at New York University.

The tide of emigration to the West seems to increase daily. . . . What an enterprising spirit characterizes the American people. . . . This . . . activity and enterprise . . . are the result of free institutions, which give an impetus to the human mind. In no other country have towns and villages sprung up so suddenly as in this. Everything seems to go ahead with railroad velocity. Well might Marryat remark that cities grow up here to more importance in ten years than they do in Europe in a century.[1]

The growth of cities is admittedly a significant aspect of the history of the West. But any precise estimate of the bearing either of urbanization upon the expansion of the American frontier or of the westward movement of population upon city growth in the United States awaits a more adequate exposition of urban development in specific sections of the country than has as yet been set forth.[2]

The migrants who poured into the Mississippi Valley in the middle of the nineteenth century built cities as well as cultivated farms. By the seventies, when the American people were first becoming conscious of the drift of population to the city, the Middle West showed a spectacular urban growth. It could then boast seven cities of more than a hundred thousand people,[3] whereas thirty years before only New Orleans had achieved that size. To be sure, the total population of the ten major midwestern cities in 1870 still fell slightly short of the more than 1,800,000 city dwellers then living in New York, Philadelphia, and Boston; but in the rate of their growth the former were putting to shame the cities of the Atlantic coast. Among these mushroom metropolises of the West, the lake cities—Buffalo, Cleveland, Detroit, Chicago, and Milwaukee—rather than the valley cities—Pittsburgh, Cincin-

nati, Louisville, Nashville, and St. Louis—showed the greatest proportional increase in numbers.[4] By 1870 the five lake cities had attained a combined population of more than sixteen times their total of 1840, although the population of the states in which they were located had barely tripled.[5]

Because of their rapid and parallel growth, a comparative analysis of these five lake cities provides a useful means of studying the nature of the emerging city in the Middle West. With striking similarity, they all limited themselves to those duties of the urban community which were common to eighteenth century cities. They all responded to the democratic movement by extending popular participation in municipal government and then by broadening the authority of the executive or administrative commission. Not only did they rely upon the individual to provide most of the services which are demanded today of the city itself but they also expected him to promote the city's growth—a promotion which in every case involved substituting the encouragement of manufacturing for an earlier emphasis on trade. And with equal uniformity they imitated the experience of one another in ordering the details of their municipal life. While it is never too wise to try to compress the variety of human behavior into patterns, the common responses of the five cities suggest the conclusion that these at least are qualities which may well be characteristic of mid-nineteenth century urbanization in the upper Middle West.

A comparative study of the charters under which the Great Lakes cities were governed between 1830 and 1870 discloses the imitation of form and limitation of function in which the powers of the urban community were at that time conceived. These charters were cut from an almost identical constitutional pattern, laid down in the spirit of eighteenth century America. Admittedly the creature of the legislative will of the state, each city nevertheless resorted frequently to the public meeting for the purpose of proposing charter changes and civic improvement.[6] With the advance to city status the meagre functions of the village period—protection against fire, opening and repairing streets, regulating markets, licensing shows, and sinking public wells—were considerably expanded. These functions were enlarged by a uniform extension of regulatory powers, services, and guarantees—additions which were, however, more boldly granted than enforced if one judges from the charges of nonenforcement levied against the city administration by the Milwaukee press.

The first city charters of Buffalo (1832), Cleveland (1836), and Chicago (1837) were strikingly similar in form. The Chicago charter is almost an identical copy of the Buffalo document save for certain local references. In the more than thirty clauses enumerating the powers of the council, the wording of the Chicago charter is different from that of Buffalo in less than half a dozen instances. The Chicago charter added provisions with respect to street lamps and ferries, but lacked the provision for the assize of bread that is found in the Buffalo framework of government. Significantly, the contemporaneous government of Milwaukee, organized at virtually the same time (1836), was still confined to the restricted duties of a village. Ten years later, however, when it emerged as a city, its citizens sought, and the state legislature granted, an expansion of powers quite similar to those of its sister cities of the Great

Lakes. The Chicago consolidation act of 1851 found an echo in a like measure for Milwaukee in 1852 and in a revision of Buffalo's charter in 1853. These charters elaborated rather than expanded the powers of the municipality in ways dictated by closer acquaintance with the problems of city government. Again the customary parallelism in form stands out both in the general pattern of the documents and in the many identical clauses, such as those setting up the fire department and compelling the removal of ill-smelling nuisances.[7]

The advance from village to city brought an extension of municipal responsibilities, but only to an extent normally resulting, especially in America, from the crowding of people into small compass. These new powers were limited in general to the protection of life and property, although the results of each extension of authority were recognized as having a bearing on the promotion of trade and hence on the prosperity of the municipality. Concern for securing property against the chronic fire hazard of the western city made possible the enactment of building restrictions and encouraged the organization of fire-fighting facilities. Concern for health prompted the authorities to establish pesthouses, to quarantine immigrants coming through the lake ports, and to abate such nuisances as stagnant pools, foul-smelling substances, and slaughter houses—reforms stimulated not so much by aesthetic considerations as by the prevailing conviction that urban filth and the spread of cholera went hand in hand. While thus exhorting cleanliness, the authorities at the same time, perhaps paradoxically, laid restrictions on wasting water and prohibited bathing in the rivers from which the city water supply was drawn.

In the interests of urban order, the city councils were empowered to provide watchmen and police; to suppress disorderly houses; to impound animals running at large; to prevent immoderate driving, rolling hoops or playing ball in the streets, and the cluttering of sidewalks with snow, dirt, firewood, awnings, or cigar store Indians; to restrain "runners" for boats and stages; and to curtail city noises. Nor were these idle grants of authority. The Cleveland council, as one of its first acts, passed an ordinance on May 9, 1836, which provided that the streets were to be swept semi-monthly on Friday mornings by the owners or occupants of property; that horses should not be fastened so as to obstruct passage in the streets nor be driven on the sidewalks; and that the huge wooden replicas of boots, saddles, and kettles with which merchants advertised their wares were not to project over three feet into the street. In addition to providing for quarantine and hospitalization of the sick poor, the health ordinances of Milwaukee required that physicians report cases of contagious diseases and that records of burials show the cause of death lest criminal or dangerous causes be left unknown; decreed a fine of ten dollars for refusal to be vaccinated on the request of a physician employed by the city council; set up barriers to the immigration of the diseased, going so far as to empower constables to call upon the aid of bystanders in forcibly keeping immigrants from landing; and banned slaughter houses within the city limits. The Buffalo council prohibited interment within certain limits and ordered that graves be not less than five feet deep. Anti-noise ordinances in Buffalo and Milwaukee prevented the playing of musical instruments on docks or wharves on Sunday, and in Milwaukee the ringing of bells or loud outcries at public sales were forbidden.

In providing for markets and the regulation of traffic in necessary commodities, these western cities followed practices by which frontier and colonial communities had attempted to protect an often insufficient food supply, prevent monopolistic practices detrimental to the public health and security, avoid the competition of foreign vendors and hucksters, and at the same time force competition upon the licensed merchants.[8] In 1849 Chicago had three markets for the retailing of perishable foods. Butchers were forced to hold stalls there until an act of 1851 permitted the establishment of meat shops outside the market.[9] City markets and strict market ordinances were justified as a means of supplying large cities with fresh and wholesome provisions, because leniency in this respect, it was felt, might encourage disease. Vendors of fresh meat, poultry, eggs, butter, lard, fruit, and vegetables were forced to sell their goods at the market during the market hours unless licensed to sell at some other place or in some other way. To guarantee the wholesomeness of the products, cleanliness of the stalls, and orderliness of the market, prohibitions were set up against pitching quoits, the presence of dogs, and the use of obscene and profane language in the vicinity of the market place. Purchasing goods at the markets for resale elsewhere or forestalling country producers for the purpose of buying their produce for resale was prohibited.[10]

Similar regulations for supervising weights and measures affected the purchase of boards, brick, coal, firewood, casks, hay, flour, tobacco, potash, and salted provisions such as fish. According to a Cleveland ordinance of May 8, 1839, vendors of hay without a certificate of weight were subject to a fine of twenty-five dollars. In 1859 Milwaukee farmers opposed as an inequitable tax the weighing charge of five cents per load of wood and twenty-five cents per load of hay—a concession sold by the city to the highest bidder.[11] The assize of bread, customary in the colonial city charter and in early charters in the West, was apparently abandoned in Chicago and for a while in Cleveland, though provided for elsewhere.[12] In these young urban communities, commerce in such necessary commodities as food, fodder, and firewood was of sufficient public interest to warrant close regulation. Other pursuits related to the public welfare were also restricted. For instance, ordinances regulating the fees of hackmen and carters were not unusual. Chapter XIII of the Buffalo ordinances of 1855 stipulated that a hackman might be fined for refusing to carry a passenger or for going by other than the shortest route. Interest in attracting immigrants prompted a Milwaukee ordinance of May 3, 1849, which fixed a maximum charge of ten cents per article on the goods of immigrants and other passengers landed on the piers of the city.

These principal activities of the mid-nineteenth century city were laid down at the inception of cityhood and were based upon the regulations commonly existing during the colonial period. Later amendments elaborated these functions of municipal government as specific problems arose, and occasionally a measure was passed which suggested an expanding concept of city government, as in the Chicago provision of 1851 with respect to planting and preserving ornamental trees along the streets and in the public grounds of the city. In general, however, the close of this middle period saw only a limited expansion of urban responsibilities beyond those assumed with the grant of the original charter. Nor did these differ in any marked way from the eighteenth century pattern of powers granted the government of New York City at the close of the colonial period.

However, in defining the political authority underlying municipal management, these cities, developing in the current of nineteenth century democracy, left eighteenth century limitations far behind. Here again is a striking uniformity of behavior in the five lake cities. Each began its career as a city with a property qualification, in addition to a residence requirement of varying length, for at least one class of voters—whites, aliens, or negroes. Detroit in 1824 required its electors to be freemen who had paid a city tax. Buffalo extended the suffrage to United States citizens but required negro voters to have a freehold estate of $250 on which taxes had been actually rated and paid. A tax qualification was prerequisite to voting in Cleveland in 1836, and Chicago in 1837 expected its voters to be householders or to have paid a city tax of not less than three dollars within the year. As late as 1846 Milwaukee exacted payment of a property tax or required highway or fire duty of male aliens who had declared their intention of becoming citizens. At the outset of cityhood in Chicago, Detroit, and Buffalo, only those owning a freehold estate were eligible for the major elective posts; Milwaukee, having demanded a similar qualification of her village trustees, abandoned this provision upon becoming a city in 1846. Chicago took the lead in a democratic movement which brought by the early fifties the abolition of property qualifications for suffrage and office holding. Milwaukeeans called a proposal to restrict the suffrage to United States citizens an "odious and anti-republican" attempt to deprive "one-half of the citizens of Milwaukee, who will be taxed for the support of the city government, of their right to a voice in electing their officers or making their laws."[13] Like the framers of the state constitutions of the middle period, these mid-western city dwellers believed in representative government closely responsive to the popular will. A proposal to allow aldermen to hold their offices for three years was opposed in Milwaukee as "placing them beyond the reach of public opinion for a time almost equal to an age in older communities."[14] Consequently, annually-elected councils were endowed with wide authority and the power of the executive office was greatly curtailed. In Buffalo the mayor was the creature of the council, and in the other cities little more than a figurehead. Chicagoans in 1840 openly resented the fact that their mayor was given a salary and pointed to Detroit and Buffalo where, they said, the mayors "in fact received nothing."[15] Adherence to the democratic principle of passing jobs around was the practice if not the provision. In Cleveland between 1836 and 1870 only five mayors succeeded themselves in office, and of the twelve available council positions the yearly average of councilmen who were reëlected was two. A study of the situation in Chicago and Milwaukee shows a similar rotation in office. In Detroit it became necessary to force men by threat or danger of fine to serve once they had been elected, although they were spe-

cifically exempted from holding the same office two years in succession. The municipal legislators served without salary, but this did not prevent many of them from amassing fortunes, especially when they held the office of street commissioner.[16] To judge from an analysis of the trades and occupations of those who were councilmen in Cleveland and Milwaukee in the first twenty years of their cityhood, commission merchants, grocers, joiners, builders, masons, and attorneys took a predominantly active part in the government of these young western cities.

Charter changes both in the early fifties and after the financial crisis of 1857 brought some decrease in the amateur management of these governments and a consequent strengthening of the executive arm. In 1852 Milwaukee was provided with an appointed comptroller, soon made elective, to manage city finances. In 1858 the state legislature devised a bicameral council for the city in the hope of retarding hasty legislation. The mayor was granted the veto power in Chicago in 1851 and in Milwaukee in 1859, a negative that was strengthened in the latter city in 1861 and in the former in 1872 by requiring two-thirds rather than a majority of the elected councilmen to override it. The major development in all the Great Lakes cities at the close of the period under discussion was in the direction of establishing boards and commissions as a means of divorcing city management from amateur direction and political interference. This trend, realized in the late sixties and early seventies, was motivated, according to the Milwaukee *Sentinel*, by a feeling that it was inefficient and costly to commit the complicated problems of street improvements and urban services to elected councilmen. It would be better, said the editor, to trust the outlay of great sums of the people's money to "three capable, honest, experienced business men . . . with a moderate compensation for their services, than take the chances under the elective principle of having men of doubtful qualities . . . without compensation . . . under the constant imputation of petty frauds and speculations upon the ward funds."[17] Vesting in the mayor the power of appointing the members of these boards and commissions is an index of the increased prestige of the executive and the decreasing influence of the legislative branch of city government at the opening of the seventies. The Great Lakes cities, growing to maturity in the environment of nineteenth century democracy, thus broadened the base of urban politics but narrowed the administration of municipal affairs.

These major cities of the Middle West did not "just grow." The promotional activities of the original speculator-founders were only the beginning of a long-time program in which newspaper editors, merchants, and citizens at large combined their efforts to attract settlers and business to a given city and away from its neighboring rivals.[18] The promoters of the embryo village on the east side of the Milwaukee river expended nearly $100,000 laying out streets and effecting other improvements designed to attract the settler. By the exertion of political influence and the donation of land they secured the county courthouse for their growing community. Across the river, the promoters of the "west side" were spending similar sums upon improvements, filling the columns of the Milwaukee *Advertiser* with glowing reports of their city's promise, and, by employ-

ing a river boat to meet the lake steamers that touched Milwaukee harbor, preëmpting immigrants possibly destined for their rivals' village. Subsequently many a subterfuge was devised by Chicago and Milwaukee in an attempt to discredit the other in the eyes of European immigrants and eastern capitalists. Only the combination of geography and the railroad left Milwaukee a tired but still confident second in the race. "Forcing" immigrants was accomplished through the use of representatives and promotional advertising in eastern cities. For example, propaganda concerning deaths from cholera, or the absence of them, figured prominently in such campaigns.[19]

The promotion of business in these cities followed a common pattern. A predominant concern for trade and commerce gave way in the middle sixties to the encouragement of manufacturing. Economic developments in Milwaukee and Cleveland substantiate this interpretation. The early interest in trade was reflected by the editor of the Milwaukee *Daily Sentinel and Gazette* in 1846: "It is . . . clearly to the interest of our merchants, millers, forwarders, and business men generally to unite upon some plan for extending and improving roads leading to Milwaukee"[20] Even before this, popular contributions had subsidized a bridge that promised to facilitate the trade of neighboring farmers with the village merchants. Plank roads and railroads were heralded as a means of tapping the markets of the hinterland. Connections by rail with the Columbia River, with the Mississippi River (completed by 1857), and with the Minnesota country, and routes eastward by steam ferry across Lake Michigan and by the Detroit and Michigan railroad were only a few of the projects. They were supported by city funds, by loans of city credit, and by popular subscription—contributions often appealed for and given as a matter of civic duty.[21] Clevelanders were equally convinced of the importance of roads and railways for prosperity. The editor of the Cleveland *Daily True Democrat* wrote in 1849: "Let us, like the wise Cincinnati merchants, spend liberally for these [plank] roads and do all to arouse our farmers and everybody to the importance of increasing our facilities for trade and travel and thus make Cleveland the center of a large region."[22] By 1856 it was asserted in the Cleveland *Leader* that railroads were responsible for the city's growth. The establishment of Boards of Trade in Buffalo (1844), Detroit (1847), Cleveland and Chicago (1848), and Milwaukee (1849); the organization and promotional excursions of merchants; the contesting of disputed trade areas through the use of runners and drummers—these activities suggest the early emphasis on trade and commerce as the key to civic prosperity. In 1857, Milwaukee merchants were urged to compete for trade in Iowa and Minnesota where

already Chicago, St. Louis, Dubuque, Galena, Cincinnati even, have their runners, posters, and advertisements scattered broadcast . . . offering tempting inducements to merchants to come and buy. . . . Now is the time for our merchants, manufacturers, and traders to . . . scatter their cards, handbills, circulars, and advertisements up and down the Mississippi. Let them dispatch some of their shrewdest clerks to La Crosse, Winona, Prescott, Hudson, St. Paul . . . and canvass thoroughly for orders.[23]

By 1855, however, Cleveland editors were sounding a warning note. Business men were blinded, they said, "by the belief that commerce alone" would make the city great. The *Leader* asserted in 1856 that "no thinking man with capital will stop here when we have only commerce to sustain us. A manufacturing town gives a man full scope for his ambitions."[24] That newspaper encouraged popular subscriptions to factory enterprises, urged the reduction of real estate prices as an inducement to capital, and agitated for the protection and consumption of home manufactures.[25] An appeal to civic duty attended this promotion as it had the earlier agitation for railroad connections. By the late sixties when Cleveland had become a manufacturing center, earlier arguments used there were being echoed in Milwaukee. Vigorous newspaper agitation, together with the organization of the Milwaukee Manufacturers Association in January 1863, excited industrial ambitions. "Commerce alone can never give us a permanent prosperity," counselled a Milwaukee editor in 1866.[26] By 1872, as a result, one-third to one-half of the working population of Milwaukee was engaged in manufacturing goods valued at $20,000,000.[27] Stimulated by the economic developments of the Civil War period, pressed by the expansion of population into areas farther west of them, and in a sense taking a cue each from the economic experiences of the other, the lake cities had turned by 1870 from an almost exclusive interest in commerce to endorse sentiments to the effect that "a thousand dollars put into manufacturing does more to gather population than a million dollars put into trade."[28]

A major source of the urban services of these young communities developed from the sense of individual responsibility which prompted thousands of city dwellers to invest their savings in the railroads and factories that were sup- posed to bring prosperity to the urban center. The mid-nineteenth century saw the Great Lakes cities in what might be called the "subscription period" of their municipal growth. Two to three days' work on the streets, for which money payments could be substituted, was expected of all able-bodied men.[29] Street and sidewalk improvements as well as the eradication of nuisances were to be taken care of individually or charged against the property benefited. For protection against theft and riot Milwaukeeans had to rely upon occasional watchmen, volunteer firemen, and members of free military companies until a night watch and a police force were organized in 1852. As late as 1855 men carried weapons for their own protection, and an ordinance of that year compelled all citizens to aid the police when called upon to do so. In 1837 the Cleveland *Herald and Gazette* referred to the "Mutual Protecting Society," and in 1839 a number of the citizens "with commendable spirit formed themselves into companies for a city watch." In 1859 the merchants of Detroit, where as early as 1825 volunteer watchmen had been mobilized by passing around a subscription paper, subscribed to the support of a patrol for the business district, and the Milwaukee Board of Trade offered a bonus for additional protection in 1860.[30] By the late fifties and early sixties police service was generally provided at city expense, and the management of the police by a commission was agitated or passed in Milwaukee (1864), Detroit (1865), and Cleveland (1866).

Fire protection came also in a major degree from individual contributions of time and money. In the middle thirties Clevelanders were fined when they refused to serve in the bucket line at fires. Local editors appealed to property owners to contribute their share of volunteer firemen and in 1840 congratulated Phoenix Company Number Four for having won the premiums offered annually by the insurance companies to stimulate competitive-minded fire fighters to efficiency and accomplishment. Milwaukeeans from all levels of society were members of the organized volunteer firemen, who met a portion of the costs of their own equipment and whose service exempted them from highway or militia duty. Donations, benefit concerts, and dinners raised $2,500 in 1851 to swell the funds by which the Ocean, Neptune, and Cataract companies of volunteer firemen carried on their work. Despite the pleas of property owners for more efficient service than unpaid volunteers could give, it was not until the appearance of the steam fire engine in the sixties that professional fire fighters were generally maintained from public funds.[31]

Aside from a meagre and inadequate tax to support almshouses and to furnish medical care for the sick poor, urban relief, too, was provided by individual donation. Invariably the cessation of navigation in the winter season brought demands from the unemployed of the city. Out of public meetings came plans for raising money and organizations for dispensing relief. Mayor D. A. J. Upham of Milwaukee expressed a general opinion in 1849 when he held that private enterprise was best equipped to meet the problem. The Cleveland *Daily True Democrat* said the poor could not be taken care of "unless individual activity and associated effort act."[32] Women's organizations, such as the Martha Washington Society of Cleveland and the Ladies

Benevolent Society of Milwaukee, were soon supplanted by more systematically managed relief groups, like the Milwaukee Provident Association and the Cleveland Relief Association. The Milwaukee group advertised its cause as a community responsibility, raised over $20,000 in the five years ending in 1867, and distributed fuel and provisions only after careful investigation of the needy. Private contributions were the chief means of support of the Chicago Relief and Aid Society, incorporated in 1857. Soup kitchens were also subsidized by private gifts and meal tickets were sold to those citizens who wished to offer them to the poor. The Milwaukee women who managed these enterprises trusted "to the benevolence of our citizens . . . for the food to be supplied."[33]

To a large extent the cultural services of the city, beyond the provision for public schools, were the result of support by subscription. Forerunners of the public libraries of the seventies were the membership libraries of such organizations as the Young Men's Associations in Chicago and Milwaukee and the Reading Room Association in Cleveland.[34] Imitating Chicago's example, and realizing that the lack of private libraries compelled "voluntary association," several Milwaukeeans organized to promote a library in 1847.[35] In canvassing for funds and members they did not neglect to stress community obligation and the example of other cities. The promotional value of good libraries to the city was "a pretty safe index of the mental advancement . . . of a city." They also emphasized the "gallantry of the Association [which] admits even ladies to a full participation of the advantages of membership, with the exception, we think, of voting."[36] Char-

tered in 1848, the Cleveland Library Association issued stock certificates and charged yearly dues. Soliciting subscriptions in 1851 for a reading room, the editor of the Cleveland *Daily True Democrat* was convinced that "nothing . . . adds so much to the reputation of a city as a good Reading Room and Library."[37]

Many other cultural activities were fostered by subscription. Local musicians and actors volunteered their services in aid of the fire department, orphan asylum, and other causes. The Milwaukee Musical Society when soliciting members in 1857 advised the public that its monthly dues of forty cents plus a two dollar initiation fee were "but a moderate tax to pay towards the support of an organization which ministers so largely to the enjoyment of our citizens and which reflects such credit upon our city."[38] The founders of academies and colleges in asking for endowments also appealed to civic duty.[39] By 1870 the beginning of public libraries[40] and the agitation for parks—following New York's example with Central Park—were slight but indicative signs of the rôle that the urban government was ultimately to play in providing aesthetic satisfaction and social and cultural benefits to its citizens.[41] A Cleveland editor went so far as to start a crusade in 1870 against city noises—"an evil rapidly becoming unendurable." He wrote: "While suppressing so rigorously all offences to the sight and smell, and punishing in general all disturbances of the peace, it would be only consistent to include in the proscription the still greater plague of noise." Yet he concluded a year later that the cure for city noises still lay in the field of individual responsibility: "We have not yet reached that point where the law will guard the nerves of the aged, the tender, and infirm from unnecessary torture."[42] Such a concept of city function did not square with the "subscription period" of city growth.

These striking parallels in the institutional history of the five major cities of the Great Lakes are to be explained in part by the contemporaneous character of their growth, by the common sources from which their population sprang, and by the similarity of the economic forces influencing their behavior. In all five cities, the foreign born provided about half the population, with natives of Germany, Ireland, and Great Britain distributing themselves in early uniform proportions, except in Milwaukee where European immigrants were more predominantly German. In the sectional origins of native Americans these cities were also similar. New York, Massachusetts, and Pennsylvania contributed most abundantly to each of the five cities save Chicago, which drew a large number from neighboring Michigan. The census of 1870 showed as well a remarkable uniformity in the percentages of people engaged in various occupational pursuits. But it was not simply a matter of similar social ingredients, for this municipal development of the Great Lakes area was apparently following a pattern or process not unusual to urban evolution elsewhere. As they grew to comparable size of the coastal cities half a century earlier. For example, after a generation of city growth the expanded powers of the lake cities in 1870, like those of the seaboard cities in 1800, represented a response more to the problems of size than to any changed philosophy of the functions of urban communities for which a difference in environment or personality

might have been responsible. By 1870 each of these lake cities was a more conscious "municipal entity" than in its village period. Commercial regulations for the common good, cooperation through taxes and subscriptions for the promotion and improvement of the city, and the recognition of some of the social responsibilities presented by the interdependence of city life certainly had fostered a group consciousness—a group attitude, however, still very largely articulated by and pivoting around the individual. The "municipal consciousness," twentieth century pattern, was more than a generation in the future. Its full development awaited the flow of population, new economic needs, and changing social philosophy of the late nineteenth and early twentieth centuries.

In these urban centers of the Middle West in the mid-nineteenth century, the houses, to one traveller's surprise, were not "wigwamified," the dress and ornament not "wampumized."[43] As Anthony Trollope said, the "general level of . . . material and intellectual wellbeing—of beef . . . and book learning" was "no doubt infinitely higher than in a European town."[44] These cities sprang from beginnings closely associated in practice and attitude with the westward expansion of the American people. As they grew, their concern for popular management and their emphasis upon the intrinsic rôle of the individual in the promotion of the physical and cultural growth of the city reveal attitudes often observed by students of the agrarian frontier. At the same time, they showed a willing dependence upon eastern sources in the transmission of culture, a studied imitation of tested forms of municipal practice and urban service, and an expanding assumption of community responsibility. Such influences suggest that in the rise of the large city in the West, as elsewhere, one sees another—perhaps equally important if less explored—side of American social history in the nineteenth century.

NOTES

1. Milwaukee *Daily Sentinel,* May 26, 1845.
2. The following are the most useful titles for making comparative studies of urban development in the Mississippi Valley. Buffalo: Robert W. Bingham, *The Cradle of the Queen City: A History of Buffalo to the Incorporation of the City* (Buffalo, 1931); Henry W. Hill, ed., *Municipality of Buffalo, New York; A History, 1720-1923* (4 vols., New York, 1923); Josephus N. Larned, *A History of Buffalo, Delineating the Evolution of the City* (2 vols., New York, 1911). Cleveland: Elroy M. Avery, *A History of Cleveland and its Environs* (3 vols., Chicago, 1918); William R. Coates, *A History of Cuyahoga County and the City of Cleveland* (3 vols., Chicago, 1924); Samuel P. Orth, *A History of Cleveland, Ohio* (3 vols., Chicago, 1910). Detroit: George B. Catlin, *The Story of Detroit* (Detroit, 1923); Clarence M. Burton, ed., *The City of Detroit, Michigan, 1701-1922* (4 vols., Chicago, 1922); Silas Farmer, *History of Detroit and Michigan* (Detroit, 1884); Arthur Pound, *Detroit, Dynamic City* (New York, 1940); Robert B. Ross and George B. Catlin, *Landmarks of Detroit* (Detroit, 1898). Milwaukee: William G. Bruce, *History of Milwaukee City and County* (3 vols., Milwaukee, 1922); John G. Gregory, *History of Milwaukee, Wisconsin* (4 vols., Chicago, 1931); Bayrd Still, "The Growth of Milwaukee as Recorded by Contemporaries," *Wisconsin Magazine of History* (Madison), XXI, 1938, pp. 262-292, and "Milwaukee, 1870-1900: the Emergence of a Metropolis," *loc. cit.,* XXIII, 1939, pp. 138-162. Chicago: Alfred T. Andreas, *History of Chicago, 1670-1885* (3 vols., Chicago, 1884-1886); J. Seymour Currey, *Chicago: Its History and Its Builders* (3 vols., Chicago, 1912); Bessie L. Pierce, *A History of Chicago* (2 vols., New

York, 1937, 1940), and *As Others See Chicago* (Chicago, 1933). Pittsburgh: Leland D. Baldwin, *Pittsburgh, the Story of a City* (Pittsburgh, 1937); George T. Fleming, *History of Pittsburgh and Environs* (5 vols., New York, 1922); Frank C. Harper, *Pittsburgh of Today, Its Resources and People* (4 vols., New York, 1931); Sarah H. Killikelly; *The History of Pittsburgh, Its Rise and Progress* (Pittsburgh, 1906). Cincinnati: Clara Chambrun, *Cincinnati: Story of the Queen City* (New York, 1939); Henry A. and Kate B. Ford, *History of Cincinnati, Ohio* (Cleveland, 1881); Charles T. Greve, *Centennial History of Cincinnati and Representative Citizens* (2 vols., Chicago, 1904). Louisville: Reuben T. Durrett, *The Centenary of Louisville* (*Filson Club Publications,* no. 8, Louisville, 1893); L. A. Williams and Co., eds., *History of the Ohio Falls Cities and their Counties* (Cleveland, 1882); J. Stoddard Johnston, ed., *Memorial History of Louisville from its first Settlement to the Year 1896* (2 vols., Chicago, n. d.). Minneapolis: Norman S. B. Gras, "The Significance of the Twin Cities for Minnesota History," *Minnesota History* (St. Paul), VII, 1926, pp. 3-17; Mildred L. Hartsough, *The Twin Cities as a Metropolitan Market: a Regional Study of the Economic Development of Minneapolis and St. Paul* (Minneapolis, 1925); Calvin F. Schmid, *Social Saga of Two Cities: An Ecological and Statistical Study of Social Trends in Minneapolis and St. Paul* (Minneapolis, 1937). St. Louis: John T. Scharf, *History of St. Louis City and County, from the Earliest Periods to the Present Day* (2 vols., Philadelphia, 1883); Walter B. Stevens, *St. Louis, the Fourth City, 1764-1911* (2 vols., St. Louis, 1911). Memphis: Gerald M. Capers, Jr., *The Biography of a River Town; Memphis: Its Heroic Age* (Chapel Hill, 1939). New Orleans: Henry Rightor, ed., *Standard History of New Orleans, Louisiana* (Chicago, 1900).
3. St. Louis, 310,864; Chicago, 298,977; Cincinnati, 216,239; New Orleans, 191,418; Pittsburgh, 139,256; Buffalo, 117,714; Louisville, 100,753. *Fifteenth Census of the United States, 1930, Population,* I, 18-19.
4. Between 1860 and 1870 the total population of the lake cities increased over 100 per cent; that of the valley cities, 60 per cent; that of New York, Philadelphia, and Boston, 20 per cent; that of the United States, 22.6 per cent. *Ibid.,* 12 *et passim.*

5. Comparative population of the Great Lakes cities:°

	1820	1830	1840	1850	1860	1870
Buffalo	2,095	8,668	18,213	42,261	81,129	117,714
Cleveland	606	1,076	6,071	17,034	43,417	92,829
Detroit	1,422	2,222	9,102	21,019	45,619	79,577
Chicago			4,470	29,963	109,260	298,977
Milwaukee			1,712	20,061	45,246	71,440

° *Ibid.,* 19. The total population of the East North Central States increased during 1840 to 1870 from 2,924,728 to 9,124,517. *Ibid.,* 11.

6. Chicago's first charter was the result of popular agitation. It was submitted to a mass meeting for popular approval, there slightly altered, and sent

to the legislature. Edmund J. James calls it a self-proposed charter, "a practical recognition of local self-government on a large scale." Edmund J. James, *The Charters of the City of Chicago* (Chicago, 1898), 23. Such local participation did not prevent imitation in selecting the form of the charter.

7. For an example of identical clauses in these city charters see *Laws of the State of New York, 1853* (Albany, 1853), p. 461; *Laws of Wisconsin, 1852* (Madison, 1852), p. 81; and *Statutes of Illinois, Private Laws, 1851* (Springfield, 1851), p. 143.

8. For colonial legislation on this subject consult Henry W. Farnam, *Chapters in the History of Social Legislation in the United States to 1860* (Washington, 1938), 92-115.

9. Bessie L. Pierce, *A History of Chicago* (New York, 1937-), II, 461, note.

10. As an example of this type of early municipal regulation see "An Ordinance Relating to the First Ward Market, and to License and regulate Butcher's Stalls, Shops and Stands for the sale of Butcher's Meat, Poultry, Game, and Fresh Fish," in *Charters and Ordinances of the City of Milwaukee* (Milwaukee, 1857), 464-465. Of similar nature is a Buffalo ordinance of April 23, 1855, and one in Cleveland, June 3, 1851.

11. Milwaukee *Sentinel*, January 4, 1859.

12. An act regulating the "Assize of Bread" seems to have been in force in Detroit as late as 1820. The price of bread was fixed according to a sliding scale based on the price of flour. George N. Fuller, *Economic and Social Beginnings in Michigan, 1805-1837* (Lansing, 1916), 126. A Massachusetts regulation, based on the price of grain plus a reasonable allowance for labor, was abandoned in 1801. Farnam, *Social Legislation to 1860*, 110. The Milwaukee ordinance regulating the manufacture and sale of bread (July 13, 1836) required registration of the baker's place of business, the use of wholesome flour, and the marking of loaves with the weight of the loaf and the initials of the baker. This was virtually the same bread legislation as that of New York in 1839 and of Boston as late as 1834. A similar provision is found in Chapter XXXVII of the Cleveland ordinances as codified in 1877.

13. Milwaukee *Courier*, January 27, 1845, quoted in Milwaukee *Evening Wisconsin*, October 15, 1895.

14. *Ibid.*

15. Pierce, *Chicago*, I, 328, note.

16. Laurence M. Larson, *A Financial and Administrative History of Milwaukee* (*Bulletin of the University of Wisconsin*, no. 242, *Economics and Political Science Series*, Vol. IV, no. 2, Madison, 1908), 27-28; Milwaukee *Sentinel*, June 27, 1857.

17. Milwaukee *Sentinel*, April 5, 1869. See also *ibid.*, March 11, 1852, and March 23, 1864; John G. Gregory, *History of Milwaukee*, *Wisconsin* (Chicago, 1931), I, 253.

18. The Cincinnati *Gazette*, quoted in the Milwaukee *Sentinel* of June 10, 1859, asserted that a newspaper served the founders of towns by acting as a kind of credential to the reality of the inchoate city, and as a light to direct the pioneer to a new home and to direct business and emigration into new channels.

19. The Boston *Chronotype*, as quoted in the Milwaukee *Daily Sentinel and Gazette*, August 29, 1846, referred to the "forcing process" as circulating "numberless libels in handbills" in the East. Milwaukeeans claimed that Chicago newspapers were libeling their health record, and Cleveland papers labored during the thirties to deny that the village was sickly.

20. Milwaukee *Daily Sentinel and Gazette*, March 11, 1846. In his inaugural address, Mayor D. A. J. Upham averred that "the improvements we most need . . . are the roads and facilities of securing trade from the country." *Ibid.*, April 12, 1849.

21. The city of Milwaukee soon substituted the issuance of bonds as loans to railroad companies for the earlier practice of buying railroad stock. Substantial security and a popular vote of authorization were required. This popular support was freely given, and by 1858 the loans to railroad companies totaled $1,614,000, all of which was ultimately repaid except two issues of $100,000 each. Larson, *Financial History of Milwaukee*, 74-75. By contrast the city of Chicago had made no railroad investments by 1870, and individual Chicagoans had not found it necessary to invest much in enterprises that eastern capitalists were eager to finance. Pierce, *Chicago*, II, 75.

22. Cleveland *Daily True Democrat*, June 1, 1849.

23. Milwaukee *Sentinel*, March 17, 1857.

24. Cleveland *Leader*, October 31, 1855, and March 10, 1856.

25. *Ibid.*, March 30, 1858.

26. Milwaukee *Sentinel*, October 20, 1866. See also *ibid.*, April 16, 1869, for an assertion by manufacturers that Milwaukeeans were still putting all their eggs in one basket.

27. Frederick Merk, *Economic History of Wisconsin During the Civil War Decade* (Madison, 1916), 127.

28. Cleveland *Leader*, April 10, 1873.

29. Chicago in 1847 required males between the ages of twenty-one and sixty to work on the streets three days each year, with commutation at the rate of fifty cents per day. Milwaukee in 1846 required two days' work with commutation at seventy-five cents per day.

30. Cleveland *Herald and Gazette*, June 28, 1837; Gregory, *Milwaukee*, II, 1123; Milwaukee *Daily Sentinel and Gazette*, April 16, May 20, 1847, and February 6, 1850; Milwaukee *Sentinel*, August 16, 1855, and January 14, 1860; Cleveland *Herald*, November 28, 1839; Clarence M. Burton, ed., *The City of Detroit, Michigan* (Detroit, 1922), I, 406.

31. Cleveland *Herald and Gazette*, December 22, 1837; Cleveland *Herald*, June 24, 1840; Cleveland *Leader*, November 25, 1862, and April 14, 1863; Milwaukee *Sentinel*, January 22, 1852, March 4, 1861, and March 4, 1862; Gregory, *Milwaukee*, II, 795 ff.; Burton, *Detroit*, I, 402.

32. Cleveland *Daily True Democrat,* December 20, 1850.

33. Milwaukee *Sentinel,* November 30, 1857. See also *ibid.,* November 23, 1857, November 12, 1866, and December 20, 1867; Milwaukee *Daily Sentinel and Gazette,* April 12, 1849; Pierce, *Chicago,* II, 445-446.

34. The Young Men's Association organized in Chicago in 1841 was modeled after a similar organization in Albany. Members were asked to donate books to the library and non-members might use the reading room at a charge of fifty cents a month. By 1847 the library had a thousand volumes, plus current newspapers. Pierce, *Chicago,* I, 286-288. The Cleveland Reading Room Association was supported by voluntary subscriptions. Elroy M. Avery, *A History of Cleveland and Its Environs* (Chicago, 1918), I, 188. Judging from an advertisement in the Cleveland *Herald,* November 30, 1836, dues were five dollars a year.

35. The charge for life members was twenty-five dollars. Regular members paid an entrance fee of two dollars and fifty cents quarterly thereafter. The sum of $1,513 was collected in the first two months. The association had 810 books at the end of the first year. The librarian donated his services, and the library was open two afternoons a week. By 1867 the association had three thousand members and more than ten thousand volumes. Gregory, *Milwaukee,* II, 1077-1078.

36. Milwaukee *Sentinel,* December 2, 1857.

37. Cleveland *Daily True Democrat,* January 29, 1851. "Lucy Ann," having come to Cleveland from the East, wrote to the editor of the Cleveland *Herald,* July 14, 1845, bemoaning the lack of a Young Men's Association or a Reading Room Association. "There are enough young men here to support a . . . library, but . . . they are more fond of riding . . . in buggies, eating ice cream,

and smoking cigars . . . than they are of obtaining worth of mind."

38. Milwaukee *Sentinel,* December 7, 1857.

39. *Ibid.,* March 4, 1852, November 26, 1853, and August 3, 1855.

40. The nucleus of Cleveland's public library was a collection of books provided under the school library law of 1853. A free public library was authorized by an act of 1867 and realized in 1869. According to the Cleveland *Leader,* March 16, 1869, "A free library is proof of the enlightened liberality in a community and of the intellectual culture and refinement thereof." Detroit's public library was formally opened in 1865. Burton, *Detroit,* I, 838. The library of the Young Men's Association of Milwaukee was transferred to the city of Milwaukee in 1878. Gregory, *Milwaukee,* II, 1078.

41. Public parks, according to the press, would counteract "the downward tendencies of city life" (Milwaukee *Daily Sentinel and Gazette,* April 24, 1845); enhance the value of property (Cleveland *Herald,* December 31, 1840); and offset urban congestion as a consequence of which "few grounds around the city remain occupied" (Milwaukee *Sentinel,* December 18, 1865). Detroit was agitating for an extensive park and Cleveland for three of them in 1865. The park question was discussed in a desultory way in Chicago during the fifties and sixties, but not until the late sixties was much accomplished. Pierce, *Chicago,* II, 339-341.

42. Cleveland *Leader,* September 3, October 18, 1870, and May 9, 1871. See also *ibid.,* May 7, 1869.

43. A narrative of Nathaniel P. Willis of 1860, quoted in Gregory, *Milwaukee,* II, 1320.

44. Anthony Trollope, *North America* (New York, 1862), I, 182.

Urban Rivalry and Internal Improvements in the Old Northwest, 1820-1860

HARRY N. SCHEIBER

At the very beginning of settlement in the Old Northwest urban communities developed in response to the commercial needs of the surrounding country. And almost as soon as they appeared, there was "urban rivalry," that is, competition among them for advantages that would promote their growth and

From *Ohio History* (October 1962), pp. 227-39, 290-92. Reprinted by permission of The Ohio Historical Society. Harry N. Scheiber is Professor of History at Dartmouth College.

enhance their attractiveness to emigrants and investors.[1] The earliest rivalries usually involved competition for advantages that government might bestow. Designation as the county seat or as the territorial or state capital marked the beginning of growth for many a rude village in the West, and the pursuit of these choice prizes was inevitably marked by keen political struggles. The presence of federal land offices, colleges and academies, or government installations such as arsenals and prisons was for many towns the only factor that permitted them to outdistance less favored rivals with equivalent natural or geographic endowments.[2] .

Sustained urban growth and economic viability were in most cases dependent upon more than initial advantages that this sort of government patronage could provide. Probably the most important single requirement for urban growth and commercial development was adequate transportation. Without reliable transport facilities connecting a town with an expanding hinterland and with outside markets, there were oppressive limitations upon growth. The struggle for internal improvements therefore became the cause of the most vigorous and persistent rivalries among western urban communities—rivalries marked by intense ambitions, deeply rooted fear of failure, and ingenious employment of the instruments of political and economic leverage at the disposal of urban leaders.[3]

The period of early urban growth in the Old Northwest coincided with the period of canal construction by the states. How, then, did urban rivalries influence state transport policy in the canal era, 1820-45? How did continued rivalry affect the planning and construction of western railroads when private promotion supplanted state enterprise, from the mid-forties to 1860? Before dealing with these questions, it must be noted that self-interested urban activities and urban consciousness cannot be strictly separated from the more embracing force of which they were manifestations, that is, from "localism," a collective consciousness and sense of common interests among the people of a given locality. The definition of common objectives and self-interest might find expression at many levels, and often urban aims and objectives were merely an intense reflection of regional aims.[4] Towns frequently spoke in state politics for the trade areas with which they were associated; yet within intrastate regions (as within interstate sections) cities might compete for hegemony. New transport facilities and redirection of trade—or even the prospect of such change—might alter drastically the regional identification of given urban centers.

The interplay of regional and local rivalries at the state level is illustrated in the history of Ohio's improvements policy. The movement for construction of a canal between Lake Erie and the Ohio River, which, it was hoped, would open eastern markets to Ohio farmers and merchants, began to gather strength about 1820 in response to construction of the Erie Canal in New York. In 1822 the Ohio legislature assigned to a special commission the task of planning such a canal. The canal commissioners soon recognized that their problem was as much one of politics as of engineering. As long as the project remained a subject of discussion in general terms, optimistic business and political leaders throughout the state gave it their support. But once the project took precise form and the commission recommended specific routes, the virtue of vagueness was lost, and the towns and regions that would be bypassed united immediately in opposition to the proposal. Spokesmen for the disappointed communities evoked the specter of oppressive taxation, argued in principle against state intervention in the economy, and denounced the commissioners for alleged corruption. Yet some of the same men had earlier been among the most outspoken advocates of a state canal project.[5]

In 1825 the Ohio canal commission recommended, and the legislature adopted, a canal program that represented a fusion of several important regional interests within the state. Two canals were authorized, rather than the single work originally contemplated. One, the Miami Canal, satisfied Cincinnati's mercantile community and southwest Ohio; it was to run sixty-seven miles from the Queen City north through the Miami Valley to Dayton, with the understanding that it would later be extended northward to the Maumee Valley and Lake Erie. The second canal, the Ohio Canal, followed a wide-sweeping reverse-S-shaped route from the Ohio River to the lake, passing first up the heavily settled Scioto Valley, then arching eastward to the headwaters of the Muskingum, there turning northward again to its terminus on the lake shore at Cleveland.[6]

This canal program gave new focus to urban and regional ambitions, which adjusted quickly to take account of inter-regional connections and new trade relationships that the canals would create. In the first place, within regions through which the canals passed, there was an intensified struggle for positions on the projected works. Everywhere

along the canal routes there was speculation in new town-sites. A Tuscarawas County promoter expressed the thoughts of hundreds like himself when he wrote to one of the canal commissioners: "I expect a new town will spring up [along the canal], which, from the great trade which must center there, from the country between us and the Ohio, must be a flourishing one. But *where* the spot is, I want *you* to tell *me*."[7] Sensitive to the potential threat to their own interests, established market towns in the interior petitioned for construction of feeder canals that would connect them with the main works. In many instances the townspeople offered to pay a portion of the cost. Several towns organized private canal companies to build feeder lines, not in expectation of direct profits, but rather to protect their commercial position.[8]

Events in the Scioto Valley, the southern route of the Ohio Canal, indicated the extremes to which localism might run. Piketon and Chillicothe had joined with other towns in the valley to support the canal bill of 1825 in the legislature. But as soon as it became necessary for the commission to set the exact canal location, each town advanced its own cause and all sense of regional unity dissolved. The Chillicothe interests were determined to obtain a canal connection. They forced through the legislature a resolution ordering the canal commission to build the canal through Chillicothe, even if it was necessary to build a dam or aqueduct across the river in order to bring the canal through the town. The canal commission complied, crossing the river to place the route through Chillicothe. To avoid further expenditure the commission decided not to re-cross the Scioto below Chillicothe. Piketon and other communities on the opposite bank downriver opposed this action bitterly, since it would prevent them from achieving a canal connection, but they were unsuccessful in their protests.[9] Ironically, the state's accommodation of Chillicothe quieted the clamor there for only a few months. Once actual construction had begun, neighborhoods within the town vied with one another in what may be termed "neighborhood rivalry," various factions demanding that a particular street or section of town be designated as the canal route. Passions ran high for several months, and the mayor finally had to hold a referendum on "the *naked* and *abstract* question" of the canal route.[10]

State officials systematically exploited such local rivalries. Where the canal might be located on either side of a river, the Ohio commissioners solicited donations of land or cash from townspeople and landowners on opposite sides of the stream, indicating that the more generous communities would be favored when the canal was located. This practice often stimulated unreasonable expectations and resulted in bitter disillusionment.[11]

Once the initial canal undertaking was approved, the "disappointed" communities—those entirely outside the region of the canals—did not give up their quest for improved transportation. On the contrary, they proposed a multitude of new projects, many of them reflecting an effort by ambitious towns to overcome the lead of commercial rivals that had obtained places on the canals. "Shall narrow views and sectional feelings withhold our assistance from a work of such evident public utility?" the promoters of one new project asked the general assembly. "Shall we, palsied by untimely fears, stop mid-way in the career of public improvement, to calculate the cost, before our fellow citizens in other parts of the State participate in their advantages?"[12]

Such new improvements schemes disrupted older regional alliances and introduced new forces into state politics. Sandusky's railroad project is a case in point. Only a few years after their town had lost to Cleveland in the struggle for designation as the lake-shore terminus of the Ohio Canal, a group of Sandusky promoters requested state aid for the Mad River and Lake Erie Railroad. The Mad River Railroad was planned in 1831 to run from Sandusky southwest to Dayton, which was then head of navigation on the Miami Canal, and ultimately to Cincinnati. When the first canal program had been debated in the legislature, six years earlier, the Miami Canal proposal had been supported by the western counties located north of Dayton—but only because of the understanding that the canal would be extended northward as soon as finances permitted. Having enjoyed the benefits of its position as head of navigation on the Miami Canal, Dayton now shifted its allegiance, and the town's representatives decided to support state aid for the Mad River Railroad instead of for extension of the canal.[13] This move threatened to strand the area to the north, and the towns in that region (especially Piqua) resented what they regarded as Dayton's treachery. "The Canal *must* be extended," Piqua's newspaper editor declared, despite "the selfish policy of those, who at a former period made such professions of friendship to us; but who, since *their* views have been accomplished, *forget* their obligations."[14]

The projects that blossomed forth in every part of the state also came into conflict with one another in the effort to secure the patronage of the legislature, which at this time commanded only limited funds. If logrolling was an important feature of the legislative process, so too was the log jam. The Ohio General Assembly was virtually stalemated for several years in the early 1830's because of conflicting demands for internal improvements.[15] The jam began to break when extension of the Miami Canal and construction of the Wabash and Erie Canal were authorized—but only because the federal government had provided land-grant aid for these projects. Finally, the pressure of local ambitions became too great to resist further. In 1836-37 the legislature approved a comprehensive system of new canals and state aid to railroad and turnpike companies, a program that within five years would bring Ohio to the verge of default on its enlarged debt. Every region had to be satisfied, it seemed; every little community able to advance half the cost was to receive state assistance in the construction of turnpikes or railways.[16]

With adoption of the enlarged improvements program, urban and regional ambitions adjusted rapidly to the new transportation developments. Many of the patterns of localism and rivalries witnessed a decade earlier now reappeared. In the Muskingum Valley, where a project to improve the river for steamboat traffic was undertaken, Zanesville and Dresden fought over which town should be the head of navigation, just as Dayton and Piqua had struggled for headship on the Miami Canal. Meanwhile, Marietta, situated at the mouth of the Muskingum, protested that the size of the locks was too limited. The vision of every town in the valley appeared to be one of infinite

optimism and boundless growth. "We look forward," a petition of Marietta merchants declared glowingly,

and [we] see our situation placed on the thoroughfare, between the Atlantic & the Medeterranean [sic] of the North, the Mississippi & the St. Lawrence. We look forward to the arrival of the Ohio & Chesapeake Canal and the Baltimore & Ohio Rail Road. . . . We look & expect to see the Ohio made slackwater by Locks & dams, from Marietta to Pittsburgh . . . & Lastly we expect to see the Locks, on the Muskingum Improvement, increased. . . . We wish to convince you, that the discriminating principle, attending the small locks, is derogatory to social Commerce, & has been discarded by all civilized nations.[17]

In the Maumee Valley, then sparsely settled, the people of several small towns—Toledo, Maumee, Perrysburg, and Manhattan—and the absentee proprietors of the towns (including several of the most prominent Ohio political leaders), all had favored construction of the Wabash and Erie Canal, a project designed to continue Indiana's Wabash and Erie Canal from the state line through the Maumee Valley to the lake. But once the Ohio legislature had decided to undertake the project, these villages competed bitterly with one another for designation as the terminus.[18] Among the instruments of rivalry employed were court injunctions, petitions to the legislature and to congress, and pressure on the United States General Land Office to limit the extent of the federal land grant by designating one of the competing towns as head of lake navigation. State officials finally decided to satisfy all the major competing points by extending the canal to the mouth of the river, with terminal locks and basins at Manhattan, Toledo, and Maumee. To equalize the conditions of rivalry the state agreed also to open all the terminal locks simultaneously.[19] Thus even after a major improvement had been authorized, the competition of rival communities could serve to increase the costs of construction.

Roughly the same patterns of localism characterized the evolution of public transport policy in the other states of the Old Northwest. During the early promotional phase of internal improvements, when state officials or private pressure groups were agitating for projects in general terms, there tended to be divisions between the great trade regions of each state. In Indiana, for example, the southern river counties viewed with suspicion the proposal for the Wabash and Erie Canal, and they coalesced to press for roads and railways from the interior to the Ohio River.[20] In Illinois, too, the region tributary to the Mississippi River and southern markets adamantly opposed state aid exclusively for the proposed canal to Chicago. The towns on the eastern lake shore in Wisconsin (still a territory) all sought canal or railroad connections with the interior; but they were prevented from realizing their objectives because of opposition in the northern region, which demanded priority for the Fox and Wisconsin river improvement project, and in the western river towns.[21]

Once specific projects had been formulated, broad regional divisions gave way under pressure for more localized objectives. "Most of the members [of the legislature] vote for nothing which does not pass through their own county," the Indiana state engineer complained in 1835. Indiana's Michigan Road, supported in a general way by all the Ohio River counties, became an object of sharp urban rivalry when designation of the southern terminus had to be made. Similarly, the program that the state's engineers submitted to the legislature in 1835 was not rendered acceptable until it had been expanded elaborately, "to buy votes," a year later.[22] In Michigan all the lake shore towns demanded connections with the interior, yet no policy could command adequate support until one embracing the objectives of every competing town had been formulated. And so Indiana, Illinois, and Michigan all adopted comprehensive state programs that overextended their resources. In both Illinois and Indiana the political strength of localism was further manifested in provisions of the law requiring simultaneous starts on all projects; in addition, each of the states' settled regions was granted representation on the boards of public works.[23] Once construction had begun, moreover, scores of proposals were put forward in each state for branch lines, feeder canals, and turnpike and railroad connections designed to satisfy the needs of towns outside the immediate areas of the main improvements.[24]

Still another feature of urban and regional rivalry as it affected state policy concerned canal tolls. Toll schedules were commonly established by state authorities on a protectionist basis. The states maintained two toll lists— one for "domestic," or in-state, manufactures and a higher schedule of tolls for "foreign," or out-of-state, commodities. In Ohio, for example, manufacturers of glassware, iron, salt, crockery, and other products were the beneficiaries of protectionist tolls.[25] As long as canals remained the sole means of cheap transport to the interior, manufacturers located inland from Lake Erie or the Ohio River enjoyed a form of tariff protection from out-of-state competition. Merchants at the terminal cities on the lake and the Ohio River condemned the protectionist policy as one which imposed artificial restrictions upon the canal commerce that was their economic lifeblood. The conflict between terminal cities and inland towns was expressed in the 1840's in a debate over wheat and flour tolls. The millers of the interior demanded tolls on unprocessed grain that were proportionally higher than tolls on flour. This, they argued, would encourage Ohio's milling industry and reduce the flow of Ohio grain to New York State mills. Merchants and millers at terminal cities opposed such action; they favored equivalent tolls on grain and flour (or even discrimination against flour) as a means of fostering the milling industry of their cities or the export of increasing quantities of grain.[26]

Similarly, merchants at Cleveland, then gateway for import of salt from the East, fought discrimination in salt tolls that protected Ohio producers in the central portion of the state. Thus within the state there was a conflict between mercantile and manufacturing interests, comparable to the division in national politics over tariff policy. The issue of canal tolls cut across party lines, and special regional alignments were fostered by this important question. State officials were forced to mediate such conflicts, with no resolution possible that could fully satisfy all contending interests.[27]

In the period of canal construction, urban and regional ambitions were directed largely toward manipulation and control of state policy. The panic of 1837 and the post-1839 depression marked the end of the era of state canals in the Old Northwest. As the depression came to an end in the mid-

forties a new internal-improvements movement gathered momentum, with a new set of conditions shaping the character of the movement. In the first place, there had been a revulsion against further large-scale construction by state government, the result of scandals in management of the public works, intolerable indebtedness, and default on their debt by several states in the depression period.[28] In the second place, the advantages of the railroad over the canal had been demonstrated. Construction of railways to meet local needs was a task that many communities believed they could undertake independently of state aid, particularly if municipal, township, or county governments extended assistance to private companies.[29] This enthusiasm for railroads was heightened by another force: the infusion of eastern capital into western railroad construction and reorganization after 1845-46. Foreign investors, too (particularly the English), showed renewed interest after 1852 in purchasing railroad bonds or local-government securities issued for railroad aid.[30] Moreover, in the canal states the railroad promised to liberate urban centers and regions that had formerly been at the mercy of geographic conditions. Limitations of terrain that had characterized canal planning were no longer relevant, a change that urban leadership was quick to comprehend. The new railroad technology reopened the critical question of which city would dominate trade in each region of the Old Northwest. As Chicago, Milwaukee, and St. Louis battled for control of the Mississippi Valley trade in the most spectacular western urban rivalry, so too in every area of the West towns competed for positions on the new railroads and for hegemony in local trade areas.[31]

Most of the projected western railroads were designed at first to serve primarily local needs and objectives. This fact explains the enthusiasm with which communities, small and large, supported private railroad companies with public aid.[32] Among the arguments of railroad promoters seeking local subscriptions and public .assistance were many that had become familiar in the canal era. Multiple market outlets were a major objective of many communities, and numerous railroad schemes were designed to free towns from "monopoly" conditions, under which they were tributary to a single market; in the same way, the state canal programs had been designed to open alternate markets to western producers formerly dependent upon the New Orleans outlet. Established metropolitan centers, such as Cleveland and Cincinnati, extended municipal aid to railroads in an effort to multiply and extend their transport radii or to obtain all-rail connections with the East. Some railroad promoters even advertised their projects as potential links in transcontinental systems that would carry the trade of Asia and the Far West through a particular town or village. And by the early fifties there had emerged the well-known competition among major cities for designation as the eastern terminus of a land-grant transcontinental railway.[33] Less pretentious communities sought places on the new railroad lines merely to survive, or else to overcome advantages enjoyed by rival towns on canals or rivers.[34]

Indicative of the emphasis upon local objectives in railroad promotion was the ambivalent western attitude toward eastern influence. The western railroad promoter was usually quite willing to accept financial assistance from established railroad companies, and he eagerly solicited eastern investment in bonds or stock. But he generally had to rely in the first instance upon local resources, public and private; and the prospect that outsiders might control the enterprise could hinder seriously his efforts to raise funds locally. One Ohio railroad organizer, for example, argued with his fellow promoters in 1851 that it was inadvisable to employ an engineer from the East to locate the line. Local people would, he said, suspect "that this Eastern man would come here with Eastern habits, feelings, associations and *interests*, the effect of which must be, to give everything an Eastern aspect."[35] In the same vein, the president of the New Albany and Salem Railroad in Indiana wrote in 1852 that because most of the stockholders lived along the route, the company was protected from "the prejudice that exists in the public mind in many places against [railroads], where they are looked upon as monopolies owned and managed by persons having no interests or sympathies in common with them."[36] Yet two of the strongest arguments employed by western railroad promoters to secure local support were that their roads might one day merge with others to form a large integrated system or that they might bring an eastern main line to the sponsoring communities.[37]

Western railroad enterpreneurs skillfully induced and exploited local rivalries, as state canal authorities had once done, by soliciting subscriptions or donations from communities on alternative routes. One may trace the routes of many early western railroads by naming the towns and counties (seldom on a straight line!) that extended public aid. Similarly, the major eastern trunk lines—notably the Pennsylvania and the Baltimore and Ohio—gave financial support to several parallel-running western railroads, thereby stimulating competition among rival communities on all the routes thus aided.[38]

Private financing and public aid at the local level were critical determinants of the pace and character of western railroad expansion. Urban rivalry continued to find expression, however, in the arena of the state legislatures. Debate over charters often involved bitter conflict over routes; and in some cases railroad interests would block altogether the chartering of rival companies.[39]

Opposition to local aid was scattered, and not until 1851 in Ohio and long afterward in other western states was it effective. Urban leaders did occasionally divide over the question of priority in allocation of funds among several companies competing for a town's patronage. A few opponents of aid took an ideological position, condemning public assistance of any kind. There were also some instances of urban-rural conflict, with farming areas opposing county aid to railroads which, they averred, would merely enhance the wealth of already affluent market towns. The farm-mortgage railroad subscriptions notorious in Wisconsin—and to a lesser extent in Illinois—testify eloquently, however, to the fact that rural opposition to railroads was by no means universal. Finally, there were some instances of rivalry involving towns within counties, with several vying for connections on the route of a railroad seeking county aid.[40]

The results of generous public and private support of western railroads were highly uneven. Whether or not their railroad stock paid dividends, many communities were amply re-

warded by commercial advantages conferred by the new transport lines.[41] But precisely because the objectives of western railway promotion had been defined within a context of local ambitions, the reaction was severe when these ambitions were frustrated. Throughout the Old Northwest the people resisted payment on bonds and subscriptions that aided railroads never built or which once built had fallen victim to bankrupt reorganization. Sometimes there was violence, as in Athens, Ohio, where townspeople tore up the tracks of the Marietta and Cincinnati Railroad, which had bypassed the town even though its citizens had voted for county aid to the company.[42] In the 1850's there appeared anti-railroad sentiment that presaged the Granger movement, a sentiment stimulated by resentment against emergent eastern dominance over railroads built initially with local aid; the outsiders often imposed rates unfavorable to the western communities that had helped build the roads.[43]

Whether or not the objectives of westerners who supported early railroads were later frustrated, the debates over transportation heightened urban community consciousness and sharpened local pride in many western towns. The issues concerning internal improvements that dominated town politics over many years constantly forced farmers and urban residents alike to re-examine their local interests, needs, and hopes in a period of rapid change in the West.

What occurred in the Old Northwest in the period 1820-60 also characterized development of the national transportation system in the pre-Civil War years: localism and regionalism were so strong that they rendered impossible any comprehensive, rational planning of

a system of internal improvements.[44] A
. . . transport map of the West in
1860 . . . [would reveal] the gross ab-
surdities of parallel lines and over-dense
construction in many areas. The highly
rational response of western leaders to
their communities' transport needs had
led to a highly irrational result. But the
western transport network included
many lines of communication, built
mainly with the resources of state and
local government, that were vital in
the development of a national economy.
And the growth of this transport network had been influenced significantly
by the effects of urban and regional
rivalry.

NOTES

1. Richard C. Wade, *The Urban Frontier: The
Rise of Western Cities, 1790-1830* (Cambridge,
Mass., 1959), *passim*, especially 322-336. It was
a signal feature of western urban rivalry in the
early nineteenth century that it often mattered
little whether competing towns were populated
or not. Given the nature of frontier politics and
town-site speculation, the "paper village" might
have great political strength in the territorial or
state legislature, or even at Washington.
2. See Francis P. Weisenburger, "The Urbanization of the Middle West: Town and Village in the
Pioneer Period," *Indiana Magazine of History*, XLI
(1945), 19-30.
3. Wade, *The Urban Frontier*, 336.
4. For useful discussions of regionalism, see Louis
Hartz, *Economic Policy and Democratic Thought:
Pennsylvania, 1776-1860* (Cambridge, Mass.,
1948), 14-21, and Louis Wirth, *Community Life
and Social Policy: Selected Papers*, edited by E.
W. Marvick and A. J. Reiss, Jr. (Chicago, 1956),
passim, especially 160-161, 166-169. See also
Harvey S. Perloff and others, *Regions, Resources,
and Economic Growth* (Baltimore, 1960). Two
seminal studies are Frederick Jackson Turner, *The
United States, 1830-1850* (New York, 1935), and
Arthur M. Schlesinger, "The City in American
History," *Mississippi Valley Historical Review*,
XXVII (1940), 43-66.
5. Harry N. Scheiber, "The Ohio Canal Movement, 1820-1825," *Ohio Historical Quarterly*,
LXIX (1960), 231-256.
6. *Ibid.*, 249-250. The Portsmouth-Cleveland canal was named the Ohio Canal in 1825; in 1849
the designation Ohio and Erie Canal became official.
7. Jacob Blickensderfer to Micajah T. Williams,
June 23, 1825. Micajah T. Williams Papers, Ohio

State Library, Columbus. See also *Senate Journal*,
31 Ohio General Assembly, 1 sess., 340.
8. Among the side cuts aided by private contributions were the Granville Feeder and the Dresden
Feeder. The Lancaster Lateral Canal, a twelve-
mile feeder from Lancaster to the Ohio and Erie
Canal, was constructed by a private company.
There is evidence in the Lancaster Lateral Canal
Company minutes that direct profits were not expected. Lancaster Lateral Canal Company Records, John T. Brasee Papers, Ohio Historical Society.
9. *House Journal*, 24 Ohio General Assembly, 1
sess., 280-281; John C. Parish, *Robert Lucas*
(Iowa City, Iowa, 1907), 91; Ebenezer Buckingham to E. A. Brown, July 21, 1828, Ethan Allen
Brown Papers, Ohio State Library.
10. William Steele to Canal Commission, January
16, 1830, Micajah T. Williams to Mayor of Chillicothe, April 5, 1830, Jesse Fulton to Alfred Kelley,
April 15, 1830, and correspondence of 1829-30,
passim, in Canal Commission Papers, State Archives, Ohio Historical Society. For a later neighborhood rivalry, albeit of a somewhat different nature, see H. J. Stratton, "The Northern Cross Railroad," *Journal of the Illinois State Historical Society*, XXVIII (1935), 17-19.
11. Scheiber, "Ohio Canal Movement," 254; B.
M. Atherton and others to Alfred Kelley, May 17,
1826, Canal Commission Papers.
12. See the report of the select committee on a
Sandusky-Dayton railroad charter in *Senate Journal*, 29 Ohio General Assembly, 1 sess., 364ff. See
also Ohio Auditor of State, *Annual Report, 1835*,
16; E. L. Bogart, *Internal Improvements and State
Debt in Ohio* (New York, 1924), 47ff.; and C. P.
McClelland and C. C. Huntington, *History of the
Ohio Canals* (Columbus, 1905), 38ff.
13. "The Dayton people are opposed to the extension of 'their Canal,'" a federal land officer reported in 1832. Thomas Van Horne to Peyton
Symmes, August 23, 1832, Miscellaneous Letters
File, Ohio Auditor's Office, Records Room. See
also Charles Anthony and Simpson Mason to Commissioners of Canal Fund, a broadside dated
March 1833, in the same place. The regional voting pattern on the issue of canal extension versus
state aid to the railroad is confirmed by a vote of
March 1, 1831, in *House Journal*, 29 Ohio General Assembly, 1 sess., 600-601. For the Mad
River Railroad, see Leola Stewart, "Sandusky:
Pionner Link Between Sail and Rail," *Ohio State
Archaeological and Historical Quarterly*, LVII
(1948), 227-236.
14. *Piqua Gazette*, March 2, 1831. The entire
controversy may be traced in the *Gazette* from
February 1831 to December 1833.
15. So reported by a member of the legislature.
Leicester King to Simon Perkins, February 11,
1835. Simon Perkins Papers, Western Reserve Historical Society, Cleveland.
16. Bogart, *Internal Improvements and State Debt
in Ohio*, 47ff. See also Carter Goodrich, *Government Promotion of American Canals and Railroads*
(New York, 1960), 134-138.

17. Joseph Barker and others to Canal Commission, August 14, 1838. Canal Commission Papers. On the Dresden-Zanesville conflict, see petition of July 31, 1838, in the same place, and Ohio Canal Commission, *15th Annual Report* (Columbus, 1839), 17-19.

18. H. S. Knapp, *History of the Maumee Valley* (Toledo, 1876), 557-558; John W. Weatherford, "The Short Life of Manhattan, Ohio," *Ohio Historical Quarterly*, LXV (1956), 381-382.

19. *Ibid.*; Micajah T. Williams to E. A. Brown, September 2, 1836, Brown Papers; Williams to Leander Ransom, August 1, 1840, Williams Papers.

20. Indiana Canal Commission to Benjamin Tappan, June 16, 1835, Canal Commission Papers; Logan Esarey, *Internal Improvements in Early Indiana* (Indiana Historical Society, *Publications*, V, No. 2, Indianapolis, 1912), 87-98.

21. I. A. Lapham, *Wisconsin: Its Geography and Topography* (Milwaukee, 1846), 46. Theodore Calvin Pease, *The Frontier State, 1818-1848* (C. W. Alvord, ed., *The Centennial History of Illinois*, II, Chicago, 1922), Chap. 10; John H. Krenkel, *Illinois Internal Improvements, 1818-1848* (Cedar Rapids, Iowa, 1958), 34ff.

22. Jesse Williams to Micajah T. Williams, January 12, 23, 1835. Micajah T. Williams Papers. See also John D. Barnhart and D. F. Carmony, *Indiana: From Frontier to Industrial Commonwealth* (New York, 1954), I, 291-292.

23. R. Carlyle Buley, *The Old Northwest: Pioneer Period, 1815-1840* (Bloomington, Ind., 1954), II, 299-300; Goodrich, *Government Promotion of Canals and Railroads,* 138-147; Esarey, *Internal Improvements in Early Indiana,* 105-106; Pease, *The Frontier State,* 216-217.

24. For the manner in which projects promoted in response to initial undertakings of the states helped produce the "long swing" characteristic of canal construction, see Carter Goodrich and others, *Canals and American Economic Development* (New York, 1962), 176-179.

25. Ohio Board of Public Works, *Special Report . . . Relative to the Toll Charged on Salt . . . January 29, 1848* (Columbus, 1948), 5. For a full discussion of this problem, see Harry N. Scheiber, "The Rate-Making Power of the State in the Canal Era: A Case Study," *Political Science Quarterly,* LXXVII (1962), 397-413.

26. Atkins & Blair to Board of Public Works, December 9, 1843; Cincinnati Chamber of Commerce petition, June 20, 1845; Collins Brown & Co. and others petition, January 1, 1848; G. W. Addams to John Waddle, February 19, 1859. Board of Public Works Papers, State Archives, Ohio Historical Society.

27. Ohio Board of Public Works, *Special Report . . . January 29, 1848,* 7; correspondence with Ohio salt manufacturers, 1840-49, *passim,* Board of Public Works Papers. See also Cleveland petition, October 2, 1858, in the same place.

28. Carter Goodrich, "The Revulsion Against Internal Improvements," *Journal of Economic History,* X (1950), 145-151.

29. For example, Alphonso Taft, *A Lecture on Cincinnati and Her Rail-Roads* (Cincinnati, 1850), 12. See also Carter Goodrich, "Local Planning of Internal Improvements," *Political Science Quarterly,* LXVI (1951), 431ff.

30. Alfred D. Chandler, Jr., "Patterns of American Railroad Finance, 1830-1850," *Business History Review,* XXVIII (1954), 258-259; Ralph W. Hidy and Muriel E. Hidy, "Anglo-American Merchant Bankers and the Railroads of the Old Northwest, 1848-1860," *ibid.,* XXXIV (1960), 154ff.

31. The St. Louis-Chicago-Milwaukee rivalry is discussed in W. W. Belcher, *The Economic Rivalry Between St. Louis and Chicago, 1850-1880* (New York, 1947), and Bayrd Still, *Milwaukee: The History of a City* (Madison, Wis., 1948). For a discussion of Cincinnati and her railroads in the 1850's, see Sherry Hessler, " 'The Great Disturbing Cause' and the Decline of the Queen City," Historical and Philosophical Society of Ohio, *Bulletin,* XX (1962), 169-185.

32. This was a national, not merely a western phenomenon. See George R. Taylor and Irene Neu, *The American Railroad Network* (Cambridge, Mass., 1956), 3-6, and Goodrich, "Local Planning of Internal Improvements," 437ff.

33. Goodrich, "Local Planning of Internal Improvements," 437-438; Herbert W. Rice, "Early Rivalry Among Wisconsin Cities for Railroads," *Wisconsin Magazine of History,* XXXV (1951), 10-15; Carrie Cropley, "When the Railroads Came to Kenosha," *ibid.,* XXXIII (1949), 189-191; Dwight L. Agnew, "Beginning of the Rock Island Lines," *Journal of the Illinois State Historical Society,* XLVI (1953), 413-415; Wylie J. Daniels, *The Village at the End of the Road* (Indianapolis, 1938), 57-58; O. Morrow and F. W. Bashore, *Historical Atlas of Paulding County, Ohio* (Madison, Wis., 1892), 24-25.

34. For an example, see Thomas D. Brock, "Paw Paw Versus the Railroads," *Michigan History,* XXXIX (1955), 129-131.

35. Samuel Carpenter to John T. Brasee, May 17, 1851. Brasee Papers.

36. Quoted in Frank F. Hargrave, *A Pioneer Indiana Railroad: The Origin and Development of the Monon* (Indianapolis, 1932), 33-34.

37. Daniel Kilgore to Thomas Swan, December 26, 1849, Kilgore Papers, Ohio Historical Society; Cleveland and Mahoning Railroad, *Annual Report, 1852* (Cleveland, 1853), 27; Fayette B. Shaw, "Transportation in the Development of Joliet and Will County," *Journal of the Illinois State Historical Society,* XXX (1937), 119ff.

38. Hargrave, *A Pioneer Indiana Railroad,* 37ff.; Walter R. Marvin, "The Steubenville and Indiana Railroad," *Ohio Historical Quarterly,* LXVI (1957), 17; William P. Smith, *The Book of the Great Railway Celebrations of 1857* (New York, 1858), *passim;* H. W. Schotter, *Growth and Development of the Pennsylvania Railroad Company* (Philadelphia, 1927), 36-38; Ohio Commissioner of Railroads, *Report, 1870,* I, 477-492; Alice E. Smith, ed., "Wisconsin's First Railroad: Linsey

Letters, 1852," *Wisconsin Magazine of History*, XXX (1947), 349.

39. Paul W. Gates, *The Illinois Central Railroad and Its Colonization Work* (Cambridge, Mass., 1934), Chap. 3; Agnew, "Beginning of the Rock Island Lines," 411; Daniels, *Village at the End of the Road*, 65-68; Victor M. Bogle, "New Albany," *Indiana Magazine of History*, L (1954), 160.

40. Kathleen B. Jacklin, "Local Aid to Railroads in Illinois, 1848-1870" (unpublished M.A. thesis, Cornell University, 1958), 68ff.; Luther M. Feeger, *The History of Transportation in Wayne County, Indiana* (reprinted from *Richmond* [Indiana] *Palladium-Item*, 1953-54), installment of September 3, 1953; Frederick Merk, *Economic History of Wisconsin During the Civil War Decade* (Madison, Wis., 1916), 238-270.

41. The citizens of Mansfield, Ohio, subscribed about $500,000 to railroad stock; nearly all of it was lost by 1870, yet a county official declared they were "unanimous in the opinion that it is money well spent." Ohio Railroad Commissioner, *Report, 1870*, II, 322.

42. Thomas W. Lewis, *History of Southeastern Ohio* (Chicago, 1928), I, 612-613. See also Ohio Railroad Commissioner, *Report, 1870*, II, 321. Estimates of the amounts of local aid extended to railroads in the Old Northwest appear in Goodrich, *Government Promotion of Canals and Railroads*, 137-148.

43. Thus the Cincinnati Chamber of Commerce complained of "the manner in which the great [railroads] discriminate against the city which helped to build them, on the ground they would help to build up her interests." William Smith, *Annual Statement of the Trade and Commerce of Cincinnati, 1860* (Cincinnati, 1860), 25. See also *Kalida* (Ohio) *Venture*, March 3, 1854, and Ohio General Assembly, Senate, *Report of the Standing Committee on Railroads* (n.p., [1861]), 2.

44. See unsigned review (by Charles Francis Adams) in *North American Review*, LI (1840), 320-321, and Goodrich, *Government Promotion of Canals and Railroads*, 45.

The Businessman as an American Institution

DANIEL J. BOORSTIN

The American businessman—a product (and a maker) of the upstart cities of the American West between the Revolution and the Civil War—was not an American version of the enterprising European city banker or merchant or manufacturer. Not an American Fugger or Medici or Rothschild or Arkwright, he was something quite different. His career and his ideals are an allegory of an American idea of community, for he was born and bred in the dynamic American urbanism in the period of our greatest growth.

The changing meaning of his very name, "businessman," gives us a clue. In 18th-century England to say someone was a "man of business" was primarily to say he engaged in public affairs. Thus David Hume in 1752 described Pericles as "a man of business." Before the end of the 18th century the expression had begun to lose this, its once primary meaning, and instead to describe a person engaged in mercantile transactions; it became a loose synonym for "merchant." But our now common word "businessman" seems to have been American in origin. It came into use around 1830 in the very period

From Daniel J. Boorstin, *The Americans: The National Experience* (New York: Random House, 1965), pp. 115-23. Copyright © 1965 by Daniel J. Boorstin. Reprinted by permission of Random House, Inc. Daniel J. Boorstin is Preston and Sterling Morton Professor of American History at the University of Chicago.

when the new Western cities were founded and were growing most rapidly. Even a casual look at this early American businessman, who he was, what he was doing, and how he thought of his work, will show how inaccurate it would be to describe him as simply a man engaged in mercantile transactions. We might better characterize him as a peculiarly American type of community maker and community leader. His starting belief was in the interfusing of public and private prosperity. Born of a social vagueness unknown in the Old World, he was a distinctive product of the New.

The new fast-growing city, where nothing had been before, a city with no history and unbounded hopes, was the American businessman's first natural habitat. In the period when he first appeared, his primary commodity was land and his secondary commodity transportation. This transformation of land rights and transport rights from political symbols and heirlooms into mere commodities was also an American phenomenon.

The businessman's characteristics would appear in the story of any one of the thousands who made their fortunes in the early 19th century. "I was born close by a saw-mill," boasted William B. Ogden (1805-77), "was early left an orphan, was cradled in a sugar-trough, christened in a mill-pond, graduated at a log-school-house, and at fourteen fancied I could do any thing I turned my hand to, and that nothing was impossible, and ever since, madame, I have been trying to prove it, and with some success." He was destined to be an upstart businessman on a heroic scale. Born into a leading local family in a small town in the Catskills in New York, he was actively dealing in real

estate before he was fifteen. Before thirty he was elected to the New York Legislature on a program to construct the New York & Erie Railroad with State aid. He was a great booster for his State, to whose growth he called the new railroad essential. "Otherwise," he argued "the sceptre will depart from Judah. The Empire State will no longer be New York. . . . Philadelphia is your great rival, and, if New York is idle, will gather in the trade of the great west."

But Ogden's enthusiasm for New York was not immovable. In 1835, the very year when the money was appropriated for the New York & Erie Railroad, he met some Eastern investors who had formed the American Land Company. They had already shown the foresight to invest heavily in Chicago real estate. One of these was Charles Butler, a politically and philanthropically minded lawyer of Albany, who married Ogden's sister. Butler himself (once a clerk in the law office of Martin Van Buren) was an energetic promoter of real estate and railroads. A man of wide public interests, he was a founder of Hobart College and of Union Theological Seminary, and an early supporter of New York University, among his other community works. He asked Ogden to go to Chicago to manage his interests. Ogden then joined in the purchase of considerable tracts there.

William B. Ogden arrived in Chicago in June, 1835. The town census showed a population of 3265, almost all of whom had come since 1832 (when the settlement had numbered under a hundred). Quickly Ogden transferred his extravagant hopes from the Empire State to the City of Chicago. In 1837, when Chicago was incorporated, Ogden was elected its first mayor, and the city census counted 4170—an increase of almost thirty per cent in two years.

"He could not forget," one of Ogden's fellow businessmen observed, "that everything which benefitted Chicago, or built up the great West, benefitted him. Why should he?" His commodity was land, whose value rose with the population. And Chicago now grew as few cities had ever grown before. The population approximately trebled, decade after decade: from 29,963 in 1850, to 109,260 in 1860, and to 298,977 in 1870. Chicago held over half a million people in 1880 and over a million by 1890, when it was already the second city on the continent. Meanwhile, real-estate values, especially in choice locations such as those Ogden was shrewd enough to buy, rose even more spectacularly. Men like Ogden proudly recorded their business success as the best evidence of their faith in their city. "In 1844," Ogden recalled, "I purchased for $8000, what 8 years thereafter, sold for 3 millions of dollars, and these cases could be extended almost indefinitely." Property he had bought in 1845 for $15,000 only twenty years later was worth ten million dollars. Successes were so common and so sudden, it was hard to know where fact ended and where fable began. Some of this purchasing was, of course, sheer speculative mania. The Chicago *American* (April 23, 1836) boasted of a piece of city property sold for $96,700 which, in romanticized arithmetic, they said had "risen in value at the rate of *one hundred per cent per* DAY, on the original cost ever since [1830], embracing a period of *five years* and a half."

Not to boost your city showed both a lack of community spirit and a lack of business sense. "Perhaps, the most striking trait of his character," a con-temporary remembered of Ogden, "was his absolute faith in Chicago. He saw in 1836, not only the Chicago of today, but in the future the great City of the continent. From that early day, his faith never wavered. Come good times—come bad times—come prosperity or adversity —Chicago booming, or Chicago in ashes, its great future was to him a fixed fact." Quite naturally Ogden became a leader in community affairs, and within a few years Chicagoans called him their "representative man."

There was hardly a public improvement in which he did not play a leading role. He built the first drawbridge across the Chicago river, laid out and opened many miles of streets in the north and west parts of the city, promoted the Illinois and Michigan Canal and advocated laws for its construction and enlargement, projected and built thousands of miles of railroads serving Chicago, and did a great deal to develop Chicago's water supply, sewage system, and parks. More than a hundred miles of streets and hundreds of bridges were built at the private expense of Ogden and his real-estate clients. He helped introduce the McCormick reaping and mowing machines into the West, and helped build the first large factory for their manufacture. He was the first president of Rush Medical College (the first institution of its kind in Chicago), a charter member of the Chicago Historical Society, president of the Board of Trustees of the first "University of Chicago," and one of the first directors of the Merchants Loan and Trust Company (1857). He was elected to the Illinois Senate by the Republicans in 1860. He supported the Theological Seminary of the Northwest, the Academy of Sciences, and the Astronomical Society. The French historian Guizot only slightly exaggerated when he said Ogden had built and owned Chicago.

Characteristic also was Ogden's interest in improving transportation. An upstart community, a community of boosters measuring itself by its rate of growth, depended on transportation in a new way. Settled communities of the Old World—Bordeaux, Lyon, Manchester, or Birmingham—especially when, as in the early 19th century, they were fast becoming industrial towns, needed transportation to feed raw materials and labor to their factories and to take away finished products. But Chicago and the other upstart cities of the American West needed it for their very lifeblood. In the Old World a city might grow or decline, prosper or languish, depending on its transportation, among other facilities. But here, without transportation there was no city at all.

An American city had to "attract" people. The primary community service was to make it easier, cheaper, and pleasanter for people to join your community. In all this, too, William B. Ogden was a paragon, for he pioneered the railroads. One of the first to run out of Chicago was the Galena & Chicago Union Railroad, built to connect Chicago with the great Mississippi River traffic. Chicago businessmen bought a controlling interest in 1846, and tried to raise money from local citizens to complete the railroad. Ogden worked hard to obtain numerous individual subscriptions in small amounts. This, its first railroad, opened a new era in the life and expansion of Chicago. Citizens subscribed its stock "as a public duty, and not as an investment." "Railroads," one of Ogden's collaborators later boasted, "were built as public enterprises, and not as money-making speculations. They were regarded as great highways con-

structed by the people, either at the expense of the government or by means of private capital, to accommodate the public, and not for the especial benefit of the stockholders." In April, 1849, the first locomotive started west from Chicago on the Galena line.

Ogden took the lead in promoting many more railroads for Chicago. In 1853 he was a director of the Pittsburg, Ft. Wayne & Chicago Railroad; in 1857, president of the Chicago, St. Paul & Fond-du-Lac Railroad which later became part of the Chicago & Northwestern Railroad, of which he was also president (1859-68). A transcontinental railroad with Chicago as the great junction was, of course, his dream. In 1850 he presided over the National Railway Convention and, on the organization of the Union Pacific Company in 1862, its first president was William B. Ogden.

The Ogden story was re-enacted a thousand times all over America—wherever there were upstart cities. Scenes were different, stakes smaller, and dimensions less heroic, but the plot everywhere was much the same. Here was a new breed: the community builder in a mushrooming city where personal and public growth, personal and public prosperity intermingled.

Another example was Dr. Daniel Drake (1785-1852), born in New Jersey, and raised in Kentucky, whose family sent him when he was only fifteen to study in the offices of a leading physician of the small town of Ft. Washington (later called Cincinnati). Within a few years he himself became the town's most prominent practitioner. He opened a drug store where, in 1816, he pioneered in the sale of artificial mineral water; soon he was also running a general store. His *Picture of Cincinnati in 1815*, with its full statistics, and its vivid account of the archaeology, topography, climate, and promise of the city, was translated and circulated widely abroad. Drake, in his own way, was as much a booster as Ogden; using subtler techniques of precise and calculated understatement, he produced the first detailed account of an upstart city. Many believed him when he concluded that small towns like Cincinnati were "destined, before the termination of the present century, to attain the rank of populous and magnificent cities." Drake had established himself in the high noon of Cincinnati prosperity, before the Panic of 1819.

Drake's boosterism was as energetic as Ogden's. Hoping to make Cincinnati a great medical center in 1819, he founded the Ohio Medical College (later the Medical College of the University of Cincinnati). He did a great deal to promote all kinds of community enterprises: the Commercial Hospital and Lunatic Asylum, the eye infirmary, the circulating library, the teacher's college. He helped plan and develop canals and he promoted railroads' leading toward the South, which included the successful municipal line, the Cincinnati Southern Railway.

Still another example with a more western habitat was General William Larimer (1809-75). Born and raised in Pennsylvania, he tried many different businesses around Pittsburgh: a general store, a freight service, horse trading, a coal company, a wholesale grocery, his father's hotel, railroads, and banking. When he lost everything in the depression of 1854, Larimer, quickly resolving to start afresh farther west, was in Nebraska the very next spring. There he too became the instantaneous booster of a town which did not yet exist. We have an intimate record in letters he sent east. On May 23, 1855:

I have taken two claims at La Platte, Nebraska Territory . . . and we are laying out a town. I am elected President of the Company, and secured ⅓ of the town. . . . I like this country very much indeed. . . . I think I can make a big raise here in a few years.

Already he claimed a good chance of being elected to Congress from Nebraska. Within a week his optimism had risen still higher: he planned to pay off his creditors with town lots, for he owned a thousand acres within the proposed city.

Now my plan is this: I intend to live in La Platte City. I intend to open up a large farm. I can raise hemp, corn or anything. . . . I will go on with the farm and if the land is ever wanted for a town it is ready. . . . I intend not only to farm simply but I will open a Commission House. I expect to supply the Territory with iron nails, lumber, etc., this will not only be profitable in itself but will be the great means of building up the city. If I go there I can build the city if I do not go only to sell lots as the city may never rise.

Larimer expected the transcontinental railroad to go through La Platte, but this proved a miscalculation. Then, after a heavy winter, the town suffered deep spring floods. "We were not long in coming to the conclusion that La Platte was doomed as a town site." The pattern of western hope was all-or-nothing.

From La Platte, Larimer moved on to Omaha. There he lived in a prefabricated house that had actually been framed in Pittsburgh, knocked down and shipped out in 1856. When Omaha, too, looked unpromising (as it did within less than two years) he moved to Leavenworth, Kansas. This was in 1858, just in time for him to learn of the discovery of gold at Cherry Creek by Pike's Peak. Unwilling to wait for the better traveling conditions of the following spring, Larimer and his son immediately made up a party and left that fall. After a forty-seven-day trip, the Larimers were among the first to arrive at the mouth of Cherry Creek, where they found two dozen cabins under construction.

This, the first settlement in Colorado, was named Auraria. Larimer's son recorded the events of November 17, 1858:

On our very first night here, my father, without consulting anyone outside of our own Leavenworth Party, packed his blankets and some provisions, left camp and crossed the Creek to pick out a new site. He left instructions for us to get up the oxen and join him, as he believed the east side of the Creek was much the best location for a town and no one in the country laid claim to it, or if so had abandoned it and left the country. . . . When we finally reached the eastern side of Cherry Creek, we found him near the bank with a camp fire awaiting us. He had 4 cottonwood poles crossed, which he called the foundation of his settlement and claimed the site for a town,—for *the* town which has now grown into the one of which Colorado is the proudest.

This time Larimer chose well. He had located on the site of Denver.

At first there was competition between the sites on either side of Cherry Creek. Then the stockholders combined and became a single city named Denver (in honor of the Virginian who had become Governor of the Kansas Territory) in 1860. "I am Denver City," Larimer wrote in a letter in February 1859. And his whole later career proved the extraordinary ability of the American businessmen of these upstart cities to fuse themselves and their destiny with that of their community—at least so long as the community remained prosperous or promising.

At the beginning Larimer had been put in charge of the town and made "Donating Agent," which authorized him to give two city lots to anyone who would build a cabin there measuring at least 16 by 16 feet. He promoted a good hotel and gave valuable shares to men "who were already or could be induced to become interested in the welfare of the city and might be influential in bringing a stage line into the country with Denver as its objective point." He encouraged the founding of drugstores, general stores, sawmills, and newspapers. Complaining that the town lacked the ultimate convenience, he finally helped organize a cemetery.

Examples could be multiplied. But even these three—Ogden, Drake, and Larimer—suggest the variety of opportunities, motives, and attitudes which created the new species *Businessman Americanus*. None of the characteristics of his American habitat was quite unique but their extreme American form and their American combination were.

Cities with no history. The upstart western cities were the rare examples of a dynamic urban environment where almost nothing had been pre-empted by history. Cities were proverbially the centers of institutions, where records were kept and the past was chronicled, hallowed, and enshrined. They were sites of palaces, cathedrals, libraries, archives, and great monuments of all kinds. The American upstart city, by contrast, had no past. At its beginning, it was free of vested interests, monopolies, guilds, skills, and "No Trespassing" signs. Here was the fluidity of the city—the spatial dimension of cosmopolitanism, movement, diversity, and change—but without the historical dimension. There were no ancient walls between classes, occupations, neighborhoods, and nationalities. The American upstart cities began without inherited neighborhood loyalties, without ghettos. "Everything," recalled Larimer, "was open to us."

Quick growth and high hopes. The pace of growth of the upstart cities fired imaginations. A town where nobody was ten years ago, but which today numbered thousands, might be expected to number tens or hundreds of thousands in a few decades. Mankind had required at least a million years to produce its first urban community of a million people; Chicagoans accomplished this feat in less than a century. Within a few days' wagon ride of Drake's Cincinnati, hundreds of towns were laid out, all guaranteed to have unrivalled advantages. Precisely one week after Larimer cut his four cottonwood poles on the future site of Denver, he wrote his wife back east that "we expect a second Sacramento City, at least." In 1834, H. M. Brackenridge noted, his Pittsburgh was changing so fast that anyone returned after ten years felt himself a stranger. He confidently foresaw that the settlement which had grown from village to big city in a quarter-century would very soon reach half a million. He could not be surprised that Cincinnati had grown from a forest to a city in thirteen years. He himself had hopes "of attaining, on the Ohio or Mississippi, distinction and wealth, with the same rapidity, and on the same scale, that those vast regions were expanding into greatness." The centennial history of St. Louis in 1876 called the city's site superior to that of any other in the world, and predicted that, when its railroad network was completed, it would outstrip Chicago and the eastern metropolises. "And yet, when this has been said, we have but commenced to tell of the wonders of a city destined in the future to equal London in its population, Athens in its philosophy, art and culture, Rome in its hotels, cathedrals, churches and grandeur, and to be the central commercial metropolis of a continent."

Community before government. On this landscape too it was normal to find communities before governments. Men in sudden urban proximity, bound together by specific, concrete purposes, first felt their common needs. Afterwards they called governments into being. From force of circumstance, then, government became functional. Early Chicagoans, and their upstart counterparts elsewhere, were not confronted with the problem of evading obsolete regulations or of transmuting time-honored tyrannies. They simply combined to provide their own water, their own sewage system, their own sidewalks, streets, bridges, and parks. They founded medical schools and universities and museums. Eager for these and other services, they created municipal governments and enlisted state and federal government aid. An upstart government had neither the odor of sanctity nor the odium of tyranny. It was a tool serving personal and community prosperity at the same time.

Intense and transferable loyalties. In upstart cities the loyalties of people were in inverse ratio to the antiquity of their communities, even to the point of absurdity. Older towns could point only to the facts of limited actual accomplishment, while the uncertain future was, of course, ever more promising. Ogden removed his enthusiasm from New York to Chicago; Larimer removed his from La Platte to Omaha to Leavenworth to Auraria to Denver. Men could do this in the twinkling of an eye, and without so much as a glance over the shoulder. Promise, not achievement, commanded loyalty and stirred the booster spirit. One was untrue to oneself and to the spirit of expanding

America if one remained enslaved to a vision which had lost its promise. The ghost town and the booster spirit were opposite sides of the same coin.

Competition among communities. The circumstances of American life in the upstart cities of the West produced a lively competitive spirit. But the characteristic and most fertile competition was a competition among communities. We have been misled by slogans of individualism. Just as the competition among colonial seaboard cities helped diffuse American culture and kept it from becoming concentrated in a European-style metropolis, so the competition among western upstart cities helped create the booster spirit. Where there had been no cities before, where all were growing fast, there was no traditional rank among urban centers. If Lexington, Kentucky, could quickly arise by 1800 to be the most populous city of the West, if St. Louis and Cincinnati and Chicago had so suddenly arisen, might not some new Lexington displace them all? Many of each community's institutions had been founded to give it a competitive advantage. Dr. Drake's medical college helped Cincinnati keep ahead of Lexington, just as Ogden's streets and bridges and parks helped Chicago lead Cincinnati. Where individual and community prosperity were so intermingled, competition among individuals was also a competition among communities.

❁   ❁   ❁

The emerging businessman of the upstart cities had much in common with the energetic American of an earlier generation. He was the Franklin of the West. He was the undifferentiated man of the colonial period, but in a more expansive setting. The new language of that day called him a "businessman"; the retrospective language of our century calls him the booster. He thrived on growth and expansion. His loyalties were intense, naive, optimistic, and quickly transferable.

Versatility was his hallmark. He usually had neither the advantages nor the disadvantages of specialized skills or monopolistic protection. In Dr. Drake's Cincinnati, physicians became merchants, clergymen became bankers, lawyers became manufacturers. "The young lawyer," H. M. Brackenridge shrewdly advised the Western seeker after fortune (in one of the first recorded uses of the word "businessman") "should think more of picking up his crumbs, than of flying like a balloon. He must be content to become a *business man,* and leave the rest to fortune." For success in this environment, the specialized skills—of lawyer, doctor, financier, or engineer—had a new unimportance. Rewards went to the organizer, the persuader, the discoverer of opportunities, the projector, the risk-taker, and the man able to attach himself quickly and profitably to some group until its promise was tested.

IV THE CITY IN THE AGE OF INDUSTRY

The emergence of the modern city, in the sixty years following the Civil War, parallels the unfolding of the Industrial Revolution in America. As Constance Green has written in her *Rise of Urban America*, "Which came first, the hen of mounting industrial strength or the egg of increasing urban influences, may be arguable, but the fact of profound change remains."

The question is not so much which came first but how they interacted with and buttressed each other. If railroads, heavy industries, and technological inventions helped build cities, urbanization in turn helped accelerate the hallmarks of industrialization: mass production, mass consumption, mass distribution of goods and services. If industrialization produced a more co-ordinated network of economic development, the network of cities became the muscles and sinews of that development—producing, selling, financing, and providing it with a market and a labor force. If industrialization meant increasing specialization, cities specialized: Cleveland with her oil, Pittsburgh with her steel, Milwaukee with her beer, Detroit with her automobiles, and Los Angeles with her sunshine. If the booming factories brought affluence along with shocking working conditions, labor violence, and corruption, the booming cities dramatized the irony of the Industrial Revolution: the collision between progress and poverty—the wealth of Wall Street, State Street, Montgomery Street, and the wretched streets of Cockroach Row, Hell's Kitchen, and the Barbary Coast. Together, the massive forces of industrialization and urbanization wrought a profound change that touched every aspect of American life: the transformation of a land of farms and villages into a nation of cities and towns. The watershed, the point of no return for an old agrarian America, was here by 1920, when the census returns showed that for the first time more than half the population lived in urban areas. Americans had moved to the city.

The city came of age in this period, but it was an era of mixed blessings for the older urban giants. New York became the Empire City, the largest city in the country. It "just growed." Philadelphia and St. Louis, like New York, fed by mass migrations, foreign and domestic, continued to expand, whereas Baltimore, Boston, and New Orleans declined. It was a boom time for the "big-little city," as Kansas City, Omaha, Denver, Birmingham, and San Francisco, began to take a more commanding position on the urban scene. If there was one city that best characterized the age of industry, it was the soaring Chicago. Only the eighth largest city in 1860, devastated by fire in 1871, it rose to become second only to New York in size and power by the last decade of the century. No one has caught the flair and fixed the image of the "City of the Big Shoulders" better than Carl Sandburg:

> Hog Butcher for the World,
> Tool Maker, Stacker of Wheat,
> Player with Railroads and the Nation's
>   Freight Handler;
> Laughing the stormy, husky, brawling
> Laughter of Youth. . . .

The emergence of the industrial city represented another stage of a phenomenon, begun in the colonial period, and extremely vital to us today, one that lies at the heart of American urban history—the city as a revolution in the nature of human settlement. This theme is fundamental to each of the following essays, and its significance and complexity is shaped as each author develops it with a different emphasis.

Leon S. Marshall uses the comparative approach, enlarging our scope and decreasing our provincialism, by contrasting the American industrial city with its English counterpart. Although he points out their important similarities, he shatters any tight analogy between the two by underscoring some of their differences. He also stresses the disruptive influences of the city as an agent for the Industrial Revolution. It was not a pretty picture, as Pittsburgh ("hell with the lid off") or Manchester ("this pell-mell of society") posed new problems and enlarged old ones for the family, working conditions, the poor, crime, disease, and immorality. Bleak as life was for many of the nineteenth-century industrial cities, a more balanced view would contrast it to the farm and village of the time, which also offered its share of poverty, drudgery, disease, and immorality.[1]

To understand the industrial city, then, it is not enough for one either to interpret its role as a promotor of social evils—important as it was—or to see it primarily in economic terms as a center for business and industry. It must also be seen, as Ralph Turner suggests, as a center for cultural change. He argues that the industrial city was a "new element" in history because it was

1. See Dorothy George's provocative *England in Transition* (London: Penguin Books, 1953).

an agent of social change, a dynamic force that caused a reorientation of the traditional cultural structure of behavior and thought.

Seeing cultural history as a clash between the old and new in action and thought, an interaction involving dislocation and assimilation, a tension between innovation and clinging to the past, Turner defines the role of the industrial city as a social and psychological force affecting several areas of cultural change, such as nineteenth-century economic thought, modern technology, the decline of localism and tradition, patterns of both conformity and diversity in human behavior, and ideas about private property. His thesis is that the city, a new kind of human settlement, churned such waves of social change that it necessitated "a reëducation of the masses," who in moving to the city brought a traditional, "peasant" mentality not adequate to cope with the changes in the labor market, machine technology, and problems of urban association. Here, then, is a variation on a theme established earlier by Carl Bridenbaugh: the city introduced us to modern times.

Hans Blumenfeld completes this chapter with an ambitious, sweeping essay. He sees the evolution of the city in terms of what went before and what may come after. By combining the approaches of an historian, an economist, an ecologist, and a city-planner, he examines three stages of "the emergence of a basically new form of human settlement," the pre-industrial city, the nineteenth-century industrial city, and the modern, sprawling metropolis of today. He attempts to answer the difficult question of what were the main forces that transformed the pre-industrial city into a modern metropolis (an urban area that "derives its identity from a single center"). To do this, he first discusses a number of crucial differences between the pre-industrial city and the metropolis and then delineates what he feels to be the major features of the metropolis—the central business area, manufacturing and related industries, housing and services, and open land—and the plans by which it may be manipulated into the city of the future.

Although he discusses the strengths and weaknesses of several schemes for the future metropolis, such as the so-called constellation, linear, and stellar metropolises, and the requirements for rational planning, he does not see the oft-accepted notion that the megalopolis is the destiny of American cities. "Megalopolis"[2]—a huge urbanized area made up of several metropolises that have expanded and grown together, such as the cities of the Ruhr in Germany or the urban strip running from Boston to Washington in the United States—is not a concept that can be applied with precision to the American scene, Blumenfeld argues, because as much as it is possible that American cities will further spill by rapid growth into one another, they will still maintain their separate identities, and, therefore, remain metropolises.

Is this too optimistic? Unlike other commentators on urban affairs, Blumen-

2. See Jean Gottman, *Megalopolis* (New York: Twentieth Century Fund, 1961).

feld is not a prophet of doom. Will the metropolis, for all its problems, be able to solve them as he suggests? Can the American city really withstand the glut of megalopolis? Can rational planning triumph over the ancient protagonists of urban sprawl—the special and vested interests of speculators, landowners, municipalities, and the free-wheeling forces of the market place?

The English and American Industrial City of the Nineteenth Century*

LEON S. MARSHALL

Cities throughout history have been the focal points of civilization; and the association of such cities as Babylon with the ancient Oriental empires, Athens with Greece, Rome with the Mediterranean empire of the Caesars and with medieval Christianity, and Venice and Florence with the Renaissance are commonplaces in history and literature. Although trite from frequent repetition, true and significant is the observation that, with all that cities have been, in no previous age has urban society had so complete domination over the life of mankind as at the present. To the student of English or American history, therefore, the rise of the industrial city of the nineteenth century is particularly important, for in that history may be found the origins of many of the critical problems troubling our own disjointed and embittered society.

The supremacy of earlier towns over their neighboring countrysides was due to the domination of commerce over

industry: that is, the facilities of the city for the distribution of productions beyond the means and requirements of household and simple agrarian economy stimulated the productive energies of the surrounding population and, in consequence, the economic needs of the city set up the pattern of economic life existing around it. In the present day, however, the economic system created by the industrial city has approached the solution of the problem of production, but has created a new set of problems arising out of that of distributing the wealth produced by this modern industrial system.

In an economic sense, an industrial city is one whose resources are almost wholly devoted or subordinated to the producing of *form* utility—the shaping of raw materials into goods for human use. London, Liverpool, and New York, where manufacturing plants are only incidental to the principal business of the city, are commercial rather than in-

From *Western Pennsylvania Historical Magazine* (September 1937), pp. 169-80. Reprinted by permission of the publisher. Leon S. Marshall is Professor of History at Kent State University.

dustrial cities since exchange (wholesale, retail, or financial) together with transportation is their chief activity. On the other hand, Manchester, Birmingham, and Pittsburgh, even though they are not now so predominantly characterized by factories and mills, are industrial cities because their wealth, population, and economic activities are largely devoted to the supplying of their factories and those of the surrounding communities with the essentials of industrial life, and their prosperity is dependent upon that of their leading industries.

In the first half of the nineteenth century, Manchester, Birmingham, and other towns in England developed into industrial cities according to a pattern which recurred in Cincinnati, Pittsburgh, and other American cities whose leading businesses were transformed by the industrial revolution. The adoption of a series of labor-saving inventions and of improved processes of manufacture led to the concentration in factories of the cotton industry around Manchester, the iron industry around Birmingham and woollen manufacture around Leeds, where facilities for labor, power, and capital were abundant. The increased prosperity and the demand for labor accompanying this concentration of industry brought in a flood of immigrants to these towns. The earlier balance in a town society composed of gentlemen, merchants, and artisans was shaken to its roots by this influx of what soon became an urban proletariat badly housed, subject to extremes of temporary affluence and poverty, and not easily adapted to the discipline of town and factory life. On the other hand, self-made capitalists accumulated fortunes by amazing combinations of luck, foresight, determination, and energy. Recognizing their im-

portance in the community and in the nation, these frequently uncultured and ruthless factory owners seized political leadership from the older dominant interests, and ultimately forced government to protect and foster the system that had enriched them. At the same time, green spaces and quaint old buildings disappeared as land was needed for offices and warehouses, and beyond the new "business districts" grimy factories pushed rows of jerry-built dwellings past the original limits of the town. Disease, poverty, crime, industrial conflict, and social animosities broke down the traditional institutions that had controlled smaller and more orderly populations, while the bewildered and alarmed inhabitants strove to erect new political and social machinery to control and refine the social revolution that was going on around them.

Wherever this pattern of development recurred, its most striking effects appeared in the growth of urban population. By 1860 more than half the people of England lived in cities and factory towns, and by 1920 more than half the population of the United States lived in urban centers. In the first fifty years of the industrial revolution, the American, as had the English cities previously, received the greatest impact of the population movement. Paterson, New Jersey, grew from 7,500 in 1840 to 68,000 in 1890; Philadelphia from less than a hundred thousand to over a million in the same period; and Pittsburgh and Allegheny from 31,000 to a third of a million fifty years later.[1] Chicago, Cincinnati, Milwaukee, Kansas City, and scores of other cities rivaled this growth, and the rise of the automobile industry produced a recurrence of this phenomenon in the twentieth century.

The influx of population was much

more rapid than the expansion of housing facilities. Congestion affected all classes, driving first the wealthy and later the middle classes to the suburbs; but for the incoming workers, too poor to afford better, the only accommodations were cheap lodging houses, and run-down tenement buildings from which absentee landlords derived as much rent with as little expense as possible while awaiting the profits of rising real-estate values. Five families living abroad and contributing little to the community in the form of taxes or improvements of their property drew most of the rentals from Pittsburgh's slums, a fact that accounts for much of the great following of Henry George's single-tax program in Pittsburgh.[2]

Until epidemics of cholera, typhoid fever, and smallpox terrified the middle classes of townspeople into attempting sanitary reforms, the disease and death lurking in the dark squalor of the slums was hardly known to the general public. Whether in England or America the discoveries made by sanitary reformers reveal a depressing similarity. Manchester with two hundred thousand inhabitants had scarcely a sewer, irregular scavengers' carts hardly touched the filth that rotted in dumps to make it more marketable as fertilizer, and until the middle of the century the town's water supply was not sufficient for more than one-third its population. Such facts as these explain why in 1841 the average expectation of life at birth in Manchester was only a few months over twenty-four years.[3] In America, a little later, few cities possessed half as many miles of sewers as of streets, and half the latter were unpaved. Fully one-third of the houses in the eighties relied upon private vaults and household utensils for the disposal of human waste. A large

part of Philadelphia's million inhabitants drank water from the Delaware River into which had been emptied daily thirteen million gallons of sewage.[4] Typhus, typhoid, and scarlet fever were the natural concomitants of such sanitary inadequacies, and Pittsburgh's share in this ghastly record consisted of the highest mortality rate for typhoid in the world between 1899 and 1907, or 1.30 per thousand.[5]

Public philanthropy tried first to stem this invasion of disease and death by erecting hospitals, of which Pittsburgh added eight between 1882 and 1895.[6] Street improvements because of the demands of traffic proceeded more rapidly than improvement in sewage, which also involved scientific knowledge as well as expense to property. Although building societies for the erection of model cottages were common in the English towns as the result of experience with congestion, only a few such attempts were made in the United States, and only where industrial corporations erected model "company houses" in the new industrial areas were these successful. Except in the new cities of the West, such as Salt Lake City, the United States lagged far behind England in city planning.

A report on a survey of Pittsburgh in 1908 pointed out as another feature of industrialism "an altogether incredible amount of overwork by everybody, reaching its extreme in the twelve-hour shift for seven days in the week in the steel mills and the railway switchyards."[7] Although the report considered the proportion of women in local industries as "menacing," Pittsburgh's mills were not so adaptable to the labor of women and children as were canning and textile factories, where light though fatiguing routine made possible their employment because of their cheapness and amenableness to discipline. In the single decade of the eighties the number of children employed increased from 1,-000,000 to 1,750,000.[8] In spite of ten-hour laws the usual working day in many industries even where women and children were employed was twelve hours. Although the labor of women and children was not new, the factory and the industrial city created new problems of family disintegration, fatigue, delinquency, and industrial superannuation, and impressed the criticalness of these problems by the vividness of the industrial scene. The public reaction to these conditions were the factory and public-health movements in England in the thirties and forties, and state agitations in America for ten-hour laws and legislation for sanitary improvements.

Legislative protection for women and children in industry in response to the demands of public opinion was achieved more rapidly in England than in America. Using as an accepted principle Sir Robert Peel's Act of 1819, which attempted to remedy abuses in the employment of children in cotton mills, societies of English humanitarians and factory workers forced Parliament to pass the Factory Act of 1834, the Mines Act of 1842, and the Ten Hours Act of 1847 in spite of the millowners' appeal to the currently accepted theory of laissez-faire in the relations between the state and industry. In America the manufacturing interests entrenched themselves in the state legislatures behind the argument that regulatory legislation would enable industries in those states not having such regulations to ruin the manufacturers of the states where the employment of women and children was limited. In spite of this opposition the

National Eight-Hour League succeeded in obtaining such laws in six states. Although the effect of these laws was greatly vitiated by lax enforcement, the enlightened opinion aroused by the agitation, the example of a few states, and the constant pressure of shorter-hours advocates brought a gradual reduction of the hours of labor and an improvement in health conditions in American factories.

The increase in leisure afforded by the shorter-hours movement and the belief that the open air of the country made the agricultural population healthier than the urban produced considerable activity in the founding of parks, and in the census of 1880 the acreage and description of such places received a prominent place in the report for each town. A Boston society in 1880 provided sand gardens for children, and by 1898 thirteen other cities in the East had established children's playgrounds.[9] Philanthropic organizations such as the Women's Christian Temperance Union, the Society for the Prevention of Cruelty to Animals, the Society for the Prevention of Cruelty to Children, the State Charities Aid Association, and the Red Cross were established to deal with other problems of industrial life.

The human animal appeared to be changing his habitat and his manner of living with all the effects known to biology of such changes in animal life. The entire effect upon human physiology of the transition in dwelling place and even in diet (particularly because of the widespread use of factory-made foods) has not even yet been determined, for historians of this period have given their attention principally to the alterations of the industrial environment by which the inhabitants of the city tried to make it a more suitable place for living. That improvements were possible was due in large part to the greater productivity of the new system of manufacture and distribution.

Startling as was the growth of population in the towns of the nineteenth century, it was far exceeded by the increase in productions. In the last half of the century American textile production increased sevenfold, agricultural implements twenty-five, packing fourteen, and iron and steel, ten. In this increased productivity, laborers as well as capitalists shared. If Professor Clapham is correct, industrial wages in England advanced forty per cent and the cost of living decreased seventeen per cent in the sixty years after 1790; Miss Coman has estimated that in the United States wages increased twelve and a half per cent and prices decreased forty between 1867 and 1900;[10] thus there were approximate net gains of seventy and eighty-six per cent for the English and American workingmen, respectively, in the margin between earnings and subsistence as compared with the initial years. While capital gains from this improved position appear in the increase of savings-bank deposits and in insurance, the mass of wage earners did not invest in either of these[11] but spent the difference upon a higher standard of living which the greater variety of manufactures made possible.

From the point of view of the city, the significant fact was that this increased economic productivity and the improved economic position of the mass of its inhabitants with respect to subsistence did not bring economic security. The replacement of skilled laborers by machinery produced a series of crises in various trades. This and the constant lowering of the limit of industrial superannuation added constantly to the number of unemployed. The competition of women and children and of immigrants of low standards of living augmented suffering and discontent. Finally, incapacitation from industrial accidents and disease completed the demoralization of a large section of labor and made poverty a norm of existence even in prosperous times. Commenting on these conditions, a French visitor to Manchester in 1844 thus compared the poverty in the old with that in the new cities, "At Paris, half the population go to the hospitals and almshouses to die. At Manchester, half the births take place in the public charities."[12]

Cyclical depression, which appeared in both England and the United States almost regularly every decade after 1815, demonstrated the failure of the new system to provide economic security to the laboring population. During the depression of 1837 a charitable society in Manchester found forty thousand pawn tickets representing an indebtedness of $27,500 at sixteen per cent in four thousand working-class homes.[13] In the United States nearly half a million were thrown out of work on the railways alone by the panic of 1873, only 400 out of 666 furnaces were in operation in the following spring, bread lines were common in every large city, and wages fell on an average of ten per cent and did not reach their former level until 1890.[14] During the panic of 1907 the surveyors of Pittsburgh reported: "Low wages for the great majority of the laborers employed by the mills, not lower than in other large cities, but low compared with prices,—so low as to be inadequate to the maintenance of a normal American standard of living; wages adjusted to the single man in the lodging house, not to the responsible head of a family."[15]

To Englishmen and Americans who remembered that under the domestic system the wage earner had owned a plot of ground to supply him with food in bad times and that in earlier days the West had offered homesteads to oppressed craftsmen, the pre-industrial era appeared as the golden age now replaced by suffering and chaos.

Of Manchester in 1844 Léon Faucher said: "At the very moment when the engines are stopped . . . moral order . . . disappears in an instant. The rich man spreads his couch amidst the beauties of the surrounding country, and abandons the town to the operatives, publicans, thieves, and prostitutes, merely taking the precaution of leaving behind him a police force whose duty it is to preserve some material order in this pell-mell of society."[16] A visitor described Pittsburgh in the eighties as "hell with the lid off." Pittsburgh, Chicago, Detroit, and Cincinnati were centers of organized crime, and in the nation the homicide rate quadrupled while the population doubled.[17] The failure of the police to cope with this growing disorder was accompanied by a series of embittered industrial disputes which appeared to be the first skirmishes of a social revolt.

Between 1816 and 1850 scarcely a year passed without a great strike in either the cotton industry or the building trades in Manchester, while these conflicts were increasingly supported by unions in other cities. The panic of 1873 produced a long strike in the New England textile mills. A ten per cent cut in wages in 1877 precipitated the first nationwide railway strike marked by battles between soldiers and workmen in Baltimore, Reading, and Pittsburgh. The workers of Baltimore foreshadowed the contemporary sit-down strike when they seized the railway yards and prevented the moving of trains, and in Pittsburgh the defeat of the militia gave control of the town to a lawless mob for two days. The bloody Homestead strike of steel workers in 1892 inaugurated an almost continuous series of strikes and lockouts lasting during the remainder of the century.

To restore order to a society that appeared near self-destruction, the philanthropically-inclined wealthy and other community leaders attempted to strengthen the church, the schools, charitable institutions, and the local government. In England, the distress uncovered during the cholera epidemic led six wealthy Manchester philanthropists to found the first statistical society in the world in 1833 "to assist in promoting the social improvement of the manufacturing population" by "collecting facts concerning the inhabitants."[18] Clergymen, merchants, and manufacturers supported monitórial schools under rival organizations in the twenties; temperance societies, mechanics' institutions, and savings banks in the thirties; and associations to promote public health, factory reform, public parks, and national education in the forties. The leaders of the new British manufacturing communities neglected few opportunities to inculcate what they believed to be the virtues of urban citizenship: knowledge of the "useful arts," temperance, industry, and thrift.

So closely parallel were the problems of the cities within the industrial pattern that the counterpart of each of the foregoing activities might be found in the history of almost any American manufacturing city. Local and national scientific and social associations took up the task of fact-finding. Washington Gladden of Columbus, Ohio, and other clergymen supported the rights of labor in its battle with capital and reorganized their congregations into "institutional churches" with charitable and educational agencies.[19] American advocates of broader educational opportunities were more successful than English in obtaining the assistance of the state to education, and illiteracy dropped from seventeen to eleven per cent in the last twenty years of the century.[20] In adult education the business genius of Redpath and Horner combined with philanthropy and local patriotism in an attempt to raise the general level of culture through the lyceum and the Chautauqua movement.

As philanthropy and mutual assistance proved at best only ameliorative, the pressure of these problems and of the interests affected by them was greatest upon government. In the 1760's the residents of Manchester had congratulated themselves on their lack of a municipal corporation, but in 1790 they began to create a series of new governmental agencies to perform tasks too complex for the traditional institutions. Beginning with watching and poor relief, the local government added before 1850 the regulation of hackney coaches (the traffic and transport problem of the day), street improvement, water supply, gas lighting, fire protection, sewage disposal, and market and public park administration. As in American municipal growth, this progress was accomplished by struggle with vested interests and against corruption: Manchester had a "boss Nadin" sixty years before New York experienced "boss Tweed."

There is not sufficient space within the limits of this article to present details illustrating the expansion of American municipal government, but the facts are sufficiently well known and

depart but little from the Manchester pattern. Whether contemporary municipal government has restored the order and security demanded by its citizens is still an open question but not a new one, for the issue has been raised in each town as it has developed into an industrial city and is inherent in its life, as, indeed, are each of the problems that have been suggested as elements in the history of English and American industrial cities in the nineteenth century.

While the conception of a pattern of development is of invaluable assistance in the study of the rise of contemporary society, the student of this history must realize that four points of differentiation between the English and American industrial revolutions make parallels and analogies not only hazardous but if not carefully done very misleading. Briefly these differences are: first, the priority of the industrial revolution in England; second, the existence in England of privileged classes strongly intrenched in government and in social influence; third, the powerful influence of the agricultural West and South in America; and fourth, the enormous proportion of foreign-born population in the United States due to immigration. In these differences, however, lie additional reasons why the American social scientist should be intimately acquainted with the evolution of the English industrial city.

The first great advantage in the study of the English pattern in the nineteenth century is that in their earliest phases the basic processes of a society undergoing industrialization appear in relative simplicity, since the historian has but to consider the impact of a relatively few new developments upon a traditional background. With the passing of the West and the industrialization of the South, those purely American differentiations will be of less importance in analyzing the continuation of the processes at the present time. Finally, the influence of foreign immigration upon the United States may not have exerted so differentiating an effect as might be supposed, and because of the present immigration policy and the rapid Americanization of the descendants of the foreign-born the greater part of this difference in conditions is bound to disappear.

The industrial revolution, it has been said, has been succeeded by a scientific revolution, industrial capitalism by finance capitalism, urbanization by metropolitanization, but the process is not yet complete, and as long as remain the problems created by the industrial revolution—the control of disease, poverty, and crime by urban communities, the raising of cultural standards necessary to urban citizenship, and the removal of economic insecurity—social scientists and historians will be interested in the American and English industrial city of the nineteenth century.

NOTES

° Presented on April 10, 1937, at the eighth annual history conference sponsored by the history department and the extension division of the University of Pittsburgh. Dr. Marshall's article is based upon researches made in the preparation of his doctoral dissertation on "The Development of Public Opinion in Manchester, 1780-1820," presented to the University of Pittsburgh in January, 1937, and of a book he is writing on "The Cultural Evolution of the First Industrial City: Manchester, 1780-1850."

1. *United States Census,* 1880, *Social Statistics,* 18:721, 733, 773, 850.
2. Robert A. Woods, "Pittsburgh: An Interpretation of Its Growth," in *The Pittsburgh District Civic Frontage,* 17 (Paul U. Kellogg, ed., *The Pittsburgh Survey,* vol. 5—New York, 1914).
3. Great Britain, Registrar General, *Seventh Annual Report,* 338 (London, 1841).
4. Allan Nevins, *The Emergence of Modern America, 1865-1878,* 321 (*A History of American Life,* vol. 8—New York, 1927).
5. Frank E. Wing, "Thirty-five Years of Typhoid," in *The Pittsburgh District Civic Frontage,* 66.
6. Sarah H. Killikelly, *The History of Pittsburgh, Its Rise and Progress,* 393-408 (Pittsburgh, 1906).
7. Edward T. Devine, "Pittsburgh the Year of the Survey," in *The Pittsburgh Civic Frontage,* 3.
8. Arthur M. Schlesinger, *The Rise of the City, 1878-1898,* 129 (*A History of American Life,* vol. 10—New York, 1933).
9. Schlesinger, *Rise of the City,* 130.
10. John H. Clapham, *The Early Railway Age, 1820-1850,* 561, 601, 602 (*An Economic History of Modern Britain,* second edition, vol. 1—Cambridge, 1930); Katharine Coman, *The Industrial History of the United States,* 306 (revised edition, New York, 1925).
11. Clapham, *Early Railway Age,* 299, 300.
12. Léon Faucher, *Manchester in 1844: Its Present Condition and Future Prospects,* 145 (London, 1844).
13. Joseph Adshead, *Distress in Manchester,* 41 (London, 1842).
14. Nevins, *Emergence of Modern America,* 299, 300, 301.
15. Devine, in *The Pittsburgh District Civic Frontage,* 3.
16. Faucher, *Manchester in 1844,* 26, 27.
17. Schlesinger, *Rise of the City,* 114.
18. Thomas S. Ashton, *Economic and Social Investigations in Manchester, 1833-1933,* 13 (London, 1934).
19. Schlesinger, *Rise of the City,* 340.
20. Schlesinger, *Rise of the City,* 171.

The Industrial City: Center of Cultural Change

RALPH E. TURNER

In 1832 the *Manchester Guardian,* commenting on an exposure of bad living conditions among the factory population, offered as an apology for their existence the following observation: "The manufacturing system as it exists in Great Britain, and the inconceivably immense towns under it, are without previous parallel in the history of the world." This recognition of the industrial city as an unprecedented phenomenon was developed, not as an apology for bad living conditions, but as an explanation of the general changes under way in society, by two English observers of early industrialism, namely, William Cooke Taylor and Robert Vaughan, both of whom, it is worth noting, were historians. Taylor wrote a general history of civilization under the title *The Natural History of Society* (1841), besides many textbooks; and Vaughan, before he became president of the Lancashire Independent College at Manchester, was professor of history at the University of London. In a sense, therefore, it may be said that the view of the industrial city as a center of cultural change belongs peculiarly to historians.

Taylor held that the industrial town was a "new element" in society, which could not develop without deranging old institutions and relationships. It exhibited, he said, "a system of social life constructed on a wholly new principle, a principle yet vague and indefinite but

developing itself by its own spontaneous force, and daily producing effects which no human foresight had anticipated." Above all, he was impressed by the formation of the urban masses who, developing new habits of thought without external aid or guidance, would ultimately, like the slow rising and gradual swelling of the ocean, "bear all elements of society aloft upon its bosom." But, although these masses lacked guidance, they were, in his opinion, no worse off than their superiors who, however educated, found little in past human experience of use in understanding the unforeseen innovations of the factory towns. The Greek verse, said Taylor, meant nothing in Manchester, and philosophy knew no circumstances like those which prevailed there.

Vaughan, who pointed out the fact, none too well recognized even today, that rural and urban populations have played different roles in the growth of civilization, argued that in the "unavoidable intercourse" of the new towns there was occurring an education of the people that would stimulate science, advance self-government, improve the arts and literature, and raise the general level of popular life. "Such, indeed, is often the astuteness acquired in the exercise of this greatest of free schools," he said, "that the smith of Sheffield, or the weaver of Manchester, would frequently prove, on any common ground,

From Carolin F. Ware, *The Cultural Approach to History* (New York: Columbia University Press, 1940), pp. 228-42. Reprinted by permission of the publisher. The late Ralph E. Turner was Professor of History at Yale University.

more than a match for a college graduate." Vaughan saw the new industrial towns as centers of "vast experiments" like those which had occurred in the cities of other lands and ages.

For us who live today in the midst of what is a chaos understood badly if at all, the views of Taylor and Vaughan may provide a point of departure for a consideration of the prevailing confusion. At least, it is clear that, if the English industrial city of the 1840's was a scene of "vast experiments," today, with similar cities having become the dominant type of community in all industrial nations, "vast experiments" have probably been carried further than they had gone in the early nineteenth century. Similarly, if, as Taylor said, the urban masses will ultimately bear all society aloft, it is probable that the tendency of this bearing is more clear today than when he noted it.

An examination of the industrial city as a center of cultural change may indicate something of these "vast experiments," may possibly show the general direction the urban masses are tending. It is the purpose of this paper to sketch the outlines of such an examination.

The postulates of the examination are to be found in the concept of culture, as developed in recent social thought, especially by anthropologists and sociologists. According to their views, "a culture" is a socially organized and transmitted structure of behavior and thought. The structure is integrated functionally, that is, its elements provide more of a unity than of a conflict of services to life and have coherence psychologically in terms of a relatively clearly focused outlook on life. The basis of this integration is a process of social interaction, through which individual interests and needs are organized into collective forms or patterns. In the growth of culture, the social process impels individuals to new modes of action and thought—innovations, they are called—and these new modes, in turn, become organized as enduring patterns, through selection in the social process. The evolution of any structure of human behavior and thought, when viewed in historical perspective, is recognizable as the evolution of a cultural tradition which, from time to time as new social conditions arise, assimilates new elements in what may be called a reorientation of the tradition. The newly assimilated elements, it may be believed, seldom outweigh those persisting from the past.

This conception of the evolution of behavior and thought also predicates that, although cultural development goes forward constantly both by the loss of old elements and by the assimilation of innovations, there may be far-reaching disturbances in a cultural tradition which, disorganizing a long-persisting integration, produces finally a new integration. At the base of such new integration, setting its pattern and tendency of growth, is the social process through which individual behavior and thought are originally organized and finally assimilated into transmitted materials. In the words of A. A. Goldenweiser,

In its constituent elements culture is psychological and, in the last analysis, comes from the individual. But as an integral entity culture is cumulative, historical, extra-individual. It comes to the individual as part of his objective experience, just as do his experiences with nature, and, like these, it is absorbed by him, thus becoming part of his psychic content.[1]

It is from the point of view of these predications that the industrial city can be seen as having special significance for cultural development. Relative to the life that prevailed in the traditional countryside and the old market and port towns, it is not difficult to understand that the industrial city tends to organize a new structure of behavior and thought. The original patterns of this structure, as they emerged in Manchester, England, have been sketched in another essay in this volume;[2] here it is important to emphasize that the industrial city, as a focus of technological, economic, political, intellectual, and esthetic changes, organized cultural influences from many sources in a social process in which the constantly increasing populations participated. Whatever the influences of industrial cities, these influences move in the social interaction that arises in city populations, as individuals carry on their occupations, pursue their interests, and obtain their satisfactions. In terms of the concept of culture, the industrial city is, then, a milieu which everywhere has the same general elements and everywhere supports the development of a structure of behavior and thought from these elements. Because it is a predication of the concept of culture that both behavior and thought, although individually expressed, are socially organized, this milieu may be conceived as bringing about, through time, the transformation of the various organizations of behavior and thought carried in the traditional culture. Thus, for example, the organizations of behavior and thought characterizing the historic sociocultural types —the peasant, the noble, and the priest— are transformed into new structures of behavior and thought, which, however different for workers, technicians, and entrepreneurs, are nevertheless the common base of their lives.

Some of the aspects of this developing structure of behavior and thought may be briefly noted. Its primary elements are evident in the intricate division of labor, which, instead of standardizing and routinizing work as commonly supposed, gives it a manifold variety of forms which make the new urban workers not a "uniform mass" but a composite of diversified types. In contrast to the historic peasants, the members of the new industrial working class possess individuality in a great variety of forms. This developing structure of thought and behavior is also evident in new social services, in new amusements, in new intellectual and artistic pursuits, as well as in new technological and economic procedures. Also the new structure of behavior and thought is embodied in new standards of consumption, in new relationships of the sexes and the members of families, in new positions of the several age groups, in new circumstances affecting health, and in new causes of death. For individuals, these aspects are elements of a changing behavior and mentality; for the industrial city milieu, they are attributes fixed upon individuals coming under its influences.

From the point of view of cultural development, it is necessary to conceive of the beginnings of this structure of behavior and thought as appearing in the early industrial cities, of its elements spreading and maturing as industrial cities have grown, and, finally, of these elements becoming integrated through an intellectual outlook upon or a feeling for life shaped in terms of the frame of reference organized in experience as it goes on among the masses who now live in industrial cities. This matter may be stated in another way. If the industrial city, considered as the social milieu of a new structure of behavior and thought, is influencing ever larger parts of national populations, this influence is evident, on the one hand, in the dislocation of old forms of behavior and thought in the several national traditions and, on the other hand, in the appearance and spread of new forms. However, at the moment, because the dislocation of the old forms intensifies the emotional attachments to them, the new ones are not recognized. If at the moment such is the case, the prevailing confusion is understandable in the feeling that, although the old modes of behavior and thought no longer serve life, there is nothing to replace them. In truth, however, the modes of behavior and thought of a *new* culture may be implicit in the industrial city, requiring only recognition and acceptance to become the basis of conscious action. In the words of Robert H. Lowie, the anthropologist, "Culture, it seems, is a matter of exceedingly slow growth until a certain 'threshold' is passed, when it darts forward, gathering momentum at an unexpected rate."[3] The present disturbed situation in western culture, where the industrial city originated and has had its fullest development, may be only the approach to such a "threshold."

Before turning to a consideration of some of the aspects of industrial-city life which may be factors at the "threshold" of a cultural change, it is well to note that no one meant to create the industrial city or, as currently designated in the United States, the "metropolitan urban area." It arose as entrepreneurs pursued their interest—profits—and engineers served that interest by technological ingenuity. But once created, it became something other than a center of business and machine industry, that is, it became a milieu having the power to organize socially a structure of behavior and thought for those coming under its influence. For this reason the industrial city may ultimately react on business and industry, giving them new forms, in spite of the interests of entrepreneurs. It seems that commonly men do two things when they perform an act, first, what they intend to do and, second, what they do not intend to do. And often the second thing is more important than the first. Certainly this seems to be the case with those persons who, while their intentional activities were chiefly concerned with making money, unknowingly created the industrial city, which, as a social milieu, is now the matrix of cultural change.

An examination of the development of industrial cities shows three classes of factors which may be considered as having significance for further cultural development. Although these factors may not have originated completely in the industrial city, their influence in contemporary life is focused in its milieu, so that they must be considered as elements of a complex of urban psychological influences. These three classes of factors may be designated: (1) the paradox of economic liberalism, (2) conditions having origin in machine technology, and (3) conditions of urban association. Each of these classes of psychological factors ramifies through contemporary society, having many manifestations and exciting many comments. However, only in the industrial city or the metropolitan urban milieu can they be viewed objectively.

By the paradox of economic liberalism, the central predications of which are too widely accepted to require statement here, is meant that entrepreneurial activity has created conditions which not only restrict the freedom of individuals but also reveal that the presumptions that universal competition promotes the automatic realization of a constantly advancing well-being are false. The restrictions on individual freedom of action have objective form in the hierarchies of employment which have appeared as technological developments have brought together ever larger units of capital. For individuals employed in these hierarchies, economic advancement is more a matter of rising from grade to grade than a shift from the status "employee" to the status "entrepreneur." Moreover, in these hierarchies economic power is exercised from the top downward. Through the "right to fire," the qualities of behavior that bring advancement become less and less those summed up in the phrase "individual initiative" and more and more those implied in the word "loyalty." Actually "conformity" rather than "initiative" is the quality desired in an ever-increasing body of individuals who occupy the status of employee. It is also important to note that economic power exerted from the top of these hierarchies upon individuals in the lower levels of employment does interfere upon occasions with the exercise of personal liberties in areas of life quite beyond that of the economic functioning of the hierarchies. The effect of this interference is to impose upon more and more individuals a regimentation in terms of private interests. Indeed, in many ways the current assertion of the doctrines of economic liberalism is merely a defense for economic power that functions as private regimentation.

Probably no more concise statement of the contradiction between the theory of economic liberalism and the fact of the private regimentation which prevails among the populations of industrial cities can be cited than the following words from Walter Lippmann's column, "How Liberty Is Lost":

> To have economic independence a man must be in a position to leave one job and go to another; he must have enough savings of some kind to exist for a considerable time without accepting the first job offered. . . . the industrial worker who has a choice between working in one factory and not working at all, the white collar intellectuals who compete savagely for the relatively few private positions and for posts in the bureaucracy—these are the people who live too precariously to exercise their liberties or to defend them. They have no savings. They have only their labor to sell, and there are very few buyers of their labor. Therefore, they have only the choice of truckling to the powerful or of perishing heroically but miserably.[4]

Who are the great to whom these workers shall truckle? The private employers or the politicians who promise jobs? The economic and political crises which have already swept away some liberal regimes, and which now threaten the remainder, root in this social soil.

In this connection, it is worth observing that, from the cultural point of view, the mere criticism of a social order cannot be the basis of social reconstruction. Indeed, if a program of social reform or amelioration can be successfully based on a critique of a social order, progress away from the conditions giving rise to the paradox of economic liberalism should have been rapid, since the rise of the early industrial cities, for the eloquence of the writers of those times on these conditions has not been surpassed by writers of the present century. But to be able to point out social evils—even, in fact, to understand their origin—is not to become adequate to deal with them. For they cannot be dealt with in terms of themselves or even in terms of the institutions which give rise to them. In other words, the evils cannot be dealt with merely as problems of distress, unemployment, and the like, or as aspects of a social order retaining the essential characteristics described in the doctrines of economic liberalism; they must be dealt with in terms of the potentialities of cultural change, implicit in the industrial city milieu. To know these potentialities involves not the emotional excitement raised by pointing to the evils, but a technique of analysis of the factors in cultural development. And to the development of this technique few social critics have made contributions.

In turning to a consideration of the two other classes of factors which are elements of the industrial city milieu, namely, conditions having their origin in machine technology and conditions of urban association, it is necessary to point out that the items listed under these headings have been arrived at in a certain way. This way has been an isolation of the repetitive, or recurring elements in industrial urban life, or, in other words, the finding of its continuously pervasive elements. This mode of analysis has been adopted on the ground that a culture, as an integrated and persisting structure of behavior and thought, is constructed psychologically upon a relatively stable order of stimuli, in terms of which patterns of reaction are developed. To such repetitive stimuli the great part of an industrial population react, and the recurring reactions become the determining tendencies of the development of the urban structure of life. Culture, it must be remembered, is both a psychological and a social phenomenon.

This way of analysis is not unfamiliar in American historiography. In fact, the classic essay, *The Significance of the Frontier in American History*, by Frederick Jackson Turner, which has received the lip, if not the mind service of a generation of students of American history, embodies it. The fundamental postulate of this essay is that a persisting underlying influence gave distinctive patterns to national life and furthermore created an intellectual outlook which unified the national culture. Certainly the following excerpts can be so understood.

The existence of an area of free land, its continuous recession, and the advance of American settlement westward explain American development.

Behind institutions, behind constitutional forms and modifications, lie the vital forces that call these organs into life and shape them to meet changing conditions. . . .

The frontier individualism has from the beginning promoted democracy. . . .

The result is that to the frontier the American intellect owes its striking characteristics. That coarseness and strength combined with acuteness and inquisitiveness, that practical inventive turn of mind, quick to find expedients, that masterful grasp of material things, lacking in the artistic but powerful to effect great ends, that restless, nervous energy, that dominant individualism, working for good and for evil, and withal that buoyancy and exuberance which comes with freedom, these are traits of the frontier, or traits called out elsewhere because of the existence of the frontier.[5]

In terms of the concept of culture, the fact of "free land" may be understood as having established patterns which, as the frontier was pushed westward, were worked into the various phases of national life and, as individual experience and behavior were organized in these patterns, came to embody a pervasive psychological reaction which was the source of the subjective tradition of the national culture. In a sense, therefore, an analysis of current American developments in cultural terms is not greatly different from the mode of thinking which led Turner to his view of national development.

In every culture the integration of man with physical nature, in terms of technology, is significant in the life of the people who carry the culture. From this integration flows the wealth which supports the social order and certain basic judgments on life that have entered always into social attitudes, religious beliefs, and moral practices. There is no need here to discuss these phenomena, as they have long existed in cultures having an agrarian base. From contemporary technology come, it seems, at least three recognizable conditions that may contribute to the shaping of new cultural forms:

First: The sense of human control. Machine technology is operated by energy produced and controlled by man; in fact, it represents the fullest expression of his rationality. He creates power, orders its flow, governs its movement, and determines its resultant. In this circumstance exists ground for the assumption that what man achieves in one field of action, he may also do in another field. As a result of man's triumph in technology, it may be that he feels more able to command his fate socially. The emergence of the concept "planned economy" roots at least partly in this circumstance.

Second: The utility of objective knowledge. That knowledge is power is appreciated by the simplest mechanic; in terms of a special body of knowledge, every machine operator or machine fixer performs his task. This circumstance boldly insists that it is knowledge which functions to give success in every situation, that myth, tradition, and special interest must give way to knowledge—and the knowledge meant is worldly, factual, and utilitarian. By implication, therefore, machine technology supports the view that social distress exists either because of lack of knowledge or because of the unwillingness to apply what is at hand.

Third: The increasing capacity to produce wealth. With the advent of machinery and applied science in agriculture and industry, man's capacity to produce wealth expanded enormously. For example, between 1920 and 1930 the agricultural population of the United States decreased by 4,000,000 persons, while agricultural production increased by 25 percent; now agricultural economists estimate that the agricultural population, not counting the backlog of persons who would have migrated to cities if jobs had been available, could be decreased by at least 3,000,000 persons without seriously affecting the agricultural production necessary to maintain national consumption at present standards. It has been estimated that since about 1870 the capacity to produce in manufacturing industries has increased 3 percent per year. Especially important is the fact that the increase of productivity has gone on steadily during the present depression decade. This fact is relevant to the present situation, which finds industrial production near the 1929 level without the employment of an equal number of workers.

These three conditions having their origin in contemporary technology—the sense of human control, the utility of objective knowledge, and the increasing capacity to produce wealth—point more and more directly to an economy in which human control, exercised with knowledge rather than with self-interest, may utilize the new capacity, to produce wealth for the support of a more secure life.

In closing this comment on the new

conditions of life that have come with contemporary technology, it should be noted that one does not need to be a philosopher in order to know them, for they run constantly in the experience of all who actually work at the production of real goods. In other words, these conditions are part and parcel of the life of the masses of industrial cities.

The conditions of urban association are certainly no less significant for setting the direction of cultural change than those arising in contemporary technology. In fact, because they have existence in social interaction, they are primary to these influences which, after all, are reactions of men to physical nature and not of men to men. Culture, it may be noted, stands between man and nature, whereas man comes to culture through the social process.

From this point of view four conditions of industrial urban association are significant:

First: The disintegration of localism and tradition. Innumerable social stimuli flow through the contemporary urban population. Newspapers, movies, and radio pour the world into their eyes and ears; from these visual and aural images there is no escape. By the number and impact of these social stimuli, local prejudices and old traditions are disintegrated. By this wearing away, the urban masses are freed to take on views which harmonize with their social environment—the industrial city as a whole, not merely as a place where labor is sold and a profit is made. Indeed, the rise of propaganda, i.e., the organized control of mass opinion, has its origin in this circumstance, for as the masses are released from local and traditional opinions, they become free to move in new directions. Propaganda is organized by special interests in order to determine this direction. In the end,

however, the movement of mass mentality will necessarily be in the direction set by the milieu which exists in the going experience of thousands of individuals.

Second: The cult of uniformity. As social stimuli flow continuously through the urban masses by way of machine-made commodities and routinized social services, manners, customs, and tastes are shaped into a wide conformity. This conformity is the necessary base of the organization of a complex social order among a large population; it makes for frictionless movement among large aggregates of individuals, who can, as a result, move together in actions not possible for them when they were embedded in local communities. Conformity serves the need for orderly coöperation in the intricate processes of urban society.

Third: The diversification of individual behavior. In communities antedating industrial cities, refinement, elegance, and taste were, in the main, attributes of small classes; to belong to these classes meant the possession of an explicit moral code, special forms of dress and manner, and particular intellectual affectations. In some respects these class attributes survive now, but among urban masses individual tastes find release from such controls. Thus there appear among urban populations innumerable groups pursuing self-selected interests, and individuals are permitted wide variations from all norms of conduct. The modern urban milieu is fostering a diversification of intellectual, artistic, and amusemental pursuits, unheard of in earlier types of communities. Individual energies are free to find expression in more ways than ever before. The industrial city well exemplifies the sociological principle that as social organization becomes more complex, individuals necessarily have more opportunity for development.

Fourth: The reorientation of the right of property. From the point of view of the concept of culture, the social rather than the economic factor is decisive in historical development. Thus it need cause no surprise that the social milieu of the industrial city is affecting the right of property—indeed, the whole relationship of men and wealth. The prevailing concept of property was derived from societies mainly agrarian in their economic and social organization. It is a concept developed mainly in terms of tangible goods, for it emphasizes possession on the ground that from possession flow the benefits of ownership. Now it appears that property in this sense has been becoming less and less important in the lives of all urban dwellers. Urban dwellers, even those having great wealth, can own very little of the property upon which their lives continually depend. The rich and the poor alike are dependent upon a continuity of services—water, food, light, heat, protection—which are maintained only through social coöperation. And they demand not ownership of these services, but their continuous functioning, regardless of ownership. Similarly, the owner of tangible property, whatever it may be, can produce little with the property that contributes to real satisfaction. His property probably functions to create any wealth that gives real satisfactions only through a minute division of labor, and such wealth is produced only through the maintenance of this division of labor. Finally, since the individual in the modern urban economy, no matter who he may be, can command few real goods through the possession of real property, he must possess some claim upon wealth

which can be executed in diverse ways; for only by such execution can he acquire the diversity of real goods which supports urban modes of living. Thus it appears that in the modern industrial city the ownership of property is far less important to the support of individual life than the maintenance of certain fundamental economic services and the establishment of some kind of claim on currently produced real goods. In fact, the elaboration of the modes of ownership through various kinds of legal claims—securities, trusts, insurance annuities, and social security claims— is an adjustment to this growing social orientation of the right of property.

However confused and clouded this exposition of the factors in the industrial urban milieu has been, it has made these factors far more clear than they are. Actually they exist today as part of the chaos previously noted. They are vaguely felt impulses, uncertain judgments, and befogged visions; they are neither defined nor oriented. However, they run in the experience of urban masses, as life goes on in terms of the labor market, machine technology, and urban association; and, as combined in a day-by-day routine, they form a frame of reference which for these masses, without conscious effort on their part, becomes the point of departure of feeling and thinking. Thus from this frame of reference issues, in the life of the masses, new attitudes toward their problems, new definitions of their interests, and new concepts of what life ought to be like. More important still in the day-by-day routine of behavior, as organized under the influence of this complex of urban forces, are the elements which may be combined in new patterns of behavior that will constitute the culture which is correlative with the modes of thinking and feeling set in this frame of reference. In other words, the frame of reference, as the subjective content of life shaped by the complex of urban forces, and the day-by-day routines of behavior, as the objective content of life shaped by this complex, together form the psychological basis for the integration of thought and behavior in a new culture.

In the concept of culture, it is postulated that at any time there are a limited number of possible modes of thinking and acting; therefore, as far as the contemporary world is concerned, if the old forms of thought and behavior are to be displaced (as, indeed, they are being displaced), the complex of urban forces which shapes this frame of reference and day-by-day routine of behavior of the urban masses fixes the possibilities for the future. It is pertinent to state here that because this frame of reference and this day-by-day routine of behavior are organized through social interaction, they affect, to some degree, the smaller specialized urban groups as well as the urban masses; for this reason contemporary cultural change is not merely an adjustment to the rise of a new social class. It is, in fact, far more fundamental, for it is touching all classes, compelling those which have been dominant to alter the forms of their control if they are to remain dominant. The twentieth century cannot have just any kind of social order; it must have one oriented in terms of the contemporary industrial urban milieu.

If one seeks a general heading under which to sum up the most significant aspect of the cultural change under way in nations whose chief communities are industrial cities or metropolitan urban areas, it would seem to be the phrase "a reëducation of the masses." Before the rise of industrial cities, the overwhelming proportion of population in all lands consisted of peasants—socially isolated, superstitious, tenacious of the land, and illiterate. As industrial cities grew, the peasant element declined and the urban masses formed. It should be recognized that, as the masses shifted to the cities, they brought with them the mentality of peasants; this has been a primary condition in their reëducation which, even today, the contrivers of propaganda know how to use. But, once in the city, the new circumstances of life—the labor market, machine technology, and urban association—began to affect their behavior and thought. It is not contended that the urban masses have been or are now conscious of this process of reëducation; it is only argued that they necessarily act and think under its effects, and that such action and thought are the elements of the cultural change now under way.

NOTES

1. A. A. Goldenweiser, *History, Psychology, and Culture* (New York, 1933), p. 59.
2. See Chap. X [of C. F. Ware's *The Cultural Approach to History*].
3. Robert H. Lowie, *Culture and Ethnology* (New York, 1917), p. 78.
4. *New York Herald Tribune*, July 16, 1938.
5. "The Significance of the Frontier in American History," *The Early Writings of Frederick Jackson Turner*, compiled by E. E. Edwards (Madison, 1938), pp. 185-229, at pp. 186, 220, 227-28.

The Modern Metropolis

. . . We [are going to] speak of the product of . . . [the] evolution [of cities] not as the modern city" but as "the modern metropolis." The change of name reflects the fact that from its long, slow evolution the city has emerged into a revolutionary stage. It has undergone a qualitative change, so that it is no longer merely a larger version of the traditional city but a new and different form of human settlement.

There is some argument about the term. Lewis Mumford objects to "metropolis" (from the Greek words for "mother" and "city"), which historically had a very different meaning; he prefers the term "conurbation," coined by Patrick Geddes, the Scottish biologist who was a pioneer in city planning. This word, however, implies formation by the fusion of several preexisting cities; most metropolises did not originate in that way. The term "megalopolis," coined by the French geographer Jean Gottmann, is generally applied to an urbanized region that contains several metropolitan areas, such as the region extending from Boston to Washington. On the whole it seems best to retain the term "metropolis," now commonly adopted in many languages as the name for a major city center and its environs.

"Metropolitan area" can be defined in various ways; the U.S. Bureau of the Census, for instance, defines it as any area containing a nuclear city of at least 50,000 population. The new phenomenon we are considering, however, is a much bigger entity with a certain minimum critical size. In agreement with the German scholar Gerhard Isenberg, I shall define a metropolis as a concentration of at least 500,000 people living within an area in which the traveling time from the outskirts to the center is no more than about 40 minutes. Isenberg and I have both derived this definition from observations of the transformation of cities into metropolises during the first half of the 20th century. At the present time—at least in North America—the critical mass that distinguishes a metropolis from the traditional city can be considerably larger—perhaps nearing one million population.

The emergence of a basically new form of human settlement is an extremely rare event in the history of mankind. For at least 5,000 years all civilizations have been characterized predominantly by just two well-marked types of settlement: the farm village and the city. Until recently the vast majority of the population lived in villages. They produced not only their own raw materials—food, fuel and fiber —but also the manufactured goods and services they required. The cities were inhabited by only a small minority of the total population, generally less than 20 percent. These people were the ruling elite—the religious, political, military and commercial leaders—and the

From *Cities* (New York: Knopf, 1965), pp. 40-57. Reprinted by permission of the publisher. Hans Blumenfeld is a lecturer in Urban and Regional Planning at the University of Toronto.

retinue of laborers, craftsmen and professionals who served them. The elite drew their subsistence and power from the work of the villagers by collecting tithes, taxes or rent. This system prevailed until the end of the 18th century, and its philosophy was well expressed by physiocrats of that time on both sides of the Atlantic, including Thomas Jefferson.

The industrial revolution dramatically reversed the distribution of population between village and city. A German contemporary of Jefferson's, Justus Moeser, foresaw at the very beginning of the revolution what was to come; he observed that "specialized division of labor forces workers to live in big cities." With increasing specialization there had to be increased cooperation of labor, both within and between establishments. The division of labor and increased productivity made concentration in cities possible, and the required cooperation of labor made it necessary, because the new system called for bringing together workers of many skills and diverse establishments that had to interchange goods and services.

The process fed on itself, growth inducing further growth. Many economists have noted that the rapid rise of productivity has been largely instrumental in bringing about a progressive shift of the main part of the labor force from the primary industry of raw-material production to the secondary industry of material processing and finally to the tertiary industry of services. Less attention has been paid to a related, equally important factor behind this shift, namely the "specializing out" of functions. The farmer's original functions of producing his own motive power (work animals), fuel (hay and oats), tools, building materials and con-

sumer goods have been specialized out to secondary industries that supply him with tractors, gasoline and his other necessities. Today, in the tertiary stage, much of the work connected with secondary industry is being specialized out to purveyors of business services (accounting, control, selling, distribution). Even the functions of the household itself (personal services, housekeeping, repairs, shopping, recreation, education) are taken over by consumer-service industries.

The dual spur of specialization and cooperation of labor started a great wave of migration from country to city all over the globe. In the advanced countries the 19th-century development of long-distance transportation by steamship and railroad and of communication by the electric telegraph made it possible for cities to draw on large regions and grow to populations of millions. For a time their growth was limited by internal restrictions. Travel within the city still had to be by foot or by hoof. A New York businessman could communicate quickly with his partners in Shanghai by cablegram, but to deliver an order to an office a few blocks away he had to send a messenger. This situation limited cities to a radius of only about three miles from the center. In the absence of elevators the city was also limited in vertical expansion. The only possible growth was interstitial, by covering every square inch of available space. Residences, factories, shops and offices all crowded close together around the center. The result was a fantastic rise in the price of city land compared with the cost of the structures that could be built on it.

This was only a transitory phase in the growth of the city, but its heritage is still with us, in structures, street patterns, institutions and concepts. We still think and talk and act in terms of "city and country" and "city and suburb," although these concepts have lost meaning in the modern metropolis and its region. The transformation was set in motion toward the end of the 19th century and early in the 20th with the invention of the telephone, the electric streetcar, the subway and the powered elevator. Even more far-reaching was the impact on the city of the automobile and the truck. With the acquisition of these aids to communication and mobility the city burst its eggshell and emerged as a metropolis. (It is worth noting that the telephone and the automobile had equally profound effects on rural life, fragmenting the old farm village and giving rise to huge, scattered farms.)

The centripetal migration from the country to the city continues unabated, but now there is an equally powerful centrifugal wave of migration from the city to the suburbs. Although on a national scale more and more of the population is becoming urban, within the urban areas there is increasing decentralization. The interaction of these two trends has produced the new form of settlement we call the metropolis. It is no longer a "city" as that institution has been understood in the past, but on the other hand it is certainly not "country" either. The fact that it is neither one nor the other has aroused nostalgic critics, who appeal for a return to "true urbanity" and to a "real countryside." But in view of the inexorable technological and economic trends that have created the metropolis these terms also require a new and different interpretation.

It has become fashionable to describe the transformation of the city into the metropolis as an "explosion." The term is misleading on two counts. The change is not destroying the city, as "explosion" implies, nor is it a sudden, unheralded event. The movement of population from the center of the city outward to an ever expanding periphery has been going on for at least a century. In the metropolitan region of New York, New Jersey and Connecticut, where the average density of population within the cities and towns of the area increased steadily up to 1860, it began to drop after that date. The outward spread of the city was nearly as strong between 1860 and 1900 as it has been since 1900. In Philadelphia the population movement away from the center of the city was actually proportionately greater in the half century between 1860 and 1910 than in the period 1900 to 1950.

Analysis of the population density in the metropolitan area of Philadelphia and that of other cities shows that the centrifugal wave of movement to the suburbs has proceeded with amazing regularity. From the center of the city out to the periphery at any one time there is a consistent decline in residential density from one zone to the next. As time has passed, the curve representing this decline has become less steep; that is, the center has lost or stood still in density while the outer areas have gained, so that the difference between them is less. Interestingly, the density gradient from the center to the periphery has also become smoother (that is, less lumped around outer towns), which seems to indicate that the center is actually strengthening its influence over the outer areas. In each zone the rise in density with time eventually flattens out, as if the density has reached a "saturation" level for that zone; this level is lower for each successive zone out to the periphery. With the passage of time the crest of the wave (the zone of fastest growth) moves outward in a regular fashion. The innermost zone at the center of the city seems to show an anomaly, in that its population density is lower than that of the surrounding area, but this merely reflects the fact that the center is occupied predominantly by stores and offices. If its daytime working population were included in the census, it would have a far higher density.

One can outline a "natural history" of the modern metropolis. The metropolis is characterized first of all by a certain measure of mutual accessibility among its various parts, which determines its total size. As I have mentioned, in most cases the area embraced by the metropolis has a radius represented by a traveling time of about 40 minutes in the principal vehicle of transportation (train or auto), or about 45 minutes from door to door. With improvement in the speed of transportation the extent of the metropolis in miles can, of course, expand. In most metropolitan areas the average travel time to work for the working population as a whole is about half an hour. No more than 15 percent of the workers spend more than 45 minutes in the daily journey to work.

This may sound surprising in view of the frequent complaints of commuters about the length of their journey. The complaints are not new. A century ago a German observer declared that the distance people on the outskirts of cities had to travel to work had reached the limit of what was bearable. Probably the range of travel times to work then was wider than it is in the metropolis today. There are strong indications, however, that the half-hour average has been more or less standard. In most

American small towns, although a majority of the workers are employed within the town, a sizable minority do travel long distances to work in other communities, usually because they cannot find a job in the hometown and must seek work elsewhere but do not wish to change their home.

It is one of the great advantages of the metropolis that people can change jobs without moving their homes. Breadth of choice—for workers, for employers and for consumers—is the essence of the metropolis. The worker has a choice of employers; the employer can find workers of a wide variety of skills, including professional and managerial. Even more important is the accessibility of a variety of goods and services on which any business enterprise depends. Only a metropolis can support the large inventories, transportation facilities and specialized services —particularly those of a financial, legal, technical and promotional nature—that are essential to modern business. Such services constitute the main source of economic strength of the metropolis—its true economic base. They are especially important to small, new and experimental enterprises. The metropolis, in particular its central area, therefore serves as an incubator for such enterprises. Contrary to a common impression, the big city is most suitably a home for small industries rather than large industrial complexes. The big plant, being more nearly self-sufficient, may often be as well off in a small town. This fact is reflected in the statistics of employment: in most metropolises the number of people that are employed in manufacturing is decreasing, relatively and sometimes absolutely, while the number that are employed in services is increasing rapidly.

What is true of business services is also true of consumer services: the metropolis attracts the consumer because it offers a wide freedom of choice. Only the large population of a metropolis can support the great proliferation of special services found in the big city: large department stores, many specialty shops, opera houses, art galleries, theaters, sports stadia, special schools, large and well-equipped institutions for medical care and adult education and a host of other necessities for the full life.

To sum up, the modern metropolis differs from the traditional city in several crucial respects: (1) it combines the function of central leadership with the functions of providing the main bulk of material production and services; (2) its population is up to 10 times larger than that of the biggest preindustrial city; (3) with modern fast transportation, which has increased its commuting radius about tenfold, it is up to 100 times larger in area than the biggest city of former times; (4) it is neither city nor country but a complex of urban districts and open areas; (5) its residential and work areas are no longer combined in one place but are located in separate districts; (6) its workers have high mobility in the choice of jobs and occupations.

The feedback cycle of metropolitan growth enlarging freedom of choice and freedom of choice in turn attracting further growth has given the metropolis amazing vitality and staying power. In the premetropolis era cities laid low by war, pestilence or loss of prestige were often abandoned or reduced to weak shadows of their former glory. Even Rome became little more than a village after it lost its empire. In contrast, all the big cities destroyed in World War II have been rebuilt, most of them to beyond their prewar size. Particularly significant is the experience of Leningrad. During the Russian Revolution and again in World War II it lost about half of its population. Moreover, the revolution ended its former role as the center of government and finance and deprived it of most of its markets and sources of supply. Yet the population of Leningrad is now four million—four times what it was in 1921. This growth is especially remarkable in view of the Soviet government's policy of restricting the growth of the major cities, a policy based on Karl Marx's condemnation of big cities because of their pollution of air, water and soil. As a metropolis Leningrad is an outstanding testament to the viability of the species.

Attempts to halt the growth of the big city have been made ever since the phenomenon first appeared on the human scene. They have been singularly unsuccessful. Elizabeth I of England and after her Oliver Cromwell tried to limit the growth of London by circling it with an enforced greenbelt, but this method failed. In any case such a device, applied to a growing city, can only lead to overcrowding. To avoid big-city problems nearly all countries today have embarked on programs of industrial decentralization, often with unsatisfactory results. In the Western nations the most far-reaching attempt at decentralization is Great Britain's "new towns" plan. This program has been eminently successful in creating new centers of industry as "growth points," but it has not availed to stop the growth of London or to limit other cities, new or old, to their planned size. Significantly, all but one of the 17 new towns built in Britain since the war are satellite towns within previously existing metropolitan regions.

The U.S.S.R., by virtue of centralized planning and ownership, has been able to carry out decentralization on a continental scale. Its program has been remarkably effective in slowing the growth of Moscow and promoting that of smaller cities. Between 1939 and 1959 the towns in the U.S.S.R. with populations of less than 200,000 grew by 84 percent; those in the 200,000-to-500,000 class grew 63 percent; those in the 500,000-to-one-million class grew 48 percent, and Moscow itself increased only 20 percent in population. Moscow has, however, gone well beyond the limit of five million that the government planned: it is now at six million, nearly four times the city's population in 1921.

In the U.S., where the forces of the market rather than central planning determine industrial locations, the growth rates in the decade 1950-1960 were 27 percent in metropolitan areas of 50,000 to 500,000 population and 35 percent in those of 500,000 to two million population. In the metropolises with a population of more than two million the average growth rate was smaller: 23 percent. This average, however, was heavily weighted by the comparatively slow-growing centers of the Northeastern sector of the nation; in Los Angeles and San Francisco, the only two metropolises of this class outside the Northeast, the growth was far above the national average for all metropolitan areas.

There is no denying that the growth of the huge metropolises has brought serious problems, chief among which are traffic congestion and the pollution of air and water by smoke, household wastes, detergents and gasoline fumes. Many cities also object that the metropolis can exist only by draining the countryside of its economic, demographic and social strength. These problems are not essentially unsolvable, however. Effective methods for control of pollution exist; they need to be applied [see "The Metabolism of Cities," by Abel Wolman, page 156]. The economic and social complaints about the metropolis seem to have little substance today. The city now repays the country in full in economic terms, as we have noted, and with the improvement in sanitation and lowering of the high 19th-century urban death rate it contributes its share of the natural population increase.

The most persistent accusation against the metropolis is that it has dissolved the family and neighborhood ties that existed in the small town and has produced anomie: the absence of any values or standards of behavior. This is questionable. A number of sociological studies in metropolises of North America and western Europe have shown that family ties remain very much alive and that a considerable amount of informal community organization can be found even in their slums.

In considering the future of the metropolis the central question is that of crowding. How much bigger can the metropolis grow? Will it eventually be "choked to death" by its own growth? Data are available for examining these questions.

It is widely believed that in a big metropolis there can only be a choice between crowding together at high densities or spending an excessive amount of time traveling to work. Actually a reasonable travel radius from a central point takes in an amazing amount of territory. At an overall travel rate of 20 miles per hour, typical for present rush-hour trips from the center to the periphery in the largest American metropolitan areas, a radius of one hour's travel describes a circle with a total area of about 1,250 square miles. No more than 312 square miles would be required to house 10 million people if they lived in single-family houses on 30-by-100-foot lots. Including streets, schools and other neighborhood facilities, the total area needed for residential use would amount to about 500 square miles. Commercial, industrial and other non-residential facilities could be accommodated amply on 150 square miles. There would be left, then, some 600 square miles, almost half of the total area within an hour's distance from the center, for parks, golf courses, forests, farms and lakes.

If the travel speed were increased to 30 miles per hour, quite feasible for both private and public transportation, the area within an hour's distance from the center could accommodate 15 million people in single-family houses on 60-by-100-foot lots, take care of all business uses and leave 1,000 square miles of open land. It may be objected that an hour is an excessive time to spend in travel to work. In practice, however, the radius from the center to the periphery would not represent the traveling distance for most workers. Relatively few would live close to the periphery, and most of these would be working at places near home rather than in the center of the city. In a metropolis of such dimensions only a small minority would have to travel more than 45 minutes to their jobs.

Evidently, then, the modern metropolis does not inherently necessitate either very high residential densities or excessively long journeys to work. The problem in planning it therefore lies in achieving a rational distribution of its components and a suitable organization of transportation facilities to connect the components.

What are the major components of the metropolis? Basically there are four: (1) the central business complex, (2) manufacturing and its allied industries, (3) housing with the attendant services and (4) open land. Let us examine each in turn.

The central area epitomizes the essence of the metropolis: mutual accessibility. It attracts particularly those functions that serve the metropolis as a whole and those that require a considerable amount of close interpersonal contact. The most conspicuous occupant of the center is diversified retail business: large department stores and specialty shops. It is surpassed in importance, however, by the closely interrelated complex of business services that occupy the giant office buildings characteristic of the central area of a metropolis: the headquarters of corporations, financial institutions and public administration and the professionals who serve them, such as lawyers, accountants and organizations engaged in promotion and public relations. Also grouped in the central area with these two categories of services are various supporting establishments, including eating and drinking places, hotels, job printers and many others.

Surprisingly, surveys show that, in spite of the recent proliferation of new office skyscrapers in the center of cities, the size of the working population in the central areas of the largest American metropolises has not actually increased over the past 30 years. Toronto, a smaller and newer metropolis, shows the same constancy in the number of central workers during the past 13 years. The explanation lies simply in the fierce competition for and the rising cost of the limited space in the center; it has caused an outward movement of those functions that can conveniently relocate farther out. Housing in the main moved out long ago; manufacturing and warehousing have tended to follow suit; so has a considerable part of the retail trade, and some of the routine business services that do not require continuous contact with their clients have also moved to less expensive locations away from the center. Modern means of communication have made this spatial separation possible. Moreover, the growth of population and purchasing power in the peripheral areas has provided bases of support there for large shopping centers, including department stores, and for many business and consumer services.

All of this indicates that the central area is undergoing a qualitative change in the direction of concentration on "higher-order" functions and at the same time is maintaining stability in quantitative terms. The forces of the market act to control overcrowding of the center. There is not much basis for the widespread fear that the metropolis will choke itself to death by uncontrolled growth.

As for manufacturing and its satellite activities, the increasing volume of production and changing technology, with a consequent requirement for more space, have made their move out to the periphery of the metropolis imperative. This is true of factories, warehouses, railroad yards, truck terminals, airports, harbor facilities and many other establishments. Three technical factors are at work: the increasing mechanization and automation of production, which calls for more floor area per worker; a switch from the traditional multistory loft building to the one-story plant, which demands more ground area; the new practice of providing open land

around the plant for parking, landscaping and plant expansion. The combined effect of these three factors has been to raise the amount of land per worker in the modern factory as much as 100 times over that occupied by the old loft building.

The next major category of land use in the metropolis—housing—accounts for the largest amount of occupied land. It also presents the greatest ills of the metropolis: slums and segregation of people by income and race.

In all metropolises the low-income families tend to be segregated in the older, high-density areas toward the center of the city. This is not by choice but because they cannot afford the prices or rents of the more spacious new homes in the outer areas. The alarming result of the centrifugal movement of new residences toward the periphery is an increasing segregation of the population by income, which in the U.S. is compounded (and partly obscured) by segregation by race. The situation is more disquieting in the metropolis than it was in the smaller city or town. There, although the poor lived in older, shabbier houses, they at least shared the schools and other public facilities with the higher-income groups. In the metropolis the people living in low-income districts, particularly the housewives and children, never even meet or come to know the rest of their fellow citizens.

Poor families are effectively prevented from moving to new housing in the suburbs not only by economic inability but also by deliberate policies of the suburban governments. Squeezed between rising expenses and inadequate tax resources, these governments have quite understandably used their power of zoning and other controls to keep out housing that does not pay its way in tax revenue. More recently the central cities have adopted policies that have much the same effect. Their programs of slum clearance and redevelopment, financed in the U.S. by the National Housing Act, have failed to replace the housing they have destroyed with sufficient new housing at rents the displaced families can afford [see "The Renewal of Cities," by Nathan Glazer, in *Cities*, Editors of *Scientific American*, eds.]. It should be obvious that housing conditions cannot be improved by decreasing the supply. Half a century ago Geddes observed: "The policy of sweeping clearance should be recognized for what I believe it is: one of the most disastrous and pernicious blunders . . . the large populations thus expelled would be . . . driven into creating worse congestion in other quarters."

Obviously the blight of slums and class segregation can be overcome only by enabling the lower-income groups to live in decent houses in desirable locations, primarily in the expanding peripheral areas, along with the middle and upper classes. The annual cost of such a program in the U.S. has been estimated at $2 billion—a modest sum compared with the amounts alloted to less constructive purposes in the national budget.

The fourth major category of metropolitan land use—open land—consists in North America at present mainly of large tracts held privately for future development. With increasing leisure there is a growing need to turn some of this land to recreational uses. In this connection we should also look at the "metropolitan region," which takes in considerably more area than the metropolis itself.

Donald J. Bogue of the University of Michigan, examining 67 metropolitan centers in the U.S., has shown that the sphere of influence of a large metropolis usually extends out to about 60 to 100 miles from the center. Typically the metropolitan region includes a number of industrial satellite towns that draw on the resources of the metropolis. The metropolis in turn looks outward to the region for various facilities, particularly recreational resorts such as large parks, lakes, summer cottages, camps, motels and lodges. In Sweden, C. F. Ahlberg, head of the Stockholm Regional Plan, has emphasized this role of the region around the capital city by naming it the "Summer Stockholm"—the widened horizon that opens up for Stockholmers when the snows have gone. Metropolises do, of course, have their winter horizons as well, typified by the ski resorts that flourish as satellites within driving distance of many an American city.

Increasingly the outer-fringe metropolitan region is becoming a popular place for retirement for people on pensions or other modest incomes who can live inexpensively in the country without being too far from the amenities of the city. This is an intriguing reversal of the ancient pattern in which the countryside was the locus of productive work and the city was the Mecca for the enjoyment of leisure.

While we are on the subject of the metropolitan region, I should like to clarify the distinction between such a region and a "conurbation" or "megalopolis." The predominant form of the metropolis is mononuclear: it derives its identity from a single center. This is the way metropolitan areas are generally organized in the U.S. and it is the only form they take in a new young settlement such as Australia, where the population is concentrated mainly in five large metropolitan areas, each centered on a single city. In the older countries of Europe, on the other hand, conurbations—metropolitan regions formed by the gradual growing together of neighboring cities—are fairly common. The outstanding examples are the cities of the Ruhr in Germany and the circle of cities that form what is known as "Randstad Holland" (including Amsterdam, Haarlem, Leiden, The Hague, Rotterdam and Utrecht). The Ruhr conurbation grew up around the coal mines. Along the French-Italian Riviera a conurbation now seems to be developing around seashore play.

There seems to be a general disposition to assume that the Boston-to-Washington axis is destined soon to become a new conurbation on a vastly larger scale than any heretofore. The available evidence does not support such a view. Each of the metropolitan areas along the seaboard remains strongly oriented to its own center. The several metropolitan regions are separated by large areas of sparse development. Conurbation can occur only when the crests of the waves of two expanding centers overlap, and except perhaps between Washington and Baltimore that is not likely to happen anywhere in North America during this century.

To get back to the problems of planning for the metropolis: How should the four main components—central business, production, residence and open land—be organized spatially? The aims here can be expressed most clearly in the form of pairs of seemingly contradictory requirements.

First, it is desirable to minimize the need for commuting to work and at the same time maximize the ability to do so. Obviously most people would like to live close to their place of work, but to seek such an arrangement as a general proposition would be unrealistic and too restrictive. It is estimated that half of all metropolitan households contain more than one gainfully employed person, and they are not likely to be employed in the same place. Furthermore, the preferred locations for residence and work do not necessarily match up. The situation in Hudson County, N.J., across the river from Manhattan, offers a striking illustration. In 1960 the county contained 244,000 jobs and 233,000 employed residents—apparently a neat balance. On analysis, however, it turns out that 35 percent of the jobs in the county were held by people who commuted from homes elsewhere, and 32 percent of the workers who lived in the county commuted out to work. Freedom of choice, both of the place to live and of the place to work, will always depend on opportunity to travel from one place to the other.

A second ideal of planning is to provide quick access to the center of the city and also quick access to the open country. Most people have tried to achieve a compromise by moving to the suburbs. The resulting pattern of urban sprawl, however, has made this move self-defeating. The more people move out to the suburbs, the farther they have to move from the city and the farther the country moves away from them.

Third, the functions of the metropolis must be integrated, yet there are also strong reasons to separate them—for example, to separate residences from factories or offices. Isolation of the functions by rigid zoning, however, threatens to break up the metropolis into barren and monotonous precincts. Evidently there is no pat answer to this problem. The optimal grain of mixture will vary with conditions.

Fourth, the social health of the metropolis requires that its people identify themselves both with their own neighborhood or group and with the metropolis as a whole. Since identification with an ingroup often leads to hostility toward outgroups, great emphasis is needed on measures that create interest and pride in the metropolis.

Fifth, the metropolis must strike a balance between continuity and receptiveness to change, between the traditions that give it identity and the flexibility necessary for growth and adaptation to new conditions.

Most of the schemes that have been proposed for shaping the future growth of the metropolis are tacitly based on these criteria, although the requirements have not generally been spelled out in precisely this form. The plans are designed to decentralize the metropolis in some way, with the dual aim of minimizing traffic congestion at the center and bringing the city closer to the countryside.

One proposal is the satellite plan I have already mentioned. In that arrangement each of the satellite towns outside the center is largely self-sufficient and more or less like the others. Another scheme somewhat similar to this is called the "constellation" plan; it would set up several widely separated units each of which would specialize in one function, such as finance, administration, cultural institutions and so on. Still another plan is the "linear" metropolis, several variants of which have been proposed. It would not be oriented toward a single center but would contain a series of them strung in a line. The advocates of this plan are attracted primarily by the possibilities it offers for

easy access to open land and for unlimited expansion. Decentralization was pushed to its ultimate conclusion in the "Broadacre City" plan suggested by Frank Lloyd Wright. He proposed to disperse the activities of the city more or less evenly over the whole metropolitan region. Such a plan would be practicable only if the time and cost of travel were reduced essentially to zero. They may approach but certainly will never reach that condition.

Probably the most realistic of the many proposals is the plan called the "stellar" or "finger" metropolis. It fingers in all directions. Each finger would retain the center and thrust out would be composed of a string of towns and would be comparable to a linear city. The towns in the string would be connected to one another and to the metropolitan center by a rapid-transit line. Between the fingers would be large wedges of open country, which would thus be easily accessible both to the fingers and to the main center. The metropolis would grow by extending the fingers. This outline is the basis of current plans for the future development of Copenhagen and Stockholm and of the "Year 2000" plan for Washington, D.C.

Any plan that seeks to control the growth of the metropolis rather than leaving it to the play of market forces will require the setting up of new forms of control. Because it inevitably entails transfers of value from one piece of land to another, planning of any sort is bound to come into conflict with the existing vested interests of landowners and municipalities. It is obvious, therefore, that the implementation of rational planning would call for: (1) the creation of an overall metropolitan government for the metropolis, (2) public ownership of all or most of the land that is to be developed, (3) tax revenues sufficient to enable the metropolitan government to acquire the land and carry out the public works required for its development, (4) a national housing policy that would eliminate segregation by providing people at all income levels with freedom of choice in the location of their dwellings.

In terms of current American political folklore these are radical measures. Each of them, however, has been carried out in varying forms and to a varying degree by more than one European nation within the framework of democratic capitalism.

In the long run the development of the metropolis is likely to be influenced most powerfully by improvements in transportation and communication and by the increase in leisure time. The first may lead to an expansion of the metropolis that will embrace a whole region. The second, depending on future developments in mankind's social structure and culture, may lead to *panem et circenses* ("bread and circuses") or to *otium cum dignitate* ("leisure with dignity"). Both are possible in the metropolis.

V THE CITY IN TRANSITION

The American city must be studied both chronologically and topically. It is not enough to see the emergence of cities as a whole, or the developing history of specific cities. We must also examine the anatomy of the city, the inner structure that reflects the characteristics of some of the key forces of urbanization that helped to make cities what they are. This chapter is devoted to such topics as social and technological developments, immigration and migration, the urban poor, and the city boss and his machine—topics that constitute some of the crucial growing pains of the city roughly between the Civil War and the New Deal.

In his broad survey of the urban world of the last quarter of the nineteenth century, ranging from impressionistic contrasts of major cities to urban crime, Arthur Schlesinger argues that as the Northern small farm and the Southern plantation were the typical institutions of the pre-Civil War period, urbanization became a "controlling factor" in American life from the 1880's on. To Schlesinger the most striking feature of urbanization was its uneven, ragged tempo, its conspicuous lack of unity and planning. Urbanization presented confounding problems in providing adequate water, sewage, fire-fighting facilities, better streets, and better housing for the poor. The response was pragmatic, experimental, and un-co-ordinated. Americans traveled the road to urban progress "groping in the dark" where the mistakes of today hopefully would be the lessons for tomorrow.

In his discussion of three vital advances in the urban world—transportation, lighting, and communication—Schlesinger suggests a theme that invites more detailed research: a relationship in a democratic society between urbanization and advances in technology.[1] Or to put it another way, how does the city promote a technology that serves the needs, conveniences, and comforts of the urban masses?

1. See Aaron Fleischer, "The Influence of Technology on Urban Forms," *Daedalus* (Winter 1961).

The United States is a nation of immigrants; her cities are populated with people propelled by two other forces of urbanization, the waves of European immigrants and the migration of native Americans. Beginning with the flood of Catholic Irish and Germans in the 1840's, a major turning point in immigration history, significant changes took place in the nature and number of newcomers who came to the United States. More stayed in the cities, fewer were Protestant and middle class, more were of rural peasant stock, desperately poor and often illiterate, especially between 1880 and 1910 when 18 million immigrants, mostly Catholics and Jews, poured in from southern and eastern Europe. Between 1840 and 1920 the immigrant helped to change the character of many American cities: Chicago with her Slavs, Milwaukee with her Germans, San Francisco with her Chinese, New Haven with her Italians, and New York, the most "foreign" city in the world, with her mulligan stew of nationalities. The ethnic clusters of "Little Europes" created an exciting diversity to urban living in language, customs, values, food, entertainment, and the arts. But the city also crystallized the plight of the immigrant: the pain of cutting old ties; the shock of alienation in and adjustment to a strange, new urban world; the hostility, contempt, bigotry, and fear of the "native" American.[2] In effect, a major theme of immigration—the difficulties of assimilation to a new culture—is the subject of the next two selections.

In a chapter from his Pulitzer prize-winning book, *The Uprooted*, Oscar Handlin presents a poignant saga of the immigrant family and its problems of assimilation, which illuminate a larger theme of urban history: the breakdown of the traditional European communal tradition in an American urban environment. According to Handlin, the immigrant brought to the New World a highly structured concept of the family, meaningful for a village community but irrelevant to the conditions of the American city. The vital cohesion of the family, sealed by the social cement of precise authority, obligations, and responsibilities, was shattered. Poverty, the language barrier, the street gang, American values regarding marriage and individualism, dissolved old familial roles and reversed others. The family roots nourished by the village soil lay scattered on the city streets. Parental authority disintegrated and with it respect; cut by shame, misunderstanding, and the hard realities of American urban life, the European heritage was shredded. The family drifted apart, wife from husband, children from parents. Handlin sums it up when he has his immigrant mother look at her family and ask, "Would the strangeness of the setting make strangers also of these her dear ones?"

Handlin does not suggest that it happened to every family, nor that all im-

2. For an analysis of both immigration policy and attitudes toward the immigrant, see John Higham, "Origins of Immigration Restriction, 1882-1897: A Social Analysis," *Mississippi Historical Review* (June 1952), and Barbara Miller Solomon, "The Intellectual Background of the Immigration Restriction Movement in New England," *New England Quarterly* (March 1952).

migrants were poor. But enough were poor to make it a bleak and tragic story.[3]

In the next essay, Nathan Glazer and Daniel Moynihan look at assimilation in a different way; indeed, they challenge it as a process and as a reality insofar as it accounts for one of America's favorite concepts of itself—the notion of the melting pot. For years the popular image of the American as a national group has been seen as the result of a kind of ethnic recipe: add a dash of French and Greek, pinches of Poles and Scandinavians, flavor heavily with English, add generous portions of Irish, Jews, and Italians and you produce a marvelous blend, the American, the tasty homogenous mixture of a variety of ethnic, religious, and national groups. This is a myth, argue Glazer and Moynihan: individuals assimilate, but cultural groups do not assimilate to the point where they produce a "seamless national web." If the metaphor of the cauldron must be used, America may be seen more as a boiling pot than a melting pot.

To fortify their argument, Glazer and Moynihan use as a test case the biggest pot of them all, New York City. They examine the recent history of the four most important subcultures that embrace the ethnic and religious pattern of New York—the Jews, Catholics, Negroes, and Puerto Ricans—and conclude that their differences and divisions rather than their melting are increasing. Their thesis is that American nationality is still brewing; it is not yet "done" and the divisive ingredients of religion and race will for the future make the American city very much a boiling pot.

The next selection shows which cities make the pot boil over and why. Gilbert Osofsky charts the making of Harlem, the nation's largest ghetto, a study of internal migration and the failure of assimilation. During the First World War the travels of the Negro from the South to the big cities in the North constituted one of the great folk wanderings in American history. If the foreign newcomer added the spice of diversity to the American city, so did the Negro as he filled the bleak pockets of the ghettos of Philadelphia, New York, Chicago, Cleveland, and Washington. If the slum of the white immigrant changed during the twentieth century, allowing many to scramble upward to the more affluent ranks of middle-class America, the ghetto of the Negro became more and more the inner city of little or no escape, a fixed eyesore of poverty and despair, a striking contradiction to democratic aspirations.

Osofsky shows that the Manhattan ghetto of today was in fact created by the 1920's. It is the ironic tale of how one of New York's most exclusive residential areas became the city's most depressed area, where one of the main

3. Does disorganization mean disaster for the family? Not necessarily, say some sociologists who argue that if the old bonds were broken, new associations arose to replace them. In effect, the family, like other institutions, responded to social change; change does not necessarily mean total disruption. See Herbert J. Gans's perceptive study of a second-generation Italian community in Boston, *The Urban Villagers* (New York: The Free Press, 1962).

industries was the undertaking business. Of particular interest is his discussion of the split within the Negro community—the cultural antagonisms between the native American Negro and the foreign-born West Indian Negro, which sapped the unity that Harlem needed so desperately during the 1920's.

The Negro was but a minority among the native masses who migrated to the city. What about the untold thousands of farm boys who migrated to the city to help shape the rank and file of the urban working class? Did they "make it" in the big city? How did their experiences compare with those of the foreign newcomer? What did the move cost them in terms of the quality of life and the opportunities they left behind?

These are just some of the questions that Stephan Thernstrom raises in his essay, "Urbanization, Migration, and Social Mobility in Late Nineteenth-Century America," where he quite rightfully argues that historians have tended to deal more with foreign immigration than with the equally important thrust of internal migration.

In a provocative attempt to set the balance straight, Thernstrom becomes a resolute revisionist, flogging cherished notions concerning the migrant, the farm *vs.* the city, the impact of industrialism upon the worker, and the American success story of rags to riches. Thus, the native migrant was no less exploited than the foreign immigrant; the farm was not superior to the city as a way of life nor as a source of opportunity, for the move to the city was "an advance of a kind . . . even the bottom of the urban heap was a step up from the farms they had left behind." Industrialism neither demoralized the urban worker nor made class lines more rigid. And finally, his major thesis: the notion of the wide-open society that permits the humble to become the elite, is largely a myth. In his discussion of three kinds of social mobility, Thernstrom argues that only a precious few entered the tiny room at the top. Those who made it were either the exceptions, like Andrew Carnegie, or the people who began in the room just below, but not in the basement. For most ex-farm urban workers, social mobility meant a rise to the *middle* of the social ladder or a drop to the lower rung. Thernstrom reminds us that mobility is, after all, a movement that can carry you either upward *or downward*, seemingly an obvious point but nonetheless one not always pinpointed by historians. Perhaps Thernstrom's most imaginative insight is his point about the restless, footloose, geographic mobility of the urbanite on the move, especially its effects upon the class consciousness of the urban worker.[4]

Thernstrom repudiates legends about social mobility and the urban working class; Daniel Bell elevates the process of social mobility to a prominent role which, he argues, illuminates much of the history of a particular element of immigrant society—the urban gangster and the rise of organized crime in America.

4. The urban worker was not of course the only constant wanderer. For a discussion of Americans as transients, see Daniel Boorstin's brilliant *The Americans: The National Experience* (New York: Random House, 1965), pp. 49-112.

According to Bell, organized crime is indigenous to American economic, ethnic, and political life. It exists and thrives, not because of an alien conspiratorial import of steely eyed Mafia "bad guys," nor primarily for the motive of gain, but because it serves the function of being a "queer ladder of social mobility" for those who seek status, prestige, and power. Crime is an American way of life because the urban gangster, despite his deviant methods, strives for the same goals as "normal" citizens in an achievement-oriented society, "gettin' ahead and goin' places" up the golden ladder to success and respectability. This, then, is the underlying, unifying drive to three forces that account for the rise of organized crime: the mainspring of gambling and its operators and its consumers, the role of various immigrant groups as leaders of organized crime, and the changing needs of the city political machine.

Like Thernstrom, Bell attacks popular beliefs. He says that no national crime organization exists, call it what you like, the Mafia, the Syndicate, or the Cosa Nostra. The dominance of the Italian-American in organized crime, according to Bell, is but another stage of ethnic succession to leadership. Crime is a means of social mobility for submerged immigrant groups. In the last half of the nineteenth century, leadership was dominated by the Irish, who shared it with east European Jews until the decade of the 1920's, when the Italians began to compete effectively for dominance.

It should be noted, however, that today many of those who are knowledgeable about organized crime would vigorously deny Bell's contention that a national crime organization is a myth. There has been more evidence to the contrary since Bell's essay appeared.[5] Many of those local, state, and federal law-enforcement officials who were skeptical about the "Syndicate" in the 1950's changed their minds in the 1960's—especially the FBI, largely because of the dynamic leadership of Robert F. Kennedy as Attorney General in the Kennedy administration.[6]

5. Bell's essay was published in the *Antioch Review* (Summer 1953) and was expanded in his book, *The End of Ideology,* published in 1960.
6. There is a vast literature on crime varying enormously in quality. Curiously, the professional scholars of the academic community, especially historians, have shown little or no interest in organized crime and its relation to and impact upon American society. They have left the subject largely to journalists and a sprinkling of social scientists and public officials. Perhaps historians feel it is not a "respectable" subject, even though for many years it has been a part of our social, cultural, and political history.
Among the recent studies that would both deny Bell's claim that there is no national crime organization and expand our knowledge about organized crime are: the President's Commission on Law Enforcement and Administration of Justice, *The Cause of Crime in a Free Society* (Washington, D.C.: U.S. Government Printing Office, 1967), and *Task Force Report: Organized Crime, Annotations and Consultants' Papers* (Washington, D.C.: U.S. Government Printing Office, 1967); the two books of Hank Messick, *Syndicate in the Sun* (New York: Macmillan, 1968), and *The Silent Syndicate* (New York: Macmillan, 1967); Alvin Moscow, *Merchants of Heroin* (New York: The Dial Press, 1968); Fred J. Cook, *The Secret Rulers* (New York: Duell, Sloan and Pearce, 1966); Wallace Turner, *Gamblers' Money* (Boston: Houghton Mifflin, 1965); Ed Reid and Ovid Demaris, *The Green Felt Jungle* (New York: Trident Press, 1963); Raymond V. Martin, *Revolt in the Mafia* (New York: Duell, Sloan and Pearce, 1963); Gus Tyler (ed.), *Organized Crime in America* (Ann

Bell's ethnic theory offers fascinating questions for the future. Who among the submerged groups will follow the Italians—the Negroes? the Puerto Ricans? And perhaps for cities in the West and Southwest, the Mexican-American? Or will they have the same trouble in assimilating and achieving social mobility within the criminal community as they have had within the larger society?

Behind any topic involving the urbanization process, be it transportation, commercial developments, housing, or the immigrant, looms the omnipresent factor—politics, defined by Edward C. Banfield as "the management of conflict." And one unique phenomenon of urban politics from the Civil War to the Second World War was the rise and decline of that peculiar American urban institution, the city boss and his political machine.

The city machine is an organization involved in politics as a business, the business of gaining political power by offering services to a number of diverse groups and inducements of power, prestige, and profit to its followers. In his heyday (a generation before World War I), the city boss could "deliver" the votes because the nature of American society permitted him to act as a broker in ethnic, economic, social, and political relations. But when significant social and political changes presented either obstacles or better services and inducements (e.g. the merit system, reforms in voting and registration methods, the rise of the labor union and the welfare state) the machine declined. Whereas the old-fashioned machine of a Richard Crocker in New York or a James Michael Curley in Boston became a thing of the past, some managed to survive by adapting to changing conditions, like the machine of Richard Daley's organization in Chicago and the city machine of Pittsburgh. Others managed to adapt but destroyed themselves through scandal, like the Pendergast machine of Kansas City.[7]

Arbor: University of Michigan Press, 1962); Robert F. Kennedy, *The Enemy Within* (New York: Harper, 1960); Earl Johnson, Jr., "Organized Crime: Challenge to the American Legal System," *Journal of Criminal Law, Criminology and Police Science* (December 1962, and January 1963); Robert T. Anderson, "From Mafia to Cosa Nostra," *American Journal of Sociology* (November 1965); and Daniel P. Moynihan, "The Private Government of Crime," *The Reporter* (July 6, 1961).

7. For an interesting account of how a city machine survived its nineteenth-century heritage and adapted to modern social change by creating new alliances, see Lyle W. Dorsett, *The Pendergast Machine* (New York: Oxford, 1968). Dorsett also disagrees with the long-accepted view that the New Deal destroyed the city machine, as does Bruce Martin Stave in his "The New Deal, the Last Hurrah, and the Building of an Urban Machine: Pittsburgh Committee Men, A Case Study," *Pennsylvania History* (October 1966). Stave, in fact, argues that for Pittsburgh, at least, the New Deal invigorated and strengthened the political machine.

With perception and skill, Zane L. Miller, *Boss Cox's Cincinnati* (New York: Oxford, 1968), correlates the processes of urbanization with the rise of bossism in Cincinnati. Another interesting and recent study of urban politics is that of Theodore J. Lowi, *At the Pleasure of the Mayor* (New York: The Free Press, 1964), who argues that the decline of the machine has not necessarily been beneficial for the city. For an excellent study of the changing twentieth-century urban machine which focusses on the emergence of "transi-

The three concluding essays of this chapter seek to interpret various aspects of the boss of the American city. In the first, Robert Merton demonstrates how sociological insights can enrich the understanding of a historical problem. He asks: How do you account for the rise of the political machine? He answers: By responding to the political needs of a motley clutch of groups whose aspirations and frustrations were not satisfied by the existing agencies of society. Merton sees the machine as an alternative to formal government. Disciplined and centralized in itself, it was an alternative to the decentralized, dispersed, overlapping authority of municipal authority, and, as such, despite its enormous waste and corruption, the city boss and his organization did serve to fulfill important social functions that society would not or could not satisfy. The machine, according to Merton, emerged because it responded especially to three groups: it humanized politics for the "deprived" classes, and through patronage, handouts, and personal relationships, it opened one of the few doors to advancement available to them; through alliances with legitimate and illegitimate business, it functioned to serve the interests of the respectable businessman and the racketeer, both of whom wanted order created out of the chaos of unrestrained competition.

Merton's argument constitutes the so-called functional theory of political behavior, one which Moisei Ostrogorski anticipated and carried forth in more detail in his analysis of how the political machine works. Written in the posh days of the city boss, this essay has withstood the test of more than half a century and remains one of the best general interpretations of the city machine in the literature of political machines.[8] Rejecting two common moral attitudes toward the boss, where the boss is either romanticized as a Robin Hood to the poor or a Robin the Hood to the "better" people, Ostrogorski shows a remarkable objectivity honed by a sharp wit as he examines the machine in all its parts—how it is built; how it operates, especially in the electoral process, the legislative bodies, the courts, the police; how it wins, why it loses; who supports it and why; and the qualities of the boss himself. Particularly astute are his evaluations of the "respectabilities," the middle and upper classes, and their roles in urban politics.

---

tional bosses," a link between the old-fashioned and modern city boss, see Harvey Wheeler, "Yesterday's Robin Hood: The Rise and Fall of Baltimore's Trenton Democratic Club," *American Quarterly* (Winter 1955). For an examination of the modern boss, see David Halberstam, "Daley of Chicago," *Harper's Magazine* (August 1968), and Blanche Blank, "The New Style Boss," *The New Republic* (September 11, 1961). See also Eric L. McKittrick, "The Study of Corruption," *Political Science Quarterly* (December 1957), which is a discussion of the changes in the twentieth-century machine with comments on two of the essays in this chapter, one by Daniel Bell and one by Robert Merton.

8. A Russian-born political scientist, Ostrogorski was a major figure in political sociology and was as well a first-rate historian. Although he was a pioneer in comparative political analysis and one of the most astute foreign students of American political behavior, his major work, published in 1902, was long neglected by both political scientists and historians.

Whereas the two preceding essays were either theoretical or general in scope, the concluding selection centers on a specific political organization, the Tweed Ring of New York, one of the most notorious city machines in American urban history. It is an analysis of a persistent theme in urban politics, the reformer *vs.* the machine, in this case, the reform movement that sought to destroy Boss Tweed and his machine, and one which culminated in one of the most dramatic elections in New York City's history. The author attempts to show how the crusade against the Tweed Ring reflected the attitudes of the reformers toward reform, the machine, corruption, the poor, and urban political institutions, and how their resounding "victory" was actually an ironic defeat.[9]

9. For a brilliant interpretation of the "liberal" mind of the late nineteenth-century reformer, see John G. Sprout, *"The Best Men": Liberal Reformers in the Gilded Age* (New York: Oxford, 1968).

The Urban World

ARTHUR M. SCHLESINGER

The clash of country and city was not a phenomenon peculiar to America. All over the civilized globe the rural regions lay under a cloud—in Great Britain, France, Germany, Russia, Italy, Belgium.[1] The introduction of farm machinery and the opening up of virgin fields in the Argentine and Australia, added to those of the new American West, rendered unprofitable much of the agricultural labor of the Old World, stirred rural conservatism into fierce discontent and enhanced the attractions of the near-by city for the peasant toilers. Everywhere there was an exodus from the soil while the trading and industrial centers waxed by leaps and bounds. Between 1881 and 1891 Prus-

sia added two million to her cities while her countryside barely increased a half million; rural France lost a half million at the same time that her urban places gained well over a million; the rural population of England and Wales declined over two hundred thousand while the towns and cities advanced by three and a quarter million.[2] By 1891 London and Paris had doubled their population of mid-century and Berlin had more than quadrupled hers.

From earliest times the painful, upward march of mankind had beaten a path through the streets of the town. The cities, not the country districts, had been—in Theodore Parker's phrase— "the fireplaces of civilization whence

From Arthur M. Schlesinger, *The Rise of the City, 1878-1898* (New York: Macmillan, 1933), pp. 78-120. Copyright 1933 by The Macmillan Company. Reprinted by permission of the publisher.

light and heat radiated out into the dark cold world." Memphis, Thebes, Nineveh, Babylon, were the great capitals of early civilized man. In Greek and Roman times the city was the state itself. The revival of a vigorous urban life in the eleventh century, along the shores of the Mediterranean and in northern Germany, hastened the breakdown of feudalism and paved the way for the Renaissance and modern times. Unregarded by all but etymologists, the age-long contrast between city and country survives in the very language we speak —that language which townsmen coined with such glib facility. The well-mannered *civis* living in *urbs* was, for that reason, civil and urbane as well as civic and urban; his manner of life was epitomized in the very word, civilization. His rude rural neighbor, on the other hand, was a pagan or a rustic (from the Latin words, *paganus* and *rusticus*, for peasant), a boor (from the Dutch *boer*, a farmer), or a heathen (that is, a dweller on the heaths).

In America in the eighties urbanization for the first time became a controlling factor in national life.[3] Just as the plantation was the typical product of the *antebellum* Southern system and the small farm of the Northern agricultural order, so the city was the supreme achievement of the new industrialism. In its confines were focused all the new economic forces: the vast accumulations of capital, the business and financial institutions, the spreading railway yards, the gaunt smoky mills, the white-collar middle classes, the motley wage-earning population. By the same token the city inevitably became the generating center for social and intellectual progress. To dwell in the midst of great affairs is stimulating and broadening; it is the source of a discontent which, if

not divine, is at least energizing. In a populous urban community like could find like; the person of ability, starved in his rural isolation, might by going there find sympathy, encouragement and that criticism which often refines talent into genius.

Moreover the new social needs created by crowded living stimulated inventors to devise mechanical remedies —appliances for better lighting, for faster communication and transit, for higher buildings—which reacted in a thousand ways on the life of urban folk. Density of population plus wealth concentration also facilitated organized effort for cultivating the life of mind and spirit.[4] In the city were to be found the best schools, the best churches, the best newspapers, and virtually all the bookstores, libraries, art galleries, museums, theaters and opera houses. It is not surprising that the great cultural advances of the time came out of the city, or that its influence should ramify to the farthest countryside.

As the cradle of progress the city, in some manner or other, seemed to favor persons born within its walls over those born on the farm. One investigator, basing his conclusions on *Who's Who in America*, found that towns of eight thousand and more people produced nearly twice as many men of distinction as their numerical importance warranted.[5] A study of the antecedents of leading American scientific men disclosed that a disproportionate number of these were likewise of city birth. "The main factors in producing scientific and other forms of intellectual performance," concluded the investigator, "seem to be density of population, wealth, opportunity, and institutions and social traditions and ideals."[6]

But the heirs of the older American

tradition did not yield the field without a struggle. To them, as to Jefferson, cities were "ulcers on the body politic." In their eyes the city spiritual was offset by the city sinister, civic splendor by civic squalor, urban virtues by urban vices, the city of light by the city of darkness. In politics they sought to preserve or restore their birthright of equality by stoutly belaboring their capitalistic foe embattled in his city fortress; but against the pervasive lure of metropolitan life, felt by their sons and daughters, they could do no better than invent sensational variations of the nursery tale of the country mouse and the city mouse. Urban growth evoked a voluminous literature of bucolic fear, typified by such titles as *The Spider and the Fly; or, Tricks, Traps, and Pitfalls of City Life by One Who Knows* (N.Y., 1873) and J. W. Buel's *Metropolitan Life Unveiled; or the Mysteries and Miseries of America's Great Cities* (St. Louis, 1882). It may be questioned, however, whether such exciting accounts with their smudgy but realistic pictures did more to repel than entice their breathless readers to partake of the life they depicted.

To traveled persons familiar with the distinctive personalities of European centers American cities presented a monotonous sameness. Apart from New York, Boston, Washington, New Orleans and a few other places Bryce believed that "American cities differ from one another only herein, that some of them are built more with brick than with wood, and others more with wood than brick."[7] Most places possessed the same checkerboard arrangement of streets lined with shade trees, the same shops grouped in much the same way, the same middle-class folk hurrying about their business, the same succes-

sion of unsightly telegraph poles, the same hotels with seedy men lounging in the dreary lobbies. Few foreign visitors stopped to think, however, that American cities were the handiwork not of many national states but of a fairly uniform continent-wide culture. If they lacked the colorful variety of ancient European foundations, they also lacked the physical inconveniences and discomforts which picturesqueness was apt to entail. But it could not be gainsaid that a tendency toward standardization, as well as toward higher standards, was one of the fruits of American urban development.

While in the European sense there was no single dominant city in America —no city both metropolis and capital— yet all agreed in according the foremost position to New York. Nowhere else were there such fine buildings, such imposing financial houses, such unusual opportunities for business and recreation. No other place had such an air of rush and bustle, the streets constantly being torn up, dug up or blown up. To New York an unending stream of visitors discovered some pretext to go each year; in it many foreign travelers, going no further, found material for pithy, if ill-informed, comments on the whole American scene. "The streets are narrow," wrote one observer in 1883, "and overshadowed as they are by edifices six or more stories in height, seem to be dwarfed into mere alley-ways."[8] At that time the well-populated district did not extend much beyond Fifty-ninth Street; and Madison Square at the intersection of Broadway and Fifth Avenue had recently supplanted Union Square as the nerve center of New York life. But the period of growth and expansion was at hand. The corporate limits, which before 1874 had not reached beyond Manhattan Island, spread rapidly until in 1898, as Greater New York, they embraced Bronx County, Kings County (Brooklyn), Richmond County (Staten Island), and a portion of Queens County (on Long Island).

As earlier, Broadway was the main artery of New York life, lending itself successively to wholesale trade, newspaper and magazine publishing, retail shopping, hotels and theaters, as it wended its way northward from the Battery. Manhattan's other famous thoroughfare, Fifth Avenue, offered a continuous pageant of "palatial hotels, gorgeous club-houses, brownstone mansions and magnificent churches."[9] Different from most American cities, the finest residences stood side by side without relief of lawn or shrubbery; only on the striking but as yet unfinished Riverside Drive, with its noble view of the Hudson, was architecture assisted by nature. Merchant princes and Wall Street millionaires vied with one another to sustain Fifth Avenue's reputation of being the most splendid thoroughfare in America, "a very alderman among streets." During the 1880's a dark brown tide swept up the avenue. The late A. T. Stewart's marble palace at the corner of Thirty-fourth Street, long a magnet for sightseers, was eclipsed by the newer brownstone mansions of the Vanderbilts and others farther up the avenue, inclosed by forbidding iron fences. In the late afternoon Fifth Avenue churned with "a torrent of equipages, returning from the races or the park: broughams, landaus, clarences, phætons, . . . equestrians in boots and corduroys, slim-waisted equestriennes with blue veils floating from tall silk hats."[10]

Yet New York was a city of contradictions, reminding one visitor of "a lady in ball costume, with diamonds in her ears, and her toes out at her boots."[11] Against the splendors of Fifth Avenue and the show places of the metropolis had to be set the rocky wastes of Shantytown, extending during the 1880's along the East Side from Forty-second to One Hundred and Tenth Street and inhabited by Irish squatters, goats and pigs living promiscuously together. Contrasting with the pillared citadels of wealth in Wall Street was the near-by slum section, a festering spot of poverty and immorality, finding a tawdry outlet for its life in the notorious Bowery.[12]

The New Yorker was already famed for his provincialism: his proud ignorance of the rest of the nation and lofty condescension toward cities of lesser note.[13] Yet foreign tourists found much to interest and detain them in these other centers, and at least one felt a native New Yorker to be "less American than many Westerners born on the banks of the Oder or on the shores of some Scandinavian *fjord*."[14] Boston charmed with the quiet tenor of her life, her atmosphere of intellectuality, her generally English appearance.[15] With the reclamation of the Back Bay, a great engineering project completed in 1881, the city acquired over a hundred acres of filled land which made possible its expansion southward and the development of straight, wide thoroughfares to Copley Square and beyond.

Even more than Boston, Philadelphia impressed her visitors as a city of homes, with row upon row of prim brick houses with white wooden shutters, owned by their occupants. "If there are few notable buildings, there are few slums."[16] In Washington the traveler found America's most beautiful city, "one of the most singularly handsome cities on the globe."[17] Its parks and wide shaped avenues, its spacious vistas, the dazzling white of its public edifices, were reminiscent of great European capitals. In the absence of an army of factory workers the general tone was one of dignified ease in pleasing contrast to the feverish anxiety typical of other cities. "The inhabitants do not rush onward as though they were late for the train . . . or as though the dinner-hour being past they were anxious to appease an irritable wife. . . ."[18]

Farther to the west lay Chicago, "the most American of American cities, and yet the most mongrel," a miracle city risen Phœnix-like from its great fire of 1871.[19] Its business and shopping district, rivaling New York's in high buildings, noise and impressiveness, was fringed by three residential areas: the north side, its broad streets lined with handsome abodes, churches and club houses overlooking the lake; the south side, a newer and hardly less aristocratic section, studded with stately mansions and spacious parks; and the vast west side, more populous than the other two combined, where dwelt the immigrants and laboring folk. Like every other great city, Chicago offered a study in contrasts: squalor matching splendor, municipal boodle contending with civic spirit; the very air now reeking with the foul stench of the stockyards, now fresh-blown from prairie or lake. A "splendid chaos" indeed, causing the roving Kipling to exclaim, "Having seen it, I urgently desire never to see it again."[20]

No better example could be found of what one contemporary called "urban imperialism." The surrounding prairie was for miles laced with railroads, and a large portion of the city and its suburbs was made up of a series of huge stations, car yards, grain elevators, cattle pens and storehouses. As the world's greatest corn, cattle and timber market Chicago completely dominated the Mississippi Valley and, to some degree, the farther West as well. Other places like Milwaukee, Kansas City, Detroit and the Twin Cities rose and flourished largely by its sufferance or favor. Even the older *entrepôts*—Cincinnati, St. Louis, New Orleans—lay under tribute to the Lake city, and Denver and San Francisco were not too remote to escape its influence.[21] Yet these and other cities had their own economic and cultural spheres of influence, and astonished Europeans found in them a level of material comfort typical only of the principal foreign centers.

Certain problems growing out of crowded living conditions vexed all municipalities, differing among them in degree rather than in kind. None was more important in 1878 than that of adequate traffic facilities. Even in the major cities streets were ill paved, if paved at all, and in the business sections were apt to be choked with rushing, jostling humanity. "The visitor is kept dodging, halting and shuffling to avoid the passing throng . . . ," asserted one timid contemporary. "The confusing rattle of 'busses and wagons over the granite pavement in Broadway almost drowns his own thoughts, and if he should desire to cross the street a thousand misgivings will assail him . . . although he sees scores of men and women constantly passing through the moving line of vehicles. . . ."[22] Cobblestones and granite blocks were the favorite paving materials in the East because of their local availability, just as wood blocks were in the Middle West.

But streets so constructed soon wore rough and uneven, and the eighties marked an era of experimentation with more satisfactory types of surfacing.[23] The discovery of natural beds of pitch on the Island of Trinidad directed attention to asphalt, already widely used in Paris and London. When Washington laid four hundred thousand square yards of it between 1878 and 1882, that city set a pace soon followed by Buffalo, Philadelphia and other places. By 1898 the United States possessed nearly thirty million square yards of asphalt paving. The imported material, however, was rivaled by a native product, brick. Charleston, West Virginia, and Bloomington, Illinois, had tried it in the previous decade, but it was not until the mid-eighties that it came into general use, notably in the Middle West. By 1898 Des Moines, Columbus and Cleveland stood first in the proportion of brick paving to population, though Philadelphia with its two million square yards had more than any other one city. In most cities macadam, a much cheaper material, was deemed sufficiently durable for residential and suburban roadways. Smaller towns contented themselves with dirt or gravel.

In the twenty years the streets of America were greatly improved, though the civic conscience did not regard it essential that good streets should be kept clean.[24] By the end of the century Washington and Buffalo had become the best-paved cities in the world while Boston and the borough of Manhattan in New York were not far behind.[25] Chicago remained the Cinderella of great American municipalities, closely rivaled by Baltimore. In 1890 only 629 of Chicago's 2048 miles of streets were paved at all, about half with wood block, the rest with macadam, gravel,

stone block, asphalt, cinders or cobblestones. Despite the civic lift given by the World's Fair of 1893 the situation was but little better at the close of the decade.

Since most large cities were intersected by waterways, the needs of rapidly growing municipalities required an adequate system of bridges. The problem appeared in its most acute form in New York where hordes of people must cross over each day to their places of work on Manhattan Island. After thirteen years in course of construction, a great bridge connecting New York with Brooklyn was completed in 1883. Its designer, John A. Roebling, had died from an injury before the work had more than started, leaving the actual construction to be directed by his son, Colonel Washington A. Roebling, who worked out the details as the enterprise proceeded.[26] All the riveting of steel in the structure was done by hand, pneumatic tools and compressed air being as yet unknown. Falling ill from overwork in December, 1872, Colonel Roebling supervised the operations from a wheel chair on the roof of his home, directing the progress with field glasses as a general might a battle.

When finished, Brooklyn Bridge was the longest suspension bridge in the world. The formal opening on May 24 was attended by President Arthur and his cabinet, the governors of near-by states and many other distinguished persons. The only discordant note in the chorus of rejoicing came from Hibernian New Yorkers who denounced the choice of Queen Victoria's birthday for the grand occasion. Majestic in the sweep of its great cables from tower to tower, the completed structure was over a mile long, with a central river span of nearly sixteen hundred feet and a passageway wide enough for two rail lines, two double carriage lanes and a footpath.

Though the traffic relief was considerable it was not sufficient. Between 1886 and 1889 Washington Bridge was built over the Harlem River, its two great steel arches each over five hundred feet in span, and in 1896 a second bridge, the Williamsburg, was begun to link Brooklyn and New York.[27] Other cities wrestled with the same problem. Thus Pittsburgh built the Seventh Street suspension bridge over the Allegheny River in 1884, Philadelphia completed a cantilever bridge carrying Market Street over the Schuylkill two years later, and Richmond, Indiana, spanned the Ohio River with a suspension bridge in 1889.[28]

Horse cars, omnibuses, cabs and other similar vehicles had suited the needs of simpler days, but the age of the great city called for swifter conveyance. The old "bobtail" cars, modeled on the stagecoach and pulled by horses or mules, did not suffice for moving an enormous mass of people to and from their places of work at about the same hours of the day. Already New York had shown the utility of an overhead railway, four-car trains being drawn by diminutive steam locomotives which scattered oil and live ashes on the heads of unwary pedestrians.[29] In 1878 a second unit, the Sixth Avenue Elevated, extending nearly the length of the island, was added to the original line. The "L" three years later was transporting one hundred and seventy-five thousand passengers daily or, if you prefer, "12,000 tons of human flesh, averaging each person at 140 lbs."[30] Under the spur of faster transit population spread rapidly northward. New lines were projected and built, reaching beyond the Harlem River into the northern suburban districts.[31] Kansas City also elevated some of her tracks in the mid-eighties and Brooklyn built an extensive system the same decade. But Chicago did not open her first line until 1892, and Boston, which meantime had begun to burrow underground, not until 1901.

The slow adoption of the overhead system was due partly to its ugliness and noise, but even more to the initial cost of construction. Of greater popularity in the eighties was the cable car, first contrived by a Scotch immigrant, Andrew S. Hallidie, in 1873 to solve the problem of transit over the hilly streets of San Francisco. The car moved by means of a grappling device which descended from the floor to an endless steel cable moving in a slotted trench between the tracks.[32] After a few years the system was taken over by cities which lacked San Francisco's peculiar need. In 1882 Charles T. Yerkes laid a cable road in Chicago, achieving not only a success for the city but a fortune for himself. Philadelphia followed the next year and New York in 1886. By the mid-nineties Eastern cities had one hundred and fifty-seven miles in operation, the Middle West two hundred and fifty-two, the Far West two hundred and seventeen and the South six.[33]

While the cable system was yet in its heyday, this generation made its most substantial contribution toward solving the problem of urban transit. For many years—at least since 1835—inventors in America and abroad had been working on the idea of an electrical railway. Until the development of a practicable dynamo in the 1870's, however, they had been baffled by the lack of an adequate supply of cheap current. The

1880's saw the launching of trial lines at points as far removed as Boston and Denver,[34] but the credit for the first American electric railway successfully operated for profit over city streets belongs to Lieutenant Frank J. Sprague. In 1887-1888 he installed two and a half miles of track in Richmond, Virginia, the cars securing their current from an overhead trolley wire fed from a central power house.

Its instant success started a veritable revolution in urban transit. Not only were electric-propelled cars fast and comfortable but they were relatively cheap to construct and maintain. Fifty-one cities installed the new system by 1890, and five years later eight hundred and fifty lines were in operation, mostly in the East and Middle West, with a total mileage of ten thousand.[35] Though horse and cable cars lingered on many streets, their doom was sealed. European cities lagged far behind those of America in adopting electric transit. At the close of the century Germany, with a trackage as great as all other European countries combined, possessed only one ninth the mileage of the United States.[36]

Traffic congestion, however, kept even pace with the new facilities for dealing with it. The tangled situation in down-town Boston, whose narrow crooked streets exemplified the old adage that one good turn deserves another, led to the final effort of this generation. Taking a leaf from the experience of London and Budapest, Boston between 1895 and 1897 constructed a subway line a mile and a half long under Tremont Street.[37] It was a notable engineering feat costing the city four and a quarter million dollars. Plans were at once made for extensions, and New York, as was fitting, projected

a much more ambitious tunnel system which, however, did not open to the public until 1904.[38] Except for these last two instances, the varied and heroic endeavors made during these twenty years to clear the city streets were all carried out under private auspices.

Hardly less urgent than the need for better transit was the need for readier communication. In 1878 the recently invented telephone was hardly more than a scientific toy.[39] To use it a person, after briskly turning a crank, screamed into a crude mouthpiece and then, if the satanic screechings and groanings of static permitted, faintly heard the return message. There was no central exchange station, telephone users being directly connected with one another by separate wires. Besides these disadvantages the sheer novelty of Bell's miracle made it unpopular. People felt "a sense of oddity, almost of foolishness," in using the instrument. "The dignity of talking consists in having a listener and there seems a kind of absurdity in addressing a piece of iron. . . ."[40] For a number of years Bell traveled about the country exhibiting his invention. On one such trip he offered Mark Twain stock in the enterprise at twenty-five, but that usually gullible humorist "didn't want it at any price," though before the year was out he put up the first telephone wire in Hartford, Connecticut, connecting his home with the *Courant* office.[41]

As population centers grew, social and business needs caused the telephone to be perfected rapidly and made the public forget its earlier prejudices. An important obstacle to success was removed in 1879 when the Western Union Telegraph Company, which had bitterly fought the Bell group by fair means and foul, came to terms and sold out its own telephone interests to the Bell Company.[42] Had the Western Union been able to invalidate Bell's claims as prior inventor before the courts, it is almost certain that the development of the telephone would have been sacrificed to that of the telegraph and hence its extension greatly retarded. Under the circumstances, however, mechanical improvements quickly ensued.[43] Francis Blake's invention of a carbon transmitter in 1881, an advance over Emile Berliner's and Edison's devices of four years before, greatly improved the carrying qualities of the voice. Two years later another young man, J. J. Carty, exorcised the mysterious noises of the wires by a simple mechanical arrangement known as the metallic-circuit system.

Hardly less important was the contriving of a central switchboard, the work largely of Charles E. Scribner who installed the first commercial board at New Haven, Connecticut, in January, 1878, for the use of twenty-one subscribers.[44] When Scribner followed this in 1885 with the invention of a multiple switchboard, the nerve center of the telephone was complete. At first boys were employed at "central," but being addicted to fighting one another and swearing at their unseen customers, they were soon superseded by girls who thus found a new vocation.[45]

The rapid expansion of the Bell system owed much to the business genius of Theodore N. Vail, general manager of the company from 1878 to 1885. Grandnephew of Stephen Vail, who had built the engines for the first transatlantic steamship, and a cousin of Alfred Vail, who had worked with Morse on the telegraph, young Vail came naturally by his interest in the latest mechanical marvel. He threw himself into the work with boundless enthusiasm, overcoming innumerable obstacles and in the end making the telephone an indispensable adjunct to every business house.[46] By insisting that equipment should be uniform and leased, not sold, to the subscriber, he saved the United States from the chaos which exists in certain other countries, notably France, where each customer buys his own instrument from a selection of about forty different varieties.

In 1880 eighty-five towns had telephone exchanges with nearly fifty thousand subscribers and about thirty-five thousand miles of wire. Ten years later the number of subscribers had grown fivefold and the wire mileage sevenfold.[47] From the first intercity line joining Boston and Lowell in 1879, the reach of the telephone grew constantly greater until by 1892 Boston and New York were talking with Washington, Pittsburgh, Chicago and Milwaukee and a few years later with Omaha.[48] As presidential candidate McKinley sat in his home at Canton, Ohio, and talked with his campaign managers in thirty-eight states. When in 1893 the monopoly held by the Bell Company expired, many independent companies sprang up, especially in the smaller towns of the Middle West where the Bell system had not found it worth while to extend its service.[49]

Nearly eight hundred thousand phones were in use by 1900, one for every ninety-five persons as compared with one for every nine hundred and twenty-three twenty years before; the United States had twice as many telephones as all Europe. In two decades Bell's invention had, from a mechanical curiosity, become a necessity of American life. That it added to the speed of living and the breaking down of personal privacy cannot be doubted. That it helped make the American people the most talkative nation in the world

is likewise clear. On the credit side of
the ledger, however, must be put the
enormous gains resulting from the facili-
tation of social and business intercourse
and from the extension of urban influences into areas of rural isolation.

Largely because of the greater utility
of the telephone the telegraph expanded
slowly during these years. In 1874 Edison had doubled the carrying capacity
of the wires by his invention of quad-
ruplex telegraphy, which allowed two
messages to be sent simultaneously from
opposite ends of the same line.[50] Actual
wire mileage, however, grew but four-
fold between 1878 and 1898. By the
mid-nineties only one telegram per person per year was being sent in the
United States while the people were
using the telephone ten times as much.[51]
The telephone far outstripped its elder
sister even for long-distance use; only
in submarine communication did the
telegraph continue to reign unchallenged. In the closing years of the decade, however, new vistas opened for
it in a field in which it was thought the
telephone could never compete. This
was wireless telegraphy, the invention
in 1896 of Guglielmo Marconi, an Italian engineer. Still in the experimental
stage, the chief use of "wireless" before
the coming of the new century was for
ocean vessels.[52]

Meantime the slower communication
afforded by the postal service had
shown steady improvement as city populations thickened.[53] In 1883 the rate
for single letters was cut from three to
two cents a half-ounce and, two years
later, to two cents an ounce, with a
provision for special-delivery service to
secure swifter transmission. In 1887
free delivery was extended to towns
with as few as ten thousand people, increasing the number of places so served
by one hundred and sixty-nine.[54] The

sale of ordinary postage stamps leaped
from seven hundred and forty-two million in 1878 to nearly two billion in
1888 and to three billion ten years
later.[55] Despite the quickened pace of
American life the post office with its
cheaper rates remained the basic means
of intercommunication, being supplemented by the faster services of the
telephone and telegraph.

Improved lighting was almost as
great a necessity as improved communication, for the new conditions of city
life required something better than the
dim rays shed from gas lamp-posts on
the streets and the yellow glow of kero-
sene lamps or open-flame gas jet indoors. For years inventors in many
countries had been seeking to harness
electricity to the service of illumination,
but success, as in the case of the trolley
car, had to await the development of
the modern dynamo.[56] Though the Russian engineer, Paul Jablochkoff, in 1876
devised an arc lamp which was used
with some success to light the boulevards of Paris, his achievement was
quickly eclipsed by the ingenuity of
Charles F. Brush, a young Ohio engineer, who in 1879 illuminated the public squares of Cleveland, Ohio, by
means of a system which could maintain sixteen arc lamps on a single wire.[57]
The superiority of the new device won
immediate public favor. Soon the his-
sing, sputtering noise of the carbons and
the brilliant glare of the lamp were
familiar sights on American city streets,
San Francisco leading the way by setting up a central power plant the same
year as the Cleveland trial. The Brush
system quickly spread across the Atlantic and presently, too, to the cities
of Japan and China.

Satisfactory as was the arc lamp for
outdoors it proved of little use for interior illumination. For this purpose

some method had to be found of minutely subdividing the electric current so as to produce lights corresponding to gas jets in size and cheapness. Inventors on both sides of the Atlantic labored at the problem;[58] but success came first to Thomas A. Edison, whose wizardry in the domain of electricity was already presaged by his improvements on the telegraph and the telephone. Edison was at this time thirty-two years old, "a pleasant looking man, of average size . . . with dark hair slightly silvered, and wonderfully piercing gray eyes," who was apt to be found "with acid-stained garments, dusty eyebrows, discolored hands and dishevelled hair."[59] Since 1876 he had been conducting his experiments in a great laboratory at Menlo Park, New Jersey; but this establishment had been acquired only after years as a tramp telegrapher and mechanical tinker had led him by devious paths from his native town of Milan, Ohio, to Boston and New York, where his inventions won generous financial backing.

The problem of incandescent lighting quickly reduced itself, in Edison's mind, to finding a suitable filament which, when sealed in a vacuum bulb, would burn more than a few hours.[60] After patiently trying many substances he succeeded in October, 1879, in getting a carbonized cotton thread to last forty-five hours. Soon after, he attained even better results from a bamboo strip torn from a palm-leaf fan. Now began a search of the world for the most suitable fiber. One of his agents made his way to the Malay Peninsula, Burma and south China; others tried Ceylon, India, the West Indies and South America. Out of six thousand specimens Edison found three varieties of bamboo and one of cane exactly suited to his pur-

pose. His incandescent lamp was patented on January 27, 1880. It not only gave a steadier, cooler and brighter light than gas, but he had also solved the problem of switching lamps off without affecting others on the same circuit.[61]

The public gazed with wonder at the new illuminant in Edison's showroom at 65 Fifth Avenue. In 1882 central lighting stations were erected in London and New York. Perhaps no mechanical invention ever spread so swiftly over the world.[62] The new light first entered American homes at the residence of J. Hood Wright in New York; it began to burn in American hotels at the Blue Mountain House in the Adirondacks; it first appeared in a theater when six hundred and fifty bulbs lighted up a performance of Gilbert and Sullivan's opera "Iolanthe" at the Bijou in Boston on December 12, 1882. The number of central electric stations for all purposes—incandescent and arc lighting, traction power, etc.—rose from thirty-eight in 1882 to nearly six hundred in 1888 and to approximately three thousand in 1898.

The greater convenience and safety of incandescent lighting put gas-light producers at a serious disadvantage, but they did what they could to meet the competition by lowering the cost of their product, at the same time improving its quality.[63] Gas made from coal was supplemented in Pennsylvania and other parts of the country by natural gas drawn from underground reservoirs. An even greater advance came in 1875 when T. S. C. Lowe discovered that a successful illuminant could be made at extremely low cost by decomposing steam and mixing it with carbonic acid and other gases. In less than a dozen years one hundred and fifty cities were using water gas, as it was called, and soon it prevailed over the other varieties. The need of achieving a steady white flame comparable to the Edison lamp was also met when Carl Auer von Welsbach of Vienna in 1885 invented a net-like conical mantle which gave forth an intense incandescent light. After the United States patent was granted in 1890, Americans developed a new skill in adjusting the fragile Welsbach mantles without breaking them. The gas-light industry, though steadily losing ground, achieved a new lease of life. Only in the field of heating, however, was it as yet able to breast electricity without fear of failure.

Improved lighting not only dispelled much of the darkness of urban night life but also many of its dangers. By helping erase the difference between day and night it lengthened the working hours for intellectual toilers, made possible continuous operation of factories and, at the same time, gave an enormous stimulus to after-dark amusements and the theater. Better illumination also meant less eye strain, though this advantage may have been offset by the constant temptation to overwork on the part of the studious. The vastly increased productivity of mind and mill in this period owes more than has ever been recognized to the services of Brush, Edison and Welsbach.

Municipalities were less successful in coping with the problem of waste elimination. Since the middle of the century and earlier, places like New York, Boston and Chicago had had public underground conduits for discharging sewage into near-by bodies of water. But their facilities lagged behind the growth of population and most other cities employed village methods of surface-draining their streets and of using private vaults and cesspools for family wastes. In 1877 Philadelphia had eighty-two thousand such vaults and cesspools, Washington fifty-six thousand and Chicago, despite its sewerage system, thirty thousand.[64] Two years later a noted sanitary engineer called proper sewage disposal "the great unanswered question of the day."[65] Its solution involved grave problems of community health, for dense populations made private uncleanliness increasingly a public concern.

In the two decades following, however, sewerage facilities were greatly extended, while important improvements were effected in sewer construction and in methods of ultimate disposal.[66] This last problem was an especially difficult one. Cities with water fronts usually discharged their sewage into sea or river with always a danger of water pollution, especially where there was a tidal backwash; elsewhere filter beds and farm irrigation systems were commonly used. Progress was very uneven. While Boston and Washington spent millions in improving their sewerage works during these years, Philadelphia and St. Louis had at the close of the period little more than half as great a mileage of sewers as of streets, and Baltimore, New Orleans and Mobile continued to rely for drainage mainly on open gutters.[67] The allied problem of garbage disposal was taken care of hardly better.[68] In New York, Boston and other ports such matter was carried in scows and barges several miles out to sea and discharged upon an outgoing tide. A common practice in inland towns was to contract for its collection by farmers who fed it to swine. Since animals so fed were subject to trichinæ, with a consequent danger to meat eaters, after 1885 furnaces began to be introduced, especially in Middle Western cities, for the reduction of garbage by fire.[69]

The growing volume of urban wastes complicated the problem of a potable water system. This generation, however, gave less heed to the quality of the water than to its quantity. Only about six hundred cities had public waterworks in 1878, but in the next two decades their number grew nearly sixfold. At the same time some of the greater cities enlarged their existing facilities.[70] Thus between 1885 and 1892 New York, at a cost of twenty-four million dollars, constructed the New Croton Aqueduct with a carrying capacity of nearly three hundred million gallons a day.

Gradually, however, as a result of European example and the advance of the germ theory of disease, attention was also given to the purity of the water. The Massachusetts board of health in 1886 was granted by law general oversight of all inland waters of the state with power to advise municipal authorities in regard to water supply, sewage disposal and methods of preventing pollution.[71] Within the next few years careful investigations were also made by the state health boards of Connecticut, Minnesota, New Jersey, New York, Ohio and Rhode Island.[72] Cities differed greatly as to the purity of their water supplies, and public-health guardians were not slow in pointing out corresponding differences as to mortality from typhoid fever. Between 1880 and 1890 about half as many people proportionately died of typhoid fever in New York and Boston, where the water was comparatively pure, as in Philadelphia and Chicago, where the supply was con-

taminated.[73] Pollution by sewage and manufacturers' wastes was especially serious in the case of cities drawing their water from rivers or other natural sources.

The activity in developing municipal water plants was in part caused by the greatly increased fire risks which resulted from the crowding together of buildings and the extensive use of electric wiring. This generation was resolved to have no such conflagrations as those of Chicago and Boston in the early seventies.[74] Though they succeeded in this aim, scarcely a year passed without one or more million-dollar fires and the waste of thousands of lives. The estimated total fire losses in 1878 were over sixty-four million dollars. In 1883 they passed permanently beyond the hundred-million-dollar mark and in 1892 and 1893 rose above one hundred and fifty million.[75]

That the situation was no worse was due to the new methods devised for combating the danger. While small towns and the more backward cities still clung to the volunteer system of fire fighting, with sometimes a nucleus of professional firemen, the large places possessed full-time paid departments, though Philadelphia's dated only from 1871 and St. Paul did not have one until ten years later.[76] With more efficient organization appeared improved apparatus and equipment.[77] Swinging harness for hitching the horses to the fire wagons came into use in the seventies, as did also the fire boat, the fire-alarm signal box and the water tower. In the next decade chemical engines were introduced in Chicago, Milwaukee, Springfield, Ohio, and elsewhere. The invention of the Grinnell automatic fire sprinkler in 1877, added to the widening use of fire-resistant building materials—concrete, terra cotta, brick, steel, asbestos—helped further to reduce fire hazards, particularly in factories and office buildings. Though wide differences continued to exist among cities, the fire departments in general compared favorably with those of any other country. Chicago, for example, had twice as many men and horses and half again as many steam fire engines as London, a city three times as populous.

Conditions of lodging varied as widely as types of people and differences in income. For well-to-do transients the great cities offered hotels constantly increasing in number, size and sumptuousness.[78] Already famous in the eighties were such hostelries as the Grand Union, Park Avenue and Murray Hill in New York, the Stratford and the Lafayette in Philadelphia, Young's and the Vendôme in Boston, the Grand Pacific, Palmer House and Auditorium in Chicago, the Brown Palace Hotel in Denver and Baldwin's in San Francisco. Among the new ones in the last decade of the century were the Plaza, Savoy and Waldorf-Astoria in New York, the Jefferson in Richmond, Virginia, and the Raleigh in Washington.

Such hotels, gorgeously decorated and furnished, with a steadily diminishing emphasis on the "steamboat style," made a special appeal with their private baths, electric elevators, electric-call service and other up-to-the-minute conveniences. Though the incessant "tinkle, tinkle, tinkle of the ice-pitcher" proved "positively nauseous" to the British compiler of Baedeker, he otherwise thought well of the American institution and had even a word of praise and commiseration for that "mannerless despot," the hotel clerk.[79] Every large city also had hotels of second and third class or of no class at all, falling as low in New York as lodging places in Chatham Street (now Park Row) and the Bowery where one could secure sleeping space for a few pennies a night.[80] In general, hotels in the South were apt to be poorer than in any other section, while in the West, even in the newer towns, they were unexpectedly good.

If the traveler did not wish to patronize his own hotel dining room, he could usually find in the larger cities excellent restaurants at hand. In Delmonico's at Fifth Avenue and Twenty-sixth Street he could eat the best meals in America, at the highest prices. There important political conferences were held, college societies celebrated their reunions and distinguished foreigners were fêted. The Brunswick and the Brevoort were hardly less fashionable, the former receiving its summer patrons in an attractive garden in the rear. While other centers were not as well served as New York, Chicago boasted of the Richelieu and Kingsley's and the French restaurants in New Orleans—Moreau's, Mme. Venn's, Flêche's, Victor's—were justly famed the country over.

City dwellers who wished to escape the drudgery and responsibility of housekeeping usually lived in boarding houses. With the opening of the Buckingham Hotel in New York in 1877, however, an increasing number of attractive apartment hotels for private families made their appearance. At the same time the swifter means of transit and communication caused a flow of population into suburban districts where shaded streets, ample lawns and neighborly friendliness gave everyday living something of a bucolic flavor. This dispersion was particularly noticeable in the last ten years of the period, far outdistancing the rapid extension of official municipal limits.[81] By the end of the nineties New York's suburbs held over a million people, one third as many as the city proper, while more people actually lived on Boston's outskirts than within her corporate confines. Pittsburgh, Providence and Cincinnati had similarly acquired strong satellite colonies.

In contrast to this agreeable picture must be placed another, that of the living conditions of the less prosperous classes and particularly of the immigrants. Of the great cities of the land Philadelphia and Chicago were least scarred by slums. Boston, Cincinnati, Jersey City and Hartford had badly diseased spots, but the evil was most deeply rooted in New York City, where land rentals were highest and the pressure of immigrants strongest.[82] In all Europe only one city district, in Prague, was half as congested as certain parts of Manhattan. Bad as conditions had been earlier in New York, they became worse in 1879 with the advent of a new type of slum, the "dumb-bell" tenement, so called because of the outline of the floor plan. This became virtually the only kind erected there in the next two decades.

Five or six stories high, the bleak narrow structure ran ninety feet back from the street, being pierced through the center by a stygian hallway less than three feet wide.[83] Each floor was honeycombed with rooms, many without direct light or air and most of them sheltering one or more families. Almost at once such barracks became foul and grimy, infested with vermin and lacking privacy and proper sanitary conveniences. The sunless, ill-smelling air shafts at the sides of the building proved a positive menace during fires by insuring the rapid spread of flames.

In rooms and hallways, on stairs and fire escapes, in the narrow streets, dirty half-clad children roamed at will, imbibing soiled thoughts from their soiled surroundings. The dense slum district bounded by Cherry, Catherine, Hamilton and Market streets was known as "lung block" because of the many deaths from tuberculosis. No wonder such rookeries were nurseries of immorality, drunkenness, disease and crime. The real surprise is, as the state tenement-house commission pointed out in 1900, that so many of the children grew up to be decent, self-respecting citizens.

In 1879 the total number of tenements in New York was estimated at twenty-one thousand, their inhabitants at more than half a million. A census taken in 1888 showed over thirty-two thousand tenements with a population exceeding a million. By 1900 the number of buildings had grown to nearly forty-three thousand and their occupants to over one and a half million.[84] From time to time philanthropic citizens like Ellen Collins and Alfred T. White built model tenements in New York and Brooklyn to demonstrate that decent lodgings for the poor comported with fair profits for the landlord. Organizations like the State Charities Association and the Association for Improving the Condition of the Poor insistently agitated for stricter housing laws. To their aid came a young Danish American, Jacob A. Riis. As police reporter on the *Sun* he had gained a firsthand knowledge of slum conditions, which he used with great literary effect in a series of newspaper and magazine articles beginning in the eighties. His first book, *How the Other Half Lives*, published in 1890, came to Theodore Roosevelt as "an enlightenment and an inspiration for which . . . I could never be too grateful."[85]

Remedial legislation, following the first tenement-house statute of 1867, was passed in 1879, 1887 and 1895.[86] But in spite of the reformers the laws contained loopholes and enforcement was sporadic. The tenement-house commission of 1900 felt that, on the whole, conditions were worse than they had been fifty years before. Yet one year later a comprehensive statute was adopted which showed that the humanitarian energies of this generation had not been spent in vain. The act of 1901 not only insured real housing reform in New York, but prompted other states and municipalities to a fundamental attack on the evil.[87]

The problem of urban lawlessness and crime was deeply rooted in that of the slums. Vile places like "Misery Row," "Poverty Lane" and "Murderers' Alley" were both continuous recruiting grounds for juvenile delinquents and hiding places for criminal bands. Lacking normal outlets for play, the tenement waifs naturally drifted into gangs in which what might have been a laudable spirit of group loyalty was twisted into an ambition to emulate the lawless exploits of their elders. Beginning as beggars, sneak thieves and pickpockets, they graduated all too quickly into the ranks of shoplifters, robbers and thugs.[88] The foreign origin of many of the slum dwellers made this transition all the easier because of prior unfamiliarity with American traditions and laws. In particular, the Irish and Italians contributed more than their proportionate share of the country's prison population, though it was the American-born immigrant children, lacking proper parental guidance and wholesome surroundings, who turned most readily to underworld life.[89] One student of the problem, observing that most of the men, women and children in the jails and penitentiaries he had visited were native-born, concluded: "We have ourselves evolved as cruel and cunning criminals as any that Europe may have foisted upon us."[90]

Other than New York the great criminal centers of the nation were Chicago, Boston, Philadelphia, Pittsburgh, Buffalo, Detroit, Cleveland, Cincinnati, St. Louis and San Francisco.[91] The freemasonry of crookdom made it possible for evildoers to pass quickly from city to city as self-preservation required, or to congregate like birds of prey when crowds gathered for such occasions as the Philadelphia Centennial or the Chicago World's Fair of 1893. In San Francisco lawlessness in the 1880's still possessed a strong frontier flavor, being characterized by the depredations of youthful hoodlums who brandished large knives and six-shooters and did not hesitate to use them.[92] In the older American centers crime for profit had fallen into the hands of professionals who constantly devised new traps for the unwary. Pickpockets, badger-game experts, knock-out-drop artists, green-goods men (who circulated worthless money), bunco steerers (swindlers), gamblers, hold-up men—all these prospered in such a hotbed of evil as New York's Tenderloin, bounded by Twenty-fourth and Fortieth streets and Fifth and Seventh avenues.[93]

In particular, New York was the national base for bank robbers. One band led by George L. Leslie was credited by Chief of Police Walling with being responsible for four fifths of the bank burglaries in America until "Western George's" murder in 1884. His greatest coup was the looting of the Manhattan

Savings Institution in New York on October 27, 1878, to the extent of nearly three million dollars, the result of three years' careful planning.[94] In order to protect the financial district from other similar maraudings Inspector Thomas Byrnes established his famous Dead Line on March 12, 1880, at Fulton Street, south of which a known criminal would be arrested on sight. While not usually of the professional ilk, absconding bank cashiers were perhaps the most elegant culprits of the time, though this form of law breaking became less frequent with the conclusion of extradition arrangements with Canada in 1889. Of the new swindles contrived during these years probably the most successful was the gold brick, introduced into New York in 1880 by Reed Waddell, a native of Springfield, Illinois. In ten years' time he is believed to have made more than two hundred and fifty thousand dollars from the sale of his gilded lead bricks and from green goods.[95]

Organized crime was the special product of the slum districts where such bands as the Hartley Mob, the Molasses Gang, the Dutch Mob, the Potashes and the Stable Gang flourished in the dives along the Bowery and its sordid byways.[96] The Whyos, the most powerful gang of all, had their principal base in Mulberry Bend whence they sallied forth on their missions of pillage and death until their own destruction in the early nineties. Fortunately for the general safety these bands spent a part of their murderous energy in fighting one another.

Criminologists and publicists pointed with alarm to the portentous increase of lawlessness in the United States. A census inquiry disclosed a fifty-per-cent rise in the number of prison inmates from 1880 to 1890.[97] Statistics collected by the *Chicago Tribune* revealed a growth of murders and homicides from 1266 during the year 1881 (24.7 to a million people) to 4290 in 1890 (or 68.5 to the million) and to 7840 in 1898 (or 107.2 to the million).[98] Such figures were all the more startling since most other civilized countries showed a declining homicide rate, the ratio in England and Germany being less than half that of the United States. Students of the subject were agreed in placing the fundamental blame on unhealthy urban growth, unrestricted immigration, the saloon and the maladjusted Negro.[99] In addition, Lombroso pointed to the lingering habits of frontier lawlessness even in the more settled states, the new opportunities for crime afforded by discoveries in chemistry and toxicology, and the evil effects of sensation-mongering newspapers. Another writer stressed the undoubted fact that violence and criminality had come to be regarded "as a sort of natural and inevitable concomitant" of every great labor disturbance.[100]

Yet it seemed to an acute observer like James Bryce that the Americans were at bottom a law-abiding people.[101] Indeed, in the absence of adequate data for earlier periods, it is possible that crime, being mainly concentrated in the cities, had become merely more conspicuous rather than greater in volume. However this may be, all agreed that the evil was accentuated by lax law enforcement. The official guardians of society only too often were in league with the antisocial elements, passively or actively. In most large centers a crook could secure police "protection" provided he agreed to hunt his prey elsewhere or, if operating locally, to share his profits with the authorities.[102] It was the opinion of the widely experienced Josiah Flynt that, from Maine to California, the aim of police departments was merely "to keep a city superficially clean, and to keep everything quiet that is likely to arouse the public to an investigation."[103] Beyond that point they felt no genuine concern.

Yet now and then conditions became intolerable, and official inquests laid bare a state of affairs almost too vile for belief. Such was the outcome of the courageous war against vice waged by the Reverend Charles H. Parkhurst, of the Madison Square Presbyterian Church in New York, with the help of the New York Society for the Prevention of Crime. The ensuing legislative inquiry, conducted in 1894 under Senator Clarence Lexow as chairman, caused the overturn of the Tammany government the following year and the appointment of Theodore Roosevelt to a strenuous administration as main police commissioner.[104] Among other things the Lexow investigation revealed that appointments and promotions in the police force were for sale and that police officials, besides collecting monthly blackmail from gamblers, saloonists and bawdyhouse keepers, exacted percentages of the profits of "street walkers," pickpockets and gun men.[105]

In various states efforts were made from time to time to divorce police administration from corrupt municipal politics, the favorite scheme being to head the city forces with officials appointed by the governor. This plan was tried in cities as widely separated as Boston, Charleston, South Carolina, Cincinnati, Detroit, Minneapolis, Omaha and Denver. But in most cases it resulted merely in transferring political control from one group of self-seeking overlords to another, without real improvement from the standpoint of the public.[106] The judiciary also shared responsibility for the bad conditions. In the opinion of one judge at least, "the greatest cause of the increase of crime is the action of the appellate courts, which . . . make the most strenuous efforts, as a rule, to see not when they can affirm but when they can reverse a case."[107]

Discouraging as was the situation, it was less so than it seemed. Individual police chiefs and officers were noted for their bravery and recitude; and every city now and then, under reform pressure, treated its wrongdoers with Draconian severity. Moreover the path of the wicked was rendered increasingly thorny by by-products of American inventive genius.[108] To overcome the difficulties presented by improvements in vault and safe construction and the constantly spreading use of Yale locks, burglars had to be ever on the alert. Likewise, electricity aided the law-abiding citizen not only by means of better-lighted streets but also through its application to burglar-alarm wiring and to emergency street boxes for summoning police help. The utility of the "rogues' gallery," in limited use since mid-century, was also greatly extended by a free exchange of photographs with other cities; and beginning in 1887 the whole method of identifying criminals was revolutionized by the introduction, first in Illinois, then in Massachusetts and elsewhere, of the Bertillon system of the Paris police, whereby detailed measurements of the culprit's body were taken and recorded.

Unfortunately urban delinquency had its repercussions on the countryside, most notoriously in the case of the "tramp evil," which had first appeared in America in the hard years following 1873.[109] While the return of prosperity after 1878 somewhat diminished the number of such vagrants, habit, uncertainties of work, difficulties of personal adjustment, *Wanderlust* and the ease of stealing rides on the railroads caused many to continue in their old ways. Pitiful caricatures of the restless hardy pioneers of earlier times, these aimless wanderers were freely spawned by the great urban centers, particularly in years of unemployment and industrial conflict like 1885-1886 and 1892-1894.[110] An unofficial tramp census taken in the year 1893 indicated that three out of five were between twenty and fifty years of age, about the same proportion were native-born and trained to skilled trades, five out of six enjoyed good health, and nearly all were literate and unmarried.[111] If, as the investigator estimated, the total number of tramps then in the nation was 45,845, they represented an army larger than Wellington's at Waterloo and their vagabondage involved the withdrawal of a quarter of one per cent of the male population from productive work, not to mention the burdens thrown on the public in the form of alms, police supervision and hospital care.

These nomads developed a manner of living, a culture, peculiar to themselves. A well-marked caste system distinguished between the hobo, forced temporarily "on the road" by lack of work, and the habitual tramp in his ascending social scale from "gay-cat" (tenderfoot) and harmless wanderer to expert criminal.[112] By cabalistic chalk marks on gate posts the elect were informed as to chances for a "hand-out"; a rigid code of ethics governed their conduct toward one another; and an argot, characterized by such expressions as doss (sleep),

elbow (detective), mooch (beg) and shack (brakeman), marked their common speech.[113]

In the 1880's a gang of itinerant criminals, known as the Lake Shore Push, working out of Cleveland, forcibly monopolized the "empties" of the Lake Shore line to the exclusion of other wanderers; and in 1886 bands, numbering a hundred or more, seized trains for temporary use in Mississippi and Tennessee. But, for the most part, tramps went about alone or by twos and threes, their occasional presence and overindulgence in drink increasing the hazards of solitary rural living. Beginning with New Jersey in 1876, a wave of anti-tramp legislation swept over the nation so that by 1893 twenty-one or more states had passed such acts.[114] Varying in severity—from a short jail sentence to public whipping or even (in two Southern states) sale into temporary servitude—these laws varied even more greatly in the degree of their enforcement. Local communities often found it necessary to improvise their own remedies; town authorities in Massachusetts attained the desired object by exacting manual work from vagrants.[115] The nuisance showed no abatement during the life of this generation; there were probably more tramps abroad at the close of the period than at its beginning.[116] Improvement awaited a better adjustment of wages and employment to available labor supply and a less indulgent attitude on the part of railroads toward the unbidden occupants of "side-door Pullmans."[117]

If we consider only the sordid aspects of urban life the American city of the period seems a cancerous growth. But the record as a whole was distinctly creditable to a generation which found itself confronted with the phenomenon of a great population everywhere clotting into towns. No other people had ever met such an emergency so promptly or, on the whole, so successfully. The basic facilities of urban living —transit, lighting and communication —were well taken care of by an outburst of native mechanical genius which helped make these years the Golden Age of Invention. Some places moved forward faster than others, of course, and all lagged in some respects while advancing in others. If the rural spirit of neighborliness was submerged in the anonymity of city life, there developed in its place a spirit of impersonal social responsibility which devoted itself, with varying earnestness and success, to questions of pure water, sewage disposal and decent housing for the poor, sometimes taking the extreme form of municipal ownership. Moreover, what the great cities felt obliged to do under the whip of necessity, smaller towns undertook in a spirit of imitation, so that the new standards affected urban life everywhere. What most impresses the historical student is the lack of unity, balance, planfulness, in the advances that were made. Urban progress was experimental, uneven, often accidental: the people were, as yet, groping in the dark. A later generation, taking stock of the past and profiting by its mistakes, would explore the possibilities of ordered city planning, not only in the interests of material welfare and community health but also with an eye to beautification.[118]

NOTES

1. See the authorities cited by A. F. Weber, *The Growth of Cities in the Nineteenth Century* (Columbia Univ., *Studies*, XI), 210-211 n.
2. Weber, *Growth of Cities*, 46, 68, 73, 82, 84.
3. For a contemporary appreciation of the dynamic rôle of the city, see F. J. Kingsbury, "The Tendency of Men to Live in Cities," *Journ. of Social Sci.*, XXXIII (1895), 1-19.
4. U. S. Commissioner of Education, *Report for 1894-95*, I, 3-8.
5. The names under the first five letters of the alphabet in *Who's Who* for 1908-1909 were analyzed. F. A. Woods, "City Boys versus Country Boys," *Science*, n.s., XXIX, 577-579. For similar conclusions, see S. S. Visher, *Geography of American Notables* (Indiana Univ., *Studies*, XV, no. 79), esp. pt. v; and R. H. Holmes, "A Study in the Origins of Distinguished Living Americans," *Am. Journ. of Sociology*, XXXIV, 670-685. Alfred Odin, *Genèse des Grands Hommes* (Paris, 1895), made a study of over six thousand French men of letters during five centuries and found that the cities produced thirteen times as many in proportion to population as the rural districts.
6. J. M. Cattell, "A Statistical Study of American Men of Science: III. The Distribution of American Men of Science," *Science*, n.s., XXIV, esp. 735.
7. James Bryce, *The American Commonwealth* (London, 1888), III, 621. See also E. Catherine Bates, *A Year in the Great Republic* (London, 1887), I, 248, and Paul Blouët (Max O'Rell, *pseud.*), *A Frenchman in America* (N. Y., 1891), 244-245.
8. Willard Glazier, *Peculiarities of American Cities* (Phila., 1883), 290. On New York, see also Paul de Rousiers, *American Life* (A. J. Herbertson, tr., Paris, 1892), chap. xiii; W. G. Marshall, *Through America* (London, 1881), chap. i; G. J. Holyoake, *Among the Americans* (Chicago, 1881), chap. ii; G. A. Sala, *America Revisited* (London, 1883), I, chaps. ii-vi; S. R. Hole, *A Little Tour in America* (N. Y., 1895), chaps. iv-vi.
9. Glazier, *Peculiarities of American Cities*, 301; J. F. Muirhead, *The Land of Contrasts* (N. Y., 1898), 193-197; H. C. Brown, *In the Golden Nineties* (*Valentine's Manual of Old New York*, XII, Hastings-on-Hudson, 1927), 25-48.
10. Raymond Westbrook, "Open Letters from New York," *Atlantic Mo.*, XLI (1878), 92.
11. Muirhead, *Land of Contrasts*, 193.
12. H. C. Brown, *New York in the Elegant Eighties* (*Valentine's Manual of Old New York*, XI, Hastings-on-Hudson, 1926), 11-16; anon., "Along the Bowery, When Vice Stalked Openly," *Police Gazette*, Nov. 29, 1930.
13. This attitude was one of the certain symptoms of *Newyorkitis*, a malady amusingly described by J. H. Girdner in a small volume so titled (N. Y., 1901).
14. Rousiers, *American Life*, 242.
15. See Emily Faithfull, *Three Visits to America* (Edinburgh, 1884), chap. viii; G. W. Steevens, *The Land of the Dollar* (N. Y., 1897), 50-53; O'Rell, *Frenchman in America*, chaps. xvi-xvii.
16. Steevens, *Land of the Dollar*, 115-116. See also Rousiers, *American Life*, 209-214, and Ephraim Turland, *Notes on a Visit to America* (Manchester, 1877), 21.
17. Muirhead, *Land of Contrasts*, 218. See also H. L. Nelson, "Social Washington," *Atlantic Mo.*,

LII (1883), 818-825; Hole, *Tour in America*, chap. xxi; Poul Blouët (Max O'Rell, *pseud.*) and Jack Allyn, *Jonathan and His Continent* (Madame Paul Blouët, tr., N. Y., 1889), 39-42; A. M. Low, "Washington: the City of Leisure," *Atlantic Mo.*, LXXXVI (1900), 767-778.

18. Hole, *Tour in America*, 246.

19. Steevens, *Land of the Dollar*, 144-145. See also Finlay Dun, *American Farming and Food* (London, 1881), chap. xii; William Archer, *America To-day* (N. Y., 1899), chap. ix; Hole, *Tour in America*, chap. xviii; Marshall, *Through America*, chap. iv; Sala, *America Revisited*, II, chap. ix; C. D. Warner, *Studies in the South and West* (N. Y., 1889), 184-186, 200-201; Glazier, *Peculiarities of American Cities*, chap. ix.

20. Rudyard Kipling, *American Notes* (Boston, 1899), esp. 91.

21. A Chicagoan of these times, being asked his opinion of New York, which he had just visited, replied, "Wal, I guess it's too far away from Chicago to do any partic'lar amount of business!" Marshall, *Through America*, 103.

22. J. W. Buel, *Metropolitan Life Unveiled* (St. Louis, 1882), 26. For similar reactions, see Rousiers, *American Life*, 240; Hole, *Tour in America*, 43-45; Marshall, *Through America*, 7.

23. G. W. Tillson, *Street Pavements and Paving Materials* (N. Y., 1900), chaps. ix-x; N. P. Lewis, "Modern City Roadways," *Pop. Sci. Mo.*, LVI (1899-1900), 524-539.

24. European cities were far ahead in the cleanliness of their streets. Emmons Clark, "Street-Cleaning in Large Cities," *Pop. Sci. Mo.*, XXXVIII (1890-1891), 748-755. However, in 1895-1898, when Colonel Waring was commissioner of street cleaning in New York under the anti-Tammany administration, he actually kept the streets clean and set an example for other American cities. Among other things, he dressed the street sweepers in white, from which the term, "white wings," derives. G. E. Waring, *Street-Cleaning* (N. Y., 1897), chaps. i-v; Charles Zueblin, *American Municipal Progress* (N. Y., 1902), 78-81.

25. J. A. Fairlie, *Municipal Administration* (N. Y., 1901), 234-235.

26. Allan Nevins, *The Emergence of Modern America* (*A History of American Life*, VIII), 80; *N. Y. Times*, May 24, 1883.

27. Anon., "The New East River Bridge," *Scientific Am.*, LXXV (1896), 213, 218.

28. For these and many other examples, see H. G. Tyrrell, *History of Bridge Engineering* (Chicago, 1911), chaps. xii-xiii.

29. Nevins, *Emergence of Modern America*, 82.

30. Marshall, *Through America*, 26. At the formal opening the trip from Trinity Church to Central Park took twenty-two minutes. *N. Y. Tribune*, May 1, 1878.

31. Bureau of the Census, *Street and Electric Railways, 1902* (*Special Rep.*), 36.

32. *Appletons' Annual Cyclopaedia*, XXVI (1886), 122-125, gives a technical description.

33. H. H. Vreeland, "The Street Railways of

America," C. M. Depew, ed., *One Hundred Years of American Commerce* (N. Y., 1895), I, 141-143.

34. By T. A. Edison at Menlo Park, C. J. Van Depoele in Chicago and elsewhere, Leo Daft in Boston and elsewhere, E. M. Bentley and W. H. Knight in Cleveland, J. C. Henry in Kansas City (where the term, trolley, probably originated), S. H. Short in Denver, and by others. Germany really led the way, Berlin having constructed a line in 1867 on the third-rail principle. T. C. Martin, "History and Development of Electric Traction," *Street and Electric Railways, 1902*, 160-167.

35. Anon., "A Retrospect of the Year 1895," *Scientific Am.*, LXXIV (1896), 2; Vreeland, "Street Railways," 144. Steps were also taken to electrify the elevated systems, though New York did not do so until 1901-1903. For an explanation, see Brown, *New York in Elegant Eighties*, 16-17.

36. Fairlie, *Municipal Administration*, 296.

37. *Street and Electric Railways, 1902*, 37-39.

38. J. B. Walker, *Fifty Years of Rapid Transit* (N. Y., 1918), chaps. xii-xiii.

39. Nevins, *Emergence of Modern America*, 88-89; G. M. Shaw, "The Telephone and How It Works," *Pop. Sci. Mo.*, XII (1877-1878), 559-569.

40. Edit., "Some Teachings of the Telephone," *Pop. Sci. Mo.*, XII (1877-1878), 626.

41. He believed it was "the *first* one that was ever used in a private house in the world." A. B. Paine, *Mark Twain* (N. Y., 1912), II, 726.

42. A. B. Paine, *In One Man's Life* (N. Y., 1921), chap. xxiii; Bureau of the Census, *Telephones and Telegraphs, 1902* (*Special Rep.*), 66-67; J. W. Stehman, *The Financial History of the American Telephone and Telegraph Company* (Boston, 1925), 13-18.

43. H. N. Casson, *The History of the Telephone* (Chicago, 1910), 118-125; E. W. Byrn, *The Progress of Invention in the Nineteenth Century* (N. Y., 1900), 82-85; Paine, *One Man's Life*, 161-162.

44. Other exchanges, established the same year, were Meriden, Connecticut, San Francisco, Albany, Chicago, Wilmington, Delaware, St. Louis, Detroit and Philadelphia. Casson, *History of the Telephone*, 143-147; anon., *Things Worth Knowing about the Telephone* (N. Y., 1929), 43.

45. Casson, *History of the Telephone*, 153-155; Katherine M. Schmitt, "I Was Your Old 'Hello' Girl," *Sat. Eve. Post*, CCV, 18 ff. (July 12, 1930).

46. Paine, *One Man's Life*, chaps. xx-xxviii.

47. Anon., "The Telephonic Exchange in the United States," *Nature*, XXIV (1880), 495; *Telephones and Telegraphs, 1902*, 5.

48. Anon., "Progress of the Bell Telephone," *Scientific Am.*, LXX (1894), 250.

49. K. B. Miller, "Merits of Independent and Industrial Telephone Systems," *Engineering Mag.*, XVIII (1900), 550-557; *Telephones and Telegraphs, 1902*, 9-11, 67.

50. F. L. Dyer and T. C. Martin, *Edison* (N. Y., 1910), I, 154-160; *Telephones and Telegraphs, 1902*, 99-105, 115.

51. T. C. Martin, "Electrical Manufacturing Interests," Depew, *American Commerce,* II, 377-378.
52. J. A. Fleming, "Scientific History and Future Uses of Wireless Telegraphy," *N. Am. Rev.,* CLXVIII (1899), 630-640; P. B. Delaney, "The Development of Wireless Telegraphy," *Engineering Mag.,* XVIII (1900), 747-754; Guglielmo Marconi, "Origin and Development of Wireless Telegraphy," *N. Am. Rev.,* CLXVIII (1899), 625-629; anon., "Recent Development of Wireless Telegraphy," *Nature,* LXI (1899), 78.
53. D. C. Roper, *The United States Post Office* (N. Y., 1917), 75, 141-142, 178, 206, 371-372.
54. Eighty-seven cities had free-carrier service in 1877-1878; 358 in 1887-1888; and 688 in 1897-1898. In the same years the number of mail carriers increased from 2275 to 6346 to 13,696. Postmaster-General, *Report for 1900,* 108-109.
55. Postmaster-General, *Report for 1878,* 6; *for 1888-89,* 704; *for 1899,* 30.
56. Bureau of the Census, *Central Electric Light and Power Stations, 1902* (*Special Rep.*), 86-92.
57. Brush has a number of American rivals in the invention of arc lighting. See Henry Schroeder, *History of the Electric Light* (*Smithsonian Miscel. Colls.,* LXXVI, no. 2), 33-41.
58. Notably Swan, Lane-Fox and Crookes in England and Edison, W. E. Sawyer, M. G. Farmer, Edward Weston and H. E. Maxim in the United States. *Central Electric Light and Power Stations, 1902,* 92-94; Schroeder, *Electric Light,* 42.
59. J. B. McClure, ed., *Edison and His Inventions* (Chicago, 1879), 15-16. See also W. H. Bishop, "A Night with Edison," *Scribner's Mo.,* XVII (1878-1879), 88-99, and F. A. Jones, *Thomas Alva Edison* (N. Y., 1908), chaps. i-vii. From 1878 to 1898 inclusive Edison took out 613 patents. Dyer and Martin, *Edison,* II, 947-965.
60. Jones, *Edison,* chap. viii; Schroeder, *Electric Light,* 43-50; Dyer and Martin, *Edison,* I, chaps. xi-xv.
61. By 1894 manufacturers were substituting cellulose for bamboo or vegetable-fiber filaments. The price of globes fell from one dollar or more apiece in the early eighties to eighteen cents in 1900. For these and other improvements, *see Central Electric Light and Power Stations, 1902,* 94-95; Byrn, *Progress of Invention,* 73; Schroeder, *Electric Light,* 50-62, 93-94.
62. Dyer and Martin, *Edison,* chaps. xvi-xvii; *Central Electric Light and Power Stations, 1902,* 7, 106-107.
63. Byrn, *Progress of Invention,* chap. xxvi.
64. Azel Ames, "Removal of Domestic Excreta," Am. Public Health Assoc., *Public Health,* IV (1877), 74.
65. G. E. Waring, "Recent Modifications in Sanitary Drainage," *Atlantic Mo.,* XLIV (1879), 62.
66. G. E. Waring, *Modern Methods of Sewage Disposal* (N. Y., 1894); G. W. Rafter and M. N. Baker, *Sewage Disposal in the United States* (N. Y., 1894).
67. Zueblin, *American Municipal Progress,* 120-126; Fairlie, *Municipal Administration,* 250-251.

68. N. S. Shaler, ed., *The United States of America* (N. Y., 1894), III, 1235-1237; M. N. Baker, *Municipal Engineering and Sanitation* (R. T. Ely, ed., *The Citizen's Library of Economics, Politics, and Sociology;* N. Y., 1901), chap. xx.
69. About ninety cities had installed furnaces by the end of 1898. W. F. Morse, *The Collection and Disposal of Municipal Waste* (N. Y., 1908), 99-116.
70. Zueblin, *American Municipal Progress,* chap. iv.
71. W. T. Sedgwick, "Notable Sanitary Experiments in Massachusetts," *Forum,* XX (1895-1896), 752-756; G. C. Whipple, *State Sanitation* (Cambridge, Mass., 1917), I, 125-128.
72. C. V. Chapin, *Municipal Sanitation in the United States* (Providence, 1901), 298.
73. The death rate per ten thousand inhabitants was: New York 3.36; Boston, 3.5; Chicago 6.25; Philadelphia 6.8. Shaler, *United States,* III, 1230.
74. See Nevins, *Emergence of Modern America,* 84-85.
75. *World Almanac for 1929,* 375. A letter of Dec. 3, 1925, from R. S. Moulton of the National Fire Protection Association, Boston, says: "During the period 1875 to 1900, while there were no large conflagrations, the total amount of the fire loss was larger in proportion to the then national wealth than it is today, being variously estimated at from three to four dollars per thousand dollars of burnable wealth as compared with from one dollar and a half to two dollars today." See also Clifford Thomson, "The Waste by Fire," *Forum,* II (1886-1887), 27-39.
76. Scranton was the only city in the hundred-thousand class which at the close of the century still relied mainly upon call men. Fairlie, *Municipal Administration,* 154-155; Zueblin, *American Municipal Progress,* 65-66.
77. Fairlie, *Municipal Administration,* 152-154; Zueblin, *American Municipal Progress,* 68; Helen Campbell and others, *Darkness and Daylight* (Hartford, 1891), chap. xxvii; P. J. McKeon, *Fire Prevention* (N. Y., 1912), esp. 6-7; C. J. H. Woodbury, "Conflagrations in Cities," Franklin Inst., *Journ.,* CXXXII (1891), 209-223.
78. Hiram Hitchcock, "The Hotels of America," Depew, *American Commerce,* I, 153-155; Alexander Craib, *America and the Americans* (London, 1892), chap. xxvii; Brown, *Golden Nineties,* 311-323.
79. Muirhead, *Land of Contrasts,* 255-257. See also [J. F. Muirhead], *The United States* (Karl Baedeker, ed., *Handbook for Travellers;* 2d rev. edn., Leipsic, 1899), xxvi-xxviii.
80. Over four and a half million cheap lodgings were provided in such houses in the single year 1888 in New York. H. L. Myrick, *The Importance of the Scientific and Practical Study of Crime* (N. Y., 1895), 25; J. A. Riis, *How the Other Half Lives* (N. Y., 1890), chap. viii.
81. *U. S. Thirteenth Census* (1910), I, 73-75; *Street and Electric Railways, 1902,* 26-29; Brown, *New York in Elegant Eighties,* 69-73; A. F.

Weber, "Suburban Annexations," *N. Am. Rev.*, CLXVI (1898), 612-617.

82. R. W. De Forest and Lawrence Veiller, eds., *The Tenement House Problem* (N. Y., 1903), I, 57, 131-170. For the situation earlier, see Nevins, *Emergence of Modern America*, 319-320.

83. A New York invention, the dumb-bell tenement was unknown in any European city. De Forest and Veiller, *Tenement House Problem*, I, 8-14, 100-102; Riis, *How the Other Half Lives*, 18-19.

84. For various estimates, see Riis, *How the Other Half Lives*, 275, 300; De Forest and Veiller, *Tenement House Problem*, I, 5, 37; II, 78.

85. Theodore Roosevelt, *An Autobiography* (N. Y., 1919), 169. Riis's *The Battle with the Slum* (N. Y., 1902) is autobiographical.

86. De Forest and Veiller, *Tenement House Problem*, I, 5, 95-116; II, 207-345.

87. H. U. Faulkner, *The Quest for Social Justice* (*A History of American Life*, XI), 158-159.

88. W. F. Howe and A. H. Hummel, *Danger!* (Buffalo, 1886), chap. iii; Campbell and others, *Darkness and Daylight*, chap. vi; Herbert Asbury, *The Gangs of New York* (N. Y., 1927), 238-246.

89. W. M. F. Round, "Immigration and Crime," *Forum*, VIII (1889-1890), 428-440; S. G. Fisher, "Immigration and Crime," *Pop. Sci. Mo.*, XLIX (1896), 625-630; F. H. Wines, *Report on Crime, Pauperism, and Benevolence in the United States* (*U. S. Eleventh Census*, 1890, XXII), I, 23-43, 131-133.

90. J. F. Willard (Josiah Flynt, *pseud.*), *Notes of an Itinerant Policeman* (Boston, 1900), 10.

91. Flynt, *Notes*, 33.

92. Marshall, *Through America*, 269-272.

93. The very name, Tenderloin, is a product of these turbulent years. Being in 1876 transferred from an obscure precinct to West Thirtieth Street, Police Captain A. S. Williams exclaimed, "I've been having chuck steak ever since I've been on the force, and now I'm going to have a bit of tenderloin." H. L. Mencken, *The American Language* (N. Y., 1919), 163, *n.* 64. Taken up by the newspapers, the term was soon applied to gay, wicked districts in any city.

94. Two of his accomplices were sentenced to long prison terms, but the police could not find enough evidence against Leslie to bring him to trial. G. W. Walling, *Recollections of a New York Chief of Police* (N. Y., 1887), chap. xix; Asbury, *Gangs of New York*, 203-211; T. F. Byrnes, *Professional Criminals of America* (N. Y., 1886), 81-82.

95. Waddell met a violent death in 1895 as a result of a thieves' quarrel. Asbury, *Gangs of New York*, 194-197.

96. Riis, *How the Other Half Lives*, chap. xix; Asbury, *Gangs of New York*, chaps. xi-xii; Howe and Hummel, *Danger!*, chap. ii; Walling, *Recollections*, chap. xxxv; Campbell and others, *Darkness and Daylight*, chap. xxiv.

97. Wines, *Report*, I, 11, 124. In general, crime statistics need to be used with considerable caution because of lack of registration in most states, divergent legal definitions of crime in the United States and abroad, differences in law enforcement as between states and from time to time within the same state, and other similar circumstances.

98. Figures cited in S. S. McClure, "The Increase of Lawlessness in the United States," *McClure's*, XXIV (1904), 168. For the same years suicides numbered 605, 2640 and 5920.

99. See, for example, H. M. Boies, *Prisoners and Paupers* (N. Y., 1893), chaps. i, vi-xi; I. C. Parker, "How to Arrest the Increase of Homicides in America," *N. Am. Rev.*, CLXII (1896), 667-673; W. D. Morrison, *Juvenile Offenders* (N. Y., 1897), esp. chap. ii; Cesare Lombroso, "Why Homicide Has Increased in the United States," *N. Am. Rev.*, CLXV (1897), 641-648; CLXVI (1898), 1-11; James O'Meara, "Concealed Weapons and Crimes," *Overland Mo.*, XVI (1890), 11-16.

100. G. C. Holt, "Lynching and Mobs," *Journ. of Social Sci.*, XXXII (1894), 76-81.

101. Bryce, *American Commonwealth*, III, 312.

102. Flynt, *Notes*, chaps. iv, vi; J. F. Willard (Josiah Flynt, *pseud.*), *The World of Graft* (N. Y., 1901), *passim*.

103. Flynt, *Notes*, 101.

104. C. H. Parkhurst, *Our Fight with Tammany* (N. Y., 1895); Roosevelt, *Autobiography*, chap. vi.

105. One woman who owned a chain of brothels testified that she paid $30,000 annually for protection. For a summary of the findings, see N. Y. State Committee Appointed to Investigate the Police Department of the City of New York, *Report and Proceedings* (Albany, 1895), I, 3-61. The commission paid by criminals in Chicago was ten per cent of their earnings, according to L. W. Moore, a reformed bank robber, in *His Own Story* (Boston, 1892), chap. xl.

106. R. B. Fosdick, *American Police Systems* (N. Y., 1920), 90-102.

107. Parker, "How to Arrest Increase of Homicides," 670.

108. B. P. Eldridge and W. B. Watts, *Our Rival, the Rascal* (Boston, 1896), chap. xviii; *Telephones and Telegraphs, 1902*, 146-148.

109. See Nevins, *Emergence of Modern America*, 301-302.

110. For the marching columns of the jobless in 1894, see D. L. McMurry, *Coxey's Army* (Boston, 1929).

111. J. J. McCook, "A Tramp Census and Its Revelations," *Forum*, XV (1893), 753-766. 1349 tramps were interviewed. Their ages averaged younger than those of tramps in England and Germany. Nearly half of them said they had taken to the road within a week of losing their last real job. Of immigrant elements the Irish were the most prominent, accounting for one fifth of all the tramps.

112. E. L. Bailey (an ex-tramp), "Tramps and Hoboes," *Forum*, XXVI (1898-1899), 217-221; Flynt, *Notes*, 49-53, 118-140; Jack London, *The Road* (N. Y., 1907).

113. J. F. Willard (Josiah Flynt, *pseud.*), *Tramp-*

ing with Tramps (N. Y., 1899), 381-398, contains a glossary with comments. This student of trampdom estimated that at least three thousand distinctive expressions had been in vogue in the previous twenty years. *Cf.* Flynt's glossary in *World of Graft,* 219-221.

114. Samuel Leavitt, "The Tramps and the Law," *Forum,* II (1886-1887), 190-200; McCook, "Tramp Census," 764-765.

115. Committee of the Massachusetts Association of Relief Officers, "Tramps and Wayfarers," Am. Stat. Assoc., *Publs.,* n.s., VII (1900), 74-84—a

report on the practices of 184 Massachusetts towns and cities.

116. Flynt in *Tramping with Tramps,* 304, estimated their number in 1898 as sixty thousand; Bailey's guess in "Tramps and Hoboes," 220, was one hundred thousand.

117. The lenience of the railroads was considered by Flynt a major factor in the situation. See *Tramping with Tramps,* 291-314, 355.

118. See P. W. Slosson, *The Great Crusade and After* (*A History of American Life,* XII), 407-408.

Generations

OSCAR HANDLIN

Sometimes at night she'd wake and turn to feel if he were there. She'd reach the space across to where he lay, sense the reassuring bulk of him. She'd hug the thought. *All else has passed away with our passing from that place. But this will never change. By holy matrimony he has made me wife and mother to his family. That* (fiercely) *we can hold intact.*

In morning's light the certainty was gone. Through the day the fear came that this most intimate part of life would not remain the same. At the stove later she paused while the long spoon in her hand continued its mechanical stirring; she looked in bewilderment at the gathering table. Would the strangeness of the setting make strangers also of these her dear ones? Resolve came back, but confidence not altogether. It would be a desperate battle to hold firm in these relationships, outside

the context that had nurtured them.

The difficulty was that formerly the family had not been a thing in itself, but an integral element of the village community. It had been fixed in a framework of numerous links and knots that held each individual within it in his place. As the functioning unit within the economy it was the means through which bread was produced and consumed. No one could live except as the member of a family.

As the medium for holding and transmitting land, its stability had been vital to social order. Every change in its structure affected the whole community. On the quality of a single marriage depended the welfare of all the brothers and sisters and less directly a widening circle of other persons. The connection with the soil had also been an element in extending these affiliations beyond

From Oscar Handlin, *The Uprooted* (Boston: Little, Brown & Co., 1051), pp. 227-58. Copyright © 1951 by Oscar Handlin. Reprinted by permission of Atlantic-Little, Brown & Co. Oscar Handlin is Charles Warren Professor of History at Harvard University.

the single household to a broad range of other kin tied together by inheritance, of blood and of possible claims to a common patrimony.

The family had therefore never been isolated. Its concerns were those of the entire village. While each home was expected to be the source of its own discipline, the community stood ready with sanctions of its own to make sure that children were obedient, that parents were good, and that relatives were helpful to each other. The network of mutual rights and obligations had thus the support of both an inner and an outer control.

Emigration took the family out of the village. The mere going was disruptive. The struggles of departure and resettlement subjected the household to a severe strain under most trying and most unusual conditions and at the same time deprived it of the counsel and assistance upon which it had traditionally depended. When so many new decisions were to be made, they had to be made alone. That alone distinguished the new family from the old.

In America also the economic unity of the common household enterprise disappeared. The minority who found their way to the farms or who, by their labors, maintained little businesses where wife and children could work along with the father, held on to the former ways. Vestiges of the old order also remained in the sweating homework system; as the father brought back the bundles that would be sewn into shirts or twisted into artificial flowers, the gathered group in the tenement room recaptured the sense of common effort familiar in recollection from the Other Side.

These were, however, but byways in the economy. In the characteristic immigrant employment, the individual was hired as an integer. He was one line in the ledger, one pair of hands on the floor, one pay envelope at the window, with no reference to who was there at home. Ultimately this pattern supplanted all others. Would they continue to take his bidding, to toil in the dim room with him, the one to pocket all, when they could go out to be their own wage earners? There was no point to it. Of what inheritance could he deprive them?

Properly speaking the family no longer had an income; there were only the combined incomes of its members. The larger unit was now a source of weakness rather than of strength. Those who could, broke away; it was madness for a man who was capable of supporting himself to maintain the ties of uncle or cousin when those ties would only draw off a share of his earnings. Those who remembered the old obligations, alas, were generally those more likely to consume than to produce—the aged, the weak, the ill. With these the circumstances, and with no outside force to assign the blame, the extensive family of the Old World disintegrated. *So it is now, a brother stabs his brother, a sister drowns her sister, for profit's sake.*

Steadily the relatives dropped away; the husband, wife, and children were left alone. Where need compelled additions to the income of this narrower household, it was better to take in boarders, tenants, on an impersonal, cash-down basis. The more compelling duties of the old extended family were treacherous here; it was safer by avoiding them to transform the relationship into one of mere occasional sociability.

The bonds to those left at home also disintegrated. There was a piece of land, and if he had not gone away it would have been his; but having gone away he ought not ask that it be sold and money set to him in America. Endless quarreling followed. Or the old folks, staying, bitterly resented the departed son who should have been the staff on which they might lean in age. *You went to make money and you forgot that you left parents; may God and your own children care for you as you for us.*

Is it the loss of income they minded, or the sadness of being abandoned? *We cannot know whether we shall yet speak with you, embrace you, at least once before our death.* It does not matter. The demands are too heavy on both emotions and purse. The old ties gradually are loosened. The family steadily tapers down to the conjugal unit, a father, a mother, and their immediate offspring. The New World has separated them from all the others who would have been one with them in the Old.

Perhaps for that reason she wished so intensely to hold together what was left. From mistress in an extensive household she had become mother of a more intimate group; that hard core she would labor to keep intact.

The early experiences of the new family entity fed her hopes. That they were cut off from all else that was familiar led the members to value each other the more. With whom else could they discuss the memories of the past and the problems of the present? Depending upon each other because there was no one else upon whom they could depend, they drew steadily together.

The very process of migration had been shared. Mostly they had come together, together faced the open road and the close quarters of the steerage. In the long lapse of time between departure and arrival, they were deprived of the busying occupations of the farm, of the comradeship of neighbors, and had for company only one another. The occasion was one for deeper understanding; and long after the final settlement, recollections would come back of the joys and tribulations of the way, come back to unite those who had made the journey together.

The warmth of participation in the enterprise of crossing cheered even those later immigrants who divided for the critical steps, husband first to make a start, wife and children after. Such a separation created problems of its own, but it did not of itself lessen the attachment of the partners to it. Though the ocean lay between, they were joined by the gravity of the common effort.

That is why, as the years passed and they thought back to the first exploratory days in America, it seemed to them that the family had been strongest and purest before its exposure to the new life. As strangers they had known no one. Evening brought them always back together. Excited with discoveries or downcast with disappointments, they communicated to one another the freshness of each occurrence. They knew then they were one like the meager loaf from which they would begin each to slice the sustenance of all. It was a tenement room or a sod hut. But it was home; and those who came to it worn out with wandering acquired for home an enduring devotion.

Only soon, the conditions of their being in the United States would break in upon them. The narrow family would not remain alone together. Individually, its members in going out would make each their own adjustments to the society about them, and coming back would be less alike. Man and woman, boy and girl, they would find for themselves new roles and establish for themselves new relationships. It would happen more quickly in the cities than on the farms where a rural environment extended the family's isolation. But ultimately it would happen everywhere. The woman meditating by the stove would resist it. But already as they took their places her heart chilled to the fear of failure.

Across the long table they confronted each other, the two who were now central to all. It was as if daily they felt the need of a fresh view of the familiar features in the light of the new experiences. In the anxious regards were mingled two questions. Is this the same being united to me those many years ago and now still unchanged? How adequate will this union be to the present demands upon it?

Indeed these were no longer the man and woman joined in wedlock at that distant date; they had never then imagined that such questions might ever arise. Their marriage had not been the product of an individual passion, but a social arrangement under the oversight of the community. She had accepted the obligations of her situation, to be obedient and faithful, to further his health and comfort, to be a good and kindly wife, the crown of her husband's life. He had taken on the responsibilities of the efficient provider who would safeguard her from degrading work, keep want away, and mildly satisfy her will. The union upon which fortune smiled was one blessed with the dignified respect of the partners for their rights and duties.

The day they turned their backs upon the old home, the relationship began to change. At the very outset, the course of the crossing led to troubles. In the long suspended period between departure and arrival, neither he nor she had duties or could expect fixed dues. They were then thrown more together than ever before, but as never before found it difficult to judge one another. The intimacy of shared miseries brought them together, but, as it were, only to be the more conscious of each other's deficiencies. A sorry figure he made, lounging about from day to day with nothing to do; while her derelictions of housewifely obligations were served up in the stale biscuits of every meal.

If migration involved a temporary separation as, after 1880, it often did, the results were more disruptive still. He went away to the sound of the children's crying; and heard it echo through the months apart. In his unaccustomed singleness, he came to miss what before he had taken for granted, the warmth of the woman's presence. *As the fish thirst for water, so I long for you.*

It is hard to know what may happen across that far dividing distance. *Only I beg you write more often.* As the letters fail to appear, for she is not familiar to the pen, worries take their place, and suspicions. Resentful, he asks a friend in the village to inform him of her doings. Does she hold to the home? At the same time the fear will rise lest she be unable to manage. The stock of grain may be too small, the labor in the field too hard. Cautionary advice covers the pages he sends home.

She has the advantage of waiting in a known place in the company of the children. But her double role is burdensome; she cannot be as he was, head of the household. The boys are unruly and, though she gives them some of the broomstick, they are snow to obey. She hires a hand to help in the field, but he is negligent; he has not for her the fear as for a master. Often she thinks of her husband and what a life he must lead there among strangers, his work heavier than a stone, his strength being drained away into a foreign soil. *The day passes in labor but in the evening I long very much and at night I cannot sleep. We can be united in heart and thought but that satisfies me not. Take us or come back; let it be so or so; as it is I exist neither upon ice nor upon water.*

Sometimes the months stretch out and the separateness widens. He sets himself a goal: I will have a thousand rubles and then send for them. But the goal is never attained. Meanwhile he is hardened in his bachelor life and puts off indefinitely the day of reunion. Or she at home grows reluctant. The dread of the new place mounts up in her and feeds off the complaints in his letters. She wishes him back—enough of this America—and when the call comes, procrastinates.

Whatever division, long or short, appeared in the transplantation was not mended in the resettlement. On the farms, the man could resume his place as head of the household enterprise; but the millions who stayed in the cities found their positions drastically altered. She could not think that he was here satisfying his obligations toward the family. No longer the sole or even the main provider, he seemed to her wanting in the most critical duty of all. Why, there were times when she herself or the children earned more than he, times when he sat home idle while they went out to bring home his bread. When he was taken on, it was not at work she understood or could respect. Away at some menial task, she could not regard him as she had that husbandman who had once managed their tiny plot and had brought up her sons to follow in his steps.

Nor could he be satisfied as to her adequacy for the life of the New World.

Deprived of the usual household chores of the garden, the needle, and the loom, she appeared often lethargic; the blood hardly ran in her veins. On the other hand management of the domestic economy under American conditions was frequently beyond her comprehension. When the results were unhappy—disorderly quarters, poor food—it was hard to draw the line between the effects of negligence and the effects of poverty and ignorance. The necessity that drove her to labor for others was the source of resentment, both because it reflected upon his own abilities and because it took her away from her proper job in the home.

Roles once thoroughly defined were now altogether confounded. The two got on under the continual strain of uncertainty as to their place in the family, as to their relationships to each other. And their experience, no longer one for the two, added constantly to that underlying uncertainty.

Sometimes it was he went out to the wide world, learned the language of the country, and grew sophisticated in the ways of the place, while she was confined to the flat and remained ignorant of the rudiments of English. *I at least know where there's an Eighth Street, and a One Hundred and Thirtieth Street with tin works, and an Eighty-fourth Street with a match factory. I know every block around the World Building and the place where the car line stops. But you know no more than if you had just landed.* Sometimes it was she, in service in some other's home, who earlier learned the ways—what food they ate and clothes they wore and how they sat of an evening in the polished sitting room. It was bitter hard to be the satisfying helpmate when one could hardly guess what wants the other had.

As the situation clarified, aspects at first hidden emerged with oppressive distinctness. In the Old World her status had been fixed by a variety of elements —whose daughter she was, what dowry she brought, into what family she married. Let her husband be unfortunate or unskillful or unthrifty, she had still a set place in the village. Here her fate was completely tied up in his success. What she was or had been mattered nothing, only what he could do. Well, it was galling to see what other, lesser women had, to watch their men push their way ahead. The utter dependence on his efforts put an acrimonious tone in her greetings as he came nightly home no better than before.

Nagging demands he could not meet confirmed his own inner doubts about himself. Was not the whole migration the story of his succession of failures? He had been unable to hold on to the land, to direct the family comfortably across the ocean or to establish it securely on this side. He felt respect ebb away and carried about a gnawing shame at his own lack of capacity. Most of all, he resented his loss of authority. Indeed he became accustomed to request, not to order, but knew it was not right it should be so; and he resented his wife's growing dominance over the household. It was a poor state of affairs when the cow showed the way to the ox.

In the secret night when her stirring waked him he did not move. Fatigue pinned him down. Yet sleep would not return. Instead an angry tension crept into his heart. Her body's presence intruded on his consciousness. Limbs rigid, he pushed the thought away; to this demand too he would not respond, by so much had he now lost his manhood.

Clenched eyelids would not keep the moonlight out. Not a beam came down the narrow airshaft; still his sight tingled to the streaks reflected from a distant meadow where they had walked amidst the long grasses, and had been young, eager for the enjoyment of each other to which marriage had opened the way. There had been no strain then; what the community had to that day forbidden, it now welcomed; and these two had been carried along by confidence in the rightness of their acts, by certainty they would each be gratified.

It was coming away that had first added wormwood to the taste. They had lost the benevolent oversight of the village which by its insistence on traditional propriety had answered every how and when. Now the deed required ever a decision; it raised ever some question; and it involved ever some clash of wills, his or hers. By leaving they had created doubts they knew not how to resolve.

He remembered the darkness of successive borrowed beds. In the enforced closeness of boardinghouses and shipboard he had stifled the groping desires. Years later, the confined warmth of many bodies would come back to assault his senses, would bring the painful recollection of urges never satisfied. And in this place that was their own it was rare that wish and opportunity coincided. In the cramped quarters they had been never alone and therefore never really together. Often there was the startling chill of interruption—the uneasy stirring of a child, the banging progress of a neighbor through the ill-lit hall. Always there was the uncertainty of when and how. Even the times when, flushed with the cheap certitude of liquor or with the passing exuberance of some new job, he had asserted his passion, there had followed inevitably an aftermath of regret and doubt. What had really been given and what received in these exchanges?

Perhaps he should not have expected more. He himself knew the dull indifference that came with being often tired. He knew too her deep fear of recurrent childbirth. Not that this was a subject of conversation between them; but it took no words to convey her dismay at each discovery of her condition. But the terms must be accepted, the price paid. Worse would follow the attempt to avoid it; often enough she had heard the stories of such a one, desperate at the approach of an eighth or ninth, who had sought the relief of self-abortion and had found only the painful death of blood poisoning.

Vaguely also they suspected that there were ways of forestalling pregnancy. But the old wives' knowledge did not extend that far; in this matter the midwife was not helpful; and, as for doctors—why, if a woman had thought of them, she would have found it difficult even to frame the terms of her inquiry. The husband had once cautiously sounded out an apothecary, but got only a jocular response: *Better sleep out on the fire escape, Joe.* Besides it all smacked of the illicit and the shameful. The law frowned on it; the priest cautioned against it; and deep inner forebodings conjured up the visions of nature's reprisals for interference with her processes.

There was, therefore, not much joy to their desiring; the shadow of the reckoning was too close. There was no blame. Only, sometimes, as she nursed her discontent, the thought came to her that, if only he had managed better, all would be otherwise. And he, reading the accusations in her eyes, felt the

pangs of a sudden guilt, the acknowledgment of his own inadequacies. At such times, a sullen anger entered the household, lingered unexpressed for days. The mornings when he went to work, he carried off a pained exasperation. Suspicions might come; the scandal of that other's wife, who with the boarder shamed her home, might cross his mind. The memory galled his wounds and, returned that night, edged his answers with acerbity. Peace then departed in an exchange of taunting words, then blows, and sad conciliation.

Some men surrendered. Confronted by intolerable burdens they deserted their families, lost themselves alone somewhere and put thus an end to this striving. Then the fatherless home, adrift, was not long from its foundering.

Mostly however they held together, the man and woman. Yes, partly it was the thought of the children that kept the family whole and partly it was the consciousness that in abandoning each other they would sever every last tie with their own past, diminish thereby their own human identity. Yes, often as they lay there, longing for escape to an undefined freedom, there was no move simply because the effort seemed too great, the means far out of reach.

But it was more than that that curbed the passing wish to flee. But it was more than that that drew them at last to each other. The old fixed order of respect between husband and wife had disappeared as the obligations on which it rested became irrelevant in the New World. Without the protective cover of well-defined roles they faced each other as individuals under the most trying conditions. That was difficult. But then as he looked upon this person who shared his bed and recalled the long way she had come, the sufferings she had borne, his heart went out to her. And then as she sensed the turning of his eyes upon her and thought of the little pleasure all his efforts brought, her heart went out to him.

It was not pity that sealed them in this attachment, but the brief glimmers of comprehension that they shared a life as they shared a bed. They were individuals, separate, two, and had been so since they left the village. But they had been two together. In those moments of recognition they knew they had been partners in a common experience and were now involved in a common situation. Only in each other could these beings find the complete understanding that would alone bring what they so desperately wanted, some reaffirmation of their own human dignity. For warmth they moved toward each other, for the warmth that came from the knowledge that here was consolation. Another knew and understood. That was a precious certainty, where all else was insecure.

About the children they can feel no certainty whatever.

This country is full of children. In the morning their clatter down the staircase fills the house. In the afternoon they occupy the streets. In the evening they pour back into the waiting flat which they quickly distend with the clamor of their ceaseless activity.

The immigrants were by no means strange to the idea of full families. The little ones had always made up a sizable part of the village population. But the spot had not been so taken up with their presence. They had had each their places, where they ought to be and where they ought not to be. They had had each their functions, what they ought to do and what they ought not

to do. They had not been, therefore, so prominent in the sight of their elders.

Perhaps it was because, in these matters as in so much else, the Old World community had been very specific in its definitions of proper behavior. What a parent owed his offspring was clear. The child was to be fed, clothed, and housed decently as befitted the status and the resources of his father. The boys and girls were to be properly brought up, taught the skills necessary for their own adulthood and imbued with the beliefs necessary for continued membership in the community. It was their due at maturity to receive the land or dowry that would permit them to take the rank their ancestors had held; and one was not unduly to be favored at the expense of his brothers and sisters.

The obligations of the young were equally plain. They were to obey their elders and particularly him who stood at the head of the family, him whom they were to approach always in fear and with respect as the source of all authority. They were to assist, to the extent they were able, in the labors of the common enterprise; every age had its appropriate tasks. Even those fully grown but without households of their own were still to work for their parents. The unmarried had strictly speaking no property, no possessions of their own; if they went out to toil for strangers they were expected still to hand over their earnings to the father.

The neat balance of rights and duties was enforced by the village as a whole. Parents delinquent in the support or the discipline of their progeny, children remiss in compliance, could expect the swift censure of the organized opinion of their neighbors. There was no breaking the pattern of these relationships without a complete break with the community. But conversely, separation from the community by emigration would altogether disrupt the relationships of parents and children.

They might suppose it was the same as they strolled to worship on a holiday, Papa, Mama, and the boys and girls, covering the paved walk in a pair of uneven rows. They were wrong. Even then they knew the momentary solidarity would disintegrate before the day was over. They no longer cohered as a family and, as individuals, could scarcely say how they stood to one another.

The divisions created by differences of experience were too great. The older ones, sedately in the rear, had been eight or nine or in their teens in the year of the crossing. They had vivid memories of the Old Country, of the troubles that drove them off, and of the hardships of the journey. They spoke their mother's language and their unaccustomed English bore a heavy accent that united them with their past. Trained under the discipline of the household that had been, they were still ready to accept obligations. Necessity had long since heaped responsibilities upon them; no doubt they had been wage earners since soon after their arrival.

There was impatience in their scrutiny of the younger ones. Before them were two to be watched, scrabbling along without regard for appearances. These had been infants or little more when the migration came; their early childhood had passed under the unsettled conditions of the transition. They had never learned the proper ways at home, and a brief attendance at the public school had confused them so they knew not where they stood. They were clumsy in the speech of both the old

land and the new; their names came from abroad but had already been corrupted into nicknames here. They were neither one thing nor the other.

At the head of the procession toddled the citizens. These more fortunate ones had been born into their environment. They had never known the Old World; they had not shared the experience of coming. They were Americans from the start, had lisped the words in English, and often received names appropriated from the older inhabitants.

It was at such times the parents were fullest of their responsibilities. As they led the way on these occasions they became gravely conscious of a disturbing uncertainty. What if the children should cease to follow, should take it into their heads to march off in some altogether strange direction! It was difficult enough to show them the right ways around the corners of the city blocks; it was infinitely more difficult to show them the right ways around the twisting curves of the new way of life.

As they consider the heaviness of their tasks, the mother and father grow somber. They remember the failures. Their minds go to that one who came to them as if on a visit, then sickened and went away. It occurs to them that they cannot possibly meet their obligations to the children. Not only that the food will hardly go around to nurture all, not only that the mended garments pass from one to another, but that by the act of migration, they, the parents, have destroyed the birthright of their sons and daughters. These boys who should be picking berries or hunting nuts, these girls who should be approaching mastery of the stove, have all been robbed and must endure the present, enter the future without their proper due. To each other, the parents acknowledge the guilt: *Yes, dear, and therefore let us sacrifice ourselves and live only for them. If there is any hope in this world, it is not for us but for them.*

It was easier to bend the neck in readiness than to be certain that the yoke would fit. With bewilderment the immigrants learned that to be willing to sacrifice was not enough, that their children must be also willing to accept the sacrifice; and of that there could be no confidence. The initial dissimilarities of experience widened with time as youngsters ventured out from the home and subjected themselves to influences foreign to their elders. The life of school and the life of street completed the separation between the generations.

If it did nothing else to the child, the school introduced into his life a rival source of authority. The day the little boy hesitantly made his way into the classroom, the image of the teacher began to compete with that of the father. The one like the other laid down a rigid code of behavior, demanded absolute obedience, and stood ready to punish infractions with swift severity. The day the youngster came back to criticize his home (*They say in school that . . .*) his parents knew they would have to struggle for his loyalty.

That was an additional reason why the immigrants labored to create educational institutions of their own; they hoped thereby to minimize the contest. But the parochial schools were expensive and spread very slowly; they accommodated at best only a small fraction of the children. The strong-minded and well-to-do could hold out against the pleas of their offspring who wished to go where everyone else went; mostly the newcomers were compelled by circumstances and by the law to depend on public instruction.

The building itself was familiar enough; this was one of the known landmarks of the neighborhood. The idea of attendance was also familiar; this had happened already to older brothers and friends. And as the lad entered the yard, even sight of the fellows playing or waiting in line had the appearance of familiarity; he recognized some from around his own block, the others were much like himself. The public school was universal, but each nevertheless reflected the quality of the homogeneous residential district within which it was situated. In effect it was Irish or Jewish or German or Polish; the first impression it made on the new scholar was that of the altogether familiar and the altogether expected.

The ringing bell broke the continuity of his life; as he walked up the cast-iron staircase he left the narrow orbit of his home and moved into the limitless world. He stood in the stiff lines and sat motionless in the formal rows of seats. He learned silence and passivity who had never before felt restraints on his actions. He came to conform to rules: there were ways of rising and of sitting, ways to come dressed, ways to leave the room on certain occasions, and ways without words to signal the need. This order would now be his life.

Mostly the boys accede, and the girls too. At least the youngest do. There are truancies, some from their stubborn will, some from their shame at the poverty of clothing, some from necessity that keeps them home or sends them out to work. But mostly they give in and come. There is vaguely an understanding that the school will help them get on; and everyone else goes, so they go along. Besides they fear the law, want no trouble.

Only often, as they sat in the torpid classrooms, their attention wandered from the drone of recitations. Through the windows, gray filmed-over, they could see the bustle of purposeful men. By contrast, the school seemed empty of achievements, empty of the possibility of achievement. For what reason were they thus confined? What could they hope to gain from all this?

They did not ask those questions. They had long ago heard the trite answers. They came in order to grow up good and useful citizens. How would the school help them? By teaching them what was in these books.

Idly the boys fingered the battered volumes from which wisdom was to flow. There was no need to open them; the bold type of their pages was familiar enough from constant drilling. THIS IS JACK. THIS IS JACK'S HOUSE. THIS IS JACK'S DADDY. JACK GOES SHOPPING. JACK GOES TO SCHOOL. ON THE WAY HE MEETS A COW. ON THE WAY HE MEETS A SHEEP. JACK COMES HOME. JACK FALLS ASLEEP.

And surely enough, across the top from page to page the brightly colored pictures show it all. Blue-eyed and blond, Jack himself stares out over the nice white collar and the neatly buttoned jacket. Across the green lawn, from the porch of the pretty yellow house, a miraculously slim mother waves. By the side of a road that dips through the fields of corn, the animals wait, each in turn to extend its greeting. There it all is, real as life.

Except that it is all a lie. There is no Jack, no house, no brightly smiling "Mummy." In the whole room there is not a boy with such a name, with such an appearance. One can walk streets without end and there will be never a glimpse of the yellow clapboards, of the close-cropped grass. Who sleeps like Jack alone in the prim room by the window to be wakened by singing birds? *Good morning, Mr. Robin.* The whole book is false because nothing in it touches on the experience of its readers and no element in their experience creeps into its pages.

Falsity runs through all their books, which all were written to be used by other pupils in other schools; even the arithmetic sets its problems in terms of the rural countryside. Falsity runs through all their education. They learn the songs their mothers never sang. They mouth the words of precepts with no meaning: *A rolling stone gathers no moss. Make hay while the sun shines.* But what stone, what moss, what hay? The time that man appeared to speak from the platform and roused them, he shook with his talk until they cheered the thin line at Bunker Hill, at Plymouth through the snow. *Our fathers' God, to Thee. . . .* Then later they thought, *Whose fathers'?* Again a deception!

They themselves compounded the enormity of the untruth by the inability to give it the lie. From the desk the teacher looked down, a challenge they dared not meet. It was foolhardy of course to question her rightness. What an arsenal was at her command to destroy them! The steel-edged ruler across the knuckles was the least of her weapons. Casually she could twist the knife of ridicule in the soreness of their sensibilities; there was so much in their accent, appearance, and manners that was open to mockery. Without effort she could make them doubt themselves; the contrast of positions was too great. As she snapped shut the closet upon the symbols of her ladyhood within—the white gloves, the rolled-up umbrella, and the sedate hat—she indicated at once the superiority of her own status. There was visible evidence of her correctness in her speech and in her bearing, in her dress, and in the frequent intimations of the quality of her upbringing.

Perhaps a few were touched with sympathy at the condition of their charges. But what these offered was pity, nobler than contempt, but to the children no more acceptable. It was rare indeed to find the dedicated woman whose understanding of her students brought a touch of love into her work. After all, it was not of this they had dreamed in normal school when they had surrendered a part of their girlhood to acquire a profession, that they would devote the rest of their lives to the surveillance of a pack of unwashed ruffians. Mostly the teachers kept their distance, kept flickering the hope that a transfer might take them to a nicer district with nicer pupils from nicer homes. When that hope died, bitterness was born; and there was thereafter more savagery than love in their instruction. To admit the least question of the rightness of what they taught would undermine the whole structure of their self-esteem. So a boy should look and be, so a home, and so a parent. Many a woman, tired with all the years of it, looked out at her "scholars" tumbling into the street, and discovered a hidden crumb of satisfaction in the thought they were not so, nor the homes to which they'd go, nor the parents who'd greet them.

It took no uncommon sagacity to learn it was better not to question the teacher's world. The wise fellow kept his mouth shut and accepted it; he came to believe in a universe, divided as it were into two realms, one for school and one for home, and each with rules and modes of behavior of it own.

Acquiescence was no solution, however. Their lives could not be so divided. As the children of the immigrants grew up, they felt increasingly the compulsion to choose between the one way and the other. For some, the vision of the yellow house was peremptory. The kindness of a teacher, taken with the earnestness of the exceptional good student, may have opened the prospect of attaining it. Or the intense will of the ambitious youngster may have done so. Or the desperate dislike of a repressive home may have made this the only tolerable alternative. In any case, this way involved the complete identification with Jack, and that meant the total rejection of the origins and the background Jack could not have had.

Only a few, however, had the ability or the desire to make the radical break. The much greater number recognized the existence of the world they saw through school, were even willing to acknowledge its superiority, but they were not willing or, perhaps, not able to enter it themselves; their ties with their families were still binding. They developed perforce a kind of life of their own, an intermediary ground from which they could enter when necessary both the life of the school and the life of the home.

The setting generally was the street, where the young were free of oversight and masters of themselves. The boys and girls of an age who played together fell spontaneously into little coteries, for the very acts of play depended upon a sense of community and upon some degree of organization. There could be no games without rules and without subjection to the sanctions that enforced them. The interests of these groups changed as their members matured, from childhood to youth to adolescence to adulthood. But with notable persistence the members held together at least until marriage made them heads of families in their own rights or until they moved out of the neighborhood.

The structure of these organizations was simple, although they were endowed with a certain formality that mirrored the associational forms of the immigrant parents. There was a consciousness of belonging; you were in the gang and that set you off from outsiders. The sense of participation was tied to a specific place, a street or a district that was their own. Within the group each individual had a role which reflected his own capacities and qualities—the leader, the fighter, the buffoon, the clever one. And the whole was held together by a code of loyalty; they were in a common situation, understood one another and felt understood, and found strength in being together. In these matters the young folk followed the behavior and adopted the standards of their elders.

But the boys in the gang had also learned something from the school and from the world it represented. The teacher had told them, and the books, that the end was to get ahead, to make good, to strive so that success might come. They must not repeat the errors of their fathers who had not made good, had not gotten ahead. The consequences of failure were everywhere apparent about them.

They could see the point of such injunctions. Only the hoary aphorisms did not ring true. A penny saved was not in their lives a penny earned; or the best policy. They were not much in demand to fill posts as office boys, so that road to a vice presidency was closed to them; and the runaway carriage of the banker's daughter came rarely into their neighborhood. The atmosphere of the street, where so much of reality was in open view, was not congenial to the ideal of the self-made businessman.

The impulse toward success found expression in terms dictated by the nature of their own group life. In childhood they strove in the competitive play of the alley, games of pursuit and capture, of sides that struggled against each other for a goal. As the boys grew older and their gangs took form, there were fighting forays in the rivalry of block against block; or (and it was not much different), where space permitted, there were savage athletic contests for the winning's sake.

The growth of professionalism gave an enormous impetus to this interest in sports which, after 1880, persisted on through adolescence to adulthood. On the baseball diamond, in the boxing ring, a lad could win fame and fortune. In these arenas, opportunity was free and only ability counted. The tone of one's name, the manners of speech and behavior, antecedents and affiliation were matters of no consequence. The pure capacity to succeed, with no other advantages, would bring the acclaim of the newspapers and wealth beyond the reach of these boys in any other way. The outstanding athletes who actually won such prizes were, of course, few in number. But each had his tremendous following of boys and young men who gained a kind of derivative satisfaction from his achievements and who sought within their own gangs to emulate his exploits. Increasingly the thoughts of the children were preoccupied with the events of the world of sport within which were played out the vivid dramas of American success and failure.

Down by the corner where the older fellows congregated another kind of game held out the excitement of winning and losing. Watching the parades at campaign time, the youngsters looked forward with anticipation to the age when they too might be old enough to carry a banner. Meanwhile on the outskirts of the crowd around the ladder, they heard the orators' stirring periods and yelled the slogans of their partisanship. Its members were not yet voters when the gang was pressed into service, performing the menial jobs that might nevertheless win it the boss's notice. Here too was the possibility of rewards and of public esteem; and here too they need not labor against the liability of their own background.

The pursuit of success might take still another form. On the same corner, or on another much like it, the same boys or others much like them waited to turn the fight within them to riches. The violence of their childish play would grow up into racketeering; there were opportunities in plenty for such efforts.

For some the chance came through politics itself; perhaps they gained a proper "in" through roughing-up intransigent voters near the polls. For others the knock came in connection with gambling, or boxing, or labor organization, or in illicit liquor dealing. In whatever form, the ability to amass force in the gang, the willingness to defy rules the binding quality of which they did not recognize, and the burning desire by whatever means to elevate themselves above their origins, led such young men into organized criminality.

There were still other ways of rising,

the professions, for instance. But sports, of course—the church, the stage, and politics, and the rackets had a larger importance even for the passive mass of the young who never ventured to be more than followers, who married and reconciled themselves to a stolid family life without the hope for success. For in these three endeavors were the closest approximations to the American standards of achievement open to persons like themselves. In no other way could the children of newcomers readily earn the appreciation of the whole society.

In the face of this whole development the immigrants were helpless. They had neither the will nor the ability to turn their offspring into other directions. The nominal authority of the fathers was only halfheartedly used; they were cruelly torn by the conflicting wishes that their sons be like themselves and yet lead better lives than they. Sensing that the school and street would tear the next generation away, the parents knew not how to counteract those forces without injuring their own flesh and blood.

If there was a serious one favored by the teachers who came home to sneer at the family ways, it was clear enough that when he could he would break away, change names, and drop all old connections. Could or should the father therefore stand in the way of his becoming a doctor?

That the brothers ran about all day with a crowd of wild ones was also disquieting. The worried parents could see no sense in the athletics, the infantile antics of grown men playing at ball. The immigrants had a deep fear of the consequences of the use of force in the rackets and an uneasy distrust of politics. But they could not deny that these were the ways to success, that these were the means of gaining the approval of the American onlookers. Even the older folk indeed derived a kind of satisfaction from the fame of men who bore names like their own, as if John L. Sullivan or Honus Wagner or Benny Leonard, somehow, testified to their own acceptance by American society. How could they then hold the youngsters to the traditional ideals of status and propriety?

In truth, the children were more in this world than they the parents. Often it was necessary for the fathers to turn for enlightenment to their sons. *We also keep a paper, but you have read more and studied in school.* The young wore their nativity like a badge that marked their superiority over their immigrant elders. It was this superiority that gave the second generation its role as mediator between the culture of the home and the culture of the wider society in the United States.

Accepting that role, the immigrants nevertheless resented it. It reversed the proper order of things. They could remember how they themselves had feared and respected the father; and they were embittered by their own failure to evoke the same fear and respect from their children. Beyond the loose behavior at the table and in the streets, these parents sensed the tones of ridicule. In their eyes the young Americans were undisciplined and ungrateful, good only at throwing stones and snow at strangers. When the boys and girls were small, it was still possible to curb their rebelliousness; the swift punishment of the strap held them temporarily in line. But as age increased their power, they were not so amenable to authority. As they grew in knowledge and in craftiness, as their earnings rose

above those of the head of the family, they ceased to bow to restraints and would no longer be ordered about.

Adolescence was therefore a time of acute crisis, and particularly for the girls. As infants they had played with their brothers, but already at seven or eight they were excluded from the society of the gang and thereafter had little to do with boys. In girlhood they stayed close to their mothers since the home was to be their place. But even they could not be shut off from the world outside. They went to school or to work, observed the American familiarity of association between men and women, and soon enough revolted against the old restrictions. They learned to dress like others, with petticoats dragging behind to shut out the air and with their waists laced up in corsets so tightly the blood could not flow; and they lost their health—or so it seemed to their elders.

The worry was that they could not be guided by the safe rules of the Old World. They knew too much, boys as well as girls. Coming down Ann Street, they could not help but notice the "jilt shops" open for the dubious satisfaction of the sailors. Sometimes they could earn pennies distributing the cards of the brothels that flourished in their neighborhoods; and it was often years before they got to understand that a hotel could be other than a house of assignation. Why, even at home, through the thin walls, through the open windows, across the narrow courts, came the revealing sights and sounds. It was all familiar enough by the time they were of an age to conduct their own exploratory operations.

Well, such a girl or boy was open to error, by betrayal or by the longing for a withheld joy. Having spent the day in the closeness of the factory, having come back to the dank room where there was no room, it was release they sought and the assertion of themselves as individuals. Everywhere crowds hemmed them in so they had never the feeling of being one, uniquely one and not one of many. And so it might happen once when the sense of inner powers would no longer tolerate constriction, and the still night offered unaccustomed privacy, and there was a yearning for identity—to be a being, to desire and be desired.

Or, it might not happen; and then only the empty wish remained, returning evening after empty evening as the moody hours went by before sleep came.

Here was the ultimate barrier between the generations: they would never understand each other's conception of marriage. Sure, the parents tried to explain the nature of this most crucial step, that this was a means of extending on in time the continuity of the family, that it involved the sacrifice of personality toward some larger end: *From a maiden you will become a married woman, from a free being a slave of your husband and fortune.* The children would not listen. For them, marriage was an act of liberation by which they cast off the family ties and expressed themselves as persons through the power to love.

Nor could the children make their parents understand the longing for individuality. To enter upon such a relationship without consultation with one's elders, to make such decisions on the basis of chance impressions, to undertake this partnership with a stranger of unknown antecedents, was a madness of the reason. To many a saddened father and mother it seemed that their

sons and daughters had moved gross passion to the center of marriage and had thereby obscured the true end of the family, perpetuation of the succession of generations.

Often enough, then, the old couple were left alone. Looking back across the years, they realized they had been incapable of controlling the course of events. Out of the village context and without the support of the community, the family as they had known it had been doomed. Though they clung to the vestige of home and urged their children to hold together, they would never recapture the essential solidarity.

Perhaps sometimes it occurred to them how much of these tribulations they would have avoided if only they had been able to find that farm and there to work united together. They need not have grieved over it. Certainly the immigrants in agriculture did not need to guard their boys and girls against the influences of the street; and there, where the father was still effective head of the household, his authority was not readily questioned. But the parents could no more keep America away in the country than in the city. As the young matured and discovered wills of their own in school and in more frequent worldly contacts, they too were rebellious and refused to be bound.

Indeed, the impact of separation, when it came, was more decisive on the farm. Lacking as rich an associational life as was possible in the urban places, the second generation had not so full a function as mediators between the cultures. The sparseness of settlement, moreover, was more likely to encourage marriage with strangers that cut the children completely off from their parents. Only here and there was an occasional township, closely knit, homogeneous, stubbornly resisting all changes in a declared antagonism to America. There the family might survive a generation in its traditional form because there the family could call on the support of communal sanctions analogous to those of the Old World. Nowhere else could it survive with its roots pulled out of the village soil.

Perhaps they never took the time to make a balance sheet of their lives, those two old ones left alone, never stopped to reckon up how much they had gained and how much lost by coming. But certainly they must occasionally have faced the wry irony of their relationships with their offspring. What hope the early seasons of their years had held was hope of efforts for their children's sake. What dreams they had had were dreams of the family transplanted, that generation after generation would bear witness to the achievement of migration.

In the end, all was tinged with vanity, with success as cruel as failure. Whatever lot their sons had drawn in this new contentious world, the family's oneness would not survive it. It was a sad satisfaction to watch the young advance, knowing that every step forward was a step away from home.

Beyond the Melting Pot

NATHAN GLAZER AND DANIEL P. MOYNIHAN

The idea of the melting pot is as old as the Republic. "I could point out to you a family," wrote the naturalized New Yorker, M-G. Jean de Crèvecoeur, in 1782, "whose grandfather was an Englishman, whose wife was Dutch, whose son married a French woman, and whose present four sons have now four wives of different nations. *He* is an American, who leaving behind him all his ancient prejudices and manners, receives new ones from the new mode of life he has embraced. . . . Here individuals of all nations are melted into a new race of men. . . ."[1] It was an idea close to the heart of the American self-image. But as a century passed, and the number of individuals and nations involved grew, the confidence that they could be fused together waned, and so

From Nathan Glazer and Daniel P. Moynihan, *Beyond the Melting Pot* (Cambridge: The M.I.T. Press, 1963, paperback edition), pp. 288-315, 346-47. Copyright © 1963 by the Massachusetts Institute of Technology and the President and Fellows of Harvard College. Reprinted by permission of the M.I.T. Press, Cambridge, Massachusetts. Nathan Glazer is Professor of Sociology at the University of California, Berkeley. Daniel P. Moynihan is Director of the Joint Center for Urban Studies of the Massachusetts Institute of Technology and Harvard University.

also the conviction that it would be a good thing if they were to be. In 1882 the Chinese were excluded, and the first general immigration law was enacted. In a steady succession thereafter, new and more selective barriers were raised until, by the National Origins Act of 1924, the nation formally adopted the policy of using immigration to reinforce, rather than further to dilute, the racial stock of the early America.

This latter process was well underway, had become in ways inexorable, when Israel Zangwill's play *The Melting Pot* was first performed in 1908. The play (quite a bad one) was an instant success. It ran for months on Broadway; its title was seized upon as a concise evocation of a profoundly significant American fact.

Behold David Quixano, the Russian Jewish immigrant—a "pogrom orphan" —escaped to New York City, exulting in the glory of his new country:

. . . America is God's Crucible, the great Melting Pot where all the races of Europe are melting and reforming! Here you stand, good folk, think I, when I see them at Ellis Island, here you stand in your fifty groups with your fifty languages and histories, and your fifty blood hatreds and rivalries, but you won't be long like that brothers, for these are the fires of God you've come to— these are the fires of God. A fig for your feuds and vendettas! German and Frenchman, Irishman and Englishman, Jews and Russians—into the Crucible with you all! God is making the American.

❋ ❋ ❋

. . . The real American has not yet arrived. He is only in the Crucible, I tell you—he will be the fusion of all the races, the coming superman.[2]

Yet looking back, it is possible to speculate that the response to *The Melting Pot* was as much one of relief as of affirmation: more a matter of reassur-ance that what had already taken place would turn out all right, rather than encouragement to carry on in the same direction.

Zangwill's hero throws himself into the amalgam process with the utmost energy; by curtainfall he has written his American symphony and won his Muscovite aristocrat: almost all concerned have been reconciled to the homogeneous future. Yet the play seems but little involved with American reality. It is a drama about Jewish separatism and Russian anti-Semitism, with a German concertmaster and an Irish maid thrown in for comic relief. Both protagonists are New Model Europeans of the time. Free thinkers and revolutionaries, it was doubtless in the power of such to merge. But neither of these doctrines was dominant among the ethnic groups of New York City in the 1900's, and in significant ways this became less so as time passed. Individuals, in very considerable numbers to be sure, broke out of their mold, but the groups remained. The experience of Zangwill's hero and heroine was *not* general. The point about the melting pot is that it did not happen.

Significantly, Zangwill was himself much involved in one of the more significant deterrents to the melting pot process. He was a Zionist. He gave more and more of his energy to this cause as time passed, and retreated from his earlier position on racial and religious mixture. Only eight years after the opening of *The Melting Pot* he was writing "It was vain for Paul to declare that there should be neither Jew nor Greek. Nature will return even if driven out with a pitchfork, still more if driven out with a dogma."[3]

We may argue whether it was "nature" that returned to frustrate continually the imminent creation of a single American nationality. The fact is that in every generation, throughout the history of the American republic, the merging of the varying streams of population differentiated from one another by origin, religion, outlook has seemed to lie just ahead—a generation, perhaps, in the future. This continual deferral of the final smelting of the different ingredients (or at least the different white ingredients) into a seamless national web as is to be found in the major national states of Europe suggests that we must search for some systematic and general causes for this American pattern of subnationalities; that it is not the temporary upsetting inflow of new and unassimilated immigrants that creates a pattern of ethnic groups within the nation, but rather some central tendency in the national ethos which structures people, whether those coming in afresh or the descendants of those who have been here for generations, into groups of different status and character.

It is striking that in 1963, almost forty years after mass immigration from Europe to this country ended, the ethnic pattern is still so strong in New York City. It is true we can point to specific causes that have served to maintain the pattern. But we know that it was not created by the great new migrations of Southern Negroes and Puerto Ricans into the city; nor by the "new" immigration, which added the great communities of East European Jews and Italians to the city; it was not even created by the great migration of Irish and Germans in the 1840's. Even in the 1830's, while the migration from Europe was still mild, and still consisted for the most part of English-speaking groups, one still finds in the politics of New York State, and of the city, the strong

impress of group differentiation. In a fascinating study of the politics of the Jacksonian period in New York State, Lee Benson concludes: "At least since the 1820's, when manhood suffrage became widespread, ethnic and religious differences have tended to be *relatively* the most widespread sources of political differences."[4]

There were ways of making distinctions among Welshmen and Englishmen, Yorkers and New Englanders, long before people speaking strange tongues and practicing strange religions came upon the scene. The group-forming characteristics of American social life—more concretely, the general expectation among those of new and old groups that group membership is significant and formative for opinion and behavior —are as old as the city. The tendency is fixed deep in American life generally; the specific pattern of ethnic differentiation, however, in every generation is created by specific events.

We can distinguish four major events or processes that have structured this pattern in New York during the past generation and whose effects will remain to maintain this pattern for some time to come—to be replaced by others we can scarcely now discern. These four formative events are the following:

First, the shaping of the Jewish community under the impact of the Nazi persecution of the Jews in Europe and the establishment of the state of Israel; second, the parallel, if less marked, shaping of a Catholic community by the reemergence of the Catholic school controversy; third, the migration of Southern Negroes to New York following World War I and continuing through the fifties; fourth, the influx of Puerto Ricans during the fifteen years following World War II.

THE JEWS

Developments within the Jewish community have had the most immediate significance. A fourth of the city is Jewish; very much more than a fourth of its wealth, energy, talent, and style is derived from the Jews. Over the past thirty years this community has undergone profound emotional experiences, centered almost entirely on the fact of Jewishness, has been measurably strengthened by immigration, and has become involved in vast Zionist enterprises, the rationale of which is exclusively Jewish. There are two aspects of these developments as they affect melting pot tendencies, one negative, the other positive.

The negative aspect has prevented a change that might otherwise have occurred. Prior to the 1930's Jews contributed significantly to the ethnic pattern of New York politics by virtue of their radicalism. This kept them apart from the Catholic establishment in the Democratic party and the Protestant regime within the Republican party but did give them a distinct role of their own. At the time of *The Melting Pot* there were, to be sure, a great many Democratic and Republican Jewish merchants and businessmen. Most East Side Jews probably voted the Tammany ticket. But indigenous Jewish politics, the politics of the *Jewish Daily Forward*, of the Workmen's Circle, and the needle-trades unions were predominantly socialist. The Russian Revolution, in which Russian Jews played a prominent role, had a strong attraction for a small but important number of their kinsmen in New York. It would appear, for example, that during the 1930's most Communist party members in New York City were Jewish.[5] It must be stressed that the vast majority of New York Jews had nothing whatever to do with Communism. Some of the strongest centers of anti-Communist activity were and are to be found within the New York Jewish community. Nonetheless there was an ethnic cast to this form of political radicalism in New York, as there had been to the earlier Socialist movement.

Both Socialism and Communism are now considerably diminished and both have lost almost entirely any ethnic base. But just at the moment when the last distinctly Jewish political activity might have disappeared, a transcendent Jewish political interest was created by the ghastly persecutions of the Nazis, the vast dislocations of World War II, and the establishment of the State of Israel. These were matters that no Jew or Christian could ignore. They were equally matters about which little could be done except through politics. From the beginnings of the Zionist movement a certain number of New York Jews have been involved on that account with the high politics of the nation. Since the mid-1930's, however, this involvement has reached deeper and deeper into the New York Jewish community. They are the one group in the city (apart from the white Protestant financial establishment) of which it may fairly be said that among the leadership echelons there is a lively, active, and effective interest in who will be the next U.S. Secretary of State but one . . . or two, or three.

In a positive sense, events of the Nazi era and its aftermath have produced an intense group consciousness among New York Jews that binds together persons of widely disparate situations and beliefs. A pronounced religious revival has occurred. Among those without formal religious ties there is a heightened sense of the defensive importance of organized Jewish activity. Among intellectuals, the feeling of Jewishness is never far from the surface.

Now, as in the past, the Jewish community in New York is the one most actively committed to the principles of racial integration and group tolerance. But open housing is something different from the melting pot. There is no reason to think that any considerable portion of the Jewish community of New York ever subscribed to Israel Zangwill's vision of a nonreligious, intermarried, homogeneous population, but it surely does not do so today. To the contrary, much of the visible activity of the community is aimed in directions that will intensify Jewish identity: Jewish elementary and secondary schools, Jewish colleges and universities, Jewish periodicals, Jewish investments in Israel, and the like. In the meantime, Jewish politicians make more (or at least not less) of the "Jewish" vote.

This is not to say the Jewish community of New York has been *created* or *maintained* by these events of the thirties or forties: that would be too narrow a view of Jewish history, and would ignore the group-making characteristics of American civilization. But the Jewish community was *shaped* by these events. Moving rapidly from working-class to middle-class occupations and styles of life, many alternative courses of development were possible. Within the frame set by these large social movements, the historical drama shaped a community intensely conscious of its Jewishness. Religion plays in many ways the smallest part of the story of American Jews. In New York City in particular the religious definition of the group explains least. Here the formal religious groups are weakest, the degree of affiliation to synagogues and temples smallest. In a city with 2,000,000 Jews, Jews need make no excuses to explain Jewishness and Jewish interests. On the one hand, there is the social and economic structure of the community; on the other, ideologies and emotions molded by the specific history of recent decades. Together they have shaped a community that itself shapes New York and will for generations to come.[6]

THE CATHOLICS

Outwardly, events since World War I have brought Catholics, notably the Irish Catholics, ever closer to the centers of power and doctrine in American life. But following a pattern common in human affairs, the process of closing the gap has heightened resentment, among some at all events, that a gap should exist. Here, as in much else concerning this general subject, it is hardly possible to isolate New York events from those of the nation generally, but because New York tends to be the center of Catholic thinking and publishing, the distinction is not crucial. The great division between the Catholic Church and the leftist and liberal groups in the city during the period from the Spanish Civil War to the era of McCarthy has been narrowed, with most elements of city politics converging on center positions. However issues of church-state relations have become considerably more difficult, and the issue of government aid to Catholic schools has become acute.

Controversy over church-state relations is nothing new to the American Catholic Church. What is new, however, and what is increasingly avowed, is the extent to which the current controversy derives from Catholic-Jewish disagreements rather than from traditional Catholic-Protestant differences. Relations between the two latter groups have steadily improved: to the point that after three centuries of separation Catholics in the 1960's began increasingly to talk of the prospects of reestablishing Christian unity. In general (there are, of course, many individual exceptions) the dominant view within Protestant and Catholic circles is that the United States is and ought to be a Christian commonwealth, to the point at very least of proclaiming "In God We Trust" on the currency and celebrating Christmas in the public schools. However, as this *rapprochement* has proceeded, within the Jewish community a contrary view has arisen which asserts that the separation of church and state ought to be even more complete than it has been, and that the "Post-Protestant era" means Post-Christian as well, insofar as government relations with religion are concerned.

The most dramatic episode of this development was the decision of the United States Supreme Court on June 25, 1962, that the recitation of an official prayer in the New York school system was unconstitutional. The case was brought by five parents of children in the public schools of the New York City suburb of New Hyde Park. Two of the parents were Jewish, one a member of the Ethical Culture Society, one a Unitarian, and one a nonbeliever. Before it concluded, however, the principal protagonists of the Catholic-Jewish controversy in New York City were involved. The attorney for the Archdiocese of New York, for example, argued in the Supreme Court for a group of parents who supported the prayer. The response to the decision could hardly

have been more diametrical. Cardinal Spellman declared, "I am shocked and frightened. . . ." The New York Board of Rabbis, on the other hand, hailed the decision: "The recitation of prayers in the public schools, which is tantamount to the teaching of prayer, is not in conformity with the spirit of the American concept of the separation of church and state. All the religious groups in this country will best advance their respective faiths by adherence to this principle." The American Jewish Committee, the American Jewish Congress, and the Anti-Defamation League of B'nai B'rith strongly supported the Court. Only among the Orthodox was there mild disagreement with the Supreme Court decision.

Although the argument could certainly be made that the American Catholic Church ought to be the first to object to the spectacle of civil servants composing government prayers, and although many Catholic commentators noted that the decision strengthened the case for private Church-sponsored schools, the general Catholic reaction was most hostile. The Jesuit publication *America*, in an editorial "To our Jewish Friends," declared that Jewish efforts to assert an ever more strict separation of church and state were painting the Jewish community into a corner, where it would be isolated from the rest of Americans.

Significantly, Protestant reaction to the decision was mixed. The Brooklyn *Tablet* took the cue, stating that the crucial question raised by the decision was "What are the Protestants going to do about it? For, although this is a national problem, it is particularly a Protestant problem, given the large Protestant enrollment in the public schools. Catholics have been fighting long—and sometimes alone—against the Church-State extremists. May we count on Protestants to supply more leadership in this case? If so, we pledge our support to join efforts against the common enemy: secularism."[7]

The subject of aid to Catholic schools is only one aspect of the more general issue of church-state relations, and here again the ethnic composition of New York City tends to produce the same alignment of opposing groups. There are elements within the Jewish community, again the Orthodox, that favor public assistance for religious schools, but the dominant view is opposed. In 1961 the New York Republican party at the state level made a tentative move toward the Catholic position by proposing a Constitutional amendment that would have permitted state construction loans to private institutions of higher learning, sectarian as well as secular. Opposition from Jewish (as well as some Protestant) groups was pronounced, and the measure was beaten at the polls.

The situation developing in this area could soberly be termed dangerous. An element of interfaith competition has entered the controversy. As the costs of education mount, it becomes increasingly difficult to maintain the quality of the education provided by private schools deprived of public assistance. It is not uncommon to hear it stated in Catholic circles that the results of national scholarship competitions already point to the weakness of Catholic education in fields such as the physical sciences. The specter is raised that a parochial education will involve sacrifice for the students as well as for their parents.

There is understandably much resentment within Catholic educational circles at the relative crudity of most such observations. At the same time this resentment is often accompanied by an unmistakable withdrawal. In a thoughtful address calling for more meticulous assessment of the qualities of Catholic education, Bishop McEntegart of the Diocese of Brooklyn went on to state that "Judgment on the effectiveness of an educational system should be something more profound and more subtle than counting heads of so-called intellectuals who happen to be named in Who's Who or the 'Social Register.' "[8]

Whether the course of the controversy will lead Catholics further into separatist views of this kind is not clear. But it is abundantly evident that so long as Catholics maintain a separate education system and the rest of the community refuses to help support it by tax funds or tax relief, a basic divisive issue will exist. This will be an ethnic issue in measure that the Catholic community continues to include the bulk of the Irish, Italian, and Polish population in the city, at least the bulk of those affiliated with organizations taking a position on the issue. If, as may very well happen, the Catholics abandon elementary and even secondary education to concentrate on their colleges and universities, the larger issue of church-state relations will no doubt subside.

But it is not the single issue of school aid, no matter how important and long-lived it is, that alone shapes the polarization between the Jewish and the emerging Catholic community. There have been other issues in the past—for example, the struggle over the legitimacy of city hospitals giving advice on birth control, which put Jews and liberal Protestants on one side and Catholics on the other. There are the recurrent disputes over government censorship of books and movies and magazines that have become freer and freer in their handling of sex and sexual perversion. This again ranges Jewish and Protestant supporters of the widest possible freedom of speech against Catholics who are more anxious about the impact of such material on young people and family life. One can see emerging such issues as the rigid state laws on divorce and abortion.[9]

Many of these issues involve Catholic *religious* doctrine. But there exists here a situation that is broader than a conflict over doctrines and the degree to which government should recognize them. What is involved is the emergence of two subcultures, two value systems, shaped and defined certainly in part by religious practice and experience and organization but by now supported by the existence of two communities. If the bishops and the rabbis were to disappear tomorrow, the subcultures and subcommunities would remain. One is secular in its attitudes, liberal in its outlook on sexual life and divorce, positive about science and social science. The other is religious in its outlook, resists the growing liberalization in sexual mores and its reflection in cultural and family life, feels strongly the tension between moral values and modern science and technology. The conflict may be seen in many ways—not least in the fact that the new disciplines such as psychoanalysis, particularly in New York, are so largely staffed by Jews.

Thus a Jewish ethos and a Catholic ethos emerge: they are more strongly affected by a specific religious doctrine in the Catholic case than in the Jewish, but neither is purely the expression of the spirit of a religion. Each is the result of the interplay of religion, ethnic group, American setting, and specific

issues. The important fact is that the differences in values and attitudes between the two groups do not, in general, become smaller with time. On the contrary: there is probably a wider gap between Jews and Catholics in New York today than in the days of Al Smith.[10]

NEGROES AND PUERTO RICANS

A close examination of Catholic-Jewish relations will reveal some of the tendency of ethnic relations in New York to be a form of class relations as well. However, the tendency is unmistakably clear with regard to the Negroes and Puerto Ricans. Some 22 per cent of the population of the city is now Negro or Puerto Rican, and the proportion will increase. (Thirty-six per cent of the births in 1961 were Negro or Puerto Rican.) To a degree that cannot fail to startle anyone who encounters the reality for the first time, the overwhelming portion of both groups constitutes a submerged, exploited, and very possibly permanent proletariat.

New York is properly regarded as the wealthiest city in the nation. Its more affluent suburbs enjoy some of the highest standards of living on earth. In the city itself white-collar wages are high, and skilled labor through aggressive trade union activity has obtained almost unprecedented standards. Bricklayers earn $5.35 an hour, plus 52¢ for pension, vacation, and insurance benefits. Electricians have a nominal twenty-five hour week and a base pay of $4.96 an hour plus fringe benefits.[11] But amidst such plenty, unbelievable squalor persists: the line of demarcation is a color line in the case of Negroes, a less definite but equally real ethnic line in the case of Puerto Ricans.

The relationship between the rise of the Negro-Puerto Rican labor supply and the decline of industrial wages is unmistakable. In 1950 there were 246,000 Puerto Ricans in the city. By 1960 this number had increased by two and one-half times to 613,000, or 8 per cent. In 1950 the average hourly earnings of manufacturing production workers in New York City ranked tenth in the nation. By 1960 they ranked thirtieth. In the same period comparable wages in Birmingham, Alabama, rose from thirty-third to tenth. In 1959 median family income for Puerto Ricans was $3,811 as against $6,091 for all the city's families (and $8,052 for suburbs of Westchester). In 1962 average weekly earnings of manufacturing production workers were 19 per cent higher in Birmingham than in New York City, 15 per cent higher in New Orleans, and almost 10 per cent higher in the nation as a whole.

These economic conditions vastly reinforce the ethnic distinctions that serve to separate the Negro community and the Puerto Rican community from the rest of the city. The Negro separation is strengthened by the fact that the colored community is on the whole Protestant, and much of its leadership comes from Protestant clergy. Thus the Negroes provide the missing element of the Protestant-Catholic-Jew triad.

Housing segregation, otherwise an intolerable offense to the persons affected, serves nonetheless to ensure the Negroes a share of seats on the City Council and in the State Legislature and Congress. This power, as well as their voting power generally, has brought Negro political leaders to positions of considerable prominence. Following the 1961 mayoralty election, Mayor Wagner appointed the talented Harlem leader,

J. Raymond Jones, as a political secretary through whom he would deal with all the Democratic party organizations of the city. Puerto Ricans have only begun to make their influence felt, but they are clearly on the way to doing so.

Their fate gives them an interest in the same issues: the housing of the poor in a city of perpetual housing shortage; the raising of the wages of the poorly paid service semiskilled occupations in which most of them work; the development of new approaches to raising motivation and capacity by means of education and training in the depressed areas of the city. They live adjacent to each other in vast neighborhoods. And they cooperate on many specific issues —for example, in fighting urban renewal programs that would displace them. But there are deeply felt differences between them. The more Americanized group is also more deeply marked by color. The furtive hope of the new group that it may move ahead as other immigrants have without the barrier of color, and the powerful links of language and culture that mark off the Puerto Ricans, suggest that, despite the fact that the two groups increasingly comprise the proletariat of the city, their history will be distinct.

Thus the cast of major characters for the next decades is complete: the Jews; the Catholics, subdivided at least into Irish and Italian components; the Negroes; the Puerto Ricans; and, of course, the white Anglo-Saxon Protestants. These latter, ranging from the Rockefeller brothers to reform district leaders in the Democratic party are, man for man, among the most influential and powerful persons in the city, and will continue to play a conspicuous and creative role in almost every aspect of the life of the metropolis.

THE ROLE OF POLITICS

The large movements of history and people which tend to reinforce the role of the ethnic groups in the city have been accompanied by new developments in political life which similarly strengthen ethnic identities. This is a complicated matter, but we can point to a number of elements. First, there is some tendency (encouraged by the development of genuine ethnic-class combinations) to substitute ethnic issues in politics for class issues. Second, there has been a decline in the vigor and creativity of politics in New York City, which seems to make New York politicians prefer to deal in terms of premelting pot verities rather than to cope with the chaotic present. Third, the development of public opinion polling would seem to have significantly strengthened the historic tendency of New York political parties to occupy the same middle ground on substantive issues, and indirectly has the effect of strengthening the ethnic component in political campaigns. As competing parties and factions use substantially the same polling techniques, they get substantially the same information about the likes and dislikes of the electorate. Hence they tend to adopt similar positions on political issues. (In much the same way, the development of marketing survey techniques in business has produced standardized commercial products such as cigarettes, automobiles, detergents, and so forth.) For the time being at least, this seems to have increased the importance of racial and ethnic distinctions that, like advertising, can still create distinctions in appearance even if little or none exist in fact. Everything we say in this field is highly speculative, but the impression that the political patterns of the city strengthen the roles of ethnic groups is overwhelming.

It is not easy to illustrate the substitution of ethnic appeals for class appeals. To the extent it occurs, those involved would hope to conceal it, always assuming the practice is deliberate. The basic fact is that for the first half of the twentieth century New York was a center of political radicalism. Faced with fierce opposition, some at least of the left wing discovered that their best tactic was to couch class appeals in ethnic terms. In such manner Vito Marcantonio, a notorious fellow traveler, flourished in the United States Congress as an Italian representative of the Italians and Puerto Ricans of East Harlem. In response to such tactics, the traditional parties have themselves employed the ethnic shorthand to deal with what are essentially class problems. Thus much was made in terms of its ethnic significance of the appointment of a Puerto Rican as a City Commissioner responsible for the relocation of families affected by urban renewal projects, but behind this significance was the more basic one that the slum-dwelling proletariat of the city was being given some control over its housing. In much the same way the balanced ticket makes it possible to offer a slate of candidates ranging across the social spectrum—rich man, poor man, beggar man, thief—but to do so in terms of the ethnic groups represented rather than the classes. In a democratic culture that has never much liked to identify individuals in terms of social classes, and does so less in the aftermath of the radical 1930's and 1940's, the ethnic shorthand is a considerable advantage.

This is of course possible only because of the splintering of traditional economic classes along ethnic lines, which tends to create class-ethnic combinations that have considerable significance at the present time in New York. The sharp division and increasing conflict between the well-paid Jewish cutters in the International Ladies' Garment Workers' Union and the low-paid Negro and Puerto Rican majority in the union have been widely publicized. One Negro cutter hailed the union before the State Commission for Human Rights and obtained a favorable decision. Similar distinctions between skilled and unskilled workers are common enough throughout the trade unions of the city. At a higher level, not dissimilar patterns can be found among the large law firms and banks, where Protestant-Catholic-Jew distinctions exist and are important even if somewhat less so than in past times.

From time to time the most significant issues of class relations assume ethnic form. Reform movements in New York City politics have invariably been class movements as well. Citing a study of Theodore Lowi, showing that reform in New York City has always meant a change in the class and ethnic background of top city appointees, James Q. Wilson summarized the phenomenon as follows:

The three "reform" mayors preceding Wagner favored upper-middle-class Yankee Protestants six to one over the Irish as appointees. Almost 40 per cent of the appointees of Seth Low were listed in the Social Register. Further, all four reform mayors—Low, Mitchel, La Guardia, and Wagner—have appointed a much larger percentage of Jews to their cabinets than their regular organizations predecessors.

In fact, of course, the problem posed by the amateur Democrats is not simply one of ethnic succession. Militant reform leaders in Manhattan get angry when they hear this "explanation" of their motives, for they reject the idea that ethnicity or religion ought to be considered at all in politics.

Although most amateur Democrats are either Jewish or Anglo-Saxon and practically none are Catholic, it is not their entry into politics so much as it is their desire to see a certain political ethic (which middle-class Jews and Yankees happen to share) implemented in local politics.[12]

The 1961 Democratic primary fight, which ended with the defeat of Carmine DeSapio and the regular Democratic organization, was a mixture of class and ethnic conflict that produced the utmost bitterness. In the mayoralty election that followed, the Democratic State Chairman, Michael H. Prendergast, in an unprecedented move, came out in support of an independent candidate, a conservative Italian Catholic, Lawrence E. Gerosa, against Mayor Wagner, who was running for reelection with the support of the middle-class reform elements within the Democratic party. In a bitter *cri de coeur*, almost inevitably his last statement as an acknowledged political leader, Prendergast lashed out at what he regarded as a leftwing conspiracy to take over the Democratic party and merge it with the Liberal party of David Dubinsky and Alex Rose, in the process excluding the traditional Catholic leadership of the city democracy. He declared:

The New York Post lays the whole plot bare in a signed column entitled "One Big Party?" in its September 27 issue. Every Democrat should read it. "The first prerequisite of the new coalition," James A. Wechsler writes, "is that Mayor Wagner win the election." He goes on to say that the new "troops" which Messrs. Dubinsky and Rose will bring to this alliance will have to fight a "rear-guard action" on the part of "Catholics of Irish descent" who, Mr. Wechsler declares, "take their temporal guidance from Patrick Scanlan and his Brooklyn Tablet propaganda sheet.

✧   ✧   ✧

It's time to call a spade a spade. The party of Al Smith's time was big enough for Democrats of all descent. The Democratic party of today is big enough for Americans of every race, creed, color or national origin.

Although much larger issues were at stake, it was natural enough for a traditionalist in politics such as Prendergast to describe the conflict in ethnic terms. And in justice it must be said that the ethnic elements of the controversy were probably much more significant than Prendergast's opponents would likely admit.

Apart from the reform movement represented by the Committee for Democratic Voters (which has yet to wield any decisive power over city—or statewide political nominations), the level of political creativity in New York politics has not been high over the past several decades. The almost pathetic tendency to follow established patterns has been reinforced by the growing practice of nominating sons and grandsons of prominent public persons. The cast of such men as Roosevelt, Rockefeller, Harriman, Wagner, and Morgenthau seems almost bent on recreating the gaslight era. In this context the balanced ticket and the balanced distribution of patronage along ethnic lines have assumed an almost fervid sanctity—to the point indeed of caricature, as in the 1961 mayoralty contest in which the Republican team of Lefkowitz, Gilhooley, and Fino faced Democrats Wagner, Screvane, and Beame, the latter victors in a primary contest with Levitt, Mackell, and Di Fede. It will be noted that each ticket consisted of a Jew, an Italian Catholic, and an Irish Catholic, or German-Irish Catholic in the case of Wagner.

The development of polling techniques has greatly facilitated the calculations—and perhaps also the illusions

—that go into the construction of a balanced ticket. It should be noted that these techniques would apply equally well, or badly, to all manner of social and economic classifications, but that so far it is the ethnic information that has attracted the interest of the political leaders and persons of influence in politics. Here, for example, is the key passage of the poll on the basis of which Robert M. Morgenthau was nominated as the Democratic candidate for governor in 1962:

The optimum way to look at the anatomy of the New York State electorate is to take three symbolic races for Governor and two for the Senate and compare them group by group. The three we will select for Governor are Screvane, Morgenthau, and Burke.[*] We select these because each represents a different fundamental assumption. Screvane makes sense as a candidate, if the election should be cast in terms of an extension of the Wagner-Rockefeller fight. This could have the advantage of potentially firming up a strong New York City vote, where, in fact, the election must be won by the Democrats. On the other hand, a Rockefeller-Screvane battle would make it more difficult to cast the election in national terms of Rockefeller vs. Kennedy which, as we shall also see, is a critical dimension to pursue.

A Morgenthau-Rockefeller race is run mainly because it represents meeting the Rockefeller-Javits ticket on its own grounds of maximum strength: among Jewish and liberal-minded voters, especially in New York City. Morgenthau is the kind of name that stands with Lehman, and, as we shall see, has undoubted appeal with Jewish voters. The question of running a moderately liberal Jewish candidate for Governor is whether this would in turn lose the Democrats some conservative Catholic voters who are not enchanted with Rockefeller and Javits to begin with, but who might normally vote Republican.

[*] Paul R. Screvane, President of the City Council, an Italian Catholic; Robert M. Morgenthau, United States Attorney for the Southern District of New York, a Jew; Adrian P. Burke, Judge of the Court of Appeals, an Irish Catholic.

	Key Group Breakdowns*				
Statewide	Democratic Candidates for Governor Pitted Against Rockefeller			Democratic Candidates for U.S. Senate Against Javits	
	Screvane %	Burke %	Morgenthau %	Bunche %	Murrow %
	47	43	49	47	46
By Area					
New York City (43%)	61	54	61	57	55
Suburbs (16%)	41	41	43	42	40
Upstate (41%)	35	35	40	40	40
By Occupation					
Business and Professional (14%)	35	22	30	57	33
White Collar (19%)	36	44	51	50	44
Sales and Service (8%)	49	49	54	42	42
Labor (34%)	56	53	57	34	52
Small Business, Shopkeeper (5%)	38	41	41	42	36
Retired and other (13%)	39	30	39	52	43
By Ethnic Groups					
White USA (29%)	35	37	36	36	40
Irish (9%)	44	49	44	48	36
English-Scotch (7%)	42	26	33	34	34
German (16%)	29	34	39	42	41
Italian (13%)	59	53	53	45	55
By Religion and Race					
White Protestant (37%)	27	27	29	35	32
White Catholic (37%)	51	54	51	42	48
White Jewish (18%)	70	56	82	81	61
Negro (8%)	70	55	68	93	74
Sex by Age					
Men (49%)	47	40	48	47	43
21-34 (15%)	42	39	40	43	34
35-49 (16%)	53	39	54	43	54
50 and over (18%)	48	43	51	55	42
Women (51%)	47	48	50	47	49
21-34 (15%)	56	56	58	55	45
35-49 (18%)	50	52	59	53	58
50 and over (18%)	39	35	36	37	41
By Union Membership					
Union Member (25%)	66	61	65	49	57
Union Family (11%)	56	59	57	52	47
Nonunion (64%)	38	35	42	45	40
By Income Groups					
Upper Middle (22%)	33	20	32	40	27
Lower Middle (64%)	47	47	52	45	48
Low (14%)	63	61	62	66	61

* Each figure gives the percentage of total vote that the proposed candidate received in the specified category. Thus, 35 per cent of the business and professional vote were recorded as saying they would vote for Screvane against Rockefeller.

The third tack that might be taken on the Governorship is to put up an outstanding Irish candidate on the assumption that with liberal Republicans Rockefeller and Javits running, the Catholic vote can be moved appreciably over to the Democratic column, especially in view of Rockefeller's divorce as a silent but powerful issue. Here, Court of Appeals Judge Adrian Burke, who far outstripped the statewide ticket in 1954 might be considered typical of this type of candidate.

Let us then look at each of these alternatives and see how the pattern of the vote varies by each. For it is certain that the key Democratic decision in 1962 must be over the candidate for Governor first, and then followed by the candidate for U.S. Senate. We also include the breakdowns by key groups for Bunche and Murrow against Javits.*

Here some fascinating and revealing patterns emerge which point the way sharply toward the kind of choice the Democrats can make optimally in their selection of Gubernatorial and Senatorial candidates for 1962 in New York:

—By area, it appears that the recent Democratic gains in the suburbs are quite solid, and a range of from 40 to 43 per cent of the vote seems wholly obtainable.

—By race and religion, we find equally revealing results. The Protestant vote is as low as it was for Kennedy in 1960, when the religious issue was running strong.

—By contrast, the Catholic vote remains relatively stable, with a slight play for Burke above the rest, and with Bunche and Murrow showing some weaknesses here. (The relative percentages, however, for a James A. Farley† race against Javits show Farley with 30 percent Protestant, a relatively lower standing; 58 percent of the Catholics, a very good showing, but with only 36 percent of the Jewish vote, a very poor result; and 67 percent of the Negro vote, only a fair showing).

The really volatile votes in this election clearly are going to be the Jewish and Negro votes. The Jewish vote ranges from a low of 56 percent (for Burke); 61 per-

* Ralph J. Bunche, United Nations official, a Negro; Edward R. Murrow, Director, United States Information Agency, a white Protestant; Jacob K. Javits, United States Senator, a Jew.

† James A. Farley, former Postmaster General, an Irish Catholic.

cent for Murrow (against Javits); 70 percent for Screvane (against Rockefeller); a very good 71 percent for Bunche (against Javits); and a thumping 82 percent for Morgenthau (against Rockefeller). Here the conclusion is perfectly obvious: by running a Lehman type of Jewish candidate against Rockefeller, the Jewish vote can be anchored well up into the high 70's and even into the 80's. By running an Irish Catholic candidate against Rockefeller, the Jewish vote comes tumbling precipitously down into the 50's. What is more, with Javits on the ticket, with strong appeal among Jews, any weakness among Jews with the Gubernatorial candidate, and the defection of the Jewish vote can be large enough to reduce the city vote to disastrously low proportions for the Democrats.

The Negro vote is only slightly less volatile. It ranges from a low of 55 percent (for Burke, again); to 68 percent for Morgenthau, not too good (an indication that Negroes will not automatically vote for a Jewish candidate, there being friction between the two groups); 70 percent for Screvane (who carried over some of the strong Wagner appeal among Negroes); 74 percent for Murrow, a good showing; and an incredibly high 93 percent for Bunche.

Observation: The conclusion for Governor seems self-evident from the results. A candidate who would run in the Wagner image, such as Screvane, would poll a powerful New York City vote, but would fade more upstate and would not pull in a full measure of the Jewish swing vote. An Irish Catholic candidate would not do appreciably better than Screvane upstate (a pattern that has been repeated throughout New York's modern political history, with Kennedy the sole exception in 1960), but with good appeal in the suburbs, yet with a disastrous showing among Jews and Negroes in New York City. A Lehman-type Jewish candidate, such as Morgenthau, by contrast, would appeal to a number of Protestants upstate (as, indeed, Lehman always did in his runs), would hold well in the suburbs, and could bring in solidly the pivotal Jewish vote in New York City.

The first choice must be a Jewish candidate for Governor of the highest caliber. (*sic.*)

There are two things to note about this poll. In the first place, the New York Jews did *not* vote solidly for Morgenthau, who lost by half a million votes. A week before the election Morgenthau headquarters received a report that a follow-up poll showed that 50 per cent of New York City Jews who had voted for the Democratic candidate Averell Harriman in 1958 were undecided about voting for Morgenthau four years later. An analysis of the vote cast in predominantly Jewish election districts shows that Rockefeller significantly improved his performance over

1958, when he had run against Averell Harriman, another white Protestant. In important areas such as Long Beach, Rockefeller went from 37.2 per cent in 1958 to 62.7 per cent in 1962, which is sufficient evidence that a Jewish name alone does not pull many votes. It could also confirm the preelection fears of the Democrats that the notoriety of their search for a "Lehman type of Jewish candidate" had produced a strong resentment within the Jewish community. The following are returns from predominantly Jewish districts:

	Rockefeller			Javits		
	1962	1958	Dif.	1962	1956	Dif.
New York City						
Bronx AD 2, School 90	27.2	20.5	+6.7	41.9	19.2	+22.7
3	21.6	18.7	+2.9	44.0	17.5	+26.5
5	26.4	19.8	+6.6	39.9	21.4	+18.5
Queens AD 7 School 164	43.8	36.5	+7.3	66.5	32.0	+34.5
Suburbs						
Jericho (part)	50.7	34.4	+16.3	60.7	36.1	+24.6
Long Beach (part)	62.7	37.2	+25.5	66.2	34.3	+31.9
Harrison (part)	71.3	69.6	+1.7	71.4	64.6	+6.8
New Rochelle Ward 4	57.8	58.8	−1.0	57.1	55.8	+1.3

These returns, which are typical enough, reveal an important fact about ethnic voting. Class interests and geographical location are the dominant influences in voting behavior, whatever the ethnic group involved. In urban, Democratic Bronx, the great majority of Jews vote Democratic. In suburban, Republican Westchester, the next county, the great majority of Jews vote Republican. But within that over-all pattern a definite ethnic swing does occur. Thus Rockefeller got barely a fifth of the vote in the third Assembly district of Democratic Bronx, while he got almost three-quarters in Harrison in Republican

Westchester, *but he improved his performance in both areas* despite the fact that his 1962 plurality was lower, statewide, than 1948. Similarly, Rockefeller got as little as 8.8 per cent on the vote in the predominantly Negro third ward of Democratic Albany, and as much as 76 per cent in upper-middle-class, Republican Rye in Westchester, but generally speaking, Rockefeller appears to have lost Negro votes in 1962 over 1958.

A second point to note is that while the poll provided detailed information on the response to the various potential candidates classified by sex, occupational status, and similar characteristics of the persons interviewed, the candidates proposed were all essentially ethnic prototypes, and the responses analyzed in the commentary were those on the ethnic line. These are terms, howsoever misleading, which are familiar to New York politics, and with which New York politicians prefer to deal.

THE FUTURE

We have tried to show how deeply the pattern of ethnicity is impressed on the life of the city. Ethnicity is more than an influence on events; it is commonly the source of events. Social and political institutions do not merely respond to ethnic interests; a great number of institutions exist for the specific purpose of serving ethnic interests. This in turn tends to perpetuate them. In many ways, the atmosphere of New York City is hospitable to ethnic groupings: it recognizes them, and rewards them, and to that extent encourages them.

This is not to say that no individual group will disappear. This, on the contrary, is a recurring phenomenon. The disappearance of the Germans is a particularly revealing case.

In terms of size or the achievements of its members, the Germans ought certainly to be included among the principal ethnic groups of the city. If never quite as numerous as the Irish, they were indisputably the second largest group in the late nineteenth century, accounting for perhaps a third of the population and enjoying the highest reputation. But today, while German influence is to be seen in virtually every aspect of the city's life, the Germans *as a group* are vanished. No appeals are made to the German vote, there are no German politicians in the

sense that there are Irish or Italian politicians, there are in fact few Germans in political life and, generally speaking, no German component in the structure of the ethnic interests of the city.

The logical explanation of this development, in terms of the presumed course of American social evolution, is simply that the Germans have been "assimilated" by the Anglo-Saxon center. To some extent this has happened. The German immigrants of the nineteenth century were certainly much closer to the old Americans than were the Irish who arrived in the same period. Many were Protestants, many were skilled workers or even members of the professions, and their level of education in general was high. Despite the language difference, they did not seem nearly so alien to the New York mercantile establishment as did the Irish. At the time of their arrival German sympathies were high in New York. (George Templeton Strong was violent in his support of doughty Prussia in its struggle with imperial, tyrannical France.) All of this greatly facilitated German assimilation.

In any event, there were obstacles to the Germans' becoming a distinct ethnic bloc. Each of the five groups we have discussed arrived with a high degree of homogeneity: in matters of education, skills, and religion the members of the group were for the most part alike. This homogeneity, as we have tried to show, invested ethnicity with meaning and importance that it would not otherwise have had. But this was not so with the Germans, who were split between Catholics and Protestants, liberals and conservatives, craftsmen and businessmen and laborers. They reflected, as it were, an entire modern society, not simply an element of one. The only things all had in common were the outward manifestations of German culture: language for a generation or two, and after that a fondness for certain types of food and drink and a consciousness of the German fatherland. This was a powerful enough bond and would very likely be visible today, except for the impact of the World Wars. The Germanophobia of America during the First World War is, of course, notorious. It had limits in New York where, for instance, German was *not* driven from the public school curriculum, but the attraction of things German was marred. This period was followed, in hardly more than a decade, by the Nazi era, during which German fascism made its appearance in Jewish New York, with what results one can imagine. The German American Bund was never a major force in the city, but it did exist. The revulsion against Nazism extended indiscriminately to things German. Thereafter, German Americans, as shocked by the Nazis as any, were disinclined to make overmuch of their national origins.

Even so, it is not clear that consciousness of German nationality has entirely ceased to exist among German-Americans in the city, or elsewhere. There is evidence that for many it has simply been submerged. In New York City, which ought logically to be producing a series of Italian and Jewish mayors, the political phenomenon of the postwar period has been Robert F. Wagner.

It is even possible that the future will see a certain resurgence of German identity in New York, although we expect it will be mild. The enemy of two world wars has become an increasingly powerful and important ally in the Cold War. Berlin has become a symbol of resistance to totalitarianism; Germany

has become an integral part of the New Europe. Significantly, the German Americans of the city have recently begun an annual Steuben Day Parade, adding for the politicians of the city yet another command performance at an ethnic outing.

Despite this mild German resurgence, it is a good general rule that except where color is involved as well the specifically *national* aspect of most ethnic groups rarely survives the third generation in any significant terms. The intermarriage which de Crèvecoeur described continues apace, so that even the strongest national traditions are steadily diluted. The groups do not disappear, however, because of their *religious* aspect which serves as the basis of a subcommunity, and a subculture. Doctrines and practices are modified to some extent to conform to an American norm, but a distinctive set of values is nurtured in the social groupings defined by religious affiliation. This is quite contrary to early expectations. It appeared to de Crèvecoeur, for example, that religious as well as national identity was being melted into one by the process of mixed neighborhoods and marriage:

. . . This mixed neighborhood will exhibit a strange religious medley, that will be neither pure Catholicism nor pure Calvinism. A very perceptible indifference even in the first generation, will become apparent; and it may happen that the daughter of the Catholic will marry the son of the seceder, and settle by themselves at a distance from their parents. What religious education will they give their children? A very imperfect one. If there happens to be in the neighborhood any place of worship, we will suppose a Quaker's meeting; rather than not shew their fine clothes, they will go to it, and some of them may attach themselves to that society. Others will remain in a perfect state of indifference; the children of these zealous parents will not be able to tell what their religious principles are, and their grandchildren still less.

Thus all sects are mixed as well as all nations; thus religious indifference is imperceptibly disseminated from one end of the continent to the other; which is at present one of the strongest characteristics of the Americans.[13]

If this was the case in the late eighteenth century, it is no longer. Religious identities are strongly held by New Yorkers, and Americans generally, and they are for the most part transmitted by blood line from the original immigrant group. A great deal of intermarriage occurs among nationality groups of the three great religious groups, of the kind Ruby Jo Kennedy described in New Haven, Connecticut, under the general term of the Triple Melting Pot,[14] but this does not weaken religious identity. When marriages occur between different religions, often one is dominant, and the result among the children is not indifference, but an increase in the numbers of one of the groups.

Religion and race seem to define the major groups into which American society is evolving as the specifically national aspect of ethnicity declines. In our large American cities, four major groups emerge: Catholics, Jews, white Protestants, and Negroes, each making up the city in different proportions. This evolution is by no means complete. And yet we can discern that the next stage of the evolution of the immigrant groups will involve a Catholic group in which the distinctions between Irish, Italian, Polish, and German Catholic are steadily reduced by intermarriage; a Jewish group, in which the line between East European, German, and Near Eastern Jews is already weak; the Negro group; and a white Protestant group, which adds to its Anglo-Saxon and

Dutch old-stock elements German and Scandinavian Protestants, as well as, more typically, the white Protestant immigrants to the city from the interior.

The white Protestants are a distinct ethnic group in New York, one that has probably passed its low point and will now begin to grow in numbers and probably also in influence. It has its special occupations, with the customary freemasonry. This involves the banks, corporation front offices, educational and philanthropic institutions, and the law offices who serve them. It has its own social world (epitomized by, but by no means confined to, the *Social Register*), its own churches, schools, voluntary organizations and all the varied institutions of a New York minority. These are accompanied by the characteristic styles in food, clothing, and drink, special family patterns, special psychological problems and ailments. For a long while political conservatism, as well as social aloofness, tended to keep the white Protestants out of the main stream of New York politics, much in the way that political radicalism tended to isolate the Jews in the early parts of the century. Theodore Roosevelt, when cautioned that none of his friends would touch New York politics, had a point in replying that it must follow that none of his friends were members of the governing classes.

There has been a resurgence of liberalism within the white Protestant group, in part based on its growth through vigorous young migrants from outside the city, who are conspicuous in the communications industry, law firms, and corporation offices of New York. These are the young people that supported Adlai Stevenson and helped lead and staff the Democratic reform movement. The influence of the white Protestant group on this city, it appears, must now grow as its numbers grow.

In this large array of the four major religio-racial groups, where do the Puerto Ricans stand? Ultimately perhaps they are to be absorbed into the Catholic group. But that is a long time away. The Puerto Ricans are separated from the Catholics as well as the Negroes by color and culture. One cannot even guess how this large element will ultimately relate itself to the other elements of the city; perhaps it will serve, in line with its own nature and genius, to soften the sharp lines that divide them.

Protestants will enjoy immunities in politics even in New York. When the Irish era came to an end in the Brooklyn Democratic party in 1961, Joseph T. Sharkey was succeeded by a troika (as it was called) of an Irish Catholic, a Jew, and a Negro Protestant. The last was a distinguished clergyman, who was at the same time head of the New York City Council of Protestant Churches. It would have been unlikely for a rabbi, unheard of for a priest, to hold such a position.

Religion and race define the next stage in the evolution of the American peoples. But the American nationality is still forming: its processes are mysterious, and the final form, if there is ever to be a final form, is as yet unknown.

NOTES

1. J. Hector St. John Crèvecoeur (Michel-Guillaume Jean de Crèvecoeur), *Letters from an American Farmer*, New York: Fox, Duffield & Co., 1904, pp. 54-55.

2. Israel Zangwill, *The Melting Pot*, New York: Macmillan, 1909, pp. 37-38.

3. Joseph Leftwich, *Israel Zangwill*, New York: Thomas Yoseloff, 1957, p. 255.

4. Lee Benson, *The Concept of Jacksonian Democracy*, Princeton, N.J.: Princeton University Press, 1961, p. 165.

5. See Nathan Glazer, *The Social Basis of American Communism*, New York: Harcourt, Brace & World, 1961, Chap. IV.

6. For the complex interplay of religious, ideological, and socioeconomic factors within the American Jewish community, see *American Judaism* by Nathan Glazer, Chicago: University of Chicago Press, 1957.

7. Quoted in the *New York Herald Tribune*, July 2, 1962.

8. *The Tablet*, February 17, 1962. In an address given in Washington on April 30, 1962, Very Reverend William F. Kelley, S.J., President of Marquette University, implicitly proposed a secondary role for Catholic education. As reported in *The Washington Post*, Father Kelley suggested that Catholic schools leave "research and the exploration for new knowledge" to "research institutes" like Hopkins, Harvard, and M.I.T., it being "perfectly respectable and professionally honorable" to concentrate on the transmission of the knowledge of the past:

It is an entirely sound plan to be trailing along at a respectable distance with a trained and educated citizenry competent to appreciate and consume the discovery of the successful investigator. Let us remember that if there are no followers, there can be no leader.

9. See *A Tale of Ten Cities*, Albert Vorspan and Eugene Lipman, New York: *Union of American Hebrew Congregations*, 1962, pp. 175 ff.

10. Gerhard Lenski, *The Religious Factor*, New York: Doubleday, 1961, gives a great deal of evidence to the effect that value differences between Catholics and white Protestants and Jews (the latter two often linked, but not always) in Detroit have increased as the groups move from working-class and immigrant generation to middle-class and later generations. Parochial schooling plays some part in these differences. For an interesting evocation of the milieu in which Jewish-Catholic political cooperation flourished, see *Al Smith*, by Oscar Handlin, Boston: Little, Brown, 1958.

11. U. S. Bureau of Labor Statistics data for October, 1962.

12. James Q. Wilson, *The Amateur Democrat*, Chicago: University of Chicago Press, 1962, p. 304.

13. de Crèvecoeur, *op. cit.*, pp. 65-66.

14. Ruby Jo Reeves Kennedy, "Single or Triple Melting Pot: Intermarriage in New Haven," *American Journal of Sociology*, Vol. 58, No. 1, July, 1952, pp. 55-66.

Harlem Tragedy: An Emerging Slum

GILBERT OSOFSKY

"I sit on my stoop on Seventh Avenue and gaze at the sunkissed folks strolling up and down and think that surely Mississippi is here in New York, in Harlem, yes, right on Seventh Avenue."

The Messenger, 1923

"I have been in places where cattle and dogs sleep with masters, but never before have I been in such a filthy house."

Judge William Blau's description of a Harlem tenement, 1922

I

The creation of a Negro community within one large and solid geographic area was unique in city history. New York had never been what realtors call an "open city"—a city in which Negroes lived wherever they chose—but the former Negro sections were traditionally only a few blocks in length, often spread across the island and generally interspersed with residences of white working-class families. Harlem, however, was a Negro world unto itself. A scattered handful of "marooned white families . . . stubbornly remained" in the Negro section, a United States census-taker recorded, but the mid-belly of Harlem was predominantly Negro by 1920.[1]

And the ghetto rapidly expanded. Between the First World War and the Great Depression, Harlem underwent radical changes. When the twenties came to an end Negroes lived as far south as One Hundred and Tenth Street—the northern boundary of Central Park; practically all the older white residents had moved away; the Russian-Jewish and Italian sections of Harlem, founded a short generation earlier, were rapidly being depopulated; and Negro Harlem, within the space of ten years, became the most "incredible slum" in the entire city. In 1920 James Weldon Johnson was able to predict a glowing future for this Negro community: "Have you ever stopped to think what the future Harlem will be?" he wrote. "It will be the greatest Negro city in the world. . . . And what a fine part of New York City [the Negro] has come into possession of!"[2] By the late 1920's and early 1930's, however, Harlem's former "high-class" homes offered, in the words of a housing expert, "the best laboratory for slum clearance . . . in the entire city." "Harlem conditions," a *New York Times* reporter concluded, are "simply deplorable."[3]

II

The Harlem slum of the twenties was the product of a few major urban developments. One of the most important was the deluge of Negro migration to New York City then. The Negro press, now largely dependent on the migrant community for support, changed its former critical attitude of migration to one openly advocating urban settlement. (The exodus was so large, a Negro minister preached, that it must have been "inspired by Almighty God.")[4] If one is looking for a dramatic turning point in the history of the urbanization of the Negro—"a race changing from farm life to city life"—it was certainly the decade of the twenties. Between 1910 and 1920 the Negro population of the city increased 66 per cent (91,709 to 152,-467); from 1920 to 1930, it expanded 115 per cent (152,467 to 327,706). In the latter year less than 25 per cent of New York City's Negro population (79,-264) was born in New York State. There were more Negroes in the city in 1930 than the combined Negro populations of Birmingham, Memphis and St. Louis. Similar population increases occurred in urban areas throughout the country.[5]

Negro migration in the twenties drew on areas of the South that had previously sent few people to New York City. The seaboard states of the Upper South —especially Virginia and the Carolinas —continued to be the main sources of New York's migrant Negro population, but people from Georgia and Florida and other Deep South states formerly under-represented also came in greater numbers: "Harlem became the symbol of liberty and the Promised Land to Negroes everywhere," the Reverend Dr. Powell wrote. "There was hardly a member of Abyssinian Church who could not count on one or more relatives among the new arrivals."[6] In 1930, some 55,000 foreign-born Negroes added to the growing diversity of the city's Negro population.

The following chart presents an exact description of the geographical origins of Negro migrants to New York City in 1930. I have selected states with 900 or more residents in the city:[7]

Negro In-Migration, New York City, 1930

Born in:	
Virginia	44,471
South Carolina	33,765
North Carolina	26,120
Georgia	19,546
Florida	8,249
Maryland	6,656
Pennsylvania	6,226
New Jersey	5,275
District of Columbia	3,358
Alabama	3,205
Massachusetts	2,329
Louisiana	2,182
Ohio	1,721
Tennessee	1,651
Texas	1,592
Kentucky	1,216
Mississippi	969
Foreign-born	54,754

The rapid settlement of a heterogeneous Negro population coincided with another population change—the migration of whites from all sections of Manhattan to other boroughs. For the first time since Dutch settlement Manhattan's population *declined* in the 1920's as first- and second-generation immigrants moved to nicer residential areas in the Bronx, Brooklyn and Queens. Many of the homes they left behind had deteriorated significantly. By 1930 a majority of New York City's foreign-born and second-generation residents lived outside Manhattan.[8] As whites moved out of Manhattan, Negroes moved in. The population of that borough declined 18 per cent in the 1920's as its Negro population increased 106 per cent. By 1930 Negroes represented 12 per cent of Manhattan's population —although they composed only 4.7 per cent of the population of the entire city.[9]

Harlem was the New York neighborhood most radically revamped by the population movements of the 1920's, although the Lower East Side also changed rapidly. Harlem underwent a revolution—what one contemporary accurately called a "stupendous upheaval." Between 1920 and 1930, 118,-792 white people left the neighborhood and 87,417 Negroes arrived.[10] Second-generation Italians and Jews were responding to the same conditions of prosperity that promoted mobility in all the immigrant neighborhoods of Manhattan—they were not *only* moving away because Negroes settled near them. Conditions of life which satisfied immigrant parents were often unacceptable to children: "The tenements which housed their parents," immigration expert Edward Corsi wrote in 1930, "are being left behind by the children. . . ." "East Harlem used to have a great deal larger population," a survey of the Mayor's Committee on City Planning during the Great Depression concluded. "Like others of the older residential districts, it has suffered by the exodus of families to newer surroundings. . . ."[11]

The city's newest migrants moved into the Harlem flats vacated by Italians and Jews. Puerto Ricans came to live in East Harlem, created community organizations, and laid the foundations for "El Barrio" of today. By 1930 some 45,000 Puerto Ricans resided in New York City and most were heavily concentrated in East Harlem.[12] Negroes moved north along St. Nicholas Avenue —"On the Heights," they called it— and south into the heart of "Little Russia," the former Jewish section. "Just Opened for Colored" signs were common in the neighborhood. Mount Olivet Baptist Church occupied, and still occupies, the once exclusive Temple Israel of Harlem. Prince Hall Masons bought a building that "was formerly a

home for aged Jews." Graham Court, a magnificent block-length apartment house on One Hundred and Sixteenth Street, with eight separate elevators and apartments of seven to ten rooms, was opened to Negroes in 1928.[13] By 1930, 164,566 Negroes, about 72 per cent of Manhattan's Negro population, lived in Harlem.[14] The Negro ghetto remained and expanded as the other ethnic ghettos disintegrated. The economic and residential mobility permitted white people in the city was, and would continue to be, largely denied Negroes. Most Negroes were "jammed together" in Harlem—even those who could afford to live elsewhere—with little possibility to escape.[15] "One notable difference appears between the immigrant and Negro populations," an important federal study of Negro housing concluded. "In the case of the former, there is the possibility of escape, with improvement in economic status, in the second generation, to more desirable sections of the city. In the case of Negroes, who remain a distinguishable group, the factor of race and certain definite racial attitudes favorable to segregation, interpose difficulties to . . . breaking physical restrictions in residence areas."[16] A rather ponderous paragraph, but a significant truth.

III

The settlement of West Indian Negroes in Harlem in the 1920's added another complicating dimension to the racial problems of this community—one that fostered discord rather than harmony among the city's Negroes. There were ten times as many foreign-born Negroes in New York City as in any other American urban area. In 1930, 54,754 foreign Negroes lived in the city—39,833 of whom resided in Manhattan. Miami, the next largest American city in terms of immigrant Negroes, was settled by only 5,512 people; Boston ranked third with 3,287 West Indians. About 25 per cent of Harlem's population in the twenties was foreign-born. Harlem was America's largest Negro melting pot.[17]

In the era of immigration restriction, West Indian Negroes came to America through what a contemporary called the "side door." The immigration laws of the 1920's seriously restricted the migration of Europeans and totally excluded Orientals but had little effect on peoples of the Caribbean. At first there were no restrictions on West Indian Negroes. After 1924, they could enter the country under quotas set aside for their mother countries. Since these quotas were never filled there was, in reality, a free flow of people from the islands to the United States in the 1920's.[18]

Although American Negroes tended to lump all the migrants together in a uniform image—"There is a general assumption," one migrant wrote, "that there is everything in common among West Indians"—it is important to recognize that Harlem's Negro immigrants represented a diverse group of peoples from dozens of different islands in the Caribbean.[19] Most Negro immigrants felt a strong attachment to their homeland. They demonstrated an "exaggerated" nationalism in America—a buffer against the strangeness of the new culture and the hostility they experienced —which was typical of white immigrant groups. It was common, for example, to find former British subjects at the office of the British consul protesting some difficulty they experienced in America.[20] Nationalistic organizations kept close check on American foreign policy in the

Caribbean and often gave banquets for and listened to addresses by West Indian dignitaries. West Indian Negroes from all countries had the lowest rate of naturalization of all immigrant groups. The people white Americans and American Negroes called "West Indians" were really individuals from Jamaica, Trinidad, Barbados, Martinique, St. Vincent, St. Lucia, Dominica, British Guiana, St. Kitts, Nevis, Montserrat, Antigua, Virgin Islands, Bermuda, the Bahamas, and so on. Although the majority spoke English, some considered French their first tongue; others Spanish; a few Dutch. The fraternal and benevolent associations they founded were not inclusive organizations for all Negro immigrants, but exclusive ones—*landmannschaften*—for people from specific islands. Danish settlers kept pictures of the King of Denmark in their homes; former British subjects held coronation pageants and balls ("Boxes, 12s. 6d.—Loges, 8s. 4d.") and flew the Union Jack in Harlem; Frenchmen had annual Bastille Day dances.[21]

Negro immigrants differed from each other in origin, yet in a broader sense they shared general experiences, desires and mores which set them apart *as a group* from their American brethren. Most came from societies in which class distinctions played a more important role in one's life than the color line—although the latter was certainly significant. Unaccustomed to common American racial slurs, they often refused to accept them without protest. The Pullman Company, for example, hesitated to employ West Indian Negroes, it was said, "because of their refusal to accept insults from passengers quietly."[22] Out of this heightened class consciousness came a small group of political and economic radicals in Harlem—"foreign-born agitators," local Negroes called them.[23] Many of Harlem's street-corner orators in the 1920's, though not all, were West Indian migrants. Hubert H. Harrison, a Virgin Islander, was among the most prominent. Harrison was a socialist, an expert in African history, a militant critic of American society and a proud defender of the "Negro's racial heritage." He conducted formal lectures in what he called the "Harlem School of Social Science," and others from street corners—his "outdoor university." A Harlem church, the Hubert H. Harrison Memorial Church, honors his memory. Others presented talks on "Socialism vs. Capitalism," organized tenants' leagues, published Marxist journals and tried to make Harlemites labor-conscious. Richard B. Moore, Frank R. Crosswaith and the Reverend Ethelred Brown—all Negro immigrants—were prominent local candidates for Board of Aldermen, Assembly and Congress on Socialist and Communist tickets—they usually polled an exceedingly small vote. Some organized rent strikes, "rent parades," lobbied for social legislation at City Hall and Albany and distributed radical literature in Harlem. "There is no West Indian slave, no American slave," the short-lived radical magazine *Challenge* commented. "You are all slaves, base, ignoble slaves."[24]

This concern with "class" led to the emergence of a broader tradition in America. What is striking about the Negro immigrant is the way his response to American conditions, such as his exaggerated sense of nationalism, was similar to the typical reactions of most European immigrants. The Negro immigrant "did not suffer from the local anesthesia of custom"[25] and he tried to create a meaningful economic position for himself within American society. Menial labor was, among most first-generation Negro immigrants, considered a sign of social degradation and looked upon with "disgust." Most were forced to accept such jobs initially, but were strongly motivated by their traditions to improve themselves. As a group, West Indians became noted for their ambition, thrift and business acumen. They were called "pushy," "the Jews of the race," "crafty," "clannish."[26] Negro journalist George S. Schuyler "admired their enterprise in business, their pushfulness."[27] "The West Indians [are] legendary in Harlem for their frugalness and thrift," one student noted. When a West Indian "got ten cents above a beggar," a common local saying ran, "he opened a business." Contemporary surveys of Negro business in Harlem and Columbus Hill demonstrate that a disproportionate number of small stores—the traditional "Race Enterprise" —were owned by Negro immigrants. Dr. P. M. H. Savory, one of the leading spokesmen of New York's foreign-born Negro community from the 1920's to his death in June 1965, owned and published the *Amsterdam News*. Many others achieved success within the racial barrier.[28]

Another significant distinction between the foreign-born Negro and the American was their attitude toward family life. Slavery initially destroyed the entire concept of family for American Negroes and the slave heritage, bulwarked by economic conditions, continued into the twentieth century to make family instability a common factor in Negro life. This had not been true for most West Indians, and they arrived in America with the orthodox respect for family ties that was traditional of rural people. The West Indian family was patriarchal in structure—contrasted with the typically matriarchal American Negro home. The father, as key worker and wage earner in the islands, ruled the household with a solid hand. It was beneath his dignity to help with domestic chores. (This led American Negroes to brand West Indian men "cruel.")[29] Children were supposed to obey their parents rigidly—American Negroes considered them strait-laced; have long and formal courtships; and receive parental approval before marriage. Illicit sexual relations were considered the worst form of moral evil.[30] These traditions began to change in the second generation, but throughout the 1920's family solidarity was a pervasive force among New York's Negro immigrants.[31]

These differences in style of life were also evident in another important institution—the church. The majority of Harlemites were Baptists and Methodists; the immigrants were predominantly Episcopalian and Catholic.[32] The beautiful St. Martin's Episcopal Church was founded in Harlem in 1928 to minister to the needs of West Indian migrants. Services in immigrant churches were generally staid and quiet; Sunday a day of prayer, rest and visiting—as it had been on the islands. Observers were impressed with the differences between the emotionalism of a typical Harlem religious service and the moderation and restraint shown in churches of the foreign-born. Negro immigrants also objected to the general frivolity and "fast ways" that were part of a typical Sunday in Harlem.[33]

All these factors combined to make Harlem in the 1920's a battleground of intraracial antagonism. American Negro nativism spilled over to taint Harlemites' reactions to the West Indian.

The Negro immigrant was ridiculed; his tropical clothing was mocked; children tossed stones at the people who looked so different; foreigners were taunted with such epithets as "monkey-chaser," "ring-tale," "king Mon," "cockney." "When a monkey-chaser dies/Don't need no undertaker/Just throw him in de Harlem River/He'll float back to Jamaica," was a verse from a Harlem ditty of the twenties. West Indians came to Harlem, ran another common saying, "to teach, open a church, or start trouble." "Bitter resentment grew on both sides." Each group called the other "aggressive." "We have . . . in Harlem," NAACP director Walter White wrote, "this strange mixture of reactions not only to prejudice from without but to equally potent prejudices from within." "If you West Indians don't like how we do things in this country," an American Negro said tersely, "you should go back where you came from. . . ."[34]

The obvious hostility of American Negroes forced Negro immigrants to unite in defense organizations larger than their individual national groups. The West Indian Committee on America, the Foreign-Born Citizens' Alliance and the West Indian Reform Association were founded in the twenties to soften these intraracial tensions and promote "cordial relations between West Indians and colored Americans." Radio programs were devoted to discussions of "Intra-Race Relations in Harlem," and immigrants were urged to become naturalized citizens. American Negroes, in turn, were asked to tone down their "considerable prejudice against West Indians." A semblance of co-operation was achieved as mass meetings were held in Harlem churches. The hatreds of the 1920's did not die, however, until West Indian Negroes stopped migrating to New York. During the Depression more immigrants left New York than entered and intraracial tensions slowly eased. Young Harlemites today, even third-generation descendants of Negro immigrants, are often unaware of these old divisions. The unique type of intraracial hostility so prominent in the twenties has never reappeared. While,it lasted, however, it served to weaken a Negro community in great need of unity. A divided Harlem confronted major social problems that desperately called for the co-operation of all.[35]

IV

The most profound change that Harlem experienced in the 1920's was its emergence as a slum. Largely within the space of a single decade Harlem was transformed from a potentially ideal community to a neighborhood with manifold social and economic problems called "deplorable," "unspeakable," "incredible." "The State would not allow cows to live in some of these apartments used by colored people . . . in Harlem," the chairman of a city housing reform committee said in 1927. The Harlem slum of today was created in the 1920's.[36]

The most important factor which led to the rapid deterioration of Harlem housing was the high cost of living in the community. Rents, traditionally high in Harlem, reached astounding proportions in the 1920's—they skyrocketed in response to the unprecedented demand created by heavy Negro migration and settlement within a restricted geographical area. "Crowded in a black ghetto," a sociologist wrote, "the Negro tenant is forced to pay exorbitant rentals because he cannot escape." In 1919 the average Harlemite paid somewhat above $21 or $22 a month for rent; by 1927 rentals had *doubled* and the "mean average market rent for Negro tenants in a typical block" was $41.77. In 1927 Harlem Negroes paid $8 more than the typical New Yorker for three-room apartments; $10 more for four rooms; and $7 more for five rooms, an Urban League survey noted.[37] Another report concluded that the typical white working-class family in New York City in the late twenties paid $6.67 per room, per month, while Harlem Negroes were charged $9.50.[38]

Realty values which had declined significantly prior to World War I *appreciated* in Harlem in the twenties.[39] Harlem experienced a slum boom. "The volume of business done in the section . . . during the last year is . . . unprecedented," *Harlem Magazine* announced in 1920. "Renting conditions have been very satisfactory to the owners and the demand for space . . . is getting keener every year [due] to the steady increase in the Negro population," a *New York Times* reporter wrote in 1923. There was, in the language of a Harlem businessman, an "unprecedented demand for Harlem real estate."[40] For landlords—Negro and white (Negro tenants continually complained that Negro landlords fleeced them with equal facility as whites)—Harlem became a profitable slum.[41]

High rents and poor salaries necessarily led to congested and unsanitary conditions. The average Negro Harlemite in the 1920's, as in the 1890's, held some menial or unskilled position which paid low wages—work which was customarily "regarded as Negro jobs." There were generally two types of businesses in New York in terms of Negro hiring policy, E. Franklin Frazier wrote: "Those that employ Negroes in menial positions and those that employ no Negroes at all." Macy's, for example, hired Negroes as elevator operators, escalator attendants and cafeteria workers; Gimbel's used none. "We have felt it inadvisable to [hire] colored people," a Metropolitan Life Insurance Company executive explained in 1930, "not because of any prejudice on the part of the company, but because . . . there would be very serious objection on the part of our white employees. . . ."[42] Throughout the city the vast majority of Negro men worked as longshoremen, elevator operators, porters, janitors, teamsters, chauffeurs, waiters and general laborers of all kinds. Negro women continued to work as domestics ("scrub women"), although in the 1920's an increasing number were employed as factory operatives in the garment industry and in laundries. Less than 20 per cent of Harlem's businesses were owned by Negroes.[43] The average Harlem family, according to President Hoover's Conference on Home Building and Home Ownership, earned $1,300 a year in the twenties; the typical white family in the city, $1,570. A variety of social investigations noted that working-class whites expended approximately 20 per cent of their income for rent, considered the proper amount by economists; Harlemites, 33 per cent and more.[44] An Urban League study of 2,160 Harlem families demonstrated that almost half (48 per cent) spent 40 or more per cent of their earnings on rent. A 1928 sample of tenement families found that Harlemites paid 45 per cent of their wages for housing. Similar conclusions were reached in a variety of local community studies.[45] Whatever the exact figure, few Negroes looked to the first of the month with expectancy.

Added to the combination of "high rents and low wages"[46] was the fact that Harlem's apartment houses and brownstones were originally built for people with radically different family structure from that of the new residents. Seventy-five per cent of Harlem's tenements had been constructed before 1900.[47] The Negro community of the twenties, like all working-class peoples in times of great migration, continued to be most heavily populated by young adults—men and women between the ages of 15 and 44. Family life had not yet begun for many Negro Harlemites —as it had for older Americans and earlier immigrants who lived in the community previously. In 1930, 66.5 per cent of Harlem Negroes were between the ages of 15 and 44, contrasted with 56.5 per cent for the general population of Manhattan and 54.4 per cent for New York City at large. Harlemites who were married had few children. In 1930, 17.5 per cent of Harlem's population was under 14; the corresponding figure for New York City was 24.5 per cent. The number of Harlemites under the age of 15 declined 14 per cent between 1920 and 1930, as whites left the neighborhood. There was a corresponding decrease of 19 per cent for those over 45 years of age.[48]

What all these statistics mean is simply that apartments of five, six, and seven rooms were suitable for older white residents with larger families and larger incomes—they obviously did not meet the needs of the Negro community in the 1920's. "The houses in the section of Harlem inhabited by the Negro were not only built for another race," E. Franklin Frazier noted, "but what is more important, for a group of different economic level, and consisting of families and households of an entirely different composition from those which now occupy these dwellings." "Unfortunately," Eugene Kinckle Jones of the Urban League stated, "the houses built before [the Negroes'] arrival were not designed to meet the needs . . . of Negroes." "The class of houses we are occupying today are not suited to our economic needs," John E. Nail said in 1921. Negro Harlemites desperately needed small apartments at low rentals: "One of the community's greatest needs [is] small apartments for small families with a reasonable rent limit. . . ."[49] Few realtors were philanthropic enough to invest their capital in new construction; older homes, properly subdivided, produced sufficient income. Only a handful of new houses were built in Harlem in the 1920's.[50]

A variety of makeshift solutions were found to make ends meet: "What you gonna do when the rent comes 'round," had been an old Negro song. The most common solution was to rent an apartment larger than one's needs and means and make up the difference by renting rooms to lodgers—"commercializing" one's home. In the twenties, approximately one white Manhattan family in nine (11.2 per cent) took in roomers, contrasted with one in four (26 per cent) for Negroes. Most lodgers were strangers people let into their homes because of economic necessity. It was difficult to separate "the respectable" from "the fast." "The most depraved Negroes lived side by side with those who were striving to live respectable lives," a contemporary complained. Urban reformers blamed many of Harlem's social problems on this "lodger evil."[51]

Every conceivable space within a home was utilized to maximum efficiency: "Sometimes even the bathtub is used to sleep on, two individuals taking turns!" Negro educator Roscoe Conkling Bruce wrote. Boardinghouses were established which rented beds by the week, day, night or hour. A large number of brownstones were converted to rooming houses: "Private residences at one time characteristic of this part of the city have been converted into tenements. . . ." One landlord transformed apartments in nine houses into one-room flats, a state commission investigating New York housing reported. Space which formerly grossed $40 a month now brought in $100 to $125. People were said to be living in "coal bins and cellars." In an extreme case, one social investigator discovered seven children sleeping on pallets on the floor of a two-room apartment. More common was the "Repeating" or "Hot Bed System"—as soon as one person awoke and left, his bed was taken over by another.[52]

An additional Harlem method devised to meet the housing crisis of the twenties was the "Rent Party." Tickets of admission were usually printed and sold for a modest price (25¢). All who wanted to come were invited to a party. Here is an example:[53]

> If you're looking for a good time,
>   don't look no more,
> Just ring my bell and I'll answer
>   the door.
> Southern Barbecue
> Given by Charley Johnson and Joe
>   Hotboy, and How hot!

Chitterlings, pigs' feet, coleslaw and potato salad were sold. Money was raised in this way to pay the rent: "The rent party," *The New York Age* editorialized in 1926, "has become a recognized means of meeting the demands of extortionate landlords. . . ." The white world saw rent parties as picturesque affairs—in reality they were a product of economic exploitation and they often degenerated into rowdy, bawdy and violent evenings.[54]

A significant part of the deterioration of the neighborhood was caused by the migrants themselves. Some needed rudimentary training in the simplest processes of good health and sanitation (Booker T. Washington, it will be remembered, preached the "gospel of the toothbrush").[55] E. Franklin Frazier called many Negro Harlemites "ignorant and unsophisticated peasant people without experience [in] urban living. . . ." They often permitted homes and buildings to remain in a state of uncleanliness and disrepair. Landlords complained that apartments were looted and fixtures stolen, that courtyards and hallways were found laden with refuse. Clothes and bedding were hung out of windows; trash sometimes thrown down air shafts; dogs walked on rooftops; profanities shouted across streets; "ragtime" played throughout the night. "Ragtime is a sufficient infliction of itself," one wag complained, "but when it keeps up all night, it becomes unbearable." "Since the so-called 'Negro invasion,'" a colored woman noted, "the streets, the property and the character of everything have undergone a change, and if you are honest, you will frankly acknowledge it has not been for the . . . improvement of the locality. . . . Are we responsible for at least some of the race prejudice which has developed since the entry of Negroes in Harlem?" Negro journals criticized "boisterous" men who laughed "hysterically" and hung around street corners, and those who used "foul language on the streets." An editorial in the *Age*, one of many, attacked "Careless Harlem Tenants": "A great deal might be said about the

necessity for training some of the tenants in the matter of common decency," it suggested. The absence of a sense of social and community responsibility, characteristic of urban life, obviously affected Negro Harlemites.[56]

All these factors combined to lead to the rapid decline of Harlem. The higher the rents, sociologists said, the greater the congestion: "Crowding is more prevalent in high-rent cities than in cities in which rent per room is more reasonable." In 1925, Manhattan's population density was 223 people per acre —in the Negro districts it was 336. Philadelphia, the second most congested Negro city in the country, had 111 Negroes to an acre of land; Chicago ranked third with 67. There were two streets in Harlem that were perhaps the most congested blocks in the entire world.[57]

People were packed together to the point of "indecency."[58] Some landlords, after opening houses to Negro tenants, lost interest in caring for their property and permitted it to run down—halls were left dark and dirty, broken pipes were permitted to rot, steam heat was cut off as heating apparatus wore out, dumb-waiters broke down and were boarded up, homes became vermin-infested. Tenants in one rat-infested building started what they called "a crusade against rats." They argued that the rats in their house were "better fed" and "better housed" than the people. Some common tenant complaints in the 1920's read: "No improvement in ten years"; "Rats, rat holes, and roaches"; "Very very cold"; "Not fit to live in"; "Air shaft smells"; "Ceilings in two rooms have fallen"; "My apartment is overrun with rats"; and so on.[59] There were more disputes between tenants and landlords in Harlem's local district court

—the Seventh District Court—than in any municipal court in the five boroughs. Traditionally, municipal courts were known as "poor-men's courts"; Harlemites called the Seventh District Court the "rent court." Occasionally, socially conscious judges of this court made personal inspections of local tenements that were subjects of litigation. Without exception what they saw horrified them: "Conditions in negro tenements in Harlem are deplorable"; "Found few fit for human habitation"; "Negro tenants are being grossly imposed upon by their landlords"; "On the whole I found a need for great reformation"; were some of their comments. One municipal official accurately called the majority of Harlem's houses "diseased properties."[60]

V

And the disease did not confine itself to houses. To touch most areas of Harlem life in the 1920's is to touch tragedy. This was especially true of the health of the community. Theoretically, a section of the city inhabited by relatively young people should have ranked below the general population in mortality and sickness rates. Just the reverse was true. Undertaking was a most profitable Harlem business.[61]

From 1923 to 1927 an Atlanta University professor made an intensive study of Harlem health. His findings were shocking. During these years Harlem's death rate, for all causes, was 42 per cent in excess of that of the entire city. Twice as many Harlem mothers died in childbirth as did mothers in other districts, and almost twice as many Harlem children "passed" as did infants in the rest of New York. Infant mortality in Harlem, 1923-1927, was 111 per thousand live births; for the city, 64.5 Families wept at the processions of "so many little white caskets." Similar statistics are recorded for deaths from tuberculosis (two and a half to three times the city rate), pneumonia, heart disease, cancer and stillbirths.[62] An astounding number of Harlemites had venereal diseases. Negro children commonly suffered from rickets—a disease of malnutrition. More women than ever reported themselves "widows" to census-takers. Negro deaths by violence increased 60 per cent between 1900 and

Health center districts, 1930 Manhattan	Infant mortality per 1,000 live births	TB mortality per 100,000 population	Pulmonary TB new case rate per 100,000 population	Other infectious diseases, rate per 100,000 population	Venereal disease new case rate per 100,000 population	General mortality rate per 1,000 population
Central Harlem	98	251	487	987	2826	15.3
Lower East Side	62	116	302	1,160	892	14.0
Kips Bay–Lenox Hill	73	75	184	937	629	12.7
East Harlem	75	137	311	1,326	913	12.0
Lower West Side	83	156	391	1,201	1,318	16.7
Riverside	64	75	196	827	778	12.3
Washington Heights	52	72	203	937	668	10.5
Total	73	122	294	1,049	1,455	13.3

1925.[63] With the single exception of the Lower West Side Health District, which included the old San Juan Hill neighborhood, Harlem was the most disease-ridden community in Manhattan.[64]

Whatever the causes of Harlem's health problems—and medical investigators continue to search for all the answers—a good deal can be laid at the door of slum environment. Urban reformers consistently showed a high correlation between poverty and congestion on the one hand and disease and death on the other. Mortality rates for infants whose mothers worked away from home, for example—and twice as many Negro women as white women in the city did—was higher than for children whose mothers remained at home; working-class families in old-law tenements (pre-1901) died at a higher-rate than those in newer houses; poverty led to the consumption of the cheapest foods, and this in turn fostered diseases of poor diet; working mothers died more readily in childbirth than unemployed women; and so on.[65] Added to all these considerations, however, was a deep strain of peasant ignorance and superstition embedded in the minds of thousands of migrants—foreign-born as well as native—who settled in Harlem. Quackery abounded in the community in the 1920's.[66]

Harlem had the reputation of a "wide-open city." Whatever you wanted, and in whatever quantity, so the impression went, could be bought there. This was certainly true for the variety of "spiritualists," "herb doctors," "African medicine men," "Indian doctors," "dispensers of snake oils," "layers-on-of-hands," "faith healers," "palmists," and phrenologists who performed a twentieth-century brand of necromancy there: "Harlem sick people are flocking to all sorts of Quacksters," an *Age* reporter noted. One man, "Professor Ajapa," sold a "herb juice" guaranteed "to cure consumption, rheumatism, and other troubles that several doctors have failed in." Powders could be purchased to keep one's wife home at night, make women fertile and men sexually appealing. "Black Herman the Magician" and "Sister P. Harreld" held séances and sold "blessed handkerchiefs," "potent powders," love charms, lodestones, amulets and "piles of roots." "Ignorance, cherished superstitions and false knowledge often govern Negroes in illness and hamper recoveries," a colored physician with the Board of Health wrote in 1926. Nine wood lice gathered in a little bag and tied around a baby's neck, some believed, would end teething. An egg fried brown on both sides and placed on a woman's abdomen would hasten labor. If a mother in the course of childbirth kicked a Bible from her bed to the floor, either she or her child would die. People had faith in the medicinal qualities of dried cobwebs, rabbit brains, "dirt-dauber tea," and something called "cockroach rum." In spite of efforts of physicians, health agencies and the Negro press to bring modern-day medical information to the community, quackery "continued to thrive with impunity in Harlem." It aggravated an already tragic situation.[67]

Accompanying the proliferation of healers, and rooted in the same rural consciousness which made quackery possible,[68] was the host of storefront churches founded in Harlem in the twenties. These were places that healed one's soul: "Jesus is the Doctor, Services on Sunday," read a sign which hung over one door. An investigator found 140 Negro churches in a 150-block area of Harlem in 1926. "Harlem is perhaps overchurched," W. E. B. DuBois said modestly. Only about a third—fifty-four —of Harlem's churches were housed in regular church buildings—and these included some of the most magnificent and costly church edifices in New York City. The rest held services in stores and homes and appealed to Harlem's least educated people. "Jack-leg preachers," "cotton-field preachers," as their critics called them, hung out their poorly printed signboards and "preached Jesus" to all who wanted to listen. One self-appointed pastor held meetings in the front room of his home and rented chairs from the local undertaker to seat his small congregation. In Harlem in the twenties one could receive the word of the Lord through such nondenominational sects as: "The Metaphysical Church of the Divine Investigation," "The Temple of the Gospel of the Kingdom," "The Church of the Temple of Love," "Holy Church of the Living God," "Temple of Luxor," "Holy Tabernacle of God," "Royal Fraternity Association," "Knights of the Rose and Cross," "Sons of God," "Sons of Christ," "Sons of Jehovah," "Sanctified Sons of the Holy Ghost," and the "Live-Ever-Die-Never" church. People not only had their worries removed in these places, a Negro clergyman wrote, but "their meager worldly goods as well."[69]

The ministers of these churches preached a fundamentalism which centered around the scheming ways of Satan, who was everywhere, and the terror and joy of divine retribution, with an emphasis on terror. One congregation expelled members who attended the theater or movies. "The devil runs every theatre," its pastor said. "He collects a tax on the souls of men and robs them of their seat in heaven." Services were fervent, loud and boisterous as members felt the spirit of the Lord and shouted and begged for His forgiveness. Tambourines sometimes kept up a rhythmic beat in the background and heightened the emotionalism to a state of frenzy. Neighbors of one storefront church sued the congregation for "conducting a public nuisance." The "weird sounds" which emanated from the building, they complained, seemed like a "jazz orchestra."[70]

Are you ready-ee? Hah!
For that great day, hah!
When the moon shall drape her face in
  mourning, hah!
And the sun drip down in blood, hah!
When the stars, hah!
Shall burst forth from their diamond
  sockets, hah!
And the mountains shall skip like lambs,
  hah!
Havoc will be there, my friends, hah!
With her jaws wide open, hah!
And the sinner-man, hah!
And cry, Oh rocks! Hah!
Hide me! Hah!
Hide me from the face of an angry God,
  hah!
Hide me, Ohhhhhh! . . .
Can't hide, sinner, you can't hide.[71]

Contemporaries were uniformly critical of these evangelists—there were many Harlem "Prophets"—and most of these preachers were probably charlatans in some form. There was at least one exception, however. A new denomination, the Church of Christ, Apostolic Faith, was founded on the streets of Harlem by the Reverend Mr. R. C. Lawson in 1919. The Reverend Mr. Lawson, of New Iberia, Louisiana, "the only real Apostolic—Holy Ghost-Bible Preacher," presented what he called the "Full Gospel" on street corners of Harlem's worst blocks. He decried the lack of emotionalism in the more established urban churches—copying "the white man's style," he said—and offered recent migrants a touch of fire and brimstone and personal Christianity characteristic of religion in the rural South:

I have found it, I have found it,
the meaning of life, life in God,
life flowing through me by the
Holy Spirit, life abundant, peace,
joy, life in its fullness.

Lawson started preaching on One Hundred and Thirty-third Street, east of Lenox Avenue. This area "was to Harlem what the Bowery is to the lower East Side," a Negro journalist recorded. From the streets, the Reverend Mr. Lawson moved into a small building and held services for those "fast drifting to a life of eternal darkness" every day and every night of the week. His Refuge Church of Christ became the founding church of the new denomination, and the Reverend Mr. Lawson its first bishop. By 1930 the Apostolic Church had some forty branches throughout the country and ran an orphanage, elementary school and "Bible Supply House"; it continues to prosper today. Annual conventions met in Refuge Church, "the most honored in the sisterhood of the Apostolic Church," and local leaders praised and publicized its good works for Harlem Negroes: "This church has had one of the most remarkable growths of any religious organizations in the country."[72]

Harlem was also a "wide-open city" in terms of vice and gambling.[73] The annual reports of the anti-vice Committee of Fourteen, founded in 1905, showed Harlem as the leading or near-leading prostitution center of Manhattan throughout the twenties. The Committee hired a Negro doctor, Ernest R. Alexander, to do a secret study of Harlem vice in 1928. His report emphasized the "openness of vice conditions in this district." Dr. Alexander personally

found sixty-one houses of prostitution in the neighborhood—more than the combined totals of four other investigators hired at the same time to survey other districts. "There is a larger amount and more open immorality in Harlem than this community has known in years," Negro alderman George W. Harris noted in 1922. "It is a house of assignation . . . this black city," Eric D. Walrond wrote bitterly in the Negro journal The Messenger.[74]

Her dark brown face
Is like a withered flower
On a broken stem.
Those kind come cheap in Harlem,
So they say.[75]

The Committee of Fourteen also disclosed that more than 90 per cent of these "daughters of joy" institutions were owned and managed by whites. Other evidence verifies this.[76]

Gambling also prevailed in the neighborhood: "Bootleggers, gamblers, and other panderers to vice have found it profitable to ply their vicious trades in this section." The poorest of the poor sought instant riches through the numbers racket. No sum was too small to bet—starting with pennies. "One can bet with plenty of takers on anything from a horse race to a mule race," the Age editorialized. Many Harlemites "would rather gamble than eat," it concluded. People selected numbers to coincide with birthdays, dreams, hymns or chapters and verses of Scripture in expectation that they would coincide with the clearing-house figures of the day. The odds were thousands to one against success, yet the smallest hope for a richer life was better than none and Negroes continued to play "policy" avidly. "The chief pastime of Harlem seems to be playing the numbers," George S. Schuyler wrote in 1925.[77]

"Buffet flats," "hooch joints," "barrel houses," and cabarets supplied Harlemites with illegal liquor, and occasionally other things, in the Prohibition era. Drugstores, cigar stores, sweetshops and delicatessens were used as "fronts" for speakeasies. "Harlem can boast of more drugstores than any similar area in the world," one Negro commented. "A plethora of delicatessen stores may be found in the Negro sections of New York, most of which are simply disguised bootlegging stores," a Harlemite concluded in 1924. "And so many confectioners! One never dreamed the Negroes were so much in need of sugar." "Speakeasies downtown are usually carefully camouflaged," a *New York Tribune* reporter noted. "In Harlem they can be spotted a hundred yards off."[78]

Poverty and family instability also led to a high incidence of juvenile delinquency. A community with fewer young teenagers should have shown a proportionally lower juvenile crime rate; as with Negro health, just the reverse was true. "The records of the Children's Court of New York for every year from 1914 to 1927 show a steady increase in the percentage of all crimes committed by Negro boys and girls," Owen R. Lovejoy of the Children's Aid Society reported. In 1914 Negro children represented 2.8 per cent of all cases before the juvenile court of New York City; in 1930 this figure rose to 11.7 per cent.[79]

Working mothers had little time to care for their children. Youngsters "with keys tied around their necks on a ribbon" wandered around the streets until families came home at night. A substantial portion were products of broken homes—families without a male head. One Harlem school principal testified that 699 of his 1,600 pupils came from families whose fathers were not living

at home. Nor did the majority of Harlem schoolchildren ever have time to accustom themselves to the regularity of school life; many families were rootless. Three-fourths of all the Negro pupils registered in one Harlem school, for example, transferred to some other before the end of one school year; some schools actually experienced a 100 per cent turnover. Pupils from the South were seriously deficient in educational training: "They are at times 14 to 15 years of age and have not the schooling of boys of eight," a Harlem principal wrote. "We cannot give a boy back seven years of wasted life. . . ." The typical Harlem school of the twenties had double and sometimes triple sessions. The "usual class size" was forty to fifty and conditions were generally "immensely over-crowded": "The school plant as a whole is old, shabby, and far from modern." In some schools 25 per cent and more of the children were overage or considered retarded.

Negro children in Harlem often led disrupted and harsh lives from the earliest years of their existence: "Testimony has been given before us as to the moral conditions among children, even of tender age," a municipal agency investigating Harlem schools recorded, "which is not to be adequately described by the word 'horrifying.' " These conditions were obviously reflected in high rates of juvenile crime but more subtly, and worst of all, in a loss of respect for oneself and for life in general. Harlem youngsters developed "a sense of subordination, of insecurity, of lack of self-confidence and self-respect, the inability . . . to stand on their own feet and face the world with open eyes and feel that [they have] as good a right as anyone else."[80]

This then was the horror of slum life

—the Harlem tragedy of the 1920's. "Court and police precinct records show," a municipal agency maintained, "that in arrests, convictions, misdemeanants, felons, female police problems and juvenile delinquencies, these areas are in the lead. . . ." It was no wonder that narcotics addiction became a serious problem then and that Harlem became "the center of the retail dope traffic of New York"; nor that local violence and hatred for the police were continually reported in the press.[81] The majority of Harlemites even during normal times lived "close to the subsistence level." Many were "under care" of charitable agencies in the period of relatively full employment. Those who needed money quickly and had no other recourse were forced to turn to loan sharks, Negro and white, who charged 30 to 40 per cent interest: Harlem "has been infested by a lot of loan sharks," a municipal magistrate who dealt with such cases stated. In one form or another the sorrow and economic deprivation of the Depression had come to Harlem in the twenties: "The reason why the Depression didn't have the impact on the Negroes that it had on the whites," George S. Schuyler said, "was that the Negroes had been in the Depression all the time."[82]

NOTES

1. The Mayor's Commission on Conditions in Harlem, "The Negro in Harlem: A Report on Social and Economic Conditions Responsible for the Outbreak of March 19, 1935" (unpublished manuscript in La Guardia Papers, Municipal Archives), p. 53. This important study, prepared under the direction of E. Franklin Frazier, will hereafter be cited as "The Negro in Harlem."
2. "The Future Harlem," The New York Age, January 10, 1920.
3. John E. Nail to James Weldon Johnson, March 12, 1934, Johnson Collection, Yale University; "Harlem Conditions Called Deplorable," The New York Times, September 6, 1927.

4. "Let Them Come," "The New Exodus," The New York Age, March 3, 1923, October 16, 1920, September 14, 1929.
5. Bureau of the Census, Fifteenth Census, 1930: Population (Washington, D.C., 1933), II, 216-218; Walter Laidlaw, Population of the City of New York, 1890-1930 (New York, 1932), p. 51.
6. Reverend Dr. Adam Clayton Powell, Sr., Against the Tide: An Autobiography (New York, 1938), pp. 70-71.
7. Bureau of the Census, Fifteenth Census, 1930: Population (Washington, D.C., 1933), II, 216-218. Note the difference in Chicago's migrant population. In order of greatest numbers Chicago Negroes came from Mississippi, Tennessee, Georgia, Alabama and Louisiana.
8. James Ford, et al., Slums and Housing: With Special Reference to New York City (Cambridge, Mass., 1936), II, 311-315.
9. Ibid., p. 317; Bureau of the Census, Negroes in the United States, 1920-1932 (Washington, D.C., 1935), p. 55.
10. Winfred B. Nathan, Health Conditions in North Harlem, 1923-1927 (New York, 1932), pp. 13-14.
11. Harlem Magazine, XIX (June 1930), 8; Mayor's Commission on City Planning, East Harlem Community Study (typescript in New York Public Library, 1937), p. 16.
12. Slums and Housing, p. 370; Antonio T. Rivera to La Guardia, June 24, 1935, La Guardia Papers; "Harlem Puerto Ricans Unite to Prove Faith," The New York Times, July 2, August 9, 16, 1926; Opportunity, IV (October 1926), 330.
13. The New York Age, August 27, 1927, March 31, 1928, January 11, 1930; The New York Times, October 19, 1924.
14. Slums and Housing, p. 314.
15. The attempt of Negroes to move into Washington Heights, Yonkers and Westchester was opposed in these sections as it had been in Harlem earlier. The Neighborhood Protective Association of Washington Heights urged landlords to sign racially restrictive covenants. Mortgage pressures from financial institutions closed down a Negro housing development in Yonkers. As a result of population pressure, however, another large ghetto was created in the Bedford-Stuyvesant section of Brooklyn in the 1920's. Of the 68,921 Negroes in Brooklyn in 1930, 47,616 lived in what is now called Bedford-Stuyvesant. "Negro Community Near Yonkers Abandoned," The New York Age, July 3, 1926, March 24, August 4, 1928, April 19, 26, 1930; Slums and Housing, p. 314. For a sketch of Brooklyn's Negro community see Ralph Foster Weld, Brooklyn Is America (New York, 1950), pp. 153-173.
16. The President's Conference on Home Building and Home Ownership, Report of the Committee on Negro Housing (Washington, D.C., 1931), p. 5.
17. Bureau of the Census, Fifteenth Census, 1930: Population (Washington, D.C., 1933), II, 70; Ira De Augustine Reid, The Negro Immigrant (New

York, 1938), pp. 248-249; Barrington Dunbar, "Factors in the Cultural Background of the American Southern Negro and the British West Indian Negro that Condition their Adjustment in Harlem" (M.A. thesis, Columbia University, 1935), *foreword*, p. 4.

18. Reid, *The Negro Immigrant*, pp. 31-35; Reid, "Negro Immigration to the United States," *Social Forces*, XVI (March 1938), 411-417; W. A. Domingo, "Restricted West Indian Immigration and the American Negro," *Opportunity*, II (October 1924), 298-299.

19. W. A. Domingo, "Gift of the Black Tropics," in Alain Locke, ed., *The New Negro: An Interpretation* (New York, 1925), p. 343.

20. *The New York Age*, July 9, 1924, February 4, 1928; Harry Robinson, "The Negro Immigrant in New York" (WPA research paper, Schomburg Collection), p. 9.

21. Garrie Ward Moore, "A Study of a Group of West Indian Negroes in New York City" (M.A. thesis, Columbia University, 1923), pp. 19-20; Reid, *The Negro Immigrant*, pp. 126-128; *The New York Age*, February 28, 1931, July 29, 1933.

22. "The Negro in New York" (unpublished WPA manuscript, Schomburg Collection), pp. 25-27; Gardner N. Jones, "The Pilgrimage to Freedom" (WPA research paper, Schomburg Collection), p. 25.

23. Reid, *The Negro Immigrant*, p. 159.

24. *Ibid.*, p. 123; "Communists in Harlem," *The New York Age*, September 21, 1929, October 2, 9, 1926, December 24, 1927, January 21, May 12, December 8, 1928, September 21, 1929.

25. Domingo, "Gift of the Black Tropics," p. 347.

26. Robinson, "Negro Immigrant in New York," pp. 21-22; Moore, "West Indian Negroes in New York City," p. 26.

27. "The Reminiscences of George S. Schuyler" (Oral History Research Office, Columbia University, 1960), p. 73.

28. Robinson, "Negro Immigrant in New York," p. 9; "The Negro in New York," p. 25; Moore, "West Indian Negroes in New York City," p. 25; Reid, *The Negro Immigrant*, p. 133; *The Messenger*, VII (September 1925), 326, 337-338; *The New York Age*, February 22, 1930; Baltimore *Afro-American*, January 9, 1932.

29. Moore, "West Indian Negroes in New York City," p. 5.

30. Dunbar, "Negro Adjustment in Harlem," pp. 14-25.

31. Reid, *The Negro Immigrant, passim.*

32. *Ibid.*, p. 125; Greater New York Federation of Churches, *Negro Churches in Manhattan* (New York, 1930).

33. Reid, *The Negro Immigrant*, p. 174; Moore, "West Indian Negroes in New York City," pp. 20-25; Dunbar, "Negro Adjustment in Harlem," chap. IV, pp. 22-23.

34. Roi Ottley, *'New World A-Coming': Inside Black America* (New York, 1943), pp. 47-48; Gardner Jones, "The Pilgrimage to Freedom"

(WPA research paper, Schomburg Collection), p. 25; Beverly Smith, "Harlem—Negro City," *New York Herald Tribune*, February 14, 1930; Reid, *The Negro Immigrant*, p. 115; *The New York Age*, July 19, 1924, March 17, 1934; Dunbar, "Negro Adjustment in Harlem," chap. III, p. 4; Walter White, "The Paradox of Color," in Alain Locke, ed., *The New Negro: An Interpretation* (New York, 1925), p. 367.

35. *The New York Age*, March 3, 24, April 21, 1928; Domingo, "The Gift of the Black Tropics," p. 344-345; Reid, *The Negro Immigrant*, p. 235.

36. "Harlem Slums," *The Crisis*, XLVIII (December 1941), 378-381; *The New York Age*, January 22, 1927.

37. New York Urban League, "Twenty-four Hundred Negro Families in Harlem: An Interpretation of the Living Conditions of Small Wage Earners" (typescript, Schomburg Collection, 1927), pp. 16-18.

38. *Report of the Committee on Negro Housing*, p. 64.

39. "Appreciation" of prices "came [when owners] remained calm. . . ." T. J. Woofter, *et al.*, *Negro Problems in Cities* (New York, 1928), p. 75. *The New York Times* printed dozens of articles on Harlem's new business prosperity.

40. "Harlem Real Estate Increasing in Value," *Harlem Magazine*, VIII (February 1920), 18b; "Unprecedented Demand for Harlem Real Estate," *ibid.*, X (November 1920), 6; "Revival of Speculative Activity on Harlem's Main Thoroughfare," *The New York Times*, January 18, 1920, July 24, 1921, June 10, 1923, February 13, 1927.

41. "Of all the gouging landlords in Harlem, the colored landlords and agents are the worst, according to the records of the Seventh District Municipal Court." "Race Landlord is Hardest on His Tenants," *The New York Age*, November 20, 1920, June 16, September 22, 1923, May 29, 1926.

42. "The Negro in Harlem," pp. 27-32; *The New York Age*, April 26, 1930.

43. Bureau of the Census, *Fourteenth Census, 1920: Population* (Washington, D.C., 1923), IV, 366-367, 1157-1179; *Fifteenth Census, 1930: Occupations* (Washington, D.C., 1933), 1130-1134; Helen B. Sayre, "Negro Women in Industry," *Opportunity*, II (August 1924), 242-244.

44. *Report of the Committee on Negro Housing*, p. 64; *Negro Problems in Cities*, p. 122.

45. "Twenty-four Hundred Negro Families in Harlem," p. 19; Sidney Axelrad, *Tenements and Tenants: A Study of 1104 Tenement Families* (New York, 1932), p. 15; New York Building and Land Utilization Committee, *Harlem Family Income Survey* (New York, 1935), p. 3; James H. Hubert, "Harlem—Its Social Problems," *Hospital Social Service*, XXI (January 1930), 44.

46. *Report of the Committee on Negro Housing*, p. vii.

47. William Wilson to La Guardia, October 6, 1944, La Guardia Papers.

48. *Health Conditions in North Harlem*, pp. 16-

17; *Fifteenth Census, 1930: Population* (Washington, D.C., 1933), II, 733-734; "The Negro in Harlem," p. 20.

49. ". . . The greatest need is the construction of model tenements. These should consist of one, two, three and four room apartments." "Modern Housing Needs," *The New York Age*, February 12, 1921, January 20, 1923, January 26, 1926, January 29, 1927; "The Negro in Harlem," p. 53; Eugene Kinckle Jones, "Negro Migration in New York State," *Opportunity*, IV (January 1926), 9.

50. Victor R. Daly, "The Housing Crisis in New York City," *The Crisis*, XXXI (December 1920), 61-62.

51. National Urban League, *Housing Conditions Among Negroes, New York City* (New York, 1915), *passim*; Ford, *et al.*, *Slums and Housing*, p. 338.

52. "Very often it is found that there are two shifts." William Wilson to La Guardia, October 6, 1944, La Guardia Papers; *The New York Age*, March 12, 1921, February 26, 1927; "Along Rainbow Row," *The New York Times*, August 15, 1921, January 27, 1922; "Twenty-four Hundred Negro Families in Harlem," *passim*; Roscoe Conkling Bruce, "The Dunbar Apartment House: An Adventure in Community Building," *The Southern Workman*, LX (October 1931), 418.

53. *New York Herald Tribune*, February 12, 13, 1930.

54. "I promoted a weekly party, to get money to pay rent." "Boisterous rent parties, flooded with moonshine, are a quick and sure resource." "The Reminiscences of Benjamin McLaurin" (Oral History Research Office, Columbia University, 1960), p. 155; *The New York Age*, August 11, 1923, June 21, December 11, 1926; Clyde Vernon Kiser, *Sea Island to City* (New York, 1932), pp. 44-45.

55. Booker T. Washington, *Up from Slavery: An Autobiography* (New York 1959), pp. 122-123. Note the following statement of a recent study: "There are many cases in which migratory workers do not understand or properly use ordinary living facilities, such as toilets, showers, bedding, kitchen appliances, and garbage cans. The result has been unnecessary damage to property and needless expense for repairs." 87th Cong., 1st Sess., *Senate Report 1098* (1961), p. 8.

56. *The New York Age*, August 1, 1912, June 5, 1920, September 16, 1922, July 14, 1928; National Urban League, *Housing Conditions Among Negroes*, pp. 9-10; "The Negro in Harlem," p. 113; Eslanda Goode Robeson, *Paul Robeson: Negro* (London, 1930), p. 46.

57. Woofter, *et al.*, *Negro Problems in Cities*, pp. 79, 84; "The Negro in Harlem," p. 53; Ernest W. Burgess, "Residential Segregation in American Cities," *The Annals*, CXL (November 1928), 105-115; Ford, *et al.*, *Slums and Housing*, p. 749.

58. Owen R. Lovejoy, *The Negro Children of New York* (New York, 1932), p. 15.

59. *The New York Age*, October 28, 1922, January 17, 1925; *Housing Conditions Among Negroes, passim*; "Twenty-four Hundred Negro Families in Harlem," *passim*.

60. "I do not think I need to say that our problem of Harlem is one of the most serious we have to face." Langdon W. Post (Chairman of New York City Housing Authority) to La Guardia, April 30, 1936, La Guardia Papers. "The Negro families of the West Harlem section have undoubtedly the most serious housing problem in the City." Ford, *et al.*, *Slums and Housing*, p. 326. *The New York Times*, September 16, 1920, October 17, 23, 1921, April 22, 1922, January 17, June 13, 1925; *The New York Age*, February 28, August 8, 1925, January 9, 1926; "Preliminary Report on the Subject of Housing (1935)," La Guardia Papers.

61. "High Cost of Dying," *The New York Age*, February 25, 1928.

62. *Health Conditions in North Harlem, passim; The Negro Children of New York*, p. 22; "Fighting the Ravages of the White Plague Among New York's Negro Population," *Opportunity*, I (January 1923), 23-24; Dr. Louis R. Wright, "Cancer as It Affects Negroes," *ibid.*, VI (June 1928), 169-170, 187; Louis I. Dublin, "The Effect of Health Education on Negro Mortality," *Proceedings of the National Conference on Social Work, 1924* (Chicago, 1924), 274-279. Hereafter cited as PNCSW.

63. ". . . Syphilitic infection is one of the most fruitful causes of stillbirths, miscarriages, and early death of infants." New York Association for Improving the Condition of the Poor, *Health Work for Mothers and Children in a Colored Community* (New York, 1924), p. 3; "The Negro's Health Progress During the Last Twenty-five Years," *Weekly Bulletin of the Department of Health*, XV (June 12, 1926), 93-96; *Fifteenth Census, 1930: Population* (Washington, D.C., 1933), II, 959; E. K. Jones, "The Negro's Struggle for Health," *PNCSW, 1923* (Chicago, 1923), 68-72.

64. Adapted from Godea J. Drolet and Louis Werner, "Vital Statistics in the Development of Neighborhood Health Centers in New York City," *Journal of Preventive Medicine*, VI (January 1932), 69.

65. In 1920, 30.3 per cent of white women in the city worked, and 57.9 per cent of colored women were employed. *Fourteenth Census, 1920: Population* (Washington, D.C., 1923), IV, 367. Robert Morse Woodbury, *Causal Factors in Infant Mortality* (Washington, D.C., 1925); L. T. Wright, "Factors Controlling Negro Health," *The Crisis*, XLII (September 1935), 264-265, 280, 284; Mildred Jane Watson, "Infant Mortality in New York City, White and Colored, 1929-1936" (M.A. thesis, Columbia University, 1938); Charles Herbert Garvin, "White Plague and Black Folk," *Opportunity*, VIII (August 1930), 232-235.

66. For "voodoo" and "devil worship" among

West Indians see Reid, *The Negro Immigrant*, pp. 48-49, 136-138.

67. ". . . Many [are] bringing with them their simple faith in roots, herbs, home remedies, [and are] imposed upon by unscrupulous venders of worthless . . . remedies," Dr. Peter Marshall Murray, "Harlem's Health," *Hospital Social Service*, XXII (October 1930), 309-313; C. V. Roman, "The Negro's Psychology and His Health," *PNCSW, 1924* (Chicago, 1924), 270-274; *Opportunity*, IV (July 1926), 206-207; *The Crisis*, XLII (August 1935), 243; *The New York Age*, September 23, 1922, February 17, July 21, August 11, 25, 1923, January 6, April 5, 1924, February 21, March 14, 1925, January 18, July 23, 1927.

68. Note the striking similarities between the medical and healing superstitions of urban Negroes in the twentieth century and those of slaves in the early nineteenth century. The following is a description of slave superstition by an ex-slave: "There is much superstition among the slaves. Many of them believe in what they call 'conjuration,' tricking, and witchcraft; and some of them pretend to understand the art, and say that by it they can prevent their masters from exercising their will over their slaves. Such are often applied to by others, to give them power to prevent their masters from flogging them. The remedy is most generally some kind of bitter root; they are directed to chew it and spit toward their masters. . . . At other times they prepare certain kinds of powders, to sprinkle their masters' dwellings." *Narrative of the Life and Adventures of Henry Bibb, An American Slave, Written by Himself* (New York, 1849), pp. 25-31.

69. Beverly Smith, "Harlem—Negro City," *New York Herald Tribune*, February 11, 1930; Ira De Augustine Reid, "Let Us Prey!" *Opportunity* IV (September 1926), 274-278; Reverend James H. Robinson, *Road Without Turning: An Autobiography* (New York, 1950), 231.

70. *The New York Age*, February 19, 1927; *The New York Times*, September 24, 1919.

71. Zora Neale Hurston, *Dust Track on a Road* (Philadelphia, 1942), pp. 279-280.

72. *The New York Age*, January 15, 1927, February 9, 1929, August 23, 1930, August 8, September 19, 1931, July 23, 1932, August 26, 1933, September 1, 1934.

73. "A Wide Open Harlem," *ibid.*, September 2, 1922.

74. Committee of Fourteen, *Annual Reports*, 1914-1930; *The Crisis*, XXXVI (November 1929), 417-418; *The Messenger*, VI (January 1924), 14.

75. Langston Hughes, "Young Prostitute," *The Crisis*, XXVI (August 1923), 162.

76. "Gambling is popular in Harlem, but the big shots of the racket are white." Fiorello La Guardia, "Harlem: Homelike and Hopeful" (unpublished manuscript, La Guardia Papers), p. 9; "A Summary of Vice Conditions in Harlem," Committee of Fourteen, *Annual Report for 1928* (New York, 1929), 31-34; *The New York Times*, February 13, 1922; *The New Age*, February 28, 1925, May 18, 1929. Although whites seemed to control most of Harlem vice, Virgin Islander Casper Holstein—well-known as a philanthropist and café owner—was reputed to be a head of the numbers racket.

77. "Harlem—The Bettor," *The New York Age*, March 7, 1925, November 6, 20, 1926, June 4, 1927, June 23, 1928; *The New York Times*, June 12, 1922, March 11, 1927; "New York: Utopia Deferred," *The Messenger*, VII (October, November 1925), 344-349, 370.

78. *The New York Age*, September 16, 1922, April 21, 1923; *New York Herald Tribune*, February 13, 1930; *The Messenger*, VI (August 1924) 247, 262.

79. Lovejoy, *The Negro Children of New York*, p. 37; *New York Herald Tribune*, February 12, 1930; Joint Committee on Negro Child Study in New York City, *A Study of Delinquent and Neglected Negro Children Before the New York City Children's Court* (New York, 1927).

80. Jacob Theobald, "Some Facts About P.S. 89, Manhattan," *The New York Age*, January 17, 1920; "Report of Subcommittee on Education," La Guardia Papers; "The Problem of Education and Recreation," *ibid.*; "The Negro in Harlem," p. 73; Lovejoy, *The Negro Children of New York*, p. 22; *The New York Age*, March 12, 1921.

81. "Results of the Crime and Delinquency Study," La Guardia Papers; *The New York Age*, January 6, February 17, June 23, 1923, June 12, 1926, December 3, 1927, July 28, 1928, January 4, 1930. A white Harlem policeman, at a later date, wrote the following: "Every one of [us] is made to feel like a soldier in an army of occupation. He is engulfed by an atmosphere of antagonism." *The Crisis*, LII (January 1945), 16-17.

82. Lovejoy, *The Negro Children of New York*, p. 15; "The Negro in Harlem," p. 110; *The New York Age*, February 9, 1929; "The Reminiscences of George S. Schuyler" (Oral History Research Office, Columbia University, 1960), p. 232.

Urbanization, Migration, and Social Mobility in Late Nineteenth-Century America

Stephan Thernstrom

The United States, it has been said, was born in the country and has moved to the city. It was during the half-century between the Civil War and World War I that the move was made. In 1860, less than a quarter of the American population lived in a city or town; by 1890, the figure had reached a third; by 1910, nearly half. By more sophisticated measures than the mere count of heads, the center of gravity of the society had obviously tilted cityward well before the last date.

If to speak of "the rise of the city" in those years is a text-book cliché, the impact of this great social transformation upon the common people of America has never been sufficiently explored. This essay is intended as a small contribution toward that task. It sketches the process by which ordinary men and women were drawn to the burgeoning cities of post-Civil War America, assesses what little we know about how they were integrated into the urban class structure, and suggests how these matters affected the viability of the political system.

I

The urbanization of late nineteenth-century America took place at a dizzying pace. Chicago, for instance, doubled its population every decade but one between 1850 and 1890, growing from 30,000 to over a million in little more than a generation. And it was not merely the conspicuous metropolitan giants but the Akrons, the Duluths, the Tacomas that were bursting at the seams; no less than 101 American communities grew by 100 percent or more in the 1880s.[1]

Why did Americans flock into these all too often unlovely places? There were some who were not pulled to the city but rather pushed out of their previous habitats and dropped there, more or less by accident. But the overriding fact is that the cities could draw on an enormous reservoir of people who were dissatisfied with their present lot and eager to seize the new opportunities offered by the metropolis.

Who were these people? It is conventional to distinguish two broad types of migrants to the American city: the immigrant from another culture, and the farm lad who moved from a rural to an urban setting within the culture. It is also conventional in historical accounts to overlook the latter type and to focus on the more exotic of the migrants, those who had to undergo the arduous process of becoming Americanized.

This is regrettable. To be sure, immigration from abroad was extremely important in the building of America's cities down to World War I. But the

From Barton J. Bernstein (ed.), *Towards a New Past: Dissenting Essays in American History* (New York: Pantheon, 1968), pp. 158-75. Copyright © 1967, 1968 by Random House, Inc. Reprinted by permission of Pantheon Books, a division of Random House, Inc. Stephan Thernstrom is Associate Professor of American History at Brandeis University.

most important source of population for the burgeoning cities was not the fields of Ireland and Austria, but those of Vermont and Iowa. The prime cause of population growth in nineteenth-century America, and the main source of urban growth, was simply the high fertility of natives living outside the city.

We tend to neglect internal migration from country to city, partly because the immigrants from abroad seem exotic and thus conspicuous, partly because of the unfortunate legacy left by Frederick Jackson Turner's frontier theory, one element of which was the notion that the open frontier served as a safety valve for urban discontent. When there were hard times in the city, according to Turner, the American worker didn't join a union or vote Socialist; he moved West and grabbed some of that free land. This theory has been subjected to the rather devastating criticism that by 1860 it took something like $1,000 capital to purchase sufficient transportation, seed equipment, livestock, and food (to live on until the first crop) to make a go of it; that it took even more than $1,000 later in the century, and that it was precisely the unemployed workmen who were least likely to have that kind of money at their command. It is estimated that for every industrial worker who became a farmer, twenty farm boys became urban dwellers.[2] There was an urban safety valve for rural discontent, and an extremely important one. The dominant form of population movement was precisely the opposite of that described by Turner.

Since scholarly attention has been focused upon immigrants from abroad, upon Oscar Handlin's "Uprooted," it will be useful to review what is known about their movement to the American city and then to ask how much the same generalizations might hold for native Americans uprooted from the countryside and plunged into the city.

Immigration is as old as America, but a seismic shift in the character of European immigration to these shores occurred in the nineteenth century, as a consequence of the commercial transformation of traditional European agriculture and the consequent displacement of millions of peasants.[3] Compared to earlier newcomers, these were people who were closer to the land and more tradition-bound, and they generally had fewer resources to bring with them than their predecessors. One shouldn't overwork this; a substantial fraction of the German and Scandinavian immigrants had enough capital to get to the West to pick up land. But some of the Germans and Scandinavians, and most men of other nationalities, had just enough cash to make it to the New World and were stuck for a time at least where they landed—New York, Boston, or wherever. They swelled the population appreciably and the relief rolls dramatically, particularly in the pre-Civil War years, when they entered cities which were basically commercial and had little use for men whose only skill in many cases was that they knew how to dig. Eventually, however, the stimulus of this vast pool of cheap labor and the demands of the growing city itself opened up a good many unskilled jobs—in the construction of roads, houses, and commercial buildings, and in the manufacturing that began to spring up in the cities.

That they were driven off the land in the Old World, that they arrived without resources, immobilized by their poverty, and that they often suffered a great deal before they secured stable employment is true enough. But these harsh facts may lead us to overlook other aspects which were extremely significant.

One is that immigration was a *selective* process. However powerful the pressures to leave, in no case did anyone in a community pull up stakes. This observation may be uncomfortably reminiscent of the popular opinion on this point: that it was the best of the Old World stock that came to the New—the most intelligent, enterprising, courageous. But this should not lead us to neglect the point altogether. The traits that led some men to leave and allowed them to survive the harrowing journey to the port, the trip itself, and the perils of the New World, could be described in somewhat different terms: substitute cunning for intelligence, for example, or ruthlessness for courage. Still, whatever the emphasis, the fact remains: as weighed in the scales of the marketplace, those who came—however driven by cruel circumstance—were better adapted to American life than those who remained in the village or died on the way.

The other main point about the immigrants, and especially those who suffered the most extreme hardships—the Irish in the 1840s and 1850s, the French Canadians in the 1870s, the Italians and various East Europeans after 1880 —is that they appraised their new situations with standards developed in peasant society. Lowell was terrible, with its cramped stinking tenements, and factory workers labored from dawn till dark for what seems a mere pittance. Children were forced to work at a brutally early age; the factories and dwellings were deathtraps. But Lowell was a damn sight better than County Cork, and men who knew from bitter experience what County Cork was like could not view their life in Lowell with quite the same simple revulsion as the middle-class reformers who judged Lowell by altogether different standards. It is not so much the objectively horrible character of a situation that goads men to action as it is a nagging discrepancy between what *is* and what is *expected*. And what one expects is determined by one's reference group—which can be a class, an ethnic or religious subculture, or some other entity which defines people's horizon of expectation.[4] Immigration provided an ever renewed stream of men who entered the American economy to fill its least attractive and least well rewarded positions, men who happen to have brought with them very low horizons of expectation fixed in peasant Europe.

That those Americans with greatest reason to feel outrageously exploited judged their situation against the dismally low standards of the decaying European village is an important clue to the stunted growth of the labor movement and the failure of American Socialism. Working in the same direction was what might be called the Tower of Babel factor. A firm sense of class solidarity was extremely difficult to develop in communities where people literally didn't speak each other's language. Even in cases where groups of immigrant workers had unusually high expectations and previous familiarity with advanced forms of collective action—such as the English artisans who led the Massachusetts textile strikes in the 1870s—they found it hard to keep the other troops in line; a clever Italian-speaking or Polish-speaking foreman could easily exploit national differences for his own ends, and if necessary there were always the most recent immigrants of all (and the

Negroes) to serve as scabs to replace the dissenters en masse.

A somewhat similar analysis applies to the migrants who left the Kansas farms for Chicago. They were linguistically and culturally set apart from many of their fellow workers; they too had low horizons of expectation fixed in the countryside and brought to the city. The latter point is often missed because of the peculiar American reverence for an idealized agrarian way of life. As we have become a nation of city dwellers, we have come more and more to believe that it is virtuous and beautiful to slave for fourteen hours a day with manure on your boots. Recently that sturdy small farmer from Johnson City, Texas, remarked that "it does not make sense on this great continent which God has blessed to have more than 70 percent of our people crammed into one percent of the land." A national "keep them down on the farm" campaign is therefore in the offing.[5] But it is damnably hard to keep them down on the farm after they've seen New York (or even Indianapolis), and it was just as hard a century ago, for the very good reason that the work is brutal, the profits are often miserably low, and the isolation is psychologically murderous. Virtuous this life may be, especially to people who don't have to live it, but enjoyable it is not—not, at least, to a very substantial fraction of our ever shrinking farm population.

This applies particularly to young men and women growing up on a farm. Their parents had a certain stake in staying where they were, even if it was a rut. And the eldest son, who would inherit the place eventually, was sometimes tempted by that. But the others left in droves, to tend machines, to dig and haul and hammer—or in the case of

the girls, to sell underwear in Marshall Field's, to mind someone else's kitchen, or in some instances to follow in the footsteps of Sister Carrie.

There were some large differences between native-born migrants to the cities and immigrants from another land, to be sure. But the familiar argument that native workmen "stood on the shoulders" of the immigrant and was subjected to less severe exploitation is somewhat misleading. The advantages enjoyed by many American-born laborers stemmed more from their urban experience than their birth, and they did not generally accrue to freshly arrived native migrants to the city. The latter were little better off than their immigrant counterparts, but then they too were spiritually prepared to endure a great deal of privation and discomfort because even the bottom of the urban heap was a step up from the farms they had left behind. The two groups were one in this respect, and perceptive employers recognized the fact. In 1875, the Superintendent of one of Andrew Carnegie's steel mills summed up his experience this way: "We must steer clear as far as we can of Englishmen, who are great sticklers for high wages, small production and strikes. My experience has shown that Germans and Irish, Swedes and what I denominate 'Buckwheats'— young American country boys, judiciously mixed, make the most honest and tractable force you can find."[6]

II

The move to the city, therefore, was an advance of a kind for the typical migrant. Were there further opportunities for advancement there, or did he then find himself crushed by circumstance and reduced to the ranks of the permanent proletariat? Did his children, whose expectations were presumably higher, discover correspondingly greater opportunities open to them? Remarkably little serious research has been devoted to these issues. Historians who see American history as a success story have been content to assume, without benefit of data, that the American dream of mobility was true, apparently on the principle that popular ideology is a sure guide to social reality. Dissenting scholars have been more inclined to the view that class barriers were relatively impassable, an assumption based upon generalized skepticism about American mythology rather than upon careful empirical study. Some recent work, however, provides the basis for a tentative reappraisal of the problem.

We know most about mobility into the most rarefied reaches of the social order regarding such elite groups as millionaires, railroad presidents, directors of large corporations, or persons listed in the *Dictionary of American Biography*. What is most impressive about the literature on the American elite is that, in spite of many variations in the way in which the elite is defined, the results of these studies are much the same. It is clear that growing up in rags is not in the least conductive to the attainment of later riches, and that it was no more so a century ago than it is today.[7] There have been spectacular instances of mobility from low down on the social scale to the very top—Andrew Carnegie, for instance. But colorful examples cannot sustain broad generalizations about social phenomena, however often they are impressed into service toward that end. Systematic investigation reveals that even in the days of Andrew Carnegie, there was little room at the top, except for those who started very close to it.

Furthermore, this seems to have been the case throughout most of American history, despite many dramatic alterations in the character of the economy. It seems perfectly plausible to assume, as many historians have on the basis of impressionistic evidence, that the precipitous growth of heavy industry in the latter half of the nineteenth century opened the doors to men with very different talents from the educated merchants who constituted the elite of the preindustrial age, that unlettered, horny-handed types like Thomas Alva Edison and Henry Ford, crude inventors and tinkerers, then came into their own; that the connection between parental wealth and status and the son's career was loosened, so that members of the business elite typically had lower social origins and less education, and were often of immigrant stock. Plausible, yes, but true, no. It helped to go to Harvard in Thomas Jefferson's America, and it seems to have helped just about as much in William McKinley's America. There were the Edisons and Fords, who rose spectacularly from low origins, but there were always a few such. Cases like these were about as exceptional in the late nineteenth century as they were earlier. The image of the great inventor springing from common soil, unspoiled by book-larnin', is a red herring. It is doubtful, to say the least, that the less you know, the more likely you are to build a better mousetrap. And in any event it was not the great inventor who raked in the money, in most cases— Henry Ford never invented anything— but rather the organizer and manipulator, whose talents seem to have been highly valued through all periods of American history.

These conclusions are interesting, but an important caution is in order. It by no means follows that if there was very little room at the top, there was little room anywhere else. It is absurd to judge the openness or lack of openness of an entire social system solely by the extent of recruitment from below into the highest positions of all. One can imagine a society in which all members of the tiny elite are democratically recruited from below, and yet where the social structure as a whole is extremely rigid with that small exception. Conversely, one can imagine a society with a hereditary ruling group at the very top, a group completely closed to aspiring men of talent but lowly birth, and yet with an enormous amount of movement back and forth below that pinnacle. Late nineteenth-century America could have approximated this latter model, with lineage, parental wealth, and education as decisive assets in the race for the very peak, as the business elite studies suggest, and yet with great fluidity at the lower and middle levels of the class structure.

Was this in fact the case? The evidence available today is regrettably scanty, but here are the broad outlines of an answer, insofar as we can generalize from a handful of studies.[8] At the lower and middle ranges of the class structure there was impressive mobility, though often of an unexpected and rather ambiguous kind. I will distinguish three types of mobility: geographical, occupational, and property, and say a little about the extent and significance of each.

First is geographical mobility, physical movement from place to place, which is tied up in an interesting way with movement through the social scale. Americans have long been thought a

restless, footloose people, and it has been assumed that the man on the move has been the man on the make; he knows that this little town doesn't provide a grand enough stage for him to display his talents, and so he goes off to the big city to win fame and fortune, or to the open frontier to do likewise. When you examine actual behavior instead of popular beliefs, however, you discover that things are more complicated than that.

It proves to be true that Americans are indeed a footloose people. In my work on Newburyport, a small industrial city, I attempted to find out what fraction of the families present in the community in the initial year of my study—1850—were still living there in the closing year, 1880, one short generation. Less than a fifth of them, it turned out—and this not in a community on the moving frontier, like Merle Curti's Trempealeau County, where you would expect a very high turnover. There the true pioneer types, who liked to clear the land, became nervous when there was another family within a half day's ride of them and sold out to the second wave of settlers (often immigrants who knew better than to try to tame the wilderness without previous experience at it). But to find roughly the same volatility in a city forty miles north of Boston suggests that the whole society was in motion.

The statistics bear out the legend that Americans are a restless people. What of the assertion that movement and success go hand in hand, that physical mobility and upward social mobility are positively correlated? Here the legend seems more questionable. It seems likely that some who pulled up stakes and went elsewhere for a new start did improve their positions; they found better land, or discovered that they possessed talents which were much more highly valued in the big city than in the place they came from. What ever would have happened to Theodore Dreiser in small-town Indiana had there been no Chicago for him to flee to?

But the point to underline, for it is less commonly understood, is that much of this remarkable population turnover was of quite a different kind. As you trace the flow of immigrants into and then out of the cities, you begin to see that a great many of those who departed did so in circumstances which make it exceedingly hard to believe that they were moving on to bigger and better things elsewhere. There is no way to be certain about this, no feasible method of tracing individuals once they disappear from the universe of the community under consideration. These questions can be explored for contemporary America by administering questionnaires to people and collecting life histories which display migration patterns, but dead men tell no tales and fill out no questionnaires, so that part of the past is irrevocably lost. But some plausible inferences can be drawn about the nature of this turnover from the fact that so many ordinary working people on the move owned no property, had no savings accounts, had acquired no special skills, and were most likely to leave when they were unemployed. They were, in short, people who had made the least successful economic adjustment to the community and who were no longer able to hang on there. At the lower reaches of the social order, getting out of town did not ordinarily mean a step up the ladder somewhere else; there is no reason to assume that in their new destinations migrant laborers found anything but more of the

same. When middle-class families, who already had a niche in the world, moved on, it was often in response to greater opportunities elsewhere; for ordinary working people physical movement meant something very different.

That is a less rosy picture than the one usually painted, but I think it is more accurate. And we should notice one very important implication of this argument: namely, that the people who were least successful and who had the greatest grievances are precisely those who never stayed put very long in any one place. Students of labor economics and trade union history have long been aware of the fact that there are certain occupations which are inordinately difficult to organize simply because they have incessant job turnover. When only 5 percent or 1 percent of the men working at a particular job in a given city at the start of the year are still employed twelve months later, as is the case with some occupations in the economic underworld today (short-order cooks or menial hospital workers, for instance), how do you build a stable organization and conduct a successful strike?

An analagous consideration applies not merely to certain selected occupations but to a large fraction of the late nineteenth-century urban working class as a whole. The Marxist model of the conditions which promote proletarian consciousness presumes not only permanency of membership in this class—the absence of upward mobility—but also, I suggest, some continuity of class membership *in one setting* so that workers come to know each other and to develop bonds of solidarity and common opposition to the ruling group above them. This would seem to entail a stable labor force in a single factory; at a minimum it assumes considerable stability in a community. One reason that a permanent proletariat along the lines envisaged by Marx did not develop in the course of American industrialization is perhaps that few Americans have *stayed* in one place, one workplace, or even one city long enough to discover a sense of common identity and common grievance. This may be a vital clue to the divergent political development of America and Western Europe in the industrial age, to the striking weakness of socialism here, as compared to Europe—though we can't be sure because we don't definitely know that the European working-class population was less volatile. I suspect that it was, to some degree, and that America was distinctive in this respect, but this is a question of glaring importance which no one has yet taken the trouble to investigate.

When I first stumbled upon this phenomenon in sifting through manuscript census schedules for nineteenth-century Newburyport, I was very doubtful that the findings could be generalized to apply to the big cities of the period. It seemed reasonable to assume that the laborers who drifted out of Newburyport so quickly after their arrival must have settled down somewhere else, and to think that a great metropolis would have offered a more inviting haven than a small city, where anonymity was impossible and where middle-class institutions of social control intruded into one's daily life with some frequency, as compared to a classic big-city lower-class ghetto, where the down-and-out could perhaps huddle together for protective warmth and be left to their own devices —for instance, those Irish wards of New York where the police made no attempt to enforce law and order until late in the century. Here if anywhere one should be able to find a continuous

lower-class population, a permanent proletariat, and I began my Boston research with great curiosity about this point.

If Boston is any example, in no American city was there a sizable lower class with great continuity of membership. You can identify some more or less continuously lower-class areas, but the crucial point is that *the same people do not stay in them*. If you take a sample of unskilled and semi-skilled laborers in Boston in 1880 and look for them in 1890, you are not much more likely to find them still in the city than was the case in Newburyport.[9]

The bottom layer of the social order in the nineteenth-century American city was thus a group of families who appear to have been permanent transients, buffeted about from place to place, never quite able to sink roots. We know very little about these people, and it is difficult to know how we can learn much about them. You get only occasional glimpses into the part of this iceberg that appears above the surface, in the person of the tramp, who first is perceived as a problem for America in the 1870s and reappears in hard times after that—in the 1890s and in the great depression most notably. But what has been said here at least suggests the significance of the phenomenon.

So much for geographical mobility. What can be said about the people who come to the city and remain there under our microscope so that we can discern what happened to them? I have already anticipated my general line of argument here in my discussion of migration out of the city—which amounted to the claim that the city was a kind of Darwinian jungle in which the fittest survived and the others drifted on to try another place. Those who did stay in the city and make their way there did, in general, succeed in advancing themselves economically and socially. There was very impressive mobility, though not always of the kind we might expect.

In approaching this matter, we must make a distinction which is obscured by applying labels like "open" or "fluid" to entire whole social structures. There are, after all, two sets of escalators in any community; one set goes down. To describe a society as enormously fluid implies that there are lots of people moving down while lots of others are moving up to take their place. This would obviously be a socially explosive situation, for all those men descending against their will would arrive at the bottom, not with low horizons of expectation set in some peasant village, but with expectations established when they were at one of the comfortable top floors of the structure.

Downward mobility is by no means an unknown phenomenon in American history. There have been socially displaced groups, especially if you take into account rather subtle shifts in the relative status of such groups as professionals.[10] But the chief generalization to make is that Americans who started their working life in a middle-class job strongly tended to end up in the middle class; sons reared in middle-class families also attained middle-class occupations in the great majority of cases. Relatively few men born into the middle class fell from there; a good many born into the working class either escaped from it altogether or advanced themselves significantly within the class. There is a well-established tradition of writing about the skilled workman, associated with such names as the Hammonds, the Lynds, Lloyd Warner, and Norman Ware, which holds the con-

trary, to be sure.[11] This tradition still has its defenders, who argue that with industrialization "class lines assumed a new and forbidding rigidity" and that "machines made obsolete many of the skilled trades of the antebellum years, drawing the once self-respecting handicraftsmen into the drudgery and monotony of factory life, where they were called upon to perform only one step in the minutely divided and automatic processes of mass production."[12] Rapid technological change doubtless did displace some skilled artisans, doubtless produced some downward mobility into semiskilled positions. But defenders of this view have built their case upon little more than scattered complaints by labor leaders, and have not conducted systematic research to verify these complaints.

Careful statistical analysis provides a very different perspective on the matter. Two points stand out. One is that as certain traditional skilled callings became obsolete, there was an enormous expansion of *other* skilled trades, and, since many of the craftsmen under pressure from technological change had rather generalized skills, they moved rapidly into these new positions and thus retained their place in the labor aristocracy.[13] Second, it is quite mistaken to assume that the sons of the threatened artisan were commonly driven down into the ranks of the factory operatives; they typically found a place either in the expanding skilled trades or in the even more rapidly expanding white-collar occupations.[14]

As for workers on the lower rungs of the occupational ladder, the unskilled and semiskilled, they had rarely drifted down from a higher beginning point. Characteristically, they were newcomers to the urban world. A substantial minority of them appear to have been able to advance themselves a notch or two occupationally, especially among the second generation; a good many of their sons became clerks, salesmen, and other petty white-collar functionaries. And the the first generation, which had less success occupationally, was commonly experiencing mobility of another kind—property mobility. Despite a pathetically low (but generally rising) wage level, despite heavy unemployment rates, many were able to accumulate significant property holdings and to establish themselves as members of the stable working class, as opposed to the drifting lower class.[15]

It may seem paradoxical to suggest that so many Americans were rising in the world and so few falling; where did the room at the top come from? The paradox is readily resolved. For one thing, our attention has been fastened upon individuals who remained physically situated in one place in which their careers could be traced; an indeterminate but substantial fraction of the population was floating and presumably unsuccessful. By no means everyone at the bottom was upwardly mobile; the point is rather that those who were not were largely invisible. Furthermore, the occupational structure itself was changing in a manner that created disproportionately more positions in the middle and upper ranges, despite the common nineteenth-century belief that industrialization was homogenizing the work force and reducing all manual employees to identical robots. The homogenizing and degrading tendencies that caught the eye of Marx and others were more than offset, it appears, by developments which made for both a more differentiated and a more top-heavy occupational structure. Third, there were

important sources of social mobility that could be attained without changing one's occupation, most notably the property mobility that was stimulated by the increases in real wages that occurred in this period. Finally, there was the so-called "demographic vacuum" created by the differential fertility of the social classes, best illustrated in the gloomy late nineteenth-century estimate that in two hundred years 1,000 Harvard graduates would have only 50 living descendants while 1,000 Italians would have 100,000. The calculation is dubious, but the example nicely clarifies the point that high-status groups failed to reproduce themselves, thus opening up vacancies which had necessarily to be filled by new men from below.

For all the brutality and rapacity which marked the American scene in the years in which the new urban industrial order came into being, what stands out most is the relative absence of collective working-class protest aimed at reshaping capitalist society. The foregoing, while hardly a full explanation, should help to make this more comprehensible. The American working class was drawn into the new society by a process that encouraged accommodation and rendered disciplined protest difficult. Within the urban industrial orbit, most of its members found modest but significant opportunities to feel that they and their children were edging their way upwards. Those who did not find such opportunities were tossed helplessly about from city to city, from state to state, alienated but invisible and impotent.

NOTES

1. C. N. Glaab and A. T. Brown, *A History of Urban America* (New York, 1967), pp. 107-11.

2. Fred Shannon, "A Post Mortem on the Labor-Safety-Valve Theory," *Agricultural History*, XIX (1954), 31-37.

3. For general accounts, see Marcus L. Hansen, *The Atlantic Migration, 1607-1860* (paperback ed.; New York, 1961); Oscar Handlin, *The Uprooted* (Boston, 1951).

4. For discussion of the sociological concepts of reference groups and the theory of relative deprivation, see Robert K. Merton, *Social Theory and Social Structure*, rev. ed. (Glencoe, Ill., 1957) and the literature cited there. The problem of assessing the level of expectations of any particular migratory group in the past is extremely complicated, and it is obvious that there have been important differences between and within groups. But the generalizations offered here seem to me the best starting point for thinking about this issue.

5. *Boston Globe*, February 5, 1967.

6. Quoted in Oscar Handlin, *Immigration as a Factor in American History* (Englewood Cliffs, N.J., 1959), pp. 66-67.

7. For a convenient review of this literature, see Seymour M. Lipset and Reinhard Bendix, *Social Mobility in Industrial Society* (Berkeley, Cal., 1959), Ch. 4.

8. The main sources for the generalizations which follow, unless otherwise indicated, are: Stephan Thernstrom, *Poverty and Progress: Social Mobility in a Nineteenth Century City* (Cambridge, Mass., 1964); Merle E. Curti, *The Making of an American Frontier Community* (Stanford, Cal., 1959); Donald B. Cole, *Immigrant City: Lawrence, Massachusetts, 1845-1921* (Chapel Hill, N.C., 1963) —for my reservations about this work, however, see my review in the *Journal of Economic History*, XXIV (1964), 259-61; Herbert G. Gutman, "Social Status and Social Mobility in 19th Century America: Paterson, N.J., A Case Study," unpublished paper for the 1964 meetings of the American Historical Association; Howard Gitelman, "The Labor Force at Waltham Watch During the Civil War Era," *Journal of Economic History*, XXV (1965), 214-43; David Brody, *Steelworkers in America: The Nonunion Era* (Cambridge, Mass., 1960); Pauline Gordon, "The Chance to Rise Within Industry" (unpublished M.A. thesis, Columbia University); Robert Wheeler, "The Fifth-Ward Irish: Mobility at Mid-Century" (unpublished seminar paper, Brown University, 1967); and the author's research in progress on social mobility in Boston over the past century, in which the career patterns of some 8,000 ordinary residents of the community are traced.

9. Recent work suggesting that even the most recent U.S. Census seriously undernumerated the Negro male population may make the critical reader wonder about the accuracy of the census and city directory canvases upon which I base my analysis. Some elaborate checking has persuaded me that these nineteenth-century sources erred primarily in their coverage—their lack of coverage, rather—of the floating working-class population. For a variety of reasons it seems clear that families which had been in the community long enough to be included in one of these canvases—and hence to be included in a sample drawn from them—were rarely left out of later canvases if they were indeed still resident in the same city. A perfect census of every soul in the community on a given day would therefore yield an even higher, not a lower, estimate of population turnover for men at the bottom, which strengthens rather than weakens the argument advanced here.

10. The assumption that discontent stemming from social displacement has been the motive force behind American reform movements has exerted great influence upon American historical writing in recent years. See for instance David Donald, "Toward a Reconsideration of Abolitionists," *Lincoln Recosidered* (New York, 1956), pp. 19-36; Richard Hofstadter, *The Age of Reform: From Bryan to F.D.R.* (New York, 1955). Donald's essay is easily demolished by anyone with the slightest acquaintance with sociological method. Hofstadter's work, while open to a very serious objection, is at least sufficiently suggestive to indicate the potential utility of the idea.

11. J. L. and Barbara Hammond, *The Town Labourer (1760-1832)* (London, 1917); Robert S. and Helen M. Lynd, *Middletown* (New York, 1929), and *Middletown in Transition* (New York, 1937); W. Lloyd Warner and J. O. Low, *The Social System of the Modern Factory* (New Haven, Conn., 1947); Norman J. Ware, *The Industrial Worker, 1840-1860* (Boston, 1924).

12. Leon Litwak, ed., *The American Labor Movement* (Englewood Cliffs, N.J., 1962), p. 3.

13. This is evident from aggregated census data and from my Boston investigation, but we badly need an American counterpart to Eric Hobsbawm's splendid essay on "The Labour Aristocracy in Nineteenth Century Britain," in *Labouring Men: Studies in the History of Labour* (London, 1964), pp. 272-315.

14. So, at least, the evidence from Boston and Indianapolis indicates; for the latter, see Natlie Rogoff, *Recent Trends in Occupational Mobility* (Glencoe, Ill., 1953).

15. The clearest demonstration of this is in Thernstrom, *Poverty and Progress*, Ch. 5. It might be thought, however, that the remarkable property mobility disclosed there depended upon the existence of an abundant stock of cheap single-family housing available for purchase. It could be that where real estate was less readily obtainable, laborers would squander the funds that were accumulated with such sacrifice in places where home ownership was an immediate possibility. It appears from Wheeler's unpublished study of nineteenth-century Providence, however, that the working-class passion for property did not require an immediate, concrete source of satisfaction like a home and a plot of land. The Irish workmen of Providence were just as successful at accumulating property holdings as their Newburyport counterparts; the difference was only that they held personal rather than real property.

Crime as an American Way of Life:
A Queer Ladder of Social Mobility

DANIEL BELL

In the 1890's the Reverend Dr. Charles Parkhurst, shocked at the open police protection afforded New York's bordellos, demanded a state inquiry. In the Lexow investigation that followed, the young and dashing William Travers Jerome staged a set of public hearings that created sensation after sensation. He badgered "Clubber" Williams, First Inspector of the Police Department, to account for wealth and property far greater than could have been saved on his salary; it was earned, the Clubber explained laconically, through land speculation "in Japan." Heavy-set Captain Schmittberger, the "collector" for the "Tenderloin precints"—Broadway's fabulous concentration of hotels, theaters, restaurants, gaming houses, and saloons—related in detail how protection money was distributed among the police force. Crooks, policemen, public officials, businessmen, all paraded across the stage, each adding his chapter to a sordid story of corruption and crime. The upshot of these revelations was reform—the election of William L. Strong, a stalwart businessman, as mayor, and the naming of Theodore Roosevelt as police commissioner.

It did not last, of course, just as previous reform victories had not lasted. Yet the ritual drama was re-enacted. Thirty years ago the Seabury investigation in New York uncovered the tin-box brigade and the thirty-three little McQuades. Jimmy Walker was ousted as Mayor and in came Fiorello LaGuardia. Tom Dewey became district attorney, broke the industrial rackets, sent Lucky Luciano to jail, and went to the governor's chair in Albany. Then reform was again swallowed up in the insatiable maw of corruption until in 1950 Kefauver and his committee counsel Rudolph Halley threw a new beam of light into the seemingly bottomless pit.

How explain this repetitious cycle? Obviously the simple moralistic distinction between "good guys" and "bad guys," so deep at the root of the reform impulse, bears little relation to the role of organized crime in American society. What, then, does?

THE QUEER LADDER

Americans have had an extraordinary talent for compromise in politics and extremism in morality. The most shameless political deals (and "steals") have been rationalized as expedient and realistically necessary. Yet in no other country have there been such spectacular attempts to curb human appetites and brand them as illicit, and nowhere else such glaring failures. From the start America was at one and the same time a frontier community where "everything goes," and the fair country of

From Daniel Bell, *The End of Ideology* (New York: The Free Press, 1960), pp. 115-36, 381-82. Reprinted by permission of the author. Daniel Bell is Professor of Sociology at Columbia University.

the Blue Laws. At the turn of the century the cleavage developed between the Big City and the small-town conscience. Crime as a growing business was fed by the revenues from prostitution, liquor, and gambling that a wide-open urban society encouraged and that a middle-class Protestant ethos tried to suppress with a ferocity unmatched in any other civilized country. Catholic cultures have rarely imposed such restrictions and have rarely suffered such excesses. Even in prim and proper Anglican England, prostitution is a commonplace of Piccadilly night life, and gambling is one of the largest and most popular industries. In America the enforcement of public morals has been a continuing feature of our history.

Some truth may lie in Max Scheler's generalization that moral indignation is a peculiar fact of middle-class phychology and represents a disguised form of repressed envy. The larger truth lies perhaps in the brawling nature of American development and in the social character of crime. Crime, in many ways, is a Coney Island mirror, caricaturing the morals and manners of a society. The jungle quality of the American business community, particularly at the turn of the century, was reflected in the mode of "business" practiced by the coarse gangster elements, most of them from new immigrant families, who were "getting ahead," just as Horatio Alger had urged. In the older, Protestant tradition the intensive acquisitiveness, such as that of Daniel Drew, was rationalized by a compulsive moral fervor. But the formal obeisance of the ruthless businessman in the workaday world to the church-going pieties of the Sabbath was one that the gangster could not make. Moreover, for the young criminal, hunting in the asphalt jungle of the crowded city, it was not the businessman with his wily manipulation of numbers but the "man with the gun" who was the American hero. "No amount of commercial prosperity," once wrote Teddy Roosevelt, "can supply the lack of the heroic virtues." The American was "the hunter, cowboy, frontiersman, the soldier, the naval hero"—and in the crowded slums, the gangster. He was a man with a gun, acquiring by personal merit what was denied him by complex orderings of stratified society. And the duel with the law was the morality play par excellence: the gangster, with whom ride our own illicit desires, and the prosecutor, representing final judgment and the force of the law.

Yet all this was acted out in a wider context. The desires satisfied in extralegal fashion were more than a hunger for the "forbidden fruits" of conventional morality. They also involved, in the complex and ever shifting structure of group, class, and ethnic stratification, which is the warp and woof of America's "open" society, such "normal" goals as independence through a business of one's own, and such "moral" aspirations as the desire for social advancement and social prestige. For crime, in the language of the sociologists, has a "functional" role in the society, and the urban rackets—the illicit activity organized for continuing profit, rather than individual illegal acts—is one of the queer ladders of social mobility in American life. Indeed, it is not too much to say that the whole question of organized crime in America cannot be understood unless one appreciates (1) the distinctive role of organized gambling as a function of a mass-consumption economy; (2) the specific role of various immigrant groups as they, one after another, became involved in marginal business and crime; and (3) the relation of crime to the changing character of the urban political machines.

GATSBY'S MODEL

As a society changes, so does, in lagging fashion, its type of crime. As American society became more "organized," as the American businessman became more "civilized" and less "buccaneering," so did the American racketeer. And just as there were important changes in the structure of business enterprise, so the "institutionalized" criminal enterprise was transformed too.

In the America of the last fifty years the main drift of society has been toward the rationalization of industry, the domestication of the crude self-made captain of industry into the respectable man of manners, and the emergence of a mass-consumption economy. The most significant transformation in the field of "institutionalized" crime in the 1940's was the increasing importance of gambling as against other kinds of illegal activity. And, as a multi-billion-dollar business, gambling underwent a transition parallel to the changes in American enterprise as a whole. This parallel was exemplified in many ways: in gambling's industrial organization (e.g., the growth of a complex technology such as the national racing-wire service and the minimization of risks by such techniques as lay-off betting); in its respectability, as was evidenced in the opening of smart and popular gambling casinos in resort towns and in "satellite" adjuncts to metropolitan areas; in its functional role in a mass-consumption economy (for sheer volume of money changing hands, nothing has ever surpassed this feverish activity

of fifty million American adults); in the social acceptance of the gamblers in the important status world of sport and entertainment, i.e., "café society."

In seeking to "legitimize" itself, gambling had quite often actually become a force against older and more vicious forms of illegal activity. In 1946, for example, when a Chicago mobster, Pat Manno, went down to Dallas, Texas, to take over gambling in the area for the Accardo-Guzik combine, he reassured the sheriff as follows: "Something I'm against, that's dope peddlers, pickpockets, hired killers. That's one thing I can't stomach, and that's one thing the fellows up there—the group won't stand for, things like that. They discourage it, they even go to headquarters and ask them why they don't do something about it."

Jimmy Cannon once reported that when the gambling raids started in Chicago the "combine" protested that, in upsetting existing stable relations, the police were only opening the way for ambitious young punks and hoodlums to start trouble. Nor is there today, as there was twenty or even forty years ago, prostitution of major organized scope in the United States. Aside from the fact that manners and morals have changed, prostitution *as an industry* doesn't pay as well as gambling. Besides, its existence threatened the tacit moral acceptance and quasi-respectability the gamblers and gambling have secured in the American way of life. It was, as any operator in the field might tell you, "bad for business."

The criminal world of the 1940's, its tone set by the captains of the gambling industry, is in startling contrast to the state of affairs in the decade before. If a Kefauver report had been written then, the main "names" would have been

Lepke and Gurrah, Dutch Schultz, Jack "Legs" Diamond, Lucky Luciano, and, reaching back a little further, Arnold Rothstein, the czar of the underworld. These men (with the exception of Luciano, who was involved in narcotics and prostitution) were in the main "industrial racketeers." Rothstein, the model for Wolfsheim the gambler in F. Scott Fitzgerald's *The Great Gatsby,* had a larger function: he was, as Frank Costello became later, the financier of the underworld, the pioneer big businessman of crime who, understanding the logic of co-ordination, sought to *organize* crime as a source of regular income. His main interest in this direction was in industrial racketeering, and his entry was through labor disputes. At one time, employers in the garment trades hired Legs Diamond and his sluggers to break strikes, and the Communists, then in control of the cloakmakers union, hired one Little Orgie to protect the pickets and beat up the scabs; only later did both sides learn that Legs Diamond and Little Orgie were working for the same man, Rothstein.

Rothstein's chief successors, Lepke Buchalter and Gurrah Shapiro, were able, in the early thirties, to dominate sections of the men's and women's clothing industries, of painting, fur dressing, flour trucking, and other fields. In a highly chaotic and cutthroat industry such as clothing, the racketeer, paradoxically, played a stabilizing role by regulating competition and fixing prices. When the NRA came in and assumed this function, the businessman found that what had once been a quasi-economic service was now pure extortion, and he began to demand police action. In other types of racketeering, such as the trucking of perishable foods and waterfront loading, where the racketeers entrenched themselves as middlemen—taking up, by default, a service that neither shippers nor truckers wanted to assume—a pattern of accommodation was roughly worked out, and the rackets assumed a quasi-legal veneer. On the waterfront, old-time racketeers perform the necessary function of loading—but at an exorbitant price—and this monopoly was recognized by both the union and the shippers, and tacitly by the government.

But in the last decade and a half, industrial racketeering has not offered much in the way of opportunity. *Like American capitalism itself, crime shifted its emphasis from production to consumption.* The focus of crime became the direct exploitation of the citizen as a consumer, largely through gambling. And while the protection of these huge revenues was inextricably linked to politics, the relation between gambling and "the mobs" became more complicated.

BIG-BUSINESS BOOKIES

Although it never showed up in the gross national product, gambling in the last decade was one of the largest industries in the United States. The Kefauver Committee estimated it as a $20 billion business. This figure had been picked up and widely quoted, but in truth no one knows what the gambling "turnover" and "take" actually is, nor how much is bet legally (parimutuel, etc.) and how much illegally. In fact, the figure cited by the committee was arbitrary and was arrived at quite sloppily. As one staff member said: "We had no real idea of the money spent. . . . The California crime commission said twelve billion. Virgil Peterson of Chicago estimated thirty billion. We picked twenty billion as a balance between the two."

If comprehensive data is not available, we do know, from specific instances, the magnitude of many of the operations. Some indication can be seen from these items culled at random:

James Carroll and the M & G syndicate did a $20 million annual business in St. Louis. This was one of the two large books in the city.

The S & G syndicate in Miami did a $26 million volume yearly; the total for all books in the Florida resort reached $40 million.

Slot machines were present in 69,786 establishments in 1951 (each paid $100 for a license to the Bureau of Internal Revenue); the usual average is three machines to a license, which would add up to 210,000 slot machines in operation in the United States. In legalized areas, where the betting is higher and more regular, the average gross "take" per machine is $50 a week.

The largest policy wheel (i.e., "numbers") in Chicago's "Black Belt" reported taxable net profits for the four-year period from 1946 through 1949, after sizable deductions for "overhead," of $3,656,968. One of the large "white" wheels reported in 1947 a gross income of $2,317,000 and a net profit of $205,-000. One CIO official estimated that perhaps 15 per cent of his union's lower-echelon officials are involved in the numbers racket (a steward, free to roam a plant, is in a perfect situation for organizing bets).

If one considers the amount of dollars bet on sports alone—an estimated six billion on baseball, a billion on football pools, another billion on basketball, six billion on horse racing—then Elmo Roper's judgment that "only the food, steel, auto, chemical, and machine-tool industries have a greater volume of business" does not seem too farfetched.

While gambling has long flourished in the United States, the influx of the big mobsters into the industry—and its expansion—started in the thirties, when repeal of Prohibition forced them to look about for new avenues of enterprise. (The change, one might say crudely, was in the "democratization" of gambling. In New York of the 1860's, 1870's, and 1880's, one found elegant establishments where the wealthy men of the city, bankers, and sportsmen gambled. The saloon was the home of the worker. The middle class of the time did not gamble. In the changing mores of America, the rise of gambling in the 1930's and 1940's meant the introduction of the middle class to gambling and casinos as a way of life.) Gambling, which had begun to flower under the nourishment of rising incomes, was the most lucrative field in sight. To a large extent the shift from bootlegging to gambling was a mere transfer of business operations. In the East, Frank Costello went into slot machines and the operation of a number of ritzy gambling casinos. He also became the "banker" for the Erickson "book," which "laid off" bets for other bookies. Joe Adonis, similarly, opened up a number of casinos, principally in New Jersey. Across the country, many other mobsters went into bookmaking. As other rackets diminished and gambling, particularly horse-race betting, flourished in the forties, a struggle erupted over the control of racing information.

Horce-race betting requires a peculiar industrial organization. The essential component is time. A bookie can operate only if he can get information on odds up to the very last minute before the race, so that he can "hedge" or "lay off" bets. With racing going on simultaneously on many tracks throughout the country, this information has to be obtained speedily and accurately. Thus, the racing wire is the nerve ganglion of race betting.

The racing-wire news service got started in the twenties through the genius of the late Moe Annenberg, who had made a fearful reputation for himself as Hearst's circulation manager in the rough-and-tough Chicago newspaper wars. Annenberg conceived the idea of a telegraphic news service which would gather information from tracks and shoot it immediately to scratch sheets, horse parlors, and bookie joints. In some instances, track owners gave Annenberg the rights to send news from tracks; more often, the news was simply "stolen" by crews operating inside or near the tracks. So efficient did this news distribution system become, that in 1942, when a plane knocked out a vital telegraph circuit which served an Air Force field as well as the gamblers, the Continental Press managed to get its racing wire service for gamblers resumed in fifteen minutes, while it took the Fourth Army, which was responsible for the defense of the entire West Coast, something like three hours.

Annenberg built up a nationwide racing information chain that not only distributed wire news but controlled suboutlets as well. In 1939, harassed by the Internal Revenue Bureau on income tax and chivvied by the Justice Department for "monopolistic" control of the wire service, the tired and aging Annenberg simply walked out of the business. He did not sell his interest or even seek to salvage some profit; he simply gave up. Yet, like any established and thriving institution, the enterprise continued, though on a decentralized basis.

James Ragen, Annenberg's operations manager and likewise a veteran of the old Chicago circulation wars, took over the national wire service through a dummy friend and renamed it the Continental Press Service.

The salient fact is that in the operation of the Annenberg and Ragen wire service, formally illegal as many of its subsidiary operations may have been (i.e., in "stealing" news, supplying information to bookies, etc.), gangsters played no part. It was a business, illicit, true, but primarily a business. The distinction between gamblers and gangsters, as we shall see, is a relevant one.

In 1946, the Chicago mob, whose main interest was in bookmaking rather than in gambling casinos, began to move in on the wire monopoly. Following repeal, the Capone lieutenants had turned, like Lepke, to labor racketeering. Murray ("The Camel") Humphries muscled in on the teamsters, the operating engineers, and the cleaning-and-dyeing, laundry, and linen-supply industries. Through a small-time punk, Willie Bioff, and union official George Browne, Capone's chief successors, Frank ("The Enforcer") Nitti and Paul Ricca, came into control of the motion-picture union and proceeded to shake down the movie industry for fabulous sums in order to "avert strikes." In 1943, when the government moved in and smashed the industrial rackets, the remaining big shots, Charley Fischetti, Jake Guzik, and Tony Accardo, decided to concentrate on gambling, and in particular began a drive to take over the racing wire.

In Chicago, the Guzik-Accardo gang, controlling a sub-distributor of the racing-news service, began tapping Continental's wires. In Los Angeles, the head of the local distribution agency for

Continental was beaten up by hoodlums working for Mickey Cohen and Joe Sica. Out of the blue appeared a new and competitive nationwide racing information and distribution service, known as Trans-American Publishing, the money for which was advanced by the Chicago mobs and Bugsy Siegel, who, at the time, held a monopoly of the bookmaking and wire-news service in Las Vegas. Many books pulled out of Continental and bought information from the new outfit; many hedged by buying from both. At the end of a year, however, the Capone mob's wire had lost about $200,000. Ragen felt that violence would erupt and went to the Cook County district attorney and told him that his life had been threatened by his rivals. Ragen knew his competitors. In June, 1946, he was killed by a blast from a shotgun.

Thereafter, the Capone mob abandoned Trans-American and got a "piece" of Continental. Through their new control of the national racing-wire monopoly, the Capone mob began to muscle in on the lucrative Miami gambling business run by the so-called S & G syndicate. For a long time S & G's monopoly over bookmaking had been so complete that when New York gambler Frank Erickson bought a three months' bookmaking concession at the expensive Roney Plaza Hotel, for $45,000, the local police, in a highly publicized raid, swooped down on the hotel; the next year the Roney Plaza was again using local talent. The Capone group, however, was tougher. They demanded an interest in Miami bookmaking and, when refused, began organizing a syndicate of their own, persuading some bookies at the big hotels to join them. Florida Governor Warren's crime investigator appeared—a friend, it seemed, of old Chicago dogtrack operator William Johnston, who had contributed $100,000 to the Governor's campaign fund—and began raiding bookie joints, but only those that were affiliated with S & G. Then S & G, which had been buying its racing news from the local distributor of Continental Press, found its service abruptly shut off. For a few days the syndicate sought to bootleg information from New Orleans, but found itself limping along. After ten days' war of attrition, the five S & G partners found themselves with a sixth partner, who, for a token "investment" of $20,000, entered a Miami business that grossed $26,000,000 in one year.

GAMBLERS AND GUYS

While Americans made gambling illegal, they did not in their hearts think of it as wicked—even the churches benefited from the bingo and lottery crazes. So they gambled—and gamblers flourished. Against this open canvas, the indignant tones of Senator Wiley and the shocked righteousness of Senator Tobey during the Kefauver investigation rang oddly. Yet it was probably this very tone of surprise that gave the activity of the Kefauver Committee its piquant quality. Here were some senators who seemingly did not know the facts of life, as most Americans did. Here, in the person of Senator Tobey, was the old New England Puritan conscience poking around in industrial America, in a world it had made but never seen. Here was old-fashioned moral indignation, at a time when cynicism was rampant in public life.

Commendable as such moralistic fervor was, it did not make for intelligent discrimination of fact. Throughout the Kefauver hearings, for example, there ran the presumption that all gamblers were invariably gangsters. This was true of Chicago's Accardo-Guzik combine, which in the past had its fingers in many kinds of rackets. It was not nearly so true of many of large gamblers in America, most of whom had the feeling that they were satisfying a basic American urge for sport and looked upon their calling with no greater sense of guilt than did many bootleggers. After all, Sherman Billingsley did start out as a speakeasy proprietor, as did the Kreindlers of the "21" Club; and today the Stork Club and the former Jack and Charlie's are the most fashionable night and dining spots in America (one prominent patron of the Stork Club: J. Edgar Hoover).

The S & G syndicate in Miami, for example (led by Harold Salvey, Jules Levitt, Charles Friedman, Sam Cohen, and Edward [Eddie Luckey] Rosenbaum), was simply a master pool of some two hundred bookies that arranged for telephone service, handled "protection," acted as bankers for those who needed ready cash on hard-hit books, and, in short, functioned somewhat analogously to the large factoring corporations in the textile field or the credit companies in the auto industry. Yet to Kefauver, the S & G men were "slippery and arrogant characters. . . . Salvey, for instance, was an old-time bookie who told us he had done nothing except engage in bookmaking or finance other bookmakers for twenty years." When, as a result of committee publicity and the newly found purity of the Miami police, the S & G syndicate went out of business, it was, as the combine's lawyer told Kefauver, because the "boys" were weary of being painted "the worst monsters in the world." "It is true," Cohen acknowledged, "that

they had been law violators." But they had never done anything worse than gambling, and "to fight the world isn't worth it."

Most intriguing of all were the opinions of James J. Carroll, the St. Louis "betting commissioner," who for years had been widely quoted on the sports pages of the country as setting odds on the Kentucky Derby winter book and the baseball pennant races. Senator Wiley, speaking like the prosecutor in Camus's novel, *The Stranger*, became the voice of official morality:

SENATOR WILEY: Have you any children?
MR. CARROLL: Yes, I have a boy.
SENATOR WILEY: How old is he?
MR. CARROLL: Thirty-three.
SENATOR WILEY: Does he gamble?
MR. CARROLL: No.
SENATOR WILEY: Would you like to see him grow up and become a gambler, either professional or amateur?
MR. CARROLL: No. . . .
SENATOR WILEY: All right. Is your son interested in your business?
MR. CARROLL: No, he is a manufacturer.
SENATOR WILEY: Why do you not get him into the business?
MR. CARROLL: Well, psychologically a great many people are unsuited for gambling.

Retreating from this gambit, the Senator sought to pin Carroll down on his contributions to political campaigns:

SENATOR WILEY: Now this morning I asked you whether you contributed any money for political candidates or parties, and you said not more than $200 at one time. I presume that does not indicate the total of your contributions in any one campaign, does it?
MR. CARROLL: Well, it might, might not, Senator. I have been an "againster" in many instances. I am a reader of *The Nation* for fifty years and they have advertisements calling for contributions for different candidates, different causes. . . . They carried an advertisement for George Norris; I contributed, I think, to that, and to the elder LaFollette.

Carroll, who admitted to having been in the betting business since 1899, was the sophisticated—but not immoral!—counterpoint to moralist Wiley. Here was a man without the stigmata of the underworld or underground; he was worldly, cynical of official rhetoric, jaundiced about people's motives; he was an "againster" who believed that "all gambling legislation originates or stems from some group or some individual seeking special interests for himself or his cause."

Asked why people gamble, Carroll distilled his experiences of fifty years with a remark that deserves a place in American social history: "I really don't know how to answer the question," he said. "I think gambling is a biological necessity for certain types. I think it is the quality that gives substance to their daydreams."

In a sense, the entire Kefauver materials, unintentionally, seem to document that remark. For what the committee revealed time and time again was a picture of gambling as a basic institution in American life, flourishing openly and accepted widely. In many of the small towns, the gambling joint is as open as a liquor establishment. The town of Havana, in Mason County, Illinois, felt miffed when Governor Adlai Stevenson intervened against local gambling. In 1950, the town had raised $15,000 of its $50,000 budget by making friendly raids on the gambling houses every month and having the owners pay fines. "With the gambling fines cut off," grumbled Mayor Clarence Chester, "the next year is going to be tough."

Apart from the gamblers, there were the mobsters. But what Senator Kefauver and company failed to understand was that the mobsters, like the gamblers, and like the entire gangdom generally, were seeking to become quasi-respectable and establish a place for themselves in American life. For the mobsters, by and large, had immigrant roots, and crime, as the pattern showed, was a route of social ascent and place in American life.

THE MYTH OF THE MAFIA

The mobsters were able, where they wished, to "muscle in" on the gambling business because the established gamblers were wholly vulnerable, not being able to call on the law for protection. The senators, however, refusing to make any distinction between a gambler and a gangster, found it convenient to talk loosely of a nationwide conspiracy of "illegal" elements. Senator Kefauver asserted that a "nationwide crime syndicate does exist in the United States, despite the protestations of a strangely assorted company of criminals, self-serving politicians, plain blind fools, and others who may be honestly misguided, that there is no such combine." The Senate committee report states the matter more dogmatically: "There is a nationwide crime syndicate known as the Mafia. . . . Its leaders are usually found in control of the most lucrative rackets in their cities. There are indications of a centralized direction and control of these rackets. . . . The Mafia is the cement that helps to bind the Costello-Adonis-Lansky syndicate of New York and the Accardo-Guzik-Fischetti syndicate of Chicago. . . . These groups have kept in touch with Luciano since his deportation from the country."

Unfortunately for a good story—and the existence of the Mafia would be a whale of a story—neither the Senate Crime Committee in its testimony, nor

Kefauver in his book, presented any real evidence that the Mafia exists as a functioning organization. One finds police officials asserting before the Kefauver committee their *belief* in the Mafia; the Narcotics Bureau *thinks* that a world-wide dope ring allegedly run by Luciano is part of the Mafia; but the only other "evidence" presented—aside from the incredulous responses both of Senator Kefauver and Rudolph Halley when nearly all the Italian gangsters asserted that they didn't know about the Mafia—is that certain crimes bear "the earmarks of the Mafia."

The legend of the Mafia has been fostered in recent years largely by the peephole writing team of Jack Lait and Lee Mortimer. In their *Chicago Confidential*, they rattled off a series of names and titles that made the organization sound like a rival to an Amos and Andy Kingfish society. Few serious reporters, however, give it much credence. Burton Turkus, the Brooklyn prosecutor who broke up the "Murder, Inc." ring, denies the existence of the Mafia. Nor could Senator Kefauver even make out much of a case for his picture of a national crime syndicate. He is forced to admit that "as it exists today [it] is an elusive and furtive but nonetheless tangible thing," and that "its organization and machinations are not always easy to pinpoint."[1] His "evidence" that many gangsters congregate at certain times of the year in such places as Hot Springs, Arkansas, in itself does not prove much; people "in the trade" usually do, and as the loquacious late Willie Moretti of New Jersey said, in explaining how he had met the late Al Capone at a race track, "Listen, well-charactered people you don't need introductions to; you just meet automatically."

Why did the Senate Crime Committee plump so hard for its theory of a Mafia and a national crime syndicate? In part, they may have been misled by their own hearsay. The Senate committee was not in the position to do original research, and its staff, both legal and investigative, was incredibly small. Senator Kefauver had begun the investigation with the attitude that with so much smoke there must be a raging fire. But smoke can also mean a smoke screen. Mob activities is a field in which busy gossip and exaggeration flourish even more readily than in a radical political sect.

There is, as well, in the American temper, a feeling that "somewhere," "somebody" is pulling all the complicated strings to which this jumbled world dances. In politics the labor image is "Wall Street" or "Big Business"; while the business stereotype was the "New Dealers." In the field of crime, the side-of-the-mouth low-down was "Costello."

The salient reason, perhaps, why the Kefauver Committee was taken in by its own myth of an omnipotent Mafia and a despotic Costello was its failure to assimilate and understand three of the more relevant sociological facts about institutionalized crime in its relation to the political life of large urban communities in America, namely: (1) the rise of the American Italian community, as part of the inevitable process of ethnic succession, to positions of importance in politics, a process that has been occurring independently but also simultaneously in most cities with large Italian constituencies—New York, Chicago, Kansas City, Los Angeles; (2) the fact that there are individual Italians who play prominent, often leading roles today in gambling and in the mobs; and (3) the fact that Italian gamblers and mobsters often possessed "status" within the Italian community itself and a "pull" in city politics.[2] These three items are indeed related—but not so as to form a "plot."

THE JEWS . . . THE IRISH . . . THE ITALIANS

The Italian community has achieved wealth and political influence much later and in a harder way than previous immigrant groups. Early Jewish wealth, that of the German Jews of the late nineteenth century, was made largely in banking and merchandising. To that extent, the dominant group in the Jewish community was outside of, and independent of, the urban political machines. Later Jewish wealth, among the East European immigrants, was built in the garment trades, though with some involvement with the Jewish gangster, who was typically an industrial racketeer (Arnold Rothstein, Lepke and Gurrah, etc.). Among Jewish lawyers, a small minority, such as the "Tammany lawyer" (like the protagonist of Sam Ornitz's *Haunch, Paunch and Jowl*), rose through politics and occasionally touched the fringes of crime. Most of the Jewish lawyers, by and large the communal leaders, climbed rapidly, however, in the opportunities that established and legitimate Jewish wealth provided. Irish immigrant wealth in the northern urban centers, concentrated largely in construction, trucking, and the waterfront, has, to a substantial extent, been wealth accumulated in and through political alliance, e.g., favoritism in city contracts.[3]

Control of the politics of the city thus has been crucial for the continuance of Irish political wealth. This alliance of Irish immigrant wealth and politics has been reciprocal; many noted Irish political figures lent their names as important window-dressing for business corporations (Al Smith, for example, who helped form the U.S. Trucking Corporation, whose executive head for many years was William J. McCormack, the alleged "Mr. Big" of the New York waterfront), while Irish businessmen have lent their wealth to further the careers of Irish politicians. Irish mobsters have rarely achieved status in the Irish community, but have served as integral arms of the politicians, as strong-arm men on election day.

The Italians found the more obvious big-city paths from rags to riches preempted. In part this was due to the character of the early Italian immigrant. Most of them were unskilled and from rural stock. Jacob Riis could remark in the nineties, "the Italian comes in at the bottom and stays there." These dispossessed agricultural laborers found jobs as ditch-diggers, on the railroads as section hands, along the docks, in the service occupations, as shoemakers, barbers, garment workers, and stayed there. Many were fleeced by the "padrone" system; a few achieved wealth from truck farming, wine growing, and marketing produce; but this "marginal wealth" was not the source of coherent and stable political power.

Significantly, although the number of Italians in the United States is about a third as high as the number of Irish, and of the thirty million Catholic communicants in the United States, about half are of Irish descent and a sixth of Italian, there is not one Italian bishop among the hundred Catholic bishops in this country or one Italian archbishop among the 21 archbishops. The Irish have a virtual monopoly. This is a factor related to the politics of the American church; but the condition also is possible because there is not significant or sufficient wealth among Italian Americans to force some parity.

The children of the immigrants, the second and third generation, became wise in the ways of the urban slums. Excluded from the political ladder—in the early thirties there were almost no Italians on the city payroll in top jobs, nor in books of the period can one find discussion of Italian political leaders— and finding few open routes to wealth, some turned to illicit ways. In the children's court statistics of the 1930's, the largest group of delinquents were the Italian; nor were there any Italian communal or social agencies to cope with these problems. Yet it was, oddly enough, the quondam racketeer, seeking to become respectable, who provided one of the major supports for the drive to win a political voice for Italians in the power structure of the urban political machines.

This rise of the Italian political bloc was connected, at least in the major northern urban centers, with another important development which tended to make the traditional relation between the politician and the protected or tolerated illicit operator more close than it had been in the past. This is the fact that the urban political machines had to evolve new forms of fund-raising, since the big business contributions, which once went heavily into municipal politics, now—with the shift in the locus of power—go largely into national affairs. (The ensuing corruption in national politics, as recent Congressional investigations show, is no petty matter; the scruples of businessmen do not seem much superior to those of the gamblers.) One way that urban political machines raised their money resembled that of the large corporations which are no longer dependent on Wall Street: by self-financing—that is, by "taxing" the large number of municipal employees who bargain collectively with City Hall for their wage increases. So the firemen's union contributed money to O'Dwyer's campaign.

A second method was taxing the gamblers. The classic example, as *Life* reported, was Jersey City, where a top lieutenant of the Hague machine spent his full time screening applicants for unofficial bookmaking licenses. If found acceptable, the applicant was given a "location," usually the house or store of a loyal precinct worker, who kicked into the machine treasury a high proportion of the large rent exacted. The one thousand bookies and their one thousand landlords in Jersey City formed the hard core of the political machine that sweated and bled to get out the votes for Hague.

A third source for the financing of these machines was the new, and often illegally earned, Italian wealth. This is well illustrated by the career of Costello and his emergence as a political power in New York. Here the ruling motive has been the search for an entree—for oneself and one's ethnic group—into the ruling circles of the big city.

Frank Costello made his money originally in bootlegging. After repeal, his big break came when Huey Long, desperate for ready cash to fight the old-line political machines, invited Costello to install slot machines in Louisiana. Costello did, and he flourished. Together with Dandy Phil Kastel, he also opened the Beverly Club, an elegant gambling establishment just outside New Orleans, at which have appeared some of the top entertainers in America. Subsequently, Costello invested his money in New York real estate (including 79 Wall Street, which he later sold), the Copacabana night club, and a leading brand of Scotch whiskey.

Costello's political opportunity came when a money-hungry Tammany, starved by lack of patronage from Roosevelt and LaGuardia, turned to him for financial support. The Italian community in New York has for years nursed a grievance against the Irish and, to a lesser extent, the Jewish political groups for monopolizing political power. They complained about the lack of judicial jobs, the small number—usually one—of Italian congressmen, the lack of representation on the state tickets. But the Italians lacked the means to make their ambition a reality. Although they formed a large voting bloc, there was rarely sufficient wealth to finance political clubs. Italian immigrants, largely poor peasants from southern Italy and Sicily, lacked the mercantile experience of the Jews and the political experience gained in the seventy-five-year history of Irish immigration.

During the Prohibition years, the Italian racketeers had made certain political contacts in order to gain protection. Costello, always the compromiser and fixer rather than the muscle-man, was the first to establish relations with Jimmy Hines, the powerful leader of the West Side in Tammany Hall. But his rival, Lucky Luciano, suspicious of the Irish and seeking more direct power, backed and elected Al Marinelli for district leader on the Lower West Side. Marinelli in 1932 was the only Italian leader inside Tammany Hall. Later, he was joined by Dr. Paul Sarubbi, a partner of gangster Johnny Torrio in a large, legitimate liquor concern. Certainly, Costello and Luciano represented no "unified" move by the Italians as a

whole for power; within the Italian community there are as many divisions as in any other group. What is significant is that different Italians, for different reasons and in various fashions, were achieving influence for the first time. Marinelli became county clerk of New York and a leading power in Tammany. In 1937, after being blasted by Tom Dewey, then running for district attorney, as a "political ally of thieves . . . and big-shot racketeers," Marinelli was removed from office by Governor Lehman. The subsequent conviction by Dewey of Luciano and Hines, and the election of LaGuardia, left most of the Tammany clubs financially weak and foundering. This was the moment Costello made his move. In a few years, by judicious financing, he controlled a bloc of "Italian" leaders in the Hall—as well as some Irish on the upper West Side and some Jewish leaders on the East Side—and was able to influence the selection of a number of Italian judges. The most notable incident, revealed by a wire tap on Costello's phone, was the "Thank you, Francisco" call in 1943 by Supreme Court judge nominee Thomas Aurelio, who gave Costello full credit for his nomination.

It was not only Tammany that was eager to accept campaign contributions from newly rich Italians, even though some of these *nouveaux riches* had "arrived" through bootlegging and gambling. Fiorello LaGuardia, the wiliest mind that melting-pot politics has ever produced, understood in the early thirties where much of his covert support came from. (So, too, did Vito Marcantonio, an apt pupil of the master: Marcantonio has consistently made deals with the Italian leaders of Tammany Hall—in 1943 he supported Aurelio and refused to repudiate him even when the

Democratic party formally did.) Joe Adonis, who had built a political following during the late twenties, when he ran a popular speakeasy, aided La-Guardia financially to a considerable extent in 1933. "The Democrats haven't recognized the Italians," Adonis told a friend. "There is no reason for the Italians to support anybody but LaGuardia; the Jews have played ball with the Democrats and haven't gotten much out of it. They know it now. They will vote for LaGuardia. So will the Italians."

Adonis played his cards shrewdly. He supported LaGuardia, but also a number of Democrats for local and judicial posts, and became a power in the Brooklyn area. His restaurant was frequented by Kenny Sutherland, the Coney Island Democratic leader; Irwin Steingut, the Democratic minority leader in Albany; Anthony DiGiovanni, later a councilman; William O'Dwyer; and Jim Moran. But, in 1937, Adonis made the mistake of supporting Royal Copeland against LaGuardia, and the irate Fiorello finally drove Adonis out of New York.[4]

LaGuardia later turned his ire against Costello, too. Yet Costello survived and reached the peak of his influence in 1942, when he was instrumental in electing Michael Kennedy leader of Tammany Hall. Despite the Aurelio fiasco, which first brought Costello into notoriety, he still had sufficient power in the Hall to swing votes for Hugo Rogers as Tammany leader in 1948. In those years many a Tammany leader came hat-in-hand to Costello's apartment or sought him out on the golf links to obtain the nomination for a judicial post.

During this period, other Italian political leaders were also coming to the fore. Generoso Pope, whose Colonial Sand and Stone Company began to prosper through political contacts, became an important political figure, especially when his purchase of the two largest Italian-language dailies (later merged into one), and of a radio station, gave him almost a monopoly of channels to Italian-speaking opinion of the city. Through Generoso Pope, and through Costello, the Italians became a major political force in New York.

That the urban machines, largely Democratic, have financed their heavy campaign costs in this fashion rather than having to turn to the "moneyed interests" explains in some part why these machines were able, in part, to support the New and Fair Deals without suffering the pressures they might have been subjected to had their source of money supply been the business groups.[5] Although he has never publicly revealed his political convictions, it is likely that Frank Costello was a fervent admirer of Franklin D. Roosevelt and his efforts to aid the common man. The basic measures of the New Deal, which most Americans today agree were necessary for the public good, would not have been possible without the support of the "corrupt" big-city machines.

THE "NEW" MONEY—AND THE OLD

There is little question that men of Italian origin appeared in most of the leading roles in the high drama of gambling and mobs, just as twenty years ago the children of East European Jews were the most prominent figures in organized crime, and before that individuals of Irish descent were similarly prominent. To some extent statistical accident and the tendency of newspapers to emphasize the few sensational figures gives a greater illusion about the domination of illicit activities by a single ethnic group than all the facts warrant. In many cities, particularly in the South and on the West Coast, the mob and gambling fraternity consisted of many other groups, and often, predominantly, of native white Protestants. Yet it is clear that in the major northern urban centers there was a distinct ethnic sequence in the modes of obtaining illicit wealth and that, uniquely in the case of the recent Italian elements, the former bootleggers and gamblers provided considerable leverage for the growth of political influence as well. A substantial number of Italian judges sitting on the bench in New York today are indebted in one fashion or another to Costello; so too are many Italian district leaders —as well as some Jewish and Irish politicians. And the motive in establishing Italian political prestige in New York was generous rather than scheming for personal advantage. For Costello it was largely a case of ethnic pride. As in earlier American eras, organized illegality became a stepladder of social ascent.

To the world at large, the news and pictures of Frank Sinatra, for example, mingling with former Italian mobsters could come somewhat as a shock. Yet to Sinatra, and to many Italians, these were men who had grown up in their neighborhoods and who were, in some instances, bywords in the community for their helpfulness and their charities. The early Italian gangsters were hoodlums —rough, unlettered, and young (Al Capone was only twenty-nine at the height of his power). Those who survived learned to dress conservatively. Their homes are in respectable suburbs. They sent their children to good schools and sought to avoid publicity.[6] Costello even went to a psychiatrist in his effort to overcome a painful feeling of inferiority in the world of manners.

As happens with all "new" money in American society, the rough and ready contractors, the construction people, trucking entrepreneurs, as well as racketeers, polished up their manners and sought recognition and respectability in their own ethnic as well as in the general community. The "shanty" Irish became the "lace curtain" Irish, and then moved out for wider recognition.[7] Sometimes acceptance came first in established "American" society, and this was a certificate for later recognition by the ethnic community, a process well illustrated by the belated acceptance in established Negro society of such figures as Sugar Ray Robinson and Joe Louis, as well as leading popular entertainers.

Yet, after all, the foundation of many a distinguished older American fortune was laid by sharp practices and morally reprehensible methods. The pioneers of American capitalism were not graduated from Harvard's School of Business Administration. The early settlers and founding fathers, as well as those who "won the West" and built up cattle, mining, and other fortunes, often did so by shady speculations and a not inconsiderable amount of violence. They ignored, circumvented, or stretched the law when it stood in the way of America's destiny and their own—or were themselves the law when it served their purposes. This has not prevented them and their descendants from feeling proper moral outrage when, under the changed circumstances of the crowded urban environments, latecomers pursued equally ruthless tactics.

THE EMBOURGEOISEMENT OF CRIME

Ironically, the social development which made possible the rise to political influence sounds, too, the knell of the rough Italian gangster. For it is the growing number of Italians with professional training and legitimate business success that both prompts and permits the Italian group to wield increasing political influence; and increasingly it is the professionals and businessmen who provide models for Italian youth today, models that hardly existed twenty years ago. Ironically, the headlines and exposés of "crime" of the Italian "gangsters" came years after the fact. Many of the top "crime" figures had long ago forsworn violence, and even their income, in large part, was derived from legitimate investments (real estate in the case of Costello, motor haulage and auto dealer franchises in the case of Adonis) or from such quasi-legitimate but socially respectable sources as gambling casinos. Hence society's "retribution" in the jail sentences for Costello and Adonis was little more than a trumped-up morality that disguised a social hypocrisy.

Apart from these considerations, what of the larger context of crime and the American way of life? The passing of the Fair Deal signalizes, oddly, the passing of an older pattern of illicit activities. The gambling fever of the past decade and a half was part of the flush and exuberance of rising incomes, and was characteristic largely of new upper-middle-class rich having a first fling at conspicuous consumption. These upper-middle-class rich, a significant new stratum in American life (not rich in the nineteenth-century sense of enormous wealth, but largely middle-sized businessmen and entrepreneurs of the service and luxury trades—the "tertiary economy" in Colin Clark's phrase—who by the tax laws have achieved sizable incomes often much higher than the managers of the super-giant corporations), were the chief patrons of the munificent gambling casinos. During the war decade when travel was difficult,

gambling and the lush resorts provided important outlets for this social class. Now they are settling down, learning about Europe and culture. The petty gambling, the betting and bingo which relieve the tedium of small-town life, or the expectation among the urban slum dwellers of winning a sizable sum by a "lucky number" or a "lucky horse," goes on. To quote Bernard Baruch: "You can't stop people from gambling on horses. And why should you prohibit a man from backing his own judgment? It's another form of personal initiative." But the lush profits are passing from gambling as the costs of co-ordination rise. And in the future it is likely that gambling, like prostitution, winning tacit acceptance as a necessary fact, will continue on a decentralized, small entrepreneur basis.

But passing, too, is a political pattern, the system of political "bosses" which in its reciprocal relation provided "protection" for, and was fed revenue from, crime. The collapse of the "boss" system was a product of the Roosevelt era. Twenty years ago Jim Farley's task was simple; he had to work only on some key state bosses. Now there is no longer such an animal. New Jersey Democracy was once ruled by Frank Hague; now there are five or six men each "top dog," for the moment, in his part of the state or faction of the party. Within the urban centers, the old Irish-dominated political machines in New York, Boston, Newark, and Chicago have fallen apart. The decentralization of the metropolitan centers, the growth of suburbs and satellite towns, the breakup of the old ecological patterns of slum and transient belts, the rise of functional groups, the increasing middle-class character of American life, all contribute to this decline.

With the rationalization and absorption of some illicit activities into the structure of the economy, the passing of an older generation that had established a hegemony over crime,[8] the general rise of minority groups to social position, and the breakup of the urban boss system, the pattern of crime we have discussed is passing as well. Crime, of course, remains as long as passion and the desire for gain remain. But the kind of big, organized city crime, as we have known it for the past seventy-five years, was based on more than these universal motives. It was based on certain characteristics of the American economy, American ethnic groups, and American politics. The changes in all these areas means that, in the form we have known it, it too will change.

NOTES

1. The accidental police discovery of a conference of Italian figures, most of them with underworld and police records, in Apalachin, New York, in November 1957, revived the talk of a Mafia. *Time* magazine assigned a reporter, Serrell Hillman, to check the story, and this is what he reported: "I spent some two weeks in New York, Washington and Chicago running down every clue to the so-called Mafia that I could find. I talked to a large number of Federal, state and local law enforcement authorities; to police, reporters, attorneys, detectives, non-profit civic groups such as the Chicago Crime Commission. Nobody from the F.B.I. and Justice Department officials on down, with the exception of a couple of Hearst crime reporters—always happy for the sake of a street sale to associate the 'Mafia' with the most routine barroom shooting —and the Narcotics Bureau believed that a Mafia exists as such. The Narcotics Bureau, which has to contend with a big problem in dope-trafficking, contends that a working alliance operates between an organized Mafia in Italy and Sicily and a U.S. Mafia. But the Bureau has never been able to submit proof of this, and the F.B.I. is skeptical. The generally held belief is that there is no tightly knit syndicate, but instead a loose "trade association" of criminals in various cities and areas, who run their own shows in their own fields but have matters of mutual interest to take up (as at the Appalachian conference). At any rate, nobody has ever been able to produce specific evidence that a Mafia is functioning."

In early 1959, Fredric Sondern, Jr., an editor of the *Reader's Digest*, published a best-selling book on the Mafia, *Brotherhood of Evil*, but a close reading of Mr. Sondern's text indicates that his sources are largely the files of the Narcotics Bureau, and his findings little more than a rehash of previously publicized material. (For a devastating review of the book, see the *Times Literary Supplement*, London, June 12, 1959, p. 351.) Interestingly enough, in May, 1959, Alvin Goldstein, a former assistant district attorney in New York, who had prosecuted racketeer Johnny Dio, conducted a crime survey of California for Governor Pat Brown and reported that he found no evidence of the existence of a Mafia in California.

2. Toward the end of his hearings, Senator Kefauver read a telegram from an indignant citizen of Italian descent, protesting against the impression the committee had created that organized crime in America was a distinctly Italian enterprise. The Senator took the occasion to state the obvious: that there are racketeers who are Italian does not mean that Italians are racketeers. However, it may be argued that to the extent the Kefauver Committee fell for the line about crime in America being organized and controlled by the Mafia, it did foster such a misunderstanding. Perhaps this is also the place to point out that insofar as the relation of ethnic groups and ethnic problems to illicit and quasi-legal activities is piously ignored, the field is left open to the kind of vicious sensationalism practiced by Mortimer and Lait.

3. A fact which should occasion little shock if one recalls that, in the nineteenth century, American railroads virtually stole 190,000,000 acres of land by bribing Congressmen, and that more recently such scandals at the Teapot Dome oil grabs during the Harding administration consummated, as the Supreme Court said, "by means of conspiracy, fraud and bribery," reached to the very doors of the White House.

4. Adonis, and associate Willie Moretti, moved across the river to Bergen County, New Jersey, where, together with the quondam racketeer Abner "Longie" Zwillman, he became one of the political powers in the state. Gambling flourished in Bergen County for almost a decade, but after the Kefauver investigation the state was forced to act. A special inquiry in 1953, headed by Nelson Stamler, revealed that Moretti had paid $286,000 to an aide of Governor Driscoll for "protection" and that the Republican state committee had accepted a $25,000 "loan" from gambler Joseph Bozzo, an associate of Zwillman. Moretti was later murdered, and Adonis deported to Italy.

5. This is an old story in American politics. Theodore Allen, a gambler and saloon keeper, whose American Mabille was an elegant music hall and bordello (he once told a Congressional investigating committee that he was the wickedest man in New York), gave Republican Boss Thurlow Weed a campaign contribution of $25,000 for the re-election of Abraham Lincoln in 1864.

6. Except at times by being overly neighborly, like Tony Accardo, who, at Yuletide 1949, in his ele-

gant River Forest home, decorated a 40-foot tree on his lawn and beneath it set a wooden Santa and reindeer, while around the yard, on tracks, electrically operated skating figures zipped merrily around while a loudspeaker poured out Christmas carols. The next Christmas, the Accardo lawn was darkened; Tony was on the lam from Kefauver.

7. The role of ethnic pride in corralling minority groups is one of the oldest pieces of wisdom in American politics; but what is more remarkable is the persistence of this identification through second and third generation descendants, a fact which, as Samuel Lubell noted in his *Future of American Politics*, was one of the explanatory keys to political behavior in recent elections. Although the Irish bloc as a solid Democratic bloc is beginning to crack, particularly as middle-class status impels individuals to identify more strongly with the GOP, the nomination in Massachusetts of Jack Kennedy for the United States Senate created a tremendous solidarity among Irish voters, and Kennedy was elected over Lodge although Eisenhower swept the state.

8. In 1959, the Justice Department set up a special group to study the "crime syndicates." The group found, in a preliminary report, that the old crime leaders have eschewed violence and "created the appearance of successful businessmen" by entering legitimate business. It is quite possible that in many of these areas (trucking, vending, restaurants, entertainment) these old mobsters are able, by various means, to gain competitive advantages. But the significant thing, sociologically, is that these new areas are legitimate business, and this may not mean, as the Justice Department construes it, the "infiltration" of mobsters into new crime areas, but their attempt to gain quasi-respectability. Significantly, when *Life* magazine, February 23, 1958, presented a large graphic demonstration of the Justice Department findings, the individuals singled out had all been in the rackets over thirty years—a point that *Life* and the Justice Department missed. There were relatively few new, younger men in crime. The original mobsters had won hegemony when they were in their early thirties and had held sway all this time. The problem of "generations" in crime has never been studied, and, in the U.S., would make a fascinating subject.

Latent Functions of the Machine

ROBERT K. MERTON

Columbia

. . . in large sectors of the American population, the political machine or the "political racket" are judged as unequivocally "bad" and "undesirable." The grounds for such moral judgment vary somewhat, but they consist substantially in pointing out that political machines violate moral codes: political patronage violates the code of selecting personnel on the basis of impersonal qualifications rather than on grounds of party loyalty or contributions to the party war-chest; bossism violates the code that votes should be based on individual appraisal of the qualifications of candidates and of political issues, and not on abiding loyalty to a feudal leader; bribery, and "honest graft" obviously offend the proprieties of property; "protection" for crime clearly violates the law and the mores; and so on.

In view of the manifold respects in which political machines, in varying degrees, run counter to the mores and at times to the law, it becomes pertinent to inquire how they manage to continue in operation. The familiar "explanations" for the continuance of the political machine are not here in point. To be sure, it may well be that if "respectable

From Robert K. Merton, *Social Theory and Social Structure* (New York: The Free Press, 1957), rev. enl. ed., pp. 71-82. Copyright 1949 by the Free Press Collier-Macmillan, Canada, Ltd., Toronto, Ontario. Copyright © 1957 by the Free Press, a corporation. Reprinted by permission of the publisher. Robert K. Merton is Professor of Sociology at Columbia University.

citizenry" would live up to their political obligations, if the electorate were to be alert and enlightened; if the number of elective officers were substantially reduced from the dozens, even hundreds, which the average voter is now expected to appraise in the course of town, county, state and national elections; if the electorate were activated by the "wealthy and educated classes without whose participation," as the not-always democratically oriented Bryce put it, "the best-framed government must speedily degenerate";—if these and a plethora of similar changes in political structure were introduced, perhaps the "evils" of the political machine would indeed be exorcized.[1] But it should be noted that these changes are often not introduced, that political machines have had the phoenix-like quality of arising strong and unspoiled from their ashes, that, in short, this structure has exhibited a notable vitality in many areas of American political life.

Proceeding from the functional view, therefore, that we should *ordinarily* (not invariably) expect persistent social patterns and social structures to perform positive functions *which are at the time not adequately fulfilled by other existing patterns and structures*, the thought occurs that perhaps this publicly maligned organization is, *under present conditions*, satisfying basic latent functions.[2] A brief examination of current analyses of this type of structure may also serve to illustrate additional problems of functional analysis.

SOME FUNCTIONS OF THE POLITICAL MACHINE

Without presuming to enter into the variations of detail marking different political machines—a Tweed, Vare, Crump, Flynn, Hague are by no means identical types of bosses—we can briefly examine the functions more or less common to the political machine, as a generic type of social organization. We neither attempt to itemize all the diverse functions of the political machine nor imply that all these functions are similarly fulfilled by each and every machine.

The key structural function of the Boss is to organize, centralize and maintain in good working condition "the scattered fragments of power" which are at present dispersed through our political organization. By this centralized organization of political power, the boss and his apparatus can satisfy the needs of diverse subgroups in the larger community which are not adequately satisfied by legally devised and culturally approved social structures.

To understand the role of bossism and the machine, therefore, we must look at two types of sociological variables: (1) the *structural context* which makes it difficult, if not impossible, for morally approved structures to fulfill essential social functions, thus leaving the door open for political machines (or their structural equivalents) to fulfill these functions and (2) the subgroups whose distinctive needs are left unsatisfied, except for the latent functions which the machine in fact fulfills.[3]

Structural Context: The constitutional framework of American political organization specifically precludes the legal possibility of highly centralized power and, it has been noted, thus "discourages the growth of effective and responsible leadership. The framers of the Constitution, as Woodrow Wilson observed, set up the check and balance system 'to keep government at a sort of mechanical equipoise by means of a standing amicable contest among its several organic parts.' They distrusted power as dangerous to liberty: and therefore they spread it thin and erected barriers against its concentration." This dispersion of power is found not only at the national level but in local areas as well. "As a consequence," Sait goes on to observe, "when *the people or particular groups* among them demanded positive action, no one had adequate authority to act. The machine provided an antidote."[4]

The constitutional dispersion of power not only makes for difficulty of effective decision and action but when action does occur it is defined and hemmed in by legalistic considerations. In consequence, there developed "a much *more human system* of partisan government, whose chief object soon became the circumvention of government by law. . . . The lawlessness of the extra-official democracy was merely the counterpoise of the legalism of the official democracy. The lawyer having been permitted to subordinate democracy to the Law, the Boss had to be called in to extricate the victim, which he did after a fashion and for a consideration."[5]

Officially, political power is dispersed. Various well-known expedients were devised for this manifest objective. Not only was there the familiar separation of powers among the several branches of the government but, in some measure, tenure in each office was limited, rotation in office approved. And the scope of power inherent in each office was severely circumscribed. Yet, observes Sait in rigorously functional terms, "Leadership is necessary; and *since* it does not develop readily within the constitutional framework, the Boss provides it in a crude and irresponsible form from the outside."[6]

Put in more generalized terms, *the functional deficiencies of the official structure generate an alternative (unofficial) structure to fulfill existing needs somewhat more effectively.* Whatever its specific historical origins, the political machine persists as an apparatus for satisfying otherwise unfulfilled needs of diverse groups in the population. By turning to a few of these subgroups and their characteristic needs, we shall be led at once to a range of latent functions of the political machine.

Functions of the Political Machine for Diverse Subgroups. It is well known that one source of strength of the political machine derives from its roots in the local community and the neighborhood. The political machine does not regard the electorate as an amorphous, undifferentiated mass of voters. With a keen sociological intuition, the machine recognizes that the voter is a person living in a specific neighborhood, with specific personal problems and personal wants. Public issues are abstract and remote; private problems are extremely concrete and immediate. It is not through the generalized appeal to large public concerns that the machine operates, but through the direct, quasi-feudal relationships between local representatives of the machine and voters in their neighborhood. Elections are won in the precinct.

The machine welds its links with ordinary men and women by elaborate networks of personal relations. Politics is transformed into personal ties. The precinct captain "must be a friend to every man, assuming if he does not feel sympathy with the unfortunate, and utilizing in his good works the resources which the boss puts at his disposal."[7] The precinct captain is forever a friend in need. In our prevailingly impersonal society, the machine, through its local agents, fulfills the important social *func-*

tion of humanizing and personalizing all manner of assistance to those in need. Foodbaskets and jobs, legal and extra-legal advice, setting to rights minor scrapes with the law, helping the bright poor boy to a political scholarship in a local college, looking after the bereaved —the whole range of crises when a feller needs a friend, and, above all, a friend who knows the score and who can do something about it,—all these find the ever-helpful precinct captain available in the pinch.

To assess this function of the political machine adequately, it is important to note not only that aid *is* provided but *the manner in which it is provided.* After all, other agencies do exist for dispensing such assistance. Welfare agencies, settlement houses, legal aid clinics, medical aid in free hospitals, public relief departments, immigration authorities—these and a multitude of other organizations are available to provide the most varied types of assistance. But in contrast to the professional techniques of the welfare worker which may typically represent in the mind of the recipient the cold, bureaucratic dispensation of limited aid following upon detailed investigation of *legal* claims to aid of the "client" are the unprofessional techniques of the precinct captain who asks no questions, exacts no compliance with legal rules of eligibility and does not "snoop" into private affairs.[8]

For many, the loss of "self-respect" is too high a price for legalized assistance. In contrast to the gulf between the settlement house workers who so often come from a different social class, educational background and ethnic group, the precinct worker is "just one of us," who understands what it's all about. The condescending lady bountiful can hardly compete with the understanding friend in need. In *this struggle between alternative structures for fulfilling the nominally same function* of providing aid and support to those who need it, is clearly the machine politician who is better integrated with the groups which he serves than the impersonal, professionalized, socially distant and legally constrained welfare worker. And since the politician can at times influence and manipulate the official organizations for the dispensation of assistance, whereas the welfare worker has practically no influence on the political machine, this only adds to his greater effectiveness. More colloquially and also, perhaps, more incisively, it was the Boston ward-leader, Martin Lomasny, who described this essential function to the curious Lincoln Steffens: "I think," said Lomasny, "that there's got to be in every ward somebody that any bloke can come to—no matter what he's done—and get help. *Help, you understand; none of your law and justice, but help.*"[9]

The "deprived classes," then, constitute one subgroup for whom the political machine satisfies wants not adequately satisfied in the same fashion by the legitimate social structure.

For a second subgroup, that of business (primarily "big" business but also "small"), the political boss serves the function of providing those political privileges which entail immediate economic gains. Business corporations, among which the public utilities (railroads, local transportation and electric light companies, communications corporations) are simply the most conspicuous in this regard, seek special political dispensations which will enable them to stabilize their situation and to near their objective of maximizing profits. Interestingly enough, corporations often want to avoid a chaos of uncontrolled competition. They want the greater security of an economic czar who controls, regulates and organizes competition, providing that this czar is not a public official with his decisions subject to public scrutiny and public control.)(The latter would be "government control," and hence taboo.) The political boss fulfills these requirements admirably.)

Examined for a moment apart from any moral considerations, the political apparatus operated by the Boss is effectively designed to perform these functions with a minimum of inefficiency. Holding the strings of diverse governmental divisions, bureaus and agencies in his competent hands, the Boss rationalizes the relations between public and private business. He serves as the business community's ambassador in the otherwise alien (and sometimes unfriendly) realm of government.) And, in strict business-like terms, he is well-paid for his economic services to his respectable business clients. In an article entitled, "An Apology to Graft," Lincoln Steffens suggested that "Our economic system, which held up riches, power and acclaim as prizes to men bold enough and able enough to buy corruptly timber, mines, oil fields and franchises and 'get away with it,' was at fault."[10] And, in a conference with a hundred or so of Los Angeles business leaders, he described a fact well known to all of them: the Boss and his machine were an *integral part* of the organization of the economy. "You cannot build or operate a railroad, or a street railway, gas, water, or power company, develop and operate a mine, or get forests and cut timber on a large scale, or run any privileged business, without corrupting or joining in the corruption of the government. You tell me privately that you must, and here I am telling you semi-

publicly that you must. And that is so all over the country. And that means that we have an organization of society in which, *for some reason*, you and your kind, the ablest, most intelligent, most imaginative, daring, and resourceful leaders of society, are and must be against society and its laws and its all-around growth."[11]

Since the demand for the services of special privileges are built into the structure of the society, the Boss fulfills diverse functions for this second subgroup of business-seeking-privilege. These "needs" of business, as presently constituted, are not adequately provided for by conventional and culturally approved social structures; consequently, the extra-legal but more-or-less efficient organization of the political machine comes to provide these services. To adopt an *exclusively* moral attitude toward the "corrupt political machine" is to lose sight of the very structural conditions which generate the "evil" that is so bitterly attacked. To adopt a functional outlook is to provide not an apologia for the political machine but a more solid basis for modifying or eliminating the machine, *providing* specific structural arrangements are introduced either for eliminating these effective demands of the business community or, if that is the objective, of satisfying these demands through alternative means.)

A third set of distinctive functions fulfilled by the political machine for a special subgroup is that of providing alternative channels of social mobility for those otherwise excluded from the more conventional avenues for personal "advancement." Both the sources of this special "need" (for social mobility) and the respect in which the political machine comes to help satisfy this need can be understood by examining the

structure of the larger culture and society. As is well known, the American
culture lays enormous emphasis on
money and power as a "success" goal
legitimate for all members of the society. By no means alone in our inven-
tory of cultural goals, it still remains
among the most heavily endowed with
positive affect and value. However, certain subgroups and certain ecological
areas are notable for the relative absence of opportunity for achieving these
(monetary and power) types of success.
They constitute, in short, sub-popula-
tions where "the cultural emphasis upon
pecuniary success has been absorbed,
but where there is *little access to conventional and legitimate* means for attaining such success. The conventional
occupational opportunities of persons in
(such areas) are almost completely
limited to manual labor. Given our cultural stigmatization of manual labor,[12]
and its correlate, the prestige of white-
collar work, it is clear that the result is
a tendency to achieve these culturally
approved objectives *through whatever
means are possible.* These people are on
the one hand, "asked to orient their
conduct toward the prospect of accumulating wealth [and power] and, on the
other, they are largely denied effective
opportunities to do so institutionally."
It is within the context of social
structure that the political machine fulfills the basic function of providing avenues of social mobility for the otherwise
disadvantaged. Within this context, even
the corrupt political machine and the
racket "represent the triumph of amoral
intelligence over morally prescribed
'failure' when the channels of vertical
mobility are closed or narrowed *in a
society which places a high premium
on economic affluence, [power] and social ascent for all its members.*"[13] As one

sociologist has noted on the basis of several years of close observation in a slum
area:

The sociologist who dismisses racket and
political organizations as deviations from
desirable standards thereby neglects some
of the major elements of slum life. . . . *He
does not discover the functions they perform for the members* [of the groupings in
the slum]. The Irish and later immigrant
peoples have had the greatest difficulty in
finding places for themselves in our urban
social and economic structure. Does anyone
believe that the immigrants and their children could have achieved their present degree of social mobility without gaining
control of the political organization of some
of our largest cities? The same is true of
the racket organization. *Politics and the
rackets have furnished an important means
of social mobility for individuals, who, because of ethnic background and low class
position,* are blocked from advancement in
the "respectable" channels.[14]

This, then, represents a third type of
function performed for a distinctive subgroup. This function, it may be noted in
passing, is fulfilled by the *sheer* existence and operation of the political machine, for it is in the machine itself that
these individuals and subgroups find
their culturally induced needs more or
less satisfied. It refers to the services
which the political apparatus provides
for its own personnel. But seen in the
wider social context we have set forth,
it no longer appears as *merely* a means
of self-aggrandizement for profit-hungry
and power-hungry *individuals,* but as
an organized provision for *subgroups*
otherwise excluded from or handicapped
in the race for "getting ahead."

Just as the political machine performs
services for "legitimate" business, so it
operates to perform not dissimilar services for "illegitimate" business: vice,
crime and rackets. Once again, the basic
sociological role of the machine in this
respect can be more fully appreciated

only if one temporarily abandons attitudes of moral indignation, to examine in all moral innocence the actual workings of the organization. In this light, it at once appears that the subgroup of the professional criminal, racketeer or gambler has basic similarities of organization, demands and operation to the subgroup of the industrialist, man of business or speculator. If there is a Lumber King or an Oil King, there is also a Vice King or a Racket King. If expansive legitimate business organizes administrative and financial syndicates to "rationalize" and to "integrate" diverse areas of production and business enterprise, so expansive rackets and crime organize syndicates to bring order to the otherwise chaotic areas of production of illicit goods and services. If legitimate business regards the proliferation of small business enterprises as wasteful and inefficient, substituting, for example, the giant chain stores for hundreds of corner groceries, so illegitimate business adopts the same businesslike attitude and syndicates crime and vice. ✳Finally, and in many respects, most important, is the basic similarity, if not near-identity, of the economic role of "legitimate" business and of "illegitimate" business. *Both are in some degree concerned with the provision of goods and services for which there is an economic demand.* Morals aside, they are both business, industrial and professional enterprises, dispensing goods and services which some people want, for which there is a market in which goods and services are transformed into commodities. And, in a prevalently market society, we should expect appropriate enterprises to arise whenever there is a market demand for certain goods or services.

As is well known, vice, crime and the rackets *are* "big business." Consider only that there have been estimated to be about 500,000 professional prostitutes in the United States of 1950, and compare this with the approximately 200,000 physicians and 350,000 professional registered nurses. It is difficult to estimate which have the larger clientele: the professional men and women of medicine or the professional men and women of vice. It is, of course, difficult to estimate the economic assets, income, profits and dividends of illicit gambling in this country and to compare it with the economic assets, income, profits and dividends of, say, the shoe industry, but it is altogether possible that the two industries are about on a par. No precise figures exist on the annual expenditures on illicit narcotics, and it is probable that these are less than the expenditures on candy, but it is also probable that they are larger than the expenditure on books.

It takes but a moment's thought to recognize that, *in strictly economic terms*, there is no relevant difference between the provision of licit and of illicit goods and services. The liquor traffic illustrates this perfectly. It would be peculiar to argue that prior to 1920 (when the 18th amendment became effective), the provision of liquor constituted an economic service, that from 1920 to 1933, its production and sale no longer constituted an economic service dispensed in a market, and that from 1934 to the present, it once again took on a serviceable aspect. Or, it would be *economically* (not morally) absurd to suggest that the sale of bootlegged liquor in the dry state of Kansas is less a response to a market demand than the sale of publicly manufactured liquor in the neighboring wet state of Missouri. Examples of this sort can of course be multiplied many times over. Can it be held that in European countries, with registered and legalized prostitution, the prostitute contributes an economic service, whereas in this country, lacking legal sanction, the prostitute provides no such service? Or that the professional abortionist is in the economic market where he is legally taboo? Or that gambling satisfies a specific demand for entertainment in Nevada, where it constitutes the largest business enterprise of the larger cities in the state, but that it differs essentially in this respect from motion pictures in the neighboring state of California?[15]

The failure to recognize that these businesses are only *morally* and not *economically* distinguishable from "legitimate" businesses has led to badly scrambled analysis. Once the economic identity of the two is recognized, we may anticipate that if the political machine performs functions for "legitimate big business" it will be all the more likely to perform not dissimilar functions for "illegitimate big business." And, of course, such is often the case.

The distinctive function of the political machine for their criminal, vice and racket clientele is to enable them to operate in satisfying the economic demands of a large market without due interference from the government. Just as big business may contribute funds to the political party war-chest to ensure a minimum of governmental interference, so with big rackets and big crime. In both instances, the political machine can, in varying degrees, provide "protection." In both instances, many features of the structural context are identical: (1) market demands for goods and services; (2) the operators' concern with maximizing gains from their enterprises; (3) the need for partial control of government which might otherwise

interfere with these activities of businessmen; (4) the need for an efficient, powerful and centralized agency to provide an effective liaison of "business" with government.

Without assuming that the foregoing pages exhaust either the range of functions or the range of subgroups served by the political machine, we can at least see that *it presently fulfills some functions for these diverse subgroups which are not adequately fulfilled by culturally approved or more conventional structures.*

Several additional implications of the functional analysis of the political machine can be mentioned here only in passing, although they obviously require to be developed at length. First, the foregoing analysis has direct implications for *social engineering.* It helps explain why the periodic efforts at "political reform," "turning the rascals out" and "cleaning political house" are typically (though not necessarily) short-lived and ineffectual. It exemplifies a basic theorem: *any attempt to eliminate an existing social structure without providing adequate alternative structures for fulfilling the functions previously fulfilled by the abolished organization is doomed to failure.* (Needless to say, this theorem has much wider bearing than the one instance of the political machine.) When "political reform" confines itself to the manifest task of "turning the rascals out," it is engaging in little more than sociological magic. The reform may for a time bring new figures into the political limelight; it may serve the casual social function of re-assuring the electorate that the moral virtues remain intact and will ultimately triumph; it may actually effect a turnover in the personnel of the political machine; it may even, for a time, so curb the activities of the machine as to leave unsatisfied the many needs it has previously fulfilled. But, inevitably, unless the reform also involves a "re-forming" of the social and political structure such that the existing needs are satisfied by alternative structures or unless it involves a change which eliminates these needs altogether, the political machine will return to its integral place in the social scheme of things. *To seek social change, without due recognition of the manifest and latent functions performed by the social organization undergoing change, is to indulge in social ritual rather than social engineering.* The concepts of manifest and latent functions (or their equivalents) are indispensable elements in the theoretic repertoire of the social engineer. In this crucial sense, these concepts are not "merely" theoretical (in the abusive sense of the term), but are eminently practical. In the deliberate enactment of social change, they can be ignored only at the price of considerably heightening the risk of failure.

A second implication of this analysis of the political machine also has a bearing upon areas wider than the one we have considered. The paradox has often been noted that the supporters of the political machine include both the "respectable" business class elements who are, of course, opposed to the criminal or racketeer and the distinctly "unrespectable" elements of the underworld. And, at first appearance, this is cited as an instance of very strange bedfellows. The learned judge is not infrequently called upon to sentence the very racketeer beside whom he sat the night before at an informal dinner of the political bigwigs. The district attorney jostles the exonerated convict on his way to the back room where the Boss has called a meeting. The big business man may complain almost as bitterly as the big racketeer about the "extortionate" contributions to the party fund demanded by the Boss. Social opposites meet—in the smoke-filled room of the successful politician.

In the light of a functional analysis all this of course no longer seems paradoxical. Since the machine serves both the businessman and the criminal man, the two seemingly antipodal groups intersect. This points to a more general theorem: *the social functions of an organization help determine the structure (including the recruitment of personnel involved in the structure), just as the structure helps determine the effectiveness with which the functions are fulfilled.* In terms of social status, the business group and the criminal group are indeed poles apart. But status does not fully determine behavior and the interrelations between groups. Functions modify these relations. Given their distinctive needs, the several subgroups in the large society are "integrated," whatever their personal desires or intentions, by the centralizing structure which serves these several needs. In a phrase with many implications which require further study, *structure affects function and function affects structure.* . . .

NOTES

1. These "explanations" are "causal" in design. They profess to indicate the social conditions under which political machines come into being. In so far as they are empirically confirmed, these explations of course add to our knowledge concerning the problem: how is it that political machines operate in certain areas and not in others? How do they manage to continue? *But these causal accounts are not sufficient.* The functional consequences of the machine, as we shall see, go far toward supplementing the causal interpretation.

2. I trust it is superfluous to add that this hypothesis is not "in support of the political machine." The question whether the dysfunctions of the ma-

chine outweigh its functions, the question whether alternative structures are not available which may fulfill its functions without necessarily entailing its social dysfunctions, still remain to be considered at an appropiate point. We are here concerned with documenting the statement that moral judgments based *entirely* on an appraisal of manifest functions of a social structure are "unrealistic" in the strict sense, *i.e.*, they do not take into account other actual consequences of that structure, consequences which may provide basic social support for the structure. As will be indicated later, "social reforms" or "social engineering" which ignore latent functions do so on pain of suffering acute disappointments and boomerang effects.

3. Again, as with preceding cases, we shall not consider the possible dysfunctions of the political machine.

4. Edward M. Sait, "Machine, Political," *Encyclopedia of the Social Sciences*, IX, 658 b [italics supplied]; *cf.* A. F. Bentley, *The Process of Government* (Chicago, 1908), Chap. 2.

5. Herbert Croly, *Progressive Democracy*, (New York, 1914), p. 254, cited by Sait, *op. cit.*, 658 b.

6. Sait, *op. cit.*, 659 a. [italics supplied].

7. *Ibid.*, 659 a.

8. Much the same contrast with official welfare policy is found in Harry Hopkins' open-handed and non-political distribution of unemployment relief in New York State under the governorship of Franklin Delano Roosevelt. As Sherwood reports: "Hopkins was harshly criticized for these irregular activities by the established welfare agencies, which claimed it was 'unprofessional conduct' to hand out work tickets without thorough investigation of each applicant, his own or his family's financial resources and probably his religious affiliations. 'Harry told the agency to go to hell,' said [Hopkins' associate, Dr. Jacob A.] Goldberg." Robert E. Sherwood, *Roosevelt and Hopkins, An Intimate History,* (New York: Harper, 1948), 30.

9. *The Autobiography of Lincoln Steffens,* (Chautauqua, New York: Chautauqua Press, 1931), 618. Deriving largely from Steffens, as he says, F. Stuart Chapin sets forth these functions of the political machine with great clarity. See his *Contemporary American Institutions* (New York: Harper, 1934), 40-54.

10. *Autobiography of Lincoln Steffens,* 570.

11. *Ibid.*, 572-3 [italics supplied]. This helps explain, as Steffens noted after Police Commissioner Theodore Roosevelt, "the prominence and respectability of the men and women who intercede for crooks" when these have been apprehended in a periodic effort to "clean up the political machine." *Cf.* Steffens, 371, and *passim*.

12. See the National Opinion Research Center survey of evaluation of occupations which firmly documents the general impression that the manual occupations rate very low indeed in the social scale of values, *even among those who are themselves engaged in manual labor.* Consider this latter point in its full implications. In effect, the cultural and social structure exacts the values of pecuniary and power success even among those who find themselves confined to the stigmatized manual occupations. Against this background, consider the powerful motivation for achieving this type of "success" by any means whatsoever. A garbage-collector who joins with other Americans in the view that the garbage-collector is "the lowest of the low" occupations can scarcely have a self-image which is pleasing to him; he is in a "pariah" occupation in the very society where he is assured that "all who have genuine merit can get ahead." Add to this, his occasional recognition that "he didn't have the same chance as others, no matter what they say," and one perceives the enormous psychological pressure upon him for "evening up the score" by finding some means, whether strictly legal or not, for moving ahead. All this provides the structural and derivatively psychological background for the "socially induced need" in *some* groups to find some accessible avenue for social mobility.

13. Merton, "Social structure and anomie," chapter IV of this volume.

14. William F. Whyte, "Social organization in the slums," *American Sociological Review*, Feb. 1943, 8, 34-39 (italics supplied). Thus, the political machine and the racket represent a special *case* of the type of organizational adjustment to the conditions described in chapter IV. It represents, note, an *organizational* adjustment: definite structures arise and operate to reduce somewhat the acute tensions and problems of individuals caught up in the described conflict between the "cultural accent on success-for-all" and the "socially structured fact of unequal opportunities for success." As chapter IV indicates, other types of *individual* "adjustment" are possible: lone-wolf crime, psychopathological states, rebellion, retreat by abandoning the culturally approved goals, etc. Likewise, other types of *organizational* adjustment sometimes occur; the racket or the political machine are not *alone* available as organized means for meeting this socially induced problem. Participation in revolutionary organizations, for example, can be seen within this context, as an alternative mode of organizational adjustment. All this bears theoretic notice here, since we might otherwise overlook the basic functional concepts of functional substitutes and functional equivalents, which are to be discussed at length in a subsequent publication.

15. Perhaps the most perceptive statement of this view has been made by Hawkins and Waller. "The prostitute, the pimp, the peddler of dope, the operator of the gambling hall, the vendor of obscene pictures, the bootlegger, the abortionist, all are productive, all produce services or goods which people desire and for which they are willing to pay. It happens that society has put these goods and services under the ban, but people go on producing them and people go on consuming them, and an act of the legislature does not make them any less a part of the economic system." "Critical notes on the cost of crime," *Journal of Criminal Law and Criminology*, 1936, 26, 679-94, at 684.

The Politicians and the Machine

MOISEI OSTROGORSKI

I

The American politician, while constituting a separate class in American society, has not a distinct origin. He is recruited from all ranks of the community, as circumstances and personal tastes happen to dictate, by a process of *natural selection.* The germ which produces the politician is the desire to obtain some public office or other. The aspirant may be a low-class attorney just as well as a small employee, an artisan, a cab-driver, a car-conductor, or even a *déclassé*, a social failure. To realize his ambition, he begins to "study politics." It is not the "Politics" of Aristotle, nor even that of Columbia College, but it is none the less a science which demands great application and certain natural aptitudes. It consists of a technical part, which includes a knowledge of the machinery of the party organization, with all its wheels within wheels,—the primaries, the committees, the various sets of conventions, —and of the legal procedure in force for making up the register and taking the vote. While learning the ostensible working of the party and of the election machinery, the future politician fathoms their inner working, the manœuvres, the dodges, and the frauds by means of which a minority, perhaps an insignificant minority, is transformed into a majority, and a semblance of popular sanction is given to the schemes of a gang of political sharpers. But all these highly useful acquirements constitute, so to speak, only the mechanical side of the politicians' art, which by itself will not carry its man very far. The principal subject-matter of his "studies" is a sort of empirical psychology. He studies the men about him and their weak points, and by trading on the latter he tries to get as large a following as possible. He begins with his immediate neighbours, who live on the same landing; he extends his advances to the inmates of the whole house, and before long to the next or the next two houses as well. When he has got acquainted with a dozen, or even half a dozen, electors, who are ready, often out of mere friendship, to join him at the elections, he is the possessor of a small political capital, which he will forthwith turn over, and which will become, perhaps, the foundation of his success, of a brilliant success, at a more or less early date. "Owning" half a dozen or a dozen votes, he is received with open arms by the local organization of the party; they make much of him, ask his advice, put him on the committee of the local branch, and even show their gratitude for the voting strength which he brings them in a less platonic fashion. His career of "ward politician" has begun.

In the popular wards of the large cities the small politician has no need

From Moisei Ostrogorski, *Democracy and the Organization of Political Parties*, Vol. II: *The United States,* edited and abridged by Seymour Martin Lipset (New York: Doubleday Anchor Paperback, 1964), pp. 179-227. Copyright © 1964 by Seymour Martin Lipset. Reprinted by permission of Doubleday & Company, Inc.

to create the political following which he forms around him; he finds it ready to hand in social life, in which neighbourly ties, and above all common tastes and mutual sympathies, give rise to small sets, groups of people who meet regularly to enjoy the pleasures of sociability and of friendship. The street corner serves them as a rendezvous as long as they are in the youthful stage. Then, when they grow older and have a few cents to spend, they meet in a drinking-saloon or in a room hired for the purpose with their modest contributions. Several "gangs" unite to found a sort of club, in which they give small parties, balls, or simply smoke, drink, and amuse themselves. This merry crew is a latent political force; when the elections come round it may furnish a compact band of voters. The small politician therefore has but to lay his hand on it. Often he has himself grown up in the gang and with it; the stirring life of the gang, with its escapades, its quarrels, and its brawls with the members of the rival gangs, frequently gave him an opportunity of displaying his superior faculties of command and of organization; his companions got into the habit of following him in everything. These qualities which he possesses and this confidence which he inspires he can turn to account as soon as he feels his vocation, as soon as he becomes a "practical politician." The agglomerations of the European immigrants offer a no less favourable soil for the growth of the political manipulator of men. Germans, Italians, or Slavs arrive without knowing the language, the manners and customs, and the institutions of the country. But thereupon they find a fellow-countryman already naturalized and at home in the New World, who puts himself fraternally at their disposal; he guides their early steps, he helps them to look out for work, he appears on their behalf before the representatives of the public authority in the ward with whom they have to deal; later on, when the legal term has expired, or even earlier, he procures their naturalization. Day by day the ties which grow up between him and them are drawn closer, he becomes for them not only a friend, an adviser, but an oracle; and full of gratitude for his friendly services, and of admiration for his intelligence, they make over to him with perfect good faith the votes which have just been given them, and which as a rule they do not know what to do with. Here again is an "owner" of votes, who will find a good investment for his modest pile in the electoral market.

When the influence of the budding politician, obtained in one way or another, asserts itself in the precinct, the Organization of the party formally invests him with the position of local leader. He becomes its official representative in the precinct (often known by the name of "captain"), and acquires an indefeasible right to a share of the profits realized by the Organization, that is, to some office suited rather to his merits as a wire-puller than to his special fitness for it. Often within the ranks of the party the budding politician meets with rivals and competitors; each has his knot of followers, and each seeks to extend his influence. The one who is most skilful in managing his fellow-creatures, in winning them by small services or promises, who best appraises each man's price, who is clever in bringing about understandings and alliances, will come out first and will transform his rivals into his trusty lieutenants. The immediate object and, to a certain extent, the arena of this "struggle for existence" is the local primary; each strives to assert himself in the primary, that is to say, to procure the election of delegates devoted to him. The competitor who succeeds in this will be "recognized" by the higher Organization of the party impassively contemplating the struggle. At the head of his gang, each of them wrangles over every inch of ground, bringing into play all his resources, from the seductiveness of his personal magnetism, of his skill as a negotiator, down to the methods of what I have called the technical portion of the art and which consists in making away with voting-papers, in voting several times under different names, preventing opponents from voting by stratagem or by violence, etc. If the competitors are numerous and pretty evenly matched, there always turns out to be one who, occupying a somewhat more advantageous position, eventually thrusts himself on the others; instead of fighting each other, they all "compromise on him," admit his authority, and follow his lead, in order to secure a more modest but safer share of the booty. Our small politician now has his lieutenants each of whom has his henchmen, and he is supreme in the primary in which delegates are elected to the local convention. His political capital has thus increased.

In the larger arena of the ward or of the district, he meets with other politicians of the same rank, and there exactly the same process of natural selection takes place, one of them achieves the position of "leader," gains an ascendency over all the "ward politicians," who place their contingents at his disposal and help him to assert his authority over the party organization in the ward, or perhaps even in more than one ward. A few of the cleverest leaders unite and form a "ring" or a "combine," to work up the electoral raw material and exploit "what there is in it." The organization of the politicians reaches the final stage of its development when the "leaders" find their master in one of their own number who commands obedience by his strength of will, his cleverness, his audacity, and his luck, and who asserts himself *per fas et nefas* in the central conventions of the party, just as his prototype, the "ward politician," asserts imself in the primary. By a common agreement which has no need to be bargained about or expressed, every one wheels into line behind this man, recognizes him as the supreme chief. He is crowned city boss or state boss, as the case may be. At the head of his adherents, he forms with them what is called the "Machine," that is to say an aggregation of individuals stretching out hierarchically from top to bottom, bound to one another by personal devotion, but mercenary, and bent solely on satisfying their appetites by exploiting the resources of a political party. The men of the "Machine" do not accept this nickname, and style themselves "the Organization," usurping the name after having usurped the thing, after having "captured" the party Organization by a series of successful operations in the primaries and the conventions. This distinction between the Machine and the Organization does not exist only in logic, but it often does in fact as well; the power of the mercenary politicians in the party Organization is not universal, there are many places which escape it more or less. Although a constant phenomenon, the Machine is not a general phenomenon. For the clearness of the narrative, I shall refer here to the Machine as if it covered the whole political area of the United States.

Sometimes an ambitious and specially gifted politician quickens or anticipates the process of natural evolution, he "builds a machine" from top to bottom; he finds out men capable of serving him as lieutenants, comes to an understanding with them, and by his manœuvres spreads his net over the whole city or the whole State. But if he succeeds in this, it is because the social and political elements of the Machine were there ready to hand. However predominant therefore the personal character of the Machine may be, it is unfair to say that its importance is no more than that of a fortuitous and temporary association. True, there are purely personal Machines to be met with which break to pieces on the disappearance of their creator, but as a rule their elements represent a permanent stock forming part of the political circulation of the country. Only one must know how to bring these elements together and keep them together. The strongest attraction and source of cohesion for the politicians are the places in the public service, from the humblest up to the highest, which bring in a little or a good deal of money. Yet most of the Machine men are paid not so much in ready money as in drafts on the future; they are a singularly confiding race, and the hopes which are held out to them suffice to keep their zeal alive for a very long time.) The material profits which the politicians receive or expect for their services are seasoned with the social pleasures which they enjoy in the gatherings of their particular circle. The "head-quarters" of the party in the locality, whether established in the premises of a drinking-saloon or elsewhere, is not only an official place of meeting, but a club where one goes to spend the evening, where one is always sure of

pleasant company because those who frequent it are united by the same interests and the same aspirations. There the politicians receive their personal friends who are not in politics, and invite them to join in their pleasures. From time to time the head politicians get up special entertainments for their men, cheap excursions, "chowder-parties" or "clam-bakes." All these gatherings are a powerful means of keeping up the loyalty of the small politicians and of developing to a high pitch the *esprit de corps* which makes them really a machine.

Each Machine being in reality composed of a number of smaller and smaller Machines which form so many microcosms within it, the respective powers as well as the rank of the chief engineers and of their fellow-workmen represent a sort of expanding ladder. This is the case in the first instance with the hierarchy of the Machine's staff: the title and the rôle of boss do not belong exclusively to the man who controls the Machine in the city or in the State; the leader is the local boss in his own district; the person in charge of the precinct is himself a little boss. The boss owes help and protection to his henchmen, he must defend them with his person, must forward their political ambitions, if they have any, ensure them a livelihood if they are not well off, as is the case with most of his lieutenants, procure them places in the public service, keep them there, however great their incompetence or their neglect of their duties. He will move heaven and earth to place his men, he will risk his influence to achieve it. This is the first reward which he claims, regardless of himself, from the boss above him, or from the head of the executive power who makes appointments. He must have a place for his henchman. If the boss is a member of the Senate he will not hesitate, in order to put pressure on the administration, to obstruct an important measure demanded by the country: he must have a place for his henchman. It is by no means out of chivalry that the boss thus devotes himself to his lieutenants, but to safeguard his own position: if he did not exert himself actively on their behalf, no one would care to "work" for such a chief; or, if with all his good will he were to become unable to get places for his men, he would undergo the same fate; he could no longer appeal to their selfish interest, nor to their imagination; the charm is broken, the prestige vanishes into thin air, and the boss ceases to be a boss. But as long as the ties which unite them to one another subsist, their mutual relations are ruled by an iron discipline. A subordinate politician must put his personal feelings completely on one side; his likes and dislikes are to order; he must be ready to exchange them one for the other without a moment's hesitation. This is the case at all grades of the Machine. The principal lieutenants themselves only wait for the word of command; even when the boss consults them, they are under no illusion as to their authority:[1] he is free to listen to their advice or not, as soon as he has given his decision not a word is spoken. The committees of the party Organization, the ward, city, State committees, simply register the will of the boss or of the respective leader, and their members are in reality only figureheads. All along the line the real power is always in the hands of a single man, the leader. The leader often does not think fit even to sit on the committee, he sends to it in his place a friend who votes according to his instructions. The great boss, the city or State boss, generally presides over the central committee, but sometimes he too puts in a lay-figure as his substitute. While devoid of real influence, the committee can depose the bosses, by electing another chairman of the committee in place of the boss or of his lay-figure. This is the formal proclamation of the deposition of the reigning boss to whom his vassals renounce allegiance.

II

The Machine is now built, the politicians are sorted and in their proper places for action. Our next step is to see them at work. For this purpose we will begin by following a politician of average importance whose intermediary position places him at the centre of action, such as a sub-boss in a large city, a "district leader" or a "ward leader" in New York, Philadelphia, or Baltimore. This "leader" presents himself to us in the first instance as the engineer-in-chief of the Machine for getting hold of the base of operations of organized parties—the nominations for elective posts. Forestalling the rôle of the primaries and the conventions, the Machine, as we know already, makes up the slate of delegates and of candidates and gets it simply registered by these party assemblies. For local elective positions, especially for municipal offices and for the delegateships of the primaries, the "leader" makes up the slate of his own authority, and on his own responsibility, that is to say, he has to choose men who are ready, after they are duly elected, to do what the Machine tells them. The slate of the higher elective posts is made up or approved by the boss himself, but it is the business of the "leader" to ensure the success of the slate at the convention, by getting docile delegates elected. Having selected his candidates, who will be presented to the people as the deliberate choice of the convention, the boss instructs the "leader" to "deliver a solid delegation" for these candidates, and the leader is bound to "deliver the goods." If the leader is unable to do so, he signs his deposition as leader. On the other hand, if the lieutenants of a boss, small or great, refuse to "deliver the goods" to him, the boss will not have the wherewithal for carrying on his trade in elective offices. The internal operations of the Machine along the whole line consist, therefore, of these deliveries: each respective leader is supposed to "deliver the delegates" to his superior, from the delegates to the county or district convention up to the delegates to the National Convention. The district leader is the first deliverer. How does he get the "goods" himself? After the delivery of the delegates, the electors must be made to vote for the candidates adopted by those delegates. The district leader again is the chief agent of this operation. How does he succeed in it?

In both cases he gains his ends by corruption and by seduction. The sinews of corruption are supplied him by the Machine; the means of seduction he derives from his own resources. He is amiable with everybody, with the lowest of the low, he is all things to all men. To offend no one, to please every one, that is his motto. He is in constant touch with all the electors of his district, he knows their ins and outs, the strong and the weak points of each man, and how to exploit them. He "understands" all his people perfectly, because he is one of them himself; he is eminently "representative" of the community on which he acts; he is on a moral and intellectual

level which is neither higher nor lower than that of the average of the inhabitants of the district: if the district is one which swarms with the dregs of the population, with frequenters of drinking-saloons, the local leader of the Machine is not much superior; on the other hand, in a well-inhabited district the leader always has a respectable appearance, his get-up and his address are gentlemanly, he speaks English correctly, he is pleasing, genial, but without being vulgar. With these apparent virtues he combines certain moral virtues, a very small stock it is true, but which ensure him esteem and general confidence: he is a man of courage, of strength of will, and above all a man of his word. No matter if he is a low wire-puller, who sticks at no fraud, or if he has committed breaches of trust in public offices,—he keeps his promises, he is a man of honour. This merit is appreciated in him to the exclusion of all the others because everybody or nearly everybody has something to ask of him; and if he is not asked for anything, he volunteers his services. All aspirants to public office who inhabit "his" district apply to him, from members of the bar who want a judgeship down to crossing-sweepers. In that district he is the sole dispenser of all the public posts at the disposal of the party Organization. The boss or the managing ring of the Machine distributes these offices among the leaders, leaving it entirely to their discretion to make the best use of them for the common cause. This "patronage" intrusted to the leader is the most important part of his ammunition, and makes him undisputed master in his territory; it draws into his orbit the whole tribe of office-seekers who realize that there is no salvation save in him. These are not only the aspirants to elective posts who cannot be elected if they are not on the slate, the slate which is in the hands of the Machine; the non-elective posts in the public departments, down to those of office messengers, are invariably given by favour; to obtain one, you must have what is called a "pull," or "pulls," occult influences which pull the official to make him do something contrary to his duty.

In addition to the places, there are a thousand and one other favours which the representative of the Machine can grant by means of his influence, favours which imply the weal or woe of the whole existence of many humble folk; permits issued by the police or by other authorities for plying some small trade or business on the public thoroughfare, such as that of costermonger, of vendor of roasted chestnuts, of seller of cooling drinks, of boot-black, etc.; a word from the leader of the Machine is enough to get the poor fellow permission to set up his improvised shop at a street-corner. It is through the leader again that one can obtain a license to open a drinking-saloon or get it refused to a competitor. The power of his pulls extends even to defying the law itself; it ensures impunity to misdemeanours, nay even to criminal offences, if the culprits are trusty followers of the Machine. Sometimes it is a case only of breaking the law with no guilty intention, such as an infringement of building regulations, but far more often the leader of the Machine uses his power to protect gaol-birds. If the offenders are notoriously supporters of the Machine, the policemen will often think twice about arresting them. When they are arrested, the leader intervenes and applies for their release on bail. Sometimes he may have to spend the whole morning at the police courts interceding for one after an-

other of his clients, arrested for being drunk and disorderly, for assaults committed in a brawl, or for other offences. The leader provides the sum fixed by the judge as bail, and then, before the hearing comes on, tries to get the judge to dismiss the case, or at all events to obtain a considerable reduction or a commutation of the penalty. Whatever the gravity of the case therefore, as soon as there is any "trouble," everybody rushes off to the leader of the Machine. He is an inverted tribune of the people, he defends the obscure and the humble against justice, he interposes between them and the arm of the law.

Many other citizens who have nothing to ask or fear from the public authorities, but who are in needy circumstances, also get help and succour from the representative of the Machine: to this one he lends a dollar; for another he obtains a railroad ticket without payment; he has coal distributed in the depth of winter; he makes other gifts in kind; he sometitmes sends poultry at Christmas time; he buys medicine for a sick person; he helps to bury the dead by procuring a coffin on credit or half price. He has a kind heart in virtue of his position and his position gives him the means of satisfying his need for kindness: the money which he distributes comes from the chest of the Machine; the latter has obtained it by the most reprehensible methods, those which we have seen practised by Tammany Hall, but no matter. With this money he can also dispense an ample hospitality in the drinking-saloons. As soon as he comes in, friends known and unknown gather round him, and he treats everybody, he orders one drink after another for the company; he is the only one who does not drink, he is on

*money by corrupt methods used to help people

duty. To the more influential electors a less intermittent hospitality is offered in the clubs of the politicians; admitted by the latter as friends, joining in their amusements, they are socially swept into the sphere of influence of the Machine. The electors who are below the favours or the civilities of the representatives of the Machine are bought right out at the market price. Each man is taken by his weak side. It is like a huge spider's web spread by the Machine over the district. Every new elector is drawn into it at once. As soon as he moves into the locality an enquiry is made about him of the representatives of the Machine in whose jurisdiction his old residence was situated, a visit is paid him, an attempt is made to win him. An answer is found in his case to the invariable question which haunts the Machine: what does he want, what would he like to have? The man who does not wish for anything, who does not ask for anything, is the most painful puzzle to the Machine; it considers him almost as a hateable being. The favours of every kind granted to those who go with the Machine, the "rewards," find a corollary in the "punishments" inflicted on those who cross its path. It deprives them of their livelihood, it persecutes and molests them with all the resources of its influence. If the man who has incurred its animosity is an employee, it gets him dismissed from his situation; if he is engaged in manufactures or trade, the leader sets the police at him who make a point of worrying him on the most futile or imaginary pretexts; at one time the sanitary conditions of his establishment are defective, at another the carriages or vans which stand outside his door impede the traffic. The tax collector makes a minute investigation into the taxes and licenses paid by the trader who is in the bad books of the Machine, and discovers that he has not been paying the proper sum.

In truth, this system of rewards and punishments cannot lay claim to originality; it is that of the Sicilian *mafia* and the Italian *camorra*, minus the stiletto and the gun, and plus the scientific method.

While bringing their efforts to bear on individual electors, the leaders of the Machine also make great exertions to cultivate the friendship of men who through their position or their business can procure them adhesions in a lump, who can serve as recruiting sergeants. For this purpose they make friends in the workmen's trade unions, in the factories and the workshops, and even descend to the lowest step in the social ladder to get useful help; they get hold of the keepers of lodging-houses, of gambling-houses, and of every kind of den frequented by the criminal or semi-criminal class, of the saloon-keepers, by ensuring them protection against the police and the law, or by paying them directly.

All this work of inveigling the electors is done both by the district leader and by the small leaders of the precincts or divisions. The latter serve as informers and finger-posts to the Machine; they are continually spying on the inhabitants of their little domain on its behalf. At the same time they operate themselves: the Machine gives them as their share some money and a few subordinate places to distribute. The relative influence attaching to their position of representative of the Machine enables them also to grant small favours and to render services of less importance. If the resources in influence and money at the disposal of the precinct leader are inadequate, he refers to the leader of the district, who almost always finds the ways and means; in cases where that is beyond the latter's powers, where an exceptionally strong "pull" or an authoritative act is required, the leader applies to the boss.

This is the proper moment for us also to transport ourselves into the higher sphere of the Machine, in which the boss reigns supreme.

III

The operations of the "leaders," which bear rather on the lower strata of the population, enable the Machine to "fix the primaries," to form the conventions of delegates to its liking, and to bring the big battalions up to the poll. But the respectable portion of the electorate would often be capable of rejecting the candidates of the Machine, for these latter are not the most deserving individuals. The Machine cannot afford the luxury of high-class candidates: they would not be able to render it the services on which it subsists; a man of independent mind and anxious to do his duty could not provide it with the pulls with which it obtains the votes of the electors.

The A B C of the strategy of the Machine is to shuffle the electoral pack, to mix up its own cause with that of the party whose flag it hoists or with the great political preoccupations of the day, and to create a confusion between the different elections themselves.) At the municipal election the issue is never the good government of the city, the state of the pavements or the drainage, but the protectionist tariff, or Cuba, or the Philippines. Why, the particular city election will predetermine the result of the impending State elections, or even

of the presidential election—is this the time to look closely into the merit of this or that local candidate? The issue is the general fate of the party in the State and in the Union, and if some electors are prepared to jeopardize it because the candidate for the city council in their ward is not the ideal of all the virtues, they will do this on their own responsibility. The Machine includes men whose political morality provokes strong animadversion; it may be so; it has governed the city or the State like a satrapy; there is, perhaps, an element of truth in this charge; but is it fair to make the party pay for the individual faults of a few of its servants? The enemy is at the gates, and it is the "life of the party," of that grand, of that noble party, which must be saved; who will lift a parricidal hand against it? Sometimes the stake is still higher; the party which the Machine claims to serve is identified with a problem which closely concerns the daily existence of the great majority of the citizens, such as the protection of the national industries or the currency; the defeat of the party means financial ruin followed by the advent of anarchy and socialism; under such circumstances what do men signify? it is the flag which must be followed. And each time the conjuncture is an exceptional one; each time it is a case of *force majeure* which makes it imperative to vote the party ticket as it stands, to vote even for a "yellow dog." The American's excitability of temperament, which inclines him to exaggeration, and his imagination, which magnifies everything, makes this game of the Machine a fairly easy one.

This card-shuffling game is very often complicated by the fact that the Machine slips spurious cards into the pack, it puts forward ornamental candidates or fictitious candidates intended to impress the electors. It selects perfectly respectable men whose reputation and social position appear to preclude the idea that they would make themselves liegemen of the Machine; but owing to their weakness of character and want of perspicacity they become, without being aware of it, tools in the hands of the astute leaders of the Machine; they do what the Machine wants, and shield it with their respectability. This category of candidates is known by the name of "figure-heads."

The skill of the heads of the Machine consists in finding out men likely to fall in with this rôle, and in managing them with the required lightness of hand by discerning the point of resistance beyond which the pressure to be put upon them must not go. The figure-head is almost a classic character, he is to be found at every stage of the political life directed by the party Organization.

The rôle of figure-head, however, is chiefly connected with important elective posts. Placed at the head of the ticket, they cover all the rest of the list with their respectability. The conspicuous office most frequently bestowed on this particular species of "prominent citizens" is that of mayor.

Another species of candidates with which the Machine hoodwinks the electors are the "dummies," the imaginary candidates. Thus the Machine, fearing that its real candidate whom it has in its mind may be rejected by the electors on account of his disreputableness, puts forward another candidate ten times more disreputable. This odious candidature provokes a revolt of the public conscience. Bowing to public opinion, the Machine humbly gives way and withdraws its man, substituting for him the other whom it had selected in petto.

It is not uncommon for the part of dummy, as confederate of the Machine, to be played by the Machine of the opposite party. If this latter has no chance of carrying its ticket against the opposite ticket, it prefers to come to terms with its rival, to help it to elect its candidates, in order to get a share of the spoils as its reward. With this object it chooses for the party which it represents candidates likely rather to repel than attract the electors; it dooms them to failure beforehand, in order to ensure the success of the pretended hostile Machine.

These Machiavellian combinations are, however, only some of the forms assumed by the co-operation of hostile Machines which, instead of fighting each other, often find it more profitable to come to terms secretly, and to make "deals." When a formidable movement of independent electors, of "reformers," breaks out, an understanding between the two Machines often seems to them the obvious course—the Machine in opposition assist the threatened Machine, not so much in order to save it as to save the Machine régime, the spoils system which supports the politicians.

When the Machine in opposition does not think it advisable to take up this attitude, the Machine attacked by the independents of its own party resorts to the "harmony" dodge: it makes fervent appeals to them in favour of concord, invites them to "harmony conferences" to induce them to disarm. It is lavish of promises of good government, subscribes to everything proposed in the way of declarations of principles, of programmes, even if they contain denunciations of the bosses and of the practices of the Machine, provided that it is allowed to have the candidates. At a pinch, it allows the recalcitrants a portion of the ticket; it is prepared to make sacrifices, for there is but one thing which it cares for—to "maintain a united party." It varies the extent of the sacrifices according to the situation; it flings the Cerberus of public opinion a few elective posts bestowed on highly respectable persons; if possible, it selects them from the class of figure-heads, otherwise it acquiesces in the complete abandonment of these offices. If the brute is savage and has sharp teeth, the Machine throws it a few more sops. Sometimes the Machine is in such danger that it consents, always "for the sake of harmony," to keep the second and third rate places only for its men. If public opinion declares with special force in favour of a certain candidature, the Machine hastens to adopt it. The flexibility with which the Machine tries to adapt itself to circumstances has no limits; it is capable, in order to mislead public opinion, of changing its skin, of becoming quite "respectable," and of appearing exclusively taken up with the public weal, of even hoisting the standard of "reform," of starting on a crusade against the corruption of the politicians, especially when that corruption is embodied in the Machine of the opposite party.

Trifling with public opinion, fencing with it or simply ignoring it when it can afford to do so, the Machine, however, always makes it believe that after all it is obliged to do what the "people" want, that it has, in reality, no power. And the "people" accepts this view with much complacency, it knows that the politicians are full of craft and guile, but it has confidence in its own strength, an ingenuous confidence which inspires it, not so much with indignation, as with indulgent contempt for the politicians whom it deems at its

mercy. The whole business of hoodwinking public opinion, to which the Machine devotes itself, is powerfully seconded by the party press. The newspapers know what's what perfectly well, but they represent in the first place an industrial concern which depends, in the United States, not so much on readers, on subscribers, as on the persons who supply the advertisements. The Machine, owing to its pulls, is able to procure the newspapers' large advertising orders. Besides this, it subsidizes individual editors or bribes them with places given to them or to their relations. In return these newspapers present the facts in a light which is favourable to the Machine, and keep out matter which is compromising for it. Often the boss prefers to secure the good offices of the reporters who regularly insert paragraphs of a few lines, insignificant in appearance, but always worded to suit the Machine, while in the same newspaper the leading articles, which hardly anyone reads, are inveighing against the Machine. Certain State bosses practise the system of "patent inside" for their requirements, and fill the local newspaper with articles and news which they get written at headquarters. Generally the small local journal is one of the powerful instruments which the Machine uses to keep public opinion in a state of coma.

IV

Being aware of the fact that the Machine holds the keys of the electoral situation, everybody whose interests are affected thereby acknowledges its power, whether they like it or not. The candidates of the party are the first to realize that they are not at liberty to attain their object independently of the Machine and still less in opposition to it. The Machine is too strong even for candidates who occupy such an exceptional position that they might, it would seem, shake it off, a man of independent character, enjoying great personal popularity, and a "military hero" to boot, whose laurels, freshly plucked in a recent war, throw the multitude into raptures, on becoming a candidate deems it nevertheless necessary to at least perform the rite of going to "see" the boss. With the great majority of candidates, the enormous election expenses and the technical complexity of the election business are quite enough to prevent them from courting the popular suffrages with their own resources; if an aspirant is not approved by the Machine of the party to which he claims to belong, he must construct a Machine for himself. Aided by the conditions with which we are familiar, the Machine has succeeded in transforming the elections into an industry, exploited like other industrial concerns, on the method of concentration of capital and labour applied to the raw material. Being able to deliver its product on the most favourable terms, it takes orders, it contracts for elections: does any one wish to become municipal councillor or member of the legislature, he has but to come to terms with the Machine, to "see" the boss and settle the price; the Machine undertakes the rest. As it enjoys a monopoly in its line of business, the Machine can refuse offers without giving any reason, that is to say, forbid an aspirant to become candidate. The boss bluntly informs an aspirant to an elective post that he cannot grant or renew his "nomination," and the applicant must bow to the decision, for the convention which makes the nomina-

tions makes them at the bidding of the boss, recruited as it is by his henchmen in the primaries, which are full of their underlings. Again, the tradition of local candidatures which excludes candidates not residing in the constituency, prevents the aspirant shown out by the boss from trying his political luck in another constituency. The boss has thus absolute power over the candidates, he can admit them into or shut them out of political life at will. It also happens that the boss compels a man to stand: in following out his ideas of election tactics, he has settled that the most suitable candidate in the particular conjuncture is So-and-so; it matters little if this individual has no wish to come forward, or if he has an appointment already, he must obey, if he does not mean to give up public life for good. The power of the Machine extends over all the branches of the government, none escape it, each serves to satisfy its wants and its appetites. The Executive, and in general the officials who are at the head of a department, are the first prey of the Machine, for they dispose of what the Machine wants above all things,—the subordinate offices in the public administrations with which it pays its henchmen and its workers. The departmental chiefs make over to it the patronage which is intrusted to them by the law. . . .

. . . Far more serious is the interference of the Machine with the legislative work in the municipal assemblies and in the State legislatures. In each legislative assembly the Machine "owns" a certain number of members whose election expenses it has paid; these tools of the Machine form a nucleus which is quickly developed by intimidation and corruption brought to bear on the independent members. The latter are swept into the net first of all by the institution of the legislative caucus, of those semi-official meetings of the members of the party in which they decide, by a majority of votes, what line shall be taken up in the full sitting of the House on each important question; on pain of apostasy, every member of the party is obliged to vote in the way agreed on. Forming a compact group which manœuvres as one man, the representatives of the Machine easily become masters of the caucus, and always thrust their decisions on it. Besides this, the members, even the most independent ones, are reduced to submission through fear of seeing all the legislative measures in which their constituencies are interested shelved. The speaker of the assembly, chosen in caucus, is a creature of the Machine, and it is he who appoints all the legislative committees, taking care to keep out the members who have shown themselves uncompromising toward the Machine. As soon as a bill brought in by one of these members is referred to the committee, it is smothered there, the committee never reports on it. The more honourable members therefore make up their minds, in despair, to vote for the most scandalous proposals, dictated by the Machine, in order to prevent the interests of their constituents from being neglected.

The Machine interferes in a similar way with municipal government. . . . It is more easy to "build a Machine" in a city than in a State: the territorial area is limited; the elements of the population on which the Machine leans are concentrated there and are more homogeneous; the spoil awaits, so to speak, the bosses are the plundering rings—contracts to be adjudged, public works to be given out, "franchises" to be granted, and sinecures to be created in the municipal departments, or rather on the pay-rolls.

The administration of justice itself does not escape the influence of the Machine, for the judges, being elective officials, are, like the others, in need of being put on the slate. The subordinate magistrates, the police justices, taken very often from among the "henchmen" of the Machine, are generally its humble servants. It is they who, together with the police, help the Machine to control the lower strata of the electors. Their duties make them the nearest and the most influential public authority, next to the police, with the masses. It is in them that the people should see embodied the majesty of the law, and they prostitute it to the Machine. Of the higher magistrates the Machine wields the most pernicious influence over the prosecuting officers, by making them, as has already been mentioned, dismiss or suspend prosecutions against its protégés. The magic effect of the "pull" is not unknown in courts of justice, especially on the occasion of the exercise of the patronage intrusted to the judges, who not only appoint the clerks, but select barristers for many lucrative berths, such as receiverships in bankruptcy, refereeships, etc. The best claim in the eyes of the judge to these appointments is not the legal knowledge and the professional dignity of the lawyer, but his relations with the boss and the Machine; it is the son or the nephew of a conspicuous politician, or a politician himself, a member of the Machine, who gets the preference.[2] The boss sits in judgment on the judges, and condemns them for the heinous offence of insubordination to the Machine; having got the judge elected the Machine considers it has "the right," as the Tammany boss put it recently, "to expect proper consideration at his hands."

Thus there is no sphere of public, political, and economic activity into which the Machine does not penetrate, in which it does not wield an influence used solely for its own interests. A detailed analysis of the resources supplied by each of these spheres to the operations and the schemes of a Machine, in a large city or in a State, would present a really formidable whole, transcending in importance all that a legitimate government, however vast its powers, can aspire to.

v   The Boss

The extraordinary powers, unparalleled under the régime of free institutions, which the Machine exercises, centre eventually in a single man—the boss. What sort of man, then, is this, who is able to wield such an authority?

Two principal species may be pointed out in the genus boss: the city boss and the State boss. The type is exactly the same, only the features differ: coarser in the one, they are often more refined in the other. The origin of the boss is always very humble, especially that of the city boss. This latter is a "self-made" man in the strict sense of the word. In the majority of cases, of foreign, Irish, extraction, the child of parents who have recently immigrated, or having himself landed on American soil at a very early age, he has begun his public career in the streets of a large city as newspaper vendor, street-car conductor, actor in a travelling circus, or, better still, waiter to a saloon-keeper, Irish like himself. There he was initiated into the mysteries of "paltics" by the conversations of the heelers and the ward politicians; he learnt to fathom the recesses of the human heart, with the insight vouchsafed into them by the generous properties of drink; and, having felt his vocation, he enlisted in the army of heelers, with the baton of boss in his knapsack. From a "repeater" (a man who votes several times over under feigned names) he quickly became head of a gang of repeaters, and then precinct leader. In the meanwhile he has, perhaps, mounted still higher on the politico-social ladder by becoming himself a saloon-keeper. Or, less fortunate, he has found his means of subsistence and his social position in a sinecure which the Machine has procured for him in the municipal administration. Extending his influence from day to day, he constructed a small local machine; with its aid he became a member of the city council, that promised land flowing with milk and honey in the form of contracts for public works or even of "franchises," of the monopolies coveted by wealthy corporations, which have the excellent habit of paying. As district leader, he swallowed up the other less able district leaders and was left without a rival. A vulgar demagogue, he got the mob on his side, and, by dealing in its votes, he became the Cæsar of the Machine and of the city. This stirring and so laborious career has sometimes been within an ace of being stopped by still more dramatic incidents, such as a criminal prosecution for homicide or less serious encounters with the law. However, he will perhaps have lost nothing by waiting; as it were by chance, justice may suddenly wake up, and, like his illustrious ancestor, Tweed, he may some day forget the cares of power in the peaceful retirement of a prison. . . .

This brilliant career of a man who from such a humble start has risen to be master of the government of a large city or of a State,—without, as a rule, filling any official position,—is, from one end to the other, the triumph of one supreme quality: skill in the management of men. The organizing genius and the *coup d'œil* of the strategist and of the tactician, which takes in vast horizons and foresees eventualities, are in the boss only the complement and the amplification of this first quality. With an inevitably limited stock of good things to be provided for an unlimited number of appetites, he performs the miracle of the loaves and fishes, discerning exactly the right slice and cutting off just the proper quantity to be given to each man. To some he offers the solid food of places, of money, and of pulls; to others the unsubstantial diet of promises. He plays with wants and appetites, with credulity and vanity, as with so many counters. He is admirably equipped for this game by his mind, which is profoundly calculating, cool, incapable of yielding to the impulse of the moment, but very capable of taking sudden and bold resolutions to meet the situation. With this uniform type of mind, which is the distinctive mark of the species, the particular temperaments vary: there is the brutal, coarse, overbearing boss; the amiable and even seductive, or "magnetic" boss; or, while devoid of personal "magnetism," mild, smooth-mannered, an "easy boss," nay, even unctuous, like a clergyman, so much so that any one who did not know him would not the least perceive the hoax if he were introduced to him as the Reverend X. Y. Z. But the affability never goes so far as expansiveness: the boss is naturally reserved, coiled up—he

has no confidant; this is wiser, at least he is sure not to be betrayed. He hardly utters his plans and his schemes to himself; he turns them over in his head and marks them by means of mental notes, which he will develop under the pressure of circumstances.

The boss often cannot even speak or write English correctly. It is said of a certain boss, who is at the head of his profession, that his whole vocabulary does not exceed three hundred words. In fact, the education which the boss has received is generally of the poorest; he has hardly attended the primary school. Yet owing to the resourceful intelligence and the dogged energy which distinguish the American, many a boss, and especially those who have risen to the position of State boss, ends by acquiring a certain polish which shows itself not only in his dress and his manners, but appears to fill the gaps of his early very defective education. He can turn this semblance of culture which he has acquired to account with the same coolness with which he exploits the varied resources of the Machine; he is capable, on the occasion of the inauguration of a political club, which brings together the pick of the Machine, of quoting the "constitution of the Athenian democracy," or of expatiating on the dangers of the American democracy like a Tocqueville on a small scale. There are bosses who have real intellectual interests. But it is a curious fact that these great manipulators of men do not turn their attention to anything living, among the things of the mind.

Cultivated or without culture, the boss is, in any event, a man of superior intelligence, but of an altogether special kind of superiority, which shows itself in a very delicate appreciation of particular situations. He is incapable of grasping principles; his ideas in politics are hard to discover: he has none, and does not need them. This is not the compass he uses, it is the wind of circumstances and of personal conjunctures which steers the course of the boss. He is incapable of stating his views on the problems of the day. He is neither a writer, nor a speaker, nor even a good talker; on the stump he would cut a poor figure. The stock of eloquence necessary for defending, by speech and by the pen, the name and style of the party under which the boss operates is supplied by others. He confines himself to turning their talents to account, just as he does those of the district leaders and other henchmen; he himself is invariably nothing more than a clever contractor. The few orators who have been discernible among the higher bosses, the senatorial bosses, even the most brilliant of these orators, were simply rhetoricians and polemists, who looked at the great questions of the day in their personal aspect, with reference to the persons who were involved in the various controversies; they never connected their name with a legislative measure or left any other lasting trace of their activity. The opportunism of which the boss is the living embodiment does not allow him to risk taking the initiative; he prefers to walk in the shadow of public opinion. Incapable of contributing to the movement of ideas, he finds it difficult to understand them, he grasps public opinion only in its crystallized state, so to speak; its aspirations and its impulses escape him, and its revolts take him by surprise. Observing and appraising mankind in detail, by their pettinesses, the boss is not qualified to appreciate the moral forces of human nature; a profound judge of

men, he does not understand man. He never credits the citizen in general with virtue and intelligence, he is not aware that these qualities exist; his skill lies in seizing on the weaknesses of men.

It must be added that the public takes pleasure, a melodramatic pleasure, in following the sayings and doings of the boss. This curiosity is not the only feeling which gains the boss his undeniable popularity. This man who, sprung from nothing, has reached the very top of the tree, strikes the imagination of the Americans and flatters it. They recognize in him a master spirit. He excites admiration like those *conquistadores* who conquered and plundered empires. Even cultivated men of high integrity cannot always resist this feeling of admiration for the favourites of fortune, honest folk or rascals, which pervades the air of the New World. One would almost think that they are proud of the bosses.

In the eyes of the great mass of the "respectable" members of the party, who do not take an active part in politics and who only hear from afar the din of the clash of arms, the boss, whose name is in every mouth, appears as a sort of paladin who is always in the breach and fighting for the good cause. The hostile cries and the objurgations which accompany the name of the boss die away as they descend further and further into the lower strata of the community, and the name alone reaches these strata encircled with a halo of notoriety. In the remote districts the *sancta simplicitas* of the people procures for the boss an attachment which sometimes is expressed in a touching and disconcerting form when one thinks of the archcorrupter and poisoners of the springs of public life who is the object of these sentiments. Yet, as a general rule, the boss does not much care to put his popularity to the test of a popular vote; he does not often stand for elective office himself.) Sometimes it is the flagrant inadequacy of his education which prevents him from filling a leading position; but more often he would run the risk of a defeat owing to his reputation of wire-puller and election jobber, whereas, if he keeps behind the scenes, he can quietly pull the strings and secure the return of the men who suit him. The State boss likes to run for the Senate of the United States, for the very reason that he can obtain this position more easily by intrigue and corruption, the Senators being elected, not by universal suffrage, but by the State Legislatures, where the boss is often supreme) In any event, it is not in the public position which the boss sometimes fills that his power resides. That power is by its nature occult and irresponsible.

Such is the boss in his public capacity. In his private sphere he is often perfectly honourable; his family life is irreproachable, he can be depended on, he is exact in the observances of religion, he has his seat in church. This holds good, also, of the subordinate politicians. The politician, great or small, simply puts in practice, without being aware of it perhaps, the doctrine of two moralities, the one for private, the other for public life. With certain bosses the divergence between the two moralities is not so wide in practice as with certain others, but one and all wield their power for their own interest and not in that of the commonwealth. The boss who uses his influence solely for the good of the party, or even for the good of the people, the virtuous boss, must be relegated to the realm of romance.

VI

The use which the boss makes of his extensive and penetrating power by no means, however, affects the whole of political life; this use is confined to his requirements as an exploiter of the industry of elections. He does not try, like the tyrants of the Greek cities or of the Italian republics, to assert his power over the *polis* in general, to control all the manifestations of political life. All his designs on the commonwealth amount, in fact, to running the elections as he likes, putting his followers in all the places, keeping out his opponents, protecting the first, making the second harmless, and realizing the material profits attaching to these places and to the influence which they procure. The line of public policy to be adopted, in itself, is a matter of indifference to the boss. The persons even of the actors on the political stage are only of moment to him in so far as they are for or against him at the elections. If he "punishes his enemies," if he brings about proscriptions, it is solely in self-defence; he never meddles with citizens who do not go out of their way to oppose him. If he is often a despot, he is so rather from necessity, as a matter of business, than from inclination. His wish is, on the contrary, to make as many friends as possible, to please everybody; for whatever the source of his power, the material substance of it is composed of the votes of the multitude given to the candidates of the boss. A really intelligent boss is never gratuitously arrogant and despotic; he wields his power of tyrant with moderation and kindliness.)

It might, however, be explained to him that it is no great merit on his part to exhibit so much moderation. That moderation is enforced on him not only by the fact which I have just brought out, namely, that his appetites and his desires are specialized by the very nature of his means of action. Even if he tried to go farther he would fall foul of the rights of the citizen, reserved by the Constitution, those rights against which all the designs of the public authorities are directed in vain) It is no use for the boss being master of the executive and the legislative, they are not omnipotent. The American Constitution has made the fundamental rights of the man and of the citizen safe from oppression by placing them under the sovereign protection of the courts, which can annul as unconstitutional not only administrative acts, but laws themselves; and the judiciary, taken as a whole, is not yet under the thumb of the bosses.) No doubt, the barrier thus erected by the pact of the Constitution, for the protection of individual rights, in marking the extreme limit beyond which it is not allowable to pass, still leaves a certain margin for possible encroachment on these rights. Being able to exploit only this margin, the boss makes it wholly and solely subservient to the interest of his electioneering business, in order to get as large a return as possible.

The point which is most exposed to the designs of the Machine is, in consequence, the municipal administration, owing to its ample resources offering abundance of loot and being, so to speak, within arm's reach. The finances of a city ruled by the Machine are always heavily burdened with useless and bloated expenditure. The departments are invariably encumbered with a very considerable number of sinecures, the sole object of which is to enable the "workers" of the Machine to draw their salaries; useful public works are knocked down at extravagant rates; the

exploitation of the monopolies in the gift of the city is granted for nothing, or for an absurdly small consideration. In a word, the results of "ring" government, which we have witnessed in the municipal history of New York, of Philadelphia, and of some other cities, are a regular feature of American cities ruled by bosses, although in a more attenuated form. The ratepayers certainly suffer from it, they have more rates to pay; but the masses who have no rates to pay have no reason to complain of this régime; they gain by it, for the public works of little or no utility which the Machine is always pressing for, in order to have opportunity for plunder, give employment to poor people, and well-paid employment, stinginess being by no means the defect of the governments carried on by the bosses. The peculation caused by the Machine is considerable, but, looking to the piratical methods which the latter practises in municipal administration, it ought logically to be even greater. After all, it often turns out that the resources of the cities which are not afflicted with a Machine are not administered much more economically. The depredations committed by the bosses are made up for, to a certain extent, by a better, more responsible administration of the municipal departments, which is due to the members of the councils of these cities and their employees being more disciplined. The Machine which selects all the candidates for public office at its good pleasure, while making them docile instruments, takes care to choose them as well as possible; and once they are installed in their posts, it sees that they do not compromise it. Instead of being responsible to the public, they are so to the Machine; the responsibility is deflected, but it is genuine, and all the more that the power of the Machine is more centralized, more personal, and more immediate.[3] If the Machine is convinced of the necessity of a certain standard of administration, it can enforce it on the persons in office more easily than the electors themselves could do. Besides this, the great mass of small employees are not dishonest; they accept their places from the Machine to earn a humble livelihood. And when they have discharged the first duty of their office, which is to serve the Machine, when this tribute on their time, their exertions, and their conscience has been taken, they honestly give the rest to the public. The municipal administration run by the most corrupt Machine —I mean Tammany Hall—affords striking proof of this state of things.

Of all the public departments in the large cities the most contaminated by the Machine is that of the police, whose co-operation is particularly valuable to it. The police in these cities is "full of politics"; and so long as it is a question of "politics," that is to say, of the operations in which the Machine is interested, the public cannot count on the protection of the police. It shields from the public the frauds committed, at the primaries and at the elections, by the followers of the Machine; it molests the Machine's opponents when they want to exercise their electoral rights; it winks at the law-breaking drinking-saloons, at the gambling-hells and houses of ill fame, which pay blackmail to the Machine. But in other respects the police really does its duty, and does it, on the whole, fairly well. But, however satisfactory the administration of the cities governed by a Machine may be as a whole, and however properly and conscientiously the employees may discharge the routine of their duties, the spirit which presides over the administration is always an unenlightened one, with no breadth or life, save in the matter of expenditure. This inferiority makes itself felt especially in educational policy; the schools are better in the cities which are not under the régime of the Machine.

Nor is legislation wholly contaminated by the Machine. The State legislatures, which vote laws, at the bidding of the boss, to swell the resources of patronage or to bestow privileges or monopolies on companies allied with the boss, also vote good laws—laws of public utility. It is even easier to obtain such a law with the help of the boss. Instead of agitating and bringing the pressure of enlightened opinion to bear on the members of the legislature, it is better to apply to the boss; the latter will give the order and the law will go through, like a letter in the post. The boss will consent to give this order if the measure, whether good or not, appears to him "popular"; in that case the passing of the law will benefit the Machine at the next election. The members of the legislative assembly, in their turn, will pass it with a readiness in which servility blends with confidence in the sagacity of the boss. The great preoccupation of the legislators who, in ordinary times, act only under pressure from outside, is to know, when others than the boss demand a measure, "who is behind them." Are they supported by numerous and influential electors? The boss's word of command reassures them. It is sometimes more useful to appeal to the boss, not only over the heads of the legislators, but even over the heads of the sovereign people. Well-meaning citizens, who are prosecuting a reform or pursuing a certain course of action, in municipal administration as well as in the government of the State, are able to convert the bosses to their views more quickly than the great mass of the electors, and with a practical effect which is at least just as certain. In these cases boss rule offers the advantages of an "enlightened despotism."

Thus, the boss acts as a disciplining force; he exerts it on the whole political community for good as well as for evil; he keeps a hold and a check on the multitude by the favours and the protection which he procures for them against the law itself, just as he keeps a hold and a check on the executive officers and the legislators.

But the boss himself is exempt from all disciplining authority; the power which he wields is not only usurped, but it is also irresponsible. He is, therefore, always liable to step out of the moderation which his character of usurper enjoins and which his mean of action, as well as the barriers of the constitution, impose on him. As with every autocrat, absolute power makes him lose his head sooner or later; he becomes wilful, arrogant, and tyrannical; he exceeds all bounds in the effrontery with which he and his men use the public resources for their own benefit. At last the public's cup of patience runs over, a revolt breaks out, and the Machine is "smashed." This is the fate of every Machine. It is only a question of time. A boss who has more self-control, more perspicacity, remains longer in power; a short-sighted and greedy boss enjoys the present hour without restraint, and precipitates his fall. The Machine which has been "smashed" is soon put together again by the same boss or by another, to meet the same fate in the end as its predecessors. It is a régime which recalls, to some extent, that which was defined by the words "a

despotism tempered by assassination." Here the assassination is only symbolical; free institutions enable the revolution to be carried out in an absolutely pacific manner, by the simple action of voting-papers. The American people have only, according to the stereotyped phrase of the stump orator, to "rise in their might and in their majesty," and everything will come right. In reality, it is not so much in their "majesty" that the people rise as in their fury. For a long time impassive and apathetic, they start up all of a sudden in a paroxysm of wrath and try to vent it on somebody or other. The sovereign people strike without pity and without discernment, guilty and innocent will all do to make up the hecatomb which they must have. Terror runs through the ranks of the politicians; the most powerful of them, the head bosses, on whose smile State Governors and legislators were hanging only the day before, bite the dust. The power of public opinion, which is supposed to weigh heavily, in the United States, on everybody and everything, reaches the politicians in the end, but it reaches them in a more or less accidental way, which excludes all regular responsibility. The authority which public opinion wields over the Machine is the authority of Judge Lynch. . . .

The most extensive limitations to which the power of the Machine and of the politicians is subject are to be found in the social and economic character of the particular community. In places where the population is more homogeneous, and forms smaller sets, in which opinion has consequently more consistency and asserts itself with more force, the Machine cannot take the liberties which it does in large cities where public spirit is smothered under the huge agglomerations of heterogeneous elements brought together promiscuously. Its proceedings do not escape the attention of the public so easily, and the Machine is from necessity more circumspect and more moderate in its desires. In places where there are no large public works to be tendered for, or important contracts to be awarded, where there are no powerful corporations with extensive interests depending on administration or legislation, in a word, where the material for plunder is not considerable, the Machine is necessarily frugal and cannot provide a sufficient livelihood for those who have no other means of subsistence. Hence the parts of the Union least contaminated by the Machine and the politicians are the country districts. There everybody knows each other. Opinion, which is more slow in forming among the rural population and that of small cities, is more solid, more durable, less spasmodic than in the large centres. The electors have both more leisure and more sense of their own value, a narrow and exacting sense, which procures them more consideration, at least in appearance. The Machine, however, does exist among these populations, but it is more respectable, more attentive to the general opinion. It does not assume the repulsive aspect of bossism, it simply appears as a trade-union of all those who live on the party or expect something from it, office-holders, aspirants to places with their relations and their friends. Comparatively speaking, this trade-union is as powerful as the Machine of the large city, and, it may be added, just as corrupt. With their eyes always fixed on the local loaves and fishes and the modest diet provided thereby, the politicians of the small rural Machine make politics subservient to these interests. It is not uncommon in the country districts and

the small cities for members of the same family to be distributed in the rival Machines. The South, which is still largely agricultural and where, according to the census of 1890, there were only two cities with a population exceeding 100,-000, and only five cities with more than 50,000 inhabitants, does not present a very favourable field for the development of the Machine. Apart from these two large cities, New Orleans and Louisville, the odious type of the boss is hardly met with in the South. In the West the Machine prospers more, while exhibiting infinite variations in the extent of its power and its misdeeds. The great hotbed of the Machine and of the bosses is still the Eastern States, which are rich and populous, and where social differentiation has made the most progress.

If on the map of the United States all the parts of the country where the Machine has developed were coloured red, the eye would at once be attracted to the right by a large blotch formed by the States of New York and Pennsylvania with a strip of the State of New Jersey on the east, with the State of Maryland on the south, and the State of Ohio on the west. This spot casts a faint shadow to the north-east over New England, while on the other side, to the west, the red will appear in more or less deep tints on the State of Illinois and will stain the neighbouring States, marking with scarlet points most of the large cities, such as St. Louis in Missouri and others of less importance, like Louisville in Kentucky or Minneapolis in Minnesota, and other still smaller ones among the large ones; then, after making a brief pause in the States of the Far West and leaving some patches there, it will flow toward the Pacific slope and deposit a thick layer of carmine on San

Francisco; and, finally, jumping right over to the Gulf of Mexico, it will cover New Orleans with a similar layer. A very considerable space will be left hardly coloured at all or will even exhibit the shot colour to be seen in certain fabrics: these are regions or cities where the Machine has no stable and regular existence; rings of mercenary politicians form in them, disappear after a short time, and re-form under favourable circumstances. A good many points again on the map will appear almost white, presenting the touching spectacle of "good Machines." But this in truth is an abuse of language, an honest Machine is not in the course of nature; it would be more correct to say that there are many local party Organizations which have not degenerated, which have not fallen into the category of Machines. Every Machine represents a party Organization, but every party Organization is not necessarily a Machine. However fair this distinction may be, it must nevertheless be admitted that, in the conditions which govern the life of American political parties, every Organization carries within it the germ of a Machine which is capable of a singularly rapid growth. A population may, so to speak, go to bed with an Organization and wake up with a Machine. Hence, the "Mushroom Machines" which are a tolerably common phenomenon. In any event, it must not be forgotten that the part of the map coloured red, while only a portion of the whole country, contains almost a third of the population of the United States and represents at least three-fifths of its economic interests. This domain of the Machine is daily growing larger. The Machine is gaining ground, especially in the West, where it is invading districts which appeared to be

free from it. It is the steady development of economic interests which paves the way for it; that development produces the wherewithal for exploitation by the Machine, and, on the other hand, it more and more absorbs individual energies and diverts the attention of the citizens from political preoccupations, while leaving still greater liberty of action to the professionals of politics.

VII

But why should this periodical necessity of "smashing" the Machines exist at all? Why is the power of the Machine, even when mitigated by the limitations and the restrictions which we have just been considering, tolerated in the full blaze of democracy? The varied materials for an answer to this question have already been disclosed to us in the course of our investigation. It now remains for us to recapitulate them in a more methodical way. The first and general condition of the Machine's existence and success is, of course, the extraordinary development of the elective régime and of the party system fostered and stimulated one by another. They have created the necessity for a highly elaborate and intricate election machinery, which can be worked only by experts. At the same time they have made the task of the ordinary citizen so difficult as to leave him bewildered and helpless, and ready to submit blindly to any guidance offered. But why should these experts be men of the stamp of "bosses," and how does it come about that they are able to keep a hold on the political machinery and exploit it so easily? What are their particular means and resources? The most common explanation given is that the Machine disposes of a large patronage, or, again, that it lives on rich corporations, and that if it had not one or the other of these resources, or both of them, it would die of inanition. This explanation is only partly true, it only deals with the material resources. Foremost among these, in fact, comes the patronage, the places in the public service of the Union, of the States, and of the municipalities; these places, supplemented by the hope of getting them, furnish the pay for maintaining the army of politicians who serve the Machine. The more places the boss has to distribute, the more firmly established will be his power.

Next come the principal direct receipts of the Machine—the assessments, the contributions paid by the candidates and by the office-holders. The percentage paid by these last yields of itself considerable sums. To give an idea of them, the case may be quoted of the assessments of the municipal employees in the city of Philadelphia: levied at the rate of two per cent, they provide, out of the $4,500,000 which the city spends in salaries, $90,000 for the benefit of the Machine. The contributions of the candidates are much higher, and no elective post escapes this tribute. The contributions given to the funds of the Machine by private individuals, by wealthy zealots of the party, important as they are, sink into insignificance beside those of the financial or industrial corporations, especially in the States of New York and Pennsylvania. There the corporations pay a regular tribute to the boss to be left in peace, to ensure themselves against the hostile designs of the legislators or of the higher executive officers. Besides this, the corporations are liable to extraordinary calls on the eve of a particularly hot election campaign,

in which the Machine will have to spend a great deal.

The enormous material resources of which the Machine thus disposes are not the only foundation of its success; it possesses also a moral stock which in fact is converted into capital like a security into cash. This moral capital consists of the deliberate or unconscious adhesion of the various elements of the community. The Machine exists and works with their consent, and by no means in spite of them. The first of these social elements on which the Machine leans is made up of its own servants and of its nearest adherents, of the social category which is consequently known by the name of "the Machine element." These people work for the Machine as they would have worked for a manufacturer, a merchant, for any one who might have employed them. They get their living in "practical politics." The work the men of the Machine do for it is undeniable; the duties of a leader, of a small precinct leader and of his lieutenants, who have to oil all the wheels of the Machine from day to day, are by no means a sinecure; they are extremely absorbing and keep the mind in a constant state of tension. The work is rather dirty; this may be, but there are so many trades which involve handling unpleasant things; every trade has its processes, and "practical politics" has its own; the use of these processes is not so much a matter of ethics as of technique. "It is perfectly idle to ask oneself if it is for good or for evil," said a member of Tammany Hall to me, who gave me a sketch of the methods of Tammany, "it is neither bad nor good, it is politics." The character of the pay, which consists of "spoils," is not objectionable either, it is almost part of the natural order of things. It is only fair that these offices should be given to the men who have "worked" for the party, and to them alone. It is a disregard of this truth which would be scandalous and would constitute a danger for the public morality, nay, even for the public order of the American democracy. A small boss once spoke to me with bitterness of the head bosses, who sometimes bestow places on persons who do not belong to the Organization, to the detriment of those who "do the work"; "if this goes on and becomes the general practice, we shall have a monarchy."

✷ It is by following this train of reasoning that the men of the Machine come to consider the independent members of the party who oppose the Machines as hateable and contemptible; these citizens not only prevent them from earning their living, but even try, while posing as champions of honesty, to get hold of the offices, without having "done the work" for the party; they are therefore hypocrites, full of "humbug and cant." The immorality is all on the side of the "reformers," who sacrifice the interests of the party to their vanity and their ambition, who do not scruple to sow discord, whereas they, the men of the Machine, sacrifice everything to "harmony." While fighting one another according to the rules of the game, the politicians of the rival Machines are often ready, not only to make common cause against the outsiders, but to help one another, to the detriment of their own parties. The considerations by which the politicians are guided in thus acting have been put into words by one of them, who said to Mr. Theodore Roosevelt, "There are no politics in politics."[4] This enigmatic utterance meant that in the world of politicians no heed is paid to the political conventions of society. Far from being utterly de-

praved men, the politicians profess rather a clan morality, which is often in opposition with the morality of society at large. The Machine, however, is but strengthened thereby: the perverted clan morality justifies the conduct and stimulates the enthusiasm of the numerous category of those who give their mercenary support to it.

✷ In addition to this category, the Machine has on its side, in the first place, the mass of the people. The criminal and semi-criminal elements, the *déclassés* of every kind, who swarm in the large cities, are devoted to the Machine, because it buys them with cash or protects them against the law. In all communities, even the best regulated ones, there is at the lowest depth a social residuum who are hostile to public order, not only from their vicious nature, but also from an inherited feeling of revolt against the State, which has dammed the torrent of individual will and passion. The Machine of the American parties has realized the unique combination which consists of protecting the low "Catilinarian existences" against the public authority by the influence which it wields over this same authority, and, while ensuring them impunity, keeping them in check by this very means.

The popular stratum which is superior in point of morality, but wretched, having only precarious means of existence, and which swells the army of the unemployed, also gets assistance from the representatives of the Machine; the boss régime, with its costly administration of the cities, does but benefit a number of humble folk. The interested philanthropy and the other attentions lavished by the politicians win them the hearts of the people. It is no use denouncing the bosses as public malefac-

Lower stratum admires the corruption

tors, laying bare the corruption of Machine rule. The people answer, "It is good enough for us." In fact, they do not see the harm done by the politicians, but they know their urbanity and their generosity. Between a couple of drinks taken at the bar, how many stories are not told of how the local leader of the Machine has got this man out of a difficulty, has given coal to another, has distributed flour among a number of neighbours, has sent wreaths to the humble obsequies of the destitute? Can it be said of such a man that he is a worthless individual? The boss Tweed, when publicly convicted of monstrous depredations and sent to prison, lost none of the esteem and admiration in which he had been held by the lower orders of New York; they were convinced that Tweed had fallen a victim to the nefarious designs of the rich, he who was so kind to the poor. It it of no consequence that the Machine prostitutes itself to the rich, to the "corporations"; its local representatives, who are close to the people, and who are themselves of the people, only get more credit from being so with the masses owing to the feeling of class antagonism which lurks in the popular mind and which is stirred by the sight of those rich; while the money received from them enables the Machine to establish itself the more firmly in the favour of the poor. Besides, the Machine does not relieve their material wretchedness only, it also relieves their moral wretchedness. The leaders of the Machine have a kindly word for the humblest inhabitants of their district; they share in their joys and in their sorrows; they find a sympathetic smile even for the halt and the maimed; they shed a ray of human brotherhood on the most miserable of creatures. They do it automatically, in the way of business, to everybody without distinction; but they none the less appear as ministers of the cult of fraternity in a higher degree than the priests of the churches and the professional philanthropists: they are nearer to the people, they come in friendly contact with them every day, and the people have confidence in them. They offer it a counterfeit of charity and fraternity, but if the people accept it so readily, the reason is that the real article is very rare in society as it at present exists. The men of higher rank who come down as it were from the moon to exhort the people to vote for honest candidates opposed to the Machine, are strangers to them, and the people have no confidence in them because they belong to another social sphere. The habits of mind and the manners of these latter, even of the most well-meaning of them, often only offer fresh food for popular prejudices; they are too gentlemanly. Few of them are able or willing to stoop to the methods of the politicians, with which it is easier to get the ear of the people. These last the people does know, they are "the nicest men," and it prefers to vote with them for dishonest candidates, who often are also "the nicest men."

Not that the lower-class elector prefers the corrupt man; he desires what is right at least as ardently as the gentleman, but he appraises honesty and justice in his own fashion. In his eyes the man who does his neighbour no harm, and who even does him good, cannot do harm to society and to the community. The lower-class elector still judges everything by the standard of private morality; he is yet incapable of rising to the height of social morality. The primitive morality of the masses delivers them into the hands of the Ma-

chine as inevitably as clan morality attaches the tribe of politicians to it. The
intelligence of the masses does not preserve them any better from the attraction exercised by the Machine.

Among the humble electors there is
a large category which, in the opinion
of many people, embodies in a special
degree this venality, this narrow morality, and this ignorance, and, for that
reason, supplies the Machine with most
of its supporters. The electoral category
thus indicated is formed by the "foreign element," that is to say, by the
immigrants. Coming from countries
with less advanced political institutions,
where they had lived in degradation
and in misery, and incapable of
promptly assimilating the spirit and the
manners of the American democracy,
these foreigners, naturalized as American citizens, whose number is counted
by millions, cannot but become an instrument of political demoralization
and lower the political level of the Republic. It would, therefore, be only too
natural that they should supply the
Machine, especially in the big cities,
with its largest following. I, for my part,
was somewhat inclined to share this
opinion when I arrived in the United
States. But a careful enquiry conducted
on the spot has made me, if not abandon it entirely, at all events qualify it
very considerably. Almost all the men
of sound judgment whom I have been
able to consult, in the East as well as in
the West, of American stock themselves
and some of them of very old stock,
protested against the theory according
to which the "ignorant foreigners" are
the great culprits in the political disorders which afflict the democracy of
America. My personal observations have
only confirmed me in their view. No
doubt, the newly naturalized citizens

are, for the most part, ignorant, but the
proportion of ignorant electors of American origin is not less great. The
wretched immigrants are easily bought,
but the poor natives of the country are
exposed to the same temptation, and
not only the poor ones.

The upshot of the matter is that the
immigrants make the task of democratic
government rather more complicated;
but the difficulty is only relative and
temporary. The rising generation is
assimilated with remarkable rapidity,
and with an abandonment of its early
associations that is often too complete
for the taste of the older generation.
The children, anxious to be the same as
their American companions, refuse to
speak the mother tongue even at home,
and the parents witness with a sore
heart the inevitable disappearance of
the last fragment of a past which is not
less dear to them because it has been
spent in tears. The influences to which
the young immigrants are subjected and
which they in their turn introduce into
daily life are those of the American environment. The movement started in the
last few years against immigration in a
country which had always welcomed
with open arms the oppressed and the
successful of the whole world, is not
so much founded on facts as due to the
calculations of the politicians who, in
order to get a little popularity, trade
on the spirit of vulgar nationalism and
on the professional envy and jealousy
which foreign competition excites in
certain sections of the working community. The bill against foreign immigration, which had been passed by Congress, was killed by President Cleveland's veto just as he was laying down
power. An American who bears a glorious name has summed up the whole
question in the following words: "Our

danger is not from the contamination of foreigners, but from the surrender of ideals upon which self-governments rest or die."[5]

VIII

The custody of these ideals is naturally entrusted to the social class which is superior to the masses by its knowledge and its wealth; but this class, which is called in the United States "the better element" because it is better off, does not fulfill its mission; it leaves the public interest to its fate, and, far from opposing obstacles to the Machine, only makes things easier for it. The abdication of the better element is due to manifold considerations which, however, may all be referred to the eminently materialistic spirit that animates the prosperous and wealthy classes. These classes, which present different grades of well-being, meet in one and the same exclusive preoccupation, that of "making money"; they embody in the highest degree the mercantile spirit of the bourgeoisie in the Old World, while exhibiting more nobility than the latter in the use made of their wealth; they measure all things by the sole criterion, "Does it pay?" Now they find that politics "do not pay," that it is not worth while neglecting one's own business to attend to public affairs; that it pays better to submit to the depredations of a Machine than to lose one's time in fighting the bosses, at least as long as they keep within the limits of comparative moderation. The race for wealth which absorbs the Americans takes up all their time, the rich allow themselves as little leisure as those who have to earn their living.

This deliberate or unconscious reasoning,—"It does not pay,"—which lies at the root of the whole passive attitude of the better element, is complicated by other considerations, some of which, resting on prejudices or sophisms, beguile the citizen who is forgetful of his duties, and appear to justify his conduct, while others promise a personal reward in return for his abstention. The chief prejudice which sways men's minds, to the greater advantage of the Machine, is party fetishism. This feeling makes many very "respectable" electors shut their eyes to the misdeeds of the Machine; they really believe that it is the other party which is a hotbed of corruption, that theirs is honest by virtue of its name. Others, more clear-sighted, groan inwardly, but take care not to kick against the Machine at elections, letting themselves be persuaded that the "life of the party is in danger," and that this is not the time to pick holes in the doings of certain representatives of the Organization; that it is not an act of civic abdication, but only a temporary sacrifice to the paramount cause of the party which is demanded of them. This temporary sacrifice is repeated every time, and every time the "good" citizens, overcoming their repugnance, "vote like men," that is to say, like so many sheep. The timorous conservatism which characterizes most of the members of the better element makes them apprehend unspeakable catastrophes if they should leave the beaten track of the party. They have an inkling that the methods of the Machine are not always clean, but they concentrate their thoughts on the great party work which the Machine performs by "getting out the vote" and descending to the lowest depths of the political community in search of it. Electors of a philosophic turn of mind take their stand on the proposition that the American government is a party government, that parties cannot exist without an organization, and that, this being so, the organization must be paid for. They refuse to see in the boss aught but the organizer of victory for their party, and do not see in him the corrupter of the Republic. In voting for the party, a good many electors vote, not so much for it as against the opposite party, which seems to them the most corrupt of the two; others are hardly under this illusion, but they none the less continue to vote for the party solely to make use of their vote: to give a vote to an independent candidate, who has no chance of being elected, appears to their materialistic mind, as a sterile act. Lastly, certain electors—and their name is legion—have not even to ask themselves if they ought to vote the party ticket or not; they are in blissful ignorance of everything that goes on within their party, of all the political scandals and the misdeeds of the politicians. They do not read the newspapers, or pay no attention to the denunciations launched by the press against the Machines and the bosses; the press has, through its own fault, lost credit with the public. The most precise charges brought home to the bosses are treated with incredulity by a great part of the public, and elicit but one reply: "It is only campaign lies." Each of them reasoning in his own way, or not reasoning at all, these electors of the better element all end by voting for the "yellow dog" run by the Machine.

What the party devotion, or the party cant professed by the better element, or ignorance and apathy do to deaden the political conscience of the great majority of this social group, is done, as regards an important section of it, by personal interest. It is no longer the unconscious or half-conscious complicity of humble electors anxious about their daily bread; it is the cool calculation of men who want things which the Machine is able to give. With the help of the Machine they can succeed better in business, as well as in the professions, and obtain honours,—honours which in the levelled society of the United States offer an irresistible attraction to a number of men. One has no idea how many there are who would like "to be something," to get a public office, sometimes for itself, sometimes to make a stepping-stone of it. Members of the bar cultivate the friendship of the bosses, do not scruple to join Tammany Hall, with a view to some position or other,—corporation counsel, prosecuting attorney, judge,—a position which will make the holder of it known to the public and extend his connection in case he is obliged to return to his profession. Men who are perfectly respectable and intelligent, but who have cast a longing glance on a public situation, look at the Machine with friendly eyes: they are thinking of the "nomination." Those even who have had an opportunity of displaying their independence and their civic indignation discover that "harmony" in the party demands sacrifices as soon as the prospect of an important post is in sight. The representatives of the corporations docilely pay their tribute as "price of the peace," holding that their first duty is to think of the interests of their share-holders.

The imperturbable optimism, which is one of the essential traits of the American character, when confronted with the disorders caused by the Machine in political life, simply says, "It will right itself." It is not even shaken by the spectacle of the material ravages inflicted by the plundering politicians, but replies, "We can stand it; you cannot ruin *this* country." So far as the material effects are concerned, the situation therefore is not supposed to present any gravity. As for the misdeeds of the Machine, considered in themselves, judged from the moral standpoint, there is no need either to make a fuss; they are part and parcel of the infirmities of human nature. Or, better still, a good many citizens, who are only too well informed, deliberately shut their eyes and stop their ears,—they deny the facts. When these citizens who assume that they know better are closely pressed and obliged to admit that the bosses are not altogether mythical beings, they declare that bossism is the inevitable outcome of all government, that without the boss there would be chaos.

Here we have the clinching argument, which expresses the real view of the members of the better element; the boss governs in their place, he relieves them of the tedious duty of governing themselves, enables them to attend to their own affairs. And here again is the true explanation of the success of the Machine: it is a government. It possesses most of the attributes of a government in a high degree, except legitimacy of origin and honesty of motive; its staff, the "leaders" and the "workers," are recruited by natural selection and not by a formal process; they are representative of the great mass of the electors; they are united to it and, above all, united among themselves by the closest ties of social cohesion, by feelings of mutual attachment and feudal loyalty toward the chiefs; individual responsibility and personal merit are the only principles which govern their relations; firmness, energy, and audacity

characterize all their acts. These virtues are exactly those which are wanting to society at large, disintegrated, split up into sets, inert and cowardly. These vital principles of government—absence of formalism, individual responsibility, and personal merit—are exactly the contrary of those which society submits to from the Machine itself, like an exoteric doctrine which, in the old days, made the vulgar an easy prey of the astute holders of the esoteric doctrine. Hence the extreme difficulty of fighting the Machine. Thanks to the party system, it is almost always necessary to dislodge the party from power in order to dislodge its boss. But when this has been done, the Organization of the opposite party is always fated to take its place; the tidal wave which has carried away the boss will only have served, after all, to bring in the rival Machine, often under the very flag of the better element which had made alliance with it; the muddy channel of public life which had just been swept clean is defiled once more. . . .

NOTES

1. I put the question to a ward boss, "Does the city boss consult you leaders?" "We call it receiving orders," was the only reply.
2. Cf. the article in the *American Law Review*, 1899, entitled "The Struggle in New York for the Independence of the Judiciary from the Control of the Party 'Boss.' "
3. The Tammany Hall boss admitted that he was in the habit of telling the municipal councillors who were slack in their attendance at the sittings of the Council to be more regular; he "regarded it as one of his functions, as a member of the executive committee of Tammany Hall, to force such attendance."
4. *Machine Politics in New York City*, reprinted in *American Ideals and other Essays*, New York, 1897, p. 122.
5. Letter from William Lloyd Garrison, of the 20th of December, 1896, to the editor of the *Evening Post* of New York.

The Crusade Against the Tweed Ring

ALEXANDER B. CALLOW, JR.

I thank my God the sun and moon
Are both stuck up so high
That no presumptuous hand can stretch
And pluck them from the sky.
If they were not, I do believe
That some reforming ass
Would recommend to take them down
And light the world with gas.

Judge James T. Brady

For five years the Tweed Ring had led a great treasury raid. The power of the Ring, like the tentacles of an octopus, encircled city government, the courts, the police, the underworld, and the State legislature. The command centers of political power from the Governor to the Board of Aldermen were controlled by the Ring and its lieutenants. The Ring ruled over an empire of patronage with thousands of the faithful on the city payrolls. Tammany Hall had been remodeled into an awesome political machine, supported by the immigrant and the native poor, and sustained on election day by a horde of Tammany warriors, repeaters, and corrupt election officials who made a mockery out of the power of the ballot. No wonder Boss Tweed could ask the reformer, "What are you going to do about it?"

Seldom have the forces of "good" government faced such a formidable opponent as they did in July 1871. Yet five months later the Tweed Ring was destroyed. Most accounts of this campaign emphasize the Ring's sensational thefts. But few questions have been raised about the crusade itself; few attempts have been made to understand the anatomy of a reform movement on a local, grass-roots level. For example, how was the crusade conducted? What was the impact of the Tweed Ring upon the reformer's imagination and in what way did the Ring reveal his attitudes toward reform, corruption, and political institutions? If the rascals were such capital rogues, why did it take so long to destroy them?

By the fall of 1871, when damning evidence was being unearthed and New York echoed from the cries of one reform rally after another, most of the press, a multitude of reform groups, and politicians from both parties were noisily scrambling after the scalps of the Tammany Ring braves. Now that the Ring was disintegrating, all vied for the heroic role of redeemer. Samuel Tilden almost reached the Presidency on the claim that he destroyed the Ring. But Tilden was a hero of last moments. A skillful general when the enemy was in retreat, he was the soul of indecision, procrastination, and lost opportunities when the Ring was in power. In those quiet days before the great uprising, only two led the crusade against the Tweed Ring: Thomas Nast of *Harper's Weekly,* and the *New York Times.* *Harper's Weekly* began in 1868 to print Thomas Nast's brilliant political cartoons, and his talent with the poisoned-

From Alexander B. Callow, Jr., *The Tweed Ring* (New York: Oxford, 1966), pp. 253-78, 298-300. Copyright © 1965, 1966 by Alexander B. Callow, Jr. Reprinted by permission of the publisher. Alexander B. Callow, Jr., is Associate Professor of American History at the University of California, Santa Barbara.

pen portrait, which could at once inspire fear and ridicule, had led many to think he was the chief wrecker of the Ring. Tweed himself thoroughly recognized Nast's artistry in making a cartoon a deadly political weapon. "I don't care a straw for your newspaper articles, my constituents don't know how to read, but they can't help seeing them damned pictures."[1]

A picture may say a thousand words, but it still took many a thousand words to excite and motivate the indignation of New Yorkers. It was the *New York Times* which published the first evidence of corruption, helped to raise the crusade to the heights of near hysteria, and therefore deserves the mantle of champion opponent of the Tweed Ring. The role played by the *Times* is a kind of case study of the enormous difficulties and stubborn persistence involved in arousing a sometimes confused and often apathetic public.

Prior to September 1870, the fight against corruption was represented by a series of angry but irregular outbursts from reform groups and newspapers. These in turn were thwarted by grand juries vulnerable to the persuasion of hard cash and lack of evidence. The Citizens' Association and the Union League, both eminent bodies of "respectabilities," had long fished in the murky waters of New York politics with only occasional luck.[2] While the reformers suspected that something was desperately wrong, the rub was in proving it. Although the Ring was organized as early as 1866, there was little awareness by reformers of either a centralized city machine or of how politics operated at the level of the ward and precinct. Instead, there was talk of a host of "rings" but uncertainty as to who were the ringleaders.

Apathy, a lack of civic conscience, and fear—which permeated every level of society—also accounted for the reformers' failure to get an audience. An absence of consensus, generated by party partisanship, divided the press and the gentry, the two groups who might have sounded the alarm and carried the fight. While the business community furnished several leaders to the reform groups, other businessmen were either afraid of the retaliatory power of Tammany Hall or they benefited from the Ring's operations, while others, too interested in making money, simply did not care.

The Tweed Ring exploited these conditions and reinforced complacency by giving something to everyone: city advertising to the press, special favors to businessmen, state aid to charitable and religious organizations, jobs and food to the poor. Tweed through his business connections and Hall through his clubs ingratiated themselves in the upper branches of society, while Sweeny and Connolly, seasoned ward leaders, were effective in the rank and file. And then there was the Astor Committee and its whitewash of the Comptroller's records, which contributed as much as any event to creating complacency.

Into this atmosphere, the champion of reform, the *New York Times,* made its "auspicious" beginning in the winter of 1870, by announcing that Messrs. Sweeny, Hall, and Hoffman were busily engaged in bringing good government to New York![3] One delicious irony was topped by another when the *Times* gave its first (and last) cheer for the Boss himself.

Senator Tweed is in a fair way to distinguish himself as a reformer. . . . From beginning to end the Tweed party has not manifested the slightest disposition to evade or prevaricate. . . . As a whole, the appointments of the heads of the various departments of the City Government . . . are far above the average in point of personal fitness, and should be satisfactory.[4]

The *Times*'s course, however, was radically altered by the summer of 1870. Ugly rumors of corruption were once again abroad, and George Jones, the *Times* publisher, apparently feeling hoodwinked and humiliated, angrily turned on the charter and its creators. An Englishman, Louis Jennings, was imported as editor. Jennings's zest for a good fight, his acerbic prose, coupled with Nast's cartoons in *Harper's Weekly*, infused the campaign with a pitch and tempo of almost evangelical fervor. For over a year, from September 20, 1870, on, there was not a day that the *Times* did not, with furious and heroic invective, assault the Tweed Ring, its organization, and allies. The *Times* begged, cajoled, scolded, and demanded that the electorate rout the rascals; nevertheless, the public, including some of the "best people," seemed to sink deeper in its apathy, and the Ring got stronger. What was wrong? Was it entirely public indifference, the usual scapegoat for corruption, or did the trouble lay partly in the nature of the crusade itself?

Two elements are necessary in any successful campaign against civic corruption: moral indignation and facts. Until July 1871, the *Times*'s attack was a grand crusade conducted without fear and without facts; it was long on denunciation, short on documentation. The slack in legal evidence was taken up in an amazing exercise of invective, the central theme of which was the wickedness of the Tweed Ring, a theme with a hundred variations on the words "thief," "rogue," and "scamp." The crusade had persistence. It had gusto. It

had all the subtlety of a sledge hammer. It was literary alchemy using the crudest of alloys. There was none of the humor or painful ridicule of a Nast cartoon, none of the dash of the *New York Herald* or the deft sarcasm of Dana's *Sun* when those two papers finally joined the bandwagon later in 1871. It was just a juggernaut of epithets, taking the edge off the crusade by dulling the reader's senses with a repetitive cry of "wolf." E. L. Godkin of *The Nation*, although admiring the newspaper's spirit, found its denunciation "tiresome."[5] Even the *Times* admitted that its readers were probably bone-tired from the constant accusations.[6] And while the *Times* spewed platitudes about political sin, the elegant Mayor of New York quipped, "Who's going to sue?"[7]

Nor was abuse heaped solely on the Ring, for the public in general, and the rich, the workingman, and the church in particular, came within the *Times*'s range as it sharpened its aim at iniquity. One major strategic device of the crusade was to arouse a feeling of guilt and shame. The public had failed its civic responsibilities. There should be a moment of self-castigation coupled with redeeming political New Year's resolutions to sweep away the apathy that allowed the monstrosities of the Tweed Ring. The rich were scorned for their complacency, hypocrisy, and lack of action.[8] They were "cowardly and effeminate," refusing to leave the comfort of their libraries for the "unpleasant smells" of the political arena.

The policy of the Ring, in fact, was to drive the honest, decent middle class out of the city and leave it to the very rich and the very poor—"the one too lazy to oppose them, and the other too ignorant."[9] If the workingman understood the elementary principles of political economy, he would not be grateful for the jobs the Ring gave him on the streets and in the parks. He should realize that the robbery of the rich was the robbery of the poor. Labor actually took the full brunt of the Ring's adventures in graft through raised rents, increased taxes, and higher priced goods.[10] As for the church, the *Times* said, at most it applauds while others fight. If only the church acted with responsibility, the public conscience would be inflamed, and the sores on the body politic would be burned out, "as if by fire."[11]

With these tactics of shock, blame, and invective, the *Times* seemed to be searching for some way to shatter the complacency of the public. An attempt was made, in a pedestrian Jeffersonian vein, to exploit the chasm between town and country, the fear—and fascination— of the city. The "hay-loft and cheese-press Democrats" were told of the moral quagmire of the Sodom-by-the-Hudson, its city-slicker politicians, its crime, its cancerous effect on the Democratic party.[12] The trouble with that approach was that upstate politicos well knew that the success of the party depended on the city Democrats' delivering a large bloc of votes, and the Tweed Ring had time and again shown it could deliver.

Perhaps an appeal to the citizens' pocketbook would help, for here lay men's hearts—"touch them there and they will wince and exhibit more sensitiveness than they will show to even the strongest appeals made to their sympathies," as the *Times* said.[13] The newspaper became choked with figures demonstrating the Ring's damage to property owners. But most of the electorate did not own real property. Columns

were devoted to an awkward analysis of city finances. But the average voter would have difficulty making sense of them. As the *Times* executed its complicated sums, apathy seemed to increase.

One reason why the crusade raged on for so long amid apparent indifference from the rest of the New York press was that the Democratic press, from the *World* on down—"or rather up, for you cannot get lower than the *World*"—(as the *Times* remarked)— were infuriated over the profound Republican partisanship of Nast and the *Times*. The *Times* was fond of repeating the adage that every Democrat was not a horse-thief, but that every horse-thief was a Democrat. Moreover, according to the *Times*, "all" Democrats were corrupt; the party had "never" undertaken a "genuine" reform.[14] Righteous moral indignation was rudely compromised when the *Times* condemned city Democrats and blithely whitewashed the Grant administration.[15]

Skepticism (and perhaps jealousy) also influenced the press. The *Times* motto should read, said one newspaper, "Print everything you please, without regard to whether it is true or false, but refuse to prove anything."[16] Horace Greeley, who puffed hot and cold throughout the campaign, even suggested that the Ring sue the *Times* for libel.[17] The *New York World*, after a brief flirtation with the Young Democracy, returned to revolve around Tammany Hall; it stoutly defended the Ring, calling the crusade as "stupid and absurd as it is wicked," and designed to introduce "a reign of anarchy."[18] Moreover, both the *Herald* and the *World* liked Oakey Hall. James Gordon Bennett of the *Herald* once said approvingly of Tweed's left-hand man, "He calls a spade a spade and Horace Greeley a humbug."[19]

Thus when Tammany wildly celebrated on July 4, 1871, it seemed that Nast's cartoons and the *Times's* river of rhetoric had produced a crusade without followers, a cause apparently lost to corruption and apathy. All had not been lost, however, for it prepared New Yorkers for what was to follow. This was made possible not by any renewed moral gusto from Tammany's "unloyal" opposition, but by a quirk of fate and an emotion common in politics—the hankering for revenge.

The first real step in the Ring's fall to disaster came on January 21, 1871, when James Watson, the trusty County Auditor and Ring bookkeeper, was killed in a sleighing accident. The Ring was to learn how indispensable he was, for the door was now open for espionage. Matthew O'Rourke was appointed County Auditor, but was not taken into the Ring's confidence. It was a fatal appointment—"a dirty traitor and a fraud," Tammany's *Leader* cried later. O'Rourke was not a happy man. He once had a claim against the city which the Ring had seen fit not to pay. A disgruntled claim-seeker could be as vicious as a woman scorned. With the patience and accuracy of a good bookkeeper, O'Rourke copied the explosive facts and figures of corruption from the Ring's account books and passed them on to the *Times*.[20]

Acting independently, Jimmy O'Brien, one of the leaders of the rebel Young Democracy, assumed the role of a political Judas. He had managed to ingratiate himself back into the good graces of the Ring, by abandoning the Young Democracy and acting as an enthusiastic trustee for the Tweed monument association. But beneath his ruddy Irish complexion, he smouldered with resentment over the Ring's refusal to pay him $300,000 in claims he collected while Sheriff. O'Brien persuaded Connolly to give one William Copeland a job in the Comptroller's office. Copeland was, in fact, O'Brien's spy, sent to obtain information to use as blackmail to get O'Brien's claims. With Watson dead, Copeland found the voucher records loosely guarded. Lush accounts, such as "County Liabilities," furnished him with a wealth of information, which he copied for O'Brien. Confronted with this political dynamite, Tweed began to pay blackmail. He paid O'Brien over $20,000 with the promise that $130,000 would be forthcoming in mortgages on prime property. O'Brien coolly pocketed the cash and turned his information over to the *Times*.[21]

The breakthrough in the crusade had come. Publisher Jones began his attack with uncommon good sense. He bought up a large block of *Times* stock, fearful the Ring might retaliate by a stock raid. And then on Saturday, July 22, 1871, the *Times* opened up with its first front-page blast: "The Secret Accounts: Proofs of Undoubted Frauds Brought to Light." Slowly and deliciously, as if opening a long-awaited Christmas package, Jones released his figures—on the armories, the courthouse, padded payrolls, judicial indiscretion—topping one horror with another.[22] On the 29th the *Times* printed a special supplement in English and German of statistics on the armory and courthouse swindles; 200,-000 copies of the first printing were quickly sold out. It was not only a sensation in New York, but it also attracted immediate national attention. For the next four months Jones never let up; front page and editorial page boiled with journalistic frenzy—and Nast drew his cartoons with even greater venom.

Now as the facts were exposed, New York stirred, rumbled, and awoke—shocked, frightened, angry. It was now time for the reformers to take more decisive action. The massive reform rally on September 4 at Cooper Union, the first of many, registered the impact of the *Times*'s exposures: the temper was explosive, the spirit was that of a back-country revival meeting. The rally was sponsored by the Committee of Seventy, whose roster bulged with some of the most distinguished names in New York, such as William F. Havemeyer, Judge James Emott, Robert Roosevelt, Charles Richard O'Conor, and Joseph H. Choate, who presented the Committee's resolutions against the Tweed Ring with the battle cry, "This is what *we* are going to do about it!"[23]

A rostrum of distinguished speakers aroused the audience to a passionate fervor: "We shall get at them. The wicked shall not always rule"; "Pitch into the boss, give it to him, he deserves it"; "There is no power like the power of the people armed, aroused, and kindled with the enthusiasm of a righteous wrath"; "What are we going to do about it?"—"Hang them," cried the voices from the audience.[24] The *Times* said afterward that if the Ring had heard the curses, hisses, and denunciations heaped on them they would have felt "too mean to live."[25]

It was evident that New York had awakened from its apathy. The Citizens' Association, the New York Council of Political Reform, and the Union League threw their weight into the crusade, and they were followed by a host of reform groups—the Young Men's Municipal Reform Association, the Apollo Hall Democracy, the Young Democracy, the German Reform Organization, and the Ward Councils of Political Reform. The press joined the chorus. Prominent businessmen and attorneys like R. A. Hunter, George W. Benster, and James Whitten met and considered forming a Vigilance Committee, but cooler heads prevailed. And Samuel Tilden entered on his somewhat gray charger. It was now expedient for him to be a reformer. The crusade reached a new dimension. It was no longer the concern of two but an issue that attracted many New Yorkers.

The impact of the Tweed Ring upon the reformer's imagination once again demonstrated the American capacity to create a morality play out of politics. Here was a drama of good versus evil. The principal characters were so wonderfully wicked that little embellishment seemed necessary. But embellished they were. While the reformers' responses were varied and often contradictory, certain dominant themes emerged.

The beginning theme, which Thomas Nast did more than anyone else to fix, was the image of the city boss, a portrait of evil. Tweed was pictured as gross, vicious, lowborn, colossally corrupt. Sweeny was the man with the black brains; Connolly was dark and oily; and Nast's favorite target, Oakey Hall, was the buffoon. These "beastly rascals" were also seen not as an indigenous product of the American urban political system, but as something sinister and alien. The corruption of the Ring was compared to the treachery of a Judas Iscariot, to the cunning of a Robespierre, the slothful greed of Oriental potentates; in tyranny and insolence they "would put their Roman predecessors to the blush."[26]

But the Boss and his ministers were

only mirrors in larger size and more evil proportions of those who flocked to their support—the Irish-Catholic immigrants. One of the most significant responses to the Tweed Ring, one which rounded out the image of evil by adding fear to it, was the revival of nativism in New York. On July 12, 1871, Protestant and Catholic Irish engaged in a bloody riot which shocked New York and revived the Know-Nothing attitudes of the 1850's and nativist fears of the 1863 draft riots. The Ring was vehemently denounced for trying to prevent the annual parade for the Orangemen, which precipitated the riot, as pacifying the Catholic Irish. When the parade was allowed, the Ring was accused of protecting the Catholic rioters. No other single event so well illustrated the tie between Tammany Hall and the Irish-Catholic voter. The cry for "clean government" now emitted the voice of nativism. There was a papal conspiracy as "Irish Catholic despotism rules the City of New York, the Metropolis of free America."[27] Letters poured into the *Times* office calling for a revival of the Native American party.[28] The Citizens' Association announced that the city had become a "common sewer" for the "dregs" of Europe; an army of ignorance was being led to the polls by the Tweed Ring.[29]

Nativism, in turn, elicited another response. The reformers, for the most part of the middle and upper class—professional men, bankers, merchants, journalists, the "better" politicians—felt a distinct loss of status since their old position of leadership had been captured by the wicked and the mob. Prior to the reign of Fernando Wood, political factions were controlled by men belonging to the upper or middle class, to whom the emoluments of office,

while desirable, were not always essential. From the days of Tweed's Forty Thieves through the Civil War, a change was occurring in New York politics, gradually, not completely, not easy to recognize; like the grin of the Cheshire Cat, sometimes it was seen, sometimes it was not. The old ruling groups, even the august Albany Regency, were being slowly displaced by a group not new, but different in numbers and the ranks from which it came—the lower-middle class, and the bottom of the social heap, the immigrant and native poor. The old ruling groups had to begin to move over and make a place for a new group, the Irish. This change found its source in the city, its growth, the changing composition of its population, the nature of its government. But the old middle- and upper-class elite, especially the reformers, who largely came from these groups, never completely understood this change and felt only bitterness toward the new and not always "respectable" elite. Republican institutions under the Tweed Ring, the reformers declared, were safe only in the "rightful" hands of the educated, the wealthy, and the virtuous. Now power had shifted to those at the bottom of society, their morals decayed, their religion Romanist, their Alma Mater the corner saloon.[30] The *Times* echoed the reformer's fears: We exist over a volcano, a vast, explosive mass of the poor and ignorant—"the dangerous classes," who "care nothing for our liberty and civilization."[31] E. L. Godkin traced the phenomenon back to the excessive democratization of the 1846 New York State Constitution.[32] Others saw it compounded by another insidious development, the rise of a new political breed, the professional politician.

As New York itself grew, politics became more centralized, more disciplined, more professionalized. While the professional politician had long been on the scene in New York politics, the impact of the Tweed Ring seemed to wipe out that memory and fix the emergence and the novelty of the professional as coinciding with the Tweed era. The *Times,* in fact, wrote of the "new profession" as if it were just making its appearance.[33] The reformer gave the professional little credit for skill in handling men or for artful political techniques at the "low" level of the ward or precinct, or for his sometimes masterful sense of organization. The reformer generally was little interested in the rude day-by-day operations of politics. His middle and upper class sensibilities were congenial to ideals and principles, not to the often rough, dreary, but necessary work of the primaries. The professional, in the reformer's eyes, was not a Robin Hood to the needy, but rather a Robin the Hood to the degenerate, wasting the taxpayers' money by giving jobs to the immigrant, bailing the drunkard out of jail, and corrupting the unemployed by giving them food and cigars—a parasite undermining the Protestant ethic of civic responsibility. The New York Council of Political Reform summed it all up. It was a contest between two forces: one made up of ruffians and desperadoes, and the other of "the delicately reared, the moral, humane, and the peace loving."[34]

Thus his sense of lost status, his contempt and fear of the masses, his nativism, his reaction to the city boss as rogue and professional politician—all indicate that the reformer's response to the Tweed Ring was more than simple moralizing about political sin. But if there was one response, a dynamic one

which gave cohesion and direction to his other reactions and provided the most powerful stimulus to reform, it was the fear that civil liberties were in danger, which to a certain degree was true. This response finally gave to the crusade a sense of genuine crisis, its *raison d'être.* The capital crime, then, was not merely the plundering of the treasury, nor the danger to the taxpayer's pocketbook; it was something more sinister than that. It was that a gang of rogues and its vicious brood, an organization alien to American life, was threatening the very bases of republican institutions—the ballot box, the schools, the church, the freedom of speech and press. "This wholesale filching and slaughter of the suffrage is a deadly thrust at the very source and fountain of our liberties . . . [we must] recover our mutilated liberties and vindicate our civil rights," shouted Joseph Choate at Cooper Union.[35] The danger to civil liberties was one of the most persistent themes of the *New York Times.*[36] Judge James Emott, Henry Clinton, Henry G. Stebbins, William Evarts, and others, all repeated the same theme: the Tweed Ring had threatened "the existence of free institutions," republicanism was "poisoned," "the glories of liberty are in danger."[37] The threat was felt even outside New York. "Democratic principles can no more carry this curse of Tammany upon them than virtue can thrive in a brothel," said the *Chicago Times.*[38]

If these fears seem exaggerated, it was because the reformers of the Tweed era were faced with their first city boss and his well-organized machine. There had been corruption in the past, but no precedent of modern city bosses to temper the reformer's idealism and sharpen his realism.

Although there were differences among the reformers, and their schemes often overlapped, there were broadly two schools of thought on how best to cleanse New York City. The largest school believed that the Ring was not a natural product of American municipal government but a political disease alien to New World representative democracy. The cure, therefore, was relatively simple. Rout the rascals, lance the boil on the body politic, and the organism would be healthy again. This prognosis reflected an implicit faith in the efficacy of American institutions. The defeat of the Tweed Ring meant the vindication of republicanism, not the questioning of it. There were, of course, minor wounds to be treated: the charter needed patching up, there were too many appointive offices, and a tight little bureaucracy should replace the Ring's bloated monster. If the Ring discredited any institution, it was the political party. Partisanship, therefore, should be replaced by efficiency, honesty, and the methods of business. "The government of a city," declared the Union League, "is altogether more a matter of business, than of statesmanship." The party system led only to "lawlessness, disorganization, pillage and anarchy."[39]

For these reformers, the cause of corruption could be the cure of corruption. The absence of the "best people" in government had allowed the wicked to rule. Thus the call was for the return to power of men with substantial wealth, education, and virtue. "The Ring could not keep its own for a day in the teeth of a combined and vigorous opposition from the men of large property."[40] New York was choked with foreigners, "many of them not pos-sessed of virtue and intelligence sufficient for self-government."[41] Therefore, what was needed, said the New York City Council of Political Reform, under the heading of "The Effectual Remedy," was for the "right-minded" to enter "into a covenant with each other . . . and the work is done."[42] If this sounded like the voice of the happy ending, it was also the voice of elitism. By implication, the "right-minded" were always the old ruling elite. It represented government of the people, for the people, by the "best people."

The second group of reformers did not share the extravagant optimism of the first. Corruption had forced them to re-examine the efficacy of democratic institutions and in so doing they found them wanting. Patchwork will not answer, wrote James Parton. The ship of state needed an overhaul from keel to taffrail, and perhaps it was necessary to "abandon the vessel and build a new one."[43] There must be some "profound defect," said C. C. P. Clark, in the American system which produced the horrors of the Tweed Ring.[44] The defect these reformers saw was one of the hallowed tenets of the American dream, universal suffrage. The comments of E. L. Godkin best illustrate this position. It was nonsense to talk about the Ring as a novelty to the American scene; it was the inevitable result of a "process of evolution," and other great cities have their "mute, inglorious Tweeds" waiting for their opportunity.[45] The curse of the city, "the great city problem," *is* the "people"—or about half of them who constitute the poor, "that huge body of ignorant and corrupt voters." The poor have no conception of self-government and choose only to live off the rich. The blight of universal suffrage is the secret of the Ring's power because it gave them an army. There can be, then, only two cures: first, suffrage should be limited, because only the propertied class, those who have a stake in society, should rule, for "we must somehow put the government into the hands of men who pay taxes." And second, the municipality should be converted into a business, stripped of political influence.[46] This program did not go far enough for Francis Leiber, James Parton, and Isaac Butts. They wanted to impose a literacy test on all New York voters.[47] It was a fine irony that those who felt their civil liberties in danger should seek to curtail the liberties of others.

From whence had come these dreams for a reformed New York? Not from the reformer's own time, for which he expressed a withering indictment. The reformer turned away from his own era, which spawned chaos and upheaval, looked back over his shoulder and found his solutions in a remembrance of things past—or what he *thought* had passed. He reached back for a lost innocence, the simplicity of an older era, the chaste republican order of a golden yesteryear. When he called for the return of the "best people," he thought of past mighties—James Kent, De Witt Clinton, Edward Livingston. His plan for a small, simplified government was the vision of the clean, honest symmetry of the town meeting, which James Welsh fondly recalled as the "natural school of American statesmanship."[48] The concept of limited suffrage, that ideological dog which had had its day, was an image of Order, a responsible aristocracy balancing a rapacious mob. The warmth of reminiscence, however, was an anesthetic to the re-

former's memory. For him the Tweed era dated the decline of political virtue. Before that ranged the long years of paradise to be found again. Forgotten were the gentlemen rogues, Fernando Wood, the Forty Thieves, and Samuel Swartwout. Nostalgia even led the reformer to tidy up the Albany Regency. Now it was remembered as an organization of "culture, integrity, and character."[49] And Thurlow Weed, an able opponent of the old, honest Regency, apparently with straight face, testified that "formerly the *suspicion* of corruption in a member [of the State legislature] would have put him 'into Coventry.' "[50] As one reform pamphlet said, "Pause here, Reader, sadly to drop a tear on the grave of departed Patriotism."[51]

As the crusade accelerated and unified both reformers and the press by early fall of 1871, the Ring, realizing it was in deep trouble, fought back like a trapped tiger and made some clumsy but typical maneuvers. George Jones was offered a bribe of $500,000 to silence the *Times*. He turned it down saying, "I don't think that the devil will ever bid higher for me than that."[52] Perhaps Thomas Nast needed a rest. He was promised $500,000 if he would leave the country and study art in Europe. "Well, I don't think I'll do it," Nast said. "I made up my mind not long ago to put some of those fellows behind the bars, *and I'm going to put them there!*"[53]

For a while Tweed remained cool and calm. A reporter for the *Missouri Republican* asked him if it were true that he had stolen money. Tweed thought a while and said, "This is not a question one gentleman ought to put to another."[54] George Templeton Strong said: "Tweed's impudent serenity is sublime. Were he not a supreme scoundrel, he would be a great man."[55] Finally, on September 8 he lost his composure and declared to a *Sun* reporter:

The *Times* has been saying all the time I have no brains. Well, I'll show Jones that I have brains. . . . I tell you, sir, if this man Jones had said the things he has said about me, twenty-five years ago, he wouldn't be alive now. But, you see, when a man has a wife and children, he can't do such a thing (clenching his fists). I would have killed him.

Nor did Mayor Hall help matters. He became ensnarled in his own contradictory statements and succeeded only in deepening the Ring's guilt. At first Hall cried innocent. The disclosures of the *Times* were "a tempest of ciphers and calumny . . . a second-hand roar about the accounts of the Supervisors and the salaries of extinct sinecures." Then he admitted some frauds were committed by the "old" Supervisors, but not by the Ring. This was interesting, because Tweed was president of the old Board of Supervisors. He said he never signed the alleged fraudulent warrants, and blamed Watson. He retracted this and admitted signing them, but only as a "ministerial act." He then claimed the signatures were forged; then retracted again and said he had signed but had been "hoodwinked." He tried sonorous prose: "When at last the smoke shall clear away, it will be seen where the political sun will clearly shine, that the proudest flag of them all, waving untorn from the highest staff of the victorious army, is that which shall never cease to be borne by Tammany Hall."[56] And naturally Hall attempted humor. "We are likely to have what befell

Adam—an early Fall."[57] In an interview with a newspaper, he showed what the *Times* called "cheek."

Reporter: "You are looking very well."
Mayor: "Oh yes, I am always cheerful. You know the true philosophy of life is to take things just as they come. How was the clever definition—let me see, I forget his name—of life? What is mind? No matter. What is matter? Never mind. That's my philosophy."[58]

Once more cupidity came to the aid of the reformers. The Committee of Seventy as well as the Citizens' Committee, composed of private citizens and Aldermen, made plans to examine Comptroller Connelly's books for further proofs of the Ring's misdeeds. On Sunday, September 10, the day before this was to happen, Connolly's office was broken into. From three small cupboards more than 3500 vouchers were stolen. It became a sensation. The Ring had panicked. The *Times* asked sarcastically why the city had spent $404,-347.72 on safes and had not given one to the Comptroller. At the same time news came from Washington that Mrs. Connolly had just put one and a half million dollars into government bonds. No longer could the *World*, *Sun*, and *Herald* spoof the *Times* on its crusade. Even Horace Greeley overcame his jealousy of the *Times* and admitted that a crusade was in order. The theft only intensified Tilden's efforts—he had now committed himself completely to the crusade—to find more proof, which he did when he investigated the accounts at the Ring's Broadway Bank. So careless was the Ring that duplicates of the stolen vouchers were found by Tilden at the bank.

The Ring at best had been untidy. Now all became a shambles. The pressure of the crusade was more than the

Ring could endure. The thieves who had traveled so far and so long together quarrelled and split into two enemy camps. Hall and Sweeny, joining forces against Tweed and Connolly, saw a chance for survival with the voucher disaster. On September 12, 1871, Hall asked Connolly to resign. Connolly, with some logic, replied to Hall that such a step would be equal to a confession, and added: "My official acts have been supervised and approved by your superior vigilance. So far as my administration is questioned equal responsibility attaches to yourself."[59]

It was now, as George Templeton Strong put it, "skunk vs. rattlesnake." Connolly, caring little for the role of sacrificial skunk, fled to the reformers. Tilden then performed a master stroke. He persuaded Connolly to step aside for four months, naming in his place Andrew Green as Acting Comptroller. Green was a distinguished public servant, and by no coincidence, a member of the Committee of Seventy.[60] Hall had made himself ridiculous by demanding Connolly's resignation, which he had no authority to do; Connolly refused and imported some of his toughs from the lower wards to guard his office. It was now skunk vs. *coiled* rattlesnake. Hall asked former General George McClellan to take Connolly's post, but McClellan, cautious in peace and war, refused. The press hooted that Hall had failed. In an interview, Hall told reporters, "Gentlemen, some of you yesterday said that I had received a severe check, and *in testimonium veritatis*, I have, so as you see, put on a check suit."[61] Connolly did deputize Green, and so one of the principal bastions of the Ring's stronghold, the Comptroller's office, was captured.

In the meantime, treason developed on the general staff. John Foley, president of one of the ward reform clubs, applied to George Barnard for an injunction to stop the Ring from paying or raising money in any way in the name of or on the credit of the County and City. Barnard, sensing the coming debacle of the Ring, responded with all the agility of a rat leaping from a sinking ship and granted the injunction. The reformers, never expecting this boon, were elated. As Tweed explained it:

So he put the injunction upon us, and in the straitened condition of our credit, which was so extended on every side, it broke us. You see our patronage had become so enormous and so costly that the injunction, which might not have troubled us at any other time, destroyed all our power to raise money from the banks or elsewhere and left us trapped.[62]

Although the injunction was later modified, government was temporarily brought to a standstill. With the city treasury nearly empty, and no recourse to raise money, city employees went for weeks without wages. Tweed gave $50,000 from his own pocket to help laborers and their families, and the *Star*, one of a few remaining journals kind to the Ring, called on the laborers to start a bread riot.[63] New Yorkers, remembering the horror of the draft riots of 1863, and the bloody Orange Parade riot of July 12, 1870, redoubled their efforts to oust the Ring.

The injunction accomplished its purpose. The main arteries of political power, money, and patronage were suddenly dried up. The thieves were fighting among themselves. With Green ruthlessly chopping off sinecure appointments, the shiny hats, stripped of place and status, were losing faith in their chiefs. With an election coming

up, *Harper's* and the *Times* were
joined by the rest of the New York
press, and the crusade reached fever
pitch. The public was daily reminded
of Tweed's arrogant, "What are you
going to do about it?" The Tweed Ring
seemed on the threshold of disaster.
But the reformers underestimated the
talents of the Boss.

For the leaders of the anti-Tammany
Democracy it seemed that victory was
in easy grasp. All that was necessary
was to control the State nominating
convention at Rochester. This did not
appear difficult in light of the disasters
that had befallen Tweed and company.
Then the reformers could elect a reform
platform, reveal the further evidence
compiled by the investigations of the
Committee of Seventy, campaign
against the horrors of the Tweed Ring,
and ride to victory in the November
election. Tilden made elaborate preparations to capture the convention by
sending out 26,000 letters to Democratic politicos asking for support with
a one-two punch: he put the name of
Charles O'Conor in nomination for
the attorney-generalship, and disputed
the right of the regular Tammany delegates to represent the city in the convention. Thus with belated courage,
Tilden arose, rallied the reformers, and
denounced the Ring. He realized the
Ring's only chance of survival lay in
renominating its henchmen for city and
state offices, and helping the election of
Republicans who had worked with it
in past legislatures—but so did the Boss.

The reformers lost some of their confidence when Tweed and his entourage,
gangs of New York toughs, arrived in
Rochester. Threats of violence were
made against anyone who should interfere with the Ring; delegates were
warned that the convention would be
broken up by force if anti-Tammany
delegates were admitted to the floor.
The reformers found themselves reliv-
ing an old story: once again they were
outmaneuvered and outwitted. Crafty
as usual, Tweed moved among the delegates and argued that the recent exposures were merely a local issue and
that an all-out fight in the convention
would undoubtedly split the party and
allow the Republicans an easy victory
in November. For the sake of party
unity he was willing to compromise. If
the reform representatives were omitted
from the roll of delegates, he would
omit the Tammany representatives.

What appeared as a compromise was
actually a victory. Even with the Tammany delegation missing, Tweed was
able to control the convention, through
lack of opposition from the reformers,
and with the help of friends won by
bribery. Charles O'Conor, who would
never have hesitated to throw the entire machinery of the state against the
Ring, was defeated for the attorney-
generalship by a large majority. A state
ticket bulging with names of the Ring's
minions was nominated. Tweed turned
against the reformers with arrogance.
He called Tilden, Horatio Seymour, and
Francis Kernan "three troublesome old
fools."[64]

Tweed had good reason to gloat. A
few days before the convention he was
re-elected chairman of the Tammany
General Committee, and at the convention he was renominated for State
Senator. He returned to New York in
triumph. At Walton House he took the
platform, removed a little Scotch tweed
cap, and told a boisterous audience:

The newspapers have already indicted,
tried, convicted and sentenced and sentenced (roars of laughter), but I feel perfectly free to appeal to a higher tribunal,

and have no fear of the result (cheers). I do not come to you, my fellow citizens, in a circuitous way, indicative of the possession of the thought of the necessity of caution engendered by fear, but directly, openly, squarely, as a man to men, and without an appeal for your sympathy other than so far as my family have suffered from the cruel indignities that have been heaped upon them for my political actions (sensation). But asking at your hands the justice and fair play that have been denied me by bitter, unrelenting, unscrupulous, prejudiced and ambitious partisan foes (deafening shouts of approval). . . .[65]

The reformers, who had once gloated, returned to New York shaken and sober. The glitter of their confidence was dulled, but their resolution was firm—even firmer. Tweed's victory at Rochester had robbed them of a valuable tactical weapon, the opportunity to proclaim themselves the regular Democratic organization. The Ring, even though quarrelling among themselves, still commanded a powerful election-day army. But failure only reinforced the reformers' determination. What had seemed after the exposures to be an easy victory was now an uphill fight. The reformers were forced to be a rival of the regular organization, and hence a third-party group, with all the difficulties a third party faced. Many of the reformers' leaders were political prima donnas— O'Conor was known for his irascibility, Tilden could be exasperatingly aloof. If thieves fell out, reformers seemed to delight in dissension and to fragment into splinter groups. If the reformers were going to battle the Tweed Ring, they needed unity, organization, and outside support. But the Republicans were notoriously weak and inept. Then, as now, thousands of eligible voters never bothered to go to the polls. There was the danger that the none-too-reputable

groups, like Mozart Hall and the Young Democracy, posing as reformers now that the Ring was embarrassed, might capture leadership from the reformers.

If the odds were formidable, the reformers were driven to work together if for no other reason than the fact that election day might be the last chance to destroy the Ring. Public indignation could not be sustained at a high pitch forever. Six days before the election, the Committee of Seventy released the evidence they unearthed from the Broadway Bank accounts. Important Republicans were persuaded to unite in a common cause by voting a straight reform ticket and not to present a separate Republican ticket to complicate matters. Young Men's Reform Associations were organized. The students of New York University, to whom Hall had recently lectured with applause, tore down the Mayor's portrait from their walls. The newspapers maintained a heavy barrage, exhorting voters to register, publicizing the facts behind the Ring's schemes, and explaining all the tactics Tammany might use to defraud the public on election day. Huge express wagons, drawn by six horses, stood ready to convey a reserve police force to any scene of disorder. Plans were made to take detected repeaters to the armories for custody to avoid the sure chance of their discharge by the courts. With a burst of excitement and energy, the reformers invaded the lower wards, the central nervous system of Tammany Hall, posting signs, passing out pamphlets, haranguing the native and immigrant poor with sidewalk speeches.

The tempo increased as the clergy of New York, pounding their pulpits, spoke out against the Tweed Ring for the first time. Dr. Henry D. Northrup of the Presbyterian Church echoed a common theme: there were but two parties, he roared, God's and the devil's. Election day "is a time when every citizen should show himself to be a man and not a sneak."[66]

The reformers who now thought they could win, called several rallies to keep things at a white heat. On November 2, a rally was held to receive the report of the Committee of Seventy. The motto over the president's chair read: "What are we going to do about it?" George Templeton Strong, pessimistic as usual, did not think they were going to do anything. "The disease of this community," he wrote in his diary, "lies too deep to be cured by meetings, resolutions, and committees. We the people are a low set, without moral virility. Our rulers, Tweed and Company, are about good enough for us."[67]

But Strong's pessimism seemed to be shared by few. The cadence of protest from the reformers, the press, the clergy, was picked up in the saloons, the restaurants, the clubs. Apathy had vanished. New York was agog with one topic of conversation, not the recent Chicago fire, not the visit of the Grand Duke Alexis, but the chance—the bare chance—that the reformers might beat the Tweed Ring on November 7th. On the eve of election day, New Yorkers waited with apprehension, and prepared themselves for one of the most important and exciting elections ever held in New York City.

Much to their own astonishment, the reformers gave Tammany Hall one of the worst defeats in its history up to that time. The scandals had finally roused New Yorkers into action. There was an unusually large turn-out, and many who previously had been apathetic, went to the polls and registered their indignation with Tammany. The reformers guarded the polling places well, and were successful in protecting themselves against excessive fraud and repeating. Moreover, several of the repeater gangs sensed the fall of the Ring and withdrew their support. The reformers elected all fifteen Aldermen, thirteen Assistant Aldermen out of twenty-one, and carried fourteen of the twenty Assembly districts. Prominent among the new Assemblymen were ex-Mayor Daniel E. Tiemann and Samuel Tilden. General Franz Siegel effectively wooed the Germans and became State Register. There were impressive upstate gains. The reformers captured four out of five Senatorial seats. The one they failed to win was the sour note. O'Donovan Rossa had once led the Irish against the British but could not do the same against Tweed in New York. The people of the Seventh District stood by the man who had served them so well with patronage and charity, and Tweed won over Rossa by over 10,000 votes. The reformers' broom swept out many of the Ring's important lieutenants. Henry Woltman was defeated by Augustus Weismann, the first German-born man to be elected to the State Senate. Timothy Campbell, Henry Genet, James Irving, and Michael Norton were all defeated. Alexander Frear and Thomas Fields were prevented from taking their seats because of election fraud. The full measure of defeat was revealed a few days later. It was announced that the annual Americus Club ball was postponed.

Once again the *Times* reported a quiet election day. It was a moot point, the newspaper said, whether this resulted from the precautions taken by the reformers or that Tammany was cowed. Of course there were some "altercations and word-combats," and "heads punched in the good old fashion so dear to the Democracy." Compared to the previous year, the reformers had won away from the regular Democrats almost 75,000 votes in the city and state, "one of the most remarkable political revolutions in the history of the country," said a contemporary, with some exaggeration.[68] The *Times* maintained that the election was won by the strong vote of the so-called neutral population, who seldom voted—"the gentlemen and quiet citizens."[69] But while there was a large registration, there were not enough neutrals to decide the election. Ironically, it was the very people the reformers despised the most, the immigrants and the native poor, who, because of their great numbers, put the reformers into office by splitting their vote between Tammany and the men running on the Democratic reform ticket.[70]

The victory over Tammany was seen as the end of a great crusade. There was much excitement. For most it meant the vindication of popular government, the triumph of the people's voice, a moral struggle where good overwhelmed evil. Under a huge headline, "New York Redeemed," the *Times* said:

The victory we have won is priceless, not only from what it gives us now, but because it will revive every man's faith in the ultimate triumph of truth and justice—because it will teach scheming politicians that the voice of the people is supreme, and that immortal principles on which this Government is founded, although they may be momentarily stifled by dishonest factions, will constantly rise triumphant, while the men who assailed them will pass away to everlasting infamy.[71]

The reformer George C. Barrett, a successful candidate, said the victory was an answer to those who had scoffed at the success of a republican form of government.[72] *Harper's Weekly* said it was one of the most significant events in the history of free governments.[73]

Only E. L. Godkin pondered whether the great "uprising" was the final and complete triumph over political corruption, whether routing the rascals was only the beginning of reform—real reform. . . .[74]

What, then, was the final reckoning of the Tweed Ring? Although Judges Barnard and McCunn were impeached, and removed from office, and Cardozo resigned but continued to practice law, none of the three were criminally prosecuted. With two exceptions, none of the Ring and its many partners in graft were ever caught or punished. Only Tweed and Ingersoll went to jail. From 1871 to 1878, Tweed spent less than half of that time in prison. Ingersoll who turned himself in, hoping for a light sentence, was sentenced to five years and seven months, but served only a few months of his term before he was pardoned by Tilden for turning State's evidence and promising to become a witness in any forthcoming Ring trials. At the time of Tweed's death sixteen suits were pending against various members of the Tweed Ring organization.[75] None came to trial. Garvey was granted immunity to appear as a witness at the Tweed and Hall trials. Although a millionaire, he never returned any of the money he made. Woodward was granted immunity for returning $155,000, although he had stolen over a million. John Keyser had the delightful gall to claim that it was the city who owed him, and he was almost successful in being awarded a $33,000 claim based on a fraudulent contract![76] Of the twenty to two hundred million dollars estimated to have been stolen by the Ring, it cost the city

$257,848.34 to recover $894,525.44, most of which came from the estates of two dead men, James Watson and James Sweeny.

The ethos of reform, however, was essentially moralistic and conservative. For some the issue was a total commitment to punishing bad men, not the examination of the institutions and conditions that made it possible for bad men to exist and thrive. To them, the cause of corruption was the work of evil men. Their optimism blinded them to the realities of a rapidly growing society, the massive growth of a great city and the effects it would have on political life. For those who questioned institutions, the answer lay not in adaptation but in a return to the good old days of rule by gentry, suffrage restrictions, tight economy, and a tiny bureaucracy. In the months, years, and decades following the Ring's fall, the reformer, imprisoned by his own social philosophy, continued to alienate the immigrant newcomer. What could have been a source of power for the reformer remained the strength of later city bosses. As the city grew and its problems multiplied, the reformer continued to turn back to that Promised Land of the good old days for his solutions to corruption, patching the charter here, passing a resolution there, always haunted by his failure to restore the profession of politics to the nobility of the Old Republic. Exposure of the Tweed Ring had given him a glimpse into the hard realities of big-city politics. But he continued to be an innocent abroad in the strange land of the professional politician and practical politics, preferring the platitude to the free cigar. He never understood the politicians who made politics their business, their appeal to the masses, their atten-

tion to the plight of the immigrant, nor, indeed, the kind of world they were living in. Thus the rascals were routed, but their supreme achievement, the city machine itself, remained essentially intact, to become a model, a legacy, to be improved upon by succeeding monarchs of New York, the Kellys, the Crokers, and the Murphys.

After all was said and done, the crusade against the Tweed Ring won the battle but lost the war. In a real sense, William Marcy Tweed had the last word, when he asked, "Well, what are you going to do about it?"

NOTES

1. Wingate, "Episode in Municipal Government," July 1875, p. 150.
2. See Citizens' Association, "An Appeal by the Citizens' Association of New York against the Abuses in the Local Government to the Legislature of the State of New York, and to the Public" (New York, 1866); "Items of Abuse in the Government of the City of New York" (New York, 1866); "Report of the Executive Council to the Honorary Council of the Citizens' Association" (New York, 1866); "Wholesale Corruption! Sale of Situations in Fourth Ward Schools" (New York, 1864); Union League Club, "Report on Cities" (New York, 1867); "The Report of the Committee on Municipal Reform" (New York, 1867).
3. Jan. 24-25, Feb. 15, 1870. The Times also reported on Mar. 9, 1870, that Richard Connolly was fighting the Ring.
4. Apr. 8, 13, 1870. See also Apr. 6, 12, and May 1, 1870.
5. July 13, 1871, quoted in the Times, July 14, 1871.
6. Apr. 3, 1872.
7. J. D. Townsend, New York in Bondage (1901), p. 73.
8. Nov. 3, 1870.
9. Ibid.
10. Ibid.; Sept. 16, 1871.
11. Dec. 4, 1870. When the celebrated Henry Ward Beecher said he pitied wicked men because their consciences would surely suffer, the Times replied in a blistering attack, saying Beecher's pity was "morbid, unwholesome, sentimental." Oct. 24, 1871.
12. Oct. 3, 1870.
13. Sept. 24, 1870.
14. Feb. 26, May 1, 1871; Oct. 3, 1870.
15. "The great strength of General Grant's Ad-

ministration . . . lies in the fact that he is believed to be honest himself, and disposed to enforce honesty and fidelity in all departments of the Government under his control." *New York Times,* Sept. 21, 1871.

16. Unidentified newspaper, *Scrapbooks of Clippings Relating to the Career of A. Oakey Hall* (New York Public Library), Vol. iv, p. 113.

17. *New York Times,* Jan. 25, 1873.

18. July 28, 31, 1871. See also *New York World,* Aug. 2, 7, 10, 1871. The *New York Sun* and *New York Evening Post* also criticized the *Times.* Bowen, *The Elegant Oakey,* p. 99. Moreover, Charles Nordhoff, the managing editor of the *Evening Post,* was fired for attacking Tweed. Lynch, *Boss Tweed,* p. 355.

19. Bowen, *The Elegant Oakey,* p. 106. See also Allan Nevins and Thomas Milton Halsey, *The Diary of George Templeton Strong,* iii (4 vols.), pp. 376, 383, 385-6.

20. Genung, *Frauds of New York,* pp. 9-13.

21. *Tweed Investigation,* pp. 50-55; Hirsch, "More Light on Boss Tweed," p. 272.

22. For a compilation of the *Times's* evidence, see *New York Times,* "How New York is Governed. Frauds of the Tammany Democrats," 1871.

23. Breen, *Thirty Years of New York Politics,* p. 337.

24. *New York Times,* Sept. 5, 1871.

25. Oct. 2, 1871.

26. *New York Times,* Oct. 10, 1870; Jan. 20, Mar. 6, 1871.

27. *New York Times,* July 12, 1871.

28. Ibid. July 16, 1871.

29. "Report of the Executive Council to the Honorary Council of the Citizens' Association" (New York, 1866), p. 21. See also "Civil Rights: A History of the New York Riot of 1871" (1871), p. 20; Nevins and Halsey, *Diary of Strong,* iv, p. 352; Thomas Nast, *Miss Columbia's School, or Will It Blow Over?,* 1871, p. 71, *passim; Harper's Weekly,* July 29, 1871. For other examples of the nativist impulse, see *The Nation,* July 20, 1871, p. 36; *New York Times,* Mar. 18, Apr. 7, July 17-18, 21, 24, Aug. 17, 1871; Wingate, "Episode in Municipal Government," Oct. 1874, pp. 378-9; Townsend, *New York in Bondage,* p. 186; Nevins and Halsey, *Diary of Strong,* iv, p. 317.

While nativism was widespread in the reformers' camp, some were anti-nativist. See A. R. Lawrence, "The Government of Cities" (New York, 1868), pp. 4-5, 11.

30. *New York Times,* Sept. 17, 1869; Jan. 7, Nov. 30, 1870; Mar. 19, 26, July 16, Sept. 17, 1871. Otto Kempner, "Boss Croker's Career," p. 6.

31. July 16, 1871. See also Sept. 17, 1869; Oct. 17, 1870; Feb. 2, Mar. 19, 1871.

32. *The Nation,* Nov. 16, 1871, p. 316.

33. Jan. 25, 1871. See also *New York Times,* Jan. 24, 1870; *New York Star,* Mar. 25, 1870; Wingate, "Episode in Municipal Government," cxix (Oct. 1874), p. 379.

34. "Statement and Plea of the New York City Council of Political Reform," p. 34.

35. *American Addresses,* pp. 61-2, 72; *New York Times,* Sept. 18, 1871; (Anon.) "Why Vote at All in '72," p. 37. Robert Roosevelt declared that the Ring "pulled away the very keystone of the arch of liberty." If the public money is stolen, wrote another reformer, "why not the public liberties too?"

36. Feb. 8, April 3, Oct. 12, 17, Nov. 3-4, 1870; Jan. 24, Feb. 24-25, Apr. 7, May 1, July 16, Sept. 5, 26-27, Oct. 27, Nov. 3, 1871.

37. Jones, *Fisk,* p. 226; *New York Times,* Sept. 4, Nov. 3, 1871. See also Abram Genung, *The Frauds of the New York City Government Exposed,* p. 41; Gustav Lening, *The Dark Side of New York,* p. 694; James Welsh, "The Root of the Municipal Evil," p. 7; Nast, *Miss Columbia's School,* pp. 39, 71; New York Council of Political Reform, "Statement and Plea," p. 40.

38. Sept. 29, 1871.

39. "Report on Municipal Reform," pp. 17-18; see also, "Why Vote at All in '72," p. 72; Welsh, "Root of the Municipal Evil," p. 5.

40. *New York Times,* Jan. 23, 1871.

41. New York City Council of Political Reform, "Report of the New York City Council of Political Reform," p. 3.

42. "Statement and Plea," p. 28. See also "Report of the New York City Council of Political Reform," pp. 4-11; The Citizens' Association, "Report of the Executive Council to the Honorary Council," p. 22; Wilson, *Memorial History,* iii, p. 562; Bryce, *American Commonwealth* (1889 ed.), ii, p. 353, (1895 ed.), ii, pp. 391, 403.

For an interesting criticism of the "best people" theory, see *The Nation,* Aug. 24, 1871, p. 125.

43. "The Government of New York," p. 451.

44. "The Commonwealth Reconstructed," p. 26.

45. *The Nation,* Apr. 18, 1878, p. 257; Nov. 9, 1871, p. 300; Nov. 27, 1873, p. 350.

46. Ibid. Nov. 4, 1875, p. 288; Oct. 18, 1877, p. 238; Nov. 27, 1873, p. 350; Apr. 18, 1878, p. 257; Oct. 12, 1871, p. 237; Nov. 4, 1875, p. 289. See also Union League, "Report on Municipal Reform," pp. 19-20, 76-7, 88; Parton, "Government of New York," p. 463.

For an attack on this position, see Charles Nordhoff, "The Mis-Government of New York, a Remedy Suggested," *North American Review,* ccxxxiii (Oct. 1871), pp. 321-43, *passim.*

47. Francis Lieber, "Reflections on the Changes Which May Seem Necessary in the Present Constitution of the State of New York," p. 4; Parton, "Government of New York," p. 460; *Rochester Union and Advertiser,* Oct. 3, 1871.

48. "Root of Municipal Evil," p. 19.

49. *New York Times,* Sept. 11, 1869.

50. Parton, "Government of New York," p. 457.

51. (Anon.), "Why Vote at All in '72," p. 29.

52. Werner, *Tammany Hall,* p. 210.

53. Albert Paine, *Thomas Nast,* 1904, p. 182.

54. *New York Times,* Aug. 24, 1871.

55. Nevins and Halsey, *Diary of Strong,* Vol. iv, p. 394.

56. For Hall's excuses, see *New York Times,* July

12, 29, Aug. 12, Sept. 11, Oct. 10, 13; *The Leader*, Aug. 19, 1871.

57. Flick, *Tilden*, p. 213; see also *New York Times*, Aug. 29, 1871.

58. *New York Times*, Sept. 22, 1871.

59. Ibid. Sept. 17, 1871.

60. Green had served thirteen years on the Park Commission, helped to plan Central Park, suggested Riverside Drive and many of the smaller parks, established the American Scenic and Historic Preservation Society, and did much to effect the merger of the Tilden, Astor, and Lennox foundation in the New York Public Libary.

61. Wingate, "Episode in Municipal Government," Oct. 1876, p. 379.

62. Lynch, *Boss Tweed*, p. 375.

63. Sept. 27, 1871.

64. Flick, *Tilden*, p. 219.

65. *New York Times*, Nov. 5, 1871.

66. Ibid. Nov. 6, 1871.

67. Nevins and Halsey, *Diary of Strong*, Vol. IV, p. 382.

68. Wingate, "Episode in Municipal Government," Oct. 1876, p. 389.

69. Nov. 11, 1871.

70. O'Connor, *Hell's Kitchen*, p. 50; Lynch, *Boss Tweed*, pp. 383-4.

71. Nov. 8, 1871.

72. Ibid.

73. Cited with no date in *New York Times*, July 12, 1872.

74. *The Nation*, Nov. 9, 1871, p. 300.

75. *Tweed Investigation*, pp. 841-5.

76. Ibid. pp. 601-85.

VI THE CITY IN THE AMERICAN MIND

The fundamental crisis of the American city, according to one knowledgeable student of urban affairs, is an intellectual crisis involving inherited attitudes and images of the city that are either distorted or no longer applicable to the reality of an urban environment. The heart of every urban problem, be it housing, poverty, transportation, or even air pollution, evokes a judgment, an attitude toward the city itself; indeed,

the action crisis of the metropolis cannot be disengaged from the intellectual crisis, for the very definition of a metropolitan problem is dependent upon one's picture of the city and the kind of life it should contain, as the choice of action to improve or revolutionize is dependent upon one's estimate of the city as an existing entity.[1]

It has been a crisis of long standing, for the intellectual history of the American city has been a battleground of conflicting attitudes of Americans, who have argued about the value of the city and the kind of life it should contain. And for good reason. As a new form of human settlement, the city broke older village and agrarian traditions and forced new adjustments, new problems, new fears, and new hopes. As a dynamic source of social change, it was seen by some as the "Hope of Democracy," by others, many of whom measured it through the lens of agrarian or small-town America, as a corruption of democracy. Thus emerged two dominant attitudes toward the city, anti-urbanism and pro-urbanism—the city as a House of Ill-Fame and as the House of God.

Morton and Lucia White have engagingly capsuled the raft of anti-urban attitudes as:

too big, too noisy, too dusky, too dirty, too smelly, too commercial, too crowded, too full of immigrants, too full of Jews, too full of Irishmen, Italians, Poles, too artificial, destructive of conversation, destructive of communication, too greedy, too capitalis-

1. Scott Greer, *The Emerging City: Myth and Reality* (New York: The Free Press, 1964), p. 21.

tic, too full of automobiles, too full of smog, too full of dust, too heartless, too intellectual, too scientific, insufficiently poetic, too lacking in manners, too mechanical,
destructive of family, tribal and patriotic feeling.[2]

On the other side of the attitudinal fence, listen to Charles Abrams's ringing
eulogy of the city:

From earliest history, the city has been linked with man's freedoms—a refuge in the
days of Cain and Joshua, the hub of a vigorous political life in Greece, the impetus to
law in Rome. When man's mind roamed free in Utopian dreams, it was the city that
was so often closest to his conception of heaven—the "Celestial City," the "Heavenly
City," the "New Jerusalem," the "Holy City," and the "City of God." Moreover, it was
the city of trade, commerce, and property that helped undermine serfdom and that
ushered in other freedoms in the process. . . . For despite its changes and challenges,
the city still contains the raw ingredients of freedom. . . . It is still the marketplace
for goods and ideas, the locus of a contractual society, the mirror for emulation, the
meeting place for diversities, the center of culture.[3]

Perhaps the best examples of the ancient confrontation of anti-urbanism and
pro-urbanism are the remark made by the poet William Cowper, "God made
the country, man made the town," and the spirited rejoiner of Oliver Wendell
Holmes, "God made the cavern and man made the house!"

But the intellectual history of the city is not adequately depicted by the
simple symmetry of pro and con. It is muddled and complex because of another dominant attitude toward the city, one of ambivalence, a mixture of
attitudes reflecting a wide variety of personal, class, ethnic, and even regional
differences. A Southerner, for example, might praise his own city but find New
York a Sodom-on-the-Hudson.

This chapter seeks to sketch the shifting currents of thought toward the
city, for what men _thought_ was just as important as what men _did_. It is a topic
vital to understanding not only the course of American urban history but also
how that history reflects, at least in part, the American's response to his society
as a whole, for the city in many ways concentrates and sharply delineates national characteristics.

Anti-urbanism in all its blatant and subtle forms is the theme of the first
two authors of this chapter. They are concerned with the views of the most
articulate and literate group of society, the philosophers, poets, and writers.

Morton and Lucia White argue that, with few exceptions, the intellectual
has been the sharpest critic of the American city.[4] Mustering an imposing intellectual varsity of some of the greatest figures in American thought, from
Thomas Jefferson to John Dewey and Frank Lloyd Wright, they analyze the

2. _The Intellectual versus the City_ (Cambridge: Harvard and The M.I.T. Press, 1962),
p. 222.
3. _Man's Struggle for Shelter in an Urbanizing World_ (Cambridge: The M.I.T. Press,
1964), p. 10.
4. Their thesis is more fully developed in _The Intellectual versus the City: From Thomas
Jefferson to Frank Lloyd Wright._

various patterns of urban hostility that distinguished Emerson from Thoreau, and Henry James and Henry Adams from earlier thinkers, such as Melville, Hawthorne, and Poe. The Whites conclude that although the intellectuals differed widely in their response to the city, they did share the basic disenchantment that the city subverted fundamental values prized by Americans throughout their history. The accumulated verdict, then, seems to be that the city was a failure, morally, esthetically, and physically.

This was also the conclusion of most of the poets who wrote about the city during the Gilded Age. According to Robert Walker's essay, the pro-urban poets were but a small voice among the bellow of the majority of poets who presented a catalog of grievances so bitter and so shrill that they created "a myth of the city formidable in its detail and frightening in its intensity."[5] Admitting that the poets dwelt only on the negative aspects of urban life, Walker interprets their hostility as the last-ditch defensive stand of a declining agrarian America. It was the lament of the once-proud, honest yeoman who, in an age of massive urban and industrial growth, became the hayseed, "fleeced, flayed, and forlorn."

Taken together, the White's and Walker's essays suggest that historically the most dominant attitude toward the city was indeed anti-urbanism. Perhaps it was. But the question is begged: were the attitudes of the intellectual community *typical* of the rest of society? The Whites feel they were. Yet they also suggest the intellectuals were alienated from the rest of their society. But alienated intellectuals can hardly be seen as being representative of a larger society which repels and in many ways rejects them. Thus some urban historians argue that anti-urbanism has been so overstated that it has obscured other important attitudes, such as the affirmations of city-boosterism and the ambivalent attitude of both liking and distrusting the city.[6]

The next two essays, in fact, point out that anti-urbanism must share a place with other attitudes that make up the complex web of ideas about the city. In "Urbanism and American Democracy," Francis E. Rourke challenges the assumption of anti-urbanism by showing that the city was more constructive than destructive in the unfolding of democracy. Whereas the other essays have emphasized the moral, esthetic, and physical accents of anti-urban thought, Rourke, finding its origins in the Jeffersonian agrarian tradition, traces anti-

5. His argument is expanded in his book, *The Poet and the Gilded Age* (Philadelphia: University of Pennsylvania Press, 1963; to be reprinted by Octagon Press). For an interesting account of how prose writers viewed New York City, see Eugene Arden, "The Evil City in American Fiction," *New York History* (July 1954).
6. Charles N. Glaab and A. Theodore Brown, *A History of Urban America* (New York: Macmillan, paperback edition, 1967), pp. 53-54. For a rejoinder to Glaab and Brown, see Jeffrey K. Hadden, Louis H. Masotti, and Calvin J. Larson (eds.), *Metropolis in Crisis* (Itasca, Ill.: F. E. Peacock Publishers, 1967), pp. 120-21.
For the enormous complexity of attitudes toward one city alone, see Bayrd Still's indispensable study of New York, *Mirror for Gotham* (New York: New York University Press, 1956) and his "The Personality of New York City," *New York Folklore Quarterly* (Summer 1958).

urbanism through American political history. He underscores an important aspect of urban thought: the skyscraper may have replaced the barn as the dominant symbol of the American landscape, but the power of agrarian thought continues through the decades of the twentieth century to our own time.[7] He suggests that many Americans still feel today that the agrarian past nourished "the roots of Americanism." Some might insist that as far as urban problems are concerned, their solutions will be found not on the prairies but on the pavements.

At this point you might be tempted to tick off the virtues of the city, weigh them against the charges of the anti-urbanists, and try to determine your own position. You might say, however, that it is not that simple and there is more to it than that. And you would be right. Anselm Strauss in his engaging essay on the variety of American attitudes shows why.

Strauss's theme is ambivalence and ambiguity as he develops the elaborate complexity of Americans' attitudes toward their cities. He sees the shifting images arising out of a number of clashes: the values of the city vs. American values in general, regionalism vs. nationalism, the old vs. the new, specialization vs. cosmopolitanism, and ruralism vs. urbanism. He shows that if one city best attests to ambivalent, ambiguous attitudes that are filled with striking contadictions, it is New York. The paradoxical nature of these attitudes is fundamentally a reflection of the ambiguities and controversies about American values themselves. To add to the complexity, he demonstrates how the image of a particular city can be remarkably changed through growth and diversification. The heart of the matter is "the strain between ideal and reality, or ideal and presumed fact [which] runs like a brilliant thread through all our antithetical thinking about America and about our cities."

Where Morton and Lucia White suggested that the earlier intellectuals anticipated the views of the modern social scientist, Scott Greer, in the final essay of this chapter, examines the ideas and methods of twentieth-century social science and finds them wanting. In a provocative, slashing attack upon political scientists, urban sociologists, and economists, he argues they have been both myth makers and myth mongers whose images of the city assert a validity, relevance, scope, and monolithic understanding not matched with the changing realities of the modern city. He criticizes particularly the theorists of the "mass society"; and he points out the built-in small-town bias which helped to lead to studies emphasizing only the extremes and the "dramatic contrasts" and which illuminated nothing of the "excluded middle" of urban life. The study of the city as a kind of human pathology, as Greer maintains, has sharply contributed to the crisis of the city. It is a crisis of myth vs. reality.

7. He may have overstated the agrarian dominance of the Ku Klux Klan and temperance movement. See Kenneth T. Jackson, *The Ku Klux Klan in the City, 1915-1930* (New York: Oxford, 1967), and James H. Timberlake, *Prohibition and the Progressive Movement: 1900-1920* (Cambridge: Harvard University Press, 1963).

The American Intellectual versus the American City[*]

MORTON AND LUCIA WHITE

Although the city has become one of the most absorbing and most intensively studied social problems in America today, and although it is now fashionable for intellectuals to express an almost tender concern for its future, to hope that its decay can be arrested, and to offer plans for its revitalization, this has not always been the attitude of our greatest American thinkers. For a variety of reasons they have expressed different degrees of hostility toward urban life in America, hostility which may be partly responsible for a feeling on the part of today's city planner and urban reformer that he has no mythology or mystique on which he can rest or depend. We have no tradition of romantic attachment to the city in our highbrow literature, nothing that remotely resembles the Greek philosopher's attachment to the *polis* or the French writer's affection for Paris. And this fits very well with the frequently defended thesis that the American writer has been more than usually alienated from the society in which he lives, that he is typically in revolt against it. Throughout the nineteenth century our society was becoming more and more urbanized, but the literary tendency to denigrate the American city hardly declined in proportion. If anything, it increased in intensity.

Faced with this fact about the history of American thought, the contemporary student of the city can take one of two opposing attitudes. He, at his peril, can turn his back on the tradition of Jefferson, Emerson, Thoreau, Hawthorne, Melville, Poe, Henry Adams, Henry James, Louis Sullivan, Frank Lloyd Wright, and John Dewey. In this case he will treat some of the American city's profoundest critics as irresponsible literary men or as idle metaphysicians who fled the city rather than face its problems. Or he can regard this critical tradition as a repository of deep, though troubling, wisdom, one which raises basic questions for any urban reformer, and some of whose premonitions and fears have been more than justified by the passage of time. There is no doubt that the second is the wiser course. He who would improve the American city can only profit by an awareness of what some of our greatest minds have said, felt, and thought about one of the most conspicuous and most troubling features of our national life.

One cannot deny, of course, that there were pro-urban literary voices like Whitman's, or that there were urban sociologists like Robert Park who tried to speak up for the city. But they are voices in "the city wilderness," never comparing in volume with the anti-urban roar in the national literary pantheon. The urbanist must face the fact that the anti-urbanist does not live only in the Kentucky hills, in the Rockies, in the Ozarks, in the Cracker country, or the bayous. He lives in the mind and heart of America as conceived by

From *Daedalus* (Winter 1961), pp. 166-79. Copyright © 1961 by Morton and Lucia White. Reprinted by permission of the authors. Morton White is Professor of Philosophy at Harvard University.

the intellectual historian. The intellect, whose home is the city, according to some sociologists, has been the American city's sharpest critic. Everyone knows that Jefferson once hoped to discourage the development of the city in America, but he was only the first of a long and varied list of critics of the city.

Jefferson despised the manners and principles of the urban "mob" as he knew it in Europe and he hoped to keep it from crossing the Atlantic intact. He certainly did not think of the city as "The Hope of Democracy," as some Progressive 'theorists did at the turn of the twentieth century. He adopted a conciliatory tone about the city in his old age when he said in 1816 that we could not possibly depend on England for manufactures, as he had originally thought, and therefore we *needed* cities. But this does not show any *love* for the city. The country and its yeomen Jefferson loved all his life; in his old age he grudgingly accepted the manufacturing city as a necessity.

The same War of 1812 which led Jefferson to reassess his views was followed by a great expansion of the American city. It inaugurated a major phase of urban civilization between the Revolution and the Civil War. By 1860 the urban population was eleven times what it had been in 1820. The early decades of the nineteenth century saw the decline of Jefferson's empiricism among American intellectuals, and the emergence of philosophical transcendentalism, but a distaste for the city persisted among American writers.

The growth of the city in the North produced an even sharper reaction in Ralph Waldo Emerson than the European city had produced in Jefferson. Emerson's first philosophical work, *Na-ture,* appeared in 1836, in the middle of that interval which witnessed an eleven-fold increase in our urban population. Its very title was a protest against what he thought was happening. Partly under the influence of English romanticism, Emerson and some of his friends took to deprecating manufacture, art, and civilization, and so it was not long before they took to criticizing the city, the greatest of artifacts. The distaste for the city as an artificial creation was associated in Emerson's mind, as it was in the case of many romantic thinkers, with doubts about the value of science as an avenue to truth. And yet Emerson agreed with the scientifically minded Jefferson about the nasty manners and principles of the city. Whereas Jefferson was given to arguing the defects of the city in common-sense political terms, Emerson sought to buttress his feelings by a metaphysical theory. Hence we may label his period as the metaphysical period of anti-urbanism. To be is to be natural for Emerson. In the wilderness he said he found "something more dear and connate than in streets or villages." The life of the city was "artificial and curtailed"; it destroyed solitude, poetry, and philosophy.

One will find passages in which Emerson extolled the application of science and the virtues of civilization, the need for sociability to educate a man's sympathies, and the advantages of specialization that allow each man to develop his own talents. This suggests a more friendly view of the industrial urban society which was emerging in his own lifetime. But he always harped on the human failings of State Street and commercialism. At times Emerson could celebrate the artifice of pure technology, but he persistently attacked the debasement of moral standards by those who pursued nothing but wealth in the cities as he knew them. One is reminded of Thorstein Veblen's praise of urban industry even as he attacked its financial captains, for it was Veblen who saw the modern industrial city as the *locus classicus* of conspicuous waste.

Thoreau went even farther than Emerson in his distaste for civilization and the city, for Thoreau also attacked the village and the farm. *Walden* is a bible of anti-urbanism, in which Thoreau celebrates the life of the isolated individual, living in Nature and free of *all* social attachments. No wonder that Thoreau refused to visit the Saturday Club, which provided one of the few values of Boston in Emerson's eyes: intellectual conversation. And when Thoreau refused, Perry Miller reminds us, he put his refusal in no uncertain terms: "The only room in Boston which I visit with alacrity is the Gentlemen's Room at the Fitchburg Depot, where I wait for cars, sometimes for two hours, in order to get out of town."[1] No wonder Henry James said that Thoreau "was essentially a sylvan personage."[2]

If Jefferson attacked the city on political grounds, and if Emerson and Thoreau may be represented as criticizing it from the point of view of transcendental metaphysics, what shall we say of Poe, Hawthorne and Melville, all of whom may be added to our list of pre-Civil War critics of the city? They were far from political theorists or metaphysicians but all of them saw the city as the scene of sin and crime. Speaking of them, Harry Levin says: "For our dreamers, America was a garden, an agrarian Eden, which was losing its innocence by becoming citified. Melville had located his City of Woe in London

or Liverpool; Poe had tracked down imaginary crimes in the streets of an imagined Paris; and Hawthorne had exposed sins most luridly among the ruins of Rome."[3] As in Jefferson's case, the urban models of extreme crime and sinfulness were not located in the United States by most of our pre-Civil War anti-urbanists, but they saw dark omens in the streets of American cities which made them fear that they might become like Paris, London, Liverpool or Rome.

The observant de Tocqueville expressed his worry about the American city in 1835, one year before Emerson's essay *Nature* appeared. He said that the fact that America as yet had no dominating metropolis was one of those circumstances which tended to maintain a democratic republic in the United States and to counteract that great danger to which all democracies are subject—the tyranny of the majority. But de Tocqueville thought that the "lower ranks" which inhabited Philadelphia (pop. 161,000) and New York (pop. 202,000) in the 1830's "constitute a rabble even more formidable than the populace of European towns. They consist of freed blacks . . . who are condemned by the laws and by public opinion to a hereditary state of misery and degradation. They also contain a multitude of Europeans who have been driven to the shore of the New World by their misfortunes or their misconduct; and they bring to the United States all our greatest vices, without any of those interests which counteract their baneful influence. As inhabitants of a country where they have no civil rights, they are ready to turn all the passions which agitate the community to their own advantage; thus, within the last few months, serious riots have broken out in Philadelphia and New York."[4] So seriously did de Tocqueville treat this matter that he said: "I look upon the size of certain American cities, and especially on the nature of their population, as a real danger which threatens the future security of the democratic republics of the New World; and I venture to predict that they will perish from this circumstance, unless the government succeeds in creating an armed force which, while it remains under the control of the majority of the nation, will be independent of the town population and able to repress its excesses."[5]

If this could be the conclusion of the most astute foreign observer ever to visit our shores, it is not surprising that some of our great literary figures might have developed less than an admiring view of our urban culture between the Revolution and the Civil War. Optimistic empiricists like Jefferson, optimistic transcendentalists like Emerson, pessimistic believers in original sin like Hawthorne and Melville, all forgot their philosophical differences when they looked upon the American city, even before it developed into the industrial jungle it was to become between the Civil War and the end of the nineteenth century.

Between 1860 and 1900 the urban population quadrupled while the rural population only doubled; and, what is more staggering and significant, between 1790 and 1890, while the total population of the country increased sixteen times, the urban population increased 139 times.[6] The great exodus from the countryside was in full force, and New England became the scene of deserted hill and village farms, while the city's problems became the great social problems of the nation. The city became the home of the elevated railroad, the trolley car, the cable car, the subway, the apartment house, the telephone, and the skyscraper, while it continued to en-

courage what one physician called "American nervousness."

Among the most influential and most fastidious observers of this development were Henry Adams and the younger Henry James. Both were men of literary genius, both were members of cultivated families with wealth in their backgrounds, and for both of them the American city provided a profound spiritual problem. Because Henry Adams and Henry James lived in the age of the city's supremacy, they did not speak of it, as Jefferson had, as a remote future phenomenon or as something existing in Europe alone. And, unlike Thoreau, they did not feel as though they had only the American city and the American wilderness to choose between. Adams and James were both refined, civilized, indeed urban men whose animadversions on the American city are made more significant precisely because they were not opposed to cities in principle. They demonstrate what a hard time the American city had at the hands of nineteenth-century intellectuals. For here at least were two *city* types who also found the American city sadly wanting. Their reaction to the American city is more esthetic, more literary, more psychological than that of their predecessors Jefferson and Emerson.

The two most important documents for an understanding of the views of Adams and James are the former's *Education* and the latter's *The American Scene*. It is significant that the great problem of the *Education of Henry Adams* was to steer a course between the poles of town and country, between the Boston and Quincy of his childhood. "Town," Adam tells us, "was restraint, law, unity. Country, only seven miles away, was liberty, diversity, outlawry, the endless delight of mere sense impressions given by nature for nothing, and breathed by boys without knowing it."[7] Adams also tells us that he spent his life trying to choose between the ways of life they represented, without ever making up his mind. And yet, in a sense, he did make up his mind, or the social forces of America made it up for him. He could not go back to the Quincy house of his grandfather Adams. And, being no Thoreau, he had to live in the American city if he was to live anywhere in America. But what was *the* American city in his mature years? Surely not Boston, but New York. And when Henry Adams looked at the New York of 1868, he tells us in a book which he wrote in 1905 that he felt swept aside by the forces pushing the country in a new direction. "His world," he lamented, "was dead. Not a Polish Jew fresh from Warsaw or Cracow—not a furtive Yaccob or Ysaac still reeking of the Ghetto, snarling a weird Yiddish to the officers of the customs—but had a keener instinct, and intenser energy, and a freer hand than he —American of Americans, with Heaven knew how many Puritans and Patriots behind him, and an education that had cost a civil war."[8] Adams felt like the dispossessed Indian and the buffalo in America after 1865, for it was a banker's, and neither a buffalo's nor a Bostonian's world. To Henry Adams, New York symbolized the spiritual confusion of America at the end of the nineteenth century.

Henry James, as one might expect, also complained about his birthplace, New York, after a period of flirtation with it. James attacked it most explicitly in *The American Scene*, published in 1907 as the report of an expatriate revisiting the country of his birth. He, too, spoke of the city's chaos, and even the New York skyline insulted his very ex-

pressively complex sensibilities. He complained of the lack of history and of the lack of time for history in a way that reminds one of his early critical work on Nathaniel Hawthorne. The buildings, he said, "never speak to you, in the manner of the builded majesties of the world . . . towers, or temples, or fortresses or palaces with the authority of things of permanence or even of things of long duration."[9] History had given way to commerce: "The great city is projected into its future as practically, a huge continuous fifty-floored conspiracy against the very idea of the ancient graces."[10] The city lacked order, structure, dignity, history. James speaks of it as "a heaped industrial battlefield" and as a scene of "the universal will to move —to move, move, move, as an end in itself, an appetite at any price."[11] He missed what he called "organic social relations,"[12] and he felt some pleasurable relief when he visited Philadelphia, because it didn't "bristle," and because "it went back."[13] In this spirit he warned: "Let not the unwary . . . visit Ellis Island"[14] as Henry Adams might have warned in *his* snobbish way. James was upset by what he called "that loud primary stage of alienism which New York most offers to sight."[15] And he dreamed "of the luxury of some such close and sweet and *whole* national consciousness as that of the Switzer and the Scot."[16] His final head-shaking conclusion was "that there was no escape from the ubiquitous alien into the future or even into the present; there was no escape but into the past."[17]

Of course, one must not forget that Henry James was a cosmopolite, a lifelong inhabitant of cities, a man who is reputed to have dined out more than any resident of London in his day. One must be mindful of the fact that his novel *The*

Princess Casamassima represents an effort to penetrate the depths of London, as does his famous admiring essay on that city. But James viewed the *American* city in an entirely different way. After his harsh handling of the Boston reformers in *The Bostonians*, the American city did not provide him with any serious material for a full-length novel because he found neither the uptown nor the downtown of the American city sufficiently interesting, as F. O. Mathiessen has pointed out.[18] And even *The Princess Casamassima* shows a greater interest in the bizarre doings of weirdly inspired misfits and aristocrats, whose philanthropic concern with the slums James satirizes, than a sustained interest in the typical life of London. With characteristic delicacy and insight he saw the crushing, oppressive defects of the British metropolis of his day, but he could never bring himself to the same kind of sympathetic concern with the American metropolis that we find in Dreiser, Crane, or Norris.

Although we are primarily concerned with recording the theme of *anti*-urbanism in American writing and thinking, it would be absurd to argue that *every* great writer or thinker in the American pantheon was hostile to urban life. The fact is that at the end of the nineteenth century there emerged a tendency to view the American city in a more friendly manner. By contrast to his brother Henry, William James had very little desire to escape from the American city into the past. His philosophy was one of hope, of optimism, of possibility —indeed, a little bit too much so—and it was this that allowed him to view the urbanization of America in a way that might encourage Americans to do something about urban problems. Unlike Henry, he did not adore the great cities of Western Europe. For ten days after his arrival in Florence in 1875 he "was so disgusted with the swarming and reeking blackness of the streets and the age of everything, that enjoyment took place under protest."[19] As for London, during his visit of 1889 he wrote his sister that he was "thoroughly sated" with it, and "never cared to see its yellow-brownness and stale spaciousness again."[20]

William James loved the country but his love of nature was tempered by a fondness for sociability, and therefore he was unable to subscribe either to Thoreau's primitivism or to the ultra-civilized sentiments of his brother. With Emerson he looked to the future, but unlike Emerson he did not think that the future excluded the possibility of a decent life in the cities of America. Many of William James's reactions to the buzzing confusion of New York of 1880 and 1900 had been unfavorable because of "the clangor, disorder and permanent earthquake conditions" which he experienced on his customary daylong visits. But in 1907 he spent a longer time there and as he says, "caught the pulse of the machine, took up the rhythm, and vibrated *mit*, and found it simply magnificent."[21] He spoke of it as an "*entirely* new New York, in soul as well as in body, from the old one, which looks like a village in retrospect. The courage, the heaven-scaling audacity of it all, and the *lightness* withal, as if there were nothing that was not easy, and the great pulses and bounds of progress, so many in directions all simultaneous that the coordination is indefinitely future, give a drumming background of life that I have never felt before. I'm sure that one *in* that movement, and at home, all other places would seem insipid."[22] This was written to his brother, of all people, after the appearance of the latter's *The American Scene*, but William had evidently read the manuscript, for he says: "I observe that your book—'The American Scene,'—dear H., is just out. I must get it and devour again the chapters relative to New York." William would not have liked them upon rereading them, and one can imagine how Henry must have winced when William exclaimed, "I'm surprised at you, Henry, not having been more enthusiastic, but perhaps the superbly powerful subway was not opened when you were there!"[23]

William James, like Walt Whitman, saw virtue and promise in the American city. Both William James and Whitman not only accept the city as an inescapable part of America, but they *enjoy* it, as Jefferson most certainly did not. The year of William James's discovery of what he called "the new New York" was 1907, when he delivered his most famous set of lectures, entitled *Pragmatism*, at Columbia. James thought his philosophy would mediate between the views of those whom he called "tenderfoot Bostonians" and those he labeled "Rocky Mountain toughs" in philosophy. It is not too fanciful to suppose that James identified the great future city, along with his pragmatic philosophy, as a blend of, a compromise between, the insipidity of Boston and the craggy brutality of the Rockies. A livable city on earth, one is temped to say, is the social counterpart of James's pragmatism, and therefore he is one of the first great American writers to associate himself with the effort to accept what is good and to root out what is bad in the American city. He does not escape to the country with Emerson and Thoreau, or to the past with his brother and Henry Adams. He revives the wisdom of the older Jefferson after a century of transcendentalism, Brook-farming and expatriation, and adds to it a love of the city. In doing so he becomes the herald of a pragmatic phase in urban thinking.

But this pragmatic phase, in which the city was joyfully described by Frederic C. Howe in 1905 as "The Hope of Democracy," did not last very long. Indeed, Howe's book contained within itself the classical argument for the central city's impending destruction. "The open fields about the city are inviting occupancy," Howe said, "and there the homes of the future will surely be. The city proper will not remain the permanent home of the people. Population must be dispersed. The great cities of Australia are spread out into the suburbs in a splendid way. For miles about are broad roads, with small houses, gardens, and an opportunity for touch with the freer, sweeter life which the country offers."[24] Howe calls the city the hope of democracy, but he is, it would appear, a suburban booster rather than a city-lover. He shares the basic inability of greater American intellectuals to go all out in their admiration for the modern American city.

A more striking illustration of the same thing may be found in the writings of John Dewey, the disciple of William James, who sympathized with so much of James's interest in the American city. In his earlier writing Dewey expressed a typically progressive interest in the city. This was part of the political liberalism of the period, with its interest in urban planning, social work, socialism, the single tax, and muck-raking. The city was not regarded as a perfect form of life, but it was seen as having promise. And, to the extent to which it showed promise, it became the concern of all sorts of people who could criticize it in a constructive spirit quite different from that which dominated the work of militant anti-urbanists from Jefferson to Henry James. For a variety of reasons Chicago became the most conspicuous locale of this new way of looking at the city. It was the home of a great university, which had opened its doors in the 'nineties and which became a center of urban sociology and, it might be said, of urban philosophy. One can understand, therefore, why William James looked to Dewey and other Chicago intellectuals as his friends, and why they regarded him as their spiritual leader. For Chicago at the turn of the century was the home of James's pupil, Robert Park, his worshipper, Jane Addams, and his disciple, John Dewey.

As early as 1899 Dewey was urging that the congregation of men into cities was one of the most conspicuous features of the modern world and that no theory of education could possibly disregard the fact of urbanization. Indeed, *the* problem of education, as Dewey saw it in his *School and Society,* was how to adjust the child to life in the city. The earlier kind of rural environment, in which he had been raised as a boy in Vermont, had its virtues, he admitted. It encouraged habits of personal orderliness, industry, and responsibility; it led to a firsthand acquaintance with nature. But, Dewey said in 1899, "it was useless to bemoan the departure of the good old days . . . if we expect merely by bemoaning and by exhortation to bring them back."[25] The problem, as Dewey saw it, was that of retaining some advantages of the older mode of life while training the child to cope with the new urban world. The school, therefore, was to be a miniature urban community, a microcosmic duplication of macrocosmic Chicago, much as Hull House was in Jane Addams' eyes. The essence of so-

ciety, said Dewey—and in this he was joined by Robert Park and other sociologists—was communication—and therefore the school was to encourage and develop this peculiarly social phenomenon, this salient feature of the urban age. Dewey's progressivism in educational theory was defined by his broad conception of communication, his idea that it takes place while children are building blocks, dancing, and cooking, as well as on the more formal level of asserting propositions.

Soon, however, a new and more critical attitude toward the city began to enter Dewey's writing. In *The Public and Its Problems* (1927) he concluded that steam and electricity, the very forces that had created modern society, that had provided it with the means of transportation and communication that made urban concentration possible, were creating a situation in which communication at its most human level was being destroyed. The very forces which brought Bangkok and Chicago closer to each other and which brought people from isolated farms to urban centers had diminished the possibility of "face-to-face" relationships. The primary group, in the phrase of the sociologist, Charles Horton Cooley, was disappearing rapidly. And while Dewey did not use our current jargon, he said, in effect, that modern society was becoming a lonely crowd of organization men.

Dewey warned: "Unless local communal life can be restored, the public cannot adequately resolve its most urgent problem: to find and identify itself."[26] But the local communal unit of which Dewey spoke now was not the enormous city as it was coming to be known in the twentieth century. It was more like the University Elementary School at the University of Chicago, or

Hull House. "Democracy must begin at home," Dewey said, "and its home is the neighborly community."[27] As a result, a curious reversal takes place in Dewey's thinking. Instead of taking the city as the model *for* the progressive school, he almost speaks as though the urban community should be modeled *on* the progressive school. Jefferson wrote at the end of his life: "As Cato concluded every speech with the words, 'Carthago delenda est,' so do I every opinion with the injunction, 'Divide the counties into wards.'" At the end of his life Dewey seemed to conclude every speech with the words, "Divide the cities into settlement houses."

It is ironic to find the most influential philosopher of the urban age in America reverting to the localism of Jefferson, but no more ironic than the anti-urbanism of Louis Sullivan and Frank Lloyd Wright, our most distinctive architects. For functionalism, like pragmatism, is one of a complex of American ideas that could not exist in a nonurban society, and yet its greatest spokesmen seem to hate the American city. Sullivan's *Autobiography* records his distaste for Boston in his childhood, and in his *Kindergarten Chats* he fulminates against New York and Chicago. "Lieber Meister," as Wright called Sullivan, bequeathed this hostility to his disciple, and the disciple, as everyone knows, added his own powerful spice to the brew of anti-urbanism. John Dewey may have reverted to Jefferson's localism, but Wright was a little more partial to Emerson. Not only are there copious references to Emerson in Wright's books, but he adds as a red-printed appendix to *The Living City* a long excerpt from Emerson's essay, "Farming," which concludes with a typically transcendental warning: "Cities force

growth and make men talkative and entertaining, but they make them artificial." And so the great American architect of the twentieth century went back spiritually to Concord, while the great American philosopher retreated to Monticello.

One moral of this tale is the city-loving urban reformers will not find much boosting or sentimental admiration of city life in the writings of those who have been canonized in our national literature and philosophy. A brief flurry of pro-urban sentiment in the late nineteenth and early twentieth century under the encouraging eye of Walt Whitman and William James was swiftly buried by the exploding megalopolis, but after it our most sensitive and gifted intellectuals went on criticizing the American city. Readers who may feel that this story is based on an excessively narrow selection of writers and thinkers should remember that other readers will find in these pages the names of our greatest political thinker, our greatest essayist, our greatest philosopher, our greatest theorist of education, our greatest novelist, our greatest autobiographer, and our greatest architect, all of them throwing up their hands about the most distinctive and most pressing features of our national life. If *their* views should not be typical of the nation's view on this topic, that in itself would be a fact that is worth recording and pondering. Moreover, it is impossible to produce a list of *pro*-urban American thinkers who remotely approach this collection in distinction and intellectual influence.

In spite of the anti-urbanism of our literary and philosophical tradition, the city planner would make a grave mistake if he were to dismiss that tradition, if he were to treat it as a point of view from which nothing could be learned, if he were to forget it and disregard it. Those who must live in today's American city or who like to live in it can profit by taking seriously the urban criticism of our great writers, for it was deep and many-sided. It was not only esthetic but also moral in character. Henry James spoke most persuasively for those who saw the city as a scene of chaos as it presented itself to "the painter's eye." It lacked order, structure, history, and dignity in 1907, and God knows that these virtues have not been miraculously supplied in the age of urban sprawl and suburban slums. But the city, as Robert Park said, is a state of mind as well as an esthetic object, and the profoundest critics of the American city have found other faults with it.

When Jefferson warned of the dangers of what he called the city mob, when Emerson complained of the city's artificiality and conventionalism, when John Dewey lamented the decline of neighborliness, all of them thought of the city as a place in which certain basic human values were being subverted, values which are cherishable today as they were in the eighteenth century of Jefferson, the nineteenth century of Emerson, and the twentieth century of Dewey. And what are these values? Jefferson's worry about the mobs of the city arose from doubt about the American city's capacity to educate its inhabitants in a way that would preserve and extend the democratic process. And when Emerson worried about the growth of artificiality and conventionalism in the city, he was thinking, as were his contemporaries, Kierkegaard and John Stuart Mill, about the increase in conformity, about the decline of individuality which was proportional to the increase of urbanization in America. Dewey's main concern was with the

improvement of human communication within the city; and by communication he did not mean the exchange of information alone. He valued the capacity to share feelings and experiences, the capacity to discuss with, to learn from and intelligently persuade others, and to *live* with them in the profoundest sense.

Who can deny in 1960, then, that the great problem of the American city is to demonstrate at least three things: first, that it can solve the problem of education for the millions of people who are entering its gates, that it can absorb the Puerto Rican, as it has other immigrant groups, into the democratic process; second, that it can foster individuality, the capacity and the right of the human being to develop into a rounded personality who is concerned with more than merely commercial values; and third, that it can be more than a vast prison of unconnected cells in which people of different occupations, color, class, or creed fail to understand one another on the basic human issues of social life, let alone agree with one another.

The moral message of the intellectual critic of the city today is not fundamentally different from what it was in the age of Jefferson, Emerson, and Dewey. For today's serious thinker must also build upon a respect for the fundamental values of education, individuality, and easy communication among men. But, unlike his predecessors, he cannot deceive himself about the *place* in which those values must be realized today. The wilderness, the isolated farm, the plantation, the self-contained New England town, the detached neighborhood are things of the past. All the world's a city now and there is no escaping urbanization, not even in outer space.

NOTES

* The argument of this essay has been developed and documented more fully in Morton and Lucia White, *The Intellectual versus the City: From Thomas Jefferson to Frank Lloyd Wright* (Cambridge: Harvard University Press and The M.I.T. Press, 1962).

1. Perry Miller (editor), *Consciousness in Concord* (Boston, 1958), p. 46.
2. Henry James, *Hawthorne* (New York, 1880), p. 80.
3. Harry Levin, *The Power of Blackness* (New York, 1958), p. 234.
4. Alexis de Tocqueville, *Democracy in America* (New York, 1945), Vol. I, p. 289, note.
5. *Ibid.*
6. Arthur M. Schlesinger, *Paths to the Present* (New York, 1949), pp. 223-225.
7. Henry Adams, *The Education of Henry Adams* (Boston, 1918), pp. 7-8.
8. *Ibid.*, p. 238.
9. Henry James, *The American Scene* (reprint, New York, 1946), p. 77.
10. *Ibid.*, p. 92.
11. *Ibid.*, p. 84.
12. *Ibid.*, p. 279.
13. *Ibid.*, pp. 275, 280.
14. *Ibid.*, p. 85.
15. *Ibid.*, p. 86.
16. *Ibid.*
17. *Ibid.*, p. 115.
18. F. O. Mathiessen, *Introduction to The American Novels and Stories of Henry James* (New York, 1947), p. x.
19. Ralph Barton Perry, *The Thought and Character of William James* (Boston, 1935), Vol. I, p. 351.
20. *Ibid.*, p. 412.
21. Henry James (editor), *The Letters of William James* (Boston, 1920), Vol. II, p. 264.
22. *Ibid.*
23. *Ibid.*
24. Frederic C. Howe, *The City: The Hope of Democracy* (New York, 1905), p. 204.
25. John Dewey, *School and Society* (Chicago, 1899), p. 9.
26. Dewey, *The Public and Its Problems* (reprint edn., Chicago, 1946), p. 216.
27. *Ibid.*, p. 213.

The Poet and the Rise of the City*

ROBERT H. WALKER

As the predominant character of Western civilization has gradually shifted from rural to urban, the force of the city has made itself felt in numerous ways and at various times. The idea of America as a city-dominated land, however, first became a topic for general public discussion in the late nineteenth century. In what spirit did America receive her new character? Accustomed to bowing toward London and Paris, did she honor her own New Yorks and Chicagos? Dedicated to technical advance, did she preen herself in the splendor of elevators and elevateds, skyscrapers and subways? Avid in her quest of progress, did she welcome the spectacular material change provided by the spreading urban giants? Or was the ghost of Jefferson too much in evidence; did the enforced collectivism of the city seem too foreign to this land of frontiersmen with their individualistic and agrarian predilections?

In the poetry of the Gilded Age there appeared with elaborate clarity the image of a new, urban America.[1] There were some poets who saw in San

From *Mississippi Valley Historical Review* (June 1962), pp. 85-99. Reprinted by permission of the publisher. Robert H. Walker is Professor of American Civilization at George Washington University.

Francisco a new Athens, in New Orleans a new Paris; there were others who hailed the American city as a technological marvel, a phenomenon of unparalleled potential usefulness. Urban promoters exulted over economic opportunities, Bohemians reveled in the stimulating heterogeneity of the metropolis, and the community-conscious pointed with pride toward new standards of civic betterment. The several cities which provided settings for the spectacular fairs and expositions of this day-of-the-diorama reaped a harvest of homage wherein they stood as symbols for the achievements of the nation at large. The image of the city, on this one facet at least, sparkled with the splendor of its rapid and dynamic growth, its marvels of engineering and transportation, its varied and often beautiful profile. The city as cynosure of wealth, learning, and opportunity received at least a modicum of recognition.

But the collective profile of the city, to judge from the poetic portrait, was far from benign and sparkling. For every verse which found something to praise, there were at least four which took an opposing view. In fact verses that praised the city for whatever reason were almost matched in number by those which opposed the city for the single reason that it contrasted unfavorably with rural life and virtue. In such verses as these one finds a demonstration not only of the strength of America's agrarian traditions but also of the defensive position of the farmer at the close of the century. Plagued by drought and debt in the West, by falling prices and inflation everywhere, the farmer fought a bitter if unsuccessful struggle against the city's lure. This battle dramatized itself in three acts, the first of which stated the source of the farmer's resentment:

A sound is heard throughout the land
Which causes vague alarms;
You hear it oft, on every hand,
"Vermont's deserted farms."

Where once the strong Green Mountain boy
Pursued his honest toil. . . .
You now behold the shattered homes
All crumbling to decay,
Like long-neglected catacombs
Of races passed away.[2]

Thanks to Madison Cawein, and to a lesser extent to Paul L. Dunbar, much of this verse pertained to the South, where "Decay and silence . . . rotting leaves" set the tone.[3] Whatever the region, the titles remained the same ("The Deserted Farm" "The Desolated Homestead"), as did the imagery of the rusted plow, the dulled scythe, the house taken over by wild creatures, and the decayed barn which once had strongly stabled the evidences of agricultural prosperity.[4]

Act two stated the argument, in the unsubtle language of propaganda, against further desertion of rural areas—"Don't Leave the Old Farm":

The city has many attractions,
But think of the vices and sins,
When once in the vortex of fashion,
How soon the course downward begins.[5]

To one having little or nothing to lose
A city life might have a charm . . .
BUT A FARMER SHOULD STICK TO HIS FARM.[6]

The dreary round of pastoral chores, over and again, was measured against the bright lights and found superior. Not only were farmers themselves urged to stay behind the plow, but special pleas were frequently directed at their offspring to "Make the dear old folks happy by staying at home."[7] Yet a third act seemed typically necessary before a fitting dénouement could be supplied. Here the country folk were observed transplanted into an urban setting, where they were plagued by strange noises and fashion's foibles, and filled with nostalgia for good country food and air, the familiarity of chores and companions.[8] Occasionally a happy adjustment was achieved; but usually the outcome depended on the farmer's coming to his senses in time to escape the disappointment of menial work after high expectations, the imprisonment in "brick and granite," which epitomized the urban trap.[9] A truly happy ending could occur only when all the denizens of crowded alleys and filthy cellars traded their lot for the "thousands of life-giving acres untilled" which America still had to offer.[10]

Aside from the main drama this conflict could also be seen in the accounts of mutual visiting between city and country dwellers. The story of the "rube" in the big city is an old one, and its retellings in the verse of this period added little to the genre except that by this time the bumpkin had to contend not only with speeding horses and falling refuse, but might even get picked up by a power shovel or snared in an elaborate piece of factory machinery.[11] Whatever the circumstances, he still returned home fleeced, flayed, and forlorn. The more frequent tale brought the "milk-white city clown" out to visit the farm.[12] Just as the farmer's openness, ignorance, and trusting nature worked against him in the city, so did the city-dweller's abstract learning, over-mannerliness, and fancy clothes invariably get him into rural scrapes. The slick drummer, the dude gambler, and the careless hunter were the stock villains of these pieces. When the urban and rural types were contrasted in a less malicious manner, it was to make the point that farm life teaches the practical whereas city life teaches the superficial.[13]

More numerous than the tale with moral appendage was the direct comparison between the two ways of life, a comparison which consistently favored the rural. In such a context were developed many of the complaints against the city which will be treated more logically below. What should be noted here is the intensity of these complaints lodged against a myriad of urban shortcomings, real and imagined, and placed against an idyllic counterfoil of rustic life—serene, secure, ennobling, healthful, direct, honest, and humble. Against one such backdrop of bucolic virtue was presented the following urban portrait:

> Contrast with this the city life
> With all its bustle and its roar;
> Its howling greed, its angry strife
> That tramples down each feeble life
> Which vainly struggles to the fore;
>
> Its brawling crime and snarling death;
> Its cries of want and wild despairs;
> Its dust and smoke which stifle breath;
> Its foul effluvia of death;
> Its catacombs of human lairs;
>
> Its seed of whirlwind, crops of tares;
> Its hells of woe, its devils' care;
> Its folly-shops of sham-faced wares;
> Its tolls, its panders and its snares . . .[14]

Personality types as well as physical and social caricatures emerged from this verse of last-ditch rural defense as it added severely and pointedly to the long list of urban evils.

Rural America, deviled by a host of problems, watched with sick heart as the frontier experience reversed itself in many areas, the wild returning to claim the cultivated and the civilized. Not only was her land given back but often her best sons, discouraged by the unfavorable social and economic contrast between town and country, defected to the urban side. Those who remained found this a bitter pill indeed; and in their poetry could be seen a bewilderment that all this should have happened in the America of Thomas Jefferson, that their virtuous agrarian birthright should have been sold so readily for a mess of pavement. It was hardly surprising that the city, which seemed to gain from rural loss at every turn, should have felt the brunt of pastoral resentment.

Yet it was not only the bitter farmer who reviled the town; poets in great number and of whatever origin and residence joined forces to compile a complaint against the city as thorough as it was lengthy, as shrewd in some cases as it was obvious in others. On the most obvious level the poets attacked the city for its unpleasant physical characteristics and for the evils that sprang directly from them. Hearing was the first of the senses to be assaulted, and the poet reacted strongly against the welter of noise which struck his ear: the "shrieking engines," the clatter of the "elevated," the "ribald song," which combined to compose a "vast unceasing din."[15] The effect of this cumulative complaint was to make "noisy" so common an epithet for "city" as practically to escape the attention.

Sight and sympathy were outraged by the prospect of "reeking slums" where "life grows fevered/With the lack of air and sun."[16] Inseparable byproducts of the overcrowded areas were disease, crime, want, and low morality. Most of the poets merely described these conditions, albeit in terms which clearly demonstrated the need for attention to these "festering" problems. Beyond description, the poet tended either to sentimentalize or to demand, rather mildly, some reform measures. Examples of both tendencies can be observed in these excerpts from a single volume:

In cities densely populated
The poor are apt to dwell,
And to describe their misery,
Is more than tongue can tell. . . .
We find no form of diction,
To adequately describe the poverty
Of a tenement-house eviction.

And thousands of such people,
In these rookeries die;
'Tis time we should pause,
And ask the reason why.
Why not condemn such places?
To exist they are a crime!
They make people old and delicate,
Who should be in their prime.[17]

To list the other poetical protests against the physical aspects of the city would be to catalogue all unpleasant or unsanitary matter—solid, liquid, or gaseous—which may have covered the ground, or polluted the water, or filled the air. One can be spared such a listing, but not without noting the intensity which characterized the reaction to such physical phenomena:

. . . the town
drench'd by a penetrant
wind-driven dust of rain,
fast-gluing to the walls soot-flakes
from grimy house-tops swept . . .
a viscous mire; compacting
the smoke-roof, propped by the towers,
spires, factory-chimneys, that threaten
under the mass enormous
to topple, and smother all life
with gloom and stifling dismay . . .
the dusk, wet, slime
of the hideous town.[18]

To the poet who wrote these lines, their impact was intended to stand for all that was repellent in our urban, industrial civilization; with less ambitious aims, other verse-writers seemed prone to revel in the ugliness which the urban scene presented to their sensitive view. The prevalence of this rather sordid school provoked one poet to chide his fellows for their addiction to this "curious cult of the Ugly" with its cheap effects produced by devotion to "Hovels where misery crouches in dull unmurmuring squalor," "black chimneyed factories," "Smut-faced factory girls . . . and the hot-lipp'd hiccoughing harlot."[19] Undoubtedly the temptation to produce an easy effect by playing up the unsavory glamour of the city was and is an appreciable one.

For the poet the city had a political and an economic identity as well as a physical one; and, although these aspects cannot be fully appreciated in this limited context, they should at least be acknowledged. Political reactions in the narrow sense—that is, comments on municipal government—were few, specific, and widely scattered both topically and geographically; the one poet who applied himself to this subject in a general way concluded that "The science of government, as applied/To cities" was "a failure."[20] In a broader sense, the political ammunition inherent in the basically economic reactions to the city was powerful and elaborate.

The core of the politico-economic protest at the end of the century rested with the inequitable distribution of wealth. Where, more obviously and more dramatically, could one observe the meeting of extremes than in the urban context?

> In a great, Christian city, died friendless, of hunger!
> Starved to death, where there's many a bright banquet hall!
> In a city of hospitals, died in a prison!
> Homeless died in a land that boasts free homes for all!
> In a city of millionaires, died without money![21]

One reads so frequently of this "want and misery/Amid the wealth and splendor of the city" that, although this theme spread far beyond the confines of the city setting, it is difficult not to

suspect that the seeds of economic resentment had been sown in asphalt and cobblestone.[22] Poetic reactions to this inequity ranged from that classic melodrama of the ill-shod and hungry newsboy with drawn face pressed against the steamy window, beyond which the wealthy sat warm and contented at the laden board, to outspoken tirades of hate addressed from poor to rich and haunting nightmares of conscience which plagued the millionaire's slumber.[23] Thus the city, as the home of the hopelessly poor, the conspicuously rich, and the aggravatingly foppish, served as a microcosm within which many a protest of larger significance was launched.

The meaning of the city to the American poet of this period cannot be fully appreciated, in some respects, without undertaking a full-scale discussion of contemporary political and economic issues, the temperance crusade, the status of women, immigration, and the theme of materialism. Yet the most remarkable aspect of this verse lies not in its contribution to the consideration of broader themes, but in the extent to which it provided a full portrait, rich and shrewd, of the urban personality and its environment. It was a portrait for the rogues' gallery, only negative and questionable features having been recorded; but it was a portrait which anticipated by decades, in its completeness as well as its perceptivity, the profile drawn by the urban sociologist.[24] In the discussion thus far, certain obvious traits have already been evinced: the city's heterogeneity, for example, its superficial character with "false front" and fashion-orientation. Besides these, there can be developed at least a dozen recognizable urban characteristics, all acknowledged by modern students of the city and all fully documented by the poets.

Poetic responses, of course, are not the same as clinical reports; one cannot expect the same detail from the bard as from the interviewer or statistician. In some cases the poetic freedom provided insights valuable beyond the laboratory atmosphere, in other cases the lack of detail robbed the portrait of its convincingness. The latter case prevailed when the poet took up his discussion of crime and delinquency, evils associated with the city as long as it has existed. Although the tendency to connect the words "crime" and "city" was as common among late nineteenth-century poets as it is among contemporary television script-writers, the annals of this putative crime wave were startlingly bare of detail. Except for a street fight or two ("De Dago cut me wid a knife") the poet kept his mysteries to himself, writing of "many a crime that is never told" or, even more vaguely, describing the city as a blossom "Where Vice and Crime conspire to fade the bloom."[25] Although the cry was generalized, it was insistent. It included the delinquent ("Young savages in city cellars reared"), and it culminated in a veritable 'clamor of crime" at all levels.[26] The crime of gambling was also noted, but this typically involved the pit and big board, rather than the dice and the punch board.

As does the prohibition campaigner, the poet also associated alcoholic overindulgence with an urban setting. One poem, entitled, "A City Incident," featured the "maniac shout . . . 'Fill the bowl!'" and ended with the child leading homeward the drunken father.[27] Another enthroned King Temperance on a rural dais while describing King Alcohol's city reign.[28] Whether the asso-

ciations with drink were pleasurable or not, and they usually were not, they were consistently identified as urban in setting.

Some evidence points to the identification of sexual deviation and promiscuity with the city, a connection the poet sought to establish by depicting a "writhing city" fraught with "dark and bestial sin."[29] Not only did the poet particularly_abhor the "red and beckoning light" of prostitution, but also the general bawdiness of attitude as portrayed by this "Red-faced" slut,

. . . her mouth all insult and lies . . .
With ribald mirth and words too vile to
    name,
A new Doll Tearsheet, glorying in her
    shame,
Armed with her Falstaff now she takes the
    town.
The flaring lights of alley-way saloons,
The reek of hideous gutters and black oaths
Of drunkenness from vice-infested dens,
Are to her senses what the silvery moon's
Chaste splendor is . . . to innocence.[30]

Secularism is another trait which sociologists ascribe to urbanites, and the poets seemed to agree here also. From the city they heard a welter of "sacrilegious babble" which showed this to be a place "where God is not."[31] True religion, as well as Christian ethics, had deserted the city, the poet found.[32] One spoke of a friend who had spent twenty years in the city: "We are pretty sure his soul, and we know his head, is grey."[33] Should Christ descend upon an American city, be it Brooklyn or Chicago, the poet prophesied another crucifixion.[34]

Not only was the city anti-religious, the poets felt, but also "anti-natural," as Lewis Mumford would say. One or two of them felt that the city man's overdependence on human control, his acceptance of artificiality, deserved drastic—if humorous—depiction. Complaining that the only sure sign of the arrival of spring in the city occurred when one's fashionable neighbor ("Saphronia") left the house without her furs, one poet went on to assert that the flowers in the park were no longer to be trusted as seasonal reminders since attendants made them bloom at the push of a button, turning them off at night.[35] Another claimed that the city-dweller needed specially developed varieties of trees and shrubs which would respond to life in small pots with wine instead of water for irrigation.[36] Natural beauty in the suburban and resort areas, many were quick to point out, had been blighted by urban commercial interests.[37] More serious, and more moving, were the poets who were made uneasy by the extent to which man-made mechanical devices had replaced natural ones. The complete dependence on such fallible media as the trolley and the elevated disturbed one poet; another condemned his own "Twentieth Century Home" because he had to reach it by trolley and then elevator.[38] In such ways did the poet make clear his accord with the sociologist who lists such urban characteristics as "artificiality" and "dependence on human control."

The idea of haste, or "time-consciousness," underlay a great deal of what was said about the city in meter. Most vividly it appeared in descriptions of living habits, such as this contemporary-seeming visit to "The Park Row Beanery":

With crash and smash and splash and slash
    the waiters sling the food
And sing and yell like merry hell, so's to be
    understood:
"Ham and!" "Draw one!" "Brown wheats!"
    "Pork n' Boston!"[39]

The degree to which the emphasis on speed had replaced the leisurely patterns admired by the poets was epitomized by the claim that a modern masculine deity, "hurry," had replaced the nine gentler female muses of old.[40] Rhyming "worry" with "hurry" the poets went on to agree with those who identify calculating and competitive characteristics with city life. Urbanites were depicted as "a curious canny folk" who "push and jostle and scheme and plot."[41] Their "artful wile" produced "snares" for a variety of unsuspecting victims.[42] More than by the canniness, the poets were oppressed by the "panting chase," the "mad conflict and unheeding crush" of the competitive strife which turned Broadway into a "mad river" where only the strong fish survived.[43]

The City's roar is rising from the street;
The old, bedraggled "types" are shuffling
    through the strife;
They plod and push, and elbow as they
    meet,
And glare and grin, and sadly call it
    "life."[44]

The "worry" which rhymed with "hurry" indicated more directly the accord of the verse-writer with social psychologists who define a city syndrome composed of insecurity, anxiety, and nervous enervation. Even to be near the city's rushing torrent, to sense its artificial impersonality, is to be robbed of peace and calm, these poets proposed. The drain of this life made people old before their time; once described a city friend, looking worried, harassed, and weak, who was then returned to strength, youth, and placidity by a removal to the country.[45] In the "tumult of the city," there was "neither rest nor peace," but a sort of mass anxiety which was summed up as the "agitations of innumerable souls."[46] With the hustle and bustle went a "shrug" of indifference; no one cared that his neighbor was racing nervously toward the end of his short, frantic life.[47]

It was this indifference, this threat to his own meaningful participation, which affected the poet most strongly; he responded subtly, elaborately, and in a manner which adumbrated most strikingly the observations of more scientific students of the city. These students tell us that urban life is characterized by social distance, by a preponderance of secondary relations, by a collectivistic rather than an individualistic frame of reference, and that these characteristics produce in the individual a sense of anonymity, often to a harmful extent. The poetry not only furnished evidence for such statements but also provided a reaction which is truly disturbing.

The idea of social distance, producing loneliness in crowded places, struck the poetic responsiveness to the paradoxical. Realizing that the city was not necessarily a warm and friendly place, for all its fire of activity, the poet pleaded for more satisfactory personal relationships:

Alone I walk in the peopled city,
Where each seems happy with his own;
O friends, I ask not for your pity—
I walk alone.[48]

He wrote of lonely bankers, lonely workers—all with plenty of people around them—and reminded his readers that it was the stranger "Alone in the City" with "no look of kind remembrance," and not the farmer, who was the isolated one.[49] The impact of this ironical solitude, of these secondary relationships, brought him to a reconsideration of values:

One of the million, that am I;
One of the million wondering why
And what it is, and if it pays,
This living in the city's ways—[50]

He pondered the impersonality of a New York hospital where people battled for life while external noises went on unheeding and uninterrupted; and sometimes he saw, in "the ceaseless lave /Of life and trade, the cities rave and jostle," the death of his own identity: "egotism's own grave/Upon the pave."[51]

The city as a "labyrinth of human ways/Where footpaths meet and cross, and meet no more" preoccupied the poet as he faced the problems of collective life.[52] The coldness of a life where no one knew his neighbor, the irony of lovers passing within feet of each other and then missing connection because of the crowds, the ease with which these same crowds could separate people who started out together—these were some of the manifestations of the city which impressed the poets with the seemingly unpredictable impersonality with which the city treated its citizens.[53] Plagued by such impressions, the poet reverted to a strange language: a "City without a face," he called it.[54] And what could this mean—city without a face? No face where there were thousands? It meant, answered the verse, the city was "jagged, formless"; it meant that the poet, his own sense of reality and identity threatened, was launching a counterattack, was attempting to take from the city those some qualities which he felt it had taken from him.

I know my Boston is a counterfeit,—
A frameless imitation, all bereft
Of living nearness, noise, and common
    speech . . .[55]

A city without noise? Certainly this was unreal. In a more sinister frame of mind he went further, calling the rush hour movement a "river flowing evermore/ Toward dim oblivion's ocean."[56]

The anonymity which the poet suffered at the hands of the city sometimes forced him into an eerie blending of the real and the unreal in framing his counterattack, plainly implying that the city itself did not exist. He coupled the "torrent of the living down Broadway" with the "myriad dead in unremembered graves" and pronounced, inscrutably, that "thousands tread/The City streets, who now are dead."[57] The occasion of hearing footsteps without seeing who made them, as one often does in the city, suggested further opportunities for blending the real and the unreal. One poet proclaimed that such sounds represented specters which raise themselves from the pavement at night to tell of foul deeds.[58] The decisive placing of the curse, the transfer of the individual's dilemma to the source, appeared as follows:

But of the City: there alone exists
True Beings and real Selves; Identities . . .
That come and go, and are not and yet are.
There also Powers . . . pass, abide, and
    brood,
And bring forth awful births.[59]

Thus was the bill of particulars laid down. Against the small voice of those who found items to praise in the relentless rise of the city was raised the deafening plaint of the urban detractors. Incited in some cases by a rural partisanship, they scored the town for its unhealthy ugliness, for its example of economic inequities, for its affinities with crime, drunkenness, sexual excesses, amorality, and artificiality. Oppressed by its killing pace, they accused it of encouraging a craftiness and overcompetitiveness which led in turn to insecurity, anxiety, and individual anonymity. With both aptitude and insistence, the poets constructed a myth of the city formidable in its detail and frightening in its intensity. Although not all of the city's critics intended to damn

it, the preponderance of negative reaction was sufficiently decisive that one may fairly summarize the content of this urban myth with lines from verses which foresaw the modern metropolis inhabited by literal satans or turned to desert and peopled only with moths.[60] Pealing the great knell of doom, the poets pointed out the city's materialistic greed and consigned it to everlasting damnation:

None shall put forth a hand and twist the
    brass
That galls the neck of Liberty, none dare
Avert the iron stigma of despair. . . .
The vengeance of the Lord has come to
    pass!
They fester in the cities who have scarred
The fact of earth until her skeleton
Is naked, and her breasts are dry and
    hard . . .[61]

Great is the City of a thousand streets,
The greatest city in the modern land.
Yet are the people blinded in their minds,
By teachings false, the vainest ways of life.
How many dream that money maketh rich.
How many judge that learning maketh
    wise.
How many cry: "Position giveth strength."
Yet it is false, and all the world is fooled.[62]

NOTes

° This subject will be discussed more fully in chapter 3 of Robert Harris Walker, *The Poet and the Guilded Age*, which is forthcoming from the Octagon Press.
1. In searching out poetic expressions of reactions to various social conditions the writer has perused some six thousand volumes of verse published between 1876 and 1905 which now form the Harris Collection of American Verse in the John Hay Library of Brown University. Both generalizations and specific citations are based on the survey of this collection, and it is believed that the coverage is sufficiently comprehensive to enable one to write with confidence of "the poet" in a collective sense. No attempt is being made here to appraise him individually on the basis of biography, aesthetic achievement, or popular esteem. The focus of the study is on the views expressed by the verse-writers as literate, articulate, and often unusually perceptive members of their contemporary community.

2. Walter M. Rogers, *Stray Leaves from a Larker's Log* (Boston, 1892), 27-28.

3. Madison J. Cawein, *Blooms of the Berry* (Louisville, 1887), 49. See also Paul L. Dunbar, *Lyrics of Lowly Life* (New York, 1896), 158, as well as lyrics throughout Cawein's collections.

4. Kate L. Wheeler, *Home Poems* (Nashua, N. H., 1897), 19-21; James H. Scott, *Poems*, 2nd ed., St. Louis, 1887), 414-17.

5. Amasa Alden, *Poems* (Wilton, Me., 1887), 34.

6. Sheldon S. Baker, *Marmondale and Other Poems* (New York, 1886), 167.

7. Belle C. Woodruff, *Collection of Wild Flowers* (Buffalo, 1894), 17.

8. See Mary M. Currier, *Among the Granite Hills* (Cambridge, Mass., 1894), 82-83; A. Fairhurst, *My Good Poems* (St. Louis, 1899), 160-65; Clara M. Tadlock, *Solomon Grinder's Christmas Eve and Other Poems* (Boston, 1885), 69-72, 106-109.

9. John W. Castelle, *Pedagogics Number One* (Chicago, 1900), 52-53; Sam Walter Foss, *Back Country Poems* (Boston, 1894), 27.

10. Cora M. Davis, *Immortelles* (New York, 1887), 113.

11. Palmer Cox, *Hans Von Pelter's Trip to Gotham* (New York, 1877).

12. James H. Morse, *Summer Haven Songs* (New York, 1886), 66.

13. Warren Boynton, *Poetry and Song, No. 2* (Rockford, Ill., 1878), 34-48.

14. Creedmore Fleenor, *In Passing Through* (Bowling Green, Ky., 1898), 61.

15. John E. Barrett, *Fugitives and Other Poems* (Buffalo, 1897), 93; Albert J. Edmunds, *Songs of Asia Sung in America: Together with Other Poems, 1800-1895* (Philadelphia, 1896), 32; A. R. Darrow, *Iphigenia and Other Poems* (Buffalo, 1888), 59; James B. Kenyon, *An Oaten Pipe* (New York, 1895), 122-24.

16. Walter Malone, *Songs of North and South* (Louisville, 1900), 40-43; Isabella H. Conant, *Field of Folk* (Boston, 1903), 48-51.

17. James McFarland, *Miscellaneous Poems* (New York, 1897), 17, 22.

18. William N. Guthrie, *Songs of American Destiny* (Cincinnati, 1900), 21.

19. Harry T. Peck, *Greystone and Porphyry* (New York, 1899), 46-62.

20. F. W. Schultz, *Course of Progress* (New York, 1892), 72.

21. Lu B. Cake, *Devil's Tea Table and Other Poems* (New York, 1898), 84.

22. D. J. Donahoe, *In Sheltered Ways* (Buffalo, 1895), 55.

23. Fanny B. Cook, *Fancy's Etchings* (San Francisco, 1892), 185; Don M. Lemon, *Ione and Other Poems* (New York, 1905), 376-78.

24. Guidance in the world of urban sociology has been obtained from summaries presented in the following current textbooks: Noel P. Gist and L. A. Halbert, *Urban Society* (New York, 1956), chap. 14; Rose Hum Lee, *The City* (Philadelphia, 1955), chap. 20; and James A. Quinn, *Urban Sociology* (New York, 1955), chap. 6. Readings collected by T. Lynn Smith and C. A. McMahan in *Sociology of Urban Life* (New York, 1951), chap. 23, were especially helpful, as were earlier treatments such as Robert E. Park, Ernest W. Burgess, and Roderick D. McKenzie, *The City* (Chicago, 1925), chap. 1; Niles Carpenter, *Sociology of City Life* (New York, 1931), chap. 6. For my purposes, the single most useful summary proved to be an article by Louis Wirth, "Urbanism as a Way of Life," *American Journal of Sociology* (Chicago), XLIV (July, 1938), 1-24. Helpful special approaches to the problem were found in Emory S. Bogardus, "Social Distance in the City," *ibid.*, XXXII (July, 1926), 40-46; Lewis Mumford, *Culture of Cities* (New York, 1938); David Riesman, *The Lonely Crowd* (New Haven, 1950).

25. George M. Major, *Lays of Chinatown and Other Verses* (New York, 1899), 23; Martha Remick, *Miscellaneous Poems* (2 vols., Malden, Mass., 1900), II, 141; Louis M. Elshemus, *Songs of Spring and Blossoms of Unrequited Love* (Buffalo, 1895), 20.

26. Malone, *Songs of North and South*, 40-43; Conant, *Field of Folk*, 48-51.

27. Belle Van Derveer, *Soul Waifs* (Buffalo, 1895), 94-96.

28. Ernest H. Crosby, *Broad-cast* (London, 1905), 93.

29. William Griffith, *Trialogues* (Kansas City, Mo., 1897), 6; Jacob Huff, *Songs of the Desert* (Williamsport, Pa., 1895), 57.

30. Remick, *Miscellaneous Poems*, II, 141; Madison J. Cawein, *Weeds by the Wall* (Louisville, 1901), 82.

31. Richard Le Gallienne, *English Poems* (2nd ed., New York, 1892), 102; Alfred J. Waterhouse, *Some Homely Little Songs* (San Francisco, 1899), 90.

32. Samuel V. Cole, *In Scipio's Gardens and Other Poems* (New York, 1901), 99-100; Lucius P. Hills, *Echoes* (Atlanta, 1892), 74-79.

33. John E. McCann and Ernest Jarrold, *Odds and Ends* (New York, 1891), 76.

34. William E. Davenport, *More Outcries from Brooklyn Hollow* (New York, n.d.), 9-11; John H. Hirt, *Second Booklet of Social Poems* (Great Falls, Mont., 1902), 44-45.

35. Edward S. Martin, *Poems and Verses* (New York, 1902), 41-43.

36. John K. Bangs, *Cobwebs from a Library Corner* (New York, 1899), 61.

37. *History of Coney Island in Rhyme* (New York, 1878); J. P. Sweet, *Day on Coney Island* (New York, 1880), 7-16.

38. James B. Elmore, *Lover in Cuba and Poems* (Alamo, Ind., 1901), 132-24; Eudorus C. Kenney, *Some More Thusettes* (Cortland, N. Y., 1905), 115-16.

39. John L. Heaton, *Quilting Bee and Other Rhymes* (New York, 1896), 137-38.

40. Edward F. Hayward, *Willoughby* (Boston, 1879), 3.

41. H. G. Watres, *Cobwebs* (Boston, 1886), 11;

Waterhouse, *Some Homely Little Songs*, 89.
42. George W. Nims, *Declining Village: or, My Old New England Home* (Boston, 1905), 22.
43. Edward D. Walker, *Poems* (New York, 1893), 16; George P. Emswiler, *Poems and Sketches* (Richmond, Ind., 1897), 42; Joe Kerr, *Jests, Jingles, and Jottings* (New York, 1893), 22.
44. Robert Bridges, *Bramble Brae* (New York, 1902), 84.
45. Clinton Collins, *Poems, Sketches* (Cincinnati, 1890), 37.
46. Denis A. McCarthy, *Round of Rimes* (Boston, 1900), 34; James E. Nesmith, *Monadnoc and Other Sketches in Verse* (Cambridge, Mass., 1888), 52.
47. May L. Gaylord, *Heart Echoes* (New York, 1895), 170.
48. O. M. Conover, *Via Solitaria: Reconciliation* (Madison, 1882), 5.
49. Laura Minkler, *Songs in the Night* (Burlington, Ia., 1891), 22.
50. Thomas W. Hall, *When Love Laughs* (New York, 1898), 12.
51. Edward A. Blount, *Poems* (Cincinnati, 1897), 28; Francis Brooks, *Poems of Francis Brooks* (Chicago, 1898), 221.
52. Lillian B. Fearing, *In the City by the Lake* (Chicago, 1892), 15.
53. Robert Grant, *Little Gods-on-wheels: or Society in Our Modern Athens* (2nd ed., Cambridge, Mass., 1879), 28; Eben J. Loomis, *Sunset Idyl and Other Poems* (Cambridge, Mass., 1903), 92-93; Paul E. More, *Great Refusal: Being Letters of a Dreamer in Gotham* (New York, 1894), 19-36.
54. Ernest H. Crosby, *Swords and Plowshares* (New York, 1902), 60.
55. Edwin A. Robinson, *Torrent and the Night Before* (Gardiner, Mo., 1896), 33-34.
56. William L. Chittenden, *Ranch Verses* (New York, 1898), 172.
57. Richard Hovey, in Bliss Carman and Hovey, *Last Songs from Vagabondia* (Boston, 1900), 52; William E. Davenport, *Visions of the City* (New York, 1884), 41.
58. Charles De Kay, *Hesperus and Other Poems* (New York, 1880), 78-80.
59. Davenport, *Visions of the City*, 9.
60. *Tour of Prince Eblis: His Rounds of Society, Church, and State* (Chicago, 1879), 11; Richard Le Gallienne, *Robert Louis Stevenson—An Elegy and Other Poems* (Boston, 1895), 9-10.
61. George C. Lodge, *Song of the Wave and Other Poems* (New York, 1898), 114.
62. William E. Davenport, *Perpetual Fire* (Brooklyn, 1886), 55.

Urbanism and American Democracy*

FRANCIS E. ROURKE

"The United States," writes Richard Hofstadter in his *Age of Reform,* "was born in the country and has moved to the city. From the beginning its political values and ideas were of necessity shaped by country life." Few could disagree with this appraisal. At the time of the first census in 1790, more than nine out of ten Americans lived in rural territory, and as late as 1860 the proportion of the population living outside of cities remained well over 75 per cent.

Thus, from the Revolution to the Civil War, agrarian dominance was a major fact of life in American politics. This was a time when rural ascendancy rested on the solid basis of numerical superiority rather than upon the legislative malapportionment and gerrymandering that have since served to shore up agrarian power against the steady erosion of population in rural areas.

What was most striking about this early system of domination by agrarian

From *Ethics*, LXXIV (July 1964), pp. 255-68. Reprinted by permission of The University of Chicago Press. Francis E. Rourke is Professor of Political Science at The Johns Hopkins University.

interests was the uncontested philosophical justification it received at the hands of Jefferson and those who followed in his wake. No such fervent ideological support was to crown the power of either of the other major groups who were in time to lay claim to supremacy in American politics—the business elite which came into prominence in the period following the Civil War, or the popular coalition which has sustained the broad outlines of the welfare state since the presidency of Franklin Roosevelt. In the days of agrarian supremacy, political power and political ideology were linked together in a neat pattern of harmony, while since that time they have often been poles apart.

Easily the most familiar protagonist of this system of agrarian democracy was Thomas Jefferson. As Griswold points out: "No one believed so implicitly as he in a causal connection between the occupation of farming and the political system of democracy, and no one, before or since his time, has given that belief a greater impetus among his countrymen."[1] Of course the doctrine of agrarian superiority which Jefferson espoused—"those who labor in the earth are the chosen people of God" —is a very old theme in Western thought. It was widely prevalent in both Greek and Roman culture, from Hesiod to Horace, and this classical view was adopted and advanced in subsequent European literature, drawing on Christian as well as pagan sources to support the comparison it drew between the virtue and vitality of the countryside and the vices and decay of urban society.

Much of this pastoral tradition stresses the physical, economic, and moral advantages of agricultural life; but throughout it there also runs the persistent theme that farming makes for better citizens as well as healthier, nobler, and more affluent men. Western intellectual history provided ample precedent for Jefferson's view that the farmer was not only the mainstay of the economy and the pillar of civil rectitude, but the backbone of the state as well: "The proportion which the aggregate of the other classes of citizens bears in any State to that of its husbandmen, is the proportion of its unsound to its healthy parts."

With the steady advance of urbanization in American society, the passages in Jefferson which retain the most telling impact today are those in which he takes specific note of what he considers to be the ill effects of cities upon the healthy functioning of a democratic society. For it was Jefferson who set the style for the treatment the city was to receive in subsequent political thought. Few statements in American political doctrine are as celebrated as his assertion that "the mobs of great cities add just so much to the support of pure government as sores do to the strength of the human body." But the view he put forward in a letter to Benjamin Rush was even more extreme. There he argued that a recent outbreak of yellow fever in coastal cities, however unfortunate its consequences in terms of human suffering, might at least have the advantage of discouraging the establishment of large urban centers in this country. For such cities, Jefferson declared, are more "pestilential" than yellow fever "to the morals, the health and the liberties of man."[2]

It has been suggested—most recently by Morton and Lucia White in their study of attitudes toward the city in American intellectual history—that Jefferson recanted these antiurban sentiments after he became president.[3] If so, this retraction was a grudging one, based largely on Jefferson's belated recognition during the Napoleonic Wars that the political independence of this country might ultimately be lost if it remained completely dependent upon the industrial cities of Europe for manufactured goods. Nor was it a permanent conversion, since Jefferson returned to his agrarian outlook in the later years of his life. Certainly there is little in Jefferson's career to support the Whites' description of him as "a great intellectual defender" of the American city.

But it is interesting to note that for a time at least the harsh realities of international politics forced Jefferson to accept some measure of urbanization, even though he regarded this development as altogether undesirable for a democratic society from a purely domestic point of view. For the individual as opposed to the state, Jefferson never lost his conviction that the highest degree of political independence rested upon the economic security provided by ownership of a small farm. But as has often been true in American history, when the requirements of foreign policy required a modification of domestic political doctrine, this modification was quickly forthcoming. The needs of national security soon overcame even Jefferson's antipathy for cities. As he himself put it in a letter to DuPont: "What is practicable must often control what is pure theory."

Jefferson's views on the negative impact of urbanization were not disputed by any of the more influential of his contemporaries. James Madison, for example, faithfully echoed the same sentiment in his own writings. "The life of the husbandman is pre-eminently suited to the comfort and happiness of the individual," he wrote. "The extremes both of want and of waste have other abodes. 'Tis not the country that peoples either the Bridewells or the Bedlams. These mansions of wretchedness are tenanted from the distresses and vices of overgrown cities."

More surprising, perhaps, than the support Jefferson received from a fellow Virginian planter like Madison was the fact that there was no dissent from his adverse judgment regarding cities on the part of leading Federalists of the day. For in principle at least these Federalists were committed to a course of economic development, the encouragement of manufacturing and commerce, which would inevitably promote the growth of urban centers. Alexander Hamilton nowhere attempted to refute the Jeffersonian point of view, however much his "report on manufactures" may have contributed to urbanization, and John Adams affirmed his belief that "agriculture is the most essential interest of America."[4]

Later on, Federalists like Chancellor Kent were even to use Jefferson's attacks on cities to buttress their own aristocratic stand against eliminating suffrage restrictions. In New York, for example, the proposal to extend the franchise stirred prolonged and bitter controversy at the state constitutional convention in 1821, and on that occasion leading Federalist spokesmen sounded warnings against the city that were thoroughly Jeffersonian in tenor:

Elisha Williams, the young Van Buren's brilliant adversary in the courts of Columbia County and chief figure in the haughty Columbia Junto, explicitly dared the Democratic delegates to confront the reasoning of their great god Jefferson on the moral influence of cities. Would Jefferson's disciples spread "the contents of those [urban] sores through the whole political body" and so expose the yeoman interest to the will of "the ring streaked and speckled population of our large towns and cities, comprising people of every kindred and tongue?" "These cities," Williams warned, "are filled with men too rich, or too poor to fraternize with the yeomen of the country." With Kent, he placed the democratic menace in the city and the future.[5]

Not the least of the paradoxical aspects of Jefferson's impact on American politics is thus the fact that his prejudice against cities ultimately became a weapon in the hands of his bitterest political opponents.

THE JEFFERSONIAN HERITAGE

Since Jefferson's antiurban views were in accord with traditional political doctrine and were expressed at a time when the overwhelming majority of all Americans lived outside of cities, these sentiments certainly did not expose him to any substantial political risk. Quite to the contrary, Jefferson's agrarian posture may be said to have served him quite well from the point of view of political advantage. Much more remarkable was the way in which this Jeffersonian attitude was to persist down through American history even into the day when the great majority of Americans had come to live in an urban environment. While Jefferson's agrarian point of view was neither risky nor original, it proved to be an extraordinarily durable part of the American political tradition.

When the Jacksonian Democrats came to power, their political base rested on the support of the labor vote in the eastern cities as well as the farmers of the West. Antagonism toward the "money power" provided the bond of unity between these two divergent

groups. And yet, Jefferson's dislike of cities continued to weave its spell over large sections of the Jacksonian movement, in part perhaps because the hated banking interests were themselves located in the cities. In his study of the Jackson era, Schlesinger points out that Jackson's followers were far from happy over the dependence of their party upon the votes it received in urban areas:

The situation in New York, where the country regularly voted Whig and the city Democratic, very much worried the *Democratic Review*, a fairly pious organ of Jeffersonianism. "As a general rule," the *Review* observed in some perplexity, we are free to confess that we prefer the suffrages of the country to those of the city. . . . The farmer is naturally a Democrat—the citizen may be so, but it is in spite of many obstacles.[6]

Other Jacksonian Democrats attempted to relieve their anxiety over the party's urban support by arguing that great cities need not necessarily be as "great sores" on the American body politic as Jefferson had originally believed.

In the decades immediately preceding the Civil War the Jeffersonian antagonism toward the city was clearly discernible in the arguments put forward by the southern apologists for slavery. This was one of the few occasions in which the proslavery argument had occasion to lean upon Jefferson's support, since Calhoun, Fitzhugh, and the other writers prominent in defense of the southern cause generally found it necessary to spend much of their time refuting Jeffersonian heresies, including the notion of the inherent equality of all mankind as expounded in the Declaration of Independence. But the defense of slavery was based in large measure on the proposition that the condition of the slave on a southern plantation was often a good deal better than the life of the wage earner in northern and European cities. And in this connection southern criticism of the odious characteristics of industrial cities bore a close resemblance to Jefferson's strictures against an urban civilization. "Large cities," wrote George Fitzhugh, "are great curses, because they impoverish a world to enrich a neighborhood."[7]

Since the Civil War hostility toward the city has also found repeated expression in the various movements of political protest which have agitated rural America, from the Grangers in the 1870's to the Farmers' Holiday Association in more recent times. Much of this antiurban sentiment is implicit rather than explicit in the literature of agrarian revolt. It is reflected in the fulsome praise lavished upon the occupation of husbandry, in dogmatic assertions regarding the indispensable role which agriculture plays in the national economy, or in persistent tirades against banking and other urban commercial interests disliked by farmers. But it is praise of agriculture which is at the center of attention rather than overt attacks on the city.

William Jennings Bryan perhaps symbolized more strikingly than any other figure the spirit of agrarian protest in American politics, and Bryan's preference for the country over the city was never left in doubt. It received its most vivid expression in his Cross of Gold speech at the 1896 Democratic national convention: "The great cities rest upon our broad and fertile prairies," said Bryan in his fervent peroration. "Burn down your cities, and leave our farms, and your cities will spring up again as if by magic; but destroy our farms and the grass will grow in the streets of every city in the country." But as a presidential candidate bidding for support

in urban as well as rural constituencies, Bryan could ill afford to reject the city altogether. In setting forth to begin the presidential campaign of 1896 in New York City, he spoke of his trip as one he was taking into the "enemy's country," but this was an area, he hastened to add, "we hope to be our country before this campaign is over."[8] Politicians like Bryan with ambitions which depended for their fulfilment upon urban as well as farm support were compelled to avoid the cruder kinds of assault upon the city in which a purely rural politician could indulge. Some of the lesser Populists were under no such inhibitions.

In its manifestations in the early part of this century, the antagonism toward cities was reinforced by two interdependent developments which exercised a major influence upon the course of American politics, the nativist movement and the drive for national prohibition. Early nativist sentiment was, as John Higham has shown in his Strangers in the Land, largely an urban rather than a rural phenomenon. The hostility toward immigrants was initially strongest in the areas where native Americans most frequently rubbed elbows with newcomers from other countries—in the great cities of the East. By the turn of the century, however, the antagonism toward the foreign-born had come to be centered in rural areas, where it blended with and helped to harden the historic agrarian prejudice against the city. The "foreign" character of American cities became one of their major liabilities in rural America—the region most aroused by the wave of nativist sentiment which swept the country in the years following World War I. Speaking of the role of the Ku Klux Klan during this period, Higham writes:

"Significantly, the Klan's home was not in the great cities. Its strength came chiefly from the towns, from the villages, and from the ordinarily tranquil countryside."

The prohibition movement was also predominantly rural in its origins, and like nativism served to sharpen hostility toward cities. The city saloon was in fact the bête noire of the temperance crusade, and the attack upon it was an effort at political as well as moral reform, since the saloon was regarded as the headquarters of, and the sustaining force behind, the system of boss rule in cities. "At the door of the saloon was laid the blame for political corruption. It was represented as the *sine qua non* of such political machines as Tammany Hall and the Cox Machine of Cincinnati, 'none of which could continue in existence for a day but for the liquor traffic.' "[9] The nativist movement likewise had the purification of city politics as a central goal in its efforts to restrict the influx of immigrants, since the support of the foreign-born was widely looked upon as a major prop upon which the power of the urban political machine rested.

The fusion between the traditional agrarian dislike of cities, nativism, and the prohibition movement came to white heat in the 1920's at both the Democratic national convention in 1924 and during the presidential campaign of 1928. In each case it was the presidential candidacy of Al Smith which triggered this reaction, since Smith was simultaneously a product of the Tammany political machine in New York City, a descendant of urban Catholic immigrants, and a "wet." It would be difficult to conceive of a less prepossessing set of qualifications from the standpoint of rural America, and the campaign against Smith became at times a crusade against the city and all that it had traditionally symbolized in American politics. Witness the viewpoint of even a liberal Republican like William Allen White: "I make no claim . . . that Smith is a Tammany plug-ugly. . . . But the Tammany system goes on to-day, as it went on 100 years ago, and, indeed, as it will go on in our American cities unless Governor Smith and the sinister forces behind him are overthrown. Tammany is indeed Tammany, and Smith is its Major Prophet."[10]

Walter Lippmann, himself a Smith supporter, explained the resistance to his candidate in these terms: "Quite apart even from the severe opposition of the prohibitionists, the objection to Tammany, the sectional objection to New York, there is an opposition to Smith which is as authentic, and, it seems to me, as poignant as his support. It is inspired by the feeling that the clamorous life of the city should not be acknowledged as the American ideal. . . . The cities exist, but they are still felt to be alien, and in this uncertainty as to what the cities might yield up, men turn to the old scenes from which the leaders they have always trusted have come."[11] And in the wake of Smith's defeat, interpretations of the 1928 election echoed the same theme. An editorial in one midwestern newspaper proclaimed that "America is not yet dominated by its great cities. Control of its destinies still remains in the smaller communities and rural regions, with their traditional conservatism and solid virtues. . . . Main Street is still the principal thoroughfare of the nation."[12]

While the agrarian prejudice against cities has thus been a continuous theme in American politics since pre-Revolutionary days, the precise nature of the danger which urbanism represents to the rural mind has varied considerably over time. During some periods it has been the propertied classes in cities—the merchants, the shippers, and the bankers—whose activities helped mold rural resentment of cities. On other occasions, and particularly in recent times, it has been the submerged proletariat which has been looked upon as the chief source of danger from urban areas—the industrial hirelings, the newly arrived immigrants, the trade union members, and, in today's metropolitan city, the non-white population.

At different times, the city has thus been regarded as a center of entrenched plutocracy and as a hotbed of radical doctrines subversive of the free-enterprise system, and it has been attacked with equal vehemence by opponents of both capitalism and socialism. Perhaps there is some reconciliation of this seeming contradiction in the fact that the farmer has, depending upon his economic circumstances, tended to regard himself both as a member of the "toiling masses" and as an entrepreneur, and these varying conceptions of the agricultural role in the economy are actually embodied in two distinct national farm organizations, the Farmer's Union and the Farm Bureau Federation.

The tendency of the city to become an odious symbol in the dialogue of American politics found its most eloquent expression in the work of Josiah Strong. Strong argued that American civilization in the closing years of the nineteenth century was confronted by a variety of perils, including immigration, Romanism, intemperance, and socialism. But it was the city which Strong identified as the focal point of all these evils. In the city, he contended, "the

dangerous elements of our civilization are each multiplied and all concentered." With Strong as with other writers, the rejection of the city was—quite apart from considerations of religious and ethnic prejudice—a negative response to the industrialization which had spawned large urban centers. For it was industrialism which was regarded as the source of the worst features of urban life, especially the great extremes in wealth—"the rich are richer and the poor are poorer in the city than elsewhere"—which appeared to be so characteristic of an urban economy.[13]

THE IMPACT OF AGRARIAN THOUGHT

There is a sense in which the recurrent note of an antagonism toward the city in American political thought may be regarded as but another illustration of the lack of congruence between political doctrine and the actual course of political events. For even as the city was being treated with such persistent disdain in the formal literature of political philosophy during the nineteenth and early twentieth centuries, the general population was simultaneously voting with its feet for urban life—moving into the city in ever increasing numbers in response to economic and other incentives. The trend toward urbanization was certainly not reversed by the hostility shown the city in the American political tradition. Indeed much of this antagonism may rather be viewed as a peevish reaction against a development that could not be prevented.

And yet it cannot be assumed that the rural assault upon the city was altogether without practical effect. For while its influence cannot be precisely measured, the argument for agrarian superiority has certainly played a useful role in providing an ideological under-pinning for the prevailing pattern of underrepresentation of the urban population that has characterized the legislative process in this country at both the state and national levels of government for better than half a century. The identification of farming with democracy may not have prevented the movement of population from rural areas, but it could and did provide rural politicians with a convenient line of defense against the impact this loss of population might otherwise have had upon their own power.

The extent of this urban underrepresentation has been underscored in numerous studies of state legislative apportionment in the United States. To be sure, this inequity has slowly been modified in recent years as a result of the exodus of population from city to suburb that has occurred since World War II. In many parts of the country today it is the suburbs rather than the cities which are most grossly discriminated against in terms of legislative apportionment. The movement of population thus tended to bring representation of urban centers in state legislatures into much closer accord with their proportionate share of the population even before the decision of the Supreme Court in *Baker* v. *Carr,* which provided cities with a judicial remedy against the traditional pattern of discrimination to which they have been subject. However, a statistical analysis of state legislative representation published in 1961 was still able to conclude that "as of 1960, the average value of the vote in the big city was less than half the average value of the vote in the open country, so far as electing members of the state legislature is concerned."[14]

In the debates which have taken place across the country over the reapportionment problem, the Jeffersonian theme of urban inferiority has often been sounded by groups interested in preserving the disproportionate influence of rural areas in state legislatures. One of the oddities of this system of underrepresentation is the fact that it has very often been given impressive support by urban residents themselves. This was the case in Michigan in 1953, where urban as well as rural residents voted in favor of continuing a system of legislative apportionment highly disadvantageous to the cities. Of course the city is far from unified from a political point of view, and there are, in fact, important urban groups which have long had a vested interest in urban underrepresentation. Many of the salient economic interests centered in cities —business concerns and public utilities, for example, have strong grounds for preferring a system of legislative representation which discriminates against cities simply because the pressure for regulatory legislation adverse to their interests may reasonably be expected to originate in urban rather than rural constituencies. In many parts of the country these business interests have been as much the beneficiary of the prevailing practice of underrepresenting cities in state legislatures as the farmers themselves.

However, it is by no means inconceivable that there is an element of honest conviction as well as self-interest in the apparent willingness of urban dwellers to resign themselves to a system of legislative representation in which they are discriminated against politically. In some cases this tolerance may simply reflect the sentimental tie of many urban residents with the rural milieu in which they were raised and which they left in order to seek their fortune in the city. Hofstadter suggests that such an ambivalent orientation was characteristic of earlier periods of American history: "Throughout the nineteenth century hundreds upon hundreds of thousands of farm-born youths . . . sang the praises of agriculture but eschewed farming as a vocation and sought their careers in the towns and cities."[15]

The most confirmed of all supporters of agrarian dominance may thus be the city resident with ancestral roots in the country, just as some of the most ardent support today for the policy of preserving wilderness areas in their primitive simplicity may come from eastern urbanites, transplanted from their native habitat in the West to the alien pavements of New York. And in point of fact the agrarian vision of the city as an infamous creation has always received considerable support from the romantic fascination with nature that has been an enduring tradition in American life. The fact that the city has been so aesthetically unappealing to urban nature lovers has not been the least of the political disadvantages under which it has labored.

REFORMING THE CITY

At its root, the Jeffersonian point of view was characterized by a fundamental antipathy toward cities. If it had been possible, some of the more fervent agrarians would unquestionably have prevented the development of cities altogether, so destructive to democracy did they regard the city as a political force. And in point of fact a great deal of energy was actually expended on efforts to keep people on the farm, or to launch "back-to-the-farm" movements when periods of temporary urban distress gave such proposals hope of success. From Jefferson to Bryan, the note of overt hostility toward cities in agrarian thought is clear and unmistakable.

However, in the decades following the Civil War, a critique of the city began to emerge which was quite different in character from this Jeffersonian point of view. The source of this new criticism was the movement for urban reform which sprang up in the latter part of the nineteenth century and has remained a salient force in municipal politics down to the present time. As a group, the reformers were highly critical of the political development of cities as it was taking place in the Gilded Age. Indeed, if the movement had a text, it was Bryce's celebrated dictum in the *American Commonwealth* that the "government of cities is the one conspicuous failure of the United States." But the reformer's orientation was one of redemption rather than antagonism, the cities were to be saved, to be lifted up, and, hopefully, even to become showcases of American democracy.

The rise of the reform movement was in direct response to the widespread corruption and mismanagement which characterized municipal government in the post-Civil War period. All of Jefferson's worst forebodings regarding the evil effects which cities would eventually have upon American democracy seemed amply justified by the exposures of the Tweed Ring in New York and the other scandals which plagued municipal governments in the nineteenth and early part of the twentieth centuries. As a matter of fact it would have been much easier for Jefferson to obtain evidence to support his condemnation of cities in the decades following the Civil War than it was during his own life time, when American cities were on the whole comparatively well governed.

The typical urban reformer did not, however, share Jefferson's pessimism regarding the city. From the reformer's point of view, there was no necessary reason why cities should have fallen to so low an estate. Frederic Howe, for example, saw cities as having great potential for improving American life. "Here life is full and eager," he wrote. "Here the industrial issues, that are fast becoming dominant in political life, will first be worked out. In the city democracy is organizing. It is becoming conscious of its powers. And as time goes on, these powers will be exercised to an increasing extent for the amelioration of those conditions that modern industrial life has created."[16] The reform creed was thus resolutely optimistic in its conviction that cities could be saved, and energetic in its pursuit of the means by which this salvation could be secured.

Within the reform movement there was widespread disagreement as to why cities had fallen upon such evil days. Some placed responsibility for municipal misgovernment upon the rapid growth of cities in the United States, and the great temptation to dishonesty that was generated by the need to develop a complex system of public works and services in urban areas within a very short space of time. Others traced the ills of urban life to the swelling tide of immigration from abroad in the decades following the Civil War and the ease with which the foreign-born population allowed itself to be exploited by corrupt political machines. And there was a strong tendency to explain the problems of cities as stemming from the failure to develop either forms of

government suitable for urban areas, or a tradition of administrative expertise in the handling of municipal affairs.

But there was also a deep conviction that the corruption of urban politics reflected a very fundamental malaise in American life, the growth of a commercial spirit and a weakening in the moral fiber of the population that was endemic in society and the economy as well as government. "The boss is not a political, he is an American institution," wrote Lincoln Steffens, and this point of view was widely shared. What was needed from the reformer's perspective was a moral regeneration of American life—a "great awakening" which would cleanse and purify not only local but national politics as well, since the movement for urban reform was only part of a much larger reform effort directed at uplifting the tone of public life in every sector of the nation's business, including the practices of private institutions where they impinged on the public interest. Symbolic of this evangelical zeal for moral improvement was the fact that a number of Protestant clergymen associated themselves with the movement for municipal reform and took a prominent part in its activities. Like abolition before it, urban reform was a moral crusade.

Moreover, in its heyday, the boss system represented an effort to govern the city through the methods of politics alone. As a result, early efforts at reform tended to place almost exclusive emphasis upon the importance of competent administration to the successful functioning of city government. In reaction against the more discreditable features of machine politics, efforts were made to "depoliticize" city government and to augment the role of the impartial expert through civil service reform, the city manager plan, and other devices. Subject as it was to simultaneous influence by doctrines of moralism and scientific management, the movement for urban reform thus sought to make city government as clean as the church and as efficient as business.

At no time did reformers lose hope that substantial improvement could be effected in the government of American cities. A great deal of this optimism was based on their knowledge of the successful operation of European cities and their conviction that American municipalities could profitably be modeled after their European counterparts. *Century Magazine* stated its belief that "we can hope for no municipal reform which shall be radical and lasting till we change our leadership to the European models." "In a score of different directions," wrote Josiah Quincy while serving as mayor of Boston, "the interests of the average citizen are better and more fully cared for, his wants more fully met, in the great city of Europe than in that of America." While recognizing the difficulty of transplanting institutions from one country to another, Richard T. Ely nevertheless argued that "what is good for Berlin is likely to be good for New York, and what answers the needs of Paris will be likely to supply a want in Chicago."[17] But there was often some discomfort attached to unfavorable comparisons of American cities with Continental cities which were political subdivisions of regimes Americans looked upon as reactionary or despotic. English cities were, therefore, the object of more unqualified admiration.

Certainly there was no doubt in the reform mind regarding the urgency of doing something to elevate urban politics, lest the corrupt city eventually corrupt the nation. Elihu Root, for example, warned his Republican colleagues that the malodorous GOP organization in Philadelphia was a source of infection in their party that could not be localized. "It is my profound conviction," he declared, "that a determined effort is necessary to save national parties from the demoralization inevitably consequent upon municipal spoliation, and, as a Republican, zealous for the welfare and reputation of my party, I advocate the foundation of a non-partisan civil movement." Unless the reform of urban politics is successful, Josiah Strong asserted, "the boss will certainly rule the city when the city rules the nation," and Strong quoted Wendell Phillips as prophesying that "the time will come when our cities will strain our institutions as slavery never did."[18]

As noted earlier, the reform perspective differed sharply from the traditional agrarian outlook inasmuch as it sought to face and solve the problems presented by the city rather than turning away in a hostile rejection of the trend toward urbanization. But it should also be remembered that much of the reform argument for the city was essentially apologetic or defensive in tone. It was conceded that the city had fallen to a very low estate politically, and the claim was simply made that the spirit and practice of urban government could —with effort—be improved. Moreover, many of the reformers were gifted publicists, and their exposures of graft and corruption in urban government, while motivated by the desire to eliminate these conditions, had also the effect of reinforcing the rural image of the city as an iniquitous environment in which the ideals of American democracy were being betrayed. In essence the reform defense of cities was based on their potentialities, not their achievements.

URBANISM AND AMERICAN DEMOCRACY

Insofar as its political reputation is concerned, the city was thus only slightly better served by reformers sympathetic to it than it was by the agrarians who looked upon it as the invariable source of political corruption. And even today, the city has still to find its philosophical protagonist, at least in the area of political thought. This is true in spite of the fact that there is an impressive amount of evidence which points to the conclusion that it is with urban America that the flowering of democracy in this country can be most clearly identified. The place of the city in the American experience has in fact been much more honorific than its position in American thought.

From a historical perspective, Arthur Schlesinger points out that it was the cities of the East which led the way in the movement for national independence which culminated in the American revolution. "Throughout the decade of controversy the seaports set the pace of resistance, supplying most of the militant leaders, conducting turbulent demonstrations at every crisis, and mobilizing farmer support when possible." In a similar vein he underlies the prominent role played by the cities in the struggle to strengthen democracy once it had been established in this country: "The first great victory for freedom of press was won by a Philadelphia lawyer defending a New York editor. . . . Faced by interstate trade restrictions, stay laws and growing social turmoil, the urban business and creditor classes feared for their future welfare and the

sanctity of property rights. The framing and ratification of the Constitution represented in considerable degree their triumph over the debtor groups and small farmers of the interior."[19]

Recent research in the general area of political behavior has also tended to refute the assumption that there is any necessary antipathy between the growth of cities and the vitality of the democratic process. In terms of some of the more obvious yardsticks that might be used to measure commitment to the norms of democracy, the urban citizen very often shows up much better than his rural counterpart. This is true, for example, with respect to two of the central attributes of democratic citizenship, an acceptance of the right of minorities to dissent from majority opinion, and an interest in the affairs of government as evidenced by participation in elections.

In a landmark study of civil liberties in the United States published in 1954, Samuel Stouffer found that rural residents were uniformly less tolerant of deviant minorities than urbanites. This rural attitude was partially explainable in terms of the operation of factors other than place of residence, especially the lower level of education which prevails in the countryside, but there nevertheless remained a residue of intolerance that was clearly associated with living in the country. As Stouffer put it:

Rural people in every region are less likely to be tolerant of non-conformists than city people, even when we compare urban and rural people with the same amount of schooling. There is something about life in a small community that makes it less hospitable to divergent opinions than is the case in our urban centers. In the anonymity of city life it is much easier for deviant behavior to flourish than in the goldfish bowl of a small community. In the large community there are sometimes so many gold-fish that nobody bothers to look at them. In the small town a lone exotic specimen can be viewed with careful critical, and occasionally devastating attention.[20]

In support of his findings, Stouffer also cites earlier studies of the degree of tolerance which prevails in various sectors of the community, including a Gallup poll conducted in 1940 which showed rural residents as being much less willing than urban dwellers to see a Catholic elected President, and a Roper study in 1947 which revealed that urbanites were far more tolerant than their rural brethren of that most unpopular minority in recent times—members of the Communist party.

Of course the fact that city people generally exhibit so much more tolerance of nonconformity than rural residents must simultaneously be weighed against the fact that cities have been quite receptive to the appeal of totalitarian ideologies, or at least have been the areas from which Communist and Fascist political groups have traditionally recruited most of their active members in this country. If the greatest threat to civil liberties is judged to come from the small ideological groups dedicated to their destruction, then the city may well be looked upon as a greater source of peril to minority rights than the country. But if the chief danger to civil liberties is rather seen as a weakening of commitment on the part of the mass of citizens to their preservation, then it is from rural America that the right to dissent has been chiefly endangered in modern times.

As far as political participation is concerned, Robert E. Lane concluded after a comprehensive survey of the literature of political behavior that residents of large cities have a much better record in this respect than citizens living in rural areas. He finds that residents of larger cities "participate in elections more than those in smaller cities" and that inhabitants of smaller cities are "more likely to vote than residents of rural areas." According to Lane, this difference in turnout mainly reflects the heightened degree of political tension in the more densely populated parts of the country. The group conflict engendered by class and ethnic rivalries in urban centers has the effect of stimulating political activity. But a variety of other factors also plays a role here, including the greater exposure of the urban citizen to stimuli from the mass media, which helps to sharpen political awareness and a sense of civic obligation in cities.

The extent to which citizens participate in politics is also related to their sense of political efficacy—the degree to which they believe such activity will have meaningful results. In this respect also Lane finds that urban citizens show up much better than rural residents: "those living in metropolitan centers have, in general, a higher sense of political efficacy than those in rural or small town areas. Perhaps because of the greater politicalization of the urbanites, their exposure to more political news and comment, their more salient class and ethnic cleavages, and their higher educational level, they are led to make politics a more significant part of their lives."[21]

It has also been suggested that urbanization has promoted the development of a two-party system in the United States, thus invigorating political discussion and activity in all parts of the country. The growth of urban population is, for example, sometimes credited with the fact that presidential elections are now closely contested in virtually all the states. However, the actual impact of urbanization upon party competition in this country is far from clear. While some studies of state politics show a correlation between the extent of urbanization and the strength of party competition, other investigations indicate that there may well be a negative relationship between the two phenomena. Certainly, there is no disputing the fact that many of the big cities in this country have become one-party enclaves.

But if such empirical evidence as exists does not always support the conclusion that democracy is inevitably strengthened by the advent of urbanization, it certainly stands in flat contradiction to the conventional agrarian assumption that rural areas are necessarily the backbone of a democratic society. Whether this evidence will seriously undermine the Jeffersonian mystique remains, however, to be seen. The force of tradition being what it is, Americans may, in the future as in the past, continue to look for the meaning of their democratic experience in the prairies rather than on the pavements. This tendency is as pronounced in the twentieth as it was in the nineteenth century: "Somewhere in our agricultural past there lie the roots of Americanism. What we. are in body and spirit is not to be discovered growing embryonically in any early city; its beginnings are to be found on the homestead or in the village, and only there."22

NOTES

° This study was undertaken under a grant from the Rockefeller Foundation, for which the author wishes to make grateful acknowledgment.
1. A. Whitney Griswold, Farming and Democracy (New York, 1948), p. 19. See also Richard Hofstadter, The Age of Reform (New York, 1960), pp. 23-36, and Henry Nash Smith, Virgin Land (New York, 1959), pp. 138-50.
2. The quotations from Jefferson are from the Writings of Thomas Jefferson (Washington, D.C., 1903), II, 229-30, and X, 173.
3. Morton and Lucia White, The Intellectual versus the City (Cambridge, Mass., 1962), pp. 17-19.
4. Madison's comment is found in The Writings of James Madison, ed. Gaillard Hunt (New York, 1906), VI, 96-98, while the statement by Adams appears in The Works of John Adams (Boston, 1852), VII, 47.
5. See Marvin Meyers, The Jacksonian Persuasion (New York, 1960), p. 240.
6. Arthur M. Schlesinger, Jr., The Age of Jackson (Boston, 1946), p. 310, n. 11.
7. George Fitzhugh, Sociology for the South (Richmond, Va., 1854), p. 139. However, there were southern writers who recognized that their region was greatly weakened by its failure to develop the commercial civilization associated with cities (see H. R. Helper, The Impending Crisis of the South [1860], esp. pp. 331-59). And Fitzhugh himself explicitly rejected the Jeffersonian prejudice in favor of an exclusively agricultural society. "Farming is the recreation of great men, the proper pursuit of dull men," he stated. "Let the ambitious South cultivate, not spurn the mechanic arts" (op. cit., pp. 156, 160).
8. See Paul W. Glad, The Trumpet Soundeth (Lincoln, Neb., 1960), p. 112. When the returns from the election of 1896 were in, they showed the core of Bryan's electoral strength as lying in the rural Midwest and mountain regions. However, there were some states, notably in New England, where Bryan received more support in urban than he did in rural areas (see William Diamond, "Urban and Rural Voting in 1896," American Historical Review, XLVI (January, 1941), 281-305.
9. Peter Odegard, Pressure Politics: The Story of the Anti-Saloon League (New York, 1928), p. 44.
10. As quoted in Edmund A. Moore, A Catholic Runs for President (New York, 1956), p. 133.
11. Walter Lippmann, Men of Destiny (New York, 1927), p. 8.
12. Quoted in Roy V. Peel and Thomas C. Donnelly, The 1928 Campaign: An Analysis (New York, 1931), p. 121.
13. See Josiah Strong, Our Country (New York, 1885), pp. 133, 130.
14. Paul T. David and Ralph Eisenberg, Devaluation of the Urban and Suburban Vote (Charlottesville, Va., 1961), p. 10.
15. Richard Hofstadter, Age of Reform (New York, 1960), pp. 31-32.
16. Frederick C. Howe, The City: The Hope of Democracy (New York, 1905), pp. 7-8.
17. "An Object Lesson in Municipal Government," Century Magazine, XXXIX (March, 1890), 792; Josiah Quincy, "The Development of American Cities," Arena, XVII (March, 1897), p. 529; and Richard T. Ely, "Model Towns," Christian Union, November 27, 1890.

18. See Robert Treat Paine, "The Elimination of National Party Designations from Municipal Ballots," in *Proceedings* of the Fifteenth Annual Meeting of the National Municipal League, 1909, p. 292; and Josiah Strong, *The Twentieth Century City* (New York, 1898), pp. 101-2.

19. Arthur M. Schlesinger, *Paths to the Present* (New York, 1949), pp. 213, 214, 215.

20. *Communism, Conformity, and Civil Liberties* (New York, 1955), p. 130.

21. Robert E. Lane, *Political Life* (Glencoe, Ill., 1959), pp. 265, 151-52.

22. Harry J. Carman and Rexford G. Tugwell, "The Significance of American Agricultural History," *Agricultural History*, XII (April, 1938), 100.

Some Varieties of American Urban Symbolism

ANSELM L. STRAUSS

Before we examine how particular populations have expressed themselves about American urbanization, it will be useful to scrutinize some persistent antitheses in American life. Those controversies—which amount to basic ambiguities of American values—involve the conflicts of sectionalism versus national centralization, of ruralism versus urbanism, of cosmopolitanism versus specialization, and of traditionalism versus modernism. Instead of discussing those antitheses and ambiguities abstractly, we shall relate them to the whole subject of American city symbolism. . . . By seeing first some of the larger issues of American valuation as they pertain to our cities, we shall better be able to understand the predominant urban symbolism of particular regions and populations.

A host of American cities, despite all differences in size, location, or composition, continually try to validate the claims that they are typical, authentic American communities. They balance what they are and what they feel they stand for against a tacitly accepted formula of American values and national purposes. But the facts and symbols of urban life become interchangeable in the course of argument, become confused in meeting the difficulties of expressing a city's hopes and achievements in a straightforward definitive fashion. They become confused, too, because of certain ambiguities in what may be assumed to be *the* American way of life.

This ambiguity of American urbanity and American values is significantly reflected in a lively contention over which city best deserves the title of "most American." The admirers of Chicago, New York, Kansas City, and Detroit, at least, claim honors for the city of their choice. Such claims are not new. As far back at least at 1851, a Baltimorian reassured a local audience that Baltimore "may be said to be an epitome of the nation itself";[1] and upon occasion critics of certain American values may point to

From Anselm L. Strauss, *Images of the American City* (New York: The Free Press, 1961), pp. 104-23, 270-71. Copyright © 1961 by the Free Press, a Corporation. Reprinted by permission of the publisher. Anselm L. Strauss is Professor of Sociology at the University of California, San Francisco, Medical Center.

one of these cities as a repulsive exemplar of those values. But a uniform, homogeneous American culture spread evenly throughout the nation would allow no city to claim more Americanness than was possessed by other cities; nor could any then base its claim upon a different set of values.

As long ago as 1891, de Rousiers described Chicago as the most American city, remarking that "It is here, indeed, that the American 'go ahead,' the idea of always going forward . . . attains its maximum intensity."[2] Some fifty-five years later, John Gunther writes that Chicago's "impact is overwhelmingly that of the United States, and it gives above all the sense that America and the Middle West are beating upon it from all sides."[3] In other words, he is stressing less its "striving" than its central position. A thousand miles away, the admirers of New York City stress rather different values. They assert that New York represents the nation at its most civilized and most creative; that it dominates the nation in every way; and that more different kinds of Americans, drawn from more regions, live in New York than in any other metropolis.[4] The proponents of Kansas City dwell upon still different aspects of American culture; George S. Perry who described that city for the *Saturday Evening Post*'s readers, saw it this way:

Kansas City is a kind of interior American crossroads and melting pot where the Southerner, the Northerner, the Easterner and the Westerner meet and become plain John American, with America unfolding . . . "in oceans of glory" in every direction. It got its start on the riches of Boston banks and Western lands and Northern furs. It is not only America's approximate geographical heart, but the center of gravity for her taste and emotion. The soap opera, movie or national magazine that doesn't "take" in Kansas City won't live long in the nation.[5]

Those who would give Detroit the honor of "most American," ignore the virtues of being of pioneer and dead-center America, and claim that Detroit best represents the spirit of modern twentieth-century America, exemplified in the city's superb system of mass production, in its drive, energy, purpose, and fusion of men and machines.[6] Pittsburgh's admirers claim similar industrial virtues for their city.[7] Indeed, a city need not even be among the largest to claim for itself, or to be proclaimed, the most typical of America. For instance:

It is a truism to say that Tulsa is the most American of American cities. All the forces that have gone into the making of a Republic have been intensified there. The successive stages through which the country as a whole has passed during three hundred years—Indian occupation, ranching, pioneering, industrial development . . . have been telescoped within the single lifetime of some of the older Tulsans. The result has been the quintessence of Americanism—its violence and strength, its buoyant optimism, its uncalculating generosity, its bumptious independence.[8]

The argument that one city best typifies America is couched in a standardized "logical" form: from a number of desirable attributes, certain ones are selected for emphasis while the remainder are ignored; and it is assumed or asserted that these selected attributes are possessed more abundantly by the admired city. In this way, many facets of American life are overlooked or given secondary status. The argument does not turn upon fact but upon value. Thus, if one values sheer quantity, then New York has most of everything; if one extolls the Midwest as the geographic heart of America and as the possessor of the most widespread and average national values, then he will deny priority to New York. In making such evaluations of their cities, Americans assess the nation's cultural assets and identify themselves with its history and destiny. When they represent a city as most American, they are conceiving it not only as unique and matchless but as the symbolic representative of esteemed national values.

Such great distinction can be claimed for few American cities; hence the citizens of the remaining urban centers must be content with a lesser assertion: namely, that their particular city represents at least one—and probably more —important aspects of American life. Thus, Iowa cities are conceived of as good places to live in because they appear to be friendly, peaceful, prosperous agricultural towns; and Fort Worth, Texas, surrounded by cattlemen's country, epitomizes the culture of that region. Such cities are parts of many Americas. The country is vast, its aspects staggeringly varied. Cities need not compete to share the nation's glory, they have only to point to those of their features wherein they typify some aspect, or aspects, of the entire American way of life.

Yet these aspects are not entirely congruent, in fact or in value. One of the most persistent clashes of value on the American scene has long been embodied in the sentimental preference of a rural existence to a thoroughly urban one. When Jefferson spoke of the danger of an American metropolitanism fated perhaps to destroy the sturdy virtues of a predominantly agricultural society, he was but expressing a dicotomy in American thought that persists to this day. Despite the continuous trend toward urbanization, our rural heritage remains potent, entering into American thought and action in increasingly subtle ways.

Eighteenth-century seaboard agriculture was not what farming became on the prairie a century later, nor what it is today in an era of large-scale mechanization. The men who worked the American soil and the life-styles that they evolved have varied greatly in place and time. Yet an American mythology grew up by which it was maintained that agricultural pursuits necessarily bred a certain kind of man. This agrarian mythology is and was a complex set of beliefs consisting of many elements, some of which developed from the several kinds of frontier conditions and others of which evolved after the Civil War in opposition to the dreadful urban conditions. The spirit of this agrarian ideology can be suggested by the following few sentences.

Rural life is slow and unhurried. Men lead natural, rich lives. People are friendly and their relationships are informal, yet orderly. The agricultural population is homogeneous in custom and culture, if not in racial stock. The round of existence is stable and the community is religious, moral, honest. Men are, thus, not motivated by purely individualistic impulses. If all farmers do not love one another, at least they understand each other and do not manipulate and exploit each other as do city dwellers. The very physical surroundings are healthy, home-like, restful, not dense with population. Not the least: the rural man is a sturdy democrat, his convictions nourished by his contact with nature itself and with the equalitarian discussion held around the crackerbarrel and in the meeting house.[9]

These conceptions are linked by affect rather than by logic. They evolved under considerably different historical circumstances, some during the development of the New England township, some when the prairie was settled, others while western farmers were castigating the railroad kings, and yet others at a time when rural migrants to cities became demoralized by conditions there. Although the country-city dichotomy has been with us for many generations, the content of the argument on either side has varied from decade to decade—as both cities and countrysides became transformed. Ideas die hard: in the formation of our rural mythology, old ideas accrued to new ones instead of disappearing entirely, despite their incongruence with fact and with each other. Probably no single rural community has ever stressed equally all elements of the entire ideological complex, for its very ambiguity allows its use as an effective resource. The town can use it as well as the village; and the small city can boast of home-like surroundings and friendly atmosphere, in an invidious contrast with the larger urban centers.

Sizeable cities can also be designated as outright embodiments of rural values—as when the citizens of Des Moines aver direct kinship with soil and farm; and in so doing, they may symbolically act in ways more farmlike than the equally business oriented farmer. The residents of most cities, perhaps, signify their association with sentimental rurality more obliquely, not always recognizing the nature of that feeling of kinship. Cities are referred to by their residents as "The City of Flowers," "The City of Trees," "The City of Homes." They draw upon the rich stock of rural imagery without directly stating their debt. Large cities as they grow to great size abandon such nicknames, which no longer seem to represent what the city has become, but may emphasize in cu-

riously subtle ways that their styles of urban life also partake of America's revered earlier heritage. Chicago—once called "The City of Gardens"—still boasts that it is the city of the prairie, and lays claim to a characteristic friendliness and informality that mark it off from, say, New York or Boston. (As George Perry says, "Chicago is a thousand times more relaxed, less 'mannered' than New York.")[10]

Like the smaller towns, the larger cities may stress one or more of the varied rural themes, thereby cashing in on a much wider ideological complex. The very statement that one's city is a "city of gardens" (albeit gardening is a far cry from farming), arouses connotations smacking of outdoor life, suggestions of qualities bred in close contact with the soil, of urbanities living a life of relaxation rather than of frantic pursuit of excessive monetary gain. The visitor to a city sometimes remarks, also, upon certain paradoxes because, while he notices that the place is marked only by a limited number of rural characteristics, he feels that these are among its important features. What he is really puzzling over is that all rural qualities are supposed to hang together; whereas in this particular city, surprisingly enough, they do not. The perception of such paradoxes is furthered by any obvious juxtaposition of rural and urban characteristics: a city nestled among beautiful mountains but marked by a high rate of crime and by horrendous slums, or a large urban center characterized by a noticeably leisured pace of life.[11] Thus about Portland, Oregon, Richard Neuberger remarks: "Torn between her peaceful past and a brawling future as the Pittsburgh of the West, Portland just can't make up her mind. . . . As a result of this strange ambivalence, Portland is a combination of the rustic and the metropolitan."[11] Similarly, Elsie Morrow writes of Springfield, Illinois, that, "At best, Springfield is a very typical American city, with a special flavor and pleasantness. At worst it is a town which has grown old without ever having grown up. It is something between a backward country settlement and a cosmopolis."[12]

The obverse of such pleasantly toned rural mythology, of course, is an affectively linked set of vices: cities are locales of demoralization, discomfort, standardization, artificiality, vulgar materialism, dishonesty, and so on through a richly invidious lexicon. But the rural-urban dichotomy allows black to be called white, and white, black. City dwellers have long characterized their cities as places of progress, opportunity, and excitement, the very image of civilization in contrast to countryside, small town, small city, in contrast, even, to those larger cities which appear provincial. Small cities and even villages have, in turn, affirmed that they participate in an urbane and urban civilization. Anyone who peruses popular urban histories will notice how very sensitive are their authors about the artistic, musical, and literary "culture" of their towns; they carefully list all "cultural" accomplishments and proclaim the progressiveness of their towns by example and assertion. A town which is not civilized, not progressive, not exciting would seem to have a narrow range of options; its citizens must balance its slight amount of urbanity with presumed rural virtues, or must assert disinterest in (un-American) urban characteristics; or, more subtly, must ignore their place in the backwash of American urbanization and remain content to be where they are.

Whatever else may be true of American cities, they are certainly a most varied lot, being neither all cosmopolitan nor all homespun. Nonetheless, particular cities become symbolized as embodiments of different facets of a cheerfully ambiguous rural-urban dichotomy. Thus, emerging styles of urban life receive relatively easy explanation or rationalization. It is as if people were to say: "We are a city like this because we grew up on the prairie, or because we are surrounded by farms, or because our main businesses were founded by farm boys, or because we have no great influx of alien peoples." Likewise, each different population within a single city can rationalize its differential mode of living by appealing to one mythology or another—or to elements of both. Moreover, a city seemingly fated by geographical position and history to be of a certain kind can be envisioned as another kind, and can be directed toward that image by strong interest groups which draw upon different sets of sustaining beliefs. Any city which unquestionably is undergoing change from a commercial to a manufacturing center, or from an agricultural town to a distributing mart, can likewise find ready interpretations to account for otherwise baffling changes in its social characteristics. All such explanations, whether vigorously contested or merely assumed, are answers to that important query: what is the meaning of this city, what kind of a place is it?

The rural-versus-urban conflict that marks American life is crosscut by another ambiguity which turns on a contrast between tradition and modernity. City adherents sometimes stress a lengthy history or a blessedly short one. Votaries of a city with a long history will tend to link its origins with those of the nation itself. Being old—the ideology runs—a long established city is less likely to be crude, vulgar, rough and ready; hence it will be more civilized, more civic-minded, more settled; its citizens will be more stable, have deeper personal and familial roots in the community; its population will be mostly native to it and its immigrants well assimilated; hence, fewer men will have been attracted there merely for opportunistic reasons. The older cities will have more cultivation of leisure, greater delicacy of human relations, and will pay more attention to matters which make for "taste" and "civilization."[13]

But the citizens of other American cities extoll the contrary virtues of youth and scant tradition. They regard their cities as relatively untrammeled by custom and convention. Just because their cities have not had time to settle down, they are supposed not to have developed rigid stances toward handling problems; they are therefore progressive and profoundly democratic, since men have fought their way to success there by their own honest efforts, benefiting neither from hereditary position nor from an elite upbringing. In these younger cities, it is believed that the lines between social classes have not yet grown into impermeable barriers; indeed, they may be denied to exist at all. A young city is conceived of as a place of freedom in still another sense. Its citizens have immigrated there of their own free will because they imagined it to be a place of considerable opportunity. Because the young community permits experimentation and the pursuit of opportunity, it is seen as an exciting place, at least more interesting than the stodgier older cities. Although the latter,

by reason of their earlier origins, may perhaps rightfully claim superiority in the arts of civilization—so the argument runs—the more recently founded communities will soon overtake or surpass them; indeed the cosmopolitanism of the older cities may only, in some instances, be a form of decadance.

Ardent speakers for both younger and older cities stress only certain elements in the total available vocabularies; they glory now in a town's experimental attitude, now in its famous traditional styles of cooking; they even combine the attributes of age and youth. Such symbolization occurs without strict regard for fact, since cities, as we have seen, may be represented as rather old when they are actually quite young, and cities of similar age may be conceived of in very different temporal terms.

Tradition and history are often given a peculiar reverse twist, so that certain eastern coastal cities are considered not to have important American qualities, while certain western centers are assigned crucial roles in the making of the nation. It is asserted or implied that there are histories and histories; but the basic history of the country concerns the clearing of the forests and settling of the frontier. The pioneer romance thus crowds out the colonial. Any city whose citizens did not participate in the pushing back of the frontier cannot, therefore, possibly possess the mystical qualities stemming from that glorious enterprise.

But the frontier is a series of conceptions, not merely a set of facts. These conceptions are linked with various rural and urban virtues, with different periods of our history, and with particular American regions as well. In those sections of the country where the frontier as a geographic reality has but recently disappeared, the frontier as a concept refers more to the mining camp and the railroad center than to pioneer agricultural settlements. The frontier was a rough and tough place, where men were men and the hardiest won out. Some of the same associations remain coupled in midwestern remembrances because of the region's boomtown tradition and because of the predominant romance of life on the open prairie. The Midwest is more than the geographic heart of the continent; many believe it to be at the core of what *is* America. Back east, the concept of the frontier has been sufficiently misted over by time so that it is referred to more obliquely ("the founders," "the settlers"), but these terms also carry a considerable charge of regional passion.

The frontier, as an idea, has also broken loose from any regional anchoring; it can be applied to endeavors in industrial, artistic, intellectual, and other non-geographic fields. Consequently, cities building upon the cumulative connotations of the frontier image can be thought of as commercial and industrial pioneers. A great metropolis like New York can strike its admirers as *the* "moving frontier" of the entire American economy and of the nation's civilization. The frontier concept allows some cities to be called currently progressive and others to be linked with the nation's slightly older history; while it may be used with relation to some cities so that it cuts both ways. An example is John Bowman's address to his fellow citizens of the Pittsburgh Chamber of Commerce, in which he reminded them of the city's great pioneer tradition:

But these qualities in men and women, you say, flared up generally among the pioneers of the time. . . . These qualities, however, did not flare up and stay flared up in any other community for so long a period nor did they reach so intense a glow as they did in Pittsburgh.

He goes on to claim that, "The significant fact now is that Pittsburgh through nearly a hundred years developed a new way of thinking, a new way of acting. These new ways became first nature in the people." And then, by simple transmutation, he views these ways as creative acts, and Pittsburgh's creativeness "was the application of creative ability to industry." This was its great contribution to Pittsburgh. And of course, "the old creativeness, developed here through a long period, is still in Pittsburgh."[14]

But when a city settles down, this turn of events is likely to be greeted by criticism—criticism mixed, however, with expressions of nostalgia and joy over the community's improvements. The citizens may perceive that certain civic characteristics derive from the original pioneer spirit which founded and built the town, however astonished the original settlers might be if they could witness the town's transformation.[15]

When residents identify a city with different rural or urban conceptions and with different kinds of romantic histories, they may also identify it with reference to another persistent American dichotomy: regionalism versus national integration. Since our cities are so widely scattered on such different landscapes, it is difficult not to associate a city with its region. Its domestic architecture, the clothing, speech, and action of some of its residents all proclaim it— and the people themselves sometimes proclaim it with belligerence. As is usual with cultural antinomies, men find ample room for ambiguity and for subtle argument. Two cities of the same region may vie for regional supremacy on symbolic as well as economic grounds. Each will claim to represent the region better; each will stress somewhat different areal attributes. Since no region is entirely homogeneous—if only because of its competing urban centers —there is plenty of room for dispute. In a rapidly changing region, such as the "New South," there may be even less agreement unless the resources of ambiguity are utilized in a way such that one city claims to represent the Old South, while the other is quite content to represent the New South (although a city like Charleston can claim to represent both).[16] A region is usually not exactly coterminous with a state; therefore, a city such as Biloxi, Mississippi, can affirm kinship with New Orleans and with bayou culture rather than with the rest of Mississippi.

Some cities, by virtue of the populations which founded them or immigrated to them later, are considered to be less typical of their regions than are their neighbors; these may compensate by claiming other important American values. Conversely, however, a city may receive great waves of foreign immigrants without serious impairment to its position as a regional standard bearer. A few cities are so new that they and their residents share little in common with the rest of the region, in history or in taste, and so are constrained to build some sort of urban history, however flimsy, or to engage in other ceremonial gestures to reaffirm their association with their region. An interesting case is Kingsport, Tennessee, a small city planned and founded by eastern bankers who were attracted to the site by abundant, cheap white labor.

Kingsport's historian, writing when the city was only eleven years old, nevertheless argues that had the village but known it, it "was sleeping only that it might awake into a beautiful prosperous city" for "the moral and mental fibre of the sturdy, resourceful people of the Kingsport community required two centuries in the making." While it "is true that the new city was incorporated and began its municipal life only eleven years ago . . . back of all this, unknown to many of the citizens themselves perhaps, is a setting which would be a pride to any of the oldest cities in the country."[17]

A few urban centers gladly spurn extensive regional affiliation. Their residents prefer to think of them as supra-national, even as "world cities," underline the city's role in the national economy, and flaunt its traits of national leadership, sophistication, cosmopolitanism, size, and other symbols of national and international placement. Some sense of the overwhelming impact of a world city is suggested by the breathless and inadequate ways its admirers attempt to sum it up. Thus, John Gunther, who first compares Chicago (the typical American city) with New York (the world city), writes that Chicago is "the greatest and most typically American of all cities. New York is bigger and more spectacular and can outmatch it in other superlatives, but it is a 'world' city, more European in some respects than American." Some pages later he writes that

now we come to New York City, the incomparable, the brilliant star city of cities, the forty-ninth state, a law unto itself, the Cyclopean paradox, the inferno with no out-of-bounds, the supreme expression of both the miseries and the splendors of contemporary civilization. . . . New York is at once the climactic synthesis of America, and yet the negation of America in that it has so many characteristics called un-American.[18]

Paul Crowell and A. H. Raskin merely say: "New York is not a city. It is a thousand cities, each with its own ninety-nine square miles."[19]

Many citizens of "world cities" make denigrating gestures toward more regionally inclined centers. They refer to those centers as less important, small-townish, hick towns, cow towns, and use other similar epithets. Consequently, these latter places may regard the more worldly centers with a suspicion that gains strength from the historic antagonism between countryside and city as well as from a regional passion against national centralization. However, no single city claims to be a national, or world, city in exactly the same way as any other does; and always regional traits are coupled with non-regional ones (even by residents of New York City).

Sectionalism is closely allied with economic specialization inasmuch as the various continental areas function differently in our national economy. Cities tend to become known for the industries, commercial enterprises, and services that are typical of the surrounding area. National cities, of course, have more varied functions; hence when New York City residents insist that it has "everything," this means more than that it performs all the important economic functions. The full significance of the claim is that all (the best—and possibly the worst) styles of life can be found in New York. But the Florida resort city, the Illinois farm city, or the New England manufacturing town can all be conceived of by their residents as simultaneously truly regional and truly American because what they manu-facture or trade or service is necessary to the nation.

Some products or services which are limited to certain cities are of sufficient national importance that those cities come to represent some particular facet of America: Pittsburgh and Detroit come readily to mind. Although not all specializations are equally praiseworthy, or even savory, nevertheless observers of such cities as Reno and Calumet City can find ample justification for believing that sex, sin, and gambling are as much a part of American life as are automobiles or opera; and Pittsburgh residents could, until recently, declare that smoke-filled air and labor troubles were the inevitable accompaniment of heavy industrialization. As George S. Perry has phrased it:

Certainly Reno is an actual and highly special aspect of American life, as much as Monte Carlo is a part of European life. . . . Many Nevadans . . . referring both to the tourist business brought in and the large amount of tax load that gambling pays . . . remark simply: "You don't shoot Santa Claus." . . . For in the American mind, Reno remains to gambling and divorces what Pittsburgh means to steel and Hollywood to movies.[20]

Cities whose range of economic function is exceedingly narrow seem frequently to lack variety of social style and suffer from deficiencies in "culture" and other civic virtues esteemed in most towns. Hence residents from other cities may make them the butts of jibes and the objects of social criticism. In the main, the outsider misses the mark for, like physicians whose identities have grown up around the practice of specific medical skills or about the "ownership" of specific bodily areas, the specialized city tends to glorify its command over special skills and resources. Two spokesmen for a pair of our most specialized cities link special skills with the spirit of America. The first is Malcolm Bingay, writing in *Detroit Is My Home Town:*

This fluidity of life, this refusal to "jell" or ever to grow old helps to explain why everything that is right or wrong which happens to our nation seems to break here first. It is that very spirit which first conceived the idea of throwing away millions upon millions of dollars of machinery as obsolete to make way for better machinery and greater speed to meet competition. This horror of obsolescence is the "Americanism" which permitted us to triumph in two great wars. . . . Other countries remained static in the sense that while they understood our standardization of parts— to a degree—they never did catch the imponderable elements of mass production in which there is nothing permanent but change.[21]

The second spokesman is Carl Crow, who, in *The City of Flint,* writes:

The history of the interesting and dynamic city of Flint has been worth recording because it is more than the chronical of an individual city. It epitomizes the history of America . . . America is a story of the industrial development which has brought us such a high standard of living.[22]

Citizens who are intensely interested in the furtherance of the arts congregate in groups and associations that many other citizens believe are less central to the life of the community than other more vigorous business, social, and cultural institutions representing the interests of the town's more typical citizens. Sometimes cultural barrenness is excused in terms of the city's symbolic age. Given sufficient time, some say, the city will grow up, develop a rich cultural life, and take its place among the civilized cities of its size—and, one might add, among some cities a tithe of its size. The residents of Chicago sometimes use this strategy to console themselves or to ward off attack, and it is probably commonly used in other cities. Here is an instance from Birmingham, Alabama:

Birmingham somehow, for all her pride in the great labors which converted a cornfield into a great metropolis in little more than the span of one man's life, Birmingham is haunted by a sense of promise unfulfilled. Her more philosophic citizens are obsessed with this thought. They brood and ponder over it, and, searching their souls and the city's history, constantly seek the reason why. They come up with many answers. One is the obvious one of her youth. . . . Another answer is . . . Birmingham is a working town. . . . Painting pictures and composing music and writing books—even the widespread appreciation of those things—all rather come with time.[23]

When a specialized city becomes economically diversified, and creates or draws to it new populations with new tastes, the imagery associated with it changes radically. It remains no longer merely a steel city, a rubber town, or an agricultural community, but is represented widely as a more cosmopolitan center.

Although every city within the United States is American in a factual sense, some cities are in some other sense denied that status from time to time. Many visitors to the Southwest would agree with John Gunther that there one may feel almost as if he is leaving the United States. ("The first thing I thought was, 'Can this possibly be North America?'")[24] But that reaction is not aroused solely by regional geography or by ethnic culture, for cities may be symbolically driven off the American landscape when they offend deeply felt standards of propriety. One critic of Pittsburgh some years ago bitterly characterized it as "A city inherited from the Middle Ages," and only partly admitted that it was one of us.[25] Reno is frequently a target for obloquy: a *Reader's Digest* article titled "Reno. Parasite on Human Weakness" is representative; its author, true to his title, could not admit that Reno is genuinely American.[26] Even Los Angeles, although it shares national characteristics conspicuously enough, seems to strike many people as odd or crazy; and, "according to its most severe critics, it is New York in purple shorts with its brains knocked out." The phrase is George S. Perry's; in less fanciful prose he sums up very well the partial denial of status to that large city when he adds that its "civilization has been declared to caricature, in one way or another, that of the entire nation."[27]

The residents of certain other cities sometimes display sensitivity to the ways in which their cities deviate from what they or outside critics conceive to be the normal national or regional urban patterns. Cincinnati has never quite recovered from Mrs. Trollope's visit nor from its reputation as a tradition-bound town located within a progressive, dynamic region.[28] When a city begins its history with a great promise but then suffers relative oblivion, it departs sufficiently from the usual regional expectations to require a set of supporting rationalizations. Thus a loyal resident of Marietta, Ohio, in 1903 mournfully took stock of a century that had passed without much progress for his town. He remarked that

a city may open the way for progress, and still not progress itself. . . . Evidently other cities . . . have excelled her [Marietta] in so many ways. . . . But at the beginning of the new century she stands young, strong, and vigorous, no longer old, except in name, with an ambition of youth and wealth of resource. . . . While it has thus taken a century of experience during which time she seems to move forward so slowly, it is well to consider that these years

were spent in laying a firm and substantial foundation whereon to build the New Marietta.[29]

In another passage, we can watch a citizen of Vincennes, Indiana, trying to puzzle out why prophesies about cities sometimes fail to materialize. Commenting on Vincennes' bustling future after "a sort of Rip Van Winkle sleep," he wrote:

This bright prospect although long delayed might have been expected from the opinions of the place and its natural advantages expressed by the missionary fathers who first visited it. . . . These men were far seeing and almost with prophetic vision foretold the future of various places they visited. . . . In no instance have their prophetic utterances failed of fruition unless it shall be in the solitary instance of Vincennes.

In urging his contemporaries on to greater civic harmony and energy, he added, "They made the same prophetic utterances with reference to Pittsburgh, Cincinnati, Louisville, Detroit, Chicago, St. Paul, St. Louis, San Francisco and many other cities. . . . And why should not their opinions with regard to Vincennes not be realized?"

The residents of most cities can escape feelings of non-typicality simply by stressing other sets of American traits, but when cities develop in astonishingly new ways, their citizens must claim, as I have already suggested, that clearly sanctioned American qualities (rurality, urbanity, sectionality) are actually present or exist in new, somewhat disguised forms.

Most curious of all is the case of New York, a city which has been passionately and repeatedly denied essential American status while its admirers have proclaimed it the greatest city in America. It is one thing to feel that this great metropolis is not the most typical of our cities, that from it foreigners receive a skewed and partial picture of the nation; but it is another matter to believe that New York as partly or wholly not American, or even "un-American." The grounds of attack and defense bring to sharp focus the ambiguity and clash of American values.[31]

In 1894 Theodore Roosevelt published an article titled, "What 'Americanism' Means" in which he argued:

There are two or three sides to the question of Americanism, and two or three senses in which the word "Americanism" can be used to express the antithesis of what is unwholesome and undesirable. In the first place we wish to be broadly American and national, as opposed to being local or sectional.[32]

In the second place, he reports, it is unwholesome for an American to become Europeanized, thus too cosmopolitan; and in the third place, the meaning pertains to those foreign immigrants who do not become quickly Americanized. These antitheses, which run through the arguments for and against New York City, can be found in another article titled "Is New York More Civilized Than Kansas?" which follows almost immediately after Roosevelt's in the same journal.[33] Kansas is defined as the more civilized (that is, as the more American) on a score of grounds, which include its homogeneity of ideal and tradition, its native population, its home life, its lack of class distinction, its religious and moral tone, and its optimal conditions for rearing children. New York is declared not to possess most of these qualities. The author even argues that Kansas is less isolated, in the civilizational as well as the geographic sense, because its greater number of railroads keep it in more intimate contact with all sections of the nation.

Through the years, New York has been accused of being too European, too suspiciously cosmopolitan, too aggressive and materialistic, too hurried and hectic, a city where family life and home life do not flourish but where—it is asserted or suspected—iniquity does. New York seems to sum up all the negative balances in the rural animus against cities, in the sectional argument against centralization and cosmopolitanism, and in the frontier bias against cities which do not share the mystic pioneer experience. No other American city is the target of such great or complete antagonism.

New York's admirers, whether they are native to the city or not, counter these arguments in two ways. They can maintain that the city is not actually deficient in these various regards. For instance, the *New York Times Magazine* makes its business the occasional publication of articles about the city which tacitly or explicitly set out to prove that New York really is a friendly place having unsuspected village-like qualities, a quiet home life, plus bits of rurality and even farming tucked away here and there. They also try to show that the large numbers of immigrants and their children, are at least as American as citizens with longer native genealogies. When New Yorkers write about themselves or about their city, their affirmation of urban identity often takes that form. (Al Smith once wrote an article titled "I Have Seven Million Neighbors.")[34]

Side by side with the outright accusation that New York fails to participate in our wholesome, rural, or village heritage runs the assertion that New York is actually our most representative city because it is our greatest. "Greatness" can be attributed on quite different grounds, for each assertion rests upon certain features of American culture judged to be of the highest importance. New York is our last frontier, the place where persons of spirit are drawn as by a magnet. It is the "moving frontier" of American culture, the most important site of progress and innovation. It is the image of America, for here the melting pot is at its most intense and here the New America—racially or culturally—is being forged rather than in the most homogeneous native American centers. Although the same theme of the urban melting pot as the epitome of American civilization is applied to other ethnically diverse cities,[35] New York is a place where all narrow local sectionalism has disappeared: because it is a great world city, as is twentieth-century America—is not this the American century! Even those who hate New York may have to admit New York's typicality on the grounds that if this is the America of today, then New York certainly best represents it. Here, for instance, is Earl Sparling's anguished summation, complete with reference to the pioneer past:

I find it an appalling place, rich for making money, poor for living. . . . But all of that is one thing. It is a different thing to shrug the whole spectacle away as something completely alien and not American. America cannot be absolved that easily. Not only is New York American, but it is the mirror in which America, after half a century of confusion, suddenly sees herself for what she is. . . . New York is the soul of America. And Americans . . . see it . . . and wonder how all this happened in a free, pioneer land.[36]

Is it any wonder that there is so much ambiguity in the symbolization of this metropolis, this New York which "is at once the climactic synthesis of America, and yet the negation of America in that it has so many characteristics called un-American?"[37] The attitude—and the bewilderment—of many Americans can be summed up in the reactions of a girl from the Midwest who, visiting New York for the first time, exclaimed that it was "just a wonderfully exciting place but so unreal; it doesn't even have trees." It is summed up also in a magnificently paradoxical set of sentences written by the editors of *Fortune* magazine, as they struggled to relate New York City to the national culture:

New York may be taken as a symbol, or it may be taken as a fact. As a symbol it is a symbol of America; its noisy, exuberant, incalculable towers rise out of the water like a man's aspirations to freedom. As a symbol it is the Gateway, the promise, the materialization of the New World. . . . But taken as a fact, New York is less Dantesque. To most Americans the fact is that "New York is not America." It is un-American in lots of ways. The concentration of power that exists among those spires is itself un-American; so are the tumultuous, vowel-twisting inhabitants who throng the sidewalks.[38]

The confusion continues. Two pages later, when the editors eloquently discuss the city's role as a great melting pot, they wrote, "In that sense New York *is* America," only to blunt the force of that assertion with "more than symbolically."

The strain between ideal and reality, or ideal and presumed fact, runs like a brilliant thread through all our antithetical thinking about America and about our cities. With a fine flair for significant ambiguities, the *Saturday Evening Post* included among more than 145 cities which it surveyed after World War II an article about "a little cow town." Its author asserted that *The Saturday Evening Post* is running a notable series of articles about American cities. All this is well enough, but . . . if we have any truly national culture, it stems from the small town and near-by farm."[39] George S. Perry, in his book, *Cities of America* could not avoid including, either, a chapter about a town of two thousand people; and, like the editors of *Fortune*, he uses those interesting terms "fact" and "symbol"—except that he applies them to a small city. "Madison, Wisconsin," he sentimentalizes,

is both a fact and a symbol that stands for many of the finest traits in the American character. It is a place where independent people get up on their hind legs and have their say. Again, it is a seat of serious learning. Moreover, it is surrounded by that basic harmony that derives from good land that has been treated intelligently and with respect. Finally, Madison's people are almost spectacularly unapathetic. They are concerned, interested, and willing to do something about almost any public question. In many ways Madison and its environs are a miniature model of the ideal America of which many of us dream.[40]

Fact and symbol, symbol and fact: it is as if the United States had developed an urbanized economy without developing a thoroughly urbanized citizen. Americans entered a great period of city building during the nineteenth century protestingly, metaphorically walking backward; and to some extent they still do, but in exceedingly subtle ways. In the various sections of the next chapter, I shall deal both with this protest against cities, and with the regional differences between American urban cultures. In the foregoing pages, we have merely scratched the surface of American urban symbolism.

NOTES

1. John P. Kennedy, "Address. Delivered before the Maryland Institute for the Promotion of the Mechanical Arts, 21st October 1851," *Occasional Addresses* (New York: Putnam & Sons, 1872), p. 244.

2. Paul de Rousiers, *American Life* (New York and Paris: Firming-Didot & Co.), p. 73.

3. John Gunther, *Inside U. S. A.* (New York: Harper & Bros., 1946), p. 369.

4. Cf. The collection of articles edited by Alexander Klein, *The Empire City, A Treasury of New York* (New York: Rinehart & Co., Inc., 1955); or Paul Crowell and A. H. Raskin, "New York, 'Greatest City in the World,'" in Robert S. Allen (ed.), *Our Fair City* (New York: Vanguard Press, Inc., 1947), esp. pp. 37-39.

5. This article was reprinted in the collection titled *Cities of America* (New York: Whittlesey House, McGraw-Hill Book Co., 1947), p. 244; see also Henry Haskell and Richard Fowler, *City of the Future. A Narrative History of Kansas City* (Kansas City: F. Glenn Publishing Company, 1950), pp. 16-17; and Darrel Garwood, *Crossroads of America. The Story of Kansas City* (New York: W. W. Norton and Co., Inc., 1948), p. 327. The latter volume especially exemplifies the conception of "crossroads" as the basis for attributing more Americanism to Kansas City than to any other city.

6. Cf. "Midwestern Birthday," *Time*, LVIII (July 30, 1951), p. 14.

7. Frank C. Harper, *Pittsburgh: Forge of the Universe* (New York: Comet Press, 1957), p. 10; and *Pittsburgh and the Pittsburgh Spirit* (Pittsburgh: Chamber of Commerce, 1928), but especially the address by John Bowman, "Pittsburgh's Contribution to Civilization," pp. 1-10.

8. Angie Debo, *Tulsa: From Creek Town to Oil Capital* (Norman, Okla.: University of Oklahoma Press, 1945), p. vii.

9. For two excellent discussions of the agrarian myth see Richard Hofstadter, *The Age of Reform* (New York: Alfred A. Knopf, Inc., 1955), esp. Part I, "The Agrarian Myth and Commercial Realities," and Part II, "The Folklore of Populism"; and Henry Nash Smith, *Virgin Land. The American West as Symbol and Myth* (New York: Vintage Books, 1955, and Cambridge: Harvard University Press, 1950), esp. Book III, "The Garden of the World," pp. 138-305.

10. Cf. G. S. Perry, "Philadelphia," *Saturday Evening Post*, CCXVIII (Sept. 14, 1946), esp. p. 82.

11. "Portland, Oregon," *Saturday Evening Post*, CCXIX (March 1, 1947), 23.

12. "Springfield, Illinois," *ibid.* (Sept. 27, 1947), p. 28.

13. This theme can be readily recognized in such books on older eastern cities as Struthers Burt, *Philadelphia* (Garden City, New York: Doubleday, Doran & Co., 1945), and Cleveland Amory, *The Proper Bostonians* (New York: E. P. Dutton & Co., 1947).

14. John Bowman, in Harper, *Pittsburgh and the Pittsburgh Spirit, op. cit.*, pp. 5-9.

15. Dorsha Hayes, *Chicago, Crossroads of American Enterprise* (New York: Julian Messner, Inc.,

1944), p. 300; and Clara de Chambrun, *Cincinnati* (New York: Charles Scribner & Sons, 1939), p. 319.

16. Cf. Robert G. Rhett, *Charleston. An Epic of Carolina* (Richmond, Va.: Garrett and Massie, 1940).

17. Howard Long, *Kingsport, A Romance of Industry* (Kingsport, Tenn.: The Sevier Press, 1928), pp. 76, 3-4.

18. *Op. cit.*, pp. 369-70, 549.

19. *Op. cit.*, p. 37.

20. "Reno," *Saturday Evening Post*, CCXXV (July 5, 1952), 70, 72.

21. (Indianapolis: Bobbs-Merrill Co., 1946), p. 19.

22. (New York: Harper & Bros., 1945), p. 205.

23. "Birmingham, Alabama," *Saturday Evening Post*, CCXX (Sept. 6, 1947), 22.

24. *Op. cit.*, pp. 886-906, esp. p. 895.

25. F. Stother, "What Kind of Pittsburgh is Detroit?" *World's Work*, LII (Oct., 1926), 633-39.

26. Anthony Abbot in *Reader's Digest*, LX (Feb., 1952), 119-22.

27. *Op. cit.*, pp. 232, 233.

28. Alvin Harlow refers to Mrs. Trollope in *The Serene Cincinnatians* (New York: Dutton and Co., 1950).

29. Thomas J. Summers, *History of Marietta* (Marietta, Ohio: Leader Publishing Company, 1903), pp. 319-20.

30. Henry Cauthorn, *A History of the City of Vincennes, Indiana* (Cleveland: Arthur H. Clark Co., 1901), p. 220.

31. For some representative statements, pro and con, see: Mark Sullivan, "Why the West Dislikes New York. The Eternal Conflict Between City and Country," *World's Work*, LXI (1926), 406-11; "New York City," *Fortune*, XX (1939), 73-75, 83-85; Charles Merz, "The Attack on New York," *Harper's*, CLXIII (1926), 81-87; Earl Sparling, "Is New York American?" *Scribner's*, LXXX (1931), 165-73; Paul Crowell and A. H. Raskin, in R. Allen (ed.), *op. cit.*, pp. 38-39; Anonymous, "What is America?" *Nation*, CXXVIII (1921), 755; and Robert Benchley, "The Typical New Yorker," in Alexander Klein (ed.), *op. cit.*, pp. 338-42.

32. *Forum*, XVII (1894), 196-200.

33. J. W. Gleed in *ibid.*, pp. 217-34.

34. *American Magazine*, CXVI (Aug., 1933), 36-38.

35. Elsie Morrow, "South Bend," *Saturday Evening Post*, CCXXIV (June 14, 1942), 87; and "Brooklyn," *ibid.*, CCXIX (Dec. 26, 1946), 14.

36. *Op. cit.*, pp. 165-73.

37. Gunther, *op. cit.*, p. 549.

38. *Op. cit.*, p. 73.

39. E. R. Jackman, "Burns, Oregon," *Saturday Evening Post*, CCXX (Jan. 31, 1948), 2.

40. *Op. cit.*, p. 221.

The City in Crisis

SCOTT GREER

Ours is an urban world. In a way that has never been true in the past we have given all of our hostages to the encompassing fortunes of great cities. Imperial Rome under the Augustans may have been as much as 10 per cent urban; America today is over 60 per cent urban and nearly half of the urbanites live in metropolitan areas with populations of over one million. Projecting these present tendencies into the future, an estimate made in 1960 indicates that four-fifths of the great increase in population expected by 1980 will be metropolitan, with the urban proportion of the total over 70 per cent.[1] Thus, there is little chance for most of us to escape from the city, even should we wish to; we had better begin to try to understand it.

This is a difficult assignment. It is very much as though we were studying

From Scott Greer, *The Emerging City* (New York: The Free Press, 1962), pp. 1-28. Copyright © 1962 by The Free Press of Glencoe, A Division of The Macmillan Company. Reprinted by permission of the publisher. Scott Greer is Professor of Political Science at Northwestern University.

the geography of the earth in the planet's early days, when cataclysmic change took place continually in response to pressure and heat, under cover of a nearly continuous cloud of vapor produced by the very changes we wished to observe. The nature of the city is changing, and the very rapidity of change is producing conflict and confusion in our images and our policy. Yet we must work out trial solutions; intellectual and political decisions are demanded every day and will not wait upon a final solution. Ironically and inescapably, our policy is one of the dynamics altering the city, and our policy rests upon our images of the city, our notions of how it works and of possible instruments for change and control.

SOME POLICY CHOICES

Our choices begin with the emerging shape of the metropolis itself. Though much is inherited, the funded energy of the past in the shape of the vast physical plant of the city does not foreclose all future choice: the projected growth for the next two decades insures that. One possibility is the retention of the general focus and structure of the city as we have inherited it. This is a more difficult job than may appear on the surface, for the original settlers, speculators, entrepreneurs, and peculators built in terms of a technology and a society that are no more. Much of the inherited city is made up of overvalued and obsolete slums, loft buildings, and nineteenth-century factories, their access barricaded by traffic. What are the possibilities of retaining such a structure for the city, what are the costs, and what are the benefits?

How should we channel new growth, and how can we do so? While urban re-

development has resulted in a few monuments and failures dedicated to the salvage of the older parts of the city, the increasing population of the metropolis has busily built and inhabited its own version of "greenbelts" in the suburbs. Most of the metropolitan growth since World War II has been suburban development, and of the population growth of sixty-four million expected by 1980, over 80 per cent will be in the suburbs. Thus, the channeling of new growth competes for attention with conservation and rebuilding of older areas.[2]

A key question for consideration by either viewpoint, and one that is frequently a bone of contention between partisans of the Utopias, is traffic and transportation. What will the circulatory system of the metropolis be? Will the increasing automobile traffic force an increase in the arteries, further adjustment to the automobile as chief carrier, and thus increasing numbers of automobiles? Such a course leads public transportation into the vicious circle of fewer passengers, greater per capita cost, poor service, higher fares, fewer passengers—and a continuous encouragement to use the automobile. On the other hand, what combination of statute and the public fisc can rechannel transportation? The last war was effective, since it literally prohibited automobile traffic through rationing. Nothing else has been effective. Those committed to public transportation point out, however, that little else has been tried—while the cities subsidize the automobile drivers and the latter flourish under such subsidy.

The automobile has, as one virtue, its great ability to increase the accessibility of scattered places on the periphery of the city: suburbia is auto-borne. Suburbia is also, preponderantly, native-born and white. Those who live in the older portions of the city (and who are, in a sense, conservatives of an older urban tradition) are of a different complexion. As their numbers increase, in absolute terms, and as they become a higher proportion of the residents and voters, they increasingly make their needs felt. The growing number of ethnic residents in the limited area of the central city has often been interpreted through the classic law of gases —and many observers await, with trepidation, the day when the central city "blows its top." Struggles to break and to hold the legal and extralegal barriers used in the war of containment are continuous—they are not unrelated to the suburban movement of the white population. These struggles create continuous policy problems in the central city —and it is no wonder that mayors and race relations commissions look with some bitterness upon the suburbanites, who profit from the total work and wealth of the metropolis but refuse to share its costs.

Yet the central city also continues to produce the classic problems of urban democracy along with the wealth from which suburbia derives its income. Few of the great public parks that grace our cities are safe at night—and many are dangerous at high noon. Entire neighborhoods are the scenes of guerilla war, with *freikorps* battling for the control of the streets. The safety of person and property is not automatically assured in the greatest cities of the wealthiest nation. The battle to naturalize the immigrant and acculturate the unwashed continues, and with it the battle to civilize, through civil service and administrative law, the political and governmental organizations of the city.

These are difficult problems, for they demand solutions considering both arguments of equity and knowledge of means. Perhaps the most encompassing statement of the urban policy choice is simply: what governmental form is best suited to contain and resolve the issues that have been lightly touched on above, as well as those not mentioned and the myriads that are surely moving toward us over the horizon of history? What is the relevant constituency? What structure can both represent the interests that demand representation and, at the same time, resolve the ineluctable conflicts inherent in the contemporary metropolis?

These are only a few of the policy choices faced by the metropolis today.

THE KALEIDOSCOPE OF IMAGES

Decisions on such topics are intimately related to the guiding image, the overall theory, with which we approach the city. How shall we effectively focus this particular "booming, buzzing confusion," this complex mass of heterogeneous and transient human action moving through time? How shall we summarize patterns in a limited set of categories, so that we can relate the parts in a meaningful way?

The development of a coherent body of thought with respect to such a large and immediate subject usually begins with a metaphor. Whether it develops into a scientifically established theory or remains a metaphor, such an image provides at least a rudimentary concept, a handle for intellectual control. With respect to the metropolis, then, we may ask: What kinds of metaphors dominate our intellectual discourse? What images stand for the totality and are, for practical purposes, "theories of the city"? We shall begin by inspecting the images used by social scientists who are concerned with the city. Political scientists, economists, and sociologists have for many decades manifested a continuing interest in the urban complex.

Political scientists typically approach the city as a governmental unit with powers and duties of a specific kind. From the concern of classical theorists with the city state, from consideration of the importance of the city in the development of modern law, and from day-to-day concern with the administrative structure of urban government, they inherit a rich body of information and concepts. The city, for the political scientist, is the corporate body, the legal personality, a little prototype of the state, preceding in history the development of the nation. It rests upon a balance of power among contending interests (including the interest of the prince) and its product is the polity: order, roads, monuments, and the "authoritative allocation of values" by those with legitimate power.

Urban sociologists emphasize a geographical image of the city. Under the influence of the ecological approach, they have constructed a two dimensional theory of the city—a sprawling map of people in places. Theirs has been a metaphor emphasizing the unplanned, "blind" development of urban concentration, the regularities in the use of space that are unlegislated but enforced by mechanisms of competition for *lebensraum*. The city, for the urban ecologist, is the mass of population, heterogeneous and dense, segregated by wealth and cultural background. It is a loose congeries with a vestigial normative structure, existing like "nature's half acre" in an ecological balance. One of the competing groups is government

itself—parties, patrons, officials. Although the early ecologists paid tribute to a moral order coexistent with the ecological order, the research and theory of urban sociology shows little concern for such a dimension. The equilibrium of their city rests upon an ecological balance among contending subgroups, and its product is a division of labor and rewards reflected on a map.

The economists, late comers to the study of the city, see it in two lights. First, as a matrix of locations for firms —a necessary translation of a national economy into space. Second, and more pertinent to our inquiry, some economists have been turning toward an image of the city as an economic unit— a kind of super firm, based upon relations between importers and exporters, contractors and subcontractors (with the household as the smallest firm) all involved in an import-export business. Thus, the economist sees the city as a center of production, trade, and distribution, whose basic units are economic organizations. Local government is itself a peculiar kind of firm. The economic city rests upon a division of labor among firms, competition, and cooperation within the framework of the market, with advantages and disadvantages in the form of location, multipliers, and marginal economies. The city as a whole is "in business," and its economic position may be estimated by the balance of trade.

All three of these images of the city betray the heavy hand of nineteenth-century liberalism. Although the political theorists concerned with the city sometimes misplaced their concreteness, mistaking a territorial jurisdiction for a general and universal social structure, when it came to business matters their city was rigorously limited to the constitutionally established powers and forms of city government in the United States. In the same fashion, the assumptions of laissez faire are built into the ecological image. Competition, conflict, accommodation and assimilation take place within a framework of rules approximately the same as those advocated by Herbert Spencer—with room for social evolution, enterprise, and the survival of those most fit to survive. The economic image is simply a verbatim translation: the city becomes a small business man.

Today, all three of these approaches suffer from the same limitation: they are far too partial. Each makes assumptions basic to its explanatory power that are never defined and tested; all focus upon the city without much concern for its environment in social space and time. In order to improve explanation and prediction in particular cases, each is extended toward the bounds of the others (frequently moving past the center of the neighboring discipline, with comic results). In the process of extension the clarity of the original image, a major virtue, is lost in the confusion of "interdisciplinary" thought. The image becomes encrusted with a mass of *ad hoc* barnacles, epicycles, and hemidemisemiquavers.

Thus, the political scientist finds that his approach leads from classic political theory to the constitutioal form of municipal government with at least moderate success, but the day to day operations of government force him to look at the nongovernmental norms that determine behavior—including the folkways and mores of avoiding the law. He is led still further afield by his concern with political parties: how can one explain governmental behavior without explaining party organization? Party organization, without economic interests? And this subject is closely related to the ecologist's concern with kinds of people in space, the conflict of group interests (including the interests of firms), the accommodations that are improvised and form the basis for tradition and, perhaps, law.

When the political scientist turns to look at the city today, he finds that the corporate body is broken into dozens of separate entities: the central city is enmeshed in a web of suburbs, a tangle of villages. Yet this is still, in some sense, "one city." Now he must consider the consequences of ecological shifts in a new light: the suburbs become overwhelmingly white, higher in social class, tending toward Republican affiliation. The central city becomes an electorate of working-class and ethnic identity. Yet each is a necessary condition for the other's existence. Furthermore, the public fisc itself is affected. The "city" may be viewed as a firm, one that can prosper or go bankrupt. Public administration theory can be related to Taylorism and the theory of the firm. Yet this firm's customers are voters, and it may be forced to do business at a constant loss.

The urban ecologist has similar problems. The urban map changes, and frequently the change forces one to look at governmental action—the moral order. Urban redevelopment, zoning, governmental autonomy in the suburbs, such matters as these change the land values of the city but cannot be explained by simple competition for space. At the same time the city, as entrepreneur, struggles to control its own economic future through promotion, redevelopment, the construction of "industrial parks." The roots of these developments lie in areas of economic and political organization that are hardly amenable to exploration through census data plotted on maps, yet they affect the maps. They represent, in some sense, an urban polity—something missing from nature's half acre.

The economist's emerging image suffers similar sea changes. He is forced to grant that zoning laws may shut off the choicest locations for industrial plants, may at an extreme impoverish a metropolitan area, while the general level of governmental services and taxes may affect the recruitment of industry to an area and hence the economic development of the city. The public fisc becomes a necessary but theoretically indigestible part of his apparatus. At the same time, if he is interested in welfare, he is forced to note that governmental services make up an area of consumption in which American urban populations frequently have static or declining products to consume. The competitive market does not produce streets, police protection, playgrounds, and parks. Here the *polity* is analogous to the market. The economist must become a student of political science in order to answer strictly economic questions.

Equally as damaging, however, as the partiality of these approaches, is the limitation in scope. A generally useful image should allow one to summarize the pertinent detail and explain cases varying widely in their surface nature; it should thus allow the interpretation of change through time. While it would be in process of continual modification and improvement, moving toward the condition of a theory, it could not be casually jettisoned. Yet Martindale, in a recent essay on Max Weber's approach to the city, indicates grave doubts as to the usefulness of the image developed by this major and influential sociologist (who was also, and originally, a political economist).

Max Weber's theory of the city, thus, leads to a rather interesting conclusion. We can grant the phenomenal increase and aggregation of modern populations as a concomitant of the industrial revolution. We should not, however, confuse physical aggregation with the growth of the city in a sociological sense. The urban community has everywhere lost its military integrity— its right to defend itself by military means. In many areas of the world it has, temporarily at least, lost its very legal and political autonomy—the same fate is possible everywhere. Meanwhile, within the city itself greater masses of residents pursue interlocal interests—as representatives of the national government, as agents in business and industries of national and international rather than of civic scope. The modern city is losing its external and formal structure. Internally it is in a state of decay while the new community represented by the nation everywhere grows at its expense. The age of the city seems to be at an end.[3]

This statement indicates one writer's belief that the utility of the legal-social definition of the city is at an end—that the city has no separate existence and therefore no interest for the social scientist. That this is not a parochial conclusion is indicated by Albert Reiss, in an introduction to one of the most authoritative collections of readings in urban sociology.

There seems to be a decline of interest in research on cities and city life, if the research in urban demography and human ecology is excluded from consideration. This is in part due to the fact that much of the research simply considers the urban community to be a *context* within which a particular kind of theoretical problem is studied, but the context itself is not often made the object of investigation. . . . A second reason for the decline in urban research activity is the fact that there has been a shift in the problem-area division of sociological knowledge so that certain of the problems formerly conceptualized as "urban sociology" now are viewed within another frame of reference or theory. This is true, for example, of what now are called the problem fields of industrial sociology, social stratification and mass communication. There is some reason to believe that the sociology of city life will limit itself largely to a consideration of urban structure (in the sense of community) during the next decade and that the fragmentation of the field will continue.[4]

Thus, Martindale counsels the abandonment of the city as a usable image of whatever kind, while for Reiss the city as an independent object of study becomes a study of community, from which concern with work, social class, mass communications, and other aspects of life in cities are eliminated. Surely this would also eliminate most of the sociological relevance of the metropolis. Ironically, at the point in time when the city has reached a societal dominance never before seen, it seems to elicit confessions of theoretical bankruptcy from its students.

For the economist, too, the city may cease to be a basic unit of analysis. Raymond Bernon concludes from a recent study of the New York Metropolitan Region that

we are a nation tending toward regional self-sufficiency in the production of goods. The plants in each region are developing increasingly complex ties with one another. And although they are not showing any increasing tendency to settle within the borders of metropolitan areas, nevertheless one of the major determinants of their location is the size and location of these metropolitan clusters.[5]

The overweening centralization of many economic activities in cities is, in this view, declining; in its place a considerably larger geographical area (without any of the classic characteristics of cities save economic interdependence), becomes the most useful unit for studying the problems of local economies.

THE CITY AND MASS SOCIETY

Thus, the images of the city deteriorate as the structure of the larger society alters through time: the economic city expands and diffuses, the political city loses autonomy and is merged in the national polity, the social city becomes indistinct from the larger whole, a context, a sample of modern society. This leads to another view of the city—that which identifies the city and nation, summarizing both under the rubric of "mass society." Such an image does not allow one to differentiate the city from all that is most characteristic of contemporary society nor, on the other hand, does it encourage one to investigate the internal structure of the city. It moves from vast changes in the nation to transformations of the individual.

Ortega, Spengler, Durkheim, Tonnies, these are some of the ideologues who saw the city as the summation of contemporary society, the end product of a long process transforming the ethnic groups of band and village into megalopolitan society.[6] Ortega saw the hierarchical orders crumbling beneath the waves of economic and political democracy, and prophesied the state of the masses; western culture would perish under the onslaught of the vulgar. Spengler spoke of the death of culture in the cities of the Autumn, social products of a loss of nerve that would lead, in the end, to Caesarism and the deification of massive power. Durkheim saw the city as epitomizing the social dust heap, the organic society unified by interdependence through the division of labor, but producing an unstable unity in which consensus and solidarity are partial and problematic. Tonnies saw community give way to the urban world in which most bonds are instrumental, negotiable, contractual, while rights and duties become separated from the age-old sanctification of the community and its rewards.

Such is the image of the city as product and producer of mass society: like the magic salt mill that sank, still grinding, to the bottom of the ocean, the city processes the culture and way of life of modern man until the entire sea has been salted. It is an image particularly congruent with American folk thought; the small-town bias of American sociologists and the important rural survivals in urban American culture led many scholars to give credence to the mass image of the urban world, even before the limitations of the various partial analyses noted had become apparent. After all, Lincoln Steffens (still a revered commentator on urban life) became famous for his study, *The Shame of the Cities* and Lord Bryce spoke of American urban government as our most conspicuous failure. Carl Sandburg immortalized an earlier Chicago as "wicked," "crooked," "brutal," while Theodore Dreiser (in his novels based upon the career of Yerkes) made dramatic and credible a view of the city as a veritable jungle in which power was evil, virtue weak, and the community notable for its absence. Such an image of the city combined the view of the countryman, the frustrated reformer, and the laissez-faire liberal of Spencerian proclivities with the powerful poetry of the ideologues.[7] Ralph Borzodi raised the flat question, *Are Cities Abnormal?* and Lewis Mumford looked back in nostalgia to the communes of the thirteenth century. This pessimistic view

attained academic respectability during the 1930's, particularly in the field called "Social Disorganization."[8]

The movement in American sociology to group the scattered studies of "social problems" in the more general field of social disorganization coincided roughly with the great depression. This approach referred all "problems" back to a general illness or incompetence of the social structure; pathological in its focus, it implicitly defined as the normal, healthy society the small town of an earlier America—or even the peasant community and the folk society. This use of a "rural-urban continuum" within which to organize and "explain" a heterogeneous mass of social problems resulted in a ubiquitous bias against the city—while the nation was rapidly becoming urbanized. Although such an approach usually paid lip service to processes of reorganization, the image of the city as the summation of social disorganization left precious little room for stability, order, and reconstruction.

The acceptance of such an image by urban sociologists was not unrelated to the ecological image of the city: it was nourished upon statistics indicating the concentration of crime, suicide, divorce, and other "social pathologies" in the cities as well as the various small studies of Chicago carried out under the direction and inspiration of Robert Park. Pictures of the urban extremes, the "Gold Coast," the slums, the "black belt," the "hobohemia," emphasized the dramatic variety of situations to be found in a metropolitan area.[9] Most important of all, however, was the celebrated essay of Louis Wirth, "Urbanism as a Way of Life," in which Wirth defines the city as a large, dense, permanent settlement of unlike groups and derives from these attributes certain likely patterns of interaction and their consequences: impersonality, isolation, the decline of primary group membership, and the dominance of formal organizations.[10] These are seen as the social characteristics of the city and, by extension, of the contemporary mass society.

Upon such a basis was the "massified" image of the city formulated and built into many urban-sociology textbooks.

Such a view was probably related to the general *weltschmerz* of the deep depression: poverty, unemployment, deficit financing at home; dictatorship, purges, and, above all, the imminence of war abroad. The doctrine of the mass society and the image of the massified city corresponded to a belief in societal determinism reciprocal to the loss of *naive* faith in individual effort. The failure of men to control history in the light of their values was evident on every hand, while Marxism and other forms of historical evolutionism focused attention upon the patterns of the failure. The dissolution of consensus and the collapse of the Republic in Germany; the dramatic quality of mass persuasion used by the demagogues of the right and the left; the power of class and race as tools for organizing social power—these were some of the regular occurrences that bulked so large in the consciousness of the 1930's. Nowhere is this stated more succinctly than in Lederer's book on Hitler, *State of the Masses*, at once a technical analysis and an appreciation of that demagogue's use of the destructive forces inherent in modern, urban society.[11] Awareness of them permeated the social thought of the thirties.

The image of the massified city during the depression was one that was closely related to an image of the total society; yet the American society of the 1930's was also one in which a variety of welfare efforts were under way; the New Deal not only publicized need, it symbolized an evolving polity that tendered means toward amelioration. Pare Lorentz and Lewis Mumford made their spectacular film, "The City," emphasizing the negative judgments of contemporary urban life—but the public-works projects poured millions of man-hours into reconstruction of the city. The mass image never served an eschatological function for American thinkers; their roots in a pragmatic and ameliorative culture were too strong for this. And, once the depression and the war had passed, the image and the reality for which it stood moved very nearly 180 degrees, from moral rejection to acceptance.

In the ten years after World War II a number of influential books appeared, dealing, again, with mass society and the city—but with what a difference! In the works of David Riesman and his associates, as well as those of William Holley White, Samuel Lubell, A. C. Spectorsky, and John R. Seeley, the image of the existing mass society very closely approaches earlier utopias.[12] While the poor remain with us, they are much fewer, and a general ebullience of tone implies their eventual disappearance. While American urban life is mobile and therefore rootless in an older sense, it appears likely that shallow roots will do the trick, even roots like those of certain water plants, which allow the plants wide latitude to drift on a liquid surface. And the political apathy, the vulnerability to charisma and manipulation, the *rassenkampf*, the resentment against the social order?

They are either cured by twenty years of economic expansion, or else made orderly and predictable by the twin engines of the mass market and the mass media. (As Wallace Stevens once wrote: ". . . Oxidia, banal suburb/ One-half of all its installments paid . . . Oxidia is Olympia.")

In all of these works the mass society is practically identified with the massified city; however, there is a striking change in focus. No longer is the older central city the arena in which good and evil grapple in a dozen matches; instead, the center of the mass is now suburbia. The mass society, the crowds of the street, are located far from the warrens of revolution and crime. They are installed, more or less securely, in the ranks of the middle classes.

This image may be called that of the "mass society in an economy of plenty," as contrasted to the "mass society of deprivation." Its principle characteristics are a continuous and easy upward mobility or, as an alternative, a secure and easy access to the goods of the mass market, for all of the population—this in combination with a wide area of choice in articles of consumption, residence, "culture," social interaction itself. The rules for obtaining the abundance of this cornucopia, however, are rather limiting at the individual level as they are not clearly understood at the societal level. In general, the resident of the massified city is portrayed as committed to (and conforming to) the bureaucratic norms in his place of work, the uncodified norms of his peer group, the continuous bombardment of norms from the mass media. He is, in short, a conformist. Riesman attempts to relate these patterns to changes in the organization of the total society, and to trace the consequences in the institutional areas of work, play, politics, and the like. Whyte emphasizes the social structure of the modern corporation and its consequences for the social character and life style of its employees. The authors of *Crestwood Heights* focus upon the interlocked mechanisms of neighborhood and school as sources of conformity. It is an image of the city that has structural components very similar to those of the "mass society" predicted by the gloomy prophets of the depression, but the over-all color and tone are very different. The degree to which this is caused by a real difference in the nature of the city and the degree to which it is colored by the eyes of the observer remain to be seen.

THE CRISIS

Some forty years after urban sociologists began their intensive study of the city and political scientists became empirical students of public administration and political behavior, our image of the city is in a process of dissolution. While we are far richer in heterogeneous concepts and partial theories, as well as information of one kind and another, in crucial ways we are curiously poverty stricken. There is little order in our theories, and our data seem largely irrelevant to them. At the very point in time when we become a metropolitan society, when the problems of the metropolis excite widespread interest, study, and action, some of the scholars studying the city lean toward the notion that it has disappeared while others proffer images so disparate and discrepant that they hardly seem to refer to the same elephant.

The city is a struggle of interest groups, an administrative hierarchy working toward the perfect machine in a curious isolation from politics, or a population whose behavior may be studied as manifestations of power at least as readily as any other aggregate. Or, it is a vast piling up of people with various characteristics, literally, a social "dust heap," organized only in the myriad competing and accommodating subgroups whose arbiter is the market. Or, it is a complex of firms, whose orientation is toward supply, production, marketing, and the advantages of location. Alternatively, it is a spatially defined segment of the total society, a sample of the mass, moving toward anarchy, anomie, revolution and dictatorship—or toward conformism, simple-minded cultural uniformity, prosperity, and bureaucratic rule. Some of these images are in direct conflict, assuming polar opposites in the behavior of the urban population. Furthermore, all of them omit a consideration of most of the routine, everyday, social order that permits a daily reprieve for the dependent millions of the urban islands.

The crisis of the city is thus, in the beginning at least, an intellectual crisis. The inherited images are no longer applicable; they are partial and based upon assumptions about the total society that are unexamined and frequently outmoded. Furthermore, the action crisis of the metropolis cannot be disengaged from the intellectual crisis, for the very definition of a metropolitan problem is dependent upon one's picture of the city and the kind of life it should contain, as the choice of action to improve or revolutionize is dependent upon one's estimate of the city as an existing entity. Those who retain the image of the city as a legal person, a corporate entity, heir to the city-states of Greece, Italy, and medieval Europe, will hardly agree with those who see it chiefly as a spatial sample of a massified society. Their notions of what is, what should be, and how it may be brought about, will tend toward the poles of possibility.

The peculiar quality of this confusion, however, is the presumption of partial validity that each image of the city elicits. While the city is not "militarily autonomous," its corporate nature cannot be dismissed. Anyone who has heard the Viziers of City Hall in a great metropolis refer proudly to "The City" is disabused of the notion. No matter how the rulers are recruited, they control a polity most immediately felt by the citizen, for they rule him "where he lives." Nor can we forget the economic basis of the city and the patterns of land use that order it in space. Where, then, does the failure of urban social science lie? It would be presumptuous to answer with more than hypotheses; however, the statement of such propositions may clarify the problem of improving our image of the city. Implied or stated in the foregoing discussions, three weaknesses in the conceptualization of urban society are baldly evident: the inadequate empirical relevance of many of these images, the partial nature of the approaches, and their limited scope and special nature.

Empirical Relevance

The failure of various images of the city to be empirically relevant may not be apparent to the casual reader; our own daily observations are so persuasive as generalities that we unconsciously validate the casual empiricism of the image maker while our own values make it easy to accept the order proffered by our favorite ideologue. Yet, if the foregoing argument has virtue, arbitration among competing images is badly needed. We must cease to think like the supposed object of study, and become the student. For this purpose, the final arbiter of social science must be the empirical argument; such an argument, however, is applicable only when the image itself may be reduced to empirically relevant theory. Failure to do so has been one cause for the multiplication of images.

Some of the images are inherently untestable as stated, for they cannot possibly be falsified. Spengler, Marx, Ortega, each assumes a natural law whose unfolding can never be foretold within the limits of test: it must be inferred after the fact. Further, such ideologues appeal also to natural right, and assume that in the long run the course of history will move toward their own judgment of human behavior. We need not multiply examples of such a position. When, however, these images of the mass society are shorn of their evolutionary presuppositions and their evaluative connotations and used as working guides, they become very different. Discounting the data from the past at the same rate we use for present observations, and eliminating proleptic prediction (or prophecy) as data, we remain with a host of hypotheses as guides to the description of social behavior in the societies and cities of today.

Such description as we have available, however, suffers from sampling bias. The early studies of Gold Coast and slum, as well as very recent reports on the new suburbia, represent a selection of polar extremes and a heightening

of dramatic contrasts through uncontrolled inference from limited observation. A theory that emphasizes extremes does not necessarily tell us anything at all about the excluded middle, which may, after all, include the vast majority of urban residents. The wealthy social circles of exurbia, the enclaves of the company men, are latter day equivalents of the "Taxi-Dance Hall" and the "Hobohemia": their use as ideal types of modern urban society is suspect indeed.

Nor can we accept, as clinching evidence in arbitrating among the images, the analysis of mass data provided by the census. It is limited indeed, and there are few postulates constructed to satisfactorily carry the argument from statistical aggregates to the nature of ongoing behavior. The rhetoric of mass statistics tells us, for example, little about the nature of metropolitan government: size, number, variety of suburban municipalities, and similar data have no self-evident connection with the nature of the political process in suburbia. Nor can we infer a great deal from the information that more crime is committed in the metropolis than the middle-sized city, in the slum than in the suburb. Ingenious and skillful analysts continue to order the data provided by the census: it is a distortion of method, leading to a distortion of theory, to presume that such data will have more than a very narrow relevance to such images of the social city as we have adduced.

But the journalist, the shrewd observer, the analyst of census data, has provided most of the evidence for and against the various images of the city. None can, in the nature of his trade, supply the data for a crucial test—none of the images can be "mapped into" a model and evaluated so easily as that.

The Partially Explicated Nature of Theory

A partially explicated theory assumes propositions in its basic explanations that are never made explicit and related to its other aspects; thus, it omits serious consideration of behavior that is crucial even to the limited aspect of things with which it deals. The advocates of scientific management in public administration focus straitly upon the formal machinery, knowing that the party structure and the various kinds of community influence constantly sway behavior away from bureaucratic norms. The urban ecologist ignores the social organization producing spatial patterns as well as that resulting from contiguity or separation. The student of public finance assumes as given, not only the economic history of his metropolis, but the mutual impact of the private enterprises and the public fisc.

To be sure, any approach must abstract; the key question, then, is the determination of criteria for exclusion or inclusion. There are two major guiding notions; first, we must include that which is necessary to the full explication of our theory (the image must be complete); second, we must move toward a closer "fit" between our theory and the delimited aspect of behavior upon which we are focused (the image must be tested). Ideally, all that is included in a given scientific approach, all that constitutes a given image of the city, must be "internal." It must make sense in the same vocabulary. An integrated approach to the urban polity does not adduce psychosomatic medicine, the technology of flood control, and the biology of fecundity into its framework *without translation.*

As the need is felt for further explanation, however, the tendency has been to add theory from every level of explanation, to mix metaphors unmercifully. Consequently, the special cases begin to outnumber the rule and social science becomes a very idiomatic language. Logically, the consequences are fatal: all can be explained after the fact, nothing can be predicted. The *ad hoc* notions from various sources become outriggers that prevent the boat from capsizing, at the cost of getting the boat in the water.

Thus, a major weakness in the various images of the city has been their lack of complete explication, and this results in a very hazy delimitation of explanatory power. The theory that is not delimited as to its application has a tendency to be continually absorbing notions at every level of generality, leaving unanswered the major question of its own internal logic, and therefore the point at which it can be profitably related to other images from other disciplines. In this light, the interdisciplinary tendency in urban studies may be a vitiating influence, for it weakens the integrity of each evolving image without uniting them in an orderly fashion.

The Limited Scope of Urban Theory

However, the images tend more and more to interpenetrate as the political scientist concerns himself with the economic growth of the city, the ecologist struggles to relate the increasingly important effects of government to the old regularities of land use, and the economist tries to deal with the corporation as a private government, the government as a public enterprise. Such shifts are not due solely to the internal dynamics of each theoretical approach; they are vitally related to the shifting relations between the great institutional areas of the society. Shrewd observers relying on personal observation note that politics may be seen as a "consumption of goods," the customer and firm as a single "organizational system," or the urban area as an "ecology of games." They are mixing their metaphors consciously; the effort is sparked by observation of the changing relations among major areas of the culture.

At the same time, the kaleidoscope of images betrays a wavering and rapidly shifting focus—where are the key structures of the city, and what changes are definitive? Are they located in the metropolitan region as a whole? the mass society? the suburbs? the central city? The spatial abstraction (the "given" image of a congestion of human activity on the face of the earth) is evidently not defining: further and other abstraction is required.

The interpenetration of images and the shifting focus both reflect the overall dynamics of the carrying society. The analysis of the city that views it as spatially abstracted eliminates (1) the relation between the city and the larger society, and therefore (2) the key dynamics in the evolving society that largely determine the relations between institutional areas and the significant organizational unit for observation. A theory limited to "the city" is too narrow in scope to explain the changing landscape of the city itself.

THE AIM OF THIS STUDY

If the above analysis is useful, it should provide directives for the reinterpretation of contemporary urban society and the reformulation of the urban image. Such a reinterpretation must have a wider scope, a more specific empirical reference, and a greater theoretical integrity than those discussed above.

It must emphasize the study of the urban complex as a structure, but a structure intimately related to the nature of the carrying society. Thus, the image of the city must be contained within an over-all picture of urban society; "urbanization" and "urbanism," in this approach, become adjectives referring to a society, not merely its population concentrations. Furthermore, such a picture must be congruent with long-term change—in the general society, in the nature of the city, and in the relations between the two.

The approach must yield an empirically relevant image, one that can be tested at many points. It must be based upon the data available, particularly those data free from the limitations of sampling bias and uncontrolled inference. It must, further, yield new vantage points from which to view old problems and create new problems with enough salience to force reconsiderations and improvements in the over-all image.

Finally, it must be guided by a concern for theoretical integrity. The focus must be delimited, the internal structure of the theory must be explicated, otherwise the image is neither clearly applicable nor testable. Consequently, however, all aspects of urban life cannot be considered. Whether those emphasized are the most useful for such an enterprise is a decision that will rest with the arbiters of improved empirical evidence and, finally, the pragmatic test of intellectual history.

NOTES

1. Philip M. Hauser, *Population Perspectives*, New Brunswick, N.J.: Rutgers University Press, 1960, "The Metropolitan Area Explosion: The Facts," Chapter 4, page 101.

2. *Ibid.*, pp. 101-106.

3. Don Martindale, "Prefatory Remarks: The Theory of the City," in Max Weber, *The City* (translated by Don Martindale and Gertrud Neuwirth), New York: The Free Press of Glencoe, 1958, p. 62.

4. Albert J. Reiss, Jr., in "Introduction: The Sociology of Urban Life, 1946-1956," in Paul K. Hatt and Albert J. Reiss, Jr. (eds.), *Cities and Society, The Revised Reader in Urban Sociology,* New York: The Free Press of Glencoe, 1957, pp. 10-11.

5. "Urban Production and Distribution," in "The Metropolis in Ferment," *Annals of the American Academy of Political and Social Science,* 314, 20-21. Donald M. Pappenfort has made a similar observation: from a conventional ecological point of view the metropolis is not a discrete entity at all, in his opinion. See "The Ecological Field and the Metropolitan Community: Manufacturing and Management," *American Journal of Sociology,* 69, 380-385.

6. For typical works see José Ortega y Gasset, *The State of the Masses;* Oswald Spengler, *Decline of the West;* Emile Durkheim, *The Division of Labor in Society* (translated by George Simpson), New York: The Free Press of Glencoe, 1949 (especially the Preface to the Second Edition); Ferdinand Tonnies, *Gemeinschaft und Gesellschaft* (translated by Charles P. Loomis as *Community and Society*), East Lansing, Mich.: Michigan State University Press, 1957.

7. For extensive and lively documentation of this melodramatic definition, see Anselm Strauss, *Images of the American City,* New York: The Free Press of Glencoe, 1961, particularly Chapter 10,

"Rural Aspects of Metropolitan Living." Closer to home is his "Appendix: A Note on Imagery in Urban Sociology."

8. For examples of this approach see Mable A. Elliott and Francis E. Merrill, *Social Disorganization,* New York: Harper and Brothers, 1941; and Robert E. L. Faris, *Social Disorganization,* New York: The Ronald Press, 1948.

9. Harvey W. Zorbaugh, *The Gold Coast and the Slum,* Chicago: University of Chicago Press, 1929; E. Franklin Frazier, *The Negro Family in Chicago,* Chicago: University of Chicago Press, 1932; Nels Anderson, *The Hobo,* Chicago: University of Chicago Press, 1923.

10. Louis Wirth, "Urbanism as a Way of Life," *American Journal of Sociology,* 44, 1-24. For a later statement more directly addressed to the mass-society hypothesis see his article on "Consensus and Mass Communications" in the *American Sociological Review,* 13, 1-15.

11. Emil Lederer, *State of the Masses.*

12. David Riesman, with Reuel Denny and Nathan Glazer, *The Lonely Crowd,* New Haven: Yale University Press, 1950; William H. Whyte, Jr., *The Organization Man,* New York: Simon and Schuster, 1956; Samuel Lubell, *The Future of American Politics,* Garden City, N. Y.: Doubleday and Company, Inc. (Anchor Edition), 1956 and *The Revolt of the Moderates,* New York: Harper and Brothers, 1956; A. C. Spectorsky, *The Exurbanites,* Philadelphia: J. B. Lippincott Company, 1955; John R. Seeley, R. Alexander Sim, and Elizabeth W. Loosly, *Crestwood Heights, A Study of the Culture of Suburban Life,* New York: Basic Books, Inc., 1955.

VII THE CITY IN NATIONAL AFFAIRS

Today it is almost a truism to say that urban problems are national problems. But many who make this point, especially journalists, politicians, and TV and radio commentators, tend to speak of the impact of the city upon national affairs as a recent phenomenon. Actually, it has a long history and there are innumerable examples in this book alone that show the direct and indirect influences that the city has had upon the national arena, socially, economically, and technologically. This chapter highlights the political impact by grouping the selections around three topics: the Progressive Era as an urban-reform movement, the relationship between the city and the federal government, and the influence of the city upon the national party system.

The Progressive Era provoked the first *national* reform movement that reflected the transition of an agrarian nation into an urban-industrialized giant. Of course the Populist movement of the 1890's was also a part of this transition, but its appeal was limited largely to the rural South and parts of the West and Midwest. The Progressive crusade, more than the Populist movement, was relevant to all geographic sections and all social classes, and it provoked a sharper response to the urban, industrial, and technological realities of the late nineteenth and early twentieth centuries. For some reformers it meant the redemption of democracy, for others an opportunity to resurrect an older and more virtuous America, and for still others the chance to transform innovations in business and technology into political action.

The seedtime of Progressivism was the 1890's; its heyday, the decade before the First World War; its impulse, an urban response to a new age. Although today most historians agree the Progressive movement was largely an urban phenomenon, there is considerable disagreement about its meaning, leadership, goals, and success that has thrown up a flurry of paradoxes.[1]

1. For an excellent bibliographical essay on the Progressive Era, see Robert Wiebe, *The Search for Order* (New York: Hill and Wang, 1967), pp. 303-24.

For the movement has been seen as liberal and conservative, a triumph and a flop, led by either the working class, the middle class, or the upper class, or a combination of politicians reflecting all classes, who either looked to the future or to the past. This debate, whose fury seems to be increasing, suggests that the Progressive movement has become a battleground for historians to argue the success or failure of the liberal tradition in the United States.

Samuel P. Hays is a good example of one who is leading a flank attack against the bastions of Progressive interpretation. His essay is both a major interpretation of Progressivism and an opportunity to review other interpretations. Hays's target is a group of revisionist historians, primarily Richard Hofstadter, who sought to revise the interpretation of the Progressive historians who saw the movement as a continuation of Jeffersonian reform—a class struggle of "the people" battling acquisitive businessmen, seeking the democratization of political institutions, fighting for an equalitarian society open to all with special privilege to none. Hofstadter in his *Age of Reform* (1955) held that the movement was actually led by reasonably affluent members of the middle class who were tormented with "status anxieties" and inspired by the values of the Protestant ethic and who sought to turn back to an older America hardly in tune with the realities of a modern urban age. Revisionism is an occupational hazard that often invites the criticism that can convert the victor into the victim. Hence, Hays attacks Hofstadter and the proponents of the "status revolution" theory to argue that Progressivism was in fact led by an upper-class group who, rather than alienated by society, were experts in the techniques of business management and the newer technological procedures and sought to introduce them into city government.[2] Hays argues that there was a striking difference between what Progressives said and what they did. They spoke as champions of the equalitarian society, enemies of special privilege, and friends of the poor. In practice, however, they destroyed a broad form of representative government, were agents of a special privileged group, and were profoundly distrustful of the lower and middle classes. The judgments come from Hays's study of the two major reforms of municipal government coming out of the Progressive period: the commission system and the city-manager plan, reforms that were in fact elitist in nature with definite anti-democratic overtones.[3]

Like many of the reformers of the Tweed Ring era, the Progressives were more concerned with introducing business efficiency in government than in measures of social justice. Unlike these reformers, however, the Progressives,

2. For an opposing view which stresses the importance of the working class, see J. Joseph Huthmacher, "Urban Liberalism and the Age of Reform," *Mississippi Valley Historical Review* (September 1962).

3. See James Weinstein, "Organized Business and the City Commission and Manager Movements," *Journal of Southern History* (May 1962), and the indictments of Lawrence J. R. Herson, "The Lost World of Municipal Government," *American Political Science Review* (June 1957).

according to Hays, were less concerned with the moral issue of "bad men" and more intent in redistributing decision-making powers and centralizing them in the hands of a select few who represented the new wealth that was spawned by the industrial advances of the last quarter of the nineteenth century. While some historians who favor a more plural approach to Progressivism might argue there was more to Progressivism than this, Professor Hays does show that reform does not always advance "progressive" and "liberal" objectives. The voice of the people can also be the voice of elitism. Employing techniques of the political scientist, he argues persuasively that political rhetoric is only one aspect of political behavior.

Another question often obscured by present-mindedness is the role of the federal government in urban affairs, the theme of the next two essays. Many students of urban affairs are concerned that the burgeoning growth of the large metropolitan areas constitute a new and drastic change in American federalism as the cities bypass the states to cement a direct federal-city relationship. Thus the old structure of federalism based on the dual arrangement of federal-state will become, like Gaul, divided into three parts: federal-state-city. Fundamental to this view is the assumption that a meaningful federal-city relationship is a fairly recent novelty, beginning in 1933 with the New Deal. In other words, the federal government employed a laissez-faire policy toward the American city until the New Deal. Daniel J. Elazar shatters these assumptions, showing: (1) The federal-city relationship is decidedly not new; discussing innumerable urban needs met by federal engagement, Elazar shows it has a long history reaching back into the earlier years of the nineteenth century.[4] (2) The new specialized demands of the large cities began not in 1933, but originated some fifteen to thirty years before the New Deal. If a watershed has to be made it should be 1913 which, according to Elazar, was the real end of the nineteenth century.

Certainly the most arresting feature of the federal pattern was the cleavage caused by the emergence of big cities as special entities, smacking of the city-state. With their different and specialized needs, they created a cleavage not only between urban and nonurban areas but within the urban world as well. For as Elazar points out, many smaller cities with a fifty thousand population or less still tend to ally themselves with rural areas and often resist, to the point of rejection, big city ideas. This and other implications that Elazar discusses necessitate a new and deeper examination of the urban impact upon the federal structure.

Whereas Elazar talks optimistically of a "co-operative federalism," Charles Abrams speaks darkly of a "bizarre federalism" which was the creature of a political heritage conspicuously inadequate for the modern urban world and its mounting aches and pains. To Abrams the necessity of an intimate, in-

4. See also Robert A. Lively, "The American System: A Review Article," *Business History Review* (March 1955).

vigorating federal-city relationship was crippled by an inconsistent federal government tripping over worn-out theories of states' rights, home rule, and local autonomy. The city is fouled in a regional and constitutional web that threatens its creative powers. Abrams accounts for the entanglement by tracing the historic factors involved, the conflicting and often unclear concepts of the public interest, the high days and key events of the New Deal that in urban housing opened a new era in federal-city relations but was dissipated by a reversion to the debilitating demands of states' rights advocates and the self-interest of suburban communities. The villain of Abrams's piece is the decentralization of decision-making powers.

In the last essay, Carl Degler asks questions that involve two critical turning points in our political history: how do you account for the dominance of the Republican party for a third of a century and the predominance of the Democratic party for most of the recent third of the twentieth century? His answers forge an intimate link between the city and national politics.

It was the "rising cities" and the receptibility of the parties to the urban voter that account for two political revolutions that occurred in little over a generation. In coming to these conclusions, Degler challenges some widely held views about the recent past and the national party system. Thus the Republicans emerged as the majority party of the nation, not in the 1870's nor in the 1880's, but in the middle of the 1890's with the critical elections of 1894 and 1896. These elections reflected conditions that were maturing in the previous decade—the rise of labor, unprecedented railroad construction, industrial output, and violent labor upheavals that together announced "the arrival of the new world of the factory, the city, and the immigrant." Thus the "watershed" thesis that sees the transition from agrarian to industrial occurring during the 1890's is invalid, since the transition actually took place in the 1880's, according to Degler. Moreover, neither changes in leadership nor the policies of the enemy, the Democrats, account for the thrust of the Republicans. Dominance was secured because the Republicans were the party most attuned to the needs and realities of the new urban industrial era. Thus, he challenges the view of the Republican party as the conservative arm of big business; on the contrary, it was the party of "energy and change."

By the same token, it is the flexibility of the Democratic party to social change and its appeal to the urban voter that accounts for the emergence of the Democrats in recent history. While many historians have believed the New Deal to be the beginning of Democratic popularity, Degler argues, it was the appeal of that "asphalt flower," Al Smith, in the campaign of 1928, and the four vital years before 1933 and the Presidency of Roosevelt.

The obvious conclusion is that for the past as well as for the future, the city has been and will be the vital hinge on which the door to party dominance opens or closes. George Mayer, an historian of the Republican party, puts it well:

The burgeoning problems of the city offer the G.O.P. more opportunity for constructive action, inasmuch as they generate antagonism between important elements of the Democratic coalition. Thus preconditions for a change in political attitudes already exist. For such a shift to materialize, the Democrats would have to take the loyalty of their dissidents for granted, and the Republicans would have to offer dynamic leadership. Otherwise, the G.O.P. seems certain to occupy its current role as a minority party for the foreseeable future.[5]

5. *The Republican Party, 1854-1966* (New York: Oxford, 1964; 1967, 2nd edition, paperback), p. 558.

The Politics of Reform in Municipal Government in the Progressive Era

SAMUEL P. HAYS

In order to achieve a more complete understanding of social change in the Progressive Era, historians must now undertake a deeper analysis of the practices of economic, political, and social groups. Political ideology alone is no longer satisfactory evidence to describe social patterns because generalizations based upon it, which tend to divide political groups into the moral and the immoral, the rational and the irrational, the efficient and the inefficient, do not square with political practice. Behind this contemporary rhetoric concerning the nature of reform lay patterns of political behavior which were at variance with it. Since an extensive gap separated ideology and practice, we can no longer take the former as an accurate description of the latter, but must reconstruct social behavior from other types of evidence.

Reform in urban government provides one of the most striking examples of this problem of analysis. The demand for change in municipal affairs, whether in terms of over-all reform, such as the commission and city-manager plans, or of more piecemeal modifications, such as the development of city-wide school boards, deeply involved reform ideology. Reformers loudly proclaimed a new structure of municipal government as more moral, more rational, and more efficient and, because it was so, self-evidently more desirable. But precisely because of this emphasis, there seemed to be no need to analyze the political forces behind change. Because the goals of reform were good, its causes were obvious; rather than being the product of particular people and particular ideas in particular situations, they were deeply imbedded in the universal impulses and truths of "progress." Consequently, historians have rarely tried to

From *Pacific Northwest Quarterly* (October 1964), pp. 157-69. Reprinted by permission of the publisher. Samuel P. Hays is Professor of American History at the University of Pittsburgh.

determine precisely who the municipal reformers were or what they did, but instead have relied on reform ideology as an accurate description of reform practice.

The reform ideology which became the basis of historical analysis is well known. It appears in classic form in Lincoln Steffens' *Shame of the Cities.* The urban political struggle of the Progressive Era, so the argument goes, involved a conflict between public impulses for "good government" against a corrupt alliance of "machine politicians" and "special interests."

During the rapid urbanization of the late 19th century, the latter had been free to aggrandize themselves, especially through franchise grants, at the expense of the public. Their power lay primarily in their ability to manipulate the political process, by bribery and corruption, for their own ends. Against such arrangements there gradually arose a public protest, a demand by the public for honest government, for officials who would act for the public rather than for themselves. To accomplish their goals, reformers sought basic modifications in the political system, both in the structure of government and in the manner of selecting public officials. These changes, successful in city after city, enabled the "public interest" to triumph.[1]

Recently, George Mowry, Alfred Chandler, Jr., and Richard Hofstadter have modified this analysis by emphasizing the fact that the impulse for reform did not come from the working class.[2] This might have been suspected from the rather strained efforts of National Municipal League writers in the "Era of Reform" to go out of their way to demonstrate working-class support for commission and city-manager governments.[3] We now know that they clutched at straws, and often erroneously, in order to prove to themselves as well as to the public that municipal reform was a mass movement.

The Mowry-Chandler-Hofstadter writings have further modified older views by asserting that reform in general and municipal reform in particular sprang from a distinctively middle-class movement. This has now become the prevailing view. Its popularity is surprising not only because it is based upon faulty logic and extremely limited evidence, but also because it, too, emphasizes the analysis of ideology rather than practice and fails to contribute much to the understanding of who distinctively were involved in reform and why.

Ostensibly, the "middle-class" theory of reform is based upon a new type of behavioral evidence, the collective biography, in studies by Mowry of California Progressive party leaders, by Chandler of a nationwide group of that party's leading figures, and by Hofstadter of four professions—ministers, lawyers, teachers, editors. These studies demonstrate the middle-class nature of reform, but they fail to determine if reformers were distinctively middle class, specifically if they differed from their opponents. One study of 300 political leaders in the state of Iowa, for example, discovered that Progressive party, Old Guard, and Cummins Republicans were all substantially alike, the Progressives differing only in that they were slightly younger than the others and had less political experience.[4] If its opponents were also middle class, then one cannot describe Progressive reform as a phenomenon, the special nature of which can be explained in terms of middle-class characteristics. One cannot explain the distinctive behavior of people in terms of characteristics which are not distinctive to them.

Hofstadter's evidence concerning professional men fails in yet another way to determine the peculiar characteristics of reformers. For he describes ministers, lawyers, teachers, and editors without determining who within these professions became reformers and who did not. Two analytical distinctions might be made. Ministers involved in municipal reform, it appears, came not from all segments of religion, but peculiarly from upper-class churches. They enjoyed the highest prestige and salaries in the religious community and had no reason to feel a loss of "status," as Hofstadter argues. Their role in reform arose from the class character of their religious organizations rather than from the mere fact of their occupation as ministers.[5] Professional men involved in reform (many of whom—engineers, architects, and doctors—Hofstadter did not examine at all) seem to have come especially from the more advanced segments of their professions, from those who sought to apply their specialized knowledge to a wider range of public affairs.[6] Their role in reform is related not to their attempt to defend earlier patterns of culture, but to the working out of the inner dynamics of professionalization in modern society.

The weakness of the "middle-class" theory of reform stems from the fact that it rests primarily upon ideological evidence, not on a thoroughgoing description of political practice. Although the studies of Mowry, Chandler, and Hofstadter ostensibly derive from behavioral evidence, they actually derive largely from the extensive expressions of middle-ground ideological position, of the reformers' own descriptions of their contemporary society, and of their expressed fears of both the lower and the upper classes, of the fright of being ground between the millstones of labor and capital.[7]

Such evidence, though it accurately portrays what people thought, does not accurately describe what they did. The great majority of Americans look upon themselves as "middle class" and subscribe to a middle-ground ideology, even though in practice they belong to a great variety of distinct social classes. Such ideologies are not rationalizations or deliberate attempts to deceive. They are natural phenomena of human behavior. But the historian should be especially sensitive to their role so that he will not take evidence of political ideology as an accurate representation of political practice.

In the following account I will summarize evidence in both secondary and primary works concerning the political practices in which municipal reformers were involved. Such an analysis logically can be broken down into three parts, each one corresponding to a step in the traditional argument. First, what was the source of reform? Did it lie in the general public rather than in particular groups? Was it middle class, working class, or perhaps of other composition? Second, what was the reform target of attack? Were reformers primarily interested in ousting the corrupt individual, the political or business leader who made private arrangements at the expense of the public, or were they interested in something else? Third, what political innovations did reformers bring about? Did they seek to expand popular participation in the governmental process?

There is now sufficient evidence to

determine the validity of these specific elements of the more general argument. Some of it has been available for several decades; some has appeared more recently; some is presented here for the first time. All of it adds up to the conclusion that reform in municipal government involved a political development far different from what we have assumed in the past.

Available evidence indicates that the source of support for reform in municipal government did not come from the lower or middle classes, but from the upper class. The leading business groups in each city and professional men closely allied with them initiated and dominated municipal movements. Leonard White, in his study of the city manager published in 1927, wrote:

The opposition to bad government usually comes to a head in the local chamber of commerce. Business men finally acquire the conviction that the growth of their city is being seriously impaired by the failures of city officials to perform their duties efficiently. Looking about for a remedy, they are captivated by the resemblance of the city-manager plan to their corporate form of business organization.[8]

In the 1930's White directed a number of studies of the origin of city-manager government. The resulting reports invariably begin with such statements as, "the Chamber of Commerce spearheaded the movement," or commission government in this city was a "businessmen's government."[9] Of thirty-two cases of city-manager government in Oklahoma examined by Jewell C. Phillips, twenty-nine were initiated either by chambers of commerce or by community committees dominated by businessmen.[10] More recently James Weinstein has presented almost irrefutable evidence that the business community, represented largely by chambers of commerce, was the overwhelming force behind both commission and city-manager movements.[11]

Dominant elements of the business community played a prominent role in another crucial aspect of municipal reform: the Municipal Research Bureau movement.[12] Especially in the larger cities, where they had less success in shaping the structure of government, reformers established centers to conduct research in municipal affairs as a springboard for influence.

The first such organization, the Bureau of Municipal Research of New York City, was founded in 1906; it was financed largely through the efforts of Andrew Carnegie and John D. Rockefeller. An investment banker provided the crucial support in Philadelphia, where a Bureau was founded in 1908. A group of wealthy Chicagoans in 1910 established the Bureau of Public Efficiency, a research agency. John H. Patterson of the National Cash Register Company, the leading figure in Dayton municipal reform, financed the Dayton Bureau, founded in 1912. And George Eastman was the driving force behind both the Bureau of Municipal Research and city-manager government in Rochester. In smaller cities data about city government was collected by interested individuals in a more informal way or by chambers of commerce, but in larger cities the task required special support, and prominent businessmen supplied it.

The character of municipal reform is demonstrated more precisely by a brief examination of the movements in Des Moines and Pittsburgh. The Des Moines Commercial Club inaugurated and carefully controlled the drive for the commission form of government.[13] In January, 1906, the Club held a so-called "mass meeting" of business and professional men to secure an enabling act from the state legislature. P. C. Kenyon, president of the Club, selected a Committee of 300, composed principally of business and professional men, to draw up a specific proposal. After the legislature approved their plan, the same committee managed the campaign which persuaded the electorate to accept the commission form of government by a narrow margin in June, 1907.

In this election the lower-income wards of the city opposed the change, the upper-income wards supported it strongly, and the middle-income wards were more evenly divided. In order to control the new government, the Committee of 300, now expanded to 530, sought to determine the nomination and election of the five new commissioners, and to this end they selected an avowedly businessman's slate. Their plans backfired when the voters swept into office a slate of anticommission candidates who now controlled the new commission government.

Proponents of the commission form of government in Des Moines spoke frequently in the name of the "people." But their more explicit statements emphasized their intent that the new plan be a "business system" of government, run by businessmen. The slate of candidates for commissioner endorsed by advocates of the plan was known as the "businessman's ticket." J. W. Hill, president of the committees of 300 and 530, bluntly declared: "The professional politician must be ousted and in his place capable business men chosen to conduct the affairs of the city." I. M. Earle, general counsel of the Bankers Life Association and a prominent figure in the movement, put the point more precisely: "When the plan was adopted it

was the intention to get businessmen to run it."

Although reformers used the ideology of popular government, they in no sense meant that all segments of society should be involved equally in municipal decision-making. They meant that their concept of the city's welfare would be best achieved if the business community controlled city government. As one businessman told a labor audience, the businessman's slate represented labor "better than you do yourself."

The composition of the municipal reform movement in Pittsburgh demonstrates its upper-class and professional as well as its business sources.[14] Here the two principal reform organizations were the Civic Club and the Voters' League. The 745 members of these two organizations came primarily from the upper class. Sixty-five per cent appeared in upper-class directories which contained the names of only 2 per cent of the city's families. Furthermore, many who were not listed in these directories lived in upper-class areas. These reformers, it should be stressed, comprised not an old but a new upper class. Few came from earlier industrial and mercantile families. Most of them had risen to social position from wealth created after 1870 in the iron, steel, electrical equipment, and other industries, and they lived in the newer rather than the older fashionable areas.

Almost half (48 per cent) of the reformers were professional men: doctors, lawyers, ministers, directors of libraries and museums, engineers, architects, private and public school teachers, and college professors. Some of these belonged to the upper class as well, especially the lawyers, ministers, and private school teachers. But for the most part

their interest in reform stemmed from
the inherent dynamics of their professions rather than from their class connections. They came from the more advanced segments of their organizations,
from those in the forefront of the
acquisition and application of knowledge. They were not the older professional men, seeking to preserve the past
against change; they were in the vanguard of professional life, actively seeking to apply expertise more widely to
public affairs.

Pittsburgh reformers included a large
segment of businessmen; 52 per cent
were bankers and corporation officials or
their wives. Among them were the presidents of fourteen large banks and officials of Westinghouse, Pittsburgh Plate
Glass, U.S. Steel and its component
parts (such as Carnegie Steel, American
Bridge, and National Tube), Jones and
Laughlin, lesser steel companies (such
as Crucible, Pittsburgh, Superior, Lock-
hart, and H. K. Porter), the H. J. Heinz
Company, and the Pittsburgh Coal
Company, as well as officials of the
Pennsylvania Railroad and the Pittsburgh and Lake Erie. These men were
not small businessmen; they directed
the most powerful banking and industrial organizations of the city. They
represented not the old business community, but industries which had developed and grown primarily within the
past fifty years and which had come to
dominate the city's economic life.

These business, professional, and
upper-class groups who dominated municipal reform movements were all involved in the rationalization and systematization of modern life; they
wished a form of government which
would be more consistent with the objectives inherent in those developments.
The most important single feature of

their perspective was the rapid expansion of the geographical scope of affairs
which they wished to influence and manipulate, a scope which was no longer
limited and narrow, no longer within
the confines of pedestrian communities,
but was now broad and city-wide, covering the whole range of activities of
the metropolitan area.

The migration of the upper class
from central to outlying areas created a
geographical distance between its residential communities and its economic
institutions. To protect the latter required involvement both in local ward
affairs and in the larger city government
as well. Moreover, upper-class cultural
institutions, such as museums, libraries,
and symphony orchestras, required an
active interest in the larger municipal
context from which these institutions
drew much of their clientele.

Professional groups, broadening the
scope of affairs which they sought to
study, measure, or manipulate, also
sought to influence the public health,
the educational system, or the physical
arrangements of the entire city. Their
concerns were limitless, not bounded by
geography, but as expansive as the professional imagination. Finally, the new
industrial community greatly broadened its perspective in governmental
affairs because of its new recognition of
the way in which factors throughout
the city affected business growth. The
increasing size and scope of industry,
the greater stake in more varied and
geographically dispersed facets of city
life, the effect of floods on many business concerns, the need to promote
traffic flows to and from work for both
blue-collar and managerial employees
—all contributed to this larger interest.
The geographically larger private perspectives of upper-class, · professional,

and business groups gave rise to a geographically larger public perspective.

These reformers were dissatisfied with existing systems of municipal government. They did not oppose corruption per se—although there was plenty of that. They objected to the structure of government which enabled local and particularistic interests to dominate. Prior to the reforms of the Progressive Era, city government consisted primarily of confederations of local wards, each of which was represented on the city's legislative body. Each ward frequently had its own elementary schools and ward-elected school boards which administered them.

These particularistic interests were the focus of a decentralized political life. City councilmen were local leaders. They spoke for their local areas, the economic interests of their inhabitants, their residential concerns, their educational, recreational, and religious interests—i.e., for those aspects of community life which mattered most to those they represented. They rolled logs in the city council to provide streets, sewers, and other public works for their local areas. They defended the community's cultural practices, its distinctive languages or national customs, its liberal attitude toward liquor, and its saloons and dance halls which served as centers of community life. One observer described this process of representation in Seattle:

The residents of the hill-tops and the suburbs may not fully appreciate the faithfulness of certain downtown ward councilmen to the interests of their constituents. . . . The people of a state would rise in arms against a senator or representative in Congress who deliberately misrepresented their wishes and imperilled their interests, though he might plead a higher regard for national good. Yet people in other parts of the city seem to forget that under the old system the ward elected councilmen with the idea of procuring service of special benefit to that ward.[15]

In short, pre-reform officials spoke for their constituencies, inevitably their own wards which had elected them, rather than for other sections or groups of the city.

The ward system of government especially gave representation in city affairs to lower- and middle-class groups. Most elected ward officials were from these groups, and they, in turn, constituted the major opposition to reforms in municipal government. In Pittsburgh, for example, immediately prior to the changes in both the city council and the school board in 1911 in which city-wide representation replaced ward representation, only 24 per cent of the 387 members of those bodies represented the same managerial, professional, and banker occupations which dominated the membership of the Civic Club and the Voters' League. The great majority (67 per cent) were small businessmen —grocers, saloonkeepers, livery-stable proprietors, owners of small hotels, druggists—white-collar workers such as clerks and bookkeepers, and skilled and unskilled workmen.[16]

This decentralized system of urban growth and the institutions which arose from it reformers now opposed. Social, professional, and economic life had developed not only in the local wards in a small community context, but also on a larger scale had become highly integrated and organized, giving rise to a superstructure of social organization which lay far above that of ward life and which was sharply divorced from it in both personal contacts and perspective.

By the late 19th century, those involved in these larger institutions found that the decentralized system of political life limited their larger objectives. The movement for reform in municipal government, therefore, constituted an attempt by upper-class, advanced professional, and large business groups to take formal political power from the previously dominant lower- and middle-class elements so that they might advance their own conceptions of desirable public policy. These two groups came from entirely different urban worlds, and the political system fashioned by one was no longer acceptable to the other.

Lower- and middle-class groups not only dominated the pre-reform governments, but vigorously opposed reform. It is significant that none of the occupational groups among them, for example, small businessmen or white-collar workers, skilled or unskilled artisans, had important representation in reform organizations thus far examined. The case studies of city-manager government undertaken in the 1930's under the direction of Leonard White detailed in city after city the particular opposition of labor. In their analysis of Jackson, Michigan, the authors of these studies wrote:

The *Square Deal*, oldest Labor paper in the state, has been consistently against manager government, perhaps largely because labor has felt that with a decentralized government elected on a ward basis it was more likely to have some voice and to receive its share of privileges.[17]

In Janesville, Wisconsin, the small shopkeepers and workingmen on the west and south sides, heavily Catholic and often Irish, opposed the commission plan in 1911 and in 1912 and the city-manager plan when adopted in 1923.[18] "In Dallas there is hardly a trace of class consciousness in the Marxian sense," one investigator declared, "yet in city elections the division has been to a great extent along class lines."[19] The commission and city-manager elections were no exceptions. To these authors it seemed a logical reaction, rather than an embarrassing fact that had to be swept away, that workingmen should have opposed municipal reform.[20]

In Des Moines working-class representatives, who in previous years might have been council members, were conspicuously absent from the "businessman's slate." Workingmen acceptable to reformers could not be found. A workingman's slate of candidates, therefore, appeared to challenge the reform slate. Organized labor, and especially the mineworkers, took the lead; one of their number, Wesley Ash, a deputy sheriff and union member, made "an astonishing run" in the primary, coming in second among a field of more than twenty candidates.[21] In fact, the strength of anticommission candidates in the primary so alarmed reformers that they frantically sought to appease labor.

The day before the final election they modified their platform to pledge both an eight-hour day and an "American standard of wages." They attempted to persuade the voters that their slate consisted of men who represented labor because they had "begun at the bottom of the ladder and made a good climb toward success by their own unaided efforts."[22] But their tactics failed. In the election of March 30, 1908, voters swept into office the entire "opposition" slate. The business and professional community had succeeded in changing the form of government, but not in securing its control. A cartoon in the leading reform newspaper illustrated their disappointment; John Q. Public sat dejectedly and muttered, "Aw, What's the Use?"

The most visible opposition to reform and the most readily available target of reform attack was the so-called "machine," for through the "machine" many different ward communities as well as lower- and middle-income groups joined effectively to influence the central city government. Their private occupational and social life did not naturally involve these groups in larger city-wide activities in the same way as the upper class was involved; hence they lacked access to privately organized economic and social power on which they could construct political power. The "machine" filled this organizational gap.

Yet it should never be forgotten that the social and economic institutions in the wards themselves provided the "machine's" sustaining support and gave it larger significance. When reformers attacked the "machine" as the most visible institutional element of the ward system, they attacked the entire ward form of political organization and the political power of lower-and middle-income groups which lay behind it.

Reformers often gave the impression that they opposed merely the corrupt politician and his "machine." But in a more fundamental way they looked upon the deficiencies of pre-reform political leaders in terms not of their personal shortcomings, but of the limitations inherent in their occupational, institutional, and class positions. In 1911 the Voters' League of Pittsburgh wrote in its pamphlet analyzing the qualifications of candidates that "a man's occupation ought to give a strong indication of his qualifications for membership on a school board."[23] Certain occupations inherently disqualified a man from serving:

Employment as ordinary laborer and in the lowest class of mill work would naturally lead to the conclusion that such men did not have sufficient education or business training to act as school directors. . . . Objection might also be made to small shopkeepers, clerks, workmen at many trades, who by lack of educational advantages and business training, could not, no matter how honest, be expected to administer properly the affairs of an educational system, requiring special knowledge, and where millions are spent each year.

These, of course, were precisely the groups which did dominate Pittsburgh government prior to reform. The League deplored the fact that school boards contained only a small number of "men prominent throughout the city in business life . . . in professional occupations . . . holding positions as managers, secretaries, auditors, superintendents and foremen" and exhorted these classes to participate more actively as candidates for office.

Reformers, therefore, wished not simply to replace bad men with good; they proposed to change the occupational and class origins of decision-makers. Toward this end they sought innovations in the formal machinery of government which would concentrate political power by sharply centralizing the processes of decision-making rather than distribute it through more popular participation in public affairs. According to the liberal view of the Progressive Era, the major political innovations of reform involved the equalization of political power through the primary, the direct election of public officials, and the initiative, referendum, and recall.

These measures played a large role in the political ideology of the time and were frequently incorporated into new municipal charters. But they provided at best only an occasional and often incidental process of decision-making. Far more important in continuous, sustained, day-to-day processes of government were those innovations which centralized decision-making in the hands of fewer and fewer people.

The systematization of municipal government took place on both the executive and the legislative levels. The strong-mayor and city-manager types became the most widely used examples of the former. In the first decade of the 20th century, the commission plan had considerable appeal, but its distribution of administrative responsibility among five people gave rise to a demand for a form with more centralized executive power; consequently, the city-manager or the commission-manager variant often replaced it.[24]

A far more pervasive and significant change, however, lay in the centralization of the system of representation, the shift from ward to city-wide election of councils and school boards. Governing bodies so selected, reformers argued, would give less attention to local and particularistic matters and more to affairs of city-wide scope. This shift, an invariable feature of both commission and city-manager plans, was often adopted by itself. In Pittsburgh, for example, the new charter of 1911 provided as the major innovation that a council of twenty-seven, each member elected from a separate ward, be replaced by a council of nine, each elected by the city as a whole.

Cities displayed wide variations in this innovation. Some regrouped wards into larger units but kept the principle of areas of representation smaller than the entire city. Some combined a majority of councilmen elected by wards with additional ones elected at large. All such innovations, however, constituted steps toward the centralization of the system of representation.

Liberal historians have not appreciated the extent to which municipal reform in the Progressive Era involved a debate over the system of representation. The ward form of representation was universally condemned on the grounds that it gave too much influence to the separate units and not enough attention to the larger problems of the city. Harry A. Toulmin, whose book, *The City Manager*, was published by the National Municipal League, stated the case:

The spirit of sectionalism had dominated the political life of every city. Ward pitted against ward, alderman against alderman, and legislation only effected by "log-rolling" extravagant measures into operation, mulcting the city, but gratifying the greed of constituents, has too long stung the conscience of decent citizenship. This constant treaty-making of factionalism has been no less than a curse. The city manager plan proposes the commendable thing of abolishing wards. The plan is not unique in this for it has been common to many forms of commission government. . . .[25]

Such a system should be supplanted, the argument usually went, with city-wide representation in which elected officials could consider the city "as a unit." "The new officers are elected," wrote Toulmin, "each to represent all the people. Their duties are so defined that they must administer the corporate business in its entirety, not as a hodgepodge of associated localities."

Behind the debate over the method of representation, however, lay a debate over who should be represented, over whose views of public policy should prevail. Many reform leaders often explicitly, if not implicitly, expressed fear that lower- and middle-income groups had too much influence in decision-making. One Galveston leader, for example, complained about the movement for initiative, referendum, and recall:

We have in our city a very large number of negroes employed on the docks; we also have a very large number of unskilled white laborers; this city also has more barrooms, according to its population, than any other city in Texas. Under these circumstances it would be extremely difficult to maintain a satisfactory city government where all ordinances must be submitted back to the voters of the city for their ratification and approval.[26]

At the National Municipal League convention of 1907, Rear Admiral F. E. Chadwick (USN Ret.), a leader in the Newport, Rhode Island, movement for municipal reform, spoke to this question even more directly:

Our present system has excluded in large degree the representation of those who have the city's well-being most at heart. It has brought, in municipalities . . . a government established by the least educated, the least interested class of citizens.

It stands to reason that a man paying $5,000 taxes in a town is more interested in the well-being and development of his town than the man who pays no taxes. . . . It equally stands to reason that the man of the $5,000 tax should be assured a representation in the committee which lays the tax and spends the money which he contributes. . . Shall we be truly democratic and give the property owner a fair show or shall we develop a tyranny of ignorance which shall crush him.[27]

Municipal reformers thus debated frequently the question of who should be represented as well as the question of what method of representation should be employed.

That these two questions were intimately connected was revealed in other reform proposals for representation, proposals which were rarely taken seriously. One suggestion was that a class system of representation be substituted for ward representation. For example, in 1908 one of the prominent candidates for commissioner in Des Moines proposed that the city council be composed of representatives of five classes: educational and ministerial organizations, manufacturers and jobbers, public utility corporations, retail merchants including liquor men, and the Des Moines Trades and Labor Assembly. Such a system would have greatly reduced the influence in the council of both middle- and lower-class groups. The proposal revealed the basic problem confronting business and professional leaders: how to reduce the influence in government of the majority of voters among middle- and lower-income groups.[28]

A growing imbalance between population and representation sharpened the desire of reformers to change from ward to city-wide elections. Despite shifts in population within most cities, neither ward district lines nor the apportionment of city council and school board seats changed frequently. Consequently, older areas of the city, with wards that were small in geographical size and held declining populations (usually lower and middle class in composition), continued to be overrepresented, and newer upper-class areas, where population was growing, became increasingly underrepresented. This intensified the reformers' conviction that the structure of government must be changed to give them the voice they needed to make their views on public policy prevail.[29]

It is not insignificant that in some cities (by no means a majority) municipal reform came about outside of the urban electoral process. The original commission government in Galveston was appointed rather than elected. The failure of previous attempts to secure an efficient city government through the local electorate made the business men of Galveston willing to put the conduct of the city's affairs in the hands of a commission dominated by state-appointed officials."[30] Only in 1903 did the courts force Galveston to elect the members of the commission, an innovation which one writer described as "an abandonment of the commission idea," and which led to the decline of the influence of the business community in the commission government.[31]

In 1911 Pittsburgh voters were not permitted to approve either the new city charter or the new school board plan, both of which provided for city-wide representation: they were a result of state legislative enactment. The governor appointed the first members of the new city council, but thereafter they were elected. The judges of the court of common pleas, however, and not the voters, selected members of the new school board.

The composition of the new city council and new school board in Pittsburgh, both of which were inaugurated in 1911, revealed the degree to which the shift from ward to city-wide representation produced a change in group representation.[32] Members of the upper class, the advanced professional men, and the large business groups dominated both. Of the fifteen members of the Pittsburgh Board of Education appointed in 1911 and the nine members of the new city council, none were small businessmen or white-collar workers. Each body contained only one person who could remotely be classified as a

blue-collar worker; each of these men filled a position specifically but unofficially designed as reserved for a "representative of labor," and each was an official of the Amalgamated Association of Iron, Steel, and Tin Workers. Six of the nine members of the new city council were prominent businessmen, and all six were listed in upper-class directories. Two others were doctors closely associated with the upper class in both professional and social life. The fifteen members of the Board of Education included ten businessmen with city-wide interests, one doctor associated with the upper class, and three women previously active in upper-class public welfare.

Lower- and middle-class elements felt that the new city governments did not represent them.[33] The studies carried out under the direction of Leonard White contain numerous expressions of the way in which the change in the structure of government produced not only a change in the geographical scope of representation, but also in the groups represented. "It is not the policies of the manager or the council they oppose," one researcher declared, "as much as the lack of representation for their economic level and social groups."[34] And another wrote:

There had been nothing unapproachable about the old ward aldermen. Every voter had a neighbor on the common council who was interested in serving him. The new councilmen, however, made an unfavorable impression on the less well-to-do voters. . . . Election at large made a change that, however desirable in other ways, left the voters in the poorer wards with a feeling that they had been deprived of their share of political importance.[35]

The success of the drive for centralization of administration and representation varied with the size of the city. In the smaller cities, business, professional, and elite groups could easily exercise a dominant influence. Their close ties readily enabled them to shape informal political power which they could transform into formal political power. After the mid-1890's the widespread organization of chambers of commerce provided a base for political action to reform municipal government, resulting in a host of small-city commission and city-manager innovations. In the larger, more heterogeneous cities, whose subcommunities were more dispersed, such community-wide action was extremely difficult. Few commission or city-manager proposals materialized here. Mayors became stronger, and steps were taken toward centralization of representation, but the ward system or some modified version usually persisted. Reformers in large cities often had to rest content with their Municipal Research Bureaus through which they could exert political influence from outside the municipal government.

A central element in the analysis of municipal reform in the Progressive Era is governmental corruption. Should it be understood in moral or political terms? Was it a product of evil men or of particular socio-political circumstances? Reform historians have adopted the former view. Selfish and evil men arose to take advantage of a political arrangement whereby unsystematic government offered many opportunities for personal gain at public expense. The system thrived until the "better elements," "men of intelligence and civic responsibility," or "right-thinking people" ousted the culprits and fashioned a political force which produced decisions in the "public interest." In this scheme of things, corruption in public

affairs grew out of individual personal failings and a deficient governmental structure which could not hold those predispositions in check, rather than from the peculiar nature of social forces. The contestants involved were morally defined: evil men who must be driven from power, and good men who must be activated politically to secure control of municipal affairs.

Public corruption, however, involves political even more than moral considerations. It arises more out of the particular distribution of political power than of personal morality. For corruption is a device to exercise control and influence outside the legal channels of decision-making when those channels are not readily responsive. Most generally, corruption stems from an inconsistency between control of the instruments of formal governmental power and the exercise of informal influence in the community. If powerful groups are denied access to formal power in legitimate ways, they seek access through procedures which the community considers illegitimate. Corrupt government, therefore, does not reflect the genius of evil men, but rather the lack of acceptable means for those who exercise power in the private community to wield the same influence in governmental affairs. It can be understood in the Progressive Era not simply by the preponderance of evil men over good, but by the peculiar nature of the distribution of political power.

The political corruption of the "Era of Reform" arose from the inaccessibility of municipal government to those who were rising in power and influence. Municipal government in the United States developed in the 19th century within a context of universal manhood suffrage which decentralized political control. Because all men, whatever their economic, social, or cultural conditions, could vote, leaders who reflected a wide variety of community interests and who represented the views of people of every circumstance arose to guide and direct municipal affairs. Since the majority of urban voters were workingmen or immigrants, the views of those groups carried great and often decisive weight in governmental affairs. Thus, as Herbert Gutman has shown, during strikes in the 1870's city officials were usually friendly to workingmen and refused to use police power to protect strikebreakers.[36]

Ward representation on city councils was an integral part of grass-roots influence, for it enabled diverse urban communities, invariably identified with particular geographical areas of the city, to express their views more clearly through councilmen peculiarly receptive to their concerns. There was a direct, reciprocal flow of power between wards and the center of city affairs in which voters felt a relatively close connection with public matters and city leaders gave special attention to their needs.

Within this political system the community's business leaders grew in influence and power as industrialism advanced, only to find that their economic position did not readily admit them to the formal machinery of government. Thus, during strikes, they had to rely on either their own private police, Pinkertons, or the state militia to enforce their use of strikebreakers. They frequently found that city officials did not accept their views of what was best for the city and what direction municipal policies should take. They had developed a common outlook, closely related to their economic activities, that the city's economic expansion should become the prime concern of municipal government, and yet they found that this view had to compete with even more influential views of public policy. They found that political tendencies which arose from universal manhood suffrage and ward representation were not always friendly to their political conceptions and goals and had produced a political system over which they had little control, despite the fact that their economic ventures were the core of the city's prosperity and the hope for future urban growth.

Under such circumstances, businessmen sought other methods of influencing municipal affairs. They did not restrict themselves to the channels of popular election and representation, but frequently applied direct influence—if not verbal persuasion, then bribery and corruption. Thereby arose the graft which Lincoln Steffens recounted in his *Shame of the Cities*. Utilities were only the largest of those business groups and individuals who requested special favors, and the franchises they sought were only the most sensational of the prizes which included such items as favorable tax assessments and rates, the vacating of streets wanted for factory expansion, or permission to operate amid antiliquor and other laws regulating personal behavior. The relationships between business and formal government became a maze of accommodations, a set of political arrangements which grew up because effective power had few legitimate means of accomplishing its ends.

Steffens and subsequent liberal historians, however, misread the significance of these arrangements, emphasizing their personal rather than their more fundamental institutional elements. To them corruption involved personal arrangements between powerful business leaders and powerful "machine" politicians. Just as they did not fully appreciate the significance of the search for political influence by the rising business community as a whole, so they did not see fully the role of the "ward politician." They stressed the argument that the political leader manipulated voters to his own personal ends, that he used constituents rather than reflected their views.

A different approach is now taking root, namely, that the urban political organization was an integral part of community life, expressing its needs and its goals. As Oscar Handlin has said, for example, the "machine" not only fulfilled specific wants, but provided one of the few avenues to success and public recognition available to the immigrant.[37] The political leader's arrangements with businessmen, therefore, were not simply personal agreements between conniving individuals; they were far-reaching accommodations between powerful sets of institutions in industrial America.

These accommodations, however, proved to be burdensome and unsatisfactory to the business community and to the upper third of socio-economic groups in general. They were expensive; they were wasteful: they were uncertain. Toward the end of the 19th century, therefore, business and professional men sought more direct control over municipal government in order to exercise political influence more effectively. They realized their goals in the early 20th century in the new commission and city-manager forms of government and in the shift from ward to city-wide representation.

These innovations did not always accomplish the objectives that the business community desired because other forces could and often did adjust to the change in governmental structure and reëstablish their influence. But businessmen hoped that reform would enable them to increase their political power, and most frequently it did. In most cases the innovations which were introduced between 1901, when Galveston adopted a commission form of government, and the Great Depression, and especially the city-manager form which reached a height of popularity in the mid-1920's, served as vehicles whereby business and professional leaders moved directly into the inner circles of government, brought into one political system their own power and the formal machinery of government, and dominated municipal affairs for two decades.

Municipal reform in the early 20th century involves a paradox: the ideology of an extension of political control and the practice of its concentration. While reformers maintained that their movement rested on a wave of popular demands, called their gatherings of business and professional leaders "mass meetings," described their reforms as "part of a world-wide trend toward popular government," and proclaimed an ideology of a popular upheaval against a selfish few, they were in practice shaping the structure of municipal government so that political power would no longer be broadly distributed, but would in fact be more centralized in the hands of a relatively small segment of the population. The paradox became even sharper when new city charters included provisions for the initiative, referendum, and recall. How does the historian cope with this paradox? Does it represent deliberate deception or simply political strategy? Or does it reflect a phenomenon which should be understood rather than explained away?

The expansion of popular involvement in decision-making was frequently a political tactic, not a political system to be established permanently, but a device to secure immediate political victory. The prohibitionist advocacy of the referendum, one of the most extensive sources of support for such a measure, came from the belief that the referendum would provide the opportunity to outlaw liquor more rapidly. The Anti-Saloon League, therefore, urged local option. But the League was not consistent. Towns which were wet, when faced with a county-wide local-option decision to outlaw liquor, demanded town or township local option to reinstate it. The League objected to this as not the proper application of the referendum idea.

Again, "Progressive" reformers often espoused the direct primary when fighting for nominations for their candidates within the party, but once in control they often became cool to it because it might result in their own defeat. By the same token, many municipal reformers attached the initiative, referendum, and recall to municipal charters often as a device to appease voters who opposed the centralization of representation and̄ executive authority. But, by requiring a high percentage of voters to sign petitions—often 25 to 30 per cent—these innovations could be and were rendered relatively harmless.

More fundamentally, however, the distinction between ideology and practice in municipal reform arose from the different roles which each played. The ideology of democratization of decision-making was negative rather than posi-

tive; it served as an instrument of attack against the existing political system rather than as a guide to alternative action. Those who wished to destroy the "machine" and to eliminate party competition in local government widely utilized the theory that these political instruments thwarted public impulses, and thereby shaped the tone of their attack.

But there is little evidence that the ideology represented a faith in a purely democratic system of decision-making or that reformers actually wished, in practice, to substitute direct democracy as a continuing system of sustained decision-making in place of the old. It was used to destroy the political institutions of the lower and middle classes and the political power which those institutions gave rise to, rather than to provide a clear-cut guide for alternative action.[38]

The guide to alternative action lay in the model of the business enterprise. In describing new conditions which they wished to create, reformers drew on the analogy of the "efficient business enterprise," criticizing current practices with the argument that "no business could conduct its affairs that way and remain in business," and calling upon business practices as the guides to improvement. As one student remarked:

The folklore of the business elite came by gradual transition to be the symbols of governmental reformers. Efficiency, system, orderliness, budgets, economy, saving, were all injected into the efforts of reformers who sought to remodel municipal government in terms of the great impersonality of corporate enterprise.[39]

Clinton Rodgers Woodruff of the National Municipal League explained that the commission form was "a simple, direct, businesslike way of administering the business affairs of the city . . . an application to city administration of that type of business organization which has been so common and so successful in the field of commerce and industry."[40] The centralization of decision-making which developed in the business corporation was now applied in municipal reform.

The model of the efficient business enterprise, then, rather than the New England town meeting, provided the positive inspiration for the municipal reformer. In giving concrete shape to this model in the strong-mayor, commission, and city-manager plans, reformers engaged in the elaboration of the processes of rationalization and systematization inherent in modern science and technology. For in many areas of society, industrialization brought a gradual shift upward in the location of decision-making and the geographical extension of the scope of the area affected by decisions.

Experts in business, in government, and in the professions measured, studied, analyzed, and manipulated ever wider realms of human life, and devices which they used to control such affairs constituted the most fundamental and far-reaching innovations in decision-making in modern America, whether in formal government or in the informal exercise of power in private life. Reformers in the Progressive Era played a major role in shaping this new system. While they expressed an ideology of restoring a previous order, they in fact helped to bring forth a system drastically new.[41]

The drama of reform lay in the competition for supremacy between two systems of decision-making. One system, based upon ward representation and growing out of the practices and ideas of representative government, involved wide latitude for the expression of grass-roots impulses and their involvement in the political process. The other grew out of the rationalization of life which came with science and technology, in which decisions arose from expert analysis and flowed from fewer and smaller centers outward to the rest of society. Those who espoused the former looked with fear upon the loss of influence which the latter involved, and those who espoused the latter looked only with disdain upon the wastefulness and inefficiency of the former.

The Progressive Era witnessed rapid strides toward a more centralized system and a relative decline for a more decentralized system. This development constituted an accommodation of forces outside the business community to the political trends within business and professional life rather than vice versa. It involved a tendency for the decision-making processes inherent in science and technology to prevail over those inherent in representative government.

Reformers in the Progressive Era and liberal historians since then misread the nature of the movement to change municipal government because they concentrated upon dramatic and sensational episodes and ignored the analysis of more fundamental political structure, of the persistent relationships of influence and power which grew out of the community's social, ideological, economic, and cultural activities. The reconstruction of these patterns of human relationships and of the changes in them is the historian's most crucial task, for they constitute the central context of historical development. History consists not of erratic and spasmodic fluctuations, of a series of random thoughts and actions, but of patterns of activity and change in which people hold thoughts and actions in common and in which there are close connections between sequences of events. These contexts give rise to a structure of human relationships which pervade all areas of life; for the political historian the most important of these is the structure of the distribution of power and influence.

The structure of political relationships however, cannot be adequately understood if we concentrate on evidence concerning ideology rather than practice. For it is becoming increasingly clear that ideological evidence is no safe guide to the understanding of practice, that what people thought and said about their society is not necessarily an accurate representation of what they did. The current task of the historian of the Progressive Era is to quit taking the reformers' own description of political practice at its face value and to utilize a wide variety of new types of evidence to reconstruct political practice in its own terms. This is not to argue that ideology is either important or unimportant. It is merely to state that ideological evidence is not appropriate to the discovery of the nature of political practice.

Only by maintaining this clear distinction can the historian successfully investigate the structure of political life in the Progressive Era. And only then can he begin to cope with the most fundamental problem of all: the relationship between political ideology and political practice. For each of these facets of political life must be understood in its own terms, through its own historical record. Each involves a distinct set of historical phenomena. The relationship between them for the Progressive Era is not now clear; it has not been in-

vestigated. But it cannot be explored until the conceptual distinction is made clear and evidence tapped which is pertinent to each. Because the nature of political practice has so long been distorted by the use of ideological evidence, the most pressing task is for its investigation through new types of evidence appropriate to it. The reconstruction of the movement for municipal reform can constitute a major step forward toward that goal.

NOTES

1. See, for example, Clifford W. Patton, *Battle for Municipal Reform* (Washington, D.C., 1940), and Frank Mann Stewart, *A Half-Century of Municipal Reform* (Berkeley, 1950).

2. George E. Mowry, *The California Progressives* (Berkeley and Los Angeles, 1951), 86-104; Richard Hofstadter, *The Age of Reform* (New York, 1955), 131-269; Alfred D. Chandler, Jr., "The Origins of Progressive Leadership," in Elting Morrison et al., eds., *Letters of Theodore Roosevelt* (Cambridge, 1951-54), VIII, Appendix III, 1462-64.

3. Harry A. Toulmin, *The City Manager* (New York, 1915), 156-68; Clinton R. Woodruff, *City Government by Commission* (New York, 1911), 243-53.

4. Eli Daniel Potts, "A Comparative Study of the Leadership of Republican Factions in Iowa, 1904-1914," M.A. thesis (State University of Iowa, 1956). Another satisfactory comparative analysis is contained in William T. Kerr, Jr., "The Progressives of Washington, 1910-12," *PNQ*, Vol. 55 (1964), 16-27.

5. Based upon a study of eleven ministers involved in municipal reform in Pittsburgh, who represented exclusively the upper-class Presbyterian and Episcopal churches.

6. Based upon a study of professional men involved in municipal reform in Pittsburgh, comprising eighty-three doctors, twelve architects, twenty-five educators, and thirteen engineers.

7. See especially Mowry, *The California Progressives.*

8. Leonard White, *The City Manager* (Chicago, 1927), ix-x.

9. Harold A. Stone et al., *City Manager Government in Nine Cities* (Chicago, 1940); Frederick C. Mosher et al., *City Manager Government in Seven Cities* (Chicago, 1940); Harold A. Stone et al., *City Manager Government in the United States* (Chicago, 1940). Cities covered by these studies include: Austin, Texas; Charlotte, North

Carolina; Dallas, Texas; Dayton, Ohio; Fredericksburg, Virginia; Jackson, Michigan; Janesville, Wisconsin; Kingsport, Tennessee; Lynchburg, Virginia; Rochester, New York; San Diego, California.

10. Jewell Cass Phillips, *Operation of the Council-Manager Plan of Government in Oklahoma Cities* (Philadelphia, 1935), 31-39.

11. James Weinstein, "Organized Business and the City Commission and Manager Movements," *Journal of Southern History*, XXVIII (1962), 166-82.

12. Norman N. Gill, *Municipal Research Bureaus* (Washington, 1944).

13. This account of the movement for commission government in Des Moines is derived from items in the Des Moines *Register* during the years from 1905 through 1908.

14. Biographical data constitutes the main source of evidence for this study of Pittsburgh reform leaders. It was found in city directories, social registers, directories of corporate directors, biographical compilations, reports of boards of education, settlement houses, welfare organizations, and similar types of material. Especially valuable was the clipping file maintained at the Carnegie Library of Pittsburgh.

15. *Town Crier* (Seattle), Feb. 18, 1911, p. 13.

16. Information derived from same sources as cited in footnote 14.

17. Stone *et al., Nine Cities*, 212.

18. *Ibid.*, 3-13.

19. *Ibid.*, 329.

20. Stone *et al., City Manager Government*, 26, 237-41, for analysis of opposition to city-manager government.

21. Des Moines *Register and Leader*, March 17, 1908.

22. *Ibid.*, March 30, March 28, 1908.

23. Voters' Civic League of Allegheny County, "Bulletin of the Voters' Civic League of Allegheny County Concerning the Public School System of Pittsburgh," Feb. 14, 1911, pp. 2-3.

24. In the decade 1911 to 1920, 43 per cent of the municipal charters adopted in eleven home rule states involved the commission form and 35 per cent the city-manager form; in the following decade the figures stood at 6 per cent and 71 per cent respectively. The adoption of city-manager charters reached a peak in the years 1918 through 1923 and declined sharply after 1933. See Leonard D. White, "The Future of Public Administration," *Public Management*, XV (1933), 12.

25. Toulmin, *The City Manager*, 42.

26. Woodruff, *City Government*, 315. The Galveston commission plan did not contain provisions for the initiative, referendum, or recall, and Galveston commercial groups which had fathered the commission plan opposed movements to include them. In 1911 Governor Colquitt of Texas vetoed a charter bill for Texarkana because it contained such provisions; he maintained that they were "undemocratic" and unnecessary to the success of commission government. *Ibid.*, 314-15.

27. *Ibid.*, 207-208.

28. Des Moines *Register and Leader*, Jan. 15, 1908.

29. Voters' Civic League of Allegheny County, "Report on the Voters' League in the Redistricting of the Wards of the City of Pittsburgh" (Pittsburgh, n.d.).

30. Horace E. Deming, "The Government of American Cities," in Woodruff, *City Government*, 167.

31. *Ibid.*, 168.

32. Information derived from same sources as cited in footnote 14.

33. W. R. Hopkins, city manager of Cleveland, indicated the degree to which the new type of government was more responsive to the business community: "It is undoubtedly easier for a city manager to insist upon acting in accordance with the business interests of the city than it is for a mayor to do the same thing." Quoted in White, *The City Manager*, 13.

34. Stone *et al., Nine Cities*, 20.

35. *Ibid.*, 225.

36. Herbert Gutman, "An Iron Workers' Strike in the Ohio Valley, 1873-74," *Ohio Historical Quarterly*, LXVIII (1959), 353-70; "Trouble on the Railroads, 1873-1874: Prelude to the 1877 Crisis," *Labor History*, II (Spring, 1961), 215-36.

37. Oscar Handlin, *The Uprooted* (Boston, 1951), 209-17.

38. Clinton Rodgers Woodruff of the National Municipal League even argued that the initiative, referendum, and recall were rarely used. "Their value lies in their existence rather than in their use." Woodruff, *City Government*, 314. It seems apparent that the most widely used of these devices, the referendum, was popularized by legislative bodies when they could not agree or did not want to take responsibility for a decision and sought to pass that responsibility to the general public, rather than because of a faith in the wisdom of popular will.

39. J. B. Shannon, "County Consolidation," *Annals of the American Academy of Political and Social Science*, Vol. 207 (January, 1940), 168.

40. Woodruff, *City Government*, 29-30.

41. Several recent studies emphasize various aspects of this movement. See, for example, Loren Baritz, *Servants of Power* (Middletown, 1960); Raymond E. Callahan, *Education and the Cult of Efficiency* (Chicago, 1962); Samuel P. Hays, *Conservation and the Gospel of Efficiency* (Cambridge, 1959); Dwight Waldo, *The Administrative State* (New York, 1948), 3-61.

Urban Problems and the Federal Government: A Historical Inquiry[*]

DANIEL J. ELAZAR

In recent years there has been a growing concern among political scientists and political practitioners alike with the evolution of the relationships between the federal government and the cities. This concern is variously directed toward federal relations with the nation's largest cities in particular toward federal relations with urban concentrations generally, or toward the need for developing a coherent pattern of relationships between the federal government and the nation's burgeoning metropolitan areas. Regardless of its immediate focus, it is based on public recognition of an obviously great increase in the dollar amounts of federal aid to the cities and a proliferation of federal programs specifically directed toward contemporary urban problems.

It is generally assumed that the federal-city relationship that is evolving is radically new in several respects: in its very concern with urban problems as such; in the fact that much of it appears to be a direct relationship, for all intents and purposes, bypassing the states insofar as active implementation of the programs is concerned; and, finally, in its overall impact on American federalism. These assumptions are based on several premises, among them that the federal government ignored the cities until recently, and that meaningful (usually taken to mean direct) federal-city relationships date back no further than the beginning of the New Deal, prior to which time the cities received such minor federal benefits as were available via the states and then only as political subdivisions of the states. As an outgrowth of these two assumptions, there is a third: that the new federal-city relationship represents a new departure for American federalism by changing the basis of the federal system from a two-level (federal-state) to a three-level (federal-state-city) relationship.[1]

In at least one sense, the foregoing assumptions are well grounded in fact. The cities (and other urban entities) in this country are indeed carving a place for themselves in the scheme of American federalism not quite like any they had before, if only because they bulk so much larger on the American scene than ever before. At the same time, to the extent that the assumptions rest on the idea that the federal-local (substituting the word "local" for "city" so as to encompass urban counties, towns, boroughs, and the like) relationship of today is a radically new one, it is necessary to examine the historical record to see if such is the case before drawing any conclusions about the course of American federalism. Only if the federal-local relationship before 1933 is properly explored and examined in light of our knowledge of the nature of American federalism as it has evolved since the adoption of the Constitution is it

From *Political Science Quarterly*, Vol. LXXXII (December 1967), pp. 505-25. Reprinted by permission of the publisher. Daniel J. Elazar is Professor of Political Science at Temple University.

possible to build an understanding of the evolution of the federal system in light of recent urbanizing trends.

This article will (1) raise some basic questions as to the character of federal-city relations in the period prior to 1933, (2) make a preliminary examination of those relations in light of the historical evidence in an effort to (3) bring the inquiry into the problem of federal-city relations today into proper historical focus and (4) to suggest some lines of further inquiry.

THE EVOLUTION OF DE FACTO ARRANGEMENTS

It would appear that the first step in an inquiry into the evolution of city-federal relationships in the United States is to determine at what point cities, as such, began to make specialized demands on the state and federal governments (past those related to simple incorporation) that differed from the demands of other local governments.

(1) Much is made of the change in city-federal relations since 1933. However, much of the supposed lack of sophisticated relations in the nineteenth century was simply due to a lack of large cities. The dates of the incorporation of today's largest cities provide one indicator of this. Table 1 (all tables follow text) reveals that prior to 1815 only seven of the nation's fifty largest cities of today were incorporated. In point of fact, they represented a majority of the incorporated cities of their time. In 1810, the nation had only forty-six urban places of more than 2,500 population, only eleven of which had more than 10,000 people and none of which reached 100,000.[2]

(2) Even when cities were established, they did not immediately develop specialized governmental needs that could not be handled to their general satisfaction within the existing structure of government. Boston, for example, the country's third largest city in the early nineteenth century, did not even see fit to incorporate until 1822, when its population was already 47,000. Until then it was governed by the same town system used in the most rural areas of New England. Admittedly, Boston was an exception. However, even after the development of incorporated municipalities, the size factor (that is, the smallness of the "cities") placed limits on the need for specialized urban services. As indicated in Tables 2 and 3, before 1840 there were no large cities in the United States and it was not until after 1900 that the medium size and large cities came to contain as much as twenty-five per cent of the nation's total population.

(3) In this regard it is also important to note that the total number of urban places (population 2,500 or more) in the United States did not exceed 1,000 for the first time until 1890 and only in that year did the urban share of the total population reach one third of the national total (Table 4). Not until 1920 did the total population of places over 2,500 exceed the total rural population. That same year the total population in cities of 100,000 and over exceeded the total population in all smaller urban places for the first time (significantly, this was reversed in 1950 as part of the suburbanizing trend).

(4) There is considerable evidence to the effect that even today virtually all cities below 50,000 in population, excepting only a few older suburban cities which face "central city"-type problems, really do not develop a "city" outlook in the political arena. As a rule, they

align themselves with the so-called "rural" areas (really a misnomer in the demographic sense today) against the "big city" in urban-rural conflict situations. Indeed, it is likely that most cities below 150,000 population (again excepting certain older suburban and industrial cities) also reject "city" ideas and align themselves in opposition to the big-city bloc on most issues. Certainly these smaller cities have not been the source of specialized city pressures on the states and demands on Washington because they have not had such demands. If the situation that prevails today can be projected backward to the period between 1790 and 1930, it is probable that widespread specialized "city" demands sufficiently differentiated from those of other local governments to create substantial intrastate urban-rural conflict did not develop until the period of the First World War, except in the cases of the very largest cities, those with present (1960) populations of over 750,000 and which then exceeded 250,000 in population. In 1910, the nineteen cities of 250,000 or more had hardly more than fifteen per cent of the nation's population. Even as late as 1930, they did not encompass a quarter of the nation's people. The big cities' desire to turn to the federal government instead of the states could not have become a national issue until then, if only because there were not enough big cities with specialized demands.

(5) This is not to imply that there were no conflicts between the states and their big cities prior to 1913, but that they were few, not uniquely urban, and not particularly unmanageable within the states until then. In Illinois, for example, the origins of the Chicago-downstate cleavage date back to the post-Civil War period and no further. Before the Civil War, the basic intrastate conflict was a sectional one between Yankee-settled northern Illinois, including Chicago, and Southern-dominated southern Illinois. The first overt conflict between the mayor of Chicago and the governor of Illinois developed in 1871 in the aftermath of the Chicago Fire, when Mayor Mason turned directly to the federal government for troops to maintain order in the gutted city even though Governor Palmer was prepared to send state militia to Chicago to do the job.[3] Still, until World War I the conflicts were few and minor and were generally resolved to the mutual satisfaction of both sides. In 1904 Chicago even obtained a limited amount of "home rule" through a constitutional amendment ratified state-wide, and in 1912 Edward Dunn, a former mayor of Chicago, was elected governor (the only time this has happened). Though his victory came in a three-way race, it and his very nomination are at least testimony to the fact that it was still considered politically feasible to nominate a Democratic mayor of Chicago for the office of governor, something which would be most unexpected today. Actually, until well after World War I, the partisan cleavage between "Democratic" Chicago and "Republican" downstate did not exist, Chicago being as Republican as the rest of northern and central Illinois.

Similar embryonic big city-outstate conflicts existed in Massachusetts, New York, Maryland, and Missouri, and perhaps elsewhere as well. But, just as in the Chicago-downstate Illinois conflict, most of those states took some steps to alleviate the situation through amendment of their constitutions to grant to their largest cities some measure of home rule of a kind not given to other cities in the same states even today. The metropolitan problems of New York City, for example, were substantially ameliorated through state assistance in the consolidation of the five boroughs in 1898. The creation of city-counties in Baltimore, Denver, Philadelphia, St. Louis, San Francisco, and other large cities at the turn of the century was also indicative of the then still existing ability and willingness of the states to assist the few large cities in meeting their relatively few specialized demands.[4] However, by 1910 or thereabouts, this option appears to have been closed off.

(6) At this point it is wise to add one caveat. Despite relative smallness in *size*, the larger pre-twentieth-century cities functioned in a more complex manner than cities of similar size today because of the magnitude of the social and economic as well as political functions that accrued to them as the largest cities of their time. Insofar as this was the case, there were "big-city" attributes present even in what today would be considered small and medium size cities. This certainly affected the major nineteenth-century cities' needs for outside aid and to some extent influenced their specific demands.

(7) One of these demands, and indeed a basic one, related to the physical growth of the cities themselves. Dynamic small and medium size cities grew to become today's large cities through annexation of adjacent lands to provide a basis for population growth. Until the late nineteenth century, annexation was, under state law and in fact, a commonly used—and an easily used—device which contributed to the internal growth of cities and met such problems of suburbanization as affected them. Annexation was often used uni-laterally by the cities to meet, directly or indirectly, problems of suburbanization and metropolitanization that today lead cities to turn to the federal and state governments for more active assistance.[5] Examples of the problems attacked by the then relatively simple device of annexation include: (a) the need for a single municipal government to serve all urban residents in a given area; (b) the provision of reasonably uniform area-wide services, few as they may have been; (c) the establishment of such area-wide regulatory standards and codes as were considered appropriate at the time; and (d) the establishment of uniform, if minimal, area-wide tax levies and revenue collections. Given the low level demands for local services in even the larger cities until relatively late in the nineteenth century, simple extension of ordinary municipal powers was usually sufficient to relax all but the most eager municipal reformers.

(8) The rise of the big city as a national entity coincides with the actual (as opposed to the chronological) end of the nineteenth century, which can be placed somewhere between 1913 and 1917. Several landmark events occurred to mark its passing: (a) Woodrow Wilson inaugurated the twentieth-century versions of "big government" and cooperative federalism, though still endowing them with a rural bias; (b) the land frontier, as expressed, for example, in the opportunity for homesteading new lands, which actually increased after 1890 for a brief period, finally ceased to exist; and (c) the United States became involved in World War I and its accompanying international entanglements. Consequently, the real line of demarcation in the history of cities' demands on the federal government— if one exists—is perhaps better drawn

at 1913 than at 1933. In the Wilson administration, however, the rural biases of the Southern- and Western-dominated Congress strictly limited the aids available to cities under the new programs.[6] Consequently, the latter year is especially significant, because it was only then that the federal government began to respond to the cities' new specialized demands.

LOCAL DEMANDS AND FEDERAL RESPONSES

What was the nature of the general demands of localities that did exist and were relevant to the cities prior to 1913? What was the nature of the responses of the federal and state governments to those demands and to such specialized demands as were then generated by the major cities? In other words, how did the federal system respond to urban needs before 1913?

The major government-oriented demands of localities prior to 1913 centered around:

(1) the development and maintenance of lines of communication with the rest of the country—particularly through the postal service;

(2) the development and maintenance of facilities for commercial intercourse locally and with the rest of the country —particularly through waterways, roads, and railroads;

(3) the development and maintenance of a limited number of local services— particularly schools, rudimentary police and fire services, rudimentary street and sanitation services, and limited welfare services (such as poor relief);

(4) contributions by extra-local governments to the local economic base to ensure prosperity and growth in a variety of specific ways, depending on the particular situation of each locality —these included items as diverse as the maintenance of federal and state institutions (and payrolls) in the locality; benefits from the federal tariff for local manufacturing establishments; state and federal contracts for locally-based businesses and various other governmental services that aided the development of local economies;

(5) outside financial assistance in some form for the support of all the above demands—particularly through grants-in-land, reimbursements of local expenditures, and distributions of the earnings of permanently endowed and earmarked funds.

Despite the considerably lower "velocity of government" (amount of government activity at all levels in relation to the total activity of society) prior to 1913, these demands were not inconsiderable. What is more, they were probably met with nearly as much relative success as the more exacting and varied demands of the twentieth century are met today.

Central to understanding the responses of the federal and state governments is an understanding of the functioning of the federal system prior to 1913. As this writer has demonstrated in *The American Partnership*, what we today call "cooperative federalism" was the dominant form of federalism even prior to the New Deal. The differences in American federalism then and now are primarily differences arising from the increased velocity of government in the twentieth century. Consequently, one may look for an absolute increase in direct federal-city relations since 1913 or 1933, but this does not necessarily imply radically new departures in federal-city relations (though this indeed may be the case in the relations between the great metropolitan centers and the federal government). It may even be that the percentage of formal federal-*local* programs in relation to the overall number of formal intergovernmental programs has not changed appreciably even as it is likely that the percentage of federal-city programs has increased as urbanization has increased. Two illustrations: (1) The direct federal-city relations created by the river and harbor improvement programs in the nineteenth century were possibly as extensive in proportion to the total amount of intergovernmental activity of the time as are direct federal-city relations in contemporary redevelopment programs. These were and are direct relations of the kinds that were later to burgeon in other fields. (2) Quasi-formal federal-county relations were developed in the post-Civil War period to conduct federal surveys of various kinds. These were federal-local relations that were not urban in character because the programs were not urban ones. Non-urban-related federal-local relations are certainly not unexpected in a generally non-urban society.

The federal response before 1913 led to city-federal relations in the following fields:

(1) Postal service was often the first governmental service of any sort demanded by residents of newly-settled local communities. Today, the extension of postal service is often overlooked as an important aspect of federal city relations because it is taken for granted. In the days of the land frontier, it was often a crucial factor influencing the possibilities for local commerce to develop and even the probability of a community's survival by providing it with: (a) a drawing card as a potential center of commerce with which to at-

tract neighboring settlers; (b) a means of communication with the outside world that made commerce possible and lessened isolation in an age when travel was difficult and expensive; (c) cash in the form of postal receipts—often the only more or less steady flow of cash available in a frontier community; and (d) freight and passenger service, which developed from stagecoach and railroad lines established as a result of obtaining mail contracts.

Nor did communities acquire postal service without exerting effort. Their leaders used pressure, political influence, and sheer public relations to gain the services of the post office, the construction of post office buildings, and the expansion of both. Among the best received new programs of Lincoln's administration were the initiation of parcel post, railway mail cars, and free delivery in cities of over fifty thousand population, all vital measures for the growth of American cities. The impact of the post office did not pass with the passing of the community's frontier stage. As the community grew, so did the post office—as a center of communication, as a business attraction, as a source of payrolls, and, most important, as a center of local politics—both as a source of political patronage and as a base of operations for local political leaders.[7]

(2) Since the close of the War 1812, the U.S. Corps of Engineers has been involved in a federal-city partnership in waterway improvement and, later, flood control. Cities actively sought federal aid in this field and were usually responsible for securing federal waterway improvements not only for themselves but for the regions (and states) they served. This was not only a matter of lobbying for federal aid, but often in-

volved joint day-to-day efforts, after the congressional appropriations were made, in carrying out projects. These efforts were usually the product of negotiations between local officials and federal administrative personnel, frequently with the assistance of the local representative in Congress. They ranged from the construction of a dredge by the City of Richmond, with federal funds, to be leased to the Army Engineers while the latter were engaged in local projects and then used by the city to maintain the improvements, to the inclusion of federal harbor services personnel on a quasi-formal Board of Harbor Improvement for the City of Boston to advise the city fathers on needed improvements so the latter could lobby for federal funds to pay for them.[8]

Cities also lobbied for and contributed toward (until forbidden to do so in most state constitutions) the construction of roads and railroads to serve their needs. Roads were either constructed by federal agencies directly or through federal land grants to the states. Railroads were constructed through federal land grants to the states or directly to federal-chartered companies. In either case, those cities competed for location of road and railroad routes and often those that lost withered away or ceased to grow. The struggle for transportation facilities involved considerable federal-city contact, collaboration, and conflict.[9]

(3) Normally there was little direct federal aid to local governmental agencies except in the earlier stages of the development of cities west of the Appalachians before the territories in which they were established achieved statehood. In those early stages, however, direct federal aid was often very significant, involving, as it did, direct grants of land for townsites and local institu-

tions, as well as the federal land survey which, as the nation's foremost effort at national planning, provided a basis for all local development in the public land states.[10] After statehood, federal aid for local services was important, but was almost invariably channeled through the states.

After the middle of the nineteenth century a new form of federal-local relations began to develop in the form of contacts between professionals in such diverse fields as education, library science, agriculture, and public welfare. These contacts were made privately and through the professional associations that began to emerge in the eighteen-forties. Over time, they grew to be a significant means of improving government services at both levels and of forging strong, if informal, cooperative lines between Washington and the localities.[11]

(4) Federal contributions to the local economic base through federal institutions, payrolls, tariffs, contracts, and the like have always been an important factor in American history. Again, their relative impact in the years before 1913 was no less than it has been since the great increase in the velocity of government in the twentieth century and may even have been greater. Though they have virtually disappeared from view today as historians have concentrated on more dramatic events of the past, the community leaders of that day were fully aware of their importance.[12] Federal military installations almost invariably were sought as contributors to local prosperity. Marine hospitals, post offices, customs offices, sub-treasuries, mints, and the like were equally sought. Military and civil construction and mail contracts were prized. Tariff concessions on particular items could make or break

particular cities which survived because of particular industries. Nineteenth-century Americans were quite conscious of this, too.

Despite the fact that the cities' demands were not much different from the demands of smaller localities, the larger cities as a general rule almost certainly benefited more than the smaller towns from the aforementioned programs. The exceptions were important because they almost invariably meant that the fortunate town would grow beyond reasonable objective expectations. Thus, in the years between 1827 and 1857 Chicago received more benefits from the federal government than St. Louis, its larger sister to the south. Most of this aid came in the form of land grants earmarked for it though channeled through the State of Illinois or directly transferred to the new city, but mail subsidies and new federal installations were also important, particularly in making the new city a center for federal activities in the Northwest. By 1860 Chicago had surpassed St. Louis in growth, no doubt aided by the extra measure of federal assistance available to the entrepreneurs who used that city as their base.[13] Almost all of these "benefits" contributed greatly to the urbanization of the United States in the long run.

Between 1913 and 1933 all of these responses were extended or modified and some new ones introduced in response to new needs.

(1) Post offices declined in importance as active elements in federal-city relations; their political importance declined, other federal agencies came into the local community, and cities grew less clearly dependent on the postal service as the primary means of communication with the outside world.

However, the establishment of postal savings banks that served the new immigrants who had flocked to the big cities of the Northeast temporarily added a new dimension to the role of the post office in urban affairs.

(2) Waterway improvements continued to be an important source of direct federal-city collaboration. Highway construction was added to the list, though as a federal-state-local program, not as a direct federal-city effort.

(3) The federal government first became involved—though only marginally —with urban housing in the eighteen-nineties when Congress became concerned with slum conditions in the great Eastern cities. Direct federal activity in the field of urban housing developed briefly during World War I, in response to the wartime situation. It lapsed after the end of hostilities.

(4) World War I also had an extraordinary though brief effect on the level of federal contributions to the local economies, urban and rural. While the cities benefited greatly from wartime industrial expansion, the agricultural areas also benefited from wartime agricultural expansion. Before and after the war, a state of "normalcy" may be said to have prevailed in the localities' search for government contributions to their economies and in the federal response, but this was not a "normalcy" of inaction.

THE EMERGENCE OF SPECIALIZED DEMANDS

In light of all this, what were the new specialized big city demands that developed between 1913 and 1933, and how did they relate to the earlier demands of the cities?

It was in the field of local services

that specialized urban demands really developed in the twentieth century. These demands originated in the late nineteenth century. They continued to develop at an accelerated rate after 1913, so that the explosion in federal-city relations that occurred during the New Deal actually did not spring full-blown from Depression-created needs but was the culmination of demands generated fifteen to thirty years earlier. These demands did not lead the cities to bypass the states for the first time. The cities had been seeking aid from the federal government in fields where pioneering programs were required for generations. Even though new urban needs were leading to new demands, few of the newly created federal programs were designed to favor urban areas over others.

The general categories we have already listed continued to be basic in the demands of both the localities generally and the new big cities after 1913, with some modifications which grew out of the changing needs of a dynamic society.

(1) Promotion of new communications facilities generally ceased to be a direct governmental concern, since post offices were already established in all but the very smallest hamlets, and telephone (like telegraph) services were developed through private enterprise. Government now became concerned with *regulation* of privately-owned communications facilities and *improvement* of postal services. Here big city needs did not appreciably differ from the general needs of all localities even after 1913, until the post-World War II years.

(2) Promotion of inter-city commercial facilities continued to involve river and harbor improvements but was also expanded into a concern for airports and highways. Needs for the former were primarily big city-oriented before World War II (since 1945 even the smaller urban places have been actively competing for navigable channels and harbor facilities) and did contribute to the cities' turning to the federal government, much in the same way that river and harbor improvements have since the War of 1812. The need for highways was more general, but, though big cities sought more federal assistance for intra-city highway connections because of the greater costs of urban highway construction, the states' primary concern with farm-to-market highways in a still half-rural nation led to congressional restrictions on the amount of federal aid which could be used for urban areas. These restrictions were not fully removed until the nineteen-forties.

(3) The need for local services increased generally, but the cities' search for federal assistance in every field (except welfare at the very end of the period under discussion) did not depart from the limited claims of localities generally. Here and there requests for assistance in urban redevelopment were heard.

(4) The demands for contributions to the local economic base were in no way diminished, nor were they specific to the big cities any more than they had been prior to 1913. If anything, the biggest cities ceased to be as dependent upon such contributions as smaller localities because of their more diverse economic bases.

Outside financial assistance, then, was sought in new ways primarily for highways and welfare, both to a limited degree. Otherwise, the previous patterns were maintained with slight modifications.

New and specialized big city demands were generated after 1913 in the fields of metropolitanization and the physical improvement of the urban environment. Both were new fields of interest that first emerged in the eighteen-nineties and were not publicly acknowledged until after 1910, and they were the demands which later evoked a response from the New Deal. Prior to 1933 little was done to meet them other than to make provision for the cities' unilateral action through permissive state legislation. This was primarily because they were expensive demands and, historically, the federal government has had to take the lead in expending large sums for the introduction of new programs managed by any level of government in the United States.

All of this points to the hardly radical conclusion that what really was occurring in the period between 1913 and 1933 was a subtle reshaping of the greater part of the range of government activities to the demands of an increasing urbanized society.

As a consequence of this reshaping of the activities of the federal-state-local partnership, virtually all cities except the largest metropolitan centers received sufficient federal and state assistance and benefits to satisfy most of their demands without leading them to take steps to alter the established patterns of federalism.

This was not the case after 1913 (and particularly after World War I) for the great metropolitan centers. They had grown so big that their needs and problems no longer fit into the same categories as those of their smaller urban sisters or of the nation's local communities, rural or urban. This change was multifaceted: On one hand, the large metropolitan centers had developed unique problems of urbanization and metropolitanization; on the other hand, the great metropolitan centers

had grown so large and socio-economically complex that they had become as self-contained and self-sufficient within the national framework (and as diverse internally) as the states of which they were parts.

Turned inward and possessing their own problems, the residents and leaders of the big metropolitan centers fell out of harmony with their states and the other urban centers within them. This estrangement led cities like New York, Chicago, Philadelphia, Detroit, Los Angeles, and others slightly smaller in population to turn to the federal government, not as constituent elements of their states advocating programs of interests to all localities (or even all cities), but as self-contained civil societies in their own right, seeking aid for their own specialized problems. At the close of the period discussed here, at least one well-known Chicagoan, Charles E. Merriam, was calling for the transformation of the large metropolitan centers into city-states. That this did not come to pass is a tribute to the stability and the flexibility of the federal system. It is also evidence that the basic cleavage in interest was not between urban and non-urban America, but between the great metropolitan centers and the rest of rapidly urbanizing America. The latter continued to appeal directly and indirectly to the federal government for aid and assistance just as they had been doing since the establishment of the Republic, but as constituent elements of their respective states, not as competing civil societies.

SOME UNANSWERED QUESTIONS

If this brief discussion has raised some of the salient questions concerning the development of city-federal relations and has presented some of the evidence and possible conclusions which may be drawn from it, it is obviously far from exhaustive. Among the important questions not discussed or only briefly mentioned are several other points of concern:

(1) *The role of the cities as participants in the political processes of federalism.* Federal aid came to the localities partly because of national necessity and partly as a result of local pressures. The latter were made manifest by the political role of the localities within the non-centralized federal system whereby their leaders and representatives could agitate for aid, mobilize support for their efforts on all levels, adapt acquired aid to local conditions, and even play the state and federal governments off against one another to their advantage.[14]

(2) *Sectional differences in federal-city relations, which seem to be quite significant.* Hints of these differences can be found in the foregoing pages— for example, in the way in which Western cities benefited primarily from federal expenditures locally. The extent of these differences appears to be more widespread, subtle, and important than such hints can indicate, reflecting, as they do, basic differences in the character of cities in the North, South, and West.

(3) *The differences in city-state relations in the several states.* The kinds of demands different cities made of the federal government and the way in which those demands were made depended, even before 1933, on the responses of their states to their special needs.

Nobody can deny that recent federal responses to urban problems have been of unprecedented scope and magnitude. At the same time, there is considerable evidence that they are not unprecedented in their roots and may not even be unprecedented in their impact. The evidence is not all in, but it should be clear that failure to understand the federal-city relationship before 1933 may lead to erroneous conclusions regarding the impact—or the proper management —of the federal-city relationship today. Such conclusions could, in turn, drastically affect the future of the American system as we know it.

Table 1

Incorporation Dates of Fifty Largest U.S. Cities by Historical Period*

I. Pre-1776 (2)	II. 1776-1815 (5)	III. 1816-1848 (22)	IV. 1849-1876 (17)	V. 1877-1912 (5)
New York (1685)	Baltimore (1797)	Atlanta (1847)	Akron (1865)	Honolulu (1909)
Philadelphia (1701)	Dayton (1805)	Boston (1822)	Birmingham (1871)	Long Beach,
	New Orleans (1805)	Buffalo (1832)	Dallas (1856)	California (1888)
	Richmond (1782)	Chicago (1837)	Denver (1861)	Miami (1896)
	San Antonio (1809)	Cincinnati (1819)	Fort Worth (1873)	Oklahoma City (1890)
		Cleveland (1836)	Indianapolis (1874)	
		Columbus (1834)	Jersey City (1855)	
		Detroit (1824)	Kansas City (1850)	
		Houston (1837)	Los Angeles (1850)	
		Jacksonville (1832)	Minneapolis (1867)	
		Louisville (1828)	Oakland (1854)	
		Memphis (1826)	Omaha (1857)	
		Milwaukee (1846)	Portland (1851)	
		Newark (1836)	St. Paul (1853)	
		Norfolk (1845)	San Diego (1850)	
		Pittsburgh (1816)	San Francisco (1850)	
		Providence (1832)	Seattle (1869)	
		Rochester (1834)		
		St. Louis (1822)		
		Syracuse (1848)		
		Toledo (1837)		
		Worcester (1848)		

* Dates are those in which cities were incorporated as cities.

Table 2

Number and Population of U.S. Cities by Category: 1790-1930

Year	Towns (2,500-10,000)		Small Cities (10,000-50,000)		Med.-Size Cities (50,000-250,000)		Large Cities (250,000-1,000,000)		Great Cities (1,000,000+)	
	No.	Total Pop. (000s)	No.	Total Pop. (000s)	No.	Total Pop. (000s)	No.	Total Pop. (000s)	No.	Total Pop. (000s)
1790	19	92	5	110						
1800	27	140	5	122	1	61				
1810	35	186	9	189	2	150				
1820	48	251	10	192	3	250				
1830	67	357	19	346	4	405				
1840	94	500	32	640	4	392	1	313		
1850	174	913	52	1,172	9	943	1	516		
1860	299	1,541	77	1,555	13	1,445	3	1,646		
1870	495	2,364	143	2,640	18	1,758	7	3,140		
1880	716	3,335	188	3,636	27	2,735	7	3,218	1	1,206
1890	994	4,661	296	5,720	47	4,809	8	3,254	3	4,468
1910	1,665	7,946	488	9,572	90	9,019	16	6,961	3	8,501
1920	1,970	9,354	608	12,110	119	11,785	22	10,764	3	10,146
1930	2,183	10,615	791	15,523	154	14,032	32	13,720	5	15,065

Source: *Historical Statistics of the United States, 1957.*

Table 3

Cities' Cumulative Per Cent of Total
Population by Size of Place:
1790-1930

Size of Place	1790	1850	1900	1930
1,000,000 plus			8.5	12.3
250,000 plus		2.2	14.4	23.4
50,000 plus		6.3	22.3	34.9
10,000 plus	2.8	11.3	31.7	47.5
2,500 plus	5.1	15.3	39.7	56.2

Source: 1950 Census of Population, Vol. II,
Characteristics of Population, Part 1.

Table 4

Distribution of U.S. Population According to Size of Place: 1790-1930

Year	Total Urban	Population Distribution Per Cent			Total Rural	Number of Urban Places by Size		
		One Million Plus	100,000 to One Million	Under 100,000		One Million Plus	100,000 to One Million	Under 100,000
1790	5.1	—	—	5.1	94.9	—	—	24
1800	6.1	—	—	6.1	93.9	—	—	33
1810	7.3	—	—	7.3	92.7	—	—	46
1820	7.2	—	1.3	5.9	92.8	—	1	60
1830	8.8	—	1.6	7.2	91.2	—	1	89
1840	10.8	—	3.0	7.8	89.2	—	3	128
1850	15.3	—	5.1	10.2	84.7	—	6	230
1860	19.8	—	8.4	11.4	80.2	—	9	383
1870	25.7	—	10.7	15.0	74.3	—	14	649
1880	28.2	2.4	10.0	15.8	71.8	1	19	919
1890	35.1	5.8	9.6	19.7	64.9	3	25	1,320
1900	39.7	8.5	10.2	21.0	60.3	3	35	1,699
1910	45.7	9.2	12.9	23.6	54.3	3	47	2,212
1920	51.2	9.6	16.3	25.3	48.8	3	65	2,654
1930	56.2	12.3	17.3	26.6	43.8	5	88	3,072

NOTES

° The bulk of the research for this article was made possible through a grant of funds from the University Research Board of the University of Illinois and of time from the Institute of Government and Public Affairs of that university. The initial hypotheses were developed and preliminary data gathered in the course of the author's other studies of nineteenth-century American federalism. See his *The American Partnership* (Chicago, 1962). Aside from the materials cited below, the author has made extensive use of documents in the State Historical Society and State Archives of Colorado, the Burton Historical Collection of the Detroit Public Library, the Barlow Collections in the Henry E. Huntington Library, the Minnesota Historical Society and State Archives of Minnesota, the Virginia State Archives, and the National Archives.

1. This viewpoint is expressed either explicitly or implicitly in recent works on federal-city relations. See, for example, *The Federal Government and the Cities* (Washington, 1962), a collection of lectures delivered at The George Washington University in 1961, of which Roscoe C. Martin's excellent "Washington and the Cities: An Introduction" is most enlightening. Two other important sources of material on the evolving federal-city relationship are Robert H. Connery and Richard H. Leach, *The Federal Government and Metropolitan Areas* (Cambridge, Mass., 1960) and "City-Federal Relations," *Proceedings of the American Municipal Congress, 1958* (Washington, 1958).

2. All statistical data are taken from U. S. Census Bureau, *Historical Statistics of the United States* (Washington, 1957) unless otherwise indicated.

3. The correspondence from that exchange was published by the State of Illinois as *Letters From Governor Palmer Concerning the Chicago Fire* (Chicago, 1873).

4. See Frank J. Goodenow, *Municipal Problems* (New York, 1897).

5. Annexation as a device declined when a sufficient number of suburban communities (including those created as suburbs or, more likely, those previously-settled towns suburbanized in the course of the expansion of the central city) began to desire to retain their "independence" and identities. They became a countervailing power within the state and were generally able to create a stalemate which served their interests. Significantly, most major annexations in recent years have taken place in the South and Southwest (Atlanta, Dallas, Houston, Nashville, Phoenix, San Antonio, Oklahoma City, to mention a few) in areas without established suburban communities to fight them. City-county consolidation and separation cases had similar histories before 1913. The *Municipal Year Book* publishes annexation data for the nation's cities annually.

6. The effects of the rural biases of the Wilson administration on the new federal grant programs are discussed in Austin F. Macdonald, *Federal Aid* (New York, 1928).

7. An abundance of documents on the role of the post office in the nineteenth century can be found in U. S. Congress, *American State Papers*. The political role of the department is discussed in Dorothy G. Fowler, *The Cabinet Politician: The Postmasters General, 1829-1909* (New York, 1943). The economic impact of postal services in cities has not been adequately treated, but Wayne E. Fuller's *RFD: The Changing Face of Rural America* (Bloomington, Ind., 1964) does much to indicate the possibilities even while focusing on rural post offices. Political studies of the extension of postal services can be found in Clyde Kelly, *United States Postal Policy* (New York, 1931) and Daniel C. Roper, *The United States Post Office* (New York, 1917).

8. *American State Papers* contains much documentary material on river and harbor improvements. Though there has been no comprehensive study of the economic impact of river and harbor improvements, there are numerous contemporary and historical studies of specific waterways and ports which deal with the question. See such standard works as E. W. Gould, *Fifty Years on the Mississippi or Gould's History of River Navigation* (St. Louis, 1889); Mildred L. Hartsough, *From Canoe to Steel Barge on the Upper Mississippi* (Minneapolis, 1934); and William E. Lass, *A History of Steamboating on the Upper Missouri River* (Lincoln, Neb., 1962). Lucille M. Kane, *The Waterfall that Built a City* (St. Paul, Minn., 1966), shows the impact of federal improvements on one major city, Minneapolis. For a brief overview of the pre-Civil War period, see Forest G. Hill, *Roads, Rails, and Waterways: The Army Engineers and Early Transportation* (Norman, Okla., 1957). For data on the appropriations and activities in every city in the United States, see U. S. House of Representatives, *Index to the Reports of the Chief of Engineers, U. S. Army, 1866-1912*, I (Rivers and Harbors) Doc. 740, 63rd Congress, 2d Session, 1914. The Richmond case is discussed in Elazar, *The American Partnership*, Chap. 16.

9. For exemplary studies of the local impact of federal aid to roads, see Philip D. Jordan, *The National Road* (Indianapolis, 1948). W. Turrentine Jackson, *Wagon Roads West* (Berkeley, 1952), Hill, Paul W. Gates, *The Illinois Central Railroad and its Colonization Work* (Cambridge, Mass., 1934), and Richard C. Overton, *Burlington West: A Colonizing History of the Burlington Railroad* (Cambridge, Mass., 1941) and undoubtedly the best studies of cities and railroad development. This writer drew extensively on the sources listed in the bibliographies of both. For overviews of federal activity, see Lewis H. Haney, *A Congressional History of Railroads in the United States, 1850-1887* (Madison, 1908, 1910), 2 Vols., and John B. Sanborn, *Congressional Grants of Land in Aid of Railways* (Madison, 1899).

10. The laws and statistics of direct federal grants

to localities are presented in Thomas C. Donaldson, *The Public Domain* (Washington, 1884), and R. M. Robbins, *Our Landed Heritage, The Public Domain, 1776-1936* (Princeton, 1942). See, also, George M. Stephenson, *The Political History of the Public Lands* (Boston, 1917).

11. Elazar, *The American Partnership*, Chap. 15.

12. The documentary evidence of federal-city relations contains many acknowledgments of the importance of these federal aids. Among the easily accessible published materials, see, for example, Thomas Hart Benton, *Thirty Years View* (New York, 1854-56). John G. Van Deusen discusses

local reactions to federal expenditures and assembles excellent fiscal data on these expenditures before the Civil War in *Economic Bases of Disunion in South Carolina* (New York, 1928).

13. Bessie L. Pierce, *A History of Chicago* (New York, 1937), 2 Vols., and James W. Putnam, *The Illinois and Michigan Canal* (Chicago, 1918).

14. See the writer's "Local Government in Intergovernmental Perspective," in *Illinois Government* (Urbana, 1961) for a brief delineation of the various roles of the localities in the federal system today, which are reasonably applicable to the period before 1933 as well.

Implications of the New Federal System

CHARLES ABRAMS

The first step is to break old patterns—to begin to think, work and plan for the development of entire metropolitan areas.

President Johnson, State of the Union Message, January 4, 1965

If the national effort to rebuild our cities limps along aimlessly and fruitlessly, an important reason is that the national power to deal with its urban problems is checked by antiquated theories of states rights, home rule, and local autonomy that no longer make sense in an era in which 70 per cent of the American people are concentrated in cities and their sprawling metropolitan formations. Though the primary responsibility for the general welfare has been conceded to the federal government since 1937,[1] and though general welfare and urban welfare are interwoven and interdependent, the state continues to check its exercise in all matters in which the welfare of urban people is involved.

Under the cloak of home rule and local autonomy, the state has passed down much of its own sovereign responsibilities to a myriad of local (mostly suburban) governments, each of which is concerned with its own welfare to the exclusion of its neighbor's. With the federal welfare power held in check by the states and the states' welfare power held in check by rural and suburban local governments, what is known as the general welfare has ceased being general.

The federal incapacity to deal directly with the urban problem has produced a system that can find no classification in political theory and no justification except as a vestige of an era that has passed. Its consequences are a national impotence to deal with the problems of poverty and substandard education, with the misery of the environment in which poor people live, and with the financial burdens and growing social costs the cities can no longer bear alone.

From Charles Abrams, *The City Is the Frontier* (New York, Harper & Row, 1965), pp. 211-12, 238-49. Copyright © 1965 by Charles Abrams. Reprinted by permission of Harper & Row, Publishers. Charles Abrams is Professor of Urban Planning at Columbia University.

The system has virtually exempted from governmental control a host of metropolitan regions composed of thousands of minor jurisdictions with common problems and with problems interlinked with those of the central city.

It has created a bizarre federalism under which the expanded general welfare state is emerging into a business welfare state.

It has ushered in a system of local financing that guarantees immunity from levy of the large aggregations of personal and corporate wealth while simultaneously socializing a growing number of enterprises formerly in the private sector.

Because the nation enjoys prosperity, we have accepted all the shortcomings of the system in the belief that those shortcomings are part of what makes it work. But the system works despite the impediments, not because of them. In a period of national prosperity, it is an anomaly that slums and poverty continue, that cities are insolvent in an age of cities, that they are ugly, unlivable, and unable politically to cope with their growing predicaments. . . .[2]

The present housing and urban renewal formulae under which the federal government bows to state sovereignty in the exercise of the welfare power and under which it carries out housing programs through local housing authorities and local renewal agencies instead of through the federal government are, in a sense, a historical accident. The same accident deters the federal government from building new towns as it did in 1936, and is responsible for the continued issuance of tax exempt bonds not only for housing and urban renewal, but for the expanding number of dubious local operations under the loose "public

benefit theory." Because I was counsel in two of the pivotal cases which effected the shift in policy, I am able to provide some of the background information.

One of the main issues after the Constitutional Convention had been whether the general welfare clause of the Constitution was intended to be an independent clause which authorized the new federal government to act in the national good or whether it was merely a qualifying clause authorizing the spending of money exclusively under the enumerated powers that preceded it (interstate commerce, war, post roads, etc.). On the side of the strong and independent federal welfare power had stood Hamilton and Monroe. They were reinforced in their view by Judge Story's conception of what had happened at the convention. Supporting the more constricted position were Madison and Jefferson, abetted in the years that followed by Presidents Polk, Pierce, and Buchanan.

Whatever may have been in the minds of the founders, all were convinced that the states would remain the dominant power in the centuries that lay ahead. Jefferson left the Convention content in the thought that the new federal government was little more than an American department of foreign affairs, while Hamilton dolefully conceded that the peoples' affections toward their own states would soon make them indifferent toward the infant nation.[3]

The feeling that the state was supreme persisted even during the century that followed. "Many people in France," wrote de Tocqueville, "imagine that a change of opinion is going on in the United States, which is favorable to a centralisation of power in the hands of the President and the Congress. I hold that a contrary tendency may distinctly be observed."[4]

Even after the state secession thesis had been shattered at Appomattox, Lord Bryce, while acknowledging a well-defined division of responsibility between the two great levels of government, thought Jefferson not unrealistic in comparing the federal government to a foreign affairs department. An American, he wrote, "may, through a long life, never be reminded of the federal government, except when he votes at presidential and congressional elections."[5] Yet if de Tocqueville and Bryce were to return for a look at America's political system today, it would appear as strange to them as Rip Van Winkle's Catskill Village looked to him after his twenty-year slumber, for the bucolic America envisioned by Jefferson has shrunk to a small remnant of its original design.

But if the old dispute over the meaning of general welfare should have been resolved by events, it remained unresolved until the New Deal, and it was not until Franklin D. Roosevelt took office that an effort was made to remove the ambiguity for all time.

THE NEW DEAL CHALLENGE TO THE CONSTRICTED WELFARE CONCEPT

Neither the states nor the cities in 1933 were in a mood to reject any federal largess on legalistic grounds, while for the federal government to close its purse on the 13 million unemployed would have been a catastrophic default. It was at this juncture that low-rent housing and other federal assistance to cities were struck upon as devices for priming an economic recovery. Harold L. Ickes, as head of the Federal Public Works Administration, was placed in charge of the federal public housing program and proceeded to buy sites for the purpose within the states' land preserves; he drew plans for his projects, built houses, and, where private land owners refused to sell their land, he boldly acquired it under a presumptive and politically (if not yet constitutionally) acceptable power of eminent domain.

Mr. Ickes was not alone in crossing the Rubicon of state police power over city affairs and over national welfare generally. The United States had simultaneously proceeded to replan the Tennessee Valley and had set up a federal Authority to prevent floods and stream pollution, provide cheap power, control the soil, and improve navigation, irrigation, and recreation.

Rexford Tugwell's dream during these trying days was the most far-reaching of all as a challenge to state power. As federal Resettlement Administrator, he had conceived a vast federal program for the building of new towns similar to Britain's Welwyn Gardens. He aimed to achieve (in Ebenezer Howard's words) "a union of city and country life in which every foot of land was planned to eliminate waste and to provide its inhabitants with pleasant and spacious living."[6] Tugwell saw a vision of such greenbelt towns around every metropolis with a

. . . chain of similar suburban communities around its borders. They would offer an opportunity for orderly efficient expansion. The greenbelts, linked together, would form continuous permanent open spaces around the city, protecting it and each suburb from overcrowding and sprawling, haphazard suburban development and encroaching industries.[7]

Tugwell studied a hundred cities and selected for his first ventures three tracts in Wisconsin, Ohio, and Maryland, all on the peripheries of busy cities. When President Roosevelt drove to Greenbelt outside Washington, D.C., he called it "an experiment that ought to be copied by every community in the United States."[8] The stage was set, it seemed, not only for a regeneration of the older cities but for a new-town movement in the areas around them. It was a direct federal assertion of national sovereignty in matters involving the nation's physical environment.

When Roosevelt visited Greenbelt, Maryland, and asked about the attitude of the local bodies, he was told that "splendid cooperation had been given by the county commission, the county and state school authorities, State Road Commission, Chamber of Commerce, Washington Suburban Sanitary Commission, county newspapers and the nearby towns. Cooperation was 'complete.' "[9]

The situation was no different in the case of Mr. Ickes' public housing projects. States which would have been expected to put up the "No Trespass" sign against federal intrusion unhesitatingly passed enabling laws authorizing cities to cooperate. Even more, when attacks were made upon Mr. Ickes' authority to invade their constitutionally protected dominions, cities and states filed briefs to support Mr. Ickes' position. Southern senators who in another day might have passionately defended the sanctity of state prerogatives became the stoutest defenders of federally initiated housing. When legal questions were raised that people occupying federal property might be under the exclusive jurisdiction of the federal government, might not be entitled to vote, sue in the state courts, or send their children to state schools, Congress quickly cooperated by enacting two laws preserving such rights.

A tradition of 150 years which had made the power over environment the preserve of the states and the forbidden territory of the federal government was thus broken. The first onslaught on the formula of state sovereignty since the Civil War was met not by the states calling out their militias, but by welcoming the invader with open arms. The states rights monolith fell quietly under the impact of emergency.

If there were some who feared the consequences of the federal intrusion, the fears subsided with the promise of local participation. When the Tennessee Valley Authority assured grass roots administration to the governments in the region, it was not long before TVA was not only welcomed but also actively supported by the states wherever cooperation was needed.

Similarly, the opposition to the federal power in housing and new-town building disappeared with the promise by Messrs. Ickes and Tugwell that the federal government would, after acquiring the land and after building the projects, dispose of them to the local communities.

"Government will withdraw," said Mr. Tugwell, "except for insisting on competent management to protect its investment and interests. Public housing authorities and other public bodies will hold and manage the properties. In drawing the original charters, care will be taken that the towns will be permanently administered as planned communities. Land and buildings will bear their full share of state and local taxation, and from these tax revenues, schools and other public services will be supported in the normal way. The government will be that which is appropriate to the size of the town under the laws of the state."[10]

Thus, up to 1936, a formula had been carved out of the necessities of the era under which the federal government had assumed the initiative and responsibility for rebuilding urban and suburban America.[11] It claimed that its authority to plan cities and grapple with the slum and housing problems was inherent in the welfare power. The government could go into cities or suburbs, build towns as England had been doing, clear slums and replan neighborhoods as it pleased. By 1937, the Public Works Administration had undertaken 51 projects in 36 cities (as well as Puerto Rico and the Virgin Islands) and had provided approximately 21,770 dwelling units for some 87,000 persons.

Had the two programs gone on unchallenged, the building of housing and new towns as well as federal influence over regional development might today have been viewed as being as laudable a federal purpose as building TVA's or Boulder Dams. Urban conservation might have taken its place of honor with soil conservation, and federal open space programs would have won the esteem held for federal parks. As Congress broadened the scope of urban aid and housing in the years that followed, it is even conceivable that the "ridiculously fragmented" region that is "more complicated than any other that mankind has yet contrived or allowed to happen,"[12] might have been set aright by the corrective federal power.

This, however, did not happen. The formula of direct federal building faded from view. The old pattern of hundreds of little autonomous districts was restored. Housing and city and regional development were returned to state and local controls. The idea of building new towns was forgotten. The federal government became the paymaster and underwriter of private risks under a string of assorted programs without theme or aim. Urban renewal was subsequently added to the amorphous string.

Federal withdrawal from direct responsibility for building and rebuilding occurred not because local operation was seen as a more efficient or more democratic formula. It was an almost fortuitous by-product of the New Deal drama during which President Roosevelt and the Supreme Court had differed on the meaning of "general welfare." At President Roosevelt's urging, Congress had enacted a succession of dramatic laws implementing his New Deal. But the conservative court of the 1930s had been paying homage to Jefferson and Madison, not Hamilton or Franklin D. Roosevelt, and in sixteen months, the old court had invalidated eight New Deal laws while sustaining only two. It was during this period that cases challenging the federal power over housing, new towns, and TVA were working their way for argument to the Supreme Court and it was in the framework of the anti-New Deal rulings of the then constituted Supreme Court that the lower courts also were rendering their anti-New Deal decisions limiting federal powers.

THE CHALLENGE TO FEDERAL JURISDICTION OVER CITIES

One of the first constitutional challenges to the New Deal advance into urban problems and state jurisdiction over them was by a stubborn Louisville citizen whose land Mr. Ickes had sought for a housing project. The general welfare power, the owner contended, was not an independent power after all, as Hamilton, Monroe, Jackson, and Story had claimed, but an *ultra vires* intrusion upon the states in contempt of Jefferson and Madison.

Yet whatever may have been in the minds of the founding fathers in their day, the fact was that since the Civil War and the industrial revolution, the federal government had exercised many more powers than the limited ones delegated to it in 1789. In fact, had it not done so, it could never have coped with the exigencies of the emerging society. It had freely embarked on such extraconstitutional deviations as appropriating money for Indian depredations in Florida and Minnesota, fires in New York City and San Francisco, tornadoes and cyclones in the South, yellow fever epidemics, grasshopper scourges, floods and droughts in many places, as well as earthquakes in Venezuela and wars or famines in Ireland, Cuba, India, or Russia. In these circumstances there would seem to have been sufficient precedent for the federal government to relieve the distress of its unemployed or its slum dwellers as well as build cities and good housing for those who needed it.

But the precedents in fact were not yet precedents in law. They had been acquiesced in during the period of limited federal sovereignty but had never been legalized. Out of necessity, but also out of an unwillingness to pass on the thorny dispute over the general welfare clause, the Supreme Court over the previous years had etched out for the "limited federal sovereignty" a devious device which had permitted the federal government to go on spending for any purpose it chose by never giving a taxpayer his day in court. The federal government, the court had held, derived its funds not only from taxes but also from the sale of its lands, and a taxpayer's action was therefore considered too "remote," "minute," "indeterminate," and not "justiciable."[13] As long as the federal government could go on spending money, however illegal the purpose, the issue could never come to a test. But the

issue could be raised if the federal government tried to affect an owner's property rights by acquiring his land. The owner's interest would then no longer be "remote" and the constitutional issue would be "justiciable."

Federal officials had therefore always scrupulously avoided putting a determinable issue before the courts. The federal government had long spent money —legally or illegally—but had carefully abstained from condemning land where its spending powers could be tested.

It was during the period in which the Supreme Court was leveling New Deal legislation piece by piece that the Louisville challenge to Mr. Ickes was working its way through the lower courts, soon to be laid before the still unchastened tribunal of last resort. The lower federal courts were unkind to Mr. Ickes. He had been enjoined from condemning the Louisville owner's land for public housing, and the Circuit Court of Appeals had upheld the injunction. Mr. Tugwell, meanwhile, had fared no better in the lower courts and was prevented from proceeding with one of his towns in New Jersey.[14]

Mr. Ickes, nevertheless, resolved to take the issue before the conservative Supreme Court and confidently filed his brief contending that the federal government had the right to clear slums, buy land for housing, or condemn it. The general welfare clause of the Constitution, he contended, gave the federal government the right to condemn land for the purpose or for any purpose related to the health and well-being of the American people.

The case, however, was never heard by the Supreme Court, for on the eve of the argument, White House officials became fearful that an unfavorable ruling by the then existing court on the general welfare clause might strike down the whole New Deal spending program. For if the federal government had no right to spend for housing under a general welfare power, what other constitutional power sanctioned its right to spend for unemployment, etc.? How the anti-New Deal Supreme Court would in fact have ruled remains in the realm of conjecture. The lower-court decisions denying the federal government's right to embark upon housing and new towns became the established law, at least for the time being.

THE MULLER CASE—A WAY
OUT IS FOUND

Meanwhile, two events worked toward salvaging the bones of Mr. Ickes' housing program. The New York City Housing Authority had proposed a project of its own on the Lower East Side, entailing the remodeling of some tenements, financed with the help of relief labor and materials. When Andrew Muller, the owner of two of the tenements, refused to sell, the local housing authority filed eminent domain proceedings and speeded the case to the state's highest court. The court sustained the local authority's right to acquire the land as a proper exercise of the state's police power.[15]

With Mr. Ickes facing a still hostile Supreme Court, it now seemed that a formula could be framed for continuing the housing program without gambling on whether the federal government could acquire land and build housing directly. Under the Muller decision, a local housing authority would now acquire land for public housing and the federal government would advance the money. Since no taxpayer could question the right of the federal government to spend

money and since no owner could challenge the right of a local authority (a state instrumentality) to condemn land, a traversable, if circuitous, path would be paved for circumventing any legal barriers raised by a taxpayer or an owner. With the Muller case as a precedent, local authorities in other states prepared for similar tests in their own state courts. A quick succession of favorable state decisions citing the Muller case as authority followed. This was the first step toward the new relationship under which the federal government was to retreat to the role of lender and spender while the local government would be the initiator and operator. The course had been marked out from necessity, not choice.

The new arrangement might have continued as a temporary expedient except that Mr. Ickes was proving a hard man for the local authorities to get along with. He had been a crusader before he had become an administrator; having exposed corruption in Chicago, he was terror-ridden lest its specter turn up in his own yard. The surest guarantee against corruption, he felt, was Mr. Ickes himself. So he proposed to do the whole job, with each local authority simply acting as his scrupulously supervised *alter ego*, condemning the land needed and then turning it over to him to do as he wished. He might ultimately turn the projects over to the authorities though he would not reveal the terms of the arrangement and the controls he would exercise.

The local housing authorities were faced with the choice of accepting surrender or finding a substitute for Mr. Ickes. Now armed with the legal sanction to do the job directly, they pressed for a new law which would set up a separate U.S. Housing Authority that

would give them federal funds to acquire the land and build housing locally.

Such a federal law was passed by
Congress in 1937. The program was decentralized with the federal government
now posited as the financier and subsi-
dizer and the local housing authorities as
the acquirers of land and the actual
builders and managers of all future projects. This remains the formula today.

THE BELATED SANCTION OF
FEDERAL POWER

By the time the new decentralized procedure had ripened, a second event—
Mr. Roosevelt's re-education of the Supreme Court—was gradually becoming
fact. Between March and June 1937 the
Court, partly reconstituted and partly
reconciled, began to ratify the New Deal
program in one decision after another. It
upheld a State Minimum Wage Law,
the Farm Mortgage Act, the amended
Railway Labor Act and, in a ruling on
the social security program, it held that
the general welfare clause of the Constitution was an independent and a substantive power rather than the constricted one of the more conservative
founding fathers.

It is too late today for the argument to be
heard with tolerance that in a crisis so extreme, the use of the moneys of the nation
to relieve the unemployed and their dependents is a use for any purpose narrower than the promotion of the general
welfare.[16]

In vain did Justice McReynolds expa-
tiate his dissent with citations from Jefferson and Madison. The judicial die was
cast and the federal government was
pushed ahead toward becoming a full-
fledged government empowered to function wherever the national welfare de-

manded it. Had Mr. Ickes been permitted to take his case to the highest
court, it is barely possible that he would
have won. Had he been able to wait, he
would certainly have won.

In any event, the stage was now set
for legalizing federally built housing,
slum clearance, new towns, and federal
aid to cities generally. The only question
that remained was whether the power
applied only during emergency periods
or generally. The test came in Ohio in
1945, where an Ickes project was challenged as not being within the power of
the federal government and hence subject to state taxation.[17] Housing, which
had been ruled by the lower courts to be
outside the federal power in the depression period, was in the period following
the recovery considered to be a federal
purpose and lawful forever after. Irrespective of emergency, the federal government was now vested with the full
right to act in the general welfare in
housing and in the building of new
towns. Had Mr. Ickes been a more judicious administrator, the federal government might conceivably have remained
(as it did in TVA) an active and effective participant in the building of a better environment for the nation's people.

By this time, however, the decentralized pattern had become firmly rooted.
The federal government was now simply
setting the general rules, approving the
contracts, and turning over the subsidies
to the local authorities. Though at last
possessing the power to build housing,
it fitted itself into the established groove
and continued to let the local governments do the job. It adopted the same
formula for urban renewal in 1949. It simultaneously helped insure mortgages
for privately developed housing, which
was being built mostly in the suburbs.

As for the new-town program, it had already been forgotten and there was by this time no pressure for its restoration.

It is not argued that if the federal government had continued clearing slums and building public housing in cities, it would have been more efficient than the local authorities. Nor is it argued that it should have resumed building government towns without using private builders or providing home ownership. But it is contended that it would have had more comprehensive jurisdiction over the nation's regions and would have been free of the petty jurisdictional limitations they prescribed. It would have made or influenced better plans for the millions of acres now sprawling throughout suburbia. By offering each jurisdiction the right to build or not to build but asserting the right to do so itself if the jurisdiction refused, it would have retained concurrent authority over the national environment and been better posed to foster its proper development, either through public or private mechanisms. It would have been able to fill the gaps where housing and new cities were needed and where it did so, dispose of it to the states or local governments. The possession of the power would, in fact, have brought better cooperation and made its exercise essential only in few cases.

THE REVERSION TO STATE HEGEMONY AND LOCAL CONFUSION

Though the federal government now had the power to plan and build new cities or rebuild old ones or to deal with cities directly without the state's veto, Congress soon elected to renounce that power by its own act. It was not merely that the procedures evolved to circum-

vent the constitutional uncertainties had become well seeded, but that new and more powerful forces had come into being between 1936 and 1949. Suburban power by this time had marshaled its forces and become more articulate. It saw the central cities as a threat and direct federal treatment with the cities as a forerunner of regional controls. By insisting upon a reversion to states rights, suburban power could better influence the course of federal policy and the flow of federal funds. In Congress, it could see to it that its peripheral smaller governments would get a greater share of the federal largess. The beneficiaries of that largess, i.e., the suburban home builders, organized to resist aid to the larger cities for public housing, community facilities, or other assistance. The states and the suburban real estate interests aligned themselves on the side of their influential suburbias.

Meanwhile, the decisions of the more liberal Supreme Court against racial restrictive covenants and school segregation, followed by the Executive Order against housing discrimination and the more recent ban on discrimination in public accommodations and the voting booth, soon brought Southern power to the side of the states rights, suburban, and real estate interests. It, too, now insisted that any federal assistance to cities shall be implemented only through the state or with the state's consent. Thus the formula that had been set for public housing in 1935 to circumvent the decisions of an irreconcilable Supreme Court and two years later to circumvent an irreconcilable federal works administrator had become in the 1950s a device for restraining constructive federal action in what were clearly welfare purposes.

THE STATES RIGHTS ENIGMA IN
THE NEW URBAN SOCIETY

In the nation of farms envisioned by Jefferson, it would have mattered little whether state boundaries were drawn by straight lines, angles, or curves. And since economies were localized and travel arduous, the states served vital and practical functions as decentralized governmental units. While no one will contend that these boundaries conform to any economic realities today, political logic and political reality do not always go together. Sensible or not, the states do exist as deeply rooted traditional actualities, and it would be impossible to reshape them without revising the whole rationale of Senate representation and geographical boundaries and without drastically revolutionizing the political system upon which the governmental process now rests.

Nor is it contended that the existence of state power is devoid of all merit. The diversity of laws and the opportunity for experimentation hold real values in that they permit the citizen to exercise choices which might not exist under a strong central government. The diversity of divorce laws between states is an example, and if Congress, under the political pressure of one influential group, were given power to enact a law as rigid as New York State's or North Carolina's, life for many might be intolerable. But this is a far cry from asserting that, in an urban society whose industrial products and people can be conveyed from one coast to another in six hours and whose problems are national in scope, a central government must subordinate its authority on nationwide and welfare problems to fifty separate jurisdictions and to thousands of smaller jurisdictions to whom the state delegates authority. The

continued failure of the states and local governments to meet their responsibilities must, in fact, lead to the greater growth of the federal power, if not ultimately to the disappearance of the states as forces in American life. The values of state power can still be salvaged by a realistic reapportionment of federal and state authority over the welfare imperatives.

NOTES

1. *Steward Machine Company v. Davis,* 301 U.S. 548 (1937).
2. [Abrams's accounts of the background for the dispute and of the constitutional issues in light of the present situation, follow.—Ed.]
3. "Upon the same principle," wrote Hamilton, "that a man is more attached to his family than to his neighborhood, to his neighborhood than to the community at large, the people of each state would be apt to feel a stronger bias toward their local governments than towards the government of the union" (*Federalist Papers,* No. 17).
4. "So far is the federal government, as it grows old, from acquiring strength, and from threatening the sovereignty of the states, that I maintain it to be growing weaker, and that the sovereignty of the union alone is in danger" (Alexis de Tocqueville, *Democracy in America,* Century, 1898, I, 535).
5. *The American Commonwealth,* Macmillan, 1895, p. 425.
6. Quoted in *Greenbelt Towns,* Resettlement Administration, September 1936.
7. *Ibid.*
8. *Prince Georgian* (a newspaper), Mount Rainier, Maryland, December 25, 1936.
9. *Ibid.*
10. *Greenbelt Towns.*
11. While the federal government had built housing on a previous occasion during World War I through the Emergency Fleet Corporation and the United States Housing Corporation, it had been done as an exercise of the war power, not the disputed general welfare power.
12. Robert C. Wood, *1400 Governments,* Harvard University Press, 1961.
13. Respondent's brief in Supreme Court in *U.S. v. Certain Lands in Louisville, Kentucky,* 78 Fed. 2nd 684 (July 15, 1935); Appeal dismissed, 297 U.S. 726 (March 30, 1936).
14. In this case, a taxpayer's suit was upheld and the incapacity of the ordinary taxpayer's right to question federal spending was distinguished as follows: "In those cases [i.e., *Frothingham v. Mellon* and *Magnano Co. v. Hamilton*] the individual was a taxpayer in the same position as millions of other citizens paying federal taxes. In the case at

bar the plaintiffs are taxpayers in a municipality having a population of only 6,500 (many of whom are not taxpayers) the chief portion of the revenues of which is derived from real estate." The taxpayer was therefore held to "suffer such a direct and immediate injury from the detachment of a large portion of the taxable property of the township and the resulting increase in taxation, as will give them a standing . . ." (*Township of Franklin* v. *Tugwell,* 85 F 2nd 208, May 18, 1936).

15. *New York City Housing Authority* v. *Muller,* 270 N.Y. 333 (March 1936).

16. *Steward Machine Co.* v. *Davis,* 301 U.S. 548 (1937), *Helvering* v. *Davis,* 301 U.S. 619 (May 24, 1937).

17. *Federal Public Housing Authority* v. *Gucken-berger,* 323 U.S. 329 (1945). In that case the Circuit Court had held that though the evils of bad housing are local in their origin, their effect may become so widespread as to create a menace to the national welfare and that Congress therefore had the right to deal with them. The Supreme Court dismissed the attack on the constitutionality with these blunt words: "Little need be said concerning the merits. Section 1 of the Housing Act declares a policy to promote the general welfare of the nation by employing its funds and credit to assist the states and their political subdivisions to relieve unemployment and safeguard health, safety and morals of the nation's citizens by improving housing conditions. . . . Challenge of the power of Congress to enact the Housing Act must fail."

American Political Parties and the Rise of the City: An Interpretation

CARL N. DEGLER

The ending of Reconstruction in 1877 deprived both Republican and Democratic parties of the issues that had sustained their rivalry for half a century. As a result, in the presidential elections from 1876 to 1892, neither party won decisively; never before nor since has popular political inertia been so noticeable.[1] More important, this indecision of the voters obscured the significant fact that the Republican party was popularly weak. For despite the preponderance of Republican presidents during these years, only James A. Garfield secured a popular plurality and his was the smallest in history. The party's weak popular base was even more evident in the congressional elections between 1874 and 1892 when the Democrats captured siz-able majorities in the House of Representatives in eight out of ten Congresses.[2] So serious was this popular weakness of the party that Republican Presidents from Rutherford B. Hayes to Benjamin Harrison, as both Vincent P. De Santis and Stanley P. Hirshson have shown, worked in a variety of ways to build up a stronger Republican party in the South, but with very limited success.[3]

Thus in the opening years of the 1890s the Republicans as a national party were in obvious trouble. The elections of 1890 and 1892 were disastrous for them as the Democrats swept into firm control of the House of Representatives and into the White House as well.[4] Despite the party's proud association

From *Journal of American History* (June 1964), pp. 41–59. Reprinted by permission of the publisher. Carl N. Degler is Professor of American History at Stanford University.

with the winning of the War for the Union, the Republicans were no more popularly based than at their founding forty years earlier; the majority of the nation's voters remained stubbornly Democratic. Moreover, with each passing election the political value of that vaunted association depreciated further as memories grew dimmer. The party seemed destined to recapitulate the history of the Whigs by serving only as a convenient alternative to the Democrats.

At that point, though, a complete reversal in party prospects took place. In the congressional election of 1894 the Republicans clearly emerged as the majority party, leaving the Democrats to wander in the political wilderness for a generation. The transfer of seats in the election of 1894 from the Democratic to the Republican side of the House was the largest in history. The Republicans gained a majority of 132, whereas in twenty-four states not a single Democrat was elected and in six others only one Democrat was returned in each. Moreover, prominent Democrats like William L. Wilson of West Virginia, William McK. Springer of Illinois, and Richard L. Bland of Missouri—men associated with important Democratic doctrines like low tariffs and free silver—lost their places.[5] This overwhelming Republican congressional victory in 1894 was confirmed two years later by what for the Republicans was to be their first decisive presidential victory without benefit of federal protection of Negro voting in the South. Measured against the margins of defeat in previous elections, William Jennings Bryan's defeat was crushing; he ran farther behind the winner than any candidate of a major party since Ulysses S. Grant trounced Horace Greeley.

Dramatic as the Republican victories

for 1894 and 1896 undoubtedly were, their enduring significance lies in the continuance of the trend they began. For the next sixteen years the Republicans, without interruption, commanded the majorities in the House and elected the presidents. Thus in the middle of the 1890s the Republicans, for the first time, emerged as the majority party of the nation.

The question which arises is: why? At the outset one can reject the hypothesis of challenging new leadership, since the party enjoyed none in the 1890s. Furthermore, since the shift in votes took place when Grover Cleveland, an acknowledged conservative, was president, and continued when a radical Democrat, Bryan, was the party's candidate, the policies of the opposition party do not offer much help in explaining the change. The only place left to look is among the voters themselves. It is their attitudes that changed as the United States passed from an agricultural to an industrial economy.

In spite of all that has been written to emphasize that the 1890s was the period during which this agrarian to industrial transition occurred, there are valid reasons for placing this momentous shift in the preceding decade.[6] It was, for example, during the 1880s that the production of manufactured goods surpassed farm goods in dollar value, and it was in this same decade that a majority of the nation's work force became engaged in non-agricultural rather than agricultural pursuits. Also during the 1880s railroad construction reached unprecedented heights, with more miles of track laid than in any other decade in American history. These were years of peak membership of the Knights of Labor, something over 700,000; the American Federation of Labor was formed, and the number of industrial strikes sharply increased.[7] It was the decade of the frightening Haymarket riot in Chicago, which, in its nationwide notoriety, epitomized the arrival of the new world of the factory, the city, and the immigrant. In fact the number of immigrants who flooded into the country in that decade exceeded that of any other similar period in the century. Furthermore, those ten years were the seedtime of the city. According to a contemporary analysis of the census, the number of cities with 8,000 or more population jumped from 286 in 1880 to 443 in 1890. Many cities doubled in size in the ten years, and some, like Chicago, had been already large at the beginning of the decade. A few made spectacular records of rapid growth. Minneapolis jumped from 47,000 to 165,000; Omaha reached 140,000 in 1890, though ten years before its population had been no more than 31,000; Denver nearly tripled its population.[8]

During that decade of transition neither the political parties nor the people were prepared by previous experience for the problems and nature of the new industrial, urban age. Hence the politics of the 1880s were sterile, uninteresting, and often trivial, as the parties and the voters rehashed stale issues and only reluctantly faced the new. Then, in the early 1890s, it would seem, the decision was made; the commitment of the voters hardened. The question then remains: why did the Republican party, which thus far had been sectionally based and numerically weak, rather than the popular Democratic party, emerge from this period of indecision as the dominant party of the nation?

A part of the answer seems to lie in the public image of the two parties. The Republican party was more suited to the needs and character of the new urban, industrial world that was beginning to dominate America. In those years the Republicans were the party of energy and change. They inherited from their antebellum beginnings as well as from the experience of Reconstruction a tradition which looked to the national authority first and to the states second. The party and its leaders had not hesitated to use the national power in behalf of economic growth by sponsoring such measures as the Homestead Act, land grants and loans to railroad construction companies, and protective tariffs. During the Civil War the Republicans demonstrated their willingness to use income and inheritance taxes, and fiat money when the nation's survival had seemed to require such novel measures. In the 1880s, it was Republican Senator Henry W. Blair who sought to employ the federal revenues and power in behalf of aid to the public schools. In each of the four times that the Blair education bill came before the Congress, Republican support always exceeded Democratic support.[9]

This nationalistic tradition and these specific measures, of course, also added up to a national image of the party that would appeal to urban voters and immigrants. As the self-proclaimed party of prosperity and economic growth, the Republicans could expect to win support from those who manned the expanding factories and crowded into the tenements of the burgeoning cities. Certainly party spokesmen made appeals to the urban working class. In 1892, for example, President Harrison told the Congress: "I believe that the protective system, which has now for something more than thirty years continuously prevailed in our legislation, has been a mighty instrument for the development of our national wealth and a most powerful agency in protecting the homes of our workingmen from the invasion of want. I have felt a most solicitous interest to preserve to our working people rates of wages that would not only give daily bread, but supply a comfortable margin for those home attractions and family comforts and enjoyments without which life is neither hopeful nor sweet."[10] Nor should such appeals be hastily brushed aside as empty rhetoric. Republican claims received substance, if not proof, from the steady rise in real wages during the last three decades of the century.[11] Moreover, foreign observers, like Friedrich Engels, who certainly could not be accused of being partial to Republican propaganda, cited the tariff as one of the principal reasons why American workingmen were better off than European. In 1893 Engels wrote to his friend Friedrich A. Sorge that "through the protective tariff system and the steadily growing domestic market the workers must have been exposed to a prosperity no trace of which has been seen here in Europe for years now. . . ."[12]

The Democratic party, to a greater extent than the Republican party, was more a congeries of state organizations than a national party. Certainly in the South and in a northern state like Illinois, there were many Democrats in the 1890s who were far from agreement with the national leadership. But even with these cautionary observations, of the two parties between 1880 and 1896, the Democrats undoubtedly presented the more conservative face to the electorate. The hallmark of the party under the dominance of Cleveland was economy, which in practice meant the paring down of government assistance to business, opposing veterans' pensions, hoarding the national resources, lowering the tariff, and, in general, stemming the Republican efforts to spur economic growth and to enhance the national power. Besides, the Democrats were ideologically unsuited to any ventures in the expansion of governmental activities. Still steeped in the Jeffersonian conception of the limited role of the federal government, the national Democrats were less likely than the Republicans to use federal powers in new ways to meet new problems. It was Cleveland, after all, who had vetoed a meager $10,000 relief appropriation for drought-stricken Texas farmers with the stern warning: "though the people support the Government the Government should not support the people."[13]

The election results of the 1880s suggest that the Republicans were even then receiving returns from their bid for working class support. Today it is axiomatic that the big cities of the country will vote Democratic, but in that period most of the large urban centers outside the South were more likely to be Republican than Democratic. It is true that cities like New York, Boston, and San Francisco were usually safely Democratic, but in the three presidential elections of the 1880s a majority of the nation's cities over 50,000 outside the South went Republican. In these three elections—even though in two of them Cleveland polled a larger vote than his Republican opponents—eastern and midwestern cities like Philadelphia, Chicago, Cleveland, Cincinnati, Buffalo, Providence, Milwaukee, Newark, Syracuse, Paterson, and Minneapolis invariably appeared in the Republican column. In the election of 1884, which was won by Democrats, the Republicans captured twenty of the thirty-three nonsouthern cities over 50,000. In 1888 the Republicans took twenty-six of the forty-four largest non-southern cities listed in the census of 1890.[14]

Furthermore, many of these Republican cities contained substantial proportions of immigrants. The 1890 census showed thirty percent or more of the population of Chicago, Milwaukee, Paterson, Cleveland, Buffalo, Pittsburgh, Providence, and Rochester to be foreign-born.[15] All of these cities voted consistently Republican in the three presidential elections of the 1880s.

But the tendency for Republicans to do better than Democrats in northern cities must not be exaggerated. The election of 1892, with its upsurge of Democratic strength in the cities, demonstrated that Republican popularity in the urban centers was neither so overwhelming nor so fixed that the popular Democracy might not reduce it.[16] Clearly some other force, some other ingredient in the mixture, was operative. That additional factor appears to be the depression of 1893.

The depression of the 1890s was an earth-shaker. Not only did it last five years or more, but it was the first economic decline since the United States had made the transition to full-scale industrialism. As a consequence its effects were felt especially in the growing cities and among the working class. A recent historian of this depression has estimated that real earnings for the population dropped eighteen percent between 1892 and 1894.[17] The single year of 1894 witnessed Coxey's army as well as other less well-known armies of unemployed workers on the march, widespread labor unrest, and the violence of the Pullman and Chicago railroad strikes. More workers went out on strike in that year than in any other in the century. The number was not equalled again until 1902.[18]

Since it is true that the Republicans for all their belief in the national power would not have taken any stronger anti-depression measures than the incumbent Democrats, the election upset of 1894 might be considered as nothing more than a case of blind, rather than calculated, reprisal against the incumbents. Furthermore, it might be said that the Republicans had been chastised in much the same fashion in 1874 when they chanced to be in power at the beginning of the depression of 1873. The objection is not as telling as it appears. In the election of 1894 there was a third party, and if simple dissent were operating, the Populists should have benefited as much from it as the Republicans. But this they did not do. Although the total Populist vote in 1894 was higher than in 1892, not a single state that year, John D. Hicks has observed, could any longer be called predominantly Populist.[19] Four western states, Kansas, Colorado, North Dakota, and Idaho, all of which had voted Populist in 1892, went Republican in 1894. In a real sense, then, the election was a victory for the Republican party and not simply a defeat for the Democrats.

If the terrible impact of the depression polarized the voting in a new way, thereby helping to explain the massive shift to the Republicans, the activities of the Democrats in 1896 could only confirm the urban voters in their belief that the Republican party was the more responsive political instrument. In their convention of 1896 the Democrats hardly noticed the cities; they had ears only for the cries of the farmers demanding currency reform. Many Populists, it is true, stood for something more than free silver, but the money issue was certainly accepted by Bryan and the vast majority of Democrats as the principal issue of the campaign. Free silver was at best uninteresting to the urban population and, at worst, anathema to them. The adoption of such a monetary policy would be inflationary and therefore contrary to the interest of all urban consumers, whether bankers, petty clerks, or factory workers. Mark Hanna, McKinley's campaign manager, sensed this defect in Bryan's appeal from the outset. Early in the campaign he said about Bryan: "He's talking silver all the time, and that's where we've got him."[20]

And they did have him. The cities, where the industrial workers were concentrated, voted overwhelmingly Republican. Only twelve of the eighty-two cities with a population of 45,000 or more went for Bryan—and seven of the twelve were in the Democratic South while two others were located in silver-producing states. Seven of the seventeen cities in the states that Bryan carried gave a majority to McKinley; on the other hand, only three of the sixty-five cities in states going to McKinley provided a majority for Bryan.[21] Bryan was hopeless in the industrial East; he did not carry a single county in all of New England, and only one in New York, and eleven rural counties in Pennsylvania. He even lost normally Democratic New York City.[22]

Taken together, the elections of 1894 and 1896 mark the emergence of the Republican party as the party of the rising cities.[23] Even a cataclysmic event like the Civil War, in which the Democrats were on the losing side, had not been able to dislodge the Democracy from its favored place in the voter's hearts. But the impact of an industrial-urban society with its new outlook and new electorate had done the trick. It is significant that several cities like San Francisco, Detroit, Indianapolis, Columbus, and St.

Paul, which had been Democratic in the 1880s and early 1890s, voted Republican in 1896 and remained Republican well into the twentieth century. None of the large cities which had been Republican in the 1880s and early 1890s, on the other hand, changed party affiliation in 1896 or for decades thereafter. Another indication of the continuity between the elections of 1894 and 1896 is that the states which showed the greatest Republican congressional gains in 1894 also showed increased Republican strength in the presidential election two years later. There were twelve states, each of which gave the Republicans four or more new seats in 1894; of these, eight were among the states which in 1896 showed the greatest number of new counties going to the Republicans. Significantly, they were mainly industrial-urban states like Illinois, New Jersey, New York, Ohio, and Pennsylvania.[24]

It is commonplace for textbooks to depict the Republican party of the late nineteenth century as the political arm of the Standard Oil Trust, but if the election returns are to be given any weight at all, that is not the way the voters saw the party in the 1890s.[25] Not only was it the party of respectability, wealth, and the Union; it was also the party of progress, prosperity, and national authority. As such it could and did enlist the support of industrial workers and immigrants as well as merchants and millionaires. As one analyst of the 1896 New England vote saw it, the Democrats may have obtained their most consistent support among the poor and the immigrants of the cities, but the Republicans gained strength there, too, "just as they did in the silk-stocking wards. . . . They were able to place the blame for unemployment upon the Democrats and to propagate successfully a doctrine that the Republican party was the party of prosperity and the 'full dinner pail.' "[26]

Ideologically, it is true, the Republican party in the 1890s had a long way to travel before it would translate its conception of the national power into an instrument for social amelioration. But it is suggestive that Robert M. La Follette in Wisconsin and Theodore Roosevelt in Washington, who are the best known of the early Progressives, were also Republicans. It is these men, and others like them in the party, who carried on the political revolution of 1894, which had first announced the Republican party as the majority party in the new America of cities and factories.

The significance of that political revolution is that the pattern of party allegiance then established continued for many years to come. To be sure, in 1912, because of a split in the Republican party, Woodrow Wilson was able to break the succession of Republican presidents. But it is also evident that the success of the Democrats in 1912 and 1916 should not be taken as a sign of a fundamental change in voter preferences. One reason for thinking so is that in 1916 Wilson was reelected by the very close margin of 600,000 popular and twenty-three electoral votes and in 1920 the Republicans swept back into the White House on a landslide. Another reason is provided by the Democratic losses in the House of Representatives after 1912. That year the democrats achieved a margin of 160 seats over the Republicans, one of the largest in congressional history, but by the mid-term elections the difference between the parties was down to 35; by 1916 it was less than 10. In 1918 the Democrats lost control of the House.

The most persuasive evidence for believing that the Republicans continued to be the majority party of the nation, despite the interruption of the Wilson administrations, is the history of elections during the 1920s. In 1920 Warren G. Harding received over 61 percent of the votes cast, a proportion of the total not achieved since the advent of universal manhood suffrage and only equalled once thereafter. Although other Republican presidential victories in the 1920s did not reach the proportions of the Harding landslide, they were all substantial. Furthermore, at no time between 1920 and 1928 was the Republican margin of strength in the House of Representatives endangered; it never went below twenty seats. In fact, near the end of the decade, Republican strength in the House was reaching out for a new high; in 1928 it was one hundred seats greater than the Democratic proportion. In the presidential election that year Herbert Hoover's majority over Alfred E. Smith was more than six million votes. In short, by the end of the 1920s the Republicans were as much the majority party of the nation as they had been in 1894 when the tide of history first turned in their favor.

Within four years, though, another political revolution had been consummated, this time returning the Democrats to the position of the majority party of the nation. In 1932 the Democrats elected their second president in forty-two years and captured the House of Representatives with a majority of unprecedented size, something like 190 seats. The true measure of the reversal of political patterns, though, did not come until 1934 and 1936. For with their overwhelming victories in those two elections, the Democrats showed that 1932 was not simply another 1912, when a large Democratic victory had been quickly eroded away in subsequent elections. Instead, in 1934 the Democrats reversed the patterns of the preceding fifty years; rather than losing seats in the House, as was customary in off-year elections, they actually added ten more to their swollen total. And then in 1936 they succeeded in reelecting Franklin D. Roosevelt by an overwhelming majority, with a proportion of votes that came very near topping Harding's landslide of 1920.

Because the Roosevelt revolution in politics coincided with the onset of the Great Depression, it is tempting to argue that it was economic adversity in 1932, much as it had been in 1894, which accounts for the shift in the voters' preferences. Certainly the impact of the depression had much to do with the long-range change; it undoubtedly accounts for the overwhelming character of the shift. But there is also much evidence to suggest that the shift which first became evident in 1932 was already in progress four years before. Beneath the surface of Hoover's victory the forces which would consummate the Roosevelt revolution were already in motion in 1928 in behalf of Alfred E. Smith.

The most obvious comment to be made about Smith's vote was its large size. Smith's 15 million votes were 6.5 million more than John D. Davis had polled in 1924, when La Follette's Progressive candidacy had drawn away some Democratic votes, and 5 million more than James M. Cox and Roosevelt had been able to capture in 1920. With this enormous gain, if by nothing else, Smith showed himself to be the most popular Democratic candidate since Bryan in 1896.

But important as Smith's ability to attract votes may have been, his contribution to the turn to the Democrats lay in something more than mere numbers.

After all, Hoover increased the Republican vote by some five million over Coolidge's total in 1924 and Harding's in 1920. What was significant was that Smith's unique combination of politically effective personal attributes was attracting a new class of voters to the Democratic party. Many years after the election, Hoover pointed out that in 1928 the candidates of both major parties had risen from small beginnings to become figures of national prominence.[27] But if this was true of the origins of Smith and Hoover, by 1928 the two men were poles apart. Unlike Hoover, or any previous presidential candidate of either party, Smith was both of lower class social background and a native of a big city. As is well known, his life and his career in politics were closely associated with New York City and the Tammany political machine. It is true that his four terms as governor of New York showed him to be progressive in thought and action as well as honest and courageous, but his loyalty to Tammany was both well known and unshakeable. Furthermore, Smith was a Roman Catholic and, thought he had no intention of making his religion a political issue, many Protestants did. In fact, in 1927, an article that gained national prominence challenged him to show that his religion would not interfere with his proper execution of the duties of president.[28] Although Smith's parents were native New Yorkers, his religion, his mother's Irish background[29] and his close association with Irish-dominated Tammany Hall stamped him as a spokesman for the urban immigrants. In short, he was the first presidential candidate to exhibit the traits of a part of the population that had never before been represented by a candidate of a majority party.

Smith's religion, which hurt him in the South and helped to explain why Hoover was able to capture four southern states, undoubtedly assisted him in the North. Massachusetts and Rhode Island, both heavily Catholic in population, went Democratic in 1928 for the first time since the Civil War. In fact, while Hoover was taking 200 southern counties from the Democrats, Smith took 122 northern counties that had been consistently Republican. Moreover, of these 122 counties, 77 were predominantly Roman Catholic; most of these 77 counties remained in the Democratic column, it is worth emphasizing, in subsequent elections.[30]

Since Roman Catholicism in America is an immigrant religion and its communicants are largely concentrated in the big cities, most of the new counties Smith gained were urban.[31] Indeed, the striking thing about Smith's candidacy was that it attracted the big city vote away from the Republicans for the first time since the 1890s. In 1920 Harding had taken all of the twelve cities with a population over 500,000, but in 1928, among these twelve, New York, Cleveland, St. Louis, Milwaukee, and San Francisco went for Smith though their states did not. Moreover, Pittsburgh and Baltimore failed to give Smith a majority by fewer than 10,000 votes each. Of the twelve cities only Los Angeles was strongly for Hoover. If the votes of all twelve cities are added together, Smith secured 38,000 more votes than Hoover; in 1920 the Republicans had carried the same cities by 1,638,000 votes.[32] In a broader sample, a recent student of the election has shown that in 1920 Harding carried all twenty-seven of the principal cities outside the South; in 1928, Smith captured eight, and made appreciable gains in the others. He ran

behind Cox and Roosevelt in only three of the twenty-seven.[33] Such a reversal was one sign that a socio-political revolution was under way.

Despite all that has been written about Smith's appeal to the voters of the big cities,[34] the significant point, often overlooked, is that his appeal was not of equal force in all cities. For example, he ran badly in southern cities, the residents of which exhibited, when compared with other southerners, the weakest commitment to the historic party principles that had made the South a stronghold of the Democrats.[35] In fact, Dallas and Houston in Texas, and Birmingham in Alabama went Republican in 1928.[36] More important was Smith's strikingly uneven attraction for the cities of the North. His attractive power was considerably stronger in those cities in which immigrant stock predominated than in those in which it was in the minority. (Immigrant stock is defined here as foreign-born whites and native whites born of one or more foreign-born parents.) According to the census of 1930, the closest to the election of 1928, there were thirty-six cities with populations in excess of a quarter of a million. In nineteen of these cities, immigrants and children of immigrants constituted 50 percent or more of the population.[37] In the presidential election of 1920, all of these nineteen cities voted Republican; in the election of 1924 all but one voted Republican. In the election of 1928, though, seven of them turned Democratic.

On the other hand, in the seventeen cities out of the thirty-six in which the native-born whites of native-born white parents constituted a majority of the population in 1930, only four went Democratic in 1928, and three of them were located in the traditionally Democratic South (Atlanta, New Orleans, and Memphis). The fourth was St. Louis. In fact, Democratic strength in these "native-white" cities actually declined in 1928, for in the 1920 and 1924 elections six of the seventeen had gone Democratic. All six of them, it should be noted, were in the Democratic South. Thus in the election of 1928 among the cities in which native whites constituted a majority, there was actually a loss in Democratic strength. In short, Smith's appeal to urban voters was not simply that he was of urban origin but that his Catholicism and Irish background stamped him as a champion of immigrants and children of immigrants. At the same time, those cities in which the immigrant stock was in the minority retained their allegiance to the Republican party—an allegiance which had been first clearly established in the 1890s for the big cities as a whole.

Yet it might be said that Smith failed, after all, to carry even a majority of the cities with a preponderance of immigrant stock. He won only seven of the nineteen cities of immigrant stock. Does not this fact call into serious question the assertion that there was a relationship between the social character of these cities and Democratic voting?

Closer analysis suggests not. As inspection of Table I makes evident, in every one of the cities with 50 percent or more immigrant stock, whether they were carried by Smith or not, the Democratic vote increased enormously in 1928

Table I

Cities with Fifty Percent or More Immigrant Stock*

City	Democratic Vote in nearest thousand		Percent Change	Republican Vote in nearest thousand		Percent Change
	1920	1928		1920	1928	
Boston	68	205	202	108	99	−7.7
Buffalo	40	126	215	100	145	45.0
Chicago	197	716	266	635	812	27.8
Cleveland	71	166	132	149	195	30.7
Detroit	52	157	201	221	265	19.9
Jersey City	63	153	143	102	100	−1.9
Los Angeles	56	210	275	178	514	189.0
Milwaukee	25	111	344	73	82	12.2
Minneapolis	143	396	178	519	561	8.1
Newark	41	118	188	116	169	45.6
New York	345	1,168	239	786	715	−9.1
Oakland	21	61	190	73	119	63.2
Philadelphia	90	276	209	308	420	36.5
Pittsburgh	40	161	301	139	216	55.5
Providence	46	97	112	80	86	7.5
Rochester	29	74	156	74	100	35.2
St. Paul	21	57	171	40	53	32.5
San Francisco	33	97	195	96	96	0.0
Seattle	17	47	176	59	96	62.9

* Two cities in this list, Oakland and Seattle, counted 47.8 and 48.2 percent respectively of immigrant stock, but they have been included here rather than in Table II, because they also have less than 50 percent of native white population. Their proportions of native white population are 46.4 and 47.7 percent respectively. The missing proportions are accounted for by colored persons.

over 1920, when the Republican majorities had been very large. In fact, in none of the cities in which immigrant stock predominated was the Democratic increase less than 100 percent, and in many it was considerably higher. In these same cities, on the other hand, the Republican vote increased as much as 100 per cent in only one of the nineteen cities and in only three did it go above 50 percent (Oakland, Pittsburgh, and Seattle). In several of the cities that Smith carried, the Republican vote actually fell from that of 1920.

If one examines the Democratic performance in those cities in which the native-white population predominated, the conclusion that there was a close association between the increase in Democratic votes and immigrant stock is further strengthened. In none of these cities was there much of an increase in either the total vote or in the vote for the Dem-

ocratic candidate. (See Table II.) Only in Denver did the Democratic vote increase as much as 75 percent; in no city did it reach as high as 100 percent as it did in every one of the cities in Table I. In five the increase was less than 25 percent and in three there was actually a loss of Democratic votes. The median value is 26.0 percent.

The Republican vote in Table II provides a revealing contrast with the Democratic vote in Table I, for now it can be seen that the "native-white" cities produced no upsurge in voting for Republicans comparable to that in the cities of immigrant stock. Except for a marked—and what turned out to be temporary—upturn in Republican strength in the southern cities of Atlanta, Birmingham, Dallas, and Houston, the increase between 1920 and 1928 in none of these cities was as much as 100 per cent. The median value is 53.2 percent.

Table II

Cities with Less than Fifty Percent of Immigrant Stock

Cities	Democratic Vote in nearest thousand		Percent Change	Republican Vote in nearest thousand		Percent Change
	1920	1928		1920	1928	
Akron	28	32	14.3	44	79	79.5
Atlanta	9	7	−22.5	3	6	100.0
Baltimore	87	126	44.8	126	135	7.3
Birmingham	25	17	−32.0	7	18	157.0
Cincinnati	78	110	41.0	113	148	31.0
Columbus	48	47	−2.3	60	92	53.2
Dallas	14	17	21.4	5	27	440.0
Denver	23	41	78.5	44	74	68.1
Houston	15	22	47.7	8	27	237.0
Indianapolis	61	73	19.7	80	110	37.4
Kansas City, Mo.	77	97	26.0	80	127	58.6
Louisville	56	64	14.3	68	98	44.3
Memphis	16	18	12.5	9	12	33.3
New Orleans	33	56	70.0	18	14	−22.2
Portland, Ore.	28	45	60.5	45	76	68.8
St. Louis	106	176	66.0	163	162	−0.68
Toledo	30	45	50.0	52	78	50.0

From this examination of the variability in the response of the cities to Smith's candidacy it seems clear that Smith brought out the immigrant vote in unprecedented numbers. Some of these voters of immigrant stock had probably been voting Republican all along and now switched to the Democrats. But many more, it would seem, voted for the first time, for otherwise one cannot explain the enormous increase in Democratic votes in the short span of eight years without a commensurate decline in Republican votes. These same people, backed by even greater numbers, would come out in 1932 to vote for Franklin Roosevelt and consummate the Roosevelt Revolution in politics. But it was Smith, the Catholic and the recognized champion of the urban-based immigrant, who first made the Democratic party the party of the cities and the immigrant.[38] This upsurge in immigrant voting in 1928 helps to explain, at least negatively, the apparent paradox of urban support for a Republican party in the 1920s that defended prohibition and pushed for restrictions on immigration. Prior to the galvanizing appearance of Smith on the political landscape, most urban immigrants just did not vote at all and many probably did not even think of themselves as part of the body politic. And to those who did vote, the Democratic party offered no candidates, other than Wilson, to lure them away from the party of national power, Theodore Roosevelt, and prosperity. Samuel Lubell has suggested, further, that the broadening educational opportunities of the 1920s also help to explain the upsurge in immigrant political participation in 1928.[39]

Despite familiarity with the connection between the cities and the Democratic party today, that connection was not forged, as far as the nation was concerned, until 1928-1932. Indeed it is the conclusion of this paper that it was the political activity of urban voters which raised the Republican party to a position of dominance in American politics for a third of a century, just as it has been the cities which have been largely responsible for the Democratic party's leading place in the nation's political life for the most recent third of this century. For Franklin Roosevelt after the landslide of 1936 continued to receive the support of the vast majority of the 37 principal cities of over 250,000 population, carrying 32 of them in 1940 and 30 in 1944.[40] Harry Truman in 1948 did about as well, even though the Dixiecrat candidate took three of the traditionally Democratic southern cities. Truman's score was 30 of the big cities against 4 for Thomas E. Dewey.

The real test of the Democratic power in the cities came in 1952 with the first campaign of Dwight D. Eisenhower, certainly the most popular Republican of the twentieth century. In that election and the next, Eisenhower made substantial inroads into the urban territory of the Democrats. In his first election, for example, he carried 21 of the 39 cities over 250,000 and in 1956 he did even better by taking 28 of them—almost as many as Franklin Roosevelt did in 1944.[41]

But there are two good reasons for seeing this resurgence of Republican strength in the cities as temporary and nothing more than a reflection of the special appeal of Eisenhower rather than as a basic shift in popular party allegiance. The first reason is that Eisenhower was able to carry a majority of the House of Representatives for his party in only the first of his four congressional elections. Indeed, his own popular vote in 1956 was greater than in 1952, but he proved unable, nonetheless, to do what every popular president since Zachary Taylor had been able to do: carry a majority of his party into the House of Representatives.

In this failure the cities played a part since many of them that voted for Eisenhower did not grant the same degree of support to the Republican congressional candidates. This tendency was most obvious in the southern cities, where he showed great strength. In 1952 he carried six of the eight southern cities[42] and in 1956 he captured all but Atlanta. Yet in the congressional races in all of these cities, Democratic congressmen, because of the South's one-party system, were almost invariably returned. More important, the same tendency could be observed in cities outside the South. For example, in the Ninth Ohio District (Toledo) a Democratic congressman was returned in all four of Eisenhower's congressional elections, though the General personally carried the city in 1952 and 1956. Although Eisenhower won Cook County, Illinois, in 1956, eight of the twelve congressional districts of the city of Chicago went Democratic. Newark and Denver, both of which supported Eisenhower in 1952 and 1956, sent only Democratic congressmen to Washington throughout the Eisenhower years. Eisenhower won Milwaukee in 1956, but the two congressmen elected from the city that year were Democrats.

The second reason for seeing Eisenhower's substantial victory as more personal than partisan is that in the election of 1960 John F. Kennedy, despite his close victory in the national popular vote, regained the cities for the Democrats. He carried 27 of the 39 cities, even though he did less well than Stevenson in 1952 among southern cities, capturing only New Orleans, San Antonio, and ever-faithful Atlanta. A large part of the explanation for Kennedy's failure to regain southern big city support commensurate with his general increase in urban backing is to be found, of course, in southern dislike of the Democratic party's stand on civil rights which began with Truman and which Kennedy went out of his way to support and advance. Nevertheless, the defection also calls attention to the quite different social character of southern, as compared with northern big cities. There are very few Catholics or children of immigrants in southern cities, so that an Al Smith and a John F. Kennedy have no religious or social appeal there as they do in the North. That this difference was influential is suggested by the return to the Democratic fold in 1960 of San Antonio and New Orleans, the only two southern cities containing substantial numbers of Catholics and children of immigrants.

In short, as the congressional strength of the Democrats throughout the Eisenhower years had suggested, the election of 1960 showed that the Democrats still retained the long-term allegiance of the big city voters, whose support had first been evident thirty-two years before in another campaign by a Roman Catholic grandson of an Irish immigrant.

NOTES

1. The following statements and all others based on voting statistics of a national character are derived from U. S. Bureau of the Census, *Historical Statistics, Colonial Times to 1957* (Washington, 1960); all figures for county returns, depending upon the years involved, are derived from the compilations of W. Dean Burnham, *Presidential Ballots, 1836-1892* (Baltimore, 1955), and Edgar Eugene Robinson, *The Presidential Vote, 1896-1932* (Stanford, 1934).

2. In 1874 Democratic strength exceeded Republican by 60 seats; in 1876 it fell to 13, then rose to 19 in 1878. In 1880 the Republicans gained an 8-seat lead over the Democrats, but in 1882 the Democrats came back with a 79-seat margin.

That lead fell off to 43 seats in 1884 and to 17 in 1886. In 1888 the Republicans won the House by 7 seats, only to lose it again in 1890, when the Democrats gained a 147-seat margin. In 1892 the Democratic lead was still 91 seats. U. S. Bureau of the Census, *Historical Statistics,* 691.

3. Vincent P. De Santis, *Republicans Face the Southern Question: The New Departure Years, 1877-1897* (Baltimore, 1959). See also, for a somewhat different emphasis but with the same conclusion, Stanley J. Hirshson, *Farewell to the Bloody Shirt: Northern Republicans & the Southern Negro, 1877-1893* (Bloomington, 1962).

4. Cortez A. M. Ewing, *Presidential Elections: From Abraham Lincoln to Franklin D. Roosevelt* (Norman, 1940), 74.

5. See *The World Almanac, 1893* (New York, 1893), 321 and *ibid., 1896* (New York, 1896), 408, for summary of results of congressional contests of 1892 and 1894. See also, Samuel P. Hays, *The Response to Industrialism, 1885-1914* (Chicago, 1957), 46-47.

6. "The decade of the nineties is the watershed of American history," Henry Steele Commager has written in *The American Mind: An Interpretation of American Thought and Character Since the 1880's* (New Haven, 1950), 41. In his preface to the same book, p. viii, Commager has a broader conception of the "watershed," including "the mid-eighties and the nineties" as the crucial years. Harold U. Faulkner, *Politics, Reform, and Expansion, 1890-1900* (New York, 1959), 1, also subscribes to the view that the nineties was the period of transition. Samuel P. Hays, *The Response to Industrialism* does not commit himself on this particular question but by implication he includes at least a part of the 1880s in the new era of industrial society.

7. In 1882, for example, there were 476 work stoppages involving 159,000 workers; in 1889 the number of strikes was 1,111 with 260,000 workers involved. Comparable figures for 1890 were 1,897 strikes and 373,000 workers. *Historical Statistics,* 99.

8. Josiah Strong, *The New Era* (New York, 1893), 197; Arthur M. Schlesinger, *The Rise of the City, 1878-1898* (New York, 1933), chs. 3-4.

9. See the full discussion in Allen J. Going, "The South and the Blair Education Bill," *Mississippi Valley Historical Review,* XLIV (Sept. 1957), 267-90.

10. William H. Michael, ed., *The Abridgement of the Message from the President of the United States to the Two Houses of Congress . . .* (Washington, 1893), 9.

11. Edward C. Kirkland, *Industry Comes of Age: Business, Labor, and Public Policy, 1860-1897* (New York, 1961), 402.

12. Karl Marx and Friedrich Engels, *Letters to Americans, 1848-1895* (New York, 1953), 258.

13. Quoted in Allan Nevins, *Grover Cleveland: A Study in Courage* (New York, 1932), 332.

14. According to the *Tribune Almanac of 1881*

there were thirty-six cities in 1880 with a population of 50,000 or more. The two southern cities of Richmond and New Orleans, and Washington, D.C., which did not possess a national vote, have been excluded from my count. In the tabulation for 1888, Memphis, Nashville, and Atlanta, as southern cities, have also been excluded in addition to the three excluded for 1880 and 1884. It might be noted for the benefit of those unfamiliar with the form of the statistics in Burnham's and Robinson's compilations of the presidential vote that the county is the smallest unit reported. Thus, my figures for the cities are actually the returns for the counties in which the cities are located and not strictly the cities themselves.

15. See table in *Eleventh Census: 1890, Population* (Washington, 1895), pt. 1, xcii. Strictly speaking, these figures are not comparable with those on voting since the immigration statistics are for the city only while the voting figures are for the county. Nevertheless, the city figures suggest the importance of the immigrant in these Republican districts and that is all that is intended.

16. In 1892, the Democrats carried twenty-four of the forty-four non-southern cities.

17. Charles Hoffman, "The Depression of the Nineties," *Journal of Economic History,* XVI (June 1956), 151.

18. *Historical Statistics,* 99.

19. *The Populist Revolt* (Minneapolis, 1931), 338.

20. Quoted in Faulkner, *Politics,* 206.

21. For these figures on urban voting I am indebted to William Diamond, "Urban and Rural Voting in 1896," *American Historical Review,* XLVI (Jan. 1941), 281-305. Diamond uses the 45,000 figure, whereas the author has used the 50,000 figure for tabulation purposes (see note 14).

22. Some historians have long given credence to the argument that Bryan did poorly in the industrial cities because employers coerced workers into voting for McKinley. See, for example, James A. Barnes, "Myths of the Bryan Campaign," *Mississippi Valley Historical Review,* XXXIV (Dec. 1947), 399-400. That argument is so weakly supported by evidence and relies so heavily upon a conspiratorial view of history that it is surprising that historians have granted it the acceptance they apparently have. Moreover, even if "the threatening employer" explanation is accepted for the election of 1896, it can no more account for the continued success of the Republicans in subsequent elections than it can explain what really cries out for explanation, that is, the great switch in 1894. Robinson, *Presidential Vote,* 7, speaks of the "revolution" of 1896, though 1894 seems to be more the beginning of the political change evident in 1896.

23. Hays, *Response to Industrialism,* 47, writes: "The Republican gains of 1894, which continued over into 1896, were largely urban. The precise nature of this new strength is not yet clear, but it

appears to have been composed largely of workers and immigrants who blamed the Democrats for the depression and who were suspicious of the economic interests and the nativist tinges of the farmers."

24. A summary of the changes in congressional seats can be found in *World Almanac, 1896*, p. 408, and the changes in county allegiances in 1896 have been derived from Robinson, *Presidential Vote*, after inspection of the election maps in C. O. Paullin, *Atlas of the Historical Geography of the United States* (Washington, 1932).

25. Samuel Hays has been one of the few writers on this period who has recognized the need for reevaluating our image of the Republican party of the late nineteenth century. See his *Response to Industrialism*, 188-89.

26. "A Theory of Critical Elections," *Journal of Politics*, XVII (Feb. 1955), 15.

27. *The Memoirs of Herbert Hoover* (2 vols., New York, 1952), II, 198.

28. Charles C. Marshall, "An Open Letter to the Honorable Alfred E. Smith," *Atlantic Monthly*, CXXXIX (April 1927), 540-49.

29. Pringle, *Smith*, 80. There seems to be no information on the national background of Smith's father. Alfred E. Smith, in his *Up to Now: An Autobiography* (New York, 1929), 3-4, says he never heard anyone speak of his father's national origins.

30. Samuel Lubell, *The Future of American Politics* (2nd ed., rev., New York, 1956), 37.

31. Not all of Smith's gains resulting from his Catholicism were urban; many Catholic rural counties also supported him. In 1928, for example, Democrats gained almost 70,000 votes in rural North Dakota, while Republicans there lost nearly 30,000. John D. Hicks, *Republican Ascendancy, 1921-1933* (New York, 1960), 213.

32. Computed from table in Samuel J. Eldersveld, "The Influence of Metropolitan Party Pluralities in Presidential Elections Since 1920: A Study of Twelve Key Cities," *American Political Science Review*, XLIII (Dec. 1949), 1196.

33. Irving Bernstein, *The Lean Years* (Boston, 1960), 79.

34. See, for example, William F. Ogburn and Nell Snow Talbot, "A Measurement of the Factors in the Presidential Election of 1928," *Social Forces*, VIII (Dec. 1929), 177, and Ray V. Peel and Thomas C. Donnelly, *The 1928 Campaign: An Analysis* (New York, 1931), 121.

35. V. O. Key, *Southern Politics in State and Nation* (New York, 1949), 318-28, observes that the cities of the South were the least strong of any southern districts for Smith and that in non-urban counties there was a high positive correlation between loyalty to the Democratic party and the proportion of Negro population. See also Bernstein, *Lean Years*, 79.

36. According to the county figures in Robinson, *Presidential Vote*, 135, 335, 338.

37. Derived from the table in Department of Commerce, *Statistical Abstract of the United States, 1931* (Washington, 1931), 22-23.

38. See also Key, "A Theory of Critical Elections," 4, and Hicks, *Republican Ascendancy*, 213.

39. Lubell, *Future of American Politics*, 38-40. As he points out, in 1900 "only one of every fifteen youngsters was going beyond the elementary school" while in 1930 "every second child of high school age was in high school."

40. The cities are those listed in Tables I and II above, but with San Antonio added since it passed 250,000 population by 1940. Conclusions about urban strength of the parties have been derived from the county voting statistics compiled in Edgar Eugene Robinson, *They Voted for Roosevelt: The Presidential Vote, 1932-1944* (Stanford, 1947) and from those in *The Political Almanac, 1952* (New York, 1952).

41. The thirty-nine cities are those listed in Tables I and II but with Fort Worth, Omaha, San Antonio, and San Diego added because they reached the 250,000 population mark by 1950 and with Providence eliminated because it fell below that level. The conclusions on the urban strength of the parties and the results of the congressional elections have been derived from Richard M. Scammon, ed., *America Votes* (4 vols., New York, 1956-1962).

42. The southern cities are: Atlanta, Birmingham, Dallas, Fort Worth, Houston, Memphis, New Orleans, and San Antonio.

VIII   THE CITY IN MODERN TIMES

The city in modern times is that giant complex, the metropolis, swallowing the hinterland with its clusters of suburban communities and satellite cities. The chief characteristic of the metropolis is decentralization, which began late in the nineteenth century and reversed the trend of centralization that characterized so many of the older cities. Accelerated by the automobile, the growth of the suburbs, and the relocation of industry and manufacturing, decentralization has boomed in the twentieth century to produce the metropolis, the super-city, which in itself represents a new phase of urban growth. Between 1900 and 1950, cities with a population of one hundred thousand or more increased from 52 to 147 per cent, which meant an increase in the total U.S. population of 32 to 56 per cent. Thus, Charles Glaab and A. Theodore Brown can conclude that "the growth of the metropolis constitutes the central theme of twentieth-century American urban history."[1]

One might add that the metropolis has also become one of the central themes of American history in general for the twentieth century, and its No. 1 domestic problem. The thread of historical continuity suggests that the metropolis, rather than having created new problems, has highlighted and intensified very old ones. After all, racism, poverty, the traffic jam, and unimaginative city planning were not born with the metropolis. The extraordinary growth of the metropolis has sharpened the demands for collective responsibility, and the resistance, apathy, and failure to meet these demands have led many Americans to forget the enormous creative powers of cities and see them, as Jefferson once did, as "sores on the body politic."

This chapter seeks to isolate certainly not all but several of the critical issues bedeviling Americans in the mid-twentieth century, such as the quality of life in the metropolis, the suburb and the slum, race and poverty, city planning and urban renewal, and what they may mean for the future.

1. *A History of Urban America,* p. 270.

481

The first two essays present sharply conflicting interpretations by two urban sociologists of a question that is fundamental to the nature of modern urban life, namely, what is urbanism—that is, what are those traits that characterize the city as a special kind of human settlement? Louis Wirth's "Urbanism as a Way of Life," is one of the most famous and influential interpretations of the modern city in our time. It is also one of the most devastating critiques in the bulky literature of the city. Using the three variables of number, density, and heterogeneity as the bony skeleton of his argument, Wirth argues that urbanism as a way of life is a portrait of social and personal disorganization. The urbanite has lost the rich, satisfying contact with the traditional primary groups which constituted social solidarity. The weakening of kinship, the declining family, the disappearance of the neighborhood, have shifted contact to formal, impersonal, superficial, transitory secondary groups. The result: a way of life characterized by loneliness, anonymity, mental breakdown, suicide, delinquency, crime, corruption—a way of life that renders the individual helpless to manipulation by symbols and stereotypes and fosters a predatory jungle of ruthless competition, aggrandizement, and mutual exploitation. This is not the hysterics of an ambitious on-the-make politician, but the cool and seemingly dispassionate analysis of a distinguished social scientist.

Written in 1938, Wirth may have reflected the frustrations and disenchantments of the 1930's, with its wars, depression, and insecurity. He may have seen the city with the bias of a rural or small-town American. Nevertheless, his persuasive and penetrating insights have a timeliness that would at once satisfy the ghost of Thomas Jefferson and the claims of the most recent urban critic.

Those like Herbert Gans who stress a social and behavioral rather than an ecological approach to the complexities of urbanism would not be satisfied, however. Writing twenty-four years after Wirth, Gans represents a group which is challenging the long dominance of the ecologist in urban sociology. The heart of Gans's argument is that ecology, the study of how humans adapt to their environment, and its lexicon of number, density, and heterogeneity, is simply not enough to explain *solely* the *social* characteristics of urbanism. The key determinants, then, are not ecological but those of class and what he calls the "life-cycle stage."

Gans's essay is a refutation of Wirth's thesis, and he brings to bear on that refutation a view that sees the city in its totality. The trouble with Wirth, he argues, is that he took the characteristics of one section of the city, the unstable transient area, and applied them to all sections of the city. Gans sees the city not with Wirth's preoccupation with the inner city, but in terms of three broad concentric circles: the inner city, the outer city, and the suburbs. Emphasizing the typical rather than the spectacular and exotic, he shows a multiplicity of social groups in *each* circle, discussing five that exist in the inner city alone. In effect, there is no one single way of life for the city and one single different way of life for the suburb.

The most provocative part of Gans's thesis is his analysis of the suburb which, like the central city, evokes ambivalent and contradictory attitudes. As Humphrey Carver sums them up,

Everyone likes to live in the suburbs. Everyone pokes fun at the suburbs. That's fair enough. Everyone respects those who made the suburbs. Everyone despises the suburbs. Everyone's friends live in the suburbs. Everyone hates the kind of people who live in the suburbs. Everyone wants bigger and better suburbs. Everyone thinks there is just too much suburbs. You and I live in the suburbs—it's lovely to have a nice home in the suburbs. The whole idea of the suburbs fills us with dismay, alarm, and frustration. Almost everyone's business is dedicated to making life in the suburbs more and more and more enjoyable. The suburbs are a crashing bore and desolating disappointment. The suburbs are exactly what we asked for. The suburbs are exactly what we've got.[2]

Gans attacks the "folklore" of the intellectuals and especially the theorists of the mass-society concept that has stereotyped the suburb as the faceless, numbing, debilitating refugee of conformity and homogeneity, so well characterized by Gertrude Stein's crack, "There is no there there." He destroys the notion that the move from city to suburb causes major behavior and personality changes. Above all, he shows that despite physical and demographic differences, there are more similarities than differences between the suburb and the city, especially between the suburb and the outer city.[3]

What Gans is saying is that the suburb *is* the city. Part of the folklore of the suburb is that it is a recent phenomenon, beginning particularly at the end of World War II, with the boom of low-cost housing, the subsidies of the Federal Housing Administration, and the soaring exodus from the central city. Urban historians have long argued that the suburb emerged well over a hundred years ago and was a part of such urbanization processes as transportation, economic developments, and population migrations.[4] As the most "modern" outer ring of the city, the suburb is, as Gans shows, an integral part of the metropolitan decentralization so characteristic of the modern super-city. Thus, to set up separate monolithic entities, such as "city" and "suburb," is only to confound the realities of modern urbanism.

The most confounding realities of modern urbanism, however, are the ancient plagues of poverty and discrimination, magnified by, but not generic to, the city. The most critical problem facing the city today concerns those at

2. *Cities in the Suburbs* (Toronto: University of Toronto Press, 1962), p. 3.
3. Confirmed suburb-baiters should pursue Gans's argument as it is expanded in his *The Levittowners: Ways of Life and Politics in a New Suburban Community* (New York: Pantheon, 1967).
4. See Sam Warner, *Streetcar Suburbs: The Process of Growth in Boston* (Cambridge: M.I.T. and Harvard University Press, 1962), a first-rate scholarly performance.

the end of the line—the urban poor, especially but not exclusively the American Negro, the most urbanized element of our society and the most deprived. In his essay in Chapter V Gilbert Osofsky argued that the ghetto of today was created by the 1920's. Jeanne R. Lowe surveys the modern ghetto from World War II to the present and shows how the ghetto-making forces of the early part of the century have been intensified and made even more critical, particularly by the changes in technology. Like Osofsky, she asks what makes a ghetto, and, after examining housing, employment, education, the family, and class differences among Negroes themselves, she shows that the answer lies in the unholy triumvirate of poverty, race discrimination, and blocked opportunity. Three parts of her interpretation need to be underscored: her criticism of urban education; the flaws in the stereotype of the Negro welfare recipient (which she should have developed more fully); and a point not always grasped by Americans confused by ghetto problems, especially the *white* offspring of former immigrant families, that is, there are significant differences between the Negro migrant and the earlier white migrant and foreign immigrant that account for the Negro's failure to seize a share of the American bonanza.[5]

The result of ghetto life—as recent history has painfully illustrated—is the violence of riots, which seem to many Americans to be the main theme of contemporary urban America. Historically, urban racial riots are nothing new in America. The new elements are their frequency, the extent of their destruction, and their impact upon the fears and hopes of both black and white America. What causes them? A blatant defiance of law and order? Underclass young hoodlums running amuck? The inflexible fortress of white racism? The so-called "revolution of rising expectations"? The answer will seriously

5. The literature about the Negro is so enormous that no attempt will be made to cite it all here, but among some of the recent books about the urban ghetto Negro, not previously cited, the following are of interest. Constance Green, *The Secret City: A History of Race Relations in the Nation's Capitol* (Princeton: Princeton University Press, 1967); Allan H. Speer, *Black Chicago: The Making of a Negro Ghetto, 1890-1920* (Chicago: University of Chicago Press, 1967); Lee Rainwater and William L. Yancey, *The Moynihan Report and the Politics of Controversy* (Cambridge: The M.I.T. Press, 1967); August Meier and Elliott M. Rudwick, *From Plantation to Ghetto: An Interpretative History of American Negroes* (New York: Hill and Wang, 1966); Karl E. and Alma F. Taeuber, *Negroes in Cities: Residential Segregation and Neighborhood Change* (Chicago: Aldine, 1965); Charles E. Silberman, *Crisis in Black and White* (New York: Knopf, 1964); Michael Harrington, *The Other America: Poverty in the United States* (New York: Macmillan, 1962); and Kenneth Clark, *The Black Ghetto* (New York: Harper & Row, 1965).

Three important books written by Negroes who grew up in the ghetto are Piri Thomas, *Down These Mean Streets* (New York: Knopf, 1967); Claude Brown, *Manchild in the Promised Land* (New York: Macmillan, 1965); and Malcolm Little, *The Autobiography of Malcolm X* (New York: Grove Press, 1965).

A study important to all phases of Negro history is Winthrop D. Jordan's brilliant *White Over Black: American Attitudes Toward the Negro, 1550-1812* (Chapel Hill: University of North Carolina Press, 1968). Although the study ends with the early nineteenth century, it is extremely relevant to twentieth-century America.

affect what is to be done with the ghetto and this in turn will affect the future history of the American city.

In a carefully executed study, Nathan S. Caplan and Jeffrey M. Paige have examined the attitudes, motives, and behavior of both Negro rioters and nonrioters in Detroit and Newark, centers for two major riots in 1967. In trying to find out why Negroes riot they tested three major theories: the "riffraff" theory, the "relative-deprivation" theory, and the "blocked opportunity" theory, which states that riots are caused by deeply rooted racial attitudes of white Americans. Their conclusions seriously question explanations of many journalists and politicians. For some, they might be obvious; for others, their findings might be shocking and unexpected, suggesting a re-evaluation of the most important and complex problem not merely for the city but for American society as a whole.[6]

Related but not exclusive to the dilemmas of race and poverty are two other confounding problems, old in their origins, new in their complexity—city planning and urban renewal. John L. Hancock examines the historical evolution of city planning in America from 1900 to 1940. He traces its origins as a professional art and science, its fits and starts, its emerging theoretical maturity—and its frustrations which defined the requirements for a city planner as "the wisdom of Solomon, the heart of a prophet, the patience of Job, and the hide of a rhinoceros."

Hancock's central theme is the discrepancy between the planner's goals and their fulfillment. On the one hand, the profession evolved in the Progressive Era from a motley crew ranging from landscape artists to lawyers, long on hope, short on theory. Increasing their skills, specializing their abilities, widening their vision from statistical projects and majestic but inadequate historic models, to the fusion of scientific and humanistic methods into generalized theories incorporating urban into regional planning, the planners built a profession. The consultant became the professional. On the other hand, public apathy, and special interest groups demanding the expediency of short-term "practical" goals, undermined attempts for meaningful city planning. Of the multitude of projects, few were completed. City planning became "city-mending"; patchwork replaced comprehensive planning. Thus

6. The literature on urban riots is growing and will continue to grow. Among the studies on the riots of the 1960's, these are important: National Advisory Commission on Civil Disorders, *The Report of the National Advisory Commission on Civil Disorders* (New York: Bantam Books, 1968); two articles by Robert Fogleston: "From Contention to Confrontation: The Police, the Negroes and the Riots of the 1960's," *Political Science Quarterly* (June 1968), and "White on Black: A Critique of the McCone Commission Report on the Los Angeles Riots," *Political Science Quarterly* (September 1967); John Hersey, *The Algiers Motel Incident* (New York: Knopf, 1968); the entire issue of *American Behavioral Scientist* (March-April 1968), which is devoted to urban violence and disorder; Paul Jacobs, *Prelude to Riot: A View of Urban America from the Bottom* (New York: Random House, 1967); and Jerome H. Skolnick, *Justice Without Trial: Law Enforcement in Democratic Society* (New York: John Wiley, 1966).

city planning has bobbed, and weaved between two legacies from the past: the goals of the Progressives of placing the group above the individual in planning for the general welfare, and the heritage of laissez faire which sacrifices over-all planning to the individual interests of commercial groups. Despite the profession's increasing sense of comprehensive planning and social responsibility, "most physical change in today's booming cities is conducted by private interests under public auspices for speculative purposes." Hancock makes it clear that the future of the American city and the quality of its life will be decided by which legacy ultimately triumphs.

The next two selections concern a critique and a rebuttal about urban renewal, the hottest controversy of city planning.[7] Herbert Gans presents a critique with a question: urban renewal for whom, the slumdwellers or the affluent white middle and upper classes? His major criticism is that most urban renewal projects have used the brawn of the federal bulldozer to tear the slums down, but have not used the federal brain to properly relocate the slumdwellers they have displaced. It is a critique built around a preposterous irony: urban renewal frequently victimizes the very people it was originally intended to benefit. Slum clearance sustains the slums. By failing to follow through with rehousing the dispossessed, urban renewal forces them into other slum areas; ergo, urban renewal often becomes slum "renewal," slums are merely shifted and made worse.

Unlike some critics of public housing, Gans does not want to burn down the barn to kill the rats. He proposes several alternative solutions, most of which hinge upon more effective federal intervention. Thus, he does not find the panacea in unrestricted private enterprise, which contributed enormously to the initial creation of the slums, nor in the simplistic doctrine that decent housing makes for the decent life. In Gans's view, there will be no fundamental improvement until a rehousing program is coupled with an effective attack upon poverty itself.

In the spirited and sometimes rancorous rebuttal that follows one can see some of the sharply divergent views on urban renewal and perhaps de-

7. In the massive literature on this subject, some of the recent and outstanding books are Scott Greer, *Urban Renewal and American Cities* (New York: Bobbs-Merrill, 1966); Charles Abrams, *The City Is the Frontier* (New York: Harper & Row, 1965); and Jane Jacobs, *The Death and Life of Great American Cities* (New York: Knopf, 1961). For an excellent critical review of Miss Jacobs's book, see Hans Blumenfeld, *The Modern Metropolis: Its Origins, Growth, Characteristics, and Planning* (Cambridge: The M.I.T. Press, 1967), pp. 180-89. In a class all its own is John W. Reps's magnificent *The Making of Urban America; A History of City Planning in the United States* (Princeton: Princeton University Press, 1965).

There are two first-rate readers which present a comprehensive view of urban renewal: Jewel Bellush and Murray Hausknecht (eds.), *Urban Renewal: People, Politics, and Planning* (Garden City: Anchor Books, 1967), and James Q. Wilson (ed.), *Urban Renewal: The Record and the Controversy* (Cambridge: The M.I.T. Press, 1967).

Although not in the "recent" category, Martin Meyerson and Edward C. Banfield, *Politics, Planning, and the Public Interest* (New York: The Free Press, 1955), is indispensable.

termine why it invokes such emotion. George M. Raymond defends urban renewal policies and argues that Gans's schemes are almost ridiculously utopian. Malcolm D. Rivkin suggests that Gans has not paid enough attention to the power of local decision-making factions. And Gans defends himself. You might ask yourself how well Gans presents and defends his case; how relevant the criticisms of his thesis are; above all, which of the three men has really found the heart of the problem.

The final selection is a summation which brings us to the present and touches upon the future. Along the theme of the difference between what we wanted and what we created, Scott Greer traces the evolution of the American city from the American Revolution to the present, restating many of the political, economical, social, ideological, and technological themes that have been presented throughout this book. His thesis is that many of us indulge in a myopic nostalgia for a kind of city that no longer exists. Just as the memory of the farm and small town once preoccupied the American imagination, we are now caught up in "the imagined central city of another era," which confounds urban renewal and municipal government, particularly. According to Greer, reality begins with the realization that the metropolis constitutes a revolution in the use of space—the decentralization of urban space. To celebrate the central city at the expense of the suburb is to forget that decentralization is, like the city, here to stay. Reality is the realization that the city is not static; it is a continually changing phenomenon which must be seen in all its parts, from the inner city to the suburb. With this in mind, argues Greer, can we determine what we want and be willing to pay for it? Or: "Do we really care about our cities?"

Do we? If we do, we will have to think through and adjust old ideas about poverty, race, central planning, and the divisions of authority between federal, state, and local authority, and make them conform to the changing realities of the city.

Urbanism as a Way of Life

Louis Wirth

I. THE CITY AND CONTEMPORARY CIVILIZATION

Just as the beginning of Western civilization is marked by the permanent settlement of formerly nomadic peoples in the Mediterranean basin, so the beginning of what is distinctively modern in our civilization is best signalized by the growth of great cities. Nowhere has mankind been farther removed from organic nature than under the conditions of life characteristic of great cities. The contemporary world no longer presents a picture of small isolated groups of human beings scattered over a vast territory, as Sumner described primitive society.[1] The distinctive feature of the mode of living of man in the modern age is his concentration into gigantic aggregations around which cluster lesser centers and from which radiate the ideas and practices that we call civilization.

The degree to which the contemporary world may be said to be "urban" is not fully or accurately measured by the proportion of the total population living in cities. The influences which cities exert upon the social life of man are greater than the ratio of the urban population would indicate, for the city is not only in ever larger degrees the dwelling-place and the workshop of modern man, but it is the initiating and controlling center of economic, political, and cultural life that has drawn the most remote parts of the world into its orbit and woven diverse areas, peoples, and activities into a cosmos.

The growth of cities and the urbanization of the world is one of the most impressive facts of modern times. Although it is impossible to state precisely what proportion of the estimated total world-population of approximately 1,-800,000,000 is urban, 69.2 per cent of the total population of those countries that do distinguish between urban and rural areas is urban.[2] Considering the fact, moreover, that the world's population is very unevenly distributed and that the growth of cities is not very far advanced in some of the countries that have only recently been touched by industrialism, this average understates the extent to which urban concentration has proceeded in those countries where the impact of the industrial revolution has been more forceful and of less recent date. This shift from a rural to a predominantly urban society, which has taken place within the span of a single generation in such industrialized areas as the United States and Japan, has been accompanied by profound changes in virtually every phase of social life. It is these changes and their ramifications that invite the attention of the sociologist to the study of the differences between the rural and the urban mode of living. The pursuit of this interest is

From *The American Journal of Sociology,* XLIV (July 1938), pp. 1-24. Reprinted by permission of The University of Chicago Press. Louis Wirth (August 28, 1897-May 3, 1952) was Professor of Sociology at The University of Chicago and a former president of the American Sociological Society and of the International Association of Sociologists.

an indispensable prerequisite for the comprehension and possible mastery of some of the most crucial contemporary problems of social life since it is likely to furnish one of the most revealing perspectives for the understanding of the ongoing changes in human nature and the social order.[3]

Since the city is the product of growth rather than of instantaneous creation, it is to be expected that the influences which it exerts upon the modes of life should not be able to wipe out completely the previously dominant modes of human association. To a greater or lesser degree, therefore, our social life bears the imprint of an earlier folk society, the characteristic modes of settlement of which were the farm, the manor, and the village. This historic influence is reinforced by the circumstance that the population of the city itself is in large measure recruited from the countryside, where a mode of life reminiscent of this earlier form of existence persists. Hence we should not expect to find abrupt and discontinuous variation between urban and rural types of personality. The city and the country may be regarded as two poles in reference to one or the other of which all human settlements tend to arrange themselves. In viewing urban-industrial and rural-folk society as ideal types of communities, we may obtain a perspective for the analysis of the basic models of human association as they appear in contemporary civilization.

II. A SOCIOLOGICAL DEFINITION OF THE CITY

Despite the preponderant significance of the city in our civilization, however, our knowledge of the nature of urbanism and the process of urbanization is mea-

ger. Many attempts have indeed been made to isolate the distinguishing characteristics of urban life. Geographers, historians, economists, and political scientists have incorporated the points of view of their respective disciplines into diverse difinitions of the city. While in no sense intended to supersede these, the formulation of a sociological approach to the city may incidentally serve to call attention to the interrelations between them by emphasizing the peculiar characteristics of the city as a particular form of human association. A sociologically significant definition of the city seeks to select those elements of urbanism which mark it as a distinctive mode of human group life.

The characterization of a community as urban on the basis of size alone is obviously arbitrary. It is difficult to defend the present census definition which designates a community of 2,500 and above as urban and all others as rural. The situation would be the same if the criterion were 4,000, 8,000, 10,000, 25,-000, or 100,000 population, for although in the latter case we might feel that we were more nearly dealing with an urban aggregate than would be the case in communities of lesser size, no definition of urbanism can hope to be completely satisfying as long as numbers are regarded as the sole criterion. Moreover, it is not difficult to demonstrate that communities of less than the arbitrarily set number of inhabitants lying within the range of influence of metropolitan centers have greater claim to recognition as urban communities than do larger ones leading a more isolated existence in a predominantly rural area. Finally, it should be recognized that census definitions are unduly influenced by the fact that the city, statistically speaking, is always an administrative concept in that the corporate limits play a decisive role in delineating the urban area. Nowhere is this more clearly apparent than in the concentrations of population on the peripheries of great metropolitan centers which cross arbitrary administrative boundaries of city, county, state, and nation.

As long as we identify urbanism with the physical entity of the city, viewing it merely as rigidly delimited in space, and proceed as if urban attributes abruptly ceased to be manifested beyond an arbitrary boundary line, we are not likely to arrive at any adequate conception of urbanism as a mode of life. The technological developments in transportation and communication which virtually mark a new epoch in human history have accentuated the role of cities as dominant elements in our civilization and have enormously extended the urban mode of living beyond the confines of the city itself. The dominance of the city, especially of the great city, may be regarded as a consequence of the concentration in cities of industrial and commercial, financial and administrative facilities and activities, transportation and communication lines; and cultural and recreational equipment such as the press, radio stations, theaters, libraries, museums, concert halls, operas, hospitals, higher educational institutions, research and publishing centers, professional organizations, and religious and welfare institutions. Were it not for the attraction and suggestions that the city exerts through these instrumentalities upon the rural population, the differences between the rural and the urban modes of life would be even greater than they are. Urbanization no longer denotes merely the process by which persons are attracted to a place called the city and incorporated into its system of life. It refers also to that cumulative accentuation of the characteristics distinctive of the mode of life which is associated with the growth of cities, and finally to the changes in the direction of modes of life recognized as urban which are apparent among people, wherever they may be, who have come under the spell of the influences which the city exerts by virtue of the power of its institutions and personalities operating through the means of communication and transportation.

The shortcomings which attach to number of inhabitants as a criterion of urbanism apply for the most part to density of population as well. Whether we accept the density of 10,000 persons per square mile as Mark Jefferson[4] proposed, or 1,000 which Willcox[5] preferred to regard as the criterion of urban settlements, it is clear that unless density is correlated with significant social characteristics it can furnish only an arbitrary basis for differentiating urban from rural communities. Since our census enumerates the night rather than the day population of an area, the locale of the most intensive urban life —the city center—generally has low population density, and the industrial and commercial areas of the city, which contain the most characteristic economic activities underlying urban society, would scarcely anywhere be truly urban if density were literally interpreted as a mark of urbanism. Nevertheless, the fact that the urban community is distinguished by a large aggregation and relatively dense concentration of population can scarcely be left out of account in a definition of the city. But these criteria must be seen as relative to the general cultural context in which cities arise and exist and are sociologically relevant only in so far as they operate as conditioning factors in social life.

The same criticisms apply to such criteria as the occupation of the inhabitants, the existence of certain physical facilities, institutions, and forms of political organization. The question is not whether cities in our civilization or in others do exhibit these distinctive traits, but how potent they are in molding the character of social life into its specifically urban form. Nor in formulating a fertile definition can we afford to overlook the great variations between cities. By means of a typology of cities based upon size, location, age, and function, such as we have undertaken to establish in our recent report to the National Resources Committee,[6] we have found it feasible to array and classify urban communities ranging from struggling small towns to thriving world-metropolitan centers; from isolated trading-centers in the midst of agricultural regions to thriving world-ports and commercial and industrial conurbations. Such differences as these appear crucial because the social characteristics and influences of these different "cities" vary widely.

A serviceable definition of urbanism should not only denote the essential characteristics which all cities—at least those in our culture—have in common, but should lend itself to the discovery of their variations. An industrial city will differ significantly in social respects from a commercial, mining, fishing, resort, university, and capital city. A one-industry city will present different sets of social characteristics from a multi-industry city, as will an industrially balanced from an imbalanced city, a suburb from a satellite, a residential suburb from an industrial suburb, a city within a metropolitan region from one lying outside, an old city from a new one, a southern city from a New England, a middle-western from a Pacific Coast city, a growing from a stable and from a dying city.

A sociological definition must obviously be inclusive enough to comprise whatever essential characteristics these different types of cities have in common as social entities, but it obviously cannot be so detailed as to take account of all the variations implicit in the manifold classes sketched above. Presumably some of the characteristics of cities are more significant in conditioning the nature of urban life than others, and we may expect the outstanding features of the urban-social scene to vary in accordance with size, density, and differences in the functional type of cities. Moreover, we may infer that rural life will bear the imprint of urbanism in the measure that through contact and communication it comes under the influence of cities. It may contribute to the clarity of the statements that follow to repeat that while the locus of urbanism as a mode of life is, of course, to be found characteristically in places which fulfil the requirements we shall set up as a definition of the city, urbanism is not confined to such localities but is manifest in varying degrees wherever the influences of the city reach.

While urbanism, or that complex of traits which makes up the characteristic mode of life in cities, and urbanization, which denotes the development and extensions of these factors, are thus not exclusively found in settlements which are cities in the physical and demographic sense, they do, nevertheless, find their most pronounced expression in such areas, especially in metropolitan cities. In formulating a definition of the city it is necessary to exercise caution in order to avoid identifying urbanism as a way of life with any specific locally or historically conditioned cultural influences which, while they may significantly affect the specific character of the community, are not the essential determinants of its character as a city.

It is particularly important to call attention to the danger of confusing urbanism with industrialism and modern capitalism. The rise of cities in the modern world is undoubtedly not independent of the emergence of modern power-driven machine technology, mass production, and capitalistic enterprise. But different as the cities of earlier epochs may have been by virtue of their development in a preindustrial and precapitalistic order from the great cities of today, they were, nevertheless, cities.

For sociological purposes a city may be defined as a relatively large, dense, and permanent settlement of socially heterogeneous individuals. On the basis of the postulates which this minimal definition suggests, a theory of urbanism may be formulated in the light of existing knowledge concerning social groups.

III. A THEORY OF URBANISM

In the rich literature on the city we look in vain for a theory of urbanism presenting in a systematic fashion the available knowledge concerning the city as a social entity. We do indeed have excellent formulations of theories on such special problems as the growth of the city viewed as a historical trend and as a recurrent process,[7] and we have a wealth of literature presenting insights of sociological relevance and empirical studies offering detailed information on a variety of particular aspects of urban life. But despite the multiplication of research and textbooks on the city, we do not as yet have a comprehensive body of compendent hypotheses which may be derived from a set of postulates implicitly contained in a sociological definition of the city, and from our general sociological knowledge which may be substantiated through empirical research. The closest approximations to a systematic theory of urbanism that we have are to be found in a penetrating essay, "Die Stadt," by Max Weber,[8] and a memorable paper by Robert E. Park on "The City: Suggestions for the Investigation of Human Behavior in the Urban Environment."[9] But even these excellent contributions are far from constituting an ordered and coherent framework of theory upon which research might profitably proceed.

In the pages that follow we shall seek to set forth a limited number of identifying characteristics of the city. Given these characteristics we shall then indicate what consequences or further characteristics follow from them in the light of general sociological theory and empirical research. We hope in this manner to arrive at the essential propositions comprising a theory of urbanism. Some of these propositions can be supported by a considerable body of already available research materials; others may be accepted as hypotheses for which a certain amount of presumptive evidence exists, but for which more ample and exact verification would be required. At least such a procedure will, it is hoped, show what in the way of systematic knowledge of the city we now have and what are the crucial and fruitful hypotheses for future research.

The central problem of the sociologist of the city is to discover the forms of social action and organization that typically emerge in relatively permanent, compact settlements of large numbers of heterogeneous individuals. We must also infer that urbanism will assume its most characteristic and extreme form in the measure in which the conditions with which it is congruent are present. Thus the larger, the more densely populated, and the more heterogeneous a community, the more accentuated the characteristics associated with urbanism will be. It should be recognized, however, that in the social world institutions and practices may be accepted and continued for reasons other than those that originally brought them into existence, and that accordingly the urban mode of life may be perpetuated under conditions quite foreign to those necessary for its origin.

Some justification may be in order for the choice of the principal terms comprising our definition of the city. The attempt has been made to make it as inclusive and at the same time as denotative as possible without loading it with unnecessary assumptions. To say that large numbers are necessary to constitute a city means, of course, large numbers in relation to a restricted area or high density of settlement. There are, nevertheless, good reasons for treating large numbers and density as separate factors, since each may be connected with significantly different social consequences. Similarly the need for adding heterogeneity to numbers of population as a necessary and distinct criterion of urbanism might be questioned, since we should expect the range of differences to increase with numbers. In defense, it may be said that the city shows a kind and degree of heterogeneity of population which cannot be wholly accounted for by the law of large numbers or adequately represented by means of a normal distribution curve. Since the pop-

ulation of the city does not reproduce itself, it must recruit its migrants from other cities, the countryside, and—in this country until recently—from other countries. The city has thus historically been the melting-pot of races, peoples, and cultures, and a most favorable breeding-ground of new biological and cultural hybrids. It has not only tolerated but rewarded individual differences. It has brought together people from the ends of the earth *because* they are different and thus useful to one another, rather than because they are homogeneous and like-minded.[10]

There are a number of sociological propositions concerning the relationship between (*a*) numbers of population, (*b*) density of settlement, (*c*) heterogeneity of inhabitants and group life, which can be formulated on the basis of observation and research.

Size of the Population Aggregate

Ever since Aristotle's *Politics*,[11] it has been recognized that increasing the number of inhabitants in a settlement beyond a certain limit will affect the relationships between them and the character of the city. Large numbers involve, as has been pointed out, a greater range of individual variation. Furthermore, the greater the number of individuals participating in a process of interaction, the greater is the *potential* differentiation between them. The personal traits, the occupations, the cultural life, and the ideas of the members of an urban community may, therefore, be expected to range between more widely separated poles than those of rural inhabitants.

That such variations should give rise to the spatial segregation of individuals according to color, ethnic heritage, economic and social status, tastes and preferences, may readily be inferred. The bonds of kinship, of neighborliness, and the sentiments arising out of living together for generations under a common folk tradition are likely to be absent or, at best, relatively weak in an aggregate the members of which have such diverse origins and backgrounds. Under such circumstances competition and formal control mechanisms furnish the substitutes for the bonds of solidarity that are relied upon to hold a folk society together.

Increase in the number of inhabitants of a community beyond a few hundred is bound to limit the possibility of each member of the community knowing all the others personally. Max Weber, in recognizing the social significance of this fact, pointed out that from a sociological point of view large numbers of inhabitants and density of settlement mean that the personal mutual acquaintanceship between the inhabitants which ordinarily inheres in a neighborhood is lacking.[12] The increase in numbers thus involves a changed character of the social relationships. As Simmel points out:

[If] the unceasing external contact of numbers of persons in the city should be met by the same number of inner reactions as in the small town, in which one knows almost every person he meets and to each of whom he has a positive relationship, one would be completely atomized internally and would fall into an unthinkable mental condition.[13]

The multiplication of persons in a state of interaction under conditions which make their contact as full personalities impossible produces that segmentalization of human relationships which has sometimes been seized upon by students of the mental life of the cities as an explanation for the "schizoid" character

of urban personality. This is not to say that the urban inhabitants have fewer acquaintances than rural inhabitants, for the reverse may actually be true; it means rather that in relation to the number of people whom they see and with whom they rub elbows in the course of daily life, they know a smaller proportion, and of these they have less intensive knowledge.

Characteristically, urbanites meet one another in highly segmental roles. They are, to be sure, dependent upon more people for the satisfactions of their life-needs than are rural people and thus are associated with a greater number of organized groups, but they are less dependent upon particular persons, and their dependence upon others is confined to a highly fractionalized aspect of the other's round of activity. This is essentially what is meant by saying that the city is characterized by secondary rather than primary contacts. The contacts of the city may indeed be face to face, but they are nevertheless impersonal, superficial, transitory, and segmental. The reserve, the indifference, and the blasé outlook which urbanites manifest in their relationships may thus be regarded as devices for immunizing themselves against the personal claims and expectations of others.

The superficiality, the anonymity, and the transitory character of urbansocial relations make intelligible, also, the sophistication and the rationality generally ascribed to city-dwellers. Our acquaintances tend to stand in a relationship of utility to us in the sense that the role which each one plays in our life is overwhelmingly regarded as a means for the achievement of our own ends. Whereas, therefore, the individual gains, on the one hand, a certain degree of emancipation or freedom from the personal and emotional controls of intimate groups, he loses, on the other hand, the spontaneous self-expression, the morale, and the sense of participation that comes with living in an integrated society. This constitutes essentially the state of *anomie* or the social void to which Durkheim alludes in attempting to account for the various forms of social disorganization in technological society.

The segmental character and utilitarian accent of interpersonal relations in the city find their institutional expression in the proliferation of specialized tasks which we see in their most developed form in the professions. The operations of the pecuniary nexus leads to predatory relationships, which tend to obstruct the efficient functioning of the social order unless checked by professional codes and occupational etiquette. The premium put upon utility and efficiency suggests the adaptability of the corporate device for the organization of enterprises in which individuals can engage only in groups. The advantage that the corporation has over the individual entrepreneur and the partnership in the urban-industrial world derives not only from the possibility it affords of centralizing the resources of thousands of individuals or from the legal privilege of limited liability and perpetual succession, but from the fact that the corporation has no soul.

The specialization of individuals, particularly in their occupations, can proceed only, as Adam Smith pointed out, upon the basis of an enlarged market, which in turn accentuates the division of labor. This enlarged market is only in part supplied by the city's hinterland; in large measure it is found among the large numbers that the city itself contains. The dominance of the city over the surrounding hinterland becomes explicable in terms of the division of labor which urban life occasions and promotes. The extreme degree of interdependence and the unstable equilibrium of urban life are closely associated with the division of labor and the specialization of occupations. This interdependence and instability is increased by the tendency of each city to specialize in those functions in which it has the greatest advantage.

In a community composed of a larger number of individuals than can know one another intimately and can be assembled in one spot, it becomes necessary to communicate through indirect mediums and to articulate individual interests by a process of delegation. Typically in the city, interests are made effective through representation. The individual counts for little, but the voice of the representative is heard with a deference roughly proportional to the numbers for whom he speaks.

While this characterization of urbanism, in so far as it derives from large numbers, does not by any means exhaust the sociological inferences that might be drawn from our knowledge of the relationship of the size of a group to the characteristic behavior of the members, for the sake of brevity the assertions made may serve to exemplify the sort of propositions that might be developed.

Density

As in the case of numbers, so in the case of concentration in limited space, certain consequences of relevance in sociological analysis of the city emerge. Of these only a few can be indicated.

As Darwin pointed out for flora and fauna and as Durkheim[14] noted in the case of human societies, an increase in numbers when area is held constant (i.e., an increase in density) tends to produce differentiation and specialization, since only in this way can the area support increased numbers. Density thus reinforces the effect of numbers in diversifying men and their activities and in increasing the complexity of the social structure.

On the subjective side, as Simmel has suggested, the close physical contact of numerous individuals necessarily produces a shift in the mediums through which we orient ourselves to the urban milieu, especially to our fellow-men. Typically, our physical contacts are close but our social contacts are distant. The urban world puts a premium on visual recognition. We see the uniform which denotes the role of the functionaries and are oblivious to the personal eccentricities that are hidden behind the uniform. We tend to acquire and develop a sensitivity to a world of artefacts and become progressively farther removed from the world of nature.

We are exposed to glaring contrasts between splendor and squalor, between riches and poverty, intelligence and ignorance, order and chaos. The competition for space is great, so that each area generally tends to be put to the use which yields the greatest economic return. Place of work tends to become dissociated from place of residence, for the proximity of industrial and commercial establishments makes an area both economically and socially undesirable for residential purposes.

Density, land values, rentals, accessibility, healthfulness, prestige, aesthetic consideration, absence of nuisances such as noise, smoke, and dirt determine the desirability of various areas of the city as places of settlement for different sections of the population. Place and nature of work, income, racial and ethnic characteristics, social status, custom, habit, taste, preference, and prejudice are among the significant factors in accordance with which the urban population is selected and distributed into more or less distinct settlements. Diverse population elements inhabiting a compact settlement thus tend to become segregated from one another in the degree in which their requirements and modes of life are incompatible with one another and in the measure in which they are antagonistic to one another. Similarly, persons of homogeneous status and needs unwittingly drift into, consciously select, or are forced by circumstances into, the same area. The different parts of the city thus acquire specialized functions. The city consequently tends to resemble a mosaic of social worlds in which the transition from one to the other is abrupt. The juxtaposition of divergent personalities and modes of life tends to produce a relativistic perspective and a sense of toleration of differences which may be regarded as prerequisites for rationality and which lead toward the secularization of life.[15]

The close living together and working together of individuals who have no sentimental and emotional ties foster a spirit of competition, aggrandizement, and mutual exploitation. To counteract irresponsibility and potential disorder, formal controls tend to be resorted to. Without rigid adherence to predictable routines a large compact society would scarcely be able to maintain itself. The clock and the traffic signal are symbolic of the basis of our social order in the urban world. Frequent close physical contact, coupled with great social distance, accentuates the reserve of unattached individuals toward one another and, unless compensated for by other opportunities for response, gives rise to loneliness. The necessary frequent movement of great numbers of individuals in a congested habitat gives occasion to friction and irritation. Nervous tensions which derive from such personal frustrations are accentuated by the rapid tempo and the complicated technology under which life in dense areas must be lived.

Heterogeneity

The social interaction among such a variety of personality types in the urban milieu tends to break down the rigidity of caste lines and to complicate the class structure, and thus induces a more ramified and differentiated framework of social stratification than is found in more integrated societies. The heightened mobility of the individual, which brings him within the range of stimulation by a great number of diverse individuals and subjects him to fluctuating status in the differentiated social groups that compose the social structure of the city, tends toward the acceptance of instability and insecurity in the world at large as a norm. This fact helps to account, too, for the sophistication and cosmopolitanism of the urbanite. No single group has the undivided allegiance of the individual. The groups with which he is affiliated do not lend themselves readily to a simple hierarchical arrangement. By virtue of his different interests arising out of different aspects of social life, the individual acquires membership in widely divergent groups, each of which functions only with reference to a single segment of his personality. Nor do these groups easily permit of a concentric arrangement so that the narrower ones fall within the circumference of the more inclusive ones, as is more likely to be the case in the rural community or in primitive societies. Rather the groups with which the person typically is affiliated are tangential to each other or intersect in highly variable fashion.

Partly as a result of the physical footlooseness of the population and partly as a result of their social mobility, the turnover in group membership generally is rapid. Place of residence, place and character of employment, income and interests fluctuate, and the task of holding organizations together and maintaining and promoting intimate and lasting acquaintanceship between the members is difficult. This applies strikingly to the local areas within the city into which persons become segregated more by virtue of differences in race, language, income, and social status, than through choice or positive attraction to people like themselves. Overwhelmingly the city-dweller is not a home-owner, and since a transitory habitat does not generate binding traditions and sentiments, only rarely is he truly a neighbor. There is little opportunity for the individual to obtain a conception of the city as a whole or to survey his place in the total scheme. Consequently he finds it difficult to determine what is to his own "best interests" and to decide between the issues and leaders presented to him by the agencies of mass suggestion. Individuals who are thus detached from the organized bodies which integrate society comprise the fluid masses that make collective behavior in the urban community so unpredictable and hence so problematical.

Although the city, through the recruitment of variant types to perform its diverse tasks and the accentuation of their uniqueness through competition and the premium upon eccentricity, novelty, efficient performance, and inventiveness, produces a highly differentiated population, it also exercises a leveling influence. Wherever large numbers of differently constituted individuals congregate, the process of depersonalization also enters. This leveling tendency inheres in part in the economic basis of the city. The development of large cities, at least in the modern age, was largely dependent upon the concentrative force of steam. The rise of the factory made possible mass production for an impersonal market. The fullest exploitation of the possibilities of the division of labor and mass production, however, is possible only with standardization of processes and products. A money economy goes hand in hand with such a system of production. Progressively as cities have developed upon a background of this system of production, the pecuniary nexus which implies the purchasability of services and things has displaced personal relations as the basis of association. Individuality under these circumstances must be replaced by categories. When large numbers have to make common use of facilities and institutions, an arrangement must be made to adjust the facilities and institutions to the needs of the average person rather than to those of particular individuals. The services of the public utilities, of the recreational, educational, and cultural institutions must be adjusted to mass requirements. Similarly, the cultural institutions, such as the schools, the movies, the radio, and the newspapers, by virtue of their mass clientele, must necessarily operate as leveling influences. The political process as it appears in urban life could not be understood without taking account of the mass appeals made through modern propaganda techniques. If the individual would participate at all in the social, political, and economic life of the city, he must subordinate some of his individuality to the demands of the larger community and in that measure immerse himself in mass movements.

IV. THE RELATION BETWEEN A THEORY OF URBANISM AND SOCIOLOGICAL RESEARCH

By means of a body of theory such as that illustratively sketched above, the complicated and many-sided phenomena of urbanism may be analyzed in terms of a limited number of basic categories. The sociological approach to the city thus acquires an essential unity and coherence enabling the empirical investigator not merely to focus more distinctly upon the problems and processes that properly fall in his province but also to treat his subject matter in a more integrated and systematic fashion. A few typical findings of empirical research in the field of urbanism, with special reference to the United States, may be indicated to substantiate the theoretical propositions set forth in the preceding pages, and some of the crucial problems for further study may be outlined.

On the basis of the three variables, number, density of settlement, and degree of heterogeneity, of the urban population, it appears possible to explain the characteristics of urban life and to account for the differences between cities of various sizes and types.

Urbanism as a characteristic mode of life may be approached empirically from three interrelated perspectives: (1) as a physical structure comprising a population base, a technology, and an ecological order; (2) as a system of social organization involving a characteristic social structure, a series of social institutions, and a typical pattern of social relationships; and (3) as a set of attitudes and ideas, and a constellation of personalities engaging in typical forms of collective behavior and subject to characteristic mechanisms of social control.

Urbanism in Ecological Perspective

Since in the case of physical structure and ecological processes we are able to operate with fairly objective indices, it becomes possible to arrive at quite precise and generally quantitative results. The dominance of the city over its hinterland becomes explicable through the functional characteristics of the city which derive in large measure from the effect of numbers and density. Many of the technical facilities and the skills and organizations to which urban life gives rise can grow and prosper only in cities where the demand is sufficiently great. The nature and scope of the services rendered by these organizations and institutions and the advantage which they enjoy over the less developed facilities of smaller towns enhances the dominance of the city and the dependence of ever wider regions upon the central metropolis.

The urban-population composition shows the operation of selective and differentiating factors. Cities contain a larger proportion of persons in the prime of life than rural areas which contain more old and very young people. In this, as in so many other respects, the larger the city the more this specific characteristic of urbanism is apparent. With the exception of the largest cities, which have attracted the bulk of foreign-born males, and a few other special types of cities, women predominate numerically over men. The heter-

ogeneity of the urban population is further indicated along racial and ethnic lines. The foreign born and their children constitute nearly two-thirds of all the inhabitants of cities of one million and over. Their proportion in the urban population declines as the size of the city decreases, until in the rural areas they comprise only about one-sixth of the total population. The larger cities similarly have attracted more Negroes and other racial groups than have the smaller communities. Considering that age, sex, race, and ethnic origin are associated with other factors such as occupation and interest, it becomes clear that one major characteristic of the urban-dweller is his dissimilarity from his fellows. Never before have such large masses of people of diverse traits as we find in our cities been thrown together into such close physical contact as in the great cities of America. Cities generally, and American cities in particular, comprise a motley of peoples and cultures, of highly differentiated modes of life between which there often is only the faintest communication, the greatest indifference and the broadest tolerance, occasionally bitter strife, but always the sharpest contrast.

The failure of the urban population to reproduce itself appears to be a biological consequence of a combination of factors in the complex of urban life, and the decline in the birth-rate generally may be regarded as one of the most significant signs of the urbanization of the Western world. While the proportion of deaths in cities is slightly greater than in the country, the outstanding difference between the failure of present-day cities to maintain their population and that of cities of the past is that in former times it was due to the exceedingly high death-rates in cities, whereas today, since cities have become more livable from a health standpoint, it is due to low birth-rates. These biological characteristics of the urban population are significant sociologically, not merely because they reflect the urban mode of existence but also because they condition the growth and future dominance of cities and their basic social organization. Since cities are the consumers rather than the producers of men, the value of human life and the social estimation of the personality will not be unaffected by the balance between births and deaths. The pattern of land use, of land values, rentals, and ownership, the nature and functioning of the physical structures, of housing, of transportation and communication facilities, of public utilities—these and many other phases of the physical mechanism of the city are not isolated phenomena unrelated to the city as a social entity, but are affected by and affect the urban mode of life.

Urbanism as a Form of Social Organization

The distinctive features of the urban mode of life have often been described sociologically as consisting of the substitution of secondary for primary contacts, the weakening of bonds of kinship, and the declining social significance of the family, the disappearance of the neighborhood, and the undermining of the traditional basis of social solidarity. All these phenomena can be substantially verified through objective indices. Thus, for instance, the low and declining urban-reproduction rates suggest that the city is not conducive to the traditional type of family life, including the rearing of children and the maintenance of the home as the locus of a whole round of vital activities. The

transfer of industrial, educational, and recreational activities to specialized institutions outside the home has deprived the family of some of its most characteristic historical functions. In cities mothers are more likely to be employed, lodgers are more frequently part of the household, marriage tends to be postponed, and the proportion of single and unattached people is greater. Families are smaller and more frequently without children than in the country. The family as a unit of social life is emancipated from the larger kinship group characteristic of the country, and the individual members pursue their own diverging interests in their vocational, educational, religious, recreational and political life.

Such functions as the maintenance of health, the methods of alleviating the hardships associated with personal and social insecurity, the provisions for education, recreation, and cultural advancement have given rise to highly specialized institutions on a community-wide, statewide, or even national basis. The same factors which have brought about greater personal insecurity also underlie the wider contrasts between individuals to be found in the urban world. While the city has broken down the rigid caste lines of pre-industrial society, it has sharpened and differentiated income and status groups. Generally, a larger proportion of the adult-urban population is gainfully employed than is the case with the adult-rural population. The white-collar class, comprising those employed in trade, in clerical, and in professional work, are proportionately more numerous in large cities and in metropolitan centers and in smaller towns than in the country.

On the whole, the city discourages an economic life in which the individual in time of crisis has a basis of subsistence to fall back upon, and it discourages self-employment. While incomes of city people are on the average higher than those of country people, the cost of living seems to be higher in the larger cities. Home ownership involves greater burdens and is rarer. Rents are higher and absorb a larger proportion of the income. Although the urban-dweller has the benefit of many communal services, he spends a large proportion of his income for such items as recreation and advancement and a smaller proportion for food. What the communal services do not furnish the urbanite must purchase, and there is virtually no human need which has remained unexploited by commercialism. Catering to thrills and furnishing means of escape from drudgery, monotony, and routine thus become one of the major functions of urban recreation, which at its best furnishes means for creative self-expression and spontaneous group association, but which more typically in the urban world results in passive spectatorism on the one hand, or sensational record-smashing feats on the other.

Being reduced to a stage of virtual impotence as an individual, the urbanite is bound to exert himself by joining with others of similar interest into organized groups to obtain his ends. This results in the enormous multiplication of voluntary organizations directed toward as great a variety of objectives as there are human needs and interests. While on the one hand the traditional ties of human association are weakened, urban existence involves a much greater degree of interdependence between man and man and a more complicated, fragile, and volatile form of mutual interrelations over many phases of which the individual as such can exert scarcely any control. Frequently there is only the most tenuous relationship between the economic position or other basic factors that determine the individual's existence in the urban world and the voluntary groups with which he is affiliated. While in a primitive and in a rural society it is generally possible to predict on the basis of a few known factors who will belong to what and who will associate with whom in almost every relationship of life, in the city we can only project the general pattern of group formation and affiliation, and this pattern will display many incongruities and contradictions.

Urban Personality and Collective Behavior

It is largely through the activities of the voluntary groups, be their objectives economic, political, educational, religious, recreational, or cultural, that the urbanite expresses and develops his personality, acquires status, and is able to carry on the round of activities that constitute his life-career. It may easily be inferred, however, that the organizational framework which these highly differentiated functions call into being does not of itself insure the consistency and integrity of the personalities whose interests it enlists. Personal disorganization, mental breakdown, suicide, delinquency, crime, corruption, and disorder might be expected under these circumstances to be more prevalent in the urban than in the rural community. This has been confirmed in so far as comparable indices are available; but the mechanisms underlying these phenomena require further analysis.

Since for most group purposes it is impossible in the city to appeal individually to the large number of discrete and differentiated individuals, and since it is only through the organizations to which men belong that their interests and resources can be enlisted for a collective cause, it may be inferred that social control in the city should typically proceed through formally organized groups. It follows, too, that the masses of men in the city are subject to manipulation by symbols and stereotypes managed by individuals working from afar or operating invisibly behind the scenes through their control of the instruments of communication. Self-government either in the economic, the political, or the cultural realm is under these circumstances reduced to a mere figure of speech or, at best, is subject to the unstable equilibrium of pressure groups. In view of the ineffectiveness of actual kinship ties we create fictional kinship groups. In the face of the disappearance of the territorial unit as a basis of social solidarity we create interest units. Meanwhile the city as a community resolves itself into a series of tenuous segmental relationships superimposed upon a territorial base with a definite center but without a definite periphery and upon a division of labor which far transcends the immediate locality and is world-wide in scope. The larger the number of persons in a state of interaction with one another the lower is the level of communication and the greater is the tendency for communication to proceed on an elementary level, i.e., on the basis of those things which are assumed to be common or to be of interest to all.

It is obviously, therefore, to the emerging trends in the communication system and to the production and distribution technology that has come into existence with modern civilization that we must look for the symptoms which will indicate the probable future development of urbanism as a mode of social life. The direction of the ongoing changes in urbanism will for good or ill transform not only the city but the world. Some of the more basic of these factors and processes and the possibilities of their direction and control invite further detailed study.

It is only in so far as the sociologist has a clear conception of the city as a social entity and a workable theory of urbanism that he can hope to develop a unified body of reliable knowledge, that which passes as "urban sociology" is certainly not at the present time. By taking his point of departure from a theory of urbanism such as that sketched in the foregoing pages to be elaborated, tested, and revised in the light of further analysis and empirical research, it is to be hoped that the criteria of relevance and validity of factual data can be determined. The miscellaneous assortment of disconnected information which has hitherto found its way into sociological treatises on the city may thus be sifted and incorporated into a coherent body of knowledge. Incidentally, only by means of some such theory will the sociologist escape the futile practice of voicing in the name of sociological science a variety of often unsupportable judgments concerning such problems as poverty, housing, city-planning, sanitation, municipal administration, policing, marketing, transportation, and other technical issues. While the sociologist cannot solve any of these practical problems—at least not by himself—he may, if he discovers his proper function, have an important contribution to make to their comprehension and solution. The prospects of doing this are brightest through a general, theoretical, rather than through an *ad hoc* approach.

NOTES

1. William Graham Sumner, *Folkways* (Boston, 1906), p. 12.

2. S. V. Pearson, *The Growth and Distribution of Population* (New York, 1935), p. 211.

3. Whereas rural life in the United States has for a long time been a subject of considerable interest on the part of governmental bureaus, the most notable case of a comprehensive report being that submitted by the Country Life Commission to President Theodore Roosevelt in 1909, it is worthy of note that no equally comprehensive official inquiry into urban life was undertaken until the establishment of a Research Committee on Urbanism of the National Resources Committee. (Cf. *Our Cities: Their Role in the National Economy* [Washington: Government Printing Office, 1937].)

4. "The Anthropogeography of Some Great Cities," *Bull. American Geographical Society*, XLI (1909), 537-66.

5. Walter F. Willcox, "A Definition of 'City' in Terms of Density," in E. W. Burgess, *The Urban Community* (Chicago, 1926), p. 119.

6. *Op. cit.*, p. 8.

7. See Robert E. Park, Ernest W. Burgess, *et al.*, *The City* (Chicago, 1925), esp. chaps. ii and iii; Werner Sombart, "Städtische Siedlung, Stadt," *Handwörterbuch der Soziologie*, ed. Alfred Vierkandt (Stuttgart, 1931); see also bibliography.

8. *Wirtschaft und Gesellschaft* (Tübingen, 1925), Part II, chap. viii, pp. 514-601.

9. Park, Burgess, *et al.*, *op. cit.*, chap. i.

10. The justification for including the term "permanent" in the definition may appear necessary. Our failure to give an extensive justification for this qualifying mark of the urban rests on the obvious fact that unless human settlements take a fairly permanent root in a locality the characteristics of urban life cannot arise, and conversely the living together of large numbers of heterogeneous individuals under dense conditions is not possible without the development of a more or less technological structure.

11. See esp. vii. 4. 4-14. Translated by B. Jowett, from which the following may be quoted:

"To the size of states there is a limit, as there is to other things, plants, animals, implements; for none of these retain their natural power when they are too large or too small, but they either wholly lose their nature, or are spoiled. . . . [A] state when composed of too few is not as a state ought to be, self-sufficing; when of too many, though self-sufficing in all mere necessaries, it is a nation and not a state, being almost incapable of constitutional government. For who can be the general of such a vast multitude, or who the herald, unless he have the voice of a Stentor?

"A state then only begins to exist when it has attained a population sufficient for a good life in the political community: it may indeed somewhat exceed this number. But, as I was saying, there must be a limit. What should be the limit will be easily ascertained by experience. For both governors and governed have duties to perform; the special functions of a governor are to command and to judge. But if the citizens of a state are to judge and to distribute offices according to merit, then they must know each other's characters; where they do not possess this knowledge, both the election to offices and the decision of lawsuits will go wrong. When the population is very large they are manifestly settled at haphazard, which clearly ought not to be. Besides, in an overpopulous state foreigners and metics will readily acquire the rights of citizens, for who will find them out? Clearly, then, the best limit of the population of a state is the largest number which suffices for the purposes of life, and can be taken in at a single view. Enough concerning the size of a city."

12. *Op. cit.*, p. 514.

13. Georg Simmel, "Die Grossstädte und das Geistesleben," *Die Grossstadt*, ed. Theodor Petermann (Dresden, 1903), pp. 187-206.

14. E. Durkheim, *De la division du travail social* (Paris, 1932), p. 248.

15. The extent to which the segregation of the population into distinct ecological and cultural areas and the resulting social attitude of tolerance, rationality, and secular mentality are functions of density as distinguished from heterogeneity is difficult to determine. Most likely we are dealing here with phenomena which are consequences of the simultaneous operation of both factors.

Urbanism and Suburbanism as Ways of Life: A Re-evaluation of Definitions *

HERBERT J. GANS

The contemporary sociological conception of cities and of urban life is based largely on the work of the Chicago School, and its summary statement in Louis Wirth's essay, "Urbanism as a Way of Life." (40) In that paper, Wirth developed a "minimum sociological definition of the city" as "a relatively large, dense and permanent settlement of socially heterogeneous individuals." (40, p. 50) From these prerequisites, he then deduced the major outlines of the urban way of life. As he saw it, number, density, and heterogeneity created a social structure in which primary-group relationships were inevitably replaced by secondary contacts that were impersonal, segmental, superficial, transitory, and often predatory in nature. As a result, the city dweller became anonymous, isolated, secular, relativistic, rational, and sophisticated. In order to function in the urban society, he was forced to combine with others to organize corporations, voluntary associations, representative forms of government, and the impersonal mass media of communications (40, pp. 54-60). These replaced the primary groups and the integrated way of life found in rural and other pre-industrial settlements.

Wirth's paper has become a classic in urban sociology, and most texts have followed his definition and description faithfully (5). In recent years, however, a considerable number of studies and essays have questioned his formulations

(1, 5, 13, 15, 17, 19, 20, 23, 24, 27, 28, 30, 35, 38, 41).[1] In addition, a number of changes have taken place in cities since the article was published in 1938, notably the exodus of white residents to low- and medium-priced houses in the suburbs, and the decentralization of industry. The evidence from these studies and the changes in American cities suggest that Wirth's statement must be revised.

There is yet another, and more important reason for such a revision. Despite its title and intent, Wirth's paper deals with urban-industrial society, rather than with the city. This is evident from his approach. Like other urban sociologists, Wirth based his analysis on a comparison of settlement types, but unlike his colleagues, who pursued urban-rural comparisons, Wirth contrasted the city to the folk society. Thus, he compared settlement types of pre-industrial and industrial society. This allowed him to include in his theory of urbanism the entire range of modern institutions which are not found in the folk society, even though many such groups (e.g., voluntary associations) are by no means exclusively urban. Moreover, Wirth's conception of the city dweller as depersonalized, atomized, and susceptible to mass movements suggests that his paper is based on, and contributes to, the theory of the mass society.

Many of Wirth's conclusions may be

From Arnold Rose (ed.), *Human Behavior and Social Processes* (Boston: Houghton Mifflin, 1962), pp. 625-48. Copyright © 1962 by Houghton Mifflin Company. Reprinted by permission of the publisher. Herbert J. Gans is with the Center for Urban Education.

504

relevant to the understanding of ways of life in modern society. However, since the theory argues that all of society is now urban, *his analysis does not distinguish ways of life in the city from those in other settlements within modern society.* In Wirth's time, the comparison of urban and pre-urban settlement types was still fruitful, but today, the primary task for urban (or community) sociology seems to me to be the analysis of the similarities and differences between contemporary settlement types.

This paper is an attempt at such an analysis; it limits itself to distinguishing ways of life in the modern city and the modern suburb. A re-analysis of Wirth's conclusions from this perspective suggests that his characterization of the urban way of life applies only—and not too accurately—to the residents of the inner city. The remaining city dwellers, as well as most suburbanites, pursue a different way of life, which I shall call "quasi-primary." This proposition raises some doubt about the mutual exclusiveness of the concepts of city and suburb and leads to a yet broader question: whether settlement concepts and other ecological concepts are useful for explaining ways of life.

THE INNER CITY

Wirth argued that number, density, and heterogeneity had two social consequences which explain the major features of urban life. On the one hand, the crowding of diverse types of people into a small area led to the segregation of homogeneous types of people into separate neighborhoods (40, p. 56). On the other hand, the lack of physical distance between city dwellers resulted in social contact between them, which

broke down existing social and cultural patterns and encouraged assimilation as well as acculturation—the melting pot effect (40, p. 52). Wirth implied that the melting pot effect was far more powerful than the tendency toward segregation and concluded that, sooner or later, the pressures engendered by the dominant social, economic, and political institutions of the city would destroy the remaining pockets of primary-group relationships (40, pp. 60-62). Eventually, the social system of the city would resemble Tönnies' *Gesellschaft*—a way of life which Wirth considered undesirable.

Because Wirth had come to see the city as the prototype of mass society, and because he examined the city from the distant vantage point of the folk society—from the wrong end of the telescope, so to speak—his view of urban life is not surprising. In addition, Wirth found support for this theory in the empirical work of his Chicago colleagues. As Greer and Kube (19, p. 112) and Wilensky (38, p. 121) have pointed out, the Chicago sociologists conducted their most intensive studies in the inner city.[2] At that time, these were slums recently invaded by new waves of European immigrants and rooming house and skid row districts, as well as the habitat of Bohemians and well-to-do Gold Coast apartment dwellers. Wirth himself studied the Maxwell Street Ghetto, an inner-city Jewish neighborhood then being dispersed by the acculturation and mobility of its inhabitants (39). Some of the characteristics of urbanism which Wirth stressed in his essay abounded in these areas.

Wirth's diagnosis of the city as *Gesellschaft* must be questioned on three counts. First, the conclusions derived from a study of the inner city cannot be generalized to the entire urban area. Second, there is as yet not enough evidence to prove—nor, admittedly, to deny—that number, density, and heterogeneity result in the social consequences which Wirth proposed. Finally, even if the causal relationship could be verified, it can be shown that a significant proportion of the city's inhabitants were, and are, isolated from these consequences by social structures and cultural patterns which they either brought to the city, or developed by living in it. Wirth conceived the urban population as consisting of heterogeneous individuals, torn from past social systems, unable to develop new ones, and therefore prey to social anarchy in the city. While it is true that a not insignificant proportion of the inner city population was, and still is, made up of unattached individuals (26), Wirth's formulation ignores the fact that this population consists mainly of relatively homogeneous groups, with social and cultural moorings that shield it fairly effectively from the suggested consequences of number, density, and heterogeneity. This applies even more to the residents of the outer city, who constitute a majority of the total city population.

The social and cultural moorings of the inner city population are best described by a brief analysis of the five types of inner city residents. These are:

1. the "cosmopolites";
2. the unmarried or childless;
3. the "ethnic villagers";
4. the "deprived"; and
5. the "trapped" and downward mobile.

The "cosmopolites" include students, artists, writers, musicians, and entertainers, as well as other intellectuals and professionals. They live in the city in order to be near the special "cultural" facilities that can only be located near the center of the city. Many cosmopolites are unmarried or childless. Others rear children in the city, especially if they have the income to afford the aid of servants and governesses. The less affluent ones may move to the suburbs to raise their children, continuing to live as cosmopolites under considerable handicaps, especially in the lower-middle-class suburbs. Many of the very rich and powerful are also cosmopolites, although they are likely to have at least two residences, one of which is suburban or exurban.

The unmarried or childless must be divided into two subtypes, depending on the permanence or transience of their status. The temporarily unmarried or childless live in the inner city for only a limited time. Young adults may team up to rent an apartment away from their parents and close to job or entertainment opportunities. When they marry, they may move first to an apartment in a transient neighborhood, but if they can afford to do so, they leave for the outer city or the suburbs with the arrival of the first or second child. The permanently unmarried may stay in the inner city for the remainder of their lives, their housing depending on their income.

The "ethnic villagers" are ethnic groups which are found in such inner city neighborhoods as New York's Lower East Side, living in some ways as they did when they were peasants in European or Puerto Rican villages (15). Although they reside in the city, they isolate themselves from significant contact with most city facilities, aside from workplaces. Their way of life differs sharply from Wirth's urbanism in its emphasis on kinship and the primary group, the lack of anonymity and secondary-group contacts, the weakness of formal organizations, and the suspicion of anything and anyone outside their neighborhood.

The first two types live in the inner city by choice; the third is there partly because of necessity, partly because of tradition. The final two types are in the inner city because they have no other choice. One is the "deprived" population: the very poor; the emotionally disturbed or otherwise handicapped; broken families; and, most important, the non-white population. These urban dwellers must take the dilapidated housing and blighted neighborhoods to which the housing market relegates them, although among them are some for whom the slum is a hiding place, or a temporary stop-over to save money for a house in the outer city or the suburbs (27).

The "trapped" are the people who stay behind when a neighborhood is invaded by non-residential land uses or lower-status immigrants, because they cannot afford to move, or are otherwise bound to their present location (27).[3] The "downward mobiles" are a related type; they may have started life in a higher class position, but have been forced down in the socio-economic hierarchy and in the quality of their accommodations. Many of them are old people, living out their existence on small pensions.

These five types all live in dense and heterogeneous surroundings, yet they have such diverse ways of life that it is hard to see how density and heterogeneity could exert a common influence. Moreover, all but the last two types are isolated or detached from their neighborhood and thus from the social consequences which Wirth described.

When people who live together have social ties based on criteria other than mere common occupancy, they can set up social barriers regardless of the physical closeness or the heterogeneity of their neighbors. The ethnic villagers are the best illustration. While a number of ethnic groups are usually found living together in the same neighborhood, they are able to *isolate* themselves from each other through a variety of social devices. Wirth himself recognized this when he wrote that "two groups can occupy a given area without losing their separate identity because each side is permitted to live its own inner life and each somehow fears or idealizes the other." (39, p. 283) Although it is true that the children in these areas were often oblivious to the social barriers set up by their parents, at least until adolescence, it is doubtful whether their acculturation can be traced to the melting pot effect as much as to the pervasive influence of the American culture that flowed into these areas from the outside.[4]

The cosmopolites, the unmarried, and the childless are *detached* from neighborhood life. The cosmopolites possess a distinct subculture which causes them to be disinterested in all but the most superficial contacts with their neighbors, somewhat like the ethnic villagers. The unmarried and childless are detached from neighborhood because of their life-cycle stage, which frees them from the routine family responsibilities that entail some relationship to the local area. In their choice of residence, the two types are therefore not concerned about their neighbors, or the availability and quality of local community facilities. Even the well-to-do can choose expensive apartments in or near poor neighborhoods, because if they have children, these are sent to special schools and summer camps which effectively isolate them from neighbors. In addition, both types, but especially the childless and unmarried, are transient. Therefore, they tend to live in areas marked by high population turnover, where their own mobility and that of their neighbors creates a universal detachment from the neighborhood.[5]

The deprived and the trapped do seem to be affected by some of the consequences of number, density, and heterogeneity. The deprived population suffers considerably from overcrowding, but this is a consequence of low income, racial discrimination, and other handicaps, and cannot be considered an inevitable result of the ecological make-up of the city.[6] Because the deprived have no residential choice, they are also forced to live amid neighbors not of their own choosing, with ways of life different and even contradictory to their own. If familial defenses against the neighborhood climate are weak, as is the case among broken families and downward mobile people, parents may lose their children to the culture of "the street." The trapped are the unhappy people who remain behind when their more advantaged neighbors move on; they must endure the heterogeneity which results from neighborhood change.

Wirth's description of the urban way of life fits best the transient areas of the inner city. Such areas are typically heterogeneous in population, partly because they are inhabited by transient types who do not require homogeneous neighbors or by deprived people who have no choice, or may themselves be quite mobile. Under conditions of transience and heterogeneity, people interact only in terms of the segmental roles necessary for obtaining local services.

Their social relationships thus display anonymity, impersonality, and superficiality.[7]

The social features of Wirth's concept of urbanism seem therefore to be a result of residential instability, rather than of number, density, or heterogeneity. In fact, heterogeneity is itself an effect of residential instability, resulting when the influx of transients causes landlords and realtors to stop acting as gatekeepers—that is, wardens of neighborhood homogeneity.[8] Residential instability is found in all types of settlements, and, presumably, its social consequences are everywhere similar. These consequences cannot therefore be identified with the ways of life of the city.

THE OUTER CITY AND THE SUBURBS

The second effect which Wirth ascribed to number, density, and heterogeneity was the segregation of homogeneous people into distinct neighborhoods,[9] on the basis of "place and nature of work, income, racial and ethnic characteristics, social status, custom, habit, taste, preference and prejudice." (40, p. 56) This description fits the residential districts of the *outer city*.[10] Although these districts contain the majority of the city's inhabitants, Wirth went into little detail about them. He made it clear, however, that the socio-psychological aspects of urbanism were prevalent there as well (40, p. 56).

Because existing neighborhood studies deal primarily with the exotic sections of the inner city, very little is known about the more typical residential neighborhoods of the outer city. However, it is evident that the way of life in these areas bears little resemblance to Wirth's urbanism. Both the studies which question Wirth's formulation and my own observations suggest that the common element in the ways of life of these neighborhoods is best described as *quasi-primary*. I use this term to characterize relationships between neighbors. Whatever the intensity or frequency of these relationships, the interaction is more intimate than a secondary contact, but more guarded than a primary one.[11]

There are actually few secondary relationships, because of the isolation of residential neighborhoods from economic institutions and workplaces. Even shopkeepers, store managers, and other local functionaries who live in the area are treated as acquaintances or friends, unless they are of a vastly different social status or are forced by their corporate employers to treat their customers as economic units (30). Voluntary associations attract only a minority of the population. Moreover, much of the organizational activity is of a sociable nature, and it is often difficult to accomplish the association's "business" because of the members' preference for sociability. Thus, it would appear that interactions in organizations, or between neighbors generally, do not fit the secondary-relationship model of urban life. As anyone who has lived in these neighborhoods knows, there is little anonymity, impersonality or privacy.[12] In fact, American cities have sometimes been described as collections of small towns.[13] There is some truth to this description, especially if the city is compared to the actual small town, rather than to the romantic construct of anti-urban critics (33).

Postwar suburbia represents the most contemporary version of the quasi-primary way of life. Owing to increases in real income and the encouragement of home ownership provided by the FHA,

families in the lower-middle class and upper working class can now live in modern single-family homes in low-density subdivisions, an opportunity previously available only to the upper and upper-middle classes (34).

The popular literature describes the new suburbs as communities in which conformity, homogeneity, and other-direction are unusually rampant (4, 32). The implication is that the move from city to suburb initiates a new way of life which causes considerable behavior and personality change in previous urbanites. A preliminary analysis of data which I am now collecting in Levittown, New Jersey, suggests, however, that the move from the city to this predominantly lower-middle-class suburb does not result in any major behavioral changes for most people. Moreover, the changes which do occur reflect the move from the social isolation of a transient city or suburban apartment building to the quasi-primary life of a neighborhood of single-family homes. Also, many of the people whose life has changed reported that the changes were intended. They existed as aspirations before the move, or as reasons for it. In other words, the suburb itself creates few changes in ways of life. Similar conclusions have been reported by Berger in his excellent study of a working-class population newly moved to a suburban subdivision (4).

A COMPARISON OF CITY AND SUBURB

If urban and suburban areas are similar in that the way of life in both is quasi-primary, and if urban residents who move out to the suburbs do not undergo any significant changes in behavior, it would be fair to argue that the differences in ways of life between the two types of settlements have been over-estimated. Yet the fact remains that a variety of physical and demographic differences exist between the city and the suburb. However, upon closer examination, many of these differences turn out to be either spurious or of little significance for the way of life of the inhabitants (34).[14]

The differences between the residential areas of cities and suburbs which have been cited most frequently are:

1. Suburbs are more likely to be dormitories.
2. They are further away from the work and play facilities of the central business districts.
3. They are newer and more modern than city residential areas and are designed for the automobile rather than for pedestrian and mass-transit forms of movement.
4. They are built up with single-family rather than multi-family structures and are therefore less dense.
5. Their populations are more homogeneous.
6. Their populations differ demographically: they are younger; more of them are married; they have higher incomes; and they hold proportionately more white collar jobs (8, p. 131).

Most urban neighborhoods are as much dormitories as the suburbs. Only in a few older inner city areas are factories and offices still located in the middle of residential blocks, and even here many of the employees do not live in the neighborhood.

The fact that the suburbs are farther from the central business district is often true only in terms of distance, not travel time. Moreover, most people make relatively little use of downtown facilities, other than workplaces (12, 21). The downtown stores seem to hold their greatest attraction for the upper-middle class (21, pp. 91-92); the same is prob-ably true of typically urban entertainment facilities. Teen-agers and young adults may take their dates to first-run movie theaters, but the museums, concert halls, and lecture rooms attract mainly upper-middle-class ticket-buyers, many of them suburban.[15]

The suburban reliance on the train and the automobile has given rise to an imaginative folklore about the consequences of commuting on alcohol consumption, sex life, and parental duties. Many of these conclusions are, however, drawn from selected high-income suburbs and exurbs, and reflect job tensions in such hectic occupations as advertising and show business more than the effects of residence (29). It is true that the upper-middle-class housewife must become a chauffeur in order to expose her children to the proper educational facilities, but such differences as walking to the corner drug store and driving to its suburban equivalent seem to me of little emotional, social, or cultural import.[16] In addition, the continuing shrinkage in the number of mass-transit users suggests that even in the city many younger people are now living a wholly auto-based way of life.

The fact that suburbs are smaller is primarily a function of political boundaries drawn long before the communities were suburban. This affects the kinds of political issues which develop and provides somewhat greater opportunity for citizen participation. Even so, in the suburbs as in the city, the minority who participate are the professional politicians, the economically concerned businessmen, lawyers and salesmen, and the ideologically motivated middle- and upper-middle-class people with better than average education.

The social consequences of differences in density and house type also seem overrated. Single-family houses on quiet streets facilitate the supervision of children; this is one reason why middle-class women who want to keep an eye on their children move to the suburbs. House type also has some effects on relationships between neighbors, insofar as there are more opportunities for visual contact between adjacent home-owners than between people on different floors of an apartment house. However, if occupants' characteristics are also held constant, the differences in actual social contact are less marked. Homogeneity of residents turns out to be more important as a determinant of sociability than proximity. If the population is heterogeneous, there is little social contact between neighbors, either on apartment-house floors or in single-family-house blocks; if people are homogeneous, there is likely to be considerable social contact in both house types. One need only contrast the apartment house located in a transient, heterogeneous neighborhood and exactly the same structure in a neighborhood occupied by a single ethnic group. The former is a lonely, anonymous building; the latter, a bustling microsociety. I have observed similar patterns in suburban areas: on blocks where people are homogeneous, they socialize; where they are heterogeneous, they do little more than exchange polite greetings (16).

Suburbs are usually described as being more homogeneous in house type than the city, but if they are compared to the outer city, the differences are small. Most inhabitants of the outer city, other than well-to-do homeowners, live on blocks of uniform structures as well —for example, the endless streets of rowhouses in Philadelphia and Balti-

more or of two-story duplexes and six-flat apartment houses in Chicago. They differ from the new suburbs only in that they were erected through more primitive methods of mass production. Suburbs are of course more predominantly areas of owner-occupied single homes, though in the outer districts of most American cities homeownership is also extremely high.

Demographically, suburbs as a whole are clearly more homogeneous than cities as a whole, though probably not more so than outer cities. However, people do not live in cities or suburbs as a whole, but in specific neighborhoods. An analysis of ways of life would require a determination of the degree of population homogeneity within the boundaries of areas defined as neighborhoods by resident's social contacts. Such an analysis would no doubt indicate that many neighborhoods in the city as well as the suburbs are homogeneous. Neighborhood homogeneity is actually a result of factors having little or nothing to do with the house type, density, or location of the area relative to the city limits. Brand new neighborhoods are more homogeneous than older ones, because they have not yet experienced resident turnover, which frequently results in population heterogeneity. Neighborhoods of low- and medium-priced housing are usually less homogeneous than those with expensive dwellings because they attract families who have reached the peak of occupational and residential mobility, as well as young families who are just starting their climb and will eventually move to neighborhoods of higher status. The latter, being accessible only to high-income people, are therefore more homogeneous with respect to other resident characteristics as well. Moreover, such areas have the economic and political power to slow down or prevent invasion. Finally, neighborhoods located in the path of ethnic or religious group movement are likely to be extremely homogeneous.

The demographic differences between cities and suburbs cannot be questioned, especially since the suburbs have attracted a large number of middle-class child-rearing families. The differences are, however, much reduced if suburbs are compared only to the outer city. In addition, a detailed comparison of suburban and outer city residential areas would show that neighborhoods with the same kinds of people can be found in the city as well as the suburbs. Once again, the age of the area and the cost of housing are more important determinants of demographic characteristics than the location of the area with respect to the city limits.

Characteristics, Social Organization, and Ecology

The preceding sections of the paper may be summarized in three propositions:

1. As concerns ways of life, the inner city must be distinguished from the outer city and the suburbs; and the latter two exhibit a way of life bearing little resemblance to Wirth's urbanism.
2. Even in the inner city, ways of life resemble Wirth's description only to a limited extent. Moreover, economic condition, cultural characteristics, life-cycle stage, and residential instability explain ways of life more satisfactorily than number, density, or heterogeneity.
3. Physical and other differences between city and suburb are often spurious or without much meaning for ways of life.

These propositions suggest that the concepts urban and suburban are

neither mutually exclusive, nor especially relevant for understanding ways of life. They—and number, density, and heterogeneity as well—are ecological concepts which describe human adaptation to the environment. However, they are not sufficient to explain social phenomena, because these phenomena cannot be understood solely as the consequences of ecological processes. Therefore, other explanations must be considered.

Ecological explanations of social life are most applicable if the subjects under study lack the ability to *make choices*, be they plants, animals, or human beings. Thus, if there is a housing shortage, people will live almost anywhere, and under extreme conditions of no choice, as in a disaster, married and single, old and young, middle and working class, stable and transient will be found side by side in whatever accommodations are available. At that time, their ways of life represent an almost direct adaptation to the environment. If the supply of housing and of neighborhoods is such that alternatives are available, however, people will make choices, and if the housing market is responsive, they can even make and satisfy explicit *demands*.

Choices and demands do not develop independently or at random; they are functions of the roles people play in the social system. These can best be understood in terms of the *characteristics* of the people involved; that is, characteristics can be used as indices to choices and demands made in the roles that constitute ways of life. Although many characteristics affect the choices and demands people make with respect to housing and neighborhoods, the most important ones seem to be *class*—in all its economic, social and cultural ramifications—and *life-cycle stage*.[17] If people have an opportunity to choose, these two characteristics will go far in explaining the kinds of housing and neighborhoods they will occupy and the ways of life they will try to establish within them.

Many of the previous assertions about ways of life in cities and suburbs can be analyzed in terms of class and life-cycle characteristics. Thus, in the inner city, the unmarried and childless live as they do, detached from neighborhood, because of their life-cycle stage; the cosmopolites, because of a combination of life-cycle stage and a distinctive but class-based subculture. The way of life of the deprived and trapped can be explained by low socio-economic level and related handicaps. The quasi-primary way of life is associated with the family stage of the life-cycle, and the norms of child-rearing and parental role found in the upper working class, the lower-middle class, and the non-cosmopolite portions of the upper-middle and upper classes.

The attributes of the so-called suburban way of life can also be understood largely in terms of these characteristics. The new suburbia is nothing more than a highly visible showcase for the ways of life of young, upper-working-class and lower-middle-class people. Ktsanes and Reissman have aptly described it as "new homes for old values." (22) Much of the descriptive and critical writing about suburbia assumes that as long as the new suburbanites lived in the city, they behaved like upper-middle-class cosmopolites and that suburban living has mysteriously transformed them (7; 14, pp. 154-162; 25; 36). The critics fail to see that the behavior and personality patterns ascribed to suburbia are in reality those of class

and age (6). These patterns could have been found among the new suburbanites when they still lived in the city and could now be observed among their peers who still reside there—if the latter were as visible to critics and researchers as are the suburbanites.

Needless to say, the concept of "characteristics" cannot explain all aspects of ways of life, either among urban or suburban residents. Some aspects must be explained by concepts of social organization that are independent of characteristics. For example, some features of the quasi-primary way of life are independent of class and age, because they evolve from the roles and situations created by joint and adjacent occupancy of land and dwellings. Likewise, residential instability is a universal process which has a number of invariate consequences. In each case, however, the way in which people react varies with their characteristics. So it is with ecological processes. Thus, there are undoubtedly differences between ways of life in urban and suburban settlements which remain after behavior patterns based on residents' characteristics have been analyzed, and which must therefore be attributed to features of the settlement (11).

Characteristics do not explain the causes of behavior; rather, they are clues to socially created and culturally defined roles, choices, and demands. A causal analysis must trace them back to the larger social, economic, and political systems which determine the situations in which roles are played and the cultural content of choices and demands, as well as the opportunities for their achievement.[18] These systems determine income distributions, educational and occupational opportunities, and in turn, fertility patterns, child-rearing methods, as well as the entire range of consumer behavior. Thus, a complete analysis of the way of life of the deprived residents of the inner city cannot stop by indicating the influence of low income, lack of education, or family instability. These must be related to such conditions as the urban economy's "need" for low-wage workers, and the housing market practices which restrict residential choice. The urban economy is in turn shaped by national economic and social systems, as well as by local and regional ecological processes. Some phenomena can be explained exclusively by reference to these ecological processes. However, it must also be recognized that as man gains greater control over the natural environment, he has been able to free himself from many of the determining and limiting effects of that environment. Thus, changes in local transportation technology, the ability of industries to be footloose, and the relative affluence of American society have given ever larger numbers of people increasing amounts of residential choice. The greater the amount of choice available, the more important does the concept of characteristics become in understanding behavior.

Consequently, the study of ways of life in communities must begin with an analysis of characteristics. If characteristics are dealt with first and held constant, we may be able to discover which behavior patterns can be attributed to features of the settlement and its natural environment.[19] Only then will it be possible to discover to what extent city and suburb are independent—rather than dependent or intervening—variables in the explanation of ways of life.

This kind of analysis might help to reconcile the ecological point of view with the behavioral and cultural one, and possibly put an end to the conflict between conceptual positions which insist on one explanation or the other (9). Both explanations have some relevance, and future research and theory must clarify the role of each in the analysis of ways of life in various types of settlement (6, p. xxii). Another important rationale for this approach is its usefulness for applied sociology—for example, city planning. The planner can recommend changes in the spatial and physical arrangements of the city. Frequently, he seeks to achieve social goals or to change social conditions through physical solutions. He has been attracted to ecological explanations because these relate behavior to phenomena which he can affect. For example, most planners tend to agree with Wirth's formulations, because they stress number and density, over which the planner has some control. If the undesirable social conditions of the inner city could be traced to these two factors, the planner could propose large-scale clearance projects which would reduce the size of the urban population, and lower residential densities. Experience with public housing projects has, however, made it apparent that low densities, new buildings, or modern site plans do not eliminate anti-social or self-destructive behavior. The analysis of characteristics will call attention to the fact that this behavior is lodged in the deprivations of low socio-economic status and racial discrimination, and that it can be changed only through the removal of these deprivations. Conversely, if such an analysis suggests residues of behavior that can be attributed to ecological processes or physical aspects of housing and neighborhoods, the planner can recommend physical changes that can really affect behavior.

A RE-EVALUATION OF DEFINITIONS

The argument presented here has implications for the sociological definition of the city. Such a definition relates ways of life to environmental features of the city qua settlement type. But if ways of life do not coincide with settlement types, and if these ways are functions of class and life-cycle stage rather than of the ecological attributes of the settlement, a sociological definition of the city cannot be formulated.[20] Concepts such as city and suburb allow us to distinguish settlement types from each other physically and demographically, but the ecological processes and conditions which they synthesize have no direct or invariate consequences for ways of life. The sociologist cannot, therefore, speak of an urban or suburban way of life.

CONCLUSION

Many of the descriptive statements made here are as time-bound as Wirth's.[21] Twenty years ago, Wirth concluded that some form of urbanism would eventually predominate in all settlement types. He was, however, writing during a time of immigrant acculturation and at the end of a serious depression, an era of minimal choice. Today, it is apparent that high-density, heterogeneous surroundings are for most people a temporary place of residence; other than for the Park Avenue or Greenwich Village cosmopolites, they are a result of necessity rather than choice. As soon as they can afford to do so, most Americans head for the single-family house and the quasi-primary way of life of the low-density neighborhood, in the outer city or the suburbs.[22]

Changes in the national economy and in government housing policy can affect many of the variables that make up housing supply and demand. For example, urban sprawl may eventually outdistance the ability of present and proposed transportation systems to move workers into the city; further industrial decentralization can forestall it and alter the entire relationship between work and residence. The expansion of present urban renewal activities can perhaps lure a significant number of cosmopolites back from the suburbs, while a drastic change in renewal policy might begin to ameliorate the housing conditions of the deprived population. A serious depression could once again make America a nation of doubled-up tenants.

These events will affect housing supply and residential choice; they will frustrate but not suppress demands for the quasi-primary way of life. However, changes in the national economy, society, and culture can affect people's characteristics—family size, educational level, and various other concomitants of life-cycle stage and class. These in turn will stimulate changes in demands and choices. The rising number of college graduates, for example, is likely to increase the cosmopolite ranks. This might in turn create a new set of city dwellers, although it will probably do no more than encourage the development of cosmopolite facilities in some suburban areas.

The current revival of interest in urban sociology and in community studies, as well as the sociologist's increasing curiosity about city planning, suggest that data may soon be available to formulate a more adequate theory of the relationship between settlements and the ways of life within them. The speculations presented in this paper are intended to raise questions; they can only be answered by more systematic data collection and theorizing.

REFERENCES

1. Axelrod, Morris. "Urban Structure and Social Participation," *American Sociological Review,* Vol. 21 (February 1956), pp. 13–18.
2. Bell, Wendell. "Social Choice, Life Styles and Suburban Residence," in William M. Dobriner (ed.), *The Suburban Community.* New York: G. P. Putnam's Sons, 1958, pp. 225–247.
3. Bell, Wendell, and Maryanne T. Force. "Urban Neighborhood Types and Participation in Formal Associations," *American Sociological Review,* Vol. 21 (February 1956), pp. 25–34.
4. Berger, Bennett. *Working Class Suburb: A Study of Auto Workers in Suburbia.* Berkeley, Calif.: University of California Press, 1960.
5. Dewey, Richard. "The Rural–Urban Continuum: Real but Relatively Unimportant," *American Journal of Sociology,* Vol. 66 (July 1960), pp. 60–66.
6. Dobriner, William M. "Introduction: Theory and Research in the Sociology of the Suburbs," in William M. Dobriner (ed.), *The Suburban Community.* New York: G. P. Putnam's Sons, 1958, pp. xiii–xxviii.
7. Duhl, Leonard J. "Mental Health and Community Planning," in *Planning 1955.* Chicago: American Society of Planning Officials, 1956, pp. 31–39.
8. Duncan, Otis Dudley, and Albert J. Reiss, Jr. *Social Characteristics of Rural and Urban Communities, 1950.* New York: John Wiley & Sons, 1956.
9. Duncan, Otis Dudley, and Leo F. Schnore. "Cultural, Behavioral and Ecological Perspectives in the Study of Social Organization," *American Journal of Sociology,* Vol. 65 (September 1959), pp. 132–155.
10. Enders, John. *Profile of the Theater Market.* New York: Playbill, undated and unpaged.
11. Fava, Sylvia Fleis. "Contrasts in Neighboring: New York City and a Suburban Community," in William M. Dobriner (ed.), *The Suburban Community.* New

York: G. P. Putnam's Sons, 1958, pp. 122–131.
12. Foley, Donald L. "The Use of Local Facilities in a Metropolis," in Paul Hatt and Albert J. Reiss, Jr. (eds.), *Cities and Society.* Glencoe, Ill.: The Free Press, 1957, pp. 237–247.
13. Form, William H., *et al.* "The Compatibility of Alternative Approaches to the Delimitation of Urban Sub-areas," *American Sociological Review,* Vol. 19 (August 1954), pp. 434–440.
14. Fromm, Erich. *The Sane Society.* New York: Rinehart & Co., Inc., 1955.
15. Gans, Herbert J. *The Urban Villagers: A Study of the Second Generation Italians in the West End of Boston.* Boston: Center for Community Studies, December 1959 (mimeographed).
16. Gans, Herbert J. "Planning and Social Life: An Evaluation of Friendship and Neighbor Relations in Suburban Communities," *Journal of the American Institute of Planners,* Vol. 27 (May 1961), pp. 134–140.
17. Greer, Scott. "Urbanism Reconsidered: A Comparative Study of Local Areas in a Metropolis," *American Sociological Review,* Vol. 21 (February 1956), pp. 19–25.
18. Greer, Scott. "The Social Structure and Political Process of Suburbia," *American Sociological Review,* Vol. 25 (August 1960), pp. 514–526.
19. Greer, Scott, and Ella Kube. "Urbanism and Social Structure: A Los Angeles Study," in Marvin B. Sussman (ed.), *Community Structure and Analysis.* New York: Thomas Y. Crowell Company, 1959, pp. 93–112.
20. Janowitz, Morris. *The Community Press in an Urban Setting.* Glencoe, Ill.: The Free Press, 1952.
21. Jonassen, Christen T. *The Shopping Center Versus Downtown.* Columbus, Ohio: Bureau of Business Research, Ohio State University, 1955.
22. Ktsanes, Thomas, and Leonard Reissmann. "Suburbia: New Homes for Old Values," *Social Problems,* Vol. 7 (Winter 1959–60), pp. 187–194.
23. Reiss, Albert J., Jr. "An Analysis of Urban Phenomena," in Robert M. Fisher (ed.), *The Metropolis in Modern Life.* Garden City, N.Y.: Doubleday & Company, Inc., 1955, pp. 41–49.
24. Reiss, Albert J., Jr. "Rural–Urban and

Status Differences in Interpersonal Contacts," *American Journal of Sociology*, Vol. 65 (September 1959), pp. 182–195.

25. Riesman, David. "The Suburban Sadness," in William M. Dobriner (ed.), *The Suburban Community*. New York: G. P. Putnam's Sons, 1958, pp. 375–408.

26. Rose, Arnold M. "Living Arrangements of Unattached Persons," *American Sociological Review*, Vol. 12 (August 1947), pp. 429–435.

27. Seeley, John R. "The Slum: Its Nature, Use and Users," *Journal of the American Institute of Planners*, Vol. 25 (February 1959), pp. 7–14.

28. Smith, Joel, William Form, and Gregory Stone. "Local Intimacy in a Middle-Sized City," *American Journal of Sociology*, Vol. 60 (November 1954), pp. 276–284.

29. Spectorsky, A. C. *The Exurbanites*. Philadelphia: J. B. Lippincott Co., 1955.

30. Stone, Gregory P. "City Shoppers and Urban Identification: Observations on the Social Psychology of City Life," *American Journal of Sociology*, Vol. 60 (July 1954), pp. 36–45.

31. Strauss, Anselm. "The Changing Imagery of American City and Suburb," *Sociological Quarterly*, Vol. 1 (January 1960), pp. 15–24.

32. Vernon, Raymond. *The Changing Economic Function of the Central City*. New York: Committee on Economic Development, Supplementary Paper No. 1, January 1959.

33. Vidich, Arthur J., and Joseph Bensman. *Small Town in Mass Society: Class, Power and Religion in a Rural Community*. Princeton, N.J.: Princeton University Press, 1958.

34. Wattell, Harold. "Levittown: A Suburban Community," in William M. Dobriner (ed.), *The Suburban Community*. New York: G. P. Putnam's Sons, 1958, pp. 287–313.

35. Whyte, William F., Jr. *Street Corner Society*. Chicago: The University of Chicago Press, 1955.

36. Whyte, William F., Jr. *The Organization Man*. New York: Simon & Schuster, 1956.

37. Wilensky, Harold L. "Life Cycle, Work, Situation and Participation in Formal Associations," in Robert W. Kleemeier, et al. (eds.), *Aging and Leisure: Research Perspectives on the Meaningful Use of Time*. New York: Oxford University Press, 1961, Chapter 8.

38. Wilensky, Harold L., and Charles Lebeaux. *Industrial Society and Social Welfare*. New York: Russell Sage Foundation, 1958.

39. Wirth, Louis. *The Ghetto*. Chicago: The University of Chicago Press, 1928.

40. Wirth, Louis. "Urbanism as a Way of Life," *American Journal of Sociology*, Vol. 44 (July 1938), pp. 1–24. Reprinted in Paul Hatt and Albert J. Reiss, Jr. (eds.), *Cities and Society*. Glencoe, Ill.: The Free Press, 1957, pp. 46–64. [All page references are to this reprinting of the article.]

41. Young, Michael, and Peter Willmott. *Family and Kinship in East London*. London: Routledge & Kegan Paul, Ltd., 1957.

NOTES

° I am indebted to Richard Dewey, John Dyckman, David Riesman, Melvin Webber, and Harold Wilensky for helpful comments on earlier drafts of this essay.

1. I shall not attempt to summarize these studies, for this task has already been performed by Dewey (5), Reiss (23), Wilensky (38), and others.

2. By the *inner city*, I mean the transient residential areas, the Gold Coasts and the slums that generally surround the central business district, although in some communities they may continue for miles beyond that district. The *outer city* includes the stable residential areas that house the working- and middle-class tenant and owner. The *suburbs* I conceive as the latest and most modern ring of the outer city, distinguished from it only by yet lower densities, and by the often irrelevant fact of the ring's location outside the city limits.

3. The trapped are not very visible, but I suspect that they are a significant element in what Raymond Vernon has described as the "gray areas" of the city (32).

4. If the melting pot has resulted from propinquity and high density, one would have expected second-generation Italians, Irish, Jews, Greeks, Slavs, etc. to have developed a single "pan-ethnic culture," consisting of a synthesis of the cultural patterns of the propinquitous national groups.

5. The corporation transients (36, 38), who provide a new source of residential instability to the suburb, differ from city transients. Since they are raising families, they want to integrate themselves into neighborhood life, and are usually able to do so, mainly because they tend to move into similar types of communities wherever they go.

6. The negative social consequences of overcrowding are a result of high room and floor density, not of the land coverage of population density which Wirth discussed. Park Avenue resi-

dents live under conditions of high land density, but do not seem to suffer visibly from overcrowding.

7. Whether or not these social phenomena have the psychological consequences Wirth suggested depends on the people who live in the area. Those who are detached from the neighborhood by choice are probably immune, but those who depend on the neighborhood for their social relationships—the unattached individuals, for example—may suffer greatly from loneliness.

8. Needless to say, residential instability must ultimately be traced back to the fact that, as Wirth pointed out, the city and its economy attract transient—and, depending on the sources of outmigration, heterogeneous—people. However, this is a characteristic of urban-industrial society, not of the city specifically.

9. By neighborhoods or residential districts I mean areas demarcated from others by distinctive physical boundaries or by social characteristics, some of which may be perceived only by the residents. However, these areas are not necessarily socially self-sufficient or culturally distinctive.

10. For the definition of *outer city,* see Footnote 2.

11. Because neighborly relations are not quite primary, and not quite secondary, they can also become *pseudo-primary;* that is, secondary ones disguised with false affect to make them appear primary. Critics have often described suburban life in this fashion, although the actual prevalence of pseudo-primary relationships has not been studied systematically in cities or suburbs.

12. These neighborhoods cannot, however, be considered as urban folk societies. People go out of the area for many of their friendships, and their allegiance to the neighborhood is neither intense not all-encompassing. Janowitz has aptly described the relationship between resident and neighborhood as one of "limited liability." (20, Chapter 7)

13. Were I not arguing that ecological concepts cannot double as sociological ones, this way of life might best be described as small-townish.

14. They may, of course, be significant for the welfare of the total metropolitan area.

15. A 1958 study of New York theater goers showed a median income of close to $10,000 and 35 per cent were reported as living in the suburbs (10).

16. I am thinking here of adults; teen-agers do suffer from the lack of informal meeting places within walking or bicycling distance.

17. These must be defined in dynamic terms. Thus, class includes also the process of social mobility, stage in the life-cycle, and the processes of socialization and aging.

18. This formulation may answer some of Duncan and Schnore's objections to socio-psychological and cultural explanations of community ways of life (9).

19. The ecologically oriented researchers who developed the Shevsky-Bell social area analysis scale have worked on the assumption that "social differences between the populations of urban neighborhoods can conveniently be summarized into differences of economic level, family characteristics and ethnicity." (3, p. 26) However, they have equated "urbanization" with a concept of life-cycle stage by using family characteristics to define the index of urbanization (3, 18, 19). In fact, Bell has identified suburbanism with familism (2).

20. Because of the distinctiveness of the ways of life found in the inner city, some writers propose definitions that refer only to these ways, ignoring those found in the outer city. For example, popular writers sometimes identify "urban" with "urbanity," i.e., "cosmopolitanism." However, such a definition ignores the other ways of life found in the inner city. Moreover, I have tried to show that these ways have few common elements, and that the ecological features of the inner city have little or no influence in shaping them.

21. Even more than Wirth's they are based on data and impressions gathered in the large Eastern and Midwestern cities of the United States.

22. Personal discussions with European planners and sociologists suggest that many European apartment dwellers have similar preferences, although economic conditions, high building costs, and the scarcity of land make it impossible for them to achieve their desires.

The End of the Line:
Race and Poverty in Cities

Jeanne Lowe

Traditionally, Americans have regarded city slums as primarily a physical problem. The federal slum clearance legislation has been written in those terms. Largely because money to get rid of urban slums was available in such programs, cities tried to eliminate their slum areas by tearing down the buildings.

During the 1950's, however, while starting to use the new government instruments of urban redevelopment and renewal, local public officials began to discover that slum elimination entailed much more than the removal of deteriorated housing and hardware—or even the substitution of low-rent dwellings. Still, most failed to acknowledge the problems that cause people to live in slums.

By the early 1960's, the changing racial-social-economic composition of central cities had magnified and vastly complicated the traditional human problems of the slums, especially in the context of a generally prospering nation. A growing portion of the city population was unable to provide for itself, and the urban community was unable or unwilling to afford that portion adequate homes and jobs in the face of changing technology and racial discrimination. Depression-born welfare and housing programs were overwhelmed; cities' fiscal resources were depleted. Northern equal-rights laws, as well as

U.S. Supreme Court decisions, became empty promises as *de facto* segregation increased in core cities that were being strangled by the suburban middle-class white noose. Meanwhile, some renewal programs, caught in the crosscurrents of minority outcries of inequity and discrimination, civil rights demonstrations, the white backlash, and some apparently irreconcilable social issues, ground to a halt or radically changed direction.

The 1960 census exposed the facts about cities' changing composition. The older core cities in the North and northern central areas had lost population during the past decade, while suburbs grew. The drop varied from a little over one per cent in New York and Baltimore to 4.5 per cent in San Francisco and 10.7 per cent in Pittsburgh. The full extent of the loss was disguised, however, by the number of "new urbanites." The twelve largest cities experienced a combined net decrease in their white population of 2,000,000, but they gained 1,800,000 non-whites. Medium-size cities, too—Rochester, Fort Wayne, San Diego—which had had few Negroes before World War II, saw their Negro populations double even as their total populations dropped. Washington D.C. became the first of America's twenty-five big cities to have a Negro majority. By the 1960's, almost as many Negroes were living in northern, borderline and western cities as in the South, and 73

From Jeanne Lowe, *Cities in a Race with Time* (New York: Random House, 1967), pp. 278-310. Copyright © 1967, by Jeanne Lowe. Reprinted by permission of Random House, Inc. Jeanne Lowe is a writer and consultant on urban affairs.

per cent of all Negroes in the country lived in cities, as compared to 73 per cent on the land only half a century before.

THE WELFARE CITY

While central cities' populations fell, their budgets continued to grow, and to grow at a much faster rate than the general rise in the cost of living or the national increase in state and local spending or revenues. In the biggest cities the disproportion was worst of all.

The largest increases in expenses were for public assistance, hospitals and health services and police. More than one third of the increase in New York City's budget from $3,000,000,000 to $4,500,000,000 in the five years from 1960-61 to 1965-66 was accounted for by these three items.[1] Health and hospitals expenditures were up 72 per cent, to $337,920,221—and one third of the city's population, over 2,500,000, qualified for a projected free health-care program on the basis of their "moderate low income" in 1966. The Police Department accounted for another $364,-120,276 in the 1965-66 budget, an increase of some $141,000,000 in the past five years; but it still lacked sufficient staff to deal with growing crime. The Welfare Department's requested allocation for 1966-67 was nearly two thirds of a billion dollars, $129,000,000, over that of the previous fiscal year.

These swelling costs were directly related to the changing population composition of central cities: more relatively young low-income families reproducing more rapidly than other metropolitan core residents; more elderly and disabled people; and the striking increase in non-white and other previously rural residents. But the latter group alone re-

ceived welfare outlays far out of proportion to their percentage. In New York, where Negroes comprise only 14 per cent of the city, they accounted for 45 per cent of those on welfare. Puerto Ricans, forming 8 per cent of the population, represented 30 per cent of the welfare load. The same pattern was repeated in other cities in the early 1960's.

The single biggest growth item in public welfare was Aid to Dependent Children—ADC. (Of the 600,000 persons to be aided by the New York Welfare Department in 1966, well over half were children under eighteen.) Particularly striking—and headline making—was the proportion of illegitimate children receiving such public assistance. In Washington D.C., where ADC accounted for 71 per cent of the entire welfare caseload, 40 per cent of the children were born out of wedlock.

Unfortunately, such statistics on mushrooming welfare costs, when brought to public attention by the press and public officials, provoked outcries against alleged abuses, demagoguery, and pressures for residency requirements and quick cures. The city manager of Newburgh, New York became a national figure (a hero to some) in the summer of 1961 with his sweeping plan for taking "bums" and "chiselers" off relief, which accounted for 12 per cent of his city's budget. Louis J. Lefkowitz, Republican candidate for Mayor of New York City that fall, proclaimed that if elected he would remove from public welfare the "wastrels" and "chiselers." National magazines ran apparently well-researched exposés of welfare abuses. The journalistic stereotype was the shiftless mother who had child after child at the public's expense to increase her relief payments rather than go to work.

The flight to the suburbs of middle-

and upper-income taxpayers was directly attributed to their having to pay these mounting city expenses. These fleeing city dwellers did not realize that a third of welfare costs are borne by the state government and another third or more by the federal government. One can run—but not far.

GETTING DOWN TO CASES

Why the enormously disproportionate growth in welfare and aid to dependent children? The Board of Commissioners of Cook County, Illinois, which pays Chicago's welfare bills, was so alarmed by the skyrocketing of ADC costs during the 1950's—up from $1,400,000 to $4,400,000—that in 1960 it appointed a thirty-five-member committee of specialists, civic leaders, businessmen and educators to investigate. The committee, in turn, retained the New York firm of Greenleigh Associates Inc., nationally known consultants to health and welfare organizations. Their year-long study was the most extensive and thorough ever made of a local public welfare program in the United States.

It is interesting that the publication of the findings attracted so little national attention compared to the alleged welfare abuses. Perhaps the report, as its title *Facts, Fallacies and Future* suggests, challenged many of the popular and comforting notions about who is on ADC and why. Indeed, no more than 3 per cent in the sample of 1,000 interviewed fit the popular stereotype. Nor did the report offer any panaceas.

The typical ADC mother in Chicago was a native of Missisippi, a Negro, in her thirties. She had been in Chicago fifteen years and had three children under fifteen, all born in Illinois. Her husband had lost his job as an unskilled laborer and had deserted her.[2] She had had an illegitimate child since. She had waited an average of a year and four months after that before applying for ADC. Generally, she was not free to remarry, but if she was, the new husband was unable to support the child. This was her first time on ADC; she stayed on the rolls less than three years; she did not want to have more children to boost her allotment. (In fact, it only allowed twenty-one cents per meal per person.)

Most women were found to feel great guilt and resentment about having an illegitimate child, but many did not know how to prevent conception. Almost all were anxious to be self-sustaining and to return to work. However, most had no marketable skill, and many could not leave home because their children were too young to go to school.

Moreover, that illegitimacy accounted for 50 per cent of ADC was found to reflect the general growing rate of illegitimacy in Cook County. But, as the report pointed out, of the illegitimate children who were adopted—and thus who did not go on ADC—almost 98.5 per cent were white and only 1.5 per cent Negro.

In 1962 Congress amended the Social Security Act largely on the basis of some proposals in the Greenleigh Report. It provided greater federal aid for rehabilitative and preventive services for adult recipients of ADC, including financing of day-care centers for children of working mothers, more counseling and reduced workloads for caseworkers; it gave aid for an unemployed second parent to keep families together and to encourage use of parents' earnings for their children's education (books, bus fares, shoes, etc.) without cutting their relief check.

But the Social Security Act, by its nature, is supportive and could not get at the basic root of dependency found by the Greenleigh study—"the marginal level of the families" before they applied for ADC, and a history of marginal subsistence, the end product of the social and economic effects of racial discrimination.

THE GHETTO DWELLERS

No doubt the welfare programs born in the depression dramatized certain traditional predicaments of any city newcomers' situation. The period of adjustment to complex urban life is a tension-fraught, often traumatic experience for almost all migrants, white or non-white, European, Asian, Appalachian-American, Puerto Rican or Mexican. Slum living, poverty, lack of marketable skills, low-level employment and frequent unemployment, high rates of reproduction, juvenile crime, family disorganization, ghettoization (self-imposed and socially reinforced), poor housekeeping—these have generally accompanied the first stages of life in cities, especially for rural newcomers, who comprise the majority of immigrants. But in the days of the last big urban influx, our government did not assume the burden for these problems; nor had it decided that slums were opposed to the public welfare.

Furthermore, one cannot overemphasize the special situation of the newly urban American Negro—who comprises the largest group of immigrants. He brings to the city extra-heavy baggage. He has not only the "badge of color" but also the ingrained burden of generations of cultural and economic deprivation. His move to the city makes painfully and inescapably apparent the effects of dependency and weak family organization which had their origins in slavery but were perpetuated after Reconstruction by the southern plantation system. This is the system that has shaped the mass of the "new urbanites," the people who comprise 20, 30, even 60 per cent of central cities' populations and who, during the 1970's, may be expected to increase their present number by 50 to 100 per cent.

The plantation system offered the Negro no experience with money, no incentive to save, no conception of time or progress—none of the basic experiences to prepare him for the urban money economy. Instead, it indoctrinated him to believe in his own inferiority, to be resigned, while it held him in a folk culture dominated by a spiritual, other-worldly, escapist outlook—in what sociologist E. Franklin Frazier called "the twilight of civilization."

Illegitimacy and the female-dominated household are not Negro traits. (Indeed, family instability is a characteristic by-product of male unemployment and poverty.) In the Negro's case, these traits were developed as a result of white southern culture and slavery, which deprived the Negro family of a legal base, and were perpetuated by the post-Civil War plantation system which kept the Negro male subservient, uneducated and economically insecure, usually out in the field or wandering the country looking for work, away from his family. Consequently his children were deprived of male authority and stable family life. But for the Negro man, who had almost no material possessions (he was always a tenant), his offspring were virtually the only tangible proof of his manhood, and the woman who would have him must accept this. Illegitimate children and their mothers were not rejected; instead, they were accommodated by the mothers, grandmothers and aunts who composed many lower-class southern Negro households.

But the city does not offer the mass of poor Negroes much opportunity to demonstrate the difference between what is racially and what is culturally or environmentally induced. City life tends to shatter the fragile structure of the lower-class Negro's family life and to accentuate, through differential employment opportunities, female dominance and masculine subordination. It also exposes the youngster, whose mother is probably out at work and whose father is either out of work, busy at two jobs or missing, to the worst influences of the slum.

These latest newcomers find few of the strengths of group pride in ethnic origin or the institutional supports that fortified the European immigrants. Not even the simple official process of "Americanization" which in five years is supposed to turn the foreigner into a citizen is available. The Negro's movement from one part of the country to another fails to supply that "shock of separation" which, as Oscar Handlin has written, precipitated the creation of new community organizations in cities by earlier immigrant groups. The individualized welfare services of the old city political machine have been preempted by impersonal government agencies, and the machine's municipal jobs for the faithful unskilled have been largely eliminated by civil service requirements or trade union restrictions. The politician does not even offer the traditional outings to the country; too often the Negro's political representative wants to keep his constituency as is.

The underworld, also, has a vested interest in preserving the minority ghetto and its hopelessness. To the despondent resident the criminal world offers "the poor man's democracy"— the chance of winning money in the numbers game. It also vends narcotics, an expensive, momentary retreat from despair, a lifetime hook that causes men to steal or kill for more and makes city streets unsafe.

The criminal world once afforded the uneducated youthful deviants in the ethnic slum illegitimate avenues to material success, but these paths are largely closed today. Crime has become as highly organized, remote and specialized as the rest of American life. Its numbers parlors are, as Richard Cloward and Lloyd Ohlin expressed it in *Delinquency and Opportunity*, like the local branch stores of a supermarket chain. The criminal hierarchy does not even provide the invisible discipline that used to hold many slum youths in line. Nor does it supply the cash that helped immigrants of earlier generations become entrepreneurs.

Even settlement houses commonly find themselves located in areas of lesser need today, because the residents whom they once served have moved away; or slum clearance and new development have altered the neighborhood. Meanwhile, vast new slum areas are neglected. Even so, settlement houses, like psychiatrically oriented social workers, are ineffective in trying to mitigate the society-induced traumas that infect the occupants of our cities' spreading black ghettos.

Meanwhile, a small group of "upper-class" Negroes, the supposed leaders and models, remain removed from and contemptuous of the masses (except for the many doctors, dentists, lawyers and businessmen who live in "golden ghettos" but enter the slum ghetto to make their living). And members of the growing middle class, who have worked their way out of the slum by dint of education and new job openings, are afraid of being dragged down by association with those still on the bottom. As the Greenleigh report noted, "upper-class Negroes are embarrassed and threatened by the public out-cry against ADC and low-income families."

This attitude, in turn, increases the alienation and frustration of the slum ghetto dweller. Speaking of the rioters at Watts in Los Angeles, a top-ranking Negro official of the federal Office of Economic Opportunity told an audience composed largely of middle-class Negroes, "Whitey isn't alone in being the object of their anger." Successful Negroes, he declared, should give the poor the benefit of their experience. But a highly placed Negro municipal employee in Los Angeles complained that he could not get other Negroes at City Hall to accompany him to the Watts area in order to persuade youngsters to get off the streets. "Why should I?" one rejoined. "I struggled for years to get out of there."

Why do middle- and upper-class Negroes fail to help their own? Primarily because the American reward system has failed to operate for them. Segregation and discrimination reinforce white stereotypes and have produced a Negro middle and upper class disproportionately small compared to the total number of Negroes, and poor compared to their white counterparts. Aside from the church, they lack the means to support their institutions. The Urban League, NAACP and CORE all rely heavily on white liberals' contributions.

His white peers have little opportunity through normal contacts and common interests to know a Negro as an individual. Practically his only civic association with white community leaders is on "interracial" committees concerned with integration or Negro rights. His isolation deprives him of the business and professional contacts and experience essential to advancing within the corporate and financial structure of American life. He does not have the extended clan that helped Europeans. Lacking entree into the American economic system, often denied credit, many Negro businessmen exploit the Negro mass as ruthlessly as do the whites. Like too many Negro doctors, lawyers, publishers and politicians, they have a vested interest in perpetuating the ghetto from which they make a living.

Ghettoization has consistently discouraged the development of a responsible elite. As Wilson wrote in *Negro Politics:* "Living in isolation from the city as a whole, . . . and desiring to differentiate himself from the [mass of disadvantaged Negroes], the middle- or upper-class Negro can see few rewards in civic leadership." Denied many of the rewards of upward mobility and the opportunity to play a serious role in American life, "the black bourgeoisie," as Frazier called them, escape into a "world of make believe," preoccupied with Negro "society" and conspicuous consumption (or else they try to earn still another Ph.D.). The Negro mass, though they may envy this elite, regards them not as models but as Uncle Toms, or as people who have been somehow "lucky in getting money"—as indeed most have been.

Who, then, is responsible for the newcomer, for easing his period of adjustment and helping him to advance?

During the late 1950's a new kind of municipal agency emerged in some cities. One of the first was Chicago's Committee on New Residents, appointed by Mayor Richard Daley as part of the city's Commission on Human Relations late in 1955 when the recent migrants' problems began to manifest themselves widely. The Committee published pamphlets and distributed thousands of simple illustrated brochures to acquaint the newcomers with the strange city and its facilities—its schools, parks, health clinics, adult educational opportunities, and even such rudimentary matters as how to use a telephone and shop at a supermarket. It organized housekeeping classes to show previously rural homemakers how to use gas stoves, incinerators and other urban novelties. It alerted other public and private agencies to the newcomers' special needs and set up field offices in "port of entry" neighborhoods.

The Committee's biggest job, however, was to find employment for the newcomers who supposedly had come in response to the siren call of industry in Chicago, traditionally a strong market for unskilled labor. The problem of finding work was twice as severe for non-white as for white newcomers.

But, as a top staff member of the Committee on New Residents commented in 1961, "In Chicago able-bodied men aren't allowed to go on relief. They assume that if you're able-bodied, you can find work. Yet there aren't jobs for the unskilled, and it's getting worse.

"In the last century, immigration was accompanied by a demand for cheap, unskilled labor. Today, you can't push a wheelbarrow or build a railroad across the country. In this highly skilled society, we can't afford to wait for the next generation. We either train them or they'll be a drag on Chicago."

One of the Committee's early acts, in 1956, had been to arrange with the city's Dunbar Vocational High School for job-training classes for newcomers. This endeavor was reported in 1959 by Ely M. Aron, chairman of the Committee, in testimony before the Board of Education calling for a larger budget.

"It seemed perfectly obvious that we only had to make known to these new residents the superb facilities . . . you had provided for trade and vocational training. Everyone—we thought—would line up to enroll in these classes, study diligently, and become a skilled worker in possibly two or three years. We sent out thousands of flyers, used every means of communication, and the result —nil.

"Now we know better. It took us a year to learn. . . . Before we can expect anyone to learn 'fine hand skills,' we must help him learn to read, understand directions, warning signals and machine dials. Today, we rejoice in the increased enrollment in the elementary school classes for adults. . . .

"It is very difficult," Aron stated, "if you're the sole head of the household, if you've moved a number of children from a rural area into a vastly complex city—it is difficult to admit that you can't read."[3]

THE BIG CHANGE

We used to have an acceptable rationalization for city slums. *Fortune* magazine, in a 1957 article on "The Enduring Slums," stated that they "are crowded because there are jobs to be had . . . sweepers at General Motors . . . scrap throwers at Inland Steel . . . handtruck pushers around New York's garment center." Slums were thus a sign of opportunity in cities, because newcomers are attracted to places of employment.

But these jobs have been disappearing. There is less and less heavy, unskilled and dirty work to be done—both in cities and on farms. During the 1950's, agricultural and fiber production increased by 27 per cent with 27 per cent fewer workers. This trend virtually forced migration to cities, especially from the newly mechanized plantation South.

It is now known that the high rate of unemployment during the late 1950's and early 1960's was caused not only by factory automation; a sluggish economy and consumer demand were also instrumental, and behind these, conservative government fiscal policies. But the fact remains, as Dorothy K. Norman wrote in the U.S. Department of Labor's *Monthly Labor Review* in 1965: "Production requirements in industry appear to have played a hoax on the Negro, by first expanding—especially during the war years of the 1940's and early 1950's—and enticing the Negroes from the farm into industrial jobs, often far from home, and then receding, as these same jobs have become increasingly vulnerable to technological and market changes.

"Industrial employment increased in a number of cities in 1964, but the totals did not rise much above 1960 levels. And in some of the largest centers—New York and Philadelphia—the downward trend persisted, the bulletin reported.

"Limited job opportunities in major centers of Negro concentration aggravate the already difficult situation in which Negroes find themselves when looking for employment. . . ."

The low-skill service jobs which untrained newcomers have traditionally filled in cities were even harder hit, relatively, by the switch to machines. For example, a great many immigrants who had never worked at any other non-farm job became elevator operators. Yet between 1957 and 1961 in New York City alone, 30,000 elevator operators' jobs were eliminated. It was anticipated that the unemployed operators could be transferred to bowling alleys. But the invention of the automatic pinsetter had eliminated thousands of these jobs as well. New mechanical cleaning processes used in many high-rise office buildings displaced still more low-skill people.

Municipal government itself, while a major growth sector for employment in recent years, has also increased use of machinery in activities that traditionally employed unskilled labor—general maintenance, street cleaning, street and road construction and administrative procedures.

The attrition in these jobs mirrors far-reaching structural shifts that have taken place in the economy since World War II. For while some jobs were disappearing, many others were being created. Between 1955 and 1965 the blue-collar work force grew only by 763,000; white-collar employment rose by 6,-540,000.

Within industry itself the big shift has been from production to non-production jobs (and smaller relative pay increases for the typical factory worker). The steel industry offers an extreme but vivid picture of the shifts. Between 1950 and 1961, its blue-collar employees dropped from 503,000 to 403,000—though production rose with automated equipment, and white-collar employment in its offices and laboratories climbed from 89,000 to 117,000. In 1946 there was one white-collar worker to every nine employed in steel; there was one in four by 1963. "The time may come when it will take a ton of paper to make a ton of steel," a bulletin of the Federal Reserve Bank observed.

The many new jobs in government are also skilled or professional. This does not mean that there is not a great deal of unskilled work to be done in public service. The work merely requires public financing. The 1966 Report of the National Commission on Technology, Automation and Economic Progress enumerated six different categories of potential jobs which could produce 5,300,000 new jobs which need to be filled in order to bring public services up to levels of acceptable operation.

In manpower utilization and national wealth, the country has been moving from a goods-producing to a service economy. This fact, in combination with the exodus of manufacturing plants from the crowded old rail centers,[4] has profound implications for cities and their residents. Not only is there relatively less wealth in locally taxable property; fewer jobs are left in cities for the new population. To reach plants now relocated in the suburbs, but which were accessible by urban public transportation, the Negro or Spanish-speaking worker who is barred from suburban residence (by income if not race) must drive many miles between home and work. Often he cannot afford to do so. (Meanwhile, suburban residents commute to office and professional jobs in center city.)

Since World War II, all net growth in jobs has occurred in the service sector, a 1965 study by Victor Fuchs of the National Bureau of Economic Research revealed. Moreover, Fuchs' study points out, growth within this service sector has been in jobs that make greater use

of workers with higher education and relatively less use of those with only limited schooling or with physical strength. The employment increase in the field of education alone between 1950 and 1960 was found to be greater than total employment in primary metal industries in both of those years. (Most dramatic postwar advance was made by professional, technical and kindred workers. This group doubled, and by 1964 numbered 8,500,000.)

Looking ahead to the 1970's, experts foresee a continuing decline in rural manpower needs. Only 10 per cent of the nation's population will be needed to feed the country and grow fiber for it. This means continued immigration from farms and plantations, though at a somewhat slower rate than in the recent past. But the number of Negroes, Puerto Ricans and other low-income, minority residents in central cities is expected to grow and be half again as large due to the young age and high birth rate of those already there.

The number of factory jobs nationally will increase—though probably not in the old manufacturing cities, and many traditional blue-collar production jobs will be upgraded in job requirements to a white-collar or skilled level. The manufacturers remaining in cities will have less need for additional, particularly for unskilled, workers. The big proportionate increase in skilled, white-collar and professional service jobs will continue in cities (as nationally), and cities may well benefit from this trend.

The U.S. Department of Labor warned in a publication on *Manpower Needs of the 1960's* (published in 1959) that "To fill these new requirements the youth who are entering the labor market will have to have much higher skills and education." The Department's 1965 publication on *Manpower Needs in 1975* reiterated the point. It stated that "The occupational groups requiring the least educational attainment are, in general, those which are expected to show the smallest employment growth and thus provide the fewest jobs for the growing labor force. . . . The demand of employers for better trained personnel appears to be insatiable."

EDUCATION—FOR WHAT?

Yet we have been breeding a new generation that is undereducated, unemployed or unemployable—the "dropouts" who by 1965 comprised almost one third of the nation's high-school-age students. They leave school usually by tenth grade, wander the streets, form gangs and get into trouble. When this postwar generation reaches adulthood in the early 70's, when 26,000,000 young people are expected to enter the labor market, about 7,500,000 teenagers will not have completed high school. About 2,500,000 million will have failed to reach eighth grade. According to the National Urban League, "A relatively high proportion of them will be nonwhite." This is particularly disturbing when it is realized that 20 percent of all the new entrants into the labor force in the late 1960's will be Negro;[5] and if present trends continue, half of them will not have had a high school education.

The prospects for these undereducated boys and girls are not bright. The recent past shows that they have three times as high an unemployment rate as graduates. They earn $27 a week less, and the disparity increases as they grow older. Their decision to quit school before graduation means a lifetime of menial jobs with meager salaries or unemployment. Indeed, many young people who dropped out of school to go to work soon found themselves out of a job and on relief. Some have recently joined the Job Corps and other new manpower training programs. Other dropouts have been adding to the urban crime wave which, during the 1960's, has seen a rise in city juvenile delinquency double the national average.

According to recent sociological studies, juvenile deviance and crime, in disproportionate amounts among the lower classes, are caused by the society that encourages certain aspirations yet withholds the possibilities of achieving these aspirations legitimately. As Cloward and Ohlin wrote in *Delinquency and Opportunity*, the cause is a discrepancy "between what lower class youth are led to want and what is actually available to them." For many young Negro males another principal cause is the early and often permanent absence of a father, as former Assistant Secretary of Labor Daniel P. Moynihan made clear in his paper on *The Negro Family*.

This combination of circumstances in ghetto areas is held to be a major cause of the recent summertime riots in Harlem, Rochester, Philadelphia, Los Angeles' Watts and other cities—circumstances to which the new government-aided anti-poverty and job training programs evidently added an extra bitter twist. The inadequately filled promise of new job opportunities and training served to exacerbate unrest in ghettos. "The Negro has gotten a much deeper sense of frustration, much deeper feelings of despair, as the gap increases between what he's actually got and what his expectations have grown to be," Dr. Philip Hauser, head of the University of Chicago's Department of Sociology, observed about the riots.

The McCone Commission, appointed by Governor Edmund Brown of California to investigate the circumstances contributing to the Watts riot, singled out inadequate schooling designed to help overcome the serious handicaps of the disadvantaged Negro child; insufficient jobs for the untrained Negro, and resentment of the police.

In a previous generation, the Italian immigrants' failure to get an education blocked their way, as they discovered too late, to economic opportunities and also led to a disproportionate rate of crime among their youth and later, among adults. For the Negro mass, moving from the twilight of civilization to cities, horizons have suddenly appeared to broaden. In cities they have achieved higher incomes and better housing conditions than in the rural South. But the newly broadened vistas of many in cities are unrealistic, considering the great obstacles.

Why should a Negro youth remain in school? Speaking primarily of the South two decades ago, the Swedish economist Gunnar Myrdal wrote in *An American Dilemma:* "Since Negroes are seldom in demand for jobs for which education is necessary, there is certainly nothing surprising in the conclusion that they, unlike whites, fail to improve their opportunities by staying in school longer." The scene has shifted more and more to northern and western city streets and their slums today.

The Negro may read in the papers about those who are succeeding. But the fact that success is news speaks for itself. What is new in today's city slum, Dr. James Conant observed in the early 1960's, is "the almost complete lack of . . . conviction" that they can ever work their way out of poverty on the part of Negro youth. "The unemployed floaters on the street are walking evidence to all youth that nothing can be accomplished by education." Conant placed a good part of the blame for the dropout problem on the discriminatory hiring practices of private companies.

Limited comfort might be derived by blaming the situation on the illiteracy and the consequent relative unemployability of the southern Negro migrant. Those who came to cities in the 1940's did have little schooling. During 1949-50 the highest migration to Chicago, for example, was of adults who had four years of education, and they subsequently bore the brunt of automation. But between 1955 and 1960, the great majority among the most mobile non-white migrants—men of twenty-five to twenty-nine years—had at least some high school training, and one fifth had a year or more of college.

Yet the percentage of unemployed Negroes during the recession of the early 1960's was two to three times as high as that of whites at *all* levels— unskilled, semiskilled and skilled. And even as the country neared "full employment" at the end of 1965, the Negro unemployment rate was still twice as high as whites, and it was even higher in the slums.[6] For Negro youth in 1966 it was 27 per cent, compared to 12 per cent for white youth. The President's Commission on Technology, Automation and Economic Progress warned in its 1966 report that "If non-whites continue to hold the same proportion of jobs in each occupation as in 1964, the non-white unemployment rate in 1975 will be more than five times that for the labor force as a whole."

The Negro has made the least advance in the growing sector of the economy—and not always for lack of education. In 1965, the Bureau of the

Census reported that "at all educational levels the Negro is less likely to be a white collar worker." According to a survey by the Census Bureau, among Negro men who had received some college training the proportion employed in lower-paid jobs was 41 per cent or twice the proportion of whites, while for male college graduates the proportion of Negroes in the lower-paid jobs was triple that of whites.

This survey stated, "Although advances have been made since 1950—the rate of progress has slowed and there remain large gaps between Negro and white achievement [even when years of schooling among Negroes are greater]. The political, economic and social issues affecting the Negro appear to arise not from lack of aspiration, but from high aspirations pressing against limited, and, in some places, declining opportunity. . . ." And fair employment laws don't help much.[7]

This highly demanding, specialized age affords the newcomer fewer of the jobs which he has traditionally filled and permits him a shorter period to become a self-sustaining member of the city economy. It also robs him of the realistic hope which served as an economic yeast for earlier generations.

The contrast is dramatized by the tale of a reunion, held in March 1962, of fifty men who had graduated half a century before from Brooklyn's now defunct Public School 43 in the "gray area" of Williamsburgh. "The gathering was a very satisfying experience," commented Nathan Smith, now a hardware merchant in Woodbridge, New Jersey, who initiated the reunion out of curiosity to learn how his classmates had turned out. "Not one of us failed to achieve at least modest success," he told a newspaper reporter who covered the

gathering. "We were mostly immigrants or children of immigrants. The only thing we had was hope and faith in the ideal of American opportunity."

The nature of that opportunity has changed. The era of the self-made, uneducated small businessman who could rise out of the slums is vanishing. He is no longer the backbone of the middle class; he is becoming part of the lower-middle class or the poor. More and more the American businessman has become an organization man; the former owner is now a manager; the clerk has been replaced by self-service. Although the current demand for new services is once again opening opportunities for small business concerns, the man who would be self-sustaining and advance on his own or in an organization must be educated.

THE PUT-OUTS

This suggests the third factor that limits the advance of the newcomers or the "culturally disadvantaged": educability. Much of this problem involves group values and cultural differences.

The lower class, whether white or non-white, differs from the middle class in its emphasis on immediate gratification and security, rather than on striving for individual status and achievement which necessitate thrift and postponement. There is practically no interest in academic education. Rather, learning is valued for immediate utility—filling out forms, applying for known civil service jobs, and so forth. Action is emphasized among the lower class; talk and reading are commonly regarded as unmasculine and are therefore eschewed.

Why should one break with one's group, become tomorrow-oriented and study hard in the expectation that doing well in school will lead to a better future? In today's slum areas, where the majority of dropouts live, many youths either see no reason to make the break or do not know how to make it.

From their earliest years, their deprived, circumscribed environment militates against the education necessary to succeed today. The family and immediate community often fail to provide the early life experiences, the sights, sounds, vocabularly and information which are necessary preschool preparations for learning; these the middle-class child receives almost automatically. Home life is crippled. The uneducated or undereducated parent speaks to the child in monosyllables and points at objects, and may even deride efforts to learn due to his own poor experience in school, or rude treatment by the child's teachers. The harassed mother shouts "Get out of my way" to too many children. There are no books, not even nursery rhymes, in the crowded noisy room or two called home. Study, even sleeping, is often impossible. The boy in the broken home (over one quarter of the Negro children live in families headed by women) is deprived of the essential male model.

Many lower-class parents are aware of the importance of education in this society. But many lack the money and time or the necessary knowledge to help their children. They may be reluctant to meet teachers because they speak poorly or dress badly; they lack the time and organizational sophistication to join PTA activities. Further, since equal opportunities and rewards are not generally available to educated Negroes, there is a tendency to protect children against rebuffs and disappointments. This is partly a defense; often it becomes a built-in lag.

Among the strongest detrimental influences on the Negro child is his negative self-image; he senses that society views him as inferior and expects inferior performance of him. This is attested by the limitations on his father and by the family's living environment, and in effect has been reinforced by the emphasis of many old-line organization Negroes on racial integration as the key to success.

This child is behind before he starts school. One out of every three children in the school systems of our fourteen biggest cities come from such "culturally deprived" backgrounds. In the 1970's, with the lower-class population explosion, there is expected to be one such child out of every two in big cities, and one out of four in many middle-size cities.

The school world has little relevance to the child's life. Its primers are illustrated with rosy-cheeked white children playing on grassy suburban lawns; his composition assignment is to describe "A Trip I Took." He may have left home without breakfast and be too hungry to concentrate. When he is confronted with a difficult problem, he abandons it quickly with a "who cares?" attitude. Teachers, unprepared for and demoralized by these students and their attitudes, spend so much time on discipline that they have little left for actual lessons.

"One of the reasons we have such a terrific discipline problem," an experienced Negro teacher in a New York "gray area" public school pointed out, "is that the children just don't care. School is a place where they are sent. Even children who are eleven and twelve years old have no ideas of their own as to what they want to get out of school." As a result, they get only one half to one third the exposure to learning that a student usually gets. The high residential mobility of many poor families compounds the inadequacies of the child's education. When he reaches high school, the situation is completely out of hand, the street takes over, and the gang.

The burden of blame for pupils' lower achievement also rests on the attitudes of teachers—on what Dr. Kenneth Clark, in *Dark Ghetto*, called their "cultural bias." A social worker who spent many years in East Harlem, a vast depressed community of 180,000 in upper Manhattan, observed: 'Teachers come in here with stereotypes. They feel the kids can't learn. So they don't learn."

But looking behind the statistics and the signs of "cultural deprivation," one discovers that the majority of the dropouts have average intelligence, and that 20 to 25 per cent even rank as culturally superior. Recent studies indicate that the "disadvantaged" child learns differently, more slowly, and responds to different stimuli; he apparently requires different teaching techniques or programs than those generally available. His disadvantage is not so much in natural gifts as in middle-class know-how—a lack which shows up in testing and teaching that is oriented to the middle-class culture.

Before many students drop out, they have dropped backward. Their progressive retardation may go back to third-grade level. And the boys do worse than the girls, who are more apt to have a suitable adult model in their mother, and more job opportunities at the white-collar level. Pupils who do not keep up with their grades are promoted nonetheless. By high school, the youngsters are so far behind in basic skills that many teachers find them uneducable.

"The teachers call them 'drop-outs,'" a field worker for Chicago's Committee on New Residents commented. "We call them 'put-outs.'"

As for the youngsters who move ahead at grade level, guidance counselors steer them away from jobs from which Negroes have been traditionally barred. When they cannot read well, they are shunted to vocational high schools to be trained for trades that have limited openings or are disappearing. Employers who decide to hire Negroes at higher levels or in kinds of work previously barred are not able to find enough who are qualified. College scholarships for qualified Negro students at many top institutions go begging. Attending college appears so impossible to many children from deprived communities that even preparing for it seems a fantasy. Because they live in such a separate community, Negro youths are unlikely to hear about the opportunities.

THE CITY SCHOOLS' PUBLIC

The changing nature of the urban population is dramatized by the two different school systems that exist in our metropolitan areas. These differ in budget and product as the two populations' pocketbooks and political power differ. The short-changing of cities by state legislatures compounds the fiscal disparity.

During the 1950's suburban parents put themselves and their communities into debt to build schools, raise salaries, expand curricula and improve teaching methods, to give their bumper crop of children the best education so they could get into college. Central cities also had an unexpectedly large number of pupils, but they were educating a generation of dropouts.

Dr. James Conant found that in the wealthy suburbs annual expenditures were often over $1,000 per pupil, compared to an average under $500 in slum schools; teacher pay was commensurate. (Between 1952 and 1962, nearly half the licensed teachers in New York City left the system.)

The financial issue was well put by Max Rubin, who served as chairman of the New York City Board of Education from 1961 to 1963. "Everybody wants good schools, but how far will the people go to pay for the schools?" he asked. "Politicians prefer to run on a low tax platform rather than on better schools and higher taxes. Without the priority on the part of the public, what can you expect of the school board and teachers? Until good schools become good politics, we will be struggling."

Negro organization leaders and many middle-class Negro parents have spent their energies and political leverage on integration. They have demanded that Negro children be bused into white-neighborhood schools (and the reverse), and have urged school pairing, rezoning and other expedients. They even oppose building new schools in ghettos. The Negro leaders have been reluctant to admit that the disadvantaged child (in big cities, many non-white and Spanish-speaking children test several grades below their white contemporaries) requires much more than school integration to improve his learning ability. They did not fight for the expensive special programs these children need, and they tended to ignore the uncomfortable fact that in integrated schools disadvantaged children have to attend separate classes because of their academic deficiencies.

Some significant experiments are under way on a metropolitan basis—in the Hartford, Connecticut, Boston and Los Angeles areas—to achieve greater racial balance by transferring some inner-city Negro pupils to white suburban schools. In Los Angeles the program is reported to be drawing mainly middle-class Negro children, and teachers say that poor children from Watts are upset by their exposure to Bel Air's wealth.

Perhaps the benefit of such pupil transfers is greater for the insulated suburban white children than for their Negro classmates. Associate Professor Preston Wilcox of the Columbia University School of Social Work, himself a Negro, has stated that emphasis on integration is probably harmful to the Negro child. "Psychologically, it's bad to tell a kid that he'll only make it if he sits next to a white," Wilcox comments.

In the big cities with huge and growing core ghettos, the integrationists are rapidly becoming crusaders without a feasible cause. In Philadelphia, Detroit, Chicago and New York, to cite just several big-city school systems, white pupils now form the minority, and the percentage of the white student population has been dropping a few points each year. In Washington D.C., public school enrollment in 1965 was 90 per cent Negro, compared to 85 per cent just the year before. Los Angeles was the only one of twenty-one big cities in which white enrollment did not drop that year. The trend is unlikely to level off or reverse itself, at least in the next decade.

Educational disadvantages are worsened by the unanticipated high densities in new ghetto-slum areas. Physical capacities have been overwhelmed. One old high school in East Brooklyn, built for 1,600 pupils, last year had an enrollment of 3,400, 85 per cent of them Negro and Puerto Rican. The school's wiring is so antiquated that it is not possible to use modern teaching devices to help the many students with reading problems. The need for three sessions means that some students start school by seven, eat lunch at 9:30 and are free by noon to roam the streets. Not surprisingly, the dropout rate is 40 per cent.

Middle-class Negro parents have become so dissatisfied with the quality of education in cities' public schools that a number who can afford it have also removed their children. (Unlike white families, many cannot withdraw to the suburbs.) In the District of Columbia in 1965, over 6 per cent of the Negro students were attending private or parochial schools, often at great financial sacrifice, and a surprising number were the sons and daughters of public schoolteachers.

Much of the insistence by Negroes on integration is doubtless based on a desire for quality education. (Commenting on parent attitudes, the director of an East Harlem settlement house observed, "In most neighborhoods, the teachers are cowed by the PTA. Here, the parents are cowed by the teacher.")

But a dramatic reversal seems to be coming about. In the summer of 1966, Livingston L. Wingate, director of Haryou-Act, the Harlem anti-poverty agency calling for the establishment of quality education in Negro ghettos, declared that "We must no longer pursue the myth that integrated education is equated with quality education." A poll of several ghetto areas in big cities showed that the great majority of parents are concerned with better education; only 2 per cent specifically with school integration.

A growing self-assurance and political awareness was evident among the par-

ents of children who were to enter a new $5,000,000 air-conditioned East Harlem elementary school in the fall of 1966. At first they insisted that the school not be opened unless it were integrated or they were given control. Slowly they shifted to a demand for control, with appointment of a Negro or Puerto Rican principal, and more Negro teachers.

But the problems of inadequate funds, insufficient teachers, old overcrowded schools and outmoded curriculum still remain, and in most ghetto areas the educational situation has been steadily deteriorating.

THE BUSINESSMEN AND THE EDUCATORS

Where have the big businessmen, the "civic leaders" of cities, been in the midst of the mounting school crisis? Strangely silent. The big worry of the businessman (as opposed to the father) is that spending more on schools will increase local taxes and scare away industry. His children do not use the public schools in central cities; few even live in the cities. Only rarely have top city leaders fought for central city school improvement in recent years or pressed state legislatures to revise school aid formulas and local school district taxing powers.[8]

Local business, industrial and financial leaders—the men who have been working for downtown revitalization, industrial redevelopment, freeway construction, metropolitan mass transit and a "quality" urban environment in order to stop the flight of industry, the white middle class and the tax base—show a strange lack of concern about the school crisis. If the present situation is allowed to continue, it seems obvious that their city will be less able to attract desirable business concerns, and the businessmen will be less able to get qualified workers for their own companies and attract white families to their redevelopments.

For at least six years, the U.S. Department of Labor has been putting up warnings. Perhaps the businessman does not perceive the implications of the inner-city school problems for his city's economic future, nor recognize that the undereducated central-city youths are likely to cause the urban manpower crisis of the 1970's. Perhaps it is hard for them to see the economic payoff in education; few even recognize the economic toll of discrimination practices.[9]

Yet the economists have been making a strong case for the return from investment in education, especially in post-industrial society. In 1960, University of Chicago economist Theodore W. Schultz, in his presidential address to the American Economic Association (and in a subsequent book on *The Economic Value of Education*), declared that "No small part of the low earnings of many Negroes, poor farm people and some older workers reflects the failure to have invested in their health and education. . . . We can ill afford to continue making the same mistake."

Schultz also observed that "If we were to treat education as pure investment, this result would suggest that the returns to education were relatively more attractive than those in non-human capital." Research has shown, he reported, that the impressive rise in real earnings per worker achieved in the past generation—the "unexplained increases" in the national income, came about "not as much through investment in capital goods, as generally assumed, but through greatly increased public and personal investment in human capital."

In 1965 the Committee for Economic Development, a national nonprofit organization of enlightened and industrial leaders, in effect endorsed his philosophy with a policy statement on *Raising Low Incomes Through Improved Education;* they urged that all possible resources, public and private, be brought to bear on adapting the educational system to the economic system, and vice versa. A CED member, William Benton, publisher of the Encyclopaedia Britannica, observed that "although education is our largest business, our factual information about the educational system, and about how best to achieve its goals, is astonishingly inadequate for the purposes of sensible planning and decision-making."

The Ford Foundation's Great Cities School Improvement Program, which in the early 1960's stimulated school systems in fourteen big cities to develop new methods and programs for teaching inner-city children, blamed the educators for public indifference. In 1963, a spokesman charged that the educators have failed to communicate the problems, and have been unwilling to evaluate the effectiveness of present methods.

"How can you expect the businessman to respond?" he asked. "He hears the Superintendent of Schools say everything is fine, and one morning he opens the paper and reads that half the students are illiterate.[10] He wonders what the schools have been doing with all the money they have.

"Educators have secured for themselves a unique isolation in American society. The majority of school systems have their own tax structure, are independent of City Hall and call themselves the answer to society's problems. The public goes along because Americans have an ingrained belief that education is the answer to everything. They tell the public what it should want and shortchange the process of planning with the people. But because the school systems refuse to evaluate themselves, they have not documented the case for what education can do, especially in central cities, and thus it becomes increasingly difficult to sell themselves. Further, their huge unwieldy administrative structure favors the status quo and penalizes the person who tries to innovate."

WHAT KIND OF EDUCATION IS THE ANSWER?

Not all educators remained oblivious to the special problems of educating inner-city children. Many were eagerly searching for new methods "to compensate for the deficiencies which hinder the disadvantaged child from taking full advantage of the conventional education program," as a 1963 bulletin of the National Education Association summarized the new movement.

New York City led the way in 1959 with its Demonstration Guidance Program, which was widely publicized as Higher Horizons. This approach offered culturally deprived children an enriched curriculum, including special counseling, more teacher attention and outings to sites of interest and cultural facilities in the larger community. Children in the pilot program responded well, and the program appealed to the general public. The new compensatory education approach was soon followed in other cities, while the program was expanded in New York schools.

There were stirrings and changes in many big-city schools, stimulated to a large extent by the millions in matching grants from the Ford Foundation. Extra personnel were added: guidance counselors, remedial reading teachers, assistant principals, "helping" teachers, community agents from school neighborhoods to provide a liaison with the community. Remedial programs in language skills were undertaken and class sizes were reduced; new teaching techniques were used; preschool classes prepared three- and four-year olds for learning; "alienated" parents were actively involved in school activities.

But federal money was required for a national program, and the civil rights ferment, ghetto riots and mounting concern for the urban poor pressured Congress into passing the unprecedented Elementary and Secondary Education Act of 1965. Under its Title I, over $1,000,000,000 was made available in the first year alone for special programs for educationally deprived children in poverty areas. The recent compensatory education programs were predominant among those eligible for Title I.

This development seemed to be the most encouraging yet. Crisis had overcome local fear of federal control of education. In 1966 many cities began Higher Horizon-type programs, team teaching methods, remedial reading programs, talent development, and "preparation for work" programs. Some were also aided by the Office of Economic Opportunity. The most popular new program was for preschool children, Project Head Start, characterized as "the infant prodigy of the Great Society." President Johnson himself hailed it as "battle-tested."

In concluding this study of American cities facing their problems, it seemed necessary to document the achievements on the great new urban education frontier, and also to find out how much more federal and local money would be required to do a saturation job.

The results were disconcerting, but instructive. As of the summer of 1966, the returns from the new urban education programs generally show that "more of the same" does not have significant effect; that the "noticeable" improvements in pupils do not last under present circumstances; and that there are almost no measurable achievements to speak of.

What seemed particularly unsettling was that the U.S. Office of Education was loathe to admit to Congress or the public the ineffectiveness of most of its billion-dollar Title I program. (I later learned that the office *was* beginning to warn the educators.) HEW Secretary John W. Gardner told Congress in April that "Great educational strides can be made by specialized educational programs," and Commissioner of Education Harold Howe testified, "Our prior experience in several cities demonstrates that such special attention in and of itself will result in improved educational performance." Yet the Office of Education could not provide me with data from local schools that showed quantifiable results. It turned out that the legislative testimony was based on publications, several years old, of early efforts in the Ford Foundation Great Cities and New York's Higher Horizons.

These publications were, indeed, optimistic about the initial results. But the Ford Foundation could direct me to none of the Great Cities schools that had found significant differences between children in compensatory and conventional education programs when tested for specific achievements.[11] (Actually, these programs lacked a research component; the main concern was to get into the schools and stimulate federal action.)

Dr. Mario Fantini, formerly director of the Great Cities program in Syracuse, New York, and now a Program Associate in the Foundation's Education Program, flatly asserted that "More of the same won't have the pay-off we expect, and I doubt we'll ever have the kind of money to do the job that way. The problem with our original approach is that the schools have assumed the kids need compensation for deficiencies and that there is nothing wrong with their program. But the schools themselves are outmoded, and we have to change the process of education. There are the beginnings of a shift in this direction. But we had to start somewhere."

Pittsburgh, another of the Great Cities, has been pushing compensatory education and team teaching in slum neighborhood schools for five years and could not show measurable improvements in children's reading scores. Officials say that high pupil turnover in slum schools has made it difficult to assess the program, and the system lacks staff for more sophisticated measurements. But teachers were confident that the improved climate would eventually be reflected in achievement scores.

Coming hard on the heels of these unsettling findings, early in July a *New York Times* article reported that the city's Board of Education had quietly closed down Higher Horizons without even a press release. An independent professional evaluation of the program's first four years (grudgingly released by the Board of Education) had found virtually no measurable effect on the achievements, IQ or reading level of enrolled pupils. It was explained that budgetary limitations had made impossible the "saturation" with additional services originally envisioned. (If the original $250 per pupil had been spent on each of the 100,000 pupils involved, $250,-000,000 would have been required annually; this is almost one quarter of Congress' first-year appropriation for Title I of the Education Act.) *The New York Times'* Education Editor, Fred Hechinger, called the results shown by some pupils "the triumphs of the lucky few."

But what of Head Start, the popular and battle-tested program? In most cities it had been offered only on a summertime basis, and one could not expect a great permanent effect. But New Haven, Connecticut, has had the pre-kindergarten program as part of the regular school year for the past six years, and could provide no data of measurable change. "Through kindergarten, there is enormous noticeable improvement, but by second grade it's all gone," a school official stated. "The children come up against the same large classes, no extra aides, the old program and teachers."

This situation supported the findings of Dr. Martin Deutsch, a psychologist and director of the Institute for Developmental Studies at New York University, who pioneered the pre-kindergarten program; he claimed that a constant follow-up in later grades is necessary if early gains are not to be lost. It also seemed to support warnings to Congress by Education Commissioner Howe that "initial gains evaporate if special education programs are not maintained," and, "Only a comprehensive long-term program . . . can overcome [disadvantaged children's] deficiencies."

THE FLAWS IN THE SYSTEM

We should not belittle the great side-benefits of the new concern and funds —the greater involvement of parents and other potential leaders in inner-city neighborhoods, the expanded role of schools in local community life, health benefits for the children. (In the first summer of Head Start, 70 per cent of the children had their first medical and dental examination. In Tampa, Florida, twelve cases of tuberculosis and fifty of nutritional deficiencies were found.) Many schools are also getting adequate libraries for the first time.

Moreover, the limited effect of the initial attempts may well point the way to more effective action, and even compensatory education is better than what was happening before.

The lack of research-proven premises behind this billion-dollar educational program probably reflects the government's desperate need to do "something" about ghetto children as much as educators' unwillingness to evaluate themselves. HEW Secretary Gardner makes known his concern about the lack of educational research. (One city has had three research directors and no research results to show for it. One director, who recently resigned, gave an oral report to the Board of Education, but wished to keep the findings unwritten until used for his own professional publication purposes.)

Title III of the Educational Act is promising. This relatively unpublicized provision finances local "centers for change" to stimulate schools to a more innovative approach that relates research to practice. Known as PACE—Projects to Advance Creativity in Education—Title III also encourages higher-education institutions and local cultural organizations to provide local schools with leadership, new kinds of talents and services. Another little-known program is Title IV, which encourages educational institutions and agencies on different levels to band together on a regional basis to establish "multi-institutional laboratories" for researching and developing new ideas. One recent example of university-school affiliation is New York University's "adoption" of a school in the Bedford-Stuyvesant area, assisted by Ford Foundation funds.

It is important to take note here of the three fundamental flaws in compensatory education, the "more of same" approach. These are mostly failures of society at large, not just of the educators. Indeed, much at fault is the basic American fallacy that education is a panacea. As in public housing, we have not considered all the determining variables.

The first problem is that the schools cannot remedy the deficits of home, family and slum environment. "Remember, the children only spend nine per cent of their time in school," one educator points out. A recent study by the U.S. Office of Education found that differences in the quality of a school had very little effect on the achievement scores of children who have a strong foundation for education at home. Children from disadvantaged homes benefit relatively more from a good school, but it does not fill the gap.

Secondly, much of the present school curriculum is irrelevant for inner-city children. As Dr. Conant observed in *Slums and Suburbs,* "What can words like 'freedom,' 'liberty' and 'equality of opportunity' mean to these young people? With what kind of zeal and dedication can we expect them to withstand . . . communism?" Psychologist Dr. Kenneth Clark has repeatedly pointed out that compensatory education will not work unless the content has more meaning for children from deprived homes. A hopeful step is the publication by major publishing houses of new textbooks and readers that show Negroes, Puerto Ricans and whites as a normal part of the American scene and also include the history of the Negro in America. On the question of whether what is taught in schools is relevant, one inner-city curriculum director observes, "We're finding out how bad what we've been doing is for *both* the white and Negro child. I'd dump 90 per cent of what we teach."

Dr. Fantini asserts that "Middle class children make the schools look good. They give back what's expected of them. But what's so good about middle class know-how? We're all disadvantaged educationally. One need only examine the drop-out rate in college, the performance of most citizens in the wider social arena, the apathy towards social injustice and our inability to exercise leadership to highlight the obsolescence of current education. The deeper issue is whether the educational system is equipping people to deal with the problems of society."

Finally, there is the basic problem of motivation and discrimination. How can we persuade disadvantaged students and their parents that it is worthwhile for the youngster to remain in school and study, to defer premature employment and make the necessary personal investment of time and effort on the premise that such efforts will be rewarded? (Well over half the estimated cost of higher education in the United States comes from income deferred by students.)

As Dr. Conant concluded in *Slums and Suburbs,* "To improve the work of the slum schools requires an improvement in the lives of the families who inhabit the slums, but without a drastic change in the employment opportunities for urban Negro youth relatively little·can be accomplished."

Our cities, the centers of the nation's economy, are also the end of the racial line in America. In cities we must proceed simultaneously and at full speed on two parallel fronts: improving environments *and* opportunities. There is no turning back.

NOTES

1. Making it larger than that of the State of New York.
2. As the report pointed out, ADC laws place "a premium on the absence of the father" by not giving assistance to families with employable fathers.
3. The Cook County Welfare Department established required literacy classes for such ablebodied, unemployed men.
4. Between 1960 and 1966 alone, New York City lost 80,000 manufacturing jobs; it is expected that it will lose 48,000 more by 1970, according to a study by the City Planning Commission.
5. The percentage in cities will be much higher.
6. A special Labor Department census in March 1966 of the poorest districts in the one hundred largest cities showed the overall Negro unemployment rate to be 9.4 per cent—compared to 3.8 per cent nationally. For Negro boys it was 31 per cent. Many in the prime-working-age group were not even looking for work, and thus not technically unemployed. In some "new" ghetto areas, the West Side of Chicago and Brooklyn's Bedford-Stuyvesant, unemployment ran an estimated 25 per cent in the summer of 1966, and statistics showed a sudden national increase in Negro joblessness.

7. In employment, as in housing, the effectiveness of anti-discrimination laws, including the Civil Rights Act of 1964, is hampered by inadequate enforcement powers, small budgets and weak administration, a Twentieth-Century Fund report has found. Another study reveals that extraordinary efforts, including aggressive recruiting campaigns by employers, are necessary to overcome Negroes' emotional blocks and inertia. Psychological tests have also been found to keep Negroes out of jobs.
8. One of the exceptions was Pennsylvania, led by Pittsburgh and Philadelphia and supported by Governor William Scranton. Recently, some southern states have come to spend a much higher percentage of their budgets on public education than have northern states—as part of the South's drive to attract industry from old northern cities.
9. The President's Council of Economic Advisers found that if discrimination in employment were eliminated and the Negro potential fully realized, at least $13,000,000,000 more in purchasing power would be placed in the hands of the bottom income groups, and current annual growth would double.
10. In October 1965, the New York City Board of Education released results of standardized achievement tests given to 626,148 pupils in second through tenth grade during 1964-65. These disclosed that more than half the city's pupils were behind their counterparts throughout the country in reading and arithmetic in second through eighth grade, and that sizable numbers were two, three and four years behind in reading.
11. An apparent exception has been the Banneker Schools in St. Louis, the one large-scale experiment where children are reported to be performing at grade level; but this was not one of the Ford programs and the Foundation had no evaluation of it. A part of the Banneker Schools' unusual success is believed to be the forceful personality of the principal and his use of every strategy to involve parents and students in the learning process.

A Study of Ghetto Rioters

NATHAN S. CAPLAN AND JEFFERY M. PAIGE

In the summer of 1964 riots broke out in the Negro ghettos of a number of major American cities. Since then rioting has occurred with increasing frequency and intensity. In 1967 there were 164 distinct disturbances; this past April, in the week following the assassination of Martin Luther King, there was violence in more than 100 communities. These disorders present a serious danger. In themselves they threaten to disrupt normal political relations and functions and to alter the quality of urban life; moreover, they are surely symptoms of deep social and economic problems.

What are those problems? Why do Negroes riot? It is important to be accurate in defining the ghetto problem because how we define it determines what we will do about it. Riots are not new in American history, and after each major outburst there have been attempts to make sense of the events by determining their causes. Formal commissions were established in 1919, 1943 and most recently in 1967 for that purpose. The reports of these commissions, the investigations of social scientists and the speculations of the press and the public have produced a number of more or less well-formulated theories as to the causes of riots. The theories differ widely in detail and more widely in degree of sophistication, but it is fair to group them into three major categories.

The first of these categories might be called the "riffraff theory." It holds that rioters are irresponsible deviants: criminals, unassimilated migrants, emotionally disturbed persons or members of an underclass. It sees the rioters as being peripheral to organized society, with no broad social or political concerns, and views the frustration that leads to rioting as simply part of a long history of personal failure.

The second category, which can be called the "relative-deprivation theory," attributes the riots to a gap between the rioters' objective economic and social situation and their expectations—which the outside observer usually considers unrealistic. These expectations are said to result either from the fact that the lot of the Negro is improving, but not rapidly enough ("the revolution of rising expectations"), or from an implicit comparison with the economic situation of whites.

The third category, the "blocked-opportunity theory," sees riots as the consequence of the prolonged exclusion of Negroes from American economic and social life. This theory views white discrimination as a constant barrier to Negro occupational mobility; the Negroes who are most likely to react violently to this barrier are those who want to better themselves and who feel that their own

From *Scientific American* (August 1968), pp. 15-21. Copyright © 1968 by Scientific American, Inc. All rights reserved. Reprinted by permission of the publisher. Nathan S. Caplan is a program associate at the Center for Research on Utilization of Scientific Knowledge, which is part of the Institute for Social Research at the University of Michigan. Jeffery M. Paige is Assistant Professor of Sociology at the University of California at Berkeley.

economic and social situation is a result of discrimination rather than of personal inadequacy. It is held that for many years the traditional stereotype of Negro inferiority provided a convenient explanation—both for whites and for blacks —of the socially inferior position of the latter, and that those Negroes who have most thoroughly rejected this stereotype are now most likely to blame white society rather than themselves for their low status and to react violently to their exclusion.

These three theories have important implications for any action taken in response to rioting. The first two theories (particularly the first), by attributing the causes of riots to individuals, relieve white institutions of most of the blame. They suggest that the antidote for rioting is to change the individual rioters through psychotherapy, social work or, if all else fails, prolonged confinement. The third theory suggests that it is not Negro rioters who must be changed but the white institutions that continue to exclude them. Changing these institutions, or the system that legitimizes them, is of course more difficult and less popular politically than establishing remedial programs.

In behalf of the National Advisory Commission on Civil Disorders (the "Kerner Commission"), our group at the Institute for Social Research at the University of Michigan undertook to test these different explanations of riots. We did this by analyzing the characteristics and attitudes of individual rioters as revealed by interview surveys conducted in two cities in which major riots took place during the summer of 1967, Detroit and Newark. In each case the sampling area consisted of the 1960 census tracts in which violence and damage had

occurred. To obtain a representative sample one must ensure that each household has an equal probability of being included, but in urban areas it is more efficient and convenient to work with only a few blocks. The best method is to see that each block has a probability of selection proportional to its size (number of dwelling units) and then to see that each unit has a probability of selection inversely proportional to the block size. Since the overall probability of selection of any dwelling unit is the product of these two probabilities, this technique ensures that each unit has a roughly equal chance of being included.

In both cities trained Negro interviewers were assigned to the selected dwelling units. In Detroit they enumerated every person above the age of 15 in each assigned dwelling and selected every other one for interviewing. In Newark they listed the Negro males between 15 and 35 and interviewed them all. The interviewers were persistent, and eventually 67 percent of the eligible respondents were interviewed in Detroit and 66 percent in Newark; the others either could not be found at home after repeated call-backs or (only about 3 percent) refused to be interviewed. These response rates are somewhat lower than those in well-conducted surveys of white middle-class populations but are comparable to rates in other recent ghetto studies.

The first objective was to identify those who had participated in the riots. Two questions were used, one more direct than the other. The indirect question simply asked if the respondent had been active during the disturbance, leaving him free to define "active" as he chose. The other question was "What did you do?" and the interviewer read off a list of behavior ranging from staying at home to sniping. Respondents were classified as "rioters" if they reported that they were active or that they had been involved in breaking windows, looting or fire-bombing and so on. Those who reported that they had stayed at home or had gone out in front of their homes to watch the disturbances were considered "nonrioters." About 11 percent of the 437 respondents in Detroit identified themselves as rioters. In Newark, where all 236 respondents were young men, the figure was 45 percent.

We checked the validity of the rioter-nonrioter classification in two ways and found a high degree of statistical support for the separation into the two categories. One method was to test for internal validity by comparing the answers of the two groups on questions that seemed likely to differentiate between them. For example, when we asked what kinds of sentence should be imposed on looters (or arsonists or snipers), respondents classified as rioters were much more likely than nonrioters to believe no penalty or a lenient one was appropriate. Similarly, more rioters than nonrioters felt that the police should have acted "more gently" when the riots began. We also had a test of external validity that supported the rioter-nonrioter designations: When we compared our respondents with 11,000 people arrested for riot activity in various cities, our rioter group resembled the arrestees more closely on the basis of a number of demographic variables than the nonrioter group did.

Satisfied as to the validity of the rioter-nonrioter categories, we went on to consider the differences in the two groups' responses to a number of questions. The data make possible empirical testing of each of the three major theories of riot participation and thus help us to begin to understand what really motivates the rioters. (In the analysis that follows the differences cited between rioters and nonrioters are statistically reliable unless otherwise noted, and they hold up after age and other relevant demographic factors are controlled.)

According to three principal varieties of the riffraff theory, the rioter is respectively a member of a deprived underclass, an unassimilated recent migrant or an emotionally disturbed person. The first hypothesis argues that the rioters are the "hard core" unemployed—often out of work for long periods of time or chronically unemployable because they lack skill or education. Having lost contact with the job market and all hope of finding work, these people are economically at the very bottom of Negro society, poorly educated even when compared with other ghetto Negroes.

The survey data do not support this hypothesis. There is no significant difference in income between rioters and nonrioters. In Detroit, where we recorded the individual income of male respondents, there was some tendency for rioters to report smaller annual incomes than nonrioters: 39 percent of the rioters and 30 percent of the nonrioters had annual incomes of less than $5,000 per year. Even this small difference disappears when the data are age-controlled, that is, when the fact that boys and young men earn less than older men is taken into account. In Newark, where we asked about family income, the economic status of the two groups is again nearly equal: 33 percent of the rioters and 29 percent of the nonrioters reported family incomes of less than $5,000. These data point up two things, both of which weigh against the riffraff theory. First, differences in economic status do not differentiate rioters from their nonrioting neighbors. Second, the rioters are not the poorest of the poor. Whereas there may be many people with very low incomes who riot, a comparable percentage of people whose incomes are just as low do not.

Among the males in both the Detroit and the Newark surveys, about 30 percent of the rioters reported that they were unemployed. The unemployment rate among the nonrioters differed in the two cities. In Detroit the unemployment rate among the nonrioters was practically identical with that for the rioters, 32 percent. Unemployment among the Newark nonrioters was lower, 19 percent. In addition we found that in Newark 61 percent of the self-reported rioters, but only 43 percent of the nonrioters, had been unemployed for a month or more during the preceding year. (Students were excluded from the analysis of employment data.) We also found that the Newark rioters more often held unskilled jobs; only 50 percent of the rioters and 60 percent of the nonrioters held jobs at the semiskilled level or better.

It is clear from these findings that the rioters are not the hard-core unemployed. In Newark, where we did find some indication of employment differences between rioters and nonrioters, the rioters are more likely to be marginally employed than truly unemployable. As a matter of fact, occupational aspiration was higher among rioters than among nonrioters in Newark. Only 29 percent of the employed rioters (compared with 44 percent of the nonrioters) said they were satisfied with their present job. Seventy-one percent of the rioters and 56 percent of the nonrioters reported that they wanted better jobs. Instead of being those at the bottom of the class structure who have given up hope, it seems that the rioters are continually on the margin

of the job market, often employed but never for long.

Nor are the rioters the least educated. In Detroit 93 percent of the rioters remained in school long enough to acquire some high school education; the comparable figure for the nonrioters is 72 percent. In Newark 98 percent of the rioters and only 86 percent of the nonrioters had attended high school. (The differences between the two cities are due to the age differences between samples, with the Newark respondents all under 35.) Probably no single finding in our data argues so strongly against the underclass theory. The finding is precisely the reverse of the prediction. There *is* a significant relation between schooling and riot activity, but it is the rioter who is the better educated! Although it is true that the rioter is likely to be a high school dropout, his nonrioting neighbor is more likely to be an elementary school dropout. Even if all the other assumptions of the underclass theory could be supported, it would require major revision or supplementation because of the finding on education.

Another riffraff hypothesis is that rioters are most likely to be found among recent migrants to the urban area. The unassimilated migrant is not accustomed to the problems of urban life and is unable to cope effectively with its complexities, it is suggested, and his bewilderment and the pressures of poverty, crime and unemployment produce frustrations that eventually lead to rioting. Certainly the facts on the movement of Negroes from the rural South to Northern cities make such a hypothesis seem reasonable. Since 1910 the proportion of Negroes living in the South has dropped from 90 percent to 55 percent. During the same period the total Negro population of the U.S. has more than doubled and the number living in cities has increased fivefold. This shift in population concentration has been felt primarily in the very Northern metropolitan centers where ghetto rioting has occurred.

In Detroit and Newark, however, we found that those most likely to riot were not the migrants but the long-term residents. In Detroit 59 percent of the rioters and 35 percent of the nonrioters had been born in the city. In Newark the discrepancy was even greater: more than half of the rioters and less than a quarter of the nonrioters were natives.

We focused more closely on the migration question by comparing the region of socialization, or upbringing, for the two riot activity groups. In both Detroit and Newark 74 percent of the rioters reported that they had been raised in the North. Among the nonrioters 64 percent in Detroit and 48 percent in Newark said they were raised in the North. It is, then, the long-term residents—those who know Northern living patterns and the city best—and not the unassimilated migrants who are most likely to riot. Again the prediction of the riffraff theory is reversed.

The third riffraff hypothesis maintains that the riots are caused when people whose personalities are vulnerable to stress lose control of their behavior; for such people rioting is a temporary aberration, an opportunity for becoming momentarily elated and free of all care. This psychiatric interpretation, like the other variations of the riffraff theory, attributes riots to people rather than to situations.

Although it is difficult to measure personality characteristics directly in surveys, the data include information about some important social determinants of adjustment. For example, the nuclear family has come to be viewed as an important influence on adult personality, and the frequent absence of the father is often cited as a cause of maladjustment among Negroes. In Newark we questioned our respondents about family structure during their childhood, asking if there was an adult male living in the home during that crucial phase of their personality development. There was essentially no difference between rioters and nonrioters in the response to this question. Almost 75 percent of the rioters and 77 percent of the nonrioters reported the presence of an adult male in their home during their childhood.

We also have several indicators of the respondents' social behavior under ordinary circumstances. In Newark, where we questioned men about their membership in organizations, we found a slight tendency for rioters to hold a larger number of group memberships and no difference between rioters and nonrioters in the types of group memberships held. In Detroit we asked about social interaction with neighbors. Again we found a slight tendency for rioters to be more active than their nonrioting neighbors: 35 percent of the rioters but only 17 percent of the nonrioters reported daily visits with their neighbors. When we questioned the Newark respondents on the regularity of their church attendance, we found no differences between the groups, rioters and nonrioters alike reporting an average attendance of two or three times a month. The information from these items does not indicate that the rioter is alienated from or peripheral to the larger Negro community.

In Detroit we had questions intended to show whether or not rioting is related to differences in support for an important American value: belief in work and the Protestant ethic. Rioters and nonrioters were virtually identical in their responses to most of these questions. For example, when we asked, "Is getting what you want out of life a matter of ability or being in the right place at the right time?" 77 percent of the rioters and 76 percent of the nonrioters said it was "ability."

We have examined the riffraff theory from a number of different viewpoints and have found that the Newark and Detroit survey data do not support it. The rioters are not the poorest of the poor. They are not the hard-core unemployed. They are not the least educated. They are not unassimilated migrants or newcomers to the city. There is no evidence that they have serious personality disturbances or are deviant in their social behavior. They do not have a different set of values. None of these factors sets the rioter off from the rest of the community in a way that justifies considering him a personal failure or an irresponsible person. In fact, on some of the "prosocial" items, such as education and occupational aspiration, the rioter compares favorably with the nonrioter or even surpasses him.

The relative-deprivation theory has two major forms. The first of these is based on a motivational finding that has been known for a long time in psychology: the closer one comes to reaching a goal, the greater the frustration of not attaining it. According to this "rising expectations" point of view, riots should take place not when things are at their worst but when things are getting better —but not fast enough. Such an explanatory model holds up well in the study of revolutions; they are usually born of hope, not despair. The French Revolution, for example, occurred during a period of unprecedented economic growth,

and it was not those in abject poverty who revolted but the rising middle class.

However serviceable this theory may be in describing the environment of revolution, it does not serve to distinguish the individual rioter. If it did, we would find that those whose economic situations had improved most dramatically were the most likely to riot. In Newark we asked respondents if things had got better or worse or had remained the same for them and their families over the past few years; we found no differences between the responses of rioters and nonrioters.

A second version of the relative-deprivation theory is based on the economic and social gap between Negroes and the majority of whites. The assumption here is that members of the black community are concerned not so much with what they have as with what they feel they deserve compared with the whites; attention to the discrepancy arouses a sense of social injustice that generates the frustration leading to rioting.

In Newark we asked: "How about the gap in income between Negroes and whites? Do you think that in Newark it is increasing, decreasing or not changing?" There was no real difference in response between the groups, with 36 percent of the rioters and 38 percent of the nonrioters reporting that the gap was increasing. On the other hand, we did find a statistically reliable difference between rioters and nonrioters when we questioned them about incomes within the Negro community. We asked respondents if they thought that "the gap between those Negroes who are better off in Newark and those who are poorer is increasing, decreasing or not changing." Thirty-nine percent of the rioters and only 27 percent of the nonrioters reported that the gap was increasing, providing support for the relative-deprivation theory in an unexpected way: Rioters are particularly sensitive to where they stand in relation to other Negroes, not to whites.

The blocked-opportunity theory, unlike the other two theories, emphasizes environmental rather than personal factors as the cause of riots. Specifically, it stresses the exclusion of Negroes from white society. If this theory accurately explains the rioting, we would expect rioters to be more sensitive to discrimination and to report that they experience it more frequently in areas of achievement such as education and employment. We would also expect them to be more likely to reject the traditional stereotype of Negro inferiority. Each of these predictions is in fact borne out by the survey data.

Asked if they felt they could find the kind of job they wanted and if not why not, rioters were more likely to say that such jobs were not available to them and that the reason was racial discrimination rather than lack of education and training. We found that 69 percent of the rioters but only 50 percent of the nonrioters in Newark said racial discrimination constituted the major obstacle to better employment. Furthermore, more than half of the rioters, as compared with less than a third of the nonrioters, felt they had been discriminated against in school.

Both the Detroit and the Newark surveys indicate that rioters have strong feelings of racial pride and even racial superiority. They not only have rejected the traditional stereotype of the Negro but also have created a positive stereotype. Asked "Who do you think are smarter people, Negroes or whites?" 53 percent of the Detroit rioters and only

26 percent of the nonrioters chose Negroes; in Newark 44 percent of the rioters and only 29 percent of the nonrioters called Negroes smarter. We also asked: "Who do you think are more dependable, Negroes or whites?" In Detroit 45 percent of the rioters but only 19 percent of the nonrioters rated Negroes more dependable, as did 39 percent of the rioters and 24 percent of the nonrioters in Newark. Similarly, the rioters were more likely to consider Negroes "braver" and "nicer" than whites.

In Newark we asked two additional items related to racial identity, and here again the responses reflect a higher level of racial pride among rioters. Significantly more rioters preferred to describe themselves as "black"—a word that has become a badge of racial pride and militancy—rather than as "Negro" or "colored." Half of the rioters and only a third of the nonrioters preferred to be called black. Similarly, we found a tendency for rioters to be stronger in the belief that all Negroes should study African history and language: 80 percent of the rioters and 68 percent of the nonrioters thought these subjects should be taught.

This group of results explains the otherwise puzzling finding that rioters are more often from the North. An analysis of the data by region of upbringing showed that those who grew up in the South had less racial pride, were much more likely to blame their failures on lack of education or training rather than on discrimination and were less likely to say they had experienced discrimination in the North. Apparently growing up within the caste system of race relations in the South produces a passive adjustment to exclusion and an acceptance of discrimination as an inevitable and unchanging part of life. The Southern-born

Negro is therefore unlikely to challenge the more subtle system of discrimination he finds in the North.

The rioter's anger at a society he views as excluding him is best expressed by the responses to this question: "If the United States got into a big world war today would you personally feel this country is worth fighting for?" Thirty-nine percent of the Detroit rioters, but only 15 percent of the nonrioters, said the country was not worth fighting for. In Newark 53 percent of the rioters and 28 percent of the nonrioters said the country was not worth fighting for.

It should be emphasized that the rioters' anger is not simply a result of hostility to whites as a racial group. Instead it seems to be a general resentment of established members of U.S. society, black and white. The survey data indicate that rioters are as resentful of more affluent Negroes as they are of whites. In Newark respondents were asked if they thought that "Negroes who make a lot of money are just as bad as white people." More than half of the rioters but only a third of the nonrioters agreed with the statement. The rioters' resentment seems to cut across racial lines.

The survey data support the blocked-opportunity theory. One is led to conclude that the continued exclusion of Negroes from American economic and social life is the fundamental cause of riots. This exclusion is a result of arbitrary racial barriers rather than of lack of ability, motivation or aspiration on the part of Negroes, and it is most galling to young Negroes who perceive it as arbitrary and unjust.

One important question remains to be answered: "Why do they riot now?" After all, the opportunity structure has been closed for 100 years. Our data suggest that Negroes who riot do so because their conception of their lives and their potential has changed without commensurate improvement in their chances for a better life. In addition to abandoning the traditional stereotype that made nonachievement and passive social adaptation seem so natural, they have developed a sense of black consciousness and a desire for a way of life in which they can feel the same pride and sense of potency they now derive from being black. Negroes are still excluded from economic opportunity and occupational advancement, but they no longer have the psychological defenses or social supports that once encouraged passive adaptation to this situation. The result has been the most serious domestic violence in this century.

Planners in the Changing American City, 1900-1940

JOHN L. HANCOCK

THE MODERN CHALLENGE

If *planning* in the broadest sense is man's attempt not to displace reality but to clarify it and bring all of its elements into harmony with human purpose,[1] then the urban planner's task has changed enormously in the past few hundred years. Cities have been uniquely unequal, functional concentrations of such reality since late neolithic times—the nexus of what we call "civilization." But the reality of man's traditional societies is fast disappearing as he learns nature is not just "out there" but is everywhere a constantly modifying state he can partially manipulate to free himself of life chiefly dependent upon human and animal labor. In the emerging transitional societies where growth and change are the normal condition, modern reality finds not just a small percentage of mankind urbanized but a world urbanizing so rapidly that most of the population will be drawn into its orbit in this century. This means great change: not discovery of preconditions for group life, but sustained mechanization, surplus economic growth, and social investment already bringing undreamed material comfort, intensive specialization, fragmentation and "leisure" for a third of the world; not hierarchial social division in segmented if similar containers but egalitarian, pragmatically interwoven diversity; not fatalistic acceptance of one's lot but "rising

expectations."[2] It means demand for new balances of community, wealth, health, beauty, privacy, identity and so on, promoting not only cultural survival, adaptability and modification, but also human enrichment. In such fluid times a "plan" is tyranny and no planning is madness. Planning becomes an agent *for enhancing life* in an ever-changing but massing world—or it is nothing.

In this context, planning's alignment with American urban policy appropriately began with AIP's charter members in the reform decade before World War I, when the nation first confronted its "new" converging culture. The city, they said, was physically urbanized but not democratically organized. "There seems to be a sort of fatalism in American cities which compels them to follow mechanically a system once inaugurated no matter what it may be," an uncontrolled spread of cities "unusually inconvenient, insanitary, wasteful, ugly, degrading, inefficient."[3] They were not the first to say so; but in adopting reformer views of cities as dynamic *human* systems whose welfare could be partially guided and enhanced by willful public action, they were the first to propose that the means include "the new social ideal of unified and comprehensive city planning."[4] Reinforced by events to 1940, the pioneer planners were instrumental in making their ambitious proposal the very essence of modern American urban policy—in theory. In fact, however, while they had

From *Journal of the American Institute of Planners*, Vol. XXXIII, No. 5 (September 1967), pp. 290-304. Reprinted by permission of the publisher. John L. Hancock is Associate Professor of the American Studies Program at the University of Kansas.

found the proper focus for our times, their record in developing it through several decades of reform and change exposes still unreconciled social aims and cultural practices in urban America.

THE AMERICAN CITY SURFACE, 1800-1940

Historic American civilization is a classic example of continuing surface change. Following the initial breakdown of traditional western society, the United States prospered in material growth and suffered much societal displacement in the 15 generations separating colonial clearings from the cities of 1900. As compared to 1790, the nation was 19 times more populous, had 72 times as many urban places (doubling per decade in the period 1840-70 when manufacturing's value began exceeding agriculture's in the gross national product), covered a domain three times as large crossed in 102 hours by train or minutes by wire. It had attained the world's highest mean (not minimum) living standard, the highest population growth rate (1800-1910) and perhaps the most blurred socially mobile society.

In the profession's early years to 1940, the GNP would quadruple again; urban places and wages double; the average work week reduce a full day; cross-country travel time reduce to a day; public works spending would extend from transportation and communication to utilities, reclamation-conservation, streets-highways, and housing-community development. Urban space needs would more than double and keep changing in character as innovations like the automobile (the largest industry by 1929) helped stimulate the construction industry (next largest), and altered town form and the whole technological net.[5]

Yet amid bountiful natural, technological, and human resources, the American *manner* of settlement and the values associated with it were profoundly disruptive, especially before the 1900's. Under pragmatically developing Crown and federal encouragement of towns "Fittest for such as can trade into England" and "for a rising nation, spread over a wide and fruitful land, traversing all the seas with the rich productions of her industry . . . advancing rapidly to destinies beyond the mortal eye," urban policy was merely commercial-expansionist, permitting any local standards and practices not in conflict with mercantile contracts or democratic constitutions from which the towns derived their charters. Thus, all cities were political wards of Crown and then states, which were loathe to broaden local powers but encouraged *de facto* sources of growth. The cities all flourished according to their ability to secure external power, market, and supply. All were dominated by profit-minded oligarchies following "settle and sell, settle and sell" boom-bust practices in pursuing growth at whatever social costs. In Andrew Carnegie's words, "The American . . . need not fear the unhealthy or abnormal growth of cities. . . . The free play of economic laws is keeping all quite right. . . . Oh, these grand, immutable, all-wise laws of natural forces, how perfectly they work if human legislators would only let them alone."[6] Most did, while pursuing happiness by a reversed golden rule.

In this narrow milieu, environmental needs—civic, health, family, personal, and so forth—were subordinated to developmental ones, usually economic, in the carrying through of "city plans" too. The fact that Savannah's plan was so rigidly maintained by her philanthropist sponsors in England despite resident demands for change (they were forbidden to sell or even to profit from the land, for example) suggests in part why she was the least prosperous, least populous colonial city by the Revolution. In contrast, Philadelphia, desiccating her "greene countrie towne" plan, became the largest, most influential commercial city in the colonies and early Republic. Similarly, planning in the best of several hundred proprietor towns built between 1775 and 1906 fell apart in a generation by inability or unwillingness of the sponsors to control peripheral or later internal growth as at Lowell, whereas those paternalists who maintained planning control but failed to anticipate or permit resident desires to flourish economically and politically suffered a similar fate in town development. (As Richard Ely said of Pullman, "It is a benevolent, all-wishing feudalism which desires the happiness of the people in such a way as shall please the authorities.") Thus American developers characteristically rejected comprehensive plans altogether and used an exploitable grid core of streets and plats—in all 50 of the SMA's of 1900 and 95 per cent of today's metro cores. The common pattern in some 200 such cities by 1900 was of identical lots, 20 to 40 per cent substandard housing with dense tenantry near the center, long before the elevator and steel frame made it so dramatic. There were few permanent open spaces or neighborhood foci. There was grade-level high speed movement on main streets well before rapid transit and cars quadrupled urban travel (1890-1920), preferential location for high-paying commercial-industrial functions, permissive public controls (little municipal land ownership), sprawling peripheral growth—these were

all superimposed on unaesthetic "once-for-all" plans without adequate provision for systematic revision or extension in advance of settlement.[7] Simple to lay out, describe, convert to many uses, and extend, the stark grid of public-private origins unquestionably was yesterday's most adaptable American plan—a meritorious one for limited purposes.

Thus, the booming city did not arise from the culture floor while our backs were turned and we were tending our gardens. As an emergent development *process*, however, it bespoke the futility of rigid *a priori* and *laissez-faire* approaches or the abnegation of direction for fluid situations—and the difficulty of trying anything else.

PRESSURE FOR REORGANIZATION AND REFORM

The haphazard physical growth and social disorder accompanying American urban development, however, stimulated increasing demands for amenity, systematic physical reorganization and social reform which preceded and helped shape the modern planning movement. Physical design by the nineteenth century's new architects and landscape architects, for example, gradually assumed "comprehensive dimension, moving beyond the context of *unit* into that of *system*." Public gardens appeared about the time that Timothy Dwight urged places where "inhabitants might always find sweet air, charming walks, fountains refreshing the atmosphere, trees encircling the sun . . . objects 'found' in the country" (1821); naturalistic suburbs and *cul-de-sac* streets by the 1830's; in-city parks by the 1850's; boulevards and garden towns, idyllic leisure-class resorts and planned industrial communities by the 1870's; metropolitan park systems by the 1890's and civic centers by the 1900's. The "utopian" Mormons put 49 agricultural-industrial satellite communities around Salt Lake City using cooperative public-private methods to establish their broad streets, superblocks focused on major cultural buildings, and reclamation of a theocratic region covering the most desolate third of the nation before federal intervention. Indeed, Robert Gourlay even recommended that the Boston "district" adopt a "science of city planning" implemented by existing public powers for large-scale land reclamation, separation of major localities by green areas, and rail ties to the hub. This was a generation before Horace Bushnell (1864), urging a "new city planning profession" of specially trained men to devise "breathing spaces" without inhibiting future needs, asked why the city should "be left to the misbegotten planning of some operator totally disqualified? . . . Nothing is to be more regretted . . . than that our American nation, having a new world to make, and a clean map on which to place it, should be sacrificing our advantage so cheaply. . . ."

More characteristic of the mainstream was designer-booster collaboration on the "city beautiful" at the Chicago world's fair (1893) whose neoclassical plan, reflecting pools, greenstrips, statuary, massive buildings, macadem roads, electrification, and hidden utilities well illustrated coordinator Daniel Burnham's remark that "Beauty has always paid better than any other commodity." Convinced that physical order equalled social order, viewers went home to plan more fairs and to plant, paint, clean, and partially rebuild their cities. The

first was Washington itself which, under the McMillan Commission, secured a Park Commission (1895); District Highway Plan (1896); the first enforceable (but not enforced) building heights and zoning laws (1899); a Planning Committee under Burnham, Frederick Law Olmsted, Sr., and others (1901); and "mapped streets" (1900-06).[8] There were just a few such works before 1900, however, most of them backed by wealthy private sponsors rarely able to continue such revitalization by themselves.

The social reformers' broader search was similar in its increasing comprehensiveness and expertise. Theodore Parker advocated planned "industrial democracy" featuring low-rent housing, and improved work and health standards in the 1830's, a generation before organized civic interest in tenement reform, public health, and migrant population control (encouraging "normal distribution in town and country," reduction of urban densities, and so on—a kind of stay-on-the-land movement in contrast to the unsuccessful "back-to-the-land" resettlement efforts of the 1900-1940 period). After the Civil War a rising chorus of voices rose with those of Henry George and Edward Bellamy to promote an "economizing of social forces"; with "Golden Rule" Jones, other reform mayors and the National Municipal League (1894) to obtain more democratic local government; and with those of Richard Ely, Simon Patten, Albion Small, and others in a few universities to secure serious urban study and research on the "new America." On the grand scale perhaps, Henry D. Lloyd (lawyer, social critic, administrator, and teacher) put many of these ideas together in his proposal to raze and transform central Chicago into a permanent cultural park focus for a regional "No Mean City" of self-contained urban-rural towns built on the latest garden city, cooperative, condemnation, and electrification methods in 1899.[9]

The merger of these interests with the more prosaic, somewhat remedial, but decidedly militant national reforms of the next generation signaled the real beginning of responsible social change in modern America. The period's very name—the *progressive era*, 1906-16 (variously dated 1900-19)—indicated the demand for orderly forward transition to a world of "social justice," "social welfare," and, as John Dewey said of the era's greatest challenge, "the possibility of constructive social engineering." It demanded that these assume primacy in the quest for human progress. The ideological response to the popular demands was a clear YES.[10] The measureable results were basic change in mood and a small but crucial reorganization of mixed-enterprise democracy, which has since broadened in scale if not purpose.

THE PROFESSION EMERGES, 1907-19

The mood and means were of vital significance to the planning profession. Progressive Republicans, reform Democrats, Socialists, and nonpartisans who had led in securing state-legislated local government changes, such as home rule, new charters, reapportionment, and so forth, also brought in the first "expert planning advisors" to lecture, show slides of work elsewhere, and in several hundred cases to survey and/or replan their cities—to show people how to rebuild cities. Given the city's increasing predominance, a *laissez-faire* past more blundering than purposeful in human

terms, and faith that man must plan (though no one really knew how) in times changing more rapidly than anyone comprehended, the era's mandate for renewal fairly cried for a new profession of urban specialists. Was the mandate important? In Franklin D. Roosevelt's words on first hearing of planning (1909), "I think from that moment on I have been interested in not the mere planning of a single city but in the larger aspects of planning. It is the way of the future."[11]

Aside from a few inspiring piecemeal reports prior to 1906, there were no surveys, general planning, or professional planners as such, and as John Nolen later recalled, "no knowledge of, no interest in city planning among the people generally." Between 1907 and 1917 over 100 towns undertook "comprehensive planning"—half the 50 largest cities, 13 per cent of all with populations over 10,000. Ninety-seven municipal planning commissions and two dozen zoning codes were enabled in a few urban states. By 1917 there were dozens of municipal information clearing houses, a shelf of technical literature, and three planning-oriented magazines "to record knowledge of intelligently and earnestly and systematically planned cities" and "the history of municipal science in the making." Eleven universities offered 23 courses on planning "principles" (subordinated to other curricula); two others gave courses on the "Economics of City Planning" and "Urban Sociology." There were four annual urban conferences (one devoted specifically to planning) plus an international meeting, planning divisions in the other design professions, and an American City Planning Institute. By the war's end practically every urban interest group in the country called for an urban cabinet post or a "Federal Bureau of Municipal Information" collating and distributing "all urban information . . . instead of confining it solely to planning."[12] The art and science of planning as a force in urban reform policies was clearly underway, then, in the progressive era.

The pivotal inaugural year was 1909 when the first National Conference on City Planning and the Problems of Congestion convened at Washington with representatives from health, housing, law, social work, engineering, gardening, real estate, government, philanthrophy, conservation, architecture, landscape architecture, and so on, all calling for reform. Supported thereafter by the Russell Sage Foundation, NCCP (last part of title having been dropped in 1910) became the chief forum for bringing the movement's emergent elements together and broadcasting them in its publications (for example, City Plan, 1915). It met in different cities each year (in Washington once during each new administration). Most importantly for the new profession, NCCP's executive and program committees were dominated by planners who used this forum to fashion their common social commitments and systematic technical approaches into a viable pattern for urban redevelopment. "What is needed in city planning?" asked Nolen, the 1909 keynoter:

Everything . . . a wiser husbanding of our aesthetic and human as well as natural resources . . . legislation that meets more meaningfully the needs of twentieth century life . . . using to our advantage science, art, skill and experience. . . . [but above all] We should no longer be content with mere increases in population and wealth. We should insist upon asking, "How do the people live, where do they work, what do they play?"

In 1910 NCCP president Frederick Law Olmsted, Jr., called this approach "the new social ideal of unified and comprehensive city planning":

City planning, applied with common sense and with due regard for human limitations of time and place, has a breadth and ramification at once inspiring and appalling. Any mind with sufficient imagination to grasp it must be stimulated by this conception of the city as one great social organism whose welfare is in part determined by the action of the people who compose the organism today, and therefore by the collective intelligence and good will that control those actions.

By 1911 president Charles Mulford Robinson called it the "science of city planning"—a decided shift from his earlier views (see Modern Civic Art, 1903). Beautification was not discussed as a major NCCP topic between 1910-20 but "planning" (rather than "plan" or "plan-making"), "system," "efficient and intelligent public controls," the "ordinary citizen," and the "common welfare" became commonplace in the idiom. Remarkably free of dogma, the planners were chiefly interested in "comprehensive planning." They discussed it as a major topic in seven of the meetings between 1910-20 along with continuing discussion of its "elements": financing and administration, zoning-planning law, and official commission practices; streets, transportation, industrial, recreation and land planning; "limited dividend" (4 per cent) low-cost housing (public-private); minimum standards (some via "model" studies); the merits of particular plans and useful European practices.[13] Finally, as the war began, they created the American City Planning Institute, a professional division within NCCP whose object "shall be to study the science and advance the art of city planning." ACPI gave full membership to trained professionals and to "others who shall have special attainments in city planning," associate membership with voting privileges to related non-professionals (no more than four of whom could sit on the 21-man Board of Governors) and a few (rare) honorary memberships.[14]

The systematization of these elements was a gradual process, of course. James Sturgis Pray introduced his seminal "Principles of City Planning" class into the landscape curriculum at Harvard in 1909, the year that Patrick Abercrombie opened the School of Civic Design at Liverpool. Benjamin Marsh's textbook *Introduction to City Planning* the same year urged government responsibility ("the most important element") for the common health and welfare, stressed housing, and termed planning "the most efficient method of projecting municipal efficiency." The planners got a most vital new perspective and preplanning tool from Shelby Harrison and Paul Kellogg's *Pittsburgh Survey* (1907-09, published 1914), whiched mapped data on population, traffic, health, housing, building (location-condition-use), property values, assessments, areas served by schools, and so on. It also appended legal-fiscal suggestions for public planning from such data. On the other hand, the most famous planning report of 1909 was Daniel Burnham and Edward Bennett's magnificently rendered, vaguely regional *Plan of Chicago*, which "quite frankly takes into consideration the fact that the American city, and Chicago preeminently, is a center of industry and traffic." It merely saluted housing needs, termed planning inexpensive (not requiring large public expenditure, taxation, or public control) but stressed

(and proved) that "aroused public sentiment; and practical men of affairs" could secure new traffic, park, and building programs giving "unity and dignity" to the city.[15]

Most comprehensive reports and several texts incorporated all these elements into the planning process by 1916. The reports, for example, generally had three major parts—preplanning surveys (mapping of physical, economic, and social data), a "General Plan" with detailed parts, and appended methods of implementation. Sometimes the latter were put into the main text for emphasis. Some surveys included evidence of the city's historic "individuality" (its achievements and deficiencies in land use, for example) so that planner and public alike might "frame a concept, an ideal of what we wish the city to be" and make it a controlling factor in the plan's development. Most specific suggestions for implementation urged better employment of existing law, more home rule and degrees of municipal authority approaching those in Europe. Few suggested planning was inexpensive or short term. ("At bottom the question is whether real values are to be had from this sort of city planning, and whether the community can provide the ways and means necessary to purchase these values.") Most spoke of spending efficiently and the major reports encouraged "equitable distribution of current taxes," increased borrowing capacity, extended bonded periods, municipal condemnation "with a much larger share for the community in increasing land values," and special tax and land incentives to encourage large-scale, low-cost housing development. No two plans were alike but the basic idea was to modernize and broaden public uses by opening up and decentralizing the city where possible so as to promote environments "having a more sensitive regard for the common welfare . . . past, present and future."

Recommendations thus included differentiated building zones and street flow, overall circulatory flow, landscaped "gateways" (such as waterfronts) for public uses, park systems covering "at least 10 per cent of the city area," rerouting or elimination of grade-level transit traffic (transit systems were encouraged in larger cities), economic "zones" (blocks) but mixed income neighborhoods (new ones grouped in park-like settings around shops or schools on the city's edges to further break the grid and reduce unplanned encroachment), downtown core of facilities, and rather formal civic groupings from which major streets radiated to the various sub-centers.[16] In a more abstract, technical manner, Robinson's *City Planning* detailed thoroughfare and residential platting standards in advance of settlement; Nelson Lewis' *Planning the Modern City* concentrated on traffic circulation and control standards, drawing heavily from his experience with New York's influential "building districts" (zoning) report; NML's *Town Planning for Small Cities* by Charles Bird (manufacturer and major Progressive Party figure in Massachusetts) recommended the reorganization of several towns of 30,000 people or less into regional districts by garden city planning principles; and NML's *City Planning* (1917) by 18 authors under Nolen, brought all such "Essential Elements of a City Plan" into one text spelling out "lines of investigation, planning and control which have been found most sound in theory and most successful in practice." These texts emphasized planning's flexibility and al-

ternatives, suggesting minimums for local work but discouraging universal, textbook solutions. They simultaneously looked toward "scientific exactness." As George Ford said in his essay on the socioeconomic factors in planning:

Satisfactory methods can be arrived at only by applying modern scientific methods. It is now realized that the city is a complex organism, so complex that no doctor is safe in prescribing for it unless he has made a thorough-going and impartial diagnosis of everything that may have even the remotest bearing on the case.[17]

If there was a definite system in this work by 1917, however, there was as yet more hope than adequate empirical data for making meaningful generalizations for this inexact science.

Who were the collaborators? All were originally trained in other fields; some formed temporary teams or permanent offices for major projects (like Ford and E. P. Goodrich's Technical Advisory Corporation). Several were Europeans working extensively in North America (like Edward Bennett, Thomas Adams, and Werner Hegemann). The 18 NML authors, for example, were almost all urban-born, lectured in the universities, wrote extensively, traveled abroad regularly, and half had worked or studied (half having at least one degree from Harvard or MIT) under men whose work was largely done before ACPI was formed. By training, their breakdown into two architects, four lawyers, five landscape architects, six engineers, a realtor, a civic reform leader, and a professor of social ethics (housing specialist) parallels that of ACPI's original 75-man roster in the first two membership categories—10 architects, 12 lawyers, 18 landscape architects, 23 engineers, 6 realtors and 7 others—with leadership unevenly divided. (Beginning with Olmsted, Sr., most ACPI presidents through 1942 were originally trained in landscape architecture or engineering.) While questions of training, ethics and leadership were frequent, however, all agreed that a "planner" was defined by his experience and focus, not by special training.[18]

In 1917 when the mood was much greater than the means for planning, actual practices were very primitive, even those that were official. Judging from 250 accounts, the work usually began with a lecture or preplanning survey of needs and opportunities in which the planner sought local support —public or private (usually a civic or commercial group, occasionally a wealthy patron). If mutually agreeable, a contract was signed making the planner responsible for all plan preparations and the sponsor responsible for eventual adoption and enforcement. This step often involved forming a larger "amalgamated" citizen group to clarify goals, assist the technical staff, review detail proposals, secure an official commission with "advisory powers," and push for planning throughout the city. During the next two to three years, field representatives collected data, encouraged the movement, reported back on its pulse, and sometimes lived in the area. The home office made all basic decisions, did the final drafting, and then presented the general program for local acceptance after an appropriate publicity program. If the plan was adopted, the planner also encouraged implementation, periodic review and cooperation with other communities (particularly contiguous ones) in the urban region. His firm often performed partial services as well—having contracts for park systems, subdivisions, campuses, industrial districts, housing programs, addi-

tional surveys not followed up and so on. The Nolen office (the largest firm between 1915 and 1925), for example, had contracts in 200 cities of which 10 were for new towns and 29 for comprehensive replanning rather evenly distributed in five basic groupings from towns of 10,000 or less to metropolitan areas of 1.5 million people or more. Less than half of the plans were implemented, a third of these with any degree of fullness—a fair average in the whole period to 1940.[19]

The climax of these early activities was the federal "emergency" wartime housing-town planning program, finally combining the expertise, standards, aims, large resources *and* public powers necessary for realization. Planner-directed teams collaborated on 67 projects averaging 25 acres in size, abandoned the grid and alleys where possible, introduced the latest technical standards, sought harmonious variety (house styles and groupings, plantings, street patterns, and so forth), preserved natural features, developed the land in large pieces to avoid economic waste and to increase pedestrian convenience, and grouped major buildings to give "definite center and point to the whole design." They did such an excellent job from the resident's point of view that there was a waiting line for purchase or occupancy up to World War II, while Congress and realtors called them "too costly" for war workers and disbanded the incompleted experiment with alacrity at the war's end. As Olmsted, Jr., saw "the very valuable lesson":

We have been convinced not only theoretically but by practical experience, that the cooperation of all those who have special knowledge in the arrangement, construction and running of towns is essential to any real "town planning" and that it is per-

fectly possible to bring about the cooperation and to apply it efficiently in actual
work.

For many of the younger collaborators
too, this experience provided "a tremendous enthusiasm to build a new and
better world," as Clarence Stein said of
himself and Henry Wright.[20]

Thus, the profession had taken some
long first steps by 1919, even if they
were steps that needed more complete
public authorization and more versatile
and imaginative planner conceptualization by today's standards. There were
definite physical changes too,—a park
system, a low-cost housing program,
better circulation, an active public
agency, occasionally all of these in one
city—but, most importantly, there was a
new intent behind this work, a new
standard of measurement. As Harland
Bartholomew put it in 1917, "The welfare of the group is . . . now generally
considered to supercede the *rights of
the individual* when questions of health,
safety and general welfare arise."[21]

FLUX AND FLOW, 1920-40
But moods change, as was indicated in
the sharp tensions distinguishing urbanization's spread in the period 1920-40.
Bracketed by wars, the opening years
assumed "prosperity" and "normalcy"
obtained with minimal public direction,
while the latter ones affirmed—perhaps
conclusively—the lie in merely voluntary
subscription to modern social responsibilities and again advanced broadly empowered public-private unions to enhance, if not insure, them. Influenced
by both attitudes, the profession's markedly improved technical, legislative,
and conceptual approaches to urban,
regional, and national problems were
more theoretical than tested until the
mid-1930's.

Cities which had begun planning

earlier were quickest to resume and expand. Major reports now commonly included more sophisticated handling of
social data, zoning and land use maps
(late 1930's), capital improvement
budgets (late 1920's), and detail and
alternate plan proposals within the
"Master Plan"—the new name for general or comprehensive plans. They were
increasingly supported by empirical research in the profession (see for example the *Harvard City Planning Series*, 1931 *ff.*), the social sciences and
federal reports making possible more
exacting scientific generalizations. *But
the record and manner of public acceptance in the 1920's was no better or
essentially different, however "official."*
Approximately one-fifth of the thousand
city planning, zoning and housing reports made in this decade—three times
as many as in the preceding one—were
actually followed through to any degree; over 95 per cent of the general
plans made were by private firms,
though now generally under city contract. Most firms were larger. They
periodically revised survey and planning data, sometimes left a field man
as local commission head, dropped
mixed transportation recommendation
(for example, rapid transit) in favor of
automated traffic planning almost exclusively, and perhaps under pressure
to be "practical" said less about the
common welfare in adjusting to what
clients would accept. Typical of the
general case, according to several studies, the largest firm (Bartholomew Associates, after 1925) dropped housing
altogether (1923-36), obscured the
priority of community over private
rights, emphasized physical elements
alone, and fitted local situations to general standards (for example, population, density, traffic projection) which
were sometimes not flexible enough to

suit rapid modern changes, although its chief remained critical of these trends (except the last) "outside the confines of his business contracts."[22]

An era affects its planners then, as everyone else. (Even Walter Lippmann wrote in 1927 that "the more or less unconscious and unplanned activities of businessmen are for once more novel, more daring and in general more revolutionary than the theories of the progressives." *Men of Destiny*. New York: Macmillan, 1927.) Consider the permissively drawn and coordinated legislative "progress." By 1935 every state had planning, zoning, plat control, or all of these written into its organic law. Public planning commissions rose from 297 in 1919 to be included in all but two of the larger cities (over 100,000 people) plus hundreds of others by 1934—95 per cent of them official, the reverse of 1919. But only a fifth had comprehensive plans, few were applying them, most were powerless advisory bodies composed of citizens often serving without pay or understanding. Massachusetts, the first state to require planning commissions (1913) had 97 by 1929, but 80 cities, including Boston, still lacked plans. Before the court approved Euclid Village's comprehensive zoning code (building and land use, height-bulk-density in "reasonable" and "substantial" relation to community safety, health, welfare, and "morals") in 1926, only 76 cities had zoning ordinances. By 1936, 1,322 or 85 per cent of the cities had them, but less than half were comprehensive, and the cities (not compelled to zone) often used them to perpetuate *status quo* discrimination and whim. Extra-territorial plat control (up to five miles, based on ACPI guidelines) permitted planning along topographical as well as jurisdictional lines in half the states by 1929,

but only a few cities adopted it, almost none in conformance with master plans. Planners approved the potential significance of these legal developments but protested their loose application and the tendency to adopt zoning *in lieu of* planning. Realtors, however, were enthusiastic after some initial doubts and real estate actually emerged as "the last great individualistic American enterprise" long after industry and finance had become large-scale, mixed corporate operations. Indeed into the early depression, national administrations urged Americans to "lay plans for making plans," provided occasional models and left everything else to local good will because "at present . . . this phrase represents a social need rather than a social capacity." Thus implementation and coordination were difficult at best, apathy was common, and expediency certain. The result, in Thomas Adams' phrase, was "city-mending."[23]

Partly because of such frustrations amid growing needs, the profession did sharpen its training, roles, and theories. With programs still subordinated to other curricula in the 80 schools (1925) offering or requiring planning courses, Harvard initiated a master's degree in Landscape Architecture in City Planning, published *City Planning Quarterly* (forerunner of the *Journal*) in 1925, and, with a Rockefeller Foundation grant, inaugurated a full three-year School of City Planning under Henry Hubbard in 1929. Columbia, Cornell, and MIT also granted the MCP degree by 1940. In courses the planner's "role" was now described as analyst, creative artist, critic, and coordinator having

above all . . . the social and civic welfare point of view, for the motive back of all city and regional planning is to improve the daily life and working conditions—to develop the "good life" . . . a difficult and elaborate process . . . [requiring] the wisdom of Solomon, the heart of a prophet, the patience of Job, and the hide of a rhinoceros.

In the new civil service category of "city planner" (created for the National Capitol Park and Planning Commission with ACPI help in 1926), the role demanded a man or woman (age 25-55) university graduate in landscape architecture with "at least five years of responsible and successful experience" or equivalent scholarship to head a staff preparing plans, recommendations, and regulations for an awesome number of physical "and other proper elements of city and regional planning." (Charles Eliot II received the first appointment.) The profession's growing belief that this was an increasingly specialized task may be seen in its exclusion of the new profession of public administrators from ACPI membership in 1924 and, as the renamed American Institute of Planners, its total separation from NCCP in 1934. NCCP (also keeping administrators off its executive board) then merged with ACA to become the American Planning and Civic Association, and the administrators formed under Walter Blucher (1935) into the American Society of Planning Officials. Thus, a mixed urban alliance divided into four rather specialized policy groups (including NML), with planners the only group eligible for all four memberships.[24]

The profession's most notable innovations in this period, however, had to do with broadening the concept of man's environment, its future and its planning. Adding psycho-biological to the earlier socioeconomic considerations of well-being, the enlarged views held that the search for and growth of individuality and diversity were as vital to existence in massing society as commonality of rights and opportunities. Refusing to plan from statistical projections or the noblest historic examples alone, the planners became less harsh in their blending of scientific and humanistic wisdom, perhaps less certain about future needs but certainly much concerned with the importance of the immediate, of what happens today, in getting there. Thus, Lewis Mumford urged NCCP in 1927 to develop "new social instruments and policies on a regional rather than an urban scale" which did not lead merely to more mechanized or congested cities. The planner's idiom increasingly contained such metaphors as "symbiosis," "human-scale," and "flow" (Mumford); the natural region," and "living" rather than "making a living" (Benton MacKaye); "excessive concentration [not as synonymous with congestion but] . . . as a psychological as well as economic and physical problem," and having "a more natural biological life under pleasanter and more natural conditions . . . to enjoy life itself." (Nolen)[25]

Several dozen elaborate experimental studies and abbreviated works resulted from these emphases. For example, Arthur Comey proposed "city-state" planning for three major cities joined by "interstate" freeways and arterial routes to surrounding towns, all separated by greenbelts, with population growth "automatically controlled" along the freeways until the region's "natural" limits had been reached. MacKaye preferred a smaller optimum-size (50,000 people each), "regional" city exercising conservation (natural, technical, human) and "commodity-flow" control in concert with requirements of other area foci. Several thick-volumed metropolitan, state, and regional studies by large staffs of planners, social scientists and officials defined joint public-private means for removing destructive socio-physical agents. They laid down advance guidelines according to natural or actual settlement instead of by arbitrary politics or economic expediency, clarified project priorities and area relationships, and prepared master plans as guides to the area's overall needs not as substitutes for local planning and development. All believed regions were the logical modern contexts for co-ordinating local and national priorities, although of course these reports lacked official sanction or enablement, as they generally still do. Similar principles were employed in the development of new towns and housing projects, notably those by the City Housing Corporation and Regional Planning Association of America (Stein, Wright, Mumford, MacKaye, Fritz Malcher, and others), whose superblocks, "steady-flow" traffic, greenbelts, and grouped housing arrangements sought stability, sociability, diversity, and (with proper enforcement and subsidized building methods) blight prevention. Failing to attract industry, technological interest in mass-housing, or private investors able to sustain the large initial costs and low unit profits, however, none of the period's 63 new towns (36 in the 1920's) was finished as planned. "Farm-city" and other rural resettlement proposals of the 1920's were not even constructed until the New Deal (and not really successfully then). And almost all of these "new towns" in city or country became half-finished upper-income suburbs little different in effect (not design) from ordinary ones[26]—going to people who already had more blessings, sunshine, and cultural insularity than anyone else.

The depression, however, made planning not only fashionable again but also imperative under the New Deal. Whereas Hoover pursued *recovery* using government's "reserve powers" to protect citizens against "forces beyond their control," Roosevelt also undertook programs for permanent *reform* on the broadest possible front, using these powers very pragmatically in the search for ways to renovate the whole cultural fabric. To guide them, he said in a popular explanation, "The time called for and still calls for planning." Indeed, as he told Congress that same year (1934):

I look forward to the time in the not too distant future, when annual appropriations, wholly covered by current revenue, will enable the work to proceed with a national *plan*. Such a plan will, in a generation or two, return many times the money spent on it; more important it will eliminate the use of inefficient tools, conserve and increase national resources, prevent waste, and enable millions of our people to take better advantage of the opportunities which God has given our country.[27]

Roosevelt (whose uncle Frederick Delano was a charter NCCP member) got many, if not most, such ideas directly from the profession. For example, upon entering office he canvassed a National Land Use Planning Committee (including ACPI members Alfred Bettman, Jacob Crane, Nolen, and Eliot II) "with reference to the technique of making planning effective." From their recommendations for a federal agency for national planning policy, research, and administration came the short-lived Civil Works Administration (1933-34), whose 10,000 employees made state and local surveys and plan studies, among other things. Another result was the seminal, *ex-officio* National Planning Board (renamed the National Resources Board in 1934, the National Resources Committee in 1935-36, and the National Resources Planning Board until Congress disbanded it in 1943). It unofficially reviewed all public policy on natural, industrial and human resources, served as a "permanent long-range commission" for research, planning, and coordinating of related private-public development; gathered the most complete data on American resources assembled through 1943; and lent professional talent and planning advice to whoever wanted it—41 states, 70 counties and regions, 400 towns and cities before 1940.[28]

The New Deal's pragmatic approach did not sweep away the *laissez-faire* past, but its massive planning began early, spanned the period, and seems to have made the difference between national chaos and general crisis—the century's continuing condition. Most development programs came out of the First Hundred Days legislation: NRPB, TVA (to 1937 it included town planning under Earle Draper and Tracy Augur), conservation and public works (CWA, Public Works Administration, and so forth), home financing and improvement (partly inspired by Hoover's Home Loan Bank), housing and slum clearance (PWA's Housing Division under Robert Kohn, Federal Housing Authority 1936, U.S. Housing Authority absorbing all town planning in 1937), and urban-rural resettlement (Subsistence Homesteads and the Greenbelt programs). Four of these programs originated in omnibus bills of 1933. Only NRPB and resettlement—perhaps the most revolutionary programs—failed to be made continuing works. All utilized professional services extensively as many of today's senior planners will attest. All were supported by enormous

expenditures as compared to the World War I period (247 millions spent on renewal in 1940, a third of it federal as opposed to one million spent by the federal government in 1917-18), and all emphasized planning for permanent social improvement this time not omitting that "one-third of a nation ill-housed, ill-clad, and ill-fed." As the Urbanism Committee described the "new" emphasis:

The prosperity and happiness of the teeming millions who dwell there are closely bound up with that of America, for if the city fails, America fails. The Nation cannot flourish without its urban-industrial centers, or without its countryside; or without a sound balance between them. City planning, county planning, rural planning, state planning, regional planning must be linked together in the higher strategy of American national policy, to the end that our national and local resources may best be conserved and developed for our human use.[29]

The nearly continuing state of war which has consumed so much of the nation's resources and attention since 1939 has perhaps unduly clouded our application of this comprehensive view of domestic development policy. But with its formal acceptance as the very center of such policy up through the national level, planners ceased to be merely semiofficial consultants and two generations of professional growth came to a close—in theory if not always in practice.

RETROSPECT: THE PAST AS INDEX OF PLANNING'S PLACE IN FUTURE POLICY

The contributions of any one group to the endless reorganization of American cities are both small and inseparably bound with the events to which they responded. Nevertheless, while contemporaries must draw their own conclusions knowing today's planning needs are more complex and the procedures more sophisticated and potent, one judges historical significance according to how well a people approach the fundamental problems of their own time, not necessarily by how well they also anticipate ours. But by either definition, certainly by the first, the profession's development of basic premises and relationships through 1940 seems critical to the organization of life-giving reality in this century. These might be summarized as follows:

1. In a massing democracy, communities built for social and personal well-being take precedence over mere economic-technological-physical growth.

2. The city's reorganization in these terms can be partially guided, unified, and enhanced by comprehensive planning which informs but does not inhibit the future.

3. Planning, the art and science of environmental development, is a process in which democratic choice can become meaningful, and capability can approach desire by identifying needs, amenities, minimum standards and so on and by implementing them in numerous designs for new communities in town and countryside which preserve and extend the most desirable features of each as appropriate to time and place.

4. Such planning requires collaboration of means, continuing reallocation of resources, full public empowerment and intelligent human subscription—a slow and gradual process whose success depends largely upon education to its human purposes—for layman and planner alike. The planner's role herein is as analyst, creative designer, critic, and coordinator, at the very least.

5. Planning of the "natural region" not the urban one alone seems the ideal

democratic context for coordinating the flow of national and local priorities, resources, and initiative, because cities overlap in needs but are deficient in means as presently constituted.

Of course, the discovery and elaboration of these ideas was more pronounced than their implementation in the period. Hence, a good part of their significance lies in prospects for the growth of such *ideas* as a departure from the past rather than in any dramatically evident humanization of the spreading cities— which was far less than one would have hoped.

How pertinent are such views in our time? Practically every close observer since reformer Frederick Howe in 1906 finds them indispensable to a world with centers but vanishing bounds, with as much disruption as convergence, with continuing economic-technological fascinations that make any planning for liveable cities difficult to obtain, although man's psychosocial needs for contact, love, privacy, beauty, greenspace and so on are "not frills or luxuries but real biological necessities," as René Dubos says.[30] Contemporary planners can point to thousands of operative public agencies; more scientific land use, economic and demographic base studies; integration of training and research with the social, behavioral, and natural sciences; and more widespread public support. But as Melvin Webber says in his AIP policy paper on "Comprehensive Planning and Social Responsibility," none of these insures our ability "to induce those patterns that will effectively increase accessibility to the diverse opportunities for productive social intercourse that are latent in an advanced civilization." Rather "Improving capacity for rationality must be joined with improving wisdom—there is no other name. It is *here* that the road forks, the one route leading to technocratic control by elites, the other to guided expansion of individual freedom." Moreover, the early planners' legacy to the present—"an egalitarian ethic and a pragmatic orientation to betterment" which Webber states and history affirms—also implies working with the events, techniques, and potentials of one's own time in pursuing and expanding the environmental vision,[31] *without* becoming mesmerized by any of them.

Who can tell what lies ahead? Obviously the city continues its rapid surface growth while its development remains sublimated to pressures unalterable even by the best planning alone. Most physical change in today's booming cities is conducted by private interests under public auspices for speculative purposes—rebuilding business centers, transport lines and suburbs where they hope the markets are; exploiting human weaknesses and upping pressures to conform—or deceive; and relocating as fast and as far from the centers for "making a living" as incomes permit. They are not villains, but our historic attachment to *a priori* decisions covering all human possibilities in yesterday's universe and to quantitative empirical standards as the only valid proof of anything combines to fill space with cheap structures, more controlling agencies than control, and a general meanness which cuts us off from one another at home and abroad. No thriving Hometown, USA, claims to be a fast-growing democracy; it invariably claims to be the fast*est* growing population or market area in its region. Unfortunately the penalties attached to such behavior include bland acceptance of affluence by most of us, alienation or intransigence by those who cannot or will not,

probably growing public wariness, loneliness and helplessness generally. Few of us escape. All these signs of imbalance on scales unknown to traditional societies indicate our need for more mix, for new definitions of *man, living,* and *community* rather than for more distinct socioeconomic categories in a free society. If our present use-and-throw away culture is weirdly appealing, it also is a commentary, then, on our unwillingness to seek and hence our inability to begin creating handsome, balanced, *many-sided* lifeways.

So planning's future in urban policy is hardly assured despite three generations of planner pressure. Thus one comes back to the millions of individual decision-makers, perhaps most of us now indifferent, who will affect any such policy; one comes back to our mutual *desire* for life lived as freely, fully, openly, and peacefully as possible. However absurd the desire, however needing restatement today—and both are considerable—it is the profession's good fortune to have been closely identified with it since near the century's turn.

NOTES

1. Lewis Mumford, *The Culture of Cities* (New York: Harcourt, Brace, 1938), pp. 374-87, 376.
2. Ernest Weissman, "The Urban Crisis in the World," *Urban Affairs Quarterly,* I (September, 1965), pp. 65-82; V. Gordon Childe, *Man Makes Himself* (New York: Mentor Books, 1951), pp. 180-88; Gideon Sjoberg, *The Preindustrial City: Past and Present* (Glencoe: Free Press, 1960), pp. 321-44; and Walter W. Rostow, *The Stages of Economic Growth* (London: Cambridge University Press, 1960), pp. 4-11.
3. John Nolen, *Replanning Reading* (Boston: G. H. Ellis, 1910), p. 3; and "Planning Problems of Industrial Cities—Niagara Falls as an Illustration," *Proceedings of the Eleventh National Conference on City Planning* (New York: NCCP, 1919), p. 23.
4. Frederick Law Olmsted, Jr., "Basic Principles of City Planning," *Proceedings . . . Second NCCP* (Boston: NCCP, 1910), pp. 3-4.

5. Donald J. Bogue, *The Population of the United States* (Glencoe: The Free Press, 1959), pp. 4-40, 126-27, 138-39; *Historical Statistics of the United States* (Washington: Government Printing Office, 1960), *passim*; Simon Kuznets and Dorthy S. Thomas, eds., *Population Distribution and Economic Growth*, 3 vols. (Philadelphia: American Philosophical Society, 1957-63) I, pp. 2-3; II, pp. 32-38, 53, 182-83, 205-71.

6. Quoted in Walter M. Whitehill, *Boston: A Topographical History* (Cambridge: Harvard University Press, 1959), p. 1; "Thomas Jefferson, 1st Inaugural Address" (1801), Inaugural Addresses of the Presidents of the United States (Washington, D.C.: Government Printing Office, 1952), pp. 11-13; Thomas Cochran and William Miller, *The Age of Enterprise* (New York: Macmillan, 1942), pp. 3-51, 252-53, 354-58, quoted 39; Andrew Carnegie, *Triumphant Democracy* (New York: Charles Scribner's Sons, 1886), pp. 47-48.

7. Richard Ely, "Pullman: A Social Study," *Harpers Magazine*, LXX (February, 1885), pp. 405-06; Daniel J. Boorstin, *The Americans: The Colonial Experience* (New York: Random House, 1958), pp. 33-96; figures from Bogue, *Population Growth in Standard Metropolitan Areas, 1900-50* (Washington D.C.: Government Printing Office, December, 1953), pp. 10-11, checked against George Ford, ed., *City Planning Progress in the United Sates, 1917* (Washington D.C.: American Institute of Architects, 1916), pp. 5-193; Richard M. Hurd, *Principles of City Land Values* (New York: The Record and Guide, 1903), pp. 1-74, 142; Homer Hoyt, *The Structure and Growth of Residential Neighborhoods in American Cities* (Washington, D.C.: Government Printing Office, 1939), pp. 101-04, 9-122; Nolen, *New Ideals in the Planning of Cities, Towns, and Villages* (New York: American City Bureau, 1919), pp. 1-19, quoted 27; John Reps, *The Making of Urban America* (Princeton: Princeton University Press, 1965), pp. 294-438.

8. Norman J. Johnston, "A Preface to the Institute," *Journal of the American Institute of Planners*, XXXI (August, 1965), pp. 198-209, quoted 201; Timothy Dwight, *Travels in New England and New York*, 4 vols. (New Haven: np, 1821-22), I, pp. 490-91; Reps, *Making of Urban America*, pp. 263-514; Leonard J. Arrington, *Great Basin Kingdom* (Cambridge: Harvard University Press, 1958), pp. 161-94, 235-414; Gourley, *Plans for Beautifying New York and Improving the City of Boston* (Boston: Saxton Pierce, 1844), pp. 1-38; Bushnell, "City Plans," *Work and Play* (New York: Charles Scribner, 1864), p. 376. (My thanks to Prof. Joseph Smeall, UND, for this source.) Ford, ed., *City Planning Progress*, pp. 183-86. There were world's fairs in Atlanta 1895, Omaha 1898, Buffalo 1901, St. Louis 1904, Seattle 1909, and San Diego-San Francisco 1914-15.

9. Quoting Parker and Lloyd in Daniel Aaron, *Men of Good Hope* (New York: Oxford University Press, 1951), pp. 45-66, 155-56, *passim;* Roy Lubove, *The Progressive and the Slums* (Pittsburgh: University of Pittsburgh Press, 1962), pp. 1-48, 217-56; B. O. Flower, *Progressive Men, Women and the Movements of the Past Twenty-Five Years* (Boston: New Arena, 1914), *passim*.

10. Dewey, *Characters and Events*, in J. Ratner ed., (New York: Henry Holt, 1929), p. 830; Woodrow Wilson, *The New Freedom* (New York: Doubleday, 1913), quoted pp. 283, 294; George Mowrey, *The Era of Theodore Roosevelt and the Birth of Modern America, 1900-1912* (New York: Harper & Brothers, 1958), pp. 16-84, 250-95; John Ihlder, "The New Civic Spirit," *American City*, IV (March, 1911), pp. 123-27.

11. "Growing Up By Plan," *Survey*, LXVII (February, 1932), p. 506.

12. Nolen, "Twenty Years of Planning Progress in the United States, 1907-27," *Proceedings . . . Nineteenth NCCP* (Boston: NCCP, 1927), pp. 1-44 quoted; editorials, *American City*, I (September, 1909), p. 3, VIII (January, 1913), p. 95, and XX (February, 1919), pp. 127-29 quoted; Robinson, "College and University Instruction in City Planning," *City Plan*, II (April, 1916), pp. 21-23; Albion W. Small, "Fifty Years of Sociology in the United States," *American Journal of Sociology*, XXI (May, 1916), pp. 734-68; Ford, ed., *City Planning Progress*, pp. 194-99; Harlan James, "Service—the Keynote of a New Cabinet Department," *Review of Reviews*, LIX (February, 1919), pp. 187-90.

13. U.S. Congress, "Hearing . . . on the Subject of City Planning," 61st Congress, 2nd Sess., 422 *Senate Documents*, LIX (1910), pp. 57-105; Flavel Shurtleff, Minutes of the Conference, the General and Executive Committees, and Correspondence, NCCP, 1910-17, and "Six Years of City Planning in the United States," *Proceedings . . . Seventh NCCP* (1915) pp. 33-41; cf. *General Index of the Proceedings of the NCCP* (Boston: University Press, 1928); Nolen, "What Is Needed in City Planning?," *Hearing*, pp. 74-75; Olmsted, Jr., "Basic Principles in City Planning," *Proceedings . . . Second NCCP* (1910), pp. 3-4; Robinson, "Problems in City Planning," *Proceedings . . . Third NCCP* (1911), pp. 217-18.

14. Pamphlet, "Constitution and By-Laws of the American City Planning Institute," 1917, quoting Article II; "Resolution Adopted by the Ninth NCCP . . . on May 9, 1917," NCCP Executive *Minutes*.

15. Frederick J. Adams and Gerald Hodge, "City Planning Instruction in the United States: The Pioneering Days, 1900-1930," *Journal of the American Institute of Planners*, XXXI (February, 1965), pp. 43-51; Marsh, *An Introduction to City Planning* with a technical chapter by George Ford (New York: np, 1909), pp. 1-2; Kellog, ed., *The Pittsburgh Survey* (New York: Survey Associates, 1914); Richard S. Childs, "What Ails Pittsburgh? A Diagnosis and Prescription," *American City*, III (July, 1910), pp. 9-12; Charles Moore, ed., *Plan*

of Chicago . . . (Chicago: Commercial Club, 1909), pp. 1-4.
16. Ford, ed., City Planning Progress, pp. 5-193; W. S. Morgan and H. M. Pollack, Modern Cities (New York: Harper and Brothers, 1913), passim; Nolen, Replanning Small Cities (Boston: B. W. Huebsh, 1912), quoted pp. 5, 28, 58-60, 155-62, passim; NCCP, "Model Plan Study," special supplement in Landscape Architecture, III (April, 1913), and comment by Olmsted, Jr., "A City Planning Program," Proceedings . . . Fifth NCCP (1913), pp. 1-16 (see winning design by F. H. Bourse, A. C. Comey, B. A. Holdemann, and J. Nolen).
17. Robinson, City Planning (New York: G. P. Putnam, 1916); Lewis, Planning the Modern City (New York: John Wiley and Sons, 1916); Bird, Town Planning for Small Cities, and Nolen, ed., City Planning, both (New York: D. Appleton for the NML, 1917, 1916), quoting p. 353.
18. Nolen, ed., City Planning, pp. xiii-xxiv; "Recommended for Membership, ACPI," ACPI Minutes, October 25, 1917, and January 23, 1918.
19. Ford, ed., City Planning Progress, quoted pp. 3-4; Norman J. Johnston, "Harland Bartholomew: His Comprehensive Plans and Science of Planning," and Hancock, "John Nolen and the American City Planning Movement: A History of Culture, Change and Community Response, 1900-1940," both unpub. Ph.D. dissertations, University of Pennsylvania, 1964, pp. 1-29, 87-133, and 231-349, respectively.
20. U.S. Bureau of Industrial Housing and Transportation, Report of the United States Housing Corporation, James Ford and Henry Hubbard, eds., 2 vols. (Washington, D.C.: Government Printing Office, 1919-20), quoting Hubbard I, pp. 70, 77, and Olmsted, Jr., II, p. 186; U.S. Shipping Board, Housing the Shipbuilders, in Frederick L. Ackerman, ed. (Philadelphia: np, 1920), pp. 1-24; E. D. Litchfield, "Yorkship Village in 1917 and 1939," American City, LIX (November, 1939), pp. 42-43; Roy Lubove, "Homes and 'A Few Well Placed Fruit Trees': An Object Lesson in Federal Housing," Social Research, MV (Winter, 1960), pp. 469-74; "Town Planning Lessons to be Learned from Government Housing Operations," Minutes of the Third ACPI Meeting, Philadelphia, January 26-27, 1919; Stein to author, June 14, 1961.
21. Problems of St. Louis (St. Louis: City Plan Commission, 1917), p. xxii (Bartholomew's italics).
22. Henry and Theodora Hubbard, Our Cities Today and Tomorrow (Cambridge: Harvard University Press, 1929), Appendix II: Thomas Adams, Outline of Town and City Planning (New York: Russell Sage Foundation, 1935), pp. 5-29, passim; Robert Walker, The Planning Function in Urban Government (Chicago: University of Chicago Press, 1941), pp. 23-26, 106-220; Hancock, "Nolen," pp. 350-607; Johnston, "Bartholomew," pp. 1-29, 134-242, quoted 183.

23. Adams, Outline, pp. 208-309, quoted 213; Hubbards, Our Cities, pp. 46-76, 142-61; Massachusetts Federation of Planning Boards, "Planning Progress in Massachusetts," Bulletin 20 (1929), pp. 1-5; Edward M. Bassett, Zoning (New York: Russell Sage Foundation, 1936), pp. 13-222; Euclid Village, Ohio, v. Ambler Realty Co., 272 U.S. 265 and 47 Sp.Ct. 114 (1926), quoted; Charles Abrams, "Economic Changes in Real Estate," New Architecture and City Planning, in Paul Zucker, ed. (New York: Philosophical Library, 1944), quoted p. 272; President's Commission, Recent Social Trends, in Wesley Mitchell, Charles Merriam et al., eds., 2 vols. (New York: Macmillan, 1933), I, quoted p. xxxi.
24. Adams and Hodge, "City Planning Instruction," pp. 43-51; John Gaus, The Graduate School of Design and the Education of Planners (Cambridge: Harvard, 1943), pp. 3-50; "Report of a Conference on a Project for Research and Instruction in City and Regional Planning," Columbia University, May 3, 1918, mimeographed; and Nolen, "Professions Concerned in City Planning," September 29, 1933, both in Nolen Papers (Harvard folders), quoting last 2-4; U.S. Civil Service, "Planner Requirements," 1926, quoted; NCCP and ACPI Minutes and member correspondence, "Report of the Committee on Reorganization of the NCCP," March 2, 1934; ACPI to members, March 19, and November 7, 1924; ACPCA, memorandum, "To the Board of Directors," May 29, 1935; American Society of Planning Officials, Newsletter (1935), p. i. Note: the Quarterly became the Planners Journal in 1934 and the Journal of the American Institute of Planners in 1944.
25. Mumford, "The Next Twenty Years in City Planning," Proceedings . . . Seventeenth NCCP (1927), pp. 45-58, quoted 56, passim; MacKaye, The New Exploration (New York: Harcourt, Brace, 1928), passim; Nolen, "Random Notes and Reactions," 1914-20, passim; letter to Olmsted, Jr., October 31, 1923, and to New York Times, November 25, 1931, all in Nolen Papers (New York Regional Plan file); cf. Regional issue of Survey, LIV (May 1, 1925).
26. Comey, "An Answer to the Garden City Challenge," American City, XXIX (July, 1923), pp. 36-38; MacKaye, New Exploration, pp. 24-30, 56-75, quoted 26, 30; Nolen, New Towns for Old (Boston: Marshall Jones, 1927), pp. 133-57, passim; and "Regional Planning," Encyclopedia of the Social Sciences, XIII (1934), pp. 205-08; Russell V. Black, "County Planning Proves Its Value," American City, XLIV (May, 1931), pp. 116-18; National Resources Committee, State Planning (Washington, D.C.: Government Printing Office, 1935, 1940), and Urbanism Committee of the NRC, Urban Planning and Land Policies and Supplementary Report, both (Washington, D.C.: Government Printing Office, 1939), pp. 45-117, and 3-161; Roy Lubove, Community Planning in the 1920's (Pittsburgh: University of Pittsburgh Press, 1963), pp. 107-27; Radburn

Garden Homes (New York: City Housing Corporation, September, 1930), brochure; *The Farm Cities Corporation* (Washington: The Corporation, nd-1923) booklet; Malcher, *The Steadyflow Traffic System* (Cambridge: Harvard University Press, 1935); Stein, *Toward New Towns for America* (New York: Rheinhold, 1957).

27. Herbert Hoover, *The Memoirs of . . .*, 3 vols. (New York: Macmillan, 1951-52), II, p. 78; Roosevelt, *On Our Way* (New York: John Day, 1934), p. xii; and *Public Papers and Messages*, in S. I. Roseman, ed., 13 vols. (New York: Random House, 1938-45), III, p. ii.

28. Crane to Nolen and L. C. Gray, April 27, 1933, quoted ("Memorandum on the Relation of Emergency Relief Work to Planning"; "Report of the National Land Use Planning Committee," February 15-18, 1932, both Nolen Papers (NRPB folder); *First Annual Report: Conference on Rural Land Utilization and Planning* (Washington: USDA, July, 1933), pp. 5-16; Federal Emergency Relief Administration, *Bulletin WD-3*, March 2, 1934; National Resources Committee, PWA, First Through Thirteenth *Circular Letters*, 1933-34; and "A Plan for Planning," *Report*, December 1, 1934.

29. NRPB, *Our Cities: Their Role in the Growth of the Nation* (Washington, D.C.: Government Printing Office, 1937), quoted p. xiii; and *Urban Planning and Land Policies*, pp. 73-309, *passim;* Francis Perkins *et al.*, *The Federal Government Today* (New York: American Council on Public Affairs, 1938), see individual reports; Paul Conkin, *Tomorrow A New World* (Ithaca: Cornell University Press for the American Historical Association, 1959), pp. 93-233, 326-31.

30. Howe, *The City: The Hope of Democracy* (New York: Charles Scribner's Sons, 1906), pp. 300-13; Charles Beard, "Conflicts in City Planning," *Yale Review* XVII (October, 1927), pp. 65-77; David Reisman *et al.*, *The Lonely Crowd* (New York: Doubleday Anchor Books, 1955), p. 348, *passim;* John K. Galbraith, *Five Speeches* (Washington: Urban America, 1966), pp. 1-6; Dubos, "Man's Unchanging Biology and Evolving Psyche," Center for the Study of Democratic Institutions, *Center Diary: 17* (March-April, 1967), pp. 38-44, quoted 41.

31. Webber, "Comprehensive Planning and Social Responsibility: Towards an AIP Consensus on the Profession's Roles and Purposes," *Journal of the American Institute of Planners*, XXIX (November, 1963), pp. 232-41, quoted 234, 236.

The Failure of Urban Renewal

HERBERT J. GANS

Suppose that the government decided that jalopies were a menace to public safety and a blight on the beauty of our highways, and therefore took them away from their drivers. Suppose, then, that to replenish the supply of automobiles, it gave these drivers a hundred dollars each to buy a good used car and also made special grants to General Motors, Ford, and Chrysler to lower the cost—although not necessarily the price—of Cadillacs, Lincolns, and Imperials by a few hundred dollars. Absurd as this may sound, change the jalopies to slum housing, and I have described, with only slight poetic license, the first fifteen years of a federal program called urban renewal.

Since 1949, this program has provided local renewal agencies with federal funds and the power of eminent domain to condemn slum neighborhoods, tear down the buildings, and resell the cleared land to private developers at a reduced price. In addition to relocating the slum dwellers in "decent, safe, and sanitary" housing, the program was intended to stimulate large-scale private rebuilding, add new tax revenues to the dwindling coffers of the cities, revitalize their downtown areas, and halt the exodus of middle-class whites to the suburbs.

For some time now, a few city planners and housing experts have been pointing out that urban renewal was not achieving its general aims, and social scientists have produced a number of critical studies of individual renewal projects. These critiques, however, have mostly appeared in academic books and journals; otherwise there has been remarkably little public discussion of the federal program. Slum-dwellers whose homes were to be torn down have indeed protested bitterly, but their outcries have been limited to particular projects; and because such outcries have rarely been supported by the local press, they have been easily brushed aside by the political power of the supporters of the projects in question. In the last few years, the civil rights movement has backed protesting slum-dwellers, though again only at the local level, while rightists have opposed the use of eminent domain to take private property from one owner in order to give it to another (especially when the new one is likely to be from out-of-town and financed by New York capital).

Slum clearance has also come under fire from several prominent architectural and social critics, led by Jane Jacobs, who have been struggling to preserve neighborhoods like Greenwich Village, with their brownstones, lofts, and small apartment houses, against the encroachment of the large high-rise projects built for luxury market and the poor alike. But these efforts have been directed mainly at private clearance outside the federal program, and their intent has been to save the city for people (intellectuals and artists, for example) who, like tourists, want jumbled diversity, antique "charm," and narrow streets for visual adventure and aesthetic pleasure. (Norman Mailer carried such thinking to its farthest point in his recent attack in the *New York Times Magazine* on the physical and social sterility of high-rise housing; Mailer's attack was also accompanied by an entirely reasonable suggestion—in fact the only viable one that could be made in this context—that the advantages of brownstone living be incorporated into skyscraper projects.)

But if criticism of the urban renewal program has in the past been spotty and sporadic, there are signs that the program as a whole is now beginning to be seriously and tellingly evaluated. At least two comprehensive studies, by Charles Abrams and Scott Greer, are nearing publication, and one highly negative analysis—by an ultra-conservative economist and often irresponsible polemicist—has already appeared: Martin Anderson's *The Federal Bulldozer*.[1] Ironically enough, Anderson's data are based largely on statistics collected by the Urban Renewal Administration. What, according to these and other data, has the program accomplished? It has cleared slums to make room for many luxury-housing and a few middle-income projects, and it has also provided inexpensive land for the expansion of colleges, hospitals, libraries, shopping areas, and other such institutions located in slum areas. As of March 1961, 126,000 dwelling units had been demolished and about 28,000 new ones built. The median monthly rental of all those erected during 1960 came to $158, and in 1962, to $192—a staggering figure for any area outside of Manhattan.

Needless to say, none of the slum-dwellers who were dispossessed in the process could afford to move into these new apartments. Local renewal agencies were supposed to relocate the dispossessed tenants in "standard" housing within their means before demolition began, but such vacant housing is scarce in most cities, and altogether unavailable in some. And since the agencies were under strong pressure to clear the land and get renewal projects going, the relocation of the tenants was impatiently, if not ruthlessly, handled. Thus, a 1961 study of renewal projects in 41 cities showed that 60 per cent of the dispossessed tenants were merely relocated in other slums; and in big cities, the proportion was even higher (over 70 per cent in Philadelphia, according to a 1958 study). Renewal sometimes even created new slums by pushing relocatees into areas and buildings which then became overcrowded and deteriorated rapidly. This has principally been the case with Negroes who, both for economic and racial reasons, have been forced to double up in other ghettos. Indeed, because almost two-thirds of the cleared slum units have been occupied by Negroes, the urban renewal program has often been characterized as Negro clearance, and in too many cities, this has been its intent.

Moreover, those dispossessed tenants who found better housing usually had to pay more rent than they could afford. In his careful study of relocation in Boston's heavily Italian West End,[2] Chester Hartman shows that 41 per cent of the West Enders lived in good housing in this so-called slum (thus suggesting that much of it should not have been torn down) and that 73 per

cent were relocated in good housing—thanks in part to the fact that the West Enders were white. This improvement was achieved at a heavy price, however, for median rents rose from $41 to $71 per month after the move.

According to renewal officials, 80 per cent of all persons. relocated now live in good housing, and rent increases were justified because many had been paying unduly low rent before. Hartman's study was the first to compare these official statistics with housing realities, and his figure of 73 per cent challenges the official claim that 97 per cent of the Boston West Enders were properly re-housed. This discrepancy may arise from the fact that renewal officials collected their data after the poorest of the uprooted tenants had fled in panic to other slums, and that officials also tended toward a rather lenient evaluation of the relocation housing of those actually studied in order to make a good record for their agency. (On the other hand, when they were certifying areas for clearance, these officials often exaggerated the degree of "blight" in order to prove their case.)

As for the substandard rents paid by slum-dwellers, this is true in only a small proportion of cases, and then mostly among whites. Real-estate economists argue that families should pay at least 20 per cent of their income for housing, but what is manageable for middle-income people is a burden to those with low incomes who pay a higher share of their earnings for food and other necessities. Yet even so, Negroes generally have to devote about 30 per cent of their income to housing, and a Chicago study cited by Hartman reports that among non-white families earning less than $3,000 a year, median rent rose from 35 per cent of income before relocation to 46 per cent afterward.

To compound the failure of urban renewal to help the poor, many clearance areas (Boston's West End is an example) were chosen, as Anderson points out, not because they had the worst slums, but because they offered the best sites for luxury housing—housing which would have been built whether the urban renewal program existed or not. Since public funds were used to clear the slums and to make the land available to private builders at reduced costs, the low-income population was in effect subsidizing its own removal for the benefit of the wealthy. What was done for the slum-dwellers in return is starkly suggested by the following statistic: *only one-half of one per cent* of all federal expenditures for urban renewal between 1949 and 1964 was spent on relocation of families and individuals; and 2 per cent if payments are included.

Finally, because the policy has been to clear a district of all slums at once in order to assemble large sites to attract private developers, entire neighborhoods have frequently been destroyed, uprooting people who had lived there for decades, closing down their institutions, ruining small businesses by the hundreds, and scattering families and friends all over the city. By removing the structure of social and emotional support provided by the neighborhood, and by forcing people to rebuild their lives separately and amid strangers elsewhere, slum clearance has often come at a serious psychological as well as financial cost to its supposed beneficiaries. Marc Fried, a clinical psychologist who studied the West Enders

after relocation, reported that 46 per cent of the women and 38 per cent of the men "give evidence of a fairly severe grief reaction or worse" in response to questions about leaving their tight-knit community. Far from "adjusting" eventually to this trauma, 26 per cent of the women remained sad or depressed even two years after they had been pushed out of the West End.[3]

People like the Italians or the Puerto Ricans who live in an intensely group-centered way among three-generation "extended families" and ethnic peers have naturally suffered greatly from the clearance of entire neighborhoods. It may well be, however, that slum clearance has inflicted yet graver emotional burdens on Negroes, despite the fact that they generally live in less cohesive and often disorganized neighborhoods. In fact, I suspect that Negroes who lack a stable family life and have trouble finding neighbors, shopkeepers, and institutions they can trust may have been hurt even more by forcible removal to new areas. This suspicion is supported by another of Fried's findings—that the socially marginal West Enders were more injured by relocation than those who had been integral members of the old neighborhood. Admittedly, some Negroes move very often on their own, but then they at least do so voluntarily, and not in consequence of a public policy which is supposed to help them in the first place. Admittedly also, relocation has made it possible for social workers to help slum-dwellers whom they could not reach until renewal brought them out in the open, so to speak. But then only a few cities have so far used social workers to make relocation a more humane process.

These high financial, social, and emotional costs paid by the slum-dwellers have generally been written off as an unavoidable by-product of "progress," the price of helping cities to collect more taxes, bring back the middle class, make better use of downtown land, stimulate private investment, and restore civic pride. But as Anderson shows, urban renewal has hardly justified these claims either. For one thing, urban renewal is a slow process the average project has taken twelve years to complete. Moreover, while the few areas suitable for luxury housing were quickly rebuilt, less desirable cleared land might lie vacant for many years because developers were—and are—unwilling to risk putting up high- and middle-income housing in areas still surrounded by slums. Frequently, they can be attracted only by promises of tax write-offs, which absorb the increased revenues that renewal is supposed to create for the city. Anderson reports that, instead of the anticipated four dollars for every public dollar, private investments have only just matched the public subsidies, and even the money for luxury housing has come forth largely because of federal subsidies. Thus, all too few of the new projects have produced tax gains and returned suburbanites, or generated the magic rebuilding boom.

Anderson goes on to argue that during the fifteen years of the federal urban renewal program, the private housing market has achieved what urban renewal has failed to do. Between 1950 and 1960, twelve million new dwelling units were built, and fully six million substandard ones disappeared—all without government action. The proportion of substandard housing in the total housing supply was reduced from 37 to 19 per cent, and even among the dwelling units occupied by non-whites,

the proportion of substandard units has dropped from 72 to 44 per cent. This comparison leads Anderson to the conclusion that the private market is much more effective than government action in removing slums and supplying new housing, and that the urban renewal program ought to be repealed.

It would appear that Anderson's findings and those of the other studies I have cited make an excellent case for doing so. However, a less biased analysis of the figures and a less tendentious mode of evaluating them than Anderson's leads to a different conclusion. To begin with, Anderson's use of nationwide statistics misses the few good renewal projects, those which have helped both the slum-dwellers and the cities, or those which brought in enough new taxes to finance other city services for the poor. Such projects can be found in small cities and especially in those where high vacancy rates assured sufficent relocation housing of standard quality. More important, all the studies I have mentioned deal with projects carried out during the 1950's, and fail to take account of the improvements in urban renewal practice under the Kennedy and Johnson administrations. Although Anderson's study supposedly covers the period up to 1963, much of his data go no further than 1960. Since then, the federal bulldozer has moved into fewer neighborhoods, and the concept of rehabilitating rather than clearing blighted neighborhoods is more and more being underwritten by subsidized loans. A new housing subsidy program —known as 221(d) (3)— for families above the income ceiling for public housing has also been launched, and in 1964, Congress passed legislation for assistance to relocatees who cannot afford their new rents.

None of this is to say that Anderson would have had to revise his findings drastically if he had taken the pains to update them. These recent innovations have so far been small in scope—only 13,000 units were financed under 211-(d)(3) in the first two years—and they still do not provide subsidies sufficient to bring better housing within the price range of the slum residents. In addition, rehabilitation unaccompanied by new construction is nearly useless because it does not eliminate overcrowding. And finally, some cities are still scheduling projects to clear away the non-white poor who stand in the path of the progress of private enterprise. Unfortunately, many cities pay little attention to federal pleas to improve the program, using the local initiative granted them by urban renewal legislation to perpetuate the practices of the 1950's. Yet even with the legislation of the 1960's, the basic error in the original design of urban renewal remains: it is still a method for eliminating the slums in order to "renew" the city, rather than a program for properly rehousing slum-dwellers.

Before going into this crucial distinction, we first need to be clear that private housing is not going to solve our slum problems. In the first place, Anderson conveniently ignores the fact that if urban renewal has benefited anyone, it is private enterprise. Bending to the pressure of the real-estate lobby, the legislation that launched urban renewal in effect required that private developers do the rebuilding, and most projects could therefore get off the drawing board only if they appeared to be financially attractive to a developer. Thus, his choice of a site and his re-

building plans inevitably took priority over the needs of the slum-dwellers.

It is true that Anderson is not defending private enterprise *per se* but the free market, although he forgets that it only exists today as a concept in reactionary minds and dated economics texts. The costs of land, capital, and construction have long since made it impossible for private developers to build for anyone but the rich, and some form of subsidy is needed to house everyone else. The building boom of the 1950's which Anderson credits to the free market was subsidized by income-tax deductions to homeowners and by F.H.A. 2nd V.A. mortgage insurance, not to mention the federal highway programs that have made the suburbs possible.

To be sure, these supports enabled private builders to put up a great deal of housing for middle-class whites. This in turn permitted well-employed workers, including some non-whites, to improve their own situation by moving into the vacated neighborhoods. Anderson is quite right in arguing that if people earn good wages, they can obtain better housing more easily and cheaply in the not-quite-private market than through urban renewal. But this market is of little help to those employed at low or even factory wages, or the unemployed, or most Negroes who, whatever their earnings, cannot live in the suburbs. In consequence, 44 per cent of all housing occupied by non-whites in 1960 was still substandard, and even with present subsidies, private enterprise can do nothing for these people. As for laissez faire, it played a major role in creating the slums in the first place.

The solution, then, is not to repeal urban renewal, but to transform it from a program of slum clearance and rehabilitation into a program of urban re-housing. This means, first, building low- and moderate-cost housing on vacant land in cities, suburbs, and new towns beyond the suburbs, and also helping slum-dwellers to move into existing housing outside the slums; and then, *after* a portion of the urban low-income population has left the slums, clearing and rehabilitating them through urban renewal. This approach is common-place in many European countries, which have long since realized that pri-vate enterprise can no more house the population and eliminate slums than it can run the post office.

Of course, governments in Europe have a much easier task than ours in developing decent low-income projects. Because they take it for granted that housing is a national rather than a local responsibility, the government agencies are not hampered by the kind of real-estate and construction lobbies which can defeat or subvert American pro-grams by charges of socialism. More-over, their municipalities own a great deal of the vacant land, and have greater control over the use of private land than do American cities. But perhaps their main advantage is the lack of popular opposition to moving the poor out of the slums and into the midst of the more affluent residents. Not only is housing desperately short for all income groups, but the European class structure, even in Western socialist countries, is still rigid enough so that low- and middle-income groups can live near each other if not next to each other, and still "know their place."

In America, on the other hand, one's house and address are major signs of social status, and no one who has any say in the matter wants people of lower income or status in his neighborhood.

Middle-class homeowners use zoning as a way of keeping out cheaper or less prestigious housing, while working-class communities employ less subtle forms of exclusion. Consequently, low-income groups, whatever their creed or color, have been forced to live in slums or near-slums, and to wait until they could acquire the means to move as a group, taking over better neighborhoods when the older occupants were ready to move on themselves.

For many years now, the only source of new housing for such people, and their only hope of escaping the worst slums, has been public housing. But this is no longer a practical alternative. Initiated during the Depression, public housing has always been a politically embattled program; its opponents, among whom the real-estate lobby looms large, first saddled it with re-strictions and then effectively crippled it. Congress now permits only 35,000 units a year to be built in the entire country.

The irony is that public housing has declined because, intended only for the poor, it faithfully carried out its man-date. Originally, sites were obtained by slum clearance; after the war, however, in order to increase the supply of low-cost housing, cities sought to build pub-lic housing on vacant land. But limited as it was to low-income tenants and thus labeled and stigmatized as an institu-tion of the dependent poor, public hous-ing was kept out of vacant land in the better neighborhoods. This, plus the high cost of land and construction, left housing officials with no other choice but to build high-rise projects on what-ever vacant land they could obtain, often next to factories or along railroad yards. Because tenants of public hous-ing are ruled by a set of strict regulations—sometimes necessary, sometimes politically inspired, but always degrading—anyone who could afford housing in the private market shunned the public projects. During the early years of the program, when fewer citizens had that choice, public housing became respectable shelter for the working class and even for the unemployed middle class. After the war, federal officials decided, and rightly so, that public housing ought to be reserved for those who had no other alternative, and therefore set income limits that admitted only the really poor. Today, public housing is home for the underclass—families who earn less than $3000-$4000 annually, many with unstable jobs or none at all, and most of them non-white.

Meanwhile the enthusiasm for public housing has been steadily dwindling and with it, badly needed political support. Newspaper reports reinforce the popular image of public-housing projects as huge nests of crime and delinquency—despite clear evidence to the contrary—and as the domicile of unregenerate and undeserving families whose children urinate only in the elevators. The position of public housing, particularly among liberal intellectuals, has also been weakened by the slurs of the social and architectural aesthetes who condemn the projects' poor exterior designs as "sterile," "monotonous," and "dehumanizing," often in ignorance of the fact that the tightly restricted funds have been allocated mainly to make the apartments themselves as spacious and livable as possible, and that the waiting lists among slum-dwellers who want these apartments remain long. Be that as it may, suburban communities and urban neighborhoods with vacant land are as hostile to public housing as ever,

and their opposition is partly responsible for the program's having been cut down to its present minuscule size.

The net result is that low-income people today cannot get out of the slums, either because they cannot afford the subsidized private market, or because the project they could afford cannot be built on vacant land. There is only one way to break through this impasse, and that is to permit them equal access to new subsidized, privately built housing by adding another subsidy to make up the difference between the actual rent and what they can reasonably be expected to pay. Such a plan, giving them a chance to choose housing like all other citizens, would help to remove the stigma of poverty and inferiority placed on them by public housing. Many forms of rent subsidy have been proposed, but the best one, now being tried in New York, is to put low- and middle-income people in the same middle-income project with the former getting the same apartments at smaller rentals.

Admittedly, this approach assumes that the poor can live with the middle class and that their presence and behavior will not threaten their neighbors' security or status. No one knows whether this is really possible, but experiments in education, job training, and social-welfare programs do show that many low-income people, when once offered *genuine* opportunities to improve their lives and given help in making use of them, are able to shake off the hold of the culture of poverty. Despite the popular stereotype, the proportion of those whom Hylan Lewis calls the clinical poor, too ravaged emotionally by poverty and deprivation to adapt to new opportunities, seems to be small. As for the rest, they only reject programs offering spurious opportunities, like job-training schemes for non-existent jobs. Further, anyone who has lived in a slum neighborhood can testify that whatever the condition of the building, most women keep their apartments clean by expenditures of time and effort inconceivable to the middle-class housewife. Moving to a better apartment would require little basic cultural change from these women, and rehousing is thus a type of new opportunity that stands a better chance of succeeding than, say, a program to inculcate new child-rearing techniques.

We have no way of telling how many slum-dwellers would be willing to participate in such a plan. However poor the condition of the flat, the slum is home, and for many it provides the support of neighboring relatives and friends, and a cultural milieu in which everyone has the same problems and is therefore willing to overlook occasional disreputable behavior. A middle-income project cannot help but have a middle-class ethos, and some lower-class people may be fearful of risking what little stability they have achieved where they are now in exchange for something new, strange, demanding, and potentially hostile. It would be hard to imagine an unwed Negro mother moving her household to a middle-income project full of married couples and far removed from the mother, sisters, and aunts who play such an important role in the female-centered life of lower-class Negroes. However, there are today a large number of stable two-parent families who live in the slums only because income and race exclude them from the better housing that is available. Families like these would surely be only too willing to leave the Harlems and Black Belts.

They would have to be helped with loans to make the move, and perhaps even with grants to buy new furniture so as not to feel ashamed in their new surroundings. They might be further encouraged by being offered income-tax relief for giving up the slums, just as we now offer such relief to people who give up being renters to become homeowners.

Undoubtedly there would be friction between the classes, and the more affluent residents would likely want to segregate themselves and their children from neighbors who did not toe the middle-class line, especially with respect to child-rearing. The new housing would therefore have to be planned to allow some voluntary social segregation for both groups, if only to make sure that enough middle-income families would move in (especially in cities where there was no shortage of housing for them). The proportion of middle- and low-income tenants would have to be regulated not only to minimize the status fears of the former, but also to give the latter enough peers to keep them from feeling socially isolated and without emotional support when problems arise. Fortunately, non-profit and limited dividend institutions, which do not have to worry about showing an immediate profit, are now being encouraged to build moderate-income housing; they can do a more careful job of planning the physical and social details of this approach than speculative private builders.

If the slums are really to be emptied and their residents properly housed elsewhere, the rehousing program will have to be extended beyond the city limits, for the simple reason that that is where most of the vacant land is located. This means admitting the low-income population to the suburbs; it also means creating new towns—self-contained communities with their own industry which would not, like the suburbs, be dependent on the city for employment opportunities, and could therefore be situated in presently rural areas. Federal support for the construction of new towns was requested as part of the 1964 Housing Act, and although Congress refused to pass it, the legislation will come up again in 1965.[4]

To be sure, white middle-class suburbanites and rural residents are not likely to welcome non-white low-income people into their communities even if the latter are no longer clearly labeled as poor. The opposition to be expected in city neighborhoods chosen for mixed-income projects would be multiplied a hundredfold in outlying areas. Being politically autonomous, and having constituencies who are not about to support measures that will threaten their security or status in the slightest, the suburbs possess the political power to keep the rehousing program out of their own vacant lots, even if they cannot stop the federal legislation that would initiate it. On the other hand, experience with the federal highway program and with urban renewal itself has demonstrated that few communities can afford to turn down large amounts of federal money. For instance, New York City is likely to build a Lower Manhattan Expressway in the teeth of considerable local opposition, if only because the federal government will pay 90 per cent of the cost and thus bring a huge sum into the city coffers. If the rehousing program were sufficiently large to put a sizable mixed-income project in every community, and if the federal government were to pick up at least 90 per cent of the tab, while also strengthening the

appeal of the program by helping to solve present transportation, school, and tax problems in the suburbs, enough political support might be generated to overcome the objections of segregationist and class-conscious whites.

Yet even if the outlying areas could be persuaded to cooperate, it is not at all certain that slum-dwellers would leave the city. Urban renewal experience has shown that for many slum-dwellers, there are more urgent needs than good housing. One is employment, and most of the opportunities for unskilled or semi-skilled work are in the city. Another is money, and some New York City slum residents recently refused to let the government inspect— much less repair—their buildings because they would lose the rent reductions they had received previously. If leaving the city meant higher rents, more limited access to job possibilities, and also separation from people and institutions which give them stability, some slum residents might very well choose overcrowding and dilapidation as the lesser of two evils.

These problems would have to be considered in planning a rehousing program beyond the city limits. The current exodus of industry from the city would of course make jobs available to the new suburbanites. The trouble is that the industries now going into the suburbs, or those that would probably be attracted to the new towns, are often precisely the ones which use the most modern machinery and the fewest unskilled workers. Thus, our rehousing plan comes up against the same obstacle—the shortage of jobs—that has frustrated other programs to help the low-income population and that will surely defeat the War on Poverty in its present form. Like so many other programs, rehousing is finally seen to depend on a step that American society is as yet unwilling to take: the deliberate creation of new jobs by government action. The building of new towns especially would have to be coordinated with measures aimed at attracting private industry to employ the prospective residents, at creating other job opportunities, and at offering intensive training for the unskilled after they have been hired. If they are not sure of a job before they leave the city, they simply will not leave.

The same social and cultural inhibitions that make slum residents hesitant to move into a mixed-income project in the city would, of course, be even stronger when it came to moving out of the city. These inhibitions might be relaxed by moving small groups of slum residents en masse, or by getting those who move first to encourage their neighbors to follow. In any case, new social institutions and community facilities would have to be developed to help the erstwhile slum-dweller feel comfortable in his new community, yet without labeling him as poor.

Despite its many virtues, a rehousing program based on the use of vacant land on either side of the city limits would not immediately clear the slums. Given suburban opposition and the occupational and social restraints on the slum-dwellers themselves, it can be predicted that if such a program were set into motion it would be small in size, and that it would pull out only the upwardly mobile—particularly the young people with stable families and incomes—who are at best a sizable minority among the poor. What can be done now to help the rest leave the slums?

The best solution is a public effort to encourage their moving into existing neighborhoods within the city and in older suburbs just beyond the city limits. Indeed, a direct rent subsidy like that now given to relocatees could enable people to obtain decent housing in these areas. This approach has several advantages. It would allow low-income people to be close to jobs and to move in groups, and it would probably attract the unwed mother who wanted to give her children a better chance in life. It would also be cheaper than building new housing, although the subsidies would have to be large enough to discourage low-income families from overcrowding—and thus deteriorating—the units in order to save on rent.

There are, however, some obvious disadvantages as well. For one thing, because non-white low-income people would be moving into presently white or partially integrated areas, the government would in effect be encouraging racial invasion. This approach would thus have the effect of pushing the white and middle-income people further toward the outer edge of the city or into suburbs. Although some whites might decide to stay, many would surely want to move, and not all would be able to afford to do so. It would be necessary to help them with rent subsidies as well; indeed, they might become prospective middle-income tenants for rehousing projects on vacant land.

Undoubtedly, all this would bring us closer to the all-black city that has already been predicted. For this reason alone, a scheme that pushes the whites further out can only be justified when combined with a rehousing program on vacant land that would begin to integrate the suburbs. But even that could not prevent a further racial imbalance between cities and suburbs.

Yet would the predominantly non-white city really be so bad? It might be for the middle class which needs the jobs, shops, and culture that the city provides. Of course, the greater the suburban exodus, the more likely it would become that middle-class culture would also move to the suburbs. This is already happening in most American cities—obvious testimony to the fact that culture (at least of the middlebrow kind represented by tent theaters and art movie-houses) does not need the city in order to flourish; and the artists who create high culture seem not to mind living among the poor even now.

Non-white low-income people might feel more positive about a city in which they were the majority, for if they had the votes, municipal services would be more attuned to their priorities than is now the case. To be sure, if poor people (of any color) were to dominate the city, its tax revenues would decrease even further, and cities would be less able than ever to supply the high quality public services that the low-income population needs so much more urgently than the middle class. Consequently, new sources of municipal income not dependent on the property tax would have to be found; federal and state grants to cities (like those already paying half the public-school costs in several states) would probably be the principal form. Even under present conditions, in fact, new sources of municipal income must soon be located if the cities are not to collapse financially.

If non-whites were to leave the slums en masse, new ghettos would eventually form in the areas to which they would move. Although this is undesirable by conventional liberal standards, the fact is that many low-income Negroes are not yet very enthusiastic about living among white neighbors. They do not favor segregation, of course; what they want is a free choice and then the ability to select predominantly non-white areas that are in better shape than the ones they live in now. If the suburbs were opened to non-whites—to the upwardly mobile ones who want integration now—free choice would become available. If the new ghettos were decent neighborhoods with good schools, and if their occupants had jobs and other opportunities to bring stability into their lives, they would be training their children to want integration a generation hence.

In short, then, a workable rehousing scheme must provide new housing on both sides of the city limits for the upwardly mobile minority, and encouragement to move into older areas for the remainder. If, in these ways, enough slum-dwellers could be enabled and induced to leave the slums, it would then be possible to clear or rehabilitate the remaining slums. Once slum areas were less crowded, and empty apartments were going begging, their profitability and market value would be reduced, and urban renewal could take place far more cheaply, and far more quickly. Relocation would be less of a problem, and with land values down, rebuilding and rehabilitation could be carried out to fit the resources of the low-income people who needed or wanted to remain in the city. A semi-suburban style of living that would be attractive to the upper-middle class could also be provided.

At this point, it would be possible to begin to remake the inner city into what it must eventually become—the hub of a vast metropolitan complex of urban neighborhoods, suburbs, and new towns, in which those institutions and functions that have to be at the center—the specialized business districts, the civil and cultural facilities, and the great hospital complexes and university campuses—would be located.

Even in such a city, there would be slums—for people who wanted to live in them, for the clinical poor who would be unable to make it elsewhere, and for rural newcomers who would become urbanized in them before moving on. But it might also be possible to relocate many of these in a new kind of public housing in which quasi-communities would be established to help those whose problems were soluble and to provide at least decent shelter for those who cannot be helped except by letting them live without harassment until we learn how to cure mental illness, addiction, and other forms of self-destructive behavior.

This massive program has much to recommend it, but we must clearly understand that moving the low-income population out of the slums would not eliminate poverty or the other problems that stem from it. A standard dwelling unit can make life more comfortable, and a decent neighborhood can discourage some anti-social behavior, but by themselves, neither can effect radical transformations. What poor people need most are decent incomes, proper jobs, better schools, and freedom from racial and class discrimination. Indeed, if the choice were between a program solely dedicated to rehousing, and a program that kept the low-income population in the city slums for another generation but provided for these needs, the latter would be preferable, for it would produce people who were able to leave the slums under their own steam. Obviously, the ideal approach is one that

coordinates the elimination of slums with the reduction of poverty.

As I have been indicating, an adequate rehousing program would be extremely costly and very difficult to carry out. Both its complexity and expense can be justified, however, on several grounds. Morally, it can be argued that no one in the Great Society should have to live in a slum, at least not involuntarily.

From a political point of view, it is urgently necessary to begin integrating the suburbs and to improve housing conditions in the city before the latter becomes an ominous ghetto of poor and increasingly angry Negroes and Puerto Ricans, and the suburbs become enclaves of affluent whites who commute fearfully to a downtown bastion of stores and offices. If the visible group tensions of recent years are allowed to expand and sharpen, another decade may very well see the beginning of open and often violent class and race warfare.

But the most persuasive argument for a rehousing program is economic. Between 50 and 60 per cent of building costs go into wages and create work for the unskilled who are now increasingly unemployable elsewhere. A dwelling unit that costs $15,000 would thus provide as much as $9000 in wages—one-and-a-half years of respectably paid employment for a single worker. Adding four-and-a-half million new low-cost housing units to rehouse half of those in substandard units in 1960 would provide almost seven million man-years of work, and the subsequent renewal of these and other substandard units yet more. Many additional jobs would also be created by the construction and operation of new shopping centers, schools, and other community facilities, as well as the highways and public transit systems that would be needed to serve the new suburbs and towns. If precedent must be cited for using a housing program to create jobs, it should be recalled that public housing was started in the Depression for precisely this reason.

The residential building industry (and the real-estate lobby) would have to be persuaded to give up their stubborn resistance to government housing programs, but the danger of future underemployment, and the opportunity of participating profitably in the rehousing scheme, should either convert present builders or attract new ones into the industry. As for the building trades unions, they have always supported government housing programs, but they have been unwilling to admit non-whites to membership. If, however, the rehousing effort were sizable enough to require many more workers than are now in the unions, the sheer demand for labor—and the enforcement of federal non-discriminatory hiring policies for public works—would probably break down the color barriers without much difficulty.

While the federal government is tooling up to change the urban renewal program into a rehousing scheme, it should also make immediate changes in current renewal practices to remove their economic and social cost from the shoulders of the slum-dwellers. Future projects should be directed at the clearance of *really harmful* slums, instead of taking units that are *run down but not demonstrably harmful* out of the supply of low-cost housing, especially for downtown revitalization and other less pressing community improvement schemes. Occupants of harmful slums, moreover, ought to be rehoused in de-

cent units they can afford. For this purpose, more public housing and 221 (d) (3) projects must be built, and relocation and rent assistance payments should be increased to eliminate the expense of moving for the slum-dweller. Indeed, the simplest way out of the relocation impasse is to give every relocatee a sizable grant, like the five-hundred dollars to one thousand dollars paid by private builders in New York City to get tenants out of existing structures quickly and painlessly. Such a grant is not only a real incentive to relocate but a means of reducing opposition to urban renewal. By itself, however, it cannot reduce the shortage of relocation housing. Where such housing now exists in plentiful supply, renewal ought to move ahead more quickly, but where there is a shortage that cannot be appreciably reduced, it would be wise to eliminate or postpone clearance and rehabilitation projects that require a large amount of relocation.

Nothing is easier than to suggest radical new programs to the overworked and relatively powerless officials of federal and local renewal agencies who must carry out the present law, badly written or not, and who are constantly pressured by influential private interests to make decisions in their favor. Many of these officials are as unhappy with what urban renewal has wrought as their armchair critics and would change the program if they could—that is, if they received encouragement from the White House, effective support in getting new legislation through Congress, and, equally important, political help at city halls to incorporate these innovations into local programs. But it should be noted that little of what I have suggested is very radical, for none of the proposals involves conflict with the entrenched American practice of subsidizing private enterprise to carry out public works at a reasonable profit. The proposals are radical only in demanding an end to our no less entrenched practice of punishing the poor. Yet they also make sure that middle-class communities are rewarded financially for whatever discomfort they may have to endure.

Nor are these suggestions very new. Indeed, only last month President Johnson sent a housing message to Congress which proposes the payment of rent subsidies as the principal method for improving housing conditions. It also requests federal financing of municipal services for tax-starved communities, and aid toward the building of new towns. These represent bold and desirable steps toward the evolution of a federal rehousing program. Unfortunately, however, the message offers little help to those who need it most. Slum-dwellers may be pleased that there will be no increase in urban renewal activity, and that relocation housing subsidies and other grants are being stepped up. But no expansion of public housing is being requested, and to make matters worse, the new rent subsidies will be available only to households above the income limits for public housing. Thus, the President's message offers no escape for the mass of the nonwhite low-income population from the ghetto slums; in fact it threatens to widen the gap between such people and the lower-middle-income population which will be eligible for rent subsidies.

On the other hand, as in the case of the War on Poverty, a new principle of government responsibility in housing is being established, and evidently the President's strategy is to obtain legislative approval for the principle by combining it with a minimal and a minimally controversial program for the first year. Once the principle has been accepted, however, the program must change quickly. It may have taken fifteen years for urban renewal even to begin providing some relief to the mass of slum-dwellers, but it cannot take that long again to become a rehousing scheme that will give them significant help. The evolution of federal policies can no longer proceed in the leisurely fashion to which politicians, bureaucrats, and middle-class voters have become accustomed, for unemployment, racial discrimination, and the condition of our cities are becoming ever more critical problems, and those who suffer from them are now considerably less patient than they have been in the past.

NOTES

1. M.I.T. Press, 272 pp., $5.95.
2. See the November 1964 issue of the *Journal of the American Institute of Planners*. The article also reviews all other relocation research and is a more reliable study of the consequences of renewal than Anderson's.
3. See "Grieving for a Lost Home," in *The Urban Condition*, edited by Leonard Duhl.
4. Meanwhile, several private developers are planning new towns (for example, James Rouse who is building Columbia near Baltimore, and Robert Simon who has already begun Reston, outside Washington) in which they propose to house some low-income people.

Urban Renewal: A Controversy

GEORGE M. RAYMOND, MALCOLM D. RIVKIN, and HERBERT J. GANS

George M. Raymond: Recognizing that all urban slums should not necessarily be replaced by low-rent or subsidized middle-income housing in the same location (which is all that the Housing Act of 1937 permitted localities to do), Congress in 1949 enacted a statute designed to make it economically feasible for cities and private enterprise to re-use the cleared land for whatever purpose local governments felt to be in the best interest of their communities. Since it was clear that many relatively disadvantaged families would be displaced in this process, the new law required them to be rehoused in decent, safe, and sanitary dwellings within their means, anywhere in the locality within convenient distance of their places of employment.

The above describes those aspects of the federal urban renewal program that concern clearance and redevelopment. It is difficult to find any similarity between what this program actually is and what Herbert J. Gans has made it seem to be in his astoundingly ill-considered attack.

Mr. Gans begins by berating urban renewal for not having built as many dwelling units as it has demolished. As a close observer of urban renewal projects, however, he must be fully aware that any comparison between the number of apartments demolished and the number subsequently erected in the same areas is totally invalid and irrelevant. Let us see why:

(1) Many areas now occupied by slum housing are unfit for continued residential use (for reasons such as their being surrounded by industry, subject to flooding, etc.).

(2) Other areas are peculiarly suited to that expansion of schools and hospitals which is so essential to their ability to supply the services demanded by our growing population.

(3) Many slum areas tightly surround our cities' obsolete business districts, and are badly needed to facilitate the expansion of the latter.

(4) Slum housing frequently needs to be removed to make way for the new schools, parks, and playgrounds that are so essential to the upgrading of our cities' vast "gray areas."

As a result of such factors, the public interest more often than not requires that less land be devoted to residential use after rebuilding than before. Furthermore, existing housing has to be demolished at least two years before new housing becomes available for occupancy. Thus, any comparison between the number of units demolished and the number built at the time of any survey will necessarily *underestimate the program's potential for creating new housing.* Any fair observer, therefore, knows that the only valid comparison between the housing supply antedating renewal and that in existence subsequently, is one that includes all housing built in the

From *Commentary* (July 1965), pp. 72-80. Copyright © 1965 by the American Jewish Committee. Reprinted by permission of the publisher. George M. Raymond is with the School of Architecture, Pratt Institute. Malcolm D. Rivkin is a writer and consultant on urban planning.

community during that period, regardless of location, as well as *all housing that has become available to people in the same income bracket as those displaced, from whatever source* (such as the migration to the suburbs of upwardly mobile white families). In Brooklyn alone, it has been estimated that between 1950 and 1960 half-a-million white persons were replaced by an equal number of generally lower-income non-whites and Puerto Ricans. The units into which these newcomers moved represented a net addition to the housing supply available to lower-income minority families. Mr. Gans has failed to take any of these well-known facts into consideration.

Strangely enough, Mr. Gans admits that the data on which he relied were supplied by Martin Anderson, author of *The Federal Bulldozer,* and characterized by Mr. Gans as "an ultra-conservative economist and often irresponsible polemicist." How, then, can he defend his use of the slanted, incomplete, and poorly digested data from such a discredited source? The answer to this question is quite clear: were Mr. Gans to use reliable data, his case against urban renewal would collapse. Let me illustrate.

An incredibly large proportion of all families displaced by urban renewal are being relocated in decent, safe, and sanitary dwellings. (Admittedly, this was not the case with many families displaced by previous programs, which were not required by law to provide relocation housing.) While local public agencies had claimed that some 84 per cent of all families had been adequately rehoused, the studies cited by Mr. Gans maintained that as many as 70 per cent were merely rehoused in other slums. However, a recently completed impar-

tial survey by the Bureau of the Census found that 94 per cent of those displaced families whose move could be traced (or more than 75 per cent of the total sample) were relocated in standard dwellings. This was accomplished even though 40 per cent of these families had an income of under $3,000! Thus it appears that the claims of local agencies were much closer to the truth than those of the detractors of urban renewal.

Mr. Gans cites a Chicago study to the effect that rents rose from 35 per cent of family income before relocation, to 46 per cent afterward. The above-mentioned Census survey, however, reported that the median proportion of income spent for rent rose by only 3 per cent, from 25 to 28 per cent. It must be noted that the Chicago study dealt with public housing, rather than urban renewal and relocation; in any event it was made in 1957, eight years ago, and long before the improved housing programs and relocation procedures —which Mr. Gans accuses the program of having spent only *one-half of one per cent* (the italics are his) of all federal expenditures for urban renewal between 1949 and 1964 on the relocation of families and individuals, but he admits that the proportion rise to 2 per cent if direct relocation payments are included. One must question the basic relevance of these figures. The one-half of one per cent represents only the cost of the local public agencies' administration of relocation programs. It does not include any of the federal subsidies involved either in the construction and operation of low-rent public housing into which many families were relocated, or in the advance of below-market interest rate loans to private builders of middle-income housing. It also omits the non-federal subsidies offered by local communities in the form of tax abatement, social services, relocation bonuses, etc. In the aggregate, these expenditures represent many times the amount claimed by Mr. Gans to be the only public assistance extended to relocated families.

Urban renewal is of no assistance to cities, Mr. Gans suggests, because "the average project has taken twelve years to complete." What he fails to point out is that a project can be 99 per cent finished, and yet be carried on the books for years as incomplete. In New York City, this is the case with such projects as Lincoln Square or Penn Station South, which have been paying taxes for years. Furthermore, in many projects, the first building erected returns many times the taxes paid by the entire project area before renewal. (A recent example is the Medical Tower office building *which occupies only 2.5 acres* of a 35-acre renewal project in Norfolk, Virginia, *and which returns twice the amount of taxes previously paid by the entire area.*) Thus, even though only partially completed, a renewal project can begin to help the city meet not only the remaining cost of the project itself, but also its many other pressing obligations.

Mr. Gans accuses urban renewal of falling short of expectations because private investments, which were to exceed public expenditures by four times, have barely matched the latter. But here again, we are confronted with a comparison made at a time when the major portion of all public expenditures designed to prepare the site for private development has already been committed, while private investment in the new buildings is only beginning to be made.

For an accurate picture of the position of private vs. public investment, one has to look at individual projects. Thus, in New Haven's Oak Street Project, *assessments* (which represent only a fraction of actual construction costs) have increased from $2 million to $16.6 million, while the total public cost has been only $5 million. (Incidentally, this project, which now pays eight times the taxes collected from the area before renewal, is still listed as "incomplete.") In Hartford, Connecticut, Constitution Plaza will be assessed at $46 million as against the previous $9 million; the total public cost is $10.4 million. Since these figures are very easy to obtain, it is strange that Mr. Gans relies on Anderson's admittedly biased data.

Between 1950 and 1960, Mr. Gans claims, "six million substandard dwellings disappeared—all without government action." The sad fact is that the decade began, and ended, with 4.1 million dilapidated units, and that some 15 million Americans continue to live in them. As a sociologist and planner, Mr. Gans should know full well that during this period the Bureau of the Census adopted a fundamental change in definitions relating to substandard housing, and that therefore his startling statistic is due to what can most charitably be described as mere sleight-of-hand, rather than to a dramatic conversion to the paths of righteousness by the nation's slum landlords.

So much for the shaky and sometimes obviously biased foundations of Mr. Gans's case against urban renewal. It is strange that he continues to beat the dead horse of the program as it was run in the 1950's, even though he recognizes that the many changes effected under the Kennedy and Johnson administrations have given it a new direction. He must surely know that the effect of new legislation on a program that takes years to mature will not be felt for four or five years. And yet, he makes no effort either to project the effect of these changes into the future, or to understand the extent to which they may vitiate much of his criticism. His constant use of data which, given his own questioning of the source, he must know to be untrue, disqualifies him as a dispassionate observer or objective scientist. For the true marks of a scientist are his ability to survive that "great tragedy of Science—the slaying of a beautiful hypothesis by an ugly fact" (T. H. Huxley), and his readiness to build a more advanced hypothesis upon its ruins. By contrast, Mr. Gans seems to be unable to abandon discredited theories, even if he has to resort to outright distortion of facts in order to hold on to them.

Before turning to Mr. Gans's proposed solution to some of the most complex and danger-laden social problems of our time, let us examine the reasons for the difficulties in the path of urban renewal. Anyone who has ever tried to set an urban renewal project in motion knows that the main reason for its bogging down is the relocation problem. By this is meant not the absence of housing or of means to develop needed housing, but the totally unbending refusal of the white community to accept any Negro settlement in its midst. The task is further complicated by the fact that many sites which are proposed for the construction of new housing are not acceptable to the Negro leadership because these sites fail to further racial integration. Under these circumstances, the only dynamic force for at least some integration in housing is a community desire to undertake urban renewal. The community is motivated by the very reasons at which Mr. Gans is so prepared to sneer, including the addition of new tax revenues to its dwindling coffers, the revitalization of its downtown areas, and the halting of the exodus of middle-class whites to the suburbs. Many early projects, begun shortly after the enactment of the basic legislation in 1949, actually did concentrate on the worst slums, as Mr. Gans would have all of them do. But instead of achieving the results he desires, these projects remained vacant for years because sites still surrounded by slums do not attract private developers.

The second major source of opposition to urban renewal are the slumlords, who frequently hide behind the arguments so generously supplied by Gans, Anderson, et al. In many communities, large and small, the poor are now exploited to the point where the shacks in which they live bring 25 to 30 per cent net profit to the owners. No wonder, therefore, that these "real-estate investors" oppose the cities' efforts at slum-clearance.

In the light of these serious difficulties, how relevant are Mr. Gans's proposals? He would like all slum-clearance efforts to be stopped until the suburbs are ready to accept in their midst "groups of slum residents en masse," together with all the "new social institutions and community facilities [needed] to help the erstwhile slum-dweller feel comfortable in his new community." Somehow, he also expects to make it possible for these "erstwhile slum-dwellers" to be moved into their new environments without being labeled as poor—which can only be interpreted to mean that they will be discreetly provided with not only housing and furniture on a par with their middle-income neighbors, but also with a continuing income equal to theirs. Given this country's traditional economic stance, it is quite doubtful that our government is about to embrace the doctrine of "from each according to his ability, to each according to his needs," which would have to provide the basis for any income policy whereby erstwhile slum-dwellers could be supplied with an instant middle-income. As for the chance of moving low-income Negroes into the suburbs, Mr. Gans himself recognizes that this would be a hundredfold more difficult than moving them into middle-income, white, city neighborhoods. Since even this, less difficult, objective has proven well-nigh impossible to accomplish, Mr. Gans's vision has all the marks of an unattainable utopia.

But the most incredible of Mr. Gans's proposals is that the federal government should accelerate the transformation of our cities into predominantly, or even exclusively, Negro enclaves. He even goes so far as to suggest that poor whites who wish to move from areas inhabited by Negroes should be given a subsidy to enable them to move to new housing on the city's outskirts! This proposal is based on the romantic notion that "non-white low-income people might feel more positive about a city in which they were the majority, for if they had the votes, municipal services would be more attuned to their priorities than is now the case." This presupposes that the City of the Poor will be governed by philosopher-kings, rather than by the kind of politician who usually rises to rule the poor and ignorant. After all, venal leadership of cities in which the poor or near-poor, of whatever color, are a majority is not a novelty on our political scene: Jersey City produced

not Woodrow Wilson, but Frank Hague. The priorities under the latter's enlightened leadership did little for the poor—except, of course, for the well-publicized turkey on Thanksgiving.

Cities deprived of their upper and middle classes, and thus composed chiefly of the poor, would inevitably entail a serious deterioration in the quality of our entire civilization, since it is the *cities*, not the suburbs, that have always carried and nurtured this precious, complex heritage. Mr. Gans's failure to grasp such a fundamental point leads him to proposals which are truly subversive, in the best sense of that word. In his legitimate concern with the problems of the poor, he is much too ready to sacrifice the city.

Furthermore, he himself admits that cities inhabited exclusively by the poor will not be able to raise the huge amounts of money required for necessary services. How realistic is it to believe that the federal government will then be ready to provide massive aid, considering that even now what is forthcoming from that source is a mere pittance when compared with the vastness of the need?

In Mr. Gans's vision of America's future city, the low-income Negroes will be able to occupy the housing in better neighborhoods vacated by all the whites and a large number of the "upwardly mobile," highly educated, and highly skilled Negroes, who will have moved to the suburbs. This process, he says, will leave so many vacant units in the old slum areas as to make it relatively easy and inexpensive to tear them down, and to turn these areas into "the hub[s] of . . . vast metropolitan complex[es] of urban neighborhoods, suburbs, and new towns. . . ." In theory, perhaps: but in real life one needs to ask a few additional questions. What would happen if the rate of new construction were to fail to keep pace with population growth? Or if the migration of the unassimilated poor to the city continued, or even increased? Would these factors not tend to keep the slums, by then fully segregated, occupied indefinitely? And at the end of the decades it would take for this process to consummate itself, what is to guarantee that the centers of cities would still be there to be salvaged? What assurance is there that the middle class, by then totally suburbanized, would continue to brave the daily trip across the angry, seething, indigent "black belt," rather than decentralize those functions which now make that trip, already excessively difficult, necessary?

As for the "hard-core," multi-problem families and socially deviant, self-destructive individuals—whose presence frequently holds up completion of renewal projects for many months, if not years, and which is, in part, responsible for the poor image of much public housing—Mr. Gans has an easy answer. For the mentally ill, the dope addict, the habitual prostitute, etc., he would either leave the existing slums, or set up "a new kind of public housing . . . quasi-communities . . . to provide at least decent shelter for those who cannot be helped . . . until we learn how to cure" their ills. This has often been advanced as the "half-way house": a settlement saturated with social services, from which families might be able to move to normal public housing if they could overcome their anti-social or self-destructive behavior. Up to now it has been rejected by those in positions of responsibility, not for lack of thought, but because it runs counter to our democratic ethos and because it much resembles the idea of "caring" for undesirables in concentration camps.

No reasonable person will resist any possible improvement of the renewal program. But notwithstanding the misleading appeal of Mr. Gans's oversimplified, hollow, and totally impractical arguments, his proposals do not amount to any program of action which lies in the realm of the possible. A clue to the nature of his confusion is furnished by his statement that "what poor people need most are decent incomes, proper jobs, better schools, and freedom from racial and class discrimination." "Indeed," he continues, "if the choice were between a program solely dedicated to rehousing, and a program that kept the low-income population in the city slums for another generation but provided for these needs, the latter would be preferable, for it would produce people who were able to leave the slums under their own steam." But unfortunately, the only choice open to us is between leaving the poor in their slums, and supplying some of them with decent housing in good neighborhoods. Dr. Robert C. Weaver, the nation's Housing Administrator and one of its foremost urban scholars, has observed that while it is true that good housing "is not itself a remedy for a family's ills . . . [it] does offer the environment in which many . . . family problems can be successfully treated." Besides, as Mr. Gans recognizes, the renewal program constantly brings problems out in the open which our society has previously been content to sweep under the rug. For example, much of the impetus for the war on poverty can be attributed to the difficulties discovered in the path of urban renewal. Also, as Mr. Gans himself points out, the construction activity which can be generated by housing and urban-renewal programs could well contribute to creating a level of employment which would include jobs for many of the unemployed poor.

Most tragically, Mr. Gans either does not know, or has forgotten, what slums are like, and what cruel effects they have on those who live in them. While doing his research for *The Urban Villagers,* he acted as a "participant observer." He may or may not have done the same in a New York City slum neighborhood. Dan Wakefiled did, and this is how he described the vast gulf between the meaning of the slum to a participant observer and to a slum-dweller:

I cannot know the slums or hate them as profoundly as Alicia does because I wasn't born there. I am able to hate them and know them in some small way because of the brief time I lived in Alicia's neighborhood. I cannot approach the abyss of her understanding because no matter what happened I knew I could always escape; I was only a visitor. There were times, though, when I tried with an effort of imagination to extend my experience to that of my neighbors. There were times when I came home tired, late at night, on 100th Street, and climbed the stairs and opened the door of my room and turned the light on and watched the sudden scurry of the cockroaches that moved on the paint-chipped kitchen wall like the scattered filings of a magnet controlled by some invisible force. I would close the door and take a deep breath of the stale, heavy air, and then suddenly I would remember that after all, this wasn't my real home—I would later move on to some clean, well-lighted place like the ones I had lived in before. But then I would close my eyes and concentrate and try to imagine that this was my home and would always be my home and that the clean, well-lighted places of the world were forever closed to me. Most of the time I could not believe it; I could feel nothing. Sometimes, though, for the

briefest instant, I could catch a flicker of the nightmare that was the only reality for every other human being beneath that roof. I could feel the enclosure of the flaking walls and see through the window the blackened reflection of the tenement across the street that blocked out the world beyond. But it was only a glimpse.

The participant observer can afford to wait for the elimination of slums. For him there is less urgency about that than about trying to make the world fit his preconceptions. Unhappily, Mr. Gans's vision of a world where poor Negroes are welcomed to the suburbs is a mirage. Thousands of years ago, a world was envisioned in which "the wolf shall dwell with the lamb, and the leopard shall lie down with the kid," but it has not yet come to pass.

Must we, then, have the slums always with us, as we seem fated to have the poor?

I do not mean to suggest that we should resign ourselves to the status quo, nor do I mean to deny that Mr. Gans is clearly motivated by a deep dedication to the cause of the downtrodden. As is well known from several millennia of experience, however, it takes more than dedication to help improve the condition of the poor. Certainly, two basic prerequisites are an ability to distinguish reality from wishful thinking, and a willingness—in the words of President Johnson—to "deal with the world as it is, if it is ever to be as we wish." That may be more difficult than spinning dreams of utopias, but it is essential if the necessary job is to be done.

Malcolm D. Rivkin: Herbert J. Gans is probably the most sensitive critic of urban renewal writing today. His measured analysis in COMMENTARY reflects intimate familiarity with the program and its problems. Unlike those critics who would scrap unban renewal, Mr. Gans sees a prospect for adapting the present machinery—with significant changes—in order to ameliorate severe social problems of contemporary urban society. His proposals for federal action are sound and realistic enough to be enacted by our urban-minded President and a cooperative Congress.

But Mr. Gans has oversimplified the solutions by seeking too hard for a *deus ex machina* in the form of federal intervention. Overstating the possibilities of the federal role in urban renewal, he diverts our attention from the real source of difficulty: the ruling elite of individual American cities. Basically, the city councils, planning boards, renewal authorities, and social institutions of our urban communities determine the kind of renewal that is effected. And regardless of any new federal legislation, these local authorities will continue to dominate the field. Mr. Gans, of course, recognizes local leadership as a problem, but he fails to emphasize the prime responsibility it bears. The following points must therefore be noted:

(1) The present urban-renewal legislation, even as it stands, is not bad legislation. It does not encourage segregation or the destruction of salvable minority-group housing. It may indeed place insufficient emphasis on rehabilitation, on combining better housing with better employment opportunities, and on other socially-motivated programs which I join Mr. Gans in desiring. But such projects can today be undertaken as part of the regular renewal activity, as special demonstration programs, or in combination with other federal and state aid programs that are already available to local municipalities. Renewal de-

pends mainly on what the *community* wants. The present legislation is broad in concept. It does set guidelines, and its accompanying administrative regulations (often cumbersome, to be sure) do establish detailed technical criteria and standards, but these guidelines and standards are applied to projects initiated by the local communities themselves. HHFA has respected the existing division between federal and local powers to a degree not commonly appreciated by the critics of "growing federal control." Before a project even comes to the federal authorities for approval and allocation of funds, it has been drafted by local planners, approved by the City Council after public hearings, and endorsed as harmonious with community interests by a "representative" advisory committee of civic leaders. It is difficult if not impossible for the federal authorities to reject out of hand a technically sound proposal that has received full support from the official and articulate elements of the community—especially when the project violates no civil-rights or other law.

I remember the genesis of one particular project in a middle-sized New England city. A small three-acre parcel of land near a well-to-do residential area had been scheduled for clearance. The renewal planners and the City Council considered a number of alternative uses for the land. It could be employed for public housing, or a limited-dividend project for middle-income families, or a high-rise, high-rent development that would bring significant revenues to the city by way of property taxes and tenant purchasing power. The federal authorities would have approved any of the feasible projects. Much citizen activity was generated, and a heated debate ensued. Finally, the local planners and the

City Council (after a public hearing) opted for the high-rent, high tax-paying alternative. As this was the local decision, endorsed by the community leadership, the project (which met all the necessary technical specifications) was approved by HHFA.

(2) Excellent, socially-motivated projects—stemming from local initiative and community leadership, not federal decree—have been accomplished under the present urban-renewal program. I am thinking particularly of New Haven, which—under the forceful guidance of Mayor Richard Lee—has both increased its tax base and provided stable middle- and lower-income housing. New Haven's techniques have included rehabilitation as well as new construction. It has pioneered in the use of rent subsidies under a demonstration grant from HHFA, and it has gone far toward using urban renewal as a means of fostering integrated neighborhoods. New Haven's success, although not complete, has occurred under the same federal legislation that has elsewhere led to excesses of clearance and luxury housing. But New Haven's leaders wanted something better for their city.

(3) Current federal activity (in the poverty program and area redevelopment) is placing more rather than less emphasis on local responsibility. This is a harbinger of things to come. The Office of Economic Opportunity requires locally staffed and planned Community Action Programs as the prerequisite for much of its assistance. Although it tries to secure the "involvement of the poor" in the framing of such programs, OEO can act only on plans produced by local agencies. Area development assistance efforts in Appalachia and elsewhere are based on the premise that the states or areas in question will themselves decide on what is needed. I do not believe that we can realistically expect any "new look" in urban renewal—no matter how enlightened it is at the federal level—to diverge from this increasing emphasis on local and state decision-making.

Nor can I agree with Mr. Gans that the carrot of heavy federal financial assistance will be so tempting that communities will lightly do away with long-held prejudices in order to collect large sums of "free" money. . . . I agree completely with Mr. Gans on the need for new federal legislation and on its content, but unless community attitudes change, this legislation will not be worth the paper on which it is printed.

The difficulty of producing this change constitutes the real roadblock to effective renewal, and leadership by federal example is at best a partial answer. At present, the fear of Negro movement into white neighborhoods is deep-rooted and strong among both suburbanites and well-to-do central city residents. Moreover, the continuing erosion of downtown tax bases and the crazy-quilt system of municipal revenue, make high tax-producing renewal projects of particular—and understandable—importance to city authorities. Until, however, integrated neighborhoods and good housing for the poor become local political issues of equal or greater significance than the tax base, very little change will occur—regardless of new federal laws. This does not mean the situation is hopeless. There are signs of growing articulateness in the Negro communities of Chicago, Washington, and other cities where Negro population and Negro incomes are both rising. This expression of concern will, one hopes, be channeled into a constructive force. The growing number of foundations and OEO-supported community action organizations, such as Community Progress in New Haven and the United Planning Organization in Washington, can certainly contribute to this process. By helping the poor to define their own needs and desires, these organizations can begin to express demands which political leaders will be unable to ignore. But the process will be slow and arduous.

One of the key forces for change is the urban university, and I am a bit surprised that it went unmentioned in Mr. Gans's otherwise comprehensive discussion. For universities—the Columbias, the Harvards, the George Washingtons, the Western Reserves—represent a major and too often aloof power in urban America. They are large landowners in the central cities, where their stake is already so great that they cannot move to suburban pastures along with the white middle class and the less heavily committed industries. They must, therefore, protect the physical and social characteristics of their surroundings. As the trainers of leadership for the Great Society, moreover, they have, or rather should have, a certain social conscience.

There are two ways in which the universities can act. First, as powerful institutions in their own communities they can press for socially responsible renewal programs, for integrated housing in middle-class areas, for an improvement in housing and job opportunities for the poor. Indeed, the universities, through skilled and willing faculty members, can provide a good deal of technical assistance to the community for performing the tasks necessary to achieve these objectives. Some schools have already accepted this role;

others are as remiss as local government itself.

Secondly, the universities have a responsibility for training the next generation of urban administrators and politicians. It is up to the schools to provide leaders of higher quality and greater sensitivity than ever before. In the course of their university experience, students can be brought face to face with the problems confronting urban America and they can be provided with both the technical skills and the values required for equitable solutions. As a new breed of sensitive planner, politician, or engineer emerges to help guide the course of urban society, the prospects for change will become greater.

None of this will be easy; nor can these problems be solved overnight—if at all. We must call on every resource. But the final outcome, whatever it may be, will depend less on Congress and the HHFA than on the people and institutions of the cities themselves.

Herbert J. Gans: Professor Raymond's argument in support of present urban renewal policies is an extremely complex one, but it may be summarized as follows. Slums ought to be cleared to meet the need for new schools, hospitals, recreational facilities, and expanded business districts. On the one hand, urban renewal can proceed without replacing the cleared units, because of the white exodus to the suburbs, and because improved relocation procedures are providing enough better housing for displaced poor non-whites. On the other hand, urban renewal cannot proceed, because whites refuse to let non-whites move into their neighborhoods and relocation is therefore impossible.

It is, however, subversive to help non-whites move into such neighborhoods, nor does the answer lie in public-housing projects, which are too much like concentration camps. Nevertheless, something ought to be done, for slums are extremely harmful to their occupants. The solution consists of "supplying some of [the slum-dwellers] with decent housing in good neighborhoods" which requires "the ability to distinguish reality from wishful thinking and a willingness . . . 'to deal with the world as it is'"—or as President Johnson says it is.

Since it is impossible to deal with such an argument, I will confine myself to comments on some of Mr. Raymond's individual charges. I did not say that urban renewal had to replace demolished low-cost housing in the same area; I merely said that in cities where such housing is in short supply, renewal ought to be halted—regardless of how many whites leave Brooklyn. Even though Mr. Raymond thinks it is more important to provide community facilities for gray areas and to build stores in downtown districts that already have too many vacancies, than it is to provide housing for displaced slum-dwellers, the latter do have to live somewhere.

Perhaps they could build shacks out of all the government reports which demonstrate the high quality of relocation procedures. The latest such document, just issued by the Bureau of the Census and cited by Mr. Raymond, may be impartial but it is also inconclusive. Unlike the studies I drew on, which describe what happened to *all* the residents of an urban renewal area after their displacement, the Census study only dealt with people who had actually been relocated by 132 local agencies during a three-month period

in 1964. However, anyone who has ever worked in an urban-renewal agency knows that many slum-dwellers flee from a project area when renewal is announced; others leave before they can be interviewed by renewal officials; and yet others depart before they can be offered relocation aid. A high proportion of all these premature movers go to other slums. According to a report of the New York City Department of Relocation, for example, 47 per cent of the slum-dwellers in the urban-renewal area of the Upper West Side left between the early months of 1963, when the city took title to the area, and at the end of the same year, when it started relocation activities. The Census report, in other words, covers only a portion of those displaced. The premature flight of so many slum-dwellers is not entirely the fault of urban-renewal procedures, but it must be taken into account in any honest evaluation of relocation.

I did not—and still do not—question the possibility that in cities where inexpensive housing is plentiful, humane relocation is taking place. But we still need reliable studies to prove this, especially in the case of big cities. Moreover, there is a similar lack of evidence concerning the amount of rent increase paid by the relocatees.

If relocation is as beneficial as local and federal officials are constantly trying to prove, why are slum dwellers—who live in blight and misery and who want better housing—so opposed to urban renewal? Is it because they are participant observers "who can afford to wait for the elimination of slums," or "socially deviant, self-destructive individuals" who enjoy holding up the completion of renewal projects? Or is it possibly because they have too many relatives and friends who have suffered from urban renewal?

And, indeed, how could it be otherwise, given the meager public-housing program, the shortage of other relocation housing, and the niggardly sums spent for relocation Mr. Raymond seems pleased that fully 2 per cent of all federal renewal funds are allocated for relocation payments, but the fact is that 1.5 per cent of these funds is spent for payments to relocated *businesses*. Displaced residents, therefore, receive only one-half of one per cent, which is what I indicated in my article. Moreover, this figure refers to actual relocation payments by the federal government, and not to local administrative costs, as Mr. Raymond claims. The other benefits he mentions accrue to middle-income relocatees, and, according to the Census report cited above, the "many families" who move into public housing turn out to be exactly 13 per cent of all those people actually relocated by local agencies.

There have, of course, been some projects which have brought higher taxes to their cities, and I said as much. I also said that federal renewal and relocation policies had improved immeasurably since the end of the Eisenhower administration. But in too many cities local agencies are still proposing renewal projects which call for the displacement of large numbers of slumdwellers into non-existent relocation housing, and—as Mr. Rivkin points out —the federal government cannot seem to stop them. I know of one Eastern city in which a luxury apartment house, built as part of an urban-renewal program, still stands almost half empty; nevertheless, there has recently been a proposal for a huge new upper-income project that will consume much of that city's federal quota of renewal funds for the next decade. In another city, rehabilitation is being used to help a Negro middle-class area oust its poor neighbors; and Columbia University has just persuaded New York City to approve a plan for the removal of many Negro and Puerto Rican residents— without adequate provision for their relocation.

If Mr. Raymond had read my article properly, he would have realized that I am quite aware of the obstacles to renewal created by white opposition to racial integration. If anything is to be done, then, about the slums occupied by non-whites, there are three possible courses of action: to rebuild within the present ghettos: to enable slum residents to move into better neighborhoods outside the ghetto, and into the suburbs as quickly as possible; or to continue the present renewal policy, which does nothing about the ghetto slums, and only lets a few upper-middle-income Negroes move into a handful of integrated projects built on renewal sites.

Mr. Raymond opts for the third solution, and this suggests how much he is really concerned about the slum-dwellers, notwithstanding his quotation from Dan Wakefield. The first solution is bitterly opposed by many Negro leaders, and is in any case impossible at present because new housing cannot be built for ghetto residents until a massive rent subsidy scheme is created for the lowest-income groups, or until the public-housing program, now virtually moribund, is expanded. Since the ghetto's principal blight is overcrowding, new housing cannot be built there without relocation, and many of its occupants will have to be helped to move into other neighborhoods.

Not only does this solution require less rent subsidy than the plan to build new housing within old ghettos, but it is also practical, for it merely assists the natural ecological process by which poor people have always bettered their housing conditions. If it entails a further white exodus to the suburbs, many cities will, to be sure, become increasingly non-white, just as a century ago, they became increasingly non-Protestant—and without resulting in the end of democracy or any of the other catastrophes predicted at the time by Mr. Raymond's ideological ancestors. I am not, then, as skeptical as he is of the ability of the poor to choose their own political leaders if they have the power to do so. They will not choose philosopher-kings any more frequently than affluent voters will, and they will rarely choose patricians like Woodrow Wilson. Their politicians might be corrupt, but even corrupt politicians respond to their constituents' demands in order to get re-elected. And since federal politicians are similarly responsive to their constituents, I am sure that the federal government will not stop funneling funds into a city merely because its voters are predominantly poor.

This brings me to the real meaning of Mr. Raymond's solution. In proposing that slum clearance continue despite the difficulties of relocation, he is really maintaining that the most important task is to provide more urban facilities for the upper and middle classes, and that we should not worry too much about the poor since they have always been with us anyway. If the city is not rebuilt for the higher income groups, he argues, there will be "a serious deterioration in the quality of our entire civi-

lization." In short, if the choice is between eliminating poverty and saving civilization, the latter comes first.

Now if this were really the choice, Mr. Raymond might have a point, although one could still argue that a civilization which allows poverty to continue in the midst of affluence is not the "precious heritage" he believes it to be. But this is *not* the choice, and Mr. Raymond is merely repeating another hoary 19th-century cliché. Culture (which is what Professor Raymond seems to mean by civilization) is not intrinsic to cities; it existed there in past centuries because the upper-income groups who supported it—and still support it—happened to live almost entirely in cities. Today this is no longer the case, for the affluent have been living in the suburbs for more than a generation. Thus, if Mr. Raymond were correct, we should now be in the midst of a serious cultural decline, but all evidence suggests the contrary. The only change I can see is that some culture is moving into the suburbs in order to be near its major supporters, and we are now witnessing the emergence of art galleries, theaters, and the like beyond the city limits. Yet no urban concert halls or museums have closed down, though their audiences are heavily suburban too.

Many of those who create culture also live in the suburbs, and there is no evidence that their creativity is thereby impaired. Moreover, the artists who live in the handful of American cities where culture is actually being created (Manhattan, Boston, Chicago, and a few others) seem to be highly productive even though their neighbors are poor and non-white in an increasing number of cases. Manhattan, a world capital rather than the typical American city I was considering, is in no danger of becoming a community of poverty-stricken non-whites. Yet even if it were, I would wager that culture would continue to flourish there, partly because the creators of culture are often poor themselves, but mainly because culture is not so fragile as to be destroyed by residential change. Moreover, if we decided to give poor non-whites an even break, they might even contribute to the creation of better culture and a better civilization.

Mr. Raymond's difficulty is that of the city planner who thinks of the city as a collection of buildings, facilities, and gray areas, but not as a place where people live. What is worse, he only wants to plan for buildings and facilities that are used by upper- and middle-income groups; ignoring the needs of the poor, he is ready to support plans that perpetuate, in Michael Harrington's inimitable phrase, "socialism for the rich and private enterprise for the poor."

One could, of course, simply attribute my disagreement with Mr. Raymond to our opposing views of priorities for governmental action; he favors the rich, and I the poor in what is for all practical purposes a latter-day class struggle. Ironically enough, however, since poverty and discrimination are the primary causes of what is wrong with our cities even by Mr. Raymond's city-planning standards, his proposal to build for the affluent cannot even achieve his own goals. After all, slums exist because too many people cannot afford or cannot get into decent housing. Urban facilities and services are so unsatisfactory because the cities must spend huge sums for welfare and for the protection of property and people

against the crime, addiction, and mental illness which are ultimately also produced by poverty and discrimination. Replacing the buildings of the city without solving the problems of their present occupants is thus a spurious proposal. This is why a serious poverty program not only has priority over urban renewal, but why it is also the most effective method of achieving the civilized and beautiful cities that Mr. Raymond, and I, and everyone else desire.

Consequently, his petulant rejection of my proposals as at best utopian and romantic is self-defeating. So, too, is his unwillingness to accept criticism of urban renewal: if it had not been for earlier critics, we might still be saddled with the urban-renewal procedures of the 1950's. His argument is also ultimately irrelevant, for whether he likes it or not, the federal government will eventually have to adopt a rehousing program. I thought I had made it perfectly clear that the change of policy will be difficult and slow, but this does not mean that our facing up to the problem now is either impractical or subversive. Rather, it is the indispensable prerequisite of proper planning.

This is also the crux of my answer to Mr. Rivkin's thoughtful remarks. He is absolutely right, of course, to suggest that the current inadequacies of urban renewal stem principally from local community decisions, and more specifically, from the failure of downtown business and real-estate interests to realize that they must use their power to improve the lot—and the purchasing power—of the low-income population, instead of continuing with useless attempts to lure the middle class back to the city.

It is also true that local autonomy in the expenditure of federal funds is not likely to decrease, although I am not as content with this trend as Mr. Rivkin seems to be. The "downtown influentials" are seldom wise enough to plan beyond their own immediate interests, and until a systematic benefit-cost analysis is made of the New Haven renewal and poverty programs, I am not sure that we can use even that city as a model of local enlightenment. Although its programs are probably the best in the country, there is some evidence that they do not provide much help to the poverty-stricken, and that they are not good enough to cope with New Haven's basic problems.

I believe that the only solution to the present impasse is more federal intervention, and since this cannot be achieved by federal control of local programs, it must be effected by the expenditure of more federal funds. Of course, federal subsidies are now accepted because of local demands and pressures for them, but the availability of new funds would create new local demands. For example, a major impetus for New York's Lower Manhattan Expressway came from the unions who want the jobs that new construction will generate. If a massive federal rehousing program were instituted, and if it were to include proper incentives for both urban and suburban demands, local support for the program would be created. Such support would not develop overnight, but if there is no new federal spending it will not develop at all.

I agree with Mr. Rivkin that local urban-renewal decisions will improve as Negro voters become more influential in city politics; even now they have exer-

cised their power to bring the program to a virtual standstill in some cities. This is of no help either to themselves or to the cities in which they live, but only a rehousing program will enroll their support in the future. I am not as sanguine as Mr. Rivkin, however, about the contribution of the urban universities. They are, among other things, real-estate operations, and when it comes to moving poor residents out of university neighborhoods, they act with the same ruthlessness as other real-estate operations. They are justifiably concerned with expanding their campuses, but they also believe, and unjustifiably so, that crime and blight can be dealt with by moving out as many low-income residents as possible, however law-abiding they may be. In this process, they pay little attention to relocation needs.

Nor am I as hopeful as Mr. Rivkin that the urban university will train the next generation of urban politicians and officials to be aware of the real problems of the cities. They will do a much better job than in the past, because they did almost nothing in the past. But up to now, much of the improvement in urban planning and research programs has been generated by funds from federal agencies and foundations, and by the greater concern with social justice and social science among the new generation of students in the field of city planning. Meanwhile, too many professors are still advocating architectural solutions that benefit mainly the upper-income groups, and Professor Raymond's remarks provide depressing evidence that progress is likely to be slow.

Waiting for Reality:
Birth of the Megalopolis

Scott Greer

The American city has always been a problem of some sort to somebody. From Jefferson's worries about the corruption of the urban masses to Johnson's concern with "renewing" our cities, there has been a presumption of failure in our urban communities. This kind of belief, however stated, has really rested upon the classical problem of social change—the dramatic disjunction between what we think we wanted, on one hand, and what we have cooperatively produced on the other.

What we have made is a society which became increasingly urban in each decade (but one) since the Revolution. We know the story but the statistics bear repeating: from less than 5 per cent urban during Washington's presidency to over 70 per cent during Johnson's. But all the time we were building an urban nation, we continued to measure it against images derived from an earlier age. The discrepancy led to moral and political efforts to reshape what was emerging in the image of that golden time.

It is conventional to attribute much of the increase in urban growth to the Civil War and its stimulation of manufacturing. However, it is important to remember that the single greatest proportionate increase of the urban population was between 1840 and 1850, when the proportion living in cities increased by nearly half. A consistent increase continued to the present, with the urban proportion rising around five per cent each decade.

The underlying cause was the increasing scale of the society. By this I mean two things: first, the increasing application of non-human energy and machines to every aspect of human work, beginning with agriculture (today our most mechanized industry); second, the increasing organization of work in large, formal structures which demand and allow spatial concentration of the factors of production and places of exchange. Increasing material wealth and increasing control over space, both resulting from the revolution in energy resources, allowed for the development of regional and national producers and markets. Around the sites of these enterprises grew the cities.

The increase of energy resources included both the development of techniques for using petrochemicals and the increase in productive lands. These latter in turn fed both national and international trade, and tended to dominate certain world markets with their produce. One result was the competitive decline in European agriculture and the movement of peasants to the cities and, in many cases, to the cities of the United States. This massive immigration shaped the basic character

From *The Nation,* ed. by David Boroff (September 1965), pp. 98-102. Copyright © 1965 by The National Centennial, Inc. Published by Prentice-Hall, Inc., Englewood Cliffs, New Jersey. Reprinted by permission of the publisher.

of American cities—differentiating them from both the cities of other nations and the remainder of American society. All cities are polyglot and heterogeneous, but American cities had more people from further and more various origins than any in history save possibly Rome.

The cities of the latter 19th century were preeminently cities of the railroad. This major breakthrough in the use of new energies, allowing the cheap movement of heavy materials across the continental nation, increased the span of productive enterprise and of the markets. However, it did little to alleviate the problem of movement *within* the city, where animal muscles (human and equine) completed the journey of goods from distant places. Movement within the city was expensive and slow; the solution was a sharp increase in density of the increasing population. This meant crowded tenements for the poor, town houses for the rich, high-rise offices, factories, and loft buildings for work. Near the terminal stood the plants and warehouses handling the heavy goods and, near them, the dwellings of the workers.

The workers were, predominantly, poor. Over the last half of the 19th century their wages rose very slowly, while they bore the brunt of "the business cycle" in unemployment without benefit of unions. Poorly educated if at all, chained to the job, polyglot and in many cases strangers from a simpler world, they constituted a majority of the people in the rapidly growing cities. Their jerry-built neighborhoods were poorly maintained (it was a sellers' market in cheap housing, as always), and they quickly deteriorated into the generic "slums." The concentration of the poorest coincided with the concentration of the criminal, the dependent, the diseased and, as a partial consequence, the revolutionary.

The American image of these cities was ambivalent. On the one hand, those who were in revolt from the village and the isolated farms looked to the city as liberator. But many others viewed it as a pit of iniquity. Anselm Strauss (in his study, *Images of the American City*) documents the intense revulsion felt for the city among those whose basic ideal was the small town life described by Riley. The Jeffersonian myth "that the country was the source of moral integrity and vigor" survived, even as millions of country boys went to the cities to gamble their futures.

These counter-images of the city are most harshly presented in the novels of Dreiser. In his series based on the career of Yerkes, the brilliant opportunities and the terrible risks of urban existence are evoked as interwoven aspects of the same whole. More important, his naturalism illuminates the weakness of public order and the free rein of chicanery and violence. Underlying this at a deeper level is a commitment on Dreiser's part to the dominant myth of American business enterprise —that social Darwinism which saw conflict, competition and survival as the "real" facts and the moral order as a mere epiphenomenon. It was "natural" that the City Council of Chicago could be controlled through bribe, as it was natural that economic aggrandizement in the person of Yerkes should integrate the transit system and thus improve the purchasing power of the worker's nickel. It amounts to saying that whatever has resulted justifies the process from which it came.

This point of view is equally evident

in the first school of American urban studies, that of the "human ecologists." Having separated the moral order from the spatially-evident community, these scholars then ignored the former to concentrate upon a description of the latter. Implicit was a social determinism which derived the existing city from the struggle for *Lebensraum* among contending interest groups of every sort. Neither moral norms nor the structure of government exerted any real influence upon the course of life in the city.

And indeed, there was much truth in such an assumption. Lincoln Steffens and his fellow muckrakers had dug up shattering evidence of corruption and compliance in City Halls throughout the nation. Politicians were handmaidens of the highest bidders among the businessmen. Plunkitt of Tammany Hall seemed a better guide to practical politics than were professors of government; his fine distinctions between honest and dishonest graft seemed at least congruent with the real rules of the game, unlike the charters, statutes and homilies of the textbooks. Nor was there anything "unnatural" about it. The irrelevant images of a small-town and rural America were held in common by those who had drafted the democratic charters. These architects assumed the farmer, the independent producer, had both the ability and the interest to govern himself through the ballot or through taking office. The reality was the mass of new urbanites, employees, entrepreneurs, hucksters from every part of the earth, often illiterate but anxious to make their way in a frightening and promising environment.

The result was the invention of the "machines"—networks of party clubs which sold favors wholesale at the top and distributed the rewards downward at retail. When such machines coincided with ethnic groups or coalitions (and this was almost always the case), the basis was laid for a politics which succeeded in relating numbers to wealth, after a fashion. It was, however, a fashion calculated to minimize the independent effect of "the public purpose" upon the business of running the city. The public treasury, the transportation system, the use of urban lands, the administration of justice—all levers capable of controlling the development of the city—were co-opted by private enterprise. The public purpose had markedly little to do with the developing layout of American cities.

Under such circumstances the energies of reformers were focused upon the creation of integrity in government. Drawn overwhelmingly from the middle-class old Americans, civic reformers were concerned with separating public purpose and private enterprise at the level of the boss, who lined his pockets, and of the voters, who bought ethnic identity and trivial privileges. The "Good Government League" fought for the short ballot, non-partisan elections, proportional representation, initiative, referendum, recall, the city manager system, and so on through a laundry list of nostrums. Their aims were "to take government out of politics."

And there were other urban reform movements. Those who could not accept with equanimity the Spencerian dictum that the weak and ignorant should perish developed the settlement-house movement, cultural missions to the poor. Those whose eyes were shocked at the urban scene resulting from the free play of the market—the maximization of profit for those with capital to invest—began to urge the creation of the "city beautiful." So pervasive, however, was the ideological climate that reformers and unregenerate exploiters alike shared a core of basic values. For those who would take government out of politics dreamed mostly of an honest administrative government, forgetting that politics is the collective determination of the future, *demanding* the representation of divergent interests. Those who were on missions to the poor forgot that under the national credo, unemployment is part of the divine scheme of free enterprise and mass poverty certain for any city. Those who planned the city beautiful ignored the dictum that nothing capable of earning a dollar should be left to government—a rule whose practical consequence was the domination of urban patterns by the money and real estate markets.

Within such limits the achievements of reformers were limited indeed. To be sure, localized planning occurred in the centers of some cities; parks were bequeathed by the wealthy; some control over new building was instituted (becoming a new source of income for the "machines"). Meanwhile, the older urban centers were flooded with new buildings throughout the latter half of the century, with huge new systems of streets and sewers accompanying them and leading to the growth of huge new fortunes. The rapid building of the urban plant used the political machine —and fed it at the same time. Yet Seth Low, Mayor of Brooklyn, in rebuttal to Lord Bryce's condemnation of our municipal government, underscored a major point: when was so much built so rapidly for so many? The antique machinery of local government provided many opportunities to stall and stalemate; it was oiled by the flow of transactions between builders, machines and officials. The society rewarded those who "got things done"—with few questions about ultimate costs.

And indeed, as the nation moved deeper into the 20th century, a determined attack on civic government as a problem began to have some successes. As the worst abuses became rare, as voting machines began to replace political machines, the image of the local official as a trained professional became increasingly applicable. Many interlinked trends underlay the change. With cessation of immigration in the early 1920s, the population became increasingly native and acclimated to American norms and beliefs; it also became better educated, more prosperous and more highly skilled as the society increased in scale. The petty rewards of the machines shrank in value along with toleration of fraud. At the same time, the sheer growth of the cities resulted in the building of huge bureaucracies having a momentum, an order, and complex problems of their own—problems requiring a level of technical competence not to be found at random among "friends of the party." With the depression and the increasing scope of the national government these bureaucracies became intricately interdependent with the larger system: the terms of federal grants gave added leverage to the emerging cadres of professional civic bureaucrats.

Ironically, the very trends which aided in the solution of older problems produced a new and equally difficult set. The increase in scale which resulted in a wealthier and better educated citizenry on one hand, and large bureaucracies producing public goods and services on the other, also increased the average citizen's control over space. Automobiles and electronic communications decreased the dependence of the population upon the small area and dense structures of the central city.

The automobile allowed residence and workplace to be separated further in space and yet remain as close in time as before. The truck allowed enterprises to locate far from the old terminals. Increasing income decreased the marginal cost of private transportation to the citizens, while vast new areas available for development on the peripheries lowered the cost of land. Spatial freedom, along with the development of lifetime mortgages, permitted the vast bulk of the population a free choice between the old high-rise city and the horizontal neighborhoods of suburbia. Their option has been overwhelmingly for the latter.

The decentralization of urban sites was not accompanied by an expansion in the jurisdiction of the older city. For one reason or another (lack of services from the city, unwillingness to be governed and identified with it), the new settlements tended to incorporate as separate municipalities. Thus the typical American metropolis became a large central city surrounded by dozens or hundreds of small suburban towns. Today over half the total population of our metropolitan area lives outside the central city.

This situation has been defined by many as a major problem—"the metropolitan problem." There is no longer any general government for the urban area as a whole. Though it produces problems due to its interdependence— problems of transportation, housing, race relations, drainage and sewerage, land use and so on (almost) indefinitely —there is no capability to act for the public welfare of the region. (Here the title of Robert Wood's book on metropolitan New York, *1400 Governments*, is a dramatic summary.) There is no decision-making body which has the fiscal and the police power to maintain an order referring to the interdependent population. There is no way the resident, as citizen of a *metropolis*, can have a say in the collective fate of the vast urban fabric.

The voices which have dramatized the problem have been, predominently, those who speak for the older central city. They are the ones who tell us that our cities are increasingly "blighted," increasingly inhabited by the segregated, the unemployed, the poor. They emphasize the increased public services necessary for such populations while the prosperous are leaving the city and industry and commerce locating in the industrial parks and shopping centers of the suburbs. The tax base is declining, while the demands for service increase.

And the older urban center deteriorates. The proud neighborhoods of the rich become converted into tenements for the poor and the segregated, great buildings and public monuments deteriorate and no new ones spring up to replace them, civic leaders and patrons of the arts move to the suburbs, leaching purpose and will from the city. The very cradle and core of civilization, the city, is deteriorating even as we become an urbanized society. This is another aspect of the metropolitan problem.

Major campaigns have been mounted for the purpose of re-establishing the cohesion of the city. Many efforts have been made to devise and put into being a new metropolitan government which could include the entire interdependent population of the great complexes. With only minor exceptions they have failed, sunk on the rock of the referendum. For, in our political culture inherited from an earlier era, the municipal corporation is virtually sacrosanct and can be changed only at the will of the citizens. And they, by and large, are not interested in one big government for the metropolis. The opposition, organized and led by the incumbent officials of the various sub-jurisdictions (including those of the central city) almost always has its way.

A second major effort addressed to the plight of the city is the national program of urban renewal. Growing out of the slum clearance and public housing programs of the depression, it has been expanded to a program to renew the cities—to do away with slums and replace them with new growth into the indefinite future. It is, then, a radical program—one aimed at controlling the growth and form of American cities in a way they have never been controlled before.

Unfortunately, the program is severely limited by the political culture and the legal structure. It is forced to share power with many agencies not necessarily committed to its goals. Thus, programs are initiated and guaranteed, indeed executed, by local government; the federal agency must deal with whatever interests the local political process has hoisted into office. The programs are also rigorously limited in what they can do; they can buy land and clear it, but aside from public buildings they cannot redevelop. All that must be undertaken by the private real estate industry. This means that the urban renewal effort can be applied only where local officials want it and where the local real estate market decrees that profits can be made. These sites may or may not be the ones most in need of redevelopment and the resulting structures may contribute as much to aesthetic blight as the ones they replaced.

An equally important limit on the program is the result of governmental fragmentation. Because the program must be a municipal effort, it cannot plan and act for the metropolitan area as a whole. Yet in respect to housing markets, industrial location, transportation and retail markets, the majority of the population outside the central city is critically important to central city developments. What happens, however, is the development of a myopic, city-focused program which ignores the major wave of metropolitan growth and development, the burgeoning suburbs, in order to fixate upon the old, second-hand acres of the central city. Here the chief effects thus far have been the destruction of low-cost housing and replacement with business and public office buildings or luxury apartments. (It is not at all certain that such buildings would not have been built anyway, without public subsidy.)

Both urban renewal and metropolitan government are programs derived from another lag between what we think we want and what we have created. Now the nostalgia is not for the small town and country, but for the imagined central city of another era. People dream of the older part of the city as "hub and symbolic center" for the metropolitan area. They decry the homogeneity of the suburbs, speak of the richness of life in the urban milieu, the heterogeneity of people and cultural experiences easily available. They point then to the "decay" at the urban core. The metropolitan problem is a problem, then, of heart's desire.

But whose heart, and whose problem? Those who set up housekeeping in the suburbs were not usually refugees from the city; they were newly formed families who chose the broad, horizontal acres as most appropriate for the style of life they wanted. It is a life centered in family, home, neighborhood, local community. They do not miss the cultural opportunities of center city, for when they and their kind lived in the center they did not take advantage of them. And besides, with television and stereo they have more access to high culture than any lot of average citizens ever had before. As for tolerance of ethnic differences—segregation of the unlike even in proximity is as possible in a central city as in the South, and has long been practiced in both milieus. In truth, tolerance is most powerfully a function of formal education and it is in the middle-class suburbs that we find the most tolerant populations—not in the polyethnic slums.

As for the "decay" of the city, it is largely an optical illusion. If we insist on seeing only the older half of the metropolis, the proportion of substandard housing, poverty, dependency, *et al*, has certainly increased in recent decades. But the reason is simply the concentration of certain types of population in certain residential areas in a city whose government, not having expanded its jurisdiction, now applies only to a minority of the total population. If we take the metropolitan population as a whole, substandard housing has decreased enormously since the 1950s. The reason is precisely the rapid building of enormous stocks of new housing in the suburbs. The increase in the Negro population is similarly explained: the concentration of the oldest (therefore cheapest) housing in the center, and the proximity of lower status and unskilled jobs, makes center-city housing inevitable for most Negroes. To be sure, formal and informal segregation forces a senseless and uneconomical concentration and density; for this, however, the major remedy is likely to come through the continual increase in vacancies among the older, but still decent, housing of the middle wards—brought about in turn by the movement of white households to the suburbs.

Our slums are products of income shortage, not housing shortage. The cure lies in education, jobs and the resulting increase in the power to control one's destiny. In the same way, participation in high culture and ethnic tolerance are products of a specific kind of experience—education—and we all do not need to move into Manhattan or the Loop in order to have such experience. (In both respects, recent national policy changes seem to result in more realistic programs.) Indeed, the spatial metaphor which leads us to focus upon the hallowed ground of "the city" probably produces more confusion than anything else.

For the city as we reconstruct it from the past no longer exists. Small towns, yes; isolation from the national network and the sharp bounds of farm land leave a tangible reality in the smaller settlements. But when we reach populations large enough to support what we think of as metropolitan functions (the arts and sciences, the specialized markets) we typically find, not an urban form, but an urban texture. Megalopolis, the strip of urban development down the Middle Atlantic seaboard, is in part an artifact of spot maps. It has little unity except contiguity. Yet that is the probable pattern of our emerging regional conurbations.

Most basic to this development is the radical change in the meaning of space. Our technologies have so developed that the entire nation can participate in moments of high solemnity more easily than could be residents of a fairly small town in the recent past; television is the new public forum. At the same time for some actors in some organizations, the entire nation is one city—Megalopolis is Main Street, the airport the major crossroads. As for the average citizen, it is likely that high significance resides, for the most part, either in a realm below that of the public (i.e., the household) or above that of the city (i.e., the national Big Screen).

If we are to exert control over the shape of our cities we must begin with a candid examination of the real nature of urban civilization today. We must take into account what John Friedman has called "interactional space," rendering the metaphors derived from maps into a useful form for this United States today. We must accept the basis in value and choice of widespread decentralization, developing an aesthetic appropriate to it—a view of "the city of a thousand places, the city on wheels," as David Crane has phrased it. Most of the difficulties of our past civic policies derived from their inappropriateness to the total round and rhythm of life in a radically changing and expanding society. With a more accurate map of what is, a more adequate explanation of why it is, we may begin to approach the major question: What do we want with enough consistency and vigor to pay the price?

Or: Do we really care about our cities?

IX EPILOGUE: THE CITY AND THE HISTORIANS

It has been said that to plan for the future one must look at the past. This last chapter is a dialogue among historians concerning the past and future of the field of American urban history.[1] With his own particular emphasis, each of the four historians reviews and criticizes the work that has been done and makes suggestions of what might be done. Together they constitute an intellectual stock-taking of a field that is relatively new as a separate discipline in American history; yet, as her older sister disciplines have had to do, urban history is groping for new subject matter, new methods of research, new kinds of evidence in order to achieve her own identity.

Although the approach and ideas of each may differ, there are some binding themes that run as common threads through each essay. (1) We need more precise definitions of what we mean by "urban," "urbanism," and the "urbanization process." (2) We need a broader, more systematic conceptual framework that embraces the city in its totality. (3) We should expand to make our methodological approach more sophisticated by incorporating into our traditional historical research methods the techniques and ideas of the social scientists—the political scientists, economists, urban sociologists, urban geographers, and cultural anthropologists.

The first selection, William Diamond's "On the Dangers of an Urban Interpretation of History," is a major essay in American urban historiography. It is of two parts. In the first section, he gives us a valuable review of the literature of the pioneer scholars in urban affairs, the urban sociologists, suggesting how their work can be useful to the historian. With this as background, he launches into a criticism of another major essay, "The City in American History" by

1. For other excellent discussions of this topic, see Anne Firor Scott, "The Study of Southern Urbanization," *Urban Affairs* (March 1966), pp. 5-14; Asa Briggs, "The Study of Cities," *Australian Journal of Adult Education*, Vol. 2 (1962); and R. Richard Wohl, "Urbanism, Urbanity, and the Historian," *University of Kansas City Review* (Autumn 1955), pp. 53-61.

Arthur M. Schlesinger (see Chapter I), and pinpoints the dangers of an urban interpretation of history by accusing Schlesinger of being imprecise in his terms and monistic in his interpretation. Schlesinger, he argues, muddled the concept "urban" by using it in so many different ways as to make it meaningless, and, worse yet, distorting. Associating "urban" too intimately with such broad phenomena as industrialism, capitalism, class and occupation differences, and the declining birth rate—*phenomena which are not necessarily generic to the city alone*—leads to the capital danger of them all: the exaggeration of the city as a causal factor in American history. Urban historians, Diamond rightfully insists, should avoid the mistake of Frederick Jackson Turner (or at least his followers) of fashioning an all-embracing theory that will only become another "bottleneck of American historiography." Ironically, perhaps, Diamond himself verges on committing a historical "sin." His strong urging for an economic approach to urban history could lead to the danger of economic determinism, another bottleneck of American historiography. Nevertheless, his warnings have a timeless relevance. He deserves to be called the gadfly of the urban historian's conscience.

Another critic of urban history is the economic historian Eric Lampard, long heard and long ignored, whose theoretical suggestions nonetheless must be taken seriously. Lampard presents a critique concerning omissions: the failure to study the societal forces that created the city; the failure to construct an adequate social history by neglecting to trace urban community life; the failure to construct a systematic conceptual scheme that would liberate the city from piecemeal examination; and the failure to distinguish between what *is* and what *is not* generic to the city. To fill the vacuum of omissions, Lampard proposes two related approaches: the study of the urbanization process which has moulded cities, with particular emphasis upon the causes and consequences of population concentration; the application of the techniques and insights of the ecological school of urban sociology to the comparative study of urban communities.[2] Buttressing urbanization and demography, as did W. Stull Holt (see Chapter I), Lampard insists that "urbanization is a phenomenon worth explaining in itself and one that may help in the explanation of other facets of social change."

Roy Lubove could not agree more. The central theme of his essay is that a study of the urbanization process and all its ramifications is essential if urban history is to become a more viable and significant discipline. Reviewing three

2. See also Eric Lampard, "Historical Aspects of Urbanization," *The Study of Urbanization,* edited by Philip M. Hauser and Leo F. Schnore (New York: John Wiley, 1965), pp. 519-54; and "The Evolving System of Cities in the United States," *Issues in Urban Economics,* edited by Harvey S. Perloff and Lowdon Wingo, Jr. (Baltimore: The Johns Hopkins Press, 1968), pp. 81-139; Everett S. Lee and Michael Lalli, "Population," *Growth of Seaport Cities,* edited by David T. Gilchrist (Charlottesville: University Press of Virginia, 1967), pp. 25-37; and Sidney Goldstein, *Patterns of Mobility, 1910-1950: The Norristown Study* (Philadelphia: University of Pennsylvania Press, 1958).

categories of urban history, Lubove is especially disenchanted with the trend of writing that loosely defines "urban" as everything that happened in cities. "If . . . we are to spare the city from becoming a kind of historical variety store—a thematic free-for-all used to explain everything, and hence nothing— it is necessary to limit or define the subject." To do this Lubove presents an approach that defines urbanization as the "city building process . . . the process of city building over time." He embraces Lampard's ideas about the ecological complex, population concentrations, and the shifting structural changes in urban communities, but goes even further. Lubove's most significant suggestion is that the objective methods of the ecologists must be balanced by the subjective approach of the behavioral school of social science. Lubove recognizes the limitations of ecology. It does not tell all. Most particularly, demographic and structural situations do not always explain why people act the way they do. The behavioralists pursue goals more elusive than and less vulnerable to the more precise and systematic analysis of the ecologists; nonetheless, their interest in attitudes, value systems, so-called cultural trait complexes, interpersonal relationships between individuals and groups is vitally important. In effect, the behavioralists tend to humanize urban studies. At present, however, there are sharp disagreements between the behavioralists and the ecologists. A reconciliation between the two schools would create a major theoretical breakthrough for all those interested in urban studies.

Another of Lubove's contributions that needs to be underscored is his development of the relationship between technology and the city, discussed by both Diamond and Lampard, but carried further by Lubove. He sees it as a broad cultural phenomenon whereby technology is stitched to invention, communications, social organization, and city-building. Curiously, the vital role of technology in the urbanization process has been largely ignored by urban historians and, even more curiously, by the historians of technology themselves.

The sharp criticism of the foregoing historians might suggest that urban history is in a state of shambles. This is not the case, as Charles N. Glaab shows in his bibliographic essay, which, combined with Lubove's bibliographical first footnote, will give one an excellent idea of the extent to which urban historiography has developed. Glaab traces the origins and rise of urban history as a field of study and demonstrates that despite its inconsistencies, endemic to any new field, urban history has come a long way since it was dominated by antiquarians, sentimentalists, and chamber of commerce enthusiasts who produced, to paraphrase Asa Briggs, history with the brains left out. Considering the newness of the field, there is already a corpus of first-rate literature, some of which can be labeled distinguished. But, as Glaab suggests, there is much more to be done. Agreeing with the previous criticisms concerning the need for sharper definitions, broader organizing ideas, and more use of social-science techniques, Glaab provides several fruitful suggestions of his own. For example, we need to know more about the smaller cities, the cities that failed and why they failed, and the dynamic period of city building from 1830 to 1860. His most important insight is the recognition that urbanization has a history of its own that does not necessarily coincide with the orthodox, fixed, and often rigid periodization of American history in general. If the city is studied only as a mirror image of national history, he argues, urban history will remain a retarded, deformed stepchild of general American history. It can and should assume a rightful place of its own. Glaab is suggesting that urban history can revitalize local and regional history to the point that it may redress some of our standard views about our national history.

Whether or not the differences between the historians represented here and the historians who write the more conventional urban history can be reconciled, remains to be seen. The dangers of the latter approach have already been cited; the dangers of the former may be that such a commitment to the urbanization process will make us lose sight of the enormous impact the city has had upon national affairs. Conflict and disagreement has, however, created a boon for American urban history: pluralism, the opportunity for choice, to wit, a variety of approaches to study of the city. This is illustrated by two recent books of outstanding quality: *A History of Urban America*, by Charles N. Glaab and A. Theodore Brown, who incorporate the techniques of the social sciences, and *The Emergence of Metropolitan America*, by Blake McKelvey,[3] who is of the "older" school and who integrates the city into the mainstream of American history. Perhaps, then, one of the key questions for the future of American urban history is whether or not we can write history that *balances* the study of the urbanization process *and* the impact of the city upon American history. Whatever the outcome, urban history, like the city itself, will continue to be one of the most difficult, yet fascinating, challenges to the historical imagination.

3. (New Brunswick, N.J.: Rutgers University Press, 1968).

On the Dangers of an Urban Interpretation of History

"There seems likely to be an urban reinterpretation of our history," Frederick Jackson Turner predicted near the end of his career.[1] Certainly the past decade has witnessed a great increase of interest in the city among students of American history. A vast number of books devoted to the history of individual cities and to the whole process of urbanization has been published. The American Historical Association has recently devoted several sessions to various aspects of urbanization. Finally, Arthur M. Schlesinger, who first used the growth of cities as a synthesizing principle around which to write part of the history of the United States, has submitted a plan for a "reconsideration of American history from the urban point of view."[2] In view of this increasing interest and of the tendency towards the use of an urban interpretation, it may be useful to reexamine the meaning of the term "city," the way in which the concept has grown among the sociologists who have studied the phenomenon, and its usefulness and validity as a synthetic principle.

Sociological interest in the city began in America towards the end of the nineteenth century. Throughout the century, in popular and scholarly literature alike, may be found evidence of a growing awareness of the city and of its dissimilarity from and antagonism to the countryside. Even the historians,

with their notoriously narrow approach to history, could not fail to note the towns and to include in their writings a few brief comments concerning them. During the last quarter of the century they began to exhibit a greater interest in the contrast of city and country, though even then they rarely went beyond a statistical enumeration of urban facts, an occasional interpolation of anecdotes of social life, and a brief discussion of the municipal problems and corruption which accompanied the emergence of an urban civilization. Of the men who wrote of America on a grand scale, only Edward Channing pointed to growing urban society as having a culture filled with significance for American history.[3] Even less frequent were the historical writers who, like Ellen Churchill Semple or Frederick Jackson Turner, concerned themselves with the conditions prerequisite to the rise of cities and to the significance of their geographic location.[4] But while the historians were writing the stories of cities primarily in terms of statistics and anecdotal antiquarianism, another group of scholars and writers were coming to the front, devoting much of their attention to the life of the city, well aware of the contrast of city and country, and interested in making the city a better place in which to live. This new point of view came in the eighties and nineties with the

From Eric F. Goldman (ed.), *Historiography and Urbanization* (Baltimore: The Johns Hopkins Press, 1941), pp. 67-108. Reprinted by permission of the publisher. William Diamond is Director of Development Finance Companies, International Finance Corporation.

municipal reform movements and the development of sociology as an autonomous science. From this view was to develop urban sociology, with which much of this essay is concerned because it is primarily the sociologist who studies "the groups, institutions, customs, traditions, attitudes, and relations which characterize the city as a type of human aggregation."[5]

Several factors contributed to bring about the simultaneous birth of the municipal reform movement and of urban sociology at this time.[6] Both developed during the period when American cities were growing with astonishing rapidity and began to dominate the nation economically and politically. Industrialization and urbanization contributed to the development of various problems whose intensity seemed to vary in proportion with the size of the city—slums, public health, bossism, and political corruption especially struck everyone who visited a big city and impressed themselves upon the minds of students and travellers alike as signs of urban degeneration. They provided ocular evidence for the dictum of Thomas Jefferson that cities are cancers on the body politic. James Bryce impressed his public with the judgment that municipal government was the one conspicuous failure of American democracy. Just as cities were seen to corrupt those who lived within them, so they appeared to enslave the non-urban inhabitants of the nation; for in the cities were centered the new power of finance, the management of railroads, and the manufacture of machinery which were revolutionizing agriculture, subjecting it to omnipotent capitalism. Upon the cities was therefore focused the hate of the rural majority of America, and at the same time to the cities flocked millions of farmers and small-towners attracted by economic opportunity, intellectual preeminence, urban social advantage, and the general "lure of the city."

At the same time, American universities were undergoing a renaissance. The universities were being freed at last from the yoke of theology, and a new generation of scholars, trained in the scientific seminars of Europe, was coming to the front. The universities of Europe, and especially of Germany, had never lost the civic tradition; and during the second half of the nineteenth century the attention of historical and political scholars was focused on the problems connected with the origins of towns and cities. American students therefore returned to the United States with greater awareness of urban life. Moreover, they had seen the beginnings of German and English municipal socialism in action, and they frequently came back with an enthusiasm for municipal ownership of public utilities as the chief cure for urban ills.

The first stage in the development of urban sociology lasted until the first decade of the twentieth century—a period when most of the writing on the city was characterized by the zeal and idealism of the reformer, whether it came from evangelical sociologists, or from "humanitarian statisticians," or from leaders of the settlement house movement. As Nels Anderson has put it, "we cannot separate the beginnings of urban sociology from the perennial battle to wipe out the slum."[7] The new study was "the rationalization of philanthropy and social reform."[8] Whether they saw the city as a blot on the American escutcheon or as "the hope of democracy," writers on the city were unanimously impressed by the urban "problem," and they described it in terms of reform and in the style of the muckraker. They generally believed utility companies and franchises were the source of urban difficulties. More often than not, there was a strong strain of ethical idealism in their thought. Almost unanimously they prescribed political reform, or education of the masses, or propaganda for the public ownership of utilities as the urban cure-all. They were militant applied sociologists. Typical of various elements in this group of writers are Josiah Strong, D. F. Wilcox, Lincoln Steffens, Richard T. Ely, and Frederic C. Howe. To these should be added Charles Zueblin, who was, in a sense, a transitional figure.

Strong, in *The Twentieth Century City*, expressed his conviction that the problem of the city was essentially an ethical one. "The sudden expansion of the city marks a profound change in civilization, the results of which will grow more and more obvious; and nowhere probably will this change be so significant as in our own country, where the twentieth century city will be decisive of national destiny."[9] For in the city social ideals undergo drastic change, and the old morality is forgotten. The "social dynamite" that produced the city was machine technology, the application of machinery to agriculture, and railroad transportation. But the only cure for the growing ills of urban society is twentieth-century Christianity; for a nation ruled by cities is a nation ruled by materialism, and in such a nation free institutions must perish. Through the teachings of Jesus, a public conscience must be developed. Then will the city become "the symbol of *heaven*—heaven on earth—the Kingdom fully come."[10]

Like Strong, Wilcox, in *The Amer-ican City: A Problem in Democracy*, declared that "the influence of cities upon the national life is quite out of proportion to their population. For the city is the distributing centre of intelligence as well as of goods." It "tends to impose its ethical and social ideals upon the whole people." "Democracy . . . has been badly damaged by its contact with city conditions." "Shall the city be permitted to destroy democracy and thereby undermine our national institutions?" he asked. "Shall the city be permitted to absorb the brains and wealth of the nation and consume them wastefully?"[11] After devoting chapters to the problems of the city street, of the control of public utilities, of civic education, municipal insurance, popular and official responsibility, Wilcox suggested remedies, but all were "ultimately dependent upon the transformation of our ethical standards."[12] Like Strong, Wilcox believed an ethical reawakening would solve the problems created by the economic and social facts which channeled city life. He believed in the efficacy of a "combined civic intelligence and civic conscience so far removed from the spirit now dominating municipal politics that it may be said to involve a radical change in human nature or in the conditions under which human nature finds expression."[13] Again in *Great Cities in America. Their Problems and Their Government*, Wilcox discussed the problems of six metropolises—each in terms of political corruption. The panacea was to be public ownership, and all who opposed it did so only because they thought government corrupt and inefficient.[14]

In *The Shame of the Cities* Lincoln Steffens took his readers through several great American cities revealing the political and social decay which lay beneath the surface.[15] Steffens may be cited as representative of the whole group of muckrakers who, from the early nineties, tried to point out the inequalities in capitalist society. His was a literature of exposure. He presented "cold facts," the result of painstaking observation; but he presented them in such a way as to arouse sympathy and indignation.

The shame of the shameless cities was pointed to by others like Steffens—by such men as Jacob Riis and Hutchins Hapgood, S. S. McClure and George Kibbe Turner, novelists Paul Leicester Ford and Alfred Henry Lewis.[16] These men wrote; others wrote and acted. "Working with the intellectual tools forged for them by Henry George, a group of old-fashioned Americans, Jeffersonians in their tastes and predilections, marched forth in the nineties and the early years of this century to face down the hosts of predatory privilege" as it appeared in cities.[17] "Golden Rule" Jones and Tom Johnson, Brand Whitlock and Newton D. Baker, above all Frederic C. Howe, saw the city, despite graft and slums, as "the hope of democracy."

Howe's study of municipal problems, entitled *The City. The Hope of Democracy*, promised a new approach to the city. This book, he wrote,

is an attempt at the Economic Interpretation of the City. It holds that the corruption, the indifference, the incompetence of the official and the apathy of the citizen, the disparity of wealth, the poverty, vice, crime, and disease, are due to causes economic and industrial. They are traceable to our Institutions rather than to the depravity of human nature. Their correction is not a matter of education or of the penal code. It is a matter of industrial democracy. The incidental conditions are personal and ethical. Whether we adopt the personal or the economic interpretation will determine our attitude towards the problems of modern city life.[18]

Howe's approach to the city seems far different from that of Josiah Strong, yet in reality the two men did not differ so greatly. Like the other municipal reformers, like Steffens and Whitlock, Howe had never learned, in John Chamberlain's words (and Howe himself admitted it later), "to pursue the truth to its ultimate lair—at bottom he was a moralist, not a realist or a scientist." Democracy was to be saved by the "best minds," like those of Richard T. Ely and Woodrow Wilson, whose lectures at the Johns Hopkins University helped rouse in him the desire to reform the city.[19]

Ely had done his graduate work in Germany and had returned to America to join the ranks of the municipal reformers. In *The Coming City* he pointed out the approaching preeminence of the city and demanded a program of reform in city government, an application of business principles to government. If religion would take municipal reform under its wing, Ely saw a bright future for the city. "If I forget thee, O Chicago, O New York, O St. Louis," he cried, "let my right hand forget her cunning."[20] It was Ely's discussions of urban problems that helped persuade young Albion W. Small to go to the Johns Hopkins University. Many years later Professor Small said of Ely's writings:

The argument was relatively novel on this side of the Atlantic, and not only in Baltimore but all over the country it was provocative of wholesome discussion. I was on the whole inclined to accept in the main Professor Ely's views about municipal control of public services, but at the same time it seemed to me that the case had been built so far too much upon mere opinion, and that a foundation should be constructed for it by penetrating into the essentials of urban life, and demonstrating the vital character of municipal activities as modes of human effort in general.[21]

Small helped start the Chicago school on its scientific urban studies.

Like Ely, Charles Zueblin was an academic man. He has been credited with the founding of the school of urban sociology at the University of Chicago, although William I. Thomas and Charles R. Henderson did much to turn Chicago's sociological interest to the study of conditions in that city.[22] In his *American Municipal Progress,* Zueblin emphasized the social activities of cities and attempted to develop a rough sociology of municipal communities.[23] In *A Decade of Civic Development,* he discussed the state of urban America at the turn of the century.[24] His book was probably the first used for courses in urban sociology. At any rate, the availability of his *American Municipal Progress* "and a number of other interesting but less comprehensive books dealing with city problems" provided some of the impetus for the appearance of "courses in urban sociology, problems of city life, and the like."[25]

Under the leadership of Henderson, Small, Thomas, and Zueblin, the department of sociology at the University of Chicago was organized in the 1890's and from then dates the beginning of the scientific study of urban sociology. Innumerable studies of various aspects of the urban environment began to appear. But it was at Columbia, not Chicago, that the first landmark in the scientific stage of the study of American cities was set up. In 1899 Adna F. Weber published *The Growth of Cities in the Nineteenth Century.*[26] It was a thorough statistical analysis of American and European cities, a study of their population and economic activities, of their growth and development, and of rural-urban migration.

Meanwhile the Chicago school, impressed by the hustle and bustle of a great city, was turning its attention to the systematic study of Chicago. It was a common belief of the time, advocated by Herbert Baxter Adams among others, that "the city offers a laboratory of social and political life in which the problems of society can be more effectively studied" than anywhere else.[27] No aspect of Chicago's environment was neglected. The way was pointed, Louis Wirth has suggested, by the publication of the *Catechism for Social Observation* by Charles Richmond Henderson and *An Introduction to the Study of Society* by Small and George Vincent, both in 1894.[28] A host of dissertations began to appear which were "modeled after the pioneer studies of American communities begun at Johns Hopkins University" under Adams, but which differed from them in being "based upon firsthand observations of life rather than the perusal of books."[29] Courses in municipal problems or municipal sociology appeared in college curricula all over the country.[30] Though urban sociology has never become a clear-cut, distinct branch of study, its outlines were separating out of the parent subject early in the century.

Coincident with the rise of the academic schools of urban sociology, a new instrument for the study of urban communities was developed—the social survey. This was one of the products of the revelations of the muckrakers, an attempt by scholars and municipal and philanthropic organizations to make more systematic, more objective the investigations of city life made by the journalists of exposure. The goal of the investigations was practical reform. In 1909, the Pittsburgh Survey was begun, the first of a long series of similar surveys of American cities which are less important to the historian for concrete results in social reform than as invaluable source material concerning American life. Like Charles Booth's monumental *Life and Labor of the People in London,* the Pittsburgh Survey suggested new approaches and new techniques in social study. Not only the city as a whole, but such aspects of urban society as religion or the slum, were subjected to the searching investigations of the social survey.[31]

With the growing use of the social survey and the increasing interest in urban sociology in the universities, more people devoted their attention to the study of various aspects of urban life. The names of Robert E. Park, Ernest W. Burgess, R. D. McKenzie, William F. Ogburn, and Louis Wirth, among others, are inseparably associated with the study of urbanism in America. In 1915, Park published his challenging essay on "The City: Suggestions for the Investigation of Human Behavior in the City Environment."[32] It was a discussion of problems to be investigated, a set of hypotheses concerning the nature of the urban environment and urban behavior. The essay, though it suggested subjects primarily for the social survey and the student of sociology, is important for the historian as well, since it pointed the questions he must ask of the city at every stage of its development. Under the impetus of Park, Burgess, and McKenzie developed a study called urban ecology, of loosely defined limits, concerned with "the relations between men and their natural environments." Its advocates have

taken over the terminology of plant and animal ecology to the study of natural areas within the city, the spatial distribution of people and institutions, ecological organization and succession, and symbiosis. The result is a vast literature of precise and detailed works on population succession and concentration, on the physical organization and growth of the city and its region, and on urban areas and personalities—such studies as Wirth's *The Ghetto,* Thrasher's *The Gang,* Zorbaugh's *The Gold Coast and the Slum,* and Anderson's *The Hobo.* Debate has raged around the concept of urban ecology. Indeed the ecologists themselves generally reject the strict environmental determinism implicit in the concept and the work they do is usually descriptive in character.[33]

Despite the vast growing literature on cities, there was no formal urban sociology until the late twenties. In 1925 appeared *The City,* a volume of essays designed to provide a frame of reference for studies on the nature of urbanism and on urban life.[34] All offer suggestions to the historian, but the most important for the historian of the American city are undoubtedly the first, Park's 1915 essay on "The City," and the last, Louis Wirth's detailed selective "Bibliography of the Urban Community." No quite so provocative, but more indicative of the character of the overwhelming bulk of urban sociological research in America, was a second volume of essays, *The Urban Community,* made up of papers read before the 1925 meeting of the American Sociological Society.[35] This, like the preceding volume, was meant to be "an introduction to an urban sociology," a "prospectus of the present state and promise of sociological research" on the city. The assumption implicit in most of these studies is that the city is a living organism; it is, therefore, studied in terms of human ecology. The first textbook in urban sociology, by Nels Anderson and Eduard C. Lindeman, appeared in 1928, and since then various systematic treatments of urbanism have been published.[36]

On the initiative of Professor Park, Charles E. Merriam, and others, the Local Community Research Committee of the University of Chicago was organized in 1923. The result was to make Chicago the most thoroughly studied city in the United States. The numberless studies of political, economic, and social life were frequently semi-historical in nature, presented a wealth of material concerning contemporary Chicago, and therefore suggested conclusions concerning the nature of urban growth throughout America. In 1929 a review of the work of the Committee was published which discussed many of its activities and provided a useful bibliography of all the work undertaken under its sponsorship.[37]

The group of scholars associated with this work has since expanded its definition of the urban community to include the entire metropolitan area of the city. This change in the focus of urban studies—common to students of the city all over the country—came in response to the fact that as new and faster means of communication and transportation developed, the style of urban growth began to change. Instead of continuously accelerating concentration, a counter-trend towards decentralization and suburbanization had set in. Population began to spill out of the municipality. The result was great sprawling conurbations of people and "the emer-

gence of metropolitan districts instead of individual cities as the actual areas of urban life."[38] The legal "city" was a unit which no longer corresponded to a real situation. Its students had therefore to concern themselves with the metropolitan area, which had no respect for political boundaries. As a consequence of this realization came such studies as Merriam's *The Government of The Metropolitan Region of Chicago*, Max R. White's *Water Supply Organization in the Chicago Region*, and Albert Lepawsky's *The Judicial System of Metropolitan Chicago*.[39] Transportation and communication had been sped up to the point, as Professor Lepawsky put it, "where the daily movement of people and of goods and the judicial conflicts arising from this movement are no longer restricted by political boundaries or jurisdictional lines."[40]

Various methods have been used to delimit the metropolitan area or the city region. The United States Census has defined "metropolitan districts" in terms of "continuous density"; all those parts of the urban environs having a certain density are considered part of the metropolitan district of the city.[41] A definition larger in extent but based on economic and social conditions has expanded the region to include "the area within which there is a large daily movement of population to and from the center for work, trade, amusement or other purposes."[42] Many criteria have been used for actually delimiting such a district—including various definitions of the trading area of a city.[43] Roughly upon such a scheme as this the Chicago Region has been defined. "It was adopted as the basis of study after a number of factors, including retail trading, commutation, telephone service, and free delivery zones, showed the fifty-mile district to be the approximate area of daily activity around the metropolis of Chicago."[44]

One of the more interesting definitions—a definition associated with one of the functions performed by the city in every culture—has been suggested by Professor Park.

People go to the city, as the farmer goes to town, not merely to market their products or their talents, as the case may be, but to meet people and to get the news. As the ultimate source of a common culture is, in a manner of speaking, common talk, the market place, wherever it is, has been, and still remains, a cultural center for the territory tributary to it.

The trade and culture areas of a city therefore coincide, Professor Park maintains, and this area may be measured by newspaper circulation. The circulation of metropolitan dailies likewise measures "the extent and degree of dependence of the suburbs upon the metropolis, and of the metropolis upon the larger region which it dominates." The "area of urban influence" may be measured in terms of the "gradients of declining newspaper circulation."[45] In the region dominated by a particular paper, "the trade routes, agencies of communication, news, and objects of attention come to focus in the metropolis. Metropolitan patterns of behavior are successively modified with increased distance from the center of dominance."[46]

Associated to some extent with the study of metropolitan regions is the rapidly growing literature of regionalism. Stemming from a revived interest in human geography, from the planning movement, and from the administrative problems of urban areas, the study of regions is generally associated in America with the names of Howard W.

Odum, Harry E. Moore, and Rupert B. Vance.[47] It is related to the whole body of literature on city and regional planning, which blossomed in the 'twenties and 'thirties and is perhaps best summed up in Lewis Mumford's comprehensive and brilliant, if occasionally erratic and unintelligible study, *The Culture of Cities*.[48] *The Regional Survey of New York and Its Environs*, which has been called the "most complete discussion of urban growth and its control," and the work of the National Resources Committee are models of the technique of city and regional planning.[49]

A step further in the determination of urban regions is involved in the study of metropolitan economy. The concept of metropolitan economy is associated with N. S. B. Gras who has pointed the way in the study of the great American cities as nuclear centers, as the economic nerve centers of huge hinterlands.[50] Various cities, through control of markets and finance and through the development of manufactures and of transportation and communication facilities, have become the "symbols" for the economic organization of huge subsidiary territories, the cores of great economic structures, rather than independent entities. For instance, Mildred L. Hartsough's analysis of *The Twin Cities as a Metropolitan Market: A Regional Study of the Economic Development of Minneapolis and St. Paul* is a discussion of those cities as the center of a great economic region.[51] This kind of region, however, is based on economic organization; it is the area of economic dominance.

These studies may be considered a part of the vast literature on ecology. Summed up in Professor Park's article, and to a lesser extent in the work of

Professor Gras, is not only a definition of the metropolitan region, but a statement as well of the ecological concepts of dominance and the gradients by which dominance is measured. The concept of dominance has been applied not only to the metropolitan region, but also to world economic organization focused in cities, by Professors Gras and McKenzie, for instance, and to local areas, such as the dominance of the downtown areas of modern cities, by Professor Burgess.[52] Such studies suggest a biological analogy.

The differentiation of areas, the distribution of institutional units [Professor Dawson says] and their complex integration take place with reference to the center of dominance somewhat after the manner in which a higher organism has its parts coordinated and controlled by means of the specialized and central cerebral cortex.[53]

The development of *The Metropolitan Community*, as well as its place in historical perspective, has been ably described by Professor McKenzie in a volume which concentrates, however, on its present nature and problems.[54] The volume discusses the factors making for concentration of people, the economic and social structure of the metropolitan community, and the institutional changes that accompanied its growth. For Professor McKenzie, the economic unity of these metropolitan regions depends upon the functional integration of territorially differentiated and specialized parts. Such an economic relationship is but the latest development in the history of the American city—a product of the bus and the automobile which permitted a tightening up of the immediate hinterland of the city. McKenzie associates the history of American settlement and urbanization with the techniques of transportation,

and sketches for each period the rise and growth of urban communities, their function and significance, and the story of interurban conflict. The emphasis is, of course, on the metropolitan organization of twentieth-century America.[55]

James A. Quinn, discussing urban sociology, has pointed out some of the methods used by the sociologist in studying city life.[56] Professor Quinn's classification includes: the historical and geographical method, whereby the location and growth of cities are investigated (thus Weber and Gras); historical and community case studies, including the social survey and the study of segregated culture areas in the city (thus the Lynds, Zorbaugh, and Reckless);[57] analysis of personal case histories (thus Wirth, Shaw, Thomas, and Cavan);[58] statistical method, stemming from the work of Franklin H. Giddings at Columbia, which has too frequently resulted in one of the great weaknesses of American sociology, in what Mumford rightfully calls "the injudicious use of irrelevant statistics" (thus the Census, Ogburn, Park, Burgess, and others on gradients within and without the city);[59] the use of maps for the study of land utilization, parks, business, recreation, and for the distribution of various economic and social data;[60] ecological organization. The new work of the Census in preparing population data by permanent census tracts "is now laying the basis for future studies of population distribution, composition and movement within large cities." Professor Quinn's classification is admittedly not exhaustive, yet it suggests to the historian of the American city the many kinds of material placed at his disposal by the urban sociologist.

Another such methodological technique, even more important for the historian, is the concept of culture, adopted by the sociologist from the work of the cultural anthropologist. The concept of culture was applied to the history of the city by Ralph Turner, at the 1939 meeting of the American Historical Association, in a provocative paper on "The Industrial City: Center of Cultural Change." Dr. Turner described the three classes of social factors—the paradox of competitive economy, the implications of machine technology, and the consequences of urban association—which are concentrated in the industrial city and make up the experience of city people. The day-to-day unconscious working of these factors has channeled the activities of urban dwellers along new lines, has changed their patterns of thought and behavior, has provided the basis for a new culture. In the industrial milieu, new institutions appeared to serve the felt needs of a new society; old institutions fought for survival, adapting themselves to the new conditions, or falling by the wayside.[61] The development of the cultural pattern of the American industrial city has similarly been very briefly sketched by Leon S. Marshall in a study of "The English and American Industrial City of the Nineteenth Century."[62]

This brief sketch of the development of sociological interest in the American city should make evident the fact that the historian of the American city has already at his disposal a wealth of literature on almost every phase of urban development. Unfortunately the great bulk of that material, since it has been produced by the sociologist, relates to the recent history of the American city; for the crowning provincialism of American urban sociology, as Lewis Mumford says, is its preoccupation with the contemporary metropolitan community.[63] Nevertheless, not much of modern urban life has been neglected, though little effort has been devoted to the development of a comprehensive theory of urbanism.[64] The literature of the city is filled with material on the economic and technological pre-conditions of urban growth; the relation of geography to the city;[65] the nature and quantity of rural-urban migration;[66] the demography of the city;[67] the social relationships of people living in the city; the breakdown of the integrity of the family; individualization; marriage and divorce; mental diseases of city people; the urban church; suicide; urban problems, from traffic to prostitution, from Americanization to zoning; the attempts to meet these problems; government and education in the city; city politics;[68] the city as a focal point of cultural activity; the conflict of urban and rural populations; the "effects" of city growth on the countryside.

The overwhelming bulk of urban bibliography is concerned with aspects of city life, yet the city is an integrated whole, each aspect of which is functionally associated with every other. Classified differently, the material offered to the historian by the sociologist runs from examinations of *Small Town Stuff* and of the culture of *Middletown* to studies of the life of the metropolitan area and of highly specialized suburban communities.[69] It is the history of the total city which the historian wishes to distil from the frequently formless, fluid mass of material available to him. Though formless, the material offers suggestions for writing a history of cities far from the sentimentality, antiquarianism, and chamber of commerce advertising that have characterized most local history.

There is nothing comparable in America to such monumental studies of European cities as those of Davidsohn and Poëte. Yet the rise of interest in cities during the past decade offers promise for the future, and already there have appeared several valuable histories of American cities. It seems that most of these studies stem from the growing interest in economic and social history, are not closely related to the thought and efforts of urban sociology, and do not attempt to integrate all aspects of the history of the city. Several such histories of individual cities are worth noting as examples. Constance M. Green's biography of *Holyoke* is a history of a product of the industrial revolution.[70] Thomas J. Wertenbaker's *Norfolk: Historic Southern Port* emphasizes the first two centuries of the story and tries to tie it in with the movement of national history.[71] Gerald M. Capers, Jr., in the *Biography of a River Town: Memphis; Its Heroic Age*, relates his history of the Tennessee town to both sectional growth and national development.[72] G. R. Leighton's miniatures of *Five Cities: The Story of Their Youth and Old Age* are only slightly marred by his occasional over-emphasis on a few individuals.[73] Several valuable studies of New York have recently appeared: Sidney I. Pomerantz, *New York: An American City, 1783-1803;*[74] Robert G. Albion, *The Rise of New York Port, 1815-1860;*[75] Ralph Foster Weld, *Brooklyn Village, 1816-1834.*[76] Bessie L. Pierce's *A History of Chicago*, not yet completed, is a synthesis of all aspects of the life of a great American city.[77]

This growing interest in the history of cities has produced two notable efforts to write the story of all urban culture in America, though both cover only a specified period of American history. In *The Rise of The City 1878-1898*, Professor Schlesinger attempted to write the history of all America in that period by focusing his attention on cities, by relating everything to the growth of cities.[78] The bulk of the volume is devoted to certain aspects of urban life but no comprehensive, integrated picture of the culture of cities emerges. In the foreword, Dixon Ryan Fox sounded a keynote for the book, when he said that the city is "the new social force" in American history.

In the ever-widening reach of its influence the author finds the key to an understanding of the most multifarious developments. . . . Aside from the part played by urban leadership in building a new structure of industry and trade . . . the city is envisaged as the dominant force of all those impulses and movements which made for a finer, more humane civilization.[79]

Professor Schlesinger himself wrote that in "America in the eighties urbanization for the first time became a controlling factor in national life."[80] "Underlying all the varied developments that made up American life was the momentous shift of the center of national equilibrium from the countryside to the city."[81]

An excellent survey of the first century of urban life in America is Carl Bridenbaugh's *Cities in the Wilderness*.[82] Professor Bridenbaugh presents the five largest towns, Boston, Newport, New York, Philadelphia, and Charles Town, as urban America, and tells the story of the changing physical appearance, the economic development, the growth of urban problems and the efforts to meet them, and social life, as a phase of general European economic history under the conditions of the American environment. The result is a skillfully done picture of urban life, perhaps overburdened at times with minute detail, but detail always to illustrate a general proposition.

The increasing attention devoted to cities has reached a new stage in the thought of Professor Schlesinger whose recent article on "The City in American History" seems to point the way to what Turner called an "urban reinterpretation" of American history. What lay below the surface in *The Rise of the City* became explicit and is deliberately stated in this recent essay.

"The true point of view in the history of this nation is not the Atlantic Coast," declared Frederick Jackson Turner in his famous paper of 1893, "it is the Great West." Professor Turner had formed his ideas in an atmosphere of profound agrarian unrest; and an announcement of the superintendent of the census in 1890 that the frontier line could no longer be traced impelled him to the conclusion that "the first period in American history" had closed. His brilliant essay necessitated a fundamental reappraisal of the springs of national development. Today, however, it seems clear that in his zeal to correct older views he overlooked the antithetical form of social organization which, coeval with the frontier, has played a significant and ever-enlarging part in American life. Turner himself wrote in a private letter in 1925, though with evident misgivings, "There seems likely to be an urban reinterpretation of our history."

A reconsideration of American history from the urban point of view need not lead to the distortion which Professor Turner feared. It should direct attention to a much neglected influence and, by so doing, help to illumine the historian's central problem: the persistent interplay of town and country in the evolution of American civilization. Recent historical writings reveal an increasing interest of scholars in the role of the city. It seems desirable, if only in broad outline, to develop certain of the larger implications of these studies and to indicate some of the further possibilities of the general subject for scholarly investigation.[83]

And out of the thread of urbanization Professor Schlesinger, in swift, broad strokes, weaves the whole fabric of American history. The essay, in short, may be an answer to the prayer of one of the critics of his earlier volume: that historians "do with the city what Turner and his students did with the frontier . . . use it as a means of explaining the problems and the pace of American life in the post-frontier period of American history."[84]

In Professor Schlesinger's essay are to be found two separate and distinct ideas. There is, in the first place, an appeal to students of American history to devote more attention to the history of cities, and it may indeed be that Professor Schlesinger meant primarily to call for such emphasis. With this there can be no quarrel. An ever-increasing number of people have come to live in cities; the city has been in this country, as in all cultures, a focal point and disseminating source of varied activity. The American city, therefore, richly deserves to have its history written.

It may be, however, that Professor Schlesinger meant to suggest not only the study of cities but also the use of the "city" as a causal factor in American history. Certainly that inference might be drawn from the introductory statement, from the treatment in the body of the essay itself, and from such statements as "cities . . . exerted an important influence on the struggle for manhood suffrage, the effort to abolish war, and the antislavery cause," or cities "sought to carve out economic dependencies and spheres of influence in the more distant country," or "southern secession was a revolt against the urban imperialism of Yankeedom," or "the city forged ahead, imposing its economic fiat on the rest of the nation," or "the urban dynamic . . . was the governing force."[85]

If the city or urbanization is to be used in a causal sense, then it is desirable to define those two terms. Anyone examining the literature on the city can hardly escape the disheartening conclusion that the "city" has been defined in many and varied ways. In his "Bibliography of the Urban Community," Professor Wirth pointed out that the "differences in standpoint and method in the various sciences show graphically in the definitions which each formulates of the same object."[86] The bibliographer, he continues, "has neither chart nor compass to guide him in his search, for the sociologist himself is not yet certain of the meaning of the concept 'city' and of the relationship of his science to the phenomenon."[87] Thus the geographers see the city as a part of the landscape; many historians, as an autonomous political unit; statisticians and most others, as a human aggregate of a certain size or density; economists, as an economic unit, a form of society "typical of a certain stage in economic development." A legal definition of the city as "an incorporated community" is obviously inadequate, for legal characteristics differ in various parts of the nation, and the growth of the metropolitan community has outmoded if not destroyed legal boundaries.[88] Using a statistical definition, Professor Bedford finds a city when certain specifically urban problems appear and uses 100,-000 as his line of demarcation.[89] But it has been pointed out that a "problem . . . may be so defined that it is present in some degree in every city."[90] Thus Professor Bridenbaugh discusses the urban problems of five colonial towns at times when they would barely

have qualified under the Census definition of a city. Recently, Professor Wirth has attempted a "sociologically significant definition" of the city, one which will "select those elements of urbanism which mark it as a distinctive mode of human group life," and he has defined the city "as a relatively large, dense, and permanent settlement of socially heterogeneous individuals." From these independent variables and their conjunction, Professor Wirth says, flow all peculiarly urban characteristics.[91]

Many students present a compound definition of a "city" by enumerating various urban characteristics. Thus Lewis Mumford defines a city as

a related collection of primary groups and purposive associations: the first, like family and neighborhood, are common to all communities, while the second are especially characteristic of city life. These varied groups support themselves through economic organizations that are likewise of a more or less corporate, or at least publicly regulated, character; they are all housed in permanent structures, within a relatively limited area. The essential physical means of a city's existence are the fixed site, the durable shelter, the permanent facilities for assembly, interchange, and storage; the essential social means are the social division of labor, whcih serves not merely the economic life but the cultural processes.[92]

Such compound definitions, which seek characteristics of cities distinguishing them from the countryside, appear in every systematic treatise on urban sociology. A close examination of these distinguishing characteristics, however, discloses the fact that they are generally based on one distinction. Thus the definition offered by Sorokin and Zimmerman in their *Principles of Rural-Urban Sociology*

is at bottom based upon a single trait, that of occupation, or more broadly, economic organization. Their principle criterion of rural society or population is occupational, the collection and cultivation of plants and animals. The urban world is engaged in manufacturing and mechanical pursuits, in trade, commerce, and the professions, in short, in non-agricultural occupations. The rural world is based primarily on an agricultural economy, the urban on an industrial and commercial. From this basis there develop those characteristics whereby size of community, density and heterogeneity of population, differentiation and stratification, mobility and interactions are correlated positively with urbanism.[93]

Adna F. Weber pointed out that this economic distinction between town and country was recognized by law in medieval times, when charters were given to wall-enclosed populations granting the privilege of engaging in commercial and industrial activities.[94] Maurice R. Davie, discussing the meaning of "city," places the basis of urban culture upon the commercial and industrial activities which "tend by their very nature to lead to a concentration of population; which produces great complexity of social relations and calls for a highly evolved type of social organization. These are the basic characteristics of urban civilization."[95] Robert M. MacIver's analysis of the difference between the urban and the rural environments is similarly based in the final analysis on differences in economic activity. Differences flow from the fact that the countryman extracts his livelihood from the soil; he lives in an intimate, immediate contact with the land and nature which is unknown to the city dweller, who derives his living from wages earned in an infinity of specialized occupations.[96]

No matter what definition of city is used, "urbanization" is generally applied to the process whereby an "urban trait" becomes increasingly characteristic of a population. Thus if size is the basis of a "city," society is urbanized as aggregations increase in size and number; if the city is defined by the presence of certain problems, a community becomes urbanized in proportion as those problems grow in intensity. Professor Wirth calls urbanization "the development and extensions" of the "complex of traits which makes up the characteristic mode of life in cities."[97] To Professor Park, urbanization is not alone the growth of great populations and the movement of people to the cities; it is also "a wider extension of industry, commerce, and of personal and social relations which have grown up with and are characteristic of great cities."[98] Professor McKenzie writes of "urbanization in a cultural . . . sense."[99] To another, urbanization is the process whereby "cities dominate greater and greater areas of hinterland populations, due especially to the multiplication of the kinds of cultural goods and the appearance of new agencies of distribution."[100] Urbanization in this case does not refer to the rise of cities, but to their influence over the countryside; and that influence is essentially the result of economic activity.

The uncertainty regarding a precise definition of the concepts under consideration has been neatly summed up by Professor Wirth, who says that "despite the preponderant significance of the city in our civilization . . . our knowledge of the nature of urbanism and the process of urbanization is meager."[101]

Which of the many meanings of "city" and "urban" Professor Schlesinger prefers is not certain, for nowhere in his essay is there an explicit definition of terms. From the context it seems that at various times different things were in the author's mind when he spoke of cities. For instance, if the city is to be considered causally relevant to the struggle over the Kansas-Nebraska act or to the widening breach between North and South in general, as Professor Schlesinger suggests, and if one is to speak of the city "imposing its economic fiat," then the city is apparently being thought of in terms of economic activity.[102] When the appearance and intensification of such problems as housing are related to the city, it is apparently being identified with a dense aggregation of people.[103] In references to "the currents of civilization flowing through the northern cities" or to cities as "nerve centers for creative cultural achievement," Professor Schlesinger seems to be thinking of the city as a nuclear center which, for various reasons, provides certain services for a wider hinterland and which, through its multiple agencies of contact, is closely connected with other such centers.[104]

To be sure the city is all of these things. But more detailed analysis will break the concept down into its components and give to each its full significance. Each of the elements may have consequences of its own, and it would only becloud the analysis to identify the city with each of them. In using the city as a causal factor to explain certain culture traits or certain events in American history, students may usefully distinguish between the city and its parts. For example, investigations of political behavior have shown that analyses in terms of economic classes give higher correlations than do analyses in terms of urban and rural interests. William F. Ogburn and Delvin Peterson have investigated the political behavior of the population of Oregon during several elections. In-

stead of merely comparing rural Oregon with Portland, they divided Portland's population into three groups which they believed corresponded with upper, middle, and lower classes, and they compared these groups with each other and with rural Oregon. Ogburn and Peterson found that the three urban classes differed greatly, rural voting generally corresponding very closely with that of the middle urban class.[105] The results of the polls of the American Institute of Public Opinion have shown time and again that "urban" is but an average, that when it is divided into various groups a broad range of opinion appears, that for political attitudes at least, economic level is probably more significant as a classification of American society than is urban or rural residence.[106]

The differentiation of classes made in modern political analysis has also been successfully applied in historical investigations and has served to reveal more precisely what is meant in many cases by "cities." Professor Schlesinger, in "The City in American History," asserts that Boston's preeminence in the revolutionary movement "may well have been due to the fact that, having recently fallen behind Philadelphia and New York as an emporium, she was resolved at any cost to stay the throttling hand of the British government."[107] As Professor Schlesinger's well-known volume on *The Colonial Merchants and the American Revolution 1763-1776* has shown, it was primarily upon the colonial merchant that "the throttling hand of the British government" fell; "the merchants of the commercial provinces were the instigators of the first discontents in the colonies."[108] In the essay itself, Professor Schlesinger points out that the "business classes rallied promptly to the defense of their interests and, heedless of the possible political consequences, enlisted the support of the artisan and mechanic groups."[109] Certainly a clearer picture of Boston's revolutionary activity emerges if the situation is described in terms of interests, such as Professor Schlesinger himself suggests.

Because of the danger of substituting a vaguely defined whole for a more precisely defined part, one may similarly challenge Professor Schlesinger's suggestion that "historians might well give greater attention to the question of the extent to which southern secession was a revolt against the urban imperialism of Yankeedom. . . . It is significant that one of the early acts of the Confederate and state authorities was to outlaw the accumulated indebtedness of many millions owing to northern merchants, bankers, and manufacturers."[110] The second sentence makes it clear that by "urban imperialism" is meant the imperialism of a certain urban class, the "merchants, bankers, and manufacturers." This was more precisely stated by the Beards in their *Rise of American Civilization*, when they suggested that the war arose from a clash of opposing economic interests. Certainly American political history is the story of the conflict and reconciliation of interests.[111] But it is doubtful whether the antagonists can be most fruitfully classified as urban and rural, for the interests of some people in the city differ from those of other urban groups as well as from those of the country population.

The fact that urban and rural populations are not homogeneous is also of importance for non-political questions. The terms "urban" and "rural" certainly cover a multitude of interests.

This is the burden of Professor MacIver's statement that "the city, especially the large city, is not only a whole environment for all its inhabitants but also a series of extremely different environments for the groups within it."[112] Much of the work done by urban ecologists has been predicated upon the existence of many environments within the city. The National Resources Committee recognized this fact as basic to its investigations. Town and country, it pointed out,

each cover a wide range of different and conflicting interests. A rural dweller may be a farm laborer, a tenant, a small owner of acres, clear or encumbered, or the possessor of a great estate. There are also holders of great blocks of mortgages upon farm lands. The city dweller may be a worker, white collar or not, a small business man, a large business man, or an industrial giant. In this sense, the interests of farmers as farmers are not always the same any more than the interests of city dwellers are always the same.[113]

The differences between various groups within the urban and the rural environments may be much greater and therefore more important than the differences between the total urban and total rural environments. The statements cited above suggest that it may be practically irrelevant to the study of American history to know that in 1890 the average wealth of families in the rural districts did not exceed $3,250 while the average wealth of city families surpassed $9,000.[114] They imply that the terms urban and rural are averages which may have less significance than the individual data or classes of data of which they are an average.

There is some evidence to support such a contention. For instance, birth rates have been declining in the United States for many years, and since cities have lower rates than the countryside, the decline is frequently ascribed to urbanization. A close examination of Census statistics has revealed the fact (which is indeed a popular commonplace) that "fertility declines rapidly as the level of living rises in all regions of the United States" and this "even when the counties are classified by density of population, in order to differentiate rural and urban areas."[115] Studies made by the Milbank Memorial Fund indicate not only that birth rates vary with occupational classes, but also that "differences in birth rates by occupational classes have been of long standing duration." Though rural women are more fertile than urban, there are marked differences within each group.[116] The importance of this intra-urban difference is evident from the fact that birth rates vary "from year to year with prosperity and depression."[117] Such studies suggest that birth rates may be more highly correlated with occupation groups and social classes than with urbanism.

Furthermore certain culture traits may not be products of a city or even of aspects of city life but rather of change in an environment. It is essential to distinguish between the characteristics of adjusted city dwellers and of rural migrants to urban centers who are in the process of adjustment. This has. been frequently pointed out, by Professor MacIver for instance, and by Professors Davie and Carpenter.[118] Thus Professor Davie notes that agnosticism and skepticism are positively correlated with cities. But, he asks, are they products of modern society which have so far gained headway in the city? Or are they the result of maladjustment to the city environment and will they therefore disappear? Or is the prevailing

conception of religion, like those of government, marriage, and the family, the product of rural life and hence destined to disappear under urban condition?[119] The same questions may be asked concerning divorce, crime, or mental breakdown, so frequently associated with cities. As Professor Carpenter puts it, "*phenomena which at the moment seem to be characteristics of urban civilization* may rather represent *transitional aspects of a population's adaptation to urbanism or the initial stages in the evolution and diffusion of new culture traits.*"[120] The distinction between effects of urbanism, of adjustment to urbanism, and of cultural change common to city and country alike is especially important for the student of American history, for the American city grew with astounding rapidity, drawing huge portions of its population from the countryside and from rural Europe.

Since American cities grew during a period of rapid technical advance, when city and country were drawing more tightly together, many of the characteristics of urban life may have been but manifestations of cultural changes that were affecting the countryside too, but more slowly. This is illustrated by a recent study of the changes in the nature of recreation in rural America. The fact that "the common denominator of these changes is a growing similarity to the recreational life of the city," led the author of the study to inquire into the possible causal relationship between the growth of cities and the increasing similarity. He found that some of the new recreational activities were the results of diffusion from the city, some came as a result of rural adaptation to city life, as when city products reached out into a rural market. Most important, however, was the fact "that certain forces that have been felt only in cities for many years past are now beginning to be felt in the country with the result that changes are occurring in rural life similar to those that developed long ago in urban life."[121] Among such forces is, of course, the introduction of machine technology with a resulting multiplication of social contacts, a greater ability to buy products, and a decreased dependence on the family and community alone for recreation.

The danger of not distinguishing between the results of urban life and those of cultural change common to both city and country, like the other difficulties involved in an urban interpretation of American history, was summed up by Professor Wirth when he warned against confusing urbanism with capitalism and industrialism.[122] Unless the concept "city" is carefully analyzed, students, in their enthusiasm for a fresh and attractive reinterpretation of American history, may make of the "city" another "frontier" and fall into the difficulties inherent in Turner's "hazy and shifting concept," which have been pointed out with increasing frequency and sharpness.[123] Students of urbanization, reading phrases like "the contrast between urban and frontier conceptions of democracy," cannot but be disturbed at the way in which the "frontier" became a bottleneck of American historiography.[124]

NOTES

1. Letter to Arthur M. Schlesinger, Madison, Wis., in Schlesinger, "The City in American History," *Mississippi Valley Historical Review* (1940), XXVII, 43.
2. *Ibid.*
3. Edward Channing, *A History of the United States* (6 vols., New York, 1905-1925), V, Ch. III, "The Urban Migration."

4. See, for instance, Ellen Churchill Semple, *American History and its Geographic Conditions* (Boston, 1903); Frederick Jackson Turner, *Rise of the New West, 1819-1829* (New York, 1906), pp. 96, 98-99, and "The Significance of the Mississippi Valley in American History," in *The Frontier in American History* (New York, 1920), pp. 194-96.
5. Stuart A. Queen and Lewis Francis Thomas, *The City: A Study of Urbanism in the United States* (New York, 1939), p. 15.
6. For discussions of the rise of urban sociology, see Nels Anderson, "The Trend of Urban Sociology," in George A. Lundberg, Read Bain, Nels Anderson, *et al.*, *Trends in American Sociology* (New York, 1929); Carle C. Zimmerman, "The Trend of Rural Sociology," *ibid.*; Floyd N. House, *The Development of Sociology* (New York, 1936), Ch. XXIX. The sketch which follows is meant merely to give an indication of the scope and range of urban sociology. There is no intention of giving a full bibliography, of giving more than a sample of trends in urban study. Nor is it possible within the range of this essay to discuss popular literature on the city, which itself has a long history and is a subject for the historian of social thought, or scholarly literature in other disciplines.
7. Anderson, "The Trend of Urban Sociology," in *Trends in American Sociology*, p. 270.
8. House, *The Development of Sociology*, the title of his chapter on the subject.
9. *The Twentieth Century City* (New York, 1898), p. 32.
10. *Ibid.*, pp. 180-81. In *The New Era or The Coming Kingdom* (New York, 1893), Strong cites a few passages from Tennyson's Locksley Hall Sixty Years After, which includes such gems as:

Is it well that while we range with Science, glorying the Time,
City children soak and blacken soul and sense in city slime?
There among the glooming alleys Progress halts on palsied feet,
Crime and hunger cast our maidens by the thousands on the street.

(p. 193)

See also Strong: *Our Country: Its Possible Future and Its Present Crisis* (New York, 1885); "Problems of the Twentieth Century City," *North American Review* (1897), CLXV, 343-49; *The Challenge of the City* (New York, 1907). See also Walter Rauschenbusch: *Christianity and the Social Crisis* (New York, 1907); "The State of the Church in the Social Movement," *American Journal of Sociology* (1897), III, 18-30. "The larger our cities grow the less hold does religion seem to have over the multitude of men and the general life. . . . For one thing, the people of our great cities are cut off from nature and from nature's God. All that they see and touch was made by man. To men in Chicago the heavens do not declare the glory of God, for they are covered with smoke. . . ." (pp. 29-30). See also L. Abbott,

Christianity and Social Problems (Boston, 1896). Though the emphasis was at first on evangelism alone, this was soon supplemented with "charity, neighborhood work and social legislation." Anderson, "The Trend of Urban Sociology," in *Trends in American Sociology*, p. 267.

11. New York, 1904, pp. 14, 21, 22.

12. *Ibid.*, p. 402.

13. *Ibid.*, p. 20.

14. New York, 1910. For a similar approach to the city, see Frank Parsons, *The City for the People; or, the Municipalization of the City Government and of Local Franchises* (Philadelphia, 1900). "The most pressing problem of the age is the problem of monopoly," and public ownership was the cure. (p. 14) "In education lies the final hope, for at bottom it is a new intelligence and a new ideal, that must be relied on to mould the real to a more perfect form." (p. 13)

15. New York, 1904. The volume was originally published as individual essays in *McClure's Magazine*.

16. See the discussion of the contents of these writings in the chapter on "The Shameless Cities," in C. C. Regier, *The Era of the Muckrakers* (Chapel Hill, 1932), and the very full bibliography of muckraking in the same volume. See also "The Shame of the Cities" and "The Search for Democracy" in Louis Filler, *Crusaders for American Liberalism* (New York, 1939). The results of the factory system, slums, poverty, transience, the mission and settlement work such as Hull House and South End House were all the subject of a voluminous literature. See, for instance, the work of Jane Addams, such as *The Spirit of Youth and the City Streets* (New York, 1914); or of Robert A. Woods, such as *The City Wilderness* (Boston, 1898).

17. John Chamberlain, *Farewell to Reform* (New York, 1932), pp. 56-57.

18. New York, 1905, pp. vii-viii.

19. Chamberlain, *Farewell to Reform*, p. 79. See also Frederic C. Howe: "The City as a Socializing Agency," *AJS* (1912), XVII, 590-601; *The Modern City and Its Problems* (New York, 1915); *The Confessions of a Reformer* (New York, 1925).

20. New York, 1902, p. 73.

21. Albion W. Small, "Fifty Years of Sociology in the United States (1865-1915)," *AJS* (1916), XXI, 734, 768.

22. Lewis Mumford, *The Culture of Cities* (New York, 1938), p. 500; Louis Wirth, "The Urban Society and Civilization," *AJS* (1940), XLV, 746; Jesse Bernard, "The History and Prospects of Sociology in the United States," in *Trends in American Sociology*, pp. 25-26.

23. *American Municipal Progress. Chapters in Municipal Sociology* (New York, 1902).

24. Chicago, 1905.

25. House, *The Development of Sociology*, p. 294.

26. Columbia University Studies in History, Economics, and Public Law, XI, New York, 1899.

27. John Martin Vincent, "Herbert B. Adams," in Howard W. Odum, ed., *American Masters of Social Science. An Approach to the Study of Social Sciences Through a Neglected Field of Biography* (New York, 1927), p. 118.

28. Wirth, "The Urban Society and Civilization," *AJS* (1940), XLV, 745-46. This article concerns primarily the work done in urban sociology at the University of Chicago from the beginning to the present.

29. *Ibid.*, p. 746.

30. See Frank L. Tolman, "The Study of Sociology in Institutions of Learning in the United States," *AJS* (1902), VII, 797-838; (1902-03), VIII, 85-121, 251-72, 531-38; L. L. Bernard, "Some Historical and Recent Trends of Sociology in the United States," *Southwestern Political and Social Science Quarterly* (1928), IX, 264-93; Harmon O. DeGraff, "The Teaching of Urban Sociology," *Social Forces* (1926), V, 248-54.

31. See Niles Carpenter, "Social Surveys," *Encyclopedia of the Social Sciences*, XIV, 162-65. For a useful history and bibliography of the social survey, see Allen Eaton and Shelby M. Harrison, *A Bibliography of Social Surveys. Reports of Fact-Finding Studies Made as a Basis for Social Action; Arranged by Subjects and Localities. Reports to January 1, 1928* (New York, 1930).

32. *AJS* (1915), XX, 577-612.

33. For a discussion of the meanings of ecology and of how it has been used, as well as for a comprehensive bibliography of the subject, see James A. Quinn, "Topical Summary of Current Literature on Human Ecology," *AJS* (1940), XLVI, 191-226. His bibliography of 347 items illustrates the range of ecological literature, from housing and mental diseases to natural areas and migration. See also R. D. McKenzie, "The Ecological Approach to the Study of the Human Community," *AJS* (1924), XXX, 287-301, and "The Field and Problems of Demography, Human Geography, and Human Ecology," in L. L. Bernard, ed., *The Fields and Methods of Sociology* (New York, 1934), pp. 52-66; C. A. Dawson, "The Sources and Methods of Human Ecology," *ibid.*, pp. 286-302.

34. By Park, Burgess, and McKenzie, with a Bibliography by Wirth (Chicago, 1925).

35. E. W. Burgess, ed. (Chicago, 1926).

36. Anderson and Lindeman, *Urban Sociology: An Introduction to the Study of Urban Communities* (New York, 1928). See for instance, Scott E. W. Bedford, *Readings in Urban Sociology* (New York, 1927), valuable for its bibliography; Maurice R. Davie, *Problems of City Life. A Study in Urban Sociology* (New York, 1932); Pitrim Sorokin and C. C. Zimmerman, *Principles of Rural-Urban Sociology* (New York, 1931), important primarily for the huge quantities of material it contains, not for its formulation of an urban-rural sociology; Niles Carpenter, *The Sociology of City Life* (New York, 1932); Noel P. Gist and L. A. Halbert, *Urban Society* (New

York, 1933); Howard Woolston, *Metropolis. A Study of Urban Communities* (New York, 1938); Stuart A. Queen and L. F. Thomas, *The City: A Study of Urbanism in the United States* (New York, 1939); Lewis Mumford, *The Culture of Cities* (New York, 1938); National Resources Committee, *Our Cities. Their Role in the National Economy* (Washington, 1937). The short sketch in the survey of *Our Cities,* the first national study of cities on a scale comparable to that of Theodore Roosevelt's Country Life Commission in 1909, presents, in brief scope, the underlying forces in the process of urbanization, the characteristics of urban populations, and the problems of cities. The emphasis is on present urban problems, but the study notes the development of those problems through the past and their importance in inducing the attitudes and institutions which characterize urban populations. A summary of the special studies undertaken by the Urbanism Committee of the NRC appears in *Our Cities,* p. 71. Historians of the American city have the advantage of the information on various aspects of urban life collected for many years by agencies of the federal government. Unfortunately that material has many and serious gaps and deficiencies. For a summary and discussion of what is available, see the section on "Federal Reporting of Urban Information," in the NRC's report on *Urban Government* (Washington, 1939).

37. T. V. Smith and Leonard D. White, *Chicago: An Experiment in Social Science Research* (Chicago, 1929). For a more recent description of the work being done on the metropolitan region of Chicago, see *AJS* (1936), XLII, 563-65.

38. NRC, *Our Cities* (Washington, 1937), pp. 10-11. This is a digest of the full report cited previously.

39. Charles E. Merriam, Spencer D. Parratt, and Albert Lepawsky (Chicago, 1933); Max R. White, *Water Supply Organization* (Chicago, 1934); Lepawsky, *The Judicial System of Metropolitan Chicago* (Chicago, 1932).

40. *Ibid.,* p. 9.

41. United States Bureau of the Census, *Metropolitan Districts. Population and Area* (Washington, 1932), p. 5. See the note on the same page concerning the efforts of United States Chamber of Commerce to define a metropolitan region.

42. Thomas H. Reed, "Metropolitan Areas," *Encyclopedia of the Social Sciences,* X, 397. See the bibliography following the article.

43. In 1927 the United States Bureau of Foreign and Domestic Commerce published an atlas in which the nation was divided into metropolitan trading regions based on wholesale grocery trading. See United States Department of Commerce, *Atlas of Wholesale Grocery Territories* (Domestic Commerce Series, No. 7, Washington, 1927). The trade area of a city has been defined as "the surrounding geographical territory economically tributary to a city and for which such city provides the chief market and financial center." John W.

Pole, Comptroller of the Currency, quoted in R. D. McKenzie, *The Metropolitan Community* (New York, 1933), p. 84.

44. Lepawsky, *The Judicial System of Metropolitan Chicago,* p. x.

45. "Urbanization as Measured by Newspaper Circulation," *AJS* (1929), XXXV, 62. See also Seldon Cowles Menefee, "Newspaper Circulation and Urban Regions," *Sociology and Social Research* (1936), XXI, 63-66; Park and Charles Newcomb, "Newspaper Circulation and Metropolitan Regions," in McKenzie, *The Metropolitan Community,* Ch. VIII.

46. Dawson, "The Sources and Methods of Human Ecology," in *The Fields and Methods of Sociology,* p. 296.

47. See the series of articles on regionalism by Shelby M. Harrison, Rupert B. Vance, William E. Cole, L. L. Bernard, Paul S. Taylor, and Louis Wirth in *Publications of the American Sociological Society* (1935), XXIX, 81-115, especially that of Vance, "Implications of the Concepts 'Region' and 'Regional Planning.' " See Howard W. Odum, *Southern Regions of the United States* (Chapel Hill, 1936), for a discussion of regionalism and of the urbanization of the South; Odum and Harry E. Moore, *American Regionalism* (New York, 1938); Vance, *Human Geography of the South. A Study in Regional Resources and Human Adequacy* (Chapel Hill, 1932), like Odum's volume, includes material on the rise of cities in the South and discussion of the differences between southern and northern towns; Benton MacKaye, *The New Exploration; A Philosophy of Regional Planning* (New York, 1928).

48. Mumford's book is one of the most stimulating and suggestive studies of urbanism published in America. It contains an excellent critical bibliography of the most important works in English, French, and German on the nature of urban life, the history of towns and cities, city planning, and regionalism.

49. *The Regional Survey of New York and Its Environs* (8 vols., New York, 1927-31), especially Volume I, R. M. Haig and R. C. McCrea, *Major Economic Factors in Metropolitan Growth and Arrangement.* See Henry Wright's important "Report on a Plan for the State of New York," in New York State, Housing and Regional Planning Commission, *Final Report* (Albany, 1926). NCR *Regional Factors in National Planning* (Washington, 1926); *Regional Planning. Part I—Pacific Northwest, Part II—St. Louis Region, Part III—New England* (Washington, 1936).

50. See N. S. B. Gras: "The Development of Metropolitan Economy in Europe and America," *American Historical Review* (1922), XXVII, 695-708; *An Introduction to Economic History* (New York, 1922); "The Rise of the Metropolitan Community," *Pub. Amer. Soc. Soc.* (1926), XX, 155-63.

51. Minneapolis, 1925. On the nature and technique of urban financial organization and of urban

economic control of the hinterland, see such studies as George Walter Woodworth, *The Detroit Money Market* (Ann Arbor, 1932) and Henrietta Larson, *The Wheat Market and the Farmer of Minnesota* (New York, 1926).

52. See, for instance, McKenzie, "The Concept of Dominance and World Organization," *AJS* (1927), XXXIII, 28-42, and Burgess, "The Determination of Gradients in the Growth of a City," *Pub. Amer. Soc. Soc.* (1927), XXI, 178-84.

53. Dawson, "The Sources and Methods of Human Ecology," in *The Fields and Methods of Sociology*, p. 295.

54. This is one of the monographs that came from the President's Research Committee on Social Trends. The report of the Committee was published as *Recent Social Trends in the United States* (2 vols., New York, 1933). This, as well as the other volumes enlarged from the report, contains valuable material on American cities.

55. McKenzie, *The Metropolitan Community*, *passim*.

56. Niles Carpenter, T. Earl Sullenger, and James A. Quinn, "The Sources and Methods of Urban Sociology," in *The Fields and Methods of Sociology*, pp. 328-45. See also the chapters on community, ecology, urban and rural sociology.

57. Robert S. and Helen M. Lynd, *Middletown* (New York, 1929), and *Middletown in Transition; A Study in Cultural Conflicts* (New York, 1937), two volumes which use the methods of cultural anthropology and which are of great importance for the study of contemporary urban life; Walter R. Reckless, *Vice in Chicago* (Chicago, 1933), a study of the spatial distribution of vice and of its relation to urban conditions.

58. Clifford R. Shaw, *The Jack Roller* (Chicago, 1930), and *The Natural History of a Delinquent Career* (Chicago, 1938); W. I. Thomas, *The Unadjusted Girl* (Boston, 1923), and the famous volumes by Thomas and Florian Znaniecki, *The Polish Peasant in Europe and America* (5 vols., Chicago, 1918-20); Ruth S. Cavan, *Suicide* (Chicago, 1928).

59. House, *The Development of Sociology*, pp. 367 ff.; Mumford, *The Culture of Cities*, p. 501; William F. Ogburn, *Social Characteristics of Cities* (Chicago, 1937).

60. See *Region of Chicago Base Map* (Chicago, 1926) and such studies of urban land utilization as Richard M. Hurd, *Principles of City Land Values* (4th ed., New York, 1924).

61. This paper is to be published this winter. The material used here comes from a copy of the MS which the author generously loaned me.

62. *Western Pennsylvania Historical Magazine* (1937), XX, 169-80.

63. *The Culture of Cities*, p. 501. See also Maurice R. Davie, "The Field and Problems of Urban Sociology," in *The Fields and Methods of Sociology*, p. 103, who points out that urban sociology "must gather more data on the history of cities and make more social historical studies of problems like city government, crime, recreation, etc. Most of its data are ultra-modern and cross-sectional."

64. Some appreciation of the volume and nature of urban studies may be secured from the two bibliographies already mentioned, and even more from an examination of the articles, book reviews, and bibliographies of the *American Journal of Sociology* (Chicago, 1895–) and other sociological journals or journals in special fields. A recent and exceedingly interesting attempt to formulate a theory of urbanism is Louis Wirth, "Urbanism as a Way of Life," *AJS* (1938), XLIV, 1-24.

65. See, for instance, M. Aurousseau, "Recent Contributions to Urban Geography: A Review," *Geographical Review* (1924), XIV, 444-55.

66. Since the city has acquired a large part of its population from rural migrants, the quantity and quality of, as well as the reasons for, rural-urban migration is of great importance for the study of the city. Although writers of popular literature wrote of the effects of migration throughout the nineteenth century, it was not until the World War that academic interest began to focus on this flow of population that has probably been as important as, if not more important than, the westward movement. The War and the immigration laws of 1921 and 1924 cut down the number of Europeans coming to America just at the time that American industry was increasing its demands for labor; the result was increased internal migration. During the twenties, too, the declining birth rate centered attention on rural-urban differentials. The depression, finally, and its effect on farmers especially, increased interest in internal migration and accelerated the flow of literature on its quantity and quality. Few issues of the sociological reviews since then lack an article on selective migration. The best introduction to the literature, and the study on which this paragraph is based, is Dorothy Swaine Thomas, *Research Memorandum on Migration Differentials* (Social Science Research Council, Bulletin No. 43, New York, 1938), which is especially valuable for its lengthy critical bibliography of studies on rural-urban migration with summaries of their conclusions. See also Vance, *Research Memorandum on Population Redistribution Within the United States* (Social Science Research Council, Bulletin No. 42, New York, 1938), and Carter Goodrich, *et al.*, *Migration and Economic Opportunity; The Report of the Study of Population Redistribution* (Philadelphia, 1936).

67. See NRC, *The Problems of a Changing Population* (Washington, 1938) and *Population Statistics, 3. Urban Data* (Washington, 1937), which discuss not only the population of cities but also the conditions that make agglomerations possible and the effects of that agglomeration.

68. On the government, administration, and politics of cities there is also a tremendous amount of literature, sprinkled with the observations and treatises of such acute students as Bryce, Goodnow, and Beard. To say more than that the litera-

ture exists is, unfortunately, beyond the scope of this paper, for the history of municipal government and politics is itself a fascinating story.

69. See, for instance, Herbert Blumenthal, *Small Town Stuff* (Chicago, 1932); H. P. Douglas, *The Suburban Trend* (New York, 1925); G. A. Lundberg, M. Komarovsky, M. A. McInery, *Leisure. A Suburban Study* (New York, 1934); Graham R. Taylor, *Satellite Cities, A Study of Industrial Suburbs* (New York, 1915).

70. *Holyoke, Massachusetts: A Case History of the Industrial Revolution in America* (New Haven, 1939).

71. Durham, 1931.

72. Chapel Hill, 1939.

73. New York, 1939.

74. Columbia University Studies in History, Economics, and Public Law, No. 442, New York, 1938.

75. New York, 1939.

76. New York, 1938.

77. 2 vols., New York, 1937—.

78. New York, 1933.

79. Schlesinger, *The Rise of the City*, p. xiv.

80. *Ibid.*, p. 79.

81. *Ibid.*, p. 435.

82. Bridenbaugh, *Cities in the Wilderness. The First Century of Urban Life in America 1625-1742* (New York, 1938). Parts of Mumford's *The Culture of Cities* concern the history of urban culture in America and are stimulating reading, as all of Mumford is.

83. "The City in American History," *Mississippi Valley Historical Review* (1940), XXVII, 43.

84. Review of *The Rise of the City* by Albert Lepawsky, *AJS* (1933), XXXIX, 253.

85. Schlesinger, in the *MVHR*, XXVII, 52, 50, 56, 61, 57.

86. Wirth, "Bibliography of the Urban Community," in Park, *The City*, p. 165.

87. *Ibid.*, p. 161.

88. Maurice R. Davie, "The Field and Problems of Urban Sociology," in *The Fields and Methods of Sociology*, pp. 98-99. This essay has an interesting discussion of the meaning (or, better, lack of meaning) of "city" and "urbanization." Much of its material is used here.

89. *Readings in Urban Sociology*, p. vii.

90. Davie, "The Field and Problems of Urban Sociology," in *The Fields and Methods of Sociology*, p. 99.

91. "Urbanism as a Way of Life," *AJS* (1933), XLIV, 4, 8.

92. Mumford, *The Culture of Cities*, p. 480.

93. Davie, "The Field and Problems of Urban Sociology," in *The Fields and Methods of Sociology*, p. 100.

94. Weber, *The Growth of Cities in the Nineteenth Century*, pp. 6 ff.

95. Davie, "The Field and Problems of Urban Sociology," in *The Fields and Methods of Sociology*, p. 101.

96. MacIver, *Society. Its Structure and Changes* (New York, 1931).

97. "Urbanism as a Way of Life," *AJS* (1938), XLIV, 7, 5.

98. "Urbanization as Measured by Newspaper Circulation," *AJS* (1929), XXXV, 69. "Specialization, the division of labor, more elaborate organization, and more effective direction and control is now taking place in agriculture, just as it formerly took place in the highly organized industries. These changes, with all that they involve, are what we properly describe as urbanization."

99. *The Metropolitan Community*, p. 25.

100. J. M. Gillette, "Urban Influence and Selection," in *Pub. Amer. Soc. Soc.* (1929), XXIII, 1.

101. "Urbanism as a Way of Life," *AJS* (1938), XLIV, 3.

102. Schlesinger in the *MVHR*, XXVII, 50-51, 55-56, 61.

103. *Ibid.*, p. 45.

104. *Ibid.*, p. 55.

105. Ogburn and Petersen, "Political Thought of Social Classes," *Political Science Quarterly* (1916), XXXI, 300-17.

106. See, for instance, Edward G. Benson and Paul Perry, "Analysis of Democratic-Republican Strength by Population Groups," *The Public Opinion Quarterly* (1940), IV, 467-68; "The Gallup Poll," Baltimore *Sun*, Sept. 27, 1940; Stuart F. Rice, *Quantitative Methods in Politics* (New York, 1928), pp. 170-72.

107. Schlesinger in the *MVHR*, XXVII, 46.

108. *The Colonial Merchants and the American Revolution* (Columbia University Studies in History, Economics, and Public Law, No. 78, New York, 1918), p. 591.

109. Schlesinger in the *MVHR*, XXVII, 46.

110. *Ibid.*, p. 55.

111. The introduction of petitions for tariff protection in the first Congress "foreshadowed a conflict of interest in the new government between city and country, which led directly to the formation of the first national parties. . . . From that day to this the chief business of American politics has been to reconcile these interests in the service of the national welfare." *Ibid.*, p. 48.

112. For example, Professor MacIver says, "If we take vital statistics alone, we find remarkable differences in birth-rates and death-rates in conditions favorable to health or to disease, for different groups and districts. A great metropolis, like London or New York, will exhibit for localized groups within it extremes of healthiness and unhealthiness, no less than of wealth and poverty, surpassing those found elsewhere in the whole countries to which they belong. The city is the home of opposites, and in these respects it is misleading to take the average figures for city and country respectively, to treat as unities for the purpose of comparison the less homogeneous and the more homogeneous." *Society*, p. 360.

113. *Our Cities*, p. v.

114. C. B. Spahr, *An Essay on the Present Distri-*

bution of Wealth in the United States (New York, 1896), pp. 46-49, cited in Schlesinger, *The Rise of the City*, p. 77. Professor Schlesinger cites Spahr's statement that "When American political parties shall again divide upon issues vitally affecting the distribution of wealth, the clearly marked line of division will not be between East and West, but between city and country."

Perhaps the great interest in studying urban-rural conflict in American history is a manifestation of the overwhelming interest of American historians in sectionalism. As a matter of fact, it is now frequently said that urban America constitutes a new section in continuous opposition to rural America. Thus Professor Bridenbaugh, examining seventeenth century America, and defining a "section" as a "social and psychological" rather than as a purely geographical entity, finds three sections: "the rural, agricultural society of the country-side; the restless, advancing society of the frontier; and the urban commercial society of the larger seaports." With other "village communities," they emerge in the eighteenth century "as a social and economic 'section'." (*Cities in the Wilderness*, p. 467.) Even the Turnerians support such a view. They have attempted to transfer the concept of the frontier to new and different conditions. Thus Percy H. Boynton, in *The Rediscovery of the Frontier* (Chicago, 1931), pp. 22-24, suggests that Frederick L. Paxson has seen the conflict of West against East blurred into or replaced

by the conflict of rural against urban; "the farmer still prolongs the life of the pioneer."

115. NRC, *The Problems of a Changing Population*, pp. 136, 137.

116. *Ibid.*, p. 142. See the entire chapter on "Social Conditions Affecting Birth Rates," prepared by Clyde V. Kiser.

117. *Ibid.*, p. 23. See also the evidence presented by William F. Ogburn and Clark Tibbitts, "Birth Rates and Social Classes," *Social Forces* (1929), VIII, 1-10.

118. See MacIver, *Society*, p. 361.

119. Davie, "The Field and Problems of Urban Sociology," in *The Fields and Methods of Sociology*, p. 106.

120. *The Sociology of City Life*, pp. 248, 217-18. Davie cites the same paragraph quoted here.

121. Edward Wilkerson Montgomery, *The Urbanization of Rural Education* (Chicago, 1936).

122. "Urbanism as a Way of Life," *AJS* (1938), XLIV, 7.

123. See, for instance, George Wilson Pierson, "The Frontier and Frontiersmen of Turner's Essays. A Scrutiny of the Foundations of the Middle Western Tradition," *The Pennsylvania Magazine of History and Biography* (1940), LXIV, 449-78; Murray Kane, "Some Considerations of the Frontier Concept of Frederick Jackson Turner," *MVHR* (1940), XXVII, 379-400.

124. Quoted phrase from Schlesinger in the *MVHR*, XXVIII, 53.

American Historians and the Study of Urbanization

Public concern with the nation's cities and their "problems" is almost as old as the cities themselves. Like beauty, however, problems exist in the eye of the beholder; they reveal more about the nature of the observer, perhaps, than about the object observed. Thus, after more than half a century of problem-oriented research on cities, it is surprising how little we know about the phenomenon of urbanization, or, to adapt Josh Billings, how much we know "that ain't so." The proliferation of undergraduate courses in urban sociology, the mushroom growth of a planning profession, and the lively interest of politicians and publicists in "the exploding metropolis" should not obscure the fact that we have neglected the study of social processes that create

From *American Historical Review* (October 1961), pp. 49-61. Reprinted by permission of the author. Eric E. Lampard is Professor of Economic History at the University of Wisconsin at Madison.

cities. A review of literature in the field, moreover, gives rise to an uneasy feeling that many of us, historians and social scientists alike, are still working with outmoded concepts and inadequate tools. Revival of public concern in recent years, therefore, provides an occasion for intellectual stock-taking which is long overdue.[1] It may be helpful to consider some of the possible shortcomings as they have affected historical studies of American cities.

Until recently historians have had little cause for satisfaction with their contributions to the field. American urban history—what there is of it—is largely the history of cities and their "problems," not the history of urbanization. Scholars have been preoccupied with biographies of particular communities, with case studies in urban rivalry, or the general "impact" of the city on society, rather than the study of urbanization as a societal process.[2] We know little beyond a bare statistical outline of the secular phenomenon of population concentration, the multiplication of points of concentration, or of relations among concentrations of different size and density in various parts of the country at different times in our history. Studies of this sort are, to be sure, the province of demographers, and historical demography is a most arcane science, yet ignorance of these fundamentals of social structure and organization has not prevented historians from speculating at length on the "significance" of westward migration nor from composing doleful accounts of urban-industrial transformation in the late nineteenth century. A serious social history of the United States ought to begin with the study of population.

Within the historical guild, only ancient and medieval scholars seem to have regarded the causes and consequences of population concentration as an essential part of the study of social change. Ancient historians often made the growth of cities coterminous with the development of civilization.[3] Prominent medievalists treated the growth of cities almost as an antibody to the rural stagnation implicit in older notions of *Naturalwirtschaft* and manorialism. Localized urban developments are thought to have accelerated the decline of medieval parochialism and to have helped energize dynamic, acquisitive communities—the forerunners of modern industrialism.[4] This kind of discourse, acceptable to the historical economists, sociologists, and geographers who once throve in the somber forests of German *Wissenschaft* and the more lucent groves of French *civilisation*, did not take root in the United States; it was decidedly out of place around the seminar tables of graduate schools of American history. After all, Americans had been taught that the United States was born in the country, that its most cherished institutions and ways of life were uniquely shaped in a rustic mold. The yeoman, the pioneer, the frontiersman, the cultivator, and their near neighbors, the independent craftsman and enterpriser, were the idealized types: the original and noblest representatives of the nation's spirit and character. This agrarian view of society was supported by much literary and statistical evidence. During the nineteenth century, it hardened into ideology. If European society was in any sense "urban," then the city was part of the bag of tricks rejected in 1776.

What American historians brought back from their pilgrimage abroad was a methodological passion for particularism and formal documentation. Up to a point this was salutary, but when historians looked for conceptual frameworks to explain American development, they mistook the phenomena of variation and difference for "uniqueness." It was easy to believe, in Frederick Jackson Turner's words, that the "true point of view" could be found in "the Great West." For all but political purposes, the historic connection between the rise of a "manufacturing civilization" in the Northeast and a "continually advancing frontier line" in the interior was ignored. The centrifugal currents of migration obscured centripetal currents from view. Although some historical studies of municipalities (largely legalistic or fiscal) had been published by Johns Hopkins University before Turner's influential paper on "the frontier," the general approach to the city had been set in 1888 when James Bryce (and his American informants Seth Low and Frank J. Goodnow) published *The American Commonwealth*. Bryce concluded that the growth of great cities was "among the most significant and least fortunate changes in the character of the population" during the first century of the Republic.[5]

The kind of socioeconomic generalization that crept in with the "new history" after the turn of the century was, from the standpoint of a history of urbanization, not a very notable advance over the older preoccupations with origins or uniqueness. Following such economists as C. H. Cooley, E. A. Ross, and A. T. Hadley, increases in the number and size of city populations were regarded as passive incidents in the growth and refinement of transportation systems or as an outcome of the Industrial Revolution of the late nine-

teenth century. Unfortunately, the conceptual framework for the analysis of urban phenomena was a peculiar compound of agrarian folklore and reformist outrage. Cities were treated almost exclusively as political and social "problems." A genuine disgust with "urban" conditions combined with an ingrained rural romanticism (a literary and political doctrine) to spread the conviction that cities were costly deviants from some natural, more verdant, order of community life. When they bothered with the subject at all, historians became absorbed in the minutiae of urban biography or explored the careers of reform movements which attempted to lift man up from his fallen "urban" condition. The only urban history was, for long, written by men with a reforming bent and the bulk of city histories by chroniclers of local fame.[6] In either case, the process of urbanization was overlooked.

In the last quarter century and, more especially, in the last decade, urban history has gained greater stature among professional historians. In 1921 Edward Channing had pointed to the "urban migration" of the years 1815-1848 as a neglected aspect of changes that accompanied the development of the trans-Appalachian West. But it was not until 1933 that urban history excited general interest with the publication of Arthur M. Schlesinger's *The Rise of the City*, in which was detailed much of the substance of urban-industrial changes in the late nineteenth century.[7] By 1952 Black McKelvey could list fifty-odd volumes devoted to one or another aspect of the nation's urban past covering the early colonial period to the present day.[8] Meanwhile the urban-industrial transformation had become part of the furniture displayed in every up-to-date textbook of United States history and in the flood of source books piled on undergraduates. The post-Civil War "impact" of the city on farm, family, church, politics, and, not least, on people is recounted in dolorous terms. It provides a necessary, disturbing overture to more reassuring harmonies achieved in the ensuing era of progressive reform. It helps fill a political void between the "End of Reconstruction" and the "Populist Revolt." Discussion centers on the conflict between an expanding urban-industrialism and a retreating rural-agrarianism in which old American values and institutions were at stake. Out of the upheaval stemmed a need for reform in government, law, economy, religion, social attitudes and relations. Thanks in part to the "progressive movement," the promise of American life was eventually made good.[9] What was essential to the old "rural" way of life was adapted, in modified form, to the new "urban" way. By the 1920's the urban-industrial matrix appears so well established that social historians take it for granted. While a few isolated pockets of "rural" America are left fighting a political rear-guard action against the twentieth century, urban-rural conflict no longer provides an adequate dialectic of change. The city drops out of the summary treatments of social history and only reappears in recent years as a point of departure for considering the rise of suburbia.[10] Needless to add, these superficial generalizations about the city were based neither on the piecemeal monographic work of urban historians nor upon any systematic study of urbanization. Apart from reducing the profession's myopic obsession with "the frontier," we doubt whether the "urban impact" school ac-

complished much of lasting importance to historiography.

The small body of professional urban historians may be exempted from many of these strictures. They place their communities in historical context and deal concretely with the growth of population, economic development, characteristics of native- and foreign-born residents, the deficiencies of municipal administration, powers, and finance. They point, moreover, to the opportunities for economic, social, and cultural improvement which a large and varied population permits. As a consequence, urban history is no longer regarded as a mere chronicle of local color and description, but as a potentially important perspective on many aspects of regional and national development. The study of particular communities and of general "urban problems" may illuminate subjects previously neglected or treated only within the "overaggregated" framework of the nation as a whole. In many respects, the United States is not a whole, and, if the thrusts of technology and pulls of opportunity tend to make people and places more alike and to reduce the divisive force of provincial influences in national affairs, the history of cities reveals how often community life has diverged from the mainstream.

It is precisely at this point, however, that historical particularism breaks down and that the potential asset becomes a present liability. We do not know enough about urbanization or "urban" characteristics in general to determine what is unique or otherwise in the experience of particular communities. The variant "facts of history" cannot be defined nor their significance appraised until they are treated in relation to larger conceptual frameworks, yet the conventional type of local history, though monumental in detail, seldom furnishes data in forms that are readily adaptable to macroscopic treatment. We lack, therefore, not only generalized frameworks of analysis but consistent and comparable data relevant to them. We need to identify the functions and characteristics that are associated with populations of different size and density countrywide, to discriminate among small towns, cities, and metropolises, and among such places in varying regional contexts over time. By such means we might secure a more systematic empirical knowledge of urbanization and its concomitants on the basis of which our particularizations about this or that community would be more pertinent and precise. As it is, the multiplication of case studies may only add to confusion, unless their findings can be related to larger and more comprehensive frames of reference.

A definition of urbanization in terms of population concentration provides a framework for the study of cities, which is relatively unambiguous. Urbanization is conceived as a societal process resulting in the formation of cities. If urbanization is sustained, the number and size of cities increase, and a larger proportion of the population comes to live in cities. Cities may continue to exist after urbanization has slackened or ceased all together. Alternatively, intensification of the process may eventually produce an urbanized society in which an overwhelming majority of the population is concentrated in and around urban centers. The entire span of American history from the seventeenth century furnishes examples of all these possibilities. At first, the process was sporadic and highly localized along the seaboards, later it accelerated,

especially in the Northeast after 1820.[11] Each subsequent phase of westward migration contributed to urbanization regionally and nationally, and, before the close of the nineteenth century, it affected every part of the continental territory in some degree. Both centrifugal and centripetal movements of population marked American history from the outset and continued long after the disappearance of "the frontier."[12] A varying rate of urbanization has been a characteristic feature of the larger settlement pattern assumed by the growing population as it organized to control, utilize, and enjoy a greater volume and variety of material goods and services. Its association with rising average levels of living has been demonstrably close.[13]

But in order for cities to grow there had to be means as well as motives. Although we may conclude from their performance that Americans have prized material achievement, we cannot use this observation to explain the achievement, let alone the pattern of community development. The motivations that give rise to organized human communities are doubtless inherent in urbanization, but are distinct from it. They are in no generic sense "urban" as opposed, say, to "rural" motivations. It is the means, therefore, that at once created the material abundance and gave form and focus to related movements of people. In the broadest sense of the word, these means have been technological. Neither population increase nor technological progress, however, is to be identified exclusively with cities, but both may give rise to urbanization and hence to cities. As Hope Tisdale has argued, technology is the *sine qua non* of urbanization, but the reverse is not true: "technology is not the exclusive property of the city; it operates in every province and pocket of society."[14]

This conclusion reveals another serious deficiency in our thinking. The generic properties of urban and nonurban communities (usually lumped together and labeled "rural") have never been adequately defined. Too often, the terms "city" and "urban" have been given circular or tautologous meanings. Urban communities are said to exist when certain "problems" or social attributes take certain forms; communities are differentiated in terms of problems, but the problems are by definition "urban." Still worse, many writers have affirmed that cities are "ways of life" or "states of mind"; they refer quite loosely to "urban" attitudes, "urban" aspirations, or "urban" behavior. Clearly, we need a more comprehensive and searching theory of "community" in order to ascertain what is generically "urban" or otherwise in the American experience. Phenomena that are found in cities are not necessarily "urban" per se, and yet this is precisely what many scholars have implied. In this regard, measuring devices have often stood surrogates for theory. The urban-rural continuum, for example, merely substituted a linear scale of demarcation for the original dichotomy of ideal types, with the opposing "urban" and "rural" type constructs placed at the poles of the continuum. The attributes of the types were reaffirmed by definition, and an assumption was made that attributes varied together with the same degree of "urban" or "rural" quality along the continuum. While this was a gesture in the direction of common-sense understanding and represented a limited improvement in measurement; it was not an advance in theory. If, as

Albert J. Reiss, Jr., has suggested, the variables selected to discriminate between "urban" and "rural" are themselves questionable, then the task of analysis remains all but insuperable.[15] Propositions about relationships among social phenomena cannot be more reliable, from a heuristic standpoint, than the concepts they purport to link.

When the problem of community types is approached from a somewhat different angle—one more congenial to historians, perhaps—by defining prerequisites for cities, the business of conceptualization is not much advanced. Preconditions for cities are by definition preurban and cannot, therefore, be attributes of urban communities as such. They may be "rural" or more likely something else again to which the adjective "rural" is attached merely to signify location, not the properties of a distinctive community type within the scope of the urban-rural dichotomy. If anything, the emergence of such conditions should be considered, as in the case of technological progress, in a broader societal or cultural framework.

Analytical confusion has been compounded, moreover, because the "urban impact" school of social historians, like its counterpart in sociology, has identified the pathological with the normative conditions of city life. As if its political shortcomings were not enough, the city milieu has been represented as a cockpit of social disorganization, anonymity, impersonality, and deviant behavior.[16] Secondary relationships among people are assumed to have multiplied at the expense of primary relationships. By implication, the country remained a place for natural, personal, and hence more "satisfying" human relationships.[17] It is curious, therefore, that, at about the time when "the city problem" was being taken over by social scientists from nineteenth-century moralizers and reformers, a new species of scientist also appeared in the country to succeed the old uplifters and grass-roots improvers. While the private inclinations and public affiliations of rural sociologists required due deference to the "agrarian myth," their professional concerns compelled them to take a more critical view of country life. They found an urgent need to reform its attitudes and ameliorate its conditions. In the country no less than in the city, health, housing, education, social relations, and even religion were found wanting.[18]

In most of these respects the "urban impact" historians seem to have been greatly influenced by the substantive writing of contemporary critics and the prescriptive writing of the early social scientists. The city is "abnormal," and rural life is presumed wholesome and sane, at least until the serpent of industrialism crept into the garden during the late nineteenth century.[19] Neither historians nor sociologists, however, developed a very clear notion of what constitutes a "normal" community by which one could judge the relevance of their findings. It was wise, perhaps, not to attempt a definition when most communities were experiencing rapid and far-reaching change.[20] Evidently much was rotten in the state of both city and country, but it seems likely that the diagnoses of both sorts of social doctor were based upon a rather artificial criterion: if not the Garden of Eden, then some romantic, corporate ideal of a preindustrial Arcadia. Both seem to have accepted the compartmentalization of society into "urban" and "rural" types and to have adopted the somewhat superficial distinctions made by economists between "industry" and "agriculture." When challenged on this, however, the historians, unlike the sociologists, were unable to fall back on the rather lame excuse that they were only talking about "ideal types."[21]

Some of these older confusions and misconceptions are still found in social science literature. Thus, when changes in technology and social organization (notably cheap electric power transmission, the automobile, and rising levels of per capita personal income) permitted some relaxation of population concentration after World War I and contributed to the reshaping of the nation's metropolitan areas, the scholars had still not decided what the proper study of community involved. Many of the vague concepts and outworn techniques were carried over into the analysis of "suburban" and "urban" phenomena. People were said to be moving out from congested cities in order to find greater personal dignity, more human relationships, and improved living conditions for themselves and their children.[22] We learn from the popular nonfiction paperbacks, nevertheless, that the 47,000,000 suburban Americans who, by 1950 enjoyed the utmost "togetherness" in an affluent society, were still this side of Paradise. Suburbanites apparently had become a lonesome crowd of other-directed organization "status-seekers," gazing out from their cracked picture windows at a wilderness of commodities and a woefully neglected "social overhead." Meanwhile, central cities crumble, and the countryside decays.

Perhaps all or much of this is so. We are not suggesting that social historians and critics have been perverse, only that in focusing so much upon "problems" they have neglected the study of process. They have not contributed much to our understanding of urbanization and urbanism in the larger context of social change. To be sure, several recent historical studies have underlined the need for more general concerns. Commentaries by W. Stull Holt, R. Richard Wohl, and Bayrd Still, among others, have intimated some of the larger processes. A timely paper by Rowland Berthoff, in so far as it points to the phenomenon of mobility, gives a further hint of the direction in which American social historians may travel.[23] The point is not that historians have labored in vain nor, necessarily, that their interpretive schemes have not been useful for particular purposes, only that different kinds of evidence can be made available and that more inclusive frames of reference must be devised.

A useful societal framework is already at hand in the concept of the "ecological complex" as developed by Amos H. Hawley, Otis Dudley Duncan, Leo F. Schnore, and other human ecologists. This group of sociologists conceives of community structure as the outcome of a changing balance between population and environment (including habitat and other populations) mediated by technology and organization. "That the community is the essential adaptive mechanism," says Hawley, "may be taken as the distinctive hypothesis of ecology." Reciprocal interaction among these four variables has recently been identified by Duncan and Schnore as "the most fundamental premise in ecological thinking."[24] The complex offers the historian a framework for the comparative study of the development and organization of interdependent communities in terms that embrace both westward and urban movements of population, changes in the spatial, occupational, and social structures of population, and of sustenance activities. It seems especially suited to the analysis of those economic and social changes which are associated with industrialization.

The complex, of course, does not explain "the world in its aspects," but it does enable the historian to explore, for example, interrelationships among currents of migration, territorial division of labor and areal differentiation, the industrialization of agriculture, manufactures, and other economic activities. Social mobility can be examined not only in terms of the career movements of individuals but in light of changes in the composition of population and structurally induced changes in the labor force, which are themselves a concomitant of industrialization. Changes in income distribution, a most pertinent index of changes in welfare, can also be linked to these structural changes in productive activities.[25] Phenomena that are associated, but not identical, with urbanization are likewise amenable to ecological analysis, for example, the emergence of bureaucratic hierarchies and other modes of functional organization that give coherence and direction to larger community systems. An economic historian may be excused, perhaps, for citing the pioneer work of N. S. B. Gras which, if vitiated in some respects by its adherence to "stage" theory, foreshadowed many of these more recent and fruitful developments in ecological thinking.[26]

Criticisms have been made of historians for their omissions: their neglect of urbanization as a societal process, their failure to establish a generic meaning for the term "urban" as a distinctive community type, and their disregard, until recently, of almost all but deviant aspects of city life. Clearly, much remains to be done if urban history is to achieve a distinctive place as a field of historical research commensurate with the place of the city in society. We will need to go beyond the present style and scope of city biographies and comparative studies. If the urban historian is to be more than a historian who happens to do his research and writing on the subject of cities, it will be necessary to show that the term "urban" explains something in history that cannot be better explained by recourse to other frames of reference. In short, "urban" must signify not subject matter alone but a scheme of conceptualization, in much the same way as "economic" or "culture" history. Viewed simply as subject matter, of course, the city is fair game for any historian, "urban" or otherwise.

To avoid indiscriminate usage on the one hand and to escape the pitfalls of ideal type construction on the other, two distinctive but related approaches to urban history have been suggested in this paper: the study of urbanization as a societal process and the comparative study of communities in a framework of human ecology. The one focuses on the phenomenon of population concentration that results in an increase in the number and size of cities, the other on the changing structure and organization of communities in terms of four specific and quantifiable references. Urbanization is a phenomenon worth explaining in itself and one that may help in the explanation of other facets of social change. Relationships within and among communities are likewise worthy of independent study and may contribute to our knowledge

of parallels and divergences that occur in the experience of larger aggregations, such as "regions" and nations. Both approaches, moreover, are designed to elucidate concrete and particular situations in terms that are also used to explore more diverse and generalized outcomes. Together, they might provide a more certain and systematic foundation for the writing of American social history.

NOTES

1. Thus, the much-advertised idea of a federal department of urban affairs goes back at least to the administrations of Taft and Wilson. Little new in substance has been added to the proposal since that time: Philip Kates, "A National Department of Municipalities," *American City*, VI (Jan. 1912), 405-407; Harlean James, "Service—The Keynote of a New Cabinet Department," *Review of Reviews*, LIX (Feb. 1919), 187-90; Charles E. Merriam, "Cities in a Changing World," *City Problems of 1934*, Annual Proceedings of US Conference of Mayors (Chicago, 1935), 73-74. For the recent discussion, see Robert H. Connery and Richard H. Leach, "Do We Need a Department of Urban Affairs?" *Western Political Quarterly*, XIII (Mar. 1960), 99-112.

2. In our use of the term "urbanization," we follow Hope Tisdale, "The Process of Urbanization," *Social Forces*, XX (Mar. 1942), 311-16.

3. Ralph E. Turner, *The Great Cultural Traditions: The Foundations of Civilization* (2 vols., New York, 1941), I, 130-31, 324-25; Herbert J. Fleure, "The Historic City in Western and Central Europe," *Bulletin of the John Rylands Library*, XX (July–Aug. 1936), 312-13. Some qualifications on the exclusiveness and persistence of the association are expressed in Stuart Piggott, "The Role of the City in Ancient Civilizations," *Metropolis in Modern Life*, ed. Robert M. Fisher (Garden City, N. Y., 1955), 5-17, and A. H. M. Jones, *The Greek City from Alexander to Justinian* (Oxford, Eng., 1940), *passim*.

4. Henri Pirenne, *Medieval Cities* (Princeton, N. J., 1925); Carl Stephenson, *Borough and Town* (Cambridge, Mass., 1933); Robert E. Dickinson, *The West European City: A Geographical Interpretation* (London, 1951); Roberto S. Lopez, "The Trade of Medieval Europe: The South," in *The Cambridge Economic History*, II, ed. Michael Postan and E. E. Rich (Cambridge, Eng., 1952), 257-354; Fritz Rörig, *Die europäische Stadt und die Kultur des Bürgertums im Mittelalter* (Göttingen, 1955). John H. Mundy and Peter Riesenberg, *The Medieval Town* (Princeton, N. J.,

1958), 9-15, 92-94, argue that: "Our teachers and our experience . . . conspire to make us exaggerate the meaning of urbanism." Nevertheless, viewing the growth of civilization over five thousand years, "this movement is that of an urban civilization that progressed from the eastern Mediterranean to Europe, and from Europe to the World." Also, Gideon Sjoberg, *The Preindustrial City, Past and Present* (Glencoe, Ill., 1960).

5. Frederick Jackson Turner, "The Significance of the Frontier in American History," 1893, as reprinted in his *The Frontier in American History* (New York, 1920), 1-3. James Bryce, *The American Commonwealth* (2 vols., New York and London, 1889), I, 593. By the nineties, agitation for "good government" and municipal reform had given rise to a number of specialized periodicals such as: *Municipal Affairs, City Government, Public Improvements, Good Government, Park & Cemetery,* and the *American Magazine of Civics.* See also "Municipal Reform Organizations," Philadelphia Publications of the National Municipal League, *Pamphlet No. 4,* 1895. For bibliography, R. T. Daland, "Political Science and the Study of Urbanism, A Bibliographical Essay," *American Political Science Review,* LI (June 1957), 491-509.

6. On the changing emphases of early city historians, see the case study by R. Richard Wohl and A. Theodore Brown, "The Usable Past: A Study of Historical Traditions in Kansas City," *Huntington Library Quarterly,* XXIII (May 1960), 237-59.

7. Edward Channing, *History of the United States* (6 vols., New York, 1905-25), V, 70-92; Arthur M. Schlesinger, *The Rise of the City, 1878-1898* (New York, 1933). By 1925, if not before, Turner himself recognized the need for "an urban reinterpretation of our history": cited by Arthur M. Schlesinger, *Paths to the Present* (New York, 1949), 210.

8. Blake McKelvey, "American Urban History Today," *American Historical Review,* LVII (July 1952), 919-29, provides the most comprehensive survey of literature in the field. Among more recent titles are: Lewis Atherton, *Main Street on the Middle Border* (Bloomington, Ind., 1954); Arthur Mann, *Yankee Reformers in the Urban Age* (Cambridge, Mass., 1954); Carl Bridenbaugh, *Cities in Revolt: Urban Life in America, 1743-1776* (New York, 1955); Nelson M. Blake, *Water for the Cities* (Syracuse, N. Y., 1956); Constance M. Green, *American Cities in the Growth of the Nation* (London and New York, 1957); Richard C. Wade, *The Urban Frontier: The Rise of Western Cities, 1790-1830* (Cambridge, Mass., 1959). Among the outstanding city histories are: Bessie L. Pierce, *A History of Chicago* (3 vols., New York, 1937, 1940, 1957); Blake McKelvey, *Rochester* (3 vols., Cambridge, Mass., 1945, 1949, 1956), and Bayrd Still, *Milwaukee, The History of a City* (Madison, Wis., 1948). The only general work on urbanization is still a comparative treatment by

Adna F. Weber, *The Growth of Cities in the Nineteenth Century* (New York, 1899).

9. See, e.g., Carl N. Degler, *Out of Our Past: The Forces That Shaped Modern America* (New York, 1959), 362. Also, Roy Lubove, "The Twentieth Century City: The Progressive as Municipal Reformer," *Mid-America,* XLI (Oct. 1959).

10. Fortunately we have been spared the full-blown "urban interpretation" of American history against which William Diamond warned: "On the Dangers of an Urban Interpretation of History," *Historiography and Urbanization,* ed. Eric F. Goldman (Baltimore, 1941), 67-108. But if one rejoices at our immunity from another variant of monism, it is necessary to add that the writing of American history has for too long been structured in terms of antithetical groups and forces in dialectical conflict: "The East" and "the frontier," the democracy against "Business" or "Government," "agriculture" and "industry," "rural" versus "urban," and so on. Such categories disclose an overly "political" view of historical change. For social historians, at least, it is necessary to explore the underlying structural and organizational changes that go much deeper than the epiphenomenal patterns of politics. Developments discussed above, for example, might be viewed as the unfolding of diverse (and sometimes contradictory) effects of a multilinear process of growth: industrialization, one of the concomitants of which, under certain technological and institutional conditions, has been the urbanization of population.

11. "The proportion between rural and town population of a country is an important fact in its interior economy and condition. It determines in a great degree, its capacity for manufactures, the extent of its commerce, and the amount of its wealth. . . . Whatever may be the good or evil tendencies of populous cities, they are the result to which all countries that are at once fertile, free, and intelligent inevitably tend." George Tucker, *The Progress of the United States in Population and Wealth in Fifty Years* (Boston, 1843), 127.

12. By the late 1840's more than half the population of Massachusetts and Rhode Island was urbanized. Before 1860 some 20 per cent of the nation's population lived in 392 urban places and, of this proportion, nearly 43 per cent lived in 9 cities of more than 100,000 inhabitants. By 1900 about 40 per cent of the United States population was resident in 1,735 urban centers. Between 1860 and 1900 the share of the United States population living in cities, 100,000 and over, rose by more than 10 percentage points; the share in cities under 10,000 increased by only 3 percentage points; and the share in the intermediate range rose by 6.6 percentage points. See also, Leon B. Truesdell, "The Development of the Urban-Rural Classification in the United States: 1874 to 1949," *Current Population Reports, Population Characteristics,* ser. p-23, No. 1 (US Department of Commerce, Bureau of the Census, Aug. 5, 1949), 1-13. Everett S. Lee and Anne S. Lee, "Internal

Migration Statistics for the United States," *Journal of the American Statistical Association*, LV (Dec. 1960), 664-97, for a discussion of concepts and sources on migration.

13. For the association between urbanization of population and per capita personal incomes nationwide, 1870-1950, see Harvey S. Perloff *et al.*, *Regions, Resources, and Economic Growth* (Baltimore, 1960), 184-90, 274-83. For an intensive local study of the same association, see Anthony M. Tang, *Economic Development in the Southern Piedmont, 1860-1950, Its Impact on Agriculture* (Chapel Hill, N. C., 1958).

14. Tisdale, "Process of Urbanization," 311-16.

15. Albert J. Reiss, Jr., "An Analysis of Urban Phenomena," in *Metropolis in Modern Life*, ed. Fisher, 41-49, argues that we have little evidence that the variables (invention and creativity, complex division of labor, agricultural activity, size of settlement, etc.) actually discriminate among communal forms; that we do not know whether such variables are independent sources of variation, or whether the discriminating variables are exhaustive sets descriptive of communal forms. Otis D. Duncan and Albert J. Reiss, Jr., *Social Characteristics of Urban and Rural Communities 1950* (New York, 1956), point out that the characteristics of populations ordered by city size along a continuum reveal a variety of patterns in relationship: that is, the relationship is not necessarily linear. The advantage of a simple demographic definition of urbanization, such as that suggested above (in terms of population concentration), is that it incorporates only two variables (population and space). Hence all other variables, for example, organizational or behavioral characteristics, may be allowed to vary independently. Thus the connection between urbanization and, say, a certain occupational structure is not prejudged.

16. Josiah Strong, *The Twentieth Century City* (New York, 1898); *id.*, *The Challenge of the City* (New York, 1907); Delos F. Wilcox, *Great Cities in America: Their Problems and Their Government* (New York, 1910); John W. Bookwalter, *Rural versus Urban: Their Conflict and Its Cause* (New York, 1911). Robert C. Brooks, *Bibliography of Municipal Problems and City Conditions* (2d ed., New York, 1901), is an invaluable guide to the contemporary discussion at home and abroad.

17. Robert E. Park *et al.*, *The City* (Chicago, 1925). While Louis Wirth thought of the city as the historic center of progress, learning, and of improved living standards, he still characterized it as the locus of poverty, crime, and social disorganization: "Urbanism as a Way of Life," *American Journal of Sociology*, XLIV (July 1938), 1-24. More recently, see *Cities Are Abnormal*, ed. Elmer T. Peterson (Norman, Okla., 1946).

18. Rural experts hoped to make country people as well off as city people were thought to be. The Country Life Movement was described by Liberty Hyde Bailey as "the working out of a desire to make rural civilization as effective and satisfying as other civilization." *The Country-Life Movement in the United States* (New York, 1911), 1-30. George W. Fiske conceded the need "to make country life as satisfying as city life and country forces as effective as city forces." *The Challenge of the Country: A Study of Country Life Opportunity* (New York and London, 1913), 1-58. Ernest R. Groves, *Rural Problems of Today* (New York, 1918), 119-36, confirmed the powerful attraction exerted by the city over "the rural mind." A more serious account of rural-urban differences was essayed by Warren H. Wilson, "Country versus City," *Papers and Proceedings, Tenth Annual Meeting of the American Sociological Society*, XI (Chicago, 1915). See also Edmund deS. Brunner, *Growth of a Science: A Half-Century of Rural Sociological Research in the United States* (New York, 1957).

19. For the urban-industrial "impact" on the old American way, see, e.g., Avery O. Craven and Walter Johnson, *The United States: Experiment in Democracy* (Boston, 1947), 441-64, 514-32; Harvey Wish, *Society and Thought in Modern America* (New York, 1952), 71-147; William E. Leuchtenburg, *The Perils of Prosperity, 1914-32* (Chicago, 1958), 2-10.

20. Municipal socialists apart, the most common standard advocated by practical-minded reformers was the model of the well-managed, efficient, business corporation. Richard E. Ely, *The Coming City* (New York, 1902), 58-61, however, suggests a better ideal was "the city as a well-ordered household." On the "efficiency movement" and the "commission government movement," see Henry Bruère, *The New City Government* (New York and London, 1913), 40-124.

21. "To set up ideal-typical polar concepts such as I have done . . . does not prove that city and country are fundamentally and necessarily different. It does not justify mistaking the hypothetical characteristics attributed to the urban and rural modes of life for established facts, as has so often been done. . . ." Louis Wirth, *Community Life and Social Policy* (Chicago, 1956), 173-74. Such compartmentalization detracts from the otherwise invaluable study of Wade, *Urban Frontier*, 341, when he concludes that by 1830 the West was divided into "two types of society—one rural and one urban." A rather mechanical application of urban sociology, aggravated by its use of literary materials, is Blanche H. Gelfant, *The American City Novel* (Norman, Okla., 1954).

22. H. Paul Douglass, *The Suburban Trend* (New York, 1925). For a less sanguine account of earlier industrial decentralization, see Graham R. Taylor, *Satellite Cities* (New York, 1915). The transformation of congested central cities into "metropolitan areas" goes back in a number of instances before the widespread use of electric power and the internal combustion engine. Half a dozen large centers were affected before the 1890's: Leo F.

Schnore, "The Timing of Metropolitan Decentralization," *Journal of American Institute of Planners,* XXV (Nov. 1959), 200-206. See also, Eric E. Lampard, "The History of Cities in the Economically Advanced Areas," *Economic Development and Cultural Change,* III (Jan. 1955), 124-26.

23. W. Stull Holt, "Some Consequences of the Urban Movement in American History," *Pacific Historical Review,* XXII (Nov. 1953), 337-51, cities the relevance to history of studies on such topics as the sources of urban population, the quality of migrants, trends in urban birth rates, urban psychology, political thought and behavior. R. Richard Wohl, "Urbanism, Urbanity, and the Historians," *University of Kansas City Review,* XXII (Autumn 1955), 53-61. Also perceptive commentary and suggestions by Bayrd Still in "Local History Contributions and Techniques in the Study of Two Colonial Cities," *Bulletin of the American Association for State and Local History,* II (Feb. 1959), 245-50. Rowland Berthoff, "The American Social Order: A Conservative Hypothesis," *American Historical Review,* LXV (Apr. 1960), 495-514. Berthoff's assertion, however, that intellectual history "both rests upon and gives form to" economic, social, and cultural history is a proposition that remains to be demonstrated.

24. Amos H. Hawley, *Human Ecology: A Theory of Community Structure* (New York, 1950), 29-31, *passim;* Otis D. Duncan and Leo F. Schnore, "Cultural, Behavioral, and Ecological Perspectives in the Study of Social Organization," *American*

Journal of Sociology, LXV (Sept. 1959), 139-46. See also Leo F. Schnore, "Social Morphology and Human Ecology," *ibid.,* LXIII (May 1958), 626-28.

25. Some of this ecological thinking is reflected in Perloff *et al., Regions, Resources, and Economic Growth,* 284-92, *passim.* On social mobility, see Elbridge Sibley, "Some Demographic Clues to Stratification," *American Sociological Review,* VII (June 1942), 322-30. It is estimated that some 150,000 workers per year on an average "ascended" from blue-collar to white-collar jobs in the period 1870-1930. If the occupational distribution of 1870 had persisted through 1930, about 9,000,000 white-collar job holders in the latter year would have been manual laborers. See also Everett S. Lee, "The Turner Thesis Reëxamined," *American Quarterly,* XIII (Spring 1961), 77-83.

26. N. S. B. Gras, "The Rise of the Metropolitan Community," *The Urban Community,* ed. Ernest W. Burgess (Chicago, 1925), 183-91. Another economic historian with an implicit ecological approach, Abbott Payson Usher, defines his subject as follows: "Economic history is concerned with the description and the analysis of the mutual transformations taking place between human societies and their environment." *A History of Mechanical Inventions* (paperback ed., Boston, 1959), 1-10. Chapters II and III of Usher's study are essential reading for social-economic historians concerned with the relation of particular events and individual efforts to the general social process.

The Urbanization Process:
An Approach to Historical Research

ROY LUBOVE

Urban history, as understood today, is virtually synonymous with everything that happened in cities. In this urban-conscious era the city threatens to substitute for the frontier, or settlement of the West, as the key to explaining the evolution of American life. This trend is encouraged by those planners and other

practitioners who seek a "usable past" to serve as a guide to current policy decisions. If, however, we are to spare the city from becoming a kind of historical variety store—a thematic free-for-all used to explain everything, and hence nothing—it is necessary to limit or define the subject. An historian once warned

From the *Journal of the American Institute of Planners,* Vol. XXXIII, No. 1 (January 1967), pp. 33-39. Reprinted by permission of the publisher. Roy Lubove is Associate Professor of American History at the University of Pittsburgh.

against an indiscriminate "urban interpretation of history." "If the city or urbanization is to be used in a causal sense," William Diamond suggested, we would have to distinguish between the "effects of urbanism, of adjustment to urbanism, and of cultural change common to city and country alike."[1] Otherwise urbanism might fallaciously be equated with broad societal trends like capitalism, industrialism, or class stratification, thus obscuring cause and effect relationships.

THE EXISTING LITERATURE

The last few years have witnessed an eruption of "urban" history, which can be divided into three broad (but not rigidly exclusive) categories.[2] Socialcultural, economic, and political studies, or some combination of them, represent one group.[3] Least satisfactory in this omnibus category are the city biographies and general accounts of urbanization. Most lack any significant conceptual framework, or fail to distinguish between urban and national history. Some are altogether episodic and trite in the antiquarian-booster tradition. The main point is that all the publications in this category deal with cities, or life in cities, but rarely with urban history as distinguished from social, economic, or political history in the context of cities.

A second group of recent publications deals with the formation of the urban environment.[4] They focus upon architecture and landscape design, housing, planning, economic development, transportation, and decisions affecting land use. Almost entirely a product of the last few years, these environmental studies provide clues to the future direction of research. A city, essentially, is an artifact, a physical container within which complex human and institutional relationships are established, and essential maintenance functions performed. This physical container or environment consists of a structure ("the spatial organization of key functional areas and essential service facilities . . . in response to certain fundamental living needs and activities of human society") and a form ("the visually perceptive features of the city which this structure produces, both the two-dimensional and three-dimensional forms created by surface, spaces, structures, and circulatory systems in a defined natural setting").[5] Urban history would benefit from much greater emphasis on environmental development: the specific decision by individuals or institutions which influenced urban form and structure, and with broader, social, economic, and technological trends which determined the nature of these decisions.

THE CITY BUILDING PROCESS

Apart from its intrinsic importance in the evolution of cities, environmental development suggests a more satisfactory definition of the field. Rather than viewing urban history as synonymous with everything that happened in cities, we might define it as the study of *the process of city-building over time*. The term "process" implies more attention to "observer-defined" issues (decision-making, organization, change mechanisms) in contrast to "actor-defined" problems (social pathologies and reform).[6] Reform, of course, can be viewed as a process. It is a legitimate subject of investigation, and part of the broader issue centering on the psychological-social impact of cities. Yet reform can be understood best in the context of the city-building process. Housing betterment efforts in the nineteenth and early twentieth centuries, for example, cannot be understood independently of building and sanitary technology, communications and transportation, design and subdivision practices, and a commodity conception of land and housing which allocated major decision-making responsibility to the private, speculative sector.

More generally, a focus upon the city-building process would provide a framework for analyzing social organization and change. The human personality is socially conditioned; it is the product of interpersonal relationships through which behavioral norms are transmitted and reinforced.[7] The spatial-temporal distribution of population, functions, and institutions plays a significant role in the patterning of these relationships. Depending on the aspirations and life styles of individuals or groups, differential environments might be accommodative or dysfunctional. Without subscribing to an environmental determinism, one can acknowledge that environment performs enabling and constraining functions. It provides or inhibits satisfactions throughout the life cycle and influences patterns of child rearing, family life, or peer group interaction. In this context it might be profitable to examine residential design practices in relation to social organization.[8] What is the social expression of low-rise as opposed to high-rise habitation; detached, row house or cluster development; superblock or grid subdivision? More feasible, perhaps, in terms of available historical data, would be local and sublocal studies dealing with the life styles of various population groups, and the enabling or constraining role of differential environments. An urban history addressed to the city-building process can, potentially, help clarify the elusive relationship be-

tween personality, social organization, and environment.[9] It provides a framework for examining both environmental and social change over time. Not least important this approach stimulates, if it does not necessitate, an urban history rooted in the behavioral and social sciences. It may never be possible to develop a sophisticated historical psychometrics, but it is worth trying.

An urban history addressed to the city-building process can certainly contribute to the evolution of a community typology. "Urbanization" or "city" is presently an umbrella term which encompasses a vast diversity of human experience and community types. There has never been, however, a single urban pattern. The range of American community types includes the commercial port towns, capitals and farm villages of the Colonial Era; the nineteenth century mill towns, communitarian settlements, industrial cities, and western speculative communities; and the twentieth century metropolitan centers, mass suburbs, and emergent new towns. These and other community types differed substantially according to function and scale, social homogeneity, nature of authority, and planning (or its absence). Thus community type can serve as an analytic tool for exploring the city-building process and specifically the relationship between environmental and social change. Similarly, rather than dealing with planning, housing, and other environmental variables as broad societal or administrative phenomena, it would be more accurate and realistic to trace their evolution in this community type context.

TECHNOLOGY: AN IMPORTANT COMPONENT

Besides its value as a framework in which to explore social organization and change (implying strong links to the behavioral and social sciences), a focus upon the city-building process mandates greater emphasis upon technological development. Technology is presently ignored in much urban history, or is mentioned in passing as a sequence of invention, or is taken for granted in the sense we all know the pre-automobile city differs in form and scale from the modern day metropolis. Not only is technology a key variable associated with "distinctive types of social structure," but the industrial-urban order essentially differs from the pre-industrial or feudal society in its dependence upon "inanimate sources of energy, a complex set of tools, and specialized scientific know-how in the production of goods and services."[10]

It is disappointing that such seminal works by Lewis Mumford as *Technics and Civilization* (1934) and *The Culture of Cities* (1938) have exerted so little influence in the writing of urban history (not to mention the sociological-anthropological tradition which treats technology as a cultural expression).[11] Mumford provided important clues for dealing with the relationship between invention and technology, social organization, and city-building. First and foremost, he interpreted technology as a cultural phenomenon which influenced and was influenced by "wishes, habits, ideas, goals." To put it another way, he explored the "translation of technical improvements into social processes" and the converse—the embodiment of social processes and norms in technology and the machine.[12] Mumford's account of the evolution of the "cult of the machine" from the Middle Ages to the seventeenth century provides a good example of his methodology. He examines the interaction of technics and culture in terms of the monastery-clock-measured

time complex; the space-distance-movement perception of the Renaissance artist and cartographer; the impact of capitalism and commercial expansion upon space-time concepts; the changing view of nature identified with experimental science; and new patterns of social regimentation epitomized in militarism and bureaucracy.[13]

Mumford's synthesis of technology and culture, applied to the city-building process, is particularly suggestive. He is concerned not only with the shaping of urban environments through architecture, building, or transportation, but with the role of changing energy sources. City-building, Mumford recognized, is profoundly influenced by what might be termed the low-yield to high-yield energy continuum. Elaborating upon the categories and terminology devised by Patrick Geddes, Mumford divides history into a sequence of eras organized around a "technological complex." Each is rooted in distinctive resources and energy systems which, in turn, produce their representative urban types. He civilization (tenth to eighteenth centhus distinguishes between eotechnic turies: wind and water, wood and glass); paleotechnic (eighteenth to nineteenth centuries: coal and steam engine, iron); and neotechnic (1880s: electricity and dynamo, new alloys and lighter metals).[14] As William Cottrell later observed, civilization is a function of energy surpluses; the "amounts and types of energy employed condition man's way of life materially and set somewhat predictable limits on what he can do and on how society will be organized."[15] In short, the city-building process, including social organization, might be examined in relation to changes in "energy converters and fuel."

The existing body of urban history

offers a surfeit of narratives about cities, and an abundance of tales about life in cities; but it largely fails to explain the city-building process in relation to technology and social organization. However, other disciplines—economics, geography, anthopology, sociology—provide insights into the nature of cities, as well as methods and concepts which might be applied to urban historical research as defined here. Space does not permit a detailed survey, but for purposes of illustration I would cite the regional studies of geographers and economists.[16] Urban history might, for example, deal with the evolution and relationship of community types, urban units, or urban-rural units over time, using the analytic tools developed by urban geographers such as "central-place" functions and "hierarchy of central places."[17] Regional economics, exemplified in the *Economic Study of the Pittsburgh Region,* suggests the use of "locational" and "economic mix" theory in tracing the history of urban development on a regional scale.[18] More specifically, it sheds light on the relationship between technology, environment, and community structure. The central theme concerns the rise and fall of an economic system superbly adapted to the coal, iron-steel, and railroad technology of the nineteenth century; and how a single locational-technological advantage—accessibility to the Connells-ville coal fields—both insured Pittsburgh's industrial preeminence after 1880, and shaped the regional community pattern of metropolis, mining village, mill town, and country hamlet. Subsequently, the life of the region was affected by the emergence of by-product coke ovens, which proved more economical when situated near the furnaces rather than the mines. Pittsburgh's competitive advantage in the production of

iron and steel was destroyed when access to the new, rapidly growing markets of the West became more important than access to a single source of coking coal. Other regions could compete when Connellsville coke declined in importance as the key differential in pig iron (and hence, steel) costs.

Pittsburgh's economic mix—centering on a limited number of heavy industries, and large plant organization—profoundly influenced the composition of the labor force and many other features of the regional community life. It ultimately created rigidities which have inhibited adaptation to twentieth century technological and market imperatives. Other communities have forged ahead in electronics, space, and diversity of service industries with all this implies for population growth or composition, and the nature of the community system. In short, transportation and communications technology have reduced in importance the kind of competitive-place advantage Pittsburgh enjoyed in the nineteenth century, and have enhanced the role of nontransportable, natural amenities in determining community evolution.[19]

It might be noted, in connection with electronics technology, that the relationship between communications and urbanization has not been systematically explored.[20] Richard Meier, for one, maintains that "research on urban communications systems seems to provide much greater rewards—in the form of more powerful explanations—than does research in the more traditional fields." The functioning of a city, he claims, can be studied in terms of the "origins, paths, contents, and destinations" of the communications network. From the perspective of social organization, "an increase in the communications rate is a prerequisite of socioeconomic growth, but overloading of communications channels causes distress and disorganization."[21] One might be skeptical of any tendency toward a communications reductionism, but the subject has played too vital a role in city-building to remain neglected.

I have suggested, thus far, that urban historiography can be divided into three categories. The first, indistinguishable from the history of everything that happened in cities, has produced some excellent social, cultural or political history, but not urban history as defined in this paper. The second category, embodied in the small nucleus of studies dealing with the creation of the urban environment, holds greater promise. It proposes a definition of urban history as the process of city-building over time. This implies a focus upon the city as a physical entity—an artifact—and the use of this framework to explore technological and social change. The third category is just emerging. Rooted in demography, statistics, and human ecology, it views urbanization as a broad societal process. It traces its lineage to Adna F. Weber's classic, *The Growth of Cities in the Nineteenth Century*.

THE ECOLOGIC COMPLEX

"The growth of cities," Weber wrote, "must be studied as a part of the question of the distribution of population, which is always dependent upon the economic organization of society—upon the constant striving to maintain as many people as possible upon a given area."[22] Since Weber, the distinctive feature of this approach to the study of cities has been its preoccupation with demographic phenomena. Human ecology, the branch of urban sociology developed by Park, Burgess, McKenzie, and others in the 1920's, devoted much attention to the spatial-temporal distribution of population aggregates.[23] According to a later formulation by Amos Hawley, the "focus of attention in ecology is upon the population which is either organized or in process of becoming organized." Ecology, and human ecology in particular, dealt basically with "population problems"; these included the "ways in which the developing community is affected by the size, composition, and rate of growth or decline of the population," as well as the "significance of migration for both the development of the community and the maintenance of community stability." In broadest terms, human ecology examined the "adjustment of population to the resources and other physical conditions of the habitat."[24]

Hope Tisdale, in the early 1940's, published an important theoretical statement on the demographic-ecological approach to urbanization. It was defined as a "process of population concentration," expressed in "multiplication of the points of concentration and the increase in size of individual concentrations." Cities, in this sense, were points or nodes of population concentration, and everything which influenced population change became relevant to the study of urbanization. Tisdale maintained that people were one of two requisites to urbanization—the other was technology. Urbanization was rooted in population movements, but technology determined the "form and focus" of the process. Two definitions of urbanization were objectionable from the Tisdale perspective. Urbanization viewed as a "process of radiation whereby ideas and practices spread out from the urban center" failed to "explain the appearance and growth of cities"; while city growth interpreted as an "increase in intensity of problems or traits or characteristics that are essentially urban" resulted in a "confusion of cause and effect, the presupposition of cities before urbanization." Most objectionable of all was the implicit corollary that "as problems are solved, as traits disappear, as characteristics change, de-urbanization sets in."[25]

In recent years a number of sociologists, notably O. D. Duncan and Leo Schnore, have labored to establish demography and ecology as the focal points of urban research. This has led to a definition of the urbanization process in terms of an "ecological complex." This complex includes, according to Duncan and Schnore, "population, environment, technology, and organization" as the key variables.[26] Although the temporal-areal distribution of population is only one element of the complex, it sems to be favored. "The logic of ecological theory" forces the "analyst to view distinctive activities—their numbers and kinds—as *properties of aggregates of populations*."[27]

Eric Lampard has consistently (and single-handedly) urged the wholesale adaptation of ecological complex theory to urban history. "Until recently," Lampard argues, "historians have had little cause for satisfaction with their contributions to the field." American urban hisory was "largely the history of cities and their 'problems,' not the history of urbanization." Seeking relief from the variety store level of conceptualization, Lampard urged a relatively "unambiguous" definition of urbanization "in terms of population concentration." Within this framework, urbanization and community structure would be interpreted as the "outcome of a changing balance between population and environment (including habitat and other populations) moderated by technology and organization."[28] In effect, the ecological complex implied an urban historiography which dealt with the "phenomenon of population concentration and certain apparent trends in social organization, structure, and behavior." Specific cities would be studied as "an accommodation of the general movement (urbanization) to a particular set of demographic, institutional, technological, and environmental circumstances—including the contingencies of events and personalities."[29]

CITY BUILDING AND ECOLOGIC
COMPLEX APPROACHES:
COMPARISONS

Both the ecological complex and what I have termed the city-building process assign a major role to technology and related economic changes. Lampard describes the ecological complex as "especially suited to the analysis of those social and economic changes which are associated with industrialization."[30] He examines these changes in one study with particular emphasis upon the impact of specialization: the *"essential link between the technical and spatial conditions of economic progress."*[31] On the question of social organization, however, the theory is somewhat ambiguous. Social organization is always included as a variable, and Lampard maintains that contingencies of events and personalities are encompassed in the formulation. Just how they are encompassed, however, is clear neither in the theory nor its application. Indeed, Duncan and Schnore are critical of any behavioral, cultural analysis of social organization which focuses on the individual, on small group or interpersonal relationships, on values, or on culture "traits." They argue that the ecologist "takes the aggregate as his frame of reference and deliberately sets out to account for the forms that social organization assumes in response to varying demographic, technological, and environmental pressures." He concentrates upon "transformations of patterns of social organization" rather than "shifts in value systems or modal character structure."[32]

In favoring the analysis of aggregates and broad societal processes, notably demography, ecological complex research has made several useful contributions. A great deal of empirical data has been synthesized (though at times one wonders if much of it is not reducible to a numbers game played with U. S. Census Reports). It has advanced our understanding of the metropolitan community—its structural, functional, and demographic differentiation, and central city-suburban relationships.[33] In minimizing the role of behavioral and subjective phenomena as change-agents, however, it limits its usefulness as a research tool. This applies to technology as well as social organization. Lewis Mumford, and more recently, Gideon Sjoberg, recognize that technology possesses a subjective dimension. Its evolution is conditioned by those very "shifts in value systems" which Schnore and Duncan relegate to the limbo of behaviorism and cultural "trait complexes." As Julius Rubin, in an important study of entrepreneurship and urban development, demonstrates, understanding of the historical process "depends as much upon the analysis of the subjective traits of groups as it does upon the analysis of the pressure of objective circumstances." Various communities, after 1825, responded differently to the challenge of the Erie Canal and emergence of the

railroad, and these "differences in behavior are to be explained by attitudinal rather than situational factors; by divergences in the history and traditions of the three regions (Boston, Philadelphia, Baltimore), which produced differences in the attitudes that the decision-making groups brought to the common problem rather than by differences in the problem itself."[34]

One important contrast between the ecological complex and what I term the city-building process centers on this issue of social organization, and the respective weight assigned to subjective, attitudinal variables. I would maintain, especially on the level of local and sublocal urban historiography, that social psychology, cultural anthopology, interpersonal psychiatry, or interactionist sociology can prove useful. They can help in explaining just how technology and environment interact with population to produce a structured behavioral-organizational field.

The two approaches differ in another way. The ecological complex interprets urbanization as a broad societal process, with singular emphasis upon the "secular phenomenon of population concentration, the multiplication of points of concentration, or of relations among concentrations of different size and density in various parts of the country at different times in our history."[35] I have used the term "city-building" rather than urbanization in order to emphasize the weight attached to the literal process of environmental formation. This implies not only a concern for what geographers call the urban "site," but for the whole range of city-building mechanisms: architecture and landscape architecture, housing and housing finance, the real estate market and realty institutions, transportation, communications, public health and sanitation, industrial technology, and business organization. In the most general sense, it implies an awareness of the city as an artifact whose form and structure are greatly determined by decisions which affect land use.[36]

The ecological complex, in practice, frequently loses sight of the city as an artifact. One learns about the flux of population aggregates and their characteristics, about demographic concentrations, diffusions and distributions—but not about the specific decisions which shaped the specific environments of specific cities, and the relationship of this "city-building complex" to technology and social organization. Urbanization, as such, is an abstraction. Cities are the entities with which one must deal, in the final analysis, and they are created by concrete decisions over time.

NOTES

1. William Diamond, "On the Dangers of an Urban Interpretation of History," in Eric F. Goldman (ed.), Historiography and Urbanization: Essays in American History in Honor of W. Stull Holt (Baltimore: Johns Hopkins Press, 1941), pp. 96, 106, 107.
2. This paper is based primarily, though not exclusively, upon publications relating to American urban history which have appeared since 1960. No effort has been made to achieve complete bibliographical coverage. Previous issues of the Urban History Group Newsletter (1954–), and a number of bibliographical essays contain more complete listings. See, Blake McKelvey, "American Urban History Today," American Historical Review, LVII (July, 1952), 919-929; Philip Dawson and Sam B. Warner, Jr., "A Selection of Works Relating to the History of Cities," in Oscar Handlin and John Burchard (eds.), The Historian and the City (Cambridge: MIT Press, 1963), pp. 270-290; Allen F. Davis, "The American Historian vs. the City," Social Studies, LVI (March, April, 1965), 91-96, 127-135; Charles N. Glaab, "The Historian and the American City: A Bibliographic Survey," in Philip M. Hauser and Leo F. Schnore, The Study of Urbanization (New York: John Wiley and Sons, 1965), pp. 53-80.
    Urbanization and historiography are examined in the following: Arthur M. Schlesinger, Sr., "The City in American History," Mississippi Valley Historical Review, XXVII (June, 1940), 43-66; William Diamond, "On the Dangers of an Urban Interpretation of History," in Eric F. Goldman (ed.), Historiography and Urbanization: Essays in American History in Honor of W. Stull Holt (Baltimore: Johns Hopkins Press, 1941), 67-108; David H. Pinkney, "Urban Studies and the Historian," Social Forces, XXVIII (May, 1950), 423-429; W. Stull Holt, "Some Consequences of the Urban Movement in American History," Pacific Historical Review, XXII (November, 1953), 337-351; R. Richard Wohl, "Urbanism, Urbanity, and the Historian," University of Kansas City Review, XXII (Autumn, 1955), 53-61; Asa Briggs, "The Study of Cities," Confluence, VII (Summer, 1958), 107-114; Mark D. Hirsch, "Reflections on Urban History and Urban Reform, 1856-1915," in Donald Sheehan and Harold C. Syrett (eds.), Essays in American Historiography: Papers Presented in Honor of Allan Nevins (New York: Columbia University Press, 1960), 109-137; Eric E. Lampard, "American Historians and the Study of Urbanization," American Historical Review, LXVII (October, 1961), 49-61; Charles N. Glaab, "The Historian and the American Urban Tradition," Wisconsin Magazine of History, XLVII (Autumn, 1963), 12-25; Oscar Handlin, "The Modern City as a Field of Historical Study," in Handlin and Burchard (eds.), The Historian and the City, 1-26.
3. The following publications are listed rather than evaluated. Many are excellent historical studies, irrespective of their relevance to the definition of urban history developed in this paper. Among the socio-cultural studies are: Moses Rischin, The Promised City: New York's Jews, 1870-1914 (Cambridge, Mass.: Harvard University Press, 1962); Morton and Lucia White, The Intellectual Versus the City: From Thomas Jefferson to Frank Lloyd Wright (Cambridge, Mass.: Harvard University Press, 1962); Seth M. Scheiner, Negro Mecca: A History of the Negro in New York City, 1865-1920 (New York: New York University Press, 1965); Gilbert Osofsky, Harlem: The Making of a Ghetto: Negro New York, 1890-1930 (New York: Harper and Row, 1966); Donald B. Cole, Immigrant City: Lawrence, Massachusetts, 1845-1921 (Chapel Hill: University of North Carolina Press, 1963); Stephan Thernstrom, Poverty and Progress: Social Mobility in a Nineteenth Century City (Cambridge, Mass.: Harvard University Press, 1964; Harold Kirker and James Kirker, Bulfinch's Boston, 1787-1817 (New York: Oxford University Press, 1964); Richard C. Wade, Slavery in the Cities: The South, 1820-1860 (New York: Oxford University Press, 1964); Alan Trachtenberg, Brooklyn Bridge: Fact and Symbol (New York: Oxford University Press, 1965). Also relevant are, George A. Dunlap, The City in the American Novel, 1789-1900 (Philadelphia: Russell, 1934); Blanche H. Gelfant, The American City Novel, 1900-1940 (Norman: University of

Oklahoma Press, 1954); Robert H. Walker, "The Poet and the Rise of the City," *Mississippi Valley Historical Review*, 49 (June, 1962), 85-99; Anselm L. Strauss, *Images of the American City* (New York: Free Press, 1961). Comparative studies include, Richard C. Wade, *The Urban Frontier: The Rise of Western Cities, 1790-1830* (Cambridge, Mass.: Harvard University Press, 1959), and Asa Briggs, *Victorian Cities* (New York: Harper and Row, 1965), orig. pub., 1963. For earlier comparative works see, Carl Bridenbaugh, *Cities in the Wilderness: The First Century of Urban Life in America, 1625-1742* (New York: Ronald Press, 1938), Bridenbaugh, *Cities in Revolt, Urban Life in America, 1743-1776* (New York: Alfred A. Knopf, 1955), and Constance M. Green, *American Cities in the Growth of the Nation* (New York: J. DeGraff, 1957).

City politics are examined in the following: Charles Garrett, *The La Guardia Years: Machine and Reform Politics in New York City* (New Brunswick: Rutgers University Press, 1961); William D. Miller, *Mr. Crump of Memphis* (Baton Rouge, Louisiana State University Press, 1964); Alex Gottfried, *Boss Cermak of Chicago: A Study of Political Leadership* (Seattle: University of Washington Press, 1962). Also political in orientation, but set apart because of its emphasis on communications networks, is Seymour J. Mandelbaum, *Boss Tweed's New York* (New York: John Wiley and Sons, 1965).

The following are economic in orientation, with particular emphasis upon entrepreneurship: Charles N. Glaab, "Business Patterns in the Growth of a Midwestern City: The Kansas City Business Community before the Civil War," *Business History Review*, XXXIII (Summer, 1959), pp. 156-174; Glaab, *Kansas City and the Railroads: Community Policy in the Growth of a Regional Metropolis* (Madison: Wisconsin State Historical Society, 1962); Julius Rubin, *Canal or Railroad? Imitation and Innovation in the Response to the Erie Canal in Philadelphia, Baltimore, and Boston* (Philadelphia: American Philosophical Society, 1961); A. Theodore Brown, *Frontier Community: Kansas City to 1870* (Columbia: University of Missouri Press, 1963). Earlier economic studies include, Vera Shlakman, *Economic History of a Factory Town: A Study of Chicopee, Massachusetts* (Northhampton, Mass., 1935); Constance M. Green, *Holyoke, Massachusetts: A Case History of the Industrial Revolution in America* (New Haven: Yale University Press, 1939); Robert G. Albion, *The Rise of New York Port, 1815-1860* (New York: The Shoe String Press, 1939); Catherine E. Reiser, *Pittsburgh's Commercial Development, 1800-1850* (Harrisburg, Pa., 1951).

Among the urban biographies are: Robert C. Reinders, *End of an Era: New Orleans, 1850-1860* (New Orleans: Pelican Pub. Co., 1965); Bayrd Still, *Milwaukee: The History of a City* (Madison: Wisconsin State Historical Society, 1948); Lawrence L. Graves (ed.), *A History of Lubbock*

(Lubbock: Texas Technological College, 1962); Constance M. Green, *Washington: Village and Capital, 1800-1878* (Princeton: Princeton University Press, 1962) and Green, *Washington: Capital City, 1869-1950* (Princeton: Princeton University Press, 1963); Thomas C. Wheeler (ed.), *A Vanishing America: The Life and Times of the Small Town* (New York: Holt, Rinehart and Winston, 1964); Edward Wagenknecht, *Chicago* (Norman: University of Oklahoma Press, 1964); Sidney Glazer, *Detroit: A Study in Urban Development* (New York: Twayne Pub., 1965). The most ambitious biographies are Blake McKelvey, *Rochester*, I. *The Water-Power City, 1812-1854*, II. *The Flower City, 1855-1890*, III. *The Quest for Quality, 1890-1925*, IV. *Rochester: An Emerging Metropolis, 1925-1961* (Cambridge: James Hineman Pub. and Rochester, N.Y., 1945-1961); and Bessie L. Pierce, *A History of Chicago*, I. *The Beginning of a City, 1673-1848*, II. *From Town to City, 1848-1871*, III. *The Rise of a Modern City, 1871-1893* (New York: Alfred H. Knopf, 1937-1957). Two examples of collective biography are, James B. Allen, *The Company Town in the American West* (Norman: University of Oklahoma Press, 1966), and Page Smith, *As a City Upon a Hill: The Town in American History* (New York, Knopf, 1966). General accounts of urbanization include, Arthur M. Schlesinger, *The Rise of the City, 1878-1898* (New York: The Macmillan Co., 1933); Constance M. Green, *The Rise of Urban America* (New York: Harper and Row, 1965); Blake McKelvey, *The Urbanization of America, 1860-1915* (New Brunswick: Rutgers University Press, 1963). A comparative, structural analysis by a sociologist is, Gideon Sjoberg, *The Preindustrial City: Past and Present* (Glencoe: The Free Press, 1960). In a class by themselves are, Lewis Mumford, *The Culture of Cities* (New York: Harcourt, Brace and World, Inc., 1938) and Mumford, *The City in History: Its Origins, Its Transformations, and Its Prospects* (New York: Harcourt, Brace and World, Inc., 1961). A number of articles deal with specialized phases of urbanization: Leon S. Marshall, "The English and American Industrial City of the Nineteenth Century," *Western Pennsylvania Historical Magazine*, XX (September, 1937), 169-180; Marshall, "The Emergence of the First Industrial City: Manchester, 1780-1850," and Ralph E. Turner, "The Industrial City: Center of Cultural Change," in Caroline F. Ware (ed.), *The Cultural Approach to History* (New York: Kennikat Press, 1940), 140-161, 228-242; Bayrd Still, "Patterns of Mid-Nineteenth Century Urbanization in the Middle West," *Mississippi Valley Historical Review*, XXVIII (September, 1941), 187-206; Francis P. Weisenburger, "The Urbanization of the Middle West: Town and Village in the Pioneer Period," *Indiana Magazine of History*, XLI (March, 1945), 19-30; Oscar O. Winther, "The Rise of Metropolitan Los Angeles," *Huntington Library Quarterly*, X (August, 1947), 391-405; Frederick D. Kershner, Jr.,

"From Country Town to Industrial City: The Urban Pattern in Indianapolis," *Indiana Magazine of History*, XLV (December, 1949), 327-338. Bessie L. Pierce, "Changing Urban Patterns in the Mississippi Valley," *Journal of the Illinois State Historical Society*, XLIII (Spring, 1950), 46-57: R. Richard Wohl and A. Theodore Brown, "The Usable Past: A Study of Historical Traditions in Kansas City," *Huntington Library Quarterly*, XXIII (May, 1960), 237-259.

4. Sam B. Warner, Jr., *Streetcar Suburbs: The Process of Growth in Boston, 1870-1900* (Cambridge: Harvard University Press, 1962); George W. Hilton and John F. Duc, *The Electric Interurban Railways in America* (Stanford, Calif.: Stanford University Press, 1960, 1964); Roy Lubove, *The Progressives and the Slums: Tenement House Reform in New York City, 1890-1917* (Pittsburgh: University of Pittsburgh Press, 1962), Lubove, *Community Planning in the 1920's: The Regional Planning Association of America* (Pittsburgh: University of Pittsburgh Press, 1963), Lubove (ed.), *H.W.S. Cleveland, Landscape Architecture as Applied to the Wants of the West* (Pittsburgh: University of Pittsburgh Press, 1965); William H. Wilson, *The City Beautiful Movement in Kansas City* (Columbia: University of Missouri Press, 1964); James E. Vance, Jr., *Geography and Urban Evolution in the San Francisco Bay Area* (Berkeley: University of California Press, 1964); Edmund H. Chapman, *Cleveland: Village to Metropolis: A Case Study of Problems of Urban Development in Nineteenth-Century America* (Cleveland: Western Reserve University Press, 1964); E. A. Gutkind, *Urban Development in Central Europe* (Glencoe: The Free Press, 1964), Vol. I., International History of City Development; Donald J. Olsen, *Town Planning in London: The Eighteenth and Nineteenth Centuries* (New Haven: Yale University Press, 1964). John W. Reps, *The Making of Urban America: A History of City Planning in the United States* (Princeton: Princeton University Press, 1965); Sumner C. Powell, *Puritan Village: The Formation of a New England Town* (Anchor edition, New York: Doubleday and Co., 1965), orig. publ., 1963; Carl W. Condit, *The Chicago School of Architecture: A History of Commercial and Public Building in the Chicago Area, 1875-1925* (Chicago: University of Chicago Press, 1964). Relevant also are; S. Giedion, *Space, Time and Architecture: The Growth of a New Tradition* (Cambridge: Harvard University Press, 1941 and subsequent editions); Lewis Mumford, *Sticks and Stones: A Study of American Architecture and Civilization*, orig. pub., 1924, *The Brown Decades: A Study of the Arts in America, 1865-1895*, orig. pub., 1931 (New York: Dover Publications Inc., 1955); John Coolidge, *Mill and Mansion: A Study of Architecture and Society in Lowell, Massachusetts, 1820-1850* (New York: Columbia University Press, 1942); David H. Pinkney, *Napoleon III and the Rebuilding of Paris* (Princeton: Princeton University Press, 1958);

Nelson M. Blake, *Water for the Cities: A History of the Urban Water Supply Problem in the United States* (Syracuse: Syracuse University Press, 1956); Paul F. Conkin, *Tomorrow a New World: The New Deal Community Program* (Ithaca: Cornell University Press, 1959); Walter M. Whitchill, *Boston: A Topographical History* (Cambridge: Harvard University Press, 1959); Lloyd Rodwin, *Housing and Economic Progress: A Study of the Housing Experience of Boston's Middle-Income Families* (Cambridge: MIT Press, 1961).

Several of the volumes cited in category one (note 2) also deal, in one way or another, with the formation of the urban physical environment. The economic studies are particularly pertinent.

In terms of the definition of urban history developed in this paper, the most satisfactory of the environmental analyses are those which attempt to relate environmental and social change. A good example is Sam B. Warner's *Streetcar Suburbs*.

5. F. Stuart Chapin, "Foundations of Urban Planning," in Werner Z. Hirsch (ed.), *Urban Life and Form* (New York: Holt, Rinehart and Winston, 1963), p. 234. Also, Kevin Lynch, *The Image of the City* (Cambridge: MIT Press, 1960); and various articles in Kevin Lynch and Lloyd Rodwin (eds.), "The Future Metropolis," *Daedalus*, XC (Winter, 1961).

6. Hugh Douglas Price, *The Metropolis and its Problems* (Syracuse: Syracuse University Press, 1960), p. 25.

7. H. S. Perry and M. L. Gawel (eds.), *Harry S. Sullivan: Interpersonal Theory of Psychiatry* (New York: Norton, 1953). The sociological equivalent, interactionism, is explored in, Arnold M. Rose (ed.), *Human Behavior and Social Processes: An Interactionist Approach* (Boston: Houghton Mifflin Co., 1962). Both theories derive, in part, from social psychology. See, Anselm Strauss (ed.), *The Social Psychology of George H. Mead* (Chicago: University of Chicago Press, 1956).

8. Leon Festinger, Stanley Schachter, and Kurt Black, *Social Pressures in Informal Groups: A Study of Human Factors in Housing* (New York: Stanford, 1950), is pertinent. Also, Anthony F. C. Wallace, *Housing and Social Structure: A Preliminary Survey, with Particular Reference to Multi-Story, Low Rent, Public Housing Projects* (Philadelphia Housing Authority, 1962); Daniel M. Wilner, et al., *The Housing Environment and Family Life: A Longitudinal Study of the Effects of Housing on Morbidity and Mental Health* (Baltimore: Johns Hopkins Press, 1963); Alvin L. Schorr, *Slums and Social Insecurity* (Washington, D. C.: Social Security Administration, 1963); Herbert Gans, *The Urban Villagers: Group and Class in the Life of Italian Americans* (Glencoe, Ill.: The Free Press, 1962) and Gans, "Urbanism and Suburbanism as Ways of Life: A Re-evaluation of Definitions," in Rose (ed.), *Human Behavior and Social Processes*, pp. 625-648; Warren A. Peterson and George K. Zollschan, "Social

Processes in the Metropolitan Community," *ibid.*, pp. 649-666.

9. Marc Fried and Peggy Gleicher, "Some Sources of Residential Satisfaction in an Urban Slum," *AIP Journal*, XXVII (November, 1961), 305-315, deals with Boston's West End. According to the authors, "the importance of localism in the West End, as well as in other working-class areas, can hardly be emphasized enough. This sense of a local spatial identity includes both local social relationships and local places." (p. 308.)

10. Sjoberg, *The Preindustrial City*, pp. 7, 12.

11. See also, Mumford, *Art and Technics* (New York: Columbia University Press, 1952). For the treatment of technology as a cultural phenomenon by sociologists and anthropologists see, "Social Aspects of Technology," *The Selected Papers of Bernhard J. Stern* (New York: 1959); Otis D. Duncan (ed.), *William F. Ogburn: On Culture and Social Change* (Chicago: University of Chicago Press, 1964) and William F. Ogburn, *Social Change with Respect to Cultural and Original Nature* (New York: Dell Pub. Co., 1966) orig. publ. 1922; Melville J. Herskovits, *Economic Anthropology: The Economic Life of Primitive Peoples* (New York: W. W. Norton and Co., 1965 (orig. publ. 1940; Leslie A. White, *The Evolution of Culture: The Development of Civilizations to the Fall of Rome* (New York: McGraw-Hill, 1959); C. Daryll Forde, *Habitat, Economy and Society* (New York: E. P. Dutton and Co., 1963) orig. publ. 1949. Relevant also by an archeologist is V. Gordon Childe, *Man Makes Himself* (New York: The New American Library of World Literature, Inc., 1951) and Childe, *What Happened in History* (Baltimore: Penguin Books, Inc., 1964).

12. Lewis Mumford, *Technics and Civilization* (New York: Harcourt, Brace and World, Inc., 1934), pp. 3, 281.

13. *Ibid.*, 9-59.

14. The paleotechnic economy, according to Mumford, appeared as a mutant during the eotechnic era in the form of the blast furnace and primitive railway. The eotechnic economy persisted as a recessive until the last quarter of the nineteenth century. Writing in the late 1930's, Mumford described the eotechnic complex as a survival, the paleotechnic as a recessive, and the neotechnic as a dominant. He refers also to an emergent "biotechnic economy" in which the "biological sciences will be freely applied to technology, and in which technology itself will be oriented toward the culture of life." Generally, the biologic and social arts will take precedence over the mechanical. Mumford, *Culture of Cities*, 495-496.

15. William F. Cottrell, *Energy and Society: The Relation between Energy, Social Change, and Economic Development* (New York: McGraw-Hill, 1955), p. 32; and Joseph Mayer, "Foreword," *Ibid.*, VII.

16. This is covered in, Hauser and Schnore, *The Study of Urbanization.*

17. See, Harold M. Mayer, "A Survey of Urban Geography," *Ibid.*, 81-113. Mayer defines the central place as a "cluster of service functions located at the point most accessible to the maximum 'profit area' which can be commanded." The hierarchy of central places is defined as the "symbiotic nesting relationship of higher- and lower-order centers." (p. 89). For an example of historical urban geography see, Robert E. Dickinson, *The West European City: A Geographical Interpretation* (New York: Humanities Press, Inc., 1962). Also by Dickinson, *City, Region and Regionalism: A Geographical Contribution to Human Ecology* (New York: Humanities Press, Inc., 1947).

18. *Pittsburgh Regional Planning Association Economic Study of the Pittsburgh Region: Region in Transition, Portrait of a Region,* and *Region with a Future* (Pittsburgh: Univ. of Pittsburgh Press, 1963). Along similar lines, see the eight volumes of the *New York Metropolitan Region Study* (Raymond Vernon, director). An example of regional economic analysis by an historian, suggesting the potentialities of this approach to urbanization and urban-rural relationships is, Julius Rubin, "City and Region in the Economic Growth of the American North and South before the Civil War," (unpublished, 1965).

19. Edward L. Ullman, "Amenities as a Factor in Regional Growth," *Geographical Review*, XLIV (January, 1954), 119-132; Melvin M. Webber, "Order in Diversity: Community without Propinquity," in Lowdon Wingo, Jr. (ed.), *Cities and Space: The Future Use of Urban Land* (Baltimore: Johns Hopkins Press, 1963), p. 47.

20. Mandelbaum, *Boss Tweed's New York,* is an exception.

21. Richard L. Meier, *A Communications Theory of Urban Growth* (Cambridge: 1962), Vol. 1, 2.

22. Adna F. Weber, *The Growth of Cities in the Nineteenth Century: A Study in Statistics,* orig. pub., 1899. (Ithaca: Cornell Univ. Press, 1963), p. 157.

23. The Burgess concentric zone hypothesis concerning urban growth became one of the best known and controversial contributions of the early ecologists. See, Ernest W. Burgess, "The Growth of the City: An Introduction to a Research Project," *Publications of the American Sociological Society,* XVIII (1924), 85-97; James A. Quinn, "The Burgess Zonal Hypothesis and its Critics," *American Sociological Review,* V (April, 1940), 210-218. Also by Quinn, *Human Ecology* (New York: J. B. Lippincott Co., 1950). Critical of the human ecologists as "positivistic, deterministic, mechanistic, and organismic," was Warner E. Gettys, "Human Ecology and Social Theory," *Social Forces,* XVIII (May, 1940), 469-476. Also, Mila A. Alihan, *Social Ecology: A Critical Analysis* (New York: Cooper Sq. Pub., 1938).

24. Amos H. Hawley, "Ecology and Human Ecology and Human Ecology," *Social Forces,* XXII (May, 1944), 403, 404, 405. A fuller account by

Hawley, is, *Human Ecology: A Theory of Com-munity Structure* (New York: Ronald, 1950). ~pe Tisdale, "The Process of Urbanization," *Social Forces*, XX (March, 1942), 311, 315.

26. Otis D. Duncan and Leo F. Schnore, "Cultural, Behavioral, and Ecological Perspectives in the Study of Social Organization," *American Journal of Sociology*, LXV (September, 1959), 135.

27. *Ibid.*, 137.

28. Lampard, "American Historians and the Study of Urbanization," pp. 49, 54, 60.

29. Eric E. Lampard, "Urbanization and Social Change: On Broadening the Scope and Relevance of Urban History," in Handlin and Burchard (eds.), *The Historian and the City*, pp. 233-234, 237. Lampard also outlines his views in "Urbanization and Urban History," *Colloquium* (Fall, 1965), pp. 12-17, 20-22.

30. Lampard, "American Historians and the Study of Urbanization," p. 60.

31. Eric E. Lampard, "The History of Cities in Economically Advanced Areas," *Economic Development and Cultural Change*, III (1954-55), 88. Specialization and the division of labor as requisites to large-scale urbanization are also stressed in, Jack P. Gibbs and Walter T. Martin, "Urbanization, Technology, and the Division of Labor: International Patterns," *American Sociological Review*, XXVII (October, 1962), 667-677. Urbanization requires that "materials be brought from great distances." Since this, in turn, depends upon specialization and technology, it follows that "the level of urbanization is contingent, at least in part, on the division of labor and technology." (p. 668.)

32. Duncan and Schnore, "Cultural, Behavioral, and Ecological Perspectives in the Study of Social Organization," pp. 144, 142. Similarly, the ecologist "is interested in the pattern of observable physical activity itself rather than the subjective expectations that individuals may entertain of their roles." (p. 137.)

33. Philip M. Hauser, "Ecological Aspects of Urban Research," in Leonard D. White (ed.), *The State of the Social Sciences* (Chicago: Univ. of Chicago Press, 1956). Along with ecological research on the metropolitan phenomenon, Hauser cites the group of studies dealing with the "specific temporal and mobility aspects of urban structure and function." (p. 237.) An example of the ecological complex approach to urbanization is, Leo F. Schnore, *The Urban Scene: Human Ecology and Demography* (New York: The Free Press, 1965).

34. Rubin, *Canal or Railroad?*, pp. 96, 9. Supporting such conclusions is, Glaab, *Kansas City and the Railroads*.

35. Lampard, "American Historians and the Study of Urbanization," p. 50.

36. William H. Form, "The Place of Social Structure in the Determination of Land Use: Some Implications for a Theory of Urban Ecology," *Social Forces*, XXXII (May, 1954), 317-323. Form argues that the "traditional ecological processes," based upon "models of eighteenth century free enterprise economics," are "no longer adequate tools to analyze changes in land use." (p. 323.) Sjoberg offers a similar criticism—"a clear account of the materialist view they espouse is definitely in order; more crucial still is the need to enumerate those premises apparently adapted from Classical Economics." Sjoberg also calls for clarification of terms, and challenges the validity of a theory of social organization and urbanism which ignores values. Gideon Sjoberg, "Theory and Research in Urban Sociology," in Hauser and Schnore, *The Study of Urbanization*, p. 66.

The Historian and the American City:
A Bibliographic Survey

CHARLES N. GLAAB

American historians came late to the study of cities, the forces that created them, and their part in the development of the United States. Turn-of-the-century scholars who led the revolt against the rigid, formalistic history of the nineteenth century, which was often little more than a narrative of past politics and diplomacy, captured the study of the American past from the gentleman-ama-

From Philip Hauser and Leo F. Schnore, *The Study of Urbanization* (New York: John Wiley & Sons, 1965), pp. 53-80. Reprinted by permission of the author and the publisher. Charles N. Glaab is a Professor of History at The University of Toledo.

teur chronicler and introduced a variety of new subects and approaches into their chosen discipline. But interest in cities and the way they had developed was not a part of the new outlook. The leaders of the movement toward a "New History" (among them James Harvey Robinson, Charles A. Beard, and Frederick Jackson Turner) focused attention on history as an instrument of social reform, on a broad kind of cultural history from which stemmed an interest in social and intellectual history, on the clash of economic interests in the past, and particularly on the creative force of the Great West—Turner's "frontier"—in shaping the unique qualities of American civilization. As the study of history penetrated graduate instruction in American universities, conflict between classes, between interest groups, or between geographic sections became fundamental dichotomies absorbed by students as readily as they acquired a respect for evidence and the exact procedures of the German seminar method. Owing in part to his enormous success as a teacher of graduate students, Turner was particularly influential. His "frontier thesis," which emphasized the continuing development of the free land of the west as the vital force in our nation's history, erected a scaffolding within which a generation of professional historians could construct craftsmanlike monographs devoted to examination of heuristic themes in the master's essays. Eventually there was reaction against his theories, but the Turnerian scheme determined the character of the dialectic. Refutation, defense, modification, or amplification of Turner is still considered a valid historical exercise.

Although Turner to some extent had always recognized the importance of the city and late in his life had even suggested the need for "an urban reinterpretation of our history," it was not until the 1930's—as an outgrowth of interest in an essentially descriptive social history concerned with the "life of the people"—that historians began to pay attention to the city. To the extent that urbanization thereafter began to work its way into general interpretations of American history, it was as part of a dramatic post-Civil War "rise of the city." This development was interpreted as an aspect of the triumph of industrialism or as part of the growth of a commercial-urban East threatening an agrarian-rural West, which represented much that was best in the American tradition. The city had created a number of new social and political problems—the slum, the machine, the political boss, the downtrodden immigrant—that were to be dealt with in future years by a new generation of Progressive reformers. Economically, the "rise of the city" exemplified the growing power of a class of exploitative capitalists, dealing in traction franchises, corrupting city governments, and oppressing workers and immigrants, but who were soon to face an aroused populace willing to enact a variety of desirable social and regulatory legislation. The Progressive Movement thus assured that under new conditions old values would be preserved with new methods; particularly in cities, as it was frequently stated, Hamiltonian means were necessary to maintain Jeffersonian ends. Although, as Eric E. Lampard has observed, an "urban-industrial transformation" has now become "part of the furniture displayed in every up-to-date textbook of United States history," there is little evidence that the substantial body of writing in urban history has influenced in any significant way general interpretations of the American past or the approaches employed by practicing American historians.[1]

In large part, this is the result of urban history's lack of academic respectability. Unlike many urban fields in the social sciences, neither the method nor the subject matter of urban history has been well defined. There are no textbooks providing a framework for inquiry, and only very recently has urban history acquired a small measure of recognition in an occasional major graduate school in American history. Only a handful of courses are taught under a variety of names, "The History of the American City," "American Urban History," or "The History of Urban Society in the United States." The content of these courses varies much more than the titles. Is urban history the history of cities, the history of urbanization, or the history of anything that takes place in an urban setting? The question has not been answered. Many studies seem customarily to be classified as urban history simply because they deal with events that have something to do with cities and cannot conveniently be fitted into one of the more formally established categories of American history. Nevertheless, there are a number of urban historians, *soi-disant*, who feel they are working within a worthwhile—and distinct enough—framework. Their scholarship is often impressive. Some of them—rather casually to be sure, but this is the fashion of the historian—have even begun to try to formulate definitions of the subject and to suggest general approaches by which more systematic future work can be conducted.[2]

THE DEVELOPMENT OF URBAN HISTORY

American historians, of course, have never ignored the city altogether.

Among the great nineteenth-century historians, even James Ford Rhodes, for all his allegiance to the traditions of conventional political history, considered some aspects of urban development in the years after the Civil War, and John Bach McMaster in his multi-volume account of the life of the people in the antebellum period occasionally provided descriptions of the growth of individual towns and cities. The fifth volume of Edward Channing's *History of the United States,* published in 1921, contained an excellent assessment of "The Urban Migration" of the years 1815-1848.[3] A formal interest in the history of American cities really dates, however, from the early 1930's with the start of publication of volumes in the famous *History of American Life* series. This series represented an ambitious attempt to write the social history of the United States. Although the volumes were generally descriptive rather than interpretative, many of them have not been superseded by anything better. In shaping the design of the study, the editors fixed on urban life as one of the important dimensions of the American social experience, and opened a new era of historical inquiry. Arthur M. Schlesinger, Sr., one of the editors, entitled his own volume on the period 1878-1898, *The Rise of the City.* Although only a portion of his work was actually devoted to the subject, Schlesinger found the growth of cities to be the unifying theme of the period. From a variety of original sources, he provided an account of population movement during the twenty-year period and described in rich detail the pattern of life in the rapidly growing American cities. His volume proved the most influential in the series in generating further research.[4]

In a bibliographical essay in *The Rise*

of the City, Schlesinger noted explicitly the lack of historical urban studies. "The American city has not yet been studied generically," he wrote, "nor do there exist any adequate social histories of particular cities."[5] In the next few years, scholars began to fill this gap. By the late 1930's, a number of studies of individual cities had appeared: Holyoke, Memphis, portions of New York's history, and the beginnings of Bessie L. Pierce's multi-volume history of Chicago. In an introduction to his study of early Memphis, Gerald M. Capers provided a defense of the new line of inquiry. The city, he argued, because of its relationship to an economic hinterland represented a much better unit for the study of sectional economic interests than did the state, which was merely an artificial political division. Pointing to the problems of trying to write American history in terms of a broad East-West division, he found that study of a city such as Memphis illuminated an important lower and upper Mississippi Valley sectional division. Capers also ringingly endorsed the principle of urban biography:

After a year's study [of Memphis], I became convinced that an adequate biography of our key cities—New York, Chicago, New Orleans, San Francisco, Kansas City, and a dozen more—would be more significant to the national epic than the biography of even so prominent a figure as Theodore Roosevelt. A large proportion of our citizens live in cities; yet how much do we actually know about the natural history of the institutional development of that political and social amoeba, the American city. This all-important task, though it interests the sociologist, the economist, the genealogist, and the literatus, is primarily and fundamentally the job of the historian —a job that he has so far neglected.[6]

As a result of this interest, Blake McKelvey in a 1952 bibliographical essay, which still provides the only general survey of scholarly writing in urban history, could cite the publication after 1930 of forty volumes of urban biography and another "dozen good books of urban history on a broader scope."[7]

The Conceptual Framework of Urban History

In 1940 Arthur M. Schlesinger, whose *Rise of the City* had stimulated much of the scholarship in urban history, published his significant essay, "The City in American History," which launched the debate on the nature of this new field.[8] Schlesinger's approach had been vaguely foreshadowed the year before when Ralph E. Turner at a meeting of the American Historical Association devoted to cultural history had presented an important paper which had turned the thesis of his more famous namesake inside out to show that the industrial city could constitute a distinct cultural environment in the same fashion as had the frontier.[9] He argued that three fundamental forces—the labor market, machine technology, and urban association—had reshaped the cultural milieu and altered the circumstances of human life. Ralph Turner was concerned with the general effect of the rise of the industrial city in the Western world. Schlesinger in his essay found a similar urban factor at work throughout the course of American history. He pointed to the growing concern of American historians with the city and called on them to devote even more attention to the subject. Without attempting to define precisely either "urbanization" or the "city," he suggested the importance of these at various stages in our history. His examples were numerous: a sense of collective responsibility and a growing spirit of nationalism had developed in the colonial towns; the framing and ratification of the Constitution represented in part a triumph of urban business and creditor classes over the small farmers of the countryside; in the nineteenth century, the breach between North and South was due in no small measure to the "urban spirit of progress animating the one section and the static, rural life of the other"; the farmers' protest movements of the late nineteenth century could be considered an agrarian reaction against urban imperialism.

Schlesinger apparently hoped that his essay might stimulate a fundamental reassessment of our history in the same fashion as had Turner's statements of "The Significance of the Frontier in American History." He made Turner his starting point, and the two essays have many organizational parallels. But in spite of its influence in focusing attention on urban themes, "The City in American History" did not cause historians to try to shape an "urban reinterpretation" of American history. A year later, William Diamond, in an excellent article which summarized the history of urban sociology and related urban studies in the United States, warned of the dangers in so doing.[10] Diamond charged that Schlesinger had failed to define his concept of the "city" and carefully showed that Schlesinger had used it in a variety of senses at different points in the essay. Diamond also argued that much that Schlesinger had attributed to urbanization could as well be the result of industrialization or of technological development. Demonstrating the influence of the Beardian school, he strongly urged that historians continue to concentrate their attention on the conflict of economic interests in our past. This in effect ended debate on method for at least a decade. In reprinting his essay in 1949, Schlesinger summarized Diamond's critique. Aside from commenting that he did not consider urban and class interpretations mutually exclusive, he suggested only that the reader judge the issues for himself.[11] Historians continued to write about cities as they had before, unconcerned for the most part about any weaknesses in their method. It is perhaps significant that most general essays on the city in American history have tended to follow the Schlesinger model.[12]

Recent theoretical pieces on urban history have emphasized two themes: (1) If urban history is to become a viable field of inquiry, historians will have to employ the more exact methods of the social sciences. (2) In writing about cities in the past, historians should take into account the findings of social sciences concerned with the present-day city. In a 1953 essay, W. Stull Holt, who had directed studies in urban history at Johns Hopkins University and who has had a long-standing interest in historical patterns of population movement, charged historians who wrote about city development with ignoring the forest for the trees, with failing to use "urbanization as the basis for a new synthesis." Holt summarized a variety of material from the social sciences and suggested the value to historians of such topics as the sources of urban population, trends in urban birth rate, and urban migration.[13]

R. Richard Wohl, a historian trained also in economics and sociology who in 1954 launched an ambitious project to write a multivolume history of Kansas City using new techniques, speculated a year later that historians ought to join social science teams in examining the history of a single city. The "full discovery of what has passed in a city's history," he wrote, "can only be called forth by cooperative, interdisciplinary inquiry." On the basis of the Kansas City example, Wohl suggested six themes that might enable historians to broaden their narrowly antiquarian inquiries into the history of a single city: (1) the cultural definition of environment; (2) the establishment of permanent communities; (3) the city's range of influence; (4) the changing shape of the culture of the city; (5) the flow of urban institutionalization; (6) targets for urbanization (that is, an examination of fits and starts in the pattern of urban development which are often shaped by a progressive redirection of the city's purposes).[14] A. Theodore Brown, who assumed direction of the History of Kansas City Project after Wohl's premature death, in a commentary on urban history expressed similar sentiments.

The history of American urbanization . . . calls for a good bit of illumination from sociology and social psychology, as well as economics. Also one could wish for more time to read nineteenth and twentieth century novels and short stories for their insights into the nature and quality of urban life. The point is that there is no sense in which I can pursue studies in city history as a practitioner of a self-sustaining "discipline" called history. If this approach is worth anything at all, it needs a great deal of re-inforcing from other so-called disciplines.[15]

The British urban historian, Asa Briggs, who has pointed out the similarity of British and American practices in his field, argued in a 1958 article that historians had not kept up with social scientists in their method. It was true that sociologists had been lacking in imagination in their approach to the city, but more recently demographers had "suggested that all studies of cities and of urbanization should begin with an analysis of population trends, and so valuable has

been that contribution that none of the other specialists have been able to neglect either their methods or their conclusions."[16]

The most fully developed argument in this vein is contained in Eric E. Lampard's recent searching and detailed critique of urban history. Lampard urged historians to begin "the study of urbanization as a societal process and the comparative study of communities in a framework of human ecology" in order to provide "a more certain and systematic foundation for the writing of American social history." Lampard argued that if urban history were to have any importance, more exact approaches were critical.

If the urban historian is to be more than a historian who happens to do his research and writing on the subject of cities, it will be necessary to show that the term "urban" explains something in history that cannot be better explained by recourse to other frames of reference. In short, "urban" must signify not subject matter alone but a scheme of conceptualization, in much the same way as "economic" or "culture" history.[17]

How much effect has this kind of exhortation had on the actual procedures of urban historians? Probably very little. At the 1961 meeting of the American Historical Association, most of the active scholars writing in the field gathered to discuss Lampard's article. The questioning revealed limited understanding of his position and less sympathy for it.[18] The role of precise definition and logically constructed theory in historical work has traditionally been minor, and so it is likely to remain. In spite of claims to objectivity, history—particularly history centering on one national state—is affected by the need of a society to maintain unifying social traditions. As long as the "agrarian myth" influences our cultural attitudes, historians are likely to continue to write about the rise of the city in the United States as a deviation from a natural agrarian order and to pose a dichotomy in the past between city and country, between rural and urban. Wohl and Brown, in a provocative case study of local historiography, have demonstrated how changing community circumstances within a framework of changing national circumstances affect the fundamental interpretations embodied in city histories written during different periods of time.[19] Their conception has larger applications and could profitably be utilized to explore other aspects of urban history. Before further instructions are issued as to what urban history ought to be, it would perhaps be profitable for critics to examine its organic relationship to the whole tradition of American historiography rather than to try to continue to delimit the extent of its divergence from the canons of the more rigorous branches of social science.

In this connection, theoretical examination to this point has perhaps not sufficiently emphasized the fact that urban history at least in its ordinary forms is as much related to the long standing tradition of local history written by amateurs with an interest in their own communities as it is to the tradition of scholarly academic history. The special research problems involved, for example, in trying to construct a city history from masses of unconventional sources and unorganized materials may interest the fox but seldom the hedgehog. In the best urban histories, minor themes are thoughtfully developed but seldom does the whole work offer an interpretative framework that could be applied to another subject. It is impossible to establish any satisfactory criteria that would

distinguish the "scholarly" urban biography from the best works produced by the amateur local historian. The urban biography does not always escape altogether tones of "sentimentality, antiquarianism, and chamber of commerce advertising." It seldom does much to illuminate the general process of urbanization. There is little concern with what the city is and little indication that the problem has been more than casually considered. The history is written around the legal unit with only limited attention to relationships with regions and hinterlands. Often the work seems to degenerate into a narrative of virtually anything going on within a city's limits which seems of interest.

But this line of criticism can be carried too far, and it often has been. An intensively localistic approach can yield rich rewards in modifying the easy generalizations that permeate the textbooks in American history. The urban biography or the comparative city history often represents the tradition of local history at its best.[20] Reviewers in the social sciences have sometimes criticized urban biographies for the very feature that many historians take to be a virtue—presentation of masses of carefully assembled facts about such matters as land speculation, town promotion, business development, and internal improvements.[21] If carefully read, these studies provide significant insights into general themes of American development. Politically, for example, the city provides a setting for political action and leadership seldom comparable to the national setting, one in which national party concerns are quite irrelevant. If the findings of a large number of urban biographies were absorbed, the ancient ideological party synthesis, which still casts its shadow over treatments of national history, would undoubtedly be seriously modified. Within another conventional division of American history, urban biographies, by enabling historians more accurately to relate ideas to typical group experience, can supply a needed perspective for intellectual history. Much of the exuberance and the rhetoric of mid-nineteenth century "manifest destiny"— to cite one example unnoted in our general histories—clearly stemmed from the projects of promoters in the towns and cities of the West. In a recent study of nineteenth-century cholera epidemics, Charles Rosenberg has imaginatively demonstrated the possibilities in relating ideology to the urban milieu.[22]

Illumination of themes in national history, however, should perhaps be considered an incidental contribution of urban history. Asa Briggs has pointed to a fundamental confusion of purpose in the historical study of individual cities. The urban historian, he writes, "has often not been sure whether he is fitting local history into a stock national framework or whether he is helping to construct a new scaffolding."[23] Briggs, among others, has suggested that urban history can perhaps make a more distinct contribution in providing new ways of looking at the nature of periodization in national history.

The stages of an individual city's history do not really reflect the received divisions of national history. Periods in community history derive from critical turning points within the community itself; it is often useful for limited purposes to regard urban communities as organic entities—developing objective needs and characteristics at different periods of their growth. A variety of examples are available from the existing histories of American cities. In the development of Kansas City, for example,

there was a premetropolitan epoch lasting from around 1850 to 1870, defined by bitter competition for predominance among several river towns. Then there was a period of rapid growth from the late 1860's into the early twentieth century with the appearance of a standard set of urban problems and strong tendencies toward social and political disorganization. There followed a period from the 1890's coming down perhaps to 1940 or later, during which bosses, transit monopoly, and some impressive city planning imposed a degree of control and regularity upon the city. Although such familiar divisions of our national history as the Civil War and the Progressive Movement marked Kansas City's history, they did not define its contours.[24] The urban biographies of Chicago, Milwaukee, and Rochester exhibit sequences of growth peculiar to those communities. A series of entrepreneurial decisions in New York City in 1817 clearly marked what its historian has called the *annus mirabilis* of the city. Similarly, the competition offered by New York's unsuccessful rivals— Baltimore, Philadelphia, and Boston— defined important stages in their histories.[25]

Turns in the course of events which change the characteristic problems a community faces change also the range of choices open to its leadership. Moreover, the age of a community and the character of its economic activities and social structure can shape its fate in rivalry with other communities. Philadelphia, an old securely established city under conservative Quaker leadership, seemed at one time unable to shift strategies rapidly enough to keep up with the much younger, more dynamic Baltimore. A prosperous and conservative group of St. Louis leaders, whose ties to the river trade were both cultural and economic, failed to match Chicago's aggressive railroad promotions and consequently lost much of the city's hinterland to the younger rival. Kansas City, in the 1850's and 1860's, was the right age to win a struggle among several towns contending for urban supremacy at the great bend of the Missouri River. St. Joseph and Independence, each a generation older, had developed specialized interest groups which opposed the community programs necessary in an age of railroad expansion. Leavenworth, Kansas City's most formidable rival, became disrupted internally as the result of the rapidity of its growth during the same period, and no unified railroad program could crystallize.[26]

Numerous other examples that point up the importance of urban history as a means of refining our understanding of social process in national development could be constructed from existing urban biographies and studies in urban rivalry. Asa Briggs, on the basis of examination of the early history of the industrial cities of Great Britain, has emphasized the same point about a different national history: "The more that one can develop these comparative studies, even within the framework of one culture, the clearer one will be, I think, about the economic and social structural differences in the rhythm and pattern of early industrial society." Briggs went on to argue that the history of the relationship between Birmingham and Manchester offered a synthesizing theme by which a history of England in the nineteenth century could be written.[27] On the basis of the published materials then available, Blake McKelvey, in his 1952 bibliographical essay, suggested a broad period scheme within which further work on the history of the city might be conducted: (1) the era of the colonial city, a period which at that date had received the most detailed scrutiny; (2) the era of the boom town as part of the westward movement of population, extending from the early part of the nineteenth century to around 1835; (3) the era of the Yankee City, 1835-1870, during which time the "enterprise and ingenuity and capital of old Americans developed more efficient trade facilities, transformed earlier handicrafts into factory industries and exploited the labor of hundreds of thousands of newcomers from across the Atlantic"; (4) the era of cosmopolitan cities from 1870 to 1915; (5) the era of emergence of metropolitan area and core cities, which had not then been examined by historians.[28]

There is little evidence that McKelvey's suggestions had much influence on subsequent writing in urban history. Injunctions to break loose from the restrictions of the national synthesis, to develop period schemes on the basis of the subject studied in terms of a broad pattern of social development and population movement have been little heeded by urban historians. It is a rare work in urban biography that does not overemphasize the impact of Civil War, First or Second World War, Progressive Movement, or New Deal on the community under consideration. The only general scholarly work available on the history of American cities, Constance Green, *American Cities in the Growth of the Nation*, though pleasantly written and valuable, is weakened by a tendency to treat individual cities as locals in which the events of national history can be examined.[29] Asa Briggs has found the same tendency in English academic urban histories and has warned of the dangers:

The historian often starts with a picture of national history, and tends to illustrate it from local information. . . . Such an approach can be stultifying. It possesses exactly the opposite dangers to those of the antiquarian. Too few facts are given value, and the opportunity to rearrange national history is missed. Urban histories which fit too easily into the conventional national framework may well mislead rather than illuminate.[30]

URBAN HISTORIES

Reading only the critiques of urban history, one might reasonably conclude that the field is so chaotic as to defy classification. Still, the body of scholarship produced in terms of a loose definition of urban history, if examined on its own merits, is often impressive. McKelvey, in his bibliographic essay, suggested the broad limits within which inquiry has taken place. "The task of urban historians," he wrote, "is to chart the interrelated streams of life active in a specific community at a given period, or to weigh the cumulative effect in time of the problems and achievements of many cities within a given society, and in both cases to measure the extent to which the ideals and aspirations of that society found expression, growth, or rebirth in urban centers."[31] The following review of writings is not based on any reasoned scheme of classification as to what should or should not be called urban history. It includes representative works which most American historians—who seldom concern themselves with these matters of definition—would probably agree belonged to the field.

The Process of Urbanization

Lampard has pointed to the major deficiency in American urban history—the lack of studies of urbanization as a process. The only general work available is still Adna F. Weber, *The Growth of Cities in the Nineteenth Century,* a comparative study first published in 1899. Its continuing value is attested by its reprinting in a new edition, which includes a biographical sketch of Weber and a bibliography of his writings.[32] There are numerous neglected nineteenth-century works which examine the movement of population toward cities. These have little statistical sophistication, but they are important historical sources reflecting contemporary attitudes toward urbanization. The force of agrarian traditions in nineteenth-century America has undoubtedly been exaggerated owing to the simple fact that historians, because of their long preoccupation with the agricultural frontier, seldom examined documents that related to the growth of cities.[33]

General Works on American Cities

The best scholarly work available on the history of American cities is Constance McLaughlin Green, *American Cities in the Growth of the Nation.*[34] Originally presented as a series of lectures in London, the study illuminates aspects of United States national history through case studies of sixteen individual cities in various periods. Christopher Tunnard and Henry Hope Reed, *American Skyline,* is an ambitious attempt to survey the development of American cities largely in terms of the urban landscape.[35] The work contains much historical background, but it is often superficial. Lewis Mumford, *The City in History,* relates the American city to the world city, but knowledge of American history is not one of Mumford's strengths.[36] Works that deal with the history of urban architecture or city planning sometimes furnish valuable general material.[37] Charles N. Glaab,

The American City: A Documentary History, is a collection that emphasizes nineteenth-century historical documents.[38]

Urban Biography

The history of the individual city has been the most productive single area of urban history. In the last two decades, support from private foundations has led to ambitious attempts to produce definitive multivolume histories of Chicago, Kansas City, and Washington, D.C.[39] These projects have provided training for a substantial number of younger historians, who have continued to maintain a scholarly interest in urban history. Urban biography has perhaps even won a measure of popular acceptance, as evidenced by Constance Green's receipt of the Pulitzer Prize in history for the first volume of her history of Washington. This is a fitting tribute, for Mrs. Green has been the most vigorous defender of the notion that an individual city has a "personality" which can be delineated through historical techniques.

In terms of this conception, the range of "personality types" represented in existing studies tends to be limited. A major proportion of the studies deal with cities in the East and in the more eastern parts of the Midwest and with cities not quite of first rank in size and importance. In addition to Pierce's *Chicago*, Blake McKelvey's recently completed *Rochester* and Bayrd Still's *Milwaukee* are outstanding examples of the genre.[40] New England cities, particularly those with an economic base in manufacturing, have received considerable attention.[41] Thomas J. Wertenbaker, *Norfolk*, is important, for it develops the history of a city with unusual natural advantages which lost to more aggressive rivals in the struggle for urban supremacy.[42] Ordinarily, the urban biography recounts a success story; a few studies of aspiring communities that failed would enlarge our understanding of the processes of city growth. Aside from an occasional isolated study such as Edgar B. Wesley's distinctive history of Owatonna, Minnesota, little work has been done on the individual histories of small American cities.[43] There are numerous scholarly studies dealing with limited periods of a city's development in the fashion of the urban biography—two studies of Memphis, one of Nashville, portions of New York's history, examinations of economic development in early Detroit and Pittsburgh, and others.[44] Through the inclusion of numerous nonacademic histories of earlier eras and works that are of popular character, many of these quite able, a bibliography of worthwhile studies of individual cities of formidable length could be compiled.[45]

Nevertheless, there are numerous cities whose histories remain almost unexamined in any serious fashion. Among eastern cities, there are no satisfactory general histories of Philadelphia or Baltimore. There is no scholarly examination of an easterly lake port, such as Toledo or Cleveland; no adequate history of St. Louis, the key city in the westward movement; no histories of a Deep South city or of New Orleans. West of the ninety-eighth meridian urban history remains all but unwritten. Aside from a recent economic history of the Latter-Day Saints, which develops the early history of Salt Lake City, there is no good example of a history of a high plains or Rocky Mountain city.[46] The Southwest and the West Coast, areas which illustrate special aspects of the historical development of American cities, are unrepresented by any scholarly urban biography.[47] The comment of a recent bibliographical guide to American studies has considerable validity:

The greatest tide in recent America, which has run for over a century but seems only to grow in strength, is the tide of urbanization. It can hardly be said that historians and geographers, as distinct from the sociologists who view it as material for abstractions, have kept abreast of it. In America there are many great urban universities whose graduate schools produce learned monographs on ancient Greek pottery or the foreign policy of Bismarck, but never dream of searching for order and significance in the prodigious developments which have been going on under their noses. And there are many great cities unrepresented here by any history or even any title, because there is no up-to-date and comprehensive history to be had.[48]

Period Studies

Owing largely to the extraordinary labors of one historian, Carl Bridenbaugh, the development of cities during the colonial period has received thorough treatment. In two monumental pieces of scholarship, Bridenbaugh has applied the techniques of urban biography to a comparative study of Boston, New York, Charleston, Philadelphia, and Newport.[49] Although critics have questioned his loose definitions of "city" and "urban," all have paid tribute to the massive task he performed in developing an unknown aspect of American history and in doing it thoroughly. Thomas J. Wertenbaker, *The Golden Age of Colonial Culture* examines Boston, New York, Philadelphia, Annapolis, Williamsburg, and Charleston as "crucibles of culture" in colonial America.[50] A major study, Richard C. Wade, *The Urban Frontier, 1790-1830*, demonstrates the impor-

tance of the Ohio Valley cities in the westward movement and supplies a needed corrective to the overemphasis in American historiography on the development of an agricultural frontier.[51]

A major deficiency among existing urban histories is the lack of any systematic study of the years from 1830 to 1860, a period of extremely rapid urbanization.[52] Although the historian is theoretically most concerned with origins, the rise of cities in the United States is ordinarily treated in general accounts as if it were almost exclusively a post-Civil War phenomenon. A thorough study of urban development in the earlier part of the century would do much to correct this faulty emphasis. Blake McKelvey's recently published *The Urbanization of America, 1860-1915* supplies a detailed treatment of the period of the growth of the modern city.[53] The work carefully synthesizes the findings of a vast amount of scholarly material dealing with this period produced in the last twenty years. The years covered by McKelvey—during which the rise of the city came to be looked upon as one of the gravest American social problems—is of course a period that is particularly rich in significant contemporary works. The Census Bureau's *Social Statistics of Cities* (1880) marked official recognition of the importance of urbanization and was the first of a number of important government documents on aspects of city life.[54] The growth of scholarly interest in the city around the turn of the century represented by the work of the economist Richard Ely at Johns Hopkins, the founding of the Chicago school of urban sociology, and the development of the social survey technique of examining community life produced a rich urban literature of great value to historians.[55]

No historian has yet attempted a general assessment of urban developments in the recent period although the writing in other urban fields, of course, has been enormous.

Urban Rivalry and Transportation

Rivalry among aspiring nineteenth-century towns and cities for trade and transportation has been the subject of a number of urban histories. "Studies in urban rivalry" could be said, in fact, to constitute a principal division of the field. Although these studies are important, they are confined largely to the discussion of economic developments in the middle part of the century. Edward C. Kirkland, *Men, Cities and Transportation: A Study in New England History, 1820-1900,* is a thorough study, which emphasizes transportation more than urban development.[56] The efforts of Boston, Baltimore, and Philadelphia to compete with the urban success of New York in the years before the Civil War have received considerable attention, notably in the previously cited works of Albion, Krout and Fox, and in the recent study by Julius Rubin.[57] Rubin demonstrates on the basis of detailed examination that local factors rather than differences in the technological or economic positions of the three communities shaped their varied responses to the Erie Canal. His emphasis that "the understanding of the historical process depends as much upon the analysis of the subjective traits of groups as it does upon the analysis of the pressure of objective circumstances" suggests a fruitful line of inquiry in urban history, which has long been affected by doctrines of objective necessity in considering the location and growth of American cities. James W. Livingood, *The Philadelphia-Baltimore Trade Rivalry, 1780-1860,* is a detailed monograph.[58] Rivalry between two smaller cities is discussed in David M. Ellis, "Albany and Troy—Commercial Rivals."[59] Wyatt W. Belcher, *The Economic Rivalry Between St. Louis and Chicago, 1850-1880,* is an excellent study of the most significant midwestern rivalry of the nineteenth century.[60] A larger study examining the relationship between the interior river and lake cities of the nineteenth century would be particularly useful. Whether the future metropolises of America would be located on lakes or rivers was a principal consideration shaping the nature of the rationales and justifications that were a part of nineteenth-century interior urban rivalries. Rivalry in Ohio and the surrounding region is examined in an article by Harry N. Scheiber, in Wisconsin by Herbert W. Rice, and in Indiana by Francis P. Weisenberger.[61] Transportation and urban rivalry in the region farther west is examined in Charles N. Glaab, *Kansas City and the Railroads.*[62] Glenn C. Quiett, *They Built the West: An Epic of Rails and Cities,* is a colorful but often inadequate popular treatment of transportation and the growth of Denver, San Francisco, Los Angeles, San Diego, Spokane, and Tacoma.[63] Historical relationships between cities, between metropolises and hinterland communities, particularly in the late nineteenth and early twentieth centuries, would seem to offer a promising subject for further attention by urban historians. The late Charles M. Gates in an unpublished paper entitled "Concept of the Metropolis in the American Westward Movement" enlarged on themes in the classic work of the economic historian N. S. B. Gras and suggested a number of ways along which such an inquiry might proceed.[64]

Special Themes in American Urban History

Histories dealing with a number of aspects of life in an urban setting are conventionally, though not necessarily logically, fitted into the field of urban history. These include studies that consider such subjects as the urban immigrant and the history of ethnic groups in American cities; histories of municipal services; urban politics and especially the urban aspects of Progressivism and twentieth-century reform movements; housing and the slum; the development of the public health movement; and the city in American thought. A great portion of these studies fall into the traditional 1860-1915 "rise-of-the-city" period. Many of them deal not with urban developments as such but with national topics considered in an urban setting. The extensive recent literature on the urban Progressive, for example, is more concerned with throwing light on the nature of Progressivism as a general political movement than in showing the part played by Progressivism in shaping the nature and direction of American urban life. One of the critical needs in urban history is for new approaches to this kind of topic that do more than merely echo the themes of national history.

Among the more important studies of urban immigration are Robert Ernst, *Immigrant Life in New York City, 1825-1863;*[65] Oscar Handlin, *Boston's Immigrants, 1790-1865;*[66] and Ralph Weld, *Brooklyn Is America.*[67] Other works not directly concerned with the subject but which contain considerable material are Marcus L. Hansen, *The Atlantic Migration, 1607-1860;*[68] Carl Wittke, *We Who Built America;*[69] Rowland T. Berthoff, *British Immigrants in Industrial America, 1790-1950;*[70] and E. P. Hutchinson, *Immigrants and Their Children, 1850-1950,*[71] which contains illuminating data on immigrant occupational patterns. The role of Jews in cities is considered in Frank Rosenthal, *The Jews of Des Moines: The First Century;*[72] Stuart E. Rosenberg, *The Jewish Community in Rochester, 1843-1925;*[73] Selig Adler and Thomas E. Connolly, *From Ararat to Suburbia: The History of the Jewish Community of Buffalo;*[74] and Moses Rischin, *The Promised City: New York's Jews, 1870-1914.*[75] Immigrant life in an industrial city is examined in Donald B. Cole, *Immigrant City: Lawrence, Massachusetts, 1845-1921.*[76] Documentary material on the urban immigrant can be found in two works by Edith Abbott (editor), *Immigration: Select Documents and Case Records*[77] and *Historical Aspects of the Immigration Problem: Select Documents.*[78]

Studies of tenements, the slum problem, and housing reform include the older works: Edith Abbott, *Tenements of Chicago, 1908-1935;*[79] R. W. De Forest and Lawrence Veiller, *The Tenement House Problem;*[80] and James Ford, et al., *Slums and Housing: With Special Reference to New York City.*[81] Roy Lubove, *The Progressive and the Slums: Tenement House Reform in New York City, 1890-1917*[82] provides a recent scholarly assessment of the subject. A significant lithographed dissertation is Gordon Atkins, *Health, Housing and Poverty in New York City, 1865-1898.*[83] A broader related study has been done by Robert H. Bremner, *From the Depths: The Discovery of Poverty in the United States.*[84]

The problem of the health of the city is treated in M. P. Ravenel (editor), *A Half Century of Public Health*[85] and in James H. Cassedy, *Charles V. Chapin and the Public Health Movement.*[86] For an earlier period the relationship between science, disease, public health, and conceptions of the urban environment is treated in Charles E. Rosenberg, *The Cholera Years.*[87]

The municipal reform movement and urban aspects of national reform are discussed in Clifford W. Patton, *The Battle for Municipal Reform, 1875-1900;*[88] Frank M. Stewart, *A Half Century of Municipal Reform: The History of the National Municipal League;*[89] Ray Ginger, *Altgeld's America,* which deals with Chicago reformers;[90] and Arthur Mann, *Yankee Reformers in the Urban Age.*[91] Richard Hofstadter, *The Age of Reform,*[92] is a convenient synthetic account which stimulated much of the current historical reevaluation of the urban bases of Progressivism. The attempt to supply an urban interpretation of twentieth-century American reform is demonstrated in J. Joseph Huthmacher, "Urban Liberalism and the Age of Reform."[93] Louis G. Geiger, "Joseph W. Folk V. Edward Butler,"[94] is a significant demur to current interpretations. A. Theodore Brown, *The Politics of Reform,*[95] provides an important case study of urban reform in a more recent period.

The place of the city in American thought has recently been assessed in Morton White and Lucia White, *The Intellectual Versus the City: From Thomas Jefferson to Frank Lloyd Wright.*[96] The Whites argue that generally the American intellectual has been opposed to the city. Although their definition of anti-urbanism sometimes becomes rather tortured and their concentration is on a limited, highly selective group of thinkers, the work is an important one. Anselm L. Strauss, *Images of the American City,*[97] attempts to develop the historical evolution of American reactions to the city through the application of techniques of social psychology. The work is original in conception, but married in sections by inadequate research in historical documents. Older documentary collections of travelers' reactions are also concerned with delimiting changing reactions to the American city.[98] The impact of the city on American literature is surveyed in George A. Dunlap, *The City in the American Novel, 1789-1900,*[99] which deals exclusively with the Eastern city, and in Blanche H. Gelfant, *The American City Novel, 1900-1940,*[100] which too rigorously applies sociological theses to the writings of Dreiser, Dos Passos, Farrell, and other novelists who have dealt with the urban scene. Robert H. Walker, "The Poet and the Rise of the City,"[101] surveys a wide variety of late nineteenth-century verse and finds that the bulk of it is critical of the place of the city in American life. Catholic thought about the city is discussed in Robert D. Cross, "The Changing Image of the City Among American Catholics."[102]

Important miscellaneous studies in urban history include the following: William Haller, Jr., *The Puritan Frontier: Town Planning in New England Colonial Development, 1630-1660;*[103] Nelson M. Blake, *Water for the Cities: A History of the Urban Water Supply Problem in the United States,*[104] an original, thoroughly researched study which should be duplicated for other municipal functions; E. Digby Baltzell, *Philadelphia Gentlemen: The Making of a National Upper Class,*[105] which traces the development of a power and class structure in Philadelphia; Lewis E. Atherton, *Main Street on the Middle Border,*[106] which thoroughly examines the midwestern small city and its cultural relationships to the metropolis; Powell A. Moore, *The Calumet Region: In-*

diana's Last Frontier,[107] a somewhat pedestrian history of a significant urban-industrial area. Aaron Abell, *The Urban Impact on American Protestantism, 1865-1900*,[108] and Henry F. May, *Protestant Churches and Industrial America*,[109] are important for the impact of the rise of the city on American churches. Paul F. Conkin, *Tomorrow a New World: The New Deal Community Program*,[110] discusses the Greenbelt towns and other New Deal experiments in community planning. Sam B. Warner, Jr., *Streetcar Suburbs: The Process of Growth in Boston, 1870-1890*,[111] is based on an unusual amount of carefully collected data, but his findings are rather unincisively presented. His appendix on the use of social statistics is an important discussion of research problems in urban history.[112]

In recent years, as the historian has turned his attention to urban themes, general series in American history have taken more account of the importance of the growth of cities. In some cases, these sections are based on original research and hence have importance as sources. The *Economic History of the United States* series might logically be expected to contain more material on urbanization than it does, but two volumes are significant: George R. Taylor, *The Transportation Revolution, 1815-1860*,[113] which considers the pre-Civil War development of cities in relation to transportation, and Edward C. Kirkland, *Industry Comes of Age: Business, Labor, and Public Policy, 1860-1897*,[114] which contains an important essay on "Building American Cities." Kirkland develops the thesis that city building was a factor stimulating continued economic growth in a period in which railroad building had been substantially completed. Among volumes in the "New American

Nation" series, Clemont Eaton, *The Growth of Southern Civilization*,[115] contains a chapter on "Town Life," Harold U. Faulkner, *Politics, Reform and Expansion, 1890-1900*,[116] considers "The Revolt of the Cities," and George E. Mowry, *The Era of Theodore Roosevelt, 1900-1912*,[117] discusses the politics of "The Cities and the States" and indicates the role of the city in the Progressive Movement. Among older single volume general studies, Roger Burlingame, *Engines of Democracy: Inventions and Society in Mature America*,[118] provides a necessary starting point for the study of urban technology and Thomas C. Cochran and William Miller, *The Age of Enterprise: A Social History of Industrial America*,[119] contains a thoughtful chapter on "Industry and the City."

CONCLUSIONS

Urban history is a relatively new and unestablished division of American history. Reflecting the long-standing interest of academic historians in sectional and economic forces and their tendency to write within the framework of an agrarian tradition, the field has only recently gained a measure of academic recognition. It is characterized by its lack of precise definition both in subject matter and method; much of the scholarship that falls within its vague limits cannot easily be disassociated from antiquarian local history. It has been attacked by social scientists, who recognize its potential value but who are revolted by its seeming chaos; it has often been dismissed by the ordinary academic historian as a gaudy frill which may desecrate an old-fashioned, humanistic discipline.

Still the United States has become an urban nation. The writing of national history reflects cultural imperatives, and urban history will become more important. In fact, a rather dramatic academic breakthrough seems imminent as a number of universities move rapidly to establish programs in urban history and as a number of textbooks are in preparation. Scholars who style themselves urban historians have made important contributions to historical knowledge; and certainly much more useful work could be done within the past framework of inquiry.[120] But there are indications that a number of younger scholars have taken some of the exhortatory analysis to heart, and as the field develops it well may move—slowly, to be sure—into closer partnership with the urban divisions of the related social sciences.

NOTES

1. Eric E. Lampard, "American Historians and the Study of Urbanization," *American Historical Review*, 67 (October 1961), p. 52.
2. The Urban History Group *Newsletter* (1954 to present) contains descriptions of courses taught in American Urban History and occasional reflections on the nature of the field.
3. (New York, 1921), pp. 70-93.
4. Arthur M. Schlesinger, Sr., and Dixon Ryan Fox (Eds.), *A History of American Life*, 13 vols. (New York, 1927-1948). Significant sections of Schlesinger's volume (New York, 1933) include "The Lure of the City," pp. 53-77 and "The Urban World," p. 78-120. For examples of urban themes in other volumes of the series, see John A. Krout and Dixon Ryan Fox, *The Completion of Independence, 1790-1830* (New York, 1944), "The Atlantic Ports," pp. 1-27, "The Day of the Merchant," pp. 212-245, and "Urban Influences," pp. 370-401; Arthur C. Cole, *The Irrepressible Conflict, 1850-1865* (New York, 1934), "Prosperity and Panic," pp. 1-33, and "Health and Happiness," pp. 179-204; Allan Nevins, *The Emergence of Modern America, 1865-1878* (New York, 1927), "Urban Living and Routes of Travel," pp. 75-100; Harold U. Faulkner, *The Quest for Social Justice, 1898-1914* (New York, 1931), "The New Democracy," pp. 81-109, and "The Decline of Laissez Faire," pp. 110-129.
5. Schlesinger, *Rise*, p. 448.
6. Gerald M. Capers, *The Biography of a River Town: Memphis, Its Heroic Age* (Chapel Hill, 1939), pp. viii-ix.
7. Blake McKelvey, "American Urban History Today," *American Historical Review*, 57 (July 1952), pp. 919-929. A more recent bibliographical essay surveying political science materials concerned with urban development also contains numerous works that are historical in nature: R. T. Daland, "Political Science and the Study of Urbanism," *American Political Science Review*, 51 (June 1957), pp. 491-509. The Urban History Group *Newsletter* (1954 to present), an irregular, mimeographed publication, surveys current bibliography in urban history and related fields. For late nineteenth-century works consult the magnificent Robert C. Brooks, "A Bibliography of Municipal Problems and City Conditions," *Municipal Affairs*, 1 (March 1897), pp. 1-234; and its revised version *Municipal Affairs*, 5 (March 1901), pp. 1-346. This work includes both American and European studies. Seemingly definitive for the period after 1880, its value diminishes as one moves further back into the nineteenth century.
8. Arthur M. Schlesinger, Sr., "The City in American History," *Mississippi Valley Historical Review*, 27 (June 1940), pp. 43-66, reprinted in revised form as "The City in American Civilization," *Paths to the Present* (New York, 1949), pp. 210-233.
9. Ralph E. Turner, "The Industrial City: Center of Cultural Change," in Caroline F. Ware (Ed.), *The Cultural Approach to History* (New York, 1940), pp. 228-242. For an earlier article which suggests some of Turner's themes, see Leon S. Marshall, "The English and American Industrial City of the Nineteenth Century," *Western Pennsylvania Historical Magazine*, 20 (September 1937), pp. 169-180.
10. William Diamond, "On the Dangers of an Urban Interpretation of History," in Eric F. Goldman (Ed.), *Historiography and Urbanization: Essays in American History in Honor of W. Stull Holt* (Baltimore, 1941), pp. 67-108.
11. Schlesinger, *Paths*, p. 297.
12. See, for example, Bayrd Still, "The History of the City in American Life," *The American Review*, 2 (May 1962), pp. 20-34; and Richard C. Wade, "The City in History—Some American Perspectives," in Werner Z. Hirsch (Ed.), *Urban Life and Form* (New York, 1963), pp. 59-77. Wade in particular emphasizes the relationship of the growth of cities to such general political developments as the struggle over slavery, Populism, and Progressivism. Other recent essays by urban historians include Blake McKelvey, "Urban Social and Economic Institutions in North America," Chap. 24 in *La Ville*, Recueils de la Societe Jean Bodic, Vol. 7 (Brussels, 1955), and Mark D. Hirsch, "Reflections on Urban History and Urban Reform 1865-1915," in D. H. Sheehan and H. C. Syrett (Eds.), *Essays in American Historiography: Papers Presented in Honor of Allan Nevins* (New York, 1960). John D. Hicks, "The Third American Revolution," *Nebraska History*, 36 (December 1955), pp. 227-245, stresses the importance of urbanization as part of a twentieth-century urban-industrial revolution.
13. W. Stull Holt, "Some Consequences of the

Urban Movement," *Pacific Historical Review*, 22 (November 1953), pp. 337-352.

14. R. Richard Wohl, "Urbanism, Urbanity, and the Historian," *University of Kansas City Review*, 22 (Autumn 1955), pp. 53-61.

15. Urban History Group *Newsletter*, No. 13 (December 1960).

16. Asa Briggs, "The Study of Cities," *Confluence*, 7 (Summer 1958), p. 107; see also p. 112.

17. Lampard, "American Historians," p. 61.

18. The meeting is reported in the Urban History Group *Newsletter*, No. 15 (April 1962).

19. R. Richard Wohl and A. Theodore Brown, "The Usable Past: A Study of Historical Traditions in Kansas City," *Huntington Library Quarterly*, 23 (May 1960), pp. 237-259.

20. For examinations of the relationship between local and urban history, see Constance McL. Green, "The Value of Local History," in Caroline F. Ware (Ed.), *The Cultural Approach to History* (New York, 1940), pp. 275-286, and Bayrd Still, "Local History Contributions and Techniques in the Study of Two Colonial Cities," *Bulletin of the American Association for State and Local History*, 2 (April 1960), pp. 495-514.

21. See, for example, review of Blake McKelvey, *Rochester: The Water Power City* in *American Journal of Sociology*, 52 (March 1947), p. 466; review of Constance McL. Green, *Naugatuck*, by C. Wendell King in *American Sociological Review*, 15 (February 1950), p. 155; review of Gerald M. Capers, Jr., *The Biography of a River Town*, by Albert Blumenthal in *American Sociological Review*, 5 (December 1940), pp. 980-981.

22. Charles E. Rosenberg, *The Cholera Years* (Chicago, 1962). The value of traditional urban history is developed more fully in an unpublished paper by A. Theodore Brown and Charles N. Glaab, "Antiquarianism Revisited: A Note on Urban History."

23. Asa Briggs, "The Study of Cities," p. 112.

24. A. Theodore Brown, "The History of Kansas City, Vol. II," unpublished manuscript.

25. Robert G. Albion, *The Rise of New York Port* (New York, 1939), p. 1; Julius Rubin, *Canal or Railroad? Imitation and Innovation in the Response to the Erie Canal in Philadelphia, Baltimore, and Boston* (Philadelphia, 1961), *passim*.

26. James W. Livingood, *The Philadelphia-Baltimore Trade Rivalry, 1780-1860* (Harrisburg, Penn., 1947), pp. 1-3, *passim;* Wyatt W. Belcher, *The Economic Rivalry Between St. Louis and Chicago, 1850-1880* (New York, 1947), pp. 72-75; Charles N. Glaab, *Kansas City and the Railroads* (Madison, 1962), *passim*.

27. Asa Briggs, "The Historian and the Study of Cities," mimeographed lecture delivered at the University of Chicago, April 6, 1956.

28. McKelvey, "American Urban History Today," pp. 921-927.

29. (New York, 1957).

30. Briggs, "The Historian and the Study of Cities."

31. McKelvey, "American Urban History Today," p. 920.

32. (New York, 1899), reprint (Ithaca, 1963).

33. Adam Seybert, *Statistical Annals . . . of the United States of America . . .* (Philadelphia, 1818) is one of the earliest attempts to assess the importance of the development of towns and cities. George Tucker, *The Progress of the United States in Population and Wealth in Fifty Years* (Boston, 1843), contains an interesting chapter analyzing the growth of cities and evaluating the weaknesses of census returns as an index to measure this development. The most systematic nineteenth-century student of urbanization was probably Jesup W. Scott (1799-1873), a Toledo newspaperman who wrote approximately fifteen articles examining the growth of cities, particularly those in the West. See, for example, his "Internal Trade of the United States," *Hunt's Merchants' Magazine*, 31 (October 1854), pp. 403-413; and "Westward the Star of Empire," *DeBow's Review*, 27 (August 1859), pp. 123-136. In general the files of the business publication, *Hunt's Merchants' Magazine*, 1839-1870, are an excellent source for the study of urban development in the first half of the nineteenth century. To a lesser extent, this is true also of the New Orleans commercial magazine, *DeBow's Review*, 1846-1864. For contemporary material on urbanization in the latter part of the nineteenth century, see the bibliographical essays in Nevins, *Emergence*, Schlesinger, *Rise*, and the Brooks bibliography.

34. (New York, 1957).

35. (Boston, 1955).

36. (New York, 1961). See also his earlier *The Culture of Cities* (New York, 1938).

37. Christopher Tunnard, *The City of Man* (New York, 1953) develops city planning and civic art in historical terms. John Burchard and Albert Bush-Brown, *The Architecture of America: A Social and Cultural History* (Boston, 1961), considers urban architecture in relation to the historical development of American cities.

38. (Homewood, Ill., 1963).

39. Bessie L. Pierce, *A History of Chicago*, in progress, I. *The Beginning of a City, 1673-1848*, II. *From Town to City, 1848-1871*, III. *The Rise of a Modern City, 1871-1893* (New York, 1937-1957); A. Theodore Brown, *The History of Kansas City*, in progress, I. *Frontier Community: Kansas City to 1870* (Columbia, Mo., 1963); Constance McL. Green, *Washington, Village and Capital, 1800-1878; Washington, Capital City, 1879-1950* (Princeton, 1962-1963).

40. Blake McKelvey, *Rochester*, 4 vols., I. *The Water-Power City, 1812-1854*, II. *The Flower City, 1855-1890*, III. *The Quest for Quality, 1890-1925*, IV. *Rochester: An Emerging Metropolis, 1925-1961* (Cambridge and Rochester, 1945-1961); Still (Madison, 1948).

41. Constance McL. Green, *Holyoke, Massachusetts* (New Haven, 1939), and *History of Nauga-*

tuck, *Connecticut* (New Haven, 1948); Vera Shlakman, *Economic History of a Factory Town* (Northampton, Mass., 1935); Rollin G. Osterweis, *Three Centuries of New Haven, 1638-1938* (New Haven, 1953).

42. Revised edition by Marvin W. Schlegel (Durham, 1962).

43. *Owatonna, The Social Development of a Minnesota Community* (Minneapolis, 1938).

44. Capers, *Biography of a River Town;* William Miller, *Memphis During the Progressive Era: 1900-1917* (Madison, 1957); Francis G. Davenport, *Cultural Life in Nashville on the Eve of the Civil War* (Chapel Hill, 1941); Albion, *Rise of New York Port;* Ralph Weld, *Brooklyn Village, 1816-1834* (New York, 1938); Harold C. Syrett, *The City of Brooklyn, 1865-1898* (New York, 1944); Sidney I. Pomerantz, *New York: An American City, 1783-1803* (New York, 1938); Allan Nevins and J. A. Krout (Eds.), *The Greater City: New York, 1898-1948* (New York, 1948); Floyd R. Dain, *Every House a Frontier: Detroit's Economic Progress, 1815-1825* (Detroit, 1956); Catherine E. Reiser, *Pittsburgh's Commercial Development, 1800-1850* (Harrisburg, 1951).

45. Works in local history of unusual value include Isaac N. P. Stokes, *The Iconography of Manhattan Island, 1498-1909,* 6 vols. (New York, 1916-1925) and Justin Winsor, *Memorial History of Boston, 1630-1880,* 4 vols. (Boston, 1880-1881). Popular works of value include Leland A. Baldwin, *Pittsburgh: The Story of a City* (Pittsburgh, 1937); Robert Molloy, *Charleston, A Gracious Heritage* (New York, 1947); Harold Sinclair, *Port of New Orleans* (New York, 1942); C. L. de Chambrun, *Cincinnati, Story of the Queen City* (New York, 1939); William G. Rose, *Cleveland, The Making of a City* (Cleveland, 1950). Detailed examination of the history of American cities requires consultation of a variety of diverse sources such as the Federal Writers' Project and the Writers' Program, *American Guide* series, 153 vols. (1935-1943), new editions and reprints (1939-1956); or of the regional studies *American Folkways,* 26 vols. (New York, 1941-1955). Volumes in these series are of such sharply varying value that it is easy to overlook the occasional worthwhile study. In the latter series, for example, see Carey McWilliams, *Southern California Country* (New York, 1946).

46. Leonard J. Arrington, *Great Basin Kingdom* (Cambridge, 1958). For popular but interesting interpretative sketches see Ray B. West (Ed.), *Rocky Mountain Cities* (New York, 1949).

47. Oscar O. Winther, "The Rise of Metropolitan Los Angeles: 1870-1910," *Huntington Library Quarterly,* 10 (August 1947), pp. 391-398, is an important article. For a popular account of the early days of the city, see Remi A. Nadeau, *City Makers* (Garden City, 1948).

48. *A Guide to the Study of the United States of America* (Washington, 1960), p. 467.

49. *Cities in the Wilderness* (New York, 1938, 1960) and *Cities in Revolt* (New York, 1955). See also Carl Bridenbaugh and Jessica Bridenbaugh, *Rebels and Gentlemen: Philadelphia in the Age of Franklin* (New York, 1942).

50. (Ithaca, 1942).

51. (Cambridge, 1959). See also his article, "Urban Life in Western America, 1790-1830," *American Historical Review,* 64 (October 1958), pp. 14-30.

52. See, however, two important articles: Bessie L. Pierce, "Changing Urban Patterns in the Mississippi Valley," *Journal of the Illinois Historical Society,* 43 (Spring 1950), pp. 46-57; and Bayrd Still, "Patterns of Mid-Nineteenth Century Urbanization in the Middle West," *Mississippi Valley Historical Review,* 28 (September 1941), pp. 187-206. Still shows the adoption by Midwestern cities of the established practices and procedures of the older urban centers of the East.

53. (New Brunswick, N. J., 1963).

54. See, for example, U. S. Bureau of the Census, *Telephones and Telegraphs* (1902), *Statistics of Cities* (1906), and *Street and Electric Railways* (1907); U. S. Senate, *Cost of Living in American Towns* (62nd Congress, 1st Session, Senate Document 22, 1911).

55. For a good short account of the history of the scholarship of American cities, see Diamond, "The Urban Interpretation," in Goldman (Ed.), *Historiography and Urbanization,* pp. 67-89. The following are important representative contemporary studies. Religiously oriented analyses of the meaning of urban life include A. D. Mayo, *The Symbols of the Capital; or Civilization in New York* (1859); E. H. Chapin, *Moral Aspects of City Life* (1853) and *Humanity in the City* (1854); Charles L. Brace, *The Dangerous Classes of New York* (1880); Josiah Strong, *Our Country* (1885), which has been called the *Uncle Tom's Cabin* of the urban reform movement, and his *The Twentieth Century City* (New York, 1898), and *The Challenge of the City* (1907); Samuel L. Loomis, *Modern Cities and Their Religious Problems* (1887); B. O. Flower, *Civilization's Inferno* (1893); William A. Stead, *If Christ Came to Chicago* (1894) and his *Satan's Invisible World Displayed* (1897). For developing conceptions of city planning and lines of defense of the city, see Frederick Law Olmsted, "Public Parks and the Enlargement of Towns," *Journal of Social Science,* 3 (November 1871); F. J. Kingsbury, "The Tendency of Men to Live in Cities," *Journal of Social Science,* 33 (November 1895); Charles M. Robinson, *The Improvement of Towns and Cities* (1901) and his *The Call of the City* (1908). For the problems of the slums, urban philanthropy and city youth, see C. D. Randall (Ed.), *History of Child Saving in the United States* (1893); C. R. Henderson, *Social Spirit in America* (1897) and his *Social Settlements* (1899); Robert A. Woods et al., *The Poor in Great Cities* (1895) and Robert A. Woods (Ed.),

Americans in Process: A Settlement Study (1902); Jacob A. Riis, *How the Other Half Lives* (1890) and his *The Children of the Poor* (1892), *Ten Years' War* (1900), *The Making of an American* (1901), and *The Battle with Slums* (1902); Jane Addams et al., *Philanthropy and Social Progress* (1893); Jane Addams, *Twenty Years at Hull House* (1910) and her *The Spirit of Youth and the City Streets* (1914); and Lillian D. Wald, *The House on Henry Street* (1915). For a statement of the rural protest against the city, see John W. Bookwalter, *Rural Versus Urban: Their Conflict and Its Cause* (1911). For consideration of the city in political and governmental terms, see Frederick C. Howe, *The City: The Hope of Democracy* (1905) and his *The Modern City and Its Problems* (1915); Richard T. Ely, *The Coming City* (1902); Delos F. Wilcox, *The American City: A Problem in Democracy* (1904) and his *Great Cities in America* (1910). For municipal functions see J. A. Fairlie, *Municipal Administration* (1901), a particularly useful study that compares the history of American and European practices; George E. Waring, *Sanitary Drainage* (1876) and his *Street-Cleaning* (1897), and *Modern Methods of Sewage Disposal* (1894); Charles Zueblin, *American Municipal Progress* (1902, 1916), both editions should be consulted as a reflection of changing attitudes toward the city; Delos F. Wilcox, *Municipal Franchises*, 2 vols. (1910); E. W. Bemis (Ed.), *Municipal Monopolies* (1899); and James B. Walker, *Fifty Years of Rapid Transit* (New York, 1917). For an important study which considers the significance of geography in the location and growth of cities, see Ellen C. Semple, *American History and Its Geographic Conditions* (1903). For two early studies of twentieth-century suburbanization, see Graham R. Taylor, *Satellite Cities* (1915) and H. Paul Douglass, *The Suburban Trend* (1925).

56. 2 vols. (Cambridge, 1948).

57. Albion, *Rise of New York Port;* Krout and Fox, ₁*The Completion of Independence;* Rubin, *Canal or Railroad?*, all previously cited.

58. Previously cited.

59. *New York History,* 24 (October 1943), pp. 484-511.

60. Previously cited.

61. Harry N. Scheiber, "Urban Rivalry and Internal Improvements in the Old Northwest, 1820-1860," *Ohio History,* 71 (October 1962), pp. 227-239; Herbert W. Rice, "Early Rivalry Among Wisconsin Cities for Railroads," *Wisconsin Magazine of History,* 35 (Autumn 1951), pp. 10-15; Francis P. Weisenburger, "The Urbanization of the Middle West: Town and Village in the Pioneer Period," *Indiana Magazine of History,* 41 (March 1954), pp. 19-30.

62. Previously cited.

63. (New York, 1934).

64. A precis of the paper along with commentaries is printed in the Urban History Group *Newsletter* No. 16 (October 1962).

65. (New York, 1949).

66. (Cambridge, 1941).

67. (New York, 1950).

68. (Cambridge, 1940).

69. (New York, 1939).

70. (Cambridge, 1953).

71. (New York, 1956).

72. (Des Moines, 1957).

73. (New York, 1953).

74. (Philadelphia, 1960).

75. (Cambridge, 1962).

76. (Chapel Hill, 1963).

77. (Chicago, 1924).

78. (Chicago, 1926).

79. (Chicago, 1936).

80. (New York, 1903).

81. (Cambridge, 1936).

82. (Pittsburgh, 1963). See also his "Lawrence Veiller and the New York State Tenement House Commission of 1900," *Mississippi Valley Historical Review,* 47 (March 1961), pp. 659-667, and "New Cities for Old: The Urban Reconstruction Program of the 1930's," *The Social Studies,* 53 (November 1962), pp. 203-212, and Robert H. Bremner, "The Big Flat: History of a New York Tenement House," *American Historical Review,* 63 (October 1958), pp. 54-62.

83. (Ann Arbor, 1947).

84. (New York, 1956).

85. (New York, 1921).

86. (Cambridge, 1962).

87. Previously cited.

88. (Washington, 1940).

89. (Berkeley, 1950).

90. (New York, 1958).

91. (Cambridge, 1954).

92. (New York, 1955).

93. *Mississippi Valley Historical Review,* 49 (September 1962), pp. 231-241.

94. *Journal of Southern History,* 28 (November 1962), pp. 438-449.

95. (Kansas City, 1958).

96. (Cambridge, 1962).

97. (New York, 1961).

98. Bessie L. Pierce (Ed.), *As Others See Chicago: Impressions of Visitors, 1673-1933* (Chicago, 1933); Bayrd Still, "The Growth of Milwaukee As Recorded by Contemporaries," *Wisconsin Magazine of History,* 21 (March 1938), pp. 262-293; Bayrd Still, *Mirror for Gotham: New York as Seen by Contemporaries from Dutch Days to the Present* (New York, 1956).

99. (Philadelphia, 1934).

100. (Norman, 1954).

101. *Mississippi Valley Historical Review,* 49 (June 1962), pp. 85-89.

102. *Catholic Historical Review,* 48 (April 1962), pp. 33-52.

103. (New York, 1951).

104. (Syracuse, 1956).

105. (Glencoe, 1958).

106. (Bloomington, 1954).

107. (Indianapolis, 1959).

108. (Cambridge, 1943).
109. (New York, 1949).
110. (Ithaca, 1959).
111. (Cambridge, 1962).
112. Reprinted as "Technical Leaflet 7, Social Studies: A Local Historian's Guide," *History News*, 18 (March 1963), pp. 67-70.
113. (New York, 1951), pp. 3-14, 348-398.
114. (New York, 1961), pp. 237-261.
115. (New York, 1961), pp. 247-260.
116. (New York, 1959), pp. 23-47.
117. (New York, 1958), pp. 59-84.
118. (New York, 1940), pp. 73-94.
119. (New York, 1942), pp. 249-272.
120. Important recent studies in urban history include Oscar Handlin and John Burchard (Eds.), *The Historian and the City* (Cambridge, Mass., 1963), a symposium which contains important theoretical material and excellent bibliographies; Lawrence L. Graves (Ed.), *A History of Lubbock* (Lubbock, Tex., 1962), a solid urban biography of a High Plains city; Richard C. Wade, *Slavery in the Cities: The South 1820-1860* (New York, 1964), broader in its treatment of Southern cities than the title might suggest; and John W. Reps, *The Making of Urban America: A History of City Planning in the United States* (Princeton, N. J., 1965), a magnificent piece of scholarship. Two important monographs on aspects of planning are Roy Lubove, *Community Planning in the 1920's: The Contribution of the Regional Planning Association of America* (Pittsburgh, 1963), and William H. Wilson, *The City Beautiful Movement in Kansas City* (Columbia, Mo., 1964).